Intercultural Communication

A Reader

Intercultural Communication

A Reader

Ninth Edition

Larry A. Samovar

San Diego State University

Richard E. Porter

California State University, Long Beach, Emeritus

Wadsworth Publishing Company

I(T)P® **An International Thomson Publishing Company**

Belmont, CA • Albany, NY • Boston • Cincinnati • Johannesberg • London • Madrid • Melbourne
Mexico City • New York • Pacific Grove, CA • Scottsdale, AZ • Singapore • Tokyo • Toronto

Executive Editor: *Deirdre Cavanaugh*
Associate Development Editor: *Megan Gilbert*
Editorial Assistants: *Dory Schaeffer & Matthew Lamb*
Project Editors: *Cathy Linberg & Howard Severson*
Permissions Editor: *Susan Walters*

Production, Copy Editing, Graphics, & Composition:
   Summerlight Creative, Eugene, OR
Text & Cover Designer: *Ellen Pettengell*
Cover Image: *Hands Touching Each Other, Jim Frazier, SIS*
Printer: *R.R. Donnelley & Sons, Crawfordsville, IN*

Printed in the United States of America
3 4 5 6 7 8 9 10

Wadsworth Publishing Company
10 Davis Drive
Belmont, CA 94002

International Thomson Editores
Seneca, 53
Colonia Polanco
11560 México D.F. México

International Thomson Publishing Europe
Berkshire House
168-173 High Holborn
London, WC1V 7AA, United Kingdom

International Thomson Publishing Asia
60 Albert Street #15-01
Albert Complex
Singapore 189969

Nelson ITP, Australia
102 Dodds Street
South Melbourne
Victoria 3205 Australia

International Thomson Publishing Japan
Hirakawa-cho Kyowa Building, 3F
2-2-1 Hirakawa-cho, Chiyoda-ku
Tokyo 102, Japan

Nelson Canada
1120 Birchmount Road
Scarborough, Ontario
Canada M1K 5G4

International Thomson Publishing Southern Africa
Building 18, Constantia Square
138 Sixteenth Road, P.O. Box 2459
Halfway House, 1685 South Africa

Library of Congress Cataloging-in-Publication Data

Intercultural communication: a reader / [edited by] Larry A. Samovar,
   Richard E. Porter. -- 9th ed.
      p.   cm.
   Includes bibliographical reference and index.
   ISBN 0-534-56241-8 (alk. paper)
      1. Intercultural communication.   I. Samovar, Larry A.
   II. Porter, Richard E.
HM1211.I57   1999
303.48'2--dc21
                        99-13103

Contents

Preface

We do not believe it is an overstatement when we assert that facility as an intercultural communicator may be one of the most important skills you will ever develop. You need only look around our world to see the need to prepare for a future in which you will interact with people who represent a wide range of cultural backgrounds. This will not be easy. You must be willing to communicate; have empathy toward foreign and alien cultures; develop a universalistic, realistic approach to the universe; and be tolerant of views that differ from your own. Intercultural communication offers the arena for this interpersonal contact. It is your ability to change, to make adjustments in your communication habits and behaviors, that supplies you with the potential to make that contact successful.

Intercultural communicative behavior not only must be void of racism and ethnocentrism, but also ought to reflect an attitude of mutual respect, trust, and worth. We emphasize that intercultural communication will not be successful if, by actions or words, communicators act in a superior or condescending manner. Every individual and every culture wants to believe it is as worthy as any other. Actions that manifest the opposite will stifle meaningful interaction. To be racist or ethnocentric is to condemn intercultural communication to failure. If you have the resolve to adopt the requisite behaviors and attitudes and the desire to overcome racism and ethnocentrism and their attendant feelings of superiority, then you can begin to know the exhilaration that comes when you have connected successfully with someone far removed from your own sphere of experience.

The occasion of this ninth edition of our book is one of excitement. The fact that we have been received with the popularity to warrant another new edition is exciting and obviously pleasing. Yet, as we proceeded, we wanted to be cautious enough to preserve the basic framework and philosophy that has sustained us through the previous eight editions. It would have been improvident of us to abandon an orientation to intercultural communication that has found wide acceptance for nearly three decades. The field as well as the authors, however, have continued to evolve. We knew, therefore, that some reshaping would be necessary.

This new edition grants us the opportunity to combine two complementary positions. First, it reflects our continued belief that the basic core of the field should not be changed for the sake of simply being novel. Such change would pilfer the book of those concepts that have been infused in all of the previous editions. Second, it reflects our belief that as our intercultural contacts change in number and intensity, there is a need to present essays that mirror that change. We have perceived each new edition as an opportunity to examine that change and to stake out new territory for the field—territory that takes into account the complexities of communicating in the 2000s.

As the field of intercultural communication has grown, we have attempted in each new edition to grow with the field and to fuse the old with the new. In 1972, the first edition contained thirty-four articles and essays. The eighth edition contained forty-six; now we include forty-five articles in our collection of readings. Some have appeared in all previous editions. In this ninth edition, we have eighteen new essays, fifteen of them prepared especially for this volume.

APPROACH

The basic energizing motive for this book has remained the same since both of us became interested in the topic of intercultural communication more than thirty years ago. We sincerely believe that the ability to communicate effectively with people from diverse cultures and co-cultures benefits each of us as individuals and has potential to benefit the more than 6 billion people with whom we share this planet. We have intentionally selected materials that will assist you in understanding those intercultural communication principles that are instrumental to your success when you interact with people from diverse cultures.

Fundamental to our approach is the conviction that communication is a social activity; it is something people do to and with one another. The activity might begin in our heads, but it is manifested in our behaviors, be they verbal or nonverbal. In both explicit and implicit ways, the information and the advice contained in this book is usable; the ideas presented can be translated into action.

USE

As in the past, we intend this anthology to be for the general reader, so we have selected materials that are broadly based, comprehensive, and suitable for both undergraduate and graduate students. Although the level of difficulty varies from essay to essay, we have not gone beyond the level found in most textbooks directed toward college and university students.

Intercultural Communication: A Reader is designed to meet three specific needs. The first comes from a canon that maintains that successful intercultural communication is a matter of highest importance if humankind and society are to survive. Events during the last thirty years have created a world that sees us linked together in a multitude of ways. From pollution to economics to health care, what happens to one culture potentially happens to all other cultures. This book, then, is designed to serve as a basic anthology for courses concerned with the issues associated with human interaction. Our intention is to make this book theoretical and practical so that the issues associated with intercultural communication can be first understood and then acted upon.

Second, the book may be used as a supplemental text to existing service and basic communication skill courses and interpersonal communication courses. The rationale is a simple one: Understanding other cultures is indispensable in this age of cross-cultural contact. It matters very little if that contact is face-to-face or on the public platform.

Third, the book provides resource material for courses in communication theory, small group communication, organizational and business communication, and mass communication, as well as for courses in anthropology, sociology, social psychology, social welfare, social policy, business, and international relations. The long list of possible uses only underscores the increased level of intercultural interaction that is characteristic of what is often now called the "global village."

ORGANIZATION

The book is organized into four closely related parts. In Part One, "Intercultural Communication: An Introduction," our purpose is twofold: We hope to acquaint you with the basic concepts of intercultural communication while at the same time arousing your interest in the topic. Hence, the essays in this part are both theoretical and philosophical. The selections explain what intercultural communication is and why it is important.

Part Two, "Sociocultural Backgrounds: What We Bring to Intercultural Communication," has two chapters that both serve the same goal: They seek to examine the influence of sociocultural forces on human interaction. Chapter 2 deals with how these forces direct the communication patterns of people from international cultures. To make this point, we have selected cultures from East Asia, India, Africa, Egypt, and Greece. Although many cultures have been left out, you will still be able to gain an appreciation of the link between culture and behavior.

Chapter 3 moves us from the international arena to co-cultures that operate within the United States. Here again space constraints have limited the total number of co-cultures we could include. Yet we believe that by having selected groups such as Latinos, African Americans, Asian Americans, Filipino Americans, the disabled, gays and lesbians, women, the deaf, and the elderly, you will get an image of the cultural diversity found in those groups with whom most of you come into contact on a regular basis. Many of these co-cultures, as well as others, are so important to the study of intercultural communication that we return to them in later chapters.

In Part Three, "Intercultural Interaction: Taking Part in Intercultural Communication," our analysis focuses on the verbal and nonverbal symbols used in intercultural communication as well as their contexts. In Chapter 4, we offer readings that will introduce you to some of the difficulties you might encounter when your intercultural partner uses a different language system. We will look at how these verbal idiosyncrasies and distinctions influence problem solving, speaking, perception, translation, interpreting, and understanding.

Chapter 5 is also concerned with symbols and explains some of the ways in which cultural diversity in nonverbal messages can influence the entire transaction. Differences in movement, facial expressions, eye contact, silence, space, time, and the like are detailed so that you might have a better appreciation of how culture and communication work in tandem.

Chapter 6 continues with the theme of how culture modifies interaction. This time, however, the interaction is examined in a specific context. The assumption is that culturally diverse rules influence how members of a culture behave in certain settings. To clarify this important issue, we have selected "places" where cultures often follow rules that differ from those found in North America. More specifically, we look at settings related to business, groups, negotiations, counseling, health care, and education.

Part Four, "Intercultural Communication: Seeking Improvement," contains two chapters that are concerned with improving intercultural communication. The readings offered in Chapter 7 are intended to provide you with knowledge about and suggestions for improving intercultural communication. Each essay presents practical recommendations.

The eighth and final chapter probes the ethical and future dimensions of intercultural communication. Essays that deal with moral issues and the future directions and challenges of intercultural communication are at the center of this chapter. Its the intent of this chapter to ask you not to conclude your study of intercultural communication with the reading of a single book or the completion of one course. We believe that the study of intercultural communication is a lifetime endeavor. Each time we want to share an idea or feeling with someone from another culture, we face a new and exhilarating learning experience. We urge everyone to seek out as many of these experiences as possible. A philosopher once wrote, "Tomorrow, when I know more, I'll recall that piece of knowledge and use it better."

ASSISTANCE

As in the past, many people have helped us rethink and reshape this project. We express appreciation to our editors Megan Gilbert and Deidre Cavanaugh, and, of course, to Rebecca Hayden, who had enough courage and insight some thirty years ago to decide that intercultural communication should and would become a viable discipline. All of these editors were stern enough to keep us in check while at the same time allowing us the flexibility to move in new directions.

In a culture that values change, this collection would not have survived for more than thirty years if we had not been fortunate enough to have so many scholars willing to contribute original essays to each edition. Here, in the ninth edition, we acknowledge the work of June Ock Yum, Nemi C. Jain, Judith N. Martin, Ellen D. Kussman, Polly A. Begley, Lisa Skow, Edith A. Folb, Dawn O. Braithwaite, Charles A. Braithwaite, Julia T. Wood, Valerie C. McKay, Shelly M. Zormeier, Mary Fong, Edwin R. McDaniel, I-Li Chao, Mitsuo Nagano, Beverly Solidon, Lucila Luna, Natalie J. Dollar, Peter Andersen, Brian H. Spitzberg, Young Yun Kim, David W. Kale, Mary Jane Collier, Aaron C. Cargile, Guo-Ming Chen, Steve Quasha, Stella Ting-Toomey, Sidney Ribeau, Sheryl Lindsley, William J. Starosta, Mohan R. Limaye, Robert Shuter, John Baldwin, Michael Hecht, Patricia Geist, Tom Bruneau, and Wen-Shu Lee. We thank all of you for letting us expose your work to thousands of other people who share your commitment to intercultural matters.

For their helpful comments and suggestions on the revision of this and earlier editions of the text, a sincere thanks go to Mark Borzi, Eastern Illinois University; Aaron Cargile, California State University, Long Beach; Hui-Ching Chang, University of Illinois at Chicago; Ling Chen, University of Oklahoma; Ni Chen, University of Maryland; Christine Colin, Carthage College; Robbin Crabtree, New Mexico State University; Randy K. Dillon, Southwest Missouri State University; Bruce Dorries, Winona State University; Joel Franks, De Anza College; Janie Fritz, Duquesne University; Bob Grant, Carthage College; Alan C. Harris, California State University, Northridge; Greg Hinckley, Seattle Central Community College; Charlotte Krolokke, Humboldt State University; Lynn Loewen, Carthage College; Jillian Pierson, University of Southern California; Gregory J. Pulliam, Illinois Institute of Technology; Margarita F   ra, Carthage College; Judith A. Sanders, California State Polytechnic University, Pomona; Nancy Eliot Parker, Embry-Riddle Aeronautical University; Erica Vora, St. Cloud University; Jerry Winsor, Central Missouri State University; and Richard L. Wiseman, California State University, Fullerton.

Finally, we express our gratitude to the countless users of previous editions who have allowed us to "talk to them" about intercultural communication. Although it may have been a rather intangible connection, we have greatly appreciated it all the same.

Larry A. Samovar
Richard E. Porter

part 1

Intercultural Interaction: An Introduction

Every tale can be told in a different way.

GREEK PROVERB

Intercultural communication is not new. It has existed as long as people from different cultures have been encountering one another. However, during the last thirty years, people have begun a systematic study of exactly what happens in intercultural contacts when the communication process involves culturally diverse people. That is to say, both here and abroad, people have accepted that cultural diversity is a fact of life. They now want to know how that diversity is reflected when people come together.

Perhaps the initial impetus for the study of intercultural communication was the knowledge that technology has produced the means of our own self-destruction. Historically, intercultural communication, more often than not, has employed a rhetoric of force rather than reason. But with the agents of change sweeping the world, perhaps we are now seeking forms of communication other than traditional force. The reason for this new study is also pragmatic. Our mobility, increased contact among cultures, a global marketplace, and the emergence of multicultural organizations and workforces require that we develop communication skills and abilities that are appropriate to a multicultural society and to life in a global village.

Traditionally, intercultural communication took place only among an extremely small proportion of the world's populace. Ministers of state and government, certain merchants, missionaries, explorers, and a few tourists were primarily the travelers and visitors to foreign lands. Until rather recently, we Americans had little contact with other cultures, even within our own country. Members of nonwhite races were segregated. Only in recent years have laws changed to foster integrated schools, workforces, and, to some extent, neighborhoods. In addition, those who made up the vast, white, middle Euro-America remained at home, rarely leaving their own county. This situation, of course, has changed markedly; we are now a mobile society among ever-increasing mobile societies.

This increased contact with other cultures and domestic co-cultures makes it imperative that we make a concerted effort to understand and get along with people who may be markedly different from us. The ability, through increased awareness and understanding, to coexist peacefully with people who do not necessarily share our backgrounds, views, beliefs, values, customs, habits, or lifestyles can benefit us in our own neighborhoods and also can be a decisive factor in forestalling international conflict.

Before we begin our inquiry, we must specify the nature of intercultural communication and recognize that people who hold various viewpoints see it somewhat differently. From what we have already said, you should suspect that the topic of intercultural communication can be explored in a variety of ways. Scholars who look at it from a mass media point of view are concerned with such issues as international broadcasting, worldwide freedom of expression, Western domination of information, and the use of modern electronic technologies for instantaneous worldwide transmission of information. Other groups investigate international communication with an emphasis on communication among nations and governments. It is the communication of diplomacy and propaganda. Still others are interested in the communication inherent in international business, which includes such diverse concerns as negotiations and communication within multicultural organizations.

Our concern is with the more personal aspects of communication: What happens when people from different cultures interact face-to-face? Hence, we identify our approach as one that examines the interpersonal dimensions of intercultural communication as it occurs in a variety of contexts. We have selected articles for this collection because they focus on those variables of both culture and communication that come into play during the communication encounter—that time when participants from different cultures are trying to share ideas, information, and feelings.

Inquiry into the nature of intercultural communication has raised many questions, but it has produced few theories and far fewer answers. Most of the inquiry has been associated with fields other than communication, primarily anthropology, international relations, social psychology, and socio- and psycholinguistics. Although the direction of research has been diverse, the knowledge has not been coordinated. Much that has emerged has been more a reaction to current sociological, racial, and ethnic concerns than an attempt to define and explain intercultural communication. But it is quite clear that knowledge of intercultural communication can help solve communication problems before they arise. School teachers who understand differences in motivation and learning styles might be better able to deal with their multicultural classrooms. Even something as simple as cultural differences in the use of eye contact might greatly improve the communication process. And perhaps those who realize that some people treat illness as a curse may be better able to deliver necessary health care. In essence, we are saying that many problems can be avoided by understanding the components of intercultural communication. This book, by applying those components to numerous cultures, seeks to contribute to that understanding.

chapter 1

Approaches to Understanding Intercultural Communication

This exploration of intercultural communication begins with a series of diverse articles that (1) introduce the philosophy underlying our concept of intercultural communication, (2) provide a general orientation and overview of intercultural communication, (3) theorize about the analysis of intercultural transactions, (4) provide insight into cultural differences, and (5) demonstrate the relationships between culture and perception. Our purpose at this point is to give you a sufficient introduction to the many wide and diverse dimensions of intercultural communication so that you will be able to approach the remainder of this volume with an appropriate frame of reference to make further inquiry interesting, informative, and useful.

We begin with an essay by the two editors of this book titled "Understanding Intercultural Communication: An Introduction and Overview." This piece attempts to introduce you to some of the specific subjects and issues associated with the study of intercultural communication. As a preface to the essay, we begin by reminding you of the importance of intercultural communication both at home and aboard. Next we discuss the purpose of culture, attempt to define it, and offer a review of the characteristics of culture. We then turn our attention to the specific areas of culture that are most germane to human communication—areas that form the field of intercultural communication. By examining these major variables (cultural values, worldview, social organizations, verbal and nonverbal language), you can better understand what happens when people of different cultures attempt to share feelings and ideas. By knowing at the outset of the book what the study of intercultural communication entails, you should have a greater appreciation for all the essays that follow.

Our second selection, by Mary Jane Collier, has the same goal as our first essay—to explain and clarify the major components of intercultural communication. As we indicated, we contend that the remainder of the book will be much more meaningful if you begin your study of intercultural communication by understanding and appreciating the basic concepts of both culture and communication. Collier seeks to contribute to that understanding by offering what she refers to as a "Ten Step Inventory." This original inventory takes the form of a series of questions. Collier answers each question by reviewing important literature in the field, illuminating the issues that must be considered by anyone attempting to study intercultural communication. In addition, Collier encourages you to take the information in her chapter and apply it to both current social problems and your own intercultural experiences.

Edward T. Hall, in "Context and Meaning," underscores the power of culture in how people perceive their surroundings, be they events or other people. He discusses the grand connection between culture and human communicative behavior by demonstrating how culture provides a highly selective screen between people and their outside worlds. This cultural filter effectively designates what people attend to as well as what they choose to ignore. This link between culture and behavior is further illustrated through Hall's discussion of high- and low-context communication; he shows how people from different cultural backgrounds learn to concentrate on certain aspects of their environment.

With the relationship between culture and communication firmly established by our first three essays, we turn to two readings that deal with the notion of ethnicity. In the first, Judith N. Martin discusses the topic of white ethnicity. In "Understanding Whiteness in the United States," she answers the question of what it means to be a white person in the United States. She provides an insight into how ethnic identities—including that of a white European American—are negotiated, co-created, reinforced, and challenged through communication. By making comparisons to other ethnic co-culture identities, Martin is able to reveal the distinctness of the white ethnic identity to better help us understand both the notion and uniqueness of ethnic identity.

In the second article about identity, Rod Janzen provides us with a viewpoint that suggests that we might conceptualize ethnic relations and ethnic identity in the United States in several different ways. In "Five Paradigms of Ethnic Relations," he traces the history of ethnic identity in the United States and provides us with a set of five possible ways of conceptualizing ethnicity as our society moves into the twenty-first century. His development of the five paradigms, or categories, of ethnicity is based upon the elements of language, religion, culture, race, and political tradition.

Understanding Intercultural Communication: An Introduction and Overview

LARRY A. SAMOVAR

RICHARD E. PORTER

Human beings draw close to one another by their common nature, but habits and customs keep them apart.

CONFUCIUS

THE IMPORTANCE OF INTERCULTURAL COMMUNICATION

The need for intercultural communication, as you might suspect is as old as human kind. From wandering tribes to traveling traders and religious missionaries, people have encountered others different from themselves. These earlier meetings, like those of today, were frequently confusing and quite often hostile. The recognition of alien differences, and the human propensity to respond malevolently to them, was expressed more than two thousand years ago by the Greek playwright Aeschylus, who wrote, "Everyone's quick to blame the alien." This sentiment is still a powerful element in today's social and political rhetoric. For instance, it is not uncommon in today's society to hear people say that most, if not all, of the social and economic problems of the United States are caused by minorities and immigrants.

Although intercultural contact has a long history, today's intercultural encounters are far more numerous and of greater importance than in any previous time in human history. So you might appreciate the

significance of the study of intercultural communication, we will pause for a moment and briefly highlight the widespread nature of cultural interaction.

New technology, in the form of transportation and communication systems, has accelerated intercultural contact. Trips once taking days, weeks, or even months are now measured in hours. Supersonic transports now make it possible for tourists, business executives, or government officials to enjoy breakfast in San Francisco and dinner in Paris—all on the same day.

Innovative communication systems have also encouraged and facilitated cultural interaction. Communication satellites, sophisticated television transmission equipment, and digital switching networks now allow people throughout the world to share information and ideas at the same time. Whether it be via the Internet, the World Wide Web, or a CNN news broadcast, electronic devices have increased cultural contact. For example, the world now has 1.2 billion television sets, which allows people, regardless of their location, to perceive the same image and message (Higgins, 1995, p. 6). As *U.S. News & World Report* noted, "Television's impact on the world community cannot be overstated" (1996, p. 48).

Globalization of the economy has further brought people together. At the conclusion of World War II, the United States emerged as the only military and economic superpower. Most of the rest of the world's economy was in disarray. Because industry in the United States was not damaged during World War II, it was the dominant economic force in the world. However, this preeminence in business is not the case as we enter the twenty-first century. For example, according to Harris and Moran (1996), there are now "more than 37,000 transnational corporations with 207,000 foreign affiliates" (p. 18). This expansion in globalization has resulted in multinational corporations participating in various international business arrangements such as joint ventures and licensing agreements. These, and countless other economic ties, mean that it would not be unusual for someone to work for an organization that does business in many countries.

Changes in immigration patterns have also contributed to the development of expanded intercultural contact. Within the boundaries of the United States, people are now redefining and rethinking the meaning of the word *American*. Neither the word nor the reality can any longer be used to describe a somewhat homogeneous group of people sharing a European heritage. We have now become, as the author Ben J. Wattenberg (1989) tells us, "the first universal nation, a truly multi-cultural society marked by unparalleled diversity" (p. 31).

The last few paragraphs have told us that, with or without our desire or consent, we are now thrust into contact with countless people who often appear alien, exotic, and perhaps even wondrous. Whether we are negotiating a major contract with the Chinese, discussing a joint venture with a German company, being supervised by someone from Mexico, counseling a young student from Cambodia, or working alongside someone who speaks no English, we encounter people with cultural backgrounds that are often strikingly different from our own. Understanding these backgrounds is essential if we want to be successful in both our social and professional lives.

COMMUNICATION AND CULTURE

Concern about cultural diversity has given rise to the marriage of culture and communication and to the recognition of intercultural communication as a unique field of study. Inherent in this fusion is the idea that intercultural communication entails the investigation of those elements of culture that most influence interaction when members of two or more cultures come together in an interpersonal setting. To better understand that influence we will first examine the essential elements of culture and then explain how these elements modify the communication process.

UNDERSTANDING CULTURE

People in Paris eat snails, but people in San Diego put poison on them. Why? People in Iran sit on the floor and pray five times each day, but people in Las Vegas stand up all night in front of slot machines. Why? Some people speak Tagalog, others speak English. Why? Some people paint and decorate their entire bodies, but others spend millions of dollars painting and decorating only their faces. Why? Some people talk to God, but others have God talk to them. Why?

The general answer to all these questions is the same. It is our culture that supplies us with the answers to these and countless other questions about what the world looks like and how we live and communicate within that world. From the instant of birth, a child is formally and informally taught how to behave. This omnipresent and commanding power of culture leads Hall (1977) to conclude that "there is not one aspect of human life that is not touched and altered by culture" (p. 14). In many ways Hall is correct: Culture is everything and everywhere. And, more important, at least for the purposes of this book, culture and communication work in tandem—they are inseparable. In fact, it is often difficult to decide which is the voice and which is the echo.

Culture helps govern and define the conditions and circumstances under which various messages may or may not be sent, noticed, or interpreted. Our entire repertory of communicative behaviors depends largely on the culture in which we have been raised. Remember, we are not born knowing how to dress, what toys to play with, what to eat, which gods to worship, or how to spend our money and our time. Culture is both teacher and textbook. From how much eye contact we make to explanations of why we get sick, culture plays a dominant role in our lives. It is the foundation of communication; and when cultures are diverse, communication practices may be different. This important point is clearly illustrated by Smith (1966), who wrote:

> In modern society different people communicate in different ways, as do people in different societies around the world; and the way people communicate is the way they live. It is their culture. Who talks with whom? How? And about what? these are questions of communication and culture. A Japanese geisha and a New England librarian send and receive different messages on different channels and in different networks. When the elements of communication differ or change, the elements of culture differ or change. Communication and culture are inseparable. (p. 1)

The Basic Function of Culture

The anthropologist Haviland (1993) suggests that "[p]eople maintain cultures to deal with problems or matters that concern them" (p. 29). It is believed that our ancestors created cultures for the same reasons. Both then and now, culture serves the basic need of laying out a predictable world in which an individual is firmly oriented. Culture enables us to make sense of our surroundings. As the English writer Thomas Fuller wrote two hundred years ago, "Culture makes all things easy." Although this view might be slightly overstated, culture does ease the transition from the womb to this new life by giving meaning to events, objects, and people in the environment. In this way culture makes the world a less frightening and mysterious place.

A Definition of Culture

It should be clear to this point that culture is ubiquitous, multidimensional, complex, and all-pervasive. Because culture is so broad, there is no single definition or central theory of what it is. Definitions range from the all-encompassing ("it is everything") to the narrow ("it is opera, art, and ballet"). For our purposes we shall define culture as the deposit of knowledge, experience, beliefs, values, attitudes, meanings, social hierarchies, religion, notions of time, roles, spatial relationships, concepts of the universe, and material objects and possessions acquired by a group of people in the course of generations through individual and group striving.

Characteristics of Culture

Regardless of the definition employed, there is general agreement about the major characteristics of culture. Examining these universal characteristics will help us understand this nebulous concept called culture, and also enable us to see how these characteristics influence communication.

Culture Is Not Innate; It Is Learned. We begin with the single most important characteristic of culture, and the one that is hardest to explain. It is the most important because it goes to the heart of what is called culture.

Without the advantages of learning from those who lived before us, we would not have culture. Therefore, you can appreciate why we said that learning was the most important of all the characteristics of culture. Babies cut off from all adult care,

training, and supervision would instinctively eat, drink, defecate, urinate, gurgle, and cry. But what they would eat, when they would eat, where they would defecate, and the like would be random. What we are saying is that all of us are born with basic needs—needs that create behavior. But how we go about meeting those needs and developing other coping behaviors are a matter of learning. As Bates and Plog (1990) note:

> Whether we feed ourselves by growing yams or hunting wild game or by herding camels and raising wheat, whether we explain a thunderstorm by attributing it to meteorological conditions or to a fight among the gods—such things are determined by what we learn as part of our enculturation. (p. 19)

Enculturation usually takes place through interaction (your parents kiss you and you learn about kissing—whom to kiss, when to kiss, and so on), observation (you watch your father do most of the driving of the family car and you learn about sex roles—what a man does, what a woman does), and imitation (you laugh at the same jokes your parents laugh at and you learn about humor—it is funny if someone slips and falls but doesn't get hurt).

Most of us would have a difficult time pointing to a specific event or experience that taught us about such things as direct eye contact, our use of silence and space, the concept and importance of attractiveness, our view of aging and the elderly, our ability to speak one language over another, our preference for activity over meditation, or why we prefer one mode of dealing with conflict over another. All of our examples show us that learning the perceptions, rules, and behaviors of cultural membership usually go on without our being aware of it.

One thing that should be clear to this point is the idea that we learn our culture in a host of ways. As many of our examples have noted, most of what we learn is communicated through our interactions with other people. Early in life we receive normative instructions from family and friends. There are, however, numerous other "teachers" that pass on the messages of culture. Let us pause a moment and look at just a few of these "instructors" and the "instructions" they offer.

A very powerful set of instructions comes from **proverbs.** Proverbs are found in nearly every culture.

Often called *maxims* or *adages*, these sayings create vivid images that are easy to learn and difficult to forget. They are repeated with such regularity as we grow up they soon become part of our belief system. Let us look at a few proverbs from various cultures and note how the specific proverbs are linked to a cultural value or belief.

"One does not make the wind blow but is blown by it." This Asian view implies that people are guided by fate rather than by their own devices.

"Order is half of life." This is a German view that stresses the value of organization, conformity, and structure.

"The mouth maintains silence in order to hear the heart talk." This Belgian saying implies the value of intuition and feelings in interaction.

"He who speaks has no knowledge and he who has knowledge does not speak." This saying from Japan demonstrates the value of silence.

"How blessed is a man who finds wisdom." This Jewish expression states the importance of learning and education.

"A zebra does not despise its stripes." From the Maasai of Africa, this saying expresses the value of accepting things as they are, of accepting oneself as one is, and of avoiding the envy of others.

"Loud thunder brings little rain." This Chinese proverb teaches the importance of being reserved instead of being boisterous.

"A man's tongue is his sword." Arabs are taught to enjoy words and use them in a powerful and forceful manner.

"A single arrow is easily broken, but not in a bunch." This proverb is found in many Asian cultures as a means of stressing the group over the individual.

"He who stirs another's porridge often burns his own." The Swedish are a very private people, and attempt to teach this value through the preceding proverb.

"The duck that quacks is the first to get shot." The Japanese proverb stresses the importance of silence.

We also learn our culture from **folk tales** and **folklore.** Whether it be ancient myths of our culture or current popular culture, folklore is value-laden and teaches and reinforces what a culture deems important. The story might be about the tough, independent, fast-shooting cowboy of the Old West or how Pinocchio's nose grew larger when he lied. Whether it be glorifying Columbus because he was daring, Abraham Lincoln learning to read by drawing letters on a shovel by the fireside, or the Saturday morning cartoon characters defending democracy and fighting for what is "right," folklore constantly reinforces our fundamental values.

We are not the only culture that "teaches" important values through folk tales. The English have their *Canterbury Tales*, which stress proper manners, courtly behavior, and dignity. The Japanese know the ancient story called *The Tale of the Forty-Seven Ronin*, which teaches them the importance of duty, obligation, and loyalty. And for the Sioux Indians, the legend of "Pushing Up the Sky" teaches what people can accomplish if they work together.

People learn about their culture even from sources as subtle as **art.** The anthropologist Nanda (1994) points out the link between art and culture when she writes: "One of the most important functions of art is to communicate, display, and reinforce important cultural themes and values" (p. 403). In Asian cultures most art depicts objects, animals, and landscapes. It seldom focuses on people. American and European art, however, emphasizes people. These differences reflect the Asian view that nature is more powerful and important than a single individual, and the American and European views that people are the center of the world.

As we conclude this section on learning, remember that large numbers of people, usually living in the same geographic area, share the experience and behaviors we have been discussing. It is this sharing that makes a culture unique. Polish poet Stanislaw said it far more eloquently when he reminded us that because of culture, "All of our separate fictions add up to a joint reality."

Culture Is Transmitted from Generation to Generation. The American philosopher Thoreau once wrote, "All the past is here." He, of course, could have been talking about culture. For cultures to exist, endure, and perpetuate, they must make sure the crucial "messages" and elements of the culture get passed on. According to Brislin (1993), "If there are values considered central to a society that have existed for many years, these must be transmitted from one generation to another" (p. 6). This characteristic adds credence to the idea that culture and communication are linked. It is communication that makes culture a continuous process. For once cultural habits, principles, values, dispositions, and the like are "invented," they are communicated to each individual within that culture. The strong need for a culture to tie each generation to past and future generations is demonstrated by Keesing (1965), who tells us, "Any break in the learning chain would lead to a culture's disappearance" (p. 28).

Culture Is Based on Symbols. The first two characteristics—that culture is learned and passed from generation to generation—leads us directly to the next idea that it is our symbol-making ability that enables us to both learn and pass on our culture from individual to individual, group to group, and generation to generation. Through language, be it verbal, nonverbal, images or icons, it is "possible to learn from cumulative, shared experience" (Smith, 1986, pp. 1–2). An excellent summary of the importance of language to culture is offered by Bates and Plog (1990):

> Language thus enables people to communicate what they would do if such-and-such happened, to organize their experiences into abstract categories ("a happy occasion," for instance, or an "evil omen"), and to express thoughts never spoken before. Morality, religion, philosophy, literature, science, economics, technology, and numerous other areas of human knowledge and belief—along with the ability to learn about and manipulate them—all depends on this type of higher-level communication. (p. 20)

The portability of symbols allows us to package and store them as well as transmit them. The mind, books, pictures, films, videos, computer disks, and the like enable a culture to preserve what it deems to be important and worthy of transmission. Hence, each individual, regardless of his or her generation, is heir to a massive "library" of information that has been collected in anticipation of his or her entry into the culture. In this sense, culture is historical as well as preservable. Each new generation might "write" more, but the notes from the past represent what we call culture. As the French novelist Proust wrote, "The past remains the present."

Culture Is Subject to Change. Cultures are a dynamic system that do not exist in a vacuum, and therefore are subject to change. From the wandering nomad thousands of years ago, to CNN's news in the 1990s, cultures are constantly being confronted with ideas and information for "outside" sources. This contact has the potential to bring change to any culture. This characteristic of change through contact is yet another example of how communication and culture are alike—both are dynamic, and both are constantly changing.

We must make two points about cultural change. First, cultures are highly adaptive. History runs over with examples of how cultures have been forced to alter their course because of natural disasters, wars, or other calamities. Events in the last few hundred years have scattered Jews throughout the world, yet their culture has adapted and survived. And think for a moment about the adjustments made by the Japanese since the end of World War II. Their government and economy were nearly destroyed during the war, yet because they could adapt, their culture endured. They are now a major economic force in the world.

Second, we would be remiss if we did not once again remind you that although many aspects of culture are subject to change, the deep structure of a culture resists major alterations. That is to say, changes in dress, food, transportation, housing, and the like, though appearing to be important, are simply attached to the existing value system. However, values associated with such things as ethics and morals, work and leisure, definitions of freedom, the importance of the past, religious practices, the pace of life, and attitudes toward gender and age are so deep in a culture that they persist generation after generation. Barnlund (1989) clearly makes this point when he writes: "The spread of Buddhism, Islam, Christianity, and Confucianism did not homogenize the societies they enveloped. It was usually the other way around: Societies insisted on adapting the religions to their own cultural traditions" (p. 192).

Culture Is Ethnocentric. The disposition toward ethnocentrism might well be the characteristic that most directly relates to intercultural communication. The important tie between ethnocentrism and communication can be seen in the definition of the term itself. Sumner (1940) is generally credited with the introduction of the term to the study of group relations and culture. He defined ethnocentrism as "the technical name for the view of things in which one's own group is the center of everything, and all others are scaled and rated with reference to it" (p. 13). In other words, ethnocentrism becomes the perceptual prism through which cultures interpret and judge all other groups. The power and impact of ethnocentrism is clearly noted by Keesing (1965): "Nearly always the folklore of a people includes myths of origin which give priority to themselves, and place the stamp of supernatural approval upon their particular customs" (p. 45). These priorities and judgments include everything from what the "out-groups" value to how they communicate. Feelings that "we are right" and "they are wrong" cover every aspect of a culture's existence. Examples range from the insignificant ("People should paint their bodies, not only their faces"), to the significant ("We must fight and die for what is right").

Our discussion thus far should not lead to the conclusion that ethnocentrism is always intentional, for it usually is not. Like culture itself, ethnocentrism is mostly learned at the unconscious level. If, for example, our schools are teaching U.S. history, geography, literature, and government, they are also, without realizing it, teaching ethnocentrism. The student, by being exposed only to this single orientation, is therefore developing the view that the United States is the center of the world, as well as learning to judge that world by North American standards—the standards he or she has been taught. If most of the authors, philosophers, scientists, composers, and political leaders you have studied are white males, then you will use the values of white males to judge other cultures. The omission of African Americans and women from most textbooks is, in a very real sense, teaching ethnocentrism.

THE ELEMENTS OF INTERCULTURAL COMMUNICATION

Culture, as we have presented the concept, is a complete pattern of living. It is elaborate, abstract, and pervasive. Countless aspects of culture help determine and guide communication behavior. Three cultural elements have the potential to affect situations in which people from different backgrounds come together: (1) perception, (2) verbal processes, and (3) nonverbal processes.

Perceptual Elements

The German novelist Hermann Hesse wrote, "There is no reality except the one contained with us." This essay has been about the manner in which our cultures help create and shape our realities. In its simplest sense, *perception* "is the process by which an individual selects, evaluates, and organizes stimuli from the external world" (Singer, 1987, p. 9). In other words, perception is an internal process whereby we convert the physical energies of the world outside of us into meaningful internal experiences. Because that world embraces everything, we can never completely know it. As Singer (1987) notes, "We experience everything in the world not as it is—but only as the world comes to us through our sensory receptors" (p. 9).

Much of what is called perception has its roots in our biology: The act of bringing the outside world to our consciousness involves a great deal of our nervous system and its complex chemistry and anatomy. Although these aspects of perception are important, for our purposes the evaluation and action dimension of perception is more pertinent. That is to say, the world looks, sounds, tastes, and feels the way it does because our culture has given us the criterion of perception.

Most communication scholars, while granting that perceptions are part of every communication event, have evolved a fairly consistent taxonomy for isolating those perceptual variables that have the potential to impede seriously the intercultural encounter. The three major sociocultural elements that directly influence perception and communication are (1) cultural values, (2) worldview (religion), and (3) social organizations (family and state).

Values. Formally, a **value** may be defined as an enduring belief that a specific mode of conduct or end-state of existence is personally or socially preferable to another (Rokeach, 1968, p. 5). They "represent a learned organization of rules for making choices and for resolving conflicts." (Rokeach, 1968, p. 161). Although each of us has a unique set of values, there also are values that tend to permeate a culture. These are called *cultural values*.

Cultural values usually are derived from the larger philosophical issues that are part of a culture's milieu. Hence, they tend to be broad-based, enduring, and relatively stable. Values generally are normative in that they inform a member of a culture about what is good and bad, right and wrong, true and false, positive and negative, and the like. Cultural values define what is worth dying for, what is worth protecting, what frightens people, what are proper subjects for study and for ridicule, and what types of events lead individuals to group solidarity. Most important, cultural values guide both perception and behavior.

As we have already indicated, values are learned; they are not universal. In many Native American cultures, where there is no written history, age is highly valued. Older people are sought out and asked to take part in many important decisions. Younger people admire them and include them in social gatherings.

Cultural values, as you would suspect, go well beyond the perception and treatment of the elderly. There are literally thousands of values found in every culture. However, most scholars agree that the cultural values that most directly influence intercultural communication relate to *individualism, family, religion, materialism, human nature, science and technology, progress and change, competition, work and leisure, equality, gender roles, nature and the environment, time, formality and informality, talk, silence, assertiveness,* and *interpersonal harmony.*

Before we move from values to worldview and social organization, it might be helpful if we pause and indicate why the institutions associated with these two elements hold such a powerful sway over the members of a particular culture.

First, the institutions of church, family, and state *carry the messages that matter most to people.* They explain to us what we should strive for (material possessions or a spiritual life), where we fit into the grand scheme of things (a belief in fate or the power of free choice), and what to expect from life (life will be easy or life will be difficult).

Second, these institutions are important because they *endure.* From the early Cro-Magnon cave drawings in southern France to the present, we can trace the strong pull of religion, family, and community.

Generation after generation is told about Moses, the Buddha, Allah, and the like. Whether it be the Eight-Fold Path, the Ten Commandments, or the Five Pillars of Islam, the messages in these writings survive. And just as Americans know about the values contained in the story of the Revolutionary War, so Mexicans are aware of the consequences of the Treaty of Guadalupe Hidalgo.

Third, *the content generated by these institutions is deeply and emotionally felt.* Think for a moment about the violent reactions that can be produced by "taking God's name in vain," calling someone's mother a "dirty name," or by setting a match to the American flag. Countries have been able to send young men to war and politicians have attempted to win elections by arousing people to the importance of "God, country, and family."

Finally, the deep structure of a culture is important because the institutions of family, church, and state *give each individual his or her unique identity.* When you think about who you are, you most likely conclude that you are a member of a family (my name is Jane Smith or Yuko Minami), that you have a religious orientation (I am a Mormon or Buddhist), and that you live in a special place (I live in the United States or I live in Japan). Regardless of their culture, all individuals perceive themselves as members of these organizations.

Worldview.   Each group of people from the earliest origins of civilization has evolved a worldview. A *worldview* is a culture's orientation toward such things as God, nature, life, death, the universe, and other philosophical issues that are concerned with the meaning of life and with "being." The link between worldview, culture, and communication is clearly stated by Pennington (1985) when she noted, "If one understands a culture's world view and cosmology, reasonable accuracy can be attained in predicting behaviors and motivations in other dimensions" (p. 32). In short, our worldview helps us locate our place and rank in the universe. Perhaps more than any other factor, it influences issues ranging from how we view other people to how we spend our time. Olayiwola (1989) argues that worldview even influences the social, economic, and political life of a nation (pp. 19–26). Reflect for just a moment on how your concepts of death, illness, and the environment often direct the choices you make and the goals you seek. The point with regard to intercultural communication should be clear: Diverse concepts produce different choices and behaviors.

As you can observe, the issues associated with worldview are timeless and represent the most fundamental basis of a culture. A Hindu, with a strong belief in reincarnation, will not only perceive time differently than a Christian, but also will have different answers to the major questions of life than will a Catholic, a Muslim, a Jew, a Taoist, or an atheist.

Worldview influences a culture at a very deep and profound level. Its effects often are quite subtle and do not reveal themselves in obvious ways. It might be helpful to think of a culture's worldview as analogous to a pebble being tossed into a pond. Just as the pebble causes ripples to spread and reverberate over the entire surface of the pond, worldview spreads itself over a culture and permeates every facet of it.

Social Organizations. The manner in which a culture organizes itself is directly related to the institutions within that culture. These institutions take a variety of configurations and can be formal or informal. The families who raise us and the governments that we associate with and hold allegiance to all help determine how we perceive the world and how we behave within that world. Let us briefly look at the institutions of family and state and see their place in any study of intercultural communication.

American author William Thayer once wrote, "As are families, so is society." His words clearly express the importance of family to both culture and each individual. The family is among the oldest and most fundamental of all human institutions. As Galvin and Brommel (1991) point out, "We are born into a family, mature in a family, form new families, and leave them at death" (p. 1). It is the family that helps the culture "teach" the child what the world looks like and his or her place in that world. Remember, it is the family that greets us in this new world once we leave the comfort of the womb. It is the family that is charged with transforming a biological organism into a human being who must spend the rest of his or her life around other human beings—human beings who expect the individual to act much like all of the other people in that culture.

The family is also important because by the time the other major cultural institutions can influence the child, the family has already exposed the individual to countless experiences. From our introduction to language to our ways of expressing love, the family is the first teacher. Just think for a moment of some of the crucial attitudes, values, and behaviors that the family first initiates. Any list would have to include self-reliance, responsibility, obedience, dominance, social skills, aggression, loyalty, sex roles, age roles, and the like. Keep in mind that at the moment of birth, a human being's development can take any number of paths. A child born in India perceives many people living together in one house and is learning about extended families. By being in the same house with elderly people, the child is also learning to value the aged. In most of Africa the entire village raises a child, and the child thus learns about the extended family.

A simple Swedish proverb and a well-known one from the United States offers us an excellent summary of the link between family and how we communicate with other people: "Children act in the village as they have learned at home," and "The apple does not fall far from the tree."

When we speak of formal and informal government as a social organization, we are talking about much more than a culture's political system. The Cuban brand of communism or the autocratic governments in some Arab countries, of course, produces a different individual than does North American or Norwegian democracy. And China's long continuous history as a country and culture will have a profound influence on the character of people raised in this country. Hence, the term *government*, as it is used in this context, also refers to one's community as well as the history of that community. The importance of government, state, or community is clearly marked by the words of historian Theodore Gochenour, who wrote, "The cultural traits of people are rooted in the history which has molded them." This observation could also serve as a definition of culture.

The history of any culture serves as the origin of the cultural values, ideals, and behaviors. History can help answer such questions as why one type of activity evolved over another. The value Mexicans place on "talk," for example, goes back in part to the socializing that was part of the marketplace during the Aztec period.

We can find countless instances of how the history of a culture determines its view of the world. For example, to comprehend the modern-day Jew, and his or her way of perceiving events and people, you would have to realize what the historian Van Doren (1991) attempted to point out when he wrote, "The history of Judaism and the Jews is a long and complicated story, full of blood and tears" (p. 16). Because of this long history of discrimination and persecution, when Jews make fundamental choices about education, freedom, war, civil rights, and the like, they rely on their history.

Japan is yet another country that vividly reflects the links between history, culture, and behavior. Because it is a series of islands, Japan has a history and character not only molded by isolation but also strongly influenced by an almost constant seismic activity and its consequences. According to Reischauer (1988), this isolation and separation "has produced in the Japanese a strong sense of self-identity and also an almost painful self-consciousness in the presence of others" (p. 32). Reischauer (1991) continues: "[I]solation has caused the Japanese to be acutely aware of anything that comes from outside" (p. 32).

As we conclude this section on the impact of history, we again remind you that thousands of examples can be found of the tandem relationships between history, worldview, and family. We have offered a handful of those as a means of demonstrating that by knowing the deep structure of culture you can better understand how that structure influences perception and communication. And we submit that the most compelling problem associated with intercultural communication is cultural diversity in perceptual processes.

Verbal Language

The importance of language to the study of intercultural communication is clearly captured in Ralph Waldo Emerson's simple sentence, "Language is the archives of history." What Emerson is telling us is that it is impossible to separate our use of language from our culture for language is not only a form of preserving culture, but also a means of sharing culture. In its most basic sense, language is an organized, generally agreed-upon, learned symbol system that is used to represent the experiences within a geographic or cultural community.

Culture teaches us both the symbol (dog) and what the symbol stands for (a furry, domesticated pet). Objects, events, experiences, and feelings have particular labels or names solely because a community of people (a culture) has arbitrarily decided to so name them.

If we extend the above notion to the intercultural setting, we can observe how different cultures can have both different symbols and different responses. Culture even influences the unadorned word *dog* we used in the last paragraph. In some areas of the world, such as Hong Kong and Korea, dogs are considered a culinary delight and often are eaten. In the United States, dogs sit on the family couch and are not cooked; hence, the word *dog* conveys a quite different meaning in the United States than it does in Hong Kong. If you take our superficial example and then apply it to every word and meaning you know, then you can begin to visualize the influence of culture on how we send and receive messages. Think for just a moment about the variety of meanings various cultures have for words such as *freedom, sexuality, trespassing, birth control, social security, leadership, assertiveness, affirmative action,* and *AIDS.*

Even the way people use language shifts from culture to culture. In the Arab tradition, "verbal language patterns that emphasize creative artistry by using rhetorical devices such as repetition, metaphor, and simile are highly valued" (Lustig, 1988, p. 102). Yet Japanese culture encourages minimum verbal communication. A Japanese proverb gives credence to this outlook by offering this advice: "By your mouth you shall perish." By multiplying this example across the countless cultures you may come into contact with, you can see how differences in language reflect differences in culture.

People living within the same geographic boundaries can also use language in ways that differ from the dominant culture. We should all be aware of the rich examples that can be drawn from African American communication. And most women, because they are raised to be polite and to focus on the other person, use language in a unique manner. They will ask more questions than men and consciously or unconsciously let men control the flow of conversation.

Nonverbal Language

As we have indicated, the ability to use words to represent feelings and ideas is universal. All human beings also use nonverbal symbols to share internal states. Although the process of using our actions to communicate is universal, the meanings for those actions often shift from culture to culture. Hence, nonverbal communication becomes yet another element that one must understand to interact effectively with people from different cultures.

We will briefly introduce you to three important nonverbal categories (bodily behavior, time, and space) that are reflected during intercultural interaction. We remind you before we begin, however, that we do not intend to expose you to the literally thousands of nonverbal behaviors found in nearly every culture, but rather, with just few simple examples, make you aware of the role of nonverbal message in the study of intercultural communication.

Bodily Behavior. Most scholars agree that other people can attach meaning to our movement (kinesics), facial expressions, eye contact and gaze, touch, concepts of time, and space. Let us briefly offer one or two examples for each element.

Body Movements. When we speak of "body movements," we are talking about both posture and specific gestures. A culture's use of both of these forms of movement can offer considerable insight into its deep structure and value system. For example, in many Asian cultures the bow is much more than a greeting. It signifies a culture's concern with status and rank. In Japan, for example, low posture during the bow indicates respect (Ishii, 1973, pp. 163–180).

The manner in which we sit also can communicate a message. In Ghana and Turkey, sitting with one's legs crossed is extremely offensive (Rich, 1989, p. 279). Thais believe that because the bottoms of the feet are the lowest part of the body, they should never be pointed at a person (Cooper & Cooper, 1994, pp. 22–23). In fact, for Thais, the feet take on so much significance that people avoid stomping with them.

Some of our most elementary gestures are culture-bound. We make a zero with our index finger and thumb as a way of "saying" everything is perfect. Yet this same gesture means money in Japan, is an insult in Malta and Greece, and is perceived as an obscene gesture in Brazil.

Even the taken-for-granted sign that we make for beckoning is culturally based. In the United States, a person who wants to signal a friend to come makes a gesture with one hand, holding the palm up and with the fingers more or less together and moving toward his or her own body. Koreans and Vietnamese express this same idea by cupping the hand with the palm down and drawing the fingers toward the palm.

Facial Expressions. Although there is general agreement that universal facial expressions do exist, cultural norms often dictate how, when, and to whom facial expressions are displayed (Porter & Samovar, 1998). In many Mediterranean cultures, people exaggerate signs of grief or sadness. It is not uncommon in this region of the world to see men crying in public. Yet in the United States, white males often suppress the desire to show these emotions. Japanese men even go so far as to hide expressions of anger, sorrow, or disgust by laughing or smiling.

There are even differences in how co-cultures employ facial expressions as a form of communication. Summarizing the research on gender differences, Pearson, West, and Turner (1995) report that, compared to men, women generally use more facial expressions and are more expressive, smile more, are more apt to return smiles, and are more attracted to others who smile (p. 123).

Touch. Instances of touch as a form of communication demonstrate how nonverbal communication is a product of culture. In Germany, both women and men shake hands at the outset of every social encounter; in the United States, women seldom shake hands. In the Arab culture, men will often greet each other by kissing and hugging. In Thailand, people do not touch in public, and to touch someone on the head is a major social transgression. Even co-cultures differ in their use of touch. In the United States, women give and receive more touch than do men, yet men tend to initiate the touch.

Concept of Time. Concepts and uses of time are also important when people of different cultures come together. Most Western cultures think of time in lineal–spatial terms. We are timebound. Our schedules and our lists dominate our lives. The Germans and the Swiss are even more aware of time than Americans. Trains, planes, and meals must always be on time. This is not true for many cultures. Activity, not a clock, determines action. Most Native American languages, for example, have no words for seconds, minutes, or hours. Hence, for American Indians, and for many other cultures, being tardy is quite different than it is for members of the dominant culture.

The pace at which a culture carries out its life also reflects its use of time. In Mexico a slower pace is valued, whether the activity be conducting a business meeting or visiting with friends. And in Africa, where a slow pace is also valued, "people who rush are suspected of trying to cheat" (Rich, 1989, p. 278).

Use of Space. We all know that Arabs and Latins tend to interact more closely than do North Americans, and we also know how uncomfortable we feel when people from these cultures get too close to us. This shows how use of space is yet another behavior that is directly related to past experience.

Distance, however, is just one aspect of the use of space as a form of communication; physical orientation is also influenced by culture. North Americans prefer to sit facing or at right angles to one another, whereas Chinese generally prefer side-by-side seating. The English and Germans are conditioned to waiting in a straight line when seeking service in public, but Arabs see nothing wrong with propelling and jostling themselves into the best possible position to secure service. This is a clear example of how the use of space can send different messages.

CONCLUSION

As our society continues to accept immigrants and refugees at a rate far greater than any other country in the world, we will only see a rapid increase in cultural diversity. If we assert the value of cultural diversity and claim to espouse and accept a multicultural global village orientation, then we must be prepared to accept and tolerate the potential conflicts embedded in cultural differences. A free, culturally diverse society can exist only if diversity is permitted to flourish without prejudice and discrimination, both of which harm all members of the village. Remember the words of Thomas Jefferson as you begin your study of intercultural communication. In just a single written sentence he was able to capture the need for all of us to be tolerant of divergent views: "It does me no injury for my neighbor to say there are twenty gods, or no God."

Reference

Barnlund, D. C. (1989). *Communicative styles of Japanese and Americans: Images and realities.* Belmont, CA: Wadsworth.

Bates, D. G., & Plog, F. (1990). *Cultural anthropology,* 3rd ed. New York: McGraw-Hill.

Brislin, R. (1993). *Understanding culture's influence on behavior.* Forth Worth, TX: Harcourt Brace Jovanovich.

Cooper, R., & Cooper, N. (1994). *Culture shock: Thailand.* Portland, OR: Graphic Arts Center.

Galvin, K. M., & Brommel, B. J. (1991). *Family communication: Cohesion and change,* 3rd ed. New York: Harper Collins.

Hall, E. T. (1977). *Beyond culture.* Garden City, NY: Anchor.

Harris, P. R., & Moran, R. T. (1996). *Managing cultural differences: Leadership strategies for a new world of business,* 4th ed. Houston, TX: Gulf Publishing.

Haviland, W. A. (1993). *Cultural anthropology,* 7th ed. Fort Worth, TX: Harcourt Brace.

Higgins, A. G. (1995, October 19). Multimedia readiness of U.S. ranked No. 1. *San Diego Union Tribune,* A-6.

Ishii, S. (1973). Characteristics of Japanese nonverbal communication. *Communication, 2,* 163–180.

Keesing, F. M. (1965). *Cultural anthropology: The science of custom.* New York: Holt, Rinehart, & Winston.

Lustig, M. W. (1988). Cultural and communications patterns of Saudi Arabians. In L. A. Samovar & R. E. Porter (Eds.), *Intercultural communication: A reader* (5th ed., p. 102). Belmont, CA: Wadsworth.

Nanda, S. (1994). *Cultural anthropology,* 5th ed. Belmont, CA: Wadsworth.

Olayiwola, R. O. (1989). The impact of Islam on the conduct of Nigerian foreign relations. *The Islamic Quarterly, 33,* 19–26.

Pearson, J. C., West, R. L., & Turner, L. H. (1995). *Gender and communication* (3rd ed). Dubuque, IA: Wm. C. Brown.

Pennington, D. L. (1985). Intercultural communication. In L. A. Samovar & R. E. Porter (Eds.), *Intercultural communication: A reader* (4th ed., p. 32). Belmont, CA: Wadsworth.

Porter, R. E., & Samovar, L. A. (1998). Cultural influences on emotional expression: Implications for intercultural communication. In P. A. Andersen & L. K. Guerrero (Eds.), *Handbook of communication and emotion: Research, theory, applications and context.* San Diego: Academic Press.

Reischauer, E. D. (1988). *The Japanese today: Change and continuity*. Cambridge, MA: Harvard University Press.

Rich, W. V. (1989). *International handbook of corporate communication*. Jefferson, NC: McFarland.

Rokeach, M. (1968). *Beliefs, values, and attitudes*. San Francisco: Jossey-Bass.

Singer, M. R. (1987). *Intercultural communication: A perceptual approach*. Englewood Cliffs, NJ: Prentice-Hall.

Smith, A. G. (Ed.). (1966). *Communication and culture: Readings in the codes of human interaction*. New York: Holt, Rinehart, & Winston.

Smith, H. (1986). *The religion of man*. New York: Harper & Row.

Sumner, W. G. (1940). *Folkways*. Boston: Ginn & Co.

Time. (Fall 1993). p. 3.

U.S. News & World Report. (1996). p. 48.

Van Doren, C. (1991). *A history of knowledge: The pivotal event, people, and achievements of world history*. New York: Ballantine Books.

Wattenberg, B. J. (1989, February 13). Tomorrow. *U.S. News & World Report*, p. 31.

Concepts and Questions

1. Samovar and Porter maintain that intercultural communication is more prevalent than ever before in recorded history. Do you believe that most people are prepared for this increase in intercultural contact? If not, why?

2. How has this increase in cultural contact touched your life?

3. Why is culture an important consideration in human interaction?

4. What is meant by the statement "culture is learned"? Can you think of examples that demonstrate this "learning" process?

5. What is the relationship between culture and perception?

6. Why is worldview important to the study of intercultural communication? How does one's worldview contribute to how one perceives the world?

7. What is meant by the phrase "cultural values"? How might these values influence intercultural communication?

8. What is meant by the statement "culture teaches both the symbol and what the symbol stands for"?

9. What aspects of nonverbal communication must we consider during intercultural communication?

Understanding Cultural Identities in Intercultural Communication: A Ten-Step Inventory

Mary Jane Collier

Let me begin by introducing myself and characterizing my experiences and background. We are beginning a conversation about intercultural communication, so becoming familiar with the fundamental assumptions I'm making about it will help you better understand why I'm making particular arguments, as well as help you evaluate the utility of my approach for your own views and conduct.

My orientation to intercultural communication is based on where I come from and where I have been—just as yours is. I am a European American, white, middle-class, middle-aged female, and I've lived on a Navajo reservation in Arizona, in small towns, and in large cities in the United States. I have been a sojourner in South Africa. I have studied national, ethnic, and gender identity and intercultural communication dealing with ethnically diverse South Africans, various British ethnic groups in England, Israelis and Palestinians in the Middle East, and African, Asian, and Latino Americans in the United States. I have participated in protests and marched for political causes. My M.A. and Ph.D. in Communication are from the University of Southern California in Los Angeles.

I have come to believe that ignoring our cultural and intercultural communication processes has profound consequences. Unless we commit our hearts, minds, and spirits to understanding what happens when people with different group identities come together, we will be doomed to approach protracted conflicts such as those in the Middle East, Bosnia, and Northern Ireland through violence and military

This original essay appears for the first time here. All rights reserved. Permission to reprint must be obtained from the author and the publisher. Mary Jane Collier teaches at the University of Denver.

action. U.S. Americans will continue political and social violence against recent immigrants and marginalized groups in California in the name of "native born Americans," as I heard recently, and forget that the United States was founded by immigrants who took the land and destroyed the lives and cultures of the indigenous peoples. We'll go on denying the kind of racism, classism, and sexism that have become more insidious and damaging now that they are hidden behind language that we call "politically correct," and those of us who are more conservative will denounce "the liberals," while those of us who are more liberal will denounce "the conservatives." We'll continue to believe that our truth is the one and only truth, rather than remembering that truths are created and molded and shaped by individuals within religious, political, and social contexts and histories.

REQUEST TO ENGAGE THE DIALOGUE

Some things you read here and then talk about will validate and confirm your ideas and identities. Some things you read here will challenge your views of yourselves and the world.

When we begin inquiry about intercultural communication, we are studying how we do, be, and know ourselves and others as cultural beings. Communication, however, is a process that occurs unconsciously or mindlessly (Langer, 1989) much or at least some of the time. Learning about things we take for granted, and seeing our lives from the perspective of people who don't live the same way or value the same things can teach us about alternative ways of interpreting and being in the world, and increase our own options. In this way, we can also know better how to engage in talk and actions that will be viewed as moral and ethical.

Please enter into this reading as if we are having a dialogue; agree, disagree, and note alternative views and examples in the margins as you read. Also, talk about the claims you read here and add or modify ideas in and outside of class.[1] Search for alternative interpretations, examples, and reactions as you discuss these issues. Please think about how your behavior looks and sounds to strangers or outsiders, and also take the time to develop understanding of the words and actions of strangers until they become

more familiar. I encourage you to continue the dialogue with each other as well as with me by using e-mail to send me your reactions and thoughts (mcollier@du.edu).

In this essay, I outline an inventory,[2] a series of steps you can use to build your understanding of an intercultural event that you observed or heard about, improve the quality of an intercultural relationship, work toward solving a social problem that is based in intercultural communication, or conduct a systematic research study. The inventory will help you focus on how people construct their cultural identities in particular situations. Some of the questions on the inventory may be more relevant to particular situations and events than others, but all questions apply and affect what you conclude.

A TEN-STEP INVENTORY

The inventory is a series of questions to help you understand and critically evaluate diverse intercultural situations. The questions can be asked before, during, or after an intercultural experience and can be applied to public or group meetings, interpersonal conversations, what you see and hear in films or television shows, read in newspapers or magazines, or come across on the Internet. The following questions can be thought of as steps that are interrelated but not necessarily sequential. In other words, when you answer the questions in Step 7 about the context of your intercultural issue, you may need to go back and revise how you answered an earlier step about cultural identities. Each step in the inventory has to do with questions that you, the "problem solver," need to ask.

1. What do I believe about communication and culture?
2. What intercultural communication question do I want to answer? Specifically, what do I want to know, understand, or change?
3. What are the cultural identity issues that are relevant to the intercultural communication problem in which I'm interested?
4. How do power and ideology emerge and affect the intercultural communication problem in which I'm interested?

5. What are the intergroup and interpersonal relationship processes that are relevant to my intercultural problem?
6. What kind of communication messages will I examine? What will be my "data"?
7. What is the context? What are the situational, historical, institutional, and social factors that impact my intercultural problem?
8. What perspective and procedures should I use to analyze or interpret the communication messages?
9. What are my preliminary interpretations and findings? What are alternative views and interpretations?
10. How can I apply my interpretations to improve the quality of my own and others' intercultural experiences?

To show how the inventory can be applied, each step will be explained and then examples will be given. Each step will be applied first to a particular intercultural problem, one based on one or more recent conflicts on college campuses across the United States. The inventory not only can be applied to analyzing a current social problem or issue, but also to help you answer a question about your own intercultural experiences or to guide a research project you conduct.

To apply the inventory to our specific campus problem, you need a little background. The current debate regarding affirmative action and policies regarding immigrants in the United States is one that is evident in political campaigns, town meetings, television talk shows, and campus organizations. On many university campuses, the debate is fueling discussion regarding the need for ethnic studies and women's studies programs, a higher percentage of faculty from underrepresented groups, separate ethnic cultural centers or international houses on campus, and separate residence halls for international students. The debate is based on whether it is best to have programs and places in which students who have particular ethnic backgrounds or backgrounds from countries outside the United States, may meet, socialize, and study in a safe environment of support; or whether it is best to offer traditional programs that emphasize how to be successful in the United States; hire faculty without attention to race, ethnicity, or sex; close the cultural centers; and streamline funding by devoting resources only to student activities that welcome all students.

This is a complex issue, and each campus, of course, is different depending on demographics and the mission of the institution. On many campuses, funding for maintaining the cultural centers and student programs comes from both administrative sources and student fees. On many campuses, costs are increasing and administrators are looking for places to downsize and save money. Take a minute to think about your own campus. Is there an ethnic studies department or program? Is there a women's studies department or program? Are there cultural centers? If you have residence halls, are any designated only for international students?

Here is the specific problem to work with and apply the steps in the inventory. An administrator on your campus has proposed closing all the cultural centers (black student alliance, Hispanic center, Native American longhouse) and international house—as well as the women's studies program and the ethnic studies program—and opening the residence hall previously designated for international students to all students. The administrator argues that separatist organizations do not prepare students to live in a culturally diverse, global society, and the centers and programs are too costly to maintain.

Answering the inventory of questions about this campus problem can help you make sense of the multiple points of view and perhaps better understand why some group members feel as they do. In the rest of this essay, each step in the inventory will be illustrated by systematically analyzing the campus problem; it will also be applied by explaining similar steps in research studies about a range of cultural groups.

STEP 1: WHAT DO I BELIEVE ABOUT COMMUNICATION AND CULTURE?

There are many ways we all commonly think of culture, and each may be more or less useful to help us understand a certain process, event, or relationship.

Approaches to Culture
Culture as Place. Often when you meet someone, the first question asked is "Where are you from?"

Sometimes this refers to a question about where the person grew up, and other times it's a question about where the person lived previously. Groups also are described in print and broadcast media, literature, and academic texts as people who are from or reside in a country or region of a country. These references become evident in everyday discourse as well when an individual says, "I'm from L. A. (Los Angeles), so . . ." implying that who she or he is can be understood through knowing where she or he lives—in this case, in Southern California, which is known for the entertainment industry, wealth, freeway commuting, and a warm coastal climate.

Places of origin or residence bring to mind different social hierarchies and norms, class distinctions, political orientations, and communication styles. Without thinking about it, we assume that people who are raised or live in a particular place probably speak the same language, hold many of the same values, and communicate in similar ways.

Culture as Ancestry and People. Another common way we think about culture is to define culture as the group of people who share the same ancestry. Ethnicity is often used as an indicator of culture. For instance, Japanese Americans are understood as a people who live in the United States whose Japanese ancestors or relatives taught them Japanese language, values, and traditions. During the Second World War, U.S. government representatives assumed that ancestry was a powerful enough force to determine their cultural alliance with Japan, and U.S. citizens of Japanese ancestry were evicted from their homes, their businesses were closed or taken over, and they were imprisoned in internment camps for the duration of the war.

An approach to culture that is also based on ancestry is that which is exemplified by linking race with culture. When people remark, "He's the white guy who lives next door to me," or when writers of newspaper accounts of crimes, for instance, include a description of the race of the alleged perpetrator, then the speaker and writer are making assumptions about racial appearance and ancestry as apparent indicators of character and identity. Scholars point out that race is a social construct, and that we cannot predict behavior, values, or beliefs—let alone content of one's character—by skin color or hair tex-

ture (Martin, 1997; Omi & Wainant, 1986; Webster, 1992). As a social construct, however, racial appearance is an everyday shorthand way to stereotype others.

Culture as Art and Artifact. Creative endeavors and expressions that represent the heart, spirit, emotions, or philosophies of a group at a particular time and place are another way we think of culture. Examples include not only what can be seen in museums and galleries, but also the artifacts and remnants of pottery, jewelry, tools, weapons left behind by groups such as the Anasazi Indians, and what is left of their dwellings in Mesa Verde.

Culture as Capital or Economic Resource. Many countries and organizations are based on economic principles of capitalism. Often we come to think of areas of the world in terms of their economic status and relative wealth. More specifically, countries or regions are thought of in terms of their buying power and developing markets; the CBS television network program "60 Minutes," for example, featured a segment on investment opportunities and expanding wealth in Russia. Approaching groups as buyers or as producers of products is to think of culture as an economic resource.

Culture as Product. We think about cultures as commodities or products when we think of the numerous toys, foods, films, videos, and music that are internationally exported and imported. The Barbie doll produced by Mattel in the United States is sold to young women all over the world. A colleague of mine who visited Beijing last year commented that the department store mannequins advertising women's clothing and accessories were, more often than not, tall and blond replicas of Barbie. When the same colleague lived with a single mother and two children in Costa Rica who were extremely poor, the daughter wanted a Barbie doll more than any other gift for the Christmas holiday.

Culture as Politics and Ideology. Another way to think of culture is to associate a country with a political ideology. In the United States, the Peace Corps was created in 1961 to give people in areas such as Central America and Africa new technologies, agricultural techniques, and democratic values. More recently, the export of U.S. democratic values through the Peace Corps has been criticized as actually exporting imperialism and colonialism.

Halualani (1998) notes that culture can be approached as the structures, ideologies, and master narratives of groups in power that are created through mediated and public forms to maintain and extend their power. The press coverage of U.S. involvement in the Persian Gulf War in 1991 has been cited as an example of government and military control of the press, and thus the coverage reflected a public-relations emphasis. The news featured the success of the United States and its allies, the spectacle of the missiles and technology, and lack of casualties (Sturken, 1995), and it did not include references to deaths caused by friendly fire or civilian casualties.

Culture as Psychology, Worldview, or Style of Thinking and Speaking.

One of the ways in which we come to know who we are is to compare our own group identities with the character of other groups (Tajfel, 1978). Often our everyday talk includes references to *they* and *we*. We learn and attribute to others, based on their group memberships, particular styles of thinking and feeling. In short, we may begin to stereotype other group members by attributing particular psychological tendencies to them (Brislin, 1986). Katz (1960) found that stereotypes become prejudiced, evaluative prejudgments about group members so that we can knowledgeably predict or explain the conduct of people in other groups, as well as serving an ego defensive function that allows us to blame others for the outcomes of events. For example, when a European American friend of mine called to tell me he was not hired for a job at a fire station, he blamed affirmative action policies that favored members of ethnic minority groups.

Culture as Performance.

Sometimes we think of culture as a kind of role we are acting in a play. Goffman (1967) created a theory of communication as performance and noted that some of our identities are "front stage" and others are more "back stage" or private. The audience affects the quality of the performance as well. Many groups such as Native American Indians have a long-standing tradition of elders sharing the oral histories and origin myths of their people at social gatherings and celebrations.

Culture as Group Identity.

We have experienced an exponential increase in access to international information due to computer technology and the Internet, far away places and people have become more accessible through more affordable and available travel, corporations are told to be multinational to be successful, and our nations and communities have become characterized by increasing diversity. In the winter of 1998, we could see the tired faces and nonverbal cues of frustration during televised interviews with United Nations representatives and national leaders as they discussed the possibility of a U.S. military strike in Iraq. Through such public and private contact with others, we come to define ourselves as members of cultural groups.

When we approach culture as group character or identity, it is essential to recognize that each group is made up of a multitude of individuals and voices and each individual has a range of group identities. McPhail (1997), for instance, discusses the range of voices and political standpoints and values making up the African American community. Halualani (1998) argues that the "American Dream" is an idealized myth that is not available to people like her who are Japanese, Hawaiian, and female. Thus, we need to recognize that cultural identities are complex and created, sustained, challenged, and contested in our contact with each other.

Culture and the Campus Problem

Stereotyping occurs on the basis of linking culture to ancestry or race, so students who experience discrimination on the basis of race may argue that they need separate cultural centers in order to have a place to meet where they can feel safe and know that people who look like them are welcome. On the other hand, European American students may argue that cultural centers or ethnic studies programs are not necessary, because these students may not value ethnicity or see why ancestry and past traditions are more important than the current American orientation.

Defining culture as ideology and politics may help you understand why members of different groups are so committed to maintaining their own cultural centers and programs, or why they wish to replace such programs. The programs are not only a source of identity reinforcement but also a source of empowerment. Finally, consider that the resources allocated to groups and programs—as well as courses focused on ethnic history, philosophy, and art—are an acknowledgment of the contribution and legitimacy of ethnic members of the U.S. American community. Thus, such programs and designated places are the site in which cultural identities are reinforced, contested, modified, and celebrated.

In my own research, I combine several approaches to culture. Currently, I define culture as a historically based, interpretive, constitutive, creative set of practices and interpretive frames that demonstrate affiliation with a group. Culture as group identity is the way I most often think of culture, although I also study the politics and ideology and the performance of the enacted group identities. A communication event or interaction becomes intercultural when different cultural identities emerge in the text or talk of interactants. I'll give several examples of the cultural groups and identity issues I study throughout the remainder of this article.

STEP 2: WHAT INTERCULTURAL COMMUNICATION QUESTION DO I WANT TO ANSWER?

Specifically, what do you want to know about the communicative event, contact, discourse, text, and situation? What is the problem you want to address? You may have had a personal experience or an intercultural conversation that left you puzzled or intrigued. Have you witnessed or been a part of an intercultural conflict that you might want to manage? Do you want to explain why members of one group seem to adapt to a new country more quickly than members of another group? Do you wish to critique how multinational corporations in developed countries influence developing nations by introducing technology and products and creating dependency? For the campus problem, you may ask: How does the social history of each "ethnic minority" group affect the standpoint taken by spokespersons of that group in the campus newspaper? How can understanding the perspective of the administrator (who

has more than one cultural identity) and the perspective of the women's studies faculty and students (who also have many cultural identities) help you identify common goals?

This is the step in which you should narrow your interests to a question that you can answer by analyzing specific messages, what you can read, see, and hear in mediated or person-to-person communication. You need to be able to answer your question through systematic empirical observation or analysis or critique of communication messages in conversations, groups, public venues, and all forms of print and broadcast media. You are acting on the premise that people construct their identities and relationships through their communication, and the study of communication messages can help us not only understand what is going on in our communication with each other, but also potentially how to improve the quality of our intercultural relationships.

STEP 3: WHAT ARE THE CULTURAL IDENTITY ISSUES THAT ARE RELEVANT?

The third set of questions points to cultural identities and how they are enacted, produced, reproduced, reinforced, contested, constructed, and reconstructed in your selected problematic situation. Listed below are several principles or assumptions about cultural identities that you may find helpful as you think about the campus problem and your own experiences and research.

Multiple Cultural Identity Types (CITs)

Many groups (though not all) form cultural systems. In some cases, shared history or geography provides commonality of worldview or lifestyle that helps create and reinforce a cultural system of communication. To create a culture, a group must first define itself as a group. This may be on the basis of nationality, ethnicity, gender, profession, geography, organization, community, physical ability or disability, or type of relationship, among others. Once the group defines itself as a unit, then a cultural system may develop. For instance, U.S. Americans define themselves as a group based on use of English as a shared code; reinforcement of democracy through political discussion and action; individual rights and freedoms of speech, press, religion, and assembly being explicitly described in the Bill of Rights and enforced in the courts; and so forth. Attorneys or sales clerks or homemakers may be linked by similarities in daily activities and standard of living.

National and Ethnic Cultures. To better understand the many different types of cultures, we can categorize them from the more general and more common to the more specific. National and ethnic cultures are fairly general. These kinds of groups base membership on heritage and history that have been handed down for generations. Their histories are based on traditions, rituals, codes of language, and norms.

Persons who share the same nationality were born in a particular country or spent a significant number of years and period of socialization in that country. Such socialization promotes and reinforces particular values, beliefs, and norms. Many people contribute to the creation of a national culture's symbols, meanings, and norms, so national culture is fairly abstract and predictions about language use and what symbols mean must be general. For instance, Japanese national culture has been described as collectivistic, high-context, high on power distance, and other-face–oriented (Gudykunst & Ting-Toomey, 1988). Not all Japanese people follow these norms in every situation; comparing Japanese to Germans, however, the Japanese as a group are more group-oriented and emphasize status hierarchies more than do the Germans as an overall group (Hofstede, 1980).

Ethnicity is a bit different in that ethnic groups share a sense of heritage and history, as well as origin from an area outside of or preceding the creation of the current nation-state of residence (Banks, 1984). In some but not all cases, ethnic groups share racial characteristics, and many have a specific history of having experienced discrimination. In the United States, ethnic groups include African Americans, Asian Americans (Japanese Americans, Chinese Americans, Vietnamese Americans, etc.), Mexican Americans, German Americans, Irish Americans, Native American Indians, and Jewish Americans.

Sex and Gender. Another common cultural group is that based on biological sex or socially constructed gender. There are many subcategories of gender cultures. Groups create, reinforce, and teach what it means to use a gender style and what is interpreted as feminine or masculine. Groups also reinforce what is appropriate or inappropriate for a good husband, good wife, feminist, chauvinist, heterosexual, gay, or lesbian. Mothers and fathers, religious leaders, teachers, and what we read and see in the media all provide information about how to be a member of a particular gender culture.

Remember that nationality, ethnicity, race, and sex are cultural group affiliations based on citizenship, heritage, and biology, and such broad memberships do not guarantee that members of those groups will automatically behave or interpret messages in the same ways. Many individuals have parents and grandparents with different backgrounds and heritages and claim more than one ethnicity and may have lived in several different countries. From the CIT perspective, cultural identity is created when a group affiliation is enacted, when an individual or group members claim membership in one or more groups. Cultural identity is based on what members of a group or community say and do and think and feel as they affiliate with others who share their history, origins, or biology. For a cultural identity to be recognized, the identity needs to be claimed and communicated in some way.

Profession. Groups of professionals sometimes create their own culture. Politicians, physicians, field workers, sales personnel, maintenance crews, bankers, and consultants share common ways of spending time, earning money, communicating with others, and sharing norms about how to be a member of their profession. For instance, most health care professionals share a commitment to health, to helping others, and to improving others' quality of life. They also share educational background, knowledge about their aspect of health care, and standards of practicing their profession.

Geographical Area. Geographical area is sometimes a boundary that contributes to the formation of a cultural group. In South Africa, the area surrounding Cape Town has its own version of spoken Afrikaans, has a higher population of coloureds (those of mixed race), and is viewed by many as a very cosmopolitan area in South Africa. The South in the United States has its own traditions, historical orientation, and Southern drawl.

Corporation. Organizational culture is yet another type of culture. The most common type is that created in large corporations such as IBM, Nike, and Xerox. Here individuals are taught the corporate symbols; the corporate myths, heroes, and legends; and what it means to be an employee. In addition, individuals are taught the proper chain of command, procedures, policies, and schedules. Finally, they are taught the norms in the corporation, who to talk to about what and at which time. Some corporations value "team players" while others value "individual initiative." Some corporations have mottoes like "Never say *no* to an assignment" or "Never be afraid to speak up if you don't have what you need."

Support groups also have their own version of organizational culture. Alcoholics Anonymous, Overeaters Anonymous, and therapy and support groups, among others, have their own sets of symbols and interpretations and norms. For example, "Let go and let God" is an important requirement in the anonymous groups, emphasizing that relinquishing individual control to a higher power is a tool in managing one's addictions. Social living groups also often create their own cultures, such as sororities and fraternities, international dormitories, and the like.

Physical Ability and Disability. Physical ability and disability is still another category of group that can become a basis for culture. Professional athletic teams teach rookies how to behave and what to do to be accepted members of the team. Persons who have physical handicaps share critical life experiences, and groups teach individuals how to accept and overcome their disabilities, as well as how to communicate more effectively with those who do not have the disability (Braithwaite, 1991).

Cultural Identification as Constituted in Communication

Cultural identity is the particular character of the group communication system that emerges when people claim group membership in a particular situation, event, or communication context. Cultural identities are negotiated, co-created, reinforced, and challenged through communication (Hecht, Collier, & Ribeau, 1993). In CIT, identity is approached from a communication perspective, which views identity as located in the communication process in which messages are constructed, reinforced, contested, and challenged. A communication perspective also includes attention to the creation of cultural identities through products or words and images that are transmitted through media or technological channels.

Group affiliation and membering occurs in multiple contexts in which insiders and outsiders enact what membership looks and sounds like. All cultures that are created are influenced by a host of social and psychological and environmental factors as well as institutions, history, and context. Latinos who wish to maintain their cultural center may argue their position more strongly at private meetings attended by members of their group and change the intensity of their tone and persuasive appeals when interacting with community representatives on their board of advisors. Identities therefore are co-created in relationship to other people. Who we are and how we are differs and emerges depending on who we are with, the cultural identities that are important to us and others, the context, the topic of conversation, and our interpretations and attributions.

Multivocality and Interpellated Cultural Identities

From an individual perspective, each person has a range of groups and cultures to which she or he belongs in a constantly changing environment. Each individual participates in many cultural systems each day, week, and year. Cultures are affected not only by changing socioeconomic and environmental conditions, but also by other cultures. As hooks (1989) reminds us, she is not only an African American, but also a woman and a college professor. To understand her conduct, one must recognize her multiple identities and voices, just as someone else must recognize *your* multiple voices and identities. It is also important to recognize that not all voices within a group sound alike.

Morgan (1996) uses the term *feminisms* to recognize multivocality within feminists as a group; some voices are more radical, some more conservative, and some both radical and conservative. *Interpellation* refers to the interrelationships among such cultural identities as sex, race, and class, and the point that one cannot understand sex without also studying race and class.

Several months ago, on my way to work, I drove by a local seminary. For several days I saw on the outside lawn a small group of women leading another larger group in prayer. I also read in the newspaper that these women were on a hunger strike and were protesting discrimination toward women faculty who were denied tenure or a voice in determining policy in the seminary. If I want an accurate picture of the issues and group standpoints, then identifying how the women leading the protest, the staff, the students, and the administrators of the seminary were defining religion, feminism, and political voice would be important, as would noticing that the individuals within each group constructed their identities and position on the issues in a unique way.

Avowal and Ascription Processes

I have used the term *multivocality* to point out that groups are made up of individuals with unique as well as similar voices. In addition, each individual may enact various cultural identities over the course of a lifetime, not to mention over the course of a day. Identities are enacted across contexts through *avowal* and *ascription* processes. Avowal has to do with what an individual portrays to others and is analogous to the face or image shown to others. In a way, avowal is the individual showing to others "This is who I am" as a member of this group or these groups.

Ascription is when individuals or group members come to know that others attribute particular identities to them as members of a group. Stereotypes and attributions that are communicated are examples. In part, identity is shaped by others' communicated views of us. For example, a black Zulu female's cultural identities in South Africa are not only shaped by her definition and image of what it means to be a black Zulu female but also by the communicated views of the white Afrikaners for whom she works, her Zulu family and relatives, the township in which she lives in poverty, her white teachers who speak Afrikaans and English, and so forth.

Another way of thinking about this is to say that cultural identities have both subjective and ascribed meanings. Some cultures emphasize ascription, or an orientation toward others. In Japan, a traditional philosophy sometimes reflected in practice is that of *amae*. Amae represents an other orientation and a sense of obligation to the group; an individual is expected to sacrifice individual needs and give to others, and others are expected to reciprocate. Thus, the harmony and cohesiveness of the group is maintained (Doi, 1989; Goldman, 1992).

Information about avowal and ascription can be useful in understanding the role others play in developing your own cultural identities. If you feel you are a member of a group that is marginalized and discriminated against or has a high need for status, then those aspects of identity may be influenced by the stereotypes or conceptions held and communicated by other groups.

Salience and Intensity Differences

Identities differ in their salience in particular contexts, and identities are enacted with different intensities at different times. The intensities provide markers of strong involvement and investment in the identity. As a white U.S. American female professor visiting Australia and being taken on a dream time walk by a male aborigine, at different times throughout the walk, I was aware of being a white minority, a U.S. American tourist who was stereotyped somewhat negatively, a college professor who was interested in culture, and an honored guest.

Salience refers to featuring one or more particular identities more strongly than others, and it certainly does not mean individuals have split personalities or need to give up one cultural identity to feature another. Some people also have less choice about what cultural identities they can feature. I have come to see that I have certain unearned privileges and choice about whether or not I choose to share my British German ethnic heritage.

Enduring and Changing Property of Identity

Cultural identities are both enduring and changing. As already mentioned, cultures have a history that is continually constructed and reconstructed with new members over time. Cultural identities change because of economic, political, social, psychological, and contextual factors, not to mention the influence of other cultural identities.

Enacting the cultural identity of being gay or lesbian in the 1990s has certain things in common with being gay in the 1980s and 1970s. Individuals who "come out of the closet" encounter similar stereotypes and ascriptions to those in earlier centuries. However, the political climate in some areas of the country in which ballot initiatives sought to limit the rights of gays or link gays with other groups such as sadomasochists also affects the cultural identity of the group. Sometimes context changes how one manifests identity and how intensely one avows an identity. For example, not all members of a gay, lesbian, and bisexual alliance may avow that identity outside of their support group.

STEP 4: WHAT IS THE ROLE OF POWER AND IDEOLOGY?

This leads us to the fourth set of questions you will want to ask about power and ideology. These include: What is power? Is it a process, a commodity, a perception or impression of influence, access, or ability to distribute resources? How do people lose or gain power?

I have noticed in my classes that members of marginalized groups are more likely to make statements such as "All intercultural communication is political" or "Power is always an issue in intercultural communication." The newer theoretical perspectives point us to identifying the extent to which power is constructed through history, institutions, and social practices; and for some of us to interrogate previously taken-for-granted assumptions and benefits we accrue on the basis of being white or male or upper class.

There are days when individually I feel somewhat powerless, and yet I, as a white, middle-class professional benefit from institutional practices in higher education and the broader political system that maintain my rights and privileges and lead me to expect to be hired, treated with respect by staff, or waited on in a department store without being shadowed or suspected of being a shoplifter. Even with affirmative-action policies, across the United States I am more likely to be hired for a corporate position or a position in higher education than my Latina, African American, or Native American Indian counterparts.

On the other hand, assuming that groups are *either* "all powerful" and totally "imperialist" *or* "powerless" and "colonized" can be an inappropriate oversimplification. Consider international contexts in which new products or ideologies are introduced by corporate representatives from developed nations to the people in less developed nations. When parents in a village in Nicaragua take a Barbie doll that was a gift from a U.N. visitor and stain the skin to be darker, dress her in indigenous clothing, and create a new ritual in which she is the voice of the ancestors sharing their stories—this is a redefinition of power.

As both group members and problem solvers, we ought to recognize that those who have some degree of power will seek to maintain it, and that there are many collective interpretations of power and resistance. McClintock (1995) notes that there exists a "diverse politics of agency, involving the dense web of relations between coercion, negotiation, complicity, refusal, dissembling, mimicry, compromise, affiliation, and revolt" (15). There are also benefits to becoming aware of taken-for-granted sources of power that have become somewhat invisible to some of us, as well as engaging in what hooks calls intercultural dialogue between those who feel oppressed and those who "exploit, oppress and dominate" (1989, p. 129) because this opens opportunities and spaces for understanding of the structures and functions of domination (Foss, 1998).

There are many related questions you may ask about power and what has endured in order to understand the historical, social, and ideological context of your intercultural problem. Such questions may address the importance of the environment, history, and institutions such as education and religion in determining how cultural identities emerge. Our own socioeconomic class affects what we deem appropriate and what we expect from others, and histories of racism, sexism, and classism, for example, influence how we all behave.

The importance of acknowledging the historical and social context in which power emerges is illustrated by the following comments. On a visit to the Middle East in the spring of 1998, a Palestinian young woman asked me, "What do you think? I am Palestinian and I live in Gaza. The Israeli government laws deny me and my brothers the right I.D. [identity] card, so I can't work in Israel, visit my aunts and uncles, or visit holy sites in Jerusalem. How can this be?" An Israeli young woman told me, "We were raised to hate them [Palestinians], to think that the men are all terrorists and the women are abused by their husbands because of Islam."

You may want to ask a more specific set of questions with regard to the power and ideology of different cultural groups in their intercultural contact. Who makes important decisions in the group, determines when and where meetings or social gatherings will take place, or speaks for the rest of the group in intercultural meetings or in public presentations? How are decisions made to allocate resources or create policy and procedures? What kinds of values and ideologies are handed down to new members?

STEP 5: WHAT ARE THE INTERGROUP AND INTERPERSONAL RELATIONSHIP PROCESSES?

Our cultural identities are constructed in relationships with others inside our own groups and with members of other groups. *Relationship process* refers to the quality of connection or bond that emerges in communication. When persons communicate with each other, their messages carry not only information, but also cues about the relationship between individuals and groups. These cues indicate who is dominant or submissive throughout the conversation or event, how much intimacy or hostility is felt, how much each partner or party trusts one another, and how much they feel included or excluded.

You could analyze the campus newspaper coverage of the debate about closing the campus centers and programs, or attend the public forum on campus where students articulate their views. Using the newspaper articles or transcriptions of the public meeting or both, you could look for relational messages that constitute the relationship, phrases that indicate friendliness such as "We support the need for safe places to meet and are open to designating additional spaces for intercultural dialogue"; or control, "How can redefining what used to be a separatist place into a place where all students can go possibly be a bad thing?"; or exclusion in the press headline "Provost Says, 'Student Input Has No Place in Closing Cultural Centers.'" You could ask intercul-

tural friends to tape-record their informal talk about the campus problem and look for what Baxter and Montgomery (1996) and Martin, Nakayama, and Flores (1997) describe as dialectic tensions in the dialogue. For instance, intercultural friends may experience contradictory tendencies to be both independent and connected, private as well as public, and dominant as well as submissive. Looking for dialectical tensions may help you guard against overly simplistic generalizations about a group's preferred mode of communication.

Sometimes people use their in-group language to reinforce their in-group status and establish distance from the out-group (Giles, Coupland, & Coupland, 1991). At other times, they may use the language of the out-group in order to adapt and align with the out-group. Some Mexican Americans speak Spanish when in neighborhood communities in order to preserve their history and roots and to reinforce their identification and bond as a people. The same persons may speak English at work because the supervisor and executives of the company demand it. They may also choose to speak Spanish in meetings to plan their response to close their cultural center, and choose English when meeting with the provost.

STEP 6: WHAT KINDS OF COMMUNICATIVE MESSAGES SHOULD I EXAMINE IN MY STUDY?

What kind of data or communication messages do you need to answer your questions? What types or forms of messages may be important? Are you interested in analyzing a series of meetings between diplomats over several years, or the speeches of one political figure in a particular period of time, or a relationship you have, or a conversation that took place yesterday? It is also important to think about what you need to examine in the way of functions or outcomes of those forms.

This set of questions deals with what kind and how much communicative data you wish to understand or explain. Some scholars study the rhetoric that is common in a century or decade, or in the letters written by an international traveler during his or her lifetime. Others choose a much more specific focus on a particular event in time or critical point in a relationship. For the campus problem, if you want to interview people from various groups, you must decide who you want to interview, what you want to ask, if you want answers to specific questions or you want to have more of a collaborative dialogue, and how many times you want to meet with them. Whether you are addressing a concrete problem or conducting a research study, you need to think about the breadth and scope of your data and what it will take to answer your question appropriately.

Form and Function of Discourse Texts

The form and function of talk with friends was the focus of a study of adolescent members of various ethnic groups in London, England (Collier & Thompson, 1997). We found that discourse among friends served dual functions: maintaining traditional and previous home cultural identity, language, and norms—and developing a new national or ethnic identity. Using in-depth group interviews, we asked questions about three contexts: home, school, and socializing with friends, and the national and ethnic identities constructed in each. We asked respondents in each context to think of a situation in which they were aware of being from different cultural backgrounds, and then we asked about who was there, what was discussed, what activities took place, and the purpose and outcome of the contact.

The adolescents were most aware of their shared national identity as British citizens at school, and they were most aware of their different ethnic backgrounds at home because that was where home language was often spoken and where narrative rituals recalling history and people were most often seen. Several respondents pointed out that these family gatherings and storytelling episodes by grandparents served to bring the family together, remind them of their past and roots, and provide a way of reinforcing transcendent values and extended family ties.

Message Patterns and Themes

Another way to analyze communication texts is to look for message patterns and themes. For example, you may wish to see how often a particular phrase or idea such as feminism comes up, around what topics, and with which conversational partners. You may also want to analyze narratives or stories and look for themes that may emerge. For example, Hecht and Ribeau (1987) and Hecht, Ribeau, and Alberts (1989) analyzed recalled conversations of African Americans with European Americans and distinguished several improvement strategies such as asserting point of view and positive self-presentation.

Modes of Expression: Labels and Norms

Labels are a way of establishing identity. The same label may vary widely in its interpretation. The term *American* is perceived as acceptable and common by many residents of the United States, as ethnocentric and self-centered by residents of Central America and Canada, and as associated with a group that is privileged, wealthy, and powerful by some developing countries. Labels used in the discourse of people involved in the campus problem can potentially reveal a great deal about identities ascribed to outsiders.

For example, *Hispanic* is a general term that many social scientists use to describe "persons of Mexican, Puerto Rican, Cuban, Central or South American or other Spanish culture of origin, regardless of race" (Marin & Marin, 1991, p. 23). Persons may choose to describe their own ethnicity with a much more specific label such as Mexican American or Chicano or Chicana. The individuals may differ on their ideas about what it means to be a member of that culture. Whether the label was created by members of the group or members of another group (e.g., *Hispanic* is a term that was originally generated by the U.S. government) provides useful information about what the label means and how it is interpreted.

Norms are explicit or inferred prescriptions of modes of appropriate and effective communication. Norms are prescriptive or evaluative because they specify appropriate and acceptable behavior, moral standards, and expectations for conduct. Norms provide cultural group members with a criteria to decide to what degree another is behaving in a competent manner. Reviewing the historical, political, and ideological context of norms and expectations that group members may bring to the public forum on campus can be helpful when assigning interpretations to the chanting and loud interruptions by members of one group.

Cultural groups create and reinforce standards for "performing the culture" appropriately and effectively. An individual is successful at enacting identity when one is accepted as a competent member of the group. For example, all those who are registered as members of Native American Indian tribes in the United States are defined as "real Indians" only when they conduct themselves in ways that insiders judge to be appropriate and acceptable for Indians (Weider & Pratt, 1990). Norms and standards for acceptable conduct are very general trends at best; they are constructed by group members and interpreted by individuals, and they change across contexts.

Affective, Cognitive, and Spiritual Components

Throughout history, many groups have felt strongly enough about the supremacy of their beliefs to conquer and convert outsiders. For instance, Jerusalem is a city that is holy to three of the world's largest religions, and Israeli control is contested by Muslim and Christian groups. Emotions and feelings are attached to identities, and these change across situation, historical context, political climate, and relationship with others. Sometimes, the avowal or featuring of a particular identity more strongly and more violently is a signal of the importance of that identity and the degree to which that identity is perceived to be threatened. When a colleague and I (Collier & Bowker, 1994) asked women friends who had different cultural identities what made a good intercultural ally, two of the African American women said that their European American friends needed to be able to hear their anger and rage about daily experiences with oppression, while their European American women friends said their feelings about the value of the friendship needed to be reciprocated.

The cognitive component of identity relates to the beliefs we have about that identity. Persons have a range of premises about each culture group to which they belong, but certain similarities become evident when you ask people to talk about what it means to be U.S. American or Thai or a member of the environmentalist group Earth First! Members of Earth First! share beliefs in the value of ancient forests, a distrust of executives who run the logging

companies, and politicians who support the lumber industry, and they view spiking trees and sabotaging logging equipment as sometimes necessary forms of protest. Such beliefs can be summarized into a core symbol, here the name of the organization—Earth First!

STEP 7: WHAT IS THE CONTEXT OF THE INTERCULTURAL PROBLEM?

How we construct identities occurs in a broad context of history, power dynamics, social norms, and specific situations. Thus, it is important to ask such questions as, What are the factors outside of the messages that can help me understand the intercultural communication? What is the physical environment? What histories and institutions (political, religious, educational, etc.) are relevant?

The site of one of my first exploratory studies of culture and communication was the Navajo reservation in Chinle, Arizona. I lived with a family and taught high school classes. I became interested in how Navajos developed and strengthened their cultural identities through family rituals and community events, and how their identities were threatened by institutions such as the Bureau of Indian Affairs schools in which students were forced to speak English.

Context includes the physical environment, for instance, where persons with different cultural identities have contact, or the location or place in which a media text, cultural product, or speech is produced, distributed, and interpreted by audiences or consumers, as well as a social and historical place in time. For example, in the campus problem, if someone argues that curriculum as well as programs of study should be based on the canons of traditional Greek knowledge as a foundation, it may be important to consider that Aristotle's ideas about rhetoric for example, were created in a time in which women were excluded from political participation, and in a place in which wealth and power were concentrated in the hands of a few of the elite.

In one of my studies, I wished to understand how young people from different cultural groups in South Africa in 1992 approached and experienced interpersonal, intercultural relationships. We (Collier &

Bornman, in press) discovered, for instance, that interethnic and interracial friendships were more common among nonwhite group members and more common in private than in public contexts. We also found that blacks, Asian Indians, and coloureds (those of mixed race) emphasized the need to acknowledge history and the consequences of the apartheid system of government, while the Afrikaners and British we interviewed emphasized the need to be present- and future-oriented.

STEP 8: WHAT PERSPECTIVES AND PROCEDURES SHOULD I USE TO STUDY THE DATA?

Epistemological Perspectives

How can you best study the communication messages in which you're interested? Whether you are trying to understand an intercultural problem, an event, or asking a research question, you will need to decide if you should be as objective as possible, ask others how they make sense of their subjective experiences, be an engaged participant, or be a more distant but knowledgeable critic. There are many perspectives to doing research that are available to you as you approach inquiry about a particular intercultural communication situation or text. Becoming familiar with them will give you a better basis from which to choose one or more perspectives in answering your own question.

Below I describe three broad perspectives to epistemology, or what and how we know what we do.[3] We will talk about these types as epistemological perspectives because each is a way in which we can view knowledge building in intercultural communication. Although I emphasize research examples, you also may adapt these approaches to practical problems from your own experience.

Positivist and Objectivist Perspectives

Positivist approaches have the longest legacy in communication because of their origins in social science. Anderson (1996) notes that objectivist theories are based in principles of **empiricism** (observation), **materialism, determinism** (cause–effect relationships), and **objectivity.** Assumptions made by researchers taking this perspective are that a materi-

al reality "out there" can be discovered, observed, measured, and operationalized, and causal relationships proven. A common assumption is that psychological states such as beliefs, feelings, attitudes, and values can be discovered and quantified through behavioral assessments such as scaled questionnaires. Further, it is assumed that behaviors (actions that can be seen and categorized) are authentic representations of psychological states (what individuals are thinking or feeling).

Perhaps as you listen to people talk about the campus problem, you begin to hypothesize that students who have friends from other cultures or who have traveled in other countries are more likely to voice their support for keeping the cultural centers and various programs. You decide to test this relationship. You could develop a set of questions that measure the extent of previous intercultural contact (living in another country, number of friends who have a different nationality or ethnicity, etc.) and measure the likelihood that a person might say or agree with someone who makes such comments as, "Programs like ethnic studies are valuable for all students" or "Women's studies courses teach issues that can be useful for men and women to learn." You would be assuming that such questions would be interpreted and mean the same things to all students, and the extent to which they agreed or disagreed with each question would represent their overall attitude. You, like social science scholars who use positivism, would want to be able to predict, for example, particular kinds of communication behavior and partly explain that behavior by looking at the variable of previous intercultural contact.

Another example of positivist research is that of Gudykunst (1994), who proposed that because Japanese people are more collectivistic and group-oriented and emphasize contextual factors such as silence in interpretation more highly than do U.S. Americans, Japanese individuals communicating with strangers will experience a higher level of anxiety than will U.S. Americans. Assumptions made in anxiety and uncertainty management theory (Gudykunst, 1994) include that national culture is a predictor and explanatory variable for intergroup behavior, and that relationships among such variables as uncertainty, anxiety, and mindfulness can predict and explain strangers' intergroup behavior.

Critical Deconstructionist Perspectives

As scholars in communication, the ways we come to know have changed dramatically over the last few centuries. One of the characteristic turns is the emergence of **skepticism** and questions about what we know, how we know, and who we are as scholars and people.

Certain overarching assumptions are shared by scholars aligned with a critical perspective. Scholars are primarily concerned with **exploitation, power,** empowerment, and the development of rhetorical tools to **deconstruct** and **critique** discourse and media texts and provide alternative interpretations. Prus (1996) characterizes the critical voice as "extreme skepticism in the viability of all forms of knowing" (p. 217).

One group of critical scholars describes the work it does as *postcolonialist.* These scholars not only criticize the use and misuse of power by particular groups, but also point out that scholars may exert power and influence on the cultural identities and conduct of the masses by deciding what is important to study and how to describe groups and social issues.

An example of the *critical perspective* is the work of van Dijk (1993) on social cognition and racism. He examines the social, political, and cultural reproduction of racism by giving attention to what he calls *microlevel interactions* and *everyday conversational talk,* along with macrostructures, socially shared strategies and representations of power, dominance, and access. He has investigated forms of racism and sexism in television news reports as well as in newspaper articles and examined how institutions are represented, how political points of view are articulated, and how economic and social policies are challenged or reinforced. Similarly, you could take a critical perspective in analyzing the newspaper reports about the campus problem and identify who is being interviewed, whose voices are featured most, what kind of examples are being quoted by members of particular groups, and the overall portrayal of particular groups.

Interpretive and Reconstructive Perspectives

A third type of epistemological perspective can be called *interpretive* because the goal is **understanding.** In most interpretive approaches, the goal of the researcher is to build understanding of how respondents come to do, be, and know (Sachs, 1984) their cultural identities. Many scholars use interpretive approaches to build understanding about the negotiation and enactment of cultural identities in particular interactional contexts.

One example of an *interpretive perspective* is CIT (Collier, 1998a,b; Collier & Thomas, 1988; Hecht, Collier, & Ribeau, 1993), which I've featured throughout this chapter. To review, one of the major premises I make is the assumption that we align with various groups, and part of what we do when we communicate with others is define who we are and distinguish ourselves as members of groups. We also construct our cultural identities as a way of developing relationships, increasing or contesting our lack of power in various situations, and creating a history that can transcend situations, periods of time, and lifetimes.

In a CIT approach, cultural identities are historical, contextual, and relational constructions; we create to some degree through our communication, our pasts, and what we hand down to new members and teach in our institutions. The historical, social, political, economic, and relational context, as well as our physical surroundings, affect who we are and who we come to be with one another. Cultural identities are commonly intelligible and accessible to group members (Carbaugh, 1990). Cultural identities emerge in everyday discourse as well as in social practices, rituals, norms, and myths that are handed down to new members.

Each perspective is based on a set of assumptions about inquiry and knowledge building. Just as our social world is characterized by rapid and complex change, so our perspectives should be open to interrogation and modification.

Researcher Perspective

Identities are constructed by and can be studied as constructions of individuals, relational partners, or group members of a community. in addition to selecting an epistemological perspective, you'll also need to select a researcher perspective. You may wish to focus on the point of view of individuals. Each person has individual interpretations of what it means to be U.S. American or Austrian or Indian, for example, and each person enacts his or her cultural identities slightly differently. If we want to understand why an individual behaves in a particular way, then we can ask the individual to talk about his or her cultural identity and experiences as a group member.

You can also study culture from a relational point of view. You can observe interaction between people, between friends, co-workers, or family members who identify themselves as members of a relationship and with different groups. Collier (1988) found that Mexican American friends emphasized the importance of their relationship in their descriptions of what is appropriate and effective—for example, meeting frequently and spending a significant portion of time together. They also described the most important characteristics of friendship to be support, trust, intimacy, and commitment to the relationship.

You may also study culture in terms of its communal properties. This is giving attention to public communication contexts and activities in communities and neighborhoods. Rituals, rites of passage, and holiday celebrations are other sources of information about how people use cultural membership to establish community.

STEP 9: WHAT ARE MY PRELIMINARY AND ALTERNATIVE INTERPRETATIONS AND CONCLUSIONS?

The ninth set of questions has to do with your interpretations. What are the patterns you are observing? What are your preliminary answers to your research questions? What are tentative conclusions?

After you formulate preliminary conclusions and answers to your questions, it will be useful to ask, What are alternative interpretations and conclusions? Who might disagree with these findings? Would your respondents (people you interviewed) or the audience for the film or newspaper articles agree or disagree with your findings? Can you ask them for further information? Are there any voices or views that have been heretofore silent and unspoken? It is also important to ask yourself, To what extent are my personal history, socialization, preferred norms of conduct, and cultural identities affecting my interpretations and conclusions? What are my personal biases that need to be identified? In the campus prob-

lem, would a student who had taken courses in women's studies, ethnic studies, or international studies have alternative interpretations of my data that might change my overall conclusions?

STEP 10: HOW CAN I APPLY MY INTERPRETATIONS?

Finally, the last set of questions asks you to pinpoint how you can apply what you learned from the intercultural problem to your own cultural identities and intercultural communication, as well as broader community, national, and international issues. Essentially, you should propose how your findings could be useful to improve your own intercultural relationships and ability to analyze critically what you read and hear, as well as how your findings may be useful for members of the cultural communities you studied or the wider community.

Sometimes what we learn has implications for similar cultural groups or intercultural interactions in a wide variety of contexts even from one country to another. How has what you learned changed how you be, do, know about intercultural communication? With whom should you share your findings? What are ethical or moral insights that you might have developed? How can you apply what you learned about the campus problem to comprehend better current political discourse about affirmative action? What do you still need to know or study?

CONCLUSIONS

The study of intercultural communication is complex and dynamic, occurs in broad historical, economic, political, and social contexts, while at the same time is characterized by distinctive social norms and practices in the particular situation. My goal is for the inventory to become a useful guide for you to build knowledge about how we co-create our cultural identities and relationships through our contact with one another. I hope the steps indicate some of the major issues that emerge in intercultural communication, such as cultural identities, power, quality of relationship, and context, as well as point you toward the many options you have to study and potentially manage intercultural problematics. Finally, I hope that the examples from the communication discourse of people in my classes and research studies encourage you to think about perspectives that are different from your own in a new way.

Learning about intercultural communication is a lifelong endeavor. It is a commitment to improving the quality of what exists now and transcends our lifetimes. Let the dialogue continue.

Endnotes

1. Melissa McCalla, Jennifer Thompson, and Charlene Belitz, doctoral students at the University of Denver, assigned a draft of this chapter in their undergraduate intercultural communication courses. The student feedback and recommendations were insightful and helpful.
2. I am grateful to Melissa McCalla for suggesting this term.
3. Please see Anderson (1996), Deetz (1994), and Mumby (1997) for additional reading about how these particular categories of knowing emerged.

References

Anderson, J. A. (1996). *Communication theory: Epistemological foundations*. New York: Guilford Press.

Banks, J. (1984). *Teaching strategies for ethnic studies* (3rd ed.). Boston: Allyn & Bacon.

Baxter, L., & Montgomery, B. (1996). *Relating: Dialogues and dialectics*. New York: Guilford Press.

Braithwaite, D. (1991). "Just how much did that wheelchair cost?" Management of privacy boundaries by persons with disabilities. *Western Journal of Speech Communication, 55*, 254–274.

Brislin, R. (1986). Prejudice and intergroup communication. In W. Gudykunst (Ed.), *Intergroup communication* (pp. 74–85). Baltimore: Edward Arnold.

Carbaugh, D. (1990). Intercultural communication. In D. Carbaugh (Ed.), *Cultural communication and intercultural contact* (pp. 151–176). Hillsdale, NJ: Lawrence Erlbaum.

Collier, M. J. (1998a). Researching cultural identity: Reconciling interpretive and post-colonial perspectives. In D. Tanno & A. Gonzalez (Eds.), *Communication and identity across cultures (International and Intercultural Communication Annual, Vol. XXI*, pp. 122–147). Thousand Oaks, CA: Sage.

———. (1998b). Intercultural friendships as interpersonal alliances. In J. Martin, T. Nakayama, & L. Flores (Eds.), *Readings in cultural contexts* (pp. 370–378). Mountain View, CA: Mayfield.

———. (1988). A comparison of conversations among and between domestic culture groups: How intra- and intercultural competencies vary. *Communication Quarterly, 36*, 122–144.

———, & Bornman, E. (In press). Core symbols in South African intercultural friendships. *International Journal of Intercultural Relations*.

———, & Bowker, J. (1994, Nov.) *U.S. American women in intercultural friendships*. Paper presented at the annual Speech Communication Association conference, New Orleans.

———, & Thomas, M. (1988). Cultural identity: An interpretive perspective. In Y. Y. Kim & W. Gudykunst (Eds.), *Theories in intercultural communication* (pp. 99–122). Newbury Park, CA: Sage.

———, & Thompson, J. (1997, May). *Intercultural adaptation among friends: Managing identities across contexts and relationships*. Paper presented at the International Conference of Language and Social Psychology, Ottawa, Canada.

Deetz, S. (1994). The future of the discipline: The challenges, the research and the social contribution. In S. Deetz (Ed.), *Communication yearbook 17* (pp. 115–147). Thousand Oaks, CA: Sage.

Doi, T. (1989). *The anatomy of dependence*. Tokyo: Kodansha Publishers.

Foss, S. K. (In preparation). bell hooks. In S. K. Foss, K. A. Foss, & C. L. Griffin (Eds.), *Feminist rhetorical theories*. Thousand Oaks, CA: Sage.

Geertz, C. (1983). *Local knowledge*. New York: Basic Books.

Giles, H., Coupland, N., & Coupland, J. (1991). Accommodation theory: Communication, contexts and consequences. In J. Giles, N. Coupland, & J. Coupland (Eds.), *Contexts of accommodation: Developments in applied sociolinguistics*. Cambridge, UK: Cambridge University Press.

Goffman, E. (1967). *Interaction ritual: Essays on face-to-face interaction*. Garden City, NY: Doubleday.

Goldman, A. (1992). *The centrality of "Ningensei" to Japanese negotiating and interpersonal relationships: Implications for U.S.–Japanese communication*. Paper presented at Speech Communication Association conference, Chicago.

Gudykunst, W. B. (1994). Anxiety/uncertainty management (AUM) theory: Current status. In R. Wiseman (Ed.), *International and Intercultural Communication Annual, Vol. XIX* (pp. 170–193). Thousand Oaks, CA: Sage.

————, & Ting-Toomey, S. (1988). *Culture and interpersonal communication*. Newbury Park: Sage.

Halualani, R. T. (1998). Seeing through the screen: A struggle of "culture." In J. Martin, T. Nakayama, & L. Flores (Eds.), *Readings in cultural contexts* (pp. 264–274). Mountain View, CA: Mayfield.

Hecht, M., & Ribeau, S. (1987). Afro-American identity labels and communicative effectiveness. *Journal of Language and Social Psychology, 6*, 319–326.

Hecht, M., Collier, M. J., & Ribeau, S. (1993). *African American communication*. Newbury Park: Sage.

Hecht, M., Larkey, L. K., Johnson, J. N., & Reinard, J. C. (1991). *A model of interethnic effectiveness*. Paper presented at the International Communication Association conference, Chicago.

Hecht, M., Ribeau, S., & Alberts, J. K. (1989). An Afro-American perspective on interethnic communication. *Communication Monographs, 56*, 385–410.

Hofstede, G. (1980). *Culture's consequences*. Newbury Park, CA: Sage.

hooks, b. (1989). *Talking back: Thinking feminist, thinking black*. Boston: South End.

Katz, E. (1960). The functional approach to the study of attitudes. *Public Opinion Quarterly, 24*, 164–204.

Langer, E. (1989). *Mindfulness*. Reading, MA: Addison-Wesley.

Marin, G., & Marin, B. V. (1991). *Research with Hispanic populations*. Newbury Park, CA: Sage.

Martin, J. (1997). Understanding whiteness in the United States. In L. Samovar & R. Porter (Eds.), *Intercultural communication: A reader* (8th ed., pp. 54–62). Belmont, CA: Wadsworth.

————, Nakayama, T. K., & Flores, L. A. (1998). A dialectical approach to intercultural communication. In J. Martin, T. Nakayama, & L. Flores (Eds.), *Readings in cultural contexts* (pp. 5–14). Mountain View, CA: Mayfield.

McClintock, A. (1995). *Imperial leather*. New York: Routledge.

McPhail, M. (1997). (Re)constructing the color line: Complicity and black conservatism. *Communication Theory, 7*, 162–177.

Morgan, R. (1996). Introduction. *Sisterhood is global*. New York: The Feminist Press.

Mumby, D. (1997). Modernism, postmodernism, and communication studies: A rereading of an ongoing debate. *Communication Theory, 7*, 1–28.

Omi, M., & Winant, H. (1986). *Racial formation in the United States*. New York: Routledge & Kegan Paul.

Prus, R. (1996). *Symbolic interaction and ethnographic research*. Albany: State University of New York Press.

Sachs, H. (1984). On doing "being ordinary." In J. M. Atkinson & J. Heritage (Eds.), *Structures of social action: Studies in conversation analysis* (pp. 413–429). Cambridge, UK: Cambridge University Press.

Sturken, M. (1995). The television image and collective amnesia: Dis(re)membering the Persian Gulf war. In P. d'Agostino & D. Tafler (Eds.), *Transmission: Toward a post-television culture* (2nd ed.) (pp. 135–150). Thousand Oaks, CA: Sage.

Tajfel, H. (1978). Interindividual and intergroup behaviour. In H. Tajfel (Ed.), *Differentiation between social groups* (pp. 27–60). London: Academic Press.

van Dijk, T. (1993). *Discourse and elite racism*. London: Routledge.

Webster, Y. (1992). *The racialization of America*. New York: St. Martin's Press.

Weider, D. L., & Pratt, S. (1990). On being a recognizable Indian among Indians. In D. Carbaugh (Ed.), *Cultural communication and intercultural contact* (pp. 45–64). Hillsdale, NJ: Lawrence Erlbaum.

Concepts and Questions

1. What is the central purpose of the "series of steps" presented by Collier?
2. Which one of Collier's "approaches to culture" do you believe most directly relates to intercultural communication?
3. How would you answer the following question: What do I want to know about the communicative event, contact, discourse, text, and situation?
4. What does Collier mean by the phrase "multiple types of cultural identities"?
5. Why is power an important variable in intercultural communication?
6. How would you answer the following question: What kinds of communicative messages should I examine to study intercultural communication?
7. How is Collier using the word *context*?
8. In what specific ways do you believe Collier's ten steps can be applied to your personal study of intercultural communication?

Context and Meaning

Edward T. Hall

One of the functions of culture is to provide a highly selective screen between man and the outside world. In its many forms, culture therefore designates what we pay attention to and what we ignore.[1] This screening function provides structure for the world and protects the nervous system from "information overload."[2] Information overload is a technical term applied to information processing systems. It describes a situation in which the system breaks down when it cannot properly handle the huge volume of information to which it is subjected. Any mother who is trying to cope with the demands of small children, run a house, enjoy her husband, and carry on even a modest social life knows that there are times when everything happens at once and the world seems to be closing in on her. She is experiencing the same information overload that afflicts business managers, administrators, physicians, attorneys, and air controllers. Institutions such as stock exchanges, libraries, and telephone systems also go through times when the demands on the system (inputs) exceed capacity. People can handle the crunch through delegating and establishing priorities; while institutional solutions are less obvious, the high-context rule seems to apply. That is, the only way to increase information-handling capacity without increasing the mass and complexity of the system is to program the memory of the system so that less information is required to activate the system, i.e., make it more like the couple that has been married for thirty-five years. The solution to the problem of coping with increased complexity and greater demands on the system seems to lie in the preprogramming of the individual or organization. This is done by means of the "contexting" process. . . .

The importance of the role of context is widely recognized in the communication fields, yet the

From Edward T. Hall, *Beyond Culture* (Garden City, NY: Doubleday & Company, 1976), pp. 85–103. Copyright © 1976, 1981 by Edward T. Hall. Reprinted by permission of Doubleday and The Lescher Agency. Professor Hall is affiliated with Northwestern University.

process is rarely described adequately, or if it is, the insights gained are not acted upon. Before dealing with context as a way of handling information overload, let me describe how I envisage the contexting process, which is an emergent function; i.e., we are just discovering what it is and how it works. Closely related to the high–low-context continuum is the degree to which one is aware of the selective screen that one places between himself and the outside world.[3] As one moves from the low to the high side of the scale, awareness of the selective process increases. Therefore, what one pays attention to, context, and information overload are all functionally related.

In the fifties, the United States government spent millions of dollars developing systems for machine translation of Russian and other languages. After years of effort on the part of some of the most talented linguists in the country, it was finally concluded that the only reliable, and ultimately the fastest, translator is a human being deeply conversant not only with the language but with the subject as well. The computers could spew out yards of printout but they meant very little. The words and some of the grammar were all there, but the sense was distorted. That the project failed was not due to lack of application, time, money, or talent, but for other reasons, which are central to the theme of this [article].

The problem lies not in the linguistic code but in the context, which carries varying proportions of the meaning. Without context, the code is incomplete since it encompasses only part of the message. This should become clear if one remembers that the spoken language is an abstraction of an event that happened, might have happened, or is being planned. As any writer knows, an event is usually infinitely more complex and rich than the language used to describe it. Moreover, the writing system is an abstraction of the spoken system and is in effect a reminder system of what somebody said or could have said. In the process of abstracting, as contrasted with measuring, people take in some things and unconsciously ignore others. This is what intelligence is: paying attention to the right things. The linear quality of a language inevitably results in accentuating some things at the expense of others. Two languages provide interesting contrasts. In English, when a man says, "It rained last night," there is no way of knowing how he arrived at that conclusion, or if he is even telling the truth, whereas a Hopi cannot talk about rain at all without signifying the nature of his relatedness to the event—firsthand experience, inference, or hearsay. This is a point made by the linguist Whorf[4] thirty years ago. However, selective attention and emphasis are not restricted to language but are characteristic of the rest of culture as well.

The rules governing what one perceives and [what one] is blind to in the course of living are not simple; at least five sets of disparate categories of events must be taken into account. These are: the subject or activity, the situation, one's status in a social system, past experience, and culture. The patterns governing juggling these five dimensions are learned early in life and are mostly taken for granted. The "subject" or topic one is engaged in has a great deal to do with what one does and does not attend. People working in the "hard" sciences, chemistry and physics, which deal with the physical world, are able to attend and integrate a considerably higher proportion of significant events observed than scientists working with living systems. The physical scientist has fewer variables to deal with; his abstractions are closer to the real events; and context is of less importance. This characterization is, of course, oversimplified. But it is important to remember that the laws governing the physical world, while relatively simple compared to those governing human behavior, may seem complex to the layman, while the complexity of language appears simple to the physicist, who, like everyone else, has been talking all his life. In these terms it is all too easy for the person who is in full command of a particular behavioral system, such as language, to confuse what he can *do* with a given system, with the unstated rules governing the way the system operates. The conceptual model I am using takes into account not only what one takes in and screens out but what one does not know about a given system even though one has mastered that system. The two are *not* the same. Michael Polanyi[5] stated this principle quite elegantly when he said, "The structure of a machine cannot be defined in terms of the laws which it harnesses."

What man chooses to take in, either consciously or unconsciously, is what gives structure and meaning to his world. Furthermore, what he perceives is "what he intends to do about it." Setting aside the other four dimensions (situation, status, past experience, and culture), theoretically it would be possible to arrange all of man's activities along a continuum ranging from those in which a very high proportion of the events influencing the outcome were consciously considered to those in which a much smaller number were considered. In the United States, interpersonal relations are frequently at the low end of the scale. Everyone has had the experience of thinking that he was making a good impression only to learn later that he was not. At times like these, we are paying attention to the wrong things or screening out behavior we should be observing. A common fault of teachers and professors is that they pay more attention to their subject matter than they do to the students, who frequently pay too much attention to the professor and not enough to the subject.

The "situation" also determines what one consciously takes in and leaves out. In an American court of law, the attorneys, the judge, and the jury are compelled by custom and legal practice to pay attention only to what is legally part of the record. Context, by design, carries very little weight. Contrast this with a situation in which an employee is trying to decipher the boss's behavior—whether he is pleased or not, and if he is going to grant a raise. Every little clue is a story in itself, as is the employee's knowledge of behavior in the past.

One's status in a social system also affects what must be attended. People at the top pay attention to different things from those at the middle or the bottom of the system. In order to survive, all organizations, whatever their size, have to develop techniques not only for replacing their leader but for switching the new leader's perceptions from the internal concerns he focused on when he was at the lower and middle levels to a type of global view that enables the head man or woman to chart the course for the institution.

The far-reaching consequences of what is attended can be illustrated by a characteristic fault in Western thinking that dates back to the philosophers of ancient Greece. Our way of thinking is quite arbitrary and causes us to look at ideas rather than events—a most serious shortcoming. Also, linearity can get in the way of mutual understanding and divert people needlessly along irrelevant tangents. The processes I am describing are particularly common in the social sciences; although the younger scientists in these fields are gradually beginning to accept the fact that when someone is talking about events on one level this does not mean that he has failed to take into account the many other events on different levels. It is just that one can talk about only a single aspect of something at any moment (illustrating the linear characteristic of language).

The results of this syndrome (of having to take multiple levels into account when using a single-level system) are reflected in a remark made by one of our most brilliant and least appreciated thinkers in modern psychiatry, H. S. Sullivan,[6] when he observed that as he composed his articles, lectures, and books the person he was writing to (whom he projected in his mind's eye) was a cross between an imbecile and a bitterly paranoid critic. What a waste. And so confusing to the reader who wants to find out what the man is really trying to say.

In less complex and fast-moving times, the problem of mutual understanding was not as difficult, because most transactions were conducted with people well known to the speaker or writer, people with similar backgrounds. It is important for conversationalists in any situation—regardless of the area of discourse (love, business, science)—to get to know each other well enough so that they realize what each person is and is not taking into account. This is crucial. Yet few are willing to make the very real effort—life simply moves too fast—which may explain some of the alienation one sees in the world today.

Programming of the sort I am alluding to takes place in all normal human transactions as well as those of many higher mammals. It constitutes the unmeasurable part of communication. This brings us to the point where it is possible to discuss context in relation to meaning, because what one pays attention to or does not attend is largely a matter of context. Remember, contexting is also an important way of handling the very great complexity of human transactions so that the system does not bog down in information overload.

Like a number of my colleagues, I have observed that meaning and context are inextricably bound up with each other. While a linguistic code can be analyzed on some levels independent of context (which is what the machine translation project tried to accomplish), *in real life the code, the context, and the*

meaning can only be seen as different aspects of a single event. What is unfeasible is to measure one side of the equation and not the others.[7]

Earlier, I said that high-context messages are placed at one end and low-context messages at the other end of a continuum. A high-context (HC) communication or message is one in which most of the information is either in the physical context or internalized in the person, while very little is in the coded, explicit, transmitted part of the message. A low-context (LC) communication is just the opposite; i.e., the mass of the information is vested in the explicit code. Twins who have grown up together can and do communicate more economically (HC) than two lawyers in a courtroom during a trial (LC), a mathematician programming a computer, two politicians drafting legislation, two administrators writing a regulation, or a child trying to explain to his mother why he got into a fight.

Although no culture exists exclusively at one end of the scale, some are high while others are low. American culture, while not on the bottom, is toward the lower end of the scale. We are still considerably above the German-Swiss, the Germans, and the Scandinavians in the amount of contexting needed in everyday life. While complex, multi-institutional cultures (those that are technologically advanced) might be thought of as inevitably LC, this is not always true. China, the possessor of a great and complex culture, is on the high-context end of the scale.

One notices this particularly in the written language of China, which is thirty-five hundred years old and has changed very little in the past three thousand years. This common written language is a unifying force tying together half a billion Chinese, Koreans, Japanese, and even some of the Vietnamese who speak Chinese. The need for context is experienced when looking up words in a Chinese dictionary. To use a Chinese dictionary, the reader must know the significance of 214 radicals (there are no counterparts for radicals in the Indo-European languages). For example, to find the word for star one must know that it appears under the sun radical. To be literate in Chinese, one has to be conversant with Chinese history. In addition, the spoken pronunciation system must be known, because there are four tones and a change of tone means a change of meaning; whereas in English, French, German, Spanish,

Italian, etc., the reader need not know how to pronounce the language in order to read it. Another interesting sidelight on the Chinese orthography is that it is also an art form.[8] To my knowledge, no low-context communication system has ever been an art form. Good art is always high-context; bad art, low-context. This is one reason why good art persists and art that releases its message all at once does not.

The level of context determines everything about the nature of the communication and is the foundation on which all subsequent behavior rests (including symbolic behavior). Recent studies in sociolinguistics have demonstrated how context-dependent the language code really is. There is an excellent example of this in the work of the linguist Bernstein,[9] who has identified what he terms "restricted" (HC) and "elaborated" (LC) codes in which vocabulary, syntax, and sounds are all altered: In the restricted code of intimacy in the home, words and sentences collapse and are shortened. This even applies to the phonemic structure of the language. The individual sounds begin to merge, as does the vocabulary, whereas in the highly articulated, highly specific, elaborated code of the classroom, law, or diplomacy, more accurate distinctions are made on all levels. Furthermore, the code that one uses signals and is consistent with the situation. A shifting of code signals a shift in everything else that is to follow. "Talking down" to someone is low-contexting him—telling him more than he needs to know. This can be done quite subtly simply by shifting from the restricted end of the code toward the elaborated forms of discourse.

From the practical viewpoint of communications strategy, one must decide how much time to invest in contexting another person. A certain amount of this is always necessary, so that the information that makes up the explicit portions of the message is neither inadequate nor excessive. One reason most bureaucrats are so difficult to deal with is that they write for each other and are insensitive to the contexting needs of the public. The written regulations are usually highly technical on the one hand, while providing little information on the other. That is, they are a mixture of different codes or else there is incongruity between the code and the people to whom it is addressed. Modern management methods, for which management consultants are largely

responsible, are less successful than they should be, because in an attempt to make everything explicit (low-contexting again) they frequently fail in their recommendations to take into account what people already know. This is a common fault of the consultant, because few consultants take the time (and few clients will pay for the time) to become completely contexted in the many complexities of the business.

There is a relationship between the worldwide activism of the sixties and where a given culture is situated on the context scale, because some are more vulnerable than others. HC actions are by definition rooted in the past, slow to change, and highly stable. Commenting on the need for the stabilizing effect of the past, anthropologist Loren Eiseley[10] takes an anti-activist position and points out how vulnerable our own culture is:

> Their world (the world of the activist), therefore, becomes increasingly the violent, unpredictable world of the first men simply because, in lacking faith in the past, one is inevitably forsaking all that enables man to be a planning animal. For man's story,[11] in brief, is essentially that of a creature who has abandoned *instinct* and replaced it with cultural tradition and the hard-won increments of contemplative thought. The lessons of the past have been found to be a reasonably secure construction for proceeding against an unknown future.[12]

Actually, activism is possible at any point in the HC–LC continuum, but it seems to have less direction or focus and becomes less predictable and more threatening to institutions in LC systems. Most HC systems, however, can absorb activism without being shaken to their foundations.

In LC systems, demonstrations are viewed as the last, most desperate act in a series of escalating events. Riots and demonstrations in the United States, particularly those involving blacks,[13] are a message, a plea, a scream of anguish and anger for the larger society to *do something*. In China (an HC culture), the Red Guard riots apparently had an entirely different significance. They were promulgated from the top of the social order, not the bottom. They were also a communication from top to bottom: first, to produce a show of strength by Mao Tse-tung; second, to give pause to the opposition and shake things up at the middle levels—a way of mobilizing society, not destroying it. Chinese friends with whom I have spoken about these riots took them much less seriously than I did. I was, of course, looking at them from the point of view of one reared in a low-context culture, where such riots can have disastrous effects on the society at large.

Wherever one looks, the influence of the subtle hand of contexting can be detected. We have just spoken of the effects of riots on high- and low-context political systems, but what about day-to-day matters of perception? On the physiological level of color perception, one sees the power of the brain's need to perceive and adjust everything in terms of context. As any interior designer knows, a powerful painting, print, or wall hanging can change the perceived color of the furnishings around it. The color psychologist Faber Birren[14] demonstrated experimentally that the perceived shade of a color depends upon the color context in which it occurs. He did this by systematically varying the color of the background surrounding different color samples.

Some of the most impressive demonstrations of the brain's ability to supply the missing information—the function of contexting—are the experiments of Edwin Land, inventor of the Land camera. Working in color photography using a single red filter, he developed a process that is simple, but the explanation for it is not. Until Land's experiments, it was believed that color prints could be made only by superimposing transparent images of three separate photographs made with the primary colors—red, blue, and yellow. Land made his color photographs with two images: a black-and-white image to give light and shadow, and a single, *red* filter for color. When these two images were projected, superimposed on a screen, even though red was the only color, they were perceived in full color with all the shades, and gradations of a three-color photograph![15] Even more remarkable is the fact that the objects used were deliberately chosen to provide no cues as to their color. To be sure that his viewers didn't unconsciously project color, Land photographed spools of plastic and wood and geometric objects whose color would be unknown to the viewer. How the eye and the visual centers of the brain function to achieve this remarkable feat of internal contexting is still only partially understood. But the actual stimulus does only part of the job.

Contexting probably involves at least two entirely different but interrelated processes—one inside the organism and the other outside. The first takes place in the brain and is a function of either past experience (programmed, internalized contexting) or the structure of the nervous system (innate contexting), or both. External contexting comprises the situation and/or setting in which an event occurs (situational and/or environmental contexting).[16]

One example of the growing interest in the relationship of external context to behavior is the widespread interest and concern about our public-housing disasters, Pruitt-Igoe Homes in St. Louis is only one example. This $26-million fiasco imposed on poor blacks is now almost completely abandoned. All but a few buildings have been dynamited, because nobody wants to live there.

Objections and defects in high-rise public housing for poor families are legion: Mothers can't supervise their children; there are usually no community service agencies nearby and no stores or markets; and quite often there is no access to any public transportation system. There are no recreation centers for teenagers and few places for young children to play. In any budget crunch, the first thing to be cut is maintenance and then the disintegration process starts; elevators and hallways turn into death traps. The case against high-rise housing for low-income families is complex and underscores the growing recognition that environments are not behaviorally neutral.

Although situational and environmental context has only recently been systematically studied, environmental effects have been known to be a factor in behavior for years. Such men as the industrialist Pullman[17] made statements that sounded very advanced at the time. He believed that if workers were supplied with clean, airy, well-built homes in pleasant surroundings, this would exert a positive influence on their health and general sense of well-being and would make them more productive as well. Pullman was not wrong in his analysis. He simply did not live up to his stated ideals. The main street of his company town, where supervisors lived, was everything he talked about. But his workers were still poorly housed. Being isolated in a company town in close proximity to the plush homes of managers made their inadequate living conditions more obvious by way of contrast, and the workers finally embarked on a violent strike. There were many other human, economic, and political needs, which Pullman had not taken into account, that led to worker dissatisfaction. Pullman's professed idealism backfired. Few were aware of the conditions under which his laborers actually lived and worked, so that the damage done to the budding but fragile environmentalist position was incalculable and gave ammunition to the "hard-nosed," "practical" types whose minds were focused on the bottom-line figures of profit and loss.

Quite often, the influence of either programmed contexting (experience) or innate contexting (which is built in) is brushed aside. Consider the individual's spatial needs and his feelings about certain spaces. For example, I have known women who needed a room to be alone in, whose husbands did not share this particular need, and they brushed aside their wives' feelings, dismissing them as childish. Women who have this experience should not let my talking about it raise their blood pressure. For it is very hard for someone who does not share an unstated, informal need with another person to experience that need as tangible and valid. Among people of northern European heritage, the only generally accepted proxemic needs are those associated with status. However, status is linked to the ego. Therefore, while people accept that the person at the top gets a large office, whenever the subject of spatial needs surfaces it is likely to be treated as a form of narcissism. The status and organizational aspects are recognized while internal needs are not.

Yet, people have spatial needs independent of status. Some people can't work unless they are in the midst of a lot of hubbub. Others can't work unless they are behind closed doors, cut off from auditory and visual distractions. Some are extraordinarily sensitive to their environments, as though they had tentacles from the body reaching out and touching everything. Others are impervious to environmental impact. It is these differences, when and if they are understood at all, that cause trouble for architects. Their primary concern is with aesthetics, and what I am talking about lies underneath aesthetics, at a much more basic level.

As often happens, today's problems are being solved in terms of yesterday's understanding. With few exceptions, most thinking on the man-environ-

ment relationship fails to make the man-environment (M–E) transaction specific, to say nothing of taking it into account. The sophisticated architect pays lip service to the M–E relationship and then goes right on with what he was going to do anyway, demonstrating once more that people's needs, cultural as well as individual—needing a room of one's own—are not seen as real. Only the building is real! (This is extension transference again.)

Of course, the process is much more complex than most people think. Until quite recently, this whole relationship had been unexplored.[18] Perhaps those who eschewed it did so because they unconsciously and intuitively recognized its complexity. Besides, it is much easier to deal with such simple facts as a balance sheet or the exterior design of a building. Anyone who begins to investigate context and contexting soon discovers that much of what is examined, even though it occurs before his eyes, is altered in its significance by many hidden factors. Support for research into these matters is picayune. What has to be studied is not only very subtle but is thought to be too fine-grained, or even trivial, to warrant serious consideration.

One hospital administrator once threw me out of his office because I wanted to study the effects of space on patients in his hospital. Not only was he not interested in the literature, which was then considerable, but he thought I was a nut to even suggest such a study. To complicate things further, proxemics research requires an inordinate amount of time. For every distance that people use, there are at least five major categories of variables that influence what is perceived as either correct or improper. Take the matter of "intrusion distance" (the distance one has to maintain from two people who are already talking in order to get attention but not intrude). How great this distance is and how long one must wait before moving in depends on: what is going on (activity), your status, your relationship in a social system (husband and wife or boss and subordinate), the emotional state of the parties, the urgency of the needs of the individual who must intrude, etc.

Despite this new information, research in the social and biological sciences has turned away from context. In fact, attempts are often made to consciously exclude context. Fortunately, there are a few exceptions, men and women who have been willing to swim against the main currents of psychological thought.

One of these is Roger Barker, who summarized twenty-five years of observations in a small Kansas town in his book *Ecological Psychology*.[19] Starting a generation ago, Barker and his students moved into the town and recorded the behavior of the citizens in a wide variety of situations and settings such as classrooms, drugstores, Sunday-school classes, basketball games, baseball games, club meetings, business offices, bars, and hangouts. Barker discovered that much of people's behavior is situation-dependent (under control of the setting), to a much greater degree than had been supposed. In fact, as a psychologist, he challenged many of the central and important tenets of his own field. In his words:

> The view is not uncommon among psychologists that the environment of behavior is a relatively unstructured, passive, probabilistic arena of objects and events upon which man behaves in accordance with the programming he carries about within himself. . . . When we look at the environment of behavior as a phenomenon worthy of investigation for itself, and not as an instrument for unraveling the behavior-relevant programming within persons, the situation is quite different. From this viewpoint the environment is seen to consist of highly structured, improbable arrangements of objects and events which coerce behavior in accordance with their own dynamic patterning. . . . We found . . . that we could predict some aspects of children's behavior more adequately from knowledge of the behavior characteristics of the drugstores, arithmetic classes, and basketball games they inhabited than from knowledge of the behavior tendencies of particular children. . . . (emphasis added) (p. 4)

Later Barker states,

> The theory and data support the view that the environment in terms of behavior settings is much more than a source of random inputs to its inhabitants, or of inputs arranged in fixed array and flow patterns. They indicate, rather, that the environment provides inputs with controls that regulate the inputs in accordance with the systemic requirements of the environment, on the one hand, and in accordance with the behavior attributes of its human components, on the other.

This means that the same environmental unit provides different inputs to different persons, and different inputs to the same person if his behavior changes; and it means, further, that the whole program of the environment's inputs changes if its own ecological properties change; if it becomes more or less populous, for example. (p. 205)[20]

Barker demonstrates that in studying man *it is impossible to separate the individual from the environment in which he functions*. Much of the work of the transactional psychologists Ames, Ittelson, and Kilpatrick,[21] as well as my earlier work,[22] leads to the same conclusion.

In summary, regardless of where one looks, one discovers that a universal feature of information systems is that meaning (what the receiver is expected to do) is made up of: the communication, the background and preprogrammed responses of the recipient, and the situation. (We call these last two the internal and external context.)

Therefore, what the receiver actually perceives is important in understanding the nature of context. Remember that what an organism perceives is influenced in four ways—by status, activity, setting, and experience. But in man one must add another crucial dimension: *culture*.

Any transaction can be characterized as high-, low-, or middle-context (Figure 1). HC transactions feature preprogrammed information that is in the receiver and in the setting, with only minimal information in the transmitted message. LC transactions are the reverse. Most of the information must be in the transmitted message in order to make up for what is missing in the context (both internal and external).

In general, HC communication, in contrast to LC, is economical, fast, efficient, and satisfying; however, time must be devoted to programming. If this programming does not take place, the communication is incomplete.

HC communications are frequently used as art forms. They act as a unifying, cohesive force, are long-lived, and are slow to change. LC communications do not unify; however, they can be changed easily and rapidly. This is why evolution by extension is so incredibly fast; extensions in their initial stages of development are low-context. To qualify this

Figure 1 *Inter-Ethnic Relationships*

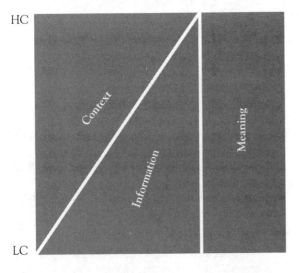

statement somewhat, some extension systems are higher on the context scale than others. A system of defense rocketry can be out of date before it is in place and is therefore very low-context. Church architecture, however, was for hundreds of years firmly rooted in the past and was the material focus for preserving religious beliefs and ideas. Even today, most churches are still quite traditional in design. One wonders if it is possible to develop strategies for balancing two apparently contradictory needs: the need to adapt and change (by moving in the low-context direction) and the need for stability (high-context). History is replete with examples of nations and institutions that failed to adapt by holding on to high-context modes too long. The instability of low-context systems, however, on the present-day scale is quite new to mankind. And furthermore, there is no reservoir of experience to show us how to deal with changes at this rate.

Extensions that now make up most of man's world are for the most part low-context. The question is, how long can man stand the tension between himself and his extensions? This is what *Future Shock*[23] and *Understanding Media*[24] are all about. Take a single example, the automobile, which completely altered the American scene in all its dimensions— exploded communities, shredded the fabric of relationships, switched the rural-urban balance, changed our sex mores and churchgoing habits, altered our

cities, crime, education, warfare, health, funerals. (One undertaker recently experimented with drive-in viewing of the corpse!) In summary:

> The screens that one imposes between oneself and reality constitute one of the ways in which reality is structured.
>
> Awareness of that structure is necessary if one is to control behavior with any semblance of rationality. Such awareness is associated with the low-context end of the scale.
>
> Yet there is a price that must be paid for awareness—instability; obsolescence, and change at a rate that may become impossible to handle and result in information overload.
>
> Therefore, as things become more complex, as they inevitably must with fast-evolving, low-context systems, it eventually becomes necessary to turn life and institutions around and move toward the greater stability of the high-context part of the scale as a way of dealing with information overload.

Notes

1. *The Hidden Dimension* discusses this quality of culture in more detail.
2. Meier (1963)
3. Man also imposes a selective screen between the conscious part of his mind and the unconscious part. Sullivan (1947) and Freud (1933)
4. Whorf (1956)
5. Polanyi (1968)
6. Sullivan (1947)
7. The linguist Noam Chomsky (1968) and his followers have tried to deal with the contexting feature of language by eliminating context and going to so-called "deep structure." The results are interesting but end up evading the main issues of communication and to an even greater extent stress ideas at the expense of what is actually going on.
8. For further information on Chinese, see Wang (1973).
9. Bernstein (1964)
10. Eiseley (1969)
11. I do not agree with Eiseley's generalizing about all of mankind, because activism, like everything else, has to be taken in context. As we will

see, LC cultures appear to be more vulnerable to violent perturbations than HC cultures.

12. Saul Bellow's (1974) article on the role of literature in a setting of changing times is also relevant to this discussion. Bellow makes the point that for some time now there has been a conscious effort on the part of avant-garde Western intellectuals to obliterate the past. "Karl Marx felt in history the tradition of all dead generations weighing like a nightmare on the brain of the living. Nietzsche speaks movingly of 'it was,' and Joyce's Stephen Daedalus also defines history as a 'nightmare from which we are trying to awaken.'" Bellow points out, however, that there is a paradox that must be met, for to do away with history is to destroy one's own part in the historical process. It is reasonably certain, however, that what these men were trying to do was to redefine context in order to reduce its influence on men's actions. Simply to do away with the past would lead to an incredibly unstable society, as we shall see.

13. Black culture is much higher on the context scale than white culture, and one would assume from our model that riots do not have the same meaning for blacks as they do to the white society in which the blacks are imbedded.

14. Birren (1961)

15. For further details on this fascinating set of experiments, see Land (1959).

16. These distinctions are completely arbitrary and are for the convenience of the writer and the reader. They do not necessarily occur in nature. The inside-outside dichotomy has been struck down many times, not only by the perceptual transactionalists (Kilpatrick, 1961) following in Dewey's footsteps but in my own writings as well. Within the brain, experience (culture) acts on the structure of the brain to produce mind. It makes little difference *how* the brain is modified; what is important is that modification does take place and is apparently continuous.

17. Buder (1967)

18. See Hall (1966) for a comprehensive treatment of man's relationship to the spaces he builds as well as a bibliography on the subject.

19. Barker (1968) and Barker and Schoggen (1973)

20. The interested reader will find it worthwhile to consult Barker's works directly.

21. Kilpatrick (1961)

22. Hall (1966)

23. Toffler (1970)

24. McLuhan (1964)

Bibliography

Barker, Roger G. *Ecological Psychology*. Stanford, Calif.: Stanford University Press, 1968.

———, and Schoggen, Phil. *Qualities of Community Life*. San Francisco: Jossey-Bass, 1973.

Bellow, Saul. "Machines and Story Books," *Harper's Magazine*, Vol. 249, pp. 48–54, August 1974.

Bernstein, Basil. "Elaborated and Restricted Codes: Their Social Origins and Some Consequences." In John J. Gumperz and Dell Hymes (eds.), The Ethnography of Communication, *American Anthropologist*, Vol. 66, No. 6, Part II, pp. 55–69, 1964.

Birren, Faber. *Color, Form and Space*. New York: Reinhold, 1961.

Buder, Stanley. "The Model Town of Pullman: Town Planning and Social Control in the Gilded Age," *Journal of the American Institute of Planners*, Vol. 33, No. 1, pp. 2–10, January 1967.

Chomsky, Noam. *Language and Mind*. New York: Harcourt, Brace & World, 1968.

Eiseley, L. "Activism and the Rejection of History," *Science*, Vol. 165, p. 129, July 11, 1969.

Freud, Sigmund. *New Introductory Lectures on Psychoanalysis*. New York: W. W. Norton & Company, 1933.

Hall, Edward T. "Art, Space and the Human Experience." In Gyorgy Kepes (ed.). *Arts of the Environment*. New York: George Braziller, Inc., 1972.

———. *The Hidden Dimension*. Garden City, N.Y.: Doubleday, 1966.

———. "Human Needs and Inhuman Cities." In *The Fitness of Man's Environment*, Smithsonian Annual II. Washington, D.C.: Smithsonian Institution Press, 1968. Reprinted in *Ekistics*, Vol. 27, No. 160, March 1969.

Kilpatrick, F. P. *Explorations in Transactional Psychology* (contains articles by Adelbert Ames, Hadley Cantril, William Ittelson, and F. P. Kilpatrick). New York: New York University Press, 1961.

McLuhan, Marshall. *Understanding Media*. New York: McGraw-Hill, 1964.

Meier, Richard. "Information Input Overload: Features of Growth in Communications-Oriented Institutions," *Libri* (Copenhagen), Vol. 13, No. 1, pp. 1–44, 1963.

Polanyi, M. "Life's Irreducible Structure," *Science*, Vol. 160, pp. 1308–12, June 21, 1968.

Sullivan, Harry Stack. *Conceptions of Modern Psychiatry.* New York: William Alanson White Psychiatric Foundation, 1947.

Toffler, Alvin. *Future Shock.* New York: Bantam Books, 1970.

Wang, William. "The Chinese Language," *Scientific American*, Vol. 228, No. 2, February 1973.

Whorf, Benjamin Lee. *Language, Thought, and Reality.* New York: The Technology Press of M.I.T. and John Wiley, 1956.

Concepts and Questions

1. What do you think Hall means when he writes "In its many forms, culture therefore designates what we pay attention to and what we ignore"?

2. Why does Hall maintain that "the rules governing what one perceives and [what one] is blind to in the course of living [are] not simple?"

3. Explain the phrase "The situation also determines what one consciously takes in and leaves out."

4. What are the major differences between high- and low-context cultures?

5. What does Hall mean when he notes that "in real life the code, the context, and the meaning can only be seen as different aspects of a single event"?

6. Why does Hall call "contexting" subtle?

7. Do you agree with Hall when he asserts that "extensions that now make up man's world are for the most part low-context"?

8. How does Hall's discussion of high- and low-context communication relate to some of the underlying premises about intercultural communication?

Understanding Whiteness in the United States

JUDITH N. MARTIN

What does it mean to be a white person in the United States? Is there such a thing as a white identity? Is it different from an ethnic identity? Is feeling white different from feeling German American or Italian American? How does being white influence the way we communicate? How is our whiteness expressed in communication?

For many people in the United States, there currently seems to be a degree of confusion and angst about racial and ethnic identity among white people. Some people never think about being white. Some think it seems all right to feel ethnic pride, but not pride in being white. Some feel that they are being forced to think about being white because of issues like affirmative action and "reverse discrimination." This essay attempts to sort out some of these issues and explore the contradictions and tensions in the notion of whiteness as an identity. We also examine how being white in the United States may influence communication, particularly in terms of how this identity develops and is reflected in the labels and words we use to refer to ourselves.

A COMMUNICATION PERSPECTIVE OF IDENTITY

Let's start with a communication perspective on identity. That is, we all have multiple identities (such as gender, religious, ethnicity, race) that make up our self-concept and how we see ourselves. Identities arise from our associations with groups, some voluntary (such as professional and religious affiliations) and some involuntary (such as age and family groups), and then develop through communication with others.

This essay first appeared here in the eighth edition. All rights reserved. Permission to reprint must be obtained from the author and the publisher. Judith Martin teaches at Arizona State University, Tempe, Arizona.

As communication scholars Michael Hecht, Mary Jane Collier, and Sidney Ribeau (1993) have noted, cultural identities are *negotiated, co-created, reinforced, and challenged through communication*. Some identities may be easier to co-create and negotiate than others. For example, does it seem easier to understand and negotiate being female than being white? How is being white negotiated and challenged through communication in today's world?

In addition, as Collier explains earlier in this chapter, our identities are expressed through *norms and labels*—the communicative behaviors and terms that reflect the core symbols or priorities of our group-associated identities. In this book, a number of essays identify the core symbols and norms of various groups like Japanese, African Americans, and Indians. Are there similar norms, labels, and core symbols that are associated with being white in the United States?

One final thing that we need to keep in mind about identities is that they are *dynamic* and *context-related*. I am not just a female, a professor, a white German American. I am all of these, and any one identity may be highlighted or suppressed depending on the situation or context. For example, in some situations, such as when I am the only white person in a conversation or when I am discussing the issue of race, my white identity is highlighted. In other conversations, my professor identity may be emphasized more. We are always in the process of becoming and unbecoming, as we negotiate, develop, and re-form our identities through communication.

Three issues need to be addressed as we apply this communication perspective to understanding white identity: the difference between white racial and ethnic identity, the characteristics of a white identity, and how whites develop a sense of being white.

WHITE RACIAL AND ETHNIC IDENTITY

Race Versus Ethnicity

What is the difference between racial and ethnic identity? Many people believe that race has to do with physical characteristics, whereas ethnicity is more a sense of a shared culture, belief system, and origin. However, most scholars now reject the bio-

logical argument in favor of a more social approach to understanding race. That is, while there may be some physiological basis for racial categories, it is the way in which these categories are constructed and the meaning attached to racial categories that have a profound influence on communication and how identities are negotiated. What are the arguments against physiological definitions?

First, racial categories vary widely in different parts of the world. One contrast is seen in the United States and South America. In the United States, there are two major racial distinctions (black and white), and this distinction is fairly rigid. People seem to have a sense of who is white and who isn't (for example, "you don't look black") and are uneasy when they are unable to categorize someone of mixed racial origin ("But are you white *or* black?"). In contrast, people in Brazil and other South American countries recognize a variety of intermediate racial categories.

A second example of how racial categories are socially constructed is that racial categories have changed throughout U.S. immigration history and some groups have been shifted from one racial category to another at particular points in history. In the eighteenth century, British immigrants struggled to preserve their base of power and even to prevent other Europeans from entering the United States. In the nineteenth century, as more and more southern Europeans immigrated, there was an attempt to classify Irish and Jewish Europeans as nonwhite. Instead, the racial line was drawn around Europe, and those outside (such as the Chinese and Japanese) were then designated as nonwhite (Omi & Winant, 1992). So while the notion of race has some basis in physiology, it probably makes more sense to talk about race *formation* and to think about race as a complex of social meanings that get interpreted through communication, rather than as something fixed, concrete, and objective.

It should also be pointed out that as socially constructed, these categories are relational, exist in relation to each other. Could there be a white without a black category? What does it mean that we tend to see race in the United States in polar categories, white and black? If people do not fit or do not want to fit into these categories, how can they negotiate their identity?

Bounded Versus Dominant/ Normative Identities

The relationship between white racial and ethnic identity can be clarified by distinguishing between bounded and dominant identities (Frankenburg, 1993; Trinh, 1986/87). Bounded cultures are those groups we belong to that are specific and not dominant or normative (such as groups defined by religion, gender, ethnicity). For most white people, connections to these groups are clear and easy to talk about. Being Irish American means we celebrate St. Patrick's Day; being Amish means we follow the *"Ordnung"* (the community rules). Growing up German American may mean working hard for the sake of working and not being very verbally expressive. It's easy to recognize and identify these cultural behaviors.

However, what it means to belong to the dominant or *normative* white culture is a much more "slippery" construct, more difficult to define, but just as real. It is not often easy to see what cultural practices or norms link white people together. For example, we usually don't think of Thanksgiving as a white American holiday. Part of the "slipperiness" of this identity is related to the dominant or normative aspect of being white.

Identity and Power

Sometimes the more powerful aspects of identity are the most unrecognized, and power is more strongly linked to aspects of identity that are ascribed, or involuntary. For example, when questioned about identity males will often not mention gender. They just don't think about it, whereas women are more likely to be aware of how gender is a part of their identity.

The same thing may be true about being white. One reason white people don't think about being white is that they may not need to. Communication scholars Tom Nakayama and Robert Krizek (1995) suggest that this lack of consciousness on the part of whites is possible only because of the power associated with being white. The experiences and communication patterns of whites are taken as the norm from which others are marked or measured. The universal norm then becomes invisible. For example, the news media refer to "black leaders" but never to "white leaders." There is "black on black violence," but

European conflicts are not referred to as "white on white violence."

What does it mean that the category "white" is seldom referred to and that whites so rarely talk about the meaning of being white? As Krizek reflects:

> I've gone through life never consciously thinking about labels. I suppose we defined ourselves as one of those people we didn't label, although nobody ever said that. We were just white, not black or brown, and I don't really know what that means. No one ever questioned it (Nakayama & Krizek, 1995, p. 292).

On the other hand, Nakayama (1993) has written about growing up in the South as a fourth-generation Japanese American, with his identity as an American consistently challenged as people frequently asked him where he was *really* from and if he spoke English.

Nakayama and Krizek attempt to show how the "invisibility" of whiteness is related to power by analyzing the "rhetoric of whiteness" or how white people talk about being white when explicitly asked. They found that people often resisted discussing how they felt about being white, which they interpret as reflecting an invisible power in which white is not a category of identity, but black African American, or Chicana is.

A second rhetorical strategy was to say that being white was based on negation, that white is "not something else (not black, brown, yellow or red)." This seems like a neutral way to talk about being white, but they point out that in this strategy white is again the universal against which other colors are marked. Another strategy confuses whiteness with nationality. Whiteness means white American. As one of their respondents noted, "A lot of times when people think of Americans, I bet you they probably think of white. They probably think it's redundant" (p. 301). What does it mean for all those Americans who are not white?

We can see how difficult it is for people to pin down the meaning of whiteness, but perhaps we'll understand intercultural communication better if we apply the same scrutiny to white identity that we apply to other cultural groups. This lack of awareness on the part of whites may be changing, as we'll discuss later. As issues of race are brought up more and more frequently in the United States (in the

O. J. Simpson trial, for example) white people are perhaps thinking more about being white than ever before, and perhaps it will become easier to identify those norms and core symbols of whiteness.

In Chapter 3 Edith Folb argues that there is a relative continuum of power in the United States associated with various identities, ranging from the more powerful groups (whites, males, Protestants, heterosexuals, middle/upper classes, the educated) to less powerful groups (racial minorities, females, religions other than Protestant, gays, the working class, the less educated). And we each may have aspects of our identity that are more or less powerful, depending on which is highlighted in any particular context. Those that are more involuntary or physically marked are more difficult and the most problematic to negotiate.

What happens when our identities are challenged? Growing up as an Amish/Mennonite young woman, I felt marginalized in many social contexts because I was physically marked by a distinctive dress and physical appearance. It was difficult to negotiate anything other than a bounded (Amish) identity. What are the communicative consequences when identities are challenged—when, for example, Asian Americans are asked "Where are you *really* from?" or "Do you speak English?" How does it affect the communication between people when the identities of some are often challenged and others (whites) are rarely challenged?

DIMENSIONS OF WHITE IDENTITY

An interesting question, then, is whether there is a set of cultural norms and symbols shared by most white people. Many scholars feel that there are uniquely white cultural patterns, but that they are often difficult to discern. Sociologist Ruth Frankenburg suggests that one way to understand whiteness is to view it not as simply a racial or ethnic category but rather as a set of three linked dimensions in which power is a key ingredient. These are modified to emphasize the communicative aspect of identity: a location of structural advantage, a standpoint from which to view ourselves and others, and a set of cultural practices (core symbols, labels, and norms).

Whiteness Is a Location of Structural Privilege

Some scholars argue that white identity is linked to the structural advantage of race privilege within the United States but that the two are not synonymous. All whites do not have power and do not have equal access to power. For example, one can point to times in U.S. history when some white cultural groups were not privileged, but rather were viewed as separate or different, as were the Irish in the early part of the twentieth century and the German Americans during World War II.

However, scholars have pointed out that the memory of marginality in these instances has outlasted the marginality. In the latter part of the twentieth century, European immigrant groups are now assimilated and are "just American." Boundaries between Americanness and whiteness have been much more fluid for "white ethnic" groups than for people of color.

How is this dimension of white identity played out in the everyday lives of white people and their communication with others? Peggy McIntosh (1995) has tried to identify the ways in which white privilege affects her daily interactions. See if you can list others:

I can, if I wish, arrange to be in the company of people of my race most of the time.

I can be fairly sure of having my voice heard in a group in which I am the only member of my race.

I can talk with my mouth full and not have people put this down to my color.

I can do well in a challenging situation without being called a credit to my race.

I am never asked to speak for all people of my racial group.

I can worry about racism without it being seen as self-interest or self-seeking.

My culture gives me little fear about ignoring the perspectives and powers of people of other races.

The question then is how does this aspect of white identity influence my communication with others? Perhaps it means that I approach most interactions with a confidence that if I'm nice, most people will be nice back to me. People won't prejudge me as untrustworthy, or "different," or "angry." Or if they see me sitting with other people who are white, they won't think this means I don't want to communicate with people who aren't white. They will judge me and communicate with me as an individual.

Several studies have, in fact, found that whites and African Americans approach interethnic conversations in different ways. Whites rarely talk about issues of power when discussing interethnic communication, whereas it is a more central issue in African American frameworks (Martin, Hecht, & Larkey, 1994). So maybe this is one aspect of being white, the fact that I don't consider power issues in conversations. Perhaps you can think of other ways that privilege may be reflected in whites' communication.

While being white in the United States may mean privilege sometimes, there seems to be an increasing perception that being white does not mean "invisible privilege." Charles A. Gallagher, who interviewed college students in a large inner-city campus found that white students thought a lot about being white and saw their whiteness not as a privilege but as a liability. They often felt that minority students were getting more breaks and more privileges. They also felt that they were prejudged by students of color as being racist because they were white.

Some whites feel that being white is not very positive, that whiteness represents blandness (like Wonder Bread), and that it is not very interesting in contrast to the cultural "richness" of other cultural groups. This sometimes leads whites to retrieve their ethnic heritage and identity (Italian American, Irish American, and so on). Ethnicity for white Americans can be almost like a garment that is put on or off at will.

Perhaps this change in identity, this growing awareness of a white identity, is occurring because the changing demographics in the United States means that whites *are beginning to perceive* themselves in the minority. Gallagher (1994) also asked students to estimate the ratio of whites to blacks on campus. Many students reported that they thought the ratio was 30 percent white students, 70 percent black students. The actual ratio was 70 percent white and 30 percent black.

The point here is not the inaccuracy of the perception, or whether whites or minorities are more privileged, but how these perceptions affect intercultural communication. How do we communicate with others if we feel that we are being prejudged as racist?

or as privileged? How are these identities negotiated and confirmed or challenged in our intercultural interactions?

Whiteness Is a "Standpoint"

A second dimension of white identity, according to Frankenburg, is a standpoint, a place from which white people look at themselves, at others, and at society. What are some perceptions shared by white people? And how do these perceptions differ from those of other cultural groups?

A dramatic example arose during the trial of the African American celebrity O. J. Simpson, accused of killing his ex-wife, Nicole Brown Simpson, and her friend Ron Goldman. An ABC News poll conducted just before the verdict was handed down showed a profound split between white and black perception: 77 percent of whites thought Simpson was guilty, 72 percent of blacks believed he was innocent (*Arizona Republic,* October 1, 1995, p. A2).

Both whites and blacks saw the same televised trial, the same evidence, heard the same legal arguments, but saw these from two different "standpoints" and arrived at two different conclusions. How could this be? Experts analyzed the two standpoints and tried to understand this dramatic difference in perception in the days immediately following the trial.

Most experts saw the roots of the different perceptions in the different life experiences of African and white Americans. As one columnist explained it:

> Most whites thought Fuhrman [the policeman accused of evidence tampering and racism] was a sick act and an exception. Most blacks, especially those in L. A. thought he was no aberration; they've known others like him. (Wilson, 1995, p. 2)

There are numerous other, perhaps less dramatic examples of how perceptions of whites contrast with those of other U.S. groups. To give just one example, according to a CBS News poll reported in the *Arizona Republic,* 38 percent of whites versus 27 percent of blacks think race relations in the United States are generally good (October 4, 1995). So something about being white influences how we view the world and ultimately how we communicate with others. As one individual reported in Nakayama and Krizek's study:

"I don't exactly know what it means to be white, but we all know don't we? I mean I never talk about it, but I know that we understand each other at some level. Like when a black guy gets on an elevator or when you have a choice to sit or stand next to a white person or a black person. You pick the white person and you look at each other, the whites and you just know that you've got it better. You don't say anything but you know. It's in the looks." (p. 298)

Of course, not all whites perceive all situations in the same way. Remember that identity is dynamic, negotiated, and context-dependent. Perhaps it is easier to see shared perceptions in dramatic situations like the Simpson trial or the Rodney King beating and the subsequent trial of white police officers. And even then, it is still difficult to understand how perceptions are related to race.

Again the question comes back to how these varying perceptions, expressions of identity, influence our communication. Are there ways to negotiate these varying perceptions?

Discussions following the O. J. Simpson trial may have presented opportunities for intercultural dialogue and finding some common ground. Blacks saw whites unanimously condemning Mark Fuhrman, and whites heard the same thing from blacks concerning Simpson's pattern of spousal abuse (*Arizona Republic*, October 1, 1995, p. A22).

Whiteness Is a Set of Core Symbols, Norms, and Labels

Core symbols are those values and priorities of a cultural group that are reflected in the norms of behavior and labels used to describe the group (Hecht, Collier, & Ribeau, 1993). Often the *norms* are unmarked; they are not made explicit, and it is hard to identify what norms are uniquely shared by whites. As noted, this difficulty comes partly from the normative and dominant aspect of being white. The dilemma is that white is everything and it is nothing. It is just there, and yet it is difficult to talk about, maybe even embarrassing.

Sometimes, these cultural practices are most clearly visible to those who are not white, to those groups who are excluded. Janet Helms (1990) and others (such as M. Asante, 1973) have attempted to outline values that are shared primarily by white people. For example, they suggest that a strong belief in individualism and an emphasis on linear thinking are two patterns that are most strongly linked to being white and are not universally shared by other cultural groups in the United States.

The *labels* we attach to ourselves and others that characterize ethnicity and/or race may be seen as a category of core symbols and are another way in which identity is expressed. Labels have meaning and are not neutral.

The questions of labels and identity has been of concern to marginalized groups for a long time. One issue revolves around who has the right to name others. Who has the right to use a label? Again power comes into play, for dominant groups can exercise power in naming others. And it is often difficult for the less powerful groups to control their own labels. It is well known that Native Americans have objected to the use of tribal terms as names for sports groups (Redskins), cars (Jeep Cherokee), and other commercial products. Some African Americans object to Aunt Jemima pancake mix and Uncle Ben's rice. It is not widely known that Quakers objected strenuously to the use of the label "Quaker" in Quaker Oats. Would we like a team called "the Fighting Honkeys"? One response of marginalized groups is to take the pejorative label and make it their own, as gay and lesbian groups did in appropriating and using the label "queer."

Dolores Tanno (1994) describes how her multiple identities are reflected in various labels (Spanish, Mexican American, Latina, Chicana). The Spanish label is one she was given by her family and designates an ancestral origin (Spain). The label Mexican American reflects two important cultures that make up her identity. Latina reflects cultural and historical connectedness with others of Spanish descent (such as Puerto Ricans and South Americans) and the Chicana label promotes political and cultural assertiveness in representing her identity. She stresses that she is all these, that each reveals a different facet of her identity: symbolic, historical, cultural, and political.

Similarly, the labels and meanings for African Americans have evolved over the years. Hecht, Collier, and Ribeau (1993) claim that the shift from black to African American as a self-preferred label is founded in issues of self-determination, strength, progress, and control.

What do white people want to be called? When we asked white college students what labels they preferred to use and preferred others to use, they consistently chose the most "normative," the least specific (Martin, Krizek, Nakayama, & Bradford, 1996). They wanted to be called white, or maybe white American, but not white Anglo-Saxon Protestant. What does it mean if whites resist being specifically "located" by geography (Anglo) or history (WASP)? Does it express the right of being the normative group, the one that names and categorizes others but is not itself categorized?

However, this may be changing as our "white" identity is being (re)negotiated and defined in contemporary U.S. society. Perhaps these issues of labels will be discussed more by whites. Perhaps we can explore the meanings for various labels—African Americans, white, European American. Or we can learn to negotiate and call people what they want to be called, as Mary Jane Collier suggests, to affirm the identity that each thinks is important.

WHITE IDENTITY DEVELOPMENT

How do we develop a sense of whiteness? This sense (just like our sense of gender) develops over time and through communication with others. There seem to be several stages of identity development, not with definite beginnings and ends, but stages nonetheless that represent different positions of understanding who we are.

In the United States, minority group members develop a sense of racial and ethnic identity much earlier than majority group members do. As psychologist Rita Hardiman (1994) describes it:

It has frequently been the case that White students enrolled in my class on racial and cultural issues in counseling expect to be taught all about the cultures of people of color and they are almost always surprised to hear that we will be discussing the White group's experience. Some students remark that they are not White; they are female, or working-class, or Catholic or Jewish, but not White. When challenged, they reluctantly admit that they are White but report that this is the first time they have had to think about what it means for them. (p. 125)

Stage 1: No Social Consciousness

In Hardiman's model, the first stage of identity development is the same for whites and minority groups; in this stage children may be aware of physical differences and some cultural differences but do not feel fearful or hostile and do not feel racially superior. However, eventually they absorb the message from the social environment (family and society) about racial groups.

Stage 2: Acceptance

The second stage, acceptance, represents the internalization of the messages about racial group membership and the acquisition of a belief in the "normalcy" (superiority) of being white. This may be either a passive acceptance or an active acceptance of the dominant socialization. An important point here is that individuals at this stage are not aware that they have been programmed to accept a particular world view about race. It is simply the way things are and is not questioned.

Passive Acceptance. In the passive acceptance stage, there is no conscious identification with being white. Whites at this stage may hold the following subtly racist views but do not see themselves as being racist. Rather, racism is seen as the holding of extreme attitudes, such as those espoused by the Klu Klux Klan.

1. Minority groups are culturally deprived and need help to assimilate.
2. Affirmative action is reverse discrimination because people of color are being given opportunities that whites have never had.
3. White culture, music, art, and literature is "classical"; works of art by people of color are primitive art, or "crafts."
4. People of color are "culturally different" whereas whites are individuals with no group identity, cultures, or shared experience of racial privilege.

People at this stage usually take one of two passive positions with respect to racial issues and interactions with people of color. They either *avoid* or adopt a *patronizing* stance. That is, they may avoid racial issues, avoid being around people of color, or be very polite when they are. Or they may take a patronizing stance, be very solicitous and try to help the less fortunate: "I really feel terrible about the few minority students in my classes. I know it's so hard for them to fit in. I really wish I could figure out some way to make things easier for them."

Active Acceptance. Those whites in the active acceptance stage are very conscious of their whiteness and may express their feelings of superiority collectively (as with a White Student Union.) There may be open resentment toward minorities who are perceived to be more advantaged: "Why do all the black students sit together in the Student Union?"

Some whites never move beyond this phase. If they do, it is usually a result of a number of cumulative events. Hardiman describes the transition of one of her students from the active acceptance stage to the next stage:

> [She took] a class in high school on African American authors. . . . She felt that the authors' experiences had happened long ago and that whatever unfairness existed then had been rectified. Later, after entering college and developing some close relationships with Asian American and African American students, she began to have other experiences that contradicted her assumptions about fairness. An incident in her residence hall involving the indiscriminate rounding up of all Black male students by police, and an ensuing protest over that incident, had a particular effect upon her. She described herself as "waking up to the reality" after this incident. (p. 127)

Stage 3: Resistance

The resistance stage represents a major attitudinal shift, from a position that blames victims for their conditions to one that names and blames a white's own dominant group as the source of racial problems. This resistance may take the form of passive resistance, with little behavioral change, or active resistance—an ownership of racism. Individuals may be embarrassed as they recognize that much of their behavior has been racist. Some may try to distance themselves from other whites or gravitate toward communities of color.

In the active resistance stage, whites believe that changing the white community is the responsibility of whites; they shift from being a good "liberal" helper to being an active agent of change. However, as they make the transition to the next stage, they realize that while they may appreciate communities of color, they are not members of those cultures and they feel a need to redefine whiteness.

Stage 4: Redefinition

In this stage, energy is refocused or redirected to redefining whiteness in nonracist terms. Whites come to see that they do not have to accept the definition of white that is placed on them by society. They can move beyond the connection to racism to see positive aspects of being European American and feel more comfortable being white. However, the difficult challenge here is to identify what white culture is. Sometimes this can be done only by coming into contact with and interacting with people of color, before moving on to redefine one's own white identity. A second task is to identify the ways in which racism is harmful to whites and to move beyond thinking that racism affects only people of color.

Stage 5: Internalization

In this stage, whites are finally able to integrate their whiteness into all other facets of their identity, and this affects other aspects of social and personal identity—sex role, religious role, and so on. At this point, there is less consciousness about identity; all aspects are internalized and manifested in spontaneous behavior.

SUMMARY

This essay attempts to initiate a dialogue about what it means to be white in the United States as we approach the twenty-first century. At this time, it seems that there are competing notions about what is involved in white identity. It is seen as both invisible and real. It is seen as both privilege and liability. It is seen as both positive and negative. And all of these dimensions are played out in our communication with others. Our identities are simultaneously shaping and being shaped by our communication.

It seems appropriate to conclude with some questions for reflection and discussion:

1. When was the first time you were aware of your racial identity? How was it talked about with your friends and family as you were growing up?
2. How did your family talk about ethnicity?
3. If you are white, in what contexts do you think about being white? Do you feel white when you are with only white people?
4. What are the communicative consequences of thinking about race in categories like black and white? What do you feel when you can't easily categorize someone as black or white?

References

Asante, M. K. (aka A. L. Smith), (1973). *Transracial Communication*. Englewood Cliffs, N.J.: Prentice-Hall.

Frankenburg, R. (1993). *White Women, Race Matters: The Social Construction of Whiteness*. Minneapolis: University of Minnesota Press.

Gallagher, C. A. (1994). White construction in the university. *Socialist Review, 1/2*, 167–187.

Hardiman, R. (1994). "White Racial Identity Development in the United States." In E. P. Salett and D. R. Koslow (Eds.), *Race, Ethnicity and Self: Identity in Multicultural Perspective*, 117–142. Washington, D.C.: National MultiCultural Institute.

Hecht, M., Collier, M. J., and Ribeau, S. (1993) *African-American Communication*. Newbury Park, Calif.: Sage.

Helms, J. E. (1990). "Toward a Model of White Racial Identity Development." In J. Helms (Ed.), *Black and White Racial Identity: Theory, Research, and Practice*, 49–66. New York: Greenwood Press.

Martin, J. N., Krizek, R. L., Nakayama, T., and Bradford, L. (1996). Labels for white Americans. *Communication Quarterly, 44*, 125–144.

Martin, J. N., Hecht, M. L., and Larkey, L. K. (1994). Conversational improvement strategies for interethnic communication: African American and European American perspectives. *Communication Monographs, 61*, 237–255.

McIntosh, P. (1995). "White Privilege and Male Privilege: A Personal Account of Coming to See Correspondences Through Work in Women's Studies." In M. L. Andersen and P. H. Collins (Eds.), *Race, Class and Gender, 76–86*. Belmont, Calif.: Wadsworth.

Nakayama, T. (1993). "Dis/orienting Identities: Asian Americans, History and Intercultural Communication." In A. Gonzalez, M. Houston, and V. Chen (Eds.), *Our Voices: Essays in Culture, Ethnicity and Communication*, 12–17. Los Angeles: Roxbury.

Nakayama, T., and Krizek, R. L. (1995). Whiteness: A strategic rhetoric. *Quarterly Journal of Speech, 81*, 291–309.

Omi, M., and Winant, H. (1992). "Racial Formations." In P. S. Rothenberg (Ed.), *Race, Class and Gender in the United States*, 26–35. New York: St. Martin's Press.

Salett, E. P., and Koslow, D. R. (Eds.). (1994). *Race, Ethnicity and Self: Identity in Multicultural Perspective*. Washington, D.C.: National MultiCultural Institute.

Tanno, D. (1994). "Names, Narratives, and the Evolution of Ethnic Identity." In A. Gonzalez, M. Houston, and V. Chen (Eds.), *Our Voices: Essays in Culture, Ethnicity and Communication*, 30–33. Los Angeles: Roxbury.

Trinh, T. M. (1986/7). Difference: A special third world women issue. *Discourse, 8*.

Wilson, S. (1995). Black and white perceptions of justice are worlds apart. *Arizona Republic*, October 4, 1995, p. A2).

Concepts and Questions

1. According to Martin, what is the role played by communication in defining one's ethnic identity?
2. How do the dimensions of white ethnic identity differ from the ethnic identity of other co-cultures in U.S. society?
3. What are the development stages of white ethnic identity? Do these stages differ in any significant way from ethnic identity development in other cultures or co-cultures?
4. Explain what Martin is asserting when she writes, "cultural identities are negotiated, co-created, reinforced, and challenged through communication."
5. How did Martin answer the following question: "What is the difference between racial and ethnic identity"?
6. How does Martin define "bounded identities"? How does she define "dominant identities"?
7. Do you believe there is a set of cultural norms and symbols shared by most white people? If yes, what are some of these norms and symbols?
8. What does Martin mean by the word *standpoint*?
9. Can you list some white "core symbols"?
10. How would you answer the following question that was posed by Martin: How do we develop a sense of whiteness?

Five Paradigms of Ethnic Relations

Rod Janzen

A major focus of contemporary American education is the nature and character of interethnic relationships. This is evident whether the analysis and debate is about global issues, the domestic multicultural agenda, or social issues in general. The views expressed in the debate reflect a diverse set of ideological assumptions, though these are often concealed rather than explicit.

The present study is based on an intensive review of the literature pertaining to interethnic relationships, as well as the author's attendance at numerous interpretive presentations on diverse forms of "multiculturalism." From this review, I have identified five different perspectives, or paradigms, on the basis of which Americans in general define ethnic relations.

Our view of different ethnic and cultural groups is conditioned by the paradigms that guide our understanding of and vision for interethnic relationships. This is the case whether one is an administrator, teacher, student, or member of the community. Educators, in particular, need to come to terms with the diversity of interethnic paradigmatic understanding. While this paper does not offer specific solutions to our national multicultural dilemma, it will hopefully help clarify some of the reasons why solutions to our problems do not come easily in this complicated time.

The first paradigm is Traditional Eurocentric Racism. In this vision, America is defined as predominantly northern and western European in its culture and institutions, with a dominant Anglo-Saxon and Protestant foundation. In this vision, which reflects the actual development of American history, other "white" Europeans are always at some point (usually within the second generation) pulled into the northern European center (Novak 1971, 114).

From *Social Education*, 1994, Volume 58, Number 6, pp. 349–353. Reprinted by permission of the National Council for the Social Sciences. Rod Janzen teaches at Fresno Pacific College, Fresno, California.

Irish immigrants, for example, initially experienced extensive discrimination due to their ethnic uniqueness and their adherence to Catholicism. Immigrants from southern Europe experienced similar bias. Because of their later date of mass immigration, they also had to deal with discrimination related to job competition with "real" Americans. The fact that many eastern Europeans were adherents of Orthodox Christianity (a tradition with which most Americans were not familiar) further complicated matters. Still, American citizens in general wanted Irish and southern and eastern European immigrants, now that they were here, to become "like" them, i.e., to become northern and western European in customs and beliefs. If one could assist in "Protestantizing" Catholic ecclesiastical and theological traditions along the way, so much the better.

Paradigm I thus describes a way of thinking and acting which brought all "white" Americans into the national fold, with one exception. Traditional Eurocentric racism never fully accepted the Jewish people because of their non-Christian religious commitment, even though Jews tended to adhere, for the most part, to northern and western European cultural traditions (Takaki 1993, 298). Jews thus found themselves occupying a quasi-purgatorial niche in American society.

According to the Paradigm I way of thinking and acting, non-Europeans were never fully accepted as "Americans." Blacks, American Indians, Asians, and Mexicans, for example, were all considered inferior peoples, culturally and intellectually. The Irish, southern Europeans, and (to a lesser extent) Jews could at some point be recognized as "real" Americans as they were assimilated (with certain stereotypical perceptions still held and acted upon), but persons in the non-European groups were never fully accepted, due to an ethnocentric bias against the cultures from which they claimed descent. Citizens of the United States wanted members of inferior ethnic groups to become "like" them with regard to customs practiced, dress, religion, and attitude toward work (though the work of the inferior peoples might be supervised by European-Americans); but they were not regarded as equals.

Paradigm I thus describes the historical American approach to latter-day non-Anglo-Saxon immigrants. This was also the approach applied to

America's indigenous peoples. It established a vision still held, in different forms, by many American citizens today who fear and do not want an America which might become darker physically, less Christian religiously, and less European with regard to its understanding of the best way to design social-political institutions. Even in the field of education, there are many who hold certain Paradigm I principles, even though they do not put their thoughts in print.

Paradigm II, Melting Pot Assimilations, offers a different point of view, and an alternative interpretation of American history. In the melting pot vision, various cultural groups from all over the world, whether they originate in Europe, Asia, the United States itself, the Middle East, Africa, or South America, are treated with essential equality in the United States. In their constant interaction—one culture crossing over into another—they begin at some point to join together to create one large heterogeneous mixture (Zangwill 1909, 37, 199).

Like the tiger who runs around a tree and turns into a stack of pancakes in the well-known folk tale, the various immigrant groups rotate ever more rapidly around whatever the central but constantly fluctuating definition of America has become. In the end, the United States itself is explained as a complete mixing together of various cultural traditions with regard to language, customs, religion, economic system, and political system.

With regard to language, for example, all immigrant groups eventually accept an Americanized form of English as a common tongue. Simultaneously, capitalism is accepted as the best economic system. Even though not all Americans belong to the same religious denomination, there is general acceptance of comparable moral principles and values. The Old Testament's Ten Commandments, for example, are valued in the Christian, Jewish, and Muslim traditions.

Through the relationship with other melting pot citizens, one ceases at some point to perceive oneself in any terms other than "American." Individual ties to ethnic groups culturally rooted in other parts of the world are not considered important or relevant. These connections in fact are seen as representing potentially disruptive forces which can give the melting pot too many distinctive and distracting ingredients, leaving citizens the sense that there is no melted-together foundational understanding of what it means to be an American. Individual immigrants are expected to discard connections to ancestral homes. Further, by marrying across ethnic boundaries in the North American "new world," they assist in the creation of a new world people, the "American people."

Paradigm II suggests that most immigrants in the past jumped into the pot voluntarily and with great enthusiasm (Fitzgerald 1980, 82), ridding themselves of many remnants of past existence. As the newly arrived cultures of the world melted into the pot, they did, of course, bring cultural traditions along with them. These customs, in various manifestations, continued to inform the debate with regard to what made someone an "American." Since everybody was equal before the law, the new immigrants could feel that they had as much ethnically based influence on what defined America as anyone who had melted into the pot at some earlier time.

Paradigm II is a description and vision for America still held by many. Indeed, a number of educators lament the fact that this model is no longer as widely accepted in the late 20th century. The melting pot paradigm does not, however, provide an accurate account of what actually transpired in American history. That story is perhaps more adequately portrayed in Paradigm I, particularly into the 1940s.

Paradigm II suggests, in a visionary sense, the melting away of all original ethnic cultures and traditions. The best part of each theoretically becomes part of what makes America a unique and great interethnic experiment. Constant interaction theoretically stirs the multicultural stew together, and a gloriously harmonious unification is the end result of such mixing.

In fact, however, most new immigrants to America found themselves pressured by the power of the institutionalized public school system and generally accepted American cultural principles to give up most ethnic traditions, unless these happened to be Anglo-Saxon Protestant in nature, and to melt into an essentially northern and western European cultural pot. Instead of melting equitably into the American soup, immigrants had first to shed essential aspects of traditional cultural belief and practice (Alba 1981, 91).

In the end, most non-Anglo-Saxon ethnic traditions were lost, with the exception of such customs as the placing of Christmas trees in American homes during the month of December and (more recently, in California) the production of tamales during that same time of year. The fact that America's large population of ethnic Germans has had so little impact on the predominant culture in the United States is perhaps the best example of the way in which the melting pot process has actually functioned. During World War I, many states even outlawed the use of German in church services (Teichroeb 1979, 96).

Paradigm II thus denotes a melting pot which in actual fact "melted away" non-Anglo-Saxon traditions. Yet this paradigm has become an integral part of mainstream American thought. It is a worldview which has been taught and promoted in American public schools both as ideal and fact, and one which has been accepted by the media in general through much of the 20th century. A large number of Americans thus still believe strongly that this is the most accurate description of historical American inter-ethnic relationships.

Both Paradigms I and II promote philosophies which are essentially assimilationist in nature. Each paradigmatic understanding assumes a common set of cultural standards which new immigrants must accept either voluntarily or by compulsion.

Many melting pot theorists today, however, call themselves "multiculturalists." They believe in the vision of a melting pot which encourages new immigrants to add to the ever-changing, melted-together, contents of the pot significant (not superficial) aspects of their traditional ethnic cultures, even as those persons are themselves transformed into ethnic "Americans" (Glazer 1991, 18).

Generally speaking, Paradigms III, IV, and V are most often used to define the multicultural way of thinking. With these paradigms we move directly into the waters of pluralism, with its emphasis on the retention and maintenance of traditional cultural beliefs and practices. There is a significant difference of opinion, however, even among advocates of pluralism, with regard to how it should be interpreted.

Paradigm III, Ethnic Nationalism, for example, suggests that each ethnic group, regardless of origin, should preserve its unique character, customs, languages, and ways of knowing without being assimilated. In this vision, the ethnic community is the principal source of one's personal and group identity.

America itself is held together, in this model, by a collective commitment to democratic institutions and practices and by the English language, which each cultural group teaches alongside other ethnic languages. Ethnic nationalism assumes the establishment of certain relationships across cultural boundaries. It expects, however, that most immigrants and Americans who have retained strong ethnic identities will focus their attention on their own cultural groups, the source of the ethnic nationalist's primary identity (Barrera 1988, 42).

Exponents of the ethnic nationalist vision often identify their ideas with the cultural mosaic concept promoted by the Canadian government. That vision was founded historically on the basis of a bicultural, French/English confrontation. Rather than being purely "multi-cultural" in nature, primary institutional support was traditionally given to two identifiable language groups (Lipset 1990, 179). Since 1971, however, the Canadian Government through its Cabinet-level Ministry of Multiculturalism and Citizenship, has encouraged every ethnic group living in Canada to retain ideological and behavioral uniqueness via substantial government-funded programs (McConaghy 1993, 190).

Pluralists who support ethnic nationalism seek to preserve special cultural and linguistic understandings and customs which have generally diminished in cosmopolitan settings. Ethnic nationalists thus emphasize the importance of retaining, in some measure, closed ethnic enclaves within American society at large. They remind us that it is not possible to express certain beliefs and feelings outside the boundaries of specific psycho-cultural-linguistic traditions. The center, in the ethnic nationalist vision is, therefore, a weak one.

Much of the Afrocentric curriculum movement fits this particular paradigm, though when it places additional emphasis on viewing the world through the lens of a myriad of cultural perspectives it might also find itself positioned within the parameters of Paradigm IV and V definitions (Hilliard 1992, 13). Persons who suggest the viability of creating semi-independent ethnic republics within the United States follow this model most closely (Barrera 1988, 160).

Table 1 *Inter-Ethnic Relationships*

Categories	Paradigm I	Paradigm II	Paradigm III	Paradigm IV	Paradigm V
Language	English	English	English/multi-lingualism	English/multi-lingualism	English/multi-lingualism
Religion	Christian (Pro-testantized)	Christian	Multireligious	Beliefs common to world religions	Multireligious
Culture	European (NW European Anglo-Saxon dominant)	European	Multicultural	World culture	Multicultural American
Race	Caucasian	Caucasian	Mixed/separate ethnic groups	Mixed	Mixed
Political Tradition	European con-stitutional democracy (NW European Anglo-Saxon domi-nant)	Constitutional democracy	Democracy responsive to ethnic needs	World democracy	Constitutional democracy

It is important to note that the Paradigm III model assumes that each national grouping contains within itself a multiplicity of ethnicities. Within the Laotian group, for example, the Hmong represent a unique group of people (traditionally semi-nomadic and illiterate). Ethnic nationalism thus has major implications for schooling if educators seek to meet the psychological needs, ways of knowing, and cultural expectancies of different native groups.

Paradigm IV, Globalism, provides a different pluralist twist by suggesting that the increasing economic, ecological, and political interconnectedness of modern life demands that we reach consensus on an international ideological and behavioral center which then forms the foundation for all world cultures, rather than thinking only in terms of what might hold Americans together (Paradigms I, II, and V) or with regard to those customs which provide communally separated cultural uniqueness (Paradigm III).

In this *Star Trek* vision, a Planet Earth melting pot is formed on the basis of continuous discussion concerning that which is common in the experience of all ethnic cultures, including common elements in the beliefs and practices of the various global religions (Fersh 1989, 17). In this model, one's own cultural identity is not of primary importance, except insofar as it provides input into the establishment of the new world order's central principles.

There is a continuous search for the center in the globalist vision, via unending discussion with regard to commonly accepted principles. The center itself draws upon the experiential and intellectual traditions of all world cultures. Global awareness, in this vision, may be promoted for social, economic, religious, or other reasons, but a central raison d'être is the importance of working together peaceably as world citizens.

While the global ideological center is being sought, that which separates and distinguishes each nationality is not simply overlooked. Through the process of constant inter-ethnic discussion, each ethnic group is given influential power with regard to the creation of the new earth culture. In order for this culture to be equitably based, in view of the world's political, economic, and demographic contexts, a tremendous amount of negotiation and discussion is demanded. One global model sometimes referred to is the United Nations, which is organized and functions in such a way that the rights of those nations which are not as strong militarily, economically, or demographically are still theoretically protected.

Paradigm IV appeals to those pluralists who fear the possibility of the inter-ethnic conflict which has sometimes accompanied ethnic nationalist emphases—in Yugoslavia or the former Soviet Union, for example—though supporters of Paradigm III counter that the underlying reason for conflict in those regions is indeed the historical attempt by some ethnic groups to destroy the cultural vitality of neighboring ethnic groups.

Ironically, if the global vision were actuated in the way its proponents seem to desire, it might ultimately establish a culture very similar to what some melting pot enthusiasts, in a more specifically nationalistic way, appear to envision for their ideological and interpretive position based on Paradigm II. The entire world, however, would now find itself melted together.

If there were, for example, nearly complete global inter-ethnic fusion, brought about in part by increased personal relationships, leading to cross-ethnic marriage en masse worldwide, it might be difficult eventually to distinguish one ethnic tradition from another. People might then rather define themselves in terms of highly idiosyncratic interests, behaviors, and beliefs. (This is what the melting pot model envisions on a national scale.) For this to happen, however, global citizens would have to begin thinking transformatively in terms of internationally recognized principles and be open to almost continuous change, over a long period of time, with regard to the agreed-upon nature of those axioms.

Paradigm V, Centered Pluralism, is a more conservative and pragmatic approach to pluralistic multiculturalism than that suggested by either ethnic nationalist or global paradigms. An underlying assumption of centered pluralism, for example, is that America needs to continue to hold itself together as a vital national system, and that this will not happen, politically or socially, unless certain established central traditions are adhered to by most citizens (Banks 1992, 32).

Centered pluralists, like ethnic nationalists, therefore insist that all Americans speak a common language (English) though they simultaneously encourage both the retention of first languages (where this is relevant) and the learning of additional official languages. Centered pluralists are also committed to democratic institutions though these are not defined from an exclusively Anglo-Saxon constitutional perspective.

In both of these emphases, centered pluralism is much more prescriptive in nature than globalism. Paradigm V also goes much further than ethnic nationalism in its general support for a commonly accepted and centrally established knowledge base. It suggests, for example, that all Americans have a common literacy foundation. This literacy base is expected to be a multicultural one, so that not all books read and studied are those written by Europeans and European-Americans, with those particular ethnic interpretations (as different as they might be). Still there are common intellectual threads, primary readings, and conventional subjects which hold Americans to similar standards of interpretation.

This paradigm also supports a national commitment to communal as well as individual socioeconomic traditions, a mixture of capitalism and socialism. Centered pluralism even allows for the possibility that democracy itself might be understood differently—and perhaps in more helpful ways—in other cultural traditions. The two-party political system and representative republicanism might therefore be reviewed with regard to operational effectiveness in the modern American context. Centered pluralism assumes, however, an underlying commitment to the kind of general principles enunciated in the United States Constitution's Bill of Rights (Haynes and Kniker 1990, 306).

Centered pluralism thus establishes a commitment to many traditional "American" beliefs and practices. At the same time, this paradigm assumes the integrity of indigenous cultural identities. A central set of beliefs and practices, previously established, undergoes continuous gradual metamorphosis through constant, desired reflective interaction between various ethnic groups and their respective traditions. In this process all ethnic communities have some impact on the slowly changing character of the American "center." Centered pluralism assumes nearly complete ethnic equality and cultural acceptance. It represents a practical response to assimilationist critics of Paradigm III who attack ethnic nationalist multiculturalism for perceived divisive tendencies.

Interestingly enough, centered pluralism, in many ways, correlates to a paradigm hinted at by Milton

Gordon in the mid-1960s (in his book, *Assimilation in American Society*). It is a vision, which, if Gordon was correct in his analysis, ultimately and paradoxically establishes a melting pot. Unlike that actuated historically, this melting pot provides full cultural equality (Gordon 1964, 158).

In this way the eventual outcome of a commitment to centered pluralism appears to be similar in nature to that predicted by melting pot multiculturalists, even as the latter do not place much emphasis on retention and maintenance of ethnic uniqueness. If, for example, all cultures are treated equally, one would expect that through direct association and intermarriage most ethnic groups would eventually melt away into one new American culture, still predominantly Anglo-Saxon in its foundation but with Arab-American, African-American, Asian-American, Pacific Islander–American, and Latin-American nuances.

Centered pluralism differs from melting pot assimilationism, however, in its willingness to support affirmative action to assist in leveling out the playing field for those ethnic groups which have experienced substantial discrimination and prejudice based on their association with certain ethnic traditions in the past. In theory, most of these are people other than non-northern, non-western Europeans; in practice, most of them are non-Europeans. Centered pluralists recognize a need to eradicate ethnocentric concepts already embedded in the American psyche and social order. Paradigm V thus envisions a melting pot which incorporates much greater ethnic diversity than that anticipated by melting pot multiculturalists.

Unlike the vision presented in the globalist Paradigm IV, centered pluralism is not international in character. Though centered pluralists speak in terms of internationalization of the curriculum, for example, their primary focus is on the United States of America.

The fact that Americans tend to view inter-ethnic relationships from the perspective of these paradigms, and that there are divergences even among those who call themselves "pluralists," makes for a very confusing situation for educators. Educators are not only asked to "multiculturalize" the curriculum but to decide, in effect, which of at least four paradigmatic understandings best describes their personal perception of multiculturalism, which then may differ from that proposed by other educators and academia. All of the paradigms discussed in this article, for example, have supporters in the public school system. Teachers are required to attend inservice workshops and often volunteer to enroll in classes which certainly expose them to some form of "multiculturalism," but which may be suggesting any one of four very different versions of that concept.

It is important to note that this article's thesis that there are five general ethnic relations paradigms does not suggest that all multiculturalists abide by these theoretical paradigms in any pure sense. They may, in fact, operate out of the perspective of one or more of these models, some rationally and with purpose, others chaotically and illogically.

In addition, teachers and educators must deal with a general public whose opinions, according to polls, are much more weighted toward assimilationist models (Paradigms I and II). It is perhaps most confusing that supporters of four of the paradigms (II through V) have representative leaders who all refer to themselves as "multiculturalists," and who all employ the same term, from Nathan Glazer to James Banks to Mario Barrera. So the following question continually arises, "Who are the real multiculturalists?" and we see constant struggle, attack, and counterattack between advocates of the various paradigmatic approaches.

It is the hope of this writer that a paradigmatic understanding of why we have reached this point of multicultural confusion will be useful in helping us to comprehend why we are doing what we are doing. Further, it will push members of the educational audience, as they listen to presentations on multiculturalism, as they read articles and curriculum documents which describe the multiculturalist vision, to be more demanding with regard to what particular philosophical position is being encouraged by presenters and writers. It is always important to know the assumptions, values, and goals of one's mentors. With this knowledge, the debate will continue with the reflective educator much more knowledgeable of the deep complexity of this issue.

References

Alba, R. D. (1981). The twilight of ethnicity among American Catholics of European ancestry. *Annals, 45*, 86–97.

Banks, J. (1992). Multicultural education: For freedom's sake. *Educational Leadership, 49*, 32–36.

Barrera, M. (1988). *Beyond Aztlan.* Notre Dame: University of Notre Dame Press.

Fersh, S. (Ed.). (1989). *Learning About Peoples and Cultures.* Evanston, Ill.: McDougal, Littel.

Fitzgerald, F. (1980). *America Revised.* New York: Vintage Press.

Glazer, N. (1991). In defense of multiculturalism. *New Republic, 205*, 18–22.

Gordon, M. (1964). *Assimilation in American Life.* New York: Oxford University Press.

Haynes, C. C., & Kniker, C. R. (1990). Religion in the classroom. *Social Education, 54*, 305, 306.

Hilliard, A. G. (1992). Why we must pluralize the curriculum. *Educational Leadership, 49*, 12–15.

Lipset, S. (1990). *Continental Divide.* New York: Routledge.

McConaghy, T. (1993). Ontario to implement antiracist policies. *Phi Delta Kappan, 75*, 190, 191.

Novak, M. (1971). *The Rise of Unmeltable Ethnics.* New York: Macmillan.

Takaki, R. (1993). *A Different Mirror.* Boston: Little, Brown.

Teichroeb, A. (Ed.). (1979). Military surveillance of Mennonites in World War I. *Mennonite Quarterly Review, 53*, 95–127.

Zangwill, I. (1909). *The Melting Pot.* New York: Macmillan.

Concepts and Questions

1. Explain what Janzen means when he writes, "Our view of different ethnic and cultural groups is conditioned by the paradigms that guide our understanding and vision for interethnic relationships"? Can you offer some examples?

2. Which of Janzen's paradigms do you believe has most shaped American culture?

3. Which of Janzen's paradigms do you believe contributes to racism? Why?

4. Can you think of categories besides the five suggested by Janzen (language, religion, culture, race, and political tradition) that are reflected in the five paradigms?

5. What are the significant differences between the five paradigms advanced by Janzen?

6. Which of the five paradigms do you believe would be the most useful model for our society in the twenty-first century? Why?

7. How would someone from a culture very different from your own respond on his or her first visit to your city? To your home?

8. If the United States emerges into a pluralistic, multicultural society, what contributions can we make as a way of preparing for this society? What problems might appear in this new society?

part 2

Sociocultural Backgrounds: What We Bring to Intercultural Communication

All persons are puzzles until at last we find in some word or act the key to the man, to the woman; straightway all their past works and actions lie in light before us.

RALPH WALDO EMERSON

One of the most important aspects of human communication is that the past experiences each participant brings to a communication event will affect his or her behavior during the encounter. It is common knowledge that each person acts according to the personal uniqueness he or she brings to the occasion. Think about those countless situations when you and some friends shared what you believed to be the same experience, yet when you started to discuss the event you soon discovered there were differences in your reactions. What you deemed dull your companions found exciting; what you considered pointless they found meaningful. The messages received were the same for all participants; yet because each of you has a unique personality and background, each person experienced a variety of feelings, sensations, and responses. Each of you brought different backgrounds to the event and, as a result, attributed individual meanings to the shared experience. In short, the event meant what it did to you because of your own unique past history.

We contend that to understand any communication encounter you must appreciate the idea that there is much more to communication than the mere analysis of messages. The messages you receive, and the responses you make to them, are products of your unique personal history. And it is those histories that often produce major differences between people.

Individual past personal histories take on added significance when we introduce the dimension of culture, for each of us is a product of our individual experiences and shaped by our culture—a culture we share with other people. As we defined it in Part 1, *culture* refers to those cumulative deposits of knowledge, beliefs, views, values, and behaviors that are acquired by a **large group** of people and passed on from one generation to the next. In this sense, culture affects you both consciously and unconsciously; it not only teaches you how and what to think about but also dictates such values as what is attractive and what is ugly, what is good and what is evil, and what is appropriate and what is not. In short, your culture tells you how to see and interpret your world. Furthermore, culture teaches you such things as how close to stand to strangers, how to greet friends, when to speak and when to remain silent, and even how to display your anger properly. When you are interacting with others and become disturbed by their actions, you can, for instance, cry, become physically violent, shout, or remain silent. Each behavior is a manifestation of what you have learned; it is largely influenced by your culture.

These cultural influences affect your ways of perceiving and acting; they contain the societal experiences and values that are passed from generation to generation. Because these behaviors are so much a part of your persona, there is a danger that you might forget that behaviors are culturally engendered and will vary among cultures. This is why a person from Japan, for example, might remain silent if disturbed by someone's actions while an Israeli or an Italian would more likely verbalize the displeasure felt.

Whatever the culture, you can better understand your behavior and the reactions of others if you realize that what you are hearing and seeing is a reflection of that culture. As you might predict, this understanding is greatly facilitated when your cultural experiences are similar to those of the people with whom you are interacting. Conversely, when different and diverse backgrounds are brought to a communication encounter, it is often difficult to share internal states and feelings. In this section, we focus on those difficulties by examining some of the experiences and perceptual backgrounds found in a variety of international cultures (Chapter 2) as well as those found in several American co-cultures (Chapter 3).

chapter 2

International Cultures: Understanding Diversity

We begin with this question: How can you understand people who come from different sections of the global village? This answer is not simple, yet it is at the very core of this book. The need for such understanding is obvious. If you look around the world at any particular moment, you will find cultures in constant contact with one another. The nightly news makes it abundantly clear that all cultures, although quite different, are linked together. Events in one part of the world influence events all over the world. Be it the global economy, concerns about pollution, or disagreements that can cause a nuclear war, no culture can remain isolated from the rest of the world.

Two things are important if you are to understand people from international cultures. First, you need to have a fund of knowledge about the people of other cultures. And second, you must learn to appreciate their diversity. This chapter offers essays that are intended to assist you with both of those assignments. You will be exposed to six essays that explore the rich diversity among cultures. Although six cultures is only a small sampling of the countless cultures found throughout the world, these six will enable you to see how people in other cultures view their world. Worldview establishes how people perceive themselves, each other, and their places in the universe, and it serves as an underlying pattern for interaction within a culture.

We begin in East Asia. One of the greatest cultural dichotomies in interaction patterns is found between North Americans and East Asians. In her article, "The Impact of Confucianism on Interpersonal Relationships and Communication Patterns in East Asia," June Ock Yum paints an intriguing picture of Confucianism's effect on how people view and interact with one another. She traces the various major components of Confucian philosophy and how they tend to determine East Asian patterns of interaction. As a counterpoint to her discussion, Yum makes continuous comparisons to prevalent North American interaction patterns so you can easily understand the differences between the two cultures.

Staying in the region of Asia, we turn to an examination of the Korean culture through an essay by James H. Robinson, "Communication in Korea: Playing Things by Eye." Robinson maintains that to engage in effective communication with Koreans we must understand the crucial Korean element of *nunch'i*. In Western terms, *nunch'i* is a keen social sense that allows Koreans to "read" other people and even grasp many of the unstated nuances often overlooked in many communication situations. According to Robinson, this acute visual perception allows Koreans to "read the eyes of others and to evaluate quickly and accurately another's emotions, attitudes, and reactions or likely reactions to a given proposal or situation." Robinson offers examples of how *nunch'i* can influence verbal messages, decision making, silence, pauses, and rhetorical questions.

Next, Nemi C. Jain and Ellen D. Kussman move us geographically and culturally as they focus on the Indian subcontinent and provide us with a glimpse of Hindu culture in their essay "Dominant Cultural Patterns of Hindus in India." Jain and Kussman demonstrate how the Hindu worldview, belief in reincarnation, concept of karma, aims of human life, paths to salvation, concept of dharma, caste system, and spirit of tolerance—which have persisted over thousands of years—permeate Indian culture. This provides a basis for the perceptual frames of reference common to much of India and a feeling for what it is to be Hindu.

Our next journey takes us to the continent of Africa. In their article "Cultural Patterns of the Maasai," Lisa Skow and Larry A. Samovar give us a unique and insightful view of the Maasai culture, which has shunned almost all Western influences and has tried to remain "pure" African. Unlike many other African cultures, it has almost completely rejected Western forms of government, dress, language, music, and religion. Skow and Samovar give us a clear view of the culture by tracing its history, values, and worldview. They then discuss Maasai verbal and nonverbal processes and show how they are influenced by the prevailing Maasai culture.

We now move from Africa to the Middle East as we explore the ancient and fascinating culture of Egypt. In an essay titled "Communication With Egyptians," Polly Begley isolates those cultural elements that are the most crucial when interacting with Egyptians. She believes that the following elements most be considered: (1) Islamic history, religious beliefs, and politics; (2) the Egyptian values of tradition, social relationships, and hierarchical structure; and (3) language and worldview. Begley offers numerous examples of how these three elements are manifested when Egyptians and non-Egyptians come together.

For our final essay, we look at the interesting culture of Greece. In "Palevome: Foundations of Struggle and Conflict in Greek Interpersonal Communication," Benjamin J. Broome demonstrates how a sense of contest and struggle permeates everyday life in Greece and how it is an essential dynamic of Greek interpersonal communication. He uses the Greek verb *palevome* (we are struggling) to illustrate the Greek perspective on conflict and its role in everyday interaction.

The Impact of Confucianism on Interpersonal Relationships and Communication Patterns in East Asia

JUNE OCK YUM

INTRODUCTION

New communication technology has removed many of the physical barriers against communication between the East and the West, but there remain philosophical and cultural barriers, which are not well understood. The increased opportunity for interaction between different cultural groups, however, has sensitized some scholars to the need to study Eastern perspectives on communication.

Most cross-cultural studies of communication simply describe foreign communication patterns and then compare them to those of North America, rarely going beneath the surface to explore the source of such differences. This paper goes beyond these limitations and explores the philosophical roots of the communication patterns in East Asian countries, before comparing them to those of North America. The assumption here is that communication is a basic social process and that, as such, it is influenced by the philosophical foundations and value systems of the society in which it is found.

There is always a danger in generalizing certain cultural patterns to large geographical areas. Even though we often refer to "Eastern" or "Asian" perspectives, there are many patterns, sometimes contradictory, within the region. For instance, the

popular notion that Asians are more spiritual than Westerners might apply to India but not to China, Korea, or Japan. Nakamura (1964) has maintained that the Chinese and the Japanese are much more nonmetaphysical than Westerners. For this reason, this paper is limited to the East Asian countries of China, Korea, and Japan, those that have been most influenced by Confucian philosophical principles. Other countries that have been influenced by Confucianism are expected to have similar characteristics. For instance, Vietnam, the only country in Southeast Asia to have been influenced more by China than India, also exhibits the strong emphasis on social relationships and devotion to the hierarchical family relations that are the essence of Confucian doctrines (Luce & Summer, 1969).

SOCIAL RELATIONSHIPS VERSUS INDIVIDUALISM

If one has to select the main difference between East Asian and North American perspectives on communication, it would be the East Asian emphasis on social relationships as opposed to the North American emphasis on individualism. According to Hofstede (1980), individualism–collectivism is one of the main dimensions that differentiate cultures. He defined individualism as the emotional independence of individual persons from groups, organizations, or other collectivities. Parsons, Shils, and Olds (1951) have suggested that self-orientation versus collectivity orientation is one of the five basic pattern variables that determine human action. Self-orientation occurs when a person gives "priority in a given situation to his own private interests, independently of their bearings on the interests or values of a given collectivity" (Parsons, Shils, & Olds, 1951, p. 81), as opposed to taking directly into account the values and interests of the collectivity before acting.

The individualism–collectivism dichotomy, however, is not identical to the difference between the East Asian emphasis on social relationships and North American emphasis on individualism. In East Asia, the emphasis is on proper social relationships and their maintenance rather than any abstract concern for a general collective body. In a sense, it is a collectivism only among those bound by social networks. For example, a recent study on the Chinese value system found that the Confucian value of reciprocity and proper relationships was not correlated with Hofstede's individualism–collectivism dimension (Chinese Culture Connection, 1987). Hui and Triandis (1986) have recommended that collectivism be treated in two different ways: (1) as a concern for a certain subset of people and (2) as a concern for a generalized collectivity of people.

In the 1830s, the French social philosopher Alexis de Tocqueville coined the term *individualism* to describe the most notable characteristic of American people. Bellah, Madsen, Sullivan, Swidler, and Tipton (1985, pp. vii, 142) agree that individualism lies at the very core of American culture, contending that "individualism . . . has marched inexorably through our history" and that "we believe in the dignity, indeed the sacredness, of the individual. Anything that would violate our right to think for ourselves, judge for ourselves, make our own decision, live our lives as we see fit, is not only morally wrong, it is sacrilegious." According to Varenne (1977), there is but one system of principles regulating interpersonal relationships in America and that is individualism.

Even though many Americans feel they must get involved, they are also committed to individualism, including the desire to cut free from the past and define one's own self. Thus, the primary mode of American involvement is choosing organizations that one can voluntarily join or voluntarily withdraw from. Varenne (1977, p. 53) said that Americans perceive social structure "not as a system made up of different groups considered to be in a symbiotic relationship, but rather of different individuals who come together to do something."

Considering this cultural orientation, it is not surprising that the dominant paradigm of communication is an individualistic one. Each communicator is perceived to be a separate individual engaging in diverse communicative activities to maximize his or her own self-interest.

In contrast, the most notable characteristic in East Asia is the emphasis on social relationships. Hall and Beadsley (1965) have maintained that, compared to East Asian countries, North America is in the Stone Age when it comes to social relationships. This East Asian preoccupation with social relationships stems from the ancient doctrines of Confucianism.

CONFUCIANISM

In the philosophical and cultural history of East Asia, Confucianism has endured as the basic social and political value system for over 1,000 years. One reason (and indication) that Confucianism has had such a profound impact is that it was adopted as the official philosophy of the Yi dynasty for 500 years in Korea, of the Tokugawa shogunate in Japan for 250 years, and of many dynasties in China.

Confucianism was institutionalized and propagated both through the formal curricula of the educational system and through the selection process of government officials. Confucian classics were required textbooks in the school systems throughout the history of China, Korea, and Japan before modern educational curricula were implemented. Government officials used to be selected through national exams that mostly examined the knowledge and the level of understanding of Confucian philosophy.

Another reason why Confucianism has exerted a much stronger impact than the other religious, philosophical systems of East Asia (such as Buddhism and Taoism) is that it is a pragmatic and present-oriented philosophy. When a student named Tzu-lu asked Confucius about serving spirits, Confucius said, "If one cannot yet serve men, how can he serve the spirits?" Asked about death, Confucius replied, "If you do not understand life, how can you understand death?" (McNaughton, 1974, p. 145). Max Weber commented, "Confucianism is extremely rationalistic since it is bereft of any form of metaphysics and in the sense that it lacks traces of nearly any religious basis. . . . At the same time, it is more realistic than any other system in the sense that it lacks and excludes all measures which are not utilitarian" (quoted by Nakamura, 1964, p. 16).

Confucianism is a philosophy of human nature that considers proper human relationships as the basis of society. In studying human nature and motivation, Confucianism sets forth four principles from which right conduct arises: *jen* (humanism), *i* (faithfulness), *li* (propriety), and *chih* (wisdom or a liberal education).

The cardinal principle, *jen* (humanism), almost defies translation since it sums up the core of Confucianism. Fundamentally it means warm human feelings between people. *Jen* is like a seed from which spring all the qualities that make up the ideal man. In addition, *jen* refers to the possession of all these qualities to a high degree. The actual practice or embodiment of *jen* in our daily lives is closely related to the concept of reciprocity. Confucius said that practicing *jen* is not to do to another man what you yourself don't want. In his own words: "If there's something that you don't like in the person to your right, don't pass it on to the person on your left. If there's something you don't like in the person to your left, don't pass it on to the person on your right" (McNaughton, 1974, p. 29).

It is suggested that Confucius himself once picked out reciprocity (*shu*) as the core of his thought. Confucius said, "There has never been a case where a man who did not understand reciprocity was able to communicate to others whatever treasures he might have had stored in himself" (McNaughton, 1974, p. 28). Therefore, practicing *jen* implies the practice of *shu*, which in turn means to know how it would feel to be the other person, to become like-hearted, and to be able to empathize with others.

The second principle of Confucianism is *i*, meaning faithfulness, loyalty, or justice. As the definition suggests, this principle also has strong implications for social relationships. Like *jen*, *i* is a difficult concept to translate. It may be easier to understand *i* through its opposite concept, which is personal or individual interest and profit. *I* is thus that part of human nature that allows us to look beyond personal, immediate profit and to elevate ourselves to the original goodness of human nature that bridges ourselves to other people (Yum, 1987). According to the principle of *i*, human relationships are not based on individual profit but rather on the betterment of the common good.

If *jen* and *i* are the contents of the Confucian ethical system, *li* (propriety, rite, respect for social forms) is its outward form. As an objective criterion of social decorum, *li* was perceived as the fundamental regulatory etiquette of human behavior. Mencius suggested that *li* originated from deference to others and reservation of oneself. Confucius said that *li* follows from

jen, that is, from being considerate to others. Only when people overcome themselves and so return to propriety can they reach humanness. On the other hand, propriety without humanness was perceived to be empty and useless.

THE IMPACT OF CONFUCIANISM ON INTERPERSONAL RELATIONSHIP PATTERNS

At least three of the four principles of Confucianism deal directly with social relationships. Under such a strong influence, East Asian countries have developed interpersonal relationship patterns that are quite different from the individualistic pattern of North America. Table 1 illustrates these five differences.

Particularistic Versus Universalistic Relationships

Human relationships under Confucianism are not universalistic but particularistic. As we described earlier, the warm human feelings of *jen* are exercised according to one's relationship with another person. Ethics in Confucian thought, therefore, are based on relationships and situations rather than on some absolute and abstract good. Instead of applying the same rule to everybody with whom they interact, East Asians differentially grade and regulate relationships according to the level of intimacy, the status of the persons involved, and the particular context. The East Asian countries have developed elaborate social interaction patterns for those whose social position and relationship to oneself is known, but there are few universal patterns that can be applied to someone who is not known.

From a North American point of view, applying different rules to different people and situations may seem to violate the sacred code of fairness and equality that accompanies the individualistic values. In North America, human relationships are not particularized. Rather, one is supposed to treat each person as an integral individual and apply general and objective rules. For instance, it is quite common in America for people to say "Hi" or "Good morning" to anybody they encounter during their morning walk,

Table 1 *Comparison Between the North American and the East Asian Orientations to Interpersonal Relationship Patterns*

East Asian Orientations	North American Orientations
1. Particularistic	Universalistic
Particular rules and interaction patterns are applied depending upon the relationship and context	General and objective rules are applied across diverse relationships and context
2. Long-term and asymmetrical reciprocity	Short-term and symmetrical reciprocity or contractual reciprocity
3. Sharp distinction between in-group and out-group members	In-group and out-group distinction is not as sharp
4. Informal intermediaries	Contractual intermediaries
Personally known intermediaries	Professional intermediaries
Frequently utilized for diverse relationships	Utilized only for specific purposes
5. Personal and public relationships often overlap	Personal and public relationships are often separate

or to strike up a conversation with another person waiting in line. If you said "Hello" or "Good morning" to a stranger in Korea, you would be looked upon as a rather odd person.

The East Asian approach suggests that it is more humanitarian to consider the particular context and the persons involved in understanding the action and behavior rather than evaluate them according to generalized rules which to a certain extent are impersonal.

Long-Term Asymmetrical Reciprocity Versus Short-Term Symmetrical or Contractual Reciprocity

Reciprocity as an embodiment of *jen* is the core concept in Confucianism, just as individualism is the core concept of the North American culture. While people may voluntarily join together for specific purposes in North America, each individual remains equal and independent; thus people join or drop out of clubs without any serious group sanctions. Commitments and obligations are often perceived as threats to one's autonomy or freedom of action. Relations are symmetrical–obligatory—that is, as nearly "paid off" as possible at any given moment—or else contractual—the obligation is to an institution or to a professional with whom one has established some contractual base (Condon & Yousef, 1975).

In contrast, Confucian philosophy views relationships as complementary or asymmetrical and reciprocally obligatory. In a sense, a person is forever indebted to others, who in turn are constrained by other debts. Dependence is not looked down upon. Rather, dependency is accepted as a necessary part of human relationships. Under this system of reciprocity, the individual does not calculate what he or she gives and receives. To calculate would be to think about immediate personal profits, which is the opposite of the principle of mutual faithfulness, *i.* It is somewhat unusual in Korea, for example, for a group of friends, colleagues, or superior and subordinates to go "Dutch" and split the bill for dinner or drinks. Rather, each person takes turns and pays for the whole group. In North America, people generally insist on "paying their own way." The practice of basing relationships on complementary obligations creates warm, lasting human relationships but also the necessity to accept the obligations accompanying such relationships.

In-Group/Out-Group Distinction

North American culture does not distinguish as strongly between in-group members and out-group members as East Asian countries do. Allegiance to a group and mobility among groups are purely voluntary, so that the longevity of membership in and loyalty to a particular group are both limited.

Mutual dependence as prescribed by the Confucian principle of *i*, however, requires that one be affiliated and identify with relatively small and tightly knit groups of people over long periods of time. These long-term relationships work because each group member expects the others to reciprocate and also because group members believe that sooner or later they will have to depend on the others. People enmeshed in this kind of network make clear distinctions between in-group and out-group members. For example, linguistic codes for in-group members are often different from those for out-group members. What is inside the group and what is outside it have drastically different meanings.

Informal Intermediaries Versus Contractual Intermediaries

Because the distinctions between in-group and out-group members are so strict, it is imperative to have an intermediary to help one initiate a new relationship in East Asia. Confucian emphasis on propriety (*li*) also dictates that one has to follow proper rituals in establishing a new relationship, and an intermediary is part of such rituals. The intermediary has an in-group relationship with both parties and so can connect them. One strategy is for the intermediary to bring up an existing relationship that links the two parties, for example, explaining that "you are both graduates of so-and-so college" or "you are both from province A." Alternatively, the intermediary can use his or her own connections with them to create an indirect sense of in-groupness, for example, explaining that one is "my junior from high school" and the other "works in the same department as I do."

Intermediaries in the United States, however, are mostly professional or contractual in nature: lawyers, negotiators, marriage counselors, and the like. The intermediary is an objective third person who does not have any knowledge of the parties' characteristics other than those directly related to the issue at hand. Also, the intermediary deals with each party as a separate, independent individual. Using personal connections to attain a desired goal does occur in the United States, but such a practice may be frowned on as nepotism and may also be perceived as giving up one's own individual freedom.

Overlap of Personal and Public Relationships

The Confucian concept of *i* leads to a strong distaste for a purely business transaction, carried out on a calculated and contractual basis. Therefore, in East Asian countries there is a tendency to mix personal with public relationships. Even though the obvious purpose of a meeting is for business, both parties feel more comfortable if the transaction occurs on a more personal, human level. According to the principles of social reciprocity, there are several steps to follow if you want to develop an effective business relationship in Korea (Lee, 1983): (1) have frequent contacts over a relatively lengthy period of time, (2) establish a personal and human relationship, (3) if possible, create some common experiences such as sports, drinking, or travel, (4) foster mutual understanding in terms of personality, personal situations, and the like, and (5) develop a certain level of trust and a favorable attitude. The goal is to diminish the clear distinction between a personal relationship and a public relationship. It is implied that if one develops a warm personal relationship, a good public relationship will follow, because it is based on trust and mutual reciprocity. Such qualities are expected to endure rather than be limited to the business deal of the moment.

In the United States, there is a rather sharp dichotomy between private and public life. Since the primary task of the individual is to achieve a high level of autonomous self-reliance, there is an effort to separate the two lives as much as possible. Since the notion of "organizational man" is contradictory to the self-reliant individual, there is a certain level of anxiety about becoming an organizational man (Bellah et al., 1985). Some also perceive private life as a haven from the pressure of individualistic, competitive public life, and as such it must be protected.

THE IMPACT OF CONFUCIANISM ON COMMUNICATION PATTERNS

Confucianism's primary concern with social relationships has strongly influenced communication patterns in East Asia. In general, it has strengthened patterns that help to build and maintain proper

Table 2 *Comparison Between the North American and the East Asian Orientations to Communication Patterns*

East Asian Orientations	North American Orientations
1. Process orientation	Outcome orientation
Communication is perceived as a process of infinite interpretation	Communication is perceived as the transference of messages
2. Differentiated linguistic codes	Less differentiated linguistic codes
Different linguistics codes are used depending upon persons involved and situations	Linguistic codes are not as extensively differentiated as East Asia
3. Indirect communication emphasis	Direct communication emphasis
The use of indirect communication is prevalent and accepted as normative	Direct communication is a norm despite the extensive use of indirect communication
4. Receiver centered	Sender centered
Meaning is in the interpretation	Meaning is in the messages created by the sender
Emphasis is on listening, sensitivity, and removal of preconception	Emphasis is on how to formulate the best messages, how to improve source credibility, and how to improve delivery skills

human relationships. Table 2 compares East Asia and North America in terms of communication patterns.

Process- Versus Outcome-Oriented Communication

Since the main function of communication under Confucian philosophy is to initiate, develop, and maintain social relationships, there is a strong emphasis on the kind of communication that promotes such relationships. For instance, it is very important in East Asia to engage in small talk before initiating business and to communicate personalized information, especially information that would help place each person in the proper context. Communication is perceived to be an infinite interpretive process (Cheng, 1987), which cannot be compartmentalized into sender, message, channel, and receiver. It presumes that each partner is engaged in an ongoing process and that the relationship is in flux.

In contrast, when the main function of communication is to actualize autonomy and self-fulfillment, as in North America, the outcome of the communication is more important than the process. With short-term, discontinuous relationships, communication is perceived to be an action that is terminated

after a certain duration and then replaced by a new communication. Tangible outcomes in terms of friends gained, opponents defeated, and self-fulfillment achieved become the primary function of communication.

Differentiated Versus Less Differentiated Linguistic Codes

East Asian languages are very complex and are differentiated according to social status, the degree of intimacy, age, sex, and the level of formality. There are also extensive and elaborate honorific linguistic systems in East Asian languages (Brown & Levinson, 1978; Ogino, Misono, & Fukushima, 1985). These differentiations are manifested not only in referential terms but also in verbs, pronouns, and nouns. They result from Confucian ethical rules that place the highest value on proper human relationships (*i*) and on propriety (*li*). McBrian (1978) has argued that language forms an integral component of social stratification systems, and the hierarchical Confucian society is well represented by the highly stratified linguistic codes in Korea.

Martin (1964) has proposed that one of the main differences between English, Japanese, and Korean is the levels of speech. In both Korean and Japanese, there are two axes of distinction: the axis of address and the axis of reference. The axis of address is divided into plain, polite, and honorific while the axis of reference is divided into humble and neutral (Martin, 1964). An honorific form is used to refer to the receiver's action, while a humble form is used to refer to the sender's action—the reverse would not be appropriate. The most deferential form of speech combines the honorific address form for receiver and the humble form of self-reference.

The English language also employs different codes depending upon intimacy and status difference between the speaker and listener. In general, however, English forms of address are reasonably well described by a single binary contrast: first name (FN) versus title plus last name (TLN) (Brown & Ford, 1964). Certain European languages also contrast the familiar and formal forms, such as *tu* and *vous* in French. The use of FN or TLN can either be reciprocal (both sides use the same form of address) or nonreciprocal (one side uses FN and the other side uses TLN). Status and intimacy also play a role in greetings. For example, "Hi" is more common to intimates and to subordinates while "Good morning" is for distant acquaintances and superiors (Brown & Ford, 1964). In contrast, Ogino, Misono, and Fukushima (1985), working in Japan, found 210 different word forms, through 8 address situations, which can be put into 20 different categories. Moreover, in modern American English practice, the distance between the mutual FN and mutual TLN represents only a very small increment of intimacy, sometimes as small as five minutes of conversation. In East Asian communication situations, the distance between very honorific languages and very informal ones is quite large and more often than not cannot be altered even after a long acquaintance.

In English, the speech level is defined mainly by address forms, while in Korean or Japanese, pronouns, verbs, and nouns all have different levels. Thus, in English "to eat" is "to eat" regardless of the person addressed. In the Korean language, however, there are three different ways of saying "to eat": *muk-da* (plain), *du-shin-da* (polite), and *chap-soo-shin-da* (honorific). Different levels of a verb are often accompanied by different levels of a noun: Rice may be *bap* (plain), *shik-sa* (polite), or *jin-ji* (honorific).

In English, the pronoun "you" is used to refer alike to the old and young, to the president of the country, and to the child next door. In East Asian languages, there are different words for "you" depending upon the level of politeness and upon the relationship. There is also the compulsory or preferential use of a term of address instead of the pronoun, as when one says: *Jeh sh Wang.Shin.shen.de shu.ma?* (Literally, "Is this Mr. Wang's book?") instead of "Is this your book?" (Chao, 1956, p. 218). Actual role terms, such as professor, aunt, student, and so forth, are used in place of the pronoun "you" even in two-partner communication because they clarify and accentuate the relationships between the two communicators better than the simple second person reference. Since Confucianism dictates that one should observe the proprieties prescribed by a social relationship, the generalized "you" does not seem to be appropriate in most communication situations in East Asian countries.

This differentiation of linguistic codes in East Asian cultures bears out the familiar psycholinguistic principle that for language communities the degree of lexical differentiation of a referent field increases with the importance of that field to the community (Brown & Ford, 1964). The importance of social relationships in Confucian societies has therefore promoted the differentiation of linguistic codes to accommodate highly differentiated relationships.

Emphasis on Indirect Communication Versus Emphasis on Direct Communication

Most cultures have both direct and indirect modes of communication. Metaphor, insinuations, innuendos, hints, and irony are only a few examples of the kinds of indirect communication that can be found in most linguistic communities. According to Searle (1969), indirect speech acts occur when the speaker communicates to the hearer more than he or she actually says by referring to some mutually shared background information and by relying on the hearer's powers of rationality and inference. Brown and Levinson (1978) have suggested that indirect speech acts are universal because they perform a basic service in strategies of politeness.

Even though the indirect mode of communication seems to be universal, however, the degree to which it is elaborated varies from culture to culture. For instance, the Malagasy speech community values an indirect style (Keenan, 1974), while certain Sabra culture prefers a straight-talking (*dugri*) style (Katriel, 1986). Rosaldo (1973) maintained that the Euro-American association of direct talk with a scientific and democratic attitude may not hold true in different cultural contexts. In Ilongot society, for example, direct talk is perceived as authoritarian and exclusionary while indirect language is perceived as accommodating and sensitive to individual wishes.

Brown and Levinson (1978) have suggested that politeness phenomena in language (indirectness is just one of them) derive from the notion of "face," the public self-image that every member wants to claim for himself or herself. According to Katriel (1986), indirect speech acts are the result of predominant concern for the other person's face. The Confucian legacy of consideration for others and concern for proper human relationships has led to the development of communication patterns that preserve one another's face. Indirect communication helps to prevent the embarrassment of rejection by the other person or disagreement among partners, leaving the relationship and each other's face intact. Lebra (1976) suggested that "defending face" is one of the main factors influencing Japanese behavior. She listed a number of concrete mechanisms for defending face, such as mediated communication (asking someone else to transmit the message), refracted communication (talking to a third person in the presence of the hearer), and acting as a delegate (conveying one's message as being from someone else), which are all indirect forms of communication.

The use of the indirect mode of communication in East Asia is pervasive and often deliberate. In comparing Japanese and American organizations, it has been noted that American employees strive to communicate with each other in a clear, precise, and explicit manner, while Japanese often deliberately communicate in a vague and indirect manner (Hirokawa, 1987; Pascale & Athos, 1981). The extensive nature of indirect communication is exemplified by the fact that there are sixteen evasive "maneuvers" that can be employed by the Japanese to avoid saying no (Imai, 1981).

It has also been suggested that there is a significant difference in the level of indirectness between North American and East Asian communication patterns. An American might say "The door is open" as an indirect way of asking the hearer to shut the door, while in Japan, instead of saying "The door is open," one often says "It is somewhat cold today." This is even more indirect, because no words refer to the door (Okabe, 1987). Operating at a still higher level of indirection, one Japanese wife communicated to her husband her discord with her mother-in-law by slight irregularities in her flower arrangements (Lebra, 1976).

One of Grice's maxims for cooperative conversation is "manner," which suggests that the speaker should avoid obscurity of expression and ambiguity (Grice, 1975). This direct communication is a norm in North America, despite the extensive use of indirect communication. Grice's principle would not be accepted as a norm, however, in East Asia. Okabe (1987) has shown that in Japan, the traditional rule of communication, which prescribes not to demand, reject, assert yourself, or criticize the listener straightforwardly, is a much more dominant principle than Grice's maxim of manner.

Reischauer (1977, p. 136) concluded that "the Japanese have a genuine mistrust of verbal skills, thinking that these tend to show superficiality in contrast to inner, less articulate feelings that are communicated by innuendo or by nonverbal means." Thus, even though both North American and East Asian communication communities employ indirect communication, its use is much more prevalent and accepted as normative in the latter than the former.

Receiver Versus Sender Centeredness

North American communication very often centers on the sender, and until recently the linear, one-way model from sender to receiver was the prevailing model of communication. Much emphasis has been placed on how senders can formulate better messages, improve source credibility, polish their delivery skills, and so forth. In contrast, the emphasis in East Asia has always been on listening and interpretation.

Cheng (1987) has identified infinite interpretation as one of the main principles of Chinese communication. The process presumes that the emphasis is on the receiver and listening rather than the sender or speech making. According to Lebra (1976, p. 123), "anticipatory communication" is common in Japan, in which, instead of the speaker's having to tell or ask for what he or she wants specifically, others guess and accommodate his or her needs, sparing him or her embarrassment in case the verbally expressed request cannot be met. In such cases, the burden of communication falls not on the message sender but on the message receiver. A person who "hears one and understands ten" is regarded as an intelligent communicator. To catch on quickly and to adjust oneself to another's position before his or her position is clearly revealed is regarded as an important communication skill. One of the common puzzles expressed by foreign students from East Asia is why they are constantly being asked what they want when they are visiting in American homes. In their own countries, the host or hostess is supposed to know what is needed and serve accordingly. The difference occurs because in North America it is important to provide individual freedom of choice; in East Asia, it is important to practice anticipatory communication and to accommodate accordingly.

With the emphasis on indirect communication, the receiver's sensitivity and ability to capture the under-the-surface meaning and to understand implicit meaning becomes critical. In North America, an effort has been made to improve the effectiveness of senders through such formal training as debate and public speech, whereas in East Asia, the effort has been on improving the receiver's sensitivity. The highest sensitivity is reached when one empties the mind of one's preconceptions and makes it as clear as a mirror (Yuji, 1984).

Recently, there has been increased interest in listening in the United States as well. Both communication scholars and practitioners recognize that listening is not only necessary from the instrumental aspect of communication (comprehension) but, more importantly, for the affective aspect (satisfaction of being listened to).

DISCUSSION

This paper compared the East Asian emphasis on social relationships with the North American emphasis on individualism. These two emphases produce very different patterns of interpersonal relationships and communication. The conclusions drawn in this paper are not absolute, however. Each culture contains both orientations to some degree. It is simply more probable that East Asians would exhibit certain patterns of communication, such as indirect communication, more often than North Americans, and vice versa.

The North American preoccupation with individualism and related concepts, such as equality, fairness, and justice, and its far-reaching influences on the whole fiber of society are well documented. On the other hand, the importance of social relationships as a key to the East Asian countries has been recognized only recently. For instance, investigations of Japanese management styles have found that one of the fundamental differences between Japanese and American management is the personalized, interdependent relationships among employees and between managers and employees in Japan. These human relationships are related to loyalty and high productivity. It is not uncommon to explain such relationships away as merely a result of other organizational practices, such as lifelong employment. If one looks under the surface, however, one realizes that it is derived from a thousand-year-old Confucian legacy, and that similar human relationship patterns are found outside of large organizations. Consequently, attempts to transplant such a management style to North America with its philosophical and cultural orientation of individualism cannot be entirely satisfactory. The culture itself would have to be modified first.

There has been increasing concern in North America about the pursuit of individualism at the expense of commitment to larger entities such as the community, civic groups, and other organizations. It has been suggested that modern individualism has progressed to such an extent that most Americans are trapped by the language of individualism itself and have lost the ability to articulate their own need to get involved (Bellah et al., 1985). Although individualism has its own strength as a value, individualism that is not accompanied by commitments to large entities eventually forces people into a state of isolation, where life itself becomes meaningless.

If human beings are fundamentally social animals, it is necessary to balance the cultural belief system of individualism with the need to get involved with others. Americans have joined voluntary associations and civic organizations more than any other citizens of the industrialized world. However, such recent phenomena as the "me" generation and young stockbrokers who pursue only personal gain at the expense of their own organizations or the society as a whole can be perceived as pathological symptoms of individualism driven to its extreme. Bellah et al. (1985, p. 284) have maintained that "social ecology is damaged not only by war, genocide, and political repression. It is also damaged by the destruction of the subtle ties that bind human beings to one another, leaving them frightened and alone." They strongly argue that we need to restore social ecology by making people aware of our intricate connectedness and interdependence.

The emphasis of Confucianism on social relationships is conducive to cooperation, warm relaxed human relations, consideration of others, and group harmony, but it has costs as well. Under such social constraints, individual initiative and innovation are slow to appear, and some individuals feel that their individuality is being suffocated. Because of the sharp distinction between in-groups and out-groups, factionalism may be inevitable. Within such well-defined sets of social relationships, people have a well-developed sense of obligation but a weak sense of duty to impersonal social entities.

Ironically, the solution for both the North American problems of excessive individualism and the excessive adherence to in-groupness in East Asia is the same: to be receptive to others. For the North Americans, this means accepting the limitations of self-reliance, becoming committed to a group, and putting the common good ahead of personal wants. For the East Asians, this means making their group boundaries more flexible and accepting outsiders with humanness and commitment to the common good.

There have been substantial changes in the East Asian societies since World War II. There has been an irrepressible influx of Western values; imported films and television programs are ubiquitous. However, it is not easy to change several hundred years of Confucian legacy. In Japan, for example, a greater proportion of young people than old expressed a preference for a boss endowed with the virtues of humanness and sympathy over a more efficient boss who would not ask for extra devotion (Dore, 1973). A similar finding was reported in Korea. When Korean workers, mostly in manufacturing plants, were asked their reasons for changing jobs, those who answered "a better human relationship and more humane treatment" still outnumbered those who answered "better payment" (Kim, 1984).

It seems inevitable, however, that the East Asian countries will see an increasing number of people who do not have traditional, binding relationships as the society moves further toward industrialization and higher mobility. The task will be to find a way for such people to cope with life without the protection of close in-group memberships and to learn to find satisfaction in expressing individual freedom and self-reliance.

References

Bellah, R., Madsen, R., Sullivan, W., Swidler, A., and Tipton, S. (1985). *Habits of the Heart: Individualism and Commitment in American Life*. New York: Harper & Row.

Brown, R. W., and Ford, M. (1964). "Address in American English." In D. Hymes (Ed.), *Language in Culture and Society*. New York: Harper & Row.

Brown, R., and Levinson, S. (1978). "Universals in Language Usage: Politeness Phenomena." In E. Goody (Ed.), *Questions and Politeness*. Cambridge: Cambridge University Press.

Chao, Y. R. (1956). Chinese terms of address. *Language*, 32, 217–241.

Cheng, C. Y. (1987). "Chinese Philosophy and Contemporary Communication Theory." In D. L. Kincaid (Ed.), *Communication Theory: Eastern and Western Perspectives*. New York: Academic Press.

Chinese Culture Connection. (1987). Chinese values and the search for culture-free dimensions of culture. *Journal of Cross-Cultural Psychology*, 18, 143–164.

Condon, J., and Yousef, F. (1975). *An Introduction to Intercultural Communication*. New York: Bobbs-Merrill.

Dore, R. (1973). *British Factory, Japanese Factory: The Origins of National Diversity in Industrial Relations*. Berkeley and Los Angeles: University of California Press.

Grice, P. H. (1975). "Logic and Conversation." In P. Cole and J. L. Morgan (Eds.), *Studies in Syntax*. Vol. 3. New York: Academic Press.

Hall, J., and Beadsley, R. (1965). *Twelve Doors to Japan*. New York: McGraw-Hill.

Hirokawa, R. (1987). "Communication Within the Japanese Business Organization." In D. L. Kincaid (Ed.), *Communication Theory: Eastern and Western Perspectives*. New York: Academic Press.

Hofstede, G. (1980). *Culture's Consequences*. Newbury Park, Calif.: Sage.

Hui, C. H., and Triandis, H. C. (1986). Individualism–collectivism: A study of cross-cultural research. *Journal of Cross-Cultural Psychology, 17*, 225–248.

Imai, M. (1981). *Sixteen Ways to Avoid Saying No*. Tokyo: Nihon Keizai Shimbun.

Katriel, T. (1986). *Talking Straight: Dugri Speech in Israeli Sabra Culture*. Cambridge: Cambridge University Press.

Keenan, E. (1974). "Norm Makers, Norm Breakers: Uses of Speech by Men and Women in a Malagasy Community." In R. Bauman and J. Sherzer (Eds.), *Explorations in the Ethnography of Speaking*. Cambridge: Cambridge University Press.

Kim, S. U. (1984). *"Kong-jang no-dong-ja-ye ee-jik iyu"* ("Reasons for Changing Jobs Among Factory Workers"). *Hankook Daily Newspaper*, May 2 (in Korean).

Lebra, T. S. (1976). *Japanese Patterns of Behavior*. Honolulu: University Press of Hawaii.

Lee, K. T. (1983). *Hankook-in ye u-shik koo-jo* (Cognitive Patterns of Korean People). Seoul: Shin-Won Moon-Wha Sa (in Korean).

Luce, D., and Sommer, J. (1969). *Viet Nam—The Unheard Voices*. Ithaca, N.Y.: Cornell University Press.

McBrian, C. (1978). Language and social stratification: The case of a Confucian society." *Anthropological Linguistics, 2*, 320–326.

McNaughton, W. (1974). *The Confucian Vision*. Ann Arbor: University of Michigan Press.

Martin, S. E. (1964). "Speech Levels in Japan and Korea." In D. Hymes (Ed.), *Language in Culture and Society*. New York: Harper & Row.

Nakamura, H. (1964). *Ways of Thinking of Eastern Peoples*. Honolulu: East-West Center Press.

Ogino, T., Misono, Y., and Fukushima, C. (1985). Diversity of honorific usage in Tokyo: A sociolinguistic approach based on a field survey." International *Journal of Sociology of Language, 55*, 23–39.

Okabe, K. (1987). "Indirect Speech Acts of the Japanese." In D. L. Kincaid (Ed.), *Communication Theory: Eastern and Western Perspectives*. New York: Academic Press.

Parsons, T., Shils, E., and Olds, J. (1951). "Categories of the Orientation and Organization of Action." In T. Parsons and E. A. Shils (Eds.), *Toward a General Theory of Action*. Cambridge, Mass.: Harvard University Press.

Pascale, R., and Athos, A. (1981). *The Art of Japanese Management: Application for American Executives*. New York: Warner Communications.

Reischauer, E. (1977). *The Japanese*. Cambridge: Harvard University Press.

Rosaldo, M. (1973). I have nothing to hide: The language of Ilongot oratory. *Language in Society, 11*, 193–223.

Searle, J. R. (1969). *Speech Acts*. Cambridge: Cambridge University Press.

Varenne, H. (1977). *Americans Together: Structured Diversity in a Midwestern Town*. New York and London: Teacher College Press.

Yuji, A. (Trans. N. Chung). (1984). *Ilbon-in ye usik koo-jo* (Japanese Thought Patterns). Seoul: Baik Yang Publishing Co. (in Korean).

Yum, J. O. (1987). Korean Philosophy and Communication. In D. L. Kincaid (Ed.), *Communication Theory: Eastern and Western Perspectives*. New York: Academic Press.

Concepts and Questions

1. According to Yum, what is one reason why Confucianism has endured?
2. In terms of communication behavior, compare an orientation toward social relationships with an orientation toward individualism.
3. What are the four Confucian principles of right conduct? How do they contribute to communication behavior?
4. How do East Asian concepts of in-group and out-group differ from those of North Americans? How might these differences affect intercultural communication?
5. How does Confucianism affect linguistic codes?
6. What are the major differences in the ways in which interpersonal bonding takes place in Eastern and Western cultures?
7. How do Eastern values concerning equality differ from Western values?
8. How does the rate of self-disclosure differ in Eastern and Western cultures?
9. What does Yum mean when she says that Confucianism is a philosophy of human nature?
10. Do you agree with Yum's observation that it is not easy to change cultural values that have been in place for several hundred years?

Communication in Korea: Playing Things by Eye

JAMES H. ROBINSON

Intercultural communication is a process full of excitement and frustration. These extremes may be especially heightened in business and professional communication, where the financial success of an enterprise is at stake. In such intercultural communication between Koreans and Westerners, the Korean concept of *nunch'i* [1] may play an important role. In Korea, *nunch'i* is a critical variable in the maintenance of social relationships. Literally, a Korean could not survive in Korea without this perceptive skill. Miscommunication between Western and Korean professionals occurs because Koreans have *nunch'i* and expect Westerners to have it too, or because Westerners do not have *nunch'i*, do not know what it is, and do not even know that anyone else expects them to have it. The following definition will outline the importance of *nunch'i* in Korean society, relate it to two other cultural concepts that predominate in East Asia, and provide concrete examples of how *nunch'i* contributes both to successful communication among Koreans and to miscommunication between Westerners and all East Asians.

NUNCH'I

In Korean, *nunch'i* means "eye measured" [2]. Martin and his colleagues define *nunch'i*'s nominative usage as "tact, savoir faire, sense, social sense, perceptiveness, an eye for social situations," and its predicate function as the attempt "to read one's mind, probe one's motives, studies one's face, grasps a situation, sees how the wind blows" [3]. More figuratively, it

From *IEEE Transactions on Professional Communication*, (September, 1996), 129–137. Copyright by the Institute of Electrical & Electronics Engineers, Inc. Reproduced by permission of the publisher. James H. Robinson teaches at St. Cloud State University.

could be translated as eye sense or playing things by eye [4]. As a Korean proverb proclaimed, "If you have a quick sense of *nunch'i*, you can even eat pickled shrimp in a Buddhist temple" [5]. As Buddhists are vegetarians, the pickling process and the eating of flesh would both be regarded as barbaric and especially so in a Buddhist temple. Consequently, the social skills required to behave in this fashion would be an example of having the quickest sense of *nunch'i*.

Scholars have referred to *nunch'i* as a nonlogical process variable that uses visual perception to discover the hidden agenda behind all forms of expression in social interaction. According to Lee [5], this *nunch'i* goes "beyond good sense or common sense." *Nunch'i* is more intuitive and sensitive than logical or rational. It does not lead to fixed decisions as one might find with good sense or common sense. As it depends on interpersonal rapport, *nunch'i* is instead a situational ethic used to solve interpersonal problems [5]. In addition, the *nun* in *nunch'i* means "eye," and so *nunch'i* is both related to using the eyes to perceive the world and to reading the eyes of others. Yum refers to *nunch'i* as "perceptiveness or sensitivity with eyes" [6]. According to Kalton, *nunch'i* is used also to read the eyes and to assess "quickly and accurately . . . another's emotions, attitudes, and reaction or likely reaction to a given proposal or situations" [7]. K. Kim states that Koreans use *nunch'i* to interpret facial expressions, words and "a mysterious 'alpha' hidden in . . . inner hearts" [8].

Because of *nunch'i*, Koreans are also very concerned about what others see and think about them: about what another's *nunch'i* tells about oneself. This concern is related to an emphasis in Confucian-influenced societies on self-control. Maturity within such a society means "controlling," "hiding," or "masking" one's emotions [9]. A negative reaction may be manifest in a face that becomes as expressionless as stone rather than in some verbal explosion. Expressions of affect are found in the eyes rather than on the face or from the whole body. Because of this emphasis on self-control, Yum says that *nunch'i* becomes crucial in understanding "minute nonverbal cues, on reading between the lines, and on hearing between the sounds" to penetrate the mask that hides one's desires. The height of the art of *nunch'i* would be to give someone something before he or she asked for it. Such behavior manifests pure genius, as it avoids the speaker's having to give a "yes" or "no" answer to a request [6, p. 80]. According to Song, " . . . nunch'i can distinguish between sincerity and falsehood, detect the good will hidden behind a grimace, uncover the villain that keeps smiling, and unmask the wolf in sheep's clothing" [10, p. 32].

In their analysis of nunch'i, S. H. Choi and S. C. Choi [11] have identified two nunch'i processes in face-to-face communication: nunch'i execution and nunch'i figuring-out. The first is an initiating action where an indirect message, which is often nonverbal, is communicated: for example, when a wife comes up and stands next to a husband who is standing by a counter, this nunch'i move means that the husband needs to move so that the wife can open a cabinet. (In U.S. culture, a more verbal move, such as "excuse me," might be expected.) A nunch'i figuring-out behavior is a response to a nunch'i execution: for example, the husband perceives the wife's proximity and moves out of the way.

In order for a nunch'i interaction to be successful, both execution and figuring-out moves are required. As in the above example, the wife has to send the correct message, and the husband has to receive it. But if the wife had executed the act without the corresponding figuring-out process by the husband, the communication act fails. The result could be (and indeed was) an argument. At the same time, if the husband initiates a figuring-out process when no nunch'i execution has been sent from the wife, the communication will also fail. Specifically, if the wife just wanted to be close to the husband and had no interest in opening the cabinet, then moving away to make room for the wife would not be a good response. In other words, proximity can have more than one meaning, and can be a nunch'i-executed move or not, and it all depends on the context or the situation.

Dualism

One cultural concept related to nunch'i is dualism. According to Song [10] and Kang [2], nunch'i can have both positive and negative sides. From the positive-side, nunch'i is foreseeing. When a mother predicts misbehavior by a child and praises the child for good behavior before the child has a chance to mis-

behave, the mother uses nunch'i as foreseeing [12]. When a foreign visitor to Korea notices that often what he or she requires is provided before even asking, this is the positive manifestation of nunch'i. This foreseeing would be the height of good behavior.

Korean scholars also describe nunch'i as having a negative side. In interactions with Korean students, this foreseeing can frustrate American educators. For example, American college administrators may encounter situations where students make an appointment, but when they arrive for what was supposed to be an important decision, the student talks of trivialities and leaves before coming to the point. Administrators may wonder what happened: with nunch'i, the student foresaw that it was not a good time to raise an important issue [7]. According to Kang [2], this negative side also encourages deception for a higher goal of harmony. Koreans would be reluctant to hurt anyone's feelings with the truth when a watering down of the truth would preserve harmony as well as face. For example, a Korean shop owner gives the customer an unrealistic time of completion for repairs because the owner's nunch'i perceives that it will make the customer feel better at least for the moment [13].

This deception that Kang describes can also result in a self-denial stance in dyadic communication. For example, Koreans will often decline the first and even a second offer of food, drink, or favors, even if they are hungry, thirsty, or in great need. In this situation, nunch'i is a strategy to negotiate the difference between a polite offer and a real offer [14]. With nunch'i, the first offer is interpreted to have two potential meanings: one, a politeness strategy used before one eats something in public, or two, an offer of food. For example, on a train, before eating a boiled egg as a snack, a person may actually offer it to others in the vicinity, but this offer is politeness if only given once, and to accept it would be unthinkable. With a second offer, the latter of these two hypotheses is reinforced although not conclusively so. With the third offer, the second hypothesis is accepted as well as the offer itself. If our train traveler made a second and then a third offer, then it would be obvious that the offer was sincere and not out of politeness and so should be accepted.

From both of these two sides, nunch'i is used to avoid unpleasantness for oneself by foreseeing the behavior of others and to avoid unpleasantness for others by using deception. While this first strategy could be very helpful in cross-cultural interactions with Americans, the second one could be misunderstood as dishonesty and result in negative stereotypes if not lead to social conflict.

Hierarchy

A second cultural concept related to *nunch'i* is hierarchy. *Nunch'i* might not exist in Korea without a hierarchical social system. Hierarchical social relations, expressed through senior–junior dyads, are manifestations of the yin–yang concept and of the five Confucian relationships. For Confucian-oriented societies, social interaction relies on the balancing of yin and yang. According to Cheng [15, p. 34], yin and yang have hierarchical characteristics: yang means the "creative, forwarding-pushing, dominating and manifest, systemic force," and yin the "receptive, recessive, dominated, hidden, informed and background force." The yin–yang dyad in social relations is also expressed through the responsibilities of each participant in the five Confucian relationships: "king–justice, subject–loyalty," "father–love, son–filiality," "husband–initiative, wife–obedience," "elder brother–brotherly love, younger brother–reverence," and "friends–mutual faith" [6, p. 77]. In Confucian societies, these relationships are dominated by the hierarchical father–son dyad, but in Western cultures, the egalitarian husband–wife dyad is the more dominant model [2].

Within these hierarchical relationships, interaction is highly ritualized, with great importance placed on the proper behavior and the proper language for both juniors and seniors. For example, juniors would very seldom drink alcohol or smoke in front of seniors. Juniors would also need to use polite–formal language to seniors, while seniors would use informal–impolite language forms with juniors for most daily interactions. At times, juniors prefer silence or a simple "yes" to attempting a verbal response to a senior within this complex hierarchical system of interaction.

In this hierarchical system, *nunch'i* can function as a social equalizer. Without it, juniors would be absolutely helpless. With it, juniors have a chance to achieve their individual needs from a very disadvan-

taged position. R. H. Kim said that *nunch'i* "is an inevitable by-product of a rigidly stratified class society where force rather than reason, class status rather than individual ability, political power rather than hard work, have been used as methods of accumulating wealth by the social elite" [14, p. 6]. In this class society, juniors must use their "quick sense" of *nunch'i* in their interactions with seniors to gain their individual needs. Argumentation, logic, and objectivity would only elicit disdain by seniors and society. When a child resorts to rational means, adults would characterize the child as "impudent" [14, p. 6].

According to C. S. Choi [12], juniors use *nunch'i* to offset the authoritarian pressures of seniors within this hierarchical social system. The end result is a "*nunch'i* culture" that operates in a "cold war" of interpersonal relations and relies heavily on covert expression or what is not said and not done more than on overt verbal or nonverbal communication. Always full of tension, the juniors or equals have to use *nunch'i* to read the mind of the senior or the equal, to manipulate the situation, and to escape any negative repercussions. Because of the infringement of seniors, one's behavior is more often than not expressed through a "silent mind." Rather than expressing oneself, this *nunch'i* culture creates a "*nunch'i* personality" that does not express individual needs. Koreans use *nunch'i* as a tactic for gathering data, as a means to analyze that data, and as a means of keeping one's own secrets. This *nunch'i* personality is that of a secret agent or a private detective [12, pp. 120–121]. For example, I was once fired from a part-time job in Korea but did not realize it until I was halfway down the hallway. The firing was marked by a really polite goodbye with an unusually deep bow. If I had used my *nunch'i*, I could have foreseen this event from the just prior conversation and either respectfully resigned or politely made an appropriate apology, which would have saved some face if not my job. In other words, my employment status was at risk, and I did not even know it until it was too late because my *nunch'i* was too slow. If it had been faster, I would have at least had a shot at changing the outcome. As it was, I was helpless.

C. S. Choi also claims that *nunch'i* is a cultural reaction to a life of pain, and oppression from seniors and invasion by outsiders. As a survival strategy or a social release valve, *nunch'i* is similar to a traditional

Korean song of the blues, a story of grief and tears [12, p. 122]. Thus a smile may mean pain, a nonplused look happiness, a polite word anger, and an impolite expression friendliness—or the other way around, depending on the situation. For international businessmen, they should realize that nunch'i was developed and perfected in Korea partly to manipulate foreigners, especially invaders. While the invaders of the past were mostly military, the present-day invader is the international businessman.

PROFESSIONAL COMMUNICATION

The second part of the paper will provide examples of how nunch'i influences professional communication. The first set of examples will explicate this communication process between Koreans. The second set will describe the miscommunication that results when Koreans expect nunch'i-related behaviors from Americans or other Westerns in communication, or, put another way, when Western businessmen enter into communication with Koreans without any cultural understanding of Korean culture.

KOREAN INTERACTIONS

S. H. Choi and S. C. Choi [11] give an example of how hidden messages that rely on nunch'i are communicated in office situations. In this situation, someone from within your office drops by, but you do not have time to talk with them because of a pressing deadline. In this Korean situation, the nunch'i-emitted verbal message would be, "What time is it now?" The visitor should then realize that the coworker knows very well what time it is and is simply providing an indirect means of communicating the fact that the visitor should leave so that the co-worker can continue with the work at hand. The visitor would then announce the intent of leaving and leave. S. H. Choi and S. C. Choi have indicated that one appropriate response would be "Oh, it's already 4 o'clock. I'd better leave now. I've an appointment at 4:15." As S. H. Choi and S. C. Choi comment:

In such a case, two parties could communicate their "real" intentions without either party indicating

knowledge of the internally transmitted message. The faces of both parties are saved by virtue of the neutrality of the Noon–Chi exchange, in an otherwise "no win" situation [11, p. 57].

If, on the other hand, the visitor had responded by referring to the surface message, the communication would have been destroyed.

The second example concerns how nunch'i can even affect the decision of when to leave the office at the end of the day. In Korea, office work does not follow the clock as much as it does the dictates of the immediate supervisor or boss. Most Korean offices are organized with a large number of desks in a large room. The supervisor or boss has a desk at the head of several rows of desks but in the same room. In short, the boss always knows who is at his or her desk. Typically, when anyone leaves, he or she announces this departure with one of several polite phrases.

In most situations, the juniors in the office cannot leave work until the boss has left. In Janelli's interview data, when he asked about coerced overtime and how one knew when one could leave work, one response was, "We have to use our nunch'i" to "appraise the mood or our superior" before leaving work [16, p. 207]. If the employee perceived that the boss was not in a good mood, the employee would stay until after the boss left. But if the boss had had a good day, then the employee could announce his departure before the boss has actually left. In this daily interaction, the mood or kibun of the boss was more important than the time clock in determining when the juniors in the office could leave the office for home, and the only means of determining the boss's kibun was through nunch'i. Without nunch'i, a junior would never be able to leave the office before the boss did.

S. H. Choi and S. C. Choi document the role of pauses and silences in nunch'i through a videotape study of the interactions between a shop owner, who is also an uncle, and the shop manager, who is a nephew, in a resort complex. In the first situation, the uncle is supervising the nephew in regard to the placement of some mats in front of the store the day after some of these mats had been stolen. The nephew is placing mats on the sidewalk in the very place where they were stolen the day before. The interaction begins:

UNCLE: Why did you put this mat in here?

NEPHEW: (2 second pause) This one? (glancing sidewise at the uncle, in fainting voice)

UNCLE: Yeah.

NEPHEW: (We're) going to use tomorrow (in fainting voice). . . . [11, p. 10]

In essence, the two-second pause by the nephew is a *nunch'i* response that expresses politeness and deference to the uncle. A direct response to the question would have been impolite. The problem of theft is communicated only through *nunch'i* in this communication and never mentioned directly. The reference to tomorrow is perhaps an indirect indication that the nephew will make sure that the mats are not stolen, in the near future at least.

In a second situation, silence as well as a pause acts as a *nunch'i* emitted message that might be characterized as a nonplused response by the nephew:

NEPHEW: (putting up a fake Christmas tree).

UNCLE: Look, that branch seems to be longer than that one at the bottom.

NEPHEW: (no response)

UNCLE: Oh maybe not?

NEPHEW: (1 sec. pause) No, it's not. [11, p. 14]

In this case, the silence by the nephew did not mean that he did not hear the uncle but that the uncle was wrong. This *nunch'i*-emitted silence was received by the uncle, who then corrected himself in a hedging manner. After a short pause, a *nunch'i*-emitted expression of politeness and deference, the nephew is then able to agree with the restatement of the uncle. As S. H. Choi and S. C. Choi relate, if the nephew's final response had followed directly after the uncle's initial statement, both the uncle and the nephew would have lost face and the interaction would have ended disastrously [11, p. 14].

In a third situation, ellipsis is used as a *nunch'i* strategy of communication. Ellipsis is a common communication strategy in which the speaker omits an element because it is understood. For example, "Been busy today?" is interpreted as a question that means, "Have you been busy today?" The first two words are simply omitted. At the sentence level in

Korea, subject ellipsis is very common in formal writing as well as oral communication. As a *nunch'i* strategy, the participant in an interaction can actually be omitted from the context. For example:

UNCLE: We haven't finished that "Doruko" painting, have we?

NEPHEW: What is Doruko painting? (as if in monologue) Which one?

UNCLE: That . . . that one which looks like a mud . . . mud . . .

NEPHEW: Oh we did, didn't we? [11, p. 20]

In this interaction, the nephew does not know what Doruko painting is and so he behaves as if the participants in the interaction were not there, he omits both his uncle and himself from the interaction by posing a rhetorical question to himself. This rhetorical response is followed by an indirect response to the uncle. If the nephew had simply confessed that he did not know what the doruko painting was, he would have lost face as an incompetent assistant to the uncle, and the uncle would have lost some degree of face, as his choice of assistant would be revealed to be less than brilliant. By omitting both interlocutors from this conversation for this brief instant to ask a rhetorical question to himself within which he then made the indirect reference to the paintings in front of them, the nephew uses a *nunch'i* strategy to cover up his ignorance and to save his face. The uncle participates in this *nunch'i* communication by defining doruko painting as a mud painting.

In these three interactions, the nephew used the three *nunch'i* strategies of pauses, silence, and ellipsis to preserve harmony in the relationship with the uncle and to maintain his face as well as that of the uncle. These strategies sent messages to the uncle that were figured out by the uncle and then responded to in kind within two channels of communication: one at the literal level and one at the meta-message level.

Intercultural Interactions

As one might imagine, *nunch'i*-related behaviors can also cause miscommunication between Americans or other Westerners and Koreans. As an Australian manager in Korea once commented, " . . . I initially found that it was difficult to elicit the 'real' views of my staff when it came to debating various sales and merchandising strategies." This Western manager continued that in " . . . my experience . . . initially you may get either 'silence' or, be told 'That won't work in Korea'." This manager stressed, "The trick is to break that invisible barrier so that you can mix in your staff's invaluable field experience and obvious cultural knowledge and gain an understanding of how your objective can still be achieved with some 'Koreanizing' of its implementation" [17]. From the Korean perspective, Janelli in his ethnography of a South Korean conglomerate wrote, "The greatest consensus in their [South Korean mid-level managers] critique of the United States appeared in their views of American interpersonal relations in business dealings" [16, p. 57]. Essentially, this criticism focused on how Americans lack a sensitivity to others in business matters. In other words, Americans are more concerned with the letter of the law or contract and less concerned with human beings. Koreans, on the other hand, tend to be more sensitive to others in both social and business interactions. *Nunch'i* is one of the causes of the invisible barrier referred to by the Australian manager, and it also creates a sensitivity gap between Koreans and Westerners. The following three examples will show how the lack of *nunch'i* on the part of Westerners in Korea can result in disastrous miscommunication.

De Mente, in his book on cross-cultural communication for Western businessmen in Korea, provides the first example. He states that "one of the extraordinary skills the foreign businessman should have to succeed in Korea is the ability to read faces—or to read *nunch'i* (noon–chee), in Korean terms" [18, p. 83]. He comments that Americans often are confronted with the statement "Things are done differently in Korea," and that these " . . . businessmen need *nunch'i* in order to understand the rationale behind 'things are done differently in Korea' and to learn a different set of 'management and negotiating skills' " [18, p. 85]. In support of this point, De Mente describes an incident involving the foreign manager of a joint-venture company in Seoul.

The firm's office was located in a very expensive but inconvenient location in Yoido, near the National Assembly Building. The foreign manager found a nice suite of offices in the downtown area of Seoul, less expensive and far more convenient for both employees and visitors. At the last moment, the Korean president refused to allow the move to take place, and would not explain his reasons to the foreign manager. The situation developed into a sticky impasse that created a great deal of ill will on both sides [18, pp. 83–84].

The office manager had explained his reasons for wanting to move the office, and believed his rationale had been understood and accepted by his point-venture partner. He had therefore proceeded in good faith. The Korean president had opposed the move from the beginning, however, and had relied upon the foreigner's ability to read *nunch'i* to understand that he was firmly against the move although he had not said so directly.

The Korean president preferred the Yoido location because it was one of the most prestigious districts in the city. It gave the company "face" on the highest government and business levels, and . . . the Yoido location had nothing to do with rent and everything to do with where the company president wanted his car to pull up in the morning [18, pp. 83–84].

The president and other Korean personnel did not simply come out and tell the foreigner that there was no way they were going to move the offices because they did not want to confront him directly with their objections and cause him to lose face in a contest he could not win. They felt it was up to him to ask the right questions and to "read" the right answers. In the end, both sides lost face in a classic case of failure in cross-cultural communications.

The second example comes from interview data collected by the author. In this situation, a Western businessman visits a Korean firm. During this visit, the Korean counterpart takes off from his office—with permission, of course—and spends as much time as necessary with his Western guest. In the course of their discussions, when the Western guest needs to send a fax back to the home office, the Korean counterpart provides this service. Entertainment is funded completely by the Korean counterpart, either through his expense account or with personal funds. But, when the Korean businessman visits his new friend in his office in England, what had been a great relationship falls apart completely. After providing great hospitality in Korea, the Korean businessman expected the same when he became the guest. But the Western businessman did not have the *nunch'i* to realize that all the hospitality in Korea had a cost. So, when the Korean businessman visits, his Western counterpart delays any interaction until after he has finished his work. After emitting several nonverbal signals of impatience, the Korean businessman emits a verbal *nunch'i* cue by asking to send a fax—thinking that this would remind the Western counterpart of one favor provided in Korea. After the Korean businessman sends his fax, he has to wait some more. In absolute frustration, he gives up and makes an excuse to leave. On his way out, insult is added to injury, as the Western counterpart finally interrupts his work to say, "But you can't go; you haven't paid for the fax."

CONCLUSION

In short, *nunch'i* is a cultural concept that Western professionals need to understand before doing business or working in Korea or with Koreans in the United States. In particular, Western professionals need to pay great attention to pauses, silences, and rhetorical questions that may appear in their interactions with Korean businessmen. These responses are examples of *nunch'i*-executed communication acts that signal disagreement or a lack of understanding.

Most importantly, the Western professional should understand that when their Korean counterpart says something such as, "We do not do it that way in Korea," this direct verbal message indicates that a series of *nunch'i*-executed messages have been previously emitted without the proper *nunch'i* figuring-out process on the part of the Western businessman. When a Korean uses this phrase, he or she is providing the contents of the message that you should have said or at least thought in response to the series of *nunch'i*-executed moves. In other words, you should have said, "Oh, this won't work in Korea?" At the least, you probably should have kept your mouth shut when encountering a seemingly

nonlogical statement or response. If you learn to perceive these *nunch'i*-executed messages and to respond properly, you have made the first step in identifying which Western business practices will and will not work in a country such as Korea.

References

[1] Throughout the text the McCune–Reischauer system of romanization is used, with the exception of direct quotes. See "Tables of the McCune–Reischauer system for the romanization of Korean." *Trans. Korean Branch Roy, Asiatic Soc.*, vol. 38, p. 121, Oct. 1961; or E. F. Klein, "Romanization of Korean: Problems, experiments, suggestions," in *Studies on Korea in Transition*. D. R. McCann *et al.* Eds. Honolulu, HI: Univ. Hawaii Press: 1979, pp. 174–199.

[2] S. P. Kang, *The East Asian Culture and Its Transformation in the West*. Seoul, Korea: Amer. Studies Inst., 1972, p. 64; and M. S. Park, *Communication Styles in Two Different Cultures: Korean and American*. Seoul, Korea: Han Shin Pub., 1979, p. 92.

[3] E. M. Martin, Y. H. Lee, and S. U. Chang, *A Korean-English Dictionary*. New Haven, CT: Yale Univ. Press, 1967.

[4] H. C. (R. H.) Kim, "Education and the Korean immigrant child," *Integrated Educ.*, vol. 15, no. 1, pp. 15–18, 1977.

[5] O. Y. Lee, *In This Earth & in That Wind*. Seoul, Korea: Roy, Asiatic Soc., Korea Branch, 1967 (translated by D. I. Steinberg).

[6] J. O. Yum, "Korean philosophy and communication," in *Communication Theory: Eastern and Western Perspectives*. D. L. Kincaid, Ed. San Diego, CA: Academic, 1987, pp. 71–86.

[7] M. Kalton, "Korean ideas and values," in *The Korea Papers: Profile in Educational Exchange*, I. Davies, Ed. Washington, DC: Nat. Assoc. for Foreign Student Affairs, vol. 23, p. 14, 1990.

[8] K. Kim, "Cross-cultural differences between American and Koreans in nonverbal behavior," in *The Korean Language: Its Structure and Social Projection*. H. Sohn, Ed. Honolulu, HI: Center for Korean Studies, Univ. Hawaii, 1975, pp. 5–18.

[9] Y. D. Cho, "Speaker's *nunch'i*: Koreans' gazing behavior in face-to-face interaction," unpublished manuscript, p. 13, 1988.

[10] Y. I. Song, "Nunch'i," *Korea J.*, vol. 11, no. 10, pp. 32, 43, 1971.

[11] S. H. Choi and S. C. Choi, "Noon–chi: An indigenous form of Koreans' politeness communication," presented at the Dept. Psychology, Univ. Hawaii, 1991, unpublished.

[12] C. S. Choi, *Han-kuk-in-oi Sa-hui-joek seong-kyok [The Social Character of Koreans]*, 2nd ed. Seoul, Korea: Gai Mun Sa, 1980, p. 122.

[13] P. S. Crane, *Korean Patterns*. Seoul, Korea: Roy, Asiatic Soc., 1967, p. 12.

[14] H. C. (R. H.) Kim, "Understanding Korean people, language, and culture," paper prepared for the Superintendent of Public Instruction, Bellington, WA, p. 5, 1979.

[15] C. Y. Cheng, "Chinese philosophy and contemporary human communication theory," in *Communication Theory: Eastern and Western Perspectives*, D. L. Kincaid, Ed. San Diego, CA: Academic Press, 1987, pp. 23–43.

[16] R. Janelli and D. Yim, *Making Capitalism: The Social and Cultural Construction of a South Korean Conglomerate*. Stanford, CA: Stanford Univ. Press, 1993.

[17] T. Bartley, "Changes . . . ? What changes!" *Korea Herald*, June 25, 1994.

[18] B. De Mente, *Korean Etiquette and Ethics in Business*. Lincolnwood, IL: Nat. Textbook, 1988.

Concepts and Questions

1. What does Robinson mean when he writes, "In order for a *nunch'i* interaction to be successful, both execution and figuring-out moves are required"?

2. Do members of the dominant culture in the United States have a concept similar to *nunch'i*? What is it?

3. How would you relate hierarchical relationships to *nunch'i*?

4. How can *nunch'i* function as a social equalizer?

5. What is the link between *nunch'i* and silence?

6. Why does Robinson suggest that *nunch'i* is a historical reaction to pain?

7. How does *nunch'i* influence the decision-making process?

8. Can you think of some ways, not mentioned by Robinson, where our lack of knowledge regarding *nunch'i* could impede intercultural communication?

Dominant Cultural Patterns of Hindus in India

NEMI C. JAIN

ELLEN D. KUSSMAN

For more than 3,000 years, the peoples of the Indian subcontinent have sought the deepest truths in order to transform limited and imperfect human life into potential greatness. Their insights and discoveries have shaped what many consider one of the world's richest and most long-lived cultures.

India has been the cradle of several religions: Hinduism, Jainism, Buddhism, and Sikhism. The great majority of her people follow Hinduism, which can be taken to mean simply "the religion of India" (Ellwood, 1992). During the last 1200 years, India has also been influenced by Islam, Christianity, and Judaism, and thus has become one of the most culturally pluralistic societies in the world. Like any other culture, Indian culture is complex and consists of many interrelated beliefs, values, norms, social systems, and artifacts. In spite of its multiethnic, multilingual, and highly stratified nature, India is united by a set of cultural patterns that is widely shared among the Hindus living in India and abroad. The term *cultural patterns* refers to "the systematic and often repetitive nature of human behavior, interaction, and organization . . . human behavior is channeled and constrained by underlying systems that impose regularity and rules on what otherwise might be random activity" (Damen, 1987, p. 110).

Hinduism is an amorphous body of beliefs, philosophies, worship practices, and codes of conduct. In its present form, Hinduism embraces many often

This essay first appeared in the seventh edition. All rights reserved. Permission to reprint must be obtained from the authors and the publisher. Professor Jain teaches in the Department of Communication and is a Research Fellow in the Center for Asian Studies at Arizona State University. Ellen Kussman teaches at the American University in Beirut, Lebanon.

contradictory beliefs and practices. Its essential spirit, however, seems to be "live and let live." The very nature of Hinduism leads to a great tolerance of other religions as followers tend to believe that the highest divine powers complement one another for the well-being of humanity and the universe. Hinduism, because of its resilience, absorption, and respect for alternative ways of reaching the same goals, has maintained vitality since its inception. As a dominant force, it influences the cultural patterns and communication behavior of over a half billion Hindus in India and abroad.

India is a most suitable culture for study because of her preeminence in Asia, her leadership role among developing nations, and her increasing participation in international affairs. In addition, Indian culture provides an instructive contrast to American cultural patterns. The purpose of this article is to discuss briefly (1) the Hindu world view; (2) belief in reincarnation; (3) the concept of *karma*; (4) the aims of human life; (5) paths to salvation; (6) the concept of *dharma*; (7) the Indian caste system; and (8) the spirit of tolerance.

Each of these cultural patterns includes numerous assumptions, beliefs, values, and norms that are overlapping and closely interrelated. Within the same culture, variations of cultural patterns normally occur. In fact, contradictions among cultural patterns are probably universal throughout societies. At times we may simplify and make firm generalizations to avoid constant use of qualifiers. Despite internal variations and contradictions, we believe these eight cultural patterns provide a useful description of Hindu Indian culture.

WORLD VIEW

World view refers to a set of interrelated assumptions and beliefs about the nature of reality, the organization of the universe, the purposes of human life, God, and other philosophical issues concerned with the concept of being (Samovar & Porter, 1991). India's great sages and philosophers have sought to understand the deepest level of reality and to satisfy the deep human longing for spiritual fulfillment. The quest generated the basic Indian wisdom that the fundamental energizing power of the cosmos and the spiritual energy of human beings are one and the same. Because of our participation in the ultimate energy and power of reality, it is possible to transform our superficial, suffering, and limited existence into a free and boundless one. This spiritual transformation has constituted the ultimate aim in life for most Indian people over the ages (Koller, 1982).

The origins and development of the Hindu world view can best be understood in terms of the following concepts: (1) undivided wholeness and ultimate reality; (2) levels of reality; and (3) the normative dimension of reality.

Undivided Wholeness and Ultimate Reality

According to Hinduism, the world of distinct and separate objects and processes is a manifestation of a more fundamental reality that is undivided and unconditional. This undivided wholeness constituting the ultimate level of reality is known by various names: *Brahman, Ātman, Puruṣa, Jīva, Allah,* and Lord. What is especially important about this belief is that, first, the ultimate reality is not seen as separate and apart from ordinary things and events, but is the inner being and energizing force of everyday existence. Initially developed in the sacred ancient Hindu scriptures, the Vedas and Upanisads, this belief is an integral part of Hinduism, Jainism, Buddhism, and Yoga (Koller, 1982).

Second, existence at the deepest level is boundless in the sense that all possibilities may coexist without excluding or comprising one another. Time, space, the number of gods and goddesses, and so on are endless. Indian mythology especially celebrates the idea that opposites not only exist together but enrich one another with all of their differences arising simultaneously in an unrestricted universe of infinite freedom.

Third, the ultimate reality is so profound that reason is incapable of apprehending it. Human reason is an effective faculty for guiding our investigations of the empirical world and for understanding the rules of our practical and theoretical activities. Since it operates by differentiating and comparing, however, it is incapable of comprehending the deepest dimensions of reality that are beyond all divisions and differences. This profound nature of reality underlies

Indian mysticism and encourages the emphasis upon Yoga and meditation (Koller, 1982).

Finally, the ultimate reality has no form and no name. What can be given a name and form is not the ultimate. From ancient Vedic times to the present, however, the ultimate reality has been symbolized by unlimited numbers of gods and goddesses who participate partially in the higher reality that they symbolize, pointing to the fullness of that reality. This is why a Hindu can say in the same breath that there are millions of gods, only one god, and no gods. The last two statements mean, respectively, that all gods symbolize the one ultimate reality and that this reality cannot be captured entirely by one symbol. But that a deity is not the ultimate reality does not mean it is unreal. On the contrary, because the deity as symbol participates in the deeper levels of reality, its reality is greater than that of our ordinary existence. Through rituals and devotion to gods and goddesses, it is believed that one can achieve a spiritual transformation of life.

Levels of Reality

Within the undivided wholeness of the totality of existence, there are various levels of reality. These range from nonexistence to empirical existence limited by space and time, to consciousness limited only by conditions of awareness, to an indescribable level beyond all conditions and limits whatsoever. The deeper the level of reality, the more fully one participates in the truth of being. One of the clearest examples of the tendency to distinguish between levels of reality occurs in the *Taittiriya Upaniṣad*, where five different levels of reality composing the "Self" are identified:

> At the lowest level the Self is material and identified with food. At the next level the Self is identified with life: "Different from and within that which consists of the essence of food is the Self consisting of life." Identifying a still higher level of reality, the text goes on to say, "Different from and within that which consists of the essence of life is the Self which consists of mind (rudimentary forms of awareness that humans share with other animals)." Next, a fourth level of reality is recognized. Here is a still deeper source of consciousness and existence: the Self said to be of the

nature of understanding *(Vijñāna)*. Finally, the Self is identified with joy as the fifth and ultimate level of reality. Joy *(ānanda)* or bliss is regarded as the root or source of all existence, the foundation of higher consciousness, lower consciousness, life, and matter (Koller, 1982, p. 101).

Normative Dimension of Reality

The deepest level of reality is normative. According to Hinduism, norms for right living are an integral part of the fabric of human existence—they are not derived from human reason and are not imposed on life from the outside. The foundation of norms is much deeper than reason; it emanates from the very nature and expression of reality at its deepest level. Human reason only interprets and applies the norms of true or right living.

In the West, norms are usually conceived as rationally derived to fulfill human needs and aspirations. In India, it is generally recognized that a person who is true to the inner norms of existence has incredible power. Human existence is regarded as a manifestation and expression of a deeper reality. The fundamental norm of the universe is the orderly coursing of this deeper reality in its central being. Moral and social rules are partial expressions of this highest norm. The normative dimensions of the interconnected reality refer to the Hindu concept of *dharma*.

BELIEF IN REINCARNATION

In Hinduism, the Supreme Being is the impersonal *Brahman*, the ultimate level of reality, a philosophical absolute, serenely blissful, beyond all ethical or metaphysical limitations. The basic Hindu view of God involves infinite being, infinite consciousness and infinite bliss. *Brahmā* is conceived of as the Supreme Soul of the universe. Every living soul is a part, a particular manifestation, of the *Brahma*. Individual souls seem to change from generation to generation, but actually only the unimportant, outer details change—a body, a face, a name, a different condition or status in life. The *Brahmā*, however, veiled behind these deceptive "realities," is continuous and indestructible. This hidden self or *ātman* is a reservoir of being that never dies, is never exhausted, and is without limit in awareness and bliss. Ātman, the ultimate level of reality at the individual level, is the infinite center of every life. Body, personality, and ātman together make up a human being (Smith, 1958).

The eternal ātman is usually buried under the almost impenetrable mass of distractions, false ideas, illusions, and self-regarding impulses that compose one's surface being. Life is ordinarily lived at a relatively superficial level, a level at which the ultimate reality is experienced only in fragmented and limited forms. These fragmented and partial forms of existence are actually forms of bondage, restricting access to the full power or energy of life flowing from the deepest level of reality. The aim of life is to cleanse the impurity from one's being to the point where its infinite center, the eternal ātman, will be fully manifest.

The Hindu belief in reincarnation affirms that individual souls enter the world and pass through a sequence of bodies or life cycles. On the subhuman level, the passage is through a series of increasingly complex bodies until at last a human one is attained. Up to this point, the soul's growth is virtually automatic. With the soul's graduation into a human body, this automatic, escalator mode of ascent comes to an end. The soul's assignment to this exalted habitation is evidence that it has reached self-consciousness, and with this state comes freedom, responsibility, and effort. Now the individual soul, as a human being, is fully responsible for its behavior through the doctrine of karma—the moral law of cause and effect. The present condition of each individual life is a product of what one did in the previous life; and one's present acts, thoughts, and decisions determine one's future states (Smith, 1958).

CONCEPT OF KARMA

Karma means basically action or activity. Actions always imply cause and effect, for nothing in this world acts or moves without an impelling cause. Karma, therefore, also refers to that chain of cause and effect, set in motion by one's deeds in the world. Sooner or later, through inexorable laws of justice built into dharma, they rebound to affect one's own future. As one sows, so one reaps (Ellwood, 1992, p. 64).

The concept of karma and the completely moral universe it implies carries two important psychologi-

cal corollaries. First, it commits the Hindu who understands it to complete personal responsibility. Each individual is wholly responsible for his or her present condition and will have exactly the future he or she is now creating. Conversely, the idea of a moral universe closes the door to all appeals to chance or accident. In this world, there is no chance or accident. Karma decrees that every decision must have its determinate consequences, but the decisions themselves are, in the last analysis, freely arrived at. Or, to approach the matter from another direction, the consequences of a person's past decisions condition his or her present lot, as a card player is dealt a particular hand but is left free to play that hand in a number of ways. This means that the general conditions of life—rank, station, position—are predetermined by one's past karma. However, individual humans as carriers of a soul are free to determine actions independently of the soul (Smith, 1958).

According to Hinduism, the ultimate aim of life is to free oneself progressively from the exclusive identification with the lower levels of the self in order to realize the most profound level of existence. Since at this deepest level, the self is identical with ultimate reality—the Brahman—once this identity has been realized, there is nothing that can defeat or destroy the self. Thus, the soul puts an end to the process of reincarnation and merges with the Brahman, from whence it originated in the first place. This state for an individual soul is called moksha, mukti, nirvana or liberation.

AIMS OF HUMAN LIFE

What do human beings want? What are the aims of human life? Hindu saints and philosophers have pondered these questions for a long time and have provided some interesting insights into human needs, wants, desires, motivations, and values. According to Hinduism, all people have four legitimate basic aims of human life: (1) kāma, pleasure or enjoyment; (2) artha, wealth or success; (3) dharma, righteousness, faithful duty or code of conduct; and (4) moksha, liberation or salvation. These four aims have constituted the basis of Indian values. Indian literature concerned with moral and social life accepts these four aims as fundamental in life. Taken together, these aims define the good life for a Hindu, giving a sense of direction to guide a person to what he or she may and may not aim at in life (Jain, 1991).

Hinduism recognizes the importance of enjoyment or *kāma* in human life. This is natural because we are all born with built-in pleasure-pain reactors and human senses. The concept of *kāma* is used in two ways in Indian literature. In the narrower sense, *kāma* is sexual desire and is symbolized by *Kāma*, the love god. *Kāma Sūtra*, along with a number of other texts, provides instructions on how to obtain the greatest sexual pleasures. As a basic human aim, however, *kāma* goes beyond this narrower sense of sexual pleasure to include all forms of enjoyment, including that of fame, fortune, and power.

A common stereotype of Indian people as so single-mindedly intent on religious salvation that there is no room for laughter, fun, or games is incorrect. Traditionally and currently, Hindus value stories, games, festivals, and parties filled with music, laughter, and fun! As a basic aim in life, *kāma* legitimizes the human pursuit of pleasure and recognizes that wealth and various goods are to be enjoyed as a way of fulfilling human nature.

India, however, has not taken pleasure as life's highest value. Hindus believe that the world holds immense possibilities for enjoyment through our senses. Moreover, there are other worlds above this one where pleasures mount by a factor of a million at each successive round; we shall experience these worlds too at later stages in our becoming (Smith, 1958). *Dharma* regulates the pursuit of pleasure at the various stages of life; for example, sexual activity is to be restricted to one's spouse and drugs and intoxicating beverages are regarded as wrong and sinful because of the injury they do. But, as long as the basic rules of morality are observed, one is free to seek all the pleasure one wishes.

The second aim of life is *artha* or worldly success (wealth, success, power, fame, and so on). Hinduism recognizes that worldly success is a worthy goal to be neither scorned nor condemned. Moreover, its satisfactions last longer than sensual pleasures. Unlike *kāma*, worldly success is a social achievement with implications for one's life, as well for one's family, relatives, caste group, and society. In this respect, it is a higher value than sensual pleasure. Although much of the Western world regards Indians as deliberately choosing poverty as a way of life, this is not true. The *Panctantra,* a popular collection of Indian wisdom states: "Wealth gives constant vigor, confidence, and power. Poverty is a curse worse than death. Virtue without wealth is of no consequence. The lack of money is the root of all evil" (Koller, 1982, p. 65).

A certain limited amount of wealth is indispensable for one's living, for upkeeping a household, raising a family, and discharging civic duties. Beyond this minimum, worldly achievements bring to many a sense of dignity and self-respect. In the end, however, these too are found wanting. Like pleasure, rewards of wealth or worldly success are transient and short-lived, Humans seek the higher goals of *dharma* and *moksha* which are more lasting and fulfilling.

Dharma, the third aim of life, refers to the faithful performance of one's duties. Hinduism abounds in directives to men and women for performing their social roles and responsibilities. It sets forth in elaborate detail the duties that go with age, stages of life, gender, disposition, caste, and social status. Like the other two aims of human life, *dharma* also yields notable rewards but fails to satisfy the human heart completely. Faithful performance of duty brings the praise and appreciation of peers. More gratifying than this, however, is the self-respect that comes from having done one's part, of having contributed to society. In the end, even this realization cannot provide joy adequate to human spirit. The final aim of human life must still lie elsewhere (Smith, 1958).

According to Hinduism, the first three aims of life—pleasure, worldly success, and faithful duty—are never ultimate goals of human life. At best they are means that we assume will take us in the direction of what we really seek. First, we want being. Everyone wants "to be" rather than "not to be." Second, we want to know, to be aware. Third, human beings seek joy, a resolution of feelings in which the basic motifs are the opposite of frustration, futility, and boredom. Not only are these the things we want, we want each in infinite degree. To state the full truth, according to Hinduism, we must then say that what humans really want is infinite being, infinite knowledge, and infinite joy. To gather them together in a single word, what human beings really want is liberation or *moksha* (or *mukti*)—complete release from the countless limitations that press so closely upon present existence (Smith, 1958).

As the ultimate aim of human life, *moksha* guides one's efforts to realize identity with the *Brahman* but does not repudiate the other aims. Indeed, it calls for fulfilling these aims as a preparation for achieving complete freedom and fulfillment. Even when the distinction between worldly and spiritual existence becomes prominent, the tendency is to see the distinction in terms of higher and lower levels of the same reality than to postulate two different and opposing realities (Smith, 1958).

Thus, pleasure, worldly success, responsible discharge of duty, and liberation are the four aims of human life. These are what humans think they want, what they really want. What human beings most want, however, are infinite being, infinite awareness, and infinite joy. According to Hinduism, they are all within one's reach and can be attained through multiple paths to salvation (Smith, 1958).

PATHS TO SALVATION

Hinduism recognizes four different types of people: "Some are basically reflective. Others are primarily emotional. Still others are essentially active. Finally, some are most accurately characterized as experimental" (Smith, 1958, p. 35). A distinct path, or *yoga*, is suitable to a person's disposition and capacity for achieving salvation or *moksha*. The four paths are: (1) *jñāna yoga*, the path of knowledge; (2) *bhakti yoga*, the path of devotion; (3) *karma yoga*, the path of work; and (4) *rāja yoga*, the path of meditation.

Jñāna yoga, intended for individuals who have philosophical and intellectual orientations, attempts to overcome ignorance through the powers of knowledge and differentiation. Through logic and reflection, individuals strive to distinguish between the surface self and the larger Self that lies behind it. *Jñāna yoga* is the shortest but steepest path to salvation, and few people have the rare combination of rationality and spirituality required for it.

Jñāna yoga consists of three steps. The first, hearing, includes the study of scriptures and other philosophical writings in order to acquaint oneself with the concepts of self, the ultimate reality, and eternal being. The second step, thinking, encompasses intensive reflection and contemplation about the distinction between the self and Self. "If the *yogi* is able and diligent, such reflections will in due time build up a lively sense of the abiding Self that underlies his phenomenal personality" (Smith, 1958, p. 38). The third step, shifting self-identification from the passing to the eternal part of being, occurs through a variety of means, such as profound reflecting and thinking of one's finite self in the third person. The latter involves observing one's activities with calm detachment from a distance.

The second path to salvation, *bhakti yoga*, relies more on emotion than reason. The most powerful and persuasive emotion is love. "People tend to become like that which they love, with the name thereof progressively written on their brows. The aim of *bhakti yoga* is to direct toward God the geyser of love that lies at the base of every heart" (Smith, 1958, p. 39).

In contrast to *jñāna yoga*, *bhakti yoga* relies on religious worship and rituals through which people attempt to achieve the virtues of gods and goddesses. Hindus cherish gods' human incarnations, such as *Rāma* and *Krishna*, because they feel that gods can be loved most readily in human form. This is the most popular path currently followed in India.

Karma yoga, the third path to salvation, is intended for action-oriented people:

> Work can be a vehicle for self-transcendence. Every deed a person does for the sake of his or her own private welfare adds another coating to the ego and in thus thickening it insulates it further from God within or without. Correlatively, every act done without thought of self diminishes self-centeredness until finally no barrier remains to cloud one from the divine (Smith, 1958, p. 45).

Depending on their dispositions, followers of *karma yoga* may choose to practice under the mode of *jnana yoga* (knowledge) or *bhakti yoga* (devotion). For example, a *karma yogi* with an intellectual bent would engage in such activities as producing, disseminating, and utilizing knowledge. On the other hand, a *karma yogi* with a devotional outlook would be involved in activities such as social worship, religious festivals, and the construction of temples.

The final path of salvation, *rāja yoga*, is considered the royal way to salvation. Followers of *rāja yoga* are experimental in nature and believe that affairs of the spirit can be approached empirically. This path is based on the belief that " . . . our true selves are vastly more wonderful than we now realize and [on] a passion for direct experience of their full reach" (Smith, 1958, p. 51). Followers engage in physical, mental, and spiritual exercises through which they reach their inner spirits.

The four paths to salvation are not exclusive, because no person is solely of one disposition—either reflective, emotional, active, or experimental. "While most persons will, on the whole, find travel on one road more satisfactory than on others and will consequently tend to keep close to it, Hinduism encourages people to test all four and combine them as best suits their needs" (Smith, 1958, pp. 60–61). Each path of salvation, however, is guided by its appropriate *dharma*.

CONCEPT OF DHARMA

Dharma defines a code of conduct that guides the life of a person both as an individual and as a member of society. It is the law of right living, the observance of which secures the double objectives of happiness on earth and *moksha*. The life of a Hindu is regulated in a very detailed manner. Personal habits, social and family ties, fasts and feasts, religious rituals, obligations of justice and morality, and even rules of personal hygiene and food preparation are all conditioned by *dharma*.

Dharma, as a social value with a strong sense of morality, accounts for the cohesion in Hindu society. Harmony is achieved when everyone follows his or her own *dharma*. It is the system of norms supported by the general opinion, conscience, or spirit of the people. *Dharma* does not force people into virtue but trains them for it. It is not a fixed code of mechanical rules but a living spirit that grows and moves in response to the development of society (Koller, 1982).

The individual and social dimensions of *dharma* are interdependent. The conscience of the individual requires a guide, and one must be taught the way to realize one's aims of life and to live according to spirit and not senses. *Dharma*, at the social level, holds all living beings in a harmonious order. Virtue is conduct contributing to social welfare, and vice is opposite (Radhakrishnan, 1979).

Dharma is usually classified according to the requirements of one's state in life and one's position in society, for these two factors determine one's own specific *dharma*. Thus, at the individual level, *asrama dharma* refers to duties attending one's particular stage in life. According to Hindu philosophy, human life consists of four stages or *āsramas*: student, householder, retiree, and renunciator (Jain, 1991, pp. 84–85). Specifically, the students' *dharma* includes obligations of sobriety, chastity, and social service. The householder stage requires marriage, raising a family, producing the goods necessary for society according to one's occupation, giving to the needy, and serving the social and political needs of the community. In the retiree stage, the individual is required to control his or her attachment to worldly possessions; it is the time for working out a philosophy for oneself, the time of transcending the sense to find and dwell at one with the timeless reality that underlies the dream of life in this world. Finally, the renunciator is a disinterested servant of humanity who finds peace in the strength of spirit and attempts to fulfill the ultimate aim of human life, *moksha* or liberation. This is also the stage of complete renunciation of worldly objects and desires.

Varna dharma, on the other hand, refers to the duties attending one's caste, social class, or position. The Hindu caste system and its relationship with *dharma* are discussed in more detail later.

Hinduism recognizes a *universal dharma* that applies to any person regardless of caste, social class, or stage in life. For example, telling the truth, avoiding unnecessary injury to others, not cheating, and so on are common *dharmas* that all human beings share. Other *dharmas* are determined by particular circumstances and therefore cannot be specified in advance. The rules for determining specific requirements of action in unusual and unpredictable situations is that the higher *dharmas* and values should always prevail. Noninjury and compassion are basic moral principles in deciding cases of conflicting moral duties, and one must never engage in behavior that is detrimental to spiritual progress (Koller, 1982).

CASTE SYSTEM

The caste system is a unique feature of Indian culture. No Indian social institution has attracted as much attention from foreign observers, nor has any other Indian institution been so grossly misunderstood, misrepresented, or maligned. Even the word *caste*, which is derived from the Portuguese *casta* (color), is a misnomer connoting some specious notion of color difference as the foundation of the system. It is a curious fact of intellectual history that caste has figured so prominently in Western thought.

The caste system began in India about 3,000 years ago. During the second millennium B.C., a host of Aryans possessing a different language and culture and different physical characteristics (tall, fair-skinned, blue-eyed, straight-haired) migrated to India. The class of differences that followed eventually established the caste system because the Aryans took for themselves the kinds of work thought to be desirable: They became the rulers, the religious leaders, the teachers, and the traders. The other people were forced to become servants for the Aryans and to do less pleasing kinds of work. The outcome of this social classification and differentiation was a society clearly divided into four castes, hierarchically, from higher to lower:

1. *Brahmins*—seers or priests who perform such duties as teaching, preaching, assisting in the sacrificial processes, giving alms, and receiving gifts
2. *Kashtryas*—administrators or rulers responsible for protecting life and treasures
3. *Vaisyas*—traders, business people, farmers, and herders
4. *Sūdras*—artisans such as carpenters, blacksmiths, and laborers

In the course of time, a fifth group developed that was ranked so low as to be considered outside and beneath the caste system itself. The members of this fifth "casteless" group are variously referred to as "untouchables," "outcastes," "scheduled castes," or (by Mahatma Gandhi) *Harijans*—"children of God." People in this group inherit the kinds of work that in India are considered least desirable, such as scavenging, slaughtering animals, leather tanning, and sweeping the streets (Chopra, 1977, pp. 27–29).

The caste system began as a straightforward, functional division of Hindu society. It was later misinterpreted by priests to be as permanent and as immutable as the word of God. Accordingly, the caste system was justified in terms of the "immutable and inborn" qualities of individuals, the unchange-

able result of "actions in previous incarnations," and the unalterable basis of Hindu religion.

The caste system applies only to the Hindu segment of Indian society. The particular caste a person belongs to is determined by birth—one is born into the caste of his or her parents. Each caste has its appropriate status, rights, duties, and *dharma*. Detailed rules regulate communication and contact among people of different castes. A caste has considerable influence on the way of life of its members; the most important relationships of life, above all marriage, usually take place within the caste.

The merit of the caste system lies in its contribution to social stability and social security. Everyone has a known role to play and a group with whom to belong. The lower castes and outcastes are not necessarily happy with their role in the system as evidenced by the numbers who converted to other religions, especially Buddhism, Islam, and Christianity—all of which allowed them to escape from caste restrictions (Terpstra, 1978).

After India's independence in 1947, discrimination based on caste was outlawed. India has launched a massive social reform movement against "untouchability." There are numerous forms of affirmative action programs and quota systems aimed at promoting the welfare of "untouchables" and lower castes. These programs have produced many benefits for disadvantaged groups in the fields of education, employment, politics, and government. Unfortunately, there is still considerable prejudice and discrimination against untouchables, especially in the rural areas which comprise approximately 75 percent of India's population (Jain, 1992).

As any American knows, legislation is not always effective in bringing about immediate changes in social behavior. Sudden changes will not occur rapidly in India either, especially with a behavior pattern sanctioned by religion and 3,000 years of tradition. In urban areas, it is more common for one to cross caste lines in choosing occupation and in marrying. In rural areas, on the other hand, caste remains a major influence in one's life.

The implications of the caste system for communication and economy are quite obvious and quite negative. To the degree that the caste system is rigidly followed, it limits communication between caste groups and hinders free flow of information. It becomes difficult to allocate human resources efficiently. If birth and caste determine work assignments, rather than ability and performance, the output of the economy suffers. Coordination and integration of the work force and management can also be hindered by caste restrictions. Occupational caste assignments derived centuries ago in an agrarian society are not likely to mesh with today's technological, urban, industrial society.

THE SPIRIT OF TOLERANCE

An outstanding feature of Indian culture is its tradition of tolerance. According to Hinduism, the reality or existence at the deepest level is boundless. No description, formula, or symbol can adequately convey the entire truth about anything. Each perspective provides a partial glimpse of reality, but none provides a complete view. Different partial—even opposing—viewpoints are regarded as complementing each other, each contributing something to a fuller understanding of reality.

Traditionally, Indian thinkers have been willing to adopt new perspectives and new positions without, however, abandoning old positions and perspectives. The new is simply added to the old, providing another dimension to one's knowledge. The new dimension may render the old less dominant or important, but it does not require the latter's rejection. The traditional storehouse of Indian ideas is like a four-thousand-year-old attic to which things were added every year but which was never once cleaned out (Koller, 1982).

Hindu culture believes in universal tolerance and accepts all religions as true. It is believed that the highest truth is too profound to allow anyone to get an exclusive grasp on it. When no beliefs can be said to be absolutely true, no beliefs can be declared absolutely false. Hindu culture is comprehensive and suits the needs of everyone, irrespective of caste, creed, color, or gender—it has universal appeal and makes room for all.

In Jainism, an offshoot of Hinduism, the theory of syādvāda, or "may be," has further developed India's spirit of tolerance. According to this theory, no absolute affirmation or denial is possible. As all knowledge is probable and relative, another person's point of view is as true as one's own. In other words, one must show restraint in making judgments—a very healthy principle. One must know that one's judgments are only partially true and can by no means be regarded as true in absolute terms. This understanding and spirit of tolerance have contributed to the advancement of Indian culture, helping to bring together the divergent groups with different languages and religious persuasions under a common culture (Murthy & Kamath, 1973).

SUMMARY

This article has discussed eight dominant cultural patterns of Hindus in India: world view, belief in reincarnation, the concept of *karma*, the aims of human life, the reincarnation to salvation, the concept of *dharma*, the caste system, and the spirit of tolerance. These patterns have been integral parts of Hinduism and Indian culture for the last 3,000 years. They have a significant influence on the personality, values, beliefs, and attitudes of Hindus in India and abroad. An understanding of Hindu cultural patterns and their influence on communication behavior will improve the quality of intercultural communication between people of India and other cultures.

References

Chopra, S. N. (1977). *India: An Area Study*. New Delhi: Vikas.

Damen, L. (1987). *Culture-Learning: The Fifth Dimension in the Language Classroom*. Reading, Mass.: Addison-Wesley.

Ellwood, R. S. (1992). *Many Peoples, Many Faiths*. 4th ed. Englewood Cliffs, N.J.: Prentice-Hall.

Jain, N. C. (1991). "World View and Cultural Patterns of India." In L. A. Samovar and R. E. Porter (Eds.), *Intercultural Communication: A Reader*, 6th ed., pp. 78–87. Belmont, Calif.: Wadsworth.

Jain, N. C. (1992). Teaching About Communicative Life in India. Paper presented at the annual meeting of the Western Speech Communication Association, Boise, Idaho, February.

Koller, J. M. (1982). *The Indian Way*. New York: Macmillan.

Murthy, H. V. S., and Kamath, S. U. (1973). *Studies in Indian Culture*. Bombay: Asia Publishing House.

Radhakrishnan, S. (1979). *Indian Religions*. New Delhi: Vision Books.

Samovar, L. A., and Porter, R. E. (1991). *Communication Between Cultures*. Belmont, Calif.: Wadsworth.

Smith, H. (1958). *The Religions of Man*. New York: Harper & Row.

Terpstra, V. (1978). *Cultural Environments of International Business*. Cincinnati: South-Western.

Concepts and Questions

1. What unique perspectives of worldview are inherent in the Hindu culture of India?

2. How might the Hindu perspective of the universe and of humankind's role in the universe affect intercultural communication between Indians and North Americans?

3. To what do Jain and Kussman refer when they discuss the Hindu spirit of tolerance? How might this spirit affect social perception and human interaction?

4. How are Jain and Kussman using the term *cultural patterns*? What are some of the patterns they mention in their chapter?

5. How would you explain the concept of undivided wholeness and ultimate reality?

6. Why do you think Westerners have such a difficult time understanding the notion of "levels of reality?"

7. Using Western concepts, how would you explain the ideas of Brahma and karma?

8. Do you believe that the Hindu view is correct when it says that all people have the same four basic aims of life? What aims would you add to that list? What aims would you delete from the Jain and Kussman list?

9. Why is dharma so hard to accomplish? What other religious codes of conduct are similar to the Hindu notion of dharma?

10. Why do Jain and Kussman maintain that an "understanding of Hindu cultural patterns and their influence on communication behavior will improve the quality of intercultural communication between the people of India and other cultures"?

Cultural Patterns of the Maasai

LISA SKOW

LARRY A. SAMOVAR

For many years critics of intercultural communication have charged that the field focuses on a handful of cultures while seriously neglecting others. For example, the literature abounds with material concerning Japan and Mexico, but there is very little to be found if one seeks to understand the cultures of India or black Africa. As economics and politics force a global interdependence, it behooves us to examine cultures that were previously excluded from our scrutiny.

The motivation for such analysis can take a variety of forms. Our desire for more information might be altruistic, as we learn that 40,000 babies die of starvation each day in developing countries. Or we may decide that we need to know about other cultures for more practical reasons. Strong ties with African countries can lead to economic, educational, and technological exchanges beneficial to individuals on both sides of the globe. Regardless of our motives, the 1990s and beyond will offer countless examples that demand that we look at cultures that we have ignored in the past. This article is an attempt to explore one of those cultures, specifically, that of the Maasai of East Africa.

If we accept the view of culture held by most anthropologists, it becomes nearly impossible to discover all there is to know about any one group of people. That is to say, how does one decide what is important about a culture if Hall (1976) is correct when he writes, "there is not one aspect of human life that is not touched and altered by culture" (p. 14)? The decision as to what to include and exclude in any analysis of a culture is usually based on the

This original article was written especially for this book. All rights reserved. Permission to reprint must be obtained from the authors and the publisher. Lisa Skow is a former Peace Corps volunteer. She currently teaches at the University of North Carolina at Chapel Hill. Larry Samovar teaches at San Diego State University.

background of the researcher. Someone interested in the music of a culture would obviously look at the portion of the culture relating to that specific topic and, in a sense, abstract only part of the total phenomenon called culture.

A researcher interested in intercultural communication is also faced with the problem of what to select from the total experiences of a people. What, in short, do we need to know if our goal is to understand the behavior of another culture? One answer to this question is found in the work of Samovar and Porter (1997). They have proposed a model of intercultural communication that can be used as a guide in selecting what aspects of culture need to be incorporated into any discussion of intercultural communication. This article will address the three major components of that model: perception, verbal processes, and nonverbal processes.

BACKGROUND

The East African countries of Kenya and Tanzania know firsthand about Western culture. They have lived through Western government, language, culture, and, unfortunately, oppression. Even today, more than two decades after each country received its independence, Western culture still has a profound influence on the people of Kenya and Tanzania. However, because there are so many different ethnic groups in these countries, it has not had the same impact and influence on each group. The Kikuyu of Kenya have adopted Western culture with such enthusiasm that one wonders what are "proper" Kikuyu traditions and customs and what are Western influences. On the other end of the Western continuum are the Maasai of southern Kenya and northern Tanzania, who have, for a number of reasons, rejected much of the culture presented by the West. They have largely shunned Western forms of government, dress, language, music, religion, and frequently even assistance. The Maasai are often referred to as "true Africans" because of their "purity"—a purity of which they are very proud.

Africa may be changing at an extraordinarily fast pace, but the Maasai are one group of people who seem content to continue their own way of life. This article hopes to offer some insight into that way of life.

PERCEPTION

One of the basic axioms of intercultural communication, and one that is part of the Samovar and Porter (1997) intercultural model, is that culture and perception work in tandem. That is to say, our cultural experiences determine, to a large extent, our view of the world. Those experiences that are most important are transmitted from generation to generation as a means of assuring that the culture will survive beyond the lifetime of its current members. Therefore, to understand any culture it is necessary to examine those experiences that are deemed meaningful enough to be carried to each generation. One way to study those experiences is through the history of a culture. The history of any culture can offer insight into the behaviors of the culture as well as explain some of the causes behind those behaviors. Let us therefore begin our analysis of the Maasai people by looking at those aspects of their history that link current perceptions to the past.

History

While the history of any culture is made up of thousands of experiences, there are often a few significant ones that serve to explain how that culture might view the world. In the case of the Maasai, there are three historical episodes that have greatly influenced their perception of themselves, other people, and events. These historical occurrences center on their creation, fierceness, and reaction to modernization.

The history of the Maasai is the history of a people with an oral tradition. Like all cultures who practice the oral tradition, the content and customs that are transmitted are largely found within the stories, poetry, and songs of the people. To the outsider they appear vague and only loosely based on facts. Some historians, along with the aid of Maasai elders, have attempted to link the stories and folklore with the available information about the Maasai's past, a past that helps explain many of the perceptions and values held by the Maasai.

Most accounts of the origin of the Maasai as a unique culture begin with the belief that they were part of a larger group that was migrating south during a severe drought (Kipury, 1983). The group found themselves trapped in a deep valley so they constructed a bridge that was to transport them out of the valley. Folk tales and history go on to tell the story of how the bridge collapsed before all the people escaped. Those who were left behind are now thought to be the Somali, Borana, and Rendile peoples. Those who managed to escape the dryness of the valley went on to be the true Maa-speaking people.

While the above rendition of early Maasai history is uncertain in answering questions regarding the origins of the Maasai, it does reveal one very important aspect of how history and perception are linked. This story helps explain how the Maasai perceive themselves compared to other tribes. It also helps an outsider understand the strong feelings of pride that are associated with the Maasai culture. For the Maasai, the story of their origin, even if it is speculation, tells them they are better than other tribes of East Africa who did not come from the north nor escape across the bridge—regardless of how long ago that arrival might have been.

The Maasai's history of warfare and conflict is yet another source of knowledge about the perception of themselves and non-Maasai. Before the advent of colonialism in the latter part of the nineteenth century, other tribes in Kenya such as the Kikuyu, Akamba, and Kalenjin were often attacked by the Maasai. The attacks were fierce and usually resulted in their enemies being forced from their lands. Some Maasai, particularly the elders, still see themselves as the conquerors of other tribes, and even today, the Maasai still have the reputation of being warlike. Non-Maasai Kenyans may warn visitors of the "terrible" Maasai and their propensity for violence. A former colleague of one of the authors often expressed her distrust of the Maasai, believing that they would harm her simply because she was from the Kikuyu tribe. She had heard about the Maasai's fierceness and their dislike of other tribes who dressed in Western clothes. Whether entirely accurate or not, this perception of them as warlike influences both the behavior of the Maasai and the behavior of those who come in contact with them.

A third historical period that has shaped the perceptions of the Maasai is the preindependence period of Kenya. Because the Maasai occupied vast areas of land in Kenya, the British colonialists turned an eye toward acquiring this valuable property. Through numerous agreements, great parcels of land were turned over to the colonialists. The Maasai were settled on new tracts of land that were much less desirable than the ones they were leaving, and they soon began to realize that not only were they giving up their prime land but they were also seeing a number of promises made by the colonialists being broken. In response to these two conclusions, the Maasai adopted an attitude of passive resistance to all Western innovations and temptations to become "modern." While most other parts of Kenya were altering their culture through education and technology, the Maasai had become disillusioned with those who were seeking to alter their way of life, and hence they refused to change (Sankan, 1971).

The rejection of cultural conversion by the Maasai has had immense consequences on them and the people around them. On one hand it has caused the government and other tribes to perceive them as stubbornly traditional, backward, uneducated, and isolated. However, for the Maasai, resistance to change is yet another indication of their strength and long history of power. Other more Westernized tribes, such as the Kikuyu, feel the Maasai are backward and not in tune with changing Kenya. Ironically, the Kikuyu seem to have a love–hate relationship with the Maasai: scorn for their refusal to be more modern yet respect for their retaining their traditional customs.

Values

What a culture values, or doesn't value, also helps determine how that culture perceives the world. Therefore, understanding what the Maasai regard as good or bad, valuable or worthless, right or wrong, just or unjust, and appropriate or inappropriate can help explain the communication behavior of their culture.

Children. For a Maasai man or woman to be without children is a great misfortune. The Maasai strongly believe that children continue the race, and more important, they will preserve the family—hence, children are highly valued. The Maasai embrace the idea that a man can "live" even after death if he has a son who can carry on his name, enjoy his wealth, and spread his reputation. In addition, they value children because they offer the senior Maasai a continuous supply of workers. The Maasai have a saying that illustrates this point: "More hands make light the work." Children supply those hands. Unfortunately, this value is in direct conflict with the Kenyan government's family planning program to curb Kenya's dangerously high population growth. While the central government tries to emphasize the need to control the population, for the Maasai the man with the most children, no matter how poor he is, is the wealthiest and happiest of all men.

Cattle. The Maasai culture revolves around the cow, on which they greatly depend for their food, clothing, housing, fuel, trade, medicine, and ceremonies. Cattle have given the Maasai their traditionally nomadic lifestyle. The more cattle a man has the more respected he is. Cattle are usually killed only on designated occasions such as for marriage and circumcision ceremonies or when special guests visit. The Maasai believe that all cattle were originally given to them by God. There is even a folk tale that tells of the Maasai descending to earth with cattle by their sides. This belief justifies their taking cattle from other tribes, even if it is in violation of the law.

Groups. Families and life-stage groups are at the core of the Maasai community. Because children are so highly valued, the family must be strong and central in their lives. An overwhelming portion of a Maasai child's education is still carried out in the home, with the grandparents, not the schools, providing the content of the culture.

Life-stage groups are specifically defined periods in the lives of all Maasai, particularly males. Traditionally, all men must go through four stages of life: childhood, adolescence (circumcision), moranship (warriorhood—junior and senior), and elderhood (junior and senior). Women must pass through childhood, circumcision, and then marriage. Each of these stages places a strong emphasis on the group. Attempts to get Maasai students to raise their hands and participate in formal classrooms are often futile. Drawing attention to oneself in a group setting is unacceptable because the tribe and the life-stage group are far more valuable than the individual (Johnstone, 1988).

Elders: Male and Female. Maasai children must give respect to any person older than themselves, whether a sibling, grandmother, or older member of the community. They must bow their heads in greeting as a sign of humility and inferiority. Even young circumcised men and women (aged fifteen to twenty-five years) must bow their heads to male elders, particularly if the elders are highly respected in the community.

The Maasai believe the older you become the wiser you become and that a wise individual deserves a great deal of deference and respect. Part of the strong emphasis placed on elders is that the Maasai hold their history in such high regard, and it is the oldest members of the tribe who know most of the history. Young people cannot know the "truth" until they progress through each of the life-stage groups.

For Maasai youths getting older indicates a change in social status. When male Maasai students return from a school holiday with their heads shaved, this indicates that they have just gone through circumcision and initiation into another life-stage. They have become men and are instantly perceived by other students and themselves as different, even older, and deserving of more respect.

Pride. Pride for the Maasai means having the virtues of obedience, honesty, wisdom, and fairness. A man may be an elder in name only, for if he does not exhibit these characteristics, he is not a respected man in the community. A woman's pride is often defined by how well she keeps her home, by whether she is an obedient wife, and by the number of children she has.

Outsiders, whether black or white, perceive the Maasai loftiness and pride as a kind of arrogance. The Maasai themselves, because they are traditionally pastoralists, still look down on strictly agricultural tribes such as the Kikuyu.

Their strong sense of pride is also fueled by their view of themselves as warriors. As noted earlier, they have always been feared by other tribes and the colonialists. Their folklore is replete with tales of their fighting with incredible fearlessness, even when their primitive weapons faced their enemies' modern bullets. For them the battles were to preserve the "true African" way of life and to protect their cattle.

Beauty. Beauty is yet another value that is important to the Maasai. Both men and women adorn themselves with elaborate beads, body paint, and other jewelry. Maasai children, especially girls, begin wearing jewelry almost from the moment of birth. One of the primary duties a woman has is to make necklaces, bracelets, bangles, belts, and earrings for their husband, children, friends, and herself. Adornment is also a way for a woman to attract a husband, and Maasai women are very meticulous in selecting jewelry for special celebrations. Maasai warriors still spend much of their day painting themselves with red ochre, and they also plait and braid their hair, which is grown long as a sign of warriorhood.

Beauty and bodily adornment are so valued in the Maasai culture that they have distinctive jewelry and dress to wear during certain periods of each life-stage. For example, one can tell if a boy has just recently been circumcised because he wears a crown of bird carcasses. Thus, we can conclude that beauty is more than superficial for the Maasai; it is a reflection of a very important value that often steers perception in one direction or another.

World View

The world view of a culture is yet another factor that greatly modifies perception. In the Samovar and Porter (1988) model, world view deals with a culture's orientation toward such things as God, humanity, the universe, death, nature, and other philosophical issues that are concerned with the concept of being. In short, it is that perception of the world that helps the individual locate his or her place and rank in the universe. It influences nearly every action in which an individual engages. Our research would tend to agree with this observation. The Maasai's world view has three components that greatly control their life and hence their perception of the universe: coexistence with nature, religion, and death.

Nature. For the Maasai, nature must always be held in the highest regard. They believe that their very existence depends solely on nature's benevolence. Their lifestyle is one that sees them interacting with the elements: Without rain their cattle will die, and in a sense so will they, for as we pointed out earlier, cattle supply most of the basic needs of the Maasai.

The Maasai also embrace the view that nature cannot be changed; it is too powerful. But they do acknowledge that nature itself changes without their intervening, and what they must do is change as nature fluctuates. Adapting to nature is most evident in the Maasai's seminomadic lifestyle. They carry coexistence to the point where they will not kill or eat wild animals unless they pose a threat or there is a severe drought. For the Maasai cultivating and hunting are seen as destructive to nature: Cultivation forces humans to deal directly with nature, changing and altering it to their specifications and needs; hunting for food is seen as something even worse, for then nature is not only being changed but it is being destroyed (Rigby, 1985).

Religion. The second aspect of world view, religion, is closely tied to the Maasai perception of nature. The Maasai have one god called "Engai," but this god has two very distinct personalities and therefore serves two purposes: "Engai Narok," the black god, is benevolent and generous and shows himself through rain and thunder; "Engai Nanyokie," the red god, is manifested in lightning. To the Maasai, God encompasses everything in nature, friendly or destructive (Saitoti and Beckwith, 1980). In fact, the word "Engai" actually means "sky." Cattle accompanied the Maasai people to earth from the sky and thus cattle are seen as mediators between humans and God as well as between humans and nature. Therefore, herding is traditionally the only acceptable livelihood, since it is God's will. Not to herd would be disrespectful to Engai and demeaning to a Maasai (Salvadon and Fedders, 1973).

There is a Maasai proverb that states, "The one chosen by God is not the one chosen by people" (Rigby, 1985, p. 92). Thus, not surprisingly, the Maasai have no priests or ministers; there is no one who represents God or purports to speak for God. There are "laiboni" who are considered the wisest of the elders and often cast curses and give blessings, but they do not represent God or preach. The Maasai have no religious writings, only oral legends, therefore the elders are important in the religious life of the people.

What is most significant is that God (Engai) is found in nature. Some Maasai households rise at dawn to pray to the sun, which is seen as a manifestation of Engai. God is found in many other forms in nature for the Maasai: rain, grass, and even a partic-

Table 1

Category	Maasai Word	Basic Meaning	Metaphorical Meaning
Object + Animal	Olmotonyi	Large bird	Eagle shoulder cape
Person + Animal	Enker	Sheep	Careless, stupid person
Person + Object	Sotua	Umbilical cord	Close friend
Quality + Object	Olpiron	Firestick	Age-set generation

ularly beautiful stone. God *is* nature and cannot be artificially symbolized in a cross or a building. Since nature is God, people must live in harmony with God and the Maasai must work together. This is a different view of God than the one offered by Christianity, in which God is separate from humans and is even from a different world.

Death. The third aspect of the Maasai world view is how they perceive death. As with most cultures, death brings sorrow to those left behind by the deceased; however, cultures differ in how they respond to death. The response of the Maasai directly coincides with their belief in the coexistence of nature and human beings; therefore, except for the "laiboni" (wise man), all corpses are left out in the open to be devoured by hyenas and other scavengers. The assumption behind this action is clear, at least to the Maasai, who believe that after they have had a full life and enjoyed the benefits of nature, it is only fitting that their bones go back to the earth so they can be used to prepare the land for future life. For the Maasai there is a circular, mutually beneficial relationship between nature and humanity.

VERBAL PROCESSES

In the most basic sense, language is an organized, generally agreed upon, learned symbol system used to represent human experiences within a geographic or cultural community. Each culture places its individual imprint on words—how they are used and what they mean.

Language is the primary vehicle by which a culture transmits its beliefs, values, and norms. Language gives people a means of interacting with other members of their culture and a means of thinking, serving both as a mechanism for communication

and as a guide to social reality. Anyone interested in studying another culture must therefore look at the way a culture uses language and also the experiences in their environment they have selected to name. Research on the Maasai culture reveals two language variables that offer a clue into the workings of this particular group of people: their use of metaphors and their reliance on proverbs.

Metaphors

Wisdom in the Maasai culture is marked not just by age and prudence but also by language use. Elders make decisions at tribal meetings based on speeches offered by various members of the group. The most successful speakers are those whose eloquence is embellished and ornate. The metaphor offers the gifted speaker a tool to demonstrate his mastery of words. Heine and Claudi (1986) explain the importance of metaphor to the Maasai when they write:

> Maa people frequently claim that their language is particularly rich in figurative speech forms. Nonliteral language, especially the use of metaphors, is in fact encouraged from earliest childhood on, and the success of a political leader depends to quite a large extent on the creative use of it (p. 17).

Because of the value placed on the metaphors, Johnstone (1988) writes, "Whenever there were big meetings to decide important matters, the men always spoke in proverbs, metaphors, and other figurative language." Messages are full of elaborate symbolism—blunt and simple words are rarely used.

The information in Table 1, developed by Heine and Claudi (1986), helps clarify some of the types of metaphors employed by the Maasai. These few examples demonstrate how most of the metaphors in the Maa language reflect what is important in their culture. For example, the use of the umbilical cord to refer to a very close friend is indicative of the value placed on childbirth and of the strong bonds between members of the same age-set. In addition, an age-set generation is formally established when a select group of elders kindles the fire on the day that a new generation of boys will be circumcised (Heine & Claudi, 1986). These age-sets form both a unique governing body and a social hierarchy in all Maasai communities.

Proverbs

Like metaphors, proverbs are an integral part of the Maasai language. Massek and Sidai (1974) noted that "a Maasai hardly speaks ten sentences without using at least one proverb" (p. 6). These proverbs have common elements and themes that are directly related to the Maasai value system.

Proverbs convey important messages to the members of a culture because they often deal with subjects that are of significance. Therefore, the assumption behind examining the proverbs is a simple one—discover the meaning of the proverb and you will understand something of what is important to its user. This axiom is exceptionally true for the Maasai, for here one encounters proverbs focusing on respect, parents, children, wisdom, and proper conduct. Let us look at some of these proverbs as a way of furthering an understanding of the Maasai culture.

1. "Meeta enkerai olopeny." (The child has no owner.) Maasai children are expected to respect all elders, not just those in the immediate family. It is very common for children to refer to older men as "Father" and to older women as "Mother."
2. "Memorataa olayoni oataa menye." (One is never a man while his father is still alive.) Even as junior elders, Maasai men do not always leave their father's homestead. It is not until a man attains the full status of senior elder that he usually establishes his own home with his wife (wives) and children. In addition, the very name of male children is indicated with the word "ole," which means "son of," placed between the first and last names. A Maasai male is very often characterized by his father's name and reputation.

3. "Eder olayioni o menye, neder entito o notanye." (A boy converses with his father while a girl converses with her mother.) This proverb is representative of both the restricted relationships between the opposite sexes in a family and the strict divisions of labor found in the Maasai culture. Young girls learn to do household chores at an early age, and by age seven their brothers are responsible for tending the family herd.
4. "Menye marrmali, menye maata." (Father of troubles, father without.) In the Maasai culture there is a conviction that a man with no children has more problems than a man with many children. They believe that even a man with a fine herd of cattle can never be rich unless he also has many children. This proverb simply serves to underscore those facts.
5. "Ideenya taa anaa osurai oota oikati." (You are as proud as lean meat with soot on it.) Being proud is a well-known characteristic of the Maasai. So strong is this value that the Maasai are often criticized by other African tribes. To sustain the reality and the perception of pride, a Maasai must always add to his accomplishments, and courageous acts and large families are two common behaviors that present an image of a proud person. It should be noted, however, that foolish pride is looked down upon as a sign of arrogance.
6. "Medany olkimojino obo elashei." (One finger does not kill a louse.) The need to cooperate is crucial to the Maasai culture, and this proverb reinforces that belief. As noted earlier, the Maasai community is a highly communal one, one that is well-structured and based on group harmony and decision making. The family unit is particularly dependent on cooperation and accord. On most occasions wives care for each other's children. Cattle are kept together and shared, with ownership only a secondary consideration.

In this section on proverbs we see the connection between what a culture talks about and what it embraces and acknowledges to be true. This link between words and behavior only serves to buttress the belief that verbal symbols represent a device by which a culture maintains and perpetuates itself.

NONVERBAL PROCESSES

Nonverbal systems represent yet another coding system that individuals and cultures use as a means of sharing their realities. Like verbal symbols, nonverbal codes are learned as part of the socialization process—that is, each culture teaches its members the symbol and the meaning for the symbol. In the case of the Maasai, there are a number of nonverbal messages that, when understood, offer the outsider some clues as to the workings of this foreign culture.

Movement and Posture

The Maasai show their pride and self-regard by the way they carry themselves. They are tall and slender and have a posture that reflects an appearance of strength and vigor. There is, at first glance, a regal air about them and at times they appear to be floating. "The morans [warriors], especially, walk very erect and relatively slowly. It's like they are in so much command of their environment that they are absolutely at ease" (Johnstone, personal correspondence, 1988).

The posture and movement of Maasai women also mirrors an attitude of pride and self-assurance. They are also tall and slender and have a gait that is slow and self-confident. Their heads are held high as a way of emphasizing their confidence and superiority over other tribes.

Paralanguage

The Maasai people utilize a number of sounds that have special meanings. The most common is the "eh" sound, which is used extensively, even though the Maasai language is ornate and metaphorical. When uttered, the sound is drawn out and can have a host of different interpretations; it can mean "yes," "I understand," or "continue." Although similar to the English regulators "uh huh" and "hmmm," "eh" is used more frequently and appears to dominate short, casual conversations among the Maasai.

Touching

While public touching between the sexes among the Maasai is usually limited to a light handshake, same-sex touching is common. Simple greetings between the sexes consist of a very light brush of the palms; in fact, so light is the touch, the hands appear barely to touch. If two women are good friends, however, they may greet each other with a light kiss on the lips. If they have not seen each other recently, they may embrace and clutch each other's upper arms. Men will frequently drape their arms around each other while conversing. When children greet an elder, they bow their heads so that the elder may place his or her hand on the young person's head, which is a sign of both respect and fondness. There is a great deal of affection to be found among the Maasai, and touching is one way of displaying that affection.

Time

The meaning cultures attach to time also reveals something of their view toward life and other people. The Maasai are unique in their treatment of time. Unlike the Westerner, for the Maasai there is always enough time: Their life is not governed by the clock; they are never in a hurry. This casual attitude produces a people who are self-possessed, calm, and most of all, *patient*.

Children are taught very early that there is never a need to rush. The vital chore of tending the family cattle requires that children stay alert and attentive to the herd's needs and safety, but such a chore also requires eight to ten hours of patient solitude.

This endless display of patience by the Maasai people is in direct contrast to time-conscious Americans. For example, public transportation in Kenya is not run on a firm schedule; buses and "matatus" (covered pick-up trucks) leave for their destinations when they are full. As do most Kenyans, the Maasai understand this. Inquiries from Americans as to when a vehicle will be departing are often answered with "just now." "Just now," however, can mean anywhere from five minutes to an hour.

Even though the present is fully enjoyed, the Maasai culture is very past-oriented. This strong tie to the past stems from the view that wisdom is found not in the present or the future, but rather in the past. The future is governed by the knowledge of the elderly, not by the discoveries of the young. The insignificance of the future is apparent in how the

Maasai perceive death: There is nothing after death unless one is a "laiboni" (wise man).

Space

Space, as it relates to land and grazing, is truly communal. Traditionally nomadic pastoralists, the Maasai did not regard any land as theirs to own but rather perceived all land as theirs to use. Rigby (1985) explains that the pastoral Maasai "do not conceive of land as 'owned' by any group, category, community or individual" (p. 124). He explains, however, that today most Maasai practice a subtle marking of territory. Each clan now has its own area and for the most part, clan boundaries are observed. Yet concepts of "land rights" and "trespassing" are still viewed as Western notions.

The Maasai's perception of private space is very different from Western perceptions. Maasai do not need or ask for much private space while in public settings. Lining up in a systematic order, and taking one's turn, is not part of the Maasai experience—public facilities, therefore, at least to the outsider, often appear disorderly. It is not uncommon to see a vehicle designed to hold fifteen packed with thirty occupants, and none of them complaining. For the Maasai, space is like time—there is always enough of it.

CONCLUSION

It has been the intent of this article to offer some observations about the Maasai culture. It is our contention that by knowing something about the perceptions and language systems of a culture, one can better understand that culture. This increased understanding provides us with a fund of knowledge that can be helpful in formulating messages directed to a group of people different from ourselves. It can also aid in interpreting the meanings behind the messages we receive from people who appear quite different from us. As Emerson wrote, "All persons are puzzled until at last we find some word or act, the key to the man, to the woman; straightaway all their past words and actions lie in light before us."

References

Hall, E. (1976). *Beyond Culture*. Garden City, N.Y.: Anchor.

Heine, B., and Claudi, U. (1986). *On the Rise of Grammatical Categories*. Berlin: Deitrich Reimer Verlag.

Johnstone, J. (1988, March 30). Personal correspondence.

Kipury, N. (1983). *Oral Literature of the Maasai*. Nairobi: Heinemann Educational Books.

Massek, A. O., and Sidai, J. O. (1974). *Eneno oo Lmaasai— Wisdom of the Maasai*. Nairobi: Transafrica Publishers.

Rigby, P. (1985). *Persistent Pastoralists: Nomadic Societies in Transition*. London: Zed Books.

Saitoti, T. O., and Beckwith, C. (1980). *Maasai*. London: Elm Tree Books.

Salvadon, C., and Fedders, A. (1973). *Maasai*. London: Collins.

Samovar, L. A., and Porter, R. E. (1997). "Approaching Intercultural Communication." In L. A. Samovar and R. E. Porter (Eds.), *Intercultural Communication: A Reader*, 8th ed. Belmont, Calif.: Wadsworth.

Sankan, S. S. O. (1971). *The Maasai*. Nairobi: Kenya Literature Bureau.

Concepts and Questions

1. What historical antecedents of Maasai culture contribute to their current worldview?
2. How does the Maasai's orientation to children affect their worldview?
3. In what ways might the Maasai worldview affect intercultural communication?
4. How does the Maasai use of metaphor differ from the North American use? How could this difference affect intercultural communication?
5. Skow and Samovar offer the following quotation by Edward T. Hall: "There is not one aspect of human life that is not touched and altered by culture." Do you agree with Hall? If so, why?
6. Why is it important to learn about the history of a culture? What aspects of the history of your culture do you deem important? Why?
7. How would you compare the values of the Maasai culture with the values of your own culture? Would a clash of these values present problems when you were communicating with a Maasai?
8. Compare three of the Maasai proverbs with three proverbs from your own culture.
9. Compare some of the Maasai's nonverbal behaviors with some of the actions found in your culture.

Communication with Egyptians

POLLY A. BEGLEY

s you step out of the Cairo airport and into a waiting taxicab, you may feel somewhat surprised and puzzled when the Egyptian driver, Mohammed, enjoins, "Now, you are in Egypt. You must think like an Egyptian—with your heart!" Every sojourner soon realizes that understanding the culture is essential to successful communication with Egyptians. And, while Mohammed's advice might be both sound and simple, the process of "thinking like an Egyptian" is complex and requires a great deal of knowledge about the culture and its historical traditions.

People have long been intrigued by Egyptian culture—mysterious pyramids, sacred temples hewn from rocky cliffs, enigmatic hieroglyphs, and five thousand years of enduring traditions. Volumes have been written about the possible purpose of ancient pyramids. Egyptologists wonder at the near-perfect preservation of writings on stones and temples that are three to four thousand years old. Villagers along the Nile cling to centuries-old traditions of conduct. In villages today, the *fellahin*, or peasants, employ the same tools and agricultural methods used during the pharaonic periods. Government experts sent to these villages are told that modern irrigation ideas and methods are unnecessary because "we have done it this way for thousands of years." Clearly, one must know a great deal about Egypt's history, customs, and traditions before he or she is prepared to appreciate fully the rich tapestry of its culture.

We cannot presume that this brief article can comprehensively cover thousands of years of history and tradition. Scholars who focus on cultural studies know that learning is a continual process. Even a lifetime of study and experience, however, would not be enough to unravel the secrets of Egyptian

civilization. The purpose of this review, then, is to seek an understanding of interactions between Egyptians and non-Egyptians by examining relevant cultural characteristics. Specifically, the primary emphasis is on those major aspects of culture that most influence intercultural communication. To this end, we will discuss the following important aspects of culture: (1) worldview and religion, (2) values, and (3) language.

EGYPTIAN WORLDVIEW AND RELIGION

Worldview represents common perception among the members of a cultural group. Samovar and Porter (1995) define it as "a culture's orientation towards God, humanity, nature, questions of existence, the universe and cosmos, life, death, sickness, and other philosophical issues that influence how its members perceive their world" (p. 114). A religion or philosophy essentially attempts to explain the unexplainable for the people of a particular community. Egyptians find solace in the religious beliefs of Islam and answer questions of existence through the sacred words of the Islamic holy book (Koran). An examination of Islamic history, principles, contemporary practices, and the role of religious beliefs within politics can provide insight into Egyptian behavioral and communicative patterns.

Islamic History

The historical roots of Islamic beliefs is important to intercultural communication because religion influences every part of everyday life in Egyptian Muslim communities. Islam began with Mohammed, who was the last of God's prophets. God spoke to Mohammed through the angel Gabriel in approximately 610 A.D., and the messages were recorded in the Koran. The Koran, the book of Islam, is the only miracle claimed by Mohammed and is considered by Muslims to be the exact words of God. This holy book contains 114 chapters (or suras) and outlines the will of God for the loyal followers of Islam (Waines, 1995, p. 23).

Although descriptions of Mohammed range from praising to condemning, no one can argue that he did not have a major impact on all of Arabia, including Egypt. Historically, the Middle East was turbulent. Vast areas, harsh deserts, warring tribes, and a precarious value placed on human life contributed to turmoil in the region. Although numerous leaders had previously attempted to create a consolidated empire, Mohammed and his followers were able to unite all of Arabia under their control. When Islam was first introduced to Egyptians, there was an established set of ancient beliefs that dated back thousands of years. These beliefs included countless deities and complicated rituals for Egyptians. In contrast, Islamic beliefs were easy to understand and follow for the common people. Islamic conquerors did not force conversion, but Egyptians were attracted by the clear and simple messages in this religion.

Today, pharaonic-era beliefs are confined to museums and tourist sites, and the number of Christians in Egyptian society has dwindled to less than 13 percent of the population. Ancient Egyptian history is considered to be anti-Islamic and has been replaced with Islamic history in Egyptian schools (Gershoni & Jankowski, 1995). A small enclave of Christians live in central Egypt, but violence plagues their relations with their Muslim neighbors. Islam effectively replaced other religious beliefs to become the prevailing worldview in Egypt.

Islamic beliefs dominate every moment from birth to death and beyond. Almost 85 to 90 percent of Egypt's population and more than one billion people worldwide are followers of Islam. Muslims seek Islam to find "the peace that comes when one's life is surrendered to God" (Smith, 1991, p. 222). This worldview reflects one of the youngest and fastest-growing major religions in the world. Some of the reasons why this religion is appealing to a large number of people can be understood by examining the principles of Islam such as tenets, pillars, and universal allure.

Islamic Principles

Four tenets are central to understanding Islam. First, it is a monotheistic religion. Second, God created the world. Third, humans are fundamentally good from birth because they are God's creations and without "original sin." Muslims believe in the innate goodness of humanity, but contemporary societies "forget" their divine origins. And, fourth, for each Muslim there will be a day of judgment when God decides whether each person will go to heaven or be condemned to hell (Smith, 1991).

Islam outlines five pillars for Muslims. First, *shahada*, or creed, is the confession of faith: *La ilaha illa 'llah* and is translated as "There is no God but God, and Muhammad is his prophet" (Smith, 1991, p. 244). Second, *salat* (prayer) is an important part of everyday life. Muslims are required to stop for prayer five times a day facing in the direction of the holy city of Mecca. Murphy (1993) described the call to prayer in Cairo, Egypt: "'God is great,' the muezzins proclaim, their words furiously amplified to rock concert proportions through the city's narrow and winding streets, a celebration of holiness at 70 decibels" (p. 1). Third, *zakat* (giving alms) to the poor is expected of each person. Fourth, *sawm* (fasting) during the month of Ramadan is required. This fast prompts Muslims to be disciplined, and it reminds them to be more charitable to the hungry and the poor within their societies. Finally, the *hajj* (pilgrimage) to Mecca is a requisite trip for those who are able to make the journey (Nigosian, 1987).

Islam possesses a universal allure, which appeals to Egyptians. This allure comes about, first, because Islam is a religion of action, not of contemplation. Second, Muslims from all cultural and ethnic groups are recognized as equal members within the religion. Believers are thus united in an international fraternity of Islam. Mohammed's words are clear on this issue: "A Muslim is the brother of a Muslim; he neither oppresses him nor does he fail him, he neither lies to him nor does he hold him in contempt" (Lippman, 1995, p. 185). Third, Islam does not require complicated rituals, or sacrifices. If one repeats the shahada creed, then he or she is a Muslim. Good Muslims follow the five pillars. This accepting simplicity of Islam unites and strengthens the people of Egypt.

Islam and Politics

Egyptian government has long recognized the power of Islam within the general populace. Each political group publicly supports the *Shari-a* (religious laws), advocates that religious principles should be taught in schools, and allows family concerns to be decided by Islamic ideologies. The constitution also declares Islam the state religion. Government support of Shari-a, however, has not prevented a rising number of secular laws. An ongoing Egyptian dilemma stems from trying to balance Islamic religious laws with attempts to bring modernization to industry and business. The introduction of new technology, as well as Western influences, has promoted lenient secular laws that are often contrary to traditional religious standards.

An increasing number of secular laws, technological advances, outside influence, population explosion, and rising unemployment has given rise to factions of religious fundamentalism. Some Egyptians believe that problems in their country are the result of society, especially the government, ignoring the principles of Islam. Fundamental religious beliefs offer the hopes of stability and orderliness during times of agitation and change. This Islamic fundamentalism has caused increased demands for a return to Shari-a (Sisk, 1992), which has resulted in increasing numbers of Egyptians following the Islamic pillars and practicing segregation by gender; more women in recent years have adopted full or partial veils in public places. In addition, fundamentalism has led to sporadic protests of foreign intrusion in several Egyptian cities.

Sojourners should be aware of Islamic religious practices while conducting business or traveling in Egypt. The Koran exhorts everyone, especially women, to cover themselves modestly. Egyptians wear less-revealing clothing and feel more comfortable communicating with others who adopt conservative attire. Egyptians also feel that it is their responsibility to help others in need. There is a long tradition of Egyptians taking anyone into their tent for sustenance or shelter from the harsh desert. Sojourners who receive help while in Egypt are told that "God wills it," as explanation for Egyptian hospitality. Travelers or business executives who display knowledge of and respect for Islamic beliefs are more likely to establish friendships and profitable business relations in Egypt. Although religious beliefs are an important part of Egyptian culture, they are but one part of understanding communication with Egyptians. In the next section we will consider Egyptian cultural values that are relevant to intercultural communication.

EGYPTIAN VALUES

Cultural values are vital areas of study for intercultural communication. Samovar and Porter (1995) state that:

> Cultural values define what is worth dying for, what is worth protecting, what frightens people, what are proper subjects for study and for ridicule, and what types of events create group solidarity. Most importantly, cultural values guide both perception and behavior. (p. 68).

If we can discover why people act a certain way, their fears, and their passions, then we can begin to understand how to improve communication between people of diverse cultures. Three important fundamental values in Egyptian culture are tradition, relationships, and hierarchical devotion.

Tradition

World histories reveal that the groups of people who have had the richest traditions have also had the longest-lived societies. Weick (1995) points out that cultures characterized by a "tradition of conduct" or that have a "well-developed folklore of action should survive longer than those that do not" (p. 126). These traditions of conduct serve to pass expertise and experience to the next generations. Because Egyptian culture is four to five thousand years old, it is not surprising that tradition is an important value.

This importance within the Egyptian population is reflected in several different ways. Egypt has a tradition of being a rural nation. The peasant farmers along the Nile are proud of their farming heritage, and they are often resistant to change. Ancient paintings depict types of donkey-powered waterwheels that are still in use today. Egyptians have survived countless epidemics, floods, droughts, and conquerors. The population has "a centuries-old capacity for letting life flow by, a little like the Nile, . . . and it is as though the present generations had inherited a seen-it-all-before attitude from their forbears" (Wayne & Simonis, 1994, p. 33). Their unity in pleasure and suffering while holding on to their traditions has contributed to the endurance of Egyptian culture for thousands of years.

Religious traditions, as previously mentioned, are an important part of life in Egypt. Ancient Egyptians thought that "every action, no matter how mundane, was in some sense a religious act: plowing, sowing, reaping, brewing, building ships, waging wars, playing games—all were viewed as earthly symbols for divine activities" (West, 1995, p. 46). Contemporary Egyptians also maintain that their religious beliefs play a pivotal role in family, politics, business, and education.

Egyptians may express polite interest in the traditions and ancestors of guests in their country. Higher regard is attributed to the person who can recite details about his or her family members from the past four to five hundred years. This strong value placed on tradition not only serves to pass on knowledge, but also can inhibit rapid changes. Visitors to Egypt should never underestimate the amount of time that it will take to establish relationships, make new contacts, and introduce technological innovations.

Relationships

Egyptians have the capability to endure, but there is still something that frightens them. The people of Egypt fear loneliness, and they wish to always be surrounded by a network of relatives and friends (Hopwood, 1982). They combat loneliness by placing great value on relationships.

Family, social, and business relationships are all taken seriously and give Egyptians great pleasure. The family is the center of society for many Middle Eastern countries. The crucial events of a person's lifetime are birth, marriage, and death. These principle daily concerns of everyday life emphasize the interconnectedness of the individual with the family. Each person represents a social collective, and sacrifices his or her needs for the greater good of that group.

Reassurance and warmth from familial relations are feelings replicated in other relationships. Kinship terms are used in various situations to reinforce positive connections among people. For example, "Egyptian politicians, from the President on down, emphasize their position as 'father figures' to the masses" (Inhorn, 1996, p. 159). The family is the basic building block of society and is a model for interactions throughout society.

The first questions that Egyptians ask guests in a conversation concern group affiliations. "Where is your family?" "Where is your father?" "Where are your classmates or co-workers?" Egyptians assume that people prefer group travel or activities. Tourists commonly report that locals never give oral directions, but always insist on accompanying them directly to their destination—no matter how far away.

A relational focus is also reflected in the blurred boundary lines between social and business interactions. Officials constantly maintain open-door policies and engage in friendly discussions with several people at one time. Building and maintaining good relations take priority over other activities in society. Egyptians often conduct lengthy business meetings without ever touching on business matters. A sojourner in Egypt realizes the power of relations after waiting at an Egyptian embassy for five hours to get a visa. Even then, there is no guarantee the paperwork will be processed before closing time. On the other hand, if good relations have been established with the family that runs the hotel, then its members may realize that one of their son's classmates works in the embassy. The visa would be delivered within half an hour to the door of the hotel after a single phone call. Relationships are a source of pleasure and are also an effective means of getting things done in a rigidly structured society.

Hierarchical Structure

Hierarchies according to age, gender, and experience are crucial in Egyptian society. Ancient traditions outline the proper place and behavior of each person in society. Interpersonal relationships are characterized by "a worldview professing the existence of a cosmic hierarchical order: The sound order of things is a descending scale of superiors and subordinates" (Yadlin, 1995, p. 157). The cosmic order begins with the major religion in Egypt. In Islam, humans submit to God's will in all matters. God is the ultimate creator, authority, and judge for all people.

The first word that visitors will learn upon arrival in Egypt is *Inshaallah*, which translates as "If God wills it." Explanations such as "God decides" or "It's when God wants it" reflect the accepted order of life. Muslims do not question their fate because God alone knows their destiny. A part of that destiny for Egyptians is fulfilling their roles in the overall social structure of society.

A strict order of social roles is also found in the family among parents and children and husband and wife. The oldest male in the family wields authority and power. This patriarch is responsible for the safety and well-being of his family members. Males and females attend separate schools, wives rarely work outside the home, and sons and daughters consider how their public behavior can influence their family. Sojourners will find that women rarely speak to outsiders when their fathers or husbands are present. The oldest son may conduct business or interactions with international contacts, but the father makes final decisions. Muslims regard these roles and practices as a natural part of life, and both women and men are staunch advocates and devotees of the traditional hierarchical order. Hierarchies are produced and reinforced through the language of family and societal communication.

EGYPTIAN LANGUAGE AND CULTURE

Language is a powerful tool. Our manner of speech can have a significant influence on another's behavior. The words that we choose reflect the way that we look at the world and perceive others. For centuries, Arabs have recognized the power of language and have used Arabic as a way to convey unity, worldview, and artistic impressions. Arabic is one of the oldest living languages in the world. It is the beautiful and flamboyant language spoken by Egyptians and other people of the Middle East.

If you venture into an Egyptian city, you will hear the rhythmic Arabic verses of the Koran chanted aloud during daily prayers. Walls of Egyptian mosques are not painted with pictures or scenes—they are covered with decorative Arabic calligraphy. A sojourner who learns a few words of Arabic will quickly gain friends in this region. Egyptians are also willing to share their knowledge of Arabic with others. On many occasions, a well-timed response of *Mish muskella* (No problem) or *Inshaallah* (If God wills it) will elicit approval and improves relations with Egyptians.

Arabic and Unity

What we say, how we say it, and why we say it are all related to our culture. Egyptians use their language to construct appropriate national identities and unity within the population. For example, Egyptians did not consider themselves Arabs until the seventh century when Arabic became the predominant way to communicate in the region (Lippman, 1995). As Egyptians adopted the new language, they were able to understand and relate to the Arabian way of life. Today, Egyptian children learn only in Arabic and are taught to memorize and proudly recite lengthy verses of the Koran. Although the Middle East comprises various countries and cultural and ethnic groups, Egyptians will readily proclaim, "But we are all Arabs!"

Arabic helps promote unity within a region just as different linguistic styles can produce disunity. For example, bargaining in Egypt is considered to be an enjoyable way to pass time and build relationships. Historically, Egyptians expect and love haggling, but for Israelis, "trading was not a pleasurable pastime, but part of a struggle for survival in a hostile environment. Thus, where bargaining has positive connotations for the Arab, for the Israeli it is reminiscent of a rejected and despised way of life" (Cohen, 1990, p. 139). Negotiations between Israel and Egypt have been taking place since 1948, and their different linguistic styles have caused more than one impasse during talks.

Arabic and Worldview

Arabic is used to convey the Islamic worldview. "Classical Arabic (which is also the written language) is sacred" because it is the dialect of the Koran (Hall, 1977, p. 31). The importance of the Koran within Islamic societies actually preserved the integrity of the classical tongue. Other major languages branched out into various dialects or became obsolete, but classical Arabic is still widely spoken among Muslims of every region. Public prayers and ceremonies worldwide are conducted in Arabic even if the Muslim adherents are not Middle Eastern Arabs.

Second, *jihad* is an Arabic word from the Koran that has often been incorrectly translated as "holy war." The mere mention of an Islamic jihad has been depicted within Western literature as religious fanatics on a killing rampage, and terrorist attacks are automatically attributed to Islamic fundamentalists (Hopfe, 1976). "Literally the word jihad means 'utmost effort' in promotion and defense of Islam, which might or might not include armed conflict with unbelievers" (Lippman, 1995, p. 113). Although there are some violent fundamentalist groups, these factions do not realistically represent the whole of Islamic followers.

Finally, Western readers of Koranic translations have reported that the holy book is repetitive, confusing, and lacks compelling features (Nigosian, 1987). Muslims maintain that these translations do not reflect the astounding beauty and rhythmic qualities of the original Arabic verses. The linguistic style of Koranic writings serve as a model for literature and speech throughout Islamic societies.

Arabic as Art

Arabic is used as an art form in Egypt. One of the foremost sights in every Egyptian city is the mosque decorated inside from top to bottom with Arabic calligraphy. Egyptian homes commonly have a scroll depicting the ninety-nine names of God in exquisite script. The mastery of spoken and written classical Arabic is indicative of education and rank in Egypt. Arabic is a language that gives pleasure to the eyes, ears, and spirits of the people. Sojourners who learn Arabic or adopt a descriptive and elegant style of speaking in another language will attain a higher level of credibility while in Egypt.

CONCLUSION

This article reviews aspects of the Islamic worldview, cultural values, and language that influence communication with Egyptians. Visitors to Egypt find that travel or business ventures are more rewarding experiences if they take the time to learn about specific cultural characteristics. If its five thousand years of history and tradition can provide a rich cultural heritage and wisdom for Egyptians, then other cultures can also learn from one of the oldest civilizations in the world.

References

Cohen, R. (1990). Deadlock: Israel and Egypt negotiate. In F. Korzenny & S. Ting-Toomey (Eds.), *Communicating for peace: Diplomacy and negotiation 14* (pp. 136–153). Newbury Park, CA: Sage.

Gershoni, I., & Jankowski, J. P. (1995). *Redefining the Egyptian nation, 1930–1945*. New York: Cambridge University.

Hall, E. T. (1977). *Beyond culture*. Garden City, NY: Anchor Books.

Hopfe, L. M. (1976). *Religions of the world*. Beverly Hills, CA: Glencoe.

Hopwood, D. (1982). *Egypt: Politics and society 1945–1981*. London: George Allen and Unwin.

Inhorn, M. C. (1996). *Infertility and patriarchy: The cultural politics of gender and family life in Egypt*. Philadelphia: University of Pennsylvania.

Lippman, T. W. (1995). *Understanding Islam: An introduction to the Muslim world* (2nd ed.). New York: Meridian.

Murphy, K. (1993, April 6). World report special edition: A new vision for Mohammed's faith. *Los Angeles Times*, p. 1.

Nigosian, S. (1987). *Islam: The way of submission*. London: Crucible.

Samovar, L. A., & Porter, R. E. (1995). *Communication between cultures* (2nd ed.). Belmont, CA: Wadsworth.

Sisk, T. D. (1992). *Islam and democracy: Religion, politics, and power in the Middle East*. Washington, DC: United States Institute of Peace Press.

Smith, H. (1991). *The world's religions: Our great wisdom traditions*. San Francisco: Harper.

Waines, D. (1995). *An introduction to Islam*. Cambridge, UK: Cambridge University Press.

Wayne, S., & Simonis, D. (1994). *Egypt and the Sudan* (3rd ed.). Hawthorn, Australia: Lonely Planet.

Weick, K. (1995). *Sensemaking in organizations*. Thousand Oaks, CA: Sage.

West, J. A. (1995). *The traveler's key to ancient Egypt: A guide to the sacred places of ancient Egypt*. Wheaton, IL: Quest Books.

Yadlin, R. (1995). The seeming duality: Patterns of interpersonal relations in a changing environment. In S. Shamir (Ed.), *Egypt from monarchy to republic: A reassessment of revolution and change* (pp. 151–170). Boulder, CO: Westview.

Concepts and Questions

1. Why does Begley say it is hard to "think like an Egyptian"?

2. What aspects of Islamic history offer insights into the Egyptian culture? What aspects of your own culture would offer valuable insights for someone wanting to study your culture?

3. Why does Begley assert that "Islamic beliefs dominate every moment from birth to death and beyond"?

4. Begley offers four tenets central to understanding Islam. What are they? Does your worldview have similar or dissimilar tenets?

5. What does Begley mean when she writes, "Islam is a religion of action, not contemplation"? Is your religion one of action or contemplation?

6. Why is Arabic language so very important to the Egyptians? What aspects of their language make it unique?

7. What does Begley imply when she talks about Arabic as art?

8. What communication patterns within your culture might present problems when communicating with someone from Egyptian culture?

Palevome: Foundations of Struggle and Conflict in Greek Interpersonal Communication

BENJAMIN J. BROOME

Conflict is most often defined as a struggle between parties who are linked in an interdependent manner over incompatible goals, interests, or resources. In Western societies the term *conflict* usually elicits negative images; it is associated with intensity of feelings, damaged relationships, and inefficient use of time and energy. Cooperation, friendly relations, and smooth transactions are put forth as ideals. Conflict signals that something is wrong and needs to be corrected. Much of the literature on conflict management and conflict resolution, published primarily in the United States, reflects this negative image of conflict (Coser, 1956; Fink, 1968; Freud, 1949; Pruitt & Lewis, 1977; Roloff, 1976).

This view of conflict is however, culture-bound. Even though many researchers recognize the possibility of productive uses of conflict (Deutsch, 1973; Folger & Poole, 1984; Kilmann & Thomas, 1977; Putman & Wilson, 1982), the existence of conflict in a relationship is usually discussed as an irregularity; relationships in conflict are "out of balance" and need to be restored to normalcy. In contrast to this view of conflict as an abnormality, other cultural groups view struggles between parties as a way of life. This is particularly true of both traditional and contemporary Hellas, better known to English language users as the country of Greece.[1]

Permeating almost every facet of everyday life in Greece is a sense of contest. To the Western mind,[2] Greece appears to be a "maddening mobile, elusive, paradoxical world, where there seems nothing solid

From the *Southern Communication Journal*, Vol. 55, No. 2 (Spring, 1990), pp. 260–275. Reprinted by permission of the Southern States Communication Association. Benjamin J. Broome teaches at George Mason University in Fairfax, Virginia.

enough to grasp save splinters, yet where no part is less than the mystical whole and where past and present, body and soul, ideal and reality blend and struggle and blend again with each other so that the most delicate scalpel can scarcely dissect them" (Holden, 1972, p. 34). However, for Greeks, this struggle can bring with it feelings of stimulation, excitement, and genuine human contact. Even the painful feelings that are often the result of conflict are not viewed as aberrations, but rather are seen as part of the natural course of human relations. In Greece, conflict is an aspect of everyday transactions that is unavoidable.

This paper discusses the Greek approach to conflict in interpersonal communication, exploring the traditional foundations of struggle as a way of life. The views presented here are based on anthropological, sociological, linguistic, and communication literature about Greece and the author's research in Greece during 1980 to 1989.

STRUGGLE AS THE ESSENCE OF LIFE: TRADITIONAL GREEK CULTURE AND ORIENTATIONS TOWARD INTERPERSONAL CONFLICT

Ernestine Friedl (1962), in describing life in a traditional Greek village at that time, reports that when one walks through the fields and inquires about how the work is going, the people generally respond with "palevome" or "we are struggling." The villagers' use of the verb *palevo* expresses the difficult conditions confronting farmers trying to make a living from the predominantly rocky soil and mountainous terrain. At the same time, it reflects the predominate worldview and orientation toward interpersonal relations characteristic of Greek reality. Triandis (1972) reports that even a positive term such as *success* is linked by Greeks with struggle, whereas for North Americans it is linked with careful planning and hard work. Nickolas Gage, author of the best-selling book *Eleni* (Gage, 1983), describes Greece as a place with "joy and tragedy straight out of Aeschylus, Sophocles, and Euripides, and it is expressed with the same classic gestures . . . the same tendency to use strong words and violent gestures; . . . the same warm heart, the disdain for time, and the delight in

life lived fully, with all the senses awake" (Gage, 1987, p. 24).

While Greece is a land of unparalleled scenic beauty, it is also a land of contrasts. Physically, the mountains and the sea meet each other throughout the country, often resulting in dramatic settings. Culturally, there are contrasts between the island inhabitants and the mountain villagers (Sanders, 1962). Historically, the Greek character has always fought over the opposing poles of a more feminine Ionian makeup and a more masculine Dorian outlook. Geographically, Greece sits between the Near East and Europe and has been invaded and occupied by forces from both, resulting in cultural influences from East and West. In politics there have been both military dictatorships and socialist governments, although the dictatorships were not the choice of the people. These contrasts and the resulting struggle between opposites are deeply embedded in the nature of Greek reality:

> . . . Greek identity as a whole (is) best seen as a constant oscillation between just such opposites as these. The spirit and the flesh, ideal and reality, triumph and despair—you name them and the Greeks suffer or enjoy them as the constant poles of their being, swinging repeatedly from one to the other and back again, often contriving to embrace both poles simultaneously, but above all never reconciled, never contented, never still. *This perennial sense of tension between diametrically opposed forces is the essence of their existence*—the one absolutely consistent feature of their identity since Greek history began. In the phrase of the Cretan novelist, Kazantzakis, they are truly double-born souls. (Holden, 1972, pp. 27–28, emphasis added)

Tension and struggle in interpersonal relations are contextually embedded in several aspects of Greek history and social reality. Traditionally, Greece has revolved around village culture, even though from pre-classical times Greeks have traveled all over the world to both satisfy their curiosity and to search for new resources. Hundreds of villages have always dotted the mostly mountainous countryside and the island ports, with relatively few urban centers.

Today the situation has changed, with the majority of the population living in three or four major cities and 40% of the population residing in Athens.

However, in many cases the suburbs of these urban centers resemble villages. The majority of the population of Athens are migrants from the villages and small towns of the countryside and the islands, and most residents of the capital were not born in that city (Campbell, 1983). More importantly, the majority of city residents remain closely tied to their traditional villages, often maintaining a village house and returning to the village for important religious occasions. Even with voting, most Greeks prefer to keep their registration in their villages rather than move it to their city of residence, maintaining their ties and status within remote villages. Thus, while externally many Greeks conform to more contemporary Western life-styles, they are psychologically and socially bound to a traditional culture that influences their lives in a myriad of ways (Triandis, 1986).

In order to understand the Greek approach to conflict and struggle as a way of life, it is necessary to explore two aspects of traditional Greek culture that have a strong influence on contemporary Greek thought and actions. The following section will discuss (a) the distinction between "ingroup" and "outgroup" in Greek society, and (b) the influence of "philotimo" on interpersonal relations.

THE CONTEXTUAL FOUNDATIONS OF INTERPERSONAL STRUGGLE

Ingroup–Outgroup Distinctions

Traditionally Greek culture is more collectivist than individualistic in nature (Doumanis, 1983) and emphasizes distinctions between ingroup and outgroup to a much larger extent than do Western societies. The major differences between ingroup behavior and outgroup behavior have been extensively examined by Triandis (1972), who describes the Greek as defining his universe in terms of the triumphs of the ingroup over the outgroup. Social behavior is strongly dependent on whether the other person is a member of the ingroup or the outgroup. This affects relations with people in a wide variety of situations, such as interaction with authority figures and with persons with whom one is in conflict.

The definition of the ingroup in traditional Greek society includes family, relatives, friends, and even friends of friends. Guest and other people who are perceived as showing appropriate warmth, acceptance, and assistance quickly become friends and thus part of the ingroup. Outgroup members include those in the community outside the immediate family, the extended family, and the network of ingroup affiliations. While a traditional village community is sharply divided into subgroups on the basis of these affiliations, the structure is not entirely rigid; people who are at one point outgroup members could become ingroup members through marriage or by establishing links of cooperative interdependence (Doumanis, 1983). An individual is attached to these different groupings with varying degrees of intimacy, ranging from total identification to outward hostility.

A great deal of commitment exists between ingroup members, requiring intimacy, concern, and good conduct. It is required that an individual behave toward members of his or her ingroup with self-sacrifice, as the well-being of the ingroup is more important than that of the individual. In the context of a highly competitive social world, the ingroup provides protection and help for its members. Feelings of trust, support, cooperation, sympathy, and admiration are exchanged frequently among members of the ingroup.

Relations with outgroup members are characterized by a great deal of suspicion and mistrust. Influence and pressure from the outgroup is rejected. The relationship between authority figures and subordinates is also dependent on ingroup/outgroup considerations. For example, in larger organizations, managers, who are usually viewed by employees in Greece as part of the outgroup, are treated with avoidance and hostility. On the other hand, managers who are identified as part of the employees' ingroup are usually given submissive acceptance and warmth.

Concealment and deception play important roles in relations with the outgroup. They serve as important means for upholding ingroup honor and prestige. In a world where ingroup honor must be protected and competition is a way of life, deception becomes a useful means of fulfilling one's duties. The phrase is often heard "You can't live without lies." For Greeks, however, the word for lies, *psemata*, does not carry with it the negative connotations assigned by most Westerners. It is used more freely and with less emotional intensity (Friedl, 1959). It does not have the overtones of morality found in English, and it is sometimes even justified on religious grounds by declaring it the desire of God (du Boulay, 1976). In fact, villagers are not humiliated because someone tries to deceive them, although they become angry if the deception succeeds (Friedl, 1962).

The suspicion and mistrust of outgroup members lead to a general lack of helpfulness toward those not part of the ingroup. This is illustrated in a study reported by Triandis (1986). Comparisons were made between how people in the United States, Europe, and Greece behave toward foreign strangers and toward strangers who are fellow nationals.[3] A number of situations were used in which either a fellow national or a foreigner interacted with a sample of local people. In one situation, where the stranger asks for help from a local person, approximately 50 percent of those asked in Europe and the United States provided the assistance, regardless as to whether the request came from a foreigner or a fellow national. However, in Greece, this degree of help was only provided to the foreigner (a potential ingroup member) requesting assistance. Only 10 percent of locals agreed to help a fellow Greek whom they did not know, as this person was clearly an outgroup member.

Even cheating, while it is completely unacceptable with the ingroup, is acceptable when it is directed toward members of the outgroup. When it occurs with the outgroup, cheating is treated in the context of competition, where it is required that the outgroup member be taken advantage of if he or she is weak. The outgroup member is expected to be on guard against cheating.

The ingroup–outgroup distinction leads to a continuous struggle between members of the two groups. Actions that are inappropriate within the ingroup are applied without hesitation to relations with the outgroup. The distinction provides for the support and safety necessary to carry on the struggle, and at the same time it provides the focus for the struggle itself. Loyalty to the ingroup and feelings ranging from mild disregard to intense animosity for the outgroup provide the background upon which many conflicts are staged.

Philotimo: The Essence of Ingroup Behavior

Perhaps the most cherished term for a Greek is *eleftheria*, which means freedom. For much of its long and sometimes glorious history, Greece has been under foreign domination. For example, the Ottoman Empire ruled Greece for 400 years, and during the Second World War it suffered tremendously under German occupation. Despite this history of domination by external forces, Greeks have always maintained a strong sense of personal freedom that transcends the circumstances. Much of this can be attributed to a central aspect of Greek self-concept called *philotimo*.

Philotimo is not translatable with a single English word; it is a concept that refers to several aspects of Greek character and social relations. First, it refers to a sense of responsibility and obligation to the ingroup, particularly to the family. The most important social unit in Greece is the family, and Greeks take their family obligations seriously. They are obliged to uphold the family honor and to provide assistance to family members. This extends in various ways to other members of the ingroup. Lee (1959) says that loyalty can only be evoked in personal relations, with the result that Greeks cannot be impartial in distributing resources that are at their disposal, whether those resources are jobs or material goods. It is one's duty to take care of family and friends first, irrespective of merit or order of priority.

Second, philotimo refers to appropriate behavior within the ingroup. As Triandis (1972) indicates, a person who is considered "philotimos" behaves toward members of his ingroup in a way that is "polite, virtuous, reliable, proud, . . . truthful, generous, self-sacrificing, tactful, respectful, and grateful" (pp. 308–309). The principle of philotimo requires a person to sacrifice himself or herself to help ingroup members and to avoid doing or saying things that reflect negatively on family or friends. Appropriate ingroup behavior should be seen and felt not only by the ingroup but by the outgroup as well, thus increasing prestige for the ingroup in the eyes of the outgroup.

Third, philotimo is strongly related to a person's sense of personal honor and self-esteem. As Lee (1959) stated: "Foremost in the Greek's view of the self is his self-esteem. It is impossible to have good relations with Greeks unless one is aware of this, the Greek philotimo. It is important to pay tribute to it, and to avoid offending it, or as the Greeks say, "molesting it" (p. 141). The Greek philotimo is easily bruised, and there is constant emphasis on both protecting the philotimo and enhancing it. Protecting one's philotimo leads to a concern with losing face, with shielding the inner core of the self from ridicule, and with avoiding actions that would cause loss of respect. There is constant guard against being outsmarted by the outgroup, and it is seldom that Greeks put themselves in a position of being in less than full control of their senses in order to avoid personal abuse and damage to the ingroup.

Offense against one's philotimo brings retaliation rather than feelings of self-criticism of self-blame. As Friedl (1962) relates, the avoidance of self-blame does not have the connotation of irresponsibility, because it is a necessary part of the maintenance of self-esteem. In the same vein, philotimo is not related to feelings of remorse or guilt, and it is not strongly tied to notions of ethical morality (Holden, 1972). If actions are taken in defense of philotimo that bring harm to outgroup members, responsibility is not accepted for what occurs following the actions. If the demands of philotimo have been satisfied, the person taking action against others is entitled to reject any blame for subsequent misfortune.

Safeguarding of philotimo promotes a sense of equality between individuals, and thus it is seldom that a Greek feels inferior to another. Even differences in status levels and role responsibilities are not cast in terms of superiority or inferiority in Greece. However, the philotimo of the Greek is very different from the notion of pride. The philotimo of the Greek is promoted by actions that bring honor and respect to the family and the ingroup, not simply to the individual. Lee (1959) points out that the expression of pride carries with it the connotation of arrogance, which is detested by the Greeks. A common proverb states that "the clever (proud) bird is caught by the nose."

In many ways, interpersonal struggle is driven by concerns of philotimo. Philotimo is the key to behavior within the ingroup, and it frames much of one's behavior toward the outgroup. Requirements of philotimo lead to actions that enhance the position of the ingroup, and at the same time trigger actions

in defense of the ingroup. Many conflicts occur because of the demands of philotimo. Perhaps it is because of the Greek's strong sense of philotimo that conflicts can continue over long periods of time and at a high level of intensity without feelings of guilt or remorse.

INTERPERSONAL STRUGGLE IN SOCIAL TRANSACTIONS

Greek social life has been described by du Boulay (1976) as a type of "see-saw," continuously in motion. Friedl (1962) used the word *tension* to capture the feelings of Greek villagers toward each other and the world, saying that a large number of social encounters feature a "sense of contest, of struggle, of agony, of a kind of pushing and pulling" (Friedl, 1962, p. 76). She used the metaphor of a "battle" to describe Greek social life in the village, arguing that the Greek search for identity in a culture that seeks so strongly to preserve ingroup honor and integrity is carried out to a large extent by pitting oneself against another. It is through contrast, with others that one learns to know oneself, and this leads to the necessity of maintaining differences and emphasizing contrasts. She says that "contrasts, and the tension contrasts create, become expected and desired" (Friedl, 1962, p. 76). Struggle and contrasts are evident in several related aspects of Greek social reality: (a) conversation style, (b) competitive nature of social relationships, and (c) process nature of relational struggle.

Conversation Style and the Role of Couvenda

The conversation style of Greeks has been described as "contrapuntal virtuosity, incisive, combative, loud" (Lee, 1959, p. 146). To the unaccustomed ear, every conversation appears to be an argument, and gentleness seems to play no part in dialogue. The substance of conversation is less important than the style because it is the process that counts (Holden, 1972). Discussion can be described as "a battle of personal opinion, and its end is neither to reach the truth nor to reach a conclusion; its end is sheer enjoyment of vigorous speech" (Lee, 1959, p. 146).

Indeed, the Western visitor to Greece is immediately struck by the intensity of the conversation:

> A city neighborhood or a village can be compared to a stage, and friends, neighbors, and kin to a Greek chorus commenting on unfolding marriages, hospitality, or sexual infidelity. No one can remain solely in the audience; however, neutrality is impossible to maintain. No one can expect to receive support of his or her reputation unless he or she defends that of allies. Manipulation of opinion depends on gossip, which in turn depends on the breaking of confidences, amusement derived from ridicule, and malicious attempts to exploit the situation. (*Greece: A Country Study*, 1985, p. 145).

Challenges, insults and attacks are, within appropriate limits, almost synonymous with conversing. Friedl (1962) says that conversation "has some of the quality of an arena in which each man displays himself as an individual and waits for an audience response. People talk at each other rather than with each other" (p. 83). It is not unusual for several monologues to be going on simultaneously at a table as different individuals struggle to hold center stage and assert their personalities.

Couvenda, or conversation, is extremely important in Greek society. As Triandis (1972) puts it, "Greeks love to discuss, to argue, and to match their wits with other debaters" (p. 323). Gage (1987) reports a conversation with a ship owner who believes that "to exercise the tongue and provoke the mind is the most fulfilling pastime of all" (p. 30). Davenport (1978) describes Athens as a city where social activity—eating out, drinking, dancing, singing and, above all, conversing—permeates everyday life to an extraordinary degree. From childhood, everyone receives a great deal of verbal stimulation, for conversation is a skill that no one can live without.

Couvenda plays a number of important functions in Greek society. First, it is through conversation that personal relationships are developed and maintained. Hirschon (1978) says that "company with others has an intrinsic value, solitude is abhorred and the personality type most approved is that of the open and warm individual, while someone described as closed is also seen as cold" (p. 77). Isolation and withdrawal, she says, are equivalent to social death;

to engage in intense verbal exchange is thus a recognition of the other's existence.

Moreover, many Greeks feel degrees of obligation toward others, even non-relatives, from their native village or surrounding area (Gage, 1987). When two strangers meet they will immediately try to discover if they share any common roots. More often than not they find they have common acquaintances or that one of their relatives is married to one of the other's relatives. Establishing this social bond through such a ritual allows each of them to place the other at least tentatively within the ingroup, thus promoting warmer feelings and a greater degree of trust.

Second, couvenda serves as a means of asserting a sense of equality in encounters with others. This equality is not necessarily related to status, education, or economic level, but rather refers to equality as a human being. As Friedl (1962) emphasizes: "The right to a certain give-and-take underlies all relationships and serves to keep each situation unique and each relationship one of equality on at least some level" (p. 83). This sense of equality is demanded by one's philotimo, and it is through couvenda that it is established and maintained. This may even lead one to present strong views on a topic with which she or he is unfamiliar and then to stubbornly defend these views even in the face of clear evidence against them. To lose an argument on the basis of the facts or logic presented by the other would show weakness and would put the person in an inferior position. Asserting one's personality by providing strong opinions and engaging in sometimes heated argument is a common means of elevating the philotimo on an individual level.

Third, couvenda provides a source of entertainment. Traditional village life is quite routine and repetitive, and especially before the advent of television it was through conversation that freshness and uniqueness were brought to commonplace events. Variation and uncertainty are imposed on aspects of life that otherwise have no intrinsically adventurous elements. Entertainment is enhanced by the rich oral tradition of the Greeks, whose language allows a precision of expression that promotes unsurpassed storytelling.

Gage (1987) shows how everyday language is rich in proverbs, myths, legends, and humor. He says that "even the most uneducated Greek sprinkles his speech liberally with proverbs, many of them reflecting the wry cynicism of a people who have become accustomed to hardship, yet have managed to retain their spiritual strength and sense of humor" (pp. 59–60). Holden (1972) shows how boasting sometimes takes the form of "apparently harmless rhetorical embroidery to make actual situations seem grander, more significant and more self-flattering than they really are" (p. 94).

Finally, couvenda is important in asserting one's personality and maintaining self-esteem. Hirschon (1978) points out that social life is vital, because prestige and reputation, which depend on the opinion of others, are the measure of both the individual's merit and that of his or her family. Friedl (1962) considers couvenda as the way men and women boast of their own and their family's achievements and as the vehicle for men to display their political knowledge and engage in political argument. Boasting is socially acceptable, and Davenport (1978) believes that it is a means of promoting philotimo.

Despite the high level of intensity reflected in couvenda, arguments, debates, and other verbal disputes are not viewed as aberrations, and they do not necessarily affect relationships negatively or lead to negative feelings within relationships. Rather, they are viewed as integral aspects of daily existence. Couvenda, while it *reflects* the interpersonal struggle that is the essence of Greek reality, functions on center stage in full view of any audience. Behind the scenes lies relational struggle in which rivalry and *competition* play key roles.

Competition and Relational Struggle

Holden (1972) writes about the "deep current of rivalry and suspicion" running between Greeks. He says that relationships are in a constant state of flux because of the competitive nature of the Greek's social orientation. Greeks tend to believe that "the friend of my enemy is my enemy, and the enemy of my enemy is my friend," so they are constantly making, dissolving, and remaking coalitions as different "enemies" appear on the scene. From Holden's (1972) viewpoint, "the prospect of life without an enemy generally seems intolerable" (p. 89), so new relational struggles are constantly developing.

The ongoing struggles in Greek social life are fueled by a competitive orientation that is different from that found in most Western societies. It is often noted that whereas in Europe and the United States people compete with each other by trying to "run faster" to get ahead of the other, the Greeks compete with each other by grabbing onto their competitor to "hold them back," thus keeping them from getting ahead. The tendency to compete by bringing down one's foe signals a very different approach to conflict that can significantly affect the manner in which conflicts are managed.

The approach to competition in Greece reflects the collectivist nature of traditional Greek culture. Whereas in individualistic cultures such as the United States and most of Europe competition is between individuals, Greek competition is primarily between the ingroup and the outgroup (Triandis, 1986). The requirements of philotimo that the Greek feels toward the ingroup help prevent forms of competition that would damage the basic ties holding the ingroup together. However, the need to defend the ingroup against harm from outside can lead to intense conflicts between the ingroup and the outgroup. Doumanis (1983) states that in traditional Greek communities "social relationships were either positive or negative, with no room for neutral gradation in between. Families were either co-operating with one another, closely and intimately, or were competing aggressively, cunningly and sometimes fiercely" (p. 28).

Process Focus of Relational Struggle

Despite the competitive nature of relations with the outgroup, the interpersonal struggle characteristic of Greek relationships is not totally focused on *outcome* but rather tends to center on *process*. Heard often is the phrase "Perazmena Ksehazmena" or "What is past is forgotten." Applying not only to unpleasant events but equally to success, it points to the short-lived nature of victory and defeat. Without a competitor, life would not be very stimulating, so new relational struggles are constantly taking shape.

It can be argued that interpersonal battles provide a great deal of personal and social satisfaction to Greeks. Friedl (1962) says that it is the continuing *aghonia* (anxiety or agony) that provides for the

Greek a feeling of being alive. Holden (1972) describes conflict as "generating the leaping spark of tension that is the only certain characteristic of Greekness. Tension, movement, change, process; these are the essence of Greek life" (p. 33).

Not only do struggles provide some degree of stimulation and satisfaction for Greeks, they also play an important role in strengthening ingroup solidarity. The hostility and opposition directed toward the outgroup serves as a complement to the cooperation necessary within the ingroup. Through competition with the outgroup, ingroup members attest to their allegiance with the ingroup. As Doumanis (1983) states: "The values of prestige and honor so central in the traditional Greek culture rested on the attention and opinion of friends *and* enemies, on the concerned interest of kin *and* the grudging acceptance of competitors" (p. 29, emphasis added).

In many ways, interpersonal communication and relationships in Greece mirror a description of the contrasts in the physical world. Just as the Greek countryside is dominated by mountainous and often rough terrain, conversations and relationships are characterized by transactions that seem to the outsider harsh and rocky. Physical, spiritual, and social struggles are built into the Greek landscape, psyche, and relationships in ways that are difficult for the Western European mind to comprehend. Although these struggles would exhaust the Westerner, they seem to invigorate the Greek. Differences such as these make the current Western notion of what constitutes conflict incomplete and perhaps inappropriate in describing cultures such as those in traditional and contemporary Hellas.

IMPLICATIONS FOR FUTURE RESEARCH

Greece is a society in transition, moving rapidly from a traditional village and island culture to a more westernized and cosmopolitan environment. While the traditional Greek cultural milieu exerts extensive influence on the communication patterns of contemporary urban Greeks, there are only a few reported studies that examine the urban environment (Campbell, 1983; Doumanis, 1983; Hirschon, 1983; Triandis, 1986).

The need exists to conduct additional field studies and empirical investigations of communication patterns in contemporary Greece. While this study has concentrated on *palevome* and its implications for interpersonal conflict in Greece, there are other cultural factors that impact on interpersonal communication. The time is ripe for studies examining phenomena such as time orientation, male and female role distinctions, and influence of religious worldviews in the context of contemporary Greece.

Research also needs to be conducted that examines the impact of Greek interpersonal communication on relations between Greeks and Western Europeans, North Americans, and other Westerners. While it is beyond the scope of this paper to explore such applications, the consequences for intercultural interaction are numerous. A concept like palevome can be instructive to both Western Europeans, North Americans, and Greeks as improved interpersonal relations are sought.

Finally, this examination points to a deficiency in the literature on conflict and conflict management. Much of the theoretical and research literature on conflict published in the United States must be reexamined and broadened. The culture-bound paradigm of conflict represented in the literature limits the extent to which the nature of this important phenomenon can be understood. While calls have been made for culture-specific research on communication processes (Broome, 1986), there are few reported studies in the communication literature that examine communication patterns in societies other than the United States (Shuter, 1990). Only through culture-specific research conducted in a culturally sensitive manner can we gain insight into the nature of a conflict and culture from a global perspective.

Notes

1. The name "Greece" comes from the Latin term given by the Romans during their occupation of Greece. Greeks refer to their country as "Hellas" or "Ellada."
2. While Greece is part of the European Economic Community and is usually included geographically as part of Europe, the culture blends the traditions of both West and East in a unique way (see

Woodhouse, 1983). Geographically, it sits between the west of Europe and the east of Turkey.

3. In Greece a foreign stranger is a potential ingroup member because of the emphasis the culture places on "philoxenia," or "kindness to strangers."

References

Area handbook for Greece. (1970). Washington, DC: American University.

Barnlund, D. C. (1975). Public and private self in Japan and the United States. Tokyo: Simul Press.

Broome, B. J. (1986). A context-based approach to teaching intercultural communication. Communication Education, 35(3), 296–306.

Campbell, J. K. (1964). Honor, family and patronage. Oxford: Clarendon Press.

Campbell, J. K. (1983). Traditional values and continuities in Greek society. In R. Clogg (Ed.), Greece in the 1980's. St. Martin's Press, 184–207.

Coser, L. (1956). The functions of conflict. New York: Free Press.

Crimes of honor still the pattern in rural Greece. New York Times, Sect. 1, February 10, 1980, 22.

Davenport, W. W. (1978). Athens. New York: Time-Life Books.

Deutsch, M. (1973). The resolution of conflict. New Haven: Yale University Press.

Doumanis, M. (1983). Mothering in Greece: From collectivism to individualism. London: Academic Press.

de Boulay, J. (1976). Lies, mockery and family integrity. In J. G. Peristiany (Ed.), Mediterranean Family Structure. Cambridge University Press, 389–406.

Fink, C. F. (1968). Some conceptual difficulties in the theory of social conflict. Journal of Conflict Resolution, 12, 412–460.

Folger, J. P., and Poole, M. S. (1984). Working through conflict: A communication perspective. Glenview, IL: Scott, Foresman.

Freud, S. (1949). An outline of psychoanalysis (J. Strachey, trans.). New York: Norton.

Friedl, E. (1962). Vasilika: A village in modern Greece. New York: Holt, Rinehart & Winston.

Gage, N. (1987). Hellas: A portrait of Greece. Athens: Efstathiadis Group.

Gage, N. (1983). Eleni. New York: Random House.

Greece: A Country Study. (1985). Washington, DC: American University.

Hirschon, R. B. (1978). Open Body/Closed Space: The Transformation of Female Sexuality. In Shirley Ardener (Ed.), Defining Females: The Nature of Women in Society. London: Croom Helm, 66–87.

Hirschon, R. B. (1983). Under one roof: Marriage, dowry, and family relations in Piraeus. In Michael Kenny and David I. Kertzer (Eds.), Urban life in Mediterranean Europe: Anthropological perspectives. Urbana: University of Illinois Press, 299–323.

Hirschon, R. B., and Gold, J. R. (1982). Territoriality and the home environment in a Greek urban community. Anthropological Quarterly, 55(2), 63–73.

Holden, D. (1972). Greece without columns: The making of the modern Greeks. Philadelphia: J. B. Lippincott, 1–36.

Kilmann, R. H., and Thomas, K. W. (1977). Developing a forced choice measure of conflict-handling behavior: The MODE instrument. Educational and Psychological Measurement, 309–325.

Lee, D. (1959). Freedom and culture. Englewood Cliffs, NJ: Prentice-Hall, Inc.

Pruitt, D., and Lewis, S. (1977). The psychology of interactive bargaining. In D. Druckman (Ed.), Negotiations. Beverly Hills: Sage.

Putman, L., and Wilson, D. E. (1982). Development of an organizational communication conflict instrument. In M. Burgoon (Ed.), Communication Yearbook (Vol. 6). Beverly Hills: Sage.

Roloff, M. E. (1976). Communication strategies, relationships, and relational changes. In G. R. Miller (Ed.), Explorations in interpersonal communication. Beverly Hills: Sage.

Sanders, I. T. (1962). Rainbow in the rock. Cambridge, MA: Harvard University Press.

Shuter, R. (Spring, 1990). The Centrality of Culture. The Southern Communication Journal, 55, 237–249.

Triandis, H. C. (1986). Education of Greek-Americans for a pluralistic society. Keynote address to the Conference on the Education of Greek Americans, New York, May.

Triandis, H. C. (1972). A comparative analysis of subjective culture. From The Analysis of Subjective Culture. New York: John Wiley & Sons, 299–335.

Woodhouse, C. M. (1983). Greece and Europe. In R. Clogg (Ed.), Greece in the 1980's. St. Martin's Press, 1–8.

Concepts and Questions

1. What significant role does conflict play in Greek interaction?

2. What are the major differences between Greek and American cultures in the relationship to and the use of conflict?

3. How would you describe the conversational style of Greek interaction?

4. What are some of the characteristics of conflict that apply to intercultural communication?

5. Does the culture you belong to treat conflict in the same manner as the Greek culture does? In what ways are they similar? In what ways do they differ?

6. What does Broome mean when he writes, "Permeating almost every facet of everyday life in Greece is a sense of contest"?

7. How would you define *philotimo* in your own words? Is there a similar concept in your culture?

8. Broome notes that the conversational style of Greeks has been described as "contrapuntal virtuosity, incisive, combative, and loud." How do these characteristics compare with the conversational style found in your culture?

chapter 3

Co-Cultures: Living in Two Cultures

In Chapter 2, we focused on international cultures—cultures that exist beyond the immediate borders of the United States. In this chapter, we turn our attention to the multicultural aspects of groups living within the United States. In most instances the people who make up these groups hold dual or multiple memberships, hence the term co-cultures. The groups that constitute these co-cultures may share a common religion, economic status, ethnic background, age, gender, sexual preference, or race. In every respect, these co-cultures share many of the same characteristics found in any culture. They often have a specialized language system, shared values, a collective worldview, and common communication patterns. These diverse co-cultures have the potential to bring new experiences and ways of interacting to a communication encounter, and many of these behaviors are often confusing and baffling to members of the dominant culture. Anyone one who is not aware of and does not understand the unique experiences of these co-cultures can experience serious communication problems.

As the United States continues its development into a pluralistic and multicultural society, there is an increased need and opportunity for effective communication between the dominant culture and the co-cultures as well as among the co-cultures themselves. Effective communication can come about only when we remove prejudice and stereotypes from our lives and develop an understanding of what each culture is really like. Frequently, prejudices and stereotypes lead to assumptions about members of co-cultures that are false, hurtful, and insulting.

Admittedly, there are many more co-cultures than we have included here. Our selection was based on three considerations. First, limited space and the necessity for efficiency prohibited a long list of co-cultures. Second, we wanted to include some social communities that are frequently in conflict with the dominant culture. And third, we wanted to emphasize the co-cultures with which you are most likely to interact. To this end, we selected a representation of the major co-cultures resident in the United States. We should add, however, that some additional co-cultures will be examined in subsequent chapters as we explore the verbal and nonverbal dimensions of intercultural communication.

In the first reading of the chapter—"Who's Got the Room at the Top?"—Edith A. Folb discusses the concept of intracultural communication, where members of the same dominant culture hold slightly different values. Folb sees the crucial characteristics of this form of communication as the interrelationships of power, dominance, and nondominance as they are manifested in the particular cultures. She carefully examines these variables as they apply to African Americans, Native Americans, Mexican Americans, women, the aged, the physically challenged, and other groups that have been "caste-marked and more often negatively identified when it comes to issues of power, dominance, and social control."

The next essay leads us to an examination of communication involving the African American co-culture. In "An African American Communication Perspective," Sidney A. Ribeau, John R. Baldwin, and Michael L. Hecht examine the communicative style of the African American. The authors are particularly concerned with identifying satisfying and dissatisfying conversational themes, conversational strategies, and communication effectiveness from an intercultural communication perspective. They identify seven issues—negative stereotypes, acceptance, personal expressiveness, authenticity, understanding, goal attainment, and power dynamics—that impact intercultural communication. They then offer several strategies for improving intercultural communication between the African American community and the dominant culture.

In recent years, it has become apparent that disabled persons are a co-culture in our society. Although there are approximately 14 million disabled Americans between the ages of 16 and 64, they often find themselves either cut off from or misunderstood by the dominant culture. Dawn O. Braithwaite and Charles A. Braithwaite look at some of the reasons for this isolation in "Understanding Communication of Persons with Disabilities as Cultural Communication." They specifically examine how disabled persons view their communication relationships with able-bodied persons. Reviewing research embracing more than one hundred in-depth interviews with physically disabled adults, the Braithwaites have discovered that these disabled people go through a process of redefinition that involves three steps: (1) redefining the self as part of a "new" culture, (2) redefining disability, and (3) redefining disability for the dominant culture. By becoming familiar with these steps, we can improve our communication with members of the disabled co-culture.

The deaf culture, although reflecting many of the characteristics that define a culture (a specialized language, values, beliefs, nonverbal communication, etc.), has only recently been fully recognized as a domestic co-culture in the United States. In an essay titled "Cultural Patterns of Deaf People," Linda A. Siple offers us valuable insights into this very special co-culture so that "conflict can be reduced and mutual respect and understanding enhanced." To contribute to that enhancement, she offers material that addresses the communication elements of perception, verbal processes, and nonverbal processes. In the area of perception, Siple examines two important topics. First, how the visual channel becomes important for the deaf. And second, she discusses the key values of the deaf culture in face-to-face communication (directness, openness, and pride). Her analysis of verbal processes includes a discussion of language, unequivocal communication, communication of sound, and names signs. To better appreciate how the deaf use nonverbal communication, Siple examines the elements of time, eye contact, and touching.

Our next essay, by Joseph P. Goodwin, is titled "Communication and Identification in the Gay Subculture." There can be little doubt that in the last two decades the gay culture has emerged as one of most vocal and visible groups on the American scene. As is the case with all co-cultures, gays have evolved a highly specialized series of communication patterns. These patterns, which help gays identify other members of the co-culture, also contribute to strong feelings of group solidarity. Goodwin highlights five of these patterns as a means of helping understand this co-culture. Specifically, he looks at gay conversation (ambiguity, puns, inversions, and double entendres), paralinguistic features (intonation, pitch, and juncture), argot, humor, and nonverbal communication (the wearing of visual cues, eye contact, and proxemics).

In the last decade, much attention has been focused on a social community previously taken for granted by many segments of American society—women. Because women are so much a part of everyone's perceptual field and daily life, very few scholars, until recently, studied this group as a co-culture. Yet the experiences of females, regardless of the culture, often produce unique ways of perceiving the world and interacting in that world. Events such as the Paula Jones sexual harassment allegations against President Clinton; successful campaigns for local, state, and national political office by women in unprecedented numbers; and the advancement of women in the business setting, have produced a situation that now confirms that the co-culture of women does indeed exist, and that society must give serious consideration to this feminine culture and how it differs from the masculine culture.

One major difference between the feminine and masculine communities is their communicative behaviors. These differences, and some of the reasons behind them, are the major concern of Julia T. Wood's essay "Gender, Communication, and Culture." Wood points out the conceptual differences between sex and gender, explains how communication contributes to the social-symbolic construction of gender, and shows how gender differences are formed very early in life and thereby constrict gender cultures. She then provides examples of men and women in conversation demonstrating how gender differences in communicative rules and purposes lead to frequent misunderstandings. She ends by providing excellent advice on how to achieve effective communication between gender cultures.

During recent congressional debates, the well-being and security of the elderly were the focus of much attention. The vocal opposition raised to proposed changes in Social Security and Medicare by this group and its advocates (such as the American Association of Retired People) has focused national attention on the co-culture of the senior citizen. In the next essay, "Understanding the Co-Culture of the Elderly," Valerie C. McKay describes the cultural dimensions and dynamics of the elderly in the United States. She introduces us to both the positive and negative stereotypes associated with the elderly and the consequences those stereotypes have on understanding the co-culture of the elderly. She then discusses the communication aspects of grandparent–grandchild relationships and the communication dynamics prevalent in this unique intergenerational relationship.

You noticed, of course, that this chapter's subtitle included the phrase "Living in Two Cultures." Perhaps you were also aware that all the groups treated in this chapter were attempting to live in two cultures. As you would suspect, maintaining "membership" in two cultures is not an easy task. Not only are there obvious differences in language and values, but also a person living in two cultures faces problems associated with defining his or her identity. Remember that a large portion of our identity comes from our culture. In our final essay, "Voicing Identities: Somewhere in the Midst of Two Worlds," we look at some of the problems faced by people who, by either chance or design, are asked to redefine or reevaluate their identities because they are "living in two cultures." Through the use of personal narratives, four college students from four different cultures help us understand some of these problems. The four stories they tell, although all different in context and setting, enable us to see the coping strategies used by people who search for their identities while "living in two cultures."

Who's Got the Room at the Top? Issues of Dominance and Nondominance in Intracultural Communication

Edith A. Folb

"If a phenomenon is important, it is perceived, and, being perceived, it is labeled." So notes Nathan Kantrowitz, sociologist and student of language behavior. Nowhere is Kantrowitz's observation more apparent than in that realm of communication studies concerned with the correlates and connections between culture and communication—what the editors of this text have termed "intercultural communication." Our contemporary technology has brought us into immediate and voyeuristic contact with diverse cultures and customs, from Stone Age dwellers of South America's rain forests to modern-age inhabitants along the information superhighway. Domestic liberation movements of the past and the diverse voices of present-day immigrants continue to focus our attention on the existence and needs of a multiplicity of groups within our own nation. So the phenomenon of culture-linked communication is pervasive among us. And, as scholars concerned with culture and communication, we have tried to identify and characterize what we see. This attempt to "label the goods," as it were, has generated, over time, a profusion of semantic labels and categories—international communication, cross-cultural communication, intercultural communication, co-cultural communication, multicultural communication, intracultural communication, interracial communication, inter-ethnic communication. What we perceive to be important, we label.

Some may chide us for our penchant for classifications—an example of Aristotelian excessiveness, they may say. However, I see it as a genuine attempt to understand what we do individually and collectively, what we focus on within the field of communication studies. I believe this effort to characterize what we do serves a useful function: It continually prods us to examine and expand our vision of what culture-linked communication is, and, at the same time, it helps us bring into sharper focus the dimensions and differences within this area of study. As Samovar and Porter (1994) remind us, "there is a need to specify the nature of intercultural communication and to recognize that various viewpoints see it somewhat differently . . . that there are a variety of ways in which the topic of intercultural communication can be explored" (p. 2). It is my intention in this essay to look at the correlates and connections between culture and communication from a particular viewpoint, one that examines the properties and issues of dominance and nondominance in communicative exchange. The essay is speculative and sometimes polemical. And the focus of my interest and discussion is the realm of intracultural communication.

THE CONCEPT OF INTRACULTURAL COMMUNICATION

The label "intracultural communication" is not unknown within the field of communication studies, although it is one that has not been widely used. Early on, Sitaram and Cogdell (1976) identified intracultural communication as "the type of communication that takes place between members of the same dominant culture, but with slightly differing values" (p. 28). They go on to explain that there are groups ("subcultures") within the dominant culture who hold a minimal number of values that differ from the mainstream, as well as from other subgroups. These differences are not sufficient to identify them as separate cultures but are diverse enough to set them apart from each other and the culture at large. "Communication between members of such subcultures is intracultural communication" (p. 28).

In another vein, Sarbaugh (1988) saw intracultural communication as an indicator of the degree of cultural experience shared (or not shared) by two people—the more culturally homogeneous the participants, the greater the level of "intraculturalness" surrounding the communicative act. For Sitaram and Cogdell, then, intracultural communication is a phenomenon that operates within a given culture among its members; for Sarbaugh, it is a measure of homogeneity that may well transcend country or culture.

More recently, Byrd (1993) has looked at intracultural communication as that which "occurs among people who are citizens of the same geopolitical system, and also hold membership in one or more tributary groups" (p. 1). Byrd goes on to identify tributary groups in terms of specific characteristics that distinguish them from the "power dominant/general population"—characteristics such as race, ethnicity, religion, gender, sexual orientation, age and ableness (p. 1).

Like Sitaram and Cogdell, I see intracultural communication as a phenomenon that functions within a single designated culture. However, like Sarbaugh, I am concerned with the particular variables within that context that importantly influence the degree and kind of cultural homogeneity or heterogeneity that can and do exist among members of the culture. Along with Byrd, the variables of particular interest to me are those which illuminate and underscore the interrelationship of power, dominance, and nondominance in a particular culture.[1] Finally, I believe that the concept of hierarchy, as it functions within a culture, has a deep impact on matters of power, dominance, and nondominance and, therefore, on both the form and content of intracultural communication.

As a backdrop for the discussion of dominance and nondominance in an intracultural context, I would like to formulate a frame of reference within which to view the discussion.

A FRAME OF REFERENCE FOR INTRACULTURAL COMMUNICATION

Society and Culture

Thomas Hobbes, the seventeenth-century political philosopher, left us an intriguing legacy in his work *Leviathan*. He posited a hypothetical starting point for humankind's march to political and social organization. He called it "the state of nature." In this presocietal state, the biggest club ruled. Kill or be killed was the prevailing modus operandi. Somewhere along the evolutionary road, our ancestors began to recognize a need to change their ways—if any of them were to survive for very long. The principle of enlightened self-interest became the name of the game. Our forebears, however grudgingly, began to curb their inclination to kill, maim, steal, or otherwise aggress upon others and joined together for mutual survival and benefit. The move was one of expediency, not altruism. "Do unto others as you would have them do unto you," whatever its religious import, is a reiteration of the principle of enlightened self-interest.

So, this aggregate of beings came together in order to survive and, in coming together, gave up certain base instincts, drives, and predilections. "Society" was formed. But it was not sufficient merely to form society; it must be maintained. Controls needed to be established to ensure its stability. Thus, the social contract was enacted. It was, indeed, the social contract that ensured mutual support, protection, welfare, and survival for the society's members—"law and order."

Those who may scoff at this postulated state of nature need only turn on their television on any given night to see it in very real terms—in Haiti, in Bosnia, on the angry streets of a riot-racked Los Angeles, in daily occurrences of drive-by-warfare. The media show us, in all too brutal detail, the rapidity with which a society's fabric can disintegrate and we can return to the force of the club.

But let us continue with the telling of humankind's tale. Social maintenance and control did not ensure the perpetuation of the society as an intact entity, carrying along its cumulative and collective experiences, knowledge, beliefs, and attitudes, as well as the emergent relationship of self to other, to the group, to the universe, to matters of time and space. That is, it did not ensure the perpetuation of society's accoutrements—its culture. Institutions and structures were needed to house, as it were, the trappings of culture. So, culture was embodied not only in the precepts passed on from one generation to another, but also in the artifacts created by society to safeguard its culture. Looked at in a different light, culture is both a blueprint for continued societal survival and the pervasive cement that holds the social mosaic together. Culture daily tells us and shows us how to be in the universe, and it informs future generations how to be.[2]

From the moment we begin life in this world, we are instructed in the cultural ways that govern and hold together our society, ways that ensure its perpetuation. Indeed, the social contract that binds us to our society and our culture from the moment of birth is neither of our own choice nor of our own design. For example, we are labeled by others almost immediately—John, Jamal, Mika, Maria. Our gender is determined at once and we are, accordingly, swaddled in appropriate colors and treated in appropriate ways.[3]

As we grow from childhood, the socialization process is stepped up and we rapidly internalize the rules of appropriate and inappropriate societal behavior. Family, religion, education, recreation, health care, and many other cultural institutions reinforce our learning and shape and regulate our behaviors and thoughts so they are orderly and comprehensible to other members of our society. Through the socialization process the human animal is transformed into the social animal. Thus, society is maintained through instruction and indoctrination in the ways of the culture.

But the question that pricks and puzzles the mind is, Whose culture is passed on? Whose social order is maintained? Whose beliefs and values are deemed appropriate? Whose norms, mores, and folkways are invoked?

Hierarchy, Power, and Dominance

In most societies, as we know them, there is a hierarchy of status and power. By its very nature, hierarchy implies an ordering process, a sense of ranking and rating of those being ordered. Our own vernacular vocabulary abounds with references to hierarchy and concomitant status and power: "top gun," "top dog," "main man," "king of the mountain," "numero uno."

High status and attendant power may be accorded to those among us who are seen or believed to be great warriors or hunters; those invested with magical, divine, or special powers; those who are deemed wise; or those who are in possession of important, valued and/or vital societal resources and goods. Of course, power and high status are not necessarily—or even usually—accorded to these specially designated members of the society in some automatic fashion. Power, control, and subsequent high status are often forcibly wrested from others and forcibly maintained. Not everyone abides by the social contract, and strong-arm rule often prevails, as conquered, colonized, and enslaved people know too well.

Whatever the basis for determining the hierarchy, the fact of its existence in a society assures the evolution and continued presence of a power elite—those at the top of the social hierarchy who accrue and possess what the society deems valuable or vital. And, in turn, the presence of a power elite ensures an asymmetrical relationship among the members of the society. In fact, power is often defined as the ability to get others to do what you want and the resources to force them to do your bidding, if they resist—the asymmetrical relationship in its extreme form.

But the perpetuation of the power elite through force is not the most effective or efficient way of ensuring one's position at the top of the hierarchy. It is considerably more effective to institute, encourage, and/or perpetuate those aspects of culture—knowledge, experiences, beliefs, values, patterns of social organization, artifacts—that subtly and manifestly reinforce and ensure the continuation of the power elite and its asymmetrical relationship within the society. Though we may dismiss Nazism as a malignant ideology, we should attend to the fact that Hitler well understood the maintenance of the power elite through the manipulation and control of culture—culture as propaganda.

Though I would not imply that all power elites maintain themselves in such an overtly manipulative way, I would at least suggest that the powerful in many societies—our own included—go to great lengths to maintain their positions of power and what those positions bring them. And to that end, they support, reinforce, and, indeed, create those particular cultural precepts and artifacts that are likely to guarantee their continued power. To the extent that the culture reflects implicitly or expressly the need and desires of the power elite to sustain itself, it becomes a vehicle for propaganda. Thus, cultural precepts and artifacts that govern such matters as social organization and behavior, values, beliefs, and the like can often be seen as rules and institutions that sustain the few at the expense of the many.

So, we come back to the question of whose rules, whose culture? I would suggest that when we in communication studies refer to the "dominant culture," we are, in fact, not talking about numbers. That is why the label "minorities" is misleading when we refer to cultural or demographic groups within the larger society. For example, women in the United States are not the numerical minority—quite the contrary. Yet they are far from being "in the majority" among the true power elite.[4] In fact, when we talk about the concept of dominant culture, we are really talking about power—those who *dominate* culture, those who historically or traditionally have had the most persistent and far-reaching impact on culture, on what we think and say, on what we believe and do in our society. We are talking about the culture of the minority and, by extension, the structures and institutions (social, political, economic, legal, religious, and so on) that maintain the power of this minority. Finally, we are talking about rules of appropriate and inappropriate behavior, thought, speech, and action for the many that preserve power for the few. Dominant culture, therefore, significantly reflects the precepts and artifacts of those who dominate culture and is not necessarily, or even usually, a reference to numbers, but rather to power. Though those who "look like" the power elite can be said to be "cultural beneficiaries" of the system, it is still those who dominate culture who call the shots—and reap the biggest rewards.

So, coming full circle, I would suggest that our socialization process, our social introduction to this aggregate of people who form society, is an introduction to a rule-governed milieu of asymmetrical societal organization and relationship, and the communicative behaviors and practices found there are likewise asymmetrical in nature. As the witticism goes, "All men (perhaps even women) are created equal—some are just more equal than others."

Given this frame of reference, I would now like to explore some definitions and concepts that, I believe, emerge from this perspective. It is my hope that the discussion will provide the reader with another way to look at intracultural communication.

A NOMENCLATURE FOR INTRACULTURAL COMMUNICATION

The Concept of Nondominance

As already indicated, I view intracultural communication as a phenomenon that operates within a given cultural context. However, my particular focus, as suggested, is not a focus on numbers but an attention to dominance, nondominance, and power in the cultural setting. That is, how do nondominant groups intersect and interact with the dominant culture membership (with those who enact the precepts and support the institutions and systems of the power elite)? For purposes of discussion and analysis, I will take most of my examples from the geopolitical configuration called the United States.

By "nondominant groups" I mean those constellations of people who have not historically or traditionally had continued access to or influence upon or within the dominant culture's social, political, legal, economic, and/or religious structures and institutions. Again, by dominant culture, I mean those who dominate culture. Nondominant groups include people of color, women, gays and lesbians, the physically challenged, and the aged poor, to name some of the most prominent. I use the expression "nondominant" to characterize these people because, as suggested, I am referring to power and dominance, not numbers and dominance. Within the United States, those most likely to hold and control positions of real—not token—power and those who have the greatest potential ease of access to power and high status are still generally white, male, able-bodied, heterosexual, and youthful in appearance, if not in age.[5]

Nondominant people are also those who, in varying degrees and various ways, have been "invisible" within the society of which they are a part and at the same time bear a visible caste mark. Furthermore, it is this mark of caste identity that is often consciously or habitually assigned low or negative status by members of the dominant culture.

The dimensions of invisibility and marked visibility are keen indicators of the status hierarchy in a given society. In his classic novel, *The Invisible Man*, Ralph Ellison instructs us in the lesson that nondominant people—in this instance, African Americans—are figuratively "invisible." They are seen by the dominant culture as no one, nobody, and therefore go unacknowledged and importantly unperceived.[6] Furthermore, nondominant peoples are often relegated to object status rather than human status. They are viewed as persons of "no consequence," literally and metaphorically. Expressions such as "If you've seen one, you've seen them all," "They all look alike to me," and "If you put a bag over their heads, it doesn't matter who you screw" attest to this level of invisibility and dehumanization of nondominant peoples (people of color or women, for instance). Indeed, one need only look at the dominant culture's slang repertory for a single nondominant group, women, to see the extent of this object status: "tail," "piece of ass," "side of beef," "hole," "gash," "slit."

At the same time that nondominant peoples are socially invisible, they are often visibly caste-marked. Though we tend to think of caste in terms, say, of East Indian culture, we can clearly apply the concept to our own culture. One of the important dimensions of a caste system is that it is hereditary—you are born into a given caste and are usually marked for life as a member. In fact, we are all born into a caste, we are all caste-marked. Indeed, some of us bear multiple caste marks. In the United States, the most visible marks of caste relate to gender, race, age, and the degree to which one is able-bodied.

As East Indians do, we also assign low to high status and privilege to people within our society. The fact that this assignment of status and privilege may be active or passive, conscious or unconscious, malicious or unthinking does not detract from the reality of the act. And one of the major determinants of status, position, and caste marking relates back to who has historically or traditionally had access to or influence upon or within the power elite and its concomitant structures and institutions. So, historically, African Americans, Native Americans, Hispanics, women, the aged poor, the physically challenged have at best been neutrally caste-marked and more often negatively identified when it comes to issues of power, dominance, and social control.

Low status has been assigned to those people whom society views as somehow "stigmatized." Indeed, we have labels to identify such stigmatiza-

tion: "deviant," "handicapped," "abnormal," "substandard," "different"—that is, different from those who dominate. As already suggested, it is the white, male, heterosexual, able-bodied, youthful person who both sets the standards for caste marking and is the human yardstick by which people within the United States still are measured and accordingly treated. As Porter and Samovar (1994) remind us, in the instance of race: "Although there has been a lessening of overt racial violence since the 1960s, the enduring racist-ethnocentric belief system has not been appreciably affected. . . . The result is a structured domination of people of color by the white Anglo power structure" (p. 6). Again, our language is a telling repository for illuminating status as it relates to subordination in the social hierarchy: "Stay in your place," "Don't get out of line," "Know your place," "A woman's place is on her back," and "Know your station in life" are just a few sample phrases.

It is inevitable that nondominant peoples will experience—indeed be subjected to and suffer from—varying degrees of fear, denial, and self-hatred of their caste marking. Frantz Fanon's (1963) vivid characterization of the "colonized native"—the oppressed native who has so internalized the power elite's perception of the norm that he or she not only serves and speaks for the colonial elite but is also often more critical and oppressive of her or his caste than is the colonial—reveals this depth of self-hatred and denial.

In a parallel vein, the concept of "passing," which relates to a person of color attempting to "pass for" white, is a statement of self-denial. Implicit in the act of passing is the acceptance, if not the belief, that "white is right" in this society, and the closer one can come to the likeness of the privileged caste, the more desirable and comfortable one's station in life will be. So, people of color have passed for white—just as Jews have passed for gentiles or gay males and lesbians have passed for straight, often with the fear of being discovered "for what they are." Physical impairment, too, has often been hidden from public view by those so challenged. Even so powerful a figure as a president of the United States—Franklin Delano Roosevelt—refused to be photographed in any way that would picture him as a "cripple."

If the act of passing is a denial of one's caste, the process of "coming out of the closet" is a conscious acceptance of one's caste. It is an important political and personal statement of power, a vivid metaphor that literally marks a rite of passage. Perhaps the most striking acknowledgment of one's caste marking in our society relates to sexual or affectional preference. For gay males or lesbians to admit their respective preferences is for them to consciously take on an identity that mainstream society has deemed abnormal and deviant—when measured against the society's standard of what is appropriate. They become, quite literally, "marked people."

In an important way, most liberation or freedom movements are devoted to having their membership come out of the closet. That is, these movements demand not only to have their people heard and empowered by the power elite, but also to have their membership reclaim and assert their identity and honor their caste. Historically, slogans embraced by domestic liberation movements in the United States have told the story of positive identification with one's caste: "Black is beautiful," "Brown power," "Sisterhood is powerful," "Gay pride," "I am an Indian and proud of it." More graphic and contemporary assertions of caste identification can be seen in the "inverting" of society's pejorative labels into positive, "in-your-face" marks of identity.[7] So, for example, there is the gay activist group, Queer Nation, or the African American rap group, NWA—Niggers With Attitude.

The nature and disposition of the social hierarchy in a given society, such as the United States, is reflected not only in the caste structure, but also in the class structure and the role prescriptions and expectations surrounding caste and class. Although the power structure in the United States is a complex and multileveled phenomenon, its predominant, generating force is economic. That is, the power elite is an elite that controls the material resources and goods in this country as well as the means and manner of production and distribution. Though one of our national fictions is that the United States is a classless society, we have, in fact, a well-established class structure based largely on economic power and control. When we talk of lower, middle, and upper classes in this country, we are not usually talking about birth or origins, but about power and control over material resources and the attendant wealth, privilege, and high status.

There is even a kind of status distinction made within the upper-class society in this country that again relates to wealth and power, but in a temporal rather than a quantitative way—how long one has had wealth, power, and high-class status. So distinctions are made between the old rich (the Harrimans, the Gores, the Pews) and the new rich (the Hunt family, Norton Simon, and their ilk).

Class, then, is intimately bound up with matters of caste. Not all, or even most, members of our society have the opportunity—let alone the caste credentials—to get a "piece of the action." It is no accident of nature that many of the nondominant peoples in this country are also poor peoples. Nor is it surprising that nondominant groups have been historically the unpaid, low-paid, and/or enslaved workforce for the economic power elite.

Finally, role prescriptions are linked to both matters of status and expectations in terms of one's perceived status, class, and caste. A role can be defined simply as a set of behaviors. The set of behaviors we ascribe to a given role is culture-bound and indicative of what has been designated as appropriate within the culture vis-à-vis that role. They are prescriptive, not descriptive, behaviors. We hold certain behavioral expectations for certain roles. It is a mark of just how culture-bound and prescriptive these roles are when someone is perceived to behave inappropriately—for example, the mother who gives up custody of her children in order to pursue her career has "stepped out of line."

Furthermore, we see certain roles as appropriate or inappropriate to a given caste. Though another of our national myths—the Horatio Alger myth—tells us that there is room at the top for the industrious, bright go-getter, the truth of the matter is that there is room at the top if you are appropriately caste-marked (that is, are white, male, able-bodied, and so on).

The resistance, even outright hostility, nondominant peoples have encountered when they aspire to or claim certain occupational roles, for example, is a mark of the power elite's reluctance to relinquish those positions that have been traditionally associated with privileged status and high caste and class ranking. The concept of the "glass ceiling," so popular in today's vocabulary, is an apt metaphor to describe not only the sense of thwarted advancement in the workplace, but also the implied resistance of the power elite to incursions from the up-and-coming "outsider." In the public arena, the idea of the presidency being held by a member of a visible, nondominant group is still just that—an idea. Whether or not a popular public figure, like Colin Powell, will or can transform idea to reality is still to be seen.[8] For that matter, even the vice-presidency has not been held by a woman or a person of color.

The cultural prescription to keep nondominant peoples "in their place" is reinforced by and reinforces what I refer to as the "subterranean self"—the culture-bound collection of prejudices, stereotypes, values, and beliefs that each of us embraces and employs to justify our world view and the place of people in that world. It is, after all, our subterranean selves that provide fuel to fire the normative in our lives—what roles people ought and ought not to perform, what and why certain individuals are ill- or well-equipped to carry out certain roles, and why people should be kept in their places, as we see them (through righteously stated rationalizations). Again, it should be remembered that those who dominate the culture reinforce and tacitly or openly encourage the perpetuation of those cultural prejudices, stereotypes, values, and beliefs that maintain the status quo; that is, the asymmetrical nature of the social hierarchy.

Those who doubt the fervent desire of the power elite to maintain things as they are need only ponder the intense and prolonged resistance to the defunct Equal Rights Amendment. If women are already "equal," why not make their equality a matter of record? Recall the hue and cry for an "English as Official Language" Amendment. After more than 200 years without such a "statement" on the books, why now? Perhaps it's a response to the perceived threat—linguistic and cultural—from the influx of "all those foreign immigrants" (read immigrants of color). And whose civil rights would be "secured" by the proposed California Civil Rights initiative?

The foregoing discussion has been an attempt to illuminate the meaning of nondominance and the position of the nondominant person within our society. By relating status in the social hierarchy to matters of caste, class, and role, it has been my intention to highlight what it means to be a nondominant person within a culture that is dominated by the cultural precepts and artifacts of a power elite. It has also been my intention to suggest that the concept of "dominant culture" is something of a fiction, as we in communication studies traditionally use it. Given my perspective, it is more accurate to talk about those who dominate a culture rather than a dominant culture per se. Finally, I have attempted to point out that cultural dominance is not necessarily, or even usually, a matter of the numbers of people in a given society, but of those who have real power in a society.

Geopolitics

The viewpoint being developed in this essay highlights still another facet of dominance and nondominance as it relates to society and the culture it generates and sustains—namely, the geopolitical aspect. The United States is not merely a territory with certain designated boundaries—a geographical entity—but is also a geopolitical configuration. It is a country whose history reflects the clear-cut interrelationship of geography, politics, economics, and the domination and control of people. For example, the westward movement and the subsequent takeover of indigenous peoples' lands and chunks of Mexico were justified by this country's doctrine of Manifest Destiny, not unlike the way Hitler's expansionism was justified by the Nazi doctrine of "geopolitik." It is not accident that the doctrine of Manifest Destiny coincides with the rapid growth and development of U.S. industrialization. The U.S. power elite wanted more land in which to expand and grow economically, so it created a rationalization to secure it.

Perhaps nowhere is a dominant culture's ethnocentrism (the ethnocentrism of those who dominate culture) more apparent than in the missionary-like work carried on by its members—whether it be to "civilize" the natives (that is, to impose the conquerors' cultural baggage on them), to "educate them in the ways of the white man," or to "Americanize" them. Indeed, the very term America is a geopolitical label as we use it. It presumes that those who inhabit the United States are the center of the Western hemisphere, indeed its only residents.[9] Identifying ourselves as "Americans" and our geopolitical entity as "America"—in light of the peoples who live to the north and south of our borders—speaks to both our economic dominance in this hemisphere and our ethnocentrism.

Identifying the United States in geopolitical terms is to identify it as a conqueror and controller of other peoples and suggests both the probability of nondominant groups of people within that territory and a polarized, even hostile, relationship between these groups and those who dominate culture. What Rich and Ogawa (1982) have pointed out in their model of interracial communication is applicable to most nondominant peoples: "As long as a power relationship exists between cultures where one has subdued and dominated the other . . . hostility, tension and strain are introduced into the communicative situation" (p. 46).

Not only were Native American lands, as well as parts of Mexico, conquered and brought under the colonial rule of the United States, but in its industrial expansionism, the United States also physically enslaved black Africans to work on the farms and plantations of the South. Throughout its short history, the United States also has economically enslaved large numbers of East European immigrants, Chinese, Irish, and Mexicans in its factories, on its railroads, and in its mines and fields through low wages and long work hours. It co-opted the cottage industries of the home and brought women and children into the factories under abysmal conditions and the lowest of wages.

And economic servitude continues today. Refugees, fleeing from war, poverty, and oppressive regimes in East and Southeast Asia, Latin America, and the Caribbean have become the invisible, low-paid nannies, maids, day laborers, and caretakers of the old and sick. So, the pool of cheap labor stays full and "in place."

Indeed, many of the nondominant peoples in this country today are the very same ones whom the powerful have historically colonized, enslaved, disenfranchised, dispossessed, discounted, and relegated to poverty and low caste and class status. The asymmetrical relationship between the conqueror and the conquered continues uninterrupted. Although the form of oppression may change through time, the fact of oppression—and coexistent nondominance—remains.

It has been my desire throughout this essay to speculate about the complex ways in which society, culture, position, and place in the societal hierarchy affect and are affected by the matters of domi-

nance, power, and social control. To this end, I have chosen to identify and characterize configurations of people within a society not only along a cultural axis but along a socioeconomic and a geopolitical axis as well. I have tried to reexamine some of the concepts and definitions employed in discussions of culture-linked communication in a particular light. And I have chosen the issues and conditions surrounding dominance and nondominance as points of departure and return. As I said at the beginning of this essay, the content is intended to encourage ongoing dialogue and exchange about the conditions and constraints surrounding intracultural communication.

Notes

1. See Folb (1980) for another perspective on the intersection of power, dominance, and nondominance as they operate within a discrete microcultural group, the world of the African American teenager, living in the inner city.

2. For a fascinating account of how and what kind of culture is transmitted from person to person, see Margaret Mead's classic text *Culture and Commitment* (1970).

3. J. T. Wood's book, *Gendered Lives: Communication, Gender and Culture* (1994), provides an informative and lively discussion of the ways in which females and males are catalogued, characterized, and compartmentalized through their communicative behavior. She focuses on the intersection of gender, culture, and communication as it affects what we say and do, as well as how others perceive us.

4. Contrary to the belief that white males are fast losing power in the United States, they are still very much in the "cat bird seat." In a *Newsweek* article (1993) entitled "White Male Paranoia," the writers bring this fact into sharp relief: "It's still a statistical piece of cake being a white man, at least in comparison with being anything else. White males make up just 39.2 percent of the population [in the U.S.], yet they account for 82.5 percent of the Forbes 400 (folks worth at least $265 million), 77 percent of Congress, 92 percent of state governors, 70 percent of tenured college faculty, almost 90 percent of daily-newspaper edi-

tors, 77 percent of TV news directors. They dominate just about everything but NOW and the NAACP" (p. 49).

5. In a country as youth conscious as the United States, advanced age is seen as a liability, not as a mark of honor and wisdom as it is in other cultures. For example, whatever other reservations people had about Ronald Reagan's political aspirations in 1980, the one most discussed was his age. His political handlers went to great lengths—as did Reagan himself—to "prove" he was young in spirit and energy, if not in years. It was important that he align himself as closely as possible with the positive mark of youth we champion and admire in this country. The same scenario is repeating itself in the 1996 election. Septuagenarian Bob Dole's handlers are trying to package him much the same as Reagan was some 16 years ago.

6. It is no mere coincidence that a common thread which binds together the domestic liberation movements of the past with the immigrant protest groups of the present in the United States is the demand to be seen, heard, and empowered.

7. Grace Sims Holt was one of the first to talk about the concept of inversion as an empowering force in language use. See her pioneering article "'Inversion' in Black Community," in Kochman (1972).

8. The issue of Colin Powell's race "will matter"—at least, according to a pre-election *Newsweek* article: "Even today the presidency is a mythic office and letting a black man be 'daddy' is a huge Freudian leap for many white Americans. (Recall that voters told pollsters in 1982 that they preferred Tom Bradley, who was black, for governor of California, but enough of them apparently changed their minds in the privacy of the polling booth to cost him the election.)" (September 25, 1995).

9. The bumper sticker, "Get the United States Out of North America," was a pointed reference to U.S. hemispheric self-centeredness.

References

Byrd, M. L. (1993). *The Intracultural Communication Book.* New York: McGraw-Hill.

Fanon, F. (1963). *Wretched of the Earth.* New York: Grove Press.

Folb, E. A. (1980). *Runnin' Down Some Lines: The Language and Culture of Black Teenagers.* Cambridge: Harvard University Press.

Holt, G. S. (1972). "'Inversion' in Black Community." In T. Kochman (Ed.), *Rappin' and Stylin' Out: Communication in Urban Black America.* Urbana: University of Illinois Press.

Porter, R. E., and Samovar, L. A. (1994). "An Introduction to Intercultural Communication." In L. A. Samovar and R. E. Porter, *Intercultural Communication: A Reader,* 7th ed., 4–26. Belmont, Calif.: Wadsworth.

Rich, A. L., and Ogawa, D. M. (1982). "Intercultural and Interracial Communication: An Analytical Approach." In L. A. Samovar and R. E. Porter (Eds.), *Intercultural Communication: A Reader,* 3d ed. Belmont, Calif.: Wadsworth.

Samovar, L. A., and Porter, R. E. (Eds.). (1994). *Intercultural Communication: A Reader,* 7th ed. Belmont, Calif.: Wadsworth.

Sarbaugh, L. E. (1988). *Intercultural Communication,* 2d ed. New Brunswick: Transaction Books.

Sitaram, K. S., and Cogdell, R. T. (1976). *Foundations of Intercultural Communication.* Columbus, Ohio: Merrill.

Wood, J. T. (1994). *Gendered Lives: Communication, Gender and Culture.* Belmont, Calif.: Wadsworth.

Concepts and Questions

1. How can you approach interaction with members of co-cultures without making erroneous assumptions that may be harmful to their sense of self-worth?

2. What does Folb mean by the term *intracultural communication?* How does this form of communication differ from intercultural communication?

3. What role or influence do hierarchy, power, and dominance have in the process of intercultural communication?

4. What does Folb mean by *nondominant groups?* How does the role or position of nondominance affect one's position in the larger culture?

5. Can you think of some co-cultures not mentioned by Folb that fall into her category of nondominant groups?

6. How do you think someone from a foreign culture would respond to one of our co-cultures? Be specific.

7. Why do you think that "in most societies there is a hierarchy of status and power"? Is this hierarchy good? Is it necessary?
8. Why does the dominant cultural control so much of what we think and believe?
9. Do you believe Folb is correct when she asserts that "it is inevitable that nondominant people will experience—indeed be subjected to and suffer from—varying degrees of fear, denial, and self-hatred of the caste marking?"
10. How would you set about trying to make people realize that their stereotypes of other cultures and co-cultures are probably false and that they need to be changed or eliminated?

An African American Communication Perspective

SIDNEY A. RIBEAU
JOHN R. BALDWIN
MICHAEL L. HECHT

African American communication is as complex as the culture from which it emerges. Taken from the shores of Africa, the enslaved captives were forced to create a means of expression consistent with an African cultural tradition, yet responsive to life in the new world. The fusion of past traditions with slavery, and post-slavery experiences in the rural South and North, created a unique ethnic culture for the group known as African Americans.

The communicative style of African American ethnic culture is captured in a number of studies that investigate linguistic characteristics, social relationships, and verbal and nonverbal messages. This early research, which is primarily descriptive, provides an introduction to a rich and promising line of inquiry. Our work expands the discussion of African American discourse to include empirical investigations of the interpersonal dimensions that characterize this unique ethnic communication system. We are particularly interested in (1) the identifications of satisfying and dissatisfying conversational themes, (2) conversational improvement strategies, and (3) communication effectiveness. A few important assumptions support our work and provide a context for this research.

This original essay first appeared in the seventh edition. All rights reserved. Permission to reprint must be obtained from the authors and the publisher. Sidney Ribeau is Vice President for Academic Affairs at California State Polytechnic University, Pomona, John R. Baldwin is a Graduate Associate at Arizona State University, and Michael L. Hecht teaches in the Department of Communication at Arizona State University.

UNDERLYING ASSUMPTIONS

We consider communication to be problematic—an interactive event during which persons assign meanings to messages and jointly create identities and social reality. This process is multi-dimensional and extremely complex. Attribution of meaning to symbols requires the interpretation of messages and negotiation of social worlds. The process is replete with the potential for failure which is magnified when ethno-cultural factors are introduced. Ethnic cultures consist of cognitive (for example, values, beliefs, norms) and material (for example, food, dress, symbols) characteristics that distinguish them from mainstream American culture. For successful communication to occur, these potential problems must be anticipated and managed.

Here we use an interpretive approach that utilizes the perceptions of cultural actors to explain their communicative behavior. The descriptions and narrative accounts provided by interactions enable one to glimpse a world normally reserved for members of the shared community. It is this world that we seek to unfold.

Culture and ethnicity are the concepts that govern our exploration of African American communication. **Culture** consists of the shared cognitive and material items that forge a group's identity and ensure its survival. Culture is created, shared, and transmitted through communication. **Ethnicity** pertains to the traditions, heritage, and ancestry that define a people. It is particularly apparent in a group's expressive forms. (We take as axiomatic the existence of ethnic cultures in America, and recognize African American culture as a fundamental element of life in America.)

Our early work is governed by the conceptual assumptions listed, and practical concern: *research on African American communication should assist the practitioner in improving relationships between African Americans and European Americans*. It is our belief that the communication discipline has much to offer the area of human relations. This line of research is intended to make a contribution to that effort. To that end we began with studies of (1) intragroup communication issues, (2) interethnic communication issues, and (3) conversational improvement

strategies. The remainder of this paper will report our findings and discuss their implications. First, however, we frame these studies within an understanding of communication effectiveness.

COMMUNICATION EFFECTIVENESS

Many scholars have provided valuable information about what behaviors and communication people believe to be effective (Martin, 1993; Martin & Hammer, 1989; Pavitt & Haight, 1985; Ruben, 1977, 1989). "Competent" or "effective" communication has been defined in many ways (Spitzberg & Cupach, 1984; Spitzberg & Hecht, 1984; Wiemann & Bradac, 1989). One way to define **effective** behavior is that which is productive and satisfying for both partners. Communication is appropriate if it follows the rules and expectations the partners have; these expectations vary depending on the context the speakers are in or the relationship between them. The positive feelings the communicators have when their expectations are met make up the "satisfying" part of our definition (Hecht, 1978, 1984). The expectations may be met because a relationship is satisfying (McLaughlin & Cody, 1982), or because the communicators were able to function effectively in a new situation (Vause & Wiemann, 1981).

In view of effective communication, we see *communication issues* as "the agenda for effective communication held in common by members of the group" (Hecht, Collier, & Ribeau, 1993, p. 127). That is, they are aspects of communication, which, if missing, pose problems for the communication; they are expectations about communication. Since different ethnic groups have different shared histories and ways of seeing the world, we believe that the unspoken, often subconscious, rules that one co-culture has for effective or satisfying communication may differ from those imposed by another. Further, given the impact of historical race and power relationships in the United States, it seems likely that African Americans (and other American cultures) would apply differing rules for measuring effective communications with in-group and out-group members.

INTRAGROUP COMMUNICATION ISSUES

We started by trying to understand how African Americans communicate among themselves. We asked African Americans, Mexican Americans, and European Americans to describe satisfying or dissatisfying conversations they had experienced with a member of their own ethnic group (Hecht & Ribeau, 1984). We found that the expectations of the groups were in some ways different, in others similar. Mexican Americans differed the most, with African Americans and European Americans responding more similarly.

Mexican Americans, for example, tended to seek closely bonded relationships, seeing the relationship itself as rewarding. Within this ethnic group, satisfying communication involved nonverbal communication and acceptance of self. In comparison, African Americans, and to a greater extent, European Americans, were self-oriented—that is, they saw the reward in something the other partner might provide for them, instead of in the existence of the relationship.

In keeping with this idea of potential reward, European Americans tended to look more to the future of the relationship. This echoes a previous study in which European Americans found communication with friends more satisfying when there were signs of intimacy that confirmed the future of the relationship (Hecht, 1984). At the same time, European Americans demonstrated less concern and interest for the partner in the conversation (other orientation) than did African Americans.

African Americans, on the other hand, found greater satisfaction in conversations where both partners were more involved in the topic. Intimacy was therapeutic and foundational to the relationship, and trust was highly important. While conversation was goal-oriented, at the same time it was important that ideas and feelings be exchanged. Where the Mexican Americans found bonding a priority for relationships, the African Americans surveyed found bonding conditional—to be established only if that exchange of ideas took place. In light of this, genuineness ("being real") and expressiveness were important, and were communicated through expressive style, passion, and deep involvement with the

topic. Helping one another was an integral part of satisfying interaction, supporting goal-oriented relationships. Because both parties may be trying to meet the same goals, it is necessary that those goals be clearly understood; thus, understanding is also important. African Americans found satisfaction when they knew where the conversation was going.

INTERGROUP COMMUNICATION ISSUES

We next sought to understand the agenda for effective interethnic communication—specifically, communication between blacks and whites (Hecht, Collier, & Ribeau, 1993, Hecht, Larkey, & Johnson, 1992; Hecht & Ribeau, 1987; Hecht, Ribeau, & Alberts, 1989; Hecht, Ribeau, & Sedano, 1990). In this research, we identified seven primary issues important to those African Americans studied: (1) negative stereotyping, (2) acceptance, (3) personal expressiveness, (4) authenticity, (5) understanding, (6) goal attainment, and (7) power dynamics. In describing these issues, we provide quotes from African American responses to interviews and surveys to illuminate the findings.

Negative Stereotyping

Negative stereotyping is "the use of rigid racial categories that distort an African American's individuality. This violates the concept of uniqueness, something research has shown to be very important to African Americans" (Hecht, Collier, & Ribeau, 1993). Negative stereotyping occurred in two ways. The first, and more obvious, was when European Americans in the study racially categorized African Americans—that is, when they treated them as a member of a group, or ascribed to them characteristics of the group, instead of treating them like individuals.

Indirect stereotyping occurred when European Americans talked to African Americans about what were seen to be "African American topics," such as sports or music. Some African Americans reported that this type of behavior made them want to withdraw, or caused them to see their conversational partner with disdain. One male African American, while seeing the introduction of such topics as an attempt to find common interests, saw those who brought them up as "patronizing or unaware," and felt that other African Americans felt the same way. Another type of indirect stereotyping is when European Americans ask or expect African Americans to speak on behalf of all African Americans. One participant *did feel satisfied* about her conversation because she "didn't feel put on the spot to speak for the whole of the black race." Another female was satisfied when the other person spoke to her "as another person and didn't let my color interfere with the conversation."

Acceptance

The second issue is *acceptance*, "the feeling that another accepts, confirms, and respects one's opinions" (Hecht, Collier, & Ribeau, 1993, p. 131). Frequently, African Americans did not feel accepted by European Americans. For example, some persons interviewed said African Americans sometimes try to make up for "cultural deprivation" and "talk rather than listen in order to cover up." They act "cool," flippant, or talkative, sometimes using stylized speech. Some of the participants saw these behaviors as responses to stereotypes, either in the sense that the African Americans were trying to control the conversation to preempt the stereotypes, or that they were trying to avoid recognizing them. One person strongly volunteered that African Americans are no longer concerned about what European Americans feel or accept. At the same time, many of those interviewed felt that acceptance was a characteristic of satisfying conversations. This acceptance might be shown by positive nonverbal behaviors, similar dress, feeling comfortable with the conversation, "mutual respect for each other's beliefs," and even, at times, acting "cool" or removed.

Personal Expressiveness

Personal expressiveness refers to the verbal and non-verbal expression of thoughts, ideas, or feelings. While many African Americans mentioned some aspect of expressiveness, how that expressiveness is played out varies from person to person. Some saw honesty, integrity, and the open sharing of ideas as

valuable; others felt it important to keep their feelings hidden in intercultural communications. For example, one African American woman expressed dissatisfaction with a conversation because "I maintained control and did not curse her out." Opinions are important, but the emphasis is on expressing feelings—"talking from the heart, not the head." In contrast, non-expressive European Americans might be seen as racist or standoffish. Interestingly, many participants—more females than males—expressed the need to portray a tough exterior. African Americans need to "be cool," and not let European Americans know what they are thinking or feeling. History had an impact here with some of the women participants, pointing out that African American women have had to be strong both in response to prejudice and often as the head of the household. A possible explanation for the contrasting answers is that some African Americans value toughness and "coolness" until barriers of fear and mistrust are broken down; then, it becomes important to express who one really is.

Authenticity

Authenticity is tied directly to the concept of being oneself, of being genuine. Both African and European Americans perceived authenticity on the part of their conversational partner when the other was seen as revealing personal information—being honest, "being real," "being themselves," or expressing personal feelings freely. One African American male complained about "so many phony conversations—white people trying to impress African Americans with their liberalness." Straightforwardness, or "telling it like it is," is one aspect of authenticity; the opposite of this is avoidance of the truth through double talking or fancy language.

At the same time, many African American males engage in self-presentation; they try to create an acceptable image of themselves through "high talk" and "stylin'." "You dress as if you had money even if you don't." Creating an acceptable self-image becomes critical when a demeaning image has been externally imposed by European American society. In this light, stylized behavior to African Americans emerges as a sign of strength, not a lack of authenticity.

Understanding

Understanding is the feeling that messages are successfully conveyed. This theme was expressed when people felt that information was adequately exchanged or learning took place. One person noted that "there was a genuine exchange of thinking, feeling, and caring." Unfortunately, understanding can be hampered by cultural differences or differences in upbringing. One female commented that "if people don't share the same life experiences, they can't be expected to truly understand each other. If whites haven't been exposed to blacks, there will be a 'fear of the unknown.'"

Goal Attainment

Goal attainment, or achieving desired ends from a conversation, was mentioned more in satisfying than in dissatisfying conversations. It is closely linked to understanding in that without some mutual understanding no goals will be met. Goals might include finding the solution to some problem, exchanging information, or finishing some project. But cultural misunderstandings can get in the way of goals. As one male responded: "Blacks and whites may come away with different meanings from a conversation because concepts aren't defined in the same way. The members of the ethnic groups tend to think in a different manner." Because of this, African Americans often find conversations with European Americans unrewarding, but those rewarding conversations are "like gates opening."

Power Dynamics

Power dynamics, the last category, contains two main themes: powerlessness and assertiveness. *Powerlessness*, a feeling of being controlled, manipulated, or trapped, resulted from behaviors that rob African American conversational partners of the right to express their ideas freely. One participant objected to the term "powerlessness" as "putting things in white terms"; the label is not as important to us as the behaviors it describes. European Americans were seen as manipulating when they tried to control the topic, tried to persuade through subtlety, or would not let the African Americans finish their thoughts.

One European American communicator "tried to carry on the conversation all by himself . . . he would keep talking and interrupted me whenever I tried to say something."

Extreme assertiveness and confrontation used by African Americans, called "Mau Mauing," by one participant is the other half of power dynamics. African Americans, it was commented, often talk with one another in a way that "whites would consider antagonistic or brutal." For this reason, many African Americans *code switch*, or change their communication style and language, when they interact with European Americans. Assertive speaking among some African Americans is exemplified by "the dozens," a put-down game in which one person puts down or makes fun of another person. It should be emphasized, however, that this type of assertiveness is by no means universal to all African Americans.

COMMUNICATION IMPROVEMENT STRATEGIES

While interethnic communication issues are characteristics or behaviors that can help or hurt these communications, the African American participants believed *improvement strategies* can enhance conversation. These are things communicators can do to help make the interaction more satisfying. While our initial research found six strategies (Hecht & Ribeau, 1987; Hecht, Ribeau, & Alberts, 1989; Martin, Larkey, & Hecht, 1991), later research has expanded the list to twelve: (1) asserting one's point of view, (2) positive self-presentation, (3) be open and friendly, (4) avoidance, (5) interaction management, (6) other-orientation, (7) inform/educate, (8) express genuineness, (9) confront, (10) internal management, (11) treat others as individuals, and (12) language management. We describe these again with quotes from African Americans to expound.

Asserting One's Point of View

Assertiveness, in both style and substance, includes using such expressions as "stress," "assert," or "emphasize my point." This strategy grew out of dissatisfying conversations and was recommended for aiding African Americans' persuasion or argumentation efforts. The purpose is not simply to inform, but to gain agreement. Examples of this point of view are expressed in these comments: "Just simply be more vocal in the conversation. This in itself will give you a sense of control or power." "I continue to put across what I believe."

Positive Self-Presentation

Two methods of positive self-presentation attempt to reverse the other person's impressions. One method of self-presentation is to deliberately contradict stereotypes: "I just make sure my actions and conversation don't fit the negative stereotype." The other method is to point out positive attributes or accomplishments: "I try to make others see what I know, that is, when I'm being talked down to I try to show my intelligence."

Be Open and Friendly

This strategy, used most often to improve dissatisfying conversations, is similar to positive self-presentation, but without the deliberate desire to impress. Again, the participants varied in their views on openness, or open-mindedness. Some respondents felt European Americans should "be more patient, not assume anything, find out first." However, some African Americans rejected openness as a European American, middle-class female attribute, preferring to present themselves as strong, more closed. Friendliness includes being considerate of the other, polite, and courteous.

Avoidance

In a dissatisfying conversation, one might avoid either the conversation itself (by leaving), or the topics that are sensitive or demeaning. The first strategy is indicated by those who "terminate the conversation," or "remove myself from the conversation." The second is used when an African American perceives that some topics just cannot be discussed with certain individuals. Possible methods of avoidance include "not bringing up the subject," or changing the subject. ("I don't think it's beneficial to try to change the other person.")

Interaction Management

Either the African or the European American can attempt to manage the flow of the interaction. This might be done to reduce problems or just to improve a conversation. Possible strategies within this category include managing immediate interaction ("take turns," "work toward a compromise"), postponing the problem ("request a time to talk it over"), or finding different means of communication ("write a note"). Sometimes the conversation can be better managed by "just talking a little more" or spending "more time" together.

Other-Orientation

A concern for or interest in the other person was a sign of satisfying relationships, and might be created in different ways. Involving the other person in the conversation or finding common ground was one method suggested: "Think or talk about something that both can identify with." Others emphasized listening to the other person's thoughts and opinions: "learn by listening," "placing them in our shoes," and "try to look at it from both sides." Either party can improve the conversation with this strategy.

Inform/Educate

Information was often shared to educate or inform the conversational partner, in contrast to "asserting one's point of view." One should "tactfully educate by giving more information," and "if the conversation is that important, try and explain whatever you feel is being misunderstood." More facts should be given, sometimes specifically citing African American history to help others understand. At the same time, African Americans sometimes mentioned the need to ask European Americans more questions. This strategy attempts to resolve the issues raised by stereotyping and lack of understanding.

Express Genuineness

This strategy, genuineness, addresses the issue of authenticity, of "being yourself." Comments in this category valued honesty and expressing feelings. Some participants opened up in hopes that their conversation partner would follow. Others saw it in terms of a need to "share your feelings of a lack of accomplishment," in attempting to have a satisfying conversation or to "ask the person to be for real." While these suggestions seem confrontational, they are geared toward moving the other into more honest expression.

Confront

Confrontation implies "either a direct confrontation of the issue or using questions to place the burden back on the other person" (Hecht, Collier, & Ribeau, 1993). Strategies in this category include "Correct misconceptions in a shrewd, effective manner," or opposing "I believe you must always confront stereotyping by saying, 'It sounds as if you are making generalizations that may not be applicable to me.'" Examples of direct questions are "Just say, 'but how do *you* feel about it?' If they don't answer, it's obvious that it at least makes them feel uncomfortable," or "Ask why and how they got that stereotype."

Internal Management

Rather than focusing on specific behaviors to improve interaction, these comments described ways for African Americans to think about or deal with the situation. Some of these suggestions included acceptance, objectivity, and nondefensiveness: "I do my best to control my thoughts," "Think first of who you are, how you feel about yourself," and "Put the situation in proper perspective, that is, lose a battle to win the war."

Treat Others as Individuals and Equals

Leave race, color, or stereotypical beliefs entirely out of the conversation some suggested: "Talk to each other without having the sense of color in the conversation." Treat people based on who they are, and nothing else: "Decisions should be made based on each individual" or "Get to know me then judge me." This strategy, voiced most often to fight the stereotyping issue, primarily advocates desired behavior by the European American conversation partner.

Language Management

A few strategies that did not fit in the other categories are grouped here including: avoid slang or jargon and use clear articulation. "Refrain from using unfamiliar jargon" and "talk the same language" are examples of comments in this area. This strategy was used to resolve problems of a lack of understanding.

Note that the African American participants recommended some of these strategies primarily as things they should do (for example, assertiveness, positive self-presentation, avoidance, internal management, inform/educate, confront, language management); some as things European Americans should do (treat others as individuals); and some as things both should do (be more open and friendly, interaction management, express genuineness, other-orientation). Second, it should be noted that within each category (for example, be more open and friendly) there is a diversity of thought among African Americans as to how or if that strategy should be used.

The African Americans we interviewed felt that these strategies might be successful for improving a conversation, but not always. When stereotyping or lack of acceptance takes place, for example, no strategies are seen as effective—it is like "bouncing off a brick wall." If African Americans "see signs of racism, patronizing behavior, or other put downs, they turn off quickly." The first few minutes of a conversation can make or break the conversation—and the relationship.

CONCLUSION

It is often tempting to state communication effectiveness theories (or others) as if they applied to the way all people behave. However, the studies described here demonstrate that rules for effective or satisfying communication behavior vary, depending on the ethnicity of the group, as well as the situation. Further, the research shows a diversity and complexity among African Americans (Hecht & Ribeau, 1991). Finally, African Americans' own descriptions reveal clear suggestions, both for African Americans and European Americans, for how to make interethnic communication more rewarding for all concerned.

References

Hecht, M. L. (1978). Toward a conceptualization of interpersonal communication satisfaction. *Quarterly Journal of Speech, 64,* 47–62.

Hecht, M. L. (1984). Satisfying communication and relationship labels: Intimacy and length of relationship as perceptual frames of naturalistic conversation." *Western Journal of Speech Communication, 48,* 201–216.

Hecht, M. L., Collier, M. J., and Ribeau, S. (1993). *African American Communication: Identity and Cultural Interpretations.* Newbury Park, Calif.: Sage.

Hecht, M. L., Larkey, L. K., and Johnson, J. N. (1992). African American and European American perceptions of problematic issues in interethnic communication effectiveness. *Human Communication Research, 19,* 209–236.

Hecht, M. L., and Ribeau, S. Ethnic communication: A comparative analysis of satisfying communication. *International Journal of Intercultural Relations, 8,* 135–151.

Hecht, M. L., and Ribeau, S. (1987). Afro-American identity labels and communicative effectiveness. *Journal of Language and Social Psychology, 6,* 319–326.

Hecht, M. L., and Ribeau, S. (1991). Sociocultural roots of ethnic identity: A look at Black America. *Journal of Black Studies, 21,* 501–513.

Hecht, M. L., Ribeau, S., and Alberts, J. K. (1989). An Afro-American perspective on interethnic communication. *Communication Monographs, 56,* 385–410.

Hecht, M. L., Ribeau, S., and Sedano, M. V. (1990). A Mexican American perspective on interethnic communication. *International Journal of Intercultural Relations, 14,* 31–55.

Martin, J. N. (1993). "Intercultural Communication Competence." In R. Wiseman and J. Koester (Eds.), *International and Intercultural Communication Annual,* 17.

Martin, J. N., Larkey, L. K., and Hecht, M. L. (February, 1991). An African American Perspective on Conversational Improvement Strategies for Interethnic Communication. Paper presented to the Intercultural and International Communication Conference, Miami, Florida.

Martin, J. N., and Hammer, M. R. (1989). Behavioral categories of intercultural communication competence: Everyday communicators' perceptions. *International Journal of Intercultural Relations, 13,* 303–332.

McLaughlin, M., and Cody, M. J. (1982). Awkward silences: Behavioral antecedents and consequences of the conversational lapse. *Human Communication Research, 8,* 229–316.

Pavitt, C., and Haight, L. (1985). The "competent communicator" as a cognitive prototype. *Human Communication Research, 12,* 225–242.

Ruben, B. D. (1977). Guidelines for cross-cultural communication effectiveness. *Group and Organizational Studies, 12,* 225–242.

Ruben, B. D. (1989). The study of cross-cultural competence: Traditions and contemporary issues. *International Journal of Intercultural Relations, 13,* 229–239.

Spitzberg, B. H. (1989). Issues in the development of a theory of interpersonal competence in the intercultural context. *International Journal of Intercultural Relations, 13,* 241–268.

Spitzberg, B. H., and Cupach, W. R. (1984). *Interpersonal Communication Competence.* Beverly Hills, Calif.: Sage.

Spitzberg, B. H., and Hecht, M. L. (1984). A component model of relational competence. *Human Communication Research, 10,* 575–600.

Vause, C. J., and Wiemann, J. M. (1981). Communication strategies for role invention. *Western Journal of Speech Communication, 45,* 241–251.

Wiemann, J. M., and Bradac, J. J. (1989). "Metatheoretical Issues in the Study of Communication Competence: Structural and Functional Approaches." In B. Dervin and M. J. Voight (Eds.), *Progress in Communication Sciences,* Vol. 9, 261–284. Norwood, N.J.: Ablex.

Concepts and Questions

1. What are the basic assumptions that Ribeau, Baldwin, and Hecht make about African American communication? Do you agree with these assumptions? Can you think of any assumptions they failed to include?

2. In what ways are culture and ethnicity alike? In what ways do they differ?

3. How do Ribeau, Baldwin, and Hecht define *effective behavior*? According to your experiences, how would you define effective behavior?

4. How do Mexican Americans differ from African Americans in their conversational styles?

5. How do Ribeau, Baldwin, and Hecht define *acceptance*?

6. Can you think of specific examples of authenticity? Understanding? Goal attainment?

7. What are the two main themes of power dynamics? How would power dynamics influence intercultural communication?

8. What recommendations do Ribeau, Baldwin and Hecht make for improving intercultural communication between whites and African Americans? How can you incorporate these recommendations into your own communication behavior?

9. Can you add other improvement strategies that go beyond the list advanced by Ribeau, Baldwin, and Hecht?

Understanding Communication of Persons with Disabilities as Cultural Communication

DAWN O. BRAITHWAITE

CHARLES A. BRAITHWAITE

Jonathan is an articulate, intelligent, thirty-five year old professional man, who has used a wheelchair since he became paraplegic when he was twenty years old. He recalls taking an ablebodied woman out to dinner at a nice restaurant. When the waitress came to take their order she looked only at his date and asked, in a condescending tone, "and what would *he* like to eat for dinner?" At the end of the meal the waitress presented Jonathan's date with the check and thanked her for her patronage.[1]

Jeff, an ablebodied student, was working with a group that included Helen, who uses a wheelchair. He related an incident that really embarrassed him. "I wasn't thinking and I said to the group, 'Let's run over to the student union and get some coffee.' I was mortified when I looked over at Helen and remembered that she can't walk. I felt like a real jerk." Helen later described the incident with Jeff, recalling,

> At yesterday's meeting, Jeff said, "Let's run over to the union" and then he looked over at me and I thought he would die. It didn't bother me at all, in fact, I use that phrase myself. I felt bad that Jeff was so embarrassed, but I didn't know what to say. Later in the group meeting I made it a point to say, "I've got to be running along now." I hope that Jeff noticed and felt OK about what he said.

Although it may seem hard to believe, these scenarios are common experiences for people with physical disabilities and are indicative of what often happens when disabled and ablebodied people communicate.

The passage of the Americans with Disabilities Act (ADA), a "bill of rights" for persons with disabilities, highlighted the fact that they are now a large, vocal, and dynamic group within the United States (Braithwaite & Labrecque, 1994; Braithwaite & Thompson, 1999). Disabled people represent one group within American culture that is growing in numbers. Persons with disabilities constitute as much as 7% of the population and are the largest minority group in certain states (Wheratt, 1988). There are two reasons for increases in the numbers of persons with disabilities. First, as the American population ages and has a longer life expectancy, more people will live long enough to develop age-related disabilities. Second, advances in medical technologies now allow persons with disabilities to survive life-threatening illnesses and injuries where survival was not possible in earlier times. For example, when actor Christopher Reeve became quadriplegic after a horse-riding accident in May 1995, newer advances in medical technology allowed him to survive his injuries and to live with a severe disability.

In the past, most people with disabilities were sheltered and many were institutionalized, but today they are very much a part of the American mainstream. Each of us will have contact with people who have disabilities within our families, among our friends, or within the workplace. Some of us will develop disabilities ourselves. Says Marie, a college student who became paralyzed after diving into a swimming pool,

> I knew there were disabled people around, but I never thought this would happen to me. I never even *knew* a disabled person before *I* became one. If before this happened, I saw a person in a wheelchair, I would have been uncomfortable and not known what to say.

Marie's comment highlights the fact that many ablebodied people feel extremely uncomfortable interacting with disabled people. As people with disabilities continue to move into mainstream culture, there is a need for both ablebodied and disabled persons to know how to communicate with one another.

DISABILITY AND CULTURAL COMMUNICATION

The goal of this essay is to focus on communication between ablebodied persons and persons with disabilities as *intercultural communication* (Carbaugh, 1990). This claim is made because, as will be demonstrated later, persons with disabilities use a distinctive speech code that implicates specific models of personhood, society, and strategic action that are qualitatively different than those models used by ablebodied persons. Because persons with disabilities are treated so differently in American society, distinctive meanings, rules, and speech habits develop that act as a powerful resource for creating and reinforcing perceptions of cultural differences between persons with disabilities and ablebodied persons. The distinctive verbal and nonverbal communication used by persons with disabilities creates a sense of cultural identity that constitutes a unique social reality.

Several researchers have described the communication of disabled and ablebodied persons as *cultural communication* (Braithwaite, 1990, 1996; Emry & Wiseman, 1987; Padden & Humphries, 1988); that is, we recognize that persons with disabilities develop certain unique communicative characteristics that are not shared by the majority of ablebodied individuals in U.S. society. In fact, except for individuals who are born with disabilities, becoming disabled means shifting from being a member of the ablebodied majority to being a member of a minority culture (Braithwaite, 1990, 1996)—that is, the onset of a physical disability requires learning new ways of talking about the self and developing new ways of engaging in interaction with others.

Adopting a cultural view in this essay, we start by introducing communication problems that can arise between persons in the ablebodied culture and those in the disabled culture. Second, we discuss some of the weaknesses of the earlier research on communication between ablebodied and disabled persons. Third, we will discuss research findings from interviews with people who have physical disabilities. Results from these interviews show that people with disabilities are engaged in a process of redefinition; that is, they critique the prevailing stereotypes about disability and they communicate strategically in order to redefine what it means to be disabled. Finally, we will talk about important contributions both scholars and students of intercultural communication can make to improving relations between disabled and ablebodied people.

CHALLENGES FOR DISABLED COMMUNICATORS

When we adopt a cultural view and attempt to understand the communicative challenges faced by people with disabilities, it is useful to distinguish between *disability* and *handicap*. Even though the two terms are often used interchangeably in everyday speech, their meanings are quite different. The two terms imply different relationships between persons with disabilities and society. People with disabilities are challenged to overcome the barriers associated with their disability as it affects all areas of their lives. Crewe and Athelstan (1985) identified five "key life functions" that may be affected by disability: (1) mobility, (2) employment, (3) self-care, (4) social relationships, and (5) communication. People are often able to compensate for physical challenges associated with the first three key life functions through assisting devices, such as wheelchairs or canes; training on how to take care of one's personal needs; and occupational therapy to find suitable employment.

A disability becomes a handicap when the physical or social environment interacts with it to impede a person in some aspect of his or her life (Crewe & Athelstan, 1985). For example, a disabled individual with paraplegia can function well in the physical environment using a wheelchair, ramps, and curb cuts, but he or she is handicapped when buildings or public transportation are not accessible to wheelchairs. When a society is willing or able to create adaptations, disabled persons have the ability to achieve increasingly independent lives (Cogswell, 1977; DeLoach & Greer, 1981). Higgins (1992) highlights the drive toward independence and the political activism of disabled people, which has resulted in laws such as the ADA. He goes on to say that disabled citizens themselves are "'standing up' . . . and working to revise the disabling practices and policies that have remade disability" (p. 249).

In fact, it is important to realize that adaptations are regularly made to the physical environment that are used by *all* people, not just people who are disabled. Most of us are unaware of just how handicapped we would be without these physical adaptations. For example, our offices are located on the second floor of a three-story building. We know that stairs take up a significant amount of space in a building. Space used for the stairwell on each level takes the place of at least one office. So, the most space-efficient way to get people to the second floor would be a climbing rope, which would necessitate relatively small opening on each floor. However, very few of us could climb a rope to reach our offices on the second story, so we would be handicapped without stairs or elevators. Similarly, physical adaptations made to accommodate people with disabilities are also useful for nondisabled people. When a parent is out with a baby in a stroller or when a student is walking with a heavy load of library books, automatic door openers, ramps, curb cuts, elevators, and larger doorways become important environmental adaptations. Physical limitations become disabilities for all of us when the physical environment cannot be adapted to preempt our shortcomings.

Challenges to Relationships Between Disabled and Ablebodied Persons

Although it is possible to identify and to cope with physical challenges associated with mobility, self-care, and employment, it is the two key life functions of *social relationships* and *communication* that are much more formidable. It is less difficult to detect and correct physical barriers than it is to deal with the insidious social barriers facing people with disabilities. Coleman and DePaulo (1991) would label social barriers as "psychological disabling," which is even more common in Western culture where "much value is placed on physical bodies and physical attractiveness" (p. 64).

When nondisabled and disabled people begin to get to know one another, the challenges of forming any new relationship are greater. For ablebodied people, this may be due to high uncertainty about how to talk with a person who is disabled. They feel uncertain about what to say or how to act because they are afraid of saying or doing the wrong thing or of hurting the disabled person's feelings. As a result, they may feel overly self-conscious, and their actions may be constrained, self-controlled, and rigid because they feel uncomfortable and uncertain (Belgrave & Mills, 1981; Braithwaite, 1990; Higgins, 1992; Weinberg, 1978). Higgins (1992) points out that the ablebodied person may try and communicate appropriately. However, "[w]ishing to act in a way acceptable to those with disabilities, they may unknowingly act offensively, patronizing disabled people with unwanted sympathy" (p. 105). Interestingly, researchers have found that the type of disability a person has does not change the way ablebodied persons react. Ablebodied persons' trepidation about communicating with a disabled person did not differ significantly across different disabilities (Fichten, Robillard, Tagalakis, & Amsel, 1991).

Even when an ablebodied person tries to "say the right thing" and communicate verbal acceptance to the person with the disability, the nonverbal behavior may communicate rejection and avoidance (Thompson, 1982). For example, disabled people often report that while an ablebodied person may talk to them, they also stand at a greater distance than usual, avoid eye contact, avoid mentioning the disability, or cut the conversation short (Braithwaite, 1990, 1991, 1996). In this case, a disability becomes a handicap in the social environment, and it can block the development of a relationship with a nondisabled person. In all, ablebodied people hold many stereotypes of people from the disabled culture. Coleman and DePaulo (1991) discuss some of these stereotypes concerning disabled people:

> For example they often perceive them as dependent, socially introverted, emotionally unstable, depressed, hypersensitive, and easily offended, especially with regard to their disability. In addition, disabled people are often presumed to differ from ablebodied people in moral character, social skills, and political orientation. . . . (p. 69)

Many ablebodied people recognize what we have described as typical communication experiences with, or attitudes toward, people who are disabled. Ablebodied persons may find themselves with conflicting advice and often do not know what is expected of them or how to act. On the one hand, they have been taught to "help the handicapped," and, on the other hand, they were told to "treat all people equally." Americans usually conceptualize persons as "individuals" who "have rights" and "make their own choices" (Carbaugh, 1988). However, when ablebodied persons encounter a person with a disability, this model of personhood creates a serious dilemma. For example, should one help persons with disabilities open doors or help them if they fall? Ablebodied persons fear saying the wrong thing, such as "See you later!" to a blind person or "Why don't you run by the store on your way home?" to a person using a wheelchair. In the end, it seems easier to avoid situations where one might interact with a disabled person rather than face discomfort and uncertainty.

People with disabilities find these situations equally problematic and are well aware of the discomfort of ablebodied people. They are able to describe in great detail both the verbal and nonverbal signals of discomfort and avoidance that ablebodied persons portray (Braithwaite, 1990, 1996). People with disabilities report that when they meet ablebodied persons, they would hope to get the discomfort "out of the way," and they want the ablebodied person to treat them as a "person like anyone else," rather than focus solely on their disability (Braithwaite, 1991, 1996).

Problems with Current Research

When we first looked at research on communication between ablebodied and disabled persons, three problems became clear. First, little is known about the communication behavior of disabled people. Although a few researchers have studied disabled persons' communication, most of them have studied the ablebodieds' reactions to disabled others. These studies on "attitudes toward disabled persons" are analogous to studies that look at majority members' attitudes toward other minority groups. A look at the intercultural literature as a whole reveals few studies from the perspective of the minority. Second, most researchers talked *about* persons with disabilities, not *with* them. Disabled persons rarely have been represented in survey data; most often these are of ablebodied people reporting their impressions of disabled people. In experimental studies, the disabled person is most often really an ablebodied person using a wheelchair.

Third, and most significantly, the research has been most often conducted from the perspective of the ablebodied person; that is, what should people with disabilities *do* to make ablebodied others feel more comfortable? From this perspective, researchers do not consider the effects on the person with the disability. For example, several studies revealed that ablebodied persons are more comfortable when disabled persons disclose about their disability, so they suggested that disabled people should self-disclose to make ablebodied others more comfortable. Braithwaite (1991) points out that these researchers have forgotten to look at how self-disclosure might affect persons who are disabled. Therefore, from much of the ablebodied-oriented research we see an *ethnocentric bias* that ignores the perspective of the disabled minority. Although there recently has been more research from the perspective of disabled interactants, we still have an incomplete picture of the communication of people who are disabled.

The remainder of this essay presents selected findings from ongoing studies done from the perspectives of disabled people about their communication with ablebodied others. More than one hundred in-depth interviews have now been completed with adults who are physically disabled. All of these people have disabilities that are visible to an observer, and none has significant communication-related disabilities (e.g., deafness, speech impairments). The goal of the research has been to describe communication with nondisabled people from the frame of reference of people who are disabled. Doing research by talking *with* disabled people helps bring out information important to them, and the researcher strives to describe patterns of responses from the interviews. These studies are a departure from what most other researchers have done because the interview format allows participants to describe their experiences in detail, and because the focus is on the perspective of the members of the disabled minority.

PROCESS OF REDEFINITION

A central theme emerging from the interviews was *redefinition*; that is, people who are disabled are critiquing the prevailing stereotypes about being disabled, and they are creating new ways of perceiving themselves and their disability. We saw three types of redefinition: (1) redefining the self as part of a "new" culture, (2) redefining the concept of disability, and (3) redefining disability for the dominant culture.

Redefining the Self as Part of the Disabled Culture

People with disabilities often discussed seeing themselves as a minority group or culture. For some interviewees, this definition crosses disability lines; that is, their definition of "disabled" includes all those who have disabilities. For others, the definition is not as broad; when they think of disability, they think exclusively about others with their own type of disability. For example, some of the people with mobility-related disabilities also talked about blind and deaf people with whom they discussed disability and others talked only about other wheelchair users. However narrowly or broadly they defined it, though, many do see themselves as part of a minority culture. For example, one interviewee described that being disabled "is like *West Side Story*. Tony and Maria; white and Puerto Rican. They were afraid of each other; ignorant of each others' cultures. People are people." Another man explained his view:

> First of all, I belong to a subculture (of disability) because of the way I have to deal with things, being in the medical system, welfare. There is the subculture. . . . I keep one foot in the ablebodied culture and one foot in my own culture. One of the reasons I do that is so that I don't go nuts.

This man's description of the "balancing act" between cultures demonstrates that membership in the disabled culture has several similarities to the experiences of other American cultural groups. Many of the interviewees have likened their own experiences to those of other cultural groups, particularly to the experiences of American ethnic minorities. Interviewees recognized the loss of status and power that comes from being disabled, and they expressed that they felt many people were uncomfortable with them simply because they are different.

When taking a cultural view, it is important to recognize that not everyone comes to the culture the same way. Some people are born with disabilities, and others acquire them later. For those people who are not born with a disability, membership in the culture is a process that emerges over time. For some, the process is an incremental one, as in the case of a person with a degenerative disease such as multiple sclerosis that develops over many years. For a person who has a sudden-onset disability, such as a broken neck in an accident or "waking up a quadriplegic," moving from the majority (a "normal" person) to the minority (a person who is disabled) may happen in a matter of seconds. This sudden transition into the disabled culture presents many challenges of redefinition and readjustment in all facets of an individual's life (Braithwaite, 1990, 1996; Goffman, 1963).

If disability is a culture, then when does one become part of that culture? Even though persons are physically disabled, how they redefine themselves from "normal" or ablebodied to disabled is a process that develops over time. Braithwaite (1990, 1996) argues that becoming physically disabled does not mean one is immediately aware of being part of the disabled culture. In fact, for most people, adjusting to disability happens in stages or phases (DeLoach & Greer, 1981; Padden & Humphries, 1988). First, after becoming disabled, the individual is focusing on rehabilitation and the physical changes and challenges he or she is experiencing. A second phase occurs when the disabled person realizes that his or her life and relationships have changed dramatically; she or he tries to find ways to minimize the disability's effects. He or she may try to return to normal routines and old relationships. This can be a frustrating phase, because often things have changed more than the person realizes. Especially when trying to reestablish old relationships the person may find that old friends are no longer comfortable with him or her or that, without shared activities, the friendships may lapse. It is at this point that the person starts to become aware that he or she is operating as a member of a different culture than before and begin to assimilate into the new culture (Braithwaite, 1990, 1996).

It is in this third phase, what DeLoach and Greer (1981) call *stigma incorporation*, that persons begin to integrate being disabled into their own definitions of self. Each person can see both positive and negative aspects of being disabled and develops ways to cope with the negative aspects (DeLoach & Greer, 1981). In this stage of adjustment, people with disabilities develop ways of behaving and communicating so that

they can function successfully in the ablebodied culture (Braithwaite, 1990; 1996). This is what Morse and Johnson (1991) call "regaining wellness," when individuals regain control of themselves and their relationships, and adapt to new ways of doing things in their lives. At this point they are able to develop communication strategies that help them live successfully in the majority culture (Braithwaite, 1990, 1991, 1996; Braithwaite & Labrecque, 1994; Emry & Wiseman, 1987; Fox, Giles, Orbe, & Bourhis, 1999).

In this phase, people incorporate the role of disability in their lives. One man said, "You're the same person you were. You just don't do the same things you did before." As another said, "If anyone refers to me as an amputee, that is guaranteed to get me madder than hell! I don't deny the leg amputation, but I am me. I am a whole person. One." During this phase people can come to terms with the negative and positive changes in their lives. One woman said:

> I find myself telling people that this has been the worst thing that has happened to me. It has also been one of the best things. It forced me to examine what I felt about myself . . . confidence is grounded in me, not in other people. As a woman, not as dependent on clothes, measurements, but what's inside me.

Finally, in an interview with Barbara Walters, four months after his accident, actor Christopher Reeve demonstrates the concept of stigma incorporation:

> You also gradually discover, as I'm discovering, that your body is not you. The mind and the spirit must take over. And that's the challenge as you move from obsessing about "Why me?" and "It's not fair" and move into "Well, what is the potential?" And, now, four months down the line I see opportunities and potential I wasn't capable of seeing back in Virginia in June . . . genuine joy and being alive means more. Every moment is more intense than it ever was.

REDEFINING DISABILITY

A third type of redefinition discussed by interviewees was *redefining* the concept of disability. For example, to help others redefine disability, one interviewee will say to them, "People will say, 'Thank God I'm not handicapped.' And I'll say, 'Let's see, how tall are you? Tell me how you get something off that shelf up there!'" His goal in this interchange is to make others see disability as one of many *characteristics* of a person. From this perspective, everyone is handicapped in one way or another, by race, sex, height, or physical attributes, and people must work to overcome their handicapping conditions. Short people may need a stool to reach something on a high shelf, and people who are very tall may be stared at and certainly will not be able to drive small, economy-sized cars. Similarly, people with disabilities will be working to adapt to the physical challenges presented to them. One interviewee, who conducts workshops in disability awareness, talked about how he helps ablebodied people redefine disability:

> I will say to people "How many of you made the clothes that you're wearing?" "How many of you grew the food that you ate yesterday?" "How many of you built the house that you live in?" Nobody raises their hand . . . and then after maybe five of those, I'll say "And I bet you think you're independent. . . . And I'll say, "I'll bet you, if we could measure how independent you feel in your life versus how independent I feel in mine, then I would rate just as high you do. And yet here I am 'depending' to have people get me dressed, undressed, on and off the john, etc. It's all in our heads, folks. Nobody is really independent." I can see them kind of go "Yeah, I never thought of it that way." And they begin to understand how it is that somebody living with this situation can feel independent. That independence really is a feeling and an attitude. It's not a physical reality.

Redefining disability can also be reflected through changing the language we use to talk about disability. One interviewee objected to being called a "handicapped person," preferring the label "persons with a handicapping condition." He explained why: "You emphasize that person's identity and then you do something about the condition." The goal is to speak in ways that emphasize the *person* rather than their disability. One interviewee who had polio as a child rejected the term "polio victim" and preferred to label herself as "a person whose arms and legs do not function very well." One way we have found to accentuate the person is to talk about "*people* with disabilities" rather than "disabled people." The goal is

to stress the person first before introducing the disability. These are all forms of strategic action that help to create and maintain a sense of unique cultural identity among persons with disabilities (Braithwaite, 1996; Braithwaite & Thompson, 1999).

Redefining disability is also reflected in sensitizing oneself to commonly used labels for being disabled, such as being a "polio victim," "arthritis sufferer," "being confined to a wheelchair," or "wheelchair bound." When trying to redefine disability as a characteristic, one could change these phrases to "a person with polio," "a person who has arthritis," or a "wheelchair user." At first glance, some may think this is no more than an attempt at political correctness, but those who study language know that the words we use do affect perception. The way people with disabilities are labeled will affect how they are seen and how they see themselves. One interviewee discussed her dislike of all the labels that negatively stereotype disabled people. She used a humorous example, talking about what is commonly referred to as "handicapped parking." She explained, "I'd like to call it 'acceptable parking' because there's nothing wrong with the parking—it's not handicapped! The point is, I'd like to stress more positive terms."

There have also been changes in the terms that refer to ablebodied people. In the interviews, it was common to refer to the majority in terms of the minority, talking about "nondisabled" or "nonhandicapped" rather than "ablebodied" or "normal." Several interviewees used the term "TABs"—temporarily ablebodied—as a humorous reference term to ablebodied people. One interviewee joked, "Everyone is a TAB. . . . I just got mine earlier than you!" Being called a TAB serves to remind ablebodied persons that no one is immune from disability. Finally, researcher Susan Fox has suggested that we avoid talking about the communication of disabled and ablebodied people and instead use the phrase "interability communication" (see Fox, Giles, Orbe, & Bourhis, 1999). However we do it, whether we are disabled or ablebodied, it is clear that the language we use both creates and reflects our view of people with disabilities.

In addition to redefining disability, the interviewees also redefined "assisting devices" such as wheelchairs or canes. For example, one man told the following story about redefining his prosthetic leg:

Now there were two girls about eight playing and I was in my shorts. And I'll play games with them and say, "Which is my good leg?" And that gets them to thinking. Well, this one (he pats artificial leg) is not nearly as old as the other one!

Another interviewee redefined assisting devices this way: "Do you know what a cane is? It's a portable railing! The essence of a wheelchair is a seat and wheels. Now, I don't know that a tricycle is not doing the exact same thing."

In these examples, the problem is not the disability or the assisting device, but how one views it. Redefining the device also helps us see how it might mean different things to disabled and ablebodied persons. Several interviewees expressed frustration with people who played with their wheelchairs. One interviewee said, "This chair is not a toy, it is *part of me*. When you touch my chair, you are touching *me*." Another woman, a business executive, elaborated: "I don't know why people who push my chair feel compelled to make car sounds as they do it."

REDEFINING DISABILITY WITHIN THE DOMINANT CULTURE

Finally, as the interviewees redefine themselves as members of a culture and what it means to have a disabling condition, they were also concerned with changing the view of disability within the larger culture (Braithwaite, 1990, 1996). The interviews revealed that most people with disabilities view themselves as public educators. People told stories about taking the time to educate children and adults on what it means to be disabled. They are actively working to change the view of themselves as helpless, as victims, or as ill and the resulting treatment of such a view. One wheelchair user said:

People do not consider you, they consider the chair first. I was in a store with my purchases on my lap and money on my lap. The clerk looked at my companion and not at me and said, "Cash or charge?"

This incident with the clerk is a story heard from *every* person interviewed in some form or another, just as it happened to Jonathan and his date at the beginning of this essay. One woman who had multi-

ple sclerosis and uses a wheelchair told of shopping for lingerie with her husband accompanying her. When they were in front of the lingerie counter, the clerk repeatedly talked only to her husband saying, "And what size does she want?" The woman told her the size and the clerk looked at the husband and said, "And what color does she want?"

Persons with disabilities recognize that ablebodied persons often see them as disabled first and as a person second (if at all). The most common theme expressed by people with disabilities in all of the interviews is that they want to be *treated like a person first*. One man explained what he thought was important to remember: "A lot of people think that handicapped people are 'less than,' and I find that it's not true at all." The interviewees rejected those things that would not lead them to being seen as persons. A man with muscular dystrophy talked about the popular Labor Day telethon:

I do not believe in those goddamned telethons. . . . They're horrible, absolutely horrible. They get into the self-pity, you know, and disabled folk do not need that. Hit people in terms of their attitudes, then try to deal with and process their feelings. And the telethons just go for the heart and leave it there.

One man suggested what he thought was a more useful approach:

What I am concerned with is anything that can do away with the "us" versus "them" distinction. Well, you and I are anatomically different, but we're two human beings! And, at the point we can sit down and communicate eyeball to eyeball; the quicker you do that, the better!

Individually and collectively, people with disabilities do identify themselves as part of a culture. They are involved in a process of redefinition of themselves and disability, and they want to help nondisabled people internalize a redefinition of people with disabilities as "people first."

CONCLUSIONS

The research we have discussed highlights the usefulness of viewing disability from a cultural perspective. People with disabilities do see themselves as members of a culture, and viewing communication between ablebodied and disabled people from this perspective sheds new light on the communication problems that exist. Emry and Wiseman (1987) argue for the usefulness of intercultural training about disability issues. They call for unfreezing old attitudes about disability and refreezing new ones. Clearly, the interviews indicate that people who have disabilities would seem to agree.

One question the interviewees answered concerned how many of them had training about communication during or after their rehabilitation. We anticipated that they had been given information to prepare them for changes in their communication and relationships due to being disabled. We speculated that this education would be especially critical for those who experience sudden-onset disabilities because their self-concepts and all of their relationships would undergo sudden, radical changes. Surprisingly, we found that less than 30% of the interviewees received disability-related communication training. Clearly, the rehabilitation process has some critical gaps, and we would argue that intercultural communication scholars have the background and experience for the kind of research and training that could smooth the transition from majority to minority (Braithwaite, 1990; Emry & Wiseman, 1987). We also believe that students of intercultural communication should have an advantage in better understanding the perspective of people with disabilities as presented in this essay and will be able to adapt to communicating with persons in this culture.

As for ablebodied persons who communicate with disabled persons, this intercultural perspective leads to the following proscriptions and prescriptions:

DO NOT:

- *assume* persons with disabilities cannot speak for themselves or cannot do things for themselves.
- *force* your help on persons with disabilities.
- *avoid* communication with persons who have disabilities simply because you are uncomfortable or unsure.
- *use terms* such as *handicapped, physically challenged, crippled, victim,* and so on unless requested to do so by persons with disabilities.
- *assume* that a disability defines a person.

DO:

- *assume* persons with disabilities can do something unless they communicate otherwise.
- *let persons with disabilities tell you* if they want something, what they want, and when they want it. If a person with a disability refuses your help, don't go ahead and help anyway. The goal is to give the person with the disability control in the situation.
- *remember* that persons with disabilities have experienced others' discomfort before and understand how you might be feeling.
- *use terms* such as "*people* with disabilities" rather than "disabled *people*." The goal is to stress the person first before introducing the disability.
- *treat* persons with disabilities as *persons first*, recognizing that you are not dealing with a disabled person but with a *person* who *has* a disability. This means actively seeking the humanity of the person you are speaking with, and focusing on the person's characteristics instead of the superficial physical appearance. Without diminishing the significance of a physical disability, you can selectively attend to many other aspects of a person during communication.

Note

1. The quotes and anecdotes in this essay come from in-depth interviews with people who have visible physical disabilities. The names of the participants in these interviews have been changed to protect their privacy.

References

Belgrave, F. Z., & Mills, J. (1981). Effect upon desire for social interaction with a physically disabled person of mentioning the disability in different contexts. *Journal of Applied Social Psychology, 11*(1), 44–57.

Braithwaite, D. O. (1990). From majority to minority: An analysis of cultural change from ablebodied to disabled. *International Journal of Intercultural Relations, 14,* 465–483.

———. (1991). Just how much did that wheelchair cost? Management of privacy boundaries by persons with disabilities. *Western Journal of Speech Communication, 55,* 254–274.

————. (1996). "I am a person first": Different perspectives on the communication of persons with disabilities. In E. B. Ray (Ed.), *Communication and disenfranchisement: Social health issues and implications* (pp. 257–272). Mahwah, NJ: Lawrence Erlbaum.

————, & Labrecque, D. (1994). Responding to the Americans with disabilities act: Contributions of interpersonal communication research and training. *Journal of Applied Communication, 22*(3), 287–294.

————, & Thompson, T. L. (Eds). (1999). *Handbook of communication and people with disabilities: Research and application*. Mahwah, NJ: Lawrence Erlbaum.

Carbaugh, D. (1988). *Talking American*. Norwood, NJ: Ablex.

————. (Ed.). (1990). *Cultural communication and intercultural contact*. Hillsdale, NJ: Lawrence Erlbaum.

Cogswell, B. E. (1977). Self-socialization: Readjustments of paraplegics in the community. In R. P. Marinelli & A. E. Dell Orto (Eds.), *The psychological and social impact of physical disability* (pp. 151–159). New York: Springer Publishing.

Coleman, L. M., & DePaulo, B. M. (1991). Uncovering the human spirit: Moving beyond disability and "missed" communications. In N. Coupland, H. Giles, & J. M. Wiemann, *Miscommunication and problematic talk* (pp. 61–84). Newbury Park, CA: Sage.

Crewe, N., & Athelstan, G. (1985). *Social and psychological aspects of physical disability*. Minneapolis: University of Minnesota, Department of Independent Study and University Resources.

DeLoach, C., & Greer, B. G. (1981). *Adjustment to severe disability*. New York: McGraw-Hill.

Emry, R., & Wiseman, R. L. (1987). An intercultural understanding of ablebodied and disabled persons' communication. *International Journal of Intercultural Relations, 11*, 7–27.

Fichten, C. S., Robillard, K., Tagalakis, V., & Amsel, R. (1991). Casual interaction between college students with various disabilities and their nondisabled peers: The internal dialogue. *Rehabilitation Psychology, 36*(1), 3–20.

Fox, S. A., Giles, H., Orbe, M., & Bourhis, R. (1999). Interability communication: Theoretical perspectives. In D. O. Braithwaite & T. L. Thompson (Eds.), *Handbook of communication and people with disabilities: Research and application*. Mahwah, NJ: Lawrence Erlbaum.

Goffman, E. (1963). *Stigma: Notes on the management of spoiled identity*. New York: Simon & Schuster.

Higgins, P. C. (1992). *Making disability: Exploring the social transformation of human variation*. Springfield, IL: Charles C. Thomas.

Morse, J. M., & Johnson, J. L. (1991). *The illness experience: Dimensions of suffering*. Newbury Park, CA: Sage.

Padden, C., & Humphries, T. (1988). *Deaf in America: Voices from a culture*. Cambridge, MA: Harvard University Press.

Thompson, T. L. (1982). Disclosure as a disability-management strategy: A review and conclusions. *Communication Quarterly, 30*, 196–202.

Weinberg, N. (1978). Modifying social stereotypes of the physically disabled. *Rehabilitation Counseling Bulletin, 22*(2), 114-124.

Wheratt, R. (August 1, 1988). Minnesota disabled to be heard. *Star Tribune*, pp. 1, 6.

Concepts and Questions

1. How does becoming disabled change a person's communication patterns?

2. What are some of the cultural problems inherent in communication between ablebodied and disabled persons?

3. Why do Braithwaite and Braithwaite believe we should learn about the communication patterns of disabled persons?

4. What do Braithwaite and Braithwaite mean when they say that "the distinctive verbal and nonverbal communication used by persons with disabilities creates a sense of cultural identity that constitutes a unique social reality"?

5. How would you distinguish between *disability* and *handicap*?

6. Why is nonverbal communication a factor when ablebodied and persons with disabilities engage in communication?

7. What problems do Braithwaite and Braithwaite see with current research being conducted on persons with disabilities?

8. What is meant by the term *redefinition*?

9. How would you answer the following question: If disability is a culture, then when does one become part of that culture?

Cultural Patterns of Deaf People

LINDA A. SIPLE

With the onset of multicultural awareness, Americans are now viewing society as a "tossed salad" of cultural diversity versus a "melting pot" of homogenized members. Even the terms we are now using reflect a changing attitude toward those many cultures that co-exist within American culture. No longer are these various cultures referred to as subcultures, implying inferiority or secondary status. The term co-culture is now being used to recognize the equal status and equal importance of the culture. Increased interest in the co-cultures of the United States has encouraged researchers to take a closer look at the cultural patterns that make these groups unique. Of late, co-cultures drawing the most attention have been the cultures of African-Americans (Weber, 1991), Latinos (Albert & Triandis, 1991), Native Americans (Madrid, 1991), and the cultural differences that exist between men and women (Tannen, 1990). Awareness of the multicultural nature of the United States has led to the identification of otherwise overlooked groups that also manifest cultural characteristics. For example, the aged (Carmichael, 1991), paraplegics (Braithwaite, 1991), and gays (Majors, 1991), to name a few, have received attention.

Deaf culture, although manifesting significant differences in language, behavior, values, and beliefs, has not been fully recognized as a domestic co-culture of the United States. The main reason for this oversight is twofold. Deafness is viewed by the majority as a disabling condition that should be corrected. From this perspective, a reasonable conclusion would be that anyone who is Deaf would like to be cured of this condition. Therefore, it does not make sense to view Deaf people as voluntarily belonging to a social system based on this identity. Second, the very nature of deafness presents a major communication obstacle. Without knowledge of Sign Language, the only avenues left to communicate are writing and speech on the part of the hearing individual, and writing, speech reading, and use of any residual hearing on the part of the Deaf person. Both modes assume the Deaf person knows English and can effectively speech read. These abilities will vary greatly depending on the Deaf individual, but, regardless of ability, communication becomes a chore instead of a naturally flowing interchange.

The view that deafness is disabling and its resulting communication barrier have both prevented the hearing majority from learning about the cultural patterns of the Deaf and, as a result, has led to stereotypes and the use of terms such as *deaf mute* or *deaf and dumb*—labels that more accurately reflect the point of view of the labeler, not the abilities of the labeled.

Viewing deafness as a disabling condition has led to seeing behavioral differences as evidence of social immaturity, eccentricities, lack of intelligence, or even signs of mental illness. According to Lane (1988), many of the studies conducted on Deaf people "reflect not the characteristics of Deaf people but the paternalistic posture of the hearing experts making these attributions" (p. 7).

Having more than 20 years experience as a Sign Language interpreter and Professor of Interpreting at the National Technical Institute for the Deaf in Rochester, New York, I have seen how these misconceptions have led to discrimination and communication conflict. By viewing the Deaf as a group with a unique culture, behavioral differences take on new meanings. This article discusses several cultural characteristics of the Deaf community in America and presents evidence for viewing Deaf people as a co-culture. The information presented within this article comes from numerous printed sources as well as personal experience interacting with the culture.

From *The Journal of Intercultural Relations*, Volume 18 (1994), 345–367. Reprinted by permission of the publisher. Linda A. Siple is affiliated with the Rochester Institute of Technology at the National Technical Institute for the Deaf Center for Sign Language and Interpreting Education.

BACKGROUND

According to the National Center for Health Statistics, there are approximately 20 million Americans who have some type of hearing loss; however, very few of these people know Sign Language or consider themselves members of Deaf culture. There are approximately 1 million Americans who use American Sign Language (ASL) and consider themselves members of Deaf culture.

Those who are deaf and do not use Sign Language tend to have enhanced visual perception; however, these individuals do not exhibit significant behavioral differences from the hearing majority. The cultural differences discussed in this article are specifically related to differences in language, behavior, values, and beliefs exhibited by the 1 million deaf individuals who make up Deaf culture.

The causes of deafness vary throughout history due to epidemics or medical advances. However, of the current population, the best estimates are that 50% of early childhood deafness is inherited. Up to 40% is recessive and 10% is dominant (Moores, 1987). "Maternal rubella was identified as the greatest cause of hearing loss in the middle 1960s and has been recognized as the major non genetic cause of deafness in school-age children in the 1980s" (Moores, 1987, p. 104). Other commonly reported causes include mother–child blood incompatibility, spinal meningitis, scarlet fever, prematurity, congenital cytomegalovirus infection (i.e., herpes virus), whooping cough, and accident or injury. Furthermore, many recent studies investigating the etiology of deafness still cite "etiology unknown" as accounting for more than 30% of the total number of reported cases (Moores, 1987; Schein & Delk, 1974; Vernon, 1968)—a surprising number given our current level of medical sophistication.

A unique aspect of Deaf culture is that most Deaf children have hearing parents, siblings, and extended family members. Less than 10% of Deaf children have Deaf parents. This is significant because if they are exposed to Deaf culture and Sign Language, it is through contact with other Deaf children and teachers at schools for the Deaf (Moores, 1987).

It is important to note that not all deaf people belong to Deaf culture. As Kannapell (1982) stated, "the degree of hearing loss is not the most important requirement for being in the Deaf community [nor is] sharing a common language . . . enough to be admitted to the Deaf community" (p. 25). Higgins (1989) stated that membership is achieved through "(1) Identification with the Deaf world, (2) shared expe-

riences that come of being Deaf, and (3) participation in the community's activities" (p. 38).

To more fully understand Deaf culture and its communication practices, it is important to discuss the sociocultural elements that make this culture distinct. Porter and Samovar (1988) proposed a model for the analysis of intercultural communication that addresses three main elements of culture: perception, verbal processes, and nonverbal processes.

PERCEPTION

Porter and Samovar (1988) defined perception as "the internal process by which we select, evaluate and organize stimuli from the external environment" (p. 24). That is to say, a culture behaves in certain ways based on how they perceive the world. To understand how a group perceives the world, we must gain an appreciation for its perceptual frames.

Visual Orientation

How one perceives the world is influenced by the communication channel used when exchanging messages. For the Deaf individual, the very nature of deafness shifts the primary channel for information exchange from auditory to visual. The visual channel becomes the mechanism for message exchange, and its use permeates the entire conversational structure. For example, turn taking, back-channel feedback, conversational repairs, and attention getting all follow visual structural rules. The auditory channel, even for those who have some hearing in the speech range, often is not an effective or reliable channel. Of the three most commonly used channels (sight, sound, and touch) the auditory channel is the least utilized. The secondary channel of communication becomes touch. As discussed later, touch serves many important conversational functions.

When channel utilization is compared between hearing individuals and individuals belonging to the Deaf culture (see Table 1), the difference is clear. However, it is not simply that different channels are used but how this difference affects perception.

The Deaf culture's primary utilization of the visual channel influences perception in two major ways. First, the visual channel is continuous whereas the

Table 1 *Channel Utilization*

	Hearing	Deaf
Visual	Secondary	Primary
Auditory	Primary	Tertiary
Tactile	Tertiary	Secondary

verbal channel is discrete. Speech starts when sound is produced and stops when vocalization ceases. However, the visual channel continues as long as two people are in each other's presence. This factor greatly influences how communication is perceived by Deaf individuals. Discussions with Deaf culture members appears to suggest that "communication" is perceived to occur even if signs are not being exchanged. The following personal experience is particularly illustrative of this point.

> While attending a lecture at a convention, I ran into a Deaf friend I had not seen for many years. We had a very brief conversation before we needed to sit down and direct our attention to the lecture. When the lecture was completed, my friend needed to leave immediately to catch a plane. I said I felt bad that we didn't have any time to talk. His response was, "We can talk on the TTY anytime, it's actually *seeing* you that is most important to me. Now I feel reconnected with you."

A second perceptual difference is that visual communication is multichanneled, whereas verbal communication is a single-channel event. Baker and Padden (1978) suggested that ASL discourse occurs in five separate visual channels: (a) the hands and arms, (b) the head, (c) the eyes, (d) the face, and (f) the total body posture. A message may be sent using all five channels simultaneously or shift from the hands, to the nose, back to the hands, and end with a change in eye gaze. This multi-channeled approach to communication is particularly evident to hearing individuals who are new to Deaf culture. One student expressed it this way: "I feel visually overwhelmed. I get tired just trying to see it all at once."

This multichanneled approach to communication is further developed in the art of storytelling. A frequent technique used by Deaf individuals when storytelling is called visual vernacular (B. Bragg, personal communication, 1974). It is a technique that makes a visually told story more dynamic through change of perspective. The effect of this technique is similar to what occurs in a movie with change of camera angle. A story may start out with a long shot of the scene, pan various characters, and then take a close-up of one particular character. The use of visual vernacular provides an interesting technique when telling a story that contains two perspectives. For example, a well-known story starts with a long shot showing a calm prairie. Then the scene is presented from the perspective of an eagle searching for food then shifts to the perspective of a rabbit, unaware of potential danger. The story continues to shift back and forth, utilizing many different camera angles, with each scene occurring faster and faster until the killing frenzy is over. The story ends with a long shot. Calm has returned to the prairie as the eagle flies farther and farther away, disappearing out of sight over a mountain (C. Baird, personal communication, 1973). . . .

Cultural Values

Porter and Samovar (1988) identified cultural values as having a direct influence on perception. Values, being the evaluative aspect of culture, inform a member what is right or wrong, which behaviors are important and which should be avoided. By analyzing the values of the Deaf culture, a deeper understanding of communication behavior can be gained.

Face-to-Face Communication. Deaf culture places much importance on face-to-face communication. Only when a Deaf person is in the presence of another Deaf person does freedom of expression exist. Given the visual nature of ASL, it is logical that this aspect of interaction has become an important value.

This value can be seen in the interaction patterns of Deaf people. For example, when two people agree to meet at a certain place and time and one is an hour late, it is not uncommon to find the first still waiting, patiently. This behavior may be influenced by restricted use of the telephone; however, the advent of telecommunication devices and telephone relay services have not significantly changed this behavior.

Face-to-face communication is so powerful within the Deaf culture it, at times, may violate "hearing" social interaction rules. For example, two Deaf people may be conversing in a theater. If the lights dim to signal that conversations are to end and attention should be directed to the stage, the conversation between two Deaf people will only cease if the lighting is insufficient to see and, if not completed, will quickly resume when the stage lights come up. Only when the conversation is completed will attention be directed to the stage.

Interfering with face-to-face communication sometimes requires a type of public apology. It has been frequently observed that when a Deaf person is conducting a workshop or group meeting and a Deaf participant gets up to leave, a one- or two-sign explanation is often subtly given. The person departing never interrupts the presenter as in "taking the turn" but recognizes that standing visually disrupts the communication, thus requiring an explanation.

One way that the value of face-to-face communication has been maintained within the culture is the existence of social and recreational clubs for the Deaf. A club for the Deaf can be found in every major city in the country. It is here that Deaf people gather to socialize, problem solve, and maintain the community. The Deaf club offers a variety of activities not found in any other place (e.g., sports activities with all Deaf teams, bingo presented in sign, card tournaments where all the players are Deaf, etc.). Captioned films were also an activity that drew many Deaf individuals to the club; however, with the advent of closed captions on many television programs and videotaped movies that can be rented, Deaf families are spending more time in the home. Although closed captioning has provided Deaf people with much greater access to hearing culture, it has changed the interaction patterns of Deaf people (K. Cagle, personal communication, October 14, 1991).

Directness. Directness for Deaf culture means being straightforward and unambiguous in the messages sent. This value can be seen in several conversational behaviors. Jankowski (1991), in her discussion of Deaf culture, compared the public speaking styles of both hearing and Deaf cultures. Hearing speakers often start a speech with a joke or some other "warm-up" technique. Only after several minutes do the listeners find out the topic of the speech. Deaf public speakers, on the other hand, use a more direct approach. The topic is clearly stated at the beginning of the speech, then each point is presented with several examples. Humor is often used to reinforce the main points of a speech.

Deaf people are more attuned to the visual environment than hearing people. They tend to notice subtle and not so subtle changes in a person's posture, stature, complexion, or overall appearance. Any major change in a person's appearance will be acknowledged in a direct manner. In general American culture, thinness, youth, and the like are valued. Comments made on physical changes toward these characteristics are seen positively; whereas physical change away from these characteristics (weight gain, aging, balding, etc.) are viewed as negative and are therefore not acknowledged.

The Deaf culture, being visually based, places more emphasis on physical characteristics, particularly unique physical characteristics (e.g., tallness, fatness, large nose, curly hair, etc.). These characteristics are not seen as good/bad or positive/negative. They are simply characteristics unique to the individual. If a person's physical appearance undergoes a change, regardless of the type of change, it would be rude not to acknowledge the change.

Openness. A third value of Deaf culture is the free exchange of information or openness. In contrast to the majority's value of privacy, Deaf culture members often freely discuss topics that might otherwise be considered too intimate for public conversation. For example, discussing a hysterectomy, mastectomy, or other intimate medical details is no more a violation of personal privacy than discussing a new car or a favorite television program. The sharing of more intimate information helps to maintain close social bonds between members. In this way, the culture functions as a support group when members need assistance.

In work environments that involve the Deaf and hearing individuals who know Sign (e.g., a school for the Deaf), the issue of open communication often is a source of conflict. When meetings occur involving both groups, hearing people will often group together and engage in spoken conversations and will not use sign. Deaf people feel this behavior is isolating and represents a deliberate attempt to exclude them from conversations. Hearing people will defend their actions, saying that the Deaf person need only to walk up to the conversation to be immediately included. This inability to overhear the conversation places the Deaf person at a conversational disadvantage in two ways: Interactants may first overhear a conversation to determine the desire to participate, and possessing a sense of context allows for ease of entry.

Pride. A fourth important value in Deaf culture is pride in being Deaf. This is often a source of confusion for hearing people who view deafness as a disabling condition. This confusion was very evident in an observed meeting with a doctor and an expectant couple. The doctor questioned the Deaf couple about their genetic history. Her conclusion was, "You'll be happy to know that I am quite sure your baby will be hearing." The couple looked very disappointed and indicated that they knew but would love the baby just the same. The doctor, convinced the interpreter misunderstood her statement, repeated it several times. The Deaf couple indicated they understood but given the choice would prefer to have a Deaf baby.

Pride in being Deaf is also seen in how Deaf people have reacted to cochlear implants. A cochlear implant is a system of electrodes that electronically stimulates the acoustic nerve. The device consists of a tiny microphone (placed in the ear canal) that picks up sound waves and transmits them to an electronic language processor that transforms the sound into electrical stimulation. The stimulating signal is applied to the acoustic nerve via a receiver coil implanted in the skull (Merzenich, 1985). Deaf culture recognizes that cochlear implantation may have a value as a biotechnical assistive device for postlingually deafened adults; however, the implants are often touted as being a medical device that can "cure" deafness, especially for children, thus continuing to promote deafness as a disabling condition. "This viewpoint denies the reality of deafness and fails to acknowledge the existence of the sizable deaf minority whose members consider themselves a viable cultural group, leading satisfying, creative and productive lives without any need for *sound*" (Canadian Cultural Society of the Deaf, 1989, p. 2).

For the hearing majority, cochlear implants are viewed much the same as corneal transplants or prosthetic devices that greatly improve the overall quality of life. A major difference is that cochlear implants do not dramatically change one's ability to hear. In addition, people who are blind or who are amputees do not belong to a separate linguistic culture. Deaf people are a minority group with a separate language and cultural identity that has resulted from their inability to hear. For this reason, some deaf people view cochlear implants as a threat to their culture.

Humor is another way Deaf pride is maintained. Deaf jokes, like humor in most cultures, show variation in topic and structure. There are puns based on visual similarity of signs, one liners, long complex narratives, and "off-color" jokes. However, the overriding theme in all Deaf jokes is that the Deaf person always comes out on top. She or he is portrayed as coming up with an ingenious solution to an impossible problem or simply outwitting a hearing person.

The following two jokes are examples involving a Deaf character from the non-Deaf as compared to the Deaf culture perspective. The value of pride can be seen in the latter whereas the former presents the Deaf character in a stereotypical "deaf-and-dumb" manner.

Non-Deaf Perspective: The Godfather was checking his books one day and found he was missing a large sum of money. He called in Tony, a deaf-mute, who was supposed to have collected the money. Tony shows up with his friend, Sam, who uses sign language and acts as Tony's interpreter. The Godfather says to Sam, "You tell Tony that I'm missing a half million dollars and I want to know where it is." Sam turns to Tony and signs the message. Tony signs back, "I don't know where it is" and Sam tells the Godfather, "He don't know where it is." The conversation goes back and forth several times more when in frustration the Godfather takes out a gun and places it at Tony's temple and says, "Tell him if he doesn't tell me in two seconds where my money is, I'll blow his head off." Sam turns to Tony and signs the message. Tony quickly signs to Sam, "OK, it's in my garage behind the wood pile." Sam tells the Godfather, "He still don't know where it is."

Deaf Culture Perspective: A Deaf couple stops at a motel for the night. About 4 o'clock in the morning the Deaf husband decides that he's thirsty and goes out to get a soda from the machine. When he starts back to his room he realizes he doesn't know which room is his. After several minutes of thought, he goes to his car and continues to honk the horn. As he does, one by one lights turn on in each room except one, the one his Deaf wife occupies.

"Success stories" are another mechanism for teaching and maintaining pride within the culture. Padden (1989), in her analysis of the values of the Deaf culture, cited the following example. A typical story may go like this:

> A deaf person grows up in an oral environment [using speech and lipreading], never having met or talked with deaf people. Later in life, the deaf person meets a deaf person who brings him to parties, teaches him Sign Language and instructs him in the way of deaf people's lives. This person becomes more and more involved, and leaves behind his past as he joins other deaf people. (p. 11).

VERBAL PROCESSES

The previous section discussed how several aspects of the sociocultural element of perception influence the communication patterns of Deaf culture. The second major grouping of sociocultural elements, as identified by Samovar and Porter (1991), fall under the category of verbal processes. These include the language used by a particular culture and the patterns of thought that exist within a culture.

Language

Language is an organized set of learned symbol systems used to represent our experiences (Samovar & Porter, 1991). For Deaf culture, their symbols are expressed in ASL. "Their language is a fully developed language which allows for a full range of human activities, from complex problem solving and social relationships to delicate and beautiful storytelling" (Higgins & Nash, 1987, p. 4).

ASL is not related to spoken English, and it is not a modern day Native American sign language. As explained earlier, linguistically, it is most closely

related to FSL. The origins of ASL point to an important feature of Sign (i.e., Sign Language is not universal). Foreign Sign Languages (e.g., British Sign Language, Japanese Sign Language, Finnish Sign Language) are similar to ASL in that they are also visual languages, but the similarity ends there. Each has its own unique phonology, vocabulary, and syntax (Sandager, 1986). That is, a Deaf person from Germany and a Deaf person from Great Britain will probably face the same communication difficulties as hearing individuals from these countries. However, Deaf people from around the world seem to strongly value face-to-face communication and many place more effort in intercultural communication than hearing individuals.

Although ASL has existed in America for quite some time, it was not recognized as a language until recently. In 1965, the publication of *A Dictionary of American Sign Language* by Stokoe, Croneberg, and Casterline first described ASL as a language separate and distinct from spoken English. For the first time, a group of linguists analyzed ASL and identified its building blocks. Cheremes, similar to phonemes, make up the three major parameters for signs. Each sign uses a particular handshape, is produced at a particular location in space, and utilizes a particular motion. In addition, signs are produced "within a highly restricted space defined by the top of the head, the waist, and the reach of the arms from side to side (with elbows bent)" (Klima & Bellugi, 1979). Figure 1 shows the space in which signs are produced.

According to Porter and Samovar (1988), "language is the primary vehicle by which a culture transmits its beliefs, values, and norms" (p. 27). ASL, being a visual-gestural language has many features that reflect these aspects of culture.

Unequivocal Communication

Directness is reflected in ASL's relatively few euphemistic phrases. Euphemisms develop when a particular term is strongly associated with being unpleasant. When this association occurs, a substitute word or euphemism develops that is free of these negative associations. In English, euphemisms are commonly developed for body parts, bodily functions, sexual acts, and death to name a few. In English, we have numerous euphemisms that function as a substitute

Figure 1. *The region in which Signs are made.*
From Technical Signs: Manual One *(p. 28)*
by F. Caccamise et al., 1982, Rochester, NY:
Rochester Institute of Technology at the National
Technical Institute for the Deaf. Copyright 1982 by
Rochester Institute of Technology at the National
Technical Institute for the Deaf. Reprinted by permission.

for the phrase, "I need to go to the bathroom" (e.g., "I need to powder my nose"; "I need to go to the little girls room"; "I have to go see a man about a horse"). In Sign Language, informants could only identify one direct way to express this message (a "T" handshape, shaken right to left, twice) and two euphemistic phrases: (a) "R-R" (meaning rest room) and (b) "I have to go make a TTY (teletypewriter) phone call." The only other euphemism identified was one frequently used by teenage girls for the term *menstruation*. This sign is rather unique in that it does not require the use of the hands. The sign is made by quickly puffing one cheek, thus, it can be secretly communicated to another girl by turning the head away from any boys who may be watching. With the exception of these three examples, euphemisms tend to be avoided by the Deaf culture because they are often vague and may lead to misunderstandings. A more direct approach is preferred.

Communication of Sound

The Sapir–Whorf hypothesis suggests that the structure of a language influences how the user of that language perceives the world. If your language requires that snow, colors, or dogs be classified in a particular way, then these objects will be perceived differently from someone who is not required to make these differentiations. ASL offers an opportunity to investigate how language may affect perception; that is, How might the users of a language based on vision (ASL) perceive and talk about a concept like *sound*?

To fully understand how sound is perceived by Deaf culture, it is helpful to first compare the concepts *quiet* and *noise*. The sign for *quiet* has two components. The first is an index finger placed over the lips, and the second involves both hands moving in a downward motion. In general, this sign is produced in a slow manner. This sign is also used for the concepts of calm, peaceful, silent, tranquil, and so forth. In contrast, the sign for *noise* involves first pointing to the ear and then both hands shaking as they move away from the signer (see Figure 2). The second component of *noise* is also used to mean *vibration*.

With Sign Language, various noises are communicated by converting the noise into its associated motion. For example, here is how Sign expresses the following noises:

A *gun shot* involves the sign for gun with the added motion depicting the kick of the gun.

A *ringing phone* involves the sign for phone with the added motion of the handset shaking with each ring.

A *scream* involves the sign for vibrations emanating from the mouth and moving out away from the signer.

Thunder (or a very loud noise) involves pointing to the ear, with the two fists producing a violent shake.

Alarm involves depicting a bell clapper hitting the side of the bell.

The culture has also modified traditions involving sound. At Deaf culture weddings, the tapping of the wineglass requesting the bride and groom to kiss is replaced with the waving of the napkin. Applause has also undergone a visual modification, particularly when the performer is Deaf. The hand clap is used for hearing performers, whereas the hand wave (both hands extended overhead and rotated back and forth) is used for Deaf performers.

Figure 2. *Comparison of the Signs for* quiet *and* noise. *From Basic Sign Communication: Vocabulary (pp. 75, 86) by W. Newell, 1983, Silver Spring, MD: National Association of the Deaf. Copyright 1983 by Rochester Institute of Technology at the National Technical Institute for the Deaf. Reprinted by permission.*

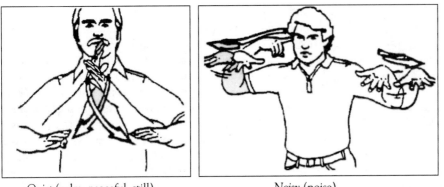

Quiet (calm, peaceful, still)   Noisy (noise)

Name Signs

Name signs, according to Supalla (1990), are the proper names of persons living within the Deaf community. All Americans are given a spoken and written name at birth; however, Deaf individuals and hearing members of the culture are also given a name sign. Name signs are most often given by a parent who is Deaf, a Deaf peer, or a Deaf teacher.

Supalla (1990) showed that a name sign can be descriptive or arbitrary. A descriptive name sign is based on a personal characteristic (e.g., large eyes, a birth mark on the cheek, curly hair) or an arbitrary name sign that involves the initials of the person and then is assigned a specific movement and location.

Mindess (1990) found that name signs reflect two major aspects of the culture: identity and solidarity. A name sign is unique in that it symbolizes a specific person. It is generally given to an individual by another Deaf person and not self-assigned. Most people have only one name sign that stays with them for life; however, some individuals may acquire a different name sign as time goes on. However, one cannot just arbitrarily decide to change one's name sign. There must be a very good reason; for example, when a woman marries, she may decide to add the initial of her husband's last name to her name sign. Another reason for changing one's name sign is if two people

in the same community happen to have the same name sign. If such a circumstance arises, one of the two must change or modify his or her sign name. However, there are social status rules associated with the change. It is generally the newer person, or if one of the two is hearing, who is expected to change.

Name signs also provide group solidarity. As Mindess (1990) pointed out, "the strongest value, which I heard expressed in many different ways, was that name signs serve as connections to the group" (p. 7). As stated earlier, one generally does not invent his or her own name sign—it is given. Deaf individuals with hearing parents received their name signs from peers or teachers when they entered the school for the Deaf. Deaf individuals who did not identify with the culture until much later in life are not given their name signs until someone in the culture feels the individual is a member. The idea that a name sign reflects identification *and* affiliation is often overlooked by hearing individuals new to Deaf culture. Students of Sign Language, like students of any foreign language, want to be able to introduce themselves using cultural conventions. In Sign Language, one's name can be expressed through finger spelling, but the student soon becomes aware that culture members have name signs. Thus, students may ask an inappropriate person for a name sign or invent one themselves. It is interesting to note that often these name signs subtly violate the structure rules of name signs. For example, a former hearing student was also an accomplished dancer. Her self-assigned name sign involved her initial plus the sign for dance. This name sign violated a structure rule in that descriptive name signs must have contact with the body. The sign for *dance* is produced in front of the signer and does not come in contact with the body. These subtle violations communicate to Deaf culture members that the owner of the name sign is probably hearing and/or may not be a bona fide member.

NONVERBAL PROCESSES

The nonverbal systems of a culture, like the verbal systems, are learned as part of the socialization process. As Porter and Samovar (1988) suggested, they may include eye gaze, touch, silence, space, time, and para-language. An analysis of some of the nonverbal processes of Deaf culture provides a deeper understanding into the culture's structure.

Time

The value of face-to-face interactions can also be analyzed from the perspective of the length of time involved in communication interactions. As Jankowski (1991) pointed out, socializing is an important Deaf culture event that extends the time required for any group meeting, in that Deaf participants must first share the latest news and renew cultural relationships. At major conventions, involving Deaf people who have not seen each other for a long period of time, conversations often continue into the wee hours of the morning. Hopper and Mowl (1987), in their description of Deaf congregations and religious services, showed how this value is incorporated throughout the service.

> The service usually begins with Deaf church members socializing for up to ten minutes. The pastor mingles as well and after about five minutes leaves to put on the vestments. . . . The worship service is participatory, often referred to as a dialogue homily, as there is interaction between the pastor conducting the service and the congregation. (p. 3)

This value is further exemplified in extended leave-taking behavior. Interactants delay the termination of a conversation by prolonging closure. "Good-bye" may be said only to be followed by the introduction of a new topic requiring several more minutes of conversation. This process may be repeated several times before the person actually departs.

This extension of time is also evident when one attempts to enter an already established conversation. When two people are engaged in conversation and a third party approaches, the third member is often left to wait on the outside of the conversational boundaries much longer than in conversations involving hearing individuals. The conversation might continue until the current topic is completed or there is a convenient place to pause and acknowledge the third party. This waiting period appears to serve two functions: It maintains the uninterrupted flow of conversation, and it permits the third party to "tune in" to the conversation before actually participating.

Eye Contact

Eye contact serves an important function for face-to-face communication. Conversations cannot start until the interactants have established eye contact. During a signed conversation, the speaker will frequently break eye contact; however, the listener cannot. This rule applies even if the listener is hearing and the speaker is a Deaf person who has good voice quality. The following quotation from a Deaf man serves as an example of this type of situation.

> Oftentimes, people tell me I speak all right and that they can understand my speech; and because of that, they often do something else while listening to me, like writing notes or reading. That really bothers me, because when they are doing that, I feel that they are not paying attention to me. I need to have eye contact with them, so that I can get some feedback about their attitudes and thoughts in response to what I am saying. (Lang & DeCaro, 1988, p. 40)

Touching

Touching serves three very important functions within the Deaf culture. First, touching is frequently used to gain attention or eye contact before a conversation can begin; second, it functions to physically connect the culture, and third, it maintains safety.

As stated earlier, a conversation cannot begin until eye contact is made. Thus, touching often precedes eye contact. For a Deaf person, a touch communicates a great deal of information. It communicates which direction to look and the urgency of communication. For example, a light, double touch on the shoulder or arm (the most frequently touched regions) simply says, "Hey, Mary." A touch that involves resting the hand on the arm communicates, "I can see you are in the middle of something, look up when you can." A hard jab or a rapidly repeating tap means, "This is very important, look immediately."

If a conversation is already in progress, a third party can gain immediate entrance to a conversation by touching the signer on the arm or gaining attention with a wave. However, this privileged entrance is only used when the interruption is absolutely necessary and what is to be communicated is important. Hearing individuals frequently violate this rule when attempting to pass through a conversation. Often, Deaf individuals will rest against the opposite sides of a hallway when conversing. This position offers the optimal distance for receiving a signed message because the face, hands, and body can all be clearly seen. Most hearing individuals assume that it is rude to walk through the conversation without first acknowledging the violation by saying "excuse me." The hearing individual believes that he or she must first get the Deaf persons' attention (i.e., a tap or wave to gain eye contact) and then sign "excuse me" or the hearing person will wait until one or both conversants stop talking and look at him or her. Once the Deaf person realizes why the conversation was interrupted, the hearing person might receive a very annoyed look accompanied with a gesture signaling to walk through quickly. From the perspective of Deaf culture, the appropriate behavior is to respect the face-to-face communication by simply passing through without interruption.

Touching also serves to physically connect culture members. Hugging is a very common part of greetings and leave taking. Rarely is a handshake used among members who know each other. Touching also occurs frequently during conversations to communicate empathy, support, or connectedness. One interesting example of this can be seen when conversations are interrupted.

> A Deaf supervisor was explaining a project to her Deaf assistant when a secretary interrupted to ask a question that needed an immediate answer. Before looking away to respond to the secretary, the supervisor placed her hand on the assistant's arm, maintaining physical contact with him, responded to the secretary using her other hand, then turning back to her assistant, removed her hand and continued the conversation.

From the perspective of the interactants, this behavior functions as a means to preserve the connectedness between conversants. When the interruption occurred, it required that eye contact be broken; thus, the physical contact served to maintain a conversational bond until eye contact could be resumed.

Touch is also used to protect interactants from harm. One of the additional duties of interactants in a signed conversation is to alert the other of any danger that may be approaching from the blind side (i.e., the region behind the respective interactants). When a potential danger approaches from the blind side, it is the other's duty to move the conversation out of the path of danger. This is often accomplished by placing the hand on the arm and gently guiding to a safe location. This activity is particularly evident when two conversants are walking and talking. It is not uncommon to see one member take the elbow of the other and guide away from a fence, chuckhole, or other potential danger. It is interesting to note that this guiding behavior is so common that conversations often continue uninterrupted.

CONCLUSION

Historically, Deaf individuals have been viewed as a disabled group. This view has led to many preconceptions and stereotypes that frequently result in negative interactions between Deaf and non-Deaf individuals. The basis for the communication conflict can be traced to two major assumptions made by non-Deaf individuals: an assumption of a deficit condition and an assumption of similarity.

The assumption that Deaf individuals are in a deficit condition because they cannot hear leads to the conclusion that they are incomplete or lacking. Underlying this assumption is the belief that given the choice Deaf individuals would prefer to hear. This assumption often creates communication that is patronizing or pitying to the Deaf individual.

The assumption of similarity is that Deaf individuals share the same cultural knowledge, experiences, and meanings as all Americans. That is, they are fluent in English, follow the same interaction rules, and hold the same cultural values. It is common for those who have undergone sensitivity training for disabled groups to believe that the only difference between Deaf and non-Deaf people is that Deaf people cannot hear. Thus, behavioral differences are often attributed to eccentric behavior, inadequate social training, or mental illness.

When Deaf individuals are viewed as a co-culture of American society, these preconceptions and stereotypes are replaced with greater tolerance for difference and respect. One is not as quick to evaluate and label behaviors that are perceived as different. Communication may not always be fully understood, but there will be a greater tendency to withhold judgments and more fully evaluate prejudices.

This article has discussed the cultural patterns of Deaf people. Evidence has been presented that Deaf culture possesses a unique set of knowledge, experience, values, and meanings. As a co-culture of American culture, Deaf culture provides a rich source for further intercultural communication research. Of great value would be a further investigation of interactional pattern differences when Deaf culture is viewed from a cultural perspective versus a disabled perspective. This line of research would provide much needed information to the non-Deaf majority, thus opening up more successful lines of communication.

References

Albert, R., & Triandis, H. (1991). Intercultural education for multicultural societies: Critical issues. In L. Samovar & R. Porter (Eds.), *Intercultural communication: A reader* (pp. 411–426). Belmont, CA: Wadsworth.

Baker, C., & Padden, C. (1978). Focusing on the non-manual components of American Sign Language. In P. Siple (Ed.), *Understanding language through Sign Language research* (pp. 27–57). New York: Academic.

Braithwaite, D. (1991). Viewing persons with disabilities as a culture. In L. Samovar & R. Porter (Eds.), *Intercultural communication: A reader* (pp. 136–142). Belmont, CA: Wadsworth.

Canadian Cultural Society of the Deaf. (1989). *The use of cochlear implants: A position paper.* Unpublished manuscript.

Carmichael, C. (1991). Intercultural perspectives of aging. In L. Samovar & R. Porter (Eds.), *Intercultural communication: A reader* (pp. 128–134). Belmont, CA: Wadsworth.

Cokely, D., & Baker, C. (1980). *American Sign Language: A teacher's resource text on grammar and culture.* Silver Spring, MD: T. J. Publishers.

Gallaudet, E. (1887). The value of the sign-language to the deaf. *American Annals of the Deaf, 32,* 141–147.

Gannon, J. (1981). *Deaf heritage.* Silver Spring, MD: National Association of the Deaf.

Gannon, J. (1989). *The week the world heard Gallaudet.* Washington, DC: Gallaudet University Press.

Groce, N. (1988). *Everyone here spoke Sign Language.* Cambridge, MA: Harvard University Press.

Higgins, P. (1989). *Outsiders in a hearing world.* Newbury Park, CA: Sage.

Higgins, P., & Nash, J. (1987). *Understanding deafness socially.* Springfield, IL: Charles Thomas.

Hopper, M., & Mowl, G. (1987, August). *United States of America Deaf culture.* Paper presented at the meeting of the Registry of Interpreters for the Deaf, St. Paul, MN.

Jankowski, K. (1991). Communicating with the deaf. In L. Samovar & R. Porter (Eds.), *Intercultural communication: A reader* (pp. 116–119). Belmont, CA: Wadsworth.

Kannapell, B. (1982). Inside the Deaf community. *The Deaf American, 34*(4), 23–26.

Klima, E., & Bellugi, U. (1979). *The signs of language.* Cambridge, MA: Harvard University Press.

Lane, H. (1984). *When the mind hears.* New York: Random House.

Lane, H. (1988). Is there a "psychology of the Deaf"? *Exceptional Children, 55*(1), 7–19.

Lang, H., & DeCaro, J. (Eds.). (1988). *Proceedings of the second convocation of faculty and staff.* Rochester, NY: National Technical Institute for the Deaf.

Madrid, A. (1991). Diversity and its discontents. In L. Samovar & R. Porter (Eds.), *Intercultural communication: A reader* (pp. 116–119). Belmont, CA: Wadsworth.

Majors, R. (1991). America's emerging gay culture. In L. Samovar & R. Porter (Eds.), *Intercultural communication: A reader* (pp. 160–166). Belmont, CA: Wadsworth.

Merzenich, M. (1985). *Cochlear implants.* New York: Raven.

Mindess, A. (1990). What name signs can tell us about Deaf culture. *Sign Language Studies, 66,* 1–21.

Moores, D. (1987). *Educating the deaf: Psychology, principles, and practices* (3rd ed.). Boston: Houghton Mifflin.

Padden, C. (1989). The Deaf community and the culture of Deaf people. In S. Wilcox (Ed.), *American Deaf culture* (pp. 1–16). Burtonsville, MD: Linstok.

Porter, R., & Samovar, L. (1988). Approaching intercultural communication. In L. Samovar & R. Porter (Eds.), *Intercultural communication: A reader* (pp. 15–30). Belmont, CA: Wadsworth.

Samovar, L., & Porter, R. (1991). *Communication between cultures.* Belmont, CA: Wadsworth.

Sandager, O. (1986). *Sign languages around the world.* North Hollywood, CA: OK Publishing.

Schein, J., & Delk, M. (1974). *The deaf population of the United States.* Silver Spring, MD: National Association of the Deaf.

Stokoe, W., Croneberg, C., & Casterline, D. (1965). *A dictionary of American Sign Language.* Washington, DC: Gallaudet College Press.

Supalla, S. (1990). The arbitrary name sign system in American Sign Language. *Sign Language Studies, 67,* 99–126.

Tannen, D. (1990). *You just don't understand.* New York: Ballantine.

Vernon, M. (1968). Current etiological factors in deafness. *American Annals of the Deaf, 113,* 106–115.

Weber, S. (1991). The need to be: The socio-cultural significance of Black language. In L. Samovar & R. Porter (Eds.), *Intercultural communication: A reader* (pp. 277–282). Belmont, CA: Wadsworth.

Woodward, J. (1973). Some characteristics of Pidgin Sign English. *Sign Language Studies, 3,* 39–46.

Woodward, J. (1978). Historical bases of American Sign Language. In P. Siple (Ed.), *Understanding language through sign language research.* New York: Academic.

Concepts and Questions

1. Why does Siple suggest that the term *co-culture* is being used instead of the term *sub-culture?* Do you agree with the shift in terminology? Why?
2. According to Siple, why has the deaf co-culture not been recognized as a domestic co-culture?
3. What characteristics of the deaf co-culture seem to make it a co-culture?
4. What are some of the "perceptual frames" discussed by Siple?
5. What are some of the differences in perceptual frames between the hearing and deaf cultures?
6. What are the major cultural values existing in the deaf co-culture? How would you compare these values with the ones held by the hearing culture?
7. Why is directness valued by the deaf?
8. Why are there very few euphemistic phrases in American Sign Language?
9. What are "name signs," and why are they important in the deaf co-culture?
10. What aspects of nonverbal communication are somewhat different when applied to the deaf co-culture?

Communication and Identification in the Gay Subculture

JOSEPH P. GOODWIN

We are constantly being bombarded by innumerable signals; we are, after all, sentient beings, and as such we receive messages in many ways. Not only do we interpret what we see and hear; odors, flavors, and physical sensations also have a bearing on our understanding of our environment and the information it contains. Virtually everything communicates. Confronted with so many messages, we filter the signals and interpret consciously only a few of them at any time. Each bit of information, however, is retained and plays an unconscious part in understanding. Thus, based upon our experiences, we give meanings to the messages we receive; we reconstruct them into information that we can understand on our own terms. These meanings may be appropriate, or they may be misinterpretations resulting from ambiguity or lack of adequate information.

A leafless tree can tell us that the season is fall or winter. The message is present even without our being there to interpret it. This example, though, illustrates the problem of ambiguity. Taken as sufficient to convey the entire message, a bare tree can mislead us. If the other trees are bare, and the ground is covered with snow, we can assume that indeed it is winter. If the air is cool, the grass and the other trees are green, the air is warm, and flowers are blooming, then we must assume that it is spring or summer and that the bare tree is either diseased or dead. We construct the complete message from a combination of details.

Since interpretation is an essential aspect of communication, a good opportunity exists for misunderstanding. To understand any message fully, we must consider both its sender and its receiver. The context of the communicative event is no less important, since we translate contextual details into parts of the message. This process presents the possibility that some messages we receive are not the messages transmitted to us. The sender's implications, our inferences, and ambiguities in the information allow us to misinterpret the communication.[1] Meaning, therefore, is doubly subjective, relying on both the sender and the receiver for parts of its content. Although the result is often confusion, these very stumbling blocks are put to good advantage by groups seeking private means of interaction. Thus gays have capitalized on the subjectivity of interpretation as one way of identifying and communicating with one another without their homosexuality becoming evident to straights.

The degree to which the gay identity is foregrounded varies according to context, as do the functions of gay folklore. The less gay the context, the more likely the folklore is to function primarily for identification and covert communication.

The gay bar communicates a number of messages; its lighting, its layout, and its ambiance all contribute to this process. Dim, colored lights convey a sense of privacy and intimacy. The floor plan generally allows the patrons easy visual access to people throughout the bar, but it also requires that, when crowded, patrons must come into close contact with one another. Indeed, the proxemics of the gay bar stand in marked contrast to those of social situations in the mainstream white American culture. Western tradition requires us to maintain a certain distance from one another and provides various coping mechanisms in case we find ourselves caught unavoidably close to someone else; in gay bars (and social situations as well), by contrast, these barriers are removed and closeness is encouraged. As one of the men Edmund White interviewed said, "This place is all about touching. . . . They kept fiddling with the design till they got it right, till everyone had to slip and slide against everyone else."[2] The gay bar makes the statement, "This place is ours; we can be ourselves; we can openly touch and express affection for one another; we can openly seek sexual partners. We can do these things because this place and this time are ours and are subject to our standards rather than straight values."

From Joseph P. Goodwin, *More Man Than You'll Ever Be* (Bloomington: Indiana University Press, 1989), pp. 11–28. Reprinted by permission of the publisher. Professor Goodwin teaches at Ball State University.

Other gay contexts include business establishments frequented primarily by homosexual people. Like the bars, these are places where gays can be open about their sexual orientation and can talk freely. Especially in larger cities, for example, there are gay restaurants that offer a safe environment more relaxed than the atmosphere of the bars. There are even entire gay neighborhoods (the "gay ghettos"). Gay social and religious organizations as well as private parties for gays offer additional opportunities for homosexual people to relate to each other *as homosexual people*. Persons present in gay contexts are usually identified by others as gay, regardless of their reasons for being there. Until otherwise informed, most gays tend to assume that all others in such places are homosexually oriented.[3]

Stores, streets, cultural events, office parties, churches, most bars, and indeed most places in our society are nongay contexts in which gays must be careful about how much information they reveal about themselves. These situations require covert communication strategies if homosexual people are to be able to recognize and communicate with one another without being discovered.

Finally, there are semigay contexts like certain parks, streets, and other places where gay people meet, but since these are public places used by many straight people as well, gays must again rely on covert strategies to avoid detection.

The American gay subculture has developed an extensive system of communication.[4] In addition to the argot, members of the community use many subtle (and not so subtle) nonverbal signals to communicate with and relate to other gays. For communication to be effective, rules must be agreed upon; people must know how to convey and interpret information. In the gay subculture there are several strategies employed in communication that are also common to other forms of gay folklore.

One such strategy is humor, which is pervasive in the gay community, a fact reflected in the language, its words, and its usage. The term *TV*, for example, means "transvestite," a simple contraction; but *transvestite*, by extension, is used to mean "television," a funny reversal typical of gay English. Place names frequently make use of such humor. Gay neighborhoods are sometimes given names like *Lavender Hill, Homo Heights, Vaseline Alley*, and the *Swish Alps*.[5] A gay bar in Bloomington is in a building that previously housed the local Moose Lodge; poking fun at the stodginess and conservatism assumed to be endemic among straight people belonging to such organizations, the owners named their bar Bullwinkle's, after the moose in the children's cartoon program. A bar frequented by men who dress in black leather, who often ride motorcycles, and who are generally presumed to prefer sadomasochistic sexual acts is called, naturally enough, a *leather bar*. If some of its patrons tend to be more effeminate than one would generally expect, the bar is referred to as a *patent leather bar*, a term that mocks the intensity associated with those who are part of the leather culture. The humor of these last two examples exhibits the essence of camp—deflating pomposity and underscoring the absurd underlying the serious.[6]

Puns are common in gay conversations. For example, a middle-aged graduate student known to have a preference for teenagers was talking about his studies. He said, "I haven't decided whether to major in American [literature] and minor in British, or major in British and minor in American." Another man said, "Well, Bill, I would have thought you'd major in minors." This type of verbal agility is quite common in the gay subculture. A sharp wit and a sharp tongue are prized possessions. Such word play requires special linguistic competence, a skill that gays develop probably because of the oral nature of the subculture and because of the pervasiveness of humor in the community.[7]

Some terms lend themselves particularly well to puns. *Fairy* and *faggot*, generally used by straights pejoratively, are two of these. Almost any time gays hear the word *fairy* (or the nearly homophonous *ferry*) used in a nongay context they turn it into a pun. S. Steinberg even used the pun in the title of his book *A Fairy Tale*, a story about a gay Jewish man and his matchmaking aunt. "Let's ride the ferry" is an obvious sexual pun. A faggot is not only a gay person; a faggot is a piece of wood to be burned, and the clipped form *fag* can mean "cigarette." *Fagged out* means "tired." *Flaming faggot* is a common phrase that takes on added meaning when someone suggests putting another log on the fire. (*Flaming* means "carrying on in a blatantly effeminate manner," and is probably derived from *flamboyant*.) The humor also has somber overtones since many gays believe that homosexual people were burned at the stake during the Middle Ages. Requesting a fag (almost always done to set up the pun, since *fag* in this sense is obsolete in the United States) may result in a response like, "I want one too!" A man bored and offering his goodbyes in a gay bar, when asked if he is leaving, may respond, "Yes, I'm about fagged out." In doing so he not only says he is tired; he is also commenting on the people in the bar, saying in effect, "I've seen enough of these people. I've leaving."

Related to puns are double entendres, which are based upon another strategy used in gay communication: ambiguity. The covert nature of many messages is created by sending an ambiguous signal; some key element necessary for a definite interpretation is missing from the communication. Ambiguous signals are used so that the message can be denied if the receiver takes offense when he interprets the information as the sender may have intended originally. The dual nature of the communication allows its originator to claim his intention is innocent and that the receiver has inferred a message that was not sent. At the same time, the gay man's dual cultural membership—gay and straight—provides him with a background from which to make double interpretations.

In the following double entendre, heard in a gay bar in Bloomington, the ambiguity is rather obvious. Feeling his attempt at finding a sexual partner for the evening to be futile, one man said, "Well, I guess I'll go home and do something constructive, like knit." Another man responded, "But you only have one needle." The first man replied, "So I'll crochet." The exchange was spontaneous and the reactions were quick; nothing was laboriously thought out. The humor goes a bit deeper than it first appears, for it plays upon the stereotype of the effeminate gay male. Both knitting and crocheting are considered boring and are associated with women. A man with only one needle (or penis) cannot engage in a cooperative endeavor like knitting, which requires two needles working together. Thus he must do with the equipment at hand: having but one needle, he must crochet (masturbate). Since this encounter took place between two men, each of whom knew the other was gay, and because it occurred within a gay context, both intended meanings were clear to those who heard the exchange. The two were simply engaging in a bit of word play. Had the men continued the conversation along similar lines, the double entendres could have been used to lay the groundwork for a sexual proposition.

John Reid, in *The Best Little Boy in the World*, gives an example of the type of nonverbal ambiguity gays are accustomed to interpreting.

> His . . . apartment sent gay bleeps into my radar, bleeps that would probably not show up on a straight screen, like the tube of K-Y in the medicine chest or the Barbra Streisand albums among his record collection. I wondered: Could Esquire be gay? I remembered the time we had played handball on his membership at the New York Athletic Club (no blacks and only twelve Jews allowed, but some faggots and lots of closet cases) and what remarkable [*sic*] good shape he was in. I wondered why he had separated from his wife and why they had had no children.[8]

The ambiguous cues were sufficient to alert the narrator that he should watch for additional hints that might confirm his suspicions regarding his friend's orientation.

Ambiguity offers another advantage. A person wishing to ignore one meaning of an ambiguous message can do so simply by taking the signal at its face value. He can in this way avoid a conversation on a topic he wishes not to talk about or resist an attempt to shift the conversation to a more intimate level.[9] The problem with ambiguity is that it can result in misinterpretation when none is intended. A speaker may wish to convey some information secretly to someone else, who misunderstands just as the outsiders do. Thus an ambiguous signal may have to be reinforced with other cues until the intended receiver no longer can have any doubt as to the message.

Inversion is a third strategy common in gay communication. Grace Sims Holt, writing about black English, says that "the phenomenon of inversion is a practical necessity for people in subordinate positions." She goes on to explain that blacks co-opted the white man's language, inverting meanings, taking pride in words whites used pejoratively in describing blacks. The whites were not aware of this word play, so it became a way in which blacks could covertly assert themselves without being punished.

The result was the blacks' maintenance of a sense of dignity and group cohesion.[10]

Not only does inversion involve a coding that provides secrecy; it also offers a means of insulting the people who are so adept at stigmatizing gays, a way of expressing contempt that frequently passes unrecognized by those who have been insulted. Inversion also conveys a defiance of heterosexual standards as well. It is a way of saying to straights, "We do not accept your morality. We have our own culture with its own ethics, and these are the rules by which we live." Drag is a highly visible form of non-verbal inversion, and as such exhibits this defiance. Drag is essentially aggressive: gay men present themselves in women's attire, in direct contravention of cultural norms.

Humor, ambiguity, and inversion are often conveyed in gay language through certain paralinguistic features worthy of a detailed study in their own right. As Maurer states in referring to argots, "[they] differ from the standard language in some aspects of structure, and especially in intonation, pitch, and juncture."[11]

Intonation is a feature played with extensively in gay English. As in standard English, many aspects of meaning are conveyed by intonation, sarcasm in particular. And since sarcasm is a form of inversion based primarily on sound rather than denotation, it is especially suited to gay intonation patterns. The word *flawless*, denoting someone who is especially attractive or something extremely well done, is pronounced with heavy emphasis on the first syllable and a falling inflection on the second. *Thank you*, spoken with a rising and then falling inflection, is an interjection expressing emphasis, a sort of oral italics. *For days* is a similar phrase, but it carries with it a sense of great quantity. "Lipstick for days!" means, "She's wearing a really thick layer of lipstick." In other words, it is similar to the English idiom *that just won't quit. Lipstick for days* is spoken beginning at a high tonal level, dropped to a low level for two syllables, and then rising to a medium level on the last syllable.

If we reduce intonation to these three tonal levels—high, medium, and low—we can make basic diagrams of the intonation patterns of these expressions. In the diagram below, dots and lines represent syllables, lines standing for syllables held longer than usual; curved lines indicate syllables beginning at one level and rising or falling to another.

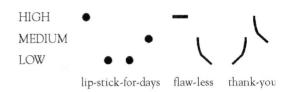

In contrast to the gay argot, *flawless* and *thank you* in standard English would be rendered more nearly as follows:

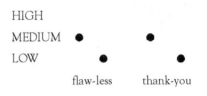

(*Lipstick for days* would not occur in standard English.) This playing with pitch and stress, the exaggeration of tonality, is basic to gay English.

Gays use their argot for secrecy, when relaxing with other gay people, and as a means of preserving and passing on much of their cultural heritage. Just as immigrants generally retain Old World traditions in their native tongues, so do gay people couch a substantial amount of their lore in the gay argot.

Many words in the gay argot are borrowed from the specialized languages of other groups, like prostitutes, drug addicts, and actors.[12] Bruce Rodgers, in *Gay Talk*, offers derivations of many of the 12,000 terms he defines. Among the languages he lists as origins are Chinese, French, Greek, Gullah, Hawaiian, Louisiana Creole, and Yiddish. A large part of the vocabulary, however, is composed of words that gays have created or to which they have applied their own meanings, such as *nelly*, a word used to describe someone who is effeminate (possibly an intensification of *nervous nelly*), and *TV*.[13] The argot is nothing if not eclectic.

A person entering the gay subculture is faced with the problem of acquiring this new language. He learns the argot in many ways. Much of it he absorbs by hearing it used again and again, an osmotic process parallel to the acquisition of one's native tongue. He adds new words to his vocabulary from time to time by asking friends what specific terms mean, and on occasion someone will volunteer information, saying, "Do you know what we call . . . ?" Sometimes the "teacher" will even suggest the reason that *x* is used to mean "*y*."

Learning occurs in many gay settings, including gay bars, which Evelyn Hooker calls "training and integration centers for the [gay] community." She goes on to say that "once he has 'come out' . . . the process of education proceeds with rapid pace. Eager and willing tutors . . . teach him the special language."[14] After learning the core word stock, the fledgling member of the community may choose to use it. If so, he may begin to use a sprinkling of words here and there, gradually becoming comfortable with the language and fluent in speaking it. At this point he has reached the fifth stage of gay acculturation: serving as a model.

The argot has spread throughout the subculture; its use is not restricted to a given part of the country. Paul H. Gebhard explains how this dissemination is possible:

> Because homosexuality cuts across all social and occupational classes its argot is enriched from many sources. A beautifully apt new term can be invented and within a short time be in the mouths of both the underworld and the socially elite. Due to mobility in the United States a standard form of the argot is nationwide, but there appear to be local colloquialisms and special usages.[15]

One type of mobility that is particularly significant in the spread of gay English is travel. Many gays travel extensively, have gay friends throughout the United States, and visit gay communities whenever possible. In doing so, they pass on new terms (and jokes, as well as other traditions) to those they visit, and in turn acquire new material from them that they bring home.

Some parts of the gay argot are as mundane as others are colorful. The following examples offer a sense of the variety the language exhibits.[16]

Active describes a man who takes the inserter role in oral or anal intercourse. He is the person who "gets done" during a sexual act. The "doer," or insertee, is *passive*. . . . Most homosexual acts are of a more mutual nature than this distinction implies. There are some men, however, who are exclusively active or passive, or who at least prefer one role to

the other. Oral intercourse is *French* and anal sex is *Greek*, these terms playing upon the stereotypes of the sexual preferences of men from France and Greece. (Edmund White wonders whether "archaeologists in the future [will] speculate about our obsessive interest in foreign verbs—French active, Greek passive.")[17] *Switch-hitters* are bisexual men; since they have sexual relations with both men and women, they are also said to be *AC/DC*. A person who is very masculine in appearance is said to be *butch*; his effeminate counterpart is *fem (femme)*. Another term for an effeminate male is *swishy*, which is almost synonymous with *nelly*. (*Swishy* carries a connotation of effeminate movements in addition to voice and mannerisms.) One who is *flaming*, behaving in an exaggeratedly and obviously effeminate way, can also be called *screaming*. *Flaming* is often used as a modifier for *faggot* (probably because of the puns possible and the alliteration created by combining the terms), and both *flaming* and *screaming* are used in tandem with *queen*.

Queen, ultimately from the Greek *gyne*, "woman" (through Indo-European *gwen-* to Old English *cwene*),[18] is a standard term used by gays in many senses. The word often carries a connotation of effeminacy (read "negative connotation") and all of its attributes: passivity, weakness, perhaps a bit of flamboyance. It is also used quite often as a term of endearment, a sort of affectionate insult. "You tired old queen" is not nearly as derogatory as it sounds. (*Tired* means "used up"—not just sexually—"jaded," "washed up," and so forth, rather than "exhausted"; it means "worn out" in the sense of having succumbed to excessive wear and tear.) Using this phrase is comparable to calling a friend who makes a silly mistake a dummy. *Queen* is used in innumerable compounds. A *drag queen* is a man who likes to go in drag; a *dinge queen* is a white man who prefers black men, and a *snow queen* is a black who prefers Caucasians. A man whose interests lie with Orientals is called a *rice queen*; he is sometimes said to have *yellow fever*.

There are many other gay terms for designating people. *Bitch* is used as both a vocative and a noun; it can, like *queen*, be used either affectionately or pejoratively. *Girl* is a standard word meaning "gay male"; its use is frequently accompanied by feminine pronouns. *Queen*, *bitch*, and *girl* are good examples of inversion. Another vocative that can be used to express affection is *Miss Thing*. The word *chicken* refers to boys, especially ones not beyond their early teens. A *chicken hawk* is an older man who prefers younger sexual partners. A *troll* is someone who is ugly and often well beyond middle age. An occasional sexual partner or a "one-night stand" is a *trick*; the man with whom one has a continuing relationship is his *lover*. Since homosexual people have been culturally sterilized, being considered to be nonreproductive, gays have adopted the word *breeders* (often occurring in the phrase "filthy breeders") to refer contemptuously to straights. *Clone* has recently been added to the gay vocabulary to designate a particular gay appearance. As White describes him, the

> Castro Street Clone . . . [has] a strongly marked
> mouth and swimming, soulful eyes (the effect of the
> mustache); a V-shaped torso by metonymy from the
> open V of the half-unbuttoned shirt above the sweaty
> chest; rounded buttocks squeezed in jeans, swelling
> out from the clinched-in waist, further emphasized by
> the charged erotic insignia of colored handkerchiefs
> and keys; a crotch instantly accessible through the
> buttons (bottom one already undone) and enlarged by
> being pressed, along with the scrotum, to one side;
> legs molded in perfect, powerful detail; the feet simpli-
> fied, brutalized and magnified by the boots.[19]

Lesbians, especially ones who are stereotypically butch to the point of being hypermasculine, are called *dykes*, *bull dykes*, and *diesel dykes*. Women, straight ones in particular, are given the extremely derogatory label *fish*, derived from the similarity of vaginal odors to those of fish. By extension, a Jewish woman is *gefilte fish*. One who is a woman by sex (as opposed to a drag queen or female impersonator) is *real*, or an *RG* (*real girl*). If she spends a great deal of time in the presence of gay men, she is called a *fag hag* or *fruit fly*, both derogatory terms and both based upon insulting epithets for gay men.

Some of these gay terms have entered standard English; *coming out* and *closet* are the most common ones to have done so. Almost everyone uses these words now, because—like many gay terms—they are especially apt for conveying certain ideas. *Closet queens* (or *closeted people*), though, fearful of being discovered, generally still refrain from using them. The majority of the vocabulary, however, is still restricted to gay usage. A good example is *tearoom*, a public restroom where homosexual encounters take place. . . . A person who is fussy about appearances and behavior almost to the point of being prissy is *piss-elegant* or *chichi* (from the French *chic*). Piss-elegance is pseudo-elegance, a dimestore version of true luxury and taste. To *dish* is to gossip, and to *read* (or *read* [someone's] *beads*) involves really chewing someone out. (*Read* is probably derived from *read the riot act to*.) A person might get read for *working deceit*, playing nasty (rather than harmless) tricks on another person, such as sabotaging a female impersonator's gown before her performance. Beads can be dropped as well as read. To *drop beads* is to drop hints about one's homosexuality. To keep from dropping beads gay people often try to avoid masculine and feminine pronouns in referring to their close friends; instead they will use various convolutions like "a friend of mine and I," "someone I know from school," and "this person I met."

As with language itself, humor can be used to elicit information from others about themselves. By telling jokes on sexual topics, for example, a narrator may obtain details about his listener's orientation from his response.[20] The response to a racist or a misogynistic anecdote can shed light on the listener's attitudes toward women and toward racial groups other than his own. The information received about a person in this way can be used to identify him as gay, or as a bigot, or as a misogynist. Of course the identification must remain tentative, for as with a leafless tree, much more must be communicated before a definite determination can be made.

Using humor as a communicative device offers certain advantages over conversation. One of the values of humor lies in its usefulness in facilitating interaction.[21] It offers us a means of quickly bringing a conversation to an intimate level, avoiding introductions and small talk. And, as John Herrick puts it, "Jokes are an easy way to win favor."[22] Humor gives our listeners insight into our personalities and their responses inform us about them. Since humor is supposedly not serious, messages that might otherwise cause offense can be couched within jokes or other forms of humorous expression. In this way, a listener is allowed to ignore the message if he finds it offensive. Should he be interested in the underlying statement, however, he is encouraged to continue the interaction, which he will generally enter through humor himself.

Regardless of our attitudes toward it, humor is a very serious medium indeed. Joking with an unfamiliar person is a delicate process, because it is an easy matter to violate the bounds of propriety if one is unfamiliar with his listener's values. Humor allows us to express ideas that are normally socially inexpressible, and in doing so we give our listeners quite a bit of insight into our thoughts and values.[23]

To function as secret communication among gays, jokes must contain a highly esoteric referent. Recognition of the humor suggests that the listener is probably homosexual. If the joke relies on ambiguity, with its humor making sense on both levels, the clue provided by the response is less definite; the secrecy of the communication is more secure, however, since the other members of the audience will probably find the joke funny too and will not be likely to ask for an explanation. Within these guidelines, humor can be employed to imply one's own homosexuality as well as to say that the narrator suspects that his listener may be gay. . . .

By providing a means of covert communication, a way of conveying potentially offensive messages, and expressing ideas common to members of the subculture, humor serves as a useful extension of language.

The same is true of personal experience narratives. Although such stories function most strongly as cohesive mechanisms, they do convey messages and attitudes. For example, Michael Monroe tells the following story to "people who are talking about whether or not they should tell their parents or [who ask] how your parents reacted to finding out you were gay." He goes on to point out that "it's an offensive story, looking back. It was a very rude thing to do to my parents. But having done it, I feel I might as well share the knowledge."

The one I tell most often is in terms of the very gradual process that I had of coming out to my parents, whereby I came home from my first semester at school, ready and armed with my new gay lingo and gestures and that sort of thing—which my parents wouldn't have identified as being gay; they just would have thought it was weird.

But then I came home for Thanksgiving maybe, one year, and picked up a trick at the bar the night

before. And he was from Dayton, so we couldn't go to his house. And I thought, "Well, it's three o'clock in the morning; surely my family will all be asleep, and [we can] go upstairs and nobody will know the difference." And I got home with him at three o'clock in the morning and *everyone* was still awake. My father was out in the garage working on his car, and my mother I guess was basting the turkey; my sister was helping my father, and my brother was—I don't know—wandering around.

And so I tried to go in the upstairs way, which would have avoided all the traffic, and I couldn't get in. The door was locked, so I had to go right through the house. And I met my brother on the stairs and he kind of gave me a funny look, like—I assumed he figured out what was going on; he didn't say anything.

But he spent the night, and in the morning I awoke to the sound of bustling around, people getting ready to go to the Thanksgiving service at church. And every time somebody ascended the staircase my heart was in my throat, with no lock on the door. And for reasons only *she* can tell you, my mother did *not* come bursting into the room. She knocked meekly on the door and said, "Michael, wake up. We're having breakfast in half an hour and we expect you to go to church with us." So I got up, and my friend got up and dressed, and I sent him out the upstairs way and he drove off, and I went down. And as I was *just* settling myself in my seat at the dining table, my mother said, "Isn't your friend staying for breakfast?"

I thought, "Well, *she's* being calm." And I stuttered and said something about, "Well, he has to be back home in a hurry." And no more was said until the end of the meal, when my mother said, "Well now, we're having lots of guests for lunch, so I want you all to come right home from church and clean up your rooms, and cleanup your bathrooms, and Michael, clean up wherever your friend stayed." He obviously had stayed with me, and I believe the door to the guest room was open, so it was apparent that he hadn't stayed there.

That night I had the audacity to ask for the car again, to go out again. And my father went through his usual song and dance about, "But it's eleven o'clock at night"—you know—"where are you going at eleven o'clock at night that—you should be coming home, not going out at this hour." And I went through *my* usual song and dance about how my friends keep late hours. And then he said, "Well, okay, you can borrow the car, but sometime we need to talk about last night."

Well, he was there working on his car with my sister and her boyfriend, so I said sure, assuming that he would choose some more appropriate moment. But he just kind of plowed ahead and said, "Well, where did your friend stay?"

And I said, "Well, upstairs."

"*Where* upstairs?"

"In my room."

"On the *floor?*" he asked.

So I took a deep breath and said, "In my bed"—which *is* a twin bed, it's not terribly large. And he seemed at that point quite taken aback—I mean he *really* had his head in the sand—and kind of choked. I think by this time my sister and her boyfriend had both stopped working on the car and were watching with interest.

And he kind of choked and said, "Well, we have plenty of beds in this house. I don't think it's necessary for you to double up. Please don't ever do that again. Now take the car and go."

And that was as much as we'd ever discussed about my life-style, my coming out. At that point I felt—well, I had no intention of bringing up the subject because I knew that—and that proved that they were—had no interest in hearing about it. They weren't going to be prepared for it. It wasn't going to be a valuable communication. So I left it like that.[24]

In that narrative Michael vividly tells his audience how his parents learned he was gay, how he dealt with their discovery by trying to avoid mentioning it, and how his parents reacted. Despite the rudeness of his actions, Michael's parents tacitly agree to accept his homosexuality as long as they are not confronted with it. Michael's message to his audience is, "I've been through letting my parents know. This is how it happened, and although it was awkward and done in a less-than-tactful way, I came through the situation successfully. My family still loves me. I did it, and so can you if you need to." Thus we see that narratives, like jokes, carry both implicit and explicit messages.

In addition to specialized language, jokes, narratives, and other aspects of verbal folklore, nonverbal cues are also used in recognition. Many gay people

claim an ability to recognize other gays on sight. Very few, however, can explain how this talent operates. One of my informants says that it is "a second sense. The majority of the time I've been right. . . . [It's] something that's born within you, something that you have no power over."[25] John Herrick gave a similar response: "Why, it's my feminine intuition," a typical gay statement employing humor that plays on the stereotype of the effeminate gay male. He then listed some of the cues that suggest a man is gay. A homosexual man who does not want to be identified as gay overcompensates, acting a bit more masculine than a heterosexual man; he stands more erectly; he has a firmer handshake. A gay man's appearance has a "finer polish" than that of a straight man, and as a gay man he will hold another man's gaze longer than a heterosexual male will."[26]

Nonverbal cues are learned in much the same way as verbal ones—through observation, asking, and being told—and gays are adept at their use. Joseph J. Hayes maintains that

gays are more sophisticated [than straights] in [using nonverbal communication], depend on it more, and know better how to manipulate it for their own ends. Moreover, their necessary involvement in role-awareness and role-playing makes them aware of [what a small amount of] important communication is actually put into words. Sophistication in nonverbal language also makes gays aware of the dangers that lurk everywhere in the use of spoken language.[27]

Drawing upon this ability, gays take note of many cues emitted by other men through their behavior, their clothing, and their jewelry and other accessories.

The range of nonverbal signals the subculture has created aids in maintaining a double identity, remaining invisible to straights and yet recognizable to other gays.[28] Some of the cues are becoming more widely recognized outside the subculture, such as the lambda and the inverted pink triangle, two of the major symbols of the gay liberation movement; both are sometimes worn as buttons, and the lambda is often worn on a necklace or used as a tie-tack.

The lowercase Greek letter λ carries several meanings. First of all, it represents scales, and thus balance. The Greeks considered balance to be the constant adjustment necessary to keep opposing forces from overcoming each other. The hook at the bottom of the right leg of the lambda represents the action required to reach and maintain balance. To the Spartans the lambda meant unity. They felt that society should never infringe on anyone's individuality and freedom. The Romans adopted the letter to represent "the light of knowledge shed into the darkness of ignorance." Finally, in physics the symbol designates an energy exchange.[29] Thus the lambda, with all its meanings, is an especially apt symbol for the gay liberation movement, which energetically seeks a balance in society and which strives through enlightenment to secure equal rights for homosexual people.

By contrast, in an unusual form of inversion, many gays have begun wearing inverted pink triangles (often with the slogan "Never again!" or in circles with diagonal lines through them) as a reminder of the oppression to which gays are still subjected. During the Holocaust the Nazis sent many non-Jews to the concentration camps, including gypsies, religious dissidents, and homosexual men and women. Untold tens of thousands of homosexual people were forced to wear the pink triangle and, like millions of Jews, were ultimately exterminated.[30]

Other visual clues are in evidence outside specifically gay contexts. Jewelry of various types functions as an identifying mark. Men's necklaces, for example, were for a long time indicators of a homosexual orientation. In the 1960s, however, members of the counterculture (and later straight men in general) co-opted this signal, decreasing its value by confusing its message.[31] The same process affected the meaning of a single earring worn by a man; although it is still an indicator of homosexuality, remnants of the drug culture, fans of punk rock music, and more recently many college students and other types of men have had their ears pierced. The "pinky ring," a ring worn on the little finger, is a third ambiguous signal. For many years gay men have used the pinky ring to signify their orientation, but as more and more straight people have begun wearing these rings, their level of ambiguity has risen greatly. Men involved in the arts often wear pinky rings with no intention of suggesting a homosexual preference. Recently some gay men have begun wearing rings on their middle fingers (and occasionally on their forefingers), but again, these signals are somewhat confused, since a few straight men wear their wedding bands on the middle fingers of their left hands.

Many gay signals are given added meaning by their placement. The left side of the body signifies active, the right side passive. Thus a pinky ring on the left hand or an earring in the left ear may indicate that the wearer prefers to take an active or dominant role in sex. Keys worn on the belt or dangling from the pocket provide the same general information.

The most specific messages are conveyed by bandanas. Again the right–left distinction is important, whether the handkerchief is carried in the back pockets or worn around the arms, wrists, or legs. When worn around the neck or as a headband the bandana indicates that the wearer is willing to take either role. The multiplicity of colors provides additional information. Although there is some variation in interpretation, there is generally a common understanding of each color's meaning. A white bandana represents a desire for masturbation; a man wearing it on the left wants to be masturbated, and one wearing it on the right is willing to perform this act for his partner as well as for himself. Light blue (robin's egg) is the color for oral intercourse, and dark blue (navy) stands for anal intercourse. A man wearing a black bandana is interested in sadomasochism. Red designates fistfucking (brachioproctic intercourse). A hustler (male prostitute) wears a green bandana on his left; a man seeking a hustler's services wears a similar handkerchief on the right. Olive green expresses an interest in military uniforms. A mustard colored bandana, worn on the left, means that the wearer is "well hung," having a penis at least eight inches long when erect; the same bandana worn on the right means that the wearer is seeking someone of such proportions. Yellow stands for watersports, wherein one partner urinates on the other, and brown is worn by those interested in scatological acts. Someone willing to do anything at any time displays an orange bandana on his left. On the right the bandana for some carries the same meaning; for others it is a statement that they are not interested in having sexual relations for the time being.[32] Another item one occasionally sees gay men carrying in their hip pockets is a teddy bear about six inches tall. The teddy bear signals a desire to cuddle or be cuddled.

Black leather is worn by a number of gay men to express a preference for sadomasochism. Charcoal brown leather indicates a neophyte's interest in exploring S&M. Other accoutrements carrying similar meanings include chains, handcuffs (used in particularly by men who enjoy B&D—bondage and discipline), and studded leather armbands, belts, and gloves.

Kenneth E. Read asserts that keys and bandanas are fads that change constantly and are not widespread.[33] Although the teddy bear may be a mere fad, the other nonverbal cues discussed above are too tenacious to be considered faddish. They become fads when, in the manner of radical chic, they are adopted by straights. They are also extremely widespread.

Another type of nonverbal communication is drag. Although most aspects of female impersonation function primarily to maintain cohesion and to aid in coping with (as well as expressing) conflict, doing drag does communicate. It can be a statement like, "I am gay, and proud of it. I can be a better woman than a real woman." In this way drag is aggressive, flouting the values of heterosexual culture by flaunting homosexuality. By inverting the meaning of the stereotype, drag imbues with pride a practice generally held in contempt. Female impersonation can, by the same method, also communicate the feminine aspects of a man's personality; it allows him to say, "I have feminine and masculine traits, and I see nothing wrong in expressing both."

Two of the most obvious nonverbal signals used by gays involve eye contact and proxemics. Among gay men, slightly sustained eye contact within a gay context indicates potential sexual interest. It may be followed (after some time) by smiles, nods, an introduction, an offer to buy a drink, an invitation to dance, or some other means of intensifying the encounter. This process is called *cruising*. When similar eye contact occurs in a nongay environment it serve as a means of recognition. Depending on the situation it may lead to cruising.[34]

One also notices among gay men an abandonment of personal space, that invisible shell we all carry around our bodies. No one is normally allowed within this area, but among gay people there is a lot of physical contact, both affectionate and sexual. This violation of personal space is more than a result of people's finding themselves in a crowded room; it is a response to the isolation homosexual people feel in heterosexual society. Everyone needs acceptance and close friends; one way the gay subculture meets this need is by eliminating the barriers normally associated with personal space.[35]

Active use of gay communication strategies is not required for acculturation. Observation of the system in action, however, begins when the gay person reaches level three of acculturation—his first association with the subculture—since at this point he inevitably becomes a passive bearer of these traditions. In addition, since much of the nonverbal communication occurs on a subconscious level, he will almost surely become an active bearer of at least this aspect of gay communication, using some of it—without his awareness—to identify others and to let them know of his orientation. If he reaches level four and begins to practice his new knowledge consciously, then the fifth stage, that of serving as a model for other newcomers, is almost sure to follow.

If gay communication did not meet the needs of the gay subculture, it would not exist. It functions in several ways, helping to define the subculture, marking both members and nonmembers; it is a medium through which the cultural heritage of the gay community can be conveyed; it is a casual, humorous way of communicating with people with whom one feels comfortable; it is a means of discussing taboo subjects openly (or semiopenly) without fear of discovery. And as David Sonenschein suggests, it is a way in which the subculture can give the gay experience meaning.[36] All of these functions of the gay argot are subsumed under one larger role the language plays: it aids in establishing and maintaining subcultural cohesion.

Notes

1. See Henry Hiż, "Logical Basis of Semiotics"; Thomas A. Sebeok, "Ecumenicalism in Semiotics"; and Rulon S. Wells, "Criteria for Semiosis," all in *A Perfusion of Signs*, ed. Thomas A. Sebeok (Bloomington: Indiana University Press, 1977).

2. Edmund White, *States of Desire: Travels in Gay America* (New York: E. P. Dutton, 1980), p. 248. See also Edward William Delph, *The Silent Community: Public Homosexual Encounters* (Beverly Hills: Sage Publications, 1978), p. 115,

and Barbara Weightman, "Gay Bars as Private Places," *Landscape* 24 (1980), passim.

3. Sherri Cavan, *Liquor License: An Ethnography of Bar Behavior* (Chicago: Aldine Publishing Co., 1966), p. 190.

4. Other gay subcultures have also developed distinctive argots. John Boswell, in *Christianity, Social Tolerance, and Homosexuality: Gay People in Western Europe from the Beginning of the Christian Era to the Fourteenth Century* (Chicago: University of Chicago Press, 1980), states that the European gay subculture of the High Middle Ages "appears to have had its own slang" (p. 253). In contemporary Greece gays speak a language of their own as well. It parallels gay English in many ways, having special meanings for words and using paralinguistic features similar to those used by American gays. As Steve A. Demakopoulos states in "The Greek Gays Have a Word for It" (*Maledicta* 2 [1978]),

> Though much of the unintelligibility of *Kaliarda* is certainly due to its esoteric vocabulary, perhaps as much can be ascribed to a very particular diction and pronunciation, as well as to an extraordinary speed of delivery. This, when accompanied by expressive gestures, mincing grimaces and feminine body movements, results in an inimitable mimicry of sound and sight. (33)

5. Evelyn Hooker, "The Homosexual Community," in *Proceedings of the XIV International Congress of Applied Psychology* (Copenhagen: Munksgaard, 1961), p. 144; Kenneth E. Read, *Other Voices: The Style of a Male Homosexual Tavern* (Novato, Calif.: Chandler & Sharp Publishers, Inc., 1980), p. 35; and White, *States of Desire*, p. 194.

6. I discuss camp [elsewhere].

7. Esther Newton, *Mother Camp: Female Impersonation in America* (Chicago: University of Chicago Press, 1972), p. 56, and Julia P. Stanley, "Homosexual Slang," *American Speech* 45 (1970): 55, touch on the significance of verbal agility among gay men.

8. John Reid, *The Best Little Boy in the World* (New York: Ballantine Books, 1973 [revised edition: 1976]), p. 192.

9. Alf H. Walle ("Getting Picked Up without Being Put Down: Jokes and the Bar Rush," *Journal of the Folklore Institute* 13 [1976]) discuss-

es the use of humor in changing the level of intimacy of a conversation.

10. Grace Sims Holt, "'Inversion' in Black Communication," in *Rappin' and Stylin' Out: Communication in Urban Black America*, ed. Thomas Kochman (Urbana: University of Illinois Press, 1972), pp. 153, 154.

11. David W. Maurer, "The Argot of Narcotic Addicts," in *Readings in American Dialectology*, ed. Harold B. Allen and Gary N. Underwood (New York: Appleton-Century-Crofts, 1971), p. 503.

12. Bruce Rodgers, *Gay Talk: A (Sometimes Outrageous) Dictionary of Gay Slang* (New York: Paragon Books, 1979), p. 14; Stanley, "Homosexual Slang," 5.

13. This fact holds, despite Stanley's contention in "Gay Slang/Gay Culture: How Are They Related?" (paper read at the 1974 annual meeting of the American Anthropological Association, in the collection of the Alfred C. Kinsey Institute for Research in Sex, Gender, and Reproduction, Indiana University, Bloomington) that "only *camp* and *closet* and their related groups of words can be said to be uniquely gay in that these sets of words have not been borrowed from other groups" (p. 8). Joseph J. Hayes repeats part of Stanley's comment verbatim (without quotation marks) in "Lesbians, Gay Men, and Their 'Languages'" (in *Gayspeak*, ed. James W. Chesebro [New York: The Pilgrim Press, 1981], p. 39).

14. Hooker, "The Homosexual Community," pp. 52, 53.

15. Paul H. Gebhard, "Homosexual Socialization," *Excerpta Medica International Congress Series No. 150* (Madrid: Proceedings of the IV World Congress of Psychiatry, 1966), p. 1029. Stanley, in "Homosexual Slang," says the rapid dissemination is a result of "the transient nature of the homosexual subculture" (46). Gays, however, seem to be no more transient than other Americans.

16. Graffiti presents an awkward problem in distinguishing between verbal and nonverbal folklore: it is verbal, and yet it is not oral. I have chosen not to deal with graffiti in any detail, because most graffiti, while homoerotic in content, is apparently written by (supposedly) straight men. There tends to be very little graffiti in the rest-

rooms of gay establishments. Gershon Legman, however, feels that "modern inscriptions . . . [are] mostly homosexual in . . . *intent*" ("Homosexuality and Toilet Inscriptions—An Analysis," unpublished manuscript, 1940–41, in the collection of the Alfred C. Kinsey Institute for Research in Sex, Gender, and Reproduction, Indiana University, Bloomington, p. T.2; emphasis added). He concludes his analysis of graffiti with the following statement:

It is perhaps worth noting that almost invariably the pictograph [accompanying an illustrated graffito] is above the inscription, signifying usually that it was drawn first—drawn, one might add, right out of the twisted, tortured mind of the frustrated and abnormal sort of creature who scratches furtive homosexual inscriptions on toilet walls. (p. T.5)

More than enough said.

17. White, *States of Desire*, p. 92.
18. John Ciardi, *A Browser's Dictionary and Native Guide to the Unknown American Language* (New York: Harper & Row, Publishers, 1980), p. 323.
19. White, *States of Desire*, p. 42. Castro Street is in the gay district in San Francisco.
20. Walle, "Getting Picked Up without Being Put Down," 201. See also Erving Goffman, *Behavior in Public Places* (London: Collier-MacMillan Ltd., The Free Press of Glencoe, 1963), pp. 245–46.
21. William H. Martineau, "A Model of the Social Functions of Humor," in *The Psychology of Humor*, ed. Jeffrey H. Goldstein and Paul H. McGhee (New York: Academic Press, 1972), p. 103.
22. Interview with John Herrick, 3 December 1981.
23. Jacob Levine, "Regression in Primitive Clowning," in *Motivation in Humor*, ed. Jacob Levine (New York: Atherton Press, 1969); Isaac Asimov, "Humor," in *Opus 200*, ed. Isaac Asimov (Boston: Houghton Mifflin Company, 1979), p. 240.
24. Interview with Michael Monroe, 1 December 1981.
25. Interview with Dorian Carr, 8 November 1981.
26. Interview with John Herrick, 3 December 1981.
27. Hayes, "Lesbians, Gay Men, and Their 'Languages,'" p. 37. See also Laud Humphreys, *Out of the Closets: The Sociology of Homosexual Liberation* (Englewood Cliffs, N.J.: Prentice-Hall, Inc., 1972), p. 67.
28. See Hal Fischer, *Gay Semiotics: A Photographic Study of Visual Coding among Homosexual Men* (San Francisco: NSF Press, 1977), passim; Hayes, "Lesbians, Gay Men, and Their 'Languages,'" pp. 37 and 42; and Edward Sagarin, "Language of the Homosexual Subculture," *Medical Aspects of Human Sexuality* 4 (1970): 40.
29. "The History of the Lambda," *Gaylife*, 27 March 1981, p. 23. See also Toby Marotta, *The Politics of Homosexuality* (Boston: Houghton Mifflin Company, 1981), p. 145n.
30. Heinz Heger, *The Men with the Pink Triangle*, trans. David Fernbach (Boston: Alyson Publications, Inc., 1980), passim.
31. Interview with Hal Parmenter; see also Lynn Ramsey, *Gigolos: The World's Best Kept Men* (Englewood Cliffs, N.J.: Prentice-Hall, Inc., 1978), p. 119. Although his work is not completely dependable, see Fischer (*Gay Semiotics*) for more information on gay nonverbal communication.
32. According to Havelock Ellis, during the early twentieth century red neckties indicated a homosexual orientation (quoted in Jonathan Katz, *Gay American History: Lesbians and Gay Men in the U.S.A.* [New York: Avon, 1976], p. 81). Fischer (*Gay Semiotics*) claims that the use of bandanas grew out of the leather culture (p. 20); Hayes ("Lesbians, Gay Men, and Their 'Languages'") suggests a more curious origin: "This custom seems to have originated in nineteenth-century Colorado mining towns, where men with pocket bandanas played 'follower' and those without played 'leader' at Friday night dances where there were few or no women present" (p. 36).
33. Read, *Other Voices*, p. 12.
34. For more about eye contact and its implications—as well as about cruising—among both gays and straights, see Cavan, *Liquor License*, p. 190; Delph, *The Silent Community*, pp. 50–51 and 121; Norine Dresser, "'The Boys in the Band Is Not Another Musical': Male Homosexuals and Their Folklore," *Western Folklore* 33 (1974): 208–209; Desmond Morris, *Manwatching: A Field Guide to Human Behavior* (New York:

Harry N. Abrams, Inc., 1977) pp. 71–72, 77, and 246; and James P. Spradley and Brenda J. Mann, *The Cocktail Waitress: Woman's Work in a Man's World* (New York: John Wiley & Sons, Inc., 1975), pp. 102 and 107.

35. Morris, *Manwatching*, pp. 130–31.

36. David Sonenschein, "The Homosexual's Language," *Sex Research* 5 (1969): 290. See also Donald Webster Cory, "The Language of the Homosexual," *Sexology* 32 (1965): 163; Maurer, "Argot of Addicts," p. 504; and Sagarin, "Language of the Homosexual Subculture," 39.

Concepts and Questions

1. What do you think Goodwin is suggesting when he notes that "we construct the complete message from a combination of details"? How would you directly relate this observation to his essay?

2. What is Goodwin referring to when he notes that "the context of the communicative event is no less important since we translate contextual details into parts of the message"?

3. How does the gay bar communicate a number of messages? What are these messages?

4. According to Goodwin, where are some places where gays are careful not to reveal too much information about themselves?

5. Why is the use of humor important in the gay community? What specific forms of humor are most often used?

6. What are double entendres, and how are they used by the gay community?

7. What are the advantages of ambiguity as it is used by the gay community?

8. What are some of the reasons gays use argot? What other co-cultures are you aware of that employ an argot? Do you know argot terms used by co-cultures? What are they? Do you know the meaning as used by the co-culture?

9. What does Goodwin mean when he notes that "to function as secret communication among gays, jokes must contain a highly esoteric referent"?

10. What are some of the nonverbal cues used by gays when sending and receiving messages within the gay community?

Gender, Communication, and Culture

JULIA T. WOOD

"MEN AND WOMEN: CAN WE GET ALONG? SHOULD WE EVEN TRY?"

Blazing across the cover of a January 1993 popular magazine, this headline announces the drama of gender, communication, and culture. Asking whether we should *even try* to get along, the magazine suggests the effort to build relationships between women and men may require more effort than it's worth. Useful as this media hype might be in selling the magazine, it's misleading in several respects. One problem is that the headline focuses on sex as the source of differences when actually, as we will see in this article, sex has very little to do with how people get along. Gender, however, has a great deal of impact on human interaction. The magazine's cover also exaggerates the difficulty of creating and sustaining satisfying relationships between the genders. If you understand why feminine and masculine cultures differ and how each communicates, it's likely you won't have a great deal of trouble getting along with people of both genders. It's also likely you'll decide it is worth the effort of trying to get along!

This article will help you understand how differences between gender cultures infuse communication. We follow the drama of culture, communication, and gender in two ways. In Act I of this drama, we consider how communication produces and reproduces cultural definitions of masculinity and femininity. Act II explores masculine and feminine cultures to discover why the genders differ in when, how, and why they use communication. To conclude, Act III offers suggestions for ways we might bridge communication gaps that sometimes interfere with effective interaction in cross-cultural gender communication.

This essay first appeared in the seventh edition. All rights reserved. Permission to reprint must be obtained from the author and the publisher. Julia T. Wood teaches at the University of North Carolina at Chapel Hill.

What makes something a culture instead of just a quality common to a number of individuals? For instance, although all people with blue eyes share a common characteristic, we don't consider them a culture. Why then would we regard masculinity and femininity as different cultures? What are feminine and masculine gender cultures, and how are they created? How do differences in gender cultures affect communication? How do we learn to translate each other's communication and to develop a second language ourselves? These are the questions we pursue in this reading.

THE SOCIAL-SYMBOLIC CONSTRUCTION OF GENDER

Perhaps you have noticed that I use the terms *feminine* and *masculine* rather than women and men. The former refer to gender and the latter to sex, which are distinct phenomena. *Women, men, male,* and *female* are words that specify sexual identities, which biology determines. In contrast, feminine and masculine designate genders, which are socially constructed meanings for sex. Before we can understand why gender is a culture, we need to clarify what gender is and how it differs from sex.

Sex

Sex is determined by genetic codes that program biological features. Of the forty-nine pairs of human chromosomes, one pair controls sex. Usually this unit has two chromosomes, one of which is always an X chromosome. If the second chromosome is a Y, the fetus is male; if it is an X, the fetus is female. (Other combinations have occurred: XYY, XXY, XO, and XXX.) During gestation, genetic codes direct the production of hormones so that fetuses receive hormones that develop genitalia and secondary sex characteristics consistent with their genetic makeup. (Again there are exceptions, usually caused by medical interventions. See Wood, 1993a for a more thorough discussion.)

Aided and abetted by hormones, genetics determine biological features that we use to classify male and female sex: external genitalia (the clitoris and vagina for a female, the penis and testes for a male)

and internal sex organs (the uterus and ovaries in females, the prostate in males). Hormones also control secondary sex characteristics such as percentage of body fat (females have more fat to protect the womb when a fetus is present), how much muscle exists, and amount of body hair. There are also differences in male and female brains. Females generally have greater specialization in the right hemisphere which controls integrative and creative thinking, while males typically have more developed left lobes, which govern analytic and abstract thought. Generally, females also have better developed corpus callosa, which are the bundles of nerves connecting the two brain lobes. This suggests women may be more able to cross to the left hemisphere than men are to cross to the right. All of these are sex differences directed by genetics and biology.

Gender

Gender is considerably more complex than sex. For starters you might think of gender as the cultural meaning of sex. A culture constructs gender by arbitrarily assigning certain qualities, activities, and identities to each sex and by then inscribing these assignments into the fabric of social life. Cultural constructions of gender are communicated to individuals through a range of structures and practices that make up our everyday world. From birth on, individuals are besieged with communication that presents cultural prescriptions for gender as natural and right. Beginning with the pink and blue blankets still used in many hospitals, gender socialization continues in interactions with parents, teachers, peers, and media. Throughout our interaction with others, we receive constant messages that reinforce females' conformity to femininity and males' to masculinity. This reveals gender is a social creation, not an individual characteristic.

The process of gender socialization is constant and thorough, so it generally succeeds in persuading individuals to adopt the gender society endorses for them. This means that individuals are not born with a gender, but we become *gendered* as we internalize and then embody our society's views of femininity and masculinity. Although some people resist gender socialization, the intensity and pervasiveness of social prescriptions for gender ensure most females will become feminine and most males will become masculine. This article should give you insight into your own gender so that you may decide whether you are masculine, feminine, or a combination of genders.

Gender refers to social beliefs and values that specify what sex *means* and what it allows and precludes in a particular society at a specific time. Because cultures vary and each one changes over time, the meaning of gender is neither universal nor stable. Instead, femininity and masculinity reflect the beliefs and values of particular cultures at certain points. The pervasive presence of socially constructed meanings of gender in our lives makes them seem natural, normal, right. Since cultures systematically normalize arbitrary definitions of gender, we seldom reflect on how *unnatural* it is that half of humans are assumed to be more passive, emotional, and interested in caring for others than the other half. If we do reflect on social definitions of masculinity and femininity, they don't make a great deal of sense (Janeway, 1971; Miller, 1986)!

In summary, gender and sex are not synonymous. Sex is biological, while gender is socially constructed. Sex is established by genetics and biology, while gender is produced and reproduced by society. Barring surgery, sex is permanent, while gender varies over time and across cultures. Sex is an individual property, while gender is a social and relational quality which gains meaning from prevailing social interests and contrast with the other gender. What we've covered so far explains the first relationship among gender, communication, and culture: We see that societies create meanings of gender that are communicated through an array of cultural structures and practices; in turn, individuals become gendered as they embody social prescriptions in their personal identities. We turn now to the second relationship, which concerns how social-symbolic constructions of gender establish codes of conduct, thought, and communication that create distinct gender cultures.

FEMININE AND MASCULINE COMMUNICATION CULTURES

Beginning in the 1970s scholars noticed that some groups of people share communication practices not common to outsiders. This led to the realization that there are distinctive speech communities, or com-

munication cultures. William Labov (1972, p. 121) defined a communication culture as existing when a set of norms regarding how to communicate is shared by a group of people. Within a communication culture, members embrace similar understandings of how to use talk and what purposes it serves.

Once scholars realized distinctive communication cultures exist, they identified many, some of which are discussed in this book: African Americans, older people, Indian Native Americans, gay men, lesbians, and people with disabilities. Members in each of these groups share perspectives that outsiders don't have, and their distinctive values, viewpoints, and experiences influence how each culture uses language. This holds true for gender cultures since women and men in general have different perspectives on why, when, and how to communicate.

Feminine and masculine communication cultures have been mapped out by a number of scholars (Aries, 1987; Beck, 1988; Coates & Cameron, 1989; Johnson, 1989; Kramarae, 1981; Spender, 1984; Tannen, 1990a, b; Treichler & Kramarae, 1983; Wood, 1993a, b, c, d; Wood & Inman, 1993). Their research reveals that most girls and women operate from assumptions about communication and use rules for communicating that differ significantly from those endorsed by most boys and men. I use the qualifying word, "most," to remind us we are discussing general differences, not absolute ones based on sex. Some women are not socialized into feminine culture or they reject it; likewise, some men do not identify with masculine culture. For the most part, however, females are socialized into feminine culture and males into masculine culture. How that transpires is our next consideration.

COMMUNICATION CONSTRUCTS GENDER CULTURES

How are different gender cultures created and sustained? At the heart of the process is human communication. It is through interaction with others that we learn what masculine and feminine mean in our society and which we are supposed to be. Communication is also the primary means by which we embody gender personally so that our ways of talking conform to and, thereby, reproduce social views of masculinity and femininity. We'll now look more closely at how boys and girls are socialized into masculine and feminine gender identities.

Clinicians and researchers have identified two primary influences on gender socialization: family communication, particularly between mothers and children, and recreational interaction among children. In each of these areas, communication reflects and reproduces gender cultures.

Psychodynamic Influences on Gender Identity

Gender is not merely a role; it is a core aspect of identity which is central to how we perceive ourselves and how we act in the world (Rakow, 1986; Zimmerman & West, 1975). In her classic book, *The Reproduction of Mothering*, psychiatrist Nancy Chodorow (1978) claims that gender identity is profoundly shaped by psychological dynamics in families and most particularly by mother–child relationships in the early years. According to Chodorow, it is significant that the primary caregiver for most children is a female, usually the mother. Mothers form different relationships with sons and daughters, and these differences cultivate masculine and feminine gender identities.

Between a mother and daughter, argue Chodorow and other clinicians (Eichenbaum & Orbach, 1983; Miller, 1986; Surrey, 1983), there is a basic identification as members of the same sex. Because daughters identify with mothers, they can develop their identities inside that primary relationship. A son, however, cannot identify fully with the mother because she is female. To develop a gender identity, sons must differentiate from mother—must pull away from the first relationship to establish selfhood. We see, then, a basic difference in the foundation of the sexes' identities: Girls tend to define self in relation to others, while boys typically define self independent of others.

Whether we think of ourselves as fundamentally connected to others (within relationship) or separate from them (independent of relationship) influences how we perceive ourselves and how we interact with others (Gilligan, 1982; Riessman, 1990; Surrey, 1983). In general, males (children and adults) maintain a greater degree of distance between themselves and others than do females. This makes sense since closeness with mothers facilitates daughters but interferes with sons in their efforts to define a self. Given these different bases of identity, it's hardly surprising that girls and women are generally comfortable building close relationships and disclosing to others, while most boys and men are reserved about involvements and disclosures (Aries, 1987; Wood, 1993a). Important as the mother–child relationship is, however, it isn't the only factor that cultivates gender identities.

The Games Children Play

Augmenting psychodynamic influences on gender identity is communication that occurs in childhood games. Insight into this area was pioneered by Daniel Maltz and Ruth Borker (1982), who studied children at play. The researchers noticed recreation was usually sex-segregated, and boys and girls tended to favor discrete kinds of games. While girls were more likely to play house, school, or jump rope, boys tended to play competitive team sports like football and baseball. Because different goals, strategies and relationships characterize girls' and boys' games, the children learned divergent rules for interaction. Engaging in play, Maltz and Borker concluded, contributes to socializing children into masculine and feminine communication cultures.

Girls' Games. Most girls' games require just two or three people so they promote personal relationships. Further, these games don't have preset or fixed rules, roles, and objectives. While touchdowns and home runs are goals in boys' games and roles such as pitcher, lineman, and blocker are clearly specified, how to play house is open to negotiation. To make their games work, girls talk with each other and agree on rules, roles, and goals: "You be the mommy and I'll be the daddy, and we'll clean house." From unstructured, cooperative play, girls learn three basic rules for how to communicate:

1. Be cooperative, collaborative, inclusive. It's important that everyone feel involved and have a chance to play.
2. Don't criticize or outdo others. Cultivate egalitarian relationships so the group is cohesive and gratifying to all.

Table 1 *Differences Between Feminine and Masculine Communication Culture*

Feminine Talk	Masculine Talk
1. Use talk to build and sustain rapport with others.	1. Use talk to assert yourself and your ideas.
2. Share yourself and learn about others through disclosing.	2. Personal disclosures can make you vulnerable.
3. Use talk to create symmetry or equality between people.	3. Use talk to establish your status and power.
4. Matching experiences with others shows understanding and empathy ("I know how you feel.")	4. Matching experiences is a competitive strategy to command attention. ("I can top that.")
5. To support others, express understanding of their feelings.	5. To support others, do something helpful—give advice or solve a problem for them.
6. Include others in conversation by asking their opinions and encouraging them to elaborate. Wait your turn to speak so others can participate.	6. Don't share the talk stage with others; wrest it from them with communication. Interrupt others to make your own points.
7. Keep the conversation going by asking questions and showing interest in others' ideas.	7. Each person is on her or his own; it's not your job to help others join in.
8. Be responsive. Let others know you hear and care about what they say.	8. Use responses to make your own points and to outshine others.
9. Be tentative so that others feel free to add their ideas.	9. Be assertive so others perceive you as confident and in command.
10. Talking is a human relationship in which details and interesting side comments enhance depth of connection.	10. Talking is a linear sequence that should convey information and accomplish goals. Extraneous details get in the way and achieve nothing.

3. Pay attention to others' feelings and needs and be sensitive in interpreting and responding to them.

In sum, girls' games occur within a gender culture that emphasizes relationships more than outcomes, sensitivity to others, and cooperative, inclusive interpersonal orientations.

Boys' Games. Unlike girls' games, those that boys tend to play involved fairly large groups (baseball requires nine players plus extras to fill in) and proceed by rules and goals that are externally established and constant. Also, boys' games allow for individual stars—MVP, for instance—and, in fact, a boy's status depends on his rank relative to others. The more structured, large, and individualized character of boys' games teaches them three rules of interaction:

1. Assert yourself. Use talk and action to highlight your ideas and to establish both your status and leadership.
2. Focus on outcomes. Use your talk and actions to make things happen, to solve problems, and achieve goals.

3. Be competitive. Vie for the talk stage. Keep attention focused on you, outdo others, and make yourself stand out.

Boys' games, then, emphasize achievement—both for the team and the individual members. The goals are to win for the team and to be the top player on it. Interaction is more an arena for negotiating power and status than for building relationships with others, and competitiveness eclipses cooperativeness as the accepted style in masculine communication cultures.

The characteristics of boys' and girls' games lead to distinctive understandings of what talk does and how we should use it. Differences Maltz and Borker identified in children's play are ones that we carry forward into adulthood so they punctuate communication between adult women and men. So divergent are some of women's and men's understandings of communication that linguist Deborah Tannen (1990b, p. 42) claims "communication between men and women can be like cross culture communication, prey to a clash of conversational styles."

In combination, psychodynamic theories and social science research offer a coherent picture of how gender cultures are produced and what they entail. Feminine socialization emphasizes relationships and sensitivity to people and the process of interaction, while masculine socialization stresses independence, power, and attention to outcomes. Table 1 summarizes how these differences in gender cultures affect communication.

MEN AND WOMEN IN CONVERSATION: CROSS-CULTURAL COMMUNICATION

As males and females learn the rules of distinctive gender cultures, they embody them in their personal identities, and this reproduces prevailing social meanings of the genders. One implication of being socialized into gendered identities is that there are generalizable differences in feminine and masculine styles of communication. These differences frequently lead to misunderstandings in cross-gender interaction.

Gender Gaps in Communication

To illustrate the practical consequences of differences we've identified, let's consider some concrete cases of cross-cultural gender communication. Following are five examples of common problems in communication between women and men. As you read them, you'll probably find that several are familiar to you.

What counts as support? Rita is really bummed out when she meets Mike for dinner. She explains that she's worried about a friend who has begun drinking heavily. When Mike advises her to get her friend into counseling, Rita repeats how worried she feels. Next, Mike tells Rita to make sure her friend doesn't drive after drinking. Rita explodes that she doesn't need advice. Irritated at her lack of appreciation for his help, Mike asks, "Then why did you ask for it?" In exasperation Rita responds, "Oh, never mind, I'll talk to Betsy. At least she cares how I feel."

Tricky feedback. Roseann and Drew are colleagues in a marketing firm. One morning he drops into her office to run an advertising play by her. As Drew discusses his ideas, Roseann nods and says "Um," "Un huh" and "Yes." When he finishes and asks what she thinks, Roseann says "I really don't think that plan will sell the product." Feeling misled, Drew demands,

"Then why were you agreeing the whole time I presented my idea?" Completely confused, Roseann responds, "What makes you think I was agreeing with you?"

Expressing care. Dedrick and Melita have been dating for two years and are very serious. To celebrate their anniversary Melita wants to spend a quiet evening in her apartment where they can talk about the relationship and be with just each other. When Dedrick arrives, he's planned a dinner and concert. Melita feels hurt that he doesn't want to talk and be close.

I'd rather do it myself. Jay is having difficulty writing a paper for his communication class, because he's not sure what the professor wants. When he mentions this to his friend Ellen, she suggests he ask the professor or a classmate to clarify directions. Jay resists, saying "I can figure it out on my own."

Can we talk about us? Anna asks her fiancé, Ben. "Can we talk about us?" Immediately Ben feels tense—another problem on the horizon. He guards himself for an unpleasant conversation and reluctantly nods assent. Anna then thanks Ben for being so supportive during the last few months when she was under enormous pressure at her job. She tells him she feels closer than ever. Then she invites him to tell her what makes him feel loved and close to her. Although Ben feels relieved to learn there isn't any crisis, he's also baffled: "If there isn't a problem, why do they need to talk about the relationship? If it's working, let it be."

You've probably been involved in conversations like these. And you've probably been confused, frustrated, hurt, or even angry when a member of the other sex didn't give you what you wanted or didn't value your efforts to be supportive. If you're a woman, you may think Mike should be more sensitive to Rita's feelings and Dedrick should cherish time alone with Melita. If you're a man, it's likely that you empathize with Mike's frustration and feel Rita is giving him a hard time when he's trying to help. Likewise, you may think Melita is lucky to have a guy willing to shell out some bucks so they can do something fun together.

Who's right in these cases? Is Rita unreasonable? Is Melita ungrateful? Are Dedrick and Mike insensitive? Is Jay stubborn? Did Roseann mislead Drew? When we focus on questions like these we fall prey to a central problem in gender communication: the tendency to judge. Because Western culture is hierarchical, we're taught to perceive differences as better and worse not simply as different. Yet, the inclination to judge one person as right and the other wrong whenever there's misunderstanding usually spells trouble for close relationships.

But judging is not the only way we *could* think about these interactions, and it's not the most constructive way if our interest is building healthy relationships. Disparaging what differs from our own style only gets in the way of effective communication and satisfying relationships. All of the energy invested in fixing fault or defending our behaviors diminishes what we can devote to learning how to communicate better. What might be more productive than judging is understanding and respecting unique styles of communication. Once we recognize there are different and distinctly valid styles of interacting, we can tune into others' perspectives and interact more constructively with them.

Understanding Cross-Gender Communication

Drawing upon earlier sections of this article, we can analyze the misunderstandings in these five dialogues and see how they grow out of the different interaction styles cultivated in feminine and masculine communication cultures. Because men and women typically rely on distinct communication rules, they have different ways of showing support, interest, and caring. This implies they may perceive the same communication in dissimilar ways.

In the first scenario, Rita's purpose in talking with Mike isn't just to tell him about her concern for her friend; she also sees communication as a way to connect with Mike (Aries, 1987; Riessman, 1990; Tannen, 1990b; Wood, 1993b). She wants him to respond to her and her feelings, because that will enhance her sense of closeness to him. Schooled in masculinity, however, Mike views communication as an instrument to do things, so he tries to help by giving advice. To Rita it seems he entirely disregards her feelings, so she doesn't feel close to Mike, which was her primary purpose in talking with him. Rita might welcome some advice, but only after Mike responds to her feelings.

In the second example, the problem arises when Drew translates Roseann's feedback according to rules of communication in masculine culture. Women learn to give lots of response cues—verbal and nonverbal behaviors to indicate interest and involvement in conversation—because that's part of using communication to build relationships with others. Masculine culture, however, focuses on outcomes more than processes, so men tend to use feedback to signal specific agreement and disagreement (Beck, 1988; Fishman, 1978; Tannen, 1990b; Wood, 1993a). When Drew hears Roseann's "ums," "uh huhs," and "yeses," he assumes she is agreeing. According to her culture's rules, however, she is only showing interest and being responsive, not signaling agreement.

Dedrick and Melita also experience culture clash in their communication. With feminine culture, talking is a way—probably the primary way—to express and expand closeness. For women there is closeness in dialogue (Aries, 1987; Riessman, 1990; Wood, 1993b). Masculine socialization, in contrast, stresses doing things and shared activities as primary ways to create and express closeness (Cancian, 1987; Swain, 1989; Wood & Inman, 1993). A man is more likely to express his caring for a woman by doing something concrete for her (washing her car, fixing an appliance) or doing something with her (skiing, a concert, tennis) than by talking explicitly about his feelings. Men generally experience "closeness in doing" (Swain, 1989). By realizing doing things is a valid way to be close, feminine individuals can avoid feeling hurt by partners who propose activities. In addition, women who want to express care in ways men value might think about what they could do for or with the men, rather than what they could say (Riessman, 1990).

Masculinity's emphasis on independence underlies Jay's unwillingness to ask others for help in understanding his assignment. As Tannen (1990b) points out rather humorously, men invariably resist asking directions when they are lost on the road while women don't hesitate to ask strangers for help. What we've discussed about gender identity helps us understand this difference. Because women initially develop identity within relationships, connections with others are generally sought and welcomed—even the casual connection made in asking for directions or help with an assignment. In contrast, men differentiated from their first relationship to develop identity, so relationships have an undertone of danger—they could jeopardize independence. So Jay's refusal to ask others for help reflects the masculine emphasis on maintaining autonomy and not appearing weak or incompetent to others. Unless Ellen realizes this difference between them, Jay will continue to baffle her.

In the final case we see a very common example of culture-clash in gender communication. Feminine culture prioritizes relationships so they are a constant source of interest, attention, and communication. In contrast, within masculine culture relationships are not as central and talk is perceived as a way to do things such as solve problems rather than a means to enhance closeness (Wood, 1993a, b, c). Given these disparate orientations, "talking about us" means radically different things to most men and women. As Tannen (1986) points out, men generally feel a relationship is going along fine if there's no need to talk about it, while women tend to feel a relationship is good as long as they are talking about it! Anna's wish to discuss the relationship because it's so good makes no sense to Ben, and his lack of interest in a conversation about the relationship hurts Anna. Again, each person errs in relying on inappropriate rules to interpret the other's communication.

Most problems in cross-cultural gender communication result from faulty translations. This happens when men interpret women according to rules of masculine culture and when women interpret men according to rules of feminine culture. Just as we wouldn't assume Western rules apply to Asian people, so we'd be wise not to imagine one gender's rules pertain to the other. When we understand there are distinct gender cultures and when we respect the logic of each one, we empower ourselves to communicate in ways that enhance our relationships.

COMMUNICATING EFFECTIVELY BETWEEN GENDER CULTURES

Whether it's a Northern American thinking someone who eats with hands is "uncouth" or a woman assuming a man is "closed" because he doesn't disclose as much as she does, we're inclined to think what differs from our customs is wrong. Ethnocentric judgments seldom improve communication or enhance relationships. Instead of debating whether feminine or masculine styles of communication are better, we should learn to see differences as merely that—differences. The information we've covered, combined with this book's emphasis on understanding and appreciating culturally diverse communication, can be distilled into six principles for effective cross-gender communication.

1. *Suspend judgment.* This is first and foremost, because as long as we are judging differences, we aren't respecting them. When you find yourself confused in cross-gender conversations, resist the tendency to judge. Instead, explore constructively what is happening and how you and your partner might better understand each other.

2. *Recognize the validity of different communication styles.* In cross-gender communication, we need to remind ourselves there is a logic and validity to both feminine and masculine communication styles. Feminine emphases on relationships, feelings, and responsiveness don't reflect inability to adhere to masculine rules for competing any more than masculine stress on instrumental outcomes is a failure to follow feminine rules for sensitivity to others. It is inappropriate to apply a single criterion —either masculine or feminine—to both genders' communication. Instead, we need to realize different goals, priorities, and standards pertain to each.

3. *Provide translation cues.* Now that you realize men and women tend to learn different rules for interaction, it makes sense to think about helping the other gender translate your communication. For instance, in the first example Rita might have said to Mike, "I appreciate your advice, but what I need first is for you to deal with my feelings." A comment such as this helps Mike interpret Rita's motives and needs. After all, there's no reason why he should automatically understand rules that aren't a part of his gender culture.

4. *Seek translation cues.* We can also improve our interactions by seeking translation cues from others. If Rita didn't tell Mike how to translate her, he could have asked "What would be helpful to you? I don't know whether you want to talk about how you're feeling or ways to help your friend. Which would be better?" This message communicates

clearly that Mike cares about Rita and he wants to support her if she'll just tell him how. Similarly, instead of blowing up when Roseann disagreed with him and assuming she had deliberately misled him, Drew might have taken a more constructive approach and said, "I thought your feedback during my spiel indicated agreement with what I was saying. What did it mean?" This kind of response would allow Drew to learn something new.

5. *Enlarge your own communication style.* Studying other cultures' communication teaches us not only about other cultures, but also about ourselves. If we're open to learning and growing, we can enlarge our own communication repertoire by incorporating skills more emphasized in other cultures. Individuals socialized into masculinity could learn a great deal from feminine culture about how to support friends. Likewise, people from feminine cultures could expand the ways they experience intimacy by appreciating "closeness in the doing" that is a masculine speciality. There's little to risk and much to gain by incorporating additional skills into our personal repertoires.

6. *Suspend judgment.* If you're thinking we already covered this principle, you're right. It's important enough, however, to merit repetition. Judgment is so thoroughly woven into Western culture that it's difficult not to evaluate others and not to defend our own positions. Yet as long as we're judging others and defending ourselves, we're probably making no headway in communicating more effectively. So, suspending judgment is the first and last principle of effective cross-gender communication.

SUMMARY

As women and men, we've been socialized into gendered identities, ones that reflect cultural constructions of femininity and masculinity. We become gendered as we interact with our families, childhood peers, and others who teach us what gender means and how we are to embody it in our attitudes, feelings, and interaction styles. This means communication produces, reflects, and reproduces gender cultures and imbues them with a taken-for-granted status that we seldom notice or question. Through an

ongoing, cyclical process communication, culture, and gender constantly recreate one another.

Because we are socialized into distinct communication cultures, women and men tend to communicate for different reasons and in different ways. When we fail to recognize that genders rely on dissimilar rules for talk, we tend to misread each other's meanings and motives. To avoid the frustration, hurt, and misunderstandings that occur when we apply one gender's rules to the other gender's communication, we need to recognize and respect the distinctive validity and value of each style.

"Men and Women: Can We Get Along? Should We Even Try?"

Chances are pretty good we will keep trying to get along. Relationships between women and men are far too exciting, frustrating, and interesting not to! What we've covered in this article provides a good foundation for the ongoing process of learning not just how to get along with members of the other gender, but to appreciate and grow from valuing the different perspectives on interaction, identity, and relationships that masculine and feminine cultures offer.

References

Aries, E. (1987). "Gender and Communication." In P. Shaver (Ed.), *Sex and Gender,* 149–176. Newbury Park, Calif.: Sage.

Beck, A. (1988). *Love Is Never Enough.* New York: Harper & Row.

Cancian, F. (1987). *Love in America.* Cambridge: Cambridge University Press.

Chodorow, N. J. (1978). *The Reproduction of Mothering: Psychoanalysis and the Sociology of Gender.* Berkeley: University of California Press.

Coates, J., and Cameron, D. (1989). *Women in Their Speech Communities: New Perspectives on Language and Sex.* London: Longman.

Eichenbaum, L., and Orbach, S. (1983). *Understanding Women: A Feminist Psychoanalytic Approach.* New York: Basic Books.

Fishman, P. M. (1978). Interaction: The work women do. *Social Problems, 25,* 397–406.

Gilligan, C. (1982). *In a Different Voice: Psychological Theory and Women's Development.* Cambridge: Harvard University Press.

Janeway, E. (1971). *Man's World, Woman's Place: A Study in Social Mythology*. New York: Dell.

Johnson, F. L. (1989). "Women's Culture and Communication: An Analytic Perspective." In C. M. Lont and S. A. Friedley (Eds.), *Beyond Boundaries: Sex and Gender Diversity in Communication*. Fairfax, Va.: George Mason University Press.

Kramarae, C. (1981). *Women and Men Speaking: Frameworks for Analysis*. Rowley, Mass.: Newbury House.

Labov, W. (1972). *Sociolinguistic Patterns*. Philadelphia: University of Pennsylvania Press.

Lakoff, R. (1975). *Language and Woman's Place*. New York: Harper & Row.

Maltz, D. N., and Borker, R. (1982). "A Cultural Approach to Male-Female Miscommunication." In J. J. Gumpertz (Ed.), *Language and Social Identity*, 196–216. Cambridge: Cambridge University Press.

Miller, J. B. (1986). *Toward a New Psychology of Women*. Boston: Beacon Press.

Rakow, L. F. (1986). Rethinking gender research in communication. *Journal of Communication, 36*, 11–26.

Riessman, J. M. (1990). *Divorce Talk: Women and Men Make Sense of Personal Relationships*. New Brunswick: Rutgers University Press.

Spender, D. (1984). *Man Made Language*. London: Routledge and Kegan Paul.

Surrey, J. L. (1983). "The Relational Self in Women: Clinical Implications." In J. V. Jordan, J. L. Surrey, and A. G. Kaplan (Speakers), *Women and Empathy: Implications for Psychological Development and Psychotherapy*, 6–11. Wellesley, Mass.: Stone Center for Developmental Services and Studies.

Swain, S. (1989). "Covert Intimacy: Closeness in Men's Friendships." In B. J. Risman and P. Schwartz (Eds.), *Gender and Intimate Realtionships*, 71–86. Belmont, Calif.: Wadsworth.

Tannen, D. (1986). *That's Not What I Meant! How Conversational Style Makes or Breaks Relationships*. New York: Ballantine.

Tannen, D. (1990a). "Gender Differences in Conversational Coherence: Physical Alignment and Topical Cohesion." In B. Dorval (Ed.), *Conversational Organization and Its Development: XXXVIII*, 167–206. Norwood, N.J.: Ablex.

Tannen, D. (1990b). *You Just Don't Understand: Women and Men in Conversation*. New York: William Morrow.

Treichler, P. A., and Kramarae, C. (1983). Women's talk in the ivory tower. *Communication Quarterly, 31*, 118–132.

Wood, J. T. (1993a). *Gendered Lives*. Belmont, Calif.: Wadsworth.

Wood, J. T. (1993b). "Engendered Relationships: Interaction, Caring, Power, and Responsibility in Close Relationships." In S. Duck (Ed.), *Processes in Close Relationships: Contexts of Close Relationships*. Vol. 3. Beverly Hills: Sage.

Wood, J. T. (1993c). "Engendered Identities: Shaping Voice and Mind Through Gender." In D. Vocate (Ed.), *Intrapersonal Communication: Different Voices, Different Minds*. Hillsdale, N.J.: Lawrence Erlbaum.

Wood, J. T. (1993d). *Who Cares?: Women, Care, and Culture*. Carbondale: Southern Illinois University Press.

Wood, J. T., and Inman, C. C. (1993). In a different mode: Masculine styles of communicating closeness. *Journal of Applied Communication Research.*

Zimmerman, D. H., and West, C. (1975). "Sex Roles, Interruptions, and Silences in Conversation." In B. Thorne and N. Henley (Eds.), *Language and Sex: Difference and Dominance*, 105–129. Rowley, Mass.: Newbury House.

Concepts and Questions

1. What does Wood mean when she asserts that communication constructs gender cultures?

2. How would you answer the following question put forth by Wood? "What makes something a culture instead of just a quality common to a number of individuals"?

3. Why should masculinity and femininity be regarded as different cultures?

4. What is the difference between a person's sex and his or her gender?

5. How would you respond to the following sentence: Research reveals that most girls and women operate from assumptions about communication and use rules for communication that differ significantly from those endorsed by most boys and men.

6. According to Wood, what are the three basic rules girls learn about how to communicate?

7. How would you explain the following sentence: As males and females learn the rules of distinctive gender cultures, they embody them in their personal identities, and this reproduces prevailing social meanings of the genders.

8. What are some differences between "feminine talk" and "masculine talk"?

9. What methods does Wood suggest to help improve understanding in cross-gender communication? From your personal experiences, can you add to her list?

Understanding the Co-Culture of the Elderly

Valerie C. McKay

On January 24, 1995, President Clinton, in his State of the Union Address, declared that "our senior citizens have made us what we are today." Who are our senior citizens? Why were they mentioned in a keynote address such as the State of the Union message? Are they deserving of a commendation such as Mr. Clinton provided, or is this simply an indication that politicians presume our senior citizens have political power that is worthy of their attention and not to be ignored? What contributions *have* our senior citizens made to the progress of our society and culture? Are they a culture of their own?

The purpose of this chapter is to illustrate, through research literature and example, the characteristics of the *culture of the elderly*. This will be accomplished first by discussing the concept of culture and why the population of senior citizens in our society can be conceptualized *culturally*; second, by noting the negative stereotypes associated with older adulthood, their origin, and their falsity; third, by reviewing current research literature describing characteristics of our senior citizens; and finally, by providing information about our senior citizens that forces us to go beyond the stereotypes and fears inherent in relations between generations.

WHAT IS CULTURE?

If we define *culture* as a "form or pattern for living," then it logically follows that the lifestyle of our senior citizens has a pattern all its own that is unique from other forms. As a co-culture, they can certainly be distinguished from the larger culture of which they are a part simply by chronological age. If our

definition becomes even more specific to include *"language, friendships, eating habits, communication practices, social acts, economic and political activities"* (Porter & Samovar, 1985, p. 19), then we must explore their lifestyle with respect to these activities even further in order to discover the culture of this singular group of citizens.

The limitation inherent in conceptualizing a culture or co-culture is the assumption of the homogeneity of the group; in other words, we assume that *most* people within the culture behave *similarly* based upon our *generalized* notion of the group. The result of this assumption is, of course, a tendency to stereotype or form "rigid preconceptions which are applied to all members of a group . . . over a period of time, regardless of individual variations" (Atkinson, Morten, & Sue, 1985, p. 172). Although some may view stereotyping as a means by which we can *generally* understand, or become familiar with, peoples of other cultures, this process often prevents us from really getting to know individual members of those same cultures. As a result, we fail to get past the uncertainty and unfamiliarity by communicating and engaging in preliminary stages of relationship (friendship) development. In many cases, the diversity (or heterogeneity) *within* a culture is greater than the diversity we find in making comparisons *between* cultures (Catchen, 1989)!

WHY SHOULD WE CONSIDER SENIOR CITIZENS TO BE A CO-CULTURE?

Although this question will be addressed in further detail later in this chapter, let's examine some preliminary evidence for the claim. Our first characteristic associated with culture is *language*. Do the elderly speak a different language? Unfortunately, there is little research that has examined singular characteristics of a language used by this particular generation; what have been examined are the patterns of discourse (talk) that occur about and within the lives of older adults (Coupland & Coupland, 1995). So, unlike many cultures that adopt jargon and terms that have meaning only among members of that culture, older adults appear to utilize language forms that coincide with the dominant culture or their culture of origin—or perhaps other forms have not been explored. What have been frequently examined are the patterns of stereotypical language used to describe older adults—both linguistically and in mediated forms of communication—and most of these patterns are commensurate with the stereotypes we hold of the elderly. This will be discussed later on in the chapter.

Now let's consider friendship and social activities. Friendships among older adults are especially significant in meeting both physical and emotional needs. They provide social support, caregiving, transportation and household help, social networking, and emotional satisfaction. Many elderly friendships are long-term—the result of many years of development and nurturance. Although elderly friendships do not differ significantly in their quality in comparison with other groups, they are especially significant for elderly women who, after the loss of their spouse, are alone, are experiencing a reduction in the quality of life, and are sometimes physically and emotionally isolated from family. In contrast, elderly men, who find themselves alone after the loss of their spouse or with the onset of retirement, are less likely to develop and maintain friendships. For some of these men, the risk of suicide increases with age, accounting for rates three times that of the general population (Perkins & Tice, 1994).

For older adults, friendships revolve around a sense of community, help (such as yard work, housekeeping, and household repairs), transportation, and emotional support. "Friendships provide important psychological and social support for the older adult in the form of companionship, mutual aid, and shared activities" (Roberto & Scott, 1989, p. 129). In rural areas, activities with friends seem to revolve more around outdoor events; in urban areas, more activities involve indoor events such as movies, performances, and so on. In fact, one nonprofit organization, Hospital Audiences, Inc., organizes trips and excursions to theater and musical performances for seniors residing in nursing homes in proximity to the New York City area (Schemo, 1994).

Another organization, the Institute of New Dimensions, provides educational opportunities to senior citizens. College-level courses are taught by volunteers, including retired academicians, community leaders, and corporate retirees. Although degrees are not awarded, the rewards are manifest by increased self-esteem and pride (Prince, 1994).

For individuals who are living alone or who are not ambulatory, senior companion programs provide assistance with household affairs, daily visitation, and friendship. Briggs (1994) reports that the Senior Companion Program (SCP) has been in operation for twenty years, and was funded by the Corporation for National Services. The program,

> [m]atches older volunteers with frail, elderly men and women who might otherwise be forced into nursing homes or hospitals. There are 185 local SCP projects spread throughout all 50 states. Companions shop, prepare meals, some monitor medication and assist with exercise, help manage household affairs—or they just simply drop by and visit (p. 260).

As a proactive community enterprise, The LIFE (Learning Informally from Elders) project was designed to (1) engage elders in dialogue and problem solving with professionals and policy makers through community forums and (2) improve the referral and communication network of professionals who serve elders. The success of this program has been the empowerment of elders in the community of New Haven, Connecticut. For example, whereas health-care providers were concerned about the numbers of elders seeking their services, participation in the LIFE forums revealed that elders' primary concerns were for their personal safety in seeking the services in clinics and health centers. One of the first solutions resulting from the LIFE forums was a meeting between project participants and police officials of the New Haven community (Pallett-Hehn & Lucas, 1994).

Organizations such as these are unique to our senior citizens, primarily because the needs of the elder community differ from those of younger people. Two issues are particularly noteworthy: (1) Our elders value their friendships in terms of both satisfying the needs of others and receiving care when needed, and (2) their lives continue to be meaningful and active—contrary to our stereotypical notions of ill health and reclusive lifestyle.

What about culture and communication practices of our older adults? Research has investigated various patterns of inter- and intragenerational talk in the lives of older adults. Some of those patterns include recall and reminiscence (Butler, 1968; Kaminsky, 1984; Lo Gerfo, 1980; Moody, 1984), storytelling

(Nussbaum & Bettini, 1994), competence and effects of aging on communicative ability (Duran, 1989), accommodation to elders (Ryan, MacLean, & Orange, 1994), intergenerational talk (Giles, Coupland, Coupland, Williams, & Nussbaum, 1992; Harwood, Giles, & Ryan, 1995; McKay, 1989, 1993), communication and loss (death) (Nussbaum, Thompson, & Robinson, 1989), communication between caregiver and elder parent (Clipp & George, 1990; Eckert & Shulman, 1996), communication between siblings (Cicirelli & Nussbaum, 1989; McKay & Caverly, 1995), and characteristics of communication in long-term marriages (Klinger-Vartabedian & Wispe, 1989; Mares & Fitzpatrick, 1995)—just to name a few. Clearly, these patterns emerge out of special interpersonal contexts in which communication within and between generations occurs. Let's consider, for example, the phenomenon of long-term marriage.

Long-term marriage is a relatively new and rare social phenomenon for two reasons: Prior to the turn of the century, most marriages ended in the death of one spouse, and *now* only one in five marriages is expected to last twenty or more years (Sporakowski & Axelson, 1989); in fact, long-term marriage may be idiosyncratic to the current elderly cohort unless the prevailing high rate of divorce drastically reduces. Consequently, there exists a paucity of research investigating the quality of long-term marriages of our older adult populations. Moreover, upon the death of a spouse, men have more opportunity to remarry than women, primarily because of the lower female mortality rate (there are more available older women than older men); but little research is available that investigates remarriage in late life.

Some communication researchers have assessed the communicative quality of marriages over the life course. For example, Sillars and Wilmot (1989) explored the *intrinsic* (implicit, idiosyncratic, and efficient communication forms developed over time), *cohort* (similar age group), and *life-stage* (developmental phases) influences on marital communication for young, middle, and older couples. These researchers found that while younger couples' communication patterns were characterized by high levels of disclosure, conflict, and problem solving, older couples appeared to be more passive, less disclosive, and confirmative (the descriptive use of "we"

and "us"). Relationships for older couples reflect commitment, shared history, ability to predict others' views, companionship, and dependence; thus, "the relationship is evaluated based on what it has been through, not on what it has the potential to become" (Sillars & Wilmot, 1989, p. 240). Interestingly, communication becomes a significant factor in couple satisfaction and happiness following the husband's retirement. Often, older wives view their husbands' retirement as an intrusion into their domestic domain, and the need to negotiate roles and responsibilities becomes essential to the satisfactory continuance of the relationship (Treas, 1983).

While early marriage is characterized by high levels of attraction and affection, later in life attraction may be substituted for affection and the development of a relationship history (Johnson, 1988). This does not mean, however, that sexuality fails to be a significant part of the marital bond or a continuing physical need for any elderly individual. "Contrary to myths accepted by many in Western society, elderly people are highly sexual beings with sexual thoughts and desires that persist into advanced age for most individuals. Unfortunately, the sexual needs of the elderly are often ignored by family members, caregivers, and society in general" (Hodson & Skein, 1994, p. 219). Congruent with our fears of aging and the aged, our tendency is to withdraw touching, affection, and other forms of intimacy in our interaction with the elderly. These authors encourage family and others (caregivers, nursing home staff, etc.) to engage in affectionate behavior with elderly companions to the degree that the relationship allows.

One more example will suffice to provide evidence of the existence of our co-culture of older adult citizens: political activity. According to Binstock (1992, p. 331), "persons 65 and older do constitute a large block of participating voters. They represent [16.7 percent to 21 percent] of those who actually voted in national elections during the 1980s. And this percentage is likely to increase in the next four decades because of projected increases in the proportion of older persons." Although an initial interpretation of this statistic might compel visions of an elderly voting conglomerate with only its self-interest in mind, the statistic itself fails to reveal the heterogeneity of the older adult constituency with regard to opinions and interest in political issues (Hess, 1992). "Diversity among older persons may be at least as great with respect to political attitudes and behavior as it is in relation to economic, social, and other characteristics" (Binstock, 1992, p. 331). Nonetheless, in relation to the total voting population, they constitute a significant proportion of participating voters.

Not surprisingly, our older adult population is well represented by interest groups whose primary goal is to reach both policy makers and the media. Moreover, given the common (mis)representation of the conflict between younger and older political interests (primarily with regard to government spending), an organization by the name of Generations United was formed to represent "both the young and the old [in] developing policy that benefits all," and it is considered a model for building bridges between generations and their respective political interests while promoting a positive image of multigenerational cooperation to the media (Coombs & Holladay, 1995, p. 335). Some of the groups involved in this coalition include AARP (American Association of Retired Persons), NCOA (National Council on the Aging), Gray Panthers, Children's Defense Fund, and the Child Welfare League of America. As noted by Coombs and Holladay (1995, p. 336):

> Aged interest groups are particularly powerful in the public agenda building, policy agenda building, and policy evaluation processes. The new challenge facing the aged interest groups is deciding how best to use their power and to whom they must communicate their political actions.

There is evidence for our claim—the elderly belong to a culture unique to their age cohort. We must remember, however, that our senior citizens are also as unique and diverse as most members of the younger population in our society perceive themselves to be (Ade-Ridder & Hennon, 1989). Unfortunately, negative stereotypes of older adulthood and our preoccupation with a youth-oriented society combine to prevent many of us from recognizing the value of the wisdom and experience our seniors have to offer. What *are* some of the stereotypical images that we as a society hold of our aging population? How would you describe a senior citizen?

What is the origin of your image of a senior citizen? Who is the model for your image of a senior citizen?

STEREOTYPES OF THE ELDERLY

As previously mentioned, stereotypes are rigid generalities that members of society impose on others with whom they are unfamiliar or whom they do not understand. Stereotypes function as a system of categorization; we often fail to recognize those individuals who do not fit the stereotype. Members of the dominant culture (in this case, our youth-oriented culture) commonly stereotype the subordinate and minority culture (the aging population) and draw negative stereotypical inferences both preceding and during intergenerational interaction (Giles et al., 1992). Two consequences of stereotyping have been noted. First, "those who have preconceived notions about minority group members may unwittingly act upon these beliefs" (Atkinson, Morten, & Sue, 1985, p. 172). Stereotyping might function to unknowingly and unintentionally impose limitations or standards upon a group of people (e.g., using elder-speak, viewing the elderly as feeble and infirm). Second, the group may engage in self-fulfilling behavior that reflects the limitations being imposed upon it (e.g., the elderly become recluse and isolated, unwilling to interact for fear of negative evaluation or embarrassment). Overcoming the tendency to stereotype, though difficult, offers us the opportunity to become familiar with and better understand members of another culture and thus avoid imposing undeserved views on a group of people.

Interestingly, social stereotypes of older adults before 1980 are in stark contrast to those after 1980. According to Rosenbaum and Button (1993), this evolution is due, in part, to the Reagan era and increased political sensitivity to the needs of our aging population. Prior to 1980, the aging were seen as frail, in need of assistance, lacking political strength, and generally a group of deserving poor that had been largely ignored given the prejudices of a youth-oriented society. After 1980 and the years of Reaganomics, the number of Baby Boomers reaching middle and older adulthood began to rise. The aging were seen as relatively well off, as a potent political force, and ready and willing to claim their portion of the federal budget with regard to health and social security benefits (Binstock, 1992).

On an interpersonal level, stereotypes of the elderly held by young, middle-aged, and older adults were investigated by Hummert, Garstka, Shaner, and Strahm (1994). While both negative and positive stereotypes emerged across all three age groups (young, middle-aged, and elderly), similarities as well as differences in stereotypical characterizations by these age groups were noted. Among the positive stereotypes, the Golden Ager is described as active, adventurous, healthy, lively, wealthy, interesting, liberal, and future-oriented (to name only a few). Perfect Grandparents are wise, kind, trustworthy, loving, understanding, and family-oriented. The John Wayne Conservative is retired, conservative, old-fashioned, nostalgic, and religious. The Activist (a stereotype identified *only* by the elderly adult subjects) is political, sexual, health conscious, and liberal. Finally, the Small Town Neighbor (also identified only by the elderly adults) is old-fashioned, quiet, conservative, tough, and nostalgic.

Hummert et al. (1994) found that all three of the age groups (young, middle-aged, and elderly) identified the Golden-Ager, Perfect Grandparent, and John Wayne Conservative as positive stereotypes of the elderly. The middle-aged group added Liberal Matriarch/Patriarch, who is described as liberal, mellow, and wealthy (is this the way individuals in middle adulthood picture their own parents?). The elderly adult group, as previously mentioned, added Activist, and Small Town Neighbor, categories comprising sexuality, political activity, health consciousness, and a strong sense of the past.

The negative stereotypes include Shrew/Curmudgeon, which is described as bored, complaining, ill-tempered, bitter, and a hypochondriac. The Despondent is depressed, hopeless, sick, neglected, and afraid. Those who are Severely Impaired are described as senile, incompetent, incoherent, feeble, sick, slow-thinking, and sexless; Mildly Impaired are tired, frustrated, worried, and lonely. The Recluse is quiet, timid, dependent, forgetful, and naive. A Self-Centered elder is greedy, miserly, snobbish, emotionless, and humorless. Finally, the Elitist (identified *only* by the elderly adults) is demanding, prejudiced, and wary.

Again, similarities in negative stereotypes across age groups were noted: All three groups identified Shrew/Curmudgeon, Despondent, Severely Impaired, and Recluse. The middle-aged group added Self-Centered; the elderly adult group, as previously mentioned, added Elitist *and* Mildly Impaired. Although these stereotypes seem harmless, and in some cases humorous, we must not fail to realize the consequences of perpetuating these positive and negative images of older adults. "Any minority community that is not well understood generates myths both in its own and the host community. These myths serve functions for both communities—they demystify, they make life more tolerable, they allow subtle discrimination to continue" (Ebrahim, 1992, p. 52). They may prevent members of one culture from getting to know members of another. How many television advertisements can you recall that depict at least one of these elderly stereotypes needing or using their products? Do you find it easy to picture an elderly individual who fits any of these stereotypes? How about one who does not?

Who or what is most responsible for perpetuating stereotypical images of our older adult population? In a study conducted by Robinson and Skill (1995, p. 386), results indicated that "the elderly continue to be infrequently seen on television and when they do appear, they occupy lead roles at about one half the rate of all other age groups;" and in attempting to provide a program that appeals to large and diverse audiences, programs are written in a way that "writers believe the target audience views that group." While the success and appeal of these stereotypical images have yet to be determined, the practice continues to be the basis for creating characters both central and peripheral to the story portrayed. As previously noted, the elderly are diverse and heterogeneous and should be represented in accordance with this fact—*just as other age and cultural groups should be*. As suggested by Robinson and Skill (1995, p. 388):

A starting point in this rather complex process might be through enhancement of elderly images in the mass media. Diverse portrayals of elderly characters may help improve societal attitudes toward the elderly . . . providing positive and negative portrayals of the elderly in all media will afford audience members of all ages the opportunity to increase their knowledge about the elderly and aging, [and] improve their attitudes toward the elderly and aging.

WHAT ARE THE CONSEQUENCES OF STEREOTYPING THE AGING?

The consequences of engaging in healthy and frequent interaction between generations have been documented in research from the early 1960s. For children with living grandparents and sometimes great-grandparents, their perceptions toward older persons, the aging process, and their own aging are enhanced by intergenerational relationships. In contrast, children who have limited contact with elders are more likely to develop stereotypical images of the elderly and increasing concern for their own aging process. Unfortunately, interaction with older adults has not been found to reduce the negative effects of stereotypical images of older adults in young children; once the stereotypes have been firmly fixed in their minds, they are difficult to eradicate. Nor surprisingly, negative stereotypes of the elderly can create fear of aging and the aged that, although unfounded, impedes and inhibits effective and quality communication between generations.

Does stereotyping function to unknowingly and unintentionally impose limitations or standards on a group of people? Does the group being stereotyped engage in self-fulfilling behavior as a consequence of the limitations being imposed upon it? Utilizing accommodation theory as the framework for analysis of accommodating behavior found in communication between generations, Ryan, MacLean, and Orange (1994, p. 273) found that "negative nonverbal behaviors were rated as significantly more likely to occur with patronizing style" and that these behaviors were frequently based on stereotyped expectations of the elderly interactants. The accommodating nonverbal behaviors included simplification and exaggeration of key components of messages, short topics, elderspeak (baby talk directed toward elders), shorter and less complex utterances, and imperatives, interrogatives, and repetitions.

Focusing on a comparison of social skills between young and old interactants, Segrin (1994) found that elders may see themselves as impaired or less skilled especially in interaction with younger people, more as a result of self-comparison than from real inability. This misperception in turn leads to lower self-esteem and perhaps less self-confidence in such interactions. These results, and those found by Ryan et al. (1994) suggest that (1) young people tend to interact with their elderly counterparts based on stereotypical notions of older adults (often in relation to perceptions of impaired physical and mental abilities), and (2) that acting on these stereotypes results in deleterious effects on the self-esteem and self-confidence of the elderly.

In fact, in a study conducted by Giles et al. (1992), intergenerational talk between young and old was explored in order to identify characteristics and effects of stereotypical images of the elderly. The study focused on the sociolinguistic behavior of both the older adults and young adults functioning in the roles of initiator and respondent in interaction. These researchers concluded that "the message transmitted (i.e., what is attended to, encoded, produced, and responded to) is affected by beliefs, assumptions, and stereotypes"; and, specifically, in the case of the aging population, the stereotypes of decrement, incompetence, and inability transcend both the way in which the message is processed and the way the response is produced (Giles et al., 1992, p. 290). Furthermore, older adults were viewed as accommodating these stereotypes by engaging in language that depicted themselves as helpless, dependent, immobile, and victims of old age. The authors refer to this behavior as "instant aging" as many of the older individuals participating in the study described themselves as active and independent prior to engaging in interaction with their youthful counterparts.

How can we transcend the barriers between cultures that stereotypes so systematically place in our way? First, we familiarize ourselves with members of the other culture; then, we try communicating with them. Who are our senior citizens? Are they really greedy, lonely, afraid, incompetent, senile, sexless, inarticulate, forgetful, depressed, stubborn, and all of the other characteristics that make up the negative stereotypes previously mentioned? One intergenerational relationship that has the potential to transcend the negative stereotypes of the aging, and perhaps even the fear of aging itself, is that which exists between grandparents and grandchildren.

THE GRANDPARENT–GRANDCHILD RELATIONSHIP

Although the nature of this relationship is as diverse as the individuals who embrace this intergenerational bond, it engenders a unique communicative character all its own. The diversity characterizing the grandparent–grandchild relationship is influenced by factors such as the age(s) of grandparent and grandchild, sex of relationship participants (as well as maternal or paternal grandparenthood), ethnicity and cultural background, grandparents' work or retirement status, geographical proximity, marital status of both parents and grandparents, and, of course, grandparents' physical health.

Two decades of research exploring the quality, individuality, and character of this distinctive relationship depicts a continuum of grandparental involvement. Early research into the nature of this relationship focused primarily on the enjoyable aspects of the relationship for grandparents, especially in relation to recreational activities and presence on holidays. Recent investigations have found some grandparents taking a more participative role in their grandchildrens' lives; this is especially evident in situations of divorce, surrogate child care, and grandparents acting as primary child care providers (e.g., grandparents as parents or GAP) (McKay, 1989, 1997; McKay & Caverly , 1995).

The intensity and degree of responsibility accepted by grandparents is largely dependent on their own life situations, their ages, and their relations with their own children. Grandparents' concern for the welfare of their grandchildren must often supersede the welfare of, or relations with, their own child (the grandchild's parent), while balancing concerns for their own health or financial status (Jendrek, 1994). Grandparents' full acceptance of responsibility for grandchild care is often the result of neglect or abuse effected by parental emotional problems, drug addiction, or alcoholism; partial acceptance from the desire to assist with child daycare (due to maternal employment), personal self-fulfillment, or the need to feel useful (Jendrek, 1994). These circumstances seem to occur across ethnic groups and geographical areas.

Focusing on the communicative nature of the grandparent–grandchild relationship, interviews with numerous grandmothers, grandfathers, grandsons, and granddaughters of various ages and ethnicities, and in several geographical areas, have provided a plethora of knowledge and understanding about this unique bond. Interestingly, the common thread, no matter what the nature of the relationship, is the desire on the part of grandparents to impart, and the desire by grandchildren to listen to, grandparents' stories of their own life experiences, family history, and advice. "Inasmuch as life stories function to help people make, shape, and preserve history, the shared stories between grandparent and grandchild provide some common ground in which to negotiate and maintain a relationship" (Nussbaum & Bettini, 1994, p. 78).

Perhaps there is no communicative event more salient to the grandparent–grandchild relationship than the sharing of stories, events, advice, or family history. The benefits intrinsic to this type of information exchange, for both grandparents and grandchildren, have been the focus of much research. For example, grandparents provide grandchildren with a source of identity development by sharing stories about their past experiences and other accounts of family history (Baranowski, 1982). Moreover, grandparents achieve a sense of continuity and satisfaction in knowing that the shared ideas, beliefs, values, and memories are carried on into the future (Mead, 1974). Of particular significance, however, is the storyteller, the grandmother or grandfather who plays an integral part in both the characterization and content of the story told (McKay, 1993). These individuals have a lifetime of wisdom and experience to impart; to be unable to do so is a loss not only to the listener, but also to the teller.

CONCLUSIONS AND IMPLICATIONS

Who are our senior citizens? To summarize, they are a co-culture of individuals who engender patterns of friendship, social activities, communication patterns, and political activity that are distinct from other forms. Their attitudes toward work and retirement vary with their needs, their life and social status, and their work histories. They are unique in that many can boast long-term marriage in contrast to a younger generation overwhelmed by high divorce rates. They are both politically active *and* politically diverse; their interest in political, economic, and social issues is heterogeneous, even though their political participation as a whole is of significant proportion. The current age cohort has participated in at least one (and possibly two) world wars, the Great Depression, and other significant historical events. They have seen dramatic innovations in electronics and technology, television, and computers. They are as varied and diverse as the younger generations perceive themselves to be.

Can we transcend the stereotypes of our aging population and reap the benefits of their wisdom and experience? The answer to this question is beyond the scope of this article. However, beginning with the grandparent–grandchild relationship, we can ask the questions and listen to the answers that may penetrate the obstacles that stereotypes of our elderly have so securely placed in our way.

One easy way to understand the culture of the elderly is to accept and perpetuate the predominantly negative stereotypes so easily accepted by our youth-oriented society. A viable alternative, however, is the recognition that, like many other cultures, there exists as much diversity within the elderly population as between it and any other group (Triandis, 1979). The objective of this chapter has been to introduce members of our elderly population, to make the reader aware of the complex and interesting lives they lead, and, at the very least, to dispel some of the negative myths and stereotypes to which our society adheres in order to avoid thinking about aging and the fear that such thoughts provoke. The communication discipline is uniquely qualified to engage in research exploring those aspects of intergenerational relations that will reveal the elderly as a valuable resource of experience and wisdom, and at the same time dispel stereotypes that have prevented the exchange of such resources in the past.

References

Ade-Ridder, L., & Hennon, C. B. (1989). Introduction: Diversity of lifestyles among the elderly. In L. Ade-Ridder and C. B. Hennon (Eds.), *Lifestyles of the elderly: Diversity in relationships, health, and caregiving* (pp. 1–8). New York: Human Sciences Press.

Atkinson, D. R., Morten, G., & Sue, D. W. (1985). Minority group counseling: An overview. In L. A. Samovar & R. E. Porter (Eds.), *Intercultural communication: A reader*. Belmont, CA: Wadsworth.

Baranowski, M. D. (1982). Grandparent–adolescent relations: Beyond the nuclear family. *Adolescence, 17,* 375–384.

Binstock, R. H. (1992). Aging, politics, and public policy. In B. B. Hess & E. W. Markson (Eds.), *Growing old in America* (pp. 325–340). New Brunswick, NJ: Transaction Publishers.

Briggs, B. (1994, October). Door-to-door friendship: The senior companion program. *Good Housekeeping,* p. 260.

Butler, R. N. (1968). The life review: An interpretation of reminiscence in the aged. In B. Neugarten (Ed.), *Middle age and aging* (pp. 486–496). Chicago: University of Chicago Press.

Catchen, H. (1989). Generational equity: Issues of gender and race. In L. Grau (Ed.), *Women in the later years: Health, social, and cultural perspectives* (pp. 21–38). New York: The Haworth Press.

Cicirelli, V. G., & Nussbaum, J. F. (1989). Relationships with siblings in late life. In J. F. Nussbaum (Ed.), *Life-span communication: Normative processes* (pp. 283–300). Hillsdale, NJ: Lawrence Erlbaum.

Clipp, E. C., & George, L. K. (1990). Caregiver needs and patterns of social support. *Journal of Gerontology, 45*(3), 102–111.

Coombs, W. T., & Holladay, S. J. (1995). The emerging political power of the elderly. In J. Nussbaum & J. Coupland (Eds.), *Handbook of communication and aging research* (pp. 317–342). Hillsdale, NJ: Lawrence Erlbaum.

Coupland, N., & Coupland, J. (1995). Discourse, identity, and aging. In J. Nussbaum & J. Coupland (Eds.), *Handbook of communication and aging research* (pp. 79–104). Hillsdale, NJ: Lawrence Erlbaum.

Duran, R. L. (1989). Social communicative competence in adulthood. In J. F. Nussbaum (Ed.), *Life-span communication: Normative processes* (pp. 195–224). Hillsdale, NJ: Lawrence Erlbaum.

Ebrahim, S. (1992). Health and ageing within ethnic minorities. In K. Morgan (Ed.), *Gerontology: Responding to an ageing society* (pp. 50–62). London: British Society of Gerontology.

Eckert, J. W., & Shulman, S. C. (1996). Daughters caring for their aging mothers: A midlife developmental process. *Journal of Gerontological Social Work, 25*(3/4), 17–32.

Giles, H., Coupland, N., Coupland, J., Williams, A., & Nussbaum, J. (1992). Intergenerational talk and communication with older people. *International Journal of Aging and Human Development, 34*(4), 271–297.

Harwood, J., Giles, H., & Ryan, E. B. (1995). Aging, communication, and Intergroup Theory: Social identity and intergenerational communication. In J. Nussbaum & J. Coupland (Eds.), *Handbook of communication and aging research* (pp. 133–160). Hillsdale, NJ: Lawrence Erlbaum.

Hess, B. B. (1992). Growing old in America in the 1990s. In B. B. Hess and E. W. Markson (Eds.), *Growing old in America* (pp. 5–22). New Brunswick, NJ: Transaction Publishers.

Hodson, D. S., & Skein, P. (1994). Sexuality and aging: The Hammerlock of myths. *Journal of Applied Gerontology, 13*(3), 219–235.

Hummert, M. L., Garstka, T. A., Shaner, J. L., & Strahm, S. (1994). Stereotypes of the elderly held by young, middle-aged, and elderly adults. *Journal of Gerontology, 49*(5), 240–249.

Jendrek, M. P. (1994). Grandparents who parent their grandchildren: Circumstances and decisions. *The Gerontologist, 34*(2), 206–216.

Johnson, C. L. (1988). Relationships among family members and friends in later life. In R. M. Milardo (Ed.), *Families and social networks* (pp. 168–169). Newbury Park, CA: Sage Publications.

———. (1994). Introduction: Social and cultural diversity of the oldest-old. *International Journal of Aging and Human Development, 38*(1), 1.

Kaminsky, M. (1984). The arts and social work: Writing and reminiscing in old age: Voices from within the process. *Journal of Gerontological Social Work, 7,* 3–18.

Klinger-Vartabedian, L., & Wispe, L. (1989). The influence of age difference in marriage on longevity. In J. F. Nussbaum (Ed.), *Life-span communication: Normative processes* (pp. 301–318). Hillsdale, NJ: Lawrence Erlbaum.

Lo Gerfo, M. (1980). Three ways of reminiscence in theory and practice. *International Journal of Aging and Human Development, 12,* 39–48.

Mares, M. L., & Fitzpatrick, M. A. (1995). The aging couple. In J. Nussbaum (Ed.), *Handbook of communication and aging* (pp. 185–206). Hillsdale, NJ: Lawrence Erlbaum.

McKay, V. C. (1989). The grandparent–grandchild relationship. In J. F. Nussbaum (Ed.), *Life-span communication: Normative processes* (pp. 257–282). Hillsdale, NJ: Lawrence Erlbaum.

———. (1993). Making connections: Narrative as the expression of continuity between generations of grandparents and grandchildren. In N. Coupland & J. Nussbaum (Eds.), *Discourse and lifespan identity* (pp. 173–185). London: Sage Publications.

———. (1997, November). *The grandparent–grandchild phenomenon: The temporary context as revealed through grandparents' discourse.* Paper presented at the annual conference of the National Communication Association, Chicago.

———, & Caverly, R. S. (1995). Relationships in later life: The nature of inter- and intragenerational ties among grandparents, grandchildren, and adult siblings. In J. Nussbaum (Ed.), *Handbook of communication and aging* (pp. 207–225). Hillsdale, NJ: Lawrence Erlbaum.

Mead, M. (1974). Grandparents as educators. *Teacher College Record, 76,* 240–249.

Moody, H. R. (1984). Reminiscence and the recovery of the public world. *Journal of Gerontological Social Work, 7,* 157–166.

Morris, R., & Bass, S. A. (1992). A new class in America: A revisionist view of retirement. In B. B. Hess & E. W. Markson (Eds.), *Growing old in America* (pp. 93–105). New Brunswick, NJ: Transaction Publishers.

Nussbaum, J., & Bettini, L. M. (1994). Shared stories of the grandparent grandchild relationship. *International Journal of Aging and Human Development, 39*(1), 67–80.

Nussbaum, J. F., Thompson, T., & Robinson, J. D. (1989). *Communication and aging.* New York: Harper & Row.

Pallett-Hehn, P., & Lucas, M. (1994). LIFE: Learning Informally from Elders. *The Gerontologist, 34*(2), 267–270.

Perkins, K., & Tice, C. (1994). Suicide and older adults: The strengths perspective in practice. *Journal of Applied Gerontology, 13*(4), 438–454.

Porter, R. E., & Samovar, L. A. (1985). Approaching intercultural communication. In L. A. Samovar & R. E. Porter (Eds.), *Intercultural communication: A reader* (pp. 15–30). Belmont, CA: Wadsworth.

Prince, R. (1994, Aug. 1). Where the elderly find learning brings its joys. *The New York Times,* p. 9.

Roberto, K. A., & Scott, J. P. (1989). Friendships in late life: A rural-urban comparison. In L. Ade-Ridder & C. B. Hennon (Eds.), *Lifestyles of the elderly: Diversity in relationships, health, and caregiving* (pp. 129–141). New York: Human Sciences Press.

Robinson, J. D., & Skill, T. (1995). Media usage and portrayals of the elderly. In J. Nussbaum (Ed.), *Handbook of communication and aging* (pp. 359–392). Hillsdale, NJ: Lawrence Erlbaum.

Rosenbaum, W. A., & Button, J. W. (1993). The unquiet future of intergenerational politics. *The Gerontologist, 33*(4), 481–490.

Ryan, E. B., MacLean, M., & Orange, J. B. (1994). Inappropriate accommodation in communication to elders: Inferences about nonverbal correlates. *International Journal of Aging and Human Development*, 39(4), 273–291.

Schemo, D. J. (1994, Sept. 5). Age cannot wither the magic of theatre. *The New York Times*, p. 9.

Segrin, C. (1994). Social skills and psychosocial problems among the elderly. *Research on Aging, 16*(3), 301–321.

Sillars, A. L., & Wilmot, W. W. (1989). Marital communication across the life-span. In J. F. Nussbaum (Ed.), *Life-span communication: Normative processes* (pp. 225–254). Hillsdale, NJ: Lawrence Erlbaum.

Sporakowski, M. J., & Axelson, L. V. (1989). Long-term marriages. In L. Ade-Ridder and C. B. Hennon (Eds.), *Lifestyles of the elderly: Diversity in relationships, health, and caregiving* (pp. 9–28). New York: Human Sciences Press.

Treas, J. (1983). Aging and the family. In D. S. Woodruff & J. E. Birren (Eds.), *Aging: Scientific perspectives and social issues*. Monterey, CA: Brooks/Cole.

Triandis, H. C. (1979). Values, attitudes, and interpersonal behavior. *Nebraska Symposium on Motivation* (pp. 195–259).

Concepts and Questions

1. How does the co-culture of the elderly differ from the dominant culture in the United States?
2. How do the elderly's personal positive and negative stereotypes differ from the stereotypes held by the younger members of the dominant culture? Do you hold any negative stereotypes? How were they developed?
3. How do stereotypes of the elderly affect intergenerational communication?
4. What social dynamics affect grandparent–grandchild communications?
5. How would you explain the following sentence: In many cases, the diversity (or heterogeneity) within a culture is greater than the diversity we find in making comparisons between cultures.
6. According to McKay, why are friendships important to older adults?
7. What are some major communication patterns existing in "inter- and intragenerational talk"?
8. What does McKay mean when she writes, "The elderly belong to a culture unique to their age cohort"?
9. How would you answer the following question: Who or what is most responsible for perpetuating stereotypical images of our adult population?

Voicing Identities Somewhere in the Midst of Two Worlds

I-Li Chao

Mitsuo Nagano

Beverly Solidon

Lucila Luna

Patricia Geist

Voices speak
Voices silence others' voices
Voices object to others' voices voicing their voice

Voicing voiceless voices
Can we?
Should we?

They can.
We should listen.

Each voice embodies doubled identities
hesitantly, confidently, tiredly, stridently, endlessly
Changing

Patricia Geist

Somewhere in the midst of two worlds, two cultures, individuals voice the challenges, dilemmas, and celebrations of their ever-changing identities. These diverse voices are encountering, interweaving, and negating the borderlands between cultures represented in their sojourns or their discovered identities. Essentially, the voices represent theories of their own adaptations, speaking concretely, experientially, emotionally, and truthfully with "tone, texture, and cadence" (Hinman, 1994, p. 329).

When we read or listen to others' voices what do we hear? What do we discover? Gilligan (1993) suggests that voice is part of a psychological immune system in the sense that it serves as a source of resistance. Voice, then, is a responsiveness to what we experience—a way of telling others the sense we are making of the order or disorder of our lives. Voicing conflicts experienced, dilemmas encountered, and consciousness raised, individuals living in the borderlands between two or more cultures tell their stories of resistance. They may resist conformity, cultural norms, and even feelings such as shame or guilt. At the same time, their voice may be one of survival, a voice of self-respect, a voice that speaks to the struggles and opportunities they face in the midst of these borderlands.

It is clear that adapting to living life in these borderlands is an ambiguous and complex process. Whether those two worlds are two different countries, two different ethnicities, or two different times in our lives, the process of reconstructing identity is an emotional, challenging, and often rewarding struggle. This article, presenting the voices of four university students, strikes at the heart of this struggle by providing us with the perspectives of both sojourners and Americans, each reconstructing his or her identity through diverse strategies. We learn from a Taiwanese woman, a Japanese man, a Filipino American woman, and a Mexican American woman about what it feels like to live somewhere between two worlds—between two identities, two cultures, two countries, and two loyalties.

I-Li Chao, a Taiwanese woman, describes the arduous and often painful challenge of missing her grandmother while coping with her guilt and fear of being so far from home. In the second story, Mitsuo Nagano, a Japanese man, voices his questioning of where he belongs as he discovers how much he has changed in the process of adapting to the United States. In the third story, Beverly Solidon, a Filipino American woman, speaks to her efforts to remember and reconnect with her Filipino roots. Finally, Lucila Luna, a Chicana, acknowledges her multiple identities, especially the diverse communities where she celebrates and feels connected to her cultural heritage.

Listen to what their voices tell us about living in the midst of two worlds.

Coping with Distance Between Two People in Two Countries

I-LI CHAO

Living in between two countries, there are struggles. I recently asked myself, "Am I an incomplete person?" By choosing between staying in my native country, Taiwan, with my eighty-year-old grandmother and my family, and my own educational goals in America. I feel like an incomplete person to have only one of them. The past six years of studying in America are fulfilling my personal challenges and part of my goal achievement. However, missing my grandmother, feeling guilty about not being with her, and having fears of not being able to see her again often become day-to-day struggles. Six years have developed some of my perspectives and values. But six years also have made me feel detached from my grandmother, not just physical detachment, but emotional detachment.

The following stories reveal the emotions and struggles I experienced while studying abroad, at the same time trying to stay connected with my family—physically, emotionally, and culturally.

GOOD-BYE! MY SWEET GREENHOUSE: JANUARY, FIRST YEAR AWAY

Nineteen years under the protection of my parents and relatives, I saw myself as a beautiful but weak flower in a greenhouse. I felt safe and thankful, but also scared and useless. "What would I be if my family could no longer support me or protect me? Could I survive?" I asked myself. A strong urge within me says no to this kind of protection. Finally, I decided to leave my "greenhouse" (my family) to study in America. It was "a road with no return."

I looked out of the car window, and tried to picture in my mind any images I saw. I felt it was my last time to see Taiwan.

A-Ma, my grandma, and I held hands for the entire time without saying a word on the way to the airport. Just by feeling her sometimes grabbing my right hand a little tighter, I knew she was worried and concerned about me being far away from home for the first time. Neither of us said a word until arriving at the airport. As always, when we stepped out of the car, I held A-Ma's arms by both of my hands, and said in Taiwanese, "A-Ma, ka-se-lee (watch your step)."

A-Ma held my hand even more tightly when we walked into the airport.

We, twelve people, looked like a baseball team leaving for another country. Actually, except for my mother who was traveling with me, the other ten people, including A-Ma, my grandpa, father, brother, sister, uncles, and aunts, just came to the airport to say "good-bye." As I said, I was a "greenhouse flower."

Standing in front of the boarding gate, I felt excitement inside of my body. After two years of preparation and persuading my parents to permit me to go to the United States, I was finally able to reach my dream, studying in America. I felt excited about the new adventure, but at the same time, sad for leaving the people I loved.

"Study hard and be safe," each of my relatives gave me their best blessing.

"Call or write us anytime, OK? Don't forget," my elder brother said.

"Watch out for your health! Don't stay up late! Since you will be away from home by yourself, you need to take care of yourself," my father reminded me.

"Je-Je, keep this." My younger sister by two years insisted on me having one of her favorite music tapes, even though she had given me many of her favorite objects in the past two weeks.

I tried to maintain my smile to my family and show no regrets about my decision. But, just when my father said, "Come back if it is too difficult to study in America. Just come back." I suddenly wept, and could not stop my tears. I held A-Ma's hands and saw the tears on her face. A-Ma still did not say a word. She just held my hands tight and looked at me with tear-filled eyes. I have never seen A-Ma cry like this.

"A-Ma . . . ," I cried, and we hugged each other tightly. Other family members tried to comfort A-Ma.

"I-Li will come back at her first break time. Don't worry. Meiyeh (my aunt who lives in California) will take care of her. Don't worry!"

My father tried to comfort me but used opposite words, "Nothing to cry about. It's your decision to study abroad. You should not cry."

I soon reminded myself that crying showed that I was still a child, not an independent adult. I wiped my tears, and avoided looking at A-Ma's face. I tried to reassure everybody about their concerns. I bit my lip and held back my tears.

"A-Ma, please take care of your health," I told A-Ma, as I quickly turned and walked through the gate with my mother. By not looking back at my family, I held all of my emotions inside until I sat in my seat in the airplane.

"A-Ma, I'm sorry!" The words have never been told.

THE EXCITING, DISHEARTENING EXPERIENCE OF DATING IN THE UNITED STATES: JULY, TWO YEARS LATER

Although I was happy that A-Ma and grandpa were visiting from Taiwan, I was overwhelmed by the excitement of being with my European American boyfriend, Christopher. One month earlier I met Christopher at a friend's party, and we had started dating (almost everyday), and our relationship had become girlfriend–boyfriend. Christopher usually made me laugh by making jokes through his nonverbal gestures. He also introduced me to many aspects of American culture which I could not learn from the textbook, such as surfing, watching football while drinking beers, American slang, and so on. This past month was the happiest time I had ever experienced. I even felt as if I could hear birds singing around me everyday.

At six thirty in the morning the day after A-Ma and grandpa had arrived in the United States, I left my aunt's house to see Christopher because he asked me to have breakfast with him today. I felt guilty not staying home and spending time with A-Ma and grandpa. However, I soon convinced myself that A-Ma and my aunt probably wanted to have a mother–daughter secret talk.

Surprisingly, when I arrived at Christopher's house, I happened to witness an incident which I had never expected to see. MY BOYFRIEND WAS SLEEPING WITH ANOTHER GIRL. The following was a series of lies, tears, and arguments between Christopher and the girl, who was actually his current girlfriend, too. Because of the shock, I did not know how to respond to the unexpected moment. I felt like my chest was being hit heavily. My whole body was unintentionally shaky. However, I just kept silent and looked at their interactions as if I were an outsider.

I held my emotions of betrayal, anger, and confusion inside until the drive home. I cried out loud without concern for other drivers staring at me. But, before I arrived home, I "cleaned up" my emotions, put more make-up on my face, and wished my family would not notice any changes in me. I especially did not want A-Ma to know because I believed she would feel disappointed with me for not spending time on my studies, and for dating a guy whom she would not approve of, an American. Now, it was even worse: The American guy cheated on me! A-Ma, if she knew, probably would shake her head for my foolishness of letting myself date a person like this. In order to show my maturity in being able to take care of myself, and to keep A-Ma from worrying, I decided to avoid any discussion of it with A-Ma and grandpa.

I did not pretend well. Just when I walked in, A-Ma asked me "What happened?" She asked me if there was someone kee-hu me (who was not nice to me and made me sad). I avoided eye-contact with A-Ma and my aunt, and replied with my unnatural smile, "A-Ma, I'm fine!"

Of course, A-Ma could tell I was not fine, but she also knew that I did not want to talk about it. I was thankful that A-Ma did not ask me further questions. However, I was too confused about the "culture shock" to hold my emotions inside. I kept wondering how a person could lie to both girls and how a person could sleep with one girl and express affection to another woman. After I "escaped" from the living room where A-Ma and my aunt were, I turned to the backyard for a discussion with my uncle. He was usually my adviser of love problems and culture shock. During the short discussion with my uncle, I was aware that A-Ma and my aunt had come to the back door many times checking on how I was.

This incident has never discussed between A-Ma and me. I later worried, "Will A-Ma think I am no longer emotionally close to her because I didn't share it with her?" I also felt guilty for putting my own pleasure, dating with Christopher, first, rather than spending time with A-Ma and my grandfather. I even imagined how sad and disappointed A-Ma would be after taking the fourteen-hour flight. I blamed myself.

ASTONISHING PHOTOS: JANUARY, FOUR YEARS LATER

Vincent, my new boyfriend, gave me a paper bag with my family's photos he brought from Taiwan. These were the pictures my family took recently. Vincent has lived with my family in Taipei for the past six months before he came to San Diego to study. We had been dating for about two and a half years. Since he planned to come to America, I asked him to take some pictures of my family before he came, and to bring them to me. I was very excited so I quickly tore the paper bag apart because I was eager to see the photos.

"Hey, relax! Relax!" Vincent said to me and smiled at me.

"Gosh! I haven't seen them for a long time." I looked at the pictures. First, I saw my elder brother's baby girl, my niece, Pin-jen's pictures, and said, "Oh! My God! She is so BIG now." I was so surprised that Pin-jen was not a "baby" any more; she had become a little girl. I could not believe how time had flown by. After seeing several photographs of Pin-jen and my parents, A-Ma's pictures came into my view.

I suddenly felt sorrow and wept over them. My tears ran down my face, and could not be stopped. I felt my whole body shake, especially my chest. I felt hardly able to breathe because my nose was plugged, and my family's pictures were dimmed by my tears.

"What happened? Are you all right?" Vincent was stunned by my reaction. He held me closer, and wanted to know what was going on. I could not answer him because I was still in a mood of sadness.

I was shocked and not able to accept what I saw in the pictures. Both of my parents have lots of gray hair and wrinkles, especially my father. His hair has become much thinner and he looks "old." It reminds me of the time I went back home one summer and I noticed how small A-Ma had become. I found I am taller than she—one head more—and I felt as if I could hold her like an adult holds a child. I am happy

"A-Ma and Me"

that I became taller, but I am sad to realize grandma's age. I looked at one picture, which A-Ma and I took together last summer. I felt warm to look at A-Ma's smile on the photo, but I felt wounded, thinking about not being with her in her old age.

"A-MA, WHERE ARE YOU?????" A SPAN OF TWO YEARS

I laughed at myself when I discovered it was only my worry and imagination. However, I have had similar kinds of dreams three times in the past two years. Each time in the dream, I experienced screaming, the feelings of grief, and the sense of loss. I did not know what to do with my "silly fear," so the only thing I did was cry by myself in the night.

I walked on a street. Suddenly, some earsplitting sounds of trumpets and percussion shocked me. I walked towards the front corner of the street where the noise came from. I found crowds there. People were talking with distressed hand gestures. They looked like they were having a serious discussion because no one smiled, and some people frowned. My curiosity pulled me to walk into the crowd to find out what had happened. People were continuously talking while I tried to walk through them. I was astonished at what I discovered, a cold body which was well-dressed laying on a wood bed. It was a funeral . . . a funeral for an old lady whose face had become dark gray-blue color. I could not believe what I saw. The cold, lifeless body in front of me was—MY . . . MY BELOVED A-MA!

My hands were shaky. No! Actually, my whole body was shaky. I felt goosebumps all over my arms and legs. My legs suddenly lost strength so that I fell to my knees beside the bed. I tried to keep myself upright by using my hands to hold on to the bed. I breathed heavily, feeling no air expand in my chest. My heart was beating fast and heavily; my cheeks were so hot that I felt like burning; my mind was totally blank. I clenched my teeth, closed my eyes which were filled with tears, and kept shaking my head. I screamed over and over, but there was no sound coming out. I could only hear myself, "ah . . . ah . . . " a weak cracky sound from my tight throat. I continuously screamed with no sound as if it were the only way to let my emotions out of my chest. I cried over and over until I lost all of my energy. Suddenly, everything around me started turning, I could not see a thing. I felt dizzy; however, I had no force to fight it back. Finally, I lost the last strength I had, and let my body sag against the bed.

Not knowing how much time had passed, I finally opened my eyes. I found myself lying on a bed with sweat all over my body. I felt thirsty and exhausted. Recognizing I was in my room, in San Diego, I wondered if what just happened was a reality or just a dream. Looking out of a window, I saw it was still dark and quiet. Three in the morning. I decided to call my family in Taiwan to check if A-Ma was fine. I quickly dialed A-Ma's number. However, my anxiety became greater and greater while the phone kept ringing longer and longer.

"What happened?" I asked myself, "A-Ma is usually there for dinner this time."

The feeling of fear started permeating me. I hung up, dialed again, hung up, and dialed again. After listening to the ringing about 50 times, I decided to call my brother's place since he lived near A-Ma.

"What's going on? Nobody answers the phone!!!" There was no one at home either. I felt like I wanted to scream because I thought probably my dream was a hint. There could be something bad really happening to A-Ma so people were with her. Was this why people were not home? I kept wondering, and different negative thoughts came into my mind while I was trying to call my aunt in Taiwan. I felt the goosebumps on my body again.

"Hello?" There was finally someone who answered the phone. It was my aunt. I felt a sense of relief, but also anxiety. I quickly asked, "Gu-Gu ("Aunt" in Chinese), I tried to call A-Ma, but no

one answers. She usually has dinner at this time. Do you know where she is?"

After my aunt told me A-Ma went to a mountain to live with her Buddhist master for a week, I finally felt relief, and laughed about my silly thoughts.

TEARS IN THE NIGHT BY MYSELF

I have never counted how many times I cried in these six years. The feelings of sadness, fear, guilt, disappointment, and helplessness are all parts of my life experiences in this "road with no return." Living in between the U.S. and Taiwan, I feel sometimes my body is here, in the United States, and my heart is there, with my family. Living in between my goals and my family, I do feel I am an incomplete person. To me, saying good-bye to my homeland is a road with no return and never-ending struggles.

Discovering and Learning from "In Between"

MITSUO NAGANO

I came to the United States to study and to accomplish my goal of becoming a fluent English speaker. It seemed like a very simple goal, but for me it has taken many years to accomplish. Even today, I feel I have not reached the goal. However, I have made progress during the three years I have lived in the United States. I have made every effort to overcome many obstacles. I have worked on my English pronunciation and have thought about the cultural differences between the United States and my native Japan.

Each of the following reveals my struggle of living and learning in between here (the United States) and there (Japan) and questioning where I belong. From my experiences in the classroom to my "visits" back to my homeland, I am now learning and how much I took for granted, how much I have changed.

THE DIFFICULT LETTERS "L" AND "R"

I came to the United States in 1994 with my excitement and enthusiasm. I went to a community college in San Diego and decided to study speech communication as a major because I thought that it would facilitate my goal of speaking English fluently. However, my English skill was not matured when I arrived at San Diego, especially, my pronunciation.

When I spoke in a discussion group in one of my classes, some native speakers looked puzzled. Furthermore, I couldn't pronounce words with the letters "L" and "R." The Japanese language doesn't require me to speak with stress and strong accents. So when I spoke English, I experienced great difficulty in pronouncing certain words. Sometimes, I wished that I could take out my tongue to form a correct pronunciation of words with the "L" and "R" shape and put it back in my mouth. Each day was very stressful and frustrating as I worked diligently to practice speaking English.

Since I was aware of the problem I had with speaking English, I decided to take an English pronunciation class. As I opened the door, I heard non-English conversations. It seemed to me that they enjoyed chatting before the class. I noticed that most of my classmates were older than I was; they were immigrants from Europe and Asia. I could imagine that they possibly had problems at their work because they could not speak English properly.

When our teacher came into the classroom, everyone said "Hello" to her in English. Then she responded with enthusiasm. She usually wrote basic English vocabularies such as verbs, days, and numbers on a blackboard. Afterward, she pronounced the words correctly and slowly, we tried to repeat what she said. When she heard a student who couldn't speak the word correctly, she came up to the student and tried to show how her mouth moved in front of their nose. One day she discovered my problem pronouncing the letter "R":

"Read," she said.

"Lead," I said incorrectly.

"No. No. NO. READ," she pronounced the word slowly.

"Lead?" I tried unsuccessfully again.

"No. Watch my mouth. READ." She spoke the word in front of my nose.

"R . . . E . . . A . . . D."

"Yes. YES."

After she was satisfied with my pronunciation, she went back to the blackboard and pronounced different words. We continued to do this type of exercise for two hours. Usually after I finished that class, I was so exhausted I felt I couldn't speak English at all.

I began to see that my pronunciation skill had improved when I took an oral interpretation class. I was assigned to read a poem and prose in front of people to express my feelings and thoughts. Obviously, I thought that it would be a tough class because I didn't have any confidence. Every time, I had a presentation I prepared long and hard with my Japanese friend who told me which words I didn't pronounce correctly.

I hated the feeling when I talked to native speakers. They always looked confused. Even though I exercised a lot to produce the sound of "L" and "R" by using my tongue, I know I didn't quite say the words correctly. Throughout the semester, I was never satisfied with my presentations because I didn't think that I could show clearly my feelings and thoughts through my words. All I did throughout the semester was practice speaking English.

On the last day of the semester, I received feedback from my professor and classmates. After the final presentations were over, my professor praised how well everyone in the class improved throughout the semester. Then she mentioned my name.

"How are you doing, Mitsuo?"

I didn't understand what she meant, so I asked her.

"What . . . do you mean?"

"I thought that you improved every time you had a presentation. Did you do anything to improve your presentation?" She pointed from low to high with her big smile.

"I just . . . did my best." I said awkwardly because I didn't anticipate her feedback on my performance in the class. Then I discovered that my classmates agreed with her opinion about me. One of my classmates gave me an unforgettable comment:

"I didn't understand what you said at the beginning of this semester, but I understand you now."

I was *happy* to hear such great feedback from my professor and classmates. After I took the oral interpretation class, I gained confidence. The stress I experienced motivated me to improve my English skills and helped me reach my goal of becoming a fluent English speaker.

RETURNING TO MY OWN CULTURE: I AM IN BETWEEN TWO CULTURES

It was December, two years from when I first arrived in the United States, when I went back to Japan for the third time. I gently put the letter from my old high school friend in my backpack. When I got this letter with an invitation card to my high school class reunion, I was so thrilled to have the chance to meet my old friends again. I had not seen them in three years.

When I arrived at Narita airport on a cold December day, I remember that I didn't even feel cold because I was so excited. I went through customs with my heavyweight suitcases containing my gifts to my friends. Before I left the United States, I bought Coca-Cola pens with a white bear logo and Hershey's candies. As I pulled my heavy cart, I searched for my parents who were supposed to pick me up at the airport. I expected to see them on time because my parents always check my flight schedule.

However, I couldn't find them. I made my way through the crowd of travelers and finally discovered the most recognized faces in the world. As I approached them, my father was still looking at a small television which indicated which flights had finished going through customs.

He didn't see me even though I came right up to him within one foot. Then I said, "Tadaima" ("I came back" in Japanese) loudly to my father. He stepped back a little and showed his awkwardness by saying, "Ah! Okaeri" ("Welcome back" in Japanese).

I have never seen such surprise on my father's face. After I met him, he called my mother to let her know he had "found his only son with hesitation." Then I asked myself why did he seem awkward or hesitant about me?

After I met both parents, my father described my hairstyle. "You look like John Lennon, I barely recognized your face."

Then he asked me a question about the boots I wore. My parents seemed surprised that I wore big toe, brown, shiny boots. I just thought that they hadn't got used to my *new* look. I repeated one phrase in my mind, "I didn't change."

As my parents continued to ask me questions about my hairstyle, my boots, and other changes, I started thinking "Did I do something wrong?" "Have I done something I should not do?" I began to feel anxiety and frustration about going to my high school reunion.

I was supposed to meet my old high school friends at the train station, which is located in my hometown. On the way to the station, I paid attention to how other people looked when they passed by me. At the station, there were many businesspeople. They looked very busy and didn't smile at all like most Americans do. Also there were many teenagers who gathered and waited for their friends. Then I searched for my friends. They should be here. It was already 6 P.M.

As I looked and walked around, I found the one group of people who looked very familiar. I started walking toward them and I didn't really think what I was going to say when I met them. I just approached them slowly and waited until they could be aware of me. One of my old friends shouted my name.

"Hey! Mitsuo. What is wrong with your hairstyle?" After you went to America, you changed." He laughed and made fun of me.

I waved my hands to them for a greeting rather than saying "How are you doing, guys?" I noticed that one of my friends suspiciously gazed at me and said nothing. Then I looked at other friends and they followed her behavior.

I just wanted to say, "How are you?" but I couldn't even say that phrase because I didn't anticipate these behaviors toward me. I also was upset and shocked. "What did I do? Why did they look at me like that without asking how have I lived in the United States for four years?" This moment indicated that I did change during four years in the United States. Simultaneously, I felt that I was isolated and segregated from my own culture. I got lost between two cultures.

After we decided which restaurant we were going to, we started walking toward our destination. As

"My Complete Adjustment"

thought to myself, I wanted her to ask me how much I have studied, I wanted her to see the papers I wrote last semester, and I wanted her to know how much I made an effort to adjust to the American culture, and reach my goals in the United States. I felt that I couldn't get together and talk with my friends like we did when we were in high school. I was disappointed and frustrated with how my friends perceived me.

I didn't try to argue with them because if I said what I have done in the United States voluntarily, I would be isolated from them completely. So I just smiled to hide my emotions and to keep harmony with them. However, I wanted them to understand me. But they kept asking me pointless questions, because they didn't have any idea how I lived in the United States and they didn't have any interest in learning about my experiences. They asked me questions like:

"Do you know an American friend whose name is Bob?"

"Do you speak English all the time?"

"Did you do any drugs?"

What does it mean to ask these questions? What did I do in the United States? I just tried to reach my goal to become a fluent English speaker. That is all. Why do they care about my hairstyle and shoes any way? I believed that I didn't do anything wrong. Did I do something which I should not do? Did I become an "Americanized" person? Did I accept differences from the American culture too much? If I did, how far can I accept and adjust to different cultures?

What I have come to know is that I didn't recognize my changes and therefore I took for granted that I had not changed. When I returned to Japan, it became a turning point. I began thinking about the ways I have been changed while living and studying in the United States. I realize now that part of my adjustment to this new culture was an abandoning of my own culture. I *have* changed. But in the process I am exploring and learning about another culture. At the same time, I am discovering how important it is to communicate with my family and friends to maintain my connection to my Japanese identity while I am developing my new identities in the United States.

time passed, it seemed to me that they started to relax and began to make conversation with me.

"I haven't seen you in like three years."

"Yeah. It was a long time," I responded softly.

"What do you do now?"

"I am a student."

"Are you a student still? Aren't you supposed to be working? How old are you?"

"I am twenty-three," I answered with hesitation. I said in my mind that she didn't have to critique about what I should be doing at my age.

"You have to work. Look at your friends. They are all working. You can't play any more at your age."

"But I study harder than when I was in high school and I enjoy studying there," I explained.

After she stopped talking, she just left me and followed our friends who were walking in front. I

Balancing Heightened Identities

BEVERLY SOLIDON

I assured myself of who I was. I was Filipino and never questioned my identity until recently. I went through life believing that eating Filipino food like pancit (similar to a Chinese chow mein dish), being Catholic, and addressing my elders as "Auntie" and "Uncle" gave me the right to call myself Filipino. Of course, these aspects are all part of the culture, but I later realized that it was much more than that.

I have taken on characteristics that are not only customary to the Philippines, like realizing the importance of religion and family, but those attributes that are American as well, such as individuality. I am making a conscious effort, not only to remember the customs and history of the Philippine culture, but also to be an active participant in the Filipino American community.

But comparing myself to those Filipino Americans who I believed had a strong sense of identity, made me feel that I did not know enough. These were people who knew not only the history of immigration of Filipinos to the United States, but also the social predicaments that many Filipino Americans face. From these people I learned about the struggle of the first Filipinos who came to America, making their livings in agriculture, only to be faced with prejudice and discrimination. I also learned of the Filipinos who fought in World War II, who were never given the benefits as the others who served the armed forces during that time. Very active in the community, these Filipino Americans who were admired and respected for their knowledge; even more so for their dedication in preparing programs to benefit the Filipino community in America. But who is to say what being Filipino or Filipino American is? I suppose it is the individual who defines his or her own identity. Even still, I find those lines of definition unclear.

Each of my life experiences have accumulated over time, creating a curiosity and sensitivity about these issues within me. But what exactly are the elements that triggered my need to find, preserve, and know my identity? I share with you the stories which have contributed to my desire of not only knowing, but balancing my identity as a Filipino American.

I reflect on my childhood. My first visit to the Philippines was too long ago for me to remember with much detail. My most colorful memory is the mosquito bites I received during my stay. It had taken me approximately sixteen years to return. Each year, for as long as I can remember, my mother and father vacationed in the Philippines, and I always opted not to go.

I can still hear my older cousins (they were only eleven years old at the time) revealing their horror stories about the Philippines which dissuaded me from visiting the country. An eight year old believes almost anything anyone tells her; at least I did.

I was born in Canada, and moved to California when I was three years old. I lived my life as an American. I attended public schools, learned about the history of George Washington, General Custer, and Susan B. Anthony. At home, my mother and father spoke to me in both Visayan (a Philippine dialect) and English. I was one of approximately five Filipinos in my entire elementary school, but that did not really bother me. But then, they referred to me as "nip" (or Asian person). "I'm not a nip. I'm Filipino!" I would snap back at all of the mean children at school.

It did not matter whether or not I visited the Philippines. I was Filipino because my parents told me so. At that time, I had no interest in going there. Or did I? Was I sensitized by the threats and comments about the islands? Did I adhere to peer pressure? This was the story of my childhood and adolescence; a cycle that remained the same for sixteen years of my life. Things could have been different, I suppose, but I cannot regret the path that was taken during those years. With my second trip to the country in 1995, I knew I needed to be more attentive.

This pivotal experience in my life as a teenager made me realize that I was equally Filipino and American; spending time with my cousins during my visit to the Philippines sixteen years later. I reflect on the curiosities that my cousins in the Philippines had about me and my life in the United States during my visit; I was suddenly their official spokesperson of

"My 'Susan B. Anthony' Speech"

"Only call-girls wear that sort of clothing," says May Ann in her conservative crisp white T-shirt and khaki shorts, proud of her natural beauty.

"Oh!" I answer, blushing as I look at the white cotton tank top I cover myself with.

At that moment, I realized that life in the United States was different from that in the Philippines; and that I still had much to learn about the Filipino culture. Then, I hear the voices of my cousins in the United States again, but this time, they are more real than before.

"They don't have running toilets, and lizards climb the walls, and the cars they drive there are real funny looking, and there are ghosts."

It rings in my ears. But I do not want to listen any longer. I really did not mind that I had to use a "tabo" or bowl and a large container of cold water to bathe. Nor did I care that lizards would sometimes find serenity on the walls of grandmother's Spanish-style home.

I reflect again, quickly recalling my departure. Was it time to return already? It is cooler, a bit windy, and the sun is concealing itself from the town. I am showered with gifts from my relatives. More importantly, comments of "Come home and visit again, Beverly! Soon!" and "Don't wait too long to come back!" embed themselves in my head, imprinted in my memory for life. "Come back? I don't even want to leave!" I say to myself. Though I am surrounded by my family, I feel very alone in the foyer of the Solidon home. I take one last look at the home where my father was reared. I memorize the features of my relatives; the hair, the eyes, the skin and the "ear-to-ear" smiles that are similar to mine, and I save those to remember them by. I smile, now seated in the back of a Toyota Wagoneer, waving good-bye and giving thanks to my family for an important cultural and life lesson. I can't help but be sad about leaving them behind. I still see them waving at me. I want to take them with me. I want to take this whole place with me. I begin to weep.

My entire outlook of the Philippines reversed itself from the naive, ethnocentric view of a child that it once was. It was not what I thought it would be. As a matter of fact, it was the complete opposite of how I envisioned it. It was not a discomfort at all. It is a part of my heritage that helped to make me who I am. Instead of seeing it as a primitive place

American culture. However, I submersed myself in everything there was to offer and felt more comfortable when my family asked me about my life as an American. I began to feel accepted.

"Do you go on dates with boys by yourself?"

"What types of cars do they drive there?"

I asked them questions as well. "Why don't you visit the U.S.?"

"Well, it's very expensive to go there," responds my cousin May Ann.

"Why do the women wear shorts and T-shirts to the beach instead of bathing suits?"

"They are very expensive. They cost the equivalent of seventeen U.S. dollars," says my Auntie Leeza.

"That's it?" I think to myself. "Do you have daylight savings time?"

They both look at me with confusion.

"Why doesn't anyone wear tank tops here?" I ask.

with nothing to offer, I found that it was a place of culture; my culture embedded with beauty, heritage, and my family. How could I allow so much time to pass without seeing, or being with them? I spent everyday with my family and became quickly attached. It rapidly passed, almost as if it was a dream.

After this visit, I thought frequently about what it meant to be Filipino American. I remember listening to a speaker at a high school conference in San Diego I attended not too long after my trip. I can still hear her off-beat, rhythmic style of speech, somewhat similar to a poet reciting his or her work in a dimly lit coffee shop, as silence falls over her audience.

"Are you Filipino because you call your elders 'Auntie' and 'Uncle'?" Some remain silent, but the others nod their heads as laughter roars from their mouths. They are beginning to really tune in and relate.

"Are you Filipino because you had to take piano lessons for the first fifteen years of your life?" I am really in tune with what she is saying. I snicker because I do call all of my elders "Auntie" and "Uncle," and I have had my share of piano lessons. She shoots her audience with more questions, her brown hands gesturing towards the audience as if to attack them.

"Are you Filipino because you know how to do the cultural dances?"

"Are you Filipino because you have a karaoke system in your home?" I do know the dances and I do have a karaoke system at home. On a more serious note she asks, her voice continuously fluctuating like the dips and climbs of a roller coaster ride, "Does it seem as if you and your parents cannot relate to each other?"

"Did your parents teach you English only and not Tagalog (the Philippines' national language) so you would be quote-unquote 'more American'?" The cessation of sound occurs once again. These questions seem to have impacted the students and me.

She continued in her deep, raspy, rhythmic voice and discussed the importance of the challenges fac-ing the young Filipino community today. I began to drown her voice out with my own pensively.

I related quite well to the questions she asked. But even still, I do not think those things make you more "Filipino." So I began to wonder if these students felt the same way. Or didn't they see that every Filipino is not a piano playing, karaoke singing, English-speaking person? There was a time when I felt comfort in knowing that I shared many of those characteristics that she spoke about. That is how I identified myself as being "Filipino." Now, because of this, combined with my experience in the Philippines, I find dissatisfaction because I believe that my Filipino heritage is much more than that.

I was in a country where those in the military found it normal to carry their artillery with them, even to eat. I was somewhere where the Church indirectly, yet greatly governed the townspeople. I was in a place where class status was distinct. I clearly remember my grandmother's maid who would accompany me on occasion to the market. I would ask her questions, frustrated when she would answer with a simple "yes ma'am" or "no ma'am" as she looked down, and even more so when she would walk a few steps behind me and not alongside of me.

Yet how normal was it for my American friends to eat rice with every meal? Did their noses cringe from the aroma of fried fish permeating throughout my home on Sunday afternoons? I know not all of my friends called all of their elders "Auntie" or "Uncle," nor did they all have a statue of the Virgin Mary sitting in their living rooms. Did they think it was weird to have to remove their shoes before entering my house?

This story I share is from the view of a Filipino American. My perspective is by one who is in the midst of two cultures neither completely Filipino nor completely American. I find it a challenge to identify with either one or the other when I have been equally influenced by both. I will accept this challenge of balancing both. I suppose I belong somewhere on this continuum—somewhere in the midst of these two lands.

Assembling My Chicano Identity

LUCILA LUNA

We all have an identity. My identity is an assemblage. I am Lucila. I am woman. An identity is a characteristic of the individual. It is feelings about self. An identity is created through the words we choose to label ourselves and others. I am a daughter. I am a sister. I am the sister of Adrian and Rose. When either one of my siblings introduces me to friends, I become Lucila, Rose's sister. My identity is linked to hers. Adrian, my brother, hates it when I introduce him as "my brother, Adrian" rather than "Adrian, my brother." He feels that by putting his name last his identity will always be linked with mine which to a certain degree is true.

Identity is something held by a group of people which, in turn, bonds the group together. As a member of a ballet folklorico I hold an identity with my dance group, Fiesta de Colores, Mexican folkloric dancers. I share my cultural pride with other Chicano students who want to keep their cultural identity alive. When I am with them my identity as a student or woman is superseded by the group's identity. The identity I share with the group members allowed me discover my cultural roots. Furthermore, Fiesta de Colors became my surrogate familia in San Diego. It filled a void that was lacking in the first year as a college student.

I am a Chicana and therefore I am part of the Chicano/Latino community. Identity in this case is held in the group as well as in the individual. This community defines a repertoire of identities that are jointly held, remembered, and taught to new members. Every Mechistas (a MEChA member) knows the struggles of Cesar Chavez and they also know not to buy grapes. The community may have a hierarchy of identities, with some more central to its notion of membership than others.

An identity provides an understanding of how individuals define themselves in general as well as in particular situations. I live on the border of two cultures: American and Mexican. At home Mexican

"Viva La Tradicion!"

things are the norm, like eating arroz and frijoles con tortillas. In my professional life the American culture rules, such as reading primarily American literature. I move between these two cultures on a daily basis, sometime with great difficulty, such as not understanding my roommate's proverbs and other times with very little effort, like when I go to Baja with my Gringo (American) boyfriend.

We "need to move from centers to 'borderland,' 'zones of difference,' and 'busy intersections' where many identities and interest are articulated with multiple others." So that these borders and boundaries cease to be barriers but rather they become bridges to other worlds. I can empathize, for examples, with struggles of African-Americans in particular with a graduate school colleague who understands the complexities of living between two worlds. He knows "what time it is!" These boundaries allow us to create our identity. This is an ongoing process that is never finished.

My identity as a Chicana is one of the most significant indicators of who I am and what I believe in. At the same time, this identity can at times conflict with my identity as an American. A perfect example of this struggle occurs every time my boyfriend joins my family for dinner. Mexican protocol requires that I serve him his dinner even if it is a buffet. My American identity says, "He can serve his own damn dinner." Therefore, my goal in sharing a few of my stories is to help others and also myself surf the borders of these two cultures more successfully.

PORQUE? (WHY?)

I am a product of the Barrio, the Chicano equivalent for "ghetto." Pulling your family out of poverty and keeping the Mexican-American culture alive are the two primary stated ideals of the Chicano student (Marin & Marin, 1991). Why do I write about being a Chicana? Chicano reflects a certain political and social consciousness for individuals who trace their family background to Mexico. By labeling myself as a Chicana, I am a participant in the political arena— a political activist, fighting for the rights of my gente (people) and my rights as a mujer (woman). Being a Chicana permeates every aspects of my life. I cannot escape it.

Chicano is a term used to voice and express an overt identity. A Chicano is a Latino or Mexican-American minus the Anglo image of himself or herself. A Chicano is a "Mexican-American who knows what's up and it really pisses him or her off" (Lopez, 1994, p. 131). Chicanismo involves a personal decision to reject assimilation into the dominant white culture and work towards the preservation of the Chicano cultural heritage. "Chicanismo results from a decision based on a political consciousness for our

Raza (Mexican, Mexican-Americans, and Chicanos), to dedicate oneself to building a Chicana/Chicano nation. Chicanismo is a concept that integrates self-awareness with cultural identity, a necessary step in developing [our] consciousness" ("El Plan de Santa Barbara, 1969, p. 3). In essence, Chicanismo reflects self-respect, dignity, self-worth, pride, and rebirth of one's ethnic and cultural background.

Acceptance of our Chicano culture is a necessary step in the building of our community. By accepting our culture, we create a definition that emphasizes those aspects central to our identity. Our identity allows us to create, with those who share it, a community that gives us a sense of belonging which is often missing from our lives when we move from our homes to a university.

We, Chicanos, find ourselves having to compete for acceptance, grades, and general resources with other students on campus. This can be alienating and emotionally unsettling for us. Embracing a clearly distinguished and recognized identity can serve as an emotional oasis, a way to alleviate our sense of alienation. Far more than merely providing us with a peer group or means of social identification, identity furnishes a way of negotiating what seems to be an increasingly competitive and alienating experience within the university. Therefore, we turn to a Chicano identity because it offers community identification: a shared history, a coherent body of ideals and values, a renewed sense of belonging and roots.

COMUNIDAD (COMMUNITY)

Why do we need a community? How else are newly arrived Latinos to deal with a new, mostly European-American environment, where the name of the university, mascot, and the buildings remind students of their rich European heritage. I still remember my brother's words as he walked around the campus: "Where are all the Mexicans?" I responded, "This isn't like home where everyone is either Asian, Black, or Brown." It is important that all Chicanos on campus feel that they belong here and that they have a feeling of familia with their Chicano brothers and sisters. This sense of community also helps reinforce cultural identity and values (Barrera, 1988).

In the early 1960s, concerned Raza came together to draw attention to the needs and concerns of Chicanos, both in the educational system and in the community. They struggled to increase educational opportunities for Chicanos and to establish academic programs for the study of the Mexican experience and providing an educational opportunity for Chicanas/Chicanos. Chicanos were committed to confronting social inequalities and rejecting assimilation into the dominant European-American society. Movimiento Estudiantil Chicano de Aztlan (MEChA) was formed to help seal this commitment; it would be fulfilled through student militant activities both on campus and in the community (Gomez-Quinones, 1978, 1990).

The first MEChA meeting I attended brought back a feeling of belonging. I felt like I was with mi familia (my family). It did not matter that I did not know many people at the meeting. Just hearing the members talk, their switching between Spanish and English so flawlessly, reminded me of home. How does Movimiento Estudiantil Chicano de Aztlan (MEChA) use identity to build a community among college students? My friend Andy tells us why he joined MEChA when he first arrived on campus:

> The first time I ever even heard of MEChA was when I came to campus. It was the end of August [when] school started. I didn't know anybody at all. Somebody told me about it in my Mexican-American class. They said it was a bunch of Mexicanos getting together to discuss issues that are facing them in the community as well as in education. I thought that was cool. So I went to a meeting. . . . I wanted to join a club or organization so I would get to know somebody at least. I was a loner!

Through this feeling of community and belonging MEChA helps retain students in higher education. Students join MEChA because it is a social club. It gives them a place to belong and people with whom they can interact.

MEChA not only constructs a community for Chicanos, it helps individuals construct a consciousness about their political identities. To empower its members groups must develop a consciousness that opposes the ideology of mainstream America. Lurdes, an active mechista, recounts how her consciousness was raised:

> I was sick with ignorance for many years. I hadn't realized my identity or my responsibilities. I settled for Hispanic and I would even call some RAZA wetbacks. [Illegal immigrants who crossed the Rio Grande into the United States.] I thought I had come over on a boat with Columbus. But, luckily I got involved in MEChA and started learning about who I really am. I realized that I am Chicana and proud. I also realized that my job . . . is to spread Chicana/Chicano pride, power, and knowledge.

Membership in MEChA spoke to this woman's sense of alienation and ignorance. MEChA helped her realize that her true identity is being a Chicana.

Chicanos negotiate ways of communicating within the group itself but also with the public at large. Negotiating an identity can be implicit, consisting of symbol or display that undermines the status quo. Chicanos, for example, have utilized code switching as means of communicating with one another. Code switching injects Spanish words into a primarily English text or conversation. By doing this, Chicanos adopt the English language to our own needs. In other words, Spanglish or code switching allows us to keep our identity by providing a form of communication that is unique. Pedro, provide us with an example of Spanglish as he rallies support for more community involvement,

> Emergency, socorro!!! We need ayuda (help) A.S.A.P. from all Mechistas. "En que?" What do you mean in what? Look around you chico/a! Your community needs you to say "si" (yes) instead of "a si puedo" (I will see if I can). Si, I know we're all committed to school, work y claro (right) that special chico or chica in our life. Pero (but) chicos, let's not forget about our communities that need our ayuda. Do you believe in la Causa? (The cause.) Well that involves assisting our people in whatever way so they can move adelante (forward). Now the question is, are YOU willing to help? (MEChA Times, 1996, p.1).

Code switching exhibits the unwillingness of Chicanos to adjust our communication patterns to those of the mainstream European-American culture. Spanglish represent Chicano pride and defiance (Barrera, 1988; Marin & Marin, 1991).

Identity is a belief in the necessity of expressing an identifiable authentic self and this belief increasingly has become the means through which individuals interpret their own experience and give it social expression. Being a Chicana means surfing the borders of the American and Mexican culture because I live on the border of these two cultures. I acknowledge and celebrate these differences as I continue to shape my different identities: Lucila the Chicana, the daughter, the friend, the girlfriend, the sister, the student, and all the other Lucilas. I know that my most intense and productive life experiences of culture take place on these boundaries.

ACCUMULATING UNDERSTANDINGS

Voicing identities is a continuous process of discovery. These four stories reveal the personal experience of what it means to live in the midst of different worlds—to live in the borderlands of two or more cultures. I-Li, Mitsuo, Beverly, and Lucila speak their truths of turning point moments in their lives when the intensity of their emotional experiences lead to discoveries. By voicing their stories in this way, at this point in time, they begin to construct their own understandings, their own theories of what it means to adapt, change, understand, and discover all of who they are, all of who they can be. In the process they discover a diversity of struggles, responsibilities, goals, political commitments, and joys.

Listening to their voices, we are invited to share in their discoveries and to consider our own process of encountering, interweaving, and engaging our multiple identities.

References

Barrera, M. (1988). *Beyond Aztlan: Ethnic autonomy in comparative perspective*. New York: Praeger.

Conquergood, D. (1991). Rethinking ethnography: Towards a critical cultural politics. *Communication Monographs, 58*, 179–194.

El plan de Santa Barbara: A Chicano plan for higher education. (1969). Oakland, CA: La Causa Publications.

Gilligan, C. (1993). *In a different voice*. Cambridge, MA: Harvard University Press.

Gomez-Quinones, J. (1990). *Chicano politics: Reality and promise 1940–1990*. Albuquerque: University of New Mexico Press.

Gomez-Quinones, J. (1978). *Mexican students por la raza; The Chicano student movement in Southern California 1967–1977*. Santa Barbara, CA: La Causa.

Hinman, L. (1994). *Ethics*. Fort Worth, TX: Harcourt Brace.

Lopez, L. (1994). Generation Mex. In E. Liu (Ed.). *Next: Young American writers on the new generation* (pp. 131–145). New York: Norton.

Marin, G., & Marin, B. V. (1991). *Research with Hispanic populations*. Newbury Park, CA: Sage.

Concepts and Questions

1. What is meant by the phrase, "Voice, then, is a responsiveness to what we experience"?
2. Do you agree with Chao when she notes the "living in between two countries, there are struggles"? What struggles is she referring to?
3. How do you believe feelings of detachment from family when away from home can be lessened?
4. Do you believe that learning the language of another culture can help with maintaining one's identity? Why?
5. Why is returning to one's culture after living in another culture such a difficult task?
6. Did you see any common problems faced by all four of the students who were "living in two cultures"? What were those problems?
7. What does Solidon mean where she says "Neither completely Filipino nor completely American. I find it a challenge to identify with either one or the other when I have been equally influenced by both."
8. What does Luna mean when she says "my identity is an assemblage"?
9. What factors do you believe have contributed to your identity?
10. Why do you believe that identities "bind a people together"?

part 3

Intercultural Interaction: Taking Part in Intercultural Communication

If we seek to understand a people we have to put ourselves, as far as we can, in that particular historical and cultural background.... One has to recognize that countries and people differ in their approach and their ways, in their approach to life and their ways of living and thinking. In order to understand them we have to understand their way of life and approach. If we wish to convince them, we have to use their language as far as we can, not language in the narrow sense of the word, but the language of the mind.

JAWAHARLAL NEHRU

In Part Three, we are concerned with participation in intercultural communication. We focus on verbal communication (Chapter 4), nonverbal forms of symbolic interaction (Chapter 5), and the social and physical context in which the interaction occurs (Chapter 6). As we pointed out in introducing Part Two, meanings reside within people, and symbols serve as stimuli to which these meanings are attributed. Meaning-evoking stimuli consist of both verbal and nonverbal behaviors. Although we consider these forms of symbolic interaction separately for convenience, we hasten to point out their interrelatedness. As nonverbal behavior accompanies verbal behavior, it becomes a unique part of the total symbolic interaction. Verbal messages often rely on their nonverbal accompaniment for cues that aid the receiver in decoding the verbal symbols. Nonverbal behaviors not only serve to amplify and clarify verbal messages but also can serve as forms of symbolic interaction without verbal counterparts. In addition, the context in which verbal and nonverbal behaviors occur adds to the evocation of meanings.

When we communicate verbally, we use words with seeming ease, because there is a high consensus of agreement about the meanings our words evoke. Our experiential backgrounds are similar enough that we share basically the same meanings for most of the word symbols we use in everyday communication. But even within our culture, we disagree over the meanings of many word symbols. As words move farther from the reality of sense data, they become more abstract, and then there is far less agreement about appropriate meanings. What do highly abstract words such as *love, freedom, equality, democracy,* and *good time* mean to you? Do they mean the same things to everyone? If you are in doubt, ask some friends; take a poll. You will surely find that people have different notions of these concepts and consequently different meanings for these words. Their experiences have been different, and they hold different beliefs, attitudes, values, concepts, and expectations. Yet all, or perhaps most, of these people are from the same culture. Their backgrounds, experiences, and concepts of the universe are really quite uniform. When cultural diversity is added to the process of decoding words, however, much larger differences in meanings and usage are found.

Culture exerts no small influence over our use of language. In fact, it strongly determines just what our language is and how we use it. In the narrowest sense, language is a set of symbols (vocabulary) that evoke more or less uniform meanings among a particular population and set of rules (grammar and syntax) for using the symbols. In the broadest sense, language is the symbolic representation of a people, and it includes their historical and cultural backgrounds as well as their approach to life and their ways of living and thinking.

What comes to be symbolized and what the symbols represent are very much functions of culture. Similarly, how we use our verbal symbols is also a function of culture. What we think about or speak with others about must be capable of symbolization, and how we speak or think about things must follow the rules we have for using our language. Because the symbols and rules are culturally determined, how and what we think or talk about are, in effect, a function of our culture. This relation between language and culture is not unidirectional, however. There is an interaction between them—what we think about and how we think about it also affects our culture.

As we can see, language and culture are inseparable. To be effective intercultural communicators requires that we be aware of the relationship between culture and language. It further requires that we learn and know about the culture of the person with whom we communicate so that we can better understand how his or her language represents that person.

Another important aspect of verbal symbols or words is that they can evoke two kinds of meanings: denotative and connotative. A *denotative* meaning indicates the referent or the "thing" to which the symbol refers. For example, the denotative meaning of the word *book* is the physical object to which it refers; or, in the case of the set of symbols *Intercultural Communication: A Reader*, the referent is the book you are now reading. Not all denotations have a physical correspondence. As we move to higher levels of abstraction, we often deal with words that represent ideas or concepts, which exist only in the mind and do not necessarily have a physical basis. For example, much communication research is directed toward changes in attitude. Yet attitude is only a hypothetical construct used to explain behavior; there is no evidence of any physical correspondence between some group of brain cells and a person's attitudes.

The second type of meaning—*connotative*—indicates a valuative dimension. Not only do we identify referents (denotative meaning), but also we place them along a valuative dimension that can be simply described as positive–neutral–negative. Where we place a word on the dimension depends on our prior experiences and how we "feel" about the referent. If we like books, we might place *Intercultural Communication: A Reader* near the positive end of the dimension. When we are dealing with more abstract symbols, we do the same thing. In fact, as the level of abstraction increases, so does our tendency to place more emphasis on connotative meanings. Most will agree that a book is the object you are holding in your hand, but whether books are good or bad or whether this particular book is good or bad or in-between is an individual judgment based on prior experience.

Culture affects both denotative and connotative meanings. Consequently, a knowledge of how these meanings can differ culturally is essential to effective intercultural communication. To make the assumption that everyone uses the same meanings is to invite communication disaster.

Culture affects language and language use in other ways. We tend to believe that our way of using language is both correct and universal and that any deviation is wrong or substandard. This belief can and does elicit many negative responses and judgments when we encounter someone from another culture whose use of language deviates from our own specifications.

What we are trying to point out with these examples should be quite obvious—language and culture are inseparable. In fact, it would be difficult to determine which is the voice and which is the echo. How we learn, employ, and respond to symbols is culturally based. In addition, the sending and the receiving of these culturally grounded symbols are what enable us to interact with people from other cultures. Hence, it is the purpose of this part of the book to highlight these verbal and non-verbal symbols: to help you understand some of the complexities, subtleties, and nuances of language and, at the same time, to acquaint you with how the social and physical contexts influence verbal and nonverbal behavior.

Communication obviously involves much more than the sending and receiving of verbal and nonverbal messages. Human interaction takes place within some social and physical setting that influences how we construct and perceive messages. The sway of context is rooted in three interrelated assumptions. First, communication is rule-governed; that is to say, each encounter has implicit and explicit rules that regulate our conduct. These rules tell us everything from what is appropriate attire to what topics can be discussed. Second, the setting helps us define what "regulations" are in operation. Reflect for a moment on your own communication behavior as you move to and from the following arenas: classroom, courtroom, church, hospital, and dance hall. Visualize yourself behaving differently as you proceed from place to place. Third, most of the communication rules we follow have been learned as part of cultural experiences. Although cultures might share the same general settings, their specific notion of proper behavior for each context manifests the values and attitudes of that culture. Concepts of turn taking, time, space, language, manners, nonverbal behavior, silence, and control of the communication flow are largely an extension of each culture.

In this part of the book, we offer readings that demonstrate the crucial link that exists between context, culture, and communication. What emerges from these essays is the realization that to understand another culture you must appreciate the rules that govern that culture's behavior in a specific setting. Although intercultural communication occurs in a variety of contexts, we have selected environments related to business, education, and health care to discuss in this part of the book.

chapter 4

Verbal Processes:
Speaking Across Cultures

Some people have suggested that, as a species, our most unique feature is our ability to receive, store, retrieve, manipulate, and generate symbols. All 5.8 billion of us deal with the past, take part in the present, and prepare for the future. By simply making certain sounds or marks on paper, we are able to share experiences with other people. Language is that simple yet complex instrument that gives us the gift of sharing ourselves with other people. This chapter looks at that gift.

It is the premise of this chapter that a culture's use of language involves much more than sounds and meanings. It also involves forms of reasoning, how conversations are carried out, specialized linguistic devices such as analogies and idioms, and ways of perceiving the world. Hence, to understand the language of any culture means you must look beyond the vocabulary, grammar, and syntax of that culture. This broad view of culture has guided us in our selection of readings. We urge you to view language from this larger perspective both as you read these articles and as you confront people from different cultures. This eclectic outlook toward language will help you understand the interaction patterns of cultures that are different from your own. The first two articles will examine this relationship between language and culture.

We begin with an essay titled "The Crossroads of Language and Culture" by Mary Fong. This selection introduces us to some fundamental ideas about the relationship between language and culture. Fong begins with a brief review of the Sapir–Whorf hypothesis, which proposed linguistic relativity and was one of the first modern observations of the relationship between language and culture. She then traces later developments in this area that have led to ethnographic research approaches to the study of language and culture. Applying these techniques in two studies of Chinese language use, Fong shows not only the ways in which ethnographic approaches are employed, but also the rich linguistic practices of the Chinese.

As we noted in the introduction to this section of the book, language involves attaching meanings to world symbols, whether they are sounds or marks on a piece of paper. If those symbols have to be translated to or from a foreign language, then numerous problems can arise. Without accurate translations, those who are trying to communicate often end up simply exchanging meaningless sounds and vague images. What usually happens is that the interpretations lack a common vocabulary and familiar referents. Our next two selections examine some of these difficulties in dealing with foreign languages. In these cases, however, communication problems occur because one of the parties is not only from a foreign culture and speaks a foreign language, but also has English as a second language. One of the most blatant examples of the problems associated with English as a second language is found in our persistent use of idioms. By their very nature, idioms can be perplexing and confusing. They are culture-bound and not readily understandable from their grammatical construction. Imagine how frustrating it would be if English were your second language and you heard someone say, "Peter has dropped the ball again by dilly-dallying over this hot potato." It is this topic of idioms that is the focus of Wen-Shu Lee in "That's Greek to Me: Between a Rock and a Hard Place in Intercultural Encounters." Lee begins by reminding us that idioms are both treacherous and important in intercultural communication because they are figurative in nature, depend on a common background for their definition, are often not explained in detail, and frequently "hold one of the keys to interpersonal closeness." To assist us, Lee advances a four-step process for using idioms: (1) cultivating a supportive conversational decorum, (2) learning to differentiate goal-oriented talk from metatalk, (3) applying the principle of double–multiple description, and (4) finding relational relevance in a speaker's life world.

In our next essay, "Language as a Mirror of Reality: Mexican American Proverbs," Shelly M. Zormeier and Larry A. Samovar consider the language of a large and prominent co-culture—that of the Mexican American. This co-culture is quite diverse, containing numerous members whose Mexican heritage precedes the fact of U.S. sovereignty over the Southwest as well as Mexicans who immigrated from Mexico within their lifetime or whose parents immigrated from Mexico. Such cultural diversity makes it difficult to perceive and understand the central values of this co-culture. We have attempted to stress the idea that language is more than words and meanings; it is also a mirror of one's cultural experience. To help us better understand the experiences of the Mexican American co-culture and to further focus our vision on the interrelationship between culture and language, Zormeier and Samovar introduce us to this culture through an examination of its proverbs.

It is in this relationship between culture and proverbs that we see how proverbs contain the values and world views of a culture. Through this examination of specific Mexican American proverbs, we gain insight into the significant values of this co-culture. This examination shows how proverbs relate to such cultural dynamics as collectivism, fatalism, present-time orientation, being orientation, and family values.

Anthropologists and sociolinguists maintain that culture and language work in tandem in three ways. First, members of cultures and co-cultures share common rules for the use and interpretation of speech. Second, one's language is a model of one's culture; language functions as a reflection of a culture's unique experiences. Third, a culture's language system allows members of the group to distinguish their communication from other cultures and co-cultures. We see all three of these characteristics in operation in "Organized Diversity Within the United States: Understanding the Houseless Youths' Code for Speaking," an essay by Natalie J. Dollar. The language community she examines is the co-culture of houseless youth. By looking at this group, and detecting how they use language differently than do members of the dominant culture, Dollar demonstrates that when members from both groups interact it is the talk and stories of the dominant culture that are heard and believed. In addition, she looks at language differences as they apply to norms for speaking; communicating identity; and divergent codes for speaking. It is Dollar's hope that an awareness of these differences can help all of us "better understand the organized diversity within cultures."

In an essay by Arron Castellan Cargile, "Language Matters," it becomes very clear that cultural misunderstandings can occur even if people speak the same language. The reason, of course, is obvious: Language involves much more than simple definitions. It is, as we noted earlier, a reflection of our experiences, and as experiences vary so does our use of language. Cargile examines three major differences (accents, vocabularies, and rates of speech) and how they might impact interaction between people from different cultures. Further, it is Cargile's contention that for some people these variations in language can contribute to negative perceptions. As a means of overcoming these harmful attitudes, Cargile concludes his essay with advice on how to keep our perceptions from impeding intercultural interaction.

We end our chapter with yet another essay that demonstrates that the manner in which a culture uses language tell us a great deal about that culture. For example, in "Irish Conversation," Martin J. Gannon provides us with an insightful look at Irish culture through an analysis of its conversational speaking. As do so many selections in this book, his begins by showing the historical roots of contemporary communication patterns. He does this by outlining the relationship between the original Irish language, Gaelic, and modern-day English. He then shows how religion (yet another historical foundation) is linked to conversation by demonstrating the Irish use of prayer as a mode of conversation. Irish hospitality is looked at so that Gannon can illustrate the free flow of conversation during Irish social activities. By examining these unique forms of conversation, Gannon helps us understand both the language patterns and culture of the Irish.

The Crossroads of Language and Culture

MARY FONG

Since the dawning of humanity, scholars have been interested in the concept of language and its relationships to human endeavor. Confucius's observation that "if language not be in accordance with the truth of things, affairs cannot be carried on to success" and Saint-Exupery's comment that "to grasp the meaning of the world of today we use a language created to express the world of yesterday" reflect this concern. In the current era, anthropologists, linguists, psychologists, and philosophers continue to try to fathom the role of language in human activity and its connection to culture. In this essay, I examine briefly some basic perspectives about the relationship between language and culture. I begin with a brief description of the Sapir–Whorf hypothesis and then review the more current ethnographic directions of culture and language research. And, then, in order to demonstrate some of the relationships between language and culture using ethnographic methodologies, I draw from research on the Chinese culture to demonstrate the intersection of language and culture in examples from both cultural interaction and intercultural interaction.

PERSPECTIVES ON LANGUAGE AND CULTURE

Sapir–Whorf Hypothesis

A major proponent of linguistic relativity and one of the first modern observations of the relationship between language and culture is the Sapir–Whorf hypothesis. This notion proposes a deterministic view that language structure is necessary in order to produce thought. In other words, language and its categories—grammar, syntax, and vocabulary—are

the only categories by which we can experience the world. Simply stated: language influences and shapes how people perceive their world, their culture. This vision dominated scholarly thinking as a point of discussion, research, and controversy for over five decades.

The Sapir–Whorf hypothesis also holds that language and thought covary with one another. That is, diversity in language categories and structure lead to cultural differences in thought and perceptions of the world. This position is known as linguistic relativity. Sapir (1951) believed that the "real world" is largely built upon the unconscious language habits of the group.

Benjamin Whorf, who was a student of Edward Sapir's in the early 1930s, initially published (Whorf, 1956) the views he and Sapir held about language and culture in a series of articles in 1940–41. He stated:

> We cut nature up, organize it into concepts, and ascribe significances as we do, largely because we are parties to an agreement to organize it in this way—an agreement that holds throughout our speech community and is codified in the patterns of our language. (p. 213)

Sapir and Whorf's ideas have been understood to mean that people who speak different languages segment their world differently. Thus, any language, such as Russian, Chinese, or German, structures a "Russian," "Chinese," or "German" reality by framing and screening what these cultural members attend to. If there is a word for "it" in their language, then cultural members know that "it" exists; and if not, "it" is nonexistent to them.

Brown (1958) in part disagreed with Sapir–Whorf and argued that a cultural member's world view is not determined by language. He held, rather, that people categorize their world by attaching labels to what is out there. People use language to do what they need it to do. Brown's position does support the idea of linguistic relativity because the perceptual categories that are frequently used receive labels, while unused or insignificant categories may not be labeled.

Several research studies on color terms and color perception tested the Sapir–Whorf hypothesis (Berlin & Kay, 1967; Bruner, Olver, & Greenfield, 1966; Greenfield & Bruner, 1966; Kay and Kempton,

1984). Eastman (1990) reviewed these studies that supported the idea of linguistic relativity and stated that "it appears to be the case that world view is a matter more of linguistic relativity than linguistic determinism" (p. 103).

Other researchers have found it difficult to test how strongly the structure of a language influences the world view of people because reliable methods for assessing the world view of a cultural people independently of the language they speak are needed (Brown, 1976; Carroll, 1967; Kay & Kempton, 1984). "In general, the Sapir–Whorf hypothesis has come to be regarded as either unconfirmable or incorrect . . . most linguists and psychologists believe that evidence offered in its support is flawed. . . . If the hypothesis can be sustained at all, it implies only a weak influence of language structure on thought" (Carroll, 1992).

ETHNOGRAPHIC RESEARCH APPROACHES

In 1974, Hymes described the development of linguistic research:

> the first half of the century was distinguished by a drive for the autonomy of language as an object of study and a focus upon description of [grammatical] structure, [while] the second half was distinguished by a concern for the integration of language in sociocultural context and a focus upon the analysis of function. (p. 208)

Hymes's description was quite accurate because the second half of the century has marked a number of qualitative research methods, such as discourse analysis, pragmatics, and ethnography of communication, as ways to investigate the interrelationship of language and culture. For some researchers, the controversy over whether language determines or reflects thought or thought determines or reflects language has not been the primary concern. To Sherzer (1987), what is at issue is the analysis of discourse as the "embodiment of the essence of culture and as constitutive of what language and culture relationship is all about." Sherzer (1987) also views discourse as the intersection where language and culture interrelate. He states, "It is discourse that

creates, recreates, focuses, modifies, and transmits both culture and language and their intersection" (p. 295).

For Sherzer (1987), culture is the organization of individuals who share rules for production and interpretation of behavior. Language represents an individual's symbolic organization of the world. Language is a medium that reflects and expresses an individual's group membership and relationships with others. Discourse analysis derives from pragmatics and speech act theory (Saville-Troike, 1989). Pragmatics or speech act theory refers to the study of the connotative (inner) and denotative (outer) meanings of "expressions when used in a conversation or a written work" (Paul, 1987, p. 101). To Silverstein (1976), pragmatics is "the study of the meaning of linguistic signs relative to their communicative functions (p. 20)." Pragmatics also entails cultural members applying their knowledge of the world to the interpretation of what is said and done in interaction (Fromkin & Rodman, 1983; Gumperz, 1982).

The ethnography of communication provides the researcher with a framework of observation and interviewing techniques to facilitate capturing interlocutors' meanings in various communicative acts both culturally and interculturally. The ethnographer endeavors to describe the communicative choices that interlocutors make. This involves describing and accounting for the interpretive systems and practices through which members construct actions and deal with behaviors.

Hymes (1962), an originator of the ethnography of communication, states that the "study of speech as a factor in cognitive and expressive behavior leads to concern with the ethnographic patterning of the uses of speech in a community" (p. 102). Investigating language and culture is finding not only linguistic structural regularities, but also regularities of usage that have motives, emotions, desires, knowledge, attitudes, and values attached to them. An essential aim of studies on language and culture using the ethnography-of-communication approach is to make implicit cultural beliefs, attitudes, values, norms of interpretation, rules of speaking, norms of interaction, and so forth explicit in order to understand and to practice communicative competence within a particular culture.

LANGUAGE STUDIES

Some of the sample findings in the cultural and intercultural studies that follow are illustrations of language and culture analysis. The qualitative methods—discourse analysis, pragmatics, and ethnography of communication—jointly provide tools and perspectives to make possible an in-depth examination of communicative phenomena.

A Cultural Study

An ethnographic study of the Chinese New Year celebration in Hong Kong (Fong, 1993) provides an example of the manner in which the Chinese employ language to reverse bad luck. By examining the speaking pattern used when someone breaks a glass object during the Chinese New Year, it is possible to understand how Chinese people "play" with words and their meanings through the use of implied statements that represent a positive idea. The unfortunate incident of breaking an object is transformed to a fortunate incident when a person orally uses a positive expression to describe the unfortunate act. The expression of the positive statement counteracts the negative occurrence. One informant from Fong's (1993) study explained:

> Be careful not to break any cups or glass things. It's bad luck to break something on the New Year. I remember seeing some old Chinese films; some child was so careless, he broke a bowl, a glass. The adult would say, "We cannot change what has happened. How can we reverse it?" By saying: /lɔk⁹ dei⁶ hɔi¹ fa¹/, which means falling down to the ground, may the flowers blossom. This expression implies /fu³ gwei³ winɲ⁴ wa⁴/, that is, being prosperous and becoming wealthy. So you see the Chinese are very clever. They would say something to change it to good. /lɔk⁹ dei⁶ hɔi¹ fa¹/ is to fall to the ground, /hɔi¹ fa¹ / is, it will blossom. /Fu³ gwei³/, will be wealthy. /Wiɲ/⁴ /wa/⁴, is prosperous. When you drop something, once it touches the floor, it blossoms up. Once the flowers blossom, you'll have wealth. This is related to the new year. [Ed. note: The author has phonetically translated Cantonese Chinese using the symbol system of the International Phonetic Alphabet. The superscript numbers indicate various tone levels found in the nine-tone Cantonese language.]

Because the expression is meant to reverse the bad luck, the positive linguistic concepts such as prosperous and wealthy contained in these expressions can be considered as good luck attributes. Possible antonyms of these linguistic concepts are misfortune and poverty, which are considered attributes of bad luck.

To understand what linguistic devices the Chinese employ, it is necessary to understand a few rules of behavior and speaking. Shimanoff (1980) proposes an "If . . . , then . . . " method of concisely stating a rule of behavior. To develop Shimanoff's method of stating behavioral rules, I will add a "because . . . , meaning . . . " sequence in order to add a meaning component to a formulation of a communication rule.

In this situation, the sequential rule statement begins with the initial linguistic "If . . . " slot, which provides information on the particular context, condition, or situation, like a speech event, speech act, or genre. It is followed by the "then . . . " slot, which refers to the speaking and/or behavioral interaction pattern discovered from the researcher's ethnographic data analysis.

The third linguistic device, the "because . . . " slot provides a concise rationale for why people of a particular culture behave the way they do. Here, an underlying belief or value system or cultural principle may be revealed to provide an explanation for a people's way of communicating. The final linguistic device, is the "meaning . . . " slot, which serves as the speaking and/or behavioral interaction pattern, a particular speech act, speech event, scene, and so forth.

These sequential rules statement provide the formula:

If . . . (context, condition, or situation like a speech event, speech act, or genre),

then . . . (speaking and/or interaction pattern)

because . . . (belief or value system or cultural principle),

meaning . . . (norm of interpretation of: a symbol, speaking pattern, interaction pattern, particular speech act, speech event, scene, etc.)

Applying these sequential rules to the Chinese custom of reversing the negative effect of an object that has been shattered can be expressed in a concise rule statement using the formula:

If a person breaks a glass item on Chinese New Year's Day,

then a Hong Kong Chinese person should say: /lɔk⁹ dei⁶ hɔi¹ fa¹/ (falling down to the ground, may the flowers blossom)

because this is believed to counteract the bad luck and to create good luck,

meaning that prosperity and wealth may come about

An Intercultural Study

An intercultural study on compliment interactions between Chinese immigrants and European Americans from the perspective of Chinese immigrants (Fong, 1994) found that both cultural groups have differing ways of speaking in compliment interactions (Chen, 1993; Chiang & Pochtrager, 1993; Fong, 1994). European Americans on the West Coast and in the Midwest generally accept a compliment (Chen, 1993; Chiang & Pochtrager, 1993; Fong, 1994). On the other hand, the literature reports that Chinese have the tendency to deny compliments in order to give an impression of modesty (Chen, 1993; Chiang & Pochtrager, 1993; Gao, 1984; Zhang, 1988). Four adaptations by Chinese immigrant participants (CIPs) to European American compliments were found. An orientation is a state or condition that is changeable from one interaction to another depending on the Chinese immigrant's adaptation to intercultural communication differences. Four orientations in which the CIP can be located are (1) intercultural shock state, (2) intercultural resistance state, (3) intercultural accommodation state, and (4) bicultural competence state. In this essay, I will examine the intercultural shock state in order to convey a sense of Chinese immigrants' thinking and speaking.

Affectively, CIPs reported feeling uncomfortable, unnatural, stressed, embarrassed, surprised, shocked, or afraid, uneasy, nervous when a European American complimented them. The situational outcome of the intercultural compliment interaction for CIPs, however, was an appreciation of receiving praise because they felt accepted, liked, and welcomed by European Americans. CIPs reported that compliments helped them to reduce some of their stress as a newcomer to the United States.

Cognitively, CIPs in the intercultural shock state have minimum knowledge of the intercultural communication differences in compliment interactions with European Americans. Prior to coming to the United States, CIPs reported that they were not familiar with the European Americans' generosity in (1) giving compliments, (2) giving compliments containing strong positive adjectives, (3) giving compliments intended to encourage a person after an unsatisfactory performance, (4) giving compliments on a wide variety of topics, (5) accepting compliments, and (6) giving compliments face-to-face in all types of relationships.

Behaviorally, five speaking patterns were found, and two examples are provided here. The first example is one type of compliment response that Chinese immigrants used: the Direct Denial + Verbal Corrective /Prescriptive response. Here is a reported intercultural compliment interaction:

(AMERICAN) ROOMMATE: You look very lovely today, Bei Sha.

(TAIWAN) ROOMMATE: Oh, no, no, no. It's not necessary to say that. I just look ordinary.

Because Chinese immigrants value indirectness and modesty in conversation, the compliment was interpreted as being direct, face-to-face, expressed openly with very positive adjectives on Bei Sha's appearance. This is contrary to the normal Chinese forms of compliment interactions. The response was made to avoid self-praise and to suggest to the American roommate that such a direct compliment should not be given.

In the second example, CIPs who were in the intercultural shock state were found to use a Silence response. Below is an intercultural compliment interaction reported to have occurred at an American host family's home during a dinner:

(AMERICAN) HOSTESS: You must be very prepared, mature to come here by yourself.

(HONG KONG) STUDENT: [silence]

Chinese immigrants highly value modesty, but they are also aware that Americans directly accept and appreciate compliments. The compliment was interpreted as being direct, face-to-face, and as expressing openly positive thoughts with very positive adjectives, which is contrary to Chinese forms of compliment interactions. The Chinese immigrant recipient reported feeling ambivalent about which cultural response to use and so remained silent.

CONCLUSION

The excerpt from the cultural study (Fong, 1993) illustrates the Chinese way of thinking and speaking. When an object is shattered during the Chinese New Year holiday, the Chinese interpret the incident as bad luck. Through speech, however, the perceived bad luck is reversed to good luck.

The intercultural compliment interaction study (Fong, 1994) sheds light on the way Chinese immigrants in the intercultural shock state reveal patterns of thinking and speaking. The denial response is a pattern of speaking that is commonly used in the intercultural shock state. CIPs in this orientation essentially perceive European Americans as being generous in giving compliments with relatively strong positive adjectives and in accepting compliments.

Current ethnographic methods hold that the best way to capture a view of language and culture is to observe the communicative phenomenon in a naturalistic setting and to have cultural members identify and classify the interaction or event as being culturally significant. The crossroads of language and culture are found in the culturally shared meaning of ideas and behaviors that are voiced as symbolic utterances, expressions, dialogue, and conversations in such various contexts as interpersonal and group interactions, research interviews, and public speaking forums.

In the two language and cultural studies described in this essay, the ways of speaking and thinking were the two primary interrelated foci that reveal and reflect the outer and inner shared substances of communications that primarily make up a speech community. To examine a speech community's patterns of speaking without also discovering the norms of interpretation or the shared sociocultural knowledge of cultural members is to silence their cultural humanness as a speech community. To study only the shared sociocultural knowledge of cultural members and not attend to how it is relevant to their way of speaking is to lose an opportunity to understand more about different cultural communication styles—potential sources of intercultural conflict.

Both examples of findings from the language and cultural studies illuminate, in part, what Hymes (1974) has suggested:

> It has often been said that language is an index to or reflection of culture. But language is not simply passive or automatic in its relation to culture. . . . Speaking is itself a form of cultural behavior, and language, like any other part of culture, partially shapes the whole; and its expression of the rest of culture is partial, selective. That selective relation, indeed, is what should be interesting to us. Why do some features of a community's life come to be named—overtly expressible in discourse—while others are not? (p. 127)

References

Berlin, B., and Kay; P. (1967). Universality and Evolution of Basic Color Terms. Working Paper #1, Laboratory for Language Behavior Research, University of California, Berkeley.

Bruner, J., Olver, R. R., and Greenfield, P. M. (1966). *Studies in Cognitive Growth*. New York: Wiley.

Brown, R. (1958). *Words and Things*. New York: Free Press.

Brown, R. (1976). Reference. In Memorial Tribute to Eric Lennenberg. *Cognition*, 4, 125–153.

Carroll, J. B. (1967). "Bibliography of the Southwest Project in Comparative Psycholinguistics." In D. Hymes (Ed.), *Studies in Southwestern Ethnolinguistics*, 452–454. The Hague: Mouton.

Carroll, J. B. (1992). "Anthropological Linguistics: An Overview." In W. Bright (Ed.), *International Encyclopedia of Linguistics*. New York: Oxford University Press.

Chen, R. (1993). Responding to compliments: A contrastive study of politeness strategies between American English and Chinese speakers. *Journal of Pragmatics*, 20, 43–75.

Chiang, F., and Pochtrager, B. (1993). A Pilot Study of Compliment Responses of American-Born English Speakers and Chinese-Born English Speakers. (available in microfiche only: ED 35GG49)

Eastman, C. M. (1990). *Aspects of language and culture*, 2d ed. Novato, Calif.: Chandler & Sharp.

Fong, M. (1993). Speaking Patterns Related to Luck During the Chinese New Year. Paper presented at the annual meeting of the Speech Communication Association, Miami, Florida.

Fong, M. (1994). Patterns of occurrences of compliment response types. In unpublished doctoral dissertation, *Chinese Immigrants' Interpretations of Their Intercultural Compliment Interactions with European-Americans*. (Chapter 6). Seattle: University of Washington.

Fromkin, V., and Rodman, R. (1983). *An Introduction to Language*, 3d ed. New York: CBS Publishing.

Gao, W. (1984). Compliment and Its Reaction in Chinese and English Cultures. *Working Papers in Discourse in English and Chinese*. Canberra: Canberra College of Advanced Education, 32–37.

Greenfield, P. M., and Bruner, J. S. (1966). Culture and cognitive growth. *International Journal of Psychology, 1*, 89–107.

Gumperz, J. J. (1982). *Discourse Strategies*. New York: Cambridge University Press.

Hymes, D. (1962). "The Ethnography of Speaking." In T. Gladwin and W. Sturtevant (Eds.), *Anthropology and Human Behavior*, 99–137. Washington, D.C.: Anthropological Society of Washington.

Hymes, D. (1964). Toward ethnographies of communication: The analysis of communicative events. *American Anthropologist, 66*, 21–41.

Hymes, D. (1974). *Foundations in Sociolinguistics: An Ethnographic Approach*. Philadelphia: University of Pennsylvania Press.

Kay, P., and Kempton, W. (1984). What is the Sapir–Whorf hypothesis? *American Anthropologist, 86*, 65–73.

Paul, A. (1987). Review of Joseph H. Greenberg, Language in the Americas. *The Chronicle of Higher Education*, July 15, p. 6.

Sapir, E. (1951). "The Status of Linguistics as a Science." In D. Mandelbaum (Ed.), *Collected Writings*. Berkeley: University of California Press.

Saville-Troike, M. (1989). *The Ethnography of Communication*, 2d ed. New York: Basil Blackwell.

Sherzer, J. (1987). A discourse-centered approach to language and culture. *American Anthropologist, 89*, 295–309.

Shimanoff, S. B. (1980). *Communication Rules: Theory and Research*. Beverly Hills: Sage.

Silverstein, M. (1976). "Shifters, Linguistic Categories, and Cultural Description." In K. H. Basso and H. A. Selby (Eds.), *Meaning in Anthropology*, 11–56. Albuquerque: University of New Mexico Press.

Whorf, B. L. (1956). *Language, thought, and reality*. Cambridge: M.I.T. Press.

Zhang, Z. (1988). A discussion of communicative culture. *Journal of Chinese Language Teacher Association, 23*, 107–112.

Concepts and Questions

1. What does Fong mean when she writes, "Language and thought vary with one another"? Do you agree?
2. Can you think of specific examples that illustrate the link between culture and language?
3. Can you explain what Fong means when she states that language influences and shapes how people perceive their world and their culture?
4. What is meant by the following phrase? "People who speak different languages segment their world differently."
5. How do Chinese immigrants and Americans differ in their ways of compliment interactions?
6. When referring to Sherzer, what does Fong mean when she writes, "Culture is the organization of individuals who share rules for production and interpretation of behavior"?
7. How do the Chinese use language to reverse bad luck?
8. In what ways do the Chinese and the Americans express themselves differently?

That's Greek to Me: Between a Rock and a Hard Place in Intercultural Encounters

WEN-SHU LEE

I t was fall 1983, my first year in the United States as a foreign student pursuing a master's degree at the Department of Communication Arts and Sciences, University of Southern California. Even after ten years of studying English to pass entrance examinations in Taiwan, I had a hard time jotting down notes in graduate seminars. To solve this problem, I would summarize what I heard in the seminar in Chinese. During a seminar break, I was frantically adding Chinese characters to my notes. One of my fellow American students watched over my shoulder and said, "That's *Greek* to me!" I promptly corrected him: "No, it's Chinese." He was shocked for about one second and then burst into laughter. We spent 20 minutes or so clarifying that "Greek" did not mean "Greek," that "Greek" meant "foreign, difficult, and mysterious stuff," and I finally *agreed* that my Chinese was "Greek" to him.

This article will address problems caused by incomprehension of idiom or slang during communication between people from different cultures. I will first explore the reasons why this is an important subject in intercultural communication. Second, I will redefine idiom incomprehension problems by integrating theories proposed by Gregory Bateson, Mikhail Bakhtin, and Jurgen Habermas. Finally, I will propose a four-step process to help people get out from between a rock and a hard place in intercultural encounters.

WHY SHOULD WE STUDY IDIOM IN INTERCULTURAL COMMUNICATION?

There are four reasons why idioms should be an important subject in intercultural communication. First, idioms are figurative in nature. Second, figurative meanings often cause comprehension problems for people from different cultures. Third, we do not explain idioms completely. Finally, idioms open up an avenue to interpersonal closeness. Let me explain these related reasons in detail for you.

Idiomatic Meaning Is Figurative

First, an idiom and its meaning often do not match because they have a *figurative* rather than a *literal* relationship. The meaning of an idiom is rarely predictable from its constituent components; consider, "bought the farm," "get your feet wet," "get your hands dirty," "a wild goose chase," "like a duck on a June bug." Like the "It's Greek to me" example, "bought the farm" has no literal relationship with "someone died," and "like a duck on a June bug" has no literal relationship with "I will confront you immediately with what you have done."

Idioms Cause Comprehension Problems for Those from Different Cultures

Second, communication breakdowns often occur when people use idioms in communicating with those who do not comprehend the idiomatic meanings. For people who use idioms "naturally," the figurative link between an idiom and its meaning often goes unnoticed. But this link becomes problematic for those who do not share the lifeworld with the idiom users.[1] This problem is more easily solved by those who speak English as a first language (hereafter, L1 speakers) than those who speak English as a second language (hereafter, L2 speakers). For example, a young college student, Susan, living in San Jose uses "Check it out, there's a stud muffin" with her friend, Jenny, while shopping with her Mom. Her mother, an L1 speaker in her fifties who does not share the lifeworld of "college life" with Susan and Jenny, may ask "What do you mean by a 'stud muffin'?" knowing that it is an expression among young people that she is not familiar with. But if Susan and

Jenny are shopping with an L2 speaker, Huei-Mei, the problem becomes more complex. She may not hear "stud muffin" clearly. Or, she may hear the idiom but remain quiet about it, suspecting that her English is not good enough. Even if she has the courage to ask for the meaning of "stud muffin," Huei-Mei may still have a hard time linking "a handsome guy" with "a male breeding horse" and "English breakfast food." Finally, even if she knows the linguistic meaning of "stud muffin," she may use it in an inappropriate relational context. For example, she may want to compliment her handsome seminar professor: "Professor Spano, you are a stud muffin." Therefore, the study of idioms is important to intercultural communication competence.

We Rarely Explain an Idiom Completely, Especially Its Relational Meaning

Third, as is apparent in the stud muffin, a complete explanation of an idiom requires a linguistic discussion about the meaning of idiom words and a relational discussion about the association between the two people who use an idiom together. Most of us engage in a linguistic explanation but leave out the relational one. For example, Susan forgets to tell Huei-Mei that "stud muffin" is used between friends (usually females) to comment on a third person, a handsome male. We do not use it with someone who has a formal, professional relationship with us. Huei-Mei, as a result, needs to know that one should not use "stud muffin" with a professor. For this reason, we need to study idiom explanations more carefully in intercultural encounters.

Idioms Enable People to Relate Closely

Finally, idioms hold one of the keys to interpersonal closeness. Idioms are commonly used in informal situations between casual acquaintances, friends, and pals (Knapp, 1984, pp. 225–228). The ability to use idioms accepted by a group may not guarantee closeness, but it can increase the possibilities of shortening interpersonal distance if so desired. That is, if people from different cultural backgrounds can use each other's idioms, formal and awkward discomfort may be replaced by a sense of informality and even closeness. This may facilitate intercultural relation-

ships in a variety of contexts—interpersonal relationships between classmates and friends, working relationships in a company, and teaching-learning relationships in the classroom.

Idioms are an important subject in intercultural communication because they create problems as well as closeness. Idioms create problems because idiom users often are unaware of the potential for confusing those who do not share their lifeworld. Idioms have the potential to create closeness because of the informality and fun associated with them. In the following sections, I will take on the most dramatic and difficult case—between L1 and L2 speakers[2]—and propose a four-step process to help them make sense of their confusion through dialogue. It is important to note that the following method may help anyone who encounters idiom problems when coming into a new environment because of marriage or relocation; when dealing with someone of a different sexual orientation; and when moving between ethnic, professional, religious groups, and so on. It is to this process I now turn.

A PROCESS FOR INTERCULTURAL UNDERSTANDING OF IDIOMS AND LIFEWORLD

This method is composed of four steps. They are based upon concrete life experiences and theories proposed by Gregory Bateson (Ruesch & Bateson, 1951; Bateson, 1972, 1979; Bateson & Bateson, 1987) and Mikhail Bakhtin (1981, 1986). The goal of these steps is to provide a guide to *a new way of talking*, remove idiom problems between L1 and L2 speakers (and those who do not share lifeworlds), and link mutually unintelligible lifeworlds through the use of dialogue.

Step 1: Establishing a New Conversational Decorum

Some L1 adult speakers live by an etiquette system which consists of tacit rules dictating how they should speak—be polite and cordial, do not comment on another's speech errors or pronunciation problems, and so on. Discussions about idioms in this case are difficult. In fact, problems with idioms are regularly ignored. Other L1 speakers may abide by a different set of rules—bolder and more honest—correcting another's speaking problems on the spot. This correction is sometimes awkward or snide, turning off the other's desire to learn.

L2 speakers also face problems regarding rules of speaking. Some L2 speakers may feel that asking questions about incomprehensible messages is a sign of weakness and stupidity, and they may turn to more private ways of learning (such as reading magazines, watching television programs, looking words up in a dictionary). This also makes discussions about idioms difficult. Other L2 speakers may be more forthright and ask for clarifications on a regular basis if they encounter problems in a conversation. At least, they start the process of learning. However, they tend to focus more on linguistic meanings than on relational meanings.

The point here is that in order to resolve idiom problems in daily conversations, both L1 and L2 speakers need to work together to establish a conversational decorum in which it is all right or socially acceptable to bring up problems. When we have a safe space to talk about idiom problems,[3] we may move next to learn how to ask questions and how to explain in a friendly and nonintimidating way. It is to this second step I will turn.

Step 2: Learning to Differentiate Goal-Oriented Talk from Metatalk

In this section, I will discuss two ways of labeling ordinary talk—metatalk and goal-oriented talk. Then I will use these labels to explain how the process of idiom explanation involves the use of metatalk to fix comprehension problems so that people can resume their goal-oriented talk to do daily business together.

People engage in *goal-oriented talk* when their shared lifeworld (that is, language and culture) is unproblematic. That is, they do not have to worry about whether they understand each other's words and meanings. They can just use language to communicate what goals they intend to accomplish. Consider an example of goal-oriented talk:

JERRY: Hey dude, whatz up?

TONY: Not much. Wanna go grab a bite?

JERRY: No. I'm under the wire. . . .

TONY: Take a chill pill. Don't worry about it so much. . . .

When lifeworld cannot be assumed, when idiomatic expressions such as "chill pill" cause comprehension problems, goal-oriented talk cannot continue. At this juncture, people need to learn to talk about talk. Talk about talk is called metatalk.[4] We use metatalk to talk about idioms. That is, we use metatalk to fix problems caused by idioms in goal-oriented talk. Ultimately, this may help people resume their goal-oriented talk. For example, the goal-oriented conversation between Jerry and Tony aim at the goals of greeting, grabbing a bite, and then calming the partner down. It may not have gone so smoothly if Tony were an L2 speaker:

JERRY: Hey dude, whatz up?

TONY: *What* did you just say?

Here Jerry and Tony find themselves between a rock and a hard place in their intercultural encounter. They need to use metatalk to get out of this dilemma. To obtain a complete knowledge of metatalk, we need to learn two sub-labels subsumed under metatalk—linguistic metatalk and relational metatalk (Bateson, 1972). They both are metatalk; however, they differ in the aspect of talk they try to deal with. Linguistic metatalk discusses talk as "linguistic codes." Relational metatalk discusses talk as "linguistic codes used by two people." Simply put, linguistic metatalk talks about words while relational metatalk talks about *relationship between the two people who use an idiom with each other*. Let me use an example to clarify these two concepts:

JERRY: Hey dude, whatz up? (*goal-oriented* talk)

TONY: What do you mean by "dude"? (*linguistic metatalk*)

JERRY: Oh, "dude" means guy, friend, a person (*linguistic metatalk*), and "Hey dude" means saying hello (*linguistic metatalk*).

TONY: What is the relationship between two people, let's say John and Steve, who use "Hey dude" with each other? (*relational metatalk*)

JERRY: Oh . . . John and Steve are younger, good pals (*relational metatalk*). This term became popular among surfers in Santa Cruz, and later, we hear it used in movies like *Wayne's World, Bill & Ted's Most Excellent Adventure*. Those who watch these movies and like them, especially young people, tend to use "Hey dude" or "most excellent" with their pals (*relational metatalk* in a historical context).

Linguistic metatalk centers on "dude" and "Hey dude," while relational metatalk focuses on "John and Steve," "surfer with pals," and "Bill & Ted." The former is talk about *words* only, while the latter is talk about *people* who use these words with each other.

This is a problem—most people, when called upon to explain an idiom, probably know about linguistic metatalk only. Most people do not know that relational metatalk is crucial for those who try to learn idioms from them. Let me give you a real case reported by my student in an intercultural communication class.

> An L2 student of mine, Ming-Huei, learned an idiom "kick the bucket." It had nothing to do with "kick" or "bucket." She learned that it meant somebody is dead. She also learned that idioms have the potential to shorten interpersonal distance. The next day, she was told that her president's father just passed away. When the president walked into the general office, Ming-Huei made a point to approach him saying, "I am so sorry that your father just kicked the bucket!"

Oh boy! Ming-Huei was linguistically correct, but relationally inappropriate. This case illustrates the importance of using both linguistic and relational metatalk to accomplish intercultural competence. There are still problems. Even if L1 speakers become aware and capable of both types of metatalk, their L2 partners may still "miss the boat" by failing to understand relational meanings, even when they are explained. The next step explains how to get across relational meanings of idioms in terms of Gregory Bateson's principle of double/multiple description.

Step 3: The Principle of Double/Multiple Description

Bateson indicates that human communication grows out of *perceived difference* (Bateson & Bateson, 1987). That is, when we say something, it is because we have perceived a "noticeable difference." For exam-

ple, if someone put a bouquet of roses on a podium in a classroom, an instructor walking into the room might say, "Oh! Roses." Following Bateson's thesis, this communication, "Oh! Roses" reflects a perceived difference between what the classroom had had (no roses) and what it had at this particular moment (roses).

Yet, human communication is predominantly single-descriptive in nature. That is, it does not spell out the comparison point. Let's juxtapose a single-descriptive talk and a double-descriptive talk to clarify the point:

PROFESSOR: Oh! Roses. (*single-descriptive talk*)

PROFESSOR: Oh! In comparison with what the room looked like before, we have roses today. (*double-descriptive talk*)

Pay attention to these examples again. We may note that single-descriptive talk seems to refer to "things"—in this case, roses. Double-descriptive talk seems to refer to "difference between two states"—in the case, the classroom before versus the classroom now. Since people, due to differences in upbringing, communication patterns, cultures, and so on may come up with different comparison points, double-descriptive talk offers a better opportunity to understand the rationale behind one's talk. That is, people may comment on the same phenomenon in a different way, not because of differences in "the single thing" observed but in differences between "two-somethings."[5]

Returning to our discussion on idioms, I want to combine double-descriptive talk with metatalk. Because relational meanings are most difficult to explain, we need to practice double-descriptive relational metatalk. Let's use "kicked the bucket" as an example. Jenny, an L1 speaker, may engage in relational metatalk and say:

> The relationship between two people, let's say Bob and Betsy, who use "kicked the bucket" to indicate that George just died, is kind of rural and informal, and their relationship with George was casual, not very respectful.

But what does Jenny mean by "rural"? "Rural" in comparison with what? "Informal" in comparison with what? "Casual" in comparison with what? And, "not very respectful" in comparison with what? To answer these questions is to reconstruct multiple ways of saying "someone just died" and to compare and contrast the similarities and differences among these relationships. For example, we may came up with the following idioms to express the same "linguistic" meaning as "kicked the bucket":

bought the farm
bit the dust
croaked
no longer with us
died
passed away

The preceding idioms together are called "alternates" (Labov, 1966; Gumperz, 1970), the term refers to different expressions/words available to a speaker to express an intent. In the preceding case, they are alternates used to express "Someone just died." The purpose of constructing a list of alternates is to enable someone explaining an idiom to do multiple-descriptive relational metatalk. Let's continue with our example. Jenny may replace her single-descriptive relational metatalk listed earlier with the following multiple/double-descriptive relational metatalk:

In comparison with the *relationship* between people who use "passed away" to indicate George's death, the *relationship* between Bob and Betsy who use "kicked the bucket" is more informal and rural.

In comparison with the *relationship* between George and those who use "no longer with us" to talk about George's death, the *relationship* between George and Bob and Betsy, who use "kicked the bucket," was not as full of respect.

"Kicked the bucket," shares a similar *relationship* assumption with "bought the farm," "bit the dust," and "croaked," while "passed away" shares a similar *relationship* assumption with "no longer with us."

By engaging in multiple/double-descriptive relational metatalk, the meanings of various relationships—"rural," "informal," and "not respectful"—become clear relative to one another. Such discussions may bring out the "heteroglossia" in a culture.[6] From dyads to families, to a work unit, to a region, a gender, sexual orientation, social class, ethnicity, state, and a certain part of a country, relational meanings vary. Linguistic metatalk gives "words" *uni-*

form meanings (for example, "They all mean 'someone died'"), the kind of meaning authorized in dictionaries and high-culture genres. Meanings here are rendered faceless, authorless, and nonidiosyncratic! Multiple/double-descriptive relational metatalk, on the other hand, gives words *idiosyncratic meanings* (for example, "Some are more rural and informal; others are used by people in more formal relationships"). An ability to engage in multiple/double-descriptive relational metatalk gives people from different cultures a more refined and contextualized understanding of each other.

But we are not out of the woods yet! To accomplish mutual intercultural understanding, we need to learn about the last step in our process.

Step 4: Finding Relevance in L2 Speakers' Lifeworld

The final step centers on the concept of "relevance." That is, it aims at making multiple-descriptive relational metatalk relevant to an L2 speaker's lifeworld. To accomplish relevance, L1 speakers need to ask their L2 partners to talk about their lifeworld back in the native land. Then, the L1 idiom explainers have to connect "an American idiom" to a specific relationship in the L2 partners' home world. If a real relationship cannot be located to link up an idiom, hypothetical relationships in the L2 partners' lifeworld may be used.

Let us continue with our "kicked the bucket" example. Jenny (L1) needs to ask Ming-Huei (L2) about a relationship in Taiwan that occurs in a rural area and in an informal situation versus a relationship in Taiwan that occurs in a metropolitan area and in a formal situation. Ming-Huei may reply:

I have an uncle who lives in Ping-Dong, which is a small rural town in southern Taiwan. My parents live in Taipei. Ping-Dong to Taipei is like Fresno to San Francisco. A rural and informal relationship would be between my uncle and my father, and a metropolitan and formal relationship would be between my father and his boss in an export-import firm.

Then Jenny should ask Ming-Huei to think of people who had died in Taiwan. One should be a person whom her father respected, and one less respected. Ming-Huei may reply,

We had a person, Mr. Wang, living in the community. He was a miser and was always very mean to people. Most of us did not like him. We did not respect him. My grandfather died when I was a fourth grader. It was about twenty-two years ago. All of us respected grandpa very much.

At this moment, Jenny has two pairs of relationships: father and uncle, and father and his boss. She also has two people who died: Mr. Wang (not respected) and grandpa (respected). Jenny may go ahead creating hypothetical situations:

When your grandpa died, your father wanted to tell his boss about it, he would say, "My father just passed away"; to your uncle, he could say, "My father died" (or "passed away" or "is no longer with us"). When Mr. Wang died, your father wanted to tell his boss about it, he could say, "Mr. Wang died"; to your uncle, he could say, "Mr. Wang bought the farm" (or "bit the dust," or "kicked the bucket," or "croaked").

At this moment, Ming-Huei may start telling Jenny about Chinese idioms used to mean "someone died," according to different relational situations. For example, the group of informal, rural, and disrespectful idioms may find their counterparts in these Chinese expressions:

pig tail pricked up[7]
went to see Yen Lwou Wang (the king of hell)[8]

The formal idioms may find their Chinese counterpart as follows:

godly[9] died
passed the world[10]
thanked the world

Alternates and multiple-descriptive relational metatalk mark the beginning of an exciting intercultural exchange. As the reader may have noticed, intercultural conversation may go off from idiom discussions to topics related to "pig tail and dynasty," "Yen Lwou Wang and heaven versus hell," and religions in China.

We can relate the preceding to our earlier discussion about lifeworld, goal-oriented talk, and metatalk. Jenny and Ming-Huei set aside their "goal-oriented talk" and used "linguistic metatalk and multiple-descriptive relational metatalk" to connect their lifeworlds (American and Taiwanese) that become problematic by various idioms concerning death. After laborious explanations in analogous situations, Ming-Huei and Jenny start to share a small portion of a common world cultivated through various idioms. They, at this moment, are prepared to resume their "goal-oriented talk," using idioms accurately and appropriately in going about their daily business. That is, they are able to move in and out of idiom explanations through the use of goal-oriented talk and metatalk.

SUMMARY

This article discusses four reasons why it is important to study idioms in intercultural communication. It provides a process for L1 and L2 speakers to work together to get out from between a rock and a hard place in intercultural communication—idiom incomprehension. It suggests four steps to accomplish this goal. First, L1 and L2 speakers need to establish a conversational decorum that facilitates the talk about idiom problems. Second, L1 and L2 speakers need to learn to differentiate goal-oriented talk from metatalk. They especially need to learn to engage in linguistic metatalk and relational metatalk. Third, to make explanations relative rather than absolute, both L1 and L2 speakers need to understand the principle of double/multiple comparison. By engaging in multiple-descriptive relational metatalk, we bring out different voices and heteroglossia in a culture. Finally, all explanations about idioms should be made relevant to the L2 speakers' lifeworld. This step finalizes the goal of having L2 speakers (or anyone coming into a new [sub]culture) learn to use idioms in a linguistically accurate and relationally appropriate way.

REFLECTIONS

Interacting with people from the same culture, we take a lot of things for granted without jeopardizing goal coordination. As habituation grows, we become increasingly incurious. Edmund Husserl (1973) calls this orientation "the natural attitude." To overcome this attitude, Husserl encouraged people to bracket various phenomena, suspend judgment, and explore phenomenologically the ultimate meaning of person-in-relation-to-the-world. Applying Husserl's thesis to intercultural encounters, we come to realize that even words (idioms, for example) cannot be taken for granted. In intercultural encounters, the shared ground of coordinated actions shrinks to the minimal. We are, therefore, forced to abandon our natural attitude. That is, intercultural encounters become involuntarily bracketed. Our four-step process may be thought of, in this context, as a heuristic guideline for a dialogical sense-making process of two "phenomenologically bracketed minds." In other words, our method helps people who have little in common to talk with each other.

This chapter suggests a radical reinterpretation of a dominant concept in intercultural communication, high- and low-context cultures (Gudykunst & Kim, 1984; Hall, 1976, 1983). When two people from different cultural backgrounds meet, whether they are labeled high-context (like Chinese culture) or low-context (like American culture), they have little to share. If the meaning of "low context" means people's sharing of tacit knowledge is low or little, intercultural encounters are inherently "low context" in nature. Explicit and elaborated communication, which often characterizes low-context cultures, becomes necessary to bridge the gap resulting from the merger of two different lifeworlds. Multiple types of talk and relevance discussed in this chapter represent the kind of intercultural talk that is conducive to the creation of sharing and, it is to be hoped, close relationships. The four-step process helps transform a "low-context" strange intercultural encounter into a qualitatively new "high-context" interaction between L1 and L2 speakers.

Idioms are central to our participation in a multicultural and multiethnic environment (including women and men, children and adults, adults and old people, professors and students, gay and straight people, Asian Americans, African Americans, Euro-Americans) at home and abroad. An ability to talk about and play with idioms means that we will be less likely to share polite smiles and later say, "It was all Greek to me" and will be more likely to have fun, ask honest questions, and share deep thoughts with each other.

Notes

1. This notion comes from Jurgen Habermas's work (1987). Lifeworld, which is also called common horizon (Todorov, 1984), means the taken-for-granted context in which people act and speak. Language and culture are part and parcel of our lifeworld. Those who share a lifeworld can leap from an idiom to a collectively intended meaning without too much trouble. Those who are not privy to this arbitrary link between idiom and its meaning are often paralyzed at the edge of idiomatic words, uncertain about where to dive in.

2. During three years of teaching idiom explanation in my intercultural communication classes, I have often encountered students amazed at the fact that their co-workers, friends, or significant others, who are L2 speakers and have been in America for a long period of time (ranging from 5 to 14 years), can speak very good English but still fail to comprehend common idioms in this culture. The project aiming at identifying and removing idiom problems often draws them closer together.

3. The new decorum called for in this chapter assumes an *ideal conversational situation*. Daily encounters are often far from perfect due to different cultural, regional, and institutional norms; assumptions about male and female relationships; sexual preferences, etc., that regualte who can speak, when, and how. That is, some people have more internal motivation and external encouragement than others to learn and practice this new/ideal decorum. Others—due to power imbalance, discrimination, or oppression—may have to work harder to achieve this ideal situation.

4. *Meta* means "about." For example, metaunderstanding means understanding about understanding. Metatalk, therefore, is a term used to mean "talk about talk."

5. For detailed definition and different forms of double description, see Bateson, 1979, pp. 69–93.

6. Heteroglossia is a concept central to Mikhail Bakhtin's work. It emphasizes the primacy of context over text. This chapter examines the

relational context surrounding a special type of text (i.e., idioms).

7. Pig tail was a male hairstyle in the Ching dynasty, the last dynasty in China (see the movie *The Last Emperor*). When a person did awful deeds, he was often beheaded, which made his pig tail prick up. Hence, "Mr. Wang's pig tail pricked up" is used to show disrespect, because he had done some awful deeds when he was alive.

8. In Chinese mythology, the person who controls hell is called "Yen Lwou Wang." He is equivalent to Satan in bibilical literature. "Mr. Wang went to see Yen Lwou Wang" means he died and went to hell.

9. Chinese culture has had tremendous tolerance for different religions (with the exception of the Cultural Revolution between 1966 and 1976). As a result, the concept of "god" may be religious as well as secular. The expression "godly died" takes on a more secular meaning. That is, "godly" (Shien) describes a person who died as *spiritual* and *desireless*. "My father godly died," therefore, is a very respectful idiom in the Chinese culture.

10. The world here means the world of the living. A person who passed or thanked the world of the living was usually one who was respected. These two idioms belong to high-culture, classic Chinese.

References

Bakhtin, M. (1981). *The Dialogic Imagination*. Austin: University of Texas Press.

Bakhtin, M. (1986). *Speech Genres and Other Late Essays*. C. Emerson & M. Holquist (Eds.). V. W. McGee (Trans.). Austin: University of Texas Press.

Bateson, G. (1972). *Steps to an Ecology of Mind*. New York: Ballantine.

Bateson, G. (1979). *Mind and Nature*. New York: Bantam.

Bateson, G., and Bateson, M. C. (1987). *Angels Fear*. New York: Macmillan.

Gudykunst, W., and Kim, Y. Y. (1984). *Communicating with Strangers*. New York: Random House.

Gumperz, J. (1970). *Sociolinguistics and Communication in Small Groups*. Working Paper No. 33, Language-Behavior Research Laboratory. Berkeley: University of California.

Habermas, J. (1987). *The Theory of Communicative Action (Vol. II): Lifeworld and System—A Critique of Functionalist Reason*. Thomas McCarthy (Trans.). Boston: Beacon Press.

Hall, E. T. (1976). *Beyond Culture*. New York: Doubleday.

Hall, E. T. (1983). *The Dance of Life*. New York: Doubleday.

Husserl, E. (1973). *Cartesian Meditations: An Introduction to Phenomenology*. D. Cairns (Trans.). The Hague: M. Nijoff.

Knapp, M. (1984). *Interpersonal Communication and Human Relationships*. Boston: Allyn & Bacon.

Labov, W. (1966). *The Social Stratification of English in New York City*. Washington, D.C.: Center for Applied Linguistics.

Ruesch, J., and Bateson, G. (1951). *Communication: The Social Matrix of Psychiatry*. New York: W. W. Norton.

Todorov, T. (1984). *Mikhail Bakhtin: The Dialogical Principle*. W. Godzich (Trans.). Minneapolis: University of Minnesota Press.

Concepts and Questions

1. Can you think of five or six common English idioms that might cause communication problems when speaking with someone who has English as a second language?

2. What is there about idioms that often make them troublesome and confusing?

3. What can we do to overcome some of the problems associated with using idioms in intercultural settings?

4. Lee asks the following question: Why should we study idioms in intercultural communication? How would you answer this question?

5. Why do idioms enable people to relate closely?

6. What does the phrase "establish a new conversational decorum" mean?

7. What is the principle of double/multiple description?

8. What would you do if confronted with idioms from a culture other than your own?

9. Why does Lee assert the following? A knowledge of idioms is "central to our participation in a multicultural environment at home and abroad."

Language as a Mirror of Reality: Mexican American Proverbs

SHELLY M. ZORMEIER

LARRY A. SAMOVAR

PROVERBS AND CULTURE

Over a century ago, the English writer Tennyson observed that "Proverbs sparkle forever." Tennyson, like countless other historians and philosophers, was fascinated by the enduring quality of proverbs. Jewish tradition even suggests that nine hundred years before Christ, Solomon (973–933 B.C.) authored more than 3,000 proverbs (Kent, 1913, p. 191). The persistent power of proverbs gives testimony to their impact on human behavior. In one or two lines and through the use of vivid images, they capture what a culture deems important. As Haskins and Butts (1973) note, "Proverbs contain the wisdom of nations" (p. 16). Regardless of the culture, proverbs teach children what to expect from life and what life extracts in return. From a very young age children are taught those proverbs that are generally accepted as true. Encased in the "truths" are important cultural values that are handed down by tradition from one generation to the next. As Campa (1947) states, "The collection of proverbs is of paramount importance in all the great literatures of the world, because they are the folklore fossils of all languages" (p. 19). They are, as the English proverb reminds us "the child of experience."

Through the wisdom of proverbs, important aspects of culture become transmissible (Samovar & Porter, 1995). The spoken word as a symbol is an excellent means of teaching because it can succinctly summarize events and predict outcomes. In this

This original essay appeared first in the eighth edition. All rights reserved. Permission to reprint must be obtained from the authors and the publisher. Shelly M. Zormeier is a consultant with Anderson Consulting in Minneapolis, Minnesota, and Larry A. Samovar teaches at San Diego State University.

way the past, present, and future are fused. Proverbs impart important messages to the members of a culture because these perceptions receive ongoing reinforcement for the most important aspects of a culture. The assumption behind examining proverbs is a simple one—discover the meaning of the proverb and you will understand something of what is important to its user. Because proverbs repeat those assumptions on which a culture operates, they offer valuable insight into the culture. Perhaps more importantly, those insights deal with meaningful cultural values.

It should be noted at the outset that while thousands of proverbs speak to specific cultural values, there are just as many values that are universal. That is to say, because proverbs describe common human experiences, many of the same proverbs can be found in nearly all cultures. In addition, through the thousands of social contacts with ancient and modern civilizations, many proverbs have been transferred from one country to another, always constituting a particular element of folklore that is common to all people. Proverbs connect the listener with his or her ancestors; they give witness to the ancient human fables that continue to plague us to this day. Even ancient philosophers have noted their importance (Sellers, 1994). Aristotle, for example, referred to proverbs as remnants and relics of the truest ancient philosophy.

Because proverbs are both universal and specific, they are normally divided into two classes (Paredes, 1970). First are those that possess a truth independent of time and place. In other words, they are universal. For instance, all cultures believe that the family is a reflection of the individual. Hence, the Chinese have a proverb that notes "Know the family and you will know the child." In the United States we hear "The apple does not fall far from the tree." In nearly every culture hard work is stressed. In Germany the proverb states "One that does not honor the penny is not worthy of the dollar." Americans are told "A penny saved is a penny earned." Most cultures place strong emphasis on honesty. Its importance can be seen in many cultural proverbs. In the Anglo culture, when someone is not honest, the proverb is stated as "Your nose is growing longer than Pinocchio's." In the Mexican culture the saying is "You grew a longer tail than a monkey." Likewise, there is the universal notion that once an event has transpired there is nothing that can be done. In the Anglo culture, this notion can be found in the proverb that states "Don't cry over spilled milk." In Mexican culture the saying is "After the rabbit is gone, why throw stones at the bush?" Yet other cross-cultural proverbs deal with the notion of taking precautions. For instance, in the Anglo culture people say "An ounce of prevention is worth a pound of cure." In the Mexican culture this proverb is stated as "Withstand the beginning; remedies come too late."

The second category into which proverbs can be divided are those that are written or spoken particularly for one culture and are transmitted to the members of that culture. We now focus on this type of proverb. More specifically, we will audit some important values of the Mexican American culture. By examining both the proverb and the message contained within the proverb, we can become aware of some of the perceptions and behaviors found within this culture.

MEXICAN AMERICAN PROVERBS

The Mexican culture has a long tradition of employing proverbs as a tool for carrying significant values. Mexican "proverbios" originated in the primitive stages of the Spanish language for conversational purposes rather than for literary purposes (Campa, 1947). They have been used to sharpen the wits, stimulate interest, test the wisdom of the learned, or entertain at festive occasions (Aranda, 1977). "They are of most ancient and honorable parentage, being the direct descendent of the oldest didactic and moral philosophy" (p. 5). Proverbs may explicitly contain advice or may describe a scene and leave the implications to be inferred. In any case, these proverbs are a large part of the Mexican American culture. They condense the wisdom, experience, and explanations of well-known truths.

In ancient times, as well as today, these proverbs can be found in Mexican American wedding songs, Christmas carols, lyrics, and poems. Since the majority of Mexican Americans are Catholic, these popular sayings can also be found within the Bible in the "Book of Proverbs," as well as in their prayers. Wherever they are found, they are primitive forms of pop-

ular art and knowledge. In them we find the fundamental elements of history, religion, and values that are important to the Mexican American culture (Campa, 1947). According to Sellers (1994), Mexican proverbs

> are the verbal property of common people. They are . . . sayings, some pithy remark from a man leaning on his plow or a woman with her elbow up on a table as she listens to the chisme-gossip of a neighbor. These sayings may inform and advise, or offer an arguable point to life. It is amusement and it is wisdom itself. It is the snappy scolding of a naughty child. It is the soothing remedy to loss and the loss of hope. . . . It is the unwritten literature and philosophy of the poor, particularly rural folk. While the wealthy and educated have Carols Fuentes and Octavio Paz, the man or woman on the street has songs, limericks, folklore, chisme, cuentos, and proverbs. (p. 6)

As a way of linking Mexican American proverbs to perception and behavior, we have selected those proverbs that represent the most important values of the Mexican American culture: collectivism, fatalism, present-time orientation, being orientation, and family. The proverbs in the following sections are located in the works of Sellers (1994).

Collectivism

The first prominent value that can be seen in Mexican American proverbs is collectivism.

Better to be a fool with the crowd than wise by oneself. In a collectivistic culture, it is much more important to show loyalty to one's in-group than to strive for individual success. It is meaningful to achieve the goals and needs of the group. Cooperation and affiliation are emphasized rather than competition or aggressiveness (Eshleman, 1985). In an individualistic culture, individuals work hard for personal accomplishments. These cultures place a strong emphasis on individual goals (Hofstede, 1980). In fact, if a person does not achieve individual success, he or she is often seen as having less academic, monetary, or social power. This is because personal identity and self-worth are derived from individual accomplishments. The opposite, of course, is the case with collectivistic cultures.

A solitary soul neither sings nor cries. People in collectivistic cultures are born into extended families and join organizations that protect them (Hofstede, 1984). "Collectivistic cultures are interdependent and as a result they work, play, live, and sleep in close proximity" (Andersen, 1989, p. 169). Therefore, it is better to be part of a collectivistic in-group because one will have others to share happiness or sorrow. An individual who is not part of a collectivistic group will have no one to rejoice with him or her in times of happiness. Likewise, there will be no one to comfort the individual during difficult times. If one belongs to a collectivistic in-group, there will always be many friends and family members who will try to understand one's feelings and provide support. Those who are not part of a collectivistic in-group will not experience the rich drama of life, which includes participating in others' joys and sorrows.

He who divides and shares is left with the best share. As part of a collectivistic society, Mexican Americans maintain a "we" consciousness. The needs of the group take precedence over individual needs. If someone is lacking a material necessity, it will be provided by others within the in-group. In this way, everyone will always be taken care of. Sharing with others will ensure that one's own needs will also be taken care of in the future.

Bewail your poverty, and not alone. Members of collectivistic societies are emotionally dependent on the institutions and organizations to which they belong. During economically difficult times, people within the Mexican American in-group will protect each other's interests. If this is not possible, at least the in-group will be able to offer support.

Fatalism

This section will discuss those proverbs that exemplify the fatalistic world view of Mexican Americans.

God gives it and God takes it away. Catholicism is manifested in the fatalistic view of Mexican Americans. They conceive of God as all-powerful and of humans as simply part of nature that is subject to His will (Schreiber & Homiak, 1981). Since God sends people to this earth, people must leave when He calls. Through creation and destruction, God maintains the balance of the world. One must suffer to deserve.

If God is going to give you something, it will come easy. Good or bad fortune is predestined. If God wishes an individual to have something, he or she will receive it. If God does not want an individual to have something, it will not be given to him or her.

He who is born to suffer will start from the cradle. God has already decided the fate of every individual (Gomez, 1972). One's fate is decided even before birth. If one's fate is to suffer, there is nothing one can do to change it. Therefore, one should submit to the allotted level of suffering.

He who is born to be a potted plant will not go beyond the porch. One has little control over the situation, environment, or world; each person has a certain place in life that cannot and should not be changed. Therefore if one's destiny is to be a "potted plant," he or she will never go beyond the porch because it was not meant to be.

Everywhere the ox goes he is put to plow; everywhere the poor man goes he must work. Also, *He who is a parrot will be green wherever he is.* These proverbs suggest that when a person is meant to do or be something in life, there is no way to change the situation. It does not matter how industrious one is, for he or she will receive only what God dictates. Just as the ox was meant to plow, the poor person will always work because it is what God has predestined. Likewise, those born to be parrots will remain parrots.

We are like well buckets, one goes up and the other comes down. Although difficulties are a part of life, the Mexican American sees a balance of opposites (Gomez, 1972). Pain is balanced by pleasure, life by death, creation by destruction, and illness by health. God maintains this balance by seeing that no extreme exists without a counterbalance. For example, "pain must follow pleasure just as a hang-over must follow a drunk" (p. 170). One must suffer to deserve. Therefore if one suffers (the well bucket comes down), God will be sure to balance this suffering with pleasure (the well bucket goes up). However, this pleasure may not be seen in this world. It may be that one's pleasure will be received after death (that is, in securing a place for oneself in heaven).

Submit to pain because it is inevitable. Difficulties are a part of life (Gomez, 1972). Everyone will experience some type of pain in life because people must suffer to deserve. People must bear illness with dignity and courage. Fate should be accepted without complaint.

Present-Time Orientation

Proverbs discussed in this section exemplify the prominence of the Mexican American present-time orientation.

Don't move the water; the river is already flooding. This proverb is interpreted to mean that one should leave matters as they are. A culture that maintains a present-time orientation is not as concerned with meeting deadlines and conforming to schedules. Acceptance and appreciation of things as they are constitute primary values. If the river is already flooding, just be content to leave it as it is.

Give time to time. One should not rush in life. There is time for everything because there is always tomorrow. While a person from a culture with a future orientation may have a clear plan of where he or she wishes to be in five or ten years, Mexican Americans are not overly concerned with obtaining a "blue print for life" (Flores, 1982). There is not as much concern for how much is accomplished today because there will eventually be time for everything.

There is more time than life. Also, *Tomorrow will be another day.* Although Mexican Americans maintain respect for the past, it is gone. Likewise, the future remains uncertain due to their fatalistic orientation. One must live for the here and now, for the moment, for that is all that can be done. If something is not completed today, do not worry because there will always be time tomorrow.

Don't do today what you can put off until tomorrow. Since the future is so uncertain and one never knows if tomorrow will really come, there is no need to rush to complete everything in one day.

Being Orientation

The being orientation is another important value in the Mexican American culture. It is therefore not surprising that many proverbs reinforce this cultural value.

He who lives a hurried life will soon die. Also, *Don't worry so much so you can last longer.* These proverbs refer to the value of focusing on the present moment. In contrast, the doing orientation is dominated by time schedules and goals, which require one to hurry to meet deadlines and complete tasks. If one is always hurrying, there will be no time for the important things in life, such as God and family.

He who gets drenched at dawn has the rest of the day to dry out. Do not be overly concerned with completing a task because there is an entire day to finish. If one gets wet in the morning, it is no problem because there is the rest of the day to dry.

He who wants everything will lose everything. Those who try to obtain everything in life will lose sight of what is really important, such as God and family. In the end, these people will be left with nothing, by neglecting God and family, people lose them. Therefore, just be content and satisfied to leave things as they are rather than focus on everything that could be gained.

Family Values

The family is of utmost importance to Mexican Americans. The traditional Mexican American family is described as patriarchal, religious, and cohesive (Eshleman, 1985). Mexican American values are taught and maintained by the family. The family teaches each person his or her responsibilities as well as characteristics and behavior appropriate for his or her gender. These responsibilities, characteristics, and behaviors can be seen in the following proverbs.

A tree that grows crooked cannot be straightened.
Mexican Americans are extremely familistic (Diaz-Guerrero, 1975). To maintain harmony in this collectivistic unit, children are taught that their responsibility is to maintain obedience and loyalty from a very young age. Children who are not taught these values from a young age and are not disciplined will never learn them.

Better to die on your feet than to live on your knees.
These proverbs relate to the concept of machismo. The value of machismo governs male behavior in almost every facet of social life but wields its greatest influence in connection with the concept of honor (Grebler, Moore, & Guzman, 1970). The conduct of a male in any social situation must support his public image as a person of honor and integrity. A situation that might compromise his image as a man is avoided at all costs.

A man is king in his home. The father is the autocratic head of the household (Murillo, 1976). Few decisions can be made without his approval or knowledge. All the other family members are expected to be respectful of him and to accede to his will. The mother must be completely devoted to her husband. Fulfillment is seen in helping her husband to achieve his goals as he sees fit.

SUMMARY

The symbols of a culture enable values to be passed from one generation to the next. The spoken word as a symbol is a way to enforce what is most important to a culture. Proverbs are unique because they contain a condensed piece of wisdom that can be easily used by anyone in that culture. These proverbs may be repeated by a mother scolding her children, a father offering advice, or even by a person singing or praying. Studying Mexican American proverbs allows one to see that the most important aspects of the Mexican American culture are collectivism, fatalism, present-time orientation, being orientation, and familism.

References

Andersen, P. A. (1989). Directions in Nonverbal Intercultural Communication Research. Paper presented to the Graduate Honors Seminar, Arizona State University, Tempe. April.

Aranda, C. (1977). *Dichos: Proverbs and Sayings from the Spanish*. New York: Greenwood Press.

Campa, A. L. (1947). Sayings and Riddles in New Mexico. *The University of New Mexico Bulletin, 15*, pp. 5–67.

Diaz-Guerrero, R. (1975). *Psychology of the Mexican*. Austin: University of Texas Press.

Eshleman, J. R. (1985). *The Family*, 4th ed. Boston: Allyn & Bacon.

Flores, Y. G. (1982). *The Impact of Acculturation of the Chicano Family*. Ann Arbor, Mich.: Xerox University Microfilms International.

Gomez, R. (1972). *Mexican-American: A Reader*. El Paso: University of Texas.

Grebler, L., Moore, J. W., and Guzman, R. C. (1970). *The Mexican American People*. Newbury Park, Calif.: Sage.

Haskins, J., and Butts, H. F. (1973). *The Psychology of Black Language*. New York: Barnes & Noble.

Hofstede, Geert (1980). *Culture's Consequences: International Differences in Work-Related Values*. Beverly Hills: Sage.

Hofstede, Geert (1984). National Cultures and Corporate Cultures. Paper presented on LIFIM Perspective Day, Helsinki, Finland, December 4, 1984.

Kent, C. F. (1913). *The Anchor Bible: Proverbs and Ecclesiastes*. Garden City, N.Y.: Doubleday.

Murillo, N. (1976). *Chicanos: Social and Psychological Perspectives*. Saint Louis: Mosby.

Paredes, Americo (1970). *Folktales of Mexico*. Chicago: University of Chicago Press.

Samovar L. A., and Porter, R. E. (1995). *Communication Between Cultures*, 2d ed. Belmont, Calif.: Wadsworth.

Schreiber, J. M., and Homiak, J. P. (1981). "Mexican-Americans." In A. Harwood (Ed.), *Ethnicity and Medical Care*, 265–335. Cambridge: Harvard University Press.

Sellers, J. M. (1994). *Folk Wisdom of Mexico*. San Francisco: Chronicle Books.

Concepts and Questions

1. How does the study of proverbs help us understand the important values of a particular culture?

2. What Mexican Americans proverbs discussed by Zormeier and Samovar can be applied to other cultures?
3. Can you think of some proverbs from your own culture and specify what values they represent?
4. What is meant by the phrase "proverbs are both universal and specific"?
5. What are your favorite proverbs? Why have you selected these?
6. What proverbs in the United States stress the value of individualism?
7. What proverbs in the United States stress the view of time held by many Americans?
8. Why are proverbs often called "the child of experience"?

Language Diversity Within the United States: Understanding the Houseless Youths' Code for Speaking

Natalie J. Dollar

As a graduate student, I became interested in understanding the diverse ways of speaking like a United States American. My first line of research in this area has focused on a speech community referred to as "Deadheads" (Dollar, 1991; forthcoming a & b). A second line, which is the focus of this article, concerns a community of speakers who call themselves "houseless" but who are known to nonmembers as "homeless" youths (Dollar, 1998; Dollar & Zimmers, 1994, forthcoming; Dollar, Zimmers, & Nichols, 1997). My primary concern in each line has been to understand the patterned use of language in social situations and the community-specific meanings associated with its use. In so doing, I aim to understand and illustrate the organized diversity within the United States, particularly the diversity in U.S. speech communities and their codes for speaking. In this article I discuss my continuing effort in terms of the houseless youth speech community. I begin with an overview of three concepts central to my research—*speech community*, *speech codes*, and *culture*. Next I describe the patterned use of two components of the houseless youths' code for speaking, namely, *communicative symbols of identity and norms for communicating with nonmember U.S. speakers*. Finally, I discuss the implications of this approach for the student who is interested in culturally diverse ways of speaking.

 Natalie J. Dollar teaches at Oregon State University, Corvallis, Oregon.

SPEECH COMMUNITIES, SPEECH CODES, AND CULTURES

Ethnographers of communication (Hymes 1962, 1972; Philipsen, 1992) have approached the study of language and culture by focusing on speech communities. According to Hymes (1972), a speech community is a "community sharing rules for the conduct and interpretation of speech, and rules for the interpretation of at least one linguistic variety" (p. 54). Individuals who share rules for the use and interpretation of speech can participate in the social activity of speaking with another. This social practice is dependent on shared rules for interpreting a linguistic variety (e.g., German, Spanish). Knowledge of interpretation rules, however, is not sufficient for socially employing the linguistic variety (e.g., discussing politics, disciplining your child, making a deposit with a bank teller, giving compliments, etc.). Just as many individuals learn to read in another language or even interpret it when spoken to them, they cannot produce meaningful utterances and engage in interaction using the language. In contrast, members of speech communities are competent in terms of both knowledge (of linguistic variety and rules for interpretation) and performance (employing linguistic variety in communicating with others).

These rules and the linguistic variety are part of a speech community's *speech code*, "a system of socially constructed symbols and meanings, premises and rules, pertaining to communicative conduct" (Philipsen, 1997, p. 126). Echoing Hymes' (1972) claim that speaking is a metaphor for social life, Philipsen (1997) posits the substance of speech codes to be "the public, discursive resources in and through which the connections between and among people are thematized, constituted or reconstituted, and managed" (p. 119). Observing and formulating a speech code allows a researcher to understand one of the many systems that make up a speech community's culture. *Culture*, in my research, refers to a system, a code, composed of symbols, meanings, premises, and rules (Geertz, 1973; Philipsen, 1997; Schneider, 1976). It is this code, this system, not a group of people or a geographical region, that I take to be culture.

The boundaries of a speech community are defined in terms of its speech code, which may not necessarily reflect community boundaries drawn in other ways. In focusing on a speech community, rather than on a national or ethnic group, for example, ethnographers of communication prioritize speaking and other forms of communication in their study of culture and language.

In this article, I continue my effort to formulate the houseless youths' code for speaking that I observed in my ethnographic studies. Note that this article alone is not suggested to support the claim for a speech code, only to illustrate some features of a code in practice, a code that is often muted by speakers employing a more powerful code for speaking. I have noticed, for instance, that the norms for communicating when houseless youths and nonmember U.S. adults interact, spontaneously and in planned contexts, overwhelmingly privileges an adult, housed voice. As such, the adult stories and realities are heard as more truthful than the houseless youths'. In this article, I illustrate what speakers and researchers continue to notice: A language does not serve all its users equally. Consider the excerpts of conversation below:

YOUTH 1 (Y1): They will not pay attention.

YOUTH 2 (Y2): Unless it's violent, sex, or drugs, they won't be there.

YOUTH 1: Yeah.

YOUTH 3 (Y3): It's not worth their time.

Continuing their walk down "the Ave," the youths' conversation moves to a discussion of writing editorials to gain "their" attention. One states that he has written published editorials, but they all agree this form of communication is not effective as a means of reaching "them," later revealed to be adults, parents, legislators, and other nonmembers. This is where we pick up the conversation below.

Y2: The only problem is the only way our voi—uh, the the only thing they hear from our voice is when our voice is coming from a pipe bomb or a . . .

Y3: Pipe bomb, or if you're pregnant and you get beat up—those type of things.

Y2: Or a twelve-gauge or chain—that's the only way they'll hear us.

Y4: Right.

Y2: They don't pay attention. They don't pay attention to walking up and talking. What they pay attention to is a raised fist holding something sharp in it, you know.

Y3: Yep.

Y2: What's one of the most—what's one of the biggest events that's happened this year? The federal building getting bombed. We don't remember, you know, so and so getting elected or so and so had a baby, you know, or triplets or something like that—something beautiful and quiet like that or a great book that was written this year, you know?

Talk continues among these youths. They note other historically violent events that have changed the world, particularly life for U.S. Americans, but agree that they would rather see changes made through nonviolent means, "the Gandhi way." As they walk away into this summer night, they return their focus to the "community forum" they just attended. Organized by a community group, a "partnership for youth," the forum was open to "everyone": parents, youth, service providers, police, volunteers, merchants, students, teachers, policy makers, and congregations were listed on the flyers publicizing the event. The flyer identified the topic for the forum: "The [name] Bill (Affecting homeless and runaway youth.) What it contains. . . ."

In both excerpts above, the youths are talking about communication problems they are having (e.g., "They will not pay attention," "the only thing they hear from our voice"). Does the community forum provide a more successful form of communicating for these youths?

Y1: They heard us, but they didn't listen to us.

Y2: It went in one ear and right out the other and right out the door.

Y3: They let maybe a grand total of five comments from kids and the rest of it was all from . . .

Y4: the adults.

Y2: The adults and . . .

Y3: the parents, the parents.

Y2: And the adults are not the ones being affected by the law. Kids are. We are.

It is at this point that we get a glimpse of who these youths are, what binds their relations, and why they attended the forum together. They are part of the "houseless" youth community, a speech community like many others in the United States whose members feel their voice is not heard by the power-holding, policy-making members of our nation. Both members of these communities and communication scholars (Chick, 1990; Kramarae, 1981; Kramarae, Thorne, & Henley, 1983) have recognized that a language is more powerful for some speakers than for others. For instance, the norms that guide the social use of English in everyday encounters serve adults' interests, particularly European American adults, better than many other U.S. American speakers such as African Americans (Houston, 1997; Kochman, 1981), Native Americans (Scollon & Wong-Scollon, 1981; 1995), and women (Kramarae, 1981). In the final excerpt above, the youths express their realization of this, noting that they were permitted to speak—although noticeably less than adults—but the adults did not "listen" to them, they did not actively reflect on and interpret the youths' speech as meaningful. In this chapter, I use my research with some street youths in two Northwestern communities—a large city and a small town—to further explore this question of language use and voice, or instances in which a speaker has been "able to speak, spoke, was heard, and was socially validated as such" (Carbaugh, 1996, p. 146).

COMMUNICATING IDENTITY: SELF AND OTHER

In 1993, a research partner of mine noticed in her work at an outreach center that many of the youths regularly use family reference terms when talking with or about other street youths, individuals with whom they have no legal or biological connection. This speech pattern—using family reference terms such as *brother* and *uncle* for persons outside of one's legal or biological family—has been noted in ethnic communities within the United States but rarely is cited as a pattern among European Americans. Some African Americans and some Mexican Americans (Gangotena, 1997), for example, use family reference terms for persons not belonging to their biological and legal families. Their patterned use and meanings associated with such use, however, differs. For example, some African Americans employ the terms loosely in reference to friends and other members of their ethnic community, while many Mexican Americans use the terms for persons outside the family but only sparingly with their closest family friends (Gangotena, 1997). Given the high number of European American street youth in the Northwest (Henning & Goldsmith, 1995), this practice is not likely to have been a speech pattern they picked up in their biological homes. Our research suggested that the referencing pattern is associated with challenges of survival, safety, trust, and acceptance that houseless youths confront on a daily basis (Dollar & Zimmers, 1994). Simply stated, families are important on the streets, too. Houseless youths acknowledge this in their patterned use of family reference terms.

Given this use of family referencing, we decided to take a closer look at some related symbols identified by researchers; the use of *family* by many U.S. American speakers evokes symbols of self, community, and nonmembers (Varenne, 1977, 1986). We focused on how street youths refer to and understand self and other or nonmember speech participant(s). In Chapter 1, Collier refers to these communication practices as *identity avowal* and *ascription*, respectively. When asked to describe *self*, many street youths cite nicknames, first names, and some variation of the phrase "a human being." Although the first two responses are meaningfully recognized by most U.S. speakers, the third is not so common. This is because some U.S. speakers have never had their humanness challenged, questioned, or denied (Nakayama & Krizek, 1995). Most street youths have! This disconfirmation is continually noted by researchers across disciplines (e.g., sociology, medicine, social work) when they argue that most youths remaining on the streets for more than a few weeks do so because they are members of street families, are fleeing abuse (mental, psychological, physical), or are "throwaways" ousted by their families (Bronstein, 1996; Hoch, 1987; Kurtz, Jarvis, & Kurtz, 1991; Nelson, 1995).

When asked to respond to nonmembers' ascription of them as "homeless," these youths claim to be "houseless, *not* homeless." The distinction, they argue, lies in their belief that a home does not have to include a legal guardian, electricity, walls, repeated occupancy, and other requirements specified in the U.S. legal housing code. So what is a "home" to these youths? They themselves explain best.

ME: Many people refer to you as "homeless." Do you agree?

Y1: Homeless, yeah, *right*. No, I'm not homeless, I'm houseless. I don't have a house that I stay in every night or hardly any night. I *do* have a home. It's wherever me and them (pointing to other youths), my brothers and sisters, are together.

Y2: See—what those people who call us homeless see is that we are here a lot. We have the right to hang out in the river park, to chill on the benches, on the sidewalks, to lay down in a park.

Y3: What they don't understand is the place they call our homes, our legal guardians' house, is not a home at all. It's where her dad rapes her when he likes (pointing to another youth) and his mom lives in filth so she can support her smack (heroin) habit (points to another youth) or where his parents live alone in a three-bedroom place since they kicked him out at twelve saying he was old enough to support himself. Sound like a fucking home to you?

Y2: Hell, *no!* A home is where you're with your family, the people you trust, where you feel safe. Just because somebody is responsible for you being born, is granted custody of you in court doesn't mean they are your family. My family is right here. You're looking at them.

A home, as illustrated in this example, is a place where you are with family and where you feel safe. It is a place where you are not sexually, mentally, physiologically, or behaviorally abused. A home is not equivalent to a legally defined house. A home is not necessarily with your legal family or guardians. "Family" is composed of your "brothers and sisters," but not necessarily your legal siblings. Your family consists of persons with whom you feel safe and a sense of trust. Each of these symbols—home, house, family, and self—arise as central to street youth identity avowals across a variety of speech scenes, both in spontaneous and planned interactions.

When these youths refer to nonmembers with whom they are speaking and ascribe identity, they often use the term *they*, or a variant of this nondescriptive third-person pronoun. When the youths are more specific, these houseless speakers rely on social categories such as "[service] providers," "adults," and "cops." These communicative symbols of identity are used both in situations among houseless youths (as in the conversation above between youths leaving the forum) and when interacting with nonmembers. When we had the opportunity to observe nonmembers interacting with houseless youths, we listened to their speech for communicative symbols of identity, particularly symbols of avowal (self) and ascription (street youth). In planned interactions between houseless youths and nonmembers, *kid, child,* and *homeless* are commonly used ascriptions for street youths. In spontaneous encounters, nonmembers tend to close these brief exchanges with evaluative ascriptions. The street youths recognize this pattern as noted by a member: "It doesn't matter if I say 'Nice day, huh?' or 'Could you spare some change?' most people get mad and start calling us 'irresponsible kids,' 'lazy scum,' or something derogatory." Although some street youths respond to these demeaning ascriptions, many of their responses are claims to being human rather than the reciprocation of evaluative ascriptions. These interactions are likely to occur in public spaces and around consumer-oriented business fronts.

When referring to self, nonmembers rely on social categories. "Parents," "successful, hardworking [U.S.] Americans," "service providers," "taxpaying citizens," and "police officer" are common identity avowals for these speakers. Unlike street youths, nonmembers use social roles as identity ascriptions. In so doing, they evoke the system of relations implied in such roles. As parents, they imply youths are kids and children. As successful and hardworking U.S. Americans, youths are cast by them as unsuccessful and lazy. This aspect of communicating identity for self—necessarily ascribing identity to other communication participants—has been noted by communication theorists and researchers (Burke, 1965; Carbaugh, 1996; Dollar, 1990).

Houseless youths' symbols for avowing identity point to two dimensions salient in speaking about self—the uniqueness (e.g., first names and nicknames) and humanness of each youth. Their use of names does not cast the nonmember into a negative role. Their claims for "humanness" do. These partic-

ular identity avowals cast nonmembers into the role of questioning, challenging, or disagreeing with the youths' humanness. The houseless youths' system for ascribing identity illustrates their recognition of "us against them," or street youths against housed persons. Their use of social categories for nonmembers reflects their understanding of the system within which they must survive, a system of U.S. social roles.

To summarize, houseless youths and nonmember U.S. interactional partners use the same linguistic variety as a basis for avowing and ascribing identity, but their situated use of this variety differs. All of the speakers express recognition of a system of social roles relevant within the United States. This system comprises "youth," "kids," "runaways" and "throwaways," "parents," "service providers," "cops" or "police," "lock-down facilities," and a host of mental and medical providers. While this list of social institutions and roles is not extensive, it does represent many of the salient social categories in street youths' interaction with nonmembers. The meaning of these identity symbols, however, differs for street youths and nonmember U.S. speakers (Dollar & Zimmers, forthcoming). Other distinctions can be noted in the norms for speaking that tend to characterize houseless youths and nonmember interaction—their interaction in both spontaneous and planned contexts. I turn now to a discussion of these norms.

NORMS FOR SPEAKING

In this section, I report data from two types of speaking scenes, *spontaneous* and *planned*. It is important to consider both in order to better understand the street youths' code for speaking with nonmember U.S. speakers. In the spontaneous category, interaction in public spaces such as sidewalks is described. A town meeting and community forum are discussed as examples of planned speech events.

Spontaneous Scenes

First, most of this interaction occurs in or on public space (e.g., sidewalks, public buildings, and parks). This aspect of these speakers' interaction arises from the houseless youths' lack of private space. These youths do not have a living room or backyard in which they can gather and interact with their friends. They are not welcome in malls because they are perceived to be unclean, likely to steal, and an overall high risk to clients and business owners. Adults not only own the private space, but also govern most of the public space (Drucker & Gumpert, 1996; Gumpert & Drucker, 1994; Lieberg, 1995). There are few places in the United States where youths can interact without an adult present. Furthermore, as youths in the United States, they speak a language that is socially designed for and by adults.

Second, this unplanned interaction does not adhere to typical "friendly" greetings exchanged between some U.S. speakers passing one another in public space. A norm for speaking recognized by many U.S. speakers is that when passing someone it is common to acknowledge the other's presence. We do so simply by glancing in other's direction and saying "Hi" or "Hello." The other reciprocates with a similar greeting. While this norm is not always followed, many U.S. speakers consider the speech norm to convey recognition and acknowledgment of another person, to connect them with another human. This is not a speech norm for interactions between street youths and nonmembers. Their interaction often takes a more conflictual form. This form is further described as I discuss the next two speaking norms.

Third, this interaction regularly involves profanity. Interestingly, members of each community use profanity differently. As noted above, nonmembers sometimes use evaluative ascriptions when referring to houseless youths. These ascriptions are one place where nonmembers accept the use of profanity. These ascriptions most often follow a street youths' attempt to initiate interaction. Some of this interaction is to ask for change, but much of it is simply an attempt to interact, to enact the greeting norm described above. Regardless, most attempts are responded to with evaluative ascriptions or nonverbal disconfirmations. The street youth is likely to respond to nonmembers' evaluations with profanity-laden claims for humanness more so than with reciprocal evaluative ascriptions of other. Unlike the nonmembers' speech, much of the youths' speech is characterized by profanity. So, while members of both communities use profanity, they do so in distinct ways. With nonmembers, it is not the norm

to do so and is only acceptable in a few contexts. For houseless youths, profanity is characteristic of their way of speaking.

Finally, much of this interaction is left incomplete as one participant walks away without the closure U.S. speakers expect. Most U.S. speakers expect some sort of verbal closing for their interactions. Researchers have identified closings as problematic for European American speakers interacting with other U.S. speakers such as Native American speakers (Scollon & Wong-Scollon, 1981). It is problematic in either the lack of a verbal closing to distinguish the end of a particular interaction or the use of different and unrecognized means of closing the interaction. For houseless youths and nonmember speakers, the lack of closings is another interactional point where their codes for speaking come into conflict.

Planned Scenes

Most planned interaction between houseless youths and nonmembers takes place in adult-oriented speech scenes. Examples include service appointments (e.g., updates with state service providers, food banks, and shelters) and organized meetings such as a town meeting designed for interactions between houseless youths and community members. In the following section, I review the most prevalent communication norms that characterize houseless youths' and nonmembers' interaction (referred to below as "housed" speakers) at two speech events, a community forum and a town meeting (Dollar, 1998; Dollar, Zimmers, & Nichols, 1998).

Many U.S. Americans recognize these speech events and the norms for communicating within each. Many, however, find them to be unsuccessful in terms of providing voice for them or their community. In the settlement of the United States, town meetings were used as speech scenes to give voice to white males while muting children, women, African Americans, and Native Americans (Zinn, 1995). The norms for speaking within the town meeting we observed continue to support an adult rather than a youth voice. This town meeting and the community forum not only support an adult voice but also their norms of speaking mute expressions by houseless youths. I illustrate this point by describing the patterns observed in these speech events.

There was a clear distinction in the speech of all participants between housed and houseless speakers. The predetermined topic of each speech event, "homeless and runaway youth," certainly contributes to this distinction. The housed speakers displayed three speech norms: *blaming*, *objectification*, and *conversational control* (Dollar, 1998; Dollar, Zimmers, & Nichols, 1998). Housed speakers used *blaming* when they spoke to the issue of why a particular law was needed and more generally to why youth run away or choose life on the streets. Many of these speakers used hedges—"for no fault of mine" and "I'm a good parent," for example—before claiming to be the parent of a runaway or street youth.

Housed speakers' *objectified* houseless youth in these speech events. They support behavioral regulations in which they "put," "place," "commit," and "lock up" houseless youths "without consent," and where the youths are "not free to leave." Their solution is to "turn the child over to law enforcement" because "children need to be contained and controlled." All of this language constructs the image of street youths as objects. Housed speakers—legislators, service providers, parents, concerned citizens, and so on—use another norm that supports objectification of these houseless youths. They speak of these youths as categories within a classification system, a scheme Dorne (1996) argues has two categories: either "perpetrators in need of state control" or the "helpless victim in need of state protection" (p. 71). All of these examples construe houseless youths to be in need of others, incapable of caring for themselves, and potentially harmful to other U.S. Americans.

Finally, housed speakers exercise a norm toward *conversational control*. The control emerges from at least two sources: norms associated with each of the U.S. speech events and the situationally enacted norms used in each. Some norms known by many U.S. Americans to be relevant to the community forum and town meeting are: (1) Each speech event has an adult moderator who selects speakers and regulates the flow of speech. (2) One person talks at a time. (3) Prechosen speakers are considered to have specialized knowledge relevant to the speech topic in each scene.

Between both of these speech events, only one prechosen speaker was a houseless youth, and the topic of both was "homeless youths." All three of

these norms support an adult, housed voice, whereas the third explicitly mutes houseless youths. In addition to using these norms to their advantage, housed speakers dismissed these youths' topics, including personal testimony. The housed speakers also successfully interrupted houseless youth speakers, while the houseless youths were unsuccessful at their interruption attempts. Finally, housed speakers held the floor more than twice the amount of time as the houseless youths.

The street youths' speech followed three norms: (1) adhere to the commonly accepted norms for these speech scenes; (2) attempt to legitimize speech by referencing specific parallels with other U.S. civil rights movements; or (3) disregard accepted speech norms and assume a houseless street style of speaking, a style characterized by profanity and emotional expression and excluded from most youth and adult interactional scenes in the United States. As noted above, when street youths use the acceptable norms for these speech events, they are unsuccessful in having their voices heard and legitimized, unsuccessful at telling their stories and having them accepted as truthful. The second norm these youths use—an attempt to gain legitimacy for their community—is a response to something denied. All three of the housed speaker norms noted above (i.e., blaming, objectifying, conversational control) undermine, challenge, and deny the houseless youths' voice, their stories, their lived reality. These youths demonstrate a better understanding of U.S. history than many of my college students as they draw explicit parallels between their struggles and other historical struggles such as the civil rights movement (African American rights, the women's movement, the gay and lesbian movement, native peoples movements, etc.) and the American Revolution. Like the second norm, the third is a reaction to their observation of the first norm (i.e., their lack of success using the accepted norms for speaking); to switch to a street youth style of speaking is an attempt by these youths to use another way of speaking as a means of gaining voice.

SPEAKING AND CULTURE

In the preceding sections, I have described ways of speaking that are demonstrated in a few U.S. social scenes. These ways of speaking are intelligible as U.S. American formulations, but they also suggest some disagreement, some diversity in speaking like a U.S. American. It is my position that the symbols and system for communicating as a houseless youth described in this chapter are part of a larger code for speaking. Although I have sketched some of the nuances of this code, its formulation is far from complete. Nonetheless, the focus on this and other speech communities provides valuable insight for students of cultural communication. I close by outlining three types of knowledge that are suggested in this approach for studying language and culture.

First, the observation and reporting of distinct codes for communicating provide valuable insight in terms of both understanding and practical application. As reportable systems, these codes for speaking can be learned and understood by those who are interested in a particular speech community. Remember that learning the code does not guarantee membership into the speech community. It may, however, provide a basis for meaningful interaction in a speech community of which you are not a member (e.g., as a traveler, as a student abroad, in a work situation).

Second, systematic study of speech communities provides another way to understand the diversity that constitutes our world. Scholars have examined the world as it is demarcated along political, economic, government, class, and other boundaries. Given the interdependence of language and culture, language and ideology, and language and identification, an approach is certainly warranted that focuses on language and its uses to explain diversity in our world. Ethnographies of communication, taking speech communities and their codes for communicating, are well suited for this type of enterprise. See Philipsen and Carbaugh (1986) for examples of a diverse range of ethnographies of communication.

Third, this approach prioritizes the relationship between communication and culture, not politics and culture, or business and culture, or nationality and culture, for example. This theoretical approach differs from other studies of culture and communication in our discipline, namely, those that take culture to be an independent variable. The focus on speech communities and their codes for communicating differs by positioning researchers and students to hear the process through which culture and communication come into contact. In addition, the speakers' conceptualization of both communication and culture are part of the set of research questions posed in ethnographies of communication. In summary, this approach for studying language and culture offers the student an opportunity to focus first and foremost on communication, the social practice, a practice that is, to borrow from Philipsen (1992), radically cultural.

References

Bronstein, L. R. (1996). Intervening with homeless youths: Direct practices without blaming the victim. *Child and Adolescent Social Work Journal, 13*(2), 127–138.

Burke, K. (1965). *Permanence and change: An anatomy of purpose.* Indianapolis: Bobbs-Merrill.

Carbaugh, D. (1996). *Situating selves: The communication of social identities in American scenes.* Albany: State University of New York Press.

Chick, J. K. (1990). The interactional accomplishment of discrimination. In D. Carbaugh's (Ed.), *Cultural communication and intercultural contact* (pp. 225–252). Hillsdale, NJ: Lawrence Erlbaum.

Dollar, N. J. (1990, April). *An analysis of altercasting in compliance-gaining discourse.* Paper presented at the meeting of the Northwest Communication Association, Coeur D'Alene, ID.

———. (1991, February). *The cultural function of Deadheads' ways of speaking.* Paper presented at the meeting of the Western States Communication Association, Boise, ID.

———. (1998). The muting of "houseless" youth: Communication scenes as critical in street youth policy. *Homeless Education: Beam, 8,* 1–4.

———. (forthcoming a). A study of diversity among some U.S. American speakers: Understanding "show" as a Deadhead speech event. In R. G. Weiner & D. D. Dodd (Eds.), *Writings on the Grateful Dead.* Westport, CT: Greenwood Press.

———. (forthcoming b). "Show talk" and communal identity: Speaking like a Deadhead. *Journal of Northwest Communication Association.*

———, & Zimmers, B. G. (1994, November). *My brothers and sisters: Homeless, free-loading, punk kids.* Paper presented at the annual meeting of the National Communication Association, New Orleans, LA.

———, & Zimmers, B. G. (forthcoming). Social identity and communicative boundaries: An analysis of youth and young adult street speakers. *Communication Research.*

————, Zimmers, B. G., & Nichols, N. (February, 1997). *The muting of "houseless" youth: An ethnography of street youth and housed persons' interaction regarding the Becca Bill.* Paper presented at the annual meeting of the Western States Communication Association meeting, Denver, CO.

Dorne, C. (1996). Helpless children or predatory delinquents? Differential backlash to "Get Tough" trends in juvenile justice. *Humanity and Society, 20*(1), 71–84.

Drucker, S., & Gumpert, G. (1996). The regulation of public social life: Communication law revisited. *Communication Quarterly, 44*(3), 280–296.

Gangotena, M. (1997). The rhetoric of *la familia* among Mexican Americans. In A. Gonzalez, M. Houston, & V. Chen (Eds.), *Our voices: Essays in culture, ethnicity and communication.* Los Angeles: Roxbury.

Geertz, C. (1973). *The interpretation of cultures: Selected essays.* New York: Basic Books.

Gumpert, G., & Drucker, S. J. (1994). Public space and urban life: Challenges in the communication landscape. *Journal of Communication, 44*(4), 169–177.

Henning, J., & Goldsmith, B. (1995). *A report on homeless youth served by the King County youth shelter system 1994.* King County Department of Community and Human Services, Community Service Division.

Hoch, C. (1987). A brief history of the homeless problem in the United States. In R. D. Bingham, R. G. Green, & S. B. White (Eds.), *The homeless in contemporary society* (pp. 16–32). Newbury Park, CA: Sage.

Houston, M. (1997). When black women talk with white women: Why dialogues are difficult. In A. Gonzalez, M. Houston, & V. Chen (Eds.), *Our voices: Essays in culture, ethnicity, and communication* (pp. 187–194). Los Angeles: Roxbury.

Hymes, D. (1962). The ethnography of speaking. In T. Gladwin & W. C. Sturtevant (Eds.), *Anthropology and human behavior* (pp. 13–53). Washington, DC: Anthropological Society of Washington.

————. (1972). Models of the interaction of language and social life. In J. Gumperz & D. Hymes (Eds.), *Directions in sociolinguistics: The ethnography of communication* (pp. 35–71). Cambridge, UK: Cambridge University Press.

Kochman, T. (1981). *Black and white: Styles in conflict.* Chicago: University of Chicago Press.

Kramarae, C. (1981). *Women and men speaking.* Rowley, MA: Newbury House.

————, Thorne, B., & Henley, N. (1983). Similarities and differences in language, speech, and nonverbal communication: An annotated bibliography. In B. Thorne, C. Kramarae, & N. Henley (Eds.), *Language, gender, and society* (pp. 151–342). Rowley, MA: Newbury House.

Kurtz, P .D., Jarvis, S. V., & Kurtz, G. L. (1991). Problems of homeless youths: Empirical findings and human services. *Social Work, 36*(4), 309–314.

Lieberg, M. (1995). Teenagers and public space. *Communication Research, 22*(6), 720–744.

Nakayama, T. K., & Krizek, R. L. (1995). Whiteness: A strategic rhetoric. *Quarterly Journal of Speech, 81,* 291–309.

Nelson, K. (1995). The child welfare response to youth violence and homelessness in the nineteenth century. *Child Welfare, 74*(1), 56–70.

Philipsen, G. (1992). *Speaking culturally: Explorations in social communication.* Albany: State University of New York Press.

————. (1997). A theory of speech codes. In G. Philipsen & T. L. Albrecht (Eds.), *Developing communication theories* (pp. 119–156). Albany: State University of New York Press.

————, & Carbaugh, D. (1986). A bibliography of fieldwork in the ethnography of communication. *Language in Society, 15,* 387–398.

Schneider, D. (1976). Notes toward a theory of culture. In K. Basso & H. Shelby (Eds.), *Meaning in anthropology* (pp. 197–220). Albuquerque: University of New Mexico Press.

Scollon, R., & Wong-Scollon, S. (1981). Athabaskan-English interethnic communication. In *Narrative, literacy, and face in interethnic communication* (pp. 11–37). Norwood, NJ: Ablex.

Scollon, R., & Wong-Scollon, S. (1995). *Intercultural communication: A discourse approach.* Cambridge, UK: Blackwell.

Varenne, H. (1977). *Americans together: Structured diversity in a midwestern town.* New York: Teachers College Press.

————. (Ed.). (1986). *Symbolizing America.* Lincoln: University of Nebraska Press.

Zinn, H. (1995). *A people's history of the United States, 1492–present.* New York: Harper-Perennial.

Concepts and Questions

1. What is Dollar referring to when she speaks of "speech communities"? Can you think of some speech communities not mentioned by Dollar?

2. How are speech communities and culture related?

3. What does Dollar mean when she writes that "speech codes reflect much of the organized diversity within any culture"?

4. How does Dollar demonstrate the idea that "a language does not serve all its users equally"?

5. Explain in your own words the following hypothesis advanced by Dollar: "Members of a common culture do not necessarily share a common code for communicating even though they share a common language."

6. How are street youths using the word *family?* Why is that word important to them?

7. In what ways does the use of profanity differ when used by the co-culture of street youth and the dominant culture?

8. How does the closing of interaction differ when the co-culture of street youths interacts with members of the dominant culture? Why does Dollar believe these differences exist?

9. How does Dollar demonstrate the points that members of the dominant culture "objectified" youth during interaction?

10. How does Dollar demonstrate differences in "conversational control"?

Language Matters

Aaron Castelan Cargile

One of the many challenges we face as participants in intercultural encounters is coping with language differences. In some cases, we may not speak the same language as our conversational partner. When not a single word in an exchange can be understood, the challenge of successful communication is quite obvious. In other cases, however, our partner may be at least competent (if not fluent) in our language, or vice versa. On these occasions, it may seem that the challenge of coping with language differences is minimal or nonexistent. Yet it must be realized that even when interacting people speak the same language, such as English, they don't always speak the same "language."

Consider, for example, a New York businessman interviewing a West Virginian job candidate who answers questions with an Appalachian drawl. Or imagine a teacher correcting her African American pupils' use of the word *hood,* or a hurried store manager addressing a complaint from a customer speaking in a slow and measured pace. In these situations, the participants may both be speaking English and their words may indeed be mutually intelligible, but these interactions can often leave them feeling misunderstood and without a sense of connection. This is because the language used in these examples, while seemingly the same, is really different: The speakers employed different accents, vocabularies, and different rates of speech than the listeners. And it is these seemingly minor language differences that usually present one of the biggest challenges to successful intercultural communication.

This original essay appears here for the first time. All rights reserved. Permission to reprint must be obtained from the author and the publisher. Aaron Cargile teaches in the Department of Communication Studies, California State University, Long Beach.

THE DIFFICULTIES OF LANGUAGE DIFFERENCES

In most instances, it is human nature to prefer similarity to difference. Research demonstrates that people tend to like others who possess attitudes and traits similar to their own, and to dislike others with dissimilar attitudes and traits (e.g., Byrne, 1971; Byrne & Clore, 1970; Clore & Byrne, 1974). Consequently, friendships are formed more readily with people perceived to be similar (Kim, 1991; Lea & Duck, 1982), and people from similar groups (e.g., culture groups, religious groups, sport team groups, etc.) are typically treated better than people from other different groups (Hinkle & Schopler, 1986; Mullen, Brown, & Smith, 1992; Turner, Brown, & Tajfel, 1979).

This preference for similarity is part of the interculturally relevant phenomenon of *ethnocentrism*. According to Sumner (1940), ethnocentrism occurs when members of a culture view themselves as the center of everything, and judge other cultures according to the standards and practices of their own culture. Of course, when others are judged relative to one's own culture, those who are most similar appear to be better. Ethnocentrism occurs naturally in people across all cultures. Unfortunately, this can be compounded when language differences are encountered.

When most people read the term *language differences*, they often think of situations in which communicators must express themselves in two different linguistic systems—for example, Japanese and French. As mentioned earlier, this situation presents an obvious challenge. To communicate without the help of a translator, participants are usually forced to use a series of grunts, gestures, or some limited vocabulary, in a struggle to convey even the most basic idea. (Try using just your body to ask a classmate, "Where is the airport?") Situations such as these may result in frustration and miscommunication, but at least participants are aware of their difficulties. In an effort to work around them, people are likely to accept, and even invite, messages or modes of expression that they would not consider "normal" otherwise (e.g., making airplane noises in an attempt to refer to the airport). These are situations in which

people generally tolerate other, comparably minor, differences between their own and another's use of language because without such tolerance, no communication could take place.

In addition to the language differences that occur when two different systems of symbolic code are used, language differences also may be present even when the same symbolic code is used—for example, when both participants speak fluent English. As described earlier, people can speak with different accents, different vocabularies, and different rates of speech, to name only a few of the many behaviors referred to by the term *language* (see Bradac, 1990). These kinds of language differences present participants with other sorts of difficulties. When the New York businessman interviews the West Virginian job applicant, he comprehends with little difficulty what is being said. Chances are, however, that he probably will not feel completely at ease during the interaction or afterward when he decides the other person's fate of employment. Sadly, these feelings may come regardless of what the applicant has said. The applicant may be thoroughly qualified for the job, and he may answer all interview questions satisfactorily, but the words running through the businessman's mind may be the same as those heard by June Tyler during a closed door meeting with a senior partner in a law firm, "Be careful about hiring anyone with a mountain accent" (Pasternak, 1994, p. A16). The discomfort felt by the businessman when faced with this fully qualified job applicant is an example of a second class of difficulties that can be brought about by language differences. These are not difficulties of comprehension; they are difficulties of fair evaluation and equal treatment, and they present a larger challenge to intercultural communication because people tend to be less aware of them.

In the above example, it could be the case that the New York businessman is consciously aware of his decision to discriminate against the job applicant based on his Appalachian accent. Though such discrimination is illegal, many people freely admit that a Southern accent is oftentimes inappropriate and will suggest that it should be abandoned in favor of other accents. For example, soon after Atlanta was awarded the 1996 summer Olympics, a column appeared in the *Atlanta Business Chronicle* encouraging citizens to "get the South out of our mouth" in order to impress the expected visitors (reported in Pearl, 1991). Unlike the open prejudice in this example, however, it is also possible that the businessman would not be aware of his discriminatory motives. Instead, he might experience only some general sense that the applicant was not quite as "sharp" as the others, and that he or she somehow did not "seem right" for the job, even though these impressions could unknowingly be fostered by the speaker's accent. Whether or not he is aware of it, the businessman's naturally developed ethnocentrism can lead him to evaluate and treat people who speak with different accents less favorably than similar sounding others.

In the case of accented speech, it is difficult to predict whether or not a listener will be consciously aware of the language difference. Depending on the person, the situation, and the specific accents involved, someone else's accent may seem as if it stands out, or it may blend in imperceptibly. When it comes to other, less complex language differences, such as those in vocabulary or speech rate, it is even less likely that the listener will hold conscious awareness of those differences. You may not often realize when someone speaks more slowly than you do, but you may still have the vague impression that they are not quite "with it." As this example suggests, awareness is not necessary for language differences to affect our judgment and treatment of other people. Sadly, this is what makes seemingly "minor" language differences particularly problematic. Unlike the earlier example in which the obviousness of the language differences held the promise of making people more tolerant of one another's behaviors, the less perceptible differences are more difficult to account for and cope with because of their relative subtlety. As a consequence, it becomes easier for us to put down and discriminate on the basis of language against someone who speaks our language differently than someone who does not speak it at all does.

Although language can be studied from a variety of behavioral perspectives, our attitudes toward language differences and their influence on intercultural communication can be traced to three major characteristics: accents, speech styles, and speech rates.

ACCENTS

Of the language behaviors that have been investigated, accent is one of the most revealing. Research has shown that listeners have clear attitudes toward those who speak "differently." American listeners who themselves speak with a standard American accent, consistently prejudge others with "Appalachian," "Spanish," "German," and "African American" vernacular-accented speech as less intelligent, poorer, less educated, and less status-possessing than standard accented speakers (Bradac & Wisegarver, 1984; Johnson & Buttny, 1982; Ryan & Carranza, 1975; Tucker & Lambert, 1969). For example, Bishop (1979) found that white female respondents evaluated African American confederates as less responsible and less desirable co-workers when they spoke "black" as opposed to "white" English. Similarly, Giles, Williams, Mackie, and Rosselli (1995) discovered that Anglo respondents rated the same bi-dialectical speaker as less literate and more lower class when he spoke English with a "Hispanic" accent, compared to an "Anglo" accent.

Surprisingly, though, standard accented listeners are not the only ones who look down on many nonstandard accented speakers. Even listeners who themselves speak with a nonstandard accent often judge that others who sound like themselves have low social standing. For example, a study by Doss and Gross (1992) revealed that African American respondents perceive same-race standard English speakers as more competent than those who spoke African American vernacular English. As this last example suggests, the complex reality of intercultural communication is not that we think badly of everyone who speaks differently. Indeed, research indicates that some "foreign" accented speakers are not perceived by Americans to be less competent or inferior—for example, British-accented English speakers (Stewart, Ryan, & Giles, 1985). Similarly, listeners who speak with a standard accent sometimes judge nonstandard-accented speakers to be equal to standard-accented speakers along some dimensions—for example, being "friendly" and "good natured" (Ryan, Hewstone, & Giles, 1984). In terms of intercultural communication, this accent attitude research makes it abundantly clear that we often prejudge others in unflattering and potentially harmful ways based on accent alone.

SPEECH STYLES

In addition to accent, a speaker's choice of words or grammatical phrase may also lead others to some potentially harmful and erroneous prejudgments. As creatures dependent on and skilled at communicating, we know that a message can be expressed in one of any number of ways. For example, one shopper may say to another, "Hey! Please hand that package of undershirts over here. Thanks." Alternatively, that same shopper might say, "[cough]. Ummm. Excuse me. You wouldn't mind passing that bag of T-shirts to me, would you? Thank you." In both instances, the same idea (or message content) is expressed. However, the speech styles are quite different. In the first message, listeners may gain the impression that the speaker is strong and confident, whereas the second message might suggest that the speaker is weak, uncertain, and, consequently, socially unattractive. Such impressions may or may not be deserved. Regardless, listeners (usually subconsciously) treat the speech styles that our messages take as accurate information about our character and abilities.

Powerful and Powerless Styles

Speech that includes features such as hesitations (e.g., "Umm"), hedges (e.g., "I sort of think so"), tag questions (e.g., "It's cold in here, isn't it?"), and polite forms (e.g., "Excuse me") are called **powerless.** On the other hand, speech styles that exhibit a relative absence of these features are called **powerful.** Powerful and powerless speech styles refer to particular forms of language usage rather than to the notion that all truly powerful and powerless people employ one style or the other. In actuality, research has shown that a significant overlap is found between a so-called powerless style and speech styles typically used by women (Crosby & Nyquist, 1977; Lakoff, 1975; Mulac & Lundell, 1986). This does not indicate, however, that all women are powerless. It simply suggests that the speech style often used by women usually leads others to perceive them as less powerful than men. Indeed, several studies have documented that whomever uses the language features included in this powerless speech style (whether a woman or a man) is thought by listeners to be both less socially attractive (e.g., less trustworthy and less likable) and less competent (e.g., less educated and less intelligent) than others not using this style (Bradac, Hemphill, & Tardy, 1981; Bradac & Mulac, 1984; Erickson, Johnson, Lind, & O'Barr, 1978). Thus, an unintentional choice of words or phrase may unknowingly, both to the speaker and the listener, lead to some unfavorable and potentially inaccurate judgments that can make any type of communication more difficult.

SPEECH RATES

Alongside accent and speech style, speech rate is another important language behavior. Speakers naturally vary in the number of words or syllables they utter per minute. This can be a function of their personality, their age, the situation, or their fluency in a nonnative language. Regardless of the actual source of the speech rate variability, (e.g., is someone speaking slow because he or she is scared, shy, old, or has just learned the language?), listeners consistently think that people who speak faster are more competent and more socially attractive than people with a relatively slow rate of speech (Brown, 1980; Street & Brady, 1982).

There is also some evidence that this relationship between speech rate and listener evaluations is affected by the rate at which the listener him- or herself speaks. As we might expect by realizing that people are ethnocentric, fast-speaking listeners especially prefer others who speak fast, and slow-speaking listeners especially prefer others who speak slow (Giles & Smith, 1979; Street, Brady, & Putman, 1983). Both instances demonstrate yet again that we do not evaluate favorably those who sound different from ourselves.

LANGUAGE-BASED DISCRIMINATION

Up to this point, we have considered evidence that points to the many ways in which language differences can lead to prejudging another's character and ability based on language use alone. These same language differences also can lead to discrimination. Oftentimes, when others sound different from ourselves, we not only think unfavorably of them, but also in many cases treat them unfairly. This fact has been most clearly demonstrated in the case of people who speak with "different" accents.

There are perhaps few contexts in which someone else's behavior is more important for our own well-being than in the employment interview or in the courtroom. In both instances, the fate of people's livelihood—or even their lives—can hang in the balance of decisions made by a selection interviewer or a jury. Because of this, it would seem especially critical to treat people equitably in these situations. Yet even here evidence points to the fact that unfair treatment can be provoked by a speaker's use of language. For example, Seggie (1983) presented standard-accented or nonstandard accented voices to listeners and told them that the speaker stood accused of one of several crimes. On the audiotapes, the speakers were heard protesting their innocence regarding the crime of which they had been accused. Listeners were then asked to make a decision regarding the probable guilt or innocence of the speaker. The results showed that standard-accented speakers were more often seen as guilty when the crime was embezzlement, whereas nonstandard-accented speakers were more often judged guilty when the crime was physical assault. Listeners thus more often associated white-collar crimes with standard-sounding defendants and crimes of violence with nonstandard-sounding defendants. Although these listeners were not actual jury members, the results plainly suggest that people can be treated differently based on their accent alone—treatment that is particularly unfair in the case of a nonstandard-accented speaker accused of a violent crime.

In the case of a job interview, in an important study by Henry and Ginzberg (1985), individuals with different ethnic or racial accents made telephone inquires about jobs advertised in a newspaper. Job applicants who spoke with a nonstandard accent were most often told that jobs had been filled. Applicants with a standard accent, however, were most often invited to appear for a personal interview, even after the nonstandard speakers were informed that applications for the position were no longer being accepted. In a similar study, de la Zerda and Hopper (1979) asked employers from San Antonio, Texas, to predict the likelihood of a speaker being hired for each of three positions: supervisor, skilled technician, and semiskilled laborer. A comparison of standard American- and (Mexican American) Spanish-accented speakers revealed that standard speakers were favored for the supervisor position, whereas Spanish-accented speakers were more likely to be hired for the semiskilled position. It would thus be doubly hard for a Spanish-accented speaker to be hired as a supervisor because he or she would be seen not only as less appropriate for this position, but also as more appropriate for the lower-skilled (and lower-waged) job. Sadly, these and other results (e.g., Giles, Wilson, & Conway, 1981; Kalin & Rayko, 1978) clearly illustrate that people can both be prejudiced against others who sound different and discriminate against these speakers in ways that may jeopardize both their livelihood and their lives.

IMPLICATIONS FOR INTERCULTURAL COMMUNICATORS

This article has shown that humans often develop unfavorable language attitudes about others who speak with accents, use different speech styles, or employ different speaking rates. In addition, we have seen that these same unfavorable attitudes occasionally develop toward similar sounding others. We have also seen how these speech-based attitudes can lead to stereotyping and prejudicial behavior. The connection between this and intercultural communication should be obvious, yet it bears further examination.

The term intercultural communication typically invokes visions of people from two (or more) different countries interacting with one another, as for example, an American customs officer talking with a French tourist. In addition, the term can be applied to interactions between people from the same nation, but from different co-cultures, as in the case of exchanges between Asian Americans and African Americans. Regardless of which type of intercultural communication is being considered, language attitudes are relevant because language use typically varies between intercultural communication participants. As we have learned, language refers to more than the formalized linguistic code used for expression (e.g., English or French); it refers also to speech styles, speech rate, and accent (among other language behaviors). Thus, even intercultural communication participants from the same nation, who grew up speaking the same language, can have systematically different ways of speaking. For example, an Asian American speaker will often have a different accent and speech style than an African American listener. Even in the rare case when language use does not vary (e.g., an African American speaking standard American English with an Anglo-American), the expectation that it will vary ensures the relevancy of language attitudes. Consequently, attitudes about language use remain important features that affect all types of intercultural communication.

When international participants do not share the same native tongue, the language differences are often striking and numerous. This situation provides many opportunities for language attitudes to influence intercultural communication. In these instances, participants not only will speak with different accents, but also may have internalized different ideas about appropriate styles of talk and different abilities to govern their language use. The American customs agent, for example, may form a steadfast and distinctly unfavorable impression of the French tourist who speaks grammatically correct English but with a French accent. To his ear, the tourist's natural accent may make her sound uneducated, her (learned) polite speech style may make her sound powerless, and her unavoidably slow speech rate (which comes when any of us first learn a second language) may make her sound unintelligent. All of these (and other) language differences can combine to create a powerfully negative impression, because attitudes about one language behavior (e.g., accent) can serve to reinforce attitudes about another (e.g., speech rate). Even if the tourist were to perform a favorably appraised language behavior (e.g., to use impressively "big" words), selective perception could cause the customs agent to ignore it. Of course, as we have seen, not all attitudes about foreign-sounding speech is negative. But because a large majority of these attitudes are, language attitudes become a critical impression-formation tool that must be managed carefully in intercultural interactions among international participants.

When participants come from the same nation but different co-cultures, the language differences may not be as striking. Even so, the ability of language attitudes to influence interaction does not diminish; in fact, they may intensify. Co-cultures can still socialize differences in all forms of language behavior. For example, Asian Americans may use polite forms of talk more than Anglo-Americans, and speakers from the South may engage in slower speech than those from the North. Because these differences appear, or because we expect them to appear, language attitudes still play an important role in intercultural communication between co-cultural group members. Consequently, responsible communicators should seek both to understand and to manage their language attitudes.

HOW DO WE MANAGE LANGUAGE ATTITUDES?

As discussed earlier, language attitudes, like many other attitudes and stereotypes, are both a natural and sometimes useful feature of social life. Language not only is a tool for expression, but also can provide valuable information about others in certain situations. For example, slow speech may actually indicate that a speaker is having difficulty organizing his or her thoughts. In other situations however, slow speech may not indicate anything about a speaker's mental processing or capacity. Thus, language attitudes can provide critical, readily available, and yet usually unreliable information about our conversational partners. Given this, how should responsible intercultural communicators manage language attitudes?

The first and most important thing to do is to recognize when your responses to others are based on language attitudes alone, and when they are based on other, more objective, and more reliable information. For example, in universities across the United States, students often respond unfavorably to foreign-born teaching assistants and professors. In fact, on some campuses more than two out of five students withdraw or switch from a class when they find out their teacher is a nonnative speaker of English (Rubin & Smith, 1988). In addition, many other students make complaints of the variety that forced Illinois to pass a fluency law for college instructors (Secter, 1987). Who is responsible for such student dissatisfaction? In some cases, there really are instructors with verifiably poor language skills. In many other cases, though, it may in fact be the stereotypical and prejudicial language attitudes developed by the students themselves that is responsible.

On first hearing an instructor's accent, students often will unknowingly make assumptions about the instructor's personality and (language) skills based solely on their own attitudes toward foreign-accented speakers (e.g., "this teacher isn't too friendly, too smart, and he doesn't speak good English"). The instructor may, in fact, be or do none of the things that the student assumes. Even so, because language attitudes have the power to initiate selective perceptions, the students may create, in their own minds, evidence to support their views. In particular, they may "hear" the instructor make grammatical mistakes that he has not really made (Cargile & Giles, 1996). Students can then, in turn, point to these "mistakes" as justification for their attitudes and a reason for responding unfavorably to the instructor. Thus, a class may end up with an instructor who is in fact friendly, smart, and who speaks grammatically correct and comprehensible English, but because students have unknowingly based their responses on their attitudes toward foreign-accented speech alone, they may feel dissatisfied with their instruction.

As the above scenario illustrates, in the end, the evaluations that we make of other speakers may be more a product of our own attitudes than the speakers' behaviors. The trouble is that we rarely realize this, and as a result we believe the other is entirely responsible for our reactions. Consequently, the first step we should take in dealing with language attitudes is to learn to recognize their role in the evaluation process. Ask yourself, "Am I thinking this about the person only because of the way that he or she speaks?" You may answer "no" to this question; thus indicating that the role that language attitudes are playing is minimal and perhaps justified. You may however answer "yes," suggesting that your attitudes about language use are exerting an undue and likely problematic influence on your behavior. Once you learn to recognize the role language attitudes play in your responses, a second step should be to seek out and integrate additional information into the evaluation process—especially when the answer to the above question is "yes." Your attitudes may lead you to believe one thing about a speaker, but your job as a responsible intercultural communicator is to test, to the best of your abilities, whether your evaluation is accurate and appropriate. For example, in the case of a nonnative English speaking instructor, find out about his or her educational background, prior teaching experience, and real English competency through patient listening (and perhaps some careful questioning) before passing the easy, ready-made judgment that this person lacks the intelligence and ability to be a successful teacher. Of course, this kind of "fact checking" and followup is effortful and never easy. It is, however, critical to managing our language attitudes well. Calling on language attitudes in intercultural interaction is nearly unavoidable. Thus, the secret is to tap their potential as a source of information without being poisoned by their power to lead listeners down a road of prejudice and discrimination.

References

Bishop, G. D. (1979). Perceived similarity in interracial attitudes and behaviors: The effects of belief and dialect style. *Journal of Applied Social Psychology, 9,* 446–465.

Bradac, J. J. (1990). Language attitudes and impression formation. In H. Giles & W. P. Robinson (Eds.), *Handbook of language and social psychology* (pp. 387–412). Chichester, UK: Wiley.

———, Hemphill, M. R., & Tardy, C. H. (1981). Language style of trial: Effects of "powerful and powerless" speech upon judgments of victims and villains. *Western Journal of Speech Communication, 45,* 327–341.

———, & Mulac, A. (1984). Attributional consequences of powerful and powerless speech styles in a crisis intervention context. *Journal of Language and Social Psychology, 3,* 1–20.

———, & Wisegarver, R. (1984). Ascribed status, lexical diversity, and accent: Determinants of perceived status, solidarity, and control of speech style. *Journal of Language and Social Psychology, 3,* 239–255.

Brown, B. L. (1980). Effects of speech rate on personality attributions and competency evaluations. In H. Giles, W. P. Robinson, & P. Smith (Eds.), *Language: Social psy-*

chological perspectives (pp. 294–300). Oxford, UK: Pergamon.

Byrne, D. E. (1971). The attraction paradigm. San Diego, CA: Academic Press.

———, & Clore, G. L. (1970). A reinforcement model of evaluative responses. Personality: An International Journal, 1, 103–128.

Cargile, A., & Giles, H. (1996, November). Language attitudes toward varieties of English: An American Japanese context. Paper presented at the Speech Communication Association annual conference, San Diego, CA.

Clore, G. L., & Byrne, D. E. (1974). A reinforcement affect model of attraction. In T. L. Huston (Ed.), Foundations of interpersonal attraction (pp. 143–170). San Diego, CA: Academic Press.

Crosby, F., & Nyquist, L. (1977). The female register: An empirical study of Lakoff's hypotheses. Language in Society, 6, 519–535.

de la Zerda, N., & Hopper, R. (1979). Employment interviewers' reactions to Mexican American speech. Communication Monographs, 46, 126–134.

Doss, R. C., & Gross, A. M. (1992). The effects of black English on stereotyping in interracial perceptions. The Journal of Black Psychology, 18, 47–58.

Erickson, B., Johnson, B. C., Lind, E. A., & O'Barr, W. (1978). Speech style and impression formation in a court setting: The effects of "powerful" and "powerless" speech. Journal of Experimental Social Psychology, 14, 266–279.

Giles, H., & Smith, P. (1979). Accommodation theory: Optimal levels of convergence. In H. Giles & R. N. S. Clair (Eds.), Language and social psychology (pp. 45–65). Baltimore, MD: University Park Press.

Giles, H., Williams, A., Mackie, D. M., & Rosselli, F. (1995). Reactions to Anglo and Hispanic American accented speakers: Affect, identity, persuasion, and the English only controversy. Language and Communication, 14, 102–123.

Giles, H., Wilson, P., & Conway, A. (1981). Accent and lexical diversity as determinates of impression formation and employment selection. Language Sciences, 3, 92–103.

Henry, F., & Ginzberg, E. (1985). Who gets the work: A test of racial discrimination in employment. Toronto: Urban Alliance on Race Relations and Social Planning Council of Metropolitan Toronto.

Hinkle, S., & Schopler, J. (1986). Bias in the evaluation of in-group and out-group performance. In S. Worchel & W. G. Austin (Eds.), Psychology of intergroup relations (pp. 196–212). Chicago: Nelson Hall.

Johnson, F. L., & Buttny, R. (1982). White listeners' responses to "sounding black" and "sounding white": The effects of message content on judgments about language. Communication Monographs, 49, 33–49.

Kalin, R., & Rayko, D. (1978). Discrimination in evaluative judgments against foreign accented job candidates. Psychological Reports, 43, 1203–1209.

Kim, H. J. (1991). Influence of language and similarity of initial intercultural attraction. In S. Ting Toomey & F. Korzenny (Eds.), Cross cultural interpersonal communication (pp. 213–229). Newbury Park, CA: Sage.

Lakoff, R. (1975). Language and woman's place. New York: Harper & Row.

Lea, M., & Duck, S. (1982). A model for the role of similarity of values in friendship development. British Journal of Social Psychology, 21, 301–310.

Mulac, A., & Lundell, T. L. (1986). Linguistic contributors to the gender-linked language effect. Journal of Language and Social Psychology, 5, 81–101.

Mullen, B., Brown, R., & Smith, C. (1992). In-group bias as a function of salience, relevance, and status: An integration. European Journal of Social Psychology, 22, 103–122.

Pasternak, J. (1994, March 29). Bias blights life outside Appalachia. Los Angeles Times, pp. A1–A16.

Pearl, D. (1991, December 13). Hush mah mouth! Some in South try to lose the drawl. Wall Street Journal, p. A1.

Rubin, D. L., & Smith, K. A. (1988). Effects of accent, ethnicity, and lecture topic on undergraduates' perceptions of nonnative English speaking teaching assistants. International Journal of Intercultural Relations, 14, 337–353.

Ryan, E. B., & Carranza, M. A. (1975). Evaluative reactions of adolescents toward speakers of standard English and Mexican American accented English. Journal of Personality and Social Psychology, 31, 855–863.

Ryan, E. B., Hewstone, M., & Giles, H. (1984). Language and intergroup attitudes. In J. Eiser (Ed.), Attitudinal Judgment (pp. 135–160). New York: Springer.

Secter, B. (1987, September 27). Foreign teachers create language gap in colleges. Los Angeles Times, pp. A1, A26–27.

Seggie, I. (1983). Attribution of guilt as a function of ethnic accent and type of crime. Journal of Multilingual and Multicultural Development, 4, 197–206.

Stewart, M. A., Ryan, E. B., & Giles, H. (1985). Accent and social class effects on status and solidarity evaluations. Personality and Social Psychology Bulletin, 11, 98–105.

Street, R. L., & Brady, R. M. (1982). Speech rate acceptance ranges as a function of evaluative domain, listener speech rate, and communication context. Communication Monographs, 49, 290–308.

Street, R. L., Brady, R. M., & Putman, W. B. (1983). The influence of speech rate stereotypes and rate similarity on listeners' evaluations of speakers. *Journal of Language and Social Psychology, 2,* 37–56.

Sumner, W. G. (1940). *Folkways.* Boston: Ginn & Co.

Tucker, G. R., & Lambert, W. E. (1969). White and Negro listeners' reactions to various American English dialects. *Social Forces, 47,* 463–468.

Turner, J. C., Brown, R. J., & Tajfel, H. (1979). Social comparison and group interest in in-group favoritism. *European Journal of Social Psychology, 9,* 187.

Concepts and Questions

1. Do you believe Cargile is correct when he notes that "research demonstrates that people tend to like others who possess attitudes and traits similar to their own and to dislike others with dissimilar attitudes and traits"?

2. How do language differences compound the problems associated with ethnocentrism?

3. Can you think of examples that illustrate Cargile's point that "language differences also may be present even when the same symbolic code is used"?

4. According to Cargile, what are examples of situations in which accents influenced someone's perception of another person? Has accent ever influenced your perception of another person? How?

5. Can you think of examples in your own life when a speaker's choice of words or grammatical phrases may have contributed to some harmful and erroneous prejudgments?

6. Why is speaking rate a variable in intercultural communication? What cultures have you interacted with that speak at a rate different than your own? Did that influence your encounter with the person?

7. In what settings do we most often see discrimination based on speech differences?

8. Do you agree with Cargile when he asserts that "when participants come from the same nation, but different co-cultures, the language differences may not be as striking"?

9. According to Cargile, how should responsible intercultural communicators manage language attitudes?

Irish Conversations

MARTIN J. GANNON

I t is a truism that the use of language is essential for the development of culture, and most, if not all, cultural groups take great pride in their native languages. Thus it is not surprising that voice is one of the four essential elements of opera, the metaphor for Italy. In the case of Ireland, it was the brutal English rule over the nation extending over several centuries that essentially made the Irish an aural people whose love of language and conversation was essential for the preservation of their heritage. More specifically, the intersection between the original Irish language, Irish Gaelic, and English has made the Irish famous for their eloquence, scintillating conversations, and unparalleled success in fields where the use of the English language is critical, such as writing, law, and teaching.

Ireland as we know it today began to emerge in 1916 when a small group of Irish patriots commandeered the old post office building in Dublin on Easter Sunday. The English executed the rebellion's 15 leaders, which sparked a war against the English that led to the modern division of Ireland into two parts: the Protestant north with a minority Catholic population and the Catholic south. The focus of this chapter is the Catholic south, which occupies five sixths of the land.

Supposedly, everybody knows everybody else's business in a country village. Ireland largely comprises such small country villages and its culture reflects this fact. Whenever the Irish meet, one of the first things they generally do is determine one another's place of origin. The conversation usually helps to identify common relatives and friends. Given the wide circle of friends and acquaintances that the Irish tend to make in their lives, it is usually not difficult to find a link.

Ireland's size is little more than 1% of that of the continental United States. It lies to the west of Great Britain, to which it is economically tied. Ireland has

From Martin J. Gannon and Associates, *Understanding Global Cultures* (Thousand Oaks, CA: Sage Publications, 1994), pp. 179–194. Reprinted by permission of Sage Publications.

four major cities: Dublin, Cork, Limerick, and Galway. In the early 1970s, more than 60% of the workforce was employed in agriculture, but today only 16% can be found in that line of work because of the transition to a more industrialized society. Although the country has modernized significantly in the past 20 years, it is still far behind many of its European neighbors. Also, many of its young people emigrate, largely because of a lack of jobs, an expensive welfare system, and a correspondingly high tax rate. Most Irish families have sons, daughters, or close relatives who have emigrated.

Because of the high level of education in modern Ireland, Irish immigrants do well in other countries, but many would like to return to Ireland simply because it is a "being" society in which the quality of life is valued more than the pursuit of monetary gain. Ireland did become part of the EC in 1973, which should help the country economically in the long run.

The importance of conversation to the Irish makes it a fitting metaphor for the nation. However, to understand the metaphor fully, we need to explore the intersection of Irish Gaelic and English, after which we can focus on an essential Irish conversation, praying to God and the saints. The free-flowing nature of Irish conversation is also one of its essential characteristics, as are the places where conversations are held.

INTERSECTION OF GAELIC AND ENGLISH

The Irish are a people who tend to enjoy simple pleasures, but the complexity of their thought patterns and culture can be baffling to outsiders. They generally have an intense love of conversation and storytelling and have been accused often of talking just to hear the sound of their own voices. The Irish use the English language in ways that are not found in any other culture. They do not just give a verbal answer, they construct a vivid mental picture that is pleasing to the mind as well as the ear. With the transition from Gaelic to English, the Irish created vivid images in Gaelic and expressed them in English; the vivid imagery of many Irish writers originated in the imaginative storytelling that was historically a critical part of social conversation. To the Irish, Gaelic was a graphic, living language that was

appropriate for expressing the wildest of ideas in a distinctive and pleasing manner.

Because of the slow arrival of electronic technology in Ireland and the country's long suppression and isolation, the talent for conversation is an art form that has not yet been lost. Among the Irish, food tends to be secondary to conversation, and a visitor will often observe that the Irish seem to forget about their food until it is almost cold. If, however, an Irishman admonishes a countryman for eating too much or too quickly, the witty reply is frequently to the effect that one never knows when the next famine will occur. This emphasis on the primacy of conversation is in contrast to the practice found in other cultures, such as the Italian and French, where not only conversation but also food is prized.

If the size of the population is taken into account, it seems that Ireland has produced many more prominent essayists, novelists, and poets than any other country since approximately 1870. This prominence reflects the intersection of the Gaelic and English languages and the aural bias of the Irish. They also have produced great musicians who combine music and words in a unique way. Conversely, the Irish have not produced a major visual artist equal to those of other European countries, and their achievements in science are modest.

There are countless examples that could be used to illustrate this intersection, but the opening words of James Joyce's (1964) *Portrait of the Artist as a Young Man*, in which he first introduced the technique of stream of consciousness, aptly serve the purpose:

> "Once upon a time and a very good time it was there was a moocow coming down along the road and this moocow that was coming down along the road met a nicens little boy named baby tuckoo."
>
> His father told him that story; his father looked at him through a glass; he had a hairy face.
>
> "He was a baby tuckoo. The moocow came down the road where Betty Byrne lived: She sold lemon platt.
>
> "O, the wild rose blossoms
> "On the little green place.
> "He sang that song. That was his song.
> "O, the green wothe botheth." (p. 1)

There are several points about this brief but pertinent passage that deserve mention. It expresses a rural bias that befits Ireland, and it reflects the vivid

Gaelic language in which Joyce was proficient. Also, it immediately captures the imagination but leaves the reader wondering what is going to happen: He must read further if he wants to capture the meaning, and it seems that the meaning will become clear only in the most circuitous way. Further, although the essence of the passage is mundane, it is expressed in a captivating manner. The reader is pleasantly surprised by the passage and eagerly awaits additional pleasant surprises. In many ways this passage is an ideal example of the manner in which Gaelic Irish and English intersect. And, although some of the modern Irish and Irish-Americans may not be aware of these historical antecedents, their patterns of speech and thought tend to reflect this intersection.

Perhaps the most imaginatively wild of the modern Irish writers to incorporate the intersection of the Gaelic and English languages in his work is Myles na gCopaleen, who also used the pseudonym Flann O'Brien. He wrote some of his novels and stories in Gaelic and others in English. Even the titles of his books are indicative of this imaginative focus: for example, *The Poor Mouth: A Bad Story About The Hard Life* (O'Brien, 1974). "Putting on the poor mouth" means making a pretense of being poor or in bad circumstances to gain advantage for oneself from creditors or prospective creditors, and the book is a satire on the rural life of western Ireland. His masterpiece, *At Swim-Two-Birds* (O'Brien, 1961), sets the scene for a confrontation between "Mad Sweeny" and "Jem Casey" in the following way:

> *Synopsis, being a summary of what has gone before,* FOR THE BENEFIT OF NEW READERS: *Dermit Trellis,* an eccentric author, conceives the project of writing a salutary book on the consequences which follow wrongdoing and creates for the purpose
>
> The Pooka Fergus MacPhellimey, a species of human Irish devil endowed with magical power. He then creates John Furriskey, a depraved character, whose task is to attack women and behave at all times in an indecent manner. By magic he is instructed by Trellis to go one night to Donnybrook where he will by arrangement meet and betray. . . . (p. 563)

The remaining characters are sequentially introduced in the same imaginative way.

In the area of music, the Chieftains, who have performed together for more than 25 years, represent the distinctive approach of the Irish to music. Their songs, played on traditional instruments, are interspersed with classic Irish dances and long dialogues that sometimes involve the audience. Similarly, Thomas Moore, who lived in the 19th century, is sometimes cited as the composer who captured the essence of the intersection of the Gaelic and English languages in such poetic songs as "Believe Me If All Those Endearing Young Charms," which he wrote for a close friend and beautiful woman whose face was badly scarred in a fire (Moore, 1857):

> Believe me, if all those endearing young charms
> Which I gaze on so fondly today
> Were to fade by tomorrow and fleet in my arms
> Like fairy gifts fading away.
> Thou woust still be ador'd
> As this moment thou art
> Let thy loveliness fade as it will.
> And upon the dear ruin
> Each wish of my heart
> Would intwine itself verdantly still. (p. 214)

A constant reminder that the Irish are radically different from the English and Americans is their brogue. When the conversion from speaking Gaelic to speaking English was occurring, this brogue was an embarrassment for many Irish. The English looked down on these "inferior" people who were unable to speak "proper" English (Waters, 1984). Today, the brogue is prized by the Irish and appreciated throughout the world.

Given that Ireland is a rural society in which unhurried conversation is prized, it should be no surprise that it is more of a "being" than a "doing" society in which there is a balanced approach to life. In fact, many of the Irish are astonished at the "doing" entrepreneurial activities of their 44 million Irish-American counterparts who have made St. Patrick's Day, which remains a holy day in Ireland, into a fun-loving time for partying that embraces all people (Milbank, 1993). The Irish generally take life much more slowly than Americans, who tend to watch the clock constantly and rush from one activity to another. No matter how rushed the Irish may be, they normally have time to stop and talk.

The Irish also tend to place more importance on strong friendships and extended family ties than do Americans. Nothing illustrates this emphasis more than the behavior of many early Irish immigrants when they first arrived in the United States. They settled near other friends or relatives who had preceded them to the United States and developed a reputation for being very clannish. But slowly the Irish love of conversation and curiosity about all things led to their interaction with others and their Americanization.

PRAYER AS CONVERSATION

Prayer or a conversation with God is one of the most important parts of an Irish life. More than 95% of the population is Roman Catholic, and regular attendance at Sunday mass is estimated at 87% of the population, the highest percentage of any country in the world. Almost every Catholic household contains crucifixes and religious pictures. These serve as outward reminders of the people's religious beliefs and duties.

Further, this prayer is accompanied by acts of good works that stem directly from the strong ethical and moral system of the Irish. They are recognized as having made the highest per capita donation to relief efforts in countries such as Ethiopia, and they are quick to donate their time, energy, and even lives to help those living in execrable conditions. The extent of the crisis in Somalia, for instance, was first reported to the United Nations by Mary Robinson, president of Ireland, and an Irish nurse was killed after arriving in Somalia to help out.

The separation between church and state found in most countries does not exist in Ireland. Until 1972 when Ireland joined the EC, a constitutional amendment guaranteed a special status to the Roman Catholic church. The Church did not oppose the removal of this amendment because it was secure in its majority (Bell, 1991). Such a secure outlook was well justified because little has changed except for the working of the constitution, and the Church plays an important role throughout the life of the Irish.

The state relies on the works of the Catholic church to support most of its social service programs. For example, most of the hospitals are run by the Catholic church rather than by the state. These hospitals are partially funded with state money and are staffed with nuns, when possible. The state has little control over how the money is spent, especially because it lacks the buildings and the power to replace the Church-run system that was in place when the state was formed.

The national school (state) system is also under the control of the various religious dominations in Ireland. It is the primary source of education for primary schoolchildren. The state funds the system, but the schools are run by local boards, which are almost always controlled by the clergy. There is a separate national school for each major religion. The local Catholic national school is managed by the local parish priest, whereas the Protestant vicar has his own separate school. Many instructors in these schools are nuns or brothers who work very inexpensively and keep the costs much lower than the state could. Conversely, in the United States it is no longer lawful even to pray in public schools. In exchange for these lower costs, the state has relinquished control. This is really the Church's last line of defense, because it has the ability to instill Catholic morality and beliefs in almost every young Irish child in the country.

In many ways the Catholic church does not actually influence the state's actions. Rather, it relies on Catholic lay groups to uphold the Church's teachings and to pressure the state. These watchdog groups can be quite vocal and often wield considerable power in their communities. Many times they are more conservative than the local parish priest. As the Irish become better educated and gain greater exposure to the rest of Europe, the preeminent position of the Church is slowly being eroded. However, as long as the Catholic church continues to control the primary school system, it will have a significant influence on the people's attitudes.

The Church also influences society by censoring books and artistic material, which has caused many Irish artists such as James Joyce and Sean O'Casey to leave Ireland to enjoy greater freedom in their work. The Irish have to travel to Britain or to Northern Ireland to purchase outlawed books or to see movies written by their Irish countrymen.

Sunday Mass is a special occasion in Ireland, and the entire family attends. On this occasion everyone wears his or her Sunday best. One Irish woman tells the story of returning home for a visit from the United States and, on Sunday morning, being asked by her mother if she did not have a better dress to wear to church; she had become lax in her church dress after spending several years in the United States. During Mass it is not unusual to see all the women and children sitting in the front of the church and the men standing or sitting in the back. This dichotomy does not mean that the Irish believe religion should be left to women and children; it only reflects the specific gender roles in Ireland, which are gradually changing, but at a rate that is slower than in other Western countries.

The Irish tend to begin and end their day with prayer. This is their opportunity to tell God their troubles and their joys. One of the more common prayers is that Ireland may one day be reunited. This act of talking to God helps to form a personal relationship between the Irish and their God. It is difficult to ignore the dictates of God, because He is such a personal and integral part of the daily Irish life. God is also present in daily life in the living personification of the numerous priests, brothers, and sisters found in Ireland. They are not shut away in cloisters, but interact with the laity throughout the day.

Entering the religious life is seen as a special calling for the Irish. In the past when families were very large, it was common for every family to give at least one son or daughter to the religious life. It was the greatest joy for an Irish mother to know that her son or daughter was in God's service, which was prized more highly than a bevy of grandchildren. Vocations to religious life have decreased in recent years, but Ireland still has many more priests per capita than most other Catholic countries.

In the Republic of Ireland there are few problems between Catholics and other religious groups, unlike the situation that exists in Northern Ireland. In fact, Catholics enjoy having Protestants in their communities, and they treat them with great respect. In one rural area where the Protestant congregation had dwindled, the Catholic parish helped Protestants with fund raising to make repairs to their church. This act of charity illustrates the great capacity for giving that the Irish possess, because generally they are not greatly attached to material possessions and are quite willing to share what they have with the world.

A FREE-FLOWING CONVERSATION: IRISH HOSPITALITY

Conversations with the Irish are known to take many strange turns, and one may end up discussing a subject and not knowing how it arose. Also, it is not only what is said that is important, but also the manner in which it is expressed. The Irish tend to be monochronic, completing one activity before going on to another, yet they cannot resist divergences and tangents in their conversations or their lives. They often feel that they are inspired by an idea that must be shared with the rest of the world regardless of what the other person may be saying. The Irish tend to respect this pattern of behavior and are quite willing to change the subject, which can account for the breadth of their conversations as well as their length.

Like their conversations, the Irish tend to be curious about all things foreign or unfamiliar, and they are quick to extend a hand in greeting and to start a conversation, usually a long one.

It is not unusual for the Irish to begin a conversation with a perfect stranger, but for most of the Irish there are no strangers—only people they have not had the pleasure of conversing with. The Irish do not usually hug in public, but this in no way reduces the warmth of their greeting. They often view Americans as too demonstrative and are uncomfortable with public displays of affection. They tend to be a very hospitable, trusting, and friendly people. Nothing illustrates this outlook more than their national greeting, "Cead mile failte" ("One hundred thousand welcomes"), which is usually accompanied by a handshake.

In addition, the Irish are famous for their hospitality toward both friends and strangers. As Delany (1974) points out: "In the olden days, anyone who had partaken of food in an Irishman's home was considered to be secure against harm or hurt from any member of the family, and no one was ever turned away" (p. 103). This spirit of hospitality still exists in Ireland. In the country, the Irish tend to keep their doors not only unlocked but also open. Whenever someone is passing by or asking for directions, it is difficult for them to leave without being asked into the house to have something to eat or drink. It is not unusual for the Irish to meet someone in the afternoon and invite him or her to their home for supper that evening, and this happens not only in the country but also the cities. They welcome people into their family and bring out their best china, linen, and the finest foods. Meals are accompanied by great conversation by both young and old.

Many of the Irish do not believe in secrets and, even if they did, it would be hard to imagine them being able to keep one. They seem quite willing to tell the world their business and expect their visitors to do the same.

However, the Irish are often unwilling to carry on superficial conversations. They enjoy a conversation that deals with something of substance, and they are well-known for breaking the often-quoted American social rule that one should not discuss politics or religion in public. The Irish enjoy nothing more than to discuss these subjects and to spark a deep philosophical conversation.

PLACES OF CONVERSATIONS: IRISH FRIENDS AND FAMILIES

There really is no place where the Irish would find it difficult to carry on a conversation. They are generally quite willing to talk about any subject at any time, but there are several places that have a special meaning for the Irish. Conversation in the home is very important for an Irish family. It is also one of the major social activities of an Irish public house or pub.

The typical Irish family is closely knit, and its members describe their activities to one another in great detail. Meal time is an event in the Irish household that should not be missed by a family member, not so much because of the food but the conversation. In fact, as noted previously, the food is really secondary to the conversation, and sometimes the Irish even forget to eat or delay doing so until the food is cold. Supper is the time of day when family members gather together to pray, eat, and update one another on their daily activities. The parents usually ask the children about their day in school and share the events of their own day.

Education and learning have always been held in high regard by the Irish. Teachers are treated with great respect in the community, and their relatively high salaries reflect their worth to the community. Ireland has a literacy rate of 99% because of compulsory national education. College education is available to all through government grants for those who cannot afford university fees. Given the dearth of employment opportunities, college students often complete a postgraduate degree before entering the job market.

The Irish who emigrate normally bring with them a well-rounded education that is valued by employers abroad. Still, even when the Irish have advanced formal training, they generally do not flaunt it.

A frequent topic of conversation at family dinners is news of extended family, friends, or neighbors. The Irish have an intense interest in the activities of their extended family and friends, but this interest is not for the pure sake of gossip. They generally are quick to congratulate on good news and even quicker to rally around in times of trouble or need. When someone is sick, it is not unusual for all of the person's friends and family to spend almost all of their time at the hospital. They help the family with necessary tasks and entertain one another with stories and remembrances. Many of the Irish have a difficult time understanding the American pattern in which the nuclear family handles emergencies and problems by itself.

This practice holds true whenever there is a death in the community. Everyone gathers together to hold an Irish wake, which combines the viewing of the body with a party that may last for two or three days. There is plenty of food, drinking, laughing, conversation, music, games, and storytelling. Presumably the practice of a wake originated because people had difficulty traveling in Ireland over poor roads and by nonmechanized means of transportation, and the wake afforded an opportunity not only to pay respect to the deceased but also to renew old friendships and reminisce. Although the problems of travel have been solved, the Irish still cling to this ancient way of saying goodbye to the deceased and uplifting the spirits of those left behind.

An event that is as important as the wake is a wedding; it is a time of celebration for the entire family and neighborhood. There is customarily a big church wedding followed by a sit-down dinner and an evening of dancing and merriment. Registry office weddings are very rare in Ireland, as might be expected in this conservative and Catholic-dominated nation. Young people usually continue to live with their parents until they are married, and then they frequently buy a home close to them.

Irish parents are generally quite strict with their children. They set down definite rules that must be followed. Irish children are given much less freedom than American children, and they usually spend all day with their parents on Sunday and may accompany them to a dance or to the pub in the evening. Parents are usually well acquainted with the families of their children's friends and believe in group activities. The tight social community in which the Irish live makes it difficult for children to do anything without their parents' knowledge. There is always a third cousin or kindly neighbor who is willing to keep tabs on the behavior of children and report back to parents, some of whom have even managed to stretch their watchful eyes across the Atlantic to keep tabs on their children living in the United States. This close control can sometimes be difficult for young people, but it creates a strong support network that is useful in times of trouble.

A frequent gathering place for men, women, and children is the local pub, because the drinking age is not enforced throughout most of Ireland. There are two sections in most pubs: The plain workingman's part and the decorated part where the cost of a pint of beer is slightly higher. In the not-too-distant past, it was seen as unbecoming for a woman to enter a pub; there are still some pubs in which women are comfortable only in the decorated part, and they typically order half-pints of beer, whereas the men order pints. Normally, the pubs do not serve food, which may reflect the Irish de-emphasis of food noted previously.

Pubs tend to be very informal, often without waiters or waitresses and with plenty of bar and table space. Young and old mingle in the pub, often conversing with one another and trading opinions. The Irish are raised with a great respect for their elders and are quite comfortable carrying on a conversation with a person of any age or background. They tend to be a democratic people by nature and, although they may not agree with a person's opinion, they will usually respect him or her for having formed one.

Irish pubs are probably the site of the most lively conversations held in Ireland. The Irish tend to be a very sociable people who generally do not believe in drinking alone. This pattern of behavior has often resulted in their reputation for being alcoholics. Many Irish drink more than they should, but the problem often appears worse than it is because almost all of their drinking takes place in public. Further, co-workers and their superiors frequently socialize in pubs, and they tend to evaluate one another in terms of not only on-the-job performance but also their ability to converse skillfully in such a setting. The favorite drink of the Irish is Guinness, a strong black stout. It is far more popular than the well-known Irish whiskey.

Even more important than a good drink in a pub is good conversation. The Irish are famous for their storytelling, and it is not unusual to find an entire pub silent while one man tells an ancient folktale or what happened to him that afternoon. It is also not unusual for someone to recite a Shakespearean play from memory in its entirety.

Besides stories, many a heated argument can erupt in a pub. The Irish seem to have a natural love of confrontation in all things, and the conversation does not even have to be about something that affects their lives. They are fond of exchanging opinions on many abstract issues and world events. It is during these sessions at the pub that the Irish sharpen their conversational skills. However, although these conversations can become heated, they rarely become violent.

Irish friends, neighbors, and families visit one another on a regular basis. As indicated above, rarely if ever is one turned away from the door. In fact, the door is usually kept open, and visitors are expected to walk right in. Family and friends know that they are always welcome and that they will be given something to eat and drink. It is not unusual for visitors to arrive late in the evening and stay until almost morning. Such visits are usually not made for any special purpose other than conversation, which is the mainstay of the Irish life no matter where it is held.

ENDING A CONVERSATION

A conversation with an Irishman can be such a long and exciting adventure that a person thinks it will never end. It will be hard to bring the conversation to a close because the Irish always seem to have the last word. Ireland is a country that welcomes its visitors and makes them feel so comfortable and accepted that it is hard to break free and return home after an afternoon or evening of conversation.

Geert Hofstede's (1980) research profiling the value orientation of 40 nations includes Ireland, and his analysis confirms many of our observations. Ireland is a masculine-oriented society in which sex roles are clearly differentiated, but the status of women clearly has improved during the past 20 years. However, it is not an acquisition-oriented society, as Hofstede's classification might suggest, but a "being-oriented" society in which the quality of life is given precedence over material rewards.

Further, Ireland clusters with those countries emphasizing individualism, as we might expect of a people who are willing and eager to explore and talk about serious and conflict-laden topics. Individualism is expressed through conversation and views on issues that affect society; major tasks are unlikely to be performed by the individual, and entrepreneurship is not a strong trait among the Irish. Individualism is also expressed in other talents such as writing, art, and music. As suggested previously, music offers its own means of conversation, and Ireland reportedly has one of the highest number of musicians per capita of all countries. Still, the Irish tend to be collectivist in their emphasis on the family, religion, a very generous welfare system, and the acceptance of strong labor unions.

Ireland also falls into the category of countries emphasizing a strong desire to meet new people and challenges (low uncertainty avoidance). And, with the possible exception of the high status accorded to the clergy, the Irish cluster with those countries that attempt to diminish social class and power differences as much as possible.

In short, the Irish tend to be an optimistic people who are ready to accept the challenges that life presents, although there is a melancholy strain in many of the Irish that is frequently attributed to the long years of English rule and the rainy weather. They usually confront things head-on and are ready to take on the world if necessary. They can be quite creative in their solutions, but also quite stubborn when asked to compromise, and they tend to be truly happy in the middle of a heated but stimulating conversation. Given their history and predilections, it is not surprising that the Irish prefer personal situations and professional fields of work where their aural-focused approach to reality can be given wide reign, even after they have spent several generations living in countries such as the United States and Australia.

References

Beckett, J. D. (1986). *A Short History of Ireland*. London: Cresset Library.

Bell, B. (1991). *Insight Guides: Ireland*. Singapore: APA Publications.

Delany, M. (1974). *Of Irish Ways*. Minneapolis: Dillon.

Hofstede, G. (1980). *Culture's Consequences*. Beverly Hills: Sage.

Joyce, J. (1964). *Portrait of the Artist as a Young Man*. New York: Viking Press.

Melbank, D. (1993). "We Make a Bit More of St. Patrick's Day Than the Irish Do." *Wall Street Journal*, March 17, pp. A1, A8.

Moore, T. (1857). *The Poetical Works of Thomas Moore*. Boston: Philips, Sampson.

O'Brien, F. (1961). "At swim-two-birds." In U. Mercier and D. Greene (Eds.), *1000 Years of Irish Prose*. New York: Grosset and Dunlap.

O'Brien, F. (1974). *The Poor Mouth: A Bad Story About the Hard Life*. New York: Seaver.

Waters, M. (1984). *The Comic Irishman*. Albany: State University of New York Press.

Concepts and Questions

1. What does Gannon mean when he suggests that "it is a truism that the use of language is essential for the development of culture"?
2. How does the intersection of Gaelic and English affect Irish culture?
3. What role does conversation have in Irish culture?
4. What influence does the Catholic church have in Irish conversation and communication patterns?
5. How might the Irish form of conversation affect intercultural communication?
6. What are some reasons why Ireland, according to Gannon, has produced so many prominent essayists, novelists, and poets since 1870?
7. Do you agree with Gannon when he asserts that "the Irish tend to place more importance on strong friendships and extended family ties than do Americans"? And if true, how is this characteristic related to the role of conversation in both cultures?
8. What does Gannon mean when he notes that "conversations with the Irish are known to take many strange turns, and one may end up discussing a subject and not knowing how it arose"? Does he give examples?
9. How do the wake and wedding contribute to the unique Irish approach to conversation?

chapter 5

Nonverbal Interaction: Action, Sound, and Silence

I t is indeed a truism that we not only communicate with our word but also with our actions. Successful participation in intercultural communication therefore requires that we recognize and understand culture's influence not only on verbal interaction but also on nonverbal interaction. Our nonverbal actions constitute a second symbol system that enables other people to gain insight into our thoughts and feelings. Because nonverbal symbols are derived from such diverse behaviors as body movements, postures, facial expressions, gestures, eye movements, physical appearance, the use and organization of space, the structuring of time, and vocal nuances, these symbolic behaviors are culturally diverse, varying from one culture to another. An awareness of the role nonverbal behaviors play during interaction is therefore crucial if we are to appreciate all aspects of intercultural communication.

Nonverbal behavior is largely unconscious. We use nonverbal symbols spontaneously, without thinking about what posture, what gesture, or what interpersonal distance is appropriate to the situation. Nonverbal behavior is critically important in intercultural communication because, as with other aspects of the communication process, these behaviors are subject to cultural diversity. In other words, culture to a large degree determines which posture, which gesture, or which interpersonal distance is appropriate in a host of social situations. This influence of culture on nonverbal behavior can be considered from two perspectives.

In the first perspective, culture tends to determine the specific nonverbal behaviors that represent or symbolize specific thoughts, feelings, or states of the communicator. Thus, what might be a sign of greeting in one culture might very well be an obscene gesture in another. Or what is considered a symbol of affirmation in one culture could be meaningless or even signify negation in another. In the second perspective, culture determines when it is appropriate to display or communicate various thoughts, feelings, or internal states; this is particularly evident in the display of emotions. Although there seems to be little cross-cultural difference in the nonverbal behaviors that represent emotional states, there can be significant cultural differences in the specification of which emotions may be displayed, who may display them, and when or where they may be displayed.

As important as verbal language is to a communication event, nonverbal communication is just as, if not more, important. Nonverbal messages can stand alone or they can tell us how other messages are to be interpreted. For example, they often indicate whether verbal messages are true, were uttered in jest, are serious or threatening, and so on. Nonverbal communication is especially important because as much as 90 percent of the social content of a message is transmitted paralinguistically—that is, nonverbally.

Chapter 5 deals with nonverbal interaction. More specifically, it deals with how one's culture influences both the perception and use of nonverbal actions. These readings will demonstrate the diversity of culturally derived nonverbal behaviors and the underlying value structures that produce these behaviors.

We begin this chapter with an overview of the topic of nonverbal communication rather than with a critique of a single culture. Peter Andersen's essay, "Cues of Culture: The Basis of Intercultural Differences in Nonverbal Communication," begins with an analysis of how culture determines our nonverbal communicative behavior. He then discusses six fundamental dimensions of cultural variability: (1) immediacy and expressiveness, (2) individualism, (3) gender, (4) power distance, (5) uncertainty, and (6) high and low context. The motivation driving Andersen's analysis is one that is at the heart of this entire book. Simply stated, if you understand the nonverbal codes used by various cultures, then you can better interact with people from those cultures.

Our next essay moves us from a discussion of cultures in general to an analysis of a specific culture. Edwin R. McDaniel, in his piece titled "Japanese Nonverbal Communication: A Reflection of Cultural Themes," examines some nonverbal communication patterns found in the Japanese culture. As a means of demonstrating the link between culture and communication, McDaniel not only examines the communication behaviors of the Japanese culture, but also traces the reasons for these behaviors. By presenting what he refers to as "cultural themes," McDaniel explains how Japan's social organizations, historical experiences, and religious orientations are directly connected to Japanese nonverbal behavior. In a propositional survey, McDaniel proposes a series of eleven propositions that tie various cultural themes to how the Japanese perceive and use kinesics (movement), oculesics (eye contact), facial expressions, proxemics, touch, personal appearance, space, time, vocalics or paralanguage, silence, and olfactics (smell).

In our next essay, "Monochronic and Polychronic Time," the anthropologist Edward T. Hall looks at the conscious and unconscious ways in which cultures use time. Hall maintains that cultures organize and respond to time in two very different ways; he has labeled them as *polychronic* (P-time) and *monochronic* (M-time). These chronological systems are not either–or categories, but the extremes of a concept dimension that offers two distinct approaches to the notion of time. People from cultures such as those found in the Mediterranean, Africa, and South America operate near the P-time end of the dimension. As the term *poly*chronic suggests, they do many things simultaneously, are more concerned with people and the present moment than with schedules, and believe that they are in command of time rather than are being controlled by it. Cultures that operate near the M-time end of the time dimension, such as those found in Northern Europe and North America, are *mono*chronic and tend toward doing only one thing at a time. They emphasize schedules, the segmentation of time, and promptness. It is easy to imagine the potential for misunderstanding when people from these diverse time orientations come together. Hall's essay helps us avoid communication problems by introducing us to the many forms these two interaction patterns may take.

As we have seen, there is a great deal of difference between cultures in terms of their nonverbal behavior. Yet, within cultures we can find, to a lesser degree, diversity in nonverbal behavior among co-cultures. One of the most important, if not *the* most important, sources of nonverbal communication diversity within a culture is gender. In our final essay, "Gender and Nonverbal Communication," Deborah Borisoff and Lisa Merrill introduce us to the role gender plays in influencing nonverbal behavior. Through an examination of women's and men's use and interpretation of space, height, touch, gestures, facial expressions, and eye contact, they explore some of the assumptions and controversies about the nonverbal aspects of gender. They provide us with rich insight into gender-based differences in the perception of nonverbal behavior by detailing how men and women differ in their awareness of and interpretation of nonverbal communication.

Cues of Culture: The Basis of Intercultural Differences in Nonverbal Communication

PETER ANDERSEN

Culture may be the central topic of the next millennium. At one time, most people spent their lives within their own culture, interacting with people from their own group. Only rarely across the generations did sojourners, traders, or warriors encounter people from other cultures—usually with disastrous effects. People with different customs were thought to be crazy, rude, sinful, promiscuous, uncivilized, or subhuman. Today, some of these attitudes toward people from other cultures still persist. In California, ballot measures have been passed that sought to restrict the rights of illegal immigrants. Among many nations, trade wars, ethnic cleansing, and genocide still take place.

As we enter the third millennium, contact between people from various cultures is increasing. International migration is at an all-time high. International trade increased 100 percent between 1985 and 1995 and nearly 400 percent between 1965 and 1995 (Brown, Kane, & Roodman, 1994). International tourism is an increasingly common phenomenon. The number of official refugees topped 18 million for the first time ever (Brown et al., 1994). In short, the amount of intercultural contact in today's world is unprecedented, making the study of intercultural communication more important than ever.

While language differences are most apparent, they are only the tips of a very large cultural iceberg. Culture is primarily an implicit nonverbal phenomenon, for most aspects of one's culture are learned through observation and imitation rather than by explicit verbal instruction or expression. The pri-

mary level of culture is communicated implicitly, without awareness, chiefly by nonverbal means (Andersen, 1988; Hall, 1984; Sapir, 1928). In most situations, intercultural interactants do not share the same language. But languages can be learned, and larger communication problems occur in the nonverbal realm. Nonverbal communication is a subtle, nonlinguistic, multidimensional, and spontaneous process (Andersen, 1986). Indeed, individuals are aware of little of their own nonverbal behavior, which is enacted mindlessly, spontaneously, and unconsciously (Andersen, 1986; Burgoon, 1985; Samovar & Porter, 1985). Because we are not usually aware of our own nonverbal behavior, it becomes extremely difficult to identify and master the nonverbal behavior of another culture. At times we feel uncomfortable in other cultures because we intuitively know something isn't right. "Because nonverbal behaviors are rarely conscious phenomena, it may be difficult for us to know exactly why we are feeling uncomfortable" (Gudykunst & Kim, 1984, p. 149). Indeed, Edward Sapir stated long ago that "We respond to gestures with an extreme alertness and, one might almost say, in accordance with an elaborate and secret code that is written nowhere, known to none and understood by all" (1928, p. 556). Indeed, culture is so basic, learned at such a tender age, and so taken-for-granted that it is often confused with human nature itself.

This article will briefly explore the subtle codes of nonverbal communication, locate culture as a part of interpersonal behavior, and then discuss six primary dimensions of cultural variation, including immediacy, individualism, gender, power distance, uncertainty–avoidance, and cultural contextualization. It is argued that each dimension explains the fundamental differences in a culture's communication, particularly its nonverbal communication.

NONVERBAL CODES

Most discussions of nonverbal intercultural communication have been anecdotal, descriptive, and atheoretical, where numerous examples of intercultural differences for each nonverbal code are discussed in detail. Recapitulation of the various nonverbal codes of intercultural communication is not a primary purpose here. Thus, the basic code of nonverbal communication will be discussed only briefly along with references that provide detailed and excellent analyses of how each nonverbal code differs interculturally.

Two of the most fundamental nonverbal differences in intercultural communication involve space and time. *Chronemics,* or the study of meanings, usage, and communication of time, is probably the most discussed and well-researched nonverbal code in the intercultural literature (Bruneau, 1979; Burgoon, Buller, & Woodall, 1989; Gudykunst & Kim, 1984; Hall, 1959, 1976, 1984; Malandro & Barker, 1983). These analyses suggest that the time frames of cultures differ so dramatically that if only chronemic differences existed, then intercultural misunderstandings would still be considerable. In the United States, time is viewed as a commodity that can be wasted, spent, saved, and used wisely. Of course, many cultures have no such concept of time. In many Third World cultures, life moves to the rhythms of nature, the day, the seasons, the year. Such human inventions as seconds, minutes, hours, and weeks have no real meaning. Things are experienced polychronically and simultaneously, whereas in Western culture time is modularized and events are scheduled sequentially, not simultaneously.

A second nonverbal code that has attracted considerable attention is *proxemics,* the communication of interpersonal space and distance. Research has documented that cultures differ substantially in their use of personal space, the distances they maintain, and their regard for territory as well as the meanings they assign to proxemic behavior (Burgoon, Buller, & Woodall, 1989; Gudykunst & Kim, 1984; Hall, 1959, 1976; Malandro & Barker, 1983; Scheflen, 1974).

Considerable intercultural differences have been reported in people's *kinesic* behavior, including their facial expressions, body movements, gestures, and conversational regulators (Burgoon, Buller, & Woodall, 1989; Gudykunst & Kim, 1984; Hall, 1976; Jensen, 1985; Malandro & Barker, 1983; Rich, 1974; Samovar, Porter, & Jain, 1981; Scheflen, 1974). Gestures differ dramatically in meaning, extensiveness, and intensity. Stories abound in the intercultural literature of gestures that signal endearment or warmth in one culture, but may be obscene or insulting in another.

Interpersonal patterns of tactile communication called *haptics* also reveal substantial intercultural differences (Andersen & Leibowitz, 1978; Malandro & Barker, 1983; Prosser, 1978; Samovar, Porter, & Jain, 1981). Recent research has shown vast differences in international and intercultural touch in amount, location, type, and public or private manifestation (Jones, 1994; McDaniel & Andersen, 1995).

Other important codes of nonverbal communication have attracted considerably less space in publications on nonverbal and intercultural communication. *Physical appearance,* the most important nonverbal code during initial encounters, is of obvious importance, because many intercultural encounters are based on stereotypes and are of short duration. Some discussions of intercultural differences in appearance are provided by Scheflen (1974) and Samovar, Porter, and Jain (1981). Though blue jeans and business suits have become increasingly accepted attire internationally, local attire still abounds. Recently, while collecting intercultural communication data at an international airport, I witnessed Tongans in multicultural ceremonial gowns, Sikhs in white turbans, Hasidic Jews in blue yarmulkes, and Africans in white dashikis—all alongside Californians in running shorts and halter tops.

Oculesics, the study of messages sent by the eyes—including eye contact, blinks, eye movements, and pupil dilation—has received only marginal attention by intercultural communication scholars (Gudykunst & Kim, 1984; Jensen, 1985; Samovar, Porter, & Jain, 1981). Because eye contact has been called an "invitation to communicate," its variation cross-culturally is an important communication topic.

Vocalics, or *paralanguage,* the nonverbal elements of the voice, also has received comparatively little attention from intercultural researchers (Gudykunst & Kim, 1984; LaBarre, 1985; Rich, 1974; Samovar, Porter, & Jain, 1981; Scheflen, 1974). Music and singing, universal forms of aesthetic communication, have been almost completely overlooked in intercultural research, except for an excellent study (Lomax, 1968) that identified several groups of worldwide cultures through differences and similarities in their folk songs. Finally, *olfactics,* the study of interpersonal communication via smell, has been virtually ignored in intercultural research despite its importance (Samovar, Porter, & Jain, 1981).

LOCATING CULTURE IN INTERPERSONAL BEHAVIOR

Culture is a critical concept to communication scholars because every communicator is a product of her or his culture. Along with traits, situations, and states, culture is one of the four primary sources of interpersonal behavior (Andersen, 1987, 1988; see Figure 1). Culture is the enduring influence of the social environment on our behavior, including our interpersonal communication behavior. Culture is a learned set of shared perceptions about beliefs, values, and needs that affect the behaviors of relatively large groups of people (Lustig & Koester, 1993). Culture exerts a considerable force on individual behavior through what Geertz (1973) called "control mechanisms—plans, recipes, rules, instructions (what computer engineers call 'programs')—for the governing of behavior" (p. 44). Culture has similar, powerful, though not identical, effects on all residents of a cultural system. "Culture can be behaviorally observed by contrasting intragroup homogeneity with intergroup heterogeneity" (Andersen, Lustig, & Andersen, 1986, p. 11).

Culture has been confused with personal traits because both are enduring phenomena (Andersen, 1987, 1988). Traits have multiple causes (Andersen, 1987), only some of which are the result of culture. Culture has also been confused with situation, for both are part of one's social environment. However, culture is an enduring phenomenon, while situation is a transient one with an observable beginning and end. Culture, along with genetics, is the most enduring, powerful, and invisible shaper of our communication behavior.

DIMENSIONS OF CULTURAL VARIATION

Thousands of anecdotes regarding nonverbal misunderstandings between persons from different cultures have been reported. Although it may be useful to know that Arabs stand closer than Americans, the Swiss are more time conscious than Italians, and Asians value silence more than Westerners, we need more than this approach. Because the number of potential pairs of cultures are huge and the number of possible nonverbal misunderstandings between

Figure 1 *Sources of influence on interpersonal behavior*

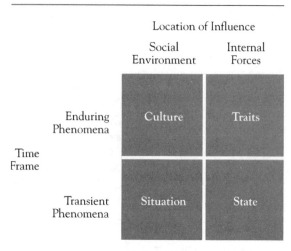

each pair of cultures is similarly large, millions of potential intercultural anecdotes are possible (Andersen, 1988). What is needed is some way to organize, explain, and understand this plethora of potential problems in intercultural communication. Some initial research has shown that cultures can be located along dimensions that help explain these intercultural differences. Most cultural differences in nonverbal behavior are a result of variations along the dimensions discussed below.

IMMEDIACY AND EXPRESSIVENESS

Immediacy behaviors are actions that simultaneously communicate warmth, closeness, and availability for communication and also signal approach rather than avoidance and closeness rather than distance (Andersen, 1985; Hecht, Andersen, & Ribeau, 1989). Examples of immediacy behaviors are smiling, touching, eye contact, closer distances, and more vocal animation. Some scholars have labeled these behaviors as "expressive" (Patterson, 1983).

Cultures that display considerable interpersonal closeness or immediacy have been labeled "contact cultures," because people in these countries stand closer together and touch more (Hall, 1966). People in low-contact cultures tend to stand apart and touch less. According to Patterson (1983):

These habitual patterns of relating to the world permeate all aspects of everyday life, but their effects on social behavior define the manner in which people relate to one another. In the case of contact cultures, this general tendency is manifested in closer approaches so that tactile and olfactory information may be gained easily. (p. 145)

Interestingly, contact cultures are generally located in warmer countries and low-contact cultures in cooler climates. Considerable research has shown that high-contact cultures comprise most Arab countries, including North Africa; the Mediterranean region, including France, Greece, Italy, Portugal, and Spain; Jews from both Europe and the Middle East; Eastern Europeans and Russians; and virtually all of Latin America (Condon & Yousef, 1983; Jones, 1994; Jones & Remland, 1982; Mehrabian, 1971; Patterson, 1983; Samovar, Porter, & Jain, 1981; Scheflen, 1972). Australians are moderate in their cultural contact level, as are North Americans, although the latter tend toward low contact (Patterson, 1983). Low-contact cultures comprise most of Northern Europe, including Scandinavia, Germany, and England; British Americans; white Anglo-Saxons (the primary culture of the United States); and virtually every Asian country, including Burma, Korea, China, Japan, Indonesia, the Philippines, Thailand, and Vietnam (Andersen, Andersen, & Lustig, 1987; Heslin & Alper, 1983; Jones, 1994; Jones & Remland, 1982; McDaniel & Andersen, 1995; Mehrabian, 1971; Patterson, 1983; Samovar, Porter, & Jain, 1981; Scheflen, 1972). Indeed, McDaniel and Andersen's data on public touch suggest the biggest difference is between Asians, who rarely touch in public, and virtually every other culture, which all manifest higher degrees of public touching. These findings are consistent with other research that suggests China and Japan are distinctly nontouch cultures (Barnland, 1978; Jones, 1994). However, two recent studies (McDaniel & Andersen, 1995; Remland, Jones, & Brinkman, 1991) report that the English engage in considerable touch and maintain relatively close distances. Indeed, both studies question whether Hall's (1966) original designation of some cultures as "low contact" is an oversimplification.

Explanations for these latitudinal variations have included energy level, climate, and metabolism

(Andersen, Lustig, & Andersen, 1990). Evidently, cultures in cooler climates tend to be more task-oriented and interpersonally "cool," whereas cultures in warmer climates tend to be more interpersonally oriented and interpersonally "warm." Even within the United States, the warmer latitudes tend to be higher-contact cultures. Andersen, Lustig, and Andersen (1990) report a .31 correlation between latitude of students' university and touch avoidance. These data suggest students at so-called Sunbelt universities are more touch-oriented. Recently, Pennebaken, Rimé, and Sproul (1994) found a correlation between latitude and expressiveness within dozens of countries. Northerners are more expressive, according to their data, in Belgium, Croatia, France, Germany, Italy, Japan, Serbia, Spain, Switzerland, and the United States, with an overall difference within the entire northern hemisphere. Pennebaken et al. (1994) conclude:

Logically, climate must profoundly affect social processes. People living in cold climates devote more time to dressing, to providing warmth, to planning ahead for food provisions during the winter months. . . . In warm climates, people are more likely to see, hear, and interact with neighbors year around. Emotional expressiveness, then would be more of a requirement. (pp. 15–16)

Similarly, Andersen, Lustig, and Andersen (1990) conclude:

In Northern latitudes societies must be more structured, more ordered, more constrained, and more organized if the individuals are to survive harsh weather forces. . . . In contrast, Southern latitudes may attract or produce a culture characterized by social extravagance and flamboyance that has no strong inclination to constrain or order their world. (p. 307)

Without a doubt, cultures differ in their immediacy. In general, northern countries, northern parts of individual countries, traditional cultures, and Asians are the least immediate and expressive. Southern people, modern countries, and non-Asian cultures are the most expressive and immediate. Obviously, these findings are painted with a fairly broad brush and will await a more detailed cultural portrait.

INDIVIDUALISM

One of the most fundamental dimensions along which cultures differ is their degree of individualism versus collectivism. This dimension determines how people live together (alone, in families, or tribes; see Hofstede, 1982), their values, and how they communicate. As we will see, Americans are individualists for better or worse. We take individualism for granted and are blind to its impact until travel brings us into contact with less individualistic, more collectivistic cultures.

Individualism has been applauded as a blessing and has been elevated to the status of a national religion in the United States. Indeed, the best and worst in our culture can be attributed to individualism. Proponents of individualism have argued that it is the basis of liberty, democracy, freedom, and economic incentive and also serves as protection against tyranny. Individualism has been blamed for our alienation from one another, loneliness, selfishness, and narcissism. Indeed, Hall (1976) has claimed that as an extreme individualist, "Western man has created chaos by denying that part of his self that integrates while enshrining the part that fragments experience" (p. 9).

There can be little doubt that individualism is one of the fundamental dimensions that distinguish cultures. Likewise, "there is little doubt that Western culture is individualistic so people rely on personal judgments. Eastern cultures emphasize harmony among people, between people and nature, and value collective judgments" (Hecht, Andersen, & Ribeau, 1989, p. 170). Tomkins (1984) demonstrated that an individual's psychological makeup is the result of this cultural dimension: "Human beings, in Western Civilization, have tended toward self-celebration, positive or negative. In Oriental thought another alternative is represented, that of harmony between man and nature" (p. 182). Prosser (1978) suggested that the Western emphasis on individuality finds its culmination in contemporary North American cultures where the chief cultural value is the role of the individual. This idea is verified in the landmark intercultural study of Hofstede (1982). In his study of individualism in forty noncommunist countries the nine most individualistic (in order) were the United States, Australia, Great Britain, Canada, Nether-lands, New Zealand, Italy, Belgium, and Denmark, all of which are Western or European cultures. The ten least individualistic (starting with the least) were Venezuela, Colombia, Pakistan, Peru, Taiwan, Thailand, Singapore, Chile, and Hong Kong, all Asian or South American cultures. Similarly, Sitaram and Codgell (1976) reported individuality to be of primary importance in Western cultures, of secondary importance in black cultures, and of lesser importance in Eastern and Muslim cultures.

Even though the United States is the most individualistic country on earth (Hofstede, 1982), some of its regions and particular ethnic groups vary in their degree of individualism. Elazar (1972) has shown that the central Midwest and the mid-Atlantic states have the most individualistic political culture, whereas the Southeast is the most traditionalistic and least individualistic. But this is all relative and, by world standards, even Mississippi is an individualistic culture. As Bellah, Madsen, Sullivan, Swidler, and Tipton (1985) stated: "Individualism lies at the very core of American culture. . . . Anything that would violate our right to think for ourselves, judge for ourselves, make our own decisions, live our lives as we see fit, is not only morally wrong, it is sacrilegious" (p. 142). Different ethnic groups may vary within a culture. African Americans, for example, place a great deal of emphasis on individualism, whereas Mexican Americans place greater emphasis on group and relational solidarity (Hecht, Andersen, & Ribeau, 1989). Indeed, our extreme individualism makes it difficult for Americans to interact with and understand people from other cultures. We are unique; all other cultures are less individualistic. As Condon and Yousef (1983) stated, "The fusion of individualism and equality is so valued and so basic that many Americans find it most difficult to relate to contrasting values in other cultures where interdependence greatly determines a person's sense of self" (p. 65).

The degree to which a culture is individualistic or collectivistic affects the nonverbal behavior of that culture in every way. First, people from individualistic cultures are more remote and distant proximally. Collectivistic cultures are interdependent; as a result, the members work, play, live, and sleep in close proximity to one another. Hofstede (1982) cites research suggesting that, as hunters and gatherers, people lived apart in individualistic, nuclear families. As agricultural societies developed, the interdependent extended family began living in close proximity in large family or tribal units. Urban–industrial societies returned to a norm of individualism, nuclear families, and lack of proximity to one's neighbors, friends, and co-workers.

Kinesic behavior tends to be more synchronized in collectivistic cultures. Where families work collectively, movements, schedules, and actions need to be highly coordinated (Argyle, 1975). In urban cultures, family members often do their "own thing," coming and going, working and playing, eating and sleeping on different schedules. People in individualistic cultures also smile more than do people in normatively oriented cultures, according to Tomkins (1984). This is probably due to the fact that individualists are responsible for their relationships and their own happiness, whereas normatively or collectively oriented people regard compliance with norms as a primary value and personal or interpersonal happiness as a secondary value (Andersen, 1988). Matsumoto (1991) contends that "collective cultures will foster emotional displays of their members that maintain and facilitate group cohesion, harmony, or cooperation, to a greater degree than individualistic cultures" (p. 132). Similarly, Lustig and Koester (1993) maintain that "people from individualistic cultures are more likely than those from collectivistic cultures to use confrontational strategies when dealing with interpersonal problems; those with a collectivist orientation are likely to use avoidance, third-party intermediaries, or other face-saving techniques" (p. 147). People in collectivistic cultures may suppress both positive and negative emotional displays that are contrary to the mood of the group, because maintaining the group is a primary value (Andersen, 1988). Recently, Bond (1993) found the Chinese culture to be lower in frequency, intensity, and duration of emotional expression. Bond asserts that "the expression of emotion is carefully regulated out of a concern for its capacity to disrupt group harmony and status hierarchies" (p. 245).

People in individualistic cultures are encouraged to express emotions because individual freedom is a paramount value. Research suggests that people in individualistic cultures are more nonverbally affiliative. Intuitively, the reason for this is not obvious, because individualism doesn't require affiliation. However, Hofstede (1982) explained that

> In less individualistic countries where traditional social ties, like those with extended family members, continue to exist, people have less of a need to make specific friendships. One's friends are predetermined by the social relationships into which one is born. In the more individualistic countries, however, affective relationships are not socially predetermined but must be acquired by each individual personally. (p. 163)

In individualistic countries such as the United States, affiliativeness, dating, flirting, small talk, smiling, and initial acquaintance are more important than in collectivistic countries where the social network is more fixed and less reliant on individual initiative. Bellah et al. (1985) maintain that for centuries in the individualistic and mobile North American society, people could meet more easily and their communication was more open. However, their relationships were usually more casual and transient.

Finally, in an impressive study of dozens of cultures, Lomax (1968) found that a country's song and dance styles were related to its level of social cohesion and collectivism. Collectivistic cultures are higher in "groupiness" and cohesion found in their singing styles. Collectivistic cultures show both more cohesiveness in singing and more synchrony in their dance style (Lomax, 1968). It isn't surprising that rock dancing, which emphasizes separateness and "doing your own thing," evolved in individualistic cultures such as England and the United States. These dances may serve as a metaphor for the whole U.S. culture, where individuality is more prevalent than in any other place (Andersen, 1988).

GENDER

The gender orientation of culture has a major impact on many aspects of nonverbal behavior. This includes the types of expressions permitted by each sex, occupational status, nonverbal aspects of power, the ability to interact with strangers or acquaintances of the opposite sex, and all aspects of interpersonal relationship between men and women. "While numerous studies have focused on gender as an individual characteristic, gender has been neglected as a cultural dimension" (Hecht, Andersen, & Ribeau, 1989, p. 171). As conceptualized here, *gender* refers to the rigidity of gender rules. In rigid cultures, masculine traits are typically attributes such as strength, assertiveness, competitiveness, and ambitiousness, whereas feminine traits are attributes such as affection, compassion, nurturance, and emotionality (Bem, 1974; Hofstede, 1982). In less rigid cultures, both men and women can express more diverse, less stereotyped sex-role behaviors. Cross-cultural research shows that young girls are expected to be more nurturant than boys, though there is considerable variation from country to country (Hall, 1984). Hofstede (1982) has measured the degree to which people of both sexes in a culture endorse masculine or feminine goals. Masculine cultures regard competition and assertiveness as important, whereas feminine cultures place more importance on nurturance and compassion. Not surprisingly, the masculinity of a culture is negatively correlated with the percentage of women in technical and professional jobs and positively correlated with segregation of the sexes in higher education (Hofstede, 1982).

Countries with the nine highest masculinity index scores, according to Hofstede (1982) are, respectively, Japan, Austria, Venezuela, Italy, Switzerland, Mexico, Ireland, Great Britain, and Germany. The nine countries with the lowest masculinity scores, respectively, are Sweden, Norway, Netherlands, Denmark, Finland, Chile, Portugal, and Thailand. Not surprisingly, high-masculinity countries have fewer women in the labor force, have only recently afforded voting privileges to women, and are less likely to consider wife rape a crime than are low masculinity countries (Seager & Olson, 1986).

Why would South American cultures not manifest the Latin pattern of machismo? Hofstede (1982) suggests that machismo is more present in the Caribbean region than in the remainder of South America. In fact, South America, as compared to Central America, has a much higher percentage of working women, much higher school attendance by girls, and more women in higher education (Seager & Olson, 1986).

Considerable research suggests that androgynous patterns of behavior (that is, both feminine and masculine) result in more self-esteem, social competence, success, and intellectual development for both

males and females (Andersen, 1988). Nonverbal styles where both men and women are free to express both masculine traits (such as dominance, anger) and feminine traits (such as warmth, emotionality) are likely to be both healthier and more effective. Buck (1984) has demonstrated that males may harm their health by internalizing emotions rather than externalizing them as women usually do. Internalized emotions that are not expressed result in more stress and higher blood pressure. Interestingly, more masculine countries show higher levels of stress (Hofstede, 1982).

Considerable research has demonstrated significant vocal differences between egalitarian and non-egalitarian countries. Countries where women are economically important and where sexual standards for women are permissive show more relaxed vocal patterns than do other countries (Lomax, 1968). Moreover, those egalitarian countries show less tension between the sexes, more vocal solidarity and coordination in their songs, and more synchrony in their movement (Lomax, 1968).

The United States tends to be a masculine country, according to Hofstede (1982), although it is not among the most masculine. Intercultural communicators should keep in mind that other countries may be either more or less sexually egalitarian than the United States. Because most countries are more feminine (that is, nurturant, compassionate), Americans of both sexes frequently seem loud, aggressive, and competitive by world standards. Likewise, Americans' attitude toward women may seem sexist in extremely feminine locations such as Scandinavia.

POWER DISTANCE

A fourth fundamental dimension of intercultural communication is power distance. *Power distance—* the degree to which power, prestige, and wealth are unequally distributed in a culture—has been measured in many cultures using Hofstede's (1982) Power Distance Index (PDI). Cultures with high PDI scores have power and influence concentrated in the hands of a few rather than more equally distributed throughout the population. Condon and Yousef (1983) distinguish among three cultural patterns: democratic, authority-centered, and authoritarian.

The PDI is highly correlated (.80) with authoritarianism (as measured by the F scale) (Hofstede, 1982).

High PDI countries, from highest to lowest, are the Philippines, Mexico, Venezuela, India, Singapore, Brazil, Hong Kong, France, and Colombia (Hofstede, 1982), all of which, except for France, are South Asian, South American, or Caribbean countries. Gudykunst and Kim (1984) report that both African and Asian cultures generally maintain hierarchical role relationships. Asian students are expected to be modest and deferent nonverbally in the presence of their instructors. Likewise, Vietnamese consider employers to be their mentor and will not question orders. Low PDI countries, lowest first, are Austria, Israel, Denmark, New Zealand, Ireland, Sweden, Norway, Finland, and Switzerland (Hofstede, 1982), all of which are European or of European origin, middle-class, and democratic and located at high latitudes. The United States is slightly lower than the median in power distance, indicating smaller status differentials than in many other countries. Cultures differ in terms of how status is acquired. In many countries, such as India, one's status is determined by class or caste. In the United States, power and status is typically determined by money and conspicuous material displays (Andersen & Bowman, 1990).

A primary determiner of power distance is the latitude of a country. Hofstede (1982) claims that latitude and climate are one of the major forces shaping a culture. He maintains that the key intervening variable is that technology is needed for survival in colder climates. This produces a chain of events in which children are less dependent on authority and learn from people other than authority figures. Hofstede (1982) reports a .65 correlation between PDI and latitude! In a study conducted at forty universities throughout the United States, Andersen, Lustig, and Andersen (1990) report a −.47 correlation between latitude and intolerance for ambiguity, and a −.45 correlation between latitude and authoritarianism. This suggests that residents of the northern United States are less authoritarian and more tolerant of ambiguity. Northern cultures may have to be more tolerant and less autocratic to ensure cooperation and survival in harsher climates.

It is obvious that power distance would affect a culture's nonverbal behavior. High PDI cultures, such as India, with a rigid caste system may severely limit interaction, as in the case of India's "untouchables." More than twenty percent of India's population are untouchables who lie at the bottom of India's five-caste system (Chinoy, 1967). Any contact with untouchables by members of other castes is strictly forbidden and considered "polluting." Certainly, tactile communication between castes is greatly curtailed in Indian culture. High PDI countries with less rigid stratification than India may still prohibit free interclass dating, marriage, and contact—all of which are taken for granted in low PDI countries.

Social systems with large power discrepancies also produce different kinesic behavior. Cultures with high power distance will foster and encourage emotions that present status differences. For instance, in high-power-distance cultures, people would be expected to show only positive emotions to high-status others and only negative emotions to low-status others (Matsumoto, 1991). According to Andersen and Bowman (1990), subordinates' bodily tension is more obvious in power-discrepant relationships. Similarly, Andersen and Bowman (1990) report that in power-discrepant circumstances, subordinates smile more in an effort to appease superiors and appear polite. The continuous smiles of many Asians are a culturally inculcated effort to appease superiors and smooth social relations, behaviors that are appropriate to a high PDI culture.

Vocalic and paralinguistic cues are also affected by the power distance in a culture. Citizens of low PDI cultures are generally less aware that vocal loudness may be offensive to others. American vocal tones are often perceived as noisy, exaggerated, and childlike (Condon & Yousef, 1983). Lomax (1968) has shown that in countries where political authority is highly centralized, singing voices are tighter and the voice box is more closed, whereas more permissive societies produce more relaxed, open, and clear sounds.

UNCERTAINTY

Uncertainty is a cultural predisposition to value risk and ambiguity (Hecht, Andersen, & Ribeau, 1989). At the individual level, this quality is often called tolerance for ambiguity (Martin & Westie, 1959).

People with intolerance of ambiguity have high levels of uncertainty avoidance and seek clear, black-and-white answers. People with tolerance of ambiguity have low levels of uncertainty avoidance and tend to be more tolerant, to accept ambiguous answers, and to see many shades of gray. Similarly, Hofstede (1982) reports that a country's neuroticism or anxiety scores are strongly correlated with uncertainty avoidance. High uncertainty avoidance is negatively correlated with risk taking and positively correlated with fear of failure.

Countries vary greatly in their tolerance for uncertainty. In some cultures, freedom leads to uncertainty, which leads to stress and anxiety. Hofstede (1982) maintained that intolerance of ambiguity and dogmatism are primarily a function of the uncertainty-avoidance dimension rather than the power-distance dimension. Countries with the highest levels of uncertainty avoidance are Greece, Portugal, Belgium, Japan, Peru, France, Chile, Spain, and Argentina (Hofstede, 1982). Southern European and South American countries dominate the list. Countries lowest in uncertainty avoidance and most tolerant are Singapore, Denmark, Sweden, Hong Kong, Ireland, Great Britain, India, the Philippines, and the United States. This list is dominated by Northern European and South Asian cultures. Hofstede (1982) also reports that Catholic countries are high in uncertainty avoidance, whereas Protestant, Hindu, and Buddhist countries tend to be more accepting of uncertainty. Eastern religions and Protestantism tend to be less "absolute," while Catholicism is a more "absolute religion." Andersen, Lustig, and Andersen (1990) report that intolerance for ambiguity is much higher in the American South than in the Northern states, tending to reflect the international pattern of latitude and tolerance.

We know relatively little about nonverbal behavior associated with uncertainty. Hofstede (1982) maintains that countries high in uncertainty avoidance tend to display emotions more than do countries low in uncertainty avoidance. Furthermore, he reports that the emotional displays of young people are tolerated less in countries with high uncertainty avoidance. Certainly, disagreement and nonconformity are not appreciated if uncertainty avoidance is high. Nonverbal behavior is more likely to be codified and rule-governed in countries with high uncer-

tainty avoidance. This seems to fit a country such as Japan, but the hypothesis remains to be tested and is somewhat speculative. Hofstede (1982) found that nations high in uncertainty avoidance report more stylized and ritual behavior, so we should expect that nonverbal behavior is more prescribed in these cultures. When people from the United States communicate with people from a country such as Japan or France (both high in uncertainty avoidance), the Americans may seem excessively nonconforming and unconventional, whereas their Japanese or French counterparts might seem too controlled and rigid to the Americans (Lustig & Koester, 1993).

HIGH AND LOW CONTEXT

A final important dimension of intercultural communication is that of context. Because nonverbal cues often provide context, this is a very important dimension. Hall (1976, 1984) has described high- and low-context cultures in considerable detail. "A high context (HC) communication or message is one in which most of the information is either in the physical context or internalized in the person, while very little is in the coded, explicit, transmitted parts of the message" (Hall, 1976, p. 91). Lifelong friends often use HC or implicit messages that are nearly impossible for an outsider to understand. The situation, a smile, or a glance provides implicit meaning that does not need to be articulated. In HC situations or cultures, information is integrated from the environment, the context, the situation, and nonverbal cues that give the message meaning that is unavailable in the explicit verbal utterance.

Low-context (LC) messages are just the opposite of HC messages; most of the information is in the explicit code (Hall, 1976). LC messages must be elaborated, clearly communicated, and highly specific. Unlike personal relationships, which are relatively high-context message systems, institutions such as courts of law and formal systems such as mathematics and computer languages require explicit LC systems, because nothing can be taken for granted (Hall, 1984).

Cultures vary considerably in the degree of context used in communication. The lowest-context cultures are probably Swiss, German, North American, and Scandinavian (Gudykunst & Kim, 1984; Hall, 1976, 1984). These cultures are preoccupied with specifics, details, literalness, and precise time schedules at the expense of context. They utilize behavior systems built around Aristotelian logic and linear thinking (Hall, 1984) and may be pathologically verbal. Cultures that have some characteristics of both HC and LC systems would include the French, English, and Italian (Gudykunst & Kim, 1984), which are somewhat less explicit than Northern European cultures.

The highest HC cultures are found in Asia. China, Japan, and Korea are extremely HC cultures (Elliott, Jensen, & McDonough, 1982; Hall, 1976, 1984). Languages are some of the most explicit communication systems, but the Chinese language is an implicit high-context system. To use a Chinese dictionary, one must understand thousands of characters that change meaning in combination with other characters. Zen Buddhism, a major influence in Asia, places a high value on silence, lack of emotional expression, and the unspoken, nonverbal parts of communication (Burgoon, Buller, & Woodall, 1989; McDaniel & Andersen, 1995). Americans frequently complain that the Japanese never "get to the point," but they fail to recognize that HC culture must provide a context and setting and let the point evolve (Hall, 1984). In a recent study of airport departures, McDaniel and Andersen (1995) found Asians to be least tactile of any cultural group on earth. The influence of Buddhism and the value placed on context rather than emotional expression probably explain this finding. American Indian cultures with ancestral migratory roots in East Asia are remarkably like contemporary Asian culture in several ways, especially in its need for high context (Hall, 1984). Not surprisingly, most Latin American cultures, a fusion of Iberian (Portuguese–Spanish) and Indian traditions, are also high-context cultures. Southern and eastern Mediterranean people such as Greeks, Turks, and Arabs tend to be HC cultures as well.

Obviously, communication is quite different in high- and low-context cultures. First, explicit forms of communication such as verbal codes are more prevalent in low-context cultures such as the United States and Northern Europe. People from LC cultures are often perceived as excessively talkative, belaboring of the obvious, and redundant. People from HC cultures may be perceived as nondisclosive, sneaky, and mysterious. Second, HC cultures do not value verbal communication the same way that LC cultures do. Elliot et al. (1982) found that more verbal people were perceived as more attractive by people in the United States, but less verbal people were perceived as more attractive in Korea, an HC culture.

A third implication for communication is that HC cultures are more reliant on and tuned in to nonverbal communication. LC cultures, particularly men in LC cultures, fail to perceive as much nonverbal communication as do members of HC cultures. Nonverbal communication provides the context for all communication (Watzlawick, Beavin, & Jackson, 1967), but people from HC cultures are particularly affected by these contextual cues. Thus, facial expressions, tensions, movements, speed of interaction, location of the interaction, and other subtle "vibes" are likely to be perceived by and have more meaning for people from high-context cultures. Finally, people in HC cultures expect more than interactants in LC cultures (Hall, 1976). People in HC cultures expect communicators to understand unarticulated feelings, subtle gestures, and environmental clues that people from low-context cultures simply do not process. Worse, both cultural extremes fail to recognize these basic differences in behavior, communication, and context and are quick to misattribute the causes for their behavior.

CONCLUSIONS

Reading about these six cultural dimensions cannot ensure competence in intercultural communication. The beauty of international travel and even travel within the United States is that it provides a unique perspective on one's own and others' behavior. Combining cognitive knowledge from intercultural readings and courses with actual encounters with people from other cultures is the best way to gain intercultural competence.

A full, practical understanding of the dimensions along which cultures differ—along with knowledge of how specific communication acts differ cross-culturally—has several practical benefits. First, such knowledge will highlight and challenge assumptions about our own behavior. The structure of our own behavior is invisible and taken for granted until it is exposed and challenged through study of cultures and actual intercultural encounters. Indeed, Hall (1976) stated that ethnic diversity in interethnic communication can be a source of strength and an asset from which one's self can be discovered.

Second, this discussion should make it clear that attributions about the nonverbal communication of people from other cultures are bound to be wrong. No dictionary or code of intercultural behavior is available. You cannot read people like books, not even people from your own culture. Understanding that someone is from a masculine, collectivistic, or high-context culture, however, will make his or her behavior less confusing and more interpretable.

Finally, understanding about intercultural communication and actually engaging in intercultural encounters is bound to reduce ethnocentrism and make strangers from other cultures seem less threatening. Fear is often based on ignorance and misunderstanding. The fact of intercultural diversity should produce joy and optimism about the number of possible ways to be human.

References

Andersen, J. F., Andersen, P. A., & Lustig, M. W. (1987). Opposite-sex touch avoidance: A national replication and extension. *Journal of Nonverbal Behavior, II*, 89–109.

Andersen, P. A. (1985). Nonverbal immediacy in interpersonal communication. In A. W. Siegman & S. Feldstein (Eds.), *Multichannel integrations of nonverbal behavior*, 1–36. Hillsdale, NJ: Lawrence Erlbaum.

———. (1986). Consciousness, cognition, and communication. *Western Journal of Speech Communication, 50*, 87–101.

———. The trait debate: A critical examination of the individual differences paradigm in intercultural communication. In B. Dervin & M. J. Voigt (Eds.), *Progress in communication sciences*, Vol. VIII, pp. 47–82. Norwood, NJ: Ablex.

———. (1988). Explaining intercultural differences in nonverbal communication. In L. A. Samovar & R. E. Porter (Eds.), *Intercultural communication: A reader*, 5th ed., pp. 272–281. Belmont, CA: Wadsworth.

———, & Bowman, L. (1990). Positions of power: Nonverbal influence in organizational communication. In J. A. DeVito & M. L. Hecht (Eds.), *The nonverbal reader*, pp. 391–411. Prospect Heights, IL: Waveland Press.

———, & Leibowitz, K. (1978). The development and nature of the construct touch avoidance. *Environmental Psychology and Nonverbal Behavior, 3*, 89–106.

———, Lustig, M. W., & Andersen, J. F. (1986). *Communication patterns among cultural regions of the United States: A theoretical perspective*. Paper presented at the annual convention of the International Communication Association, Chicago.

———, Lustig, R., & Andersen, J. F. (1990). Changes in latitude, changes in attitude: The relationship between climate and interpersonal communication predispositions. *Communication Quarterly, 38*, 291–311.

Argyle, M. (1975). *Bodily communication*. New York: International Universities Press.

Barnland, D. C. (1978). Communication styles in two cultures: Japan and the United States. In A. Kendon, R. M. Harris, & M. R. Key (Eds.), *Organization of behavior in face to face interaction*, pp. 427–456. The Hague: Mouton.

Bellah, R. N., Madsen, R., Sullivan, W. M., Swidler, A., & Tipton, S. (1985). *Habits of the heart: Individualism and commitment in American life*. New York: Harper & Row.

Bem, S. L. (1974). The measurement of psychological androgny. *Journal of Consulting and Clinical Psychology, 42*, 155–162.

Bond, M. H. (1993). Emotions and their expression in Chinese culture. *Journal of Nonverbal Behavior, 17*, 245–262.

Brown. L. R., Kane, H., & Roodman, D. M. (1994). *Vital signs 1994: The trends that are shaping our future*. New York: W. W. Norton.

Bruneau, T. (1979). The time dimension in intercultural communication. In D. Nimmo (Ed.), *Communication yearbook 3*, pp. 423–433. New Brunswick, NJ: Transaction Books.

Buck, R. (1984). *The communication of emotion*. New York: Guilford Press.

Burgoon, J. K. (1985). Nonverbal signals. In M. L. Knapp & G. R. Miller (Eds.), *Handbook of interpersonal communication*, pp. 344–390. Beverly Hills, CA: Sage.

———, Buller, D. B., & Woodall, W. G. (1989). *Nonverbal communication: The unspoken dialogue*. New York: Harper & Row.

Chinoy, E. (1967). *Society*. New York: Random House.

Condon, J. C., & Yousef, F. (1983). *An introduction to intercultural communication*. Indianapolis: Bobbs-Merrill.

Elazar, D. J. (1972). *American federalism: A view from the states*. New York: Thomas P. Crowell.

Elliot, S., Scott, M. D., Jensen, A. D., & McDonough, M. (1982). Perceptions of reticence: A cross-cultural investigation. In M. Burgoon (Ed.), *Communication yearbook 5*, pp. 591–602. New Brunswick, NJ: Transaction Books.

Geertz, C. (1973). *The interpretation of cultures*. New York: Basic Books.

Gudykunst, W. B., & Kim, Y. Y. (1984). *Communicating with strangers: An approach to intercultural communication*. New York: Random House.

Hall, E. T. (1959). *The silent language*. New York: Doubleday.

———. (1966). A system of the notation of proxemic behavior. *American Anthropologist, 65*, 1003–1026.

———. (1976). *Beyond culture*. Garden City, NY: Anchor.

———. (1984). *The dance of life: The other dimension of time*. Garden City, NY: Anchor.

Hecht, M. L., Andersen, P. A., & Ribeau, S. A. (1989). The cultural dimensions of nonverbal communication. In M. K. Asante & W. B. Gudykunst (Eds.), *Handbook of international and intercultural communication*, pp. 163–185. Newbury Park, CA: Sage.

Heslin, R., & Alper, T. (1983). "Touch: A bonding gesture." In J. M. Wiemann & R. Harrison (Eds.), *Nonverbal Interaction*, 47–75. Beverly Hills, CA: Sage.

Hofstede, G. (1982). *Culture's consequences*, abridged ed. Beverly Hills, CA: Sage.

Jensen, J. V. (1985). Perspectives on nonverbal intercultural communication. In L. A. Samovar & R. E. Porter (Eds.), *Intercultural communication: A reader*, 4th ed., pp. 256–272. Belmont, CA: Wadsworth.

Jones, S. E. (1994). *The right touch: Understanding and using the language of physical contact*. Cresshill, NJ: Hampton Press.

Jones, T. S., & Remland, M. S. (1982, May). *Cross-cultural differences in self-reported touch avoidance*. Paper presented at the annual convention of the Eastern Communication Association, Hartford, CT.

LaBarre, W. (1985). Paralinguistics, kinesics, and cultural anthropology. In L. A. Samovar & R. E. Porter (Eds.), *Intercultural communication: A reader*, pp. 272–279. Belmont, CA: Wadsworth.

Lomax, A. (1968). *Folk song style and culture*. New Brunswick, NJ: Transaction Books.

Lustig, M. L., & Koester, J. (1993). *Intercultural competence: Interpersonal communication across culture*. New York: HarperCollins.

Malandro, L. A., & Barker, L. (1983). *Nonverbal communication*. Reading, MA: Addison-Wesley.

Martin, J. G., & Westie, F. R. (1959). The intolerant personality. *American Sociological Review, 24*, 521–528.

Matsumoto, D. (1991). Cultural influences on facial expressions of emotion. *Southern Communication Journal, 56*, 128–137.

McDaniel, E. R., & Andersen, P. A. (1995, May). *Inter-cultural variations in tactic communication: An empirical field study*. Paper presented at the International Communication Association Convention, Albuquerque, NM.

Mehrabian, A. (1971). *Silent messages*. Belmont, CA: Wadsworth.

Patterson, M. L. (1983). *Nonverbal behavior: A functional perspective*. New York: Springer-Verlag.

Pennebaken, J. W., Rimé, B., & Sproul, G. (1994). *Stereotype of emotional expressiveness of Northerners and Southerners: A cross-cultural test of Montesquieu's hypotheses*. Unpublished paper, Southern Methodist University, Dallas, TX.

Prosser, M. H. (1978). *The cultural dialogue: An introduction to intercultural communication*. Boston: Houghton Mifflin.

Remland, M. S., Jones, T. S., & Brinkman, H. (1991). Proxemic and haptic behavior in three European countries. *Journal of Nonverbal Behavior, 15*, 215–232.

Rich, A. L. (1974). *Interracial communication*. New York: Harper & Row.

Samovar, L. A., & Porter, R. E. (1985). Nonverbal interaction. In L. A. Samovar & R. E. Porter (Eds.), *Intercultural communication: A reader*. Belmont, CA: Wadsworth.

Samovar, P. A., Porter, R. E., & Jain, N. C. (1981). *Understanding intercultural communication*. Belmont, CA: Wadsworth.

Sapir, E. (1928). The unconscious patterning of behavior in society. In E. S. Drummer (Ed.), *The unconscious*, pp. 114–142. New York: Knopf.

Scheflen, A. E. (1972). *Body language and the social order*. Englewood Cliffs, NJ: Prentice-Hall.

———. (1974). *How behavior means*. Garden City, NY: Anchor.

Seager, J., & Olson, A. (1986). *Women in the world atlas*. New York: Simon & Schuster.

Sitaram, K. S., & Codgell, R. T. (1976). *Foundations of intercultural communication*. Columbus, OH: Charles E. Merrill.

Tomkins, S. S. (1984). Affect theory. In K. R. Scherer & P. Ekman (Eds.), *Approaches to emotion*, pp. 163–195. Hillsdale, NJ: Lawrence Erlbaum.

Watzlawick, P., Beavin, J. H., & Jackson, D. D. (1967). *Pragmatics of human communication*. New York: W. W. Norton.

Concepts and Questions

1. What does Andersen mean when he writes "the primary level of culture is communicated implicitly, without awareness, by primarily nonverbal means"?

2. Do you agree with Andersen that two of the most fundamental nonverbal differences in intercultural communication involve space and time? From your experiences, what two nonverbal areas have you found most troublesome when interacting with people from different cultures?

3. From your personal experiences, can you think of different ways in which people in various cultures greet, show emotion, and beckon?

4. Do you believe that intercultural communication problems are more serious when they involve nonverbal communication or verbal communication?

5. What is *kinesic* behavior? How does it vary from one culture to another? What types of communication problems can be caused by cultural differences in *kinesic* behavior?

6. The term *hoptics* refers to patterns of tactile communication. How does tactile communication differ between cultures? Can you think of examples of how tactile communication differs among members of co-cultures? What type of communication problems might arise when people with different touching orientations interact?

7. How does physical appearance affect first impressions during interaction? How are expectations of physical appearance related to the informal–formal dimension of culture?

8. How does immediacy affect interpersonal interaction? What differences in behaviors would you expect from high- and low-contact cultures? In what way would violations of immediacy expectations affect intercultural communication?

9. How is the degree of individualism within cultures manifest in nonverbal behavior?

10. What is the relationship between power distance and kinesic behavior? How is high-power distance displayed? How is low-power distance displayed?

Japanese Nonverbal Communication: A Reflection of Cultural Themes

EDWIN R. MCDANIEL

Modern technological advances have made the world a much smaller place, promoting increased interactions between peoples of different nations and cultures. Growing international economic interdependencies and expanding multi-national security alliances have significantly increased the importance of effective intercultural encounters. Individuals from diverse cultures are interacting with each other more and more frequently—in professional, diplomatic, and social venues.

The most critical aspect of this burgeoning transnational intercourse is, of course, communication. The ability to understand and be understood is central to successful cross-cultural activities. Comprehension, however, must go beyond a topical awareness of another culture's communicative practices and behaviors. An appreciation of the cultural antecedents and motivations shaping an individual's communication conventions is necessary for understanding *how* and *why* a particular practice is used.

An established method of explaining the cultural motivations of human behavior is to identify and isolate consistent themes among a social grouping. Anthropological writings have posited that each culture manifests a "limited number of dynamic affirmations" (Opler, 1945, p. 198), referred to as themes. According to Opler (1945), these cultural themes promote and regulate human behavioral activities that are societally encouraged and condoned. To illustrate this approach, Opler (1945) used an examination of the social relations of the Lipan Apaches to demonstrate how thematic study could provide insight to cultural beliefs and behaviors.

In communication studies, the concept of thematic commonality has been utilized by Burgoon and Hale (1984, 1987) to help explicate relational communications. They conceptualized a series of "interrelated message themes" (Burgoon & Hale, 1987, p. 19), which have purported application to both verbal and nonverbal exchanges. These proposed themes, or *topi*, have become a supposition cited in studies of interpersonal relations communication (e.g., Buller & Burgoon, 1986; Coker & Burgoon, 1987; Spitzberg, 1989).

Burgoon and Hale's (1984) concept of identifying consistent themes to assist in the explanation of a communication process possesses significant utility for additional, more comprehensive employment. The innovation has clear application to the study of culture-specific communication predispositions.

Using the Japanese as a cultural model, this essay makes practical application of the thematic consistency concept advanced by Opler (1945, 1946) and Burgoon and Hale (1984, 1987). The objective is to illustrate how nonverbal communication practices function as a reflection, or representation, of societal cultural themes. Employing a standard taxonomy of nonverbal communication codes and addressing each individually, cultural themes influencing and manifested by the code are discussed in a propositional format. Additionally, the essay strives to demonstrate how cultural influences can subtly shape a society's communication conventions.

JAPANESE CULTURAL THEMES

Japan's predominantly homogeneous population embodies a particularly rich array of cultural themes. The more prevalent themes include group affiliation (collectivism), hierarchy, social balance or harmony (*wa*), empathy, mutual-dependency, *gaman* (perseverance and sacrifice), humility, and formality (ritual, tradition, and protocol) (Caudill, 1973; Lebra, 1976; Reischauer, 1988).

Confucian based collectivism exerts a significant influence on Japanese communication patterns. The nation's racial and cultural homogeneity creates a strong identity bond and facilitates intragroup and interpersonal familiarity. This societal closeness promotes an instinctive, nonverbal understanding between Japanese people. Their cultural similitude abets an intuitive, nonverbal comprehension by diminishing the requirement to orally specify numerous details (Barnlund, 1989; Ishii, 1984; Kinosita, 1988; Kitao & Kitao, 1985; Morsbach, 1988a; Nakane, 1970; Westwood & Vargo, 1985; Yum, 1988).

The Japanese concept of collectivism is epitomize by their usage of the term *nihonjinron* to express self-perceived uniqueness as both a nation and a people. This idea of distinctive originality provides the Japanese a focus for social cohesiveness. Their propensity for group affiliation has created a social context referred to as *uchi-soto*, or inside–outside. This context can also be viewed as in-group (possessing membership) and out-group (no involvement). Within the security of their respective in-group (*uchi*), the Japanese can be quite expressive and display considerable nonverbal affiliation with other members. Much less interaction will occur in an out-group (*soto*) situation (Gudykunst & Nishida, 1984; Gudykunst, Nishida, & Schmidt, 1989; Gudykunst, Yoon, & Nishida, 1987; Lebra, 1976, 1993).

The hierarchical nature of Japanese society and an inexorable compulsion for social balance or harmony (*wa*) increases the reliance on nonverbal behaviors and concomitantly discourages verbal exchanges. A hierarchy exists in every instance of group or interpersonal interaction. In this superior–subordinate environment, the junior is socially compelled to assume a passive role, awaiting and hopefully anticipating the senior's desires or actions. The senior, desiring to exemplify humility and avoid any social or personal discord, will endeavor to nonverbally ascertain the junior's expectations.

The cultural pressure for social balance dictates the course of all Japanese activities and creates a pervasive acceptance of ambiguity and vagueness during any communication endeavor. Reluctant to arbitrarily advance personal opinions or attitudes, the Japanese will draw on the situational context and attempt to instinctively discern what the other person is thinking (Hall & Hall, 1990; Ishii, 1984; Ishii & Bruneau, 1991; Kitao & Kitao, 1985; Lebra, 1976; Morsbach, 1988a; Munakata, 1986; Reischauer, 1988).

The cultural trait of empathy (*omoiyari*) also lessens the Japanese reliance on verbal exchanges. In Japan, considerable value is placed on an individual's ability to empathetically determine the needs of another person. During interpersonal encounters, the Japanese will frequently use indirect or vague statements and depend on the other person's sensitivity to ascertain the desired meaning of the interaction (Doi, 1988; Ishii, 1984; Lebra, 1976).

PROPOSITIONAL SURVEY

Considered in isolation, a nonverbal code normally provides only partial interpretation of the intended message. This study, however, is not concerned with the code's proposed message, but instead attempts to demonstrate how the code is culturally based and motivated. To this end, in each of the following propositions, specific nonverbal communication codes are shown to reflect one or more cultural themes common to Japanese society.

P1: *Japanese kinesics reflect the cultural themes of (1) group orientation, (2) hierarchy, (3) social balance, (4) formality, and (5) humility.*

The Japanese enjoy a wide array of kinesic activities, especially gestures (Caudill & Weinstein, 1969; March, 1990; Seward, 1983). Usage, however, is situational and often limited to males (Richie, 1987). A Japanese manager, for instance, might rely on gestures to communicate with work subordinates (Sethi, 1974), thereby demonstrating the cohesive familiarity common among in-group (*uchi*) members.

The Japanese are more relaxed and expressive within their in-group. Away from the in-group, however, the use of body language is usually remarkably restrained (Cohen, 1991; Ishii, 1975). In public, it is quite common to see both Japanese men and women sitting quietly and unobtrusively, with hands folded (March, 1990). This self-restraint of body movement in out-group (*soto*) environments is designed to avoid attention and maintain situational harmony or balance.

As another example of concern for social balance, Japanese hand gestures are never used in reference to a person who is present at the time. Instead, they are employed when referring to some absent party

(Richie, 1987). This, quite naturally, reduces the opportunity for offending anyone present and helps sustain contextual harmony.

The most common activity associated with Japanese kinesics is the bow, an integral and repetitive part of daily social interaction. The Japanese bow when meeting someone, when asking for something, while apologizing, when offering congratulations, when acknowledging someone else, and when departing, to mention just a few instances. Historically a sign of submission, the bow is a contemporary ritual that continues to convey respect and denote hierarchical status. The junior person bows first, lowest, and longest. An improperly executed bow can be interpreted as a significant insult (Hendry, 1989; Ishii, 1975; Kitao & Kitao, 1987, 1989; Morsbach, 1988b; Ramsey, 1979; Richie, 1987; Ruch, 1984).

Traditional Japanese women exhibit a very distinct kinesic activity by obscuring facial areas with their hands or some object[1] (Ishii, 1975; Ramsey, 1981). Ramsey's (1981) investigation of this phenomenon concluded that women utilized these adaptors for impression management. A very explicit intent of these actions is to evoke a perception of humility when in the presence of a social superior.

P2: *Japanese oculesics reflect the cultural themes of (1) hierarchy, (2) social balance, and (3) humility.*

In Japan, prolonged eye contact is considered rude, threatening, and disrespectful.[1] The Japanese are taught, from childhood, to avert their gaze or look at a person's throat. When one is part of an audience, looking away, or simply sitting silently with eyes closed indicates attention to, and possibly agreement with, the speaker. Direct, sustained eye contact is normally avoided, unless a superior wants to admonish a subordinate (Hall & Hall, 1990; Ishii, 1975; Kasahara, 1986; Kitao & Kitao, 1987, 1989; March, 1990; Morsbach, 1973; Richie, 1987; Ruch, 1984; Watson, 1970).

By avoiding eye contact, the participants in communication simultaneously evince an air of humility and sustain situational *wa*. The employment of direct eye contact by a superior is a clear exercise of hierarchical prerogative (March, 1990).

P3: *Japanese facial expressions reflect the cultural themes of (1) social balance and (2) gaman.*

As is common to all aspects of their social behavior, the Japanese do not normally evince any significant emotion through public facial displays. The most commonly observed expressions are either a placid, unrevealing countenance or a nondescript smile, whose actual meaning, or intent, may be totally indecipherable. A smile can indicate happiness or serve as a friendly acknowledgement. Alternatively, it may be worn to mask negative emotions, especially displeasure, anger, or grief (Gudykunst & Nishida, 1993; Kitao & Kitao, 1987, 1989; Matsumoto, 1996; Morsbach, 1973).

For the Japanese, the smile is simply a part of social etiquette, designed to help sustain harmony. In a social environment, the Japanese would consider it unpardonable to burden someone else with an outward show of elation, irritation, or anguish. Eschewing any external display of negative emotion is an example of perseverance or self-sacrifice (gaman) to avoid disrupting the social balance (wa). The smile is also used to avoid conflict; a Japanese might simply smile in order to avoid answering an awkward question or giving a negative answer (Ishii, 1975; Kitao & Kitao, 1987, 1989; Nakane, 1970; Ruch, 1984; Seward, 1972).

P4: *Japanese proxemic behaviors reflect the cultural themes of (1) in-group affinity, (2) hierarchy, and (3) balance.*

The Japanese attitude toward personal space is, on the surface, quite complex and often seemingly contradictory. In uncrowded situations, they assiduously strive to maintain personal space intervals that are even greater than those maintained by Americans. Conversely, when on a train or bus they offer no resistance to frequent or even prolonged body contact with total strangers. Personal space is also very close among friends or family members (Hall, 1990; Richie, 1987).

This apparent dichotomy is the result of their societal group orientation, vertical structure, and constant concern for social balance. In an uncrowded out-group environment, the Japanese maintain their personal space, which also provides a psychological barrier against the unknown, such as the hierarchical status and group affiliation of others (Ishii, 1975; Morsbach, 1973; Watson, 1970). If forced into close proximity with an out-group member, the Japanese will assume a facade of unperturbable passivity in an effort to maintain situational harmony. I have often observed the Japanese projecting an air of composed detachment while being subjected to suffocating conditions in a crowded Tokyo subway car.

Among in-group members, where strong social ties exist, personal space is dramatically reduced. Traditionally, family members commonly slept in the same room, within easy touching distance of each other (Caudill & Plath, 1966). Male white-collar co-workers (salarimen) sitting close together and patting each other on the back during after-work drinking excursions are a common sight in Japanese bars.

Japanese proxemic behavior has been the subject of several investigations. In a study involving status manipulation, Japanese subjects exhibited signs of anxiety in reaction to an interviewer's forward lean (Bond & Shiraishi, 1974). Iwata's (1979) study of Japanese female students disclosed that individuals with high self-esteem evinced a negative reaction to crowding. This is consistent with the Japanese concept of hierarchy. Self-esteem would be proportional with social status, which would predicate greater interpersonal distance in out-group situations.

P5: *Japanese tactile conventions reflect the cultural themes of (1) in-group affinity and (2) social balance.*

Studies of Japanese maternal care have disclosed that children experience considerable touch from their mothers (Caudill & Plath, 1966; Caudill & Weinstein, 1969). Even today, parents and their young children very often share the same bed. The amount of public tactile interaction drops dramatically, however, after childhood, and the individual is expected to conform to societal nontouch standards (Barnlund, 1975; McDaniel & Andersen, 1998; Montague, 1978). Indeed, adult Japanese actively avoid public displays of interpersonal physical expressiveness[1] (Barnlund, 1989; Malandro & Barker, 1983) unless in a close-knit in-group setting.

For adults, in-group (uchi) touching is quite acceptable (Lebra, 1976). This is especially evident when male co-workers are drinking (Miyamoto, 1994). In an out-group (soto) situation, touch is very uncommon unless it results inadvertently from crowding, and then it is simply ignored (Ishii, 1975; Morsbach, 1973; Ramsey, 1985). These conventions are again indicative of the value placed on group affiliation and harmony.

P6: *Japanese personal appearance reflects the cultural themes of (1) collectivism, (2) group affiliation, (3) social balance, and (4) hierarchy.*

The central theme of Japanese external appearance is, quite simply, group identity and status. The ubiquitous dark suit dominates the business world, and everyone, both men and women, normally opt for conservative styles. Small lapel pins or badges identifying the individual's company are frequently worn.[2] Blue-collar workers normally wear a uniform (such as coveralls or smocks) distinctive to their corporation (Condon & Yousef, 1983; Hall, 1981; Harris & Moran, 1979; March, 1990; Morsbach, 1973; Ruch, 1984).

The general proclivity for conservative dress styles and colors emphasizes the nation's collectivism and, concomitantly, lessens the potential for social disharmony arising from nonconformist attire. Lapel pins and uniforms signal a particular group affiliation, which in turn helps in determining a person's social position.

While not specifically nonverbal, the Japanese business card, or *meshi*, must be discussed. It exerts considerable influence on Japanese nonverbal behavior and communication in general. The initial impression of an individual is derived from his or her *meshi*. The card must be of the appropriate size and color and in addition to the individual's name, list the person's company and position. This facilitates rapid determination of the individual's group affiliation and personal station, which dictates the correct deportment and appropriate speech levels for participants engaging in interpersonal dialogue (Craft, 1986; Morsbach, 1973; Ruch, 1984).

P7: *Japanese use of space reflects the cultural themes of (1) hierarchy and (2) group orientation.*

The Japanese hierarchical contextualization of space is best exemplified by the standard spatial array of governmental and corporate offices. Numerous desks, occupied by lower-level employees, are lined, facing each other, hierarchically in rows in a large, common room, absent of walls or partitions. The supervisors and managers are positioned at the head of each row. This organization encourages the exchange of information, facilitates multitask accomplishment, promotes group cooperation and solidarity, and facilitates rapid discernment of the work-center rank structure. Seating arrangements at any formal or semi-formal function are also based on hierarchy (Hamabata, 1990; Ramsey, 1979; Ramsey & Birk, 1983; Ruch, 1984; Takamizawa, 1988).

In explaining the Japanese perception of space as a hierarchical concept, Hall (1990) offers an insightful illustration. Neighborhood houses in Japan are numbered in the order they are constructed, regardless of actual location along the street.

P8: *Japanese use of time reflects the cultural themes of (1) hierarchy, (2) group orientation, and (3) social balance.*

Hall and Hall (1990) have indicted that the Japanese use time polychronically among themselves and monochronically when conducting business with foreigners. The rigid adherence to schedules when dealing with foreigners is in contrast with the temporal flexibility exhibited during interactions with other Japanese. This demonstrates an ability to adjustment to dynamic situations. For example, schedules may have to be altered in order to accommodate the desires of a senior, which reflects hierarchical sensitivities.

The Japanese decision-making process characterizes the influence of group orientation and social balance on the usage of time. In almost every interpersonal context, it is necessary to build a consensus before announcing a decision. This process, concerned with maintaining social balance among group members, can take days, weeks, or even months (Hall, 1988; Nakane, 1970; Stewart, 1993).

P9: *Japanese vocalics reflect the cultural themes of (1) hierarchy, (2) social balance, and (3) empathy.*

The Japanese make ample use of paralanguage in their conversations. During interpersonal discussions, the Japanese will constantly use small, culturally unique, gestures (*aizuchi*) and utterances (e.g., *hai, soo, un*, or *ee*) to demonstrate their attentiveness (Harris & Moran, 1979; Nishida, 1996). These vocalics possess a cultural motivation. Hierarchy is demonstrated by the adjustment of voice tone and pitch to fit the speaker's position of junior or senior (Morsbach, 1973). Additionally, the feedback stream indicates that the listener is paying attention to the speaker, which serves to help maintain positive social relations (*wa*) between the two individuals.

For the Japanese, laughter can possess a variety of meanings. Laughter can signal joy, of course, but it is also used to disguise embarrassment, sadness, or even anger (Seward, 1972). Use of laughter in the latter modes is designed to maintain situational harmony and avoid any potential for interpersonal discord.

In a 1989 study, White analyzed tape-recorded English-language conversations of Americans and native Japanese. The Japanese participants employed significantly more feedback responses than did the Americans. Unable to ascertain a linguistic reason for this greater use of vocalics, White (1989) concluded it was a cultural influence. The listener was believed to be exhibiting a sensitivity to the speaker's viewpoint and feelings (in other words, was expressing empathy).

P10: *Japanese use of silence reflects the cultural themes of (1) hierarchy, (2) social balance, and (3) empathy.*

The salient role of silence in the Japanese communication process is attributed to a general mistrust of spoken words and an emphasis on emotionally discerning the other person's intentions (empathy). Silence is considered a virtue as well as a sign of respectability and trustworthiness (Buruma, 1985; Cohen, 1991; Hall & Hall, 1990; Ishii, 1975, 1984; Lebra, 1976, 1993; Morsbach, 1988a).

A pronounced feature of Japanese conversations is the many short pauses or breaks, referred to as *ma*. According to Matsumoto (1988), the Japanese closely attend to these brief conversational breaks. The pauses may convey meaning, demonstrate respect, or be an attempt to assess the other person or the situation (Di Mare, 1990; Doi, 1973, 1988).

Instances of *ma* in Japanese discourse can impart a variety of messages, with the context supplying the actual meaning. Silence is employed to tactfully signal disagreement, nonacceptance, or an uncomfortable dilemma. A period of silence can be used to consider an appropriate response or formulate an opinion. Also, a junior may remain silent in deference to a senior (Graham & Herberger, 1983; Morsbach, 1973; Ramsey & Birk, 1983; Ueda, 1974).

P11: *The Japanese use of olfactics reflects the cultural theme of social balance.*

Little information is available concerning the Japanese attitude toward odors. Kasahara (1986) asserted that the Japanese propensity for cleanliness creates a preference for an environment totally absent of odors. Although there is no supporting evidence, the near ritualistic traditional of frequent baths and the desire to refrain from personal offense lends credence to this supposition.

CONCLUSIONS

The preceding propositions suggest that the use of, and reliance on, nonverbal communication is actually a part of Japanese behavioral psychology motivated by cultural imperatives. If this concept is accepted, the benefits of employing cultural motivations to investigate a society's nonverbal communication habits, or other communication patterns, becomes self-evident. Application of cultural themes to communicative dispositions could provide a salient methodology for examining, and better understanding, both cultural-specific and intercultural communication phenomena.

Potential benefits derived from practical application of this approach are especially promising. Greater appreciation of the cultural imperatives behind communicative behaviors would directly enhance intercultural communication competence. An individual engaged in an intercultural communication exchange would better understand both *what* the other person was doing and *why* they were doing it.

The suggested design is not, however, free of limitations. Several perceived impediments exist that require additional investigation and clarification before implementation of wider theoretical application.

A particularly important aspect that demands greater inquiry relates to the identification of cultural themes. As earlier discussed, Japan presents an unusually homogeneous culture when compared with other nations. This societal similitude facilitates discernment of both cultural themes and their motivations. Moreover, the cultural themes can then be reliably applied across almost all dimensions of Japanese society. [3]

Other societies, such as the United States, do not enjoy the degree of cultural congruency extant in Japan. For these cases, identification and application of consistent cultural themes to the composite ethnicities is fraught with considerable difficulty and potential peril. Any motivation to stereotype themes across an entire heterogeneous populace must be tempered by a resolve to treat ethnic divisions as both separate entities and as integral parts of the greater societal whole.

Another dilemma requiring meditation concerns units of measurement. The nonverbal communication patterns of a culture are, for the most part, observable and measurable. Culture, as an entity itself and as a motivator of communication behaviors, is not, however, readily quantifiable. The majority of studies dealing with cultural influences have relied on recounts of personal experiences and observations (anecdotal documentation).

Many studies incorporate "culture" as a somewhat ethereal, abstract manifestation of humankind's imagination. Others have approached "culture" empirically and attempted to employ scientific measurements. Hofstede, for instance, used survey questionnaires and statistical analysis in an effort to determine the role of culture in the formation of value systems which affect "human thinking, organizations, and institutions in predictable ways" (1980, p. 11). Similarly, Osgood, May, and Miron have made noteworthy progress in statistically quantifying intangible attributes, what they term "subjective culture" (1975, p. 4).

The progress of Hofstede (1980) and Osgood, May, and Miron (1975) suggest that culture is not entirely beyond the scope of objective quantification. Their achievements provide benchmarks for empirical examination of the influence of cultural themes on communication behaviors.

Thematic universality is also an area of potential peril for theoretical application of cultural themes to communicative practices. Specifically, the investigator must not axiomatically assume that similar themes beget similar behaviors when moving between cultures. A theme prompting a specific behavioral action in one culture may generate an entirely different pattern in another cultural environment. To obviate this possible pitfall, each culture must be examined as a unique entity. The identification of common cultural themes and communication practices across a substantial number of societies is needed before theoretical application can be made on unexamined cultures.

Further investigation is also needed to determine if any of the cultural themes are codependent. For example, if hierarchy is manifested by a culture, will formality or another theme also be present?

The preceding constraints should not be interpreted as a repudiation of the proposed approach to explaining communicative practices. Rather, they are simply areas of concern that must be investigated and clarified before cultural themes can be reliably employed to help discern and understand societal communication predispositions. Resolution of these concerns will only serve to instill the concept with increased application, additional rigor, and greater parsimony.

Notes

1. Although sometimes moving at a seemingly glacial pace, culture is actually a dynamic process. As individuals avail themselves to modern technologies they are exposed to, and often adopt, different social practices. This diffusion of cultural behaviors can and does exert change. With this in mind, we must recognize that the nonverbal communicative behaviors of the Japanese, as discussed in this article, are undergoing change. For example, except in rural areas, one seldom sees young Japanese women place their hand over their mouth. Direct eye contact is becoming increasingly common, especial in interactions with Westerners. Public touch is becoming more acceptable, and young Japanese couples can be seen cuddling in Tokyo's parks.

2. Even this established tradition is undergoing change. A recent article in a Japanese business newspaper bemoaned the fact that many of the younger employees were eschewing the company's lapel pins.

3. This is not to suggest that the Japanese are a wholly homogenous group uninfluenced by other cultures. For example, Japan has three large minority groups—Koreans, Ainu, and Burakumin—which possess distinct cultural characteristics. In recent years, the urban areas of Japan have

also experienced a growing influx of foreign workers, coming from all parts of the globe. These immigrants bring their own values, beliefs, and behaviors, some of which are diffused, in varying degrees, into the Japanese culture.

References

Barnlund, D. (1975). *Public and private self in Japan and United States*. Tokyo: Simul.

———. (1989). *Communicative styles of Japanese and Americans*. Belmont, CA: Wadsworth.

Buller, D. B., & Burgoon, J. K. (1986). The effects of vocalics and nonverbal sensitivity on compliance. *Human Communication Research, 13*(1), 126–144.

Burgoon, J. K., & Hale, J. L. (1984). The fundamental topi of relational communication. *Communication Monographs, 51*, 193–214.

———. (1987). Validation and measurement of the fundamental themes of relational communication. *Communication Monographs, 54*, 19–62.

Buruma, I. (1985). *A Japanese mirror*. New York: Penguin Books.

Caudill, W. (1973). General culture: The influence of social structure and culture on human behavior in modern Japan. *The Journal of Nervous and Mental Disease, 157*, 240–257.

———, & Plath, D. (1966). Who sleeps with whom? Parent–child involvement in urban Japanese families. *Psychiatry, 29*, 344–366.

———, & Weinstein, H. (1969). Maternal care and infant behavior in Japan and America. *Psychiatry, 32*, 12–43.

Cohen, R. (1991). *Negotiating across cultures*. Washington, D.C.: United States Institute of Peace.

Coker, D. A., & Burgoon, J. K. (1987). The nature of conversational involvement and nonverbal encoding patterns. *Human Communication Research, 13*(4), 463–494.

Condon, J. C., & Yousef, F. (1983). *An introduction to intercultural communication*. Indianapolis, IN: Bobbs-Merrill.

Craft, L. (1986). All in the cards: The mighty *meishi*. *TOKYO Business Today*. May, 61–64.

Di Mare, L. (1990). Ma and Japan. *Southern Communication Journal, 55*(3), 319–328.

Doi, T. (1973). The Japanese patterns of communication and the concept of *amae*. *The Quarterly Journal of Speech, 59*, 180–185.

———. (1988). Dependency in human relationships. In D. I. Okimoto & T. P. Rohlen (Eds.), *Inside the Japanese system: Readings on contemporary society and political economy* (pp. 20–25). Stanford, CA: Stanford University Press.

Graham, J. L., & Herberger, R. A. (1983). Negotiations abroad: Don't shoot from the hip. *Harvard Business Review, 83*(4), pp. 160–168.

Gudykunst, W. B., & Nishida, T. (1984). Individual and cultural influences on uncertainty reduction. *Communication Monographs, 51*, 23–36.

———. (1993). Interpersonal and intergroup communication in Japan and the United States. In W. B. Gudykunst (Ed.), *Communication in Japan and the United States* (pp. 149–214). Albany: State University of New York Press.

———, & Schmidt, K. (1989). The influence of culture, relational, and personality factors on uncertainty reduction processes. *Western Journal of Speech Communication, 53*, 13–29.

Gudykunst, W. B., Yoon, Y. C., & Nishida, T. (1987). The influence of individualism–collectivism on perceptions of communication in ingroup and outgroup relationships. *Communication Monographs, 54*, 295–306.

Hall, E. T. (1981). *Beyond culture*. New York: Anchor Books, Doubleday. (Original work published 1976.)

———. (1988). The hidden dimensions of time and space in today's world. In F. Poyatos (Ed.), *Cross-cultural perspectives in nonverbal communication* (pp. 145–152). Lewiston, NY: C. J. Hogrefe.

———. (1990). *The hidden dimension*. New York: Anchor Books, Doubleday. (Original work published 1966.)

———, & Hall, M. R. (1990). *Hidden differences: Doing business with the Japanese*. New York: Anchor Books, Doubleday. (Original work published 1987.)

Hamabata, M. M. (1990). *Crested kimono: Power and love in the Japanese business family*. Ithaca, NY: Cornell University Press.

Harris, P. R., & Moran, R. T. (1979). *Managing cultural differences*. Houston, TX: Gulf Publishing.

Hendry, J. (1989). *Becoming Japanese: The world of the preschool child*. Honolulu: University of Hawaii Press. (Originally published in 1986.)

Hofstede, G. (1980). *Culture's consequence: International differences in work-related values*. Newbury Park, CA: Sage.

Ishii, S. (1975). Characteristics of Japanese nonverbal communicative behavior. *Occasional Papers in Speech*. Honolulu: Department of Speech, University of Hawaii.

———. (1984). *Enyro–Sasshi* communication: A key to understanding Japanese interpersonal relations. *Cross Currents, 11*, 49–58.

———, & Bruneau, T. (1991) Silence and silences in cross-cultural perspective: Japan and the United States.

In L. A. Samovar and R. E. Porter (Eds), *Intercultural communication: A reader* (6th ed.) (pp. 314–319). Belmont, CA: Wadsworth.

Iwata, O. (1979). Selected personality traits as determinants of the perception of crowding. *Japanese Psychological Research, 21,* 1–9.

Kasahara, Y. (1986). Fear of eye-to-eye confrontation among neurotic patients in Japan. In T. S. Lebra & W. P. Lebra (Ed.), *Japanese culture and behavior: Selected readings* (rev. ed.) (pp. 379–387). Honolulu: University of Hawaii Press.

Kinosita, K. (1988). Language habits of the Japanese. *Bulletin of the Association for Business Communication, 51*(3), 35–40.

Kitao, K., & Kitao, S. K. (1985). *Effects of social environment on Japanese and American communication.* (ERIC Document Reproduction Service No. ED 260 579)

———. (1987). *Differences in the kinesic codes of Americans and Japanese.* East Lansing, MI: Department of Communication, Michigan State University. (ERIC Document Reproduction Service No. ED 282 400)

———. (1989). *Intercultural communication between Japan and the United States.* Tokyo: Eichosha Shinsha Co. (ERIC Document Reproduction Service No. ED 321 303)

Lebra, T. S. (1976). *Japanese patterns of behavior.* Honolulu: University of Hawaii Press.

———. (1993). Culture, self, and communication in Japan and the United States. In W. B. Gudykunst (Ed.), *Communication in Japan and the United States* (pp. 51–87). Albany: State University of New York Press.

Malandro, L. A., & Barker, L. L. (1983). *Nonverbal communication.* Menlo Park, CA: Addison-Wesley.

March, R. M. (1990). *The Japanese negotiator: Subtlety and strategy beyond Western logic.* New York: Kondansha. (Original work published 1989.)

Matsumoto, D. (1996). *Unmasking Japan: Myths and realities about the emotions of the Japanese.* Stanford, CA: Stanford University Press.

Matsumoto, M. (1988). *The unspoken way: "Haragei": Silence in Japanese business and society.* New York: Kondansha. (Original work published 1984 in Japanese under the title *Haragei.*)

McDaniel, E. R., & Andersen, P. A. (1998). International patterns of tactile communication: A field study. *Journal of Nonverbal Behavior, 22,* 59–75.

Miyamoto, M. (1994). *Straitjacket society: An insider's irreverent view of bureaucratic Japan.* New York: Kodansha International.

Montague, A. (1978). *Touching: The human significance of the skin* (2nd ed.). New York: Harper & Row.

Morsbach, H. (1973). Aspects of nonverbal communication in Japan. *Journal of Nervous and Mental Disease, 157,* 262–277.

———. (1988a). The importance of silence and stillness in Japanese nonverbal communication: A cross-cultural approach. In F. Poyatos (Ed.), *Cross-cultural perspectives in nonverbal communication* (pp. 201–215). Lewiston, NY: C. J. Hogrefe.

———. (1988b). Nonverbal communication and hierarchical relationships: The case of bowing in Japan. In F. Poyatos (Ed.), *Cross-cultural perspectives in nonverbal communication* (pp. 189–199). Lewiston, NY: C. J. Hogrefe.

Munakata, T. (1986). Japanese attitudes toward mental illness and mental health care. In T. S. Lebra & W. P. Lebra (Ed.), *Japanese culture and behavior: Selected readings* (rev. ed.) (pp. 369–378). Honolulu: University of Hawaii Press.

Nakane, C. (1970). *Japanese society.* Berkeley: University of California Press.

Nishida, T. (1996). Communications in personal relationships in Japan. In W. B. Gudykunst, S. Ting-Toomey, & T. Nishida (Eds.), *Communication in personal relationships across cultures* (pp. 102–117). Thousand Oaks, CA: Sage.

Opler, M. E. (1945). Themes as dynamic forces in culture. *American Journal of Sociology, 51,* 198–206.

———. (1946). An application of the theory of themes in culture. *Journal of the Washington Academy of Sciences, 36*(5), 137–166.

Osgood, C. E., May, W. H., & Miron, M. S. (1975). *Cross-cultural universals of affective meaning.* Urbana: University of Illinois Press.

Ramsey, S. J. (1979). Nonverbal behavior: An intercultural perspective. In M. K. Asante, E. Newmark, & C. A. Blake (Eds.), *Handbook of intercultural communication* (pp. 105–143). Beverly Hills, CA: Sage.

———. (1981). The kinesics of femininity in Japanese women. *Language Sciences, 3*(1), 104–123.

———. (1985). To hear one and understand ten: Nonverbal behavior in Japan. In L. A. Samovar & R. E. Porter (Eds.), *Intercultural communication: A reader* (4th ed., pp. 307–321). Belmont, CA: Wadsworth.

———, & Birk, J. (1983). Training North Americans for interaction with Japanese: Considerations of language and communication style. In D. Landis & R. W. Brislin (Eds.), *The handbook of intercultural training: Vol. III. Area studies in intercultural training* (pp. 227–259). New York: Pergamon Press.

Reischauer, E. O. (1988). *The Japanese today: Change and continuity.* Cambridge, MA: Belknap Press of Harvard University.

Richie, D. (1987). *A lateral view: Essays on contemporary Japan*. Tokyo: The Japan Times.

Ruch, W. (1984). *Corporate communication: A comparison of Japanese and American practices*. Westport, CT: Quorum Books.

Sethi, S. P. (1974). Japanese management practices: Part I. *Columbia Journal of World Business*, 9(4), 94–104.

Seward, J. (1972). *The Japanese*. New York: William Morrow.

———. (1983). *Japanese in action* (rev. ed.). New York: Weatherhill.

Spitzberg, B. H. (1989). Issues in the development of a theory of interpersonal competence in the intercultural context. *International Journal of Intercultural Relations*, 13, 241–268.

Stewart, L. P. (1993). Organizational communication in Japan and the United States. In W. B. Gudykunst (Ed.), *Communication in Japan and the United States* (pp. 215–248). Albany: State University of New York Press.

Takamizawa, H. (1988). *Business Japanese: A guide to improved communication*. New York: Kondansha International.

Ueda, T. (1974). Sixteen ways to avoid saying "no" in Japan. In J. C. Condon & M. Saito (Eds.), *Intercultural encounters with Japan* (pp. 185–192). Tokyo: Simul Press.

White, S. (1989). Backchannels across cultures: A study of Americans and Japanese. *Language in Society*, 18(1), 59–76.

Watson, M. O. (1970). *Proxemic behavior: A cross-cultural study*. The Hague: Mouton.

Westwood, M. J., & Vargo, J. W. (1985). Counselling double-minority status clients. In R. J. Samuda (Ed.), *Intercultural counselling and assessment: Global perspectives* (pp. 303–313). Lewiston, NY: C. J. Hogrefe.

Yum, Y. (1988). The impact of Confucianism on interpersonal relationship and communication patterns in East Asia. *Communication Monographs*, 55, 374–388.

Concepts and Questions

1. What are "cultural themes" and how may we benefit from their study?

2. What are the major Japanese cultural themes that influence intercultural communication?

3. Can you think of any American cultural themes that might influence how Americans use nonverbal communication?

4. How does the Confucian-based collectivism help control Japanese nonverbal communication?

5. What cultural themes are seen as the basis for Japanese kinesic behavior? Are the same or different themes active in U.S. American nonverbal behavior?

6. What are the most obvious activities associated with Japanese kinesic behavior? What would be a U.S. American counterpart?

7. How does culture influence personal appearance in Japanese and U.S. American culture?

8. What are the cultural underpinnings of silence in Japan? How does the Japanese manipulation of silence affect intercultural communication?

9. Describe differences in the use of *vocalics* or paralanguage in Japan and the United States. How might these differences lead to misunderstandings during intercultural communication?

Monochronic and Polychronic Time

EDWARD T. HALL

Lorenzo Hubbell, trader to the Navajo and the Hopi, was three quarters Spanish and one quarter New Englander, but culturally he was Spanish to the core. Seeing him for the first time on government business transactions relating to my work in the 1930s, I felt embarrassed and a little shy because he didn't have a regular office where people could talk in private. Instead, there was a large corner room—part of his house adjoining the trading post—in which business took place. Business covered everything from visits with officials and friends, conferences with Indians who had come to see him, who also most often needed to borrow money or make sheep deals, as well as a hundred or more routine transactions with store clerks and Indians who had not come to see Lorenzo specifically but only to trade. There were long-distance telephone calls to his warehouse in Winslow, Arizona, with cattle buyers, and his brother, Roman, at Ganado, Arizona—all this and more (some of it quite personal), carried on in public, in front of our small world for all to see and hear. If you wanted to learn about the life of an Indian trader or the ins and outs of running a small trading empire (Lorenzo had a dozen posts scattered throughout northern Arizona), all you had to do was to sit in Lorenzo's office for a month or so and take note of what was going on. Eventually all the different parts of the pattern would unfold before your eyes, as eventually they did before mine, as I lived and worked on that reservation over a five-year period.

I was prepared for the fact that the Indians do things differently from [Anglo-European] (AE) cultures because I had spent part of my childhood on the Upper Rio Grande River with the Pueblo Indi-

From Edward T. Hall, *The Dance of Life: The Other Dimension of Time* (New York: Doubleday and Company, 1983), pp. 42–54. Copyright ©1983 by Edward T. Hall. Used by permission of Doubleday, a division of Bantam, Doubleday, Dell Publishing Group, Inc.

ans as friends. Such differences were taken for granted. But this public, everything-at-once, mélange way of conducting business made an impression on me. There was no escaping it, here was another world, but in this instance, although both Spanish and Anglos had their roots firmly planted in European soil, each handled time in radically different ways.

It didn't take long for me to accustom myself to Lorenzo's business ambiance. There was so much going on that I could hardly tear myself away. My own work schedule won out, of course, but I did find that the Hubbell store had a pull like a strong magnet, and I never missed an opportunity to visit with Lorenzo. After driving through Oraibi, I would pull up next to his store, park my pickup, and go through the side door to the office. These visits were absolutely necessary because without news of what was going on life could become precarious. Lorenzo's desert "salon" was better than a newspaper, which, incidentally, we lacked.

Having been initiated to Lorenzo's way of doing business, I later began to notice similar mutual involvement in events among the New Mexico Spanish. I also observed the same patterns in Latin America, as well as in the Arab world. Watching my countrymen's reactions to this "many things at a time" system I noted how deeply it affected the channeling and flow of information, the shape and form of the networks connecting people, and a host of other important social and cultural features of the society. I realized that there was more to this culture pattern than one might at first suppose.

Years of exposure to other cultures demonstrated that complex societies organize time in at least two different ways: events scheduled as separate items—one thing at a time—as in North Europe, or following the Mediterranean model of involvement in several things at once. The two systems are logically and empirically quite distinct. Like oil and water, they don't mix. Each has its strengths as well as its weaknesses. I have termed doing many things at once: polychronic, P-time. The North European system—doing one thing at a time—is monochronic, M-time. P-time stresses involvement of people and completion of transactions rather than adherence to preset schedules. Appointments are not taken as seriously and, as a consequence, are frequently broken. P-time is treated as less tangible than M-time.

For polychronic people, time is seldom experienced as "wasted," and is apt to be considered a point rather than a ribbon or a road, but that point is often sacred. An Arab will say, "I will see you before one hour," or "I will see you after two days." What he means in the first instance is that it will not be longer than an hour before he sees you and at least two days in the second instance. These commitments are taken quite seriously as long as one remains in the P-time pattern.

Once, in the early '60s, when I was in Patras, Greece, which is in the middle of the P-time belt, my own time system was thrown in my face under rather ridiculous but still amusing circumstances. An impatient Greek hotel clerk, anxious to get me and my ménage settled in some quarters which were far from first-class, was pushing me to make a commitment so he could continue with his siesta. I couldn't decide whether to accept this rather forlorn "bird in the hand" or take a chance on another hotel that looked, if possible, even less inviting. Out of the blue, the clerk blurted, "Make up your mind. After all, time is money!" How would you reply to that at a time of day when literally nothing was happening? I couldn't help but laugh at the incongruity of it all. If there ever was a case of time not being money, it was in Patras during siesta in the summer.

Though M-time cultures tend to make a fetish out of management, there are points at which M-time doesn't make as much sense as it might. Life in general is at times unpredictable; and who can tell exactly how long a particular client, patient, or set of transactions will take. These are imponderables in the chemistry of human transactions. What can be accomplished one day in ten minutes may take twenty minutes on the next. Some days people will be rushed and can't finish; on others, there is time to spare, so they "waste" the remaining time.

In Latin America and the Middle East, North Americans can frequently be psychologically stressed. Immersed in a polychronic environment in the markets, stores, and souks of Mediterranean and Arab countries, one is surrounded by other customers all vying for the attention of a single clerk who is trying to wait on everyone at once. There is no recognized order as to who is to be served next, no queue or numbers to indicate who has been waiting the longest. To the North European or American, it appears that confusion and clamor abound. In a different context, the same patterns can be seen operating in the governmental bureaucracies of Mediterranean countries: A typical office layout for important officials frequently includes a large reception area (an ornate version of Lorenzo Hubbell's office), outside the private suite, where small groups of people can wait and be visited by the minister or his aides. These functionaries do most of their business outside in this semipublic setting, moving from group to group conferring with each in turn. The semiprivate transactions take less time, give others the feeling that they are in the presence of the minister as well as other important people with whom they may also want to confer. Once one is used to this pattern, it is clear that there are advantages, which frequently outweigh the disadvantages of a series of private meetings in the inner office.

Particularly distressing to Americans is the way in which polychronic people handle appointments. Being on time simply doesn't mean the same thing as it does in the United States. Matters in a polychronic culture seem in a constant state of flux. Nothing is solid or firm, particularly plans for the future; even important plans may be changed right up to the minute of execution.

In contrast, people in the Western world find little in life exempt from the iron hand of M-time. Time is so thoroughly woven into the fabric of existence that we are hardly aware of the degree to which it determines and coordinates everything we do, including the molding of relations with others in many subtle ways. In fact, social and business life, even one's sex life, is commonly schedule-dominated. By scheduling, we compartmentalize; this makes it possible to concentrate on one thing at a time, but it also reduces the context. Since scheduling by its very nature selects what will and will not be perceived and attended, and permits only a limited number of events within a given period, what gets scheduled constitutes a system for setting priorities for both people and functions. Important things are taken up first and allotted the most time; unimportant things are left to last or omitted if time runs out.

M-time is also tangible; we speak of it as being saved, spent, wasted, lost, made up, crawling, killed, and running out. These metaphors must be taken seriously. M-time scheduling is used as a classification system that orders life. The rules apply to everything except birth and death. It should be mentioned, that without schedules or something similar to the M-time system, it is doubtful that our industrial civilization could have developed as it has. There are other consequences. Monochronic time seals off one or two people from the group and intensifies relationships with one other person or, at most, two or three people. M-time in this sense is like a room with a closed door ensuring privacy. The only problem is that you must vacate the "room" at the end of the allotted fifteen minutes or an hour, a day, or a week, depending on the schedule, and make way for the next person in line. Failure to make way by intruding on the time of the next person is not only a sign of extreme egocentrism and narcissism, but [also] just plain bad manners.

Monochronic time is arbitrary and imposed, that is, learned. Because it is so thoroughly learned and so thoroughly integrated into our culture, it is treated as though it were the only natural and logical way of organizing life. Yet, it is not inherent in man's biological rhythms or his creative drives, nor is it existential in nature.

Schedules can and frequently do cut things short just when they are beginning to go well. For example, research funds run out just as the results are beginning to be achieved. How often has the reader had the experience of realizing that he is pleasurably immersed in some creative activity, totally unaware of time, solely conscious of the job at hand, only to be brought back to "reality" with the rude shock of realizing that other, frequently inconsequential previous commitments are bearing down on him?

Some Americans associate schedules with reality, but M-time can alienate us from ourselves and from others by reducing context. It subtly influences how we think and perceive the world in segmented compartments. This is convenient in linear operations but disastrous in its effect on nonlinear creative tasks. Latino peoples are an example of the opposite. In Latin America, the intelligentsia and the academicians frequently participate in several fields at once—fields which the average North American academician, business, or professional person thinks of as antithetical. Business, philosophy, medicine, and poetry, for example, are common, well-respected combinations.

Polychronic people, such as the Arabs and Turks, who are almost never alone, even in the home, make very different uses of "screening" than Europeans do. They interact with several people at once and are continually involved with each other. Tight scheduling is therefore difficult, if not impossible.

Theoretically, when considering social organization, P-time systems should demand a much greater centralization of control and be characterized by a rather shallow or simple structure. This is because the leader deals continually with many people, most of who stay informed as to what is happening. The Arab fellah can always see his sheik. There are no intermediaries between man and sheik or between man and God. The flow of information as well as people's need to stay informed complement each other. Polychronic people are so deeply immersed in each other's business that they feel a compulsion to keep in touch. Any stray scrap of a story is gathered in and stored away. Their knowledge of each other is truly extraordinary. Their involvement in people is the very core of their existence. This has bureaucratic implications. For example, delegation of authority and a buildup in bureaucratic levels are not required to handle high volumes of business. The principal shortcoming of P-type bureaucracies is that as functions increase, there is a proliferation of small bureaucracies that really are not set up to handle the problems of outsiders. In fact, outsiders traveling or residing in Latin American or Mediterranean countries find the bureaucracies unusually cumbersome and unresponsive. In polychronic countries, one has to be an insider or have a "friend" who can make things happen. All bureaucracies are oriented inward, but P-type bureaucracies are especially so.

There are also interesting points to be made concerning the act of administration as it is conceived in these two settings. Administration and control of polychronic peoples in the Middle East and Latin America is a matter of job analysis. Administration consists of taking each subordinate's job and identifying the activities that go to make up the job. These are then labeled and frequently indicated on the elaborate charts with checks to make it possible for the administrator to be sure that each function has been performed. In this way, it is felt that absolute control is maintained over the individual. Yet scheduling how and when each activity is actually performed is left up to the employee. For an employer to schedule a subordinate's work for him would be considered a tyrannical violation of his individuality—an invasion of the self.

In contrast, M-time people schedule the activity and leave the analysis of the activities of the job to the individual. A P-type analysis, even though technical by its very nature, keeps reminding the subordinate that his job is not only a system but also part of a larger system. M-type people, on the other hand, by virtue of compartmentalization, are less likely to see their activities in context as part of the larger whole. This does not mean that they are unaware of the "organization"—far from it—only that the job itself or even the goals of the organization are seldom seen as a whole.

Giving the organization a higher priority than the functions it performs is common in our culture. This is epitomized in television, where we allow the TV commercials, the "special message," to break the continuity of even the most important communication. There is a message all right, and the message is that art gives way to commerce—polychronic advertising agencies impose their values on a monochronic population. In monochronic North European countries, where patterns are more homogeneous, commercial interruptions of this sort are not tolerated. There is a strict limit as to the number as well as the times when commercials can be shown. The average American TV program has been allotted one or two hours, for which people have set aside time, and is conceived, written, directed, acted, and played as a unity. Interjecting commercials throughout the body of the program breaks that continuity and flies in the face of one of the core systems of the culture. The polychronic Spanish treat the main feature as a close friend or relative who should not be disturbed and let the commercials mill around in the antechamber outside. My point is not that one system is superior to another, it's just that the two don't mix. The effect is disruptive, and reminiscent of what the English are going through today, now that the old monochronic queuing patterns have broken down as a consequence of a large infusion of polychronic peoples from the colonies.

Both M-time and P-time systems have strengths as well as weaknesses. There is a limit to the speed with which jobs can be analyzed, although once analyzed, proper reporting can enable a P-time administrator to handle a surprising number of subordinates. Nevertheless, organizations run on the polychronic model are limited in size, they depend on having gifted people at the top, and are slow and cumbersome when dealing with anything that is new or different. Without gifted people, a P-type bureaucracy can be a disaster. M-type organizations go in the opposite direction. They can and do grow much larger than the P-type. However, they combine bureaucracies instead of proliferating them, e.g., with consolidated schools, the business conglomerate, and the new superdepartments we are developing in government.

The blindness of the monochronic organization is to the humanity of its members. The weakness of the polychronic type lies in its extreme dependence on the leader to handle contingencies and stay on top of things. M-type bureaucracies, as they grow larger, turn inward; oblivious to their own structure, they grow rigid and are apt to lose sight of their original purpose. Prime examples are the Army Corps of Engineers and the Bureau of Reclamation, which wreak havoc on our environment in their dedicated efforts to stay in business by building dams or aiding the flow of rivers to the sea.

At the beginning of this chapter, I stated that "American time is monochronic." On the surface, this is true, but in a deeper sense, American (AE) time is both polychronic and monochronic. M-time dominates the official worlds of business, government, the professions, entertainment, and sports. However, in the home—particularly the more traditional home in which women are the core around which everything revolves—one finds that P-time takes over. How else can one raise several children at once, run a household, hold a job, be a wife, mother, nurse, tutor, chauffeur, and general fixer-upper? Nevertheless, most of us automatically equate P-time with informal activities and with the multiple tasks and responsibilities and ties of women to networks of people. At the preconscious level, M-time is male time and P-time is female time, and the ramifications of this difference are considerable.

In the conclusion of an important book, *Unfinished Business*, Maggie Scarf vividly illustrates this point. Scarf addresses herself to the question of why it is that depression (the hidden illness of our age) is three to six times more prevalent in women than it is in men. How does time equate with depression in women? It so happens that the time system of the dominant culture adds another source of trauma and alienation to the already overburdened psyches of many American women. According to Scarf, depression comes about in part as a consequence of breaking significant ties that make up most women's worlds. In our culture, men as a group tend to be more task-oriented, while women's lives center on networks of people and their relations with people. Traditionally, a woman's world is a world of human emotions, of love, attachment, envy, anxiety, and hate. This is a little difficult for late-twentieth-century people to accept because it implies basic differences between men and women that are not fashionable at the moment. Nevertheless, for most cultures around the world, the feminine mystique is intimately identified with the development of the human relations side of the personality rather than the technical, cortical left-brain occupational side. In the United States, AE women live in a world of peoples and relationships and their egos become spread out among those who are closest to them by a process we call *identification*. When the relationships are threatened or broken or something happens to those to whom one is close, there are worries and anxieties, and depression is a natural result.

Polychronic cultures are by their very nature oriented to people. Any human being who is naturally drawn to other human beings and who lives in a world dominated by human relationships will be either pushed or pulled toward the polychronic end of the time spectrum. If you value people, you must hear them out and cannot cut them off simply because of a schedule.

M-time, on the other hand, is oriented to tasks, schedules, and procedures. As anyone who has had experience with our bureaucracies knows, schedules and procedures take on a life all their own without reference to either logic or human needs. And it is this set of written and unwritten rules—and the consequences of these rules—that is at least partially responsible for the reputation of American business being cut off from human beings and unwilling to recognize the importance of employee morale. Morale may well be the deciding factor in whether a given company makes a profit or not. Admittedly, American management is slowly, very slowly, getting the message. The problem is that modern management has accentuated the monochronic side at the expense of the less manageable, and less predictable, polychronic side. Virtually everything in our culture works for and rewards a monochronic view of the world. But the antihuman aspect of M-time is alienating, especially to women. Unfortunately, too many women have "bought" the M-time world, not realizing that unconscious sexism is part of it. The pattern of an entire system of time is too large, too diffuse, and too ubiquitous for most to identify its patterns. Women sense there is something alien about the way in which modern organizations handle time, beginning with how the workday, the week, and the year are set up. Such changes as flextime do not alter the fact that as soon as one enters the door of the office; one becomes immediately locked into a monochronic, monolithic structure that is virtually impossible to change.

There are other sources of tension between people who have internalized these two systems. Keep in mind that polychronic individuals are oriented toward people, human relationships, and the family, which is the core of their existence. Family takes precedence over everything else. Close friends come next. In the absence of schedules, when there is a crisis the family always comes first. If a monochronic woman has a polychronic hairdresser, there will inevitably be problems, even if she has a regular appointment and is scheduled at the same time each week. In circumstances like these, the hairdresser (following his or her own pattern) will inevitably feel compelled to "squeeze people in." As a consequence, the regular customer, who has scheduled her time very carefully (which is why she has a standing appointment in the first place), is kept waiting and feels put down, angry, and frustrated. The hairdresser is also in a bind because if he does not accommodate his relative or friend regardless of the schedule, the result is endless repercussions within his family circle. Not only must he give preferential treatment to relatives, but the degree of accommodation and who is pushed aside or what is pushed aside is itself a communication!

The more important the customer or business that is disrupted, the more reassured the hairdresser's polychronic Aunt Nell will feel. The way to ensure the message that one is accepted or loved is to call up at the last minute and expect everyone to rearrange everything. If they don't, it can be taken as a clear signal that they don't care enough. The M-time individual caught in this P-time pattern has the feeling either that he is being pressured or that he simply doesn't count. There are many instances where culture patterns are on a collision course and there can be no resolution until the point of conflict is identified. One side or the other literally gives up. In the instance cited above, it is the hairdresser who usually loses a good customer. Patterns of this variety are what maintain ethnicity. Neither pattern is right, only different, and it is important to remember that they do not mix.

Not all M-times and P-times are the same. There are tight and loose versions of each. The Japanese, for example, in the official business side of their lives where people do not meet on a highly personalized basis, provide us an excellent example of tight M-time. When an American professor, business person, technical expert, or consultant visits Japan, he may find that his time is like a carefully packed trunk—so tightly packed, in fact, that it is impossible to squeeze one more thing into the container. On a recent trip to Japan, I was contacted by a well-known colleague who had translated one of my earlier books. He wanted to see me and asked if he could pick me up at my hotel at twelve-fifteen so we could have lunch together. I had situated myself in the lobby a few minutes early as the Japanese are almost always prompt. At twelve-seventeen, I could see his tense figure darting through the crowd of arriving business people and politicians who had collected near the door. Following greetings, he ushered me outside to the ubiquitous black limousine with chauffeur, with white doilies covering the arms and headrests. The door of the car had hardly closed when he started outlining our schedule for the lunch period by saying that he had an appointment at three o'clock to do a TV broadcast. That set the time limit and established the basic parameters in which everyone knew where he would be at any given part of the agenda. He stated these limits—a little over two hours—taking travel time into account.

My colleague next explained that not only were we to have lunch, but he wanted to tape an interview for a magazine. That meant lunch and an interview, which would last thirty to forty minutes. What else? Ah, yes. He hoped I wouldn't mind spending time with Mr. X, who had published one of my earlier books in Japanese, because Mr. X was very anxious to pin down a commitment on my part to allow him to publish my next book. He was particularly eager to see me because he missed out on publishing the last two books, even though he had written me in the United States. Yes, I did remember that he had written, but his letter arrived after my agent had made the decision on the Japanese publisher. That, incidentally, was the very reason why he wanted to see me personally. Three down and how many more to go? Oh, yes, there would be some photographers there and he hoped I wouldn't mind if pictures were taken? The pictures were to be both formal group shots, which were posed, and informal, candid shots during the interview, as well as pictures taken with Mr. X. As it turned out, there were at least two sets of photographers as well as a sound man, and while it wasn't "60 Minutes," there was quite a lot of confusion (the two sets of photographers each required precious seconds to straighten things out). I had to hand it to everyone—they were not only extraordinarily skilled and well organized, but also polite and considerate. Then, he hoped I wouldn't mind but there was a young man who was studying communication who had scored over 600 on an examination, which I was told put him 200 points above the average. This young man would be joining us for lunch. I didn't see how we were going to eat anything, much less discuss issues of mutual interest. In situations such as these, one soon learns to sit back, relax, and let the individual in charge orchestrate everything. The lunch was excellent, as I knew it would be—hardly leisurely, but still very good.

All the interviews and the conversation with the student went off as scheduled. The difficulties came when I had to explain to the Japanese publisher that I had no control over my own book—that once I had written a book and handed it in to my publisher, the book was marketed by either my publisher or my agent. Simply being first in line did not guarantee anything. I had to try to make it clear that I was tied into an already existing set of relationships with attached obligations and that there were other people who made these decisions. This required some explaining, and I then spent considerable time trying to work out a method for the publisher to get a hearing with my agent. This is sometimes virtually impossible because each publisher and each agent in the United States has its own representative in Japan. Thus an author is in their hands, too.

We did finish on time—pretty much to everyone's satisfaction, I believe. My friend departed on schedule as the cameramen were putting away their equipment and the soundman was rolling up his wires and disconnecting his microphones. The student drove me back to my hotel on schedule, a little after 3 P.M.

The pattern is not too different from schedules for authors in the United States. The difference is that in Japan the tightly scheduled monochronic pattern is applied to foreigners who are not well enough integrated into the Japanese system to be able to do things in a more leisurely manner, and where emphasis is on developing a good working relationship.

All cultures with high technologies seem to incorporate both polychronic as well as monochronic functions. The point is that each does it in its own way. The Japanese are polychronic when looking and working inward, toward themselves. When dealing with the outside world, they have adopted the dominant time system, which characterizes that world. That is, they shift to the monochronic mode and, characteristically, since these are technical matters, they outshine us. . . .

Concepts and Questions

1. How might cultural differences in time conceptualization lead to intercultural communication problems?
2. How have you seen Hall's concept of monochronic time reflected in your culture?

3. What difficulties might an M-time–oriented person experience when interacting with someone who follows a P-time orientation? What feelings might emerge during this interaction?
4. What difficulties might a P-time–oriented person experience when interacting with someone who follows an M-time orientation? What feelings might emerge during this interaction?
5. What does Hall imply by the statement "there are points at which M-time doesn't make as much sense as it might"?
6. How does an M-time orientation affect perception?
7. What problems arise in a P-time–oriented society as bureaucratic levels increase? How does a P-time society adjust to a bureaucratic buildup?
8. How is administrative scheduling affected by M-time and P-time orientations?
9. What does Hall mean by his statement that "European-American (EA) time is both polychronic and monochronic"?
10. Hall notes that "both M-time and P-time systems have strengths as well as weaknesses." What are some of these strengths and weaknesses?

Gender and Nonverbal Communication

DEBORAH BORISOFF

LISA MERRILL

The effect of gender is produced through the stylization of the body and, hence, must be understood as the mundane way in which bodily gestures, movements, and styles of various kinds constitute the illusion of an abiding gendered self.

JUDITH BUTLER, GENDER TROUBLE

There's language in her eye, her cheek, her lip; Nay, her foot speaks; Her wanton spirits look out at every joint and motive of her body.

WILLIAM SHAKESPEARE, TROILUS AND CRESSIDA

According to Judith Butler (1990), what we know as gender is a set of "acts" or social performances which people are repeatedly compelled to enact so that, over time, they "produce the appearance of substance, of a natural sort of being" (p. 33). For example, young girls are intentionally taught to "sit like a lady" with legs close together; young boys are instructed not to cry or express fear. Erving Goffman (1979) has called these nonverbal behaviors a form of "gender display." There are frequently severe social penalties for those who act in violation of their culture's accepted gender "script." The gender-differentiated nonverbal behaviors that result from this socialization are learned rather than innate, and they become part of an individual's experience as a "gendered self." As a result, many people conclude that men "naturally" take up more space than do women or that women are "naturally" more emotionally expressive than men, although the prescriptions for how men and women should act vary from culture to culture.

Reprinted by permission of Waveland Press, Inc. from Deborah Borisoff and Lisa Merrill, *The Power to Communicate: Gender Differences as Barriers*, 3d ed. (Prospect Heights, IL: Waveland Press, Inc., 1998). All rights reserved. Deborah Borisoff teaches at New York University, and Lisa Merrill teaches at Hofstra University.

Nonverbal messages have a *presentational dimension;* it is through demeanor, gestures, expressions, and artifacts that communicators present aspects of their socially constructed—and gendered—selves to others. It is through our nonverbal behaviors that we express and display our emotions and our experience of gender, ethnicity, sexuality, and socioeconomic class identifications. Each of these variables influences the others. For example, every culture formulates its own display rules that dictate when, how, and with what consequences nonverbal expressions will be exhibited. In some cultures, heterosexual male friends, family members, or colleagues routinely walk hand-in-hand and kiss each other upon greeting and leave-taking; but in other cultures men who engage in these behaviors are considered homosexual. In some cultures, women are taught that it is not "ladylike" to run, to meet a man's gaze directly, or to expose one's arms, legs, or face to the gaze of male strangers in public. In other cultures, women engage in athletics and wear slacks and shirts with short sleeves, clothing that is not differentiated from that worn by men.

In this article, we will examine some of the assumptions and controversies about the nonverbal performance of gender as well as explore women's and men's use and interpretation of such nonverbal variables as space, height, touch, gesture, facial expressions, and eye contact. Further, because sensitivity to the nonverbal messages of others is both a learned skill and related to a given society's gender expectations, we will consider whether men and women differ in their perception of and ability to decode nonverbal messages accurately.

SPACE, OR "BIGGER IS BETTER"

In North American culture, space is a signifier of power, and individuals who have command over greater amounts of space and territory are often considered to have greater power. Women and lower-status persons of both sexes are afforded and expected to take up less space than males and higher-status persons. In addition, people in subordinate positions cannot control others from entering the space available to them. The boss can enter the worker's space, lean on the employee's desk, or tower over the subordinate. Only with the supervisor's invitation can the subordinate enter into the supervisor's space. In public and in private, in the workplace and in the streets, women constantly experience space encroachment. Gender-differentiated proxemic patterns appear even in childhood when young boys are encouraged and permitted to play outdoors while play for young girls is more frequently centered within the home (Graebner, 1982; Harper and Sanders, 1975; Thorne, 1993; Valentine, 1997).

Learned behavior patterns inform beliefs about entitlement to space and affect how individuals interpret the use of space—especially when expected spatial norms are violated. In the animal kingdom and among human beings, subordinates yield space to dominants. Frank Willis (1966) performed studies in which he measured the initial distance set by an approaching person. He established that both sexes approach women more closely than they do men. In a review of many such research studies on nonverbal sex differences in interpersonal distance, Judith Hall (1984) also found that females are approached more closely than are males. When women's space is intruded upon, they are apt to acquiesce to the intrusion—just as they frequently acquiesce to interruptions. Jeanette Silveira's research (1972) indicated that when men and women walked toward each other on the sidewalk, the woman moved out of the man's way in twelve out of nineteen cases. Knapp and Hall (1997) speculate that acquiescing or ceding space to males may be linked, in part, to associating male behavior with the potential for threatening aggression. They further hypothesize that acquiescence to "invasions" of personal space may be attributed to societal norms for maintaining "appropriate" distance; "people expect men to keep larger distances, and when they do not, it may be disturbing" (p. 168). Yet as we have seen, societal norms and expectations serve dominant interests.

Women are encouraged to sit and move in ways that intensify the lesser amount of space available to them. For example, women when involved in a dyadic or small-group communication interaction may sit poised on the edge of a chair, eagerly leaning forward rather than "taking up" space. "Feminine" clothes also contribute to a nonverbal image of female weakness and reconfigure the bodies that wear them. Tight skirts and tight slacks restrict movement. High heels force women to take small

steps. In the late 1800s economist Thorstein Veblen (1899) asserted that "the high heel, the skirt, the impracticable bonnet, the corset, and the general disregard of the wearer's comfort which is an obvious feature of all civilized women's apparel, are so many items of evidence to the effect that in the modern civilized scheme of life the woman is still, in theory, the economic dependent of the man." Veblen noted that middle-class women were not just restricted in their movements, they, and their relative powerlessness, were literally "on display" (pp. 126–127).

In the United States, contemporary women are still socialized to take up less space than men. They are taught to sit with their legs together and elbows to their sides and to walk with smaller steps. Contemporary women's fashion, such as tight clothing, short skirts, and high heels, discourages women who wear it from sitting and moving expansively, as do men. While seated, men spread their legs and put their arms on the armrests of chairs. They walk with longer strides. We know that these stereotypical ways of moving are not anatomically based, because men in Asia, for example, sit with their legs as closely together and cross their legs as do Western women. Yet in the United States, men who retreat into such little available space may not be considered "masculine," while women who sit and stand with open movements and walk with long strides may be regarded as "unfeminine."

Culture as well as gender exerts a determining force on the degree of personal space individuals use in interaction with each other. Members of many cultures tend, in general, to interact at closer distances than do white North Americans. As Carol Zinner Dolphin (1988) has established, "use of personal space as influenced by the sex(es) of interacting individuals tends to differ dramatically from one culture to another" (p. 28). Dolphin found that proximity was influenced by a given culture's expectations for male or female behavior. Thus, while one culture may expect physical closeness and contact between men, in another this may be largely forbidden. Some cultures may expect women to maintain larger distances from each other than are expected of men from each other, while members of other cultures may interpret such behavior between women as a sign of coldness or disinterest. While some cultures allow for a degree of close physical proximity in mixed-sex interactions, others prohibit it and proscribe greater amounts of distance between men and women.

Jeffrey Sanders and his colleagues (1985) studied the degrees of personal distance maintained between same- and mixed-sex dyads of North American and Arab students. Sanders found that mixed-sex pairs of Arab women and men interacted at a much greater distance than did either same-sex pairs of Arab students or same- or mixed-sex North American pairs. Robert Shuter's (1976) study of proxemics and touch in men and women from three Latin American cultures (Costa Rica, Colombia, and Panama) found that same-sex female dyads in all three cultures interacted the most closely—at significantly smaller distances and with greater amounts of physical contact—than same-sex male or opposite-sex dyads. In these two cases, respectively, the greater distance between men and women and the greater closeness between women are cultural expectations, constituting part of the construction and performance of gender in the cultures studied.

Within most cultures, the closer people feel to each other emotionally, the more they are likely to allow each other to be close in proximity. Thus, the distance between communicators in an interaction may be influenced by gender, culture, power, and the degree of intimacy and reciprocity. There is no one meaning for any given nonverbal message. In some cases, close interpersonal distances between people are a result of warmth and affiliation; in others, they reflect an abuse of status differences. Distance between partners in an interaction may be an expression of respect and deference—or disinterest and hostility.

Lombardo's (1986) study of sex-roles and personal distance has led him to suggest that the sex of communicators and their orientation toward particular sex roles exerts a considerable impact over how individuals use space, their perceptions of spatial needs, and the invasions of their personal space. For example, if the feeling of emotional closeness or affiliation between individuals is not reciprocal, an undesired intrusion into others' personal space may be considered a gross abuse of power. Our discussion of sexual harassment will be informed by an awareness of the complex components involved in such nonverbal behavior as negotiating personal space. According to Bochner (1982), the "meanings" attached to the use of personal space are determined by a range of variables, including the relationship between the individuals involved, their relative status and power, their degree of intimacy, and the type of activity in which they are engaged.

TOUCH, OR "JUST A FRIENDLY PAT ON THE BACK?"

Touch, like physical closeness, may be considered an expression of affection, support, or sexual attraction. However, touch may be used to express and maintain an asymmetrical relationship as well as a reciprocal one. For example, as a gesture of comfort, the doctor may touch the patient, but the patient may not initiate physical contact with the doctor. Similarly, upon entering the secretary's cubicle, the department head might pat the secretary on the back and inquire about her or his family. However, this apparently "friendly" gesture is not as benign as it appears as long as the secretary does not have an equal right to initiate the same pat on the back and elicit similar personal information from the department head.

In the mid-1970s, Nancy Henley performed observational studies investigating the relationship between touch and socioeconomic status, sex, and age. Henley (1973, 1977) found that, in interactions between people not romantically involved with each other, higher-status persons (individuals of higher socioeconomic status, male, and older) touched lower-status persons significantly more often. In their review of gender and touching behavior between romantic partners, Knapp and Hall (1997) report "inconsistent" findings on "which sex touches the other more, overall" (p. 303). In these situations, as a relationship becomes more intimate and committed, sex differences in the initiation of touch between partners appears less evident. Yet even in such relationships, Knapp and Hall contend that "observers seem to *perceive* the initiator [of touch] as the person with greater power" (p. 304). These findings have important implications for both women and men. Individuals of both sexes should guard against using touch to assert authority. We should avoid initiating touch in situations where either the other individual is not desirous of the gesture or where the higher-status person would not accept a reciprocal touch.

What about when the gesture is reciprocal? Coworkers must be aware of outsiders possibly misconstruing the sexual implications of touch. In the 1984 Mondale–Ferraro campaign for the United States presidency, newscasters mentioned a distinction from previous campaigns. Whereas male candidates for president and vice-president traditionally linked inner arms and waved their raised outer arms, Mondale and Ferraro waved outer arms with their inner arms at their sides. They did not touch each other. The sexism and heterosexism in our society impose restrictions on behavior. Until people become accustomed to perceiving women as competent professionals in their own right rather than as potential sexual objects, they will have difficulty imagining a collegial relationship between men and women without sexual implications. Consequently, at present, women and men who work together will continue to be subject to greater scrutiny than same-sex pairs.

Within same-sex dyads in the United States, women are generally much freer than men to touch one another. Women friends and relatives may walk arm-in-arm, dance together, and hug one another. Touch between heterosexual males is generally more restricted. As Barrie Thorne (1993) found in her ethnographic study of elementary school boys and girls, young girls regularly engage in such gestures of intimacy with each other as stroking or combing their friends' hair, whereas touch among boys is rarely relaxed and affectionate—limited primarily to a ritual handslap and the mock violence of pushing, poking, and grabbing (p. 94). Outside of the sporting arena, many North American men do not feel free to exchange much more than a slap on the back without their behavior being construed as having sexual connotations.

It is important to remember that the notion of "appropriate" touch, like that of "comfortable" interpersonal distance between communicators, is largely culturally determined. In some cultures same-sex male dyads have a greater latitude of haptic expression with each other. They may commonly hug or kiss each other on both cheeks, for example, while women friends or family members are much more restricted in their socially sanctioned ability to touch one another. In some cultures, all touch between men and women who are not related to each other by family or by marriage is strictly forbidden. In these circumstances, uninvited touch may be experienced as an abuse of power that takes the form of cultural as well as sexual oppression.

HEIGHT, OR "WHOM DO YOU LOOK UP TO?"

Height is also a nonverbal variable that may be manipulated, thereby either empowering or impeding an individual. We say, "I look up to you" to indicate respect or admiration. "Higher," like "bigger," is often used to mean "better" or "more" (as in "higher class," "high opinion").

In hierarchies, the individual with greater power frequently is perceived as taller than he or she is. Paul R. Wilson (1968) reported that undergraduates who were asked to estimate the height of a man who was described as any one of five academic ranks increased their estimation of his height when his ascribed status was increased. In some environments—for example, in courtrooms, in the military, in some religious practices—deference is enforced by norms of courtesy and respect which dictate, for example, who may sit and who may stand when status unequals interact.

While men as a group may be somewhat taller than women, in individual mixed-sex dyads, these differences may be minimal or reversed. However, there are behaviors which make males appear taller. Social dyads in which the woman is appreciably taller than the man are frequently subject to ridicule, as though they are subverting gender and power expectations. In a world in which height equals power and women are not supposed to be more powerful than men, taller women may attempt to diminish themselves, to slouch and round their shoulders so as to retreat or to occupy as little space as possible.

Traditional female facial expressions of coyness and flirtation may reinforce the height and power differential between the sexes. For example, women frequently exhibit their femininity by tilting their heads to the side and looking upward when talking to male conversational partners. Although the head tilt is a gesture which indicates attentive listening in either sex, women are apt to employ this more frequently in mixed-sex pairs than men, thus reinforcing the notion that, in addition to listening, the woman is "looking up to" the man.

We must guard against using height to control or to influence. Superiors need not tower over subordinates in the workplace. Tall individuals should be encouraged neither to use their height in an intimidating fashion nor to attempt to diminish themselves by denying their personal power. Power need not be used as power *over* others.

FACIAL EXPRESSIONS, OR "YOU LOOK SO PRETTY WHEN YOU SMILE"

White, middle-class women in the United States are expected to be highly expressive emotionally. One of the hallmarks of the feminine stereotype for this group is to be facially expressive, and a woman's face is believed to reflect her emotional state. The most common and easily discernible facial expression is the smile.

From childhood, white female children are admonished to smile. They are taught to smile not as an expression of their own pleasure, but because it is pleasing to others. Hence a smile may be considered a gesture of appeasement or deference. Women are told that they are more attractive when they smile and appear happy. The key word in the previous sentence is "appear." As long as women and other subordinates are concerned with pleasing others, they are not considered threatening to their superiors. African-American women are not expected to perform their "femininity" within their cultures in exactly the same manner. As a result, Halberstadt and Saitta (1987) found African-American women to be less deferential than white women and, therefore, less inclined to smile merely because it is expected of them. Consequently, some of the racism to which women of color are exposed is a result of whites misinterpreting an absence of facial gestures of deference as hostility, arrogance, unfriendliness, or disinterest. As long as one *seems* to be satisfied with the position that has been allotted, the hierarchical system is reinforced. Smiles, therefore, can function as genuine or artificial signs of satisfaction.

In addition to functioning as an expression of pleasure, pleasantness, or a desire for approval, smil-

ing may also reflect the smiler's nervousness. In a number of service occupations, smiling is not only preferred behavior, it is *required*. In Arlie Russell Hochschild's (1983) article "Smile Wars: Counting the Casualties of Emotional Labor," she discussed the emotional labor required of flight attendants. According to Hochschild, the flight attendant, receptionist, waitress, and salesperson often pay a psychological price for their requisite smiles. When a smile is an *expected* part of the job, it becomes a commodity to be given. Women in these and other occupations frequently are required to "give" male patrons or superiors a smile. The constant feigned smile is an expression of duplicity. (And it must be feigned, for obviously no one can be happy all the time.) An individual engaging in this behavior cuts him- or herself off from the expression of his or her own emotions. The smile becomes a mask, a form of "make up," constructed to gain the approval of one who has power. Subordinates are expected to smile at superiors. When the boss walks into the room, the secretaries are expected to smile and warmly greet him or her.

Moreover, dominant members of a hierarchy are less likely to smile or disclose their feelings nonverbally. They typically withhold verbal and nonverbal expressions of emotions. Instead, they are often encouraged to maintain a "poker face," to appear neutral and impassive, and to disclose as little about themselves as possible. However, in some contexts, rather than smiling to gain others' approval, superiors are apt to assume facial expressions which imply that they are judging others. One such example, according to Gerald I. Nierenberg and Henry H. Calero (1971), is the disapproving attitude conveyed by raised eyebrows, a partially twisted head, and a look of doubt. (According to Webster's Dictionary, the word *supercilious* comes from Latin meaning "disdain or haughtiness as expressed by raising the eyebrows.")

Little difference has been found in the smiling behavior of female and male infants and young children. However, as white North American girls grow up, they smile significantly more frequently than do white North American boys. In one study, preschool boys' spontaneous facial expressions were found to decrease dramatically from age four to six (Buck, 1977). According to Hall (1984), "this suggests that socialization, pressure or modeling induces boys during this period to reduce expression of emotion via the face" (p. 54). The social pressure to present a "more masculine" face (less smiling) may be operative for boys at this age since they are likely to be in school starting at age four or five.

As we stated earlier, women are believed to be more facially expressive (Hall 1984; Leathers 1986) than men. In analyses of numerous studies of expression accuracy, Hall (1984) found that "females were better expressors, that is their expressions were more accurately judged by decoders" (p. 53). Perhaps one of the ways to account for women's greater expressiveness is to consider to what extent the performance of femininity in the United States depends upon heightened or exaggerated facial expression.

Zuckerman and his colleagues (1982) conducted three separate studies which related the legibility of an individual's facial expressions to signifiers of masculinity and femininity. The studies revealed that the very concept of femininity implies clear and willing expression of nonverbal cues. According to Marianne La France and Nancy Henley (1994) the pressure on women to develop and to "perform" these nonverbal cues is reinforced and perpetuated by men's "greater social power relative to women in everyday social interactions" (p. 290). Borisoff and Hahn (1997a) contend that to the extent that initial attractiveness and heterosexual relationship satisfaction remain associated with women's nonverbal expressiveness, women "are destined to be the arbiters of affective nonverbal display" (p. 65). Of course, nonverbal signifiers of "masculinity" or "femininity" are culturally determined, rather than innate. In those cultures and subcultures in which being facially expressive is an integral component in the collection of behaviors that are seen as markers of "femininity," males may resist both the nonverbal display of expression and attentiveness to others in order to appear more masculine.

As Buck (1979) has noted, people whose faces express their emotional states have lower levels of electrothermal response than do people whose faces do not display emotion. Higher electrothermal responses indicate suppressed emotions and have been considered possible contributors to heart disease and other stress-related conditions which are more prevalent in men than women. Thus, men may be paying with their lives for withholding emotional expression (see Borisoff and Merrill, 1991).

As we will see in the following chapters, in homes, schools, and workplaces we need to be aware of ways in which expressions of emotions serve to establish or maintain a power differential. Women and other subordinates should evaluate the need to engage in overeager smiles for approval or to offer smiles that are expected of them. Men and dominant members of hierarchies should also reevaluate their tendency to withhold or mask emotional expressiveness and equate the appearance of pleasing expressions with compliance due them. They might also allow themselves to engage more openly in genuine, mutual expressions of pleasure and approval.

GAZE, OR "ARE YOU LOOKING AT ME?"

Direct eye contact between individuals may be interpreted in several different ways. Looking directly into another person's eyes can connote an aggressive threat, a sexual invitation, or a desire for honest and open communication. For many contemporary theorists, the "gaze" is a metaphor for power, where a seeing subject—frequently assumed to be male—takes the position of an active spectator when regarding another person as a passive object. This notion of objectification, where one person looks while another "is looked at," is at the root of many interpretations of and reactions to eye contact.

A number of years ago, actor Robert DeNiro portrayed a psychopathic murderer in the film *Taxi Driver*. Posed in front of a mirror, DeNiro glared at his own reflection, taunting an imaginary assailant whom he envisioned to be staring at him. Menacingly, he asked, " . . . You talkin' to me? Who do you think you're talkin' to?" DeNiro's character interpreted a glance as an attempt at dominance. Researchers Ellsworth, Carlsmith, and Henson (1972) tell us that a stare may have this function. Ellsworth and her colleagues have reported studies that relate staring in humans to primate threat displays. For most individuals, a glance that catches another person's eye for several seconds is relatively insignificant. If, however, eye contact is maintained beyond several seconds, a nonverbal power contest may ensue in which the person with less power ultimately averts her or his eyes.

Thus, gaze has been proven to be related to status and power as well as to gender. In a number of cultures, children are taught that to look adults in the eyes is a sign of disrespect. Submission is indicated by a bowed head and an averted glance. In mixed-sex pairs, women are more likely than men to avert their eyes. Judith Hall's (1984) analysis established that "the more dominant individual gazes more while speaking and relatively less while listening; while the less dominant individual gazes more while listening and relatively less while speaking" (p. 73). Further, Ellyson and his colleagues' 1980 study on visual dominance behavior in female dyads found that while women with relatively high status gazed an equivalent amount of time while speaking and listening, lower-status female subjects gazed significantly more while listening than when speaking. In her book *Body Politics*, Nancy Henley attempted to differentiate between subordinate attentiveness and dominant staring. Henley (1977) claimed that women and other subordinates look at others more but avert their eyes when looked at. Both of these behaviors are indicative of submissiveness. Status exerts a powerful influence on gaze and affects the behavior of research subjects of both sexes. Knapp and Hall (1997) reported that in studies where the variable of assigned status was removed "the male tends to use the gaze pattern typically used by higher-status people, while the female tends to use the gaze pattern typically used by lower-status people" (p. 456).

In any discussion of nonverbal communication, it is important not to interpret behavior in an ethnocentric fashion. Eye contact, like all other nonverbal behavior, has different connotations in different cultural contexts. There are cultures in which direct eye contact between men and women is regarded as a sexual invitation and is, therefore, to be avoided in "polite" society. For individuals from these backgrounds, averting one's eyes in a mixed-sex dyad may be a sign of respect, modesty, or disinterest, rather than inattentiveness or submissiveness. In Curt and Nine's (1983) study of nonverbal communication among Hispanic couples, they found that many Puerto Rican wives never looked directly at their husbands.

Because of differing expectations and interpretations for behavior, there is the potential for much misunderstanding in mixed-sex and intercultural communication exchanges. Women and men need to be able to identify very precisely those behaviors which seem intrusive or inappropriate and their connection with power inequities in specific social contexts.

GESTURE AND DEMEANOR, OR "ACT LIKE A LADY"

It is through our bearing, demeanor, and gestural mannerisms that we perform much of the behavior that is associated with gender identities. But the gestures of communicators, the ways they "carry themselves," and the meanings associated with those nonverbal behaviors are also, in part, culturally specific, and they have changed over time.

In a nineteenth-century English etiquette manual entitled *The Habits of Good Society: A Handbook for Ladies and Gentlemen* (1870), readers who desired "good manners" were warned that "Foreigners talk with their arms and hands as auxiliaries to the voice. The custom is considered vulgar by us calm Englishmen. . . . You have no need to act with the hands, but if you use them at all, it should be very slightly and gracefully, never bringing down your fist upon the table, nor slapping one hand upon the other, nor poking your fingers at your interlocutor" (pp. 284–285). Yet, while appearing "calm" and "graceful" might signify appropriate "manly" gentility to the Englishman of one hundred years ago, those same qualities of graceful restraint are liable to be read as "feminine" to contemporary North American communicators who have been taught to equate forcefulness with "masculinity" rather than vulgarity. Class and cultural biases are apparent in this warning not to "talk with one's hands." Similar gender biases and stereotypes are operative when women are told that it is "ladylike" to stand up straight and hold one's body rigid, rather than to appear to be "loose" and "easy," as if a woman's deportment signified her sexual availability.

ARTIFACTUAL MESSAGES, OR "WHAT YOU WEAR SPEAKS VOLUMES"

Artifacts are objects. When worn, they have been used to signify a wearer's gender, culture, and socio-economic class. From the moment at which families or hospitals assign infants pink or blue blankets, arti-facts announce and contribute to the shaping of children's experience of gender. As Julia Wood (1994) has noted, clothing is a form of artifactual communication that "manifest[s] and promote[s] cultural definitions of masculinity and femininity" (p. 159). In earlier centuries sumptuary laws regulated "appropriate" dress, and it was literally against the law for women to wear men's breeches, for men to appear in women's dress, or for anyone to dress above their appropriate "station" in life by wearing the clothes of others more privileged than they, except in the special province of the theatre (Garber, 1992; Merrill, 1998 in press).

Elizabeth Grosz (1994) has asserted that "through exercises and habitual patterns of movement, through negotiating its environment . . . and through clothing and make-up, the body is more or less marked, constituted as an appropriate, or, as the case may be, inappropriate body for its cultural requirements." Grosz contend that these procedures are more than adornment; rather, the "norms and ideals governing beauty and health" in a given culture and time literally shape the bodies of those who ascribe to them (p. 142). Consider the nineteenth-century woman tightly lacing herself into a corset designed to reduce her waist to a then-fashionable eighteen inches, and so transforming her body into an artificial hourglass shape, or the contemporary man using steroids to build his muscles into a body type currently fashionable. In both cases norms of "beauty" and people's complicity in or resistance to them send complex messages about gender and cultural values. What do the bodies of bodybuilders or anorexics "communicate" about the desirability of hard, pumped-up muscles or excessively thin, childlike bodies to those who witness them?

Like other forms of nonverbal communication, our bodies and the ways we clothe them are liable to be interpreted to signify things that the communicator may not have intended. For example, women are frequently seen and evaluated largely in terms of how they appear to others. Whether or not women's bodies are clothed in such a way as to intentionally draw attention to female body parts, sex-differentiated clothing (such as low-cut blouses, tightly fitted garments, short skirts, and high heels), rather than merely reflecting an individual's taste and sense of personal aesthetics, reinforces cultural values. Men's looser fitting clothing, ample pockets, and flat shoes afford those who wear them a greater freedom of movement than most women's clothes.

DECODING NONVERBAL MESSAGES, OR "I CAN SEE WHAT YOU MEAN"

In Judith Hall's (1984) extensive review of studies of differences in decoding nonverbal messages, women were found to be significantly better decoders of nonverbal cues than were men. Women were found to be most skilled in decoding facial expressions. Hall based her review on seventy-five studies of sex differences in nonverbal decoding skills and fifty subsequent studies (1984) as well as her work with Robert Rosenthal on the design of the PONS (Profile of Nonverbal Sensitivity) Test. Regardless of age, white and African-American women exceeded men in the ability to ascertain emotions expressed nonverbally. Although differences in men's and women's scores on the PONS Test were small, they were consistent. Recent research, according to Knapp and Hall (1997) suggests no discernible differences in the ability to determine solely from nonverbal cues whether or not an individual is lying. The only emotion Knapp and Hall found men to be more adept at identifying was anger in other men.

To what can we attribute this facility? Several different hypotheses have been offered. Rosenthal and his colleagues (1979) hypothesized that women's greater accuracy in decoding facial expressions may be related to the fact that women gaze at others' faces more in interaction and that "one decodes better what one is paying attention to at the moment" (Hall 1984, p. 34). Related to this is the claim that women's experience with young children and their sensitivity as caregivers necessitate their accurate reading of nonverbal messages (Rosenthal et al., 1979).

Hall proposed a relationship between the amount of time that women gaze at their conversational partners and women's greater accuracy in decoding facial expressions. She suggested that "women may seek cues of approval or disapproval or cues that indicate how contented others are from moment to moment as part of a general motive to maintain harmonious relationships" (1984, pp. 34–35). Furthermore, research findings support a positive correlation between an individual's successful decoding of nonverbal cues and that individual's own expression accuracy in depicting messages nonverbally. Thus, women, who themselves are expected to be more nonverbally expressive, may be more accurate in reading the messages of others.

Nancy Henley (1973, 1977) offered the "oppression" theory. She posited that women, and others who have less power, must learn to "read" the nonverbal messages of those who have power over them. People who are oppressed have heightened needs to anticipate and to understand others' nonverbal messages. Henley claims that this is the reason for the greater interpersonal sensitivity of women and other less dominant persons. We suspect, therefore, that as women and men continue to negotiate and redefine their social roles and economic positions in society, these changes are likely to influence acuity in decoding nonverbal messages. At this point, however, Hall and her colleagues' findings that women far exceeded men in their ability to ascertain emotions expressed nonverbally remains largely uncontested in the research literature.

It appears impossible to provide one definitive explanation for women's greater facility with decoding nonverbal messages. Basically, all of the explanations offered to date fall into two categories: theorists who relate women's greater nonverbal decoding skills to needs which arise out of their subordinate status and theorists who attribute women's nonverbal skills to their greater tendency toward affiliation with others. However, as Hall contends:

> ... it is ... difficult to disentangle these two basic explanations—dominance and affiliation—because of the possibility that women's lower status reduces their ability to challenge or threaten anyone, which in turn enables or requires them to act warm and nice. (1984, p. 84)

In any case, nonverbal factors such as touch, space, height, gaze, and facial expressions exert a potent influence on our interactions with others. Although frequently unacknowledged, many of our notions of masculinity and femininity rest on the nonverbal messages we display and those we decode. We are often unaware of our nonverbal behavior and of how it is being interpreted by others. This can present obstacles in professional as well as personal settings. Certainly one cannot work effectively if being ogled or ignored, leered at or laughed at. We need to monitor our own behavior responsibly and to provide feedback to others about what we perceive to be their reactions to us.

References

Bochner, S. (1982). The social psychology of cross-cultural relations. In S. Bochner (Ed.), *Cultures in Contact*, 5–44. New York: Pergamon Press.

Borisoff, D., and Hahn, D. F. (1997). The mirror in the window: Displaying our gender biases. In S. J. Drucker and G. Gumpert (Eds.), *Voices in the Street: Explorations in Gender, Media, and Public Space*, 101–107. Cresskill, NJ: Hampton Press.

Borisoff, D., and Merrill, L. (1991). Gender issues and listening. In D. Borisoff and M. Purdy (Eds.), *Listening in Everyday Life: A Personal and Professional Approach*, 59–85. Lanham, MD: University Press of America.

Buck, R. (1977). Nonverbal communication of affect in preschool children: Relationships with personality and skin conductance. *Journal of Personality and Social Psychology*, 35: 225–236.

Butler, J. (1990). *Gender Trouble: Feminism and the Subversion of Identity*. New York: Routledge.

Curt, C., and Nine, J. (1983). Hispanic-Anglo conflicts in nonverbal communication. In I. Albino (Ed.), *Perspectives Pedagogicas*. San Juan: Universidad de Puerto Rico.

Dolphin, C. Z. (1988). Beyond Hall: Variables in the use of personal space. *Howard Journal of Communications*, 1: 23–38.

Ellsworth, P. C., Carlsmith, J. M., and Hensen, A. (1972). The stare as a stimulus to flight in human subjects: A series of field experiments. *Journal of Personality and Social Psychology*, 21: 302–311.

Ellyson, S. L., Dovidio, J. F., Corson, R. L., and Vinicur, D. L. (1980). Visual dominance behavior in female dyads: Situational and personality factors. *Social Psychology Quarterly*, 42: 328–336.

Goffman, E. (1979). *Gender Advertisements*. New York: Harper & Row.

Graebner, A. (1982). Growing up female. In L. A. Samovar and R. E. Porter (Eds.), *Intercultural Communication: A Reader*. Belmont, CA: Wadsworth Publishing.

Grosz, E. (1994). *Volatile Bodies: Toward a Corporeal Feminism*. Bloomington: Indiana University Press.

Halberstadt, A., and Saitta, M. (1987). Gender, nonverbal behavior and perceived dominance: A test of the theory. *Journal of Personality and Social Psychology*, 53: 257–272.

Hall, J. (1984). *Nonverbal Sex Differences: Communication Accuracy and Expressive Style*. Baltimore, Johns Hopkins University Press.

Harper, L. V., and Sanders, K. M. (1975). Preschool children's use of space: Sex differences in outdoor play. *Developmental Psychology*, 11: 119.

Henley, N. M. (1973). Status and sex: Some touching observations. *Bulletin of the Psychonomic Society*, 2: 91–93.

———. (1977). *Body Politics: Power, Sex, and Nonverbal Communication*. Englewood Cliffs, NJ: Prentice-Hall.

Hochschild, A. H. (1997, April 20). There's no place like work. *New York Times Sunday Magazine*, 51–55, 81, 84.

LaFrance, M., and Henley, N. M. (1994). On oppressing hypotheses: Or differences in nonverbal sensitivity revisited. In H. L. Radke and H. J. Stam (Eds.), *Power/Gender: Social Relations in Theory and Practice*, 287–311. Thousand Oaks, CA: Sage Publications.

Leathers, D. (1986). *Successful Nonverbal Communication*. New York: Macmillan.

Lombardo, J. P. (1986). Interaction of sex and sex role response to violations of preferred seating arrangements. *Sex Roles*, 15: 173–183.

Nierenberg, G. I., and Calero, H. H. (1971). *How to Read a Person Like a Book*. New York: Hawthorne.

Rosenthall, R., Hall, J., DiMatteo, M. R., Rogers, R. S., and Archer, D. (1979). *Sensitivity to Nonverbal Communication: The PONS Test*. Baltimore: Johns Hopkins University Press.

Sanders, J., et al. (1985). Personal space amongst Arabs and Americans. *International Journal of Psychology*, 20 (1): 13–17.

Shuter, R., (1976). Nonverbal communication: Proxemics and tactility in Latin America. *Journal of Communication*, 26(3): 46-52.

Silveira, J. (1972, February). Thoughts on the politics of touch. *Women's Press*, 1: 13.

Thorne, B. (1993). *Gender Play: Girls and Boys in School*. New Brunswick, NJ: Rutgers University Press.

Valentine, G. (1997). "My son's a bit ditzy." "My wife's a bit soft": Gender, children and cultures of parenting. *Gender, Place and Culture*, 4(1): 37–62.

Veblen, T. (1899). *Theory of the Leisure Class*. Reprint. New York: New American Library, 1953.

Willis, F. (1966). Initial speaking distance as a function of the speaker's relationship. *Psychonomic Science*, 5: 221–222.

Wilson, P. R. (1968). Perceptual distortion of height as a function of ascribed academic status. *Journal of Social Psychology*, 74: 97–192.

Wood, J. T. (1994). *Gendered Lives: Communication, Gender, and Culture*. Belmont, CA: Wadsworth.

Zuckerman, M., DeFrank, R. S., Spiegel, N. H., and Larrance, D. T. (1982). Masculinity–femininity and the encoding of nonverbal cues. *Journal of Personality and Social Psychology*, 42: 548–556.

Concepts and Questions

1. How is gender manifested as a set or series of social acts? What implications can you draw from this perspective?

2. What do Borisoff and Merrill mean when they say that nonverbal messages have a *presentational* dimension?

3. How does space define power? How does the use of space by men and women affect perceptions of power and influence behavior by women and men?

4. How do gender differences in the use of personal space during interaction affect individual behavior?

5. What feelings may be evoked by touch? Are these feelings the same for women as they are for men? How might misperceptions of touch affect communication between men and women?

6. How does individual height function as a nonverbal variable? How does height reflect power status between men and women?

7. In what manner does smiling behavior differ between women and men among white, middle-class Americans? Do the same behaviors hold for African American women and men? If not, why?

8. How do facial expressions function to signify masculinity or femininity? In what manner might gender differences in the facial expressions of males and females affect communication between men and women?

9. How may direct eye contact between individuals be interpreted? Is it the same for women as for men? What might be the consequences of eye aversion rather than direct eye contact in a male–female dyadic interaction?

10. In the decoding of nonverbal messages, which gender tends to be the better decoder? Why does this seem to be the case?

chapter 6

Cultural Contexts:
The Influence of the Setting

All human interaction takes place within a social setting or context that affects the communication event. Whether you are in a classroom, dance hall, doctor's office, business meeting, or church, the context or social environment influences how you communicate. How you dress, what you talk about, whom you talk to, and even the volume level of that talk are in some way determined by the context in which you find yourself. We call attention to this social context because the setting is never neutral; it always influences, to some degree, how the communication participants behave. We have all learned appropriate patterns of communicative behavior for the various social contexts in which we normally find ourselves. But, as with other aspects of intercultural communication, the patterns of behavior appropriate to social contexts are culturally diverse. When we find ourselves in an unfamiliar context without an internalized set of rules to govern our behavior or when we are interacting with someone who has internalized a different set of rules, communication problems often arise. This chapter is about those communication problems and about the resolution of those problems. To help us better engage in intercultural communication, we will examine contextual dynamics as they apply to the business, health care, and educational settings.

The growth of international business during the last thirty years has been startling. Overseas transactions that generated millions of dollars annually just a few decades ago are now multibillion-dollar operations. Furthermore, the international business community has become multinational, with culturally diverse organizational units. Understanding how communication operates in this setting is becoming increasingly important. In fact, the study of international business and the multinational organization has now become an important topic within the fields of intercultural and organizational communication. People who function successfully in the arenas of international business and world markets have had to learn how to deal effectively with approaches to business that are often quite different from their own.

Because of worldwide economic growth and the internationalization of business, people no longer have the luxury of dealing exclusively with those who possess the same cultural background and experiences. One's associates, clients, subordinates, and even supervisors are frequently from different countries and cultures. Such aspects of business life as methods of negotiation, decision making, policy formulation, marketing techniques, management structure, human resource management, gift giving, and patterns of communication are now subject to culturally diverse influences.

While the globalization of business was taking place, changes also were occurring within the United States: The country has become a pluralistic, multicultural society. As a result, the cultural diversity of both the U.S. population and the U.S. workforce has increased, and we now often find ourselves engaged in intercultural communication in a variety of domestic communication contexts. The workplace, schools, social service agencies, and health services, among others, are contexts that have become especially intercultural. Consequently, intercultural interaction within the United States continues to increase.

As we have indicated, the readings in this chapter deal with cultural diversity in communication contexts. We focus on a combination of international and domestic settings in which knowledge and appreciation of cultural diversity are important if successful intercultural communication is to occur.

We begin with essays that involve a setting that is truly international—the business setting. It is obvious that all business activities encompass many forms of communication, and those forms reflect the attitudes, values, and communication patterns unique to each culture. Hence, our first four essays examine how culture touches and alters organizational communication, managerial styles, negotiation strategies, human relations, and interpersonal relations.

Business between the United States and Asia has been an important element in the American economy for several decades. Recent economic difficulties in Asia, especially in Japan, Hong Kong, Indonesia, Taiwan, and South Korea, have affected the U.S. economy and stock market. Future successful economic dealings in Asia will require an increased understanding of how Asian culture impacts business practices. To this end, we begin with two essays that focus on doing business with Asian cultures.

Our first business-oriented essay focuses on a series of cultures that are often referred to as the Five Asian Dragons (Hong Kong, Japan, Singapore, South Korea, and Taiwan). In "'The Five Asian Dragons': Management Behaviors and Organizational Communication," Guo-Ming Chen and Jensen Chung maintain that to communicate effectively with people from these cultures it is crucial to appreciate the role of Confucianism in interpersonal communication. According to Chen and Chung, this Confucian worldview, which emphasizes hierarchical relationships, family systems, benevolence, and education, helps explain the manner in which these five cultures engage in managerial behaviors and organizational communication.

In our second essay dealing with Asia, Edwin R. McDaniel and Steve Quasha share their experiences gained from more than 30 years of living, studying, and working with the Japanese. In their essay "The Communicative Aspects of Doing Business in Japan," they first lead us through a historical overview of the formation of both Japanese and U.S. cultural patterns that govern communication in the business context. Next, they use selected interactions from the Japanese business environment to illustrate the diverse communicative behaviors of both Japanese and U.S. business representatives. In many respects, McDaniel and Quasha take us on a tour of the Japanese business environment and guide us through the maze of diverse communication behaviors and expectations encountered when dealing with initial meetings, the Japanese concept of face, decision making, negotiations, conflict management, and the use of language interpreters. Their keen insights provide us a unique opportunity to discover, understand, and appreciate the complex differences in business communication practices as well as gain a glimpse of how knowledgeable one must be to function successfully as a U.S. representative in the Japanese business environment.

Business practices in Europe, while not as diverse as in Asia, are often quite different than those found in the United States. As the European community continues with its economic consolidation and adoption of a single European currency, competition for a share of European markets is going to increase. Simultaneously, the merger of American and European companies are adding to the cultural diversity of the business world. For instance, on May 7, 1998, the *Seattle Times* reported, "Chrysler is being acquired by Germany's Daimler-Benz . . . in a deal that weds two companies whose image and corporate cultures are vastly different" (p. D3). Understanding how communication can operate successfully in these environments is a major concern in continuing international business. To help us gain insight into the differences in culture and communication practices between American and German cultures and companies, we turn to Robert A. Friday's article, "Contrasts in Discussion Behaviors of German and American Managers." Here Friday traces cultural expectations of both German and American managers across several dimensions, pointing out the differences and how they may lead to misunderstandings and ineffective communication. Specifically, he is concerned with cultural differences as they relate to (1) the perception of business, (2) interpersonal credibility, (3) assertiveness and fair play, (4) problem solving, and (5) education and training. Friday ends his essay by offering suggestions that he believes will increase cultural understanding when German and American managers share a common environment.

Although there is major American involvement in both European and Asian marketplaces, there are still many intercultural communication concerns relative to the business world closer to home. With the advent of the North American Free Trade Agreement (NAFTA), working relationships between the United States and Mexico have increased dramatically. Both in terms of trade negotiations between the United States and Mexico and in the operation of U.S. businesses in Mexico, the need for better understanding of Mexican culture and the differences in U.S.–Mexican business practices increases daily. In her essay "U.S. Americans and Mexicans Working Together: Five Core Concepts for Enhancing Effectiveness," Sheryl Lindsley provides us with valuable insights into Mexican culture as it applies to the business environment. Here Lindsley discusses five shared cultural patterns or core concepts common to doing business in Mexico. These are *confianza, simpatía, palanca, estabilidad,* and *mañana;* these are not mutually exclusive categories, but overlapping concepts reflecting deeply held values for many Mexicans. As these shared values make their way into the business environment, effective American business managers and representatives will be aware of their influence on behavior and communication.

A multicultural society strongly affects the health care setting because cultural beliefs about health and disease can differ significantly. Such a simple question as

"How do you catch a cold?" can elicit a variety of answers ranging from standing in a draft to being the victim of a supernatural spirit or spell, depending on one's cultural background. In her article, "Communicating Health and Understanding in the Borderlands of Co-Cultures," Patricia Geist examines the complex and dynamic features of communication in the health care context. She begins by linking culture, health, and communication. She then provides a cultural sensitivity model of health care communication for educating health care providers, for clinical practice, and for patient empowerment. Next, Geist examines specific case examples that demonstrate the problems found by both providers and patients when culturally specific beliefs and practices of patients are ignored during diagnosis and treatment. Finally, she concludes with proposed avenues for overcoming the obstacles revealed in programs for expanding our notions of culture and culturally sensitive health care.

Education in a multicultural society is the final context we will consider. Classrooms are a most important setting where the sway of culture must be considered. Although educational practices at any educational level of a multicultural society are affected by the cultural diversity found in each classroom, it is in the university setting that cultural diversity may have its strongest influence. Here, students not only reflect the cultural diversity of the host society, but also the diversity of many other nations and cultures because of students participating in international education programs.

In their essay "Intercultural Communication in the University Classroom," Lisa M. Skow and Laurie Stephan enable us to see the role culture plays in the learning and teaching processes. After establishing the increasing growth rate of international students in U.S. college classrooms, they show us how culture affects the classroom setting by looking at how cultural values influence intercultural communication. They next examine how culture can determine different learning and teaching styles inherent in the university classroom. Finally, they relate how culture-specific verbal and nonverbal ways of speaking influence communication between students and teachers.

The "Five Asian Dragons": Management Behaviors and Organizational Communication

GUO-MING CHEN

JENSEN CHUNG

T he progress of technology has made global markets more accessible and the business world more interrelated and more international in the last decade. As Adler (1983) indicates, the increasing internationalization of business means an increasing multiculturalism within organizations and an increasing interaction between managers and employees of different cultures. This increasing multiculturalism in organizations calls for understandings among cultures and new strategies for organizational operations. From Adler's perspective the influence of Confucianism on modern Asian organizations is a case that deserves further investigation by communication scholars.

In the Pacific basin nations, the internationalization of business has occurred and in recent years in this region several newly industrializing nations have emerged in East Asia. Among these Asian nations five have been experiencing what is called an "economic miracle." These political entities, dubbed "Five Dragons," include Hong Kong, Japan, Singapore, South Korea, and Taiwan. According to a World Bank report (1988), between 1980 and 1986, the average annual growth rate of per capita gross national product (GNP) was 6.1% for Hong Kong, 3.7% for Japan, 5.3% for Singapore, 8.2% for South Korea, and 6.8% for Taiwan, while only 1.8% for European countries and 3.1% for the United States.

From *Communication Quarterly* (Spring 1994), 93–105. Copyright by the Speech Communication Association. Reprinted by permission of the publisher. Professor Chen teaches at the University of Rhode Island. Professor Chung teaches at San Francisco State University.

Why are these particular countries so successful economically? Many scholars have attempted to answer this question from different perspectives, including the value of economic growth and the fast response to the international market (e.g., Chan, 1990; Wu, 1988). Although different scholars provide various factors to explain the unexpected economic growth of the Five Dragons, most of them agree that, for the root cause, one must turn to the domain of culture. It is the purpose of this inquiry to examine the impact of cultural environment on the economic success of the Asian Five Dragons. Because these economically successful nations in Northeast Asia share the same cultural heritage of Confucianism, this inquiry aims at investigating how Confucianism as a cultural factor contributes to the success of these nations. More specifically, this study explores the impact of Confucianism on the organizational life and organizational communication in these nations.

CULTURAL MODIFIERS

To what degree do the cultural factors of a society influence its organizational life? Child (1981) indicates that different cultural orientations will lead to specific organizational effects. Gorden (1984) summarizes five hypotheses regarding the relationship between cultural orientations and organizational effects specified by Child: (1) If the society considers human nature as good, then the organizations will advocate employee autonomy and reliance on intrinsic motivation; (2) if the society believes that the human being is the master of nature, then the organizations will lead to adventurous and proactive management; (3) if the society orients to the future, then the organizations will emphasize long-term planning, workforce planning, and assessment centers; (4) if the society is "being" oriented, then the organizations will emphasize interpersonal sensitivity, and concern about morale and communication climate; and (5) if the society orients to individualism, then the organizations will minimize authority and hierarchy.

Hofstede's (1980) large-scale study shows the consistent relationship between cultural orientations and organizational life. The results of Hofstede's

Table 1 *Confucian Principles of Interpersonal Communication*

Four Principles	Contents
Hierarchical relationship	Particularistic relationship Complementary social reciprocity Ingroup/outgroup distinction Essential intermediary and formality Overlap of personal and public relationships
Family system	Private relationship Paternalistic leadership Harmony is the first virtue Distrust of outgroup members Loyalty and commitment
Jen	*Jen*—benevolence, self-discipline, filial piety, brotherly love, and trust *Yi*—righteousness, faithfulness, and justice in social interaction *Li*—propriety, rite, and respect for social norms
Education emphasis	Providing education for all people without discrimination Ethical teachings

national value surveys from a multinational company in some 40 different countries reveal four dimensions of cultural values that are related to the organizational life: power distance, individualism, masculinity, and uncertainty avoidance.

Furthermore, the Chinese Culture Connection (1987) also has collected data from 22 countries and found four dimensions of cultural values that show influence on organizational life, especially in Asian countries. Three of the four dimensions are similar to Hofstede's power distance, individualism, and masculinity. The fourth one is labeled "Confucian Work Dynamism." The Chinese Culture Connection not only argues that it is this dimension that distinguishes the cultural orientation between Western and Eastern organizations, but also finds that this dimension is strongly related to the economic growth of the Asian Five Dragons over the period between 1965 and 1985. These studies indicate that a strong connection between cultural factors and the logic of organizing exists.

"Neo-Confucianism," rooted in the teachings of Confucius, is used by Kahn (1979) to describe the cultural traits of East Asian nations. According to Kahn, East Asian nations have common cultural roots that can be traced to Confucianism. This shared cultural heritage has contributed to the economic success of these nations in the international market over the past 30 years.

Confucius was born in China around 500 B.C. His teachings are mainly concerned with practical ethics of daily life without any addition of religion elements. Confucianism includes a set of pragmatic rules for the daily behaviors of common people. Hofstede and Bond (1988) indicate that the teachings of Confucius are comprised of four key principles; the hierarchical relationship among people, the family as a basic unit, *Jen*, and the emphasis on education. We now use these principles as a framework to explain how Confucianism influences interpersonal relationships and organizational lives in the Asian Five Dragons (see Table 1).

THE DOMINANT CULTURE OF THE FIVE DRAGONS

It is a common belief that specific nations possess specific cultural traits that are resistant to change.

HIERARCHICAL RELATIONSHIP

According to Confucius, human relationships should be regulated by the Five Codes of Ethics, *Wu Lun*, which is based on the five basic relationships:

ruler/subject, father/son, husband/wife, older brother/younger brother, and between friends. These relationships are assumed to be unequal and complementary. Condon (1977) indicates that complementary relationships tend to "maximize differences in age, sex, role, or status and serve to encourage the mutuality of the relationship, the interdependency" (p. 54). Juniors are required to owe their seniors respect and obedience, and seniors owe their juniors consideration and protection. In other words, the Confucian Five Code of Ethics stipulates that the ruler has to show justice, and the subject shows loyalty; father shows love, and son shows filial piety; husband shows initiation, and wife shows obedience; the older brother shows brotherly love, and younger brother shows reverence in return; and friends show mutual faith to each other.

The application of *Wu Lun* to the organizational life shows five types of ordering relationships: particularistic relationships, complementary social reciprocity, ingroup/outgroup distinction, essential intermediary and formality, and overlap of personal and public relationships (Yum, 1988). Particularistic relationships are relatively predictable. They are governed by a set of specific communication rules and patterns that provide individuals with directions concerning interaction. This kind of relationship may be extended to friends, family, co-workers, or superior/subordinate, along with many other relationships. The function of maintaining a particularistic relationship is a way for East Asians to avoid embarrassing encounters or serious conflicts (Hwang, 1988; Jacobs, 1979). Moreover, particularistic relationships are often used as a social resource, which is a "potential power in persuasion, influence, and control" in the organizational life (Chung, 1991, p. 9).

Complementary social reciprocity, the second type of orderly relationship resulting from the Five Code of Ethics, refers to the process of give-and-take in a social interaction. Based on the hierarchical relationship, Confucian philosophy views interpersonal relationships as asymmetrical and reciprocally obligatory in which people always feel indebted to others. When East Asians receive a gift from others, for example, they show a deep appreciation and heartily try to find an opportunity to return the favor (Shiang, 1982). This obligation of returning the favor to others is also strongly reflected in the superior/subordinate relationship in an organization. Usually, a superior has certain responsibilities or obligations, such as protection and a holistic concern for subordinates; employees, in turn, have obligations, such as loyalty or commitment to a superior.

With the Confucian teaching of interpersonal relationships, another must define the existence of an individual in East Asian societies. This characteristic of mutual interdependence between people leads to a sharp distinction between ingroup and outgroup members. Such interdependence "requires that one be affiliated with relatively small and tightly knit groups of people and have a relatively long identification with those groups" (Yum, 1987, p. 94). Individuals who join the group or an organization are assigned different positional roles, and are required to fulfill certain obligations. Moreover, they are subordinate to the group in which commitments and loyalty are required. Due to these requirements for group members, people are only able to belong to a limited number of organizations throughout their lives. This long-term, reciprocal relationship between the individual and the group is further developed into the lifetime employment system in Japanese organizations.

The Confucian principles of *Yi* (righteousness) and *Li* (propriety) dictate that individuals must follow a proper way and a proper ritual in a social interaction. An intermediary is a product of this requirement. It is a popular practice in East Asia to use an intermediary to help people initiate a new relationship or solve a conflict. This kind of indirect interaction and the formality of social life is considered a way of avoiding an embarrassing confrontation, a way of "saving face." A smooth and predictable verbal and nonverbal interaction is usually reached through the value of indirect communication and formality, factors which explain why it is very common for the East Asians to use formal codes of conduct, titles, honorifics in their interactions with others.

Finally, the Confucian idea of social reciprocity leads to a vague boundary between personal and public relationships. According to Yum (1988), this orientation leads to a strong taste for a pure business transaction in which people try to develop a personal rather than a business-like atmosphere. To build a good and warm personal relationship is the key to success in a business transaction. In Japan, for example, consensus is often reached before a meeting is summoned. Similarly, in other East Asian nations, one must develop a mutual understanding, establish a personal relationship, keep frequent contacts, develop personal trust, and build mutual interests in social activities with one's counterpart to develop an effective business relationship.

THE FAMILY SYSTEM

Confucian teachings consider "family" the prototype of all social organizations. Confucianism is like social cement that fixes family members in the network of their appropriate hierarchical relationships. Furthermore, concepts such as loyalty, obedience, and filial piety practiced in the family are transferred to social organizations in which habits of disciplined subordination and acceptance of authority are fostered (MacFarquhar, 1980).

Three discernible value orientations influenced by Confucian teachings can be identified within the family system: a lineal structure of relational orientation, a specific positional role behavior, and an authoritarian orientation (Chen, 1988). According to Hwang (1989), this collectivistic sense of the family structure that is applied to social organizations is one of the main reasons for the economic success of the Asian Five Dragons. Within this collectivistic family system, one becomes only a member of a family in which one must learn to restrain oneself, to subdue individuality in order to maintain the harmony in the family (Hofstede & Bond, 1988). The extension of the family system to business produces a popular practice of "family enterprise" in the Asian Five Dragons. Chen (1991) stipulates five characteristics of "family enterprise" that are heavily influenced by Confucian teachings:

1. Private relationship. The private relationship is based on the concept of "similarity" or "affinity," and it includes: (1) blood relationships—consisting of one's own family, relatives outside the household, wife's relatives, and relatives of different surnames (Chen, 1988); (2) demographic relationships—for those who are from the same area of the country; (3) colleague relationships—

for those who work in the same organization; (4) teacher-student relationships; and (5) classmate relationships (Chiao, 1988).
2. Paternalistic leadership. In this kind of organization a manager always acts like a father who expresses concern for employees with families and the quality of the products the employees produce. This makes it difficult for workers to separate their personal and professional lives.
3. Harmony, the first virtue. Only harmony among group members can produce fortune. It is believed that personal harmony is the best way to maintain dignity, self-respect, and prestige.
4. Distrust of outgroup members. This characteristic shows that most high and middle management are selected from the network of the private relationships.
5. Relative loyalty and commitment between managers and employees. The concern with employee's personal benefit from top management usually requires the unconditional loyalty or spirit of sacrifice from employees.

Jen (Benevolence)

Jen is one of the cardinal concepts of Confucian teachings. It is a collective concept, which is comprised of various virtues, but "love" is the core meaning of Jen. To oneself, Jen is self-restraint and self-discipline; to others, benevolence; to parents, filial piety; to elders, brotherly love; to personal duty, loyalty; and to interpersonal behaviors, trust (Chen, 1987). Jen is like a seed from which all the virtuous qualities of the ideal humans are originated.

Basically, the concept of Jen interweaves with two other cardinal concepts of Confucian teachings: Yi (righteousness) and Li (propriety). Only through Yi and Li is the meaning of Jen rectified. Yi is the binding force of social interaction; it refers to the righteousness, faithfulness, loyalty, and justice in the process of social interaction. Yi serves two major functions: guidance of behavior and connection of all appropriate behaviors. As a directive behavior Yi stipulates what one ought and ought not do. In this sense, Yi is the internal criterion of appropriateness of Jen, which affects all human behaviors.

Li is the external form of Jen. It refers to propriety, rite, and respect for social norms, and it is "the rule of the universe and the fundamental regulatory etiquette of human behavior" (Yum, 1988, p. 378). The practice of *Li* allows the intimate connections of individual character and social duties by means of rules, including propriety of conduct, propriety of speech, and propriety of example.

Based on Confucian teachings, "reciprocity," referring to mutual expectations of social responsibility among people, is the yardstick of propriety of conduct. Confucian teachings place the performance of duties due others above all other duties and treat this performance as a necessary means of self-development. Confucius explicates this idea by indicating that in order to confirm or enlarge oneself, one has to confirm and enlarge others.

Confucian teachings admonish followers to be cautious about their speech, because the "smartness" of speech elicits hatred from others. One's speech should be simple, direct, and to the point. In other words, one should express the precise meaning rather than what seems to be said or variant from it. Straightforwardness or too much candor during discourse, however, is dangerous, since it is often not regulated by the rule of appropriateness. Confucius warns that straightforwardness, without the rules of propriety, will often lead to rudeness.

Confucian teachings also emphasize the important role of a listener in the process of discourse. A listener must be able to understand accurately what a person says, because it is impossible to know men without knowing the force of words. Moreover, the ability to know when to speak and the ability to read a speaker's facial expression are also important to the listener, especially when communicating with a superior. Confucius uses "impetuousness" to describe those who speak before spoken to; "reticence" for those who do not reply when spoken to; and "blindness" for those who speak without observing the superior's facial expression. Finally, Confucian teachings urge a superior to be cautious when giving commands to subordinates. Confucius indicates that once commands are issued, they must be carried into effect and cannot be retracted.

Lastly, the propriety of example refers to the kind of people with whom a person should associate. Confucian teachings indicate that three kinds of friends will benefit a person: the upright, the devoted, and the learned. In contrast, three kinds of friends will harm a person: the fawning, the flattering, and the too eloquent. Confucius repeatedly utters the admonition for being with those who employ artful speeches and insinuating looks. He considers that words and an insinuating appearance are barriers for being virtuous. Prudence, in regard to conversation and association with others, is strongly recommended in Confucian teachings.

An admonition to a friend or superior is encouraged in Confucian teachings, but the admonition must be regulated by appropriateness. Confucius further warns against unnecessary admonitions, because frequent remonstrances and reproofs often lead to disgrace. All these Confucian ideas provide a set of rules that guide the behaviors and relationships between superiors and subordinates in modern organizations of the Asian Five Dragons. More influences are discussed in the next section.

THE EMPHASIS ON EDUCATION

The perfectibility and educability of human beings is central to Confucian thinking. This emphasis on education has become one of the most important characteristics of Chinese culture, and the tradition is carried over to every Asian nation, especially the Asian Five Dragons. The World Bank reports that in 1985 the number in secondary school as percentage of age group in the Asian Five Dragons is: Hong Kong, 69%; Japan, 96%; Singapore, 71%; South Korea, 94%; and Taiwan, 99%. According to Tai (1989), the Confucian emphasis on education is considered a substantial facilitator to the process of economic modernization, which underlines a rudimentary economic principle: "Human resource development is a slow, long-term, and costly process, but the benefit is great, cumulative, and nearly always outweighs the cost" (p. 25). Only the skillful and intelligent human beings are able to use the economic resources productively.

The philosophy of Confucian education is based on the idea of "providing education for all people without discrimination," and completely emphasizes the teaching of ethics; thus, the purpose of education is to help students develop an ideal personality. Through this educational system, virtues with regard to one's tasks in life are integrated. Those virtues

Table 2 *Confucian Influence on Management/Leadership*

Ideal State of Management	Leadership
To develop a secure working environment for all employees in the organization	Rectification of name—a process for a leader to correctly perceive his/her role behavior and the legitimate authority from it
Humanistic management: 1. Human nature is mutable 2. A committed employee is able to adapt to the changing environment 3. Mutual understanding between superior and subordinate is a key to organizational success	Sincerity—honesty to one's self and truthfulness toward employees: (1) five virtues to be pursued, and (2) five evils to be avoided

attributing to the economic growth of the Asian Five Dragons include skill acquisition, hard work, moderation, patience, and perseverance.

The four key principles of Confucian teachings show a direct impact on organizational communication, especially on the principle of management and interpersonal relationship and communication in the Asian Five Dragons.

THE IMPACT OF CONFUCIANISM ON ORGANIZATIONAL COMMUNICATION

A conclusion that can be drawn from the previous discussion of the four key principles of Confucian teachings is that "human" is the focal point of Confucian teachings. When applied to the process of management, the Confucian style of management is therefore termed "humanistic management" or "ethical management" (Tseng, 1991). The humanistic emphasis of Confucian teachings is parallel to the Human Relations Model of organizing developed in the West. As Conrad (1989) points out, the Human Relations Model focuses on the "individual identities and needs of employees and looks to improvements in personal relations and interpersonal communication as a way of simultaneously meeting organizational needs for control and coordination and employee needs for predictability, creativity, autonomy, and sociability" (p. 157). This section examines the influence of Confucian teachings on management principles and interpersonal relationships and communication in the organizations of Asian Five Dragons.

INFLUENCE ON MANAGEMENT PRINCIPLES

Two aspects of management are discussed: the ideal state of management and leadership (see Table 2). Based on Confucian principles, the ideal state of management is to develop a secure working environment for all employees in the organization through the process of self-cultivation and self-improvement. Tseng (1986) labels this thought as "M theory." M represents three concepts: men, medium, and management. M theory indicates that management is a process of making a harmonious balance among people. M theory entails three assumptions. First, human nature is mutable. The responsibility of a manager is to lead employees to a perfect working environment through the practice of *Jen*. Second, a committed employee is able to adapt to changing environments. A manager has to inform employees clearly about the goal of and behavioral criteria in the company. The adaptability to contingencies is regulated by *Yi*. Third, the mutual understanding between a superior and subordinate is a key to organizational success. This assumption is based on the understanding of one's role and position in the organization. A manager needs to specify role behaviors and to expect the fulfillment of those role behaviors. The achievement of this goal is regulated by cooperation, reciprocity, and mutual trust, as originated from the concept of *Li*. The ideal state of management, therefore, is the integration of practicing the three core concepts of Confucian teaching: *Jen*, *Yi*, and *Li*.

Although the hierarchical structure of interpersonal relationships between a superior and subordi-

Table 3 *Confucian Influence on Communication in the Organization*

Interpersonal Relationship	Organizational Life
Explicit communication rules	Reduced uncertainty in organizational communication
Complimentary relationship	Socio-emotional communication prevails
Ingroup/outgroup distinction	Team building; life-time employment
Intermediary	Non-confrontational communication
Vague boundary between personal and public relationships	Conflict avoidance; consensus building; trust
Similar communication context	Facilitate communication and training

nate makes Asian social groups function smoothly with more authoritarian interaction patterns, Confucian teachings specify that an effective leadership must follow two requirements: "cheng ming" (rectification of name) and "cheng" (sincerity). Only when terms are correctly used for the positional roles of leadership and understood by employees can the reality of organizing be described. The rectification of name is a process for leaders to correctly perceive the role behaviors and gain the legitimate authority from it (Hsieh & Fang, 1991).

Sincerity is referred to as honesty to self and truthfulness toward employees. According to Chan (1952), the function of sincerity is to exercise fully one's native intelligence and good knowledge, conscience, and native ability to do good. Confucian teachings indicate that a sincere mind is the precursor of "Kan Ying" (influence and response). Sincerity is the basis for receiving from employees a positive response to a manager's influence. The practice of sincerity in leadership reveals the abilities of "esteeming the five virtues" and "avoiding the four evils" indicated by Confucius. The five virtues are: (1) To treat as advantageous what employees find advantageous, (2) to put only those able employees to work, (3) to have desires for achieving humanness-at-its-best without greed, (4) to be dignified but not proud regarding quantity and size of property, and (5) to inspire awe from employees without being brutal. The four evils to be avoided are: (1) cruelty—to punish employees for the lack of instructions, (2) outrageousness—to expect accomplishment from employees without proper advisement, (3) deterioration—to insist upon completion after instruction to proceed slow-

ly, and (4) pettiness—to promise a reward but to begrudge its payment.

INFLUENCE ON RELATIONSHIP AND COMMUNICATION

Based on the foregoing discussions, six characteristics of interpersonal relationships and communication as a result of the Confucian influence can be identified in the organizations of the Asian Five Dragons: Explicit communication rules, complementary relationships, ingroup and outgroup distinction, use of an intermediary, vague boundary between personal and public relationships, and similar communication contexts. These characteristics and their influences on the organizational life and communication cost are discussed as follows (see Table 3):

First, explicit communication rules are predominant in interpersonal communication. Because human relationships in Confucian societies are regulated by the Five Code of Ethics (*Wu Lun*), interpersonal relationships are governed by a set of explicit communication rules and are, thus, relatively predictable. Many rules in interpersonal communication are transferred to the organizational setting. The hierarchical ruler/subject and father/son relationships, for example, are applied to the superior/subordinate relationships. Since these rules are explicit, learning rules becomes important and necessary for the group members. Following these rules would lead to safer communication which minimizes uncertainty and guesswork in the organization. Communication cost is then reduced.

The hierarchical superior/subordinate relationship is especially reflected in Korean and Japanese organizations. For example, according to Klopf (1991), in a Japanese business setting the relationships are usually based on rank, which is determined by sex, age, educational background, and length of service in the company. Moreover, the hierarchical structure of relationship requires strict communication patterns. This explains why subordinates use honorifics and become more restrained when talking to superiors.

Second, since interpersonal relationships are complementary, the management or the superiors in the organization give holistic and fraternalistic concerns to employees or subordinates in exchange for their loyalty. Socio-emotional functions of communication are almost inherent in the management–employee or superior–subordinate relationships. For example, Chung (1992) indicates that superiors in Taiwanese and Japanese companies often get involved in the resolution of subordinates' family problems. In Japan, "when an employee dies on the job, the company would hire his wife, although not necessarily to do the same job in the same company" (p. 7). The cost of socio-emotional communication may be great, but many frustrations, dissatisfactions, or conflicts are then prevented.

Third, due to the tendency of clearly distinguishing ingroup and outgroup members, organizational members are easier to motivate toward the goal of team building, and commitment to the group can be easily transferred to the organization as a whole. Organizational climate then is more supportive. The Japanese term *kaisha* well displays the concept of "ingroup" in Japanese organizations. According to Nakane (1970), kaisha is

> "my" or "our" company, the community to which one belongs primarily; and which is all-important in one's life. Thus in most cases the company provides the whole social existence of a person, has authority over all aspects of his life; he is deeply involved in the association. (p. 4)

The clear distinction between ingroup and outgroup and the "we" feeling among group members also affect management-employee relationship and control system. As Rehder (1981) points out, when comparing the traditional American and Japanese organizations, Japanese organizations rely on high group motivation and standards with social work control, while, in American organizations, employment commitment depends on economic conditions and performance. As a result of this group motivation, many Japanese workers proudly identify themselves as their "company's man" (Goldhaber, 1993). The advantage of "easy motivating within group" is not without cost. Ingroup motivation is usually accomplished at the expense of outgroup exclusion. This is why, in Confucianism-influenced societies and organizations, outsiders or foreigners have greater difficulty being accepted. The input from the environment is, thus, reduced to a minimum, resulting in a relatively closed communication system.

Fourth, because an intermediary is customarily used for initiating a new relationship or resolving a conflict, communication styles become nonconfrontational. This code would reduce conflicts and, thus, minimize communication costs. The nonconfrontational communication style is based on the Confucian concept *Ho* (harmony). According to Chung (1992), in Chinese organizations conflict is considered harmful and leads to a negative result in the organization. For example, a superior's disciplinary action to a subordinate in the Chinese organization is usually practiced by following the saying "Extol the merit in public hall; rectify the wrongdoing in the private room."

Fifth, the vague boundary between personal and public relationships in Confucian societies makes contact with organizational members more frequent. This, in turn, functions to identify mutual interests, expand overlapping communication contexts, build trust, and reach consensus. For example, Japanese superiors often invite subordinates to have a drink or to engage in other social situations after work. These socio-emotional communication activities on a relatively personal level characteristically create a common culture, which reduces uncertainty and conflict and increases morale and effectiveness.

Lastly, the heavy emphasis on education and equal opportunity of education has produced educated communicators who can communicate within more similar contexts than if education gaps are wide. The cost of education may be enormous, but education could facilitate communication, especially

Table 4 *The Preventive Communication Cost and Compensation in Confucianism-Influenced Organizations*

Preventive Communication Cost	Compensation
Rule-learning cost	Reduced guesswork and uncertainty
Long-term interaction cost	Reduced apprehension and increased liking and mutual respect
Outgroup exclusion cost	Easier motivation
Intermediary cost	Reduced conflict
Personal contact cost	Loyalty and commitment
Education cost	Reduced misunderstanding and clarification efforts

in terms of the organizational socialization and organizational training. The previous discussions of emphasis on education in the Asian Five Dragons have explained the impact of education on the organizational life.

The six characteristics present a general picture of the Confucianism-influenced organizational communication, resembling the Human Relations School of organizational thought developed in the West. The emphasis on interpersonal relationships in Confucian teachings, for example, is also advocated by Follett and Barnard, the pioneers of the Human Relations School (Bostdorff, 1985). The emphasis on human relationship in Confucianism-influenced organizational communication is also echoed by Mayo, the main pioneer of the human relations theory of organization. Some of his assumptions, as summarized by Eisenberg and Goodall (1993), include that employees are motivated by social needs and obtain the sense of self-identity through interactions with others.

The Human Relations School, however, does not adequately explain why communication can boost effectiveness or productivity. This investigation of Confucianism with respect to organizational communication identifies an Eastern version of "The Human Relations School." This version provides abundant information about how an emphasis on interpersonal relationships might boost effectiveness, especially through the approach of communication cost.

Inferring from what was discussed above, the Confucian societies and organizations invest heavily in communication through rule learning, long-term interaction, outgroup exclusion, intermediary, personal contact, and education. The investment on these aspects of organizational communication is related to communication cost. "The rule-learning cost" is paid off by the reduced guesswork and uncertainty. "The long-term interaction" cost can reduce communication apprehension and increase liking and mutual respect. "The outgroup exclusion cost" may help motivation. "The intermediary" cost can reduce conflict or smooth the conflict-resolution process. "The personal contact cost" is paid back by loyalty and commitment, and, finally, "the education cost" is compensated by the reduced communication gap, misunderstanding and clarification effort. In view of this model (see Table 4), all these costs are in problem prevention rather than in problem solution. This emphasis on employees' satisfaction with the social and interpersonal relationships of peers has been found to influence significantly the organization's productivity (Carey, 1967).

As can be observed from this analysis, in Confucianism-influenced organizations the human aspect of the employee's problem is the focus of attention. This is a feature of high-producing organizations indicated by Likert (1961). Confucianism-influenced organizational communication, therefore, implies positive contributions to lower employee turnover, smaller number of grievances, more easily aroused company morale, and stronger employment commitment. These organizational characteristics are some of the measures of organizational effectiveness (Goldhaber, 1993).

Finally, this analysis identifies a new dimension of communication cost study. Most previous studies on communication costs are from the space perspective emphasizing the relationships between office location and costs maintaining contacts, especially by those employees who are relocated (Goddard, 1975; Pye, 1976; Thorngren, 1970). This study points out a direction toward the human relation aspect of communication cost. It may not be easily quantified from this perspective, but the significance and impact are apparently greater than those of the space perspective.

CONCLUSIONS

In this essay, we delineate Confucianism as the cultural root of the Asian Five Dragons. The impressive economic and social progress has been remarkable over the past three decades in the areas of the Asian Five Dragons. The process of this development is complicated, and many articles and books about the development of the Five Dragons have been published. Although a number of general economic factors are used to interpret the success of the Asian Five Dragons, most scholars agree that cultural influence based on Confucianism is a major factor contributing to the success. Confucius develops a code of ethics that guides the interpersonal relationships of the familistic organizations. The acceptance of Confucian teachings by the Asian Five Dragons shapes a human-oriented workforce. It not only relatively reduces the communication cost, but also generates a greater organizational effectiveness.

The characteristics of Confucianism-influenced organizational communication identified in this study imply several strategies for effective organizational communication. These strategies are basically investing in preventive, as opposed to problem-solving, measures for organizational effectiveness.

First, organizations can facilitate rule learning of employees by investing more in orientation programs for new employees. These rule-learning programs can be based on the assumption that employees will stay and are encouraged to stay for a relatively long period of time.

Second, socio-emotional communication activities need to be geared toward establishing long term relationships among employees. For example, superficial conversations at cocktail parties can be complemented with group activities that require more personal contacts and interdependent effort. The quality control circle, for instance, is an old but long-neglected tool to this effect. Third, motivational communication efforts can be based on themes that emphasize external competition and promote internal "we" feelings.

Some of these suggestions may not be totally new. Some of them, the quality control circle, for example, have become popular after Japanese success stories in production management were widely recognized. Unfortunately, these programs are not broadly valued in the western organizations. The above strategies may become more evidently powerful when organizations go international or multicultural such as culturally diversified organizations, multinational corporations, overseas subsidiaries from the West to the East, and vice versa.

As implied in the analysis above, the Confucianism-influenced organizational communication also displays certain weak spots. The ingroup/outgroup distinction, for example, may make the organization clannish and may reduce the possibility of communicating with the external environments and in turn reinforces the homogeneity and hurts the creativity. Nevertheless, this can hardly emerge as a problem in the Western organizations, given the high mobility, heterogeneity, and individualism in the Western society as a context. It will be interesting for future research to continue this line of research.

References

Adler, N. (1983). Cross-cultural management research: The ostrich and the trend. *Academy of Management Review, 8,* 226–232.

Bostdorff, D. (1985, November). *Mary Parker Follett.* Paper presented at the annual meeting of the Speech Communication Association, Denver, CO.

Carey, A. (1967). The Hawthorne studies: A radical criticism. *American Sociological Review, 32,* 403–416.

Chan, S. (1990). *East Asian Dynamism.* Boulder, CO: Westview.

Chan, W. T. (1952). Basic Chinese philosophical concepts. *Philosophy East and West, 2,* 166–170.

Chen, D. C. (1987). *Confucius thoughts.* Taipei: Cheng Chuong.

Chen, G. M. (1988, November). *A comparative study of value orientations of Chinese and American families: A communication view*. Paper presented at the annual meeting of the Speech Communication Association, New Orleans, Louisiana.

Chen, M. C. (1991). Family culture and management. In G. S. Yang & C. S. Tseng (Eds.), *A Chinese perspective of management* (pp. 189–212). Taipei: Kwei Kwan.

Chiao, C. (1988). A study of Guan Hsi. In K. S. Yang (Ed.), *The psychology of the Chinese people* (pp. 105–122). Taipei: Kwei Kuan.

Child, J. (1981). Culture, contingency and capitalism in the cross-national study of organizations. In L. L. Cummings & B. M. Shaw (Eds.), *Research in organizational behavior* (pp. 303–356). Greenwich, CT: JAI.

Chinese Culture Connection (1987). Chinese values and the search for culture-free dimensions of culture. *Journal of Cross-Cultural Psychology, 18*, 143–164.

Chung, J. (1991, April). *Seniority and particularistic ties in a Chinese conflict resolution process*. Paper presented at the annual conference of the Eastern Communication Association, Pittsburgh, Pennsylvania.

Chung, J. (1992, November). *Equilibrium in the Confucianism-influenced superior–subordinate communication system*. Paper presented at the annual meeting of the Speech Communication Association, Chicago, Illinois.

Condon, J. C. (1977). *Interpersonal Communication*. New York: Macmillan.

Conrad, C. (1989). *Strategic Organizational Communication*. Chicago: Holt, Rinehart and Winston.

Eisenberg, E. M., & Goodall, H. L. (1993). *Organizational Communication: Balancing Creativity and Constant*. New York: St. Martin's.

Goddard, J. (1975). Organizational information flows and the urban system. *Economic Appliquee*, 125–164.

Goldhaber, G. (1993). *Organizational Communication*. Dubuque, IA: William C. Brown.

Gorden, W. I. (1984, May/June). Organizational imperatives and culture modifiers. *Business Horizons*, 76–83.

Hofstede, G. (1980). *Culture's Consequences: International Differences in Work-Related Values*. Beverly Hills, CA: Sage.

———, & Bond, M. H. (1988). The Confucius connection: From cultural roots to economic growth. *Organizational Dynamics, 16*, 5–21.

Hsieh, C. H. & Fang, C. F. (1991). The Confucian idea of management in Analects. In K. S. Yang and S. C. Tseng (Eds.), *A Chinese perspective of management* (pp. 95–114). Taipei: Kwei Kuan.

Hwang, K. K. (1988). Renqin and face: The Chinese power game. In K. K. Hwang (Ed.), *The Chinese Power Game* (pp. 7–56). Taipei: Giren.

———. (1989). Confucian thoughts and modernization: Theory analysis and empirical study. *China Tribune, 319*, 7–24.

Jacobs, B. J. (1979). A preliminary model of particularistic ties in Chinese political alliances: Kan-ching and Kuan-hsi in a rural Taiwanese township. *China Quarterly, 78*, 237–273.

Kahn, H. (1979). *World Economic Development: 1979 and Beyond*. Boulder, CO: Westview.

Likert, R. (1961). *New Patterns of Management*. New York: McGraw Hill.

MacFarquhar, R. (1980, February 9). The post-Confucian challenge. *The Economist*, 65–72.

Nakane, C. (1970). *Japanese Society*. Berkeley: Center for Japanese and Korean Studies.

Pye, R. (1976). Effect of telecommunication on the location of office employment. *OMEQA*, 289–300.

Rehder, R. (1981, April). What American and Japanese managers are learning from each other. *Business Horizons*, 63–70.

Shiang, T. C. (1982). *A Study of Chinese Character*. Taipei: Shang Wu.

Tai, H. C. (1989). The oriental alternative: An hypothesis on culture and economy. In H. C. Tai (Ed.), *Confucianism and Economic Development: An Oriental Alternative?* Washington, DC: Washington Institute.

Thorngren, B. (1970). How do contact systems affect regional involvement? *Environment and Planning, 2*, 409–427.

Tseng, S. C. (1986). *The Chinese Idea of Administration*. Taipei: Lien Ching.

———. (1991). Chinese management: A Confucian perspective. In K. S. Yang & S. C. Tseng (Eds.), *A Chinese Perspective of Management* (pp. 75–94). Taipei: Kwei Kuan.

World Bank (1988). *World Development Reports*. New York: Oxford.

Wu, R. I. (1988). The distinctive features of Taiwan's development. In P. L. Berger & H. H. M. Hsiao (Eds.), *In Search of an East Asian Development Model* (pp. 179–196). New Brunswick: Transaction.

Yum, J. O. (1987). The practice of Uye-Ri in interpersonal relationships. In D. L. Kincaid (Ed.), *Communication Theory: Eastern and Western Perspectives* (pp. 87–100). New York: Academic.

———. (1988). The impact of Confucianism on interpersonal relationships and communication patterns in East Asia. *Communication Monographs, 55*, 374–388.

Concepts and Questions

1. Why do you suppose many scholars agree that culture has been the root cause of the economic success of the Asian "Five Dragons"?
2. How does "Confucian Work Dynamism" differ from the cultural dimensions of power distance, individualism, and masculinity?
3. What are the Confucian principles of interpersonal communication?
4. How are the Confucian five codes of ethics manifest in modern Asian business organizations?
5. How does the Confucian concept of social reciprocity function in Asian business organizations? Does it have a counterpart in U.S. business cultures?
6. In what manner does Confucian teaching about family systems affect contemporary Asian business organizational structures? Can you think of similar situations in American business?
7. How do Confucian teachings influence communication? What communication behaviors are expected and what types are to be avoided?
8. Based on Confucian principles, what is the goal of the ideal state of management? How does M-theory relate to this goal?
9. What six characteristics of interpersonal relationships and communication result from Confucian influences? How are these manifest in the "Five Dragons" organizational behavior?
10. What distinctions can you draw between the Confucian-influenced organizational communication strategies and those apparent in U.S. business organizations?

The Communicative Aspects of Doing Business in Japan

Edwin R. McDaniel
Steve Quasha

Contemporary communicative behaviors practiced in Japan and the United States are a product of very different and often contradictory cultural antecedents. Contrasting historical events, which shaped the enduring values and beliefs of the two nations, also laid the foundation for the subconscious premises behind their varying communication practices. These cultural differences become especially salient in the Japan–U.S. business setting.

The numerous volumes found in the international business section of any Barnes and Noble or Borders bookstore attest to the important role that competent cross-cultural communication plays in successful commercial ventures. Despite this wealth of information, some of which is quite good, representatives from both Japan and the United States continue to profess that they do not understand the business practices of the other nation. An appreciation of the different cultural values and how they influence each nation's respective communicative practices will not prevent commercial conflicts between Japan and the United States, but awareness will lessen the potential for discord and create a basis for enhanced understanding.

The objective of this essay is to offer a cultural perspective on different communication behaviors that often lead to contentious relations in the Japanese–U.S. business environment. The first section provides a historical overview of the formation of each nation's more discernible cultural patterns and examines how these values govern communication in a business context. In the second part, selected

This original article appears here for the first time. All rights reserved. Permission to reprint must be obtained from the authors and the publisher. Edwin McDaniel is affiliated with Arizona State University. Steve Quasha teaches at Gifu University, Gifu, Japan.

interactions from the Japanese business environment are used to illustrate the varying culturally patterned communication behaviors of Japanese and U.S. business representatives.

HISTORICAL FORMATION OF CONTEMPORARY JAPANESE AND U.S. CULTURAL PATTERNS

Contemporary Japanese and U.S. cultural patterns are products of very different historical frameworks. Even the geographical setting of the two nations stands in marked contrast. Japan is a relatively small, insular, densely populated country with a somewhat homogeneous society. On the other hand, overall vastness, significant distance between population centers, and a multicultural populace characterize the United States. These diverse geographic and demographic features, coupled with contrasting historical events, have given rise to quite different social beliefs and values.

The origin of cultural values most evident in Japan today can be traced to the Tokugawa Era (1600–1868). In the early 1600s, Japan was consolidated under the leadership of a military style governor (*shogun*). Most Japanese resided in castle towns, and society was divided into four specific, hierarchical groups—*samurai*, farmer, artisan, and merchant—each with its own subgroups and hierarchy. The central government proscribed strict protocols regulating the conduct of every aspect of personal and public life. The objective of these conventions, grounded in Confucian orthodoxy, was to ensure external peace and internal group harmony by subordinating the individual to the greater social order. Social **stability** was the paramount objective (Hirschmeiier & Yui, 1981).

Unlike the Japanese, early U.S. settlers were imbued with the concept of personal freedom. By migrating to the United States, they had escaped the feudalistic and monarchistic institutions that shaped the European social order. Often living alone, in sparsely populated areas, or in widely separated cities, U.S. settlers were constantly pushing the frontier westward. In contrast to Japan, **change** was constant in the United States as individuals and organizations sought to acquire new lands and profits. The role of

the U.S. government was not to regulate or control the population, but to help construct an infrastructure that would assist citizens in expanding the frontier and thereby facilitate individual accumulation of wealth (LaFeber, 1997).

The distinct physical conditions, demographics, and historical circumstances that shaped contemporary Japanese and U.S. social orders also gave rise to quite different culturally patterned beliefs, values, and behaviors; these have been further influenced by intergenerational evolution. Japan's early experience under Tokugawa rule, for example, instilled a continuing sense of collectivism, or group orientation, and hierarchy. Regimentation of the population into distinct groupings with separate social standings inculcated the Japanese with an acceptance of power differentiation. Proscribed protocols for almost every aspect of social conduct has been translated into an enduring dedication to social and organizational formality (i.e., a single correct way of doing things).

The emphasis that Tokugawa rulers placed on social stability also has been translated into contemporary deportment. Today, this desire to maintain social balance is called *wa*, which is commonly translated as "harmony." The meaning, however, is much more complex and can be extended to include social balance, stability, teamwork, or group spirit (Goldman, 1994; Gudykunst & Nishida, 1994). At the core of *wa* lies the philosophy of subordinating the individual to the needs of the greater whole—family, in-group, organization, nation.

As with its history, population, and geography, the enduring values of the United States stand in striking contrast to those of Japan. The rugged frontier mentality continues to influence standards of conduct in the United States, where conformity frequently carries a negative connotation. The ideal that every person is born free and equal, with the inherent right of individual choice, leaves U.S. citizens with little respect, and even less tolerance, for hierarchical social orderings. Equality and fairness exert a strong influence on all undertakings and have produced a highly informal society. Indeed, in the United States, an adherence to or emphasis on formalities can precipitate discordant relations.

During the United States' formative period, the constant westward push into new territories produced a positive orientation toward change, and change is now equated with progress. The ability to conceive new ideas and innovative ways of doing things is regarded as a highly desirable attribute. Consistency lies in the expectation of frequent changes designed to improve both conditions and products.

Each nation's respective experiences have coalesced to create enduring cultural patterns that result in contrasting philosophies and values toward the conduct of business and toward communication within business organizations. For example, the quest to maximize profit is usually the overriding concern of every U.S. corporate endeavor. Consideration for employee relations is frequently secondary, and interactions with the government are often adversarial.

Profit is, of course, also a salient consideration in Japanese businesses, but it is usually a secondary concern. Gaining market share and the well-being of company employees are the primary motivations for Japanese businessmen, who see corporate–employee relations and corporate–government interactions as a series of mutual obligations, the fulfillment of which will benefit everyone. Accordingly, Japanese business executives will sometimes subordinate corporate profit to maintain harmony within the organization, the market, or the nation (De Mente, 1993; Japan, 1998).

From a communication perspective, March (1992) has described Japan as a "culture of command" (p. 219). Japanese businessmen work in an environment that places little value on verbal give-and-take between seniors and juniors. Subordinates are expected to obey directives issued by superiors without the need for discussions. The subordinates are, however, allowed considerable latitude in devising appropriate measures for implementing the directive.

In the United States, verbal interaction between superiors and subordinates is an expected norm, and constructive criticism of proposals is actively sought. This tendency has led March (1992) to characterize the United States as a "culture of persuasive argumentation" (p. 219). In many instances, however, subordinates may expect to receive detailed guidance on how to discharge their responsibilities.

"Command" and "argumentation" are but two aspects of business communication that set Japan and the United States apart. The influence of the four different cultural patterns (see Table 1) discussed earlier can be isolated in any number of different commercial settings, as the following section will illustrate.

COMMUNICATION IN THE JAPANESE BUSINESS ENVIRONMENT

The record of modern Japanese–U.S. business interactions is replete with examples of culturally inappropriate behaviors that resulted in failed efforts. From the early 1970s and into the 1980s, a frequent but sadly true scenario saw American business representatives arriving in Tokyo and Osaka with the expectation of concluding all aspects of the desired deal in just a few days. It was also common that these same Americans returned home empty-handed, frustrated, and with little understanding of what had gone wrong. Hall and Hall (1987) have characterized these events as a play that continues to repeat the first act. Fortunately, as a result of greater economic integration between the two nations, things have improved somewhat in recent years, but eager U.S. business representatives still arrive in Japan with little or no appreciation of the cultural and communicative aspects of Japanese business.

As a means of illustrating the cultural patterning of Japanese business communication, we will describe a typical first meeting between Japanese and U.S. business representatives.[1] We will step through the various stages, beginning with introductions and moving through negotiations, decision making, and conflict. In each stage, the cultural determinants of the various communicative behaviors will be discussed.

Initial Meetings

The first meeting between Japanese and U.S. business counterparts represents a critical period for communication and impression management. Without prior knowledge of Japanese business practices, U.S. Americans will usually expect to begin substantive discussions soon after introductions. Too frequently, they assume that their Japanese counterparts are already aware of the U.S. firm's reputation. Conversely, the Japanese expect the initial meeting to

Table 1 *Contemporary Japanese and U.S. Cultural Patterns*

Japan	United States
Collectivistic	Individualistic
Hierarchical	Egalitarian
Formal	Informal
Social stability (*wa*)	Change

focus on the two sides getting acquainted. Unlike the United States, commerce in Japan is based on relationships, and these relationships are maintained during both strong and weak markets.

One basis for this variation in business philosophies can be traced to the collectivism–individualism continuum. American companies see themselves in competition with every other corporation. In Japan, however, businesses commonly form groups (large holding companies called *keiretsu*) that cooperate among themselves and compete against other groups. Thus, while the U.S. representatives consider the initial meeting to be the first step in the quest for joint profits, the Japanese want to glean information that will help in making a decision about the suitability and sustainability of a long-term relationship.

In the absence of prior interactions, U.S. companies should ensure that at least one senior executive heads the delegation for the first meeting. To the status-conscious and formal Japanese, this communicates that the U.S. organization considers the proposed venture to be one of importance. The executive may or may not engage in the actual negotiations, but the benefits from his or her presence at the initial round of introductions will frequently prove advantageous during this crucial early phase of the relationship.

The senior U.S. representative at the meetings should serve as the delegation's primary spokesperson. In this instance, hierarchy and social balance (*wa*) play a determining role in communication. For the Japanese, the senior representative will present the consensus of the group. Public dissent or open disagreement among delegation members would signal that a prior consensus had not been achieved and may prove disruptive to group cohesion. Therefore, U.S. members should avoid the egalitarian practice of open, intragroup debate.

Greeting Behaviors. The most senior U.S. delegate should enter the room first and greet the head of the Japanese side. Most Japanese international businessmen[2] have adopted the handshake as a greeting protocol, but U.S. business representatives can gain a degree of credibility by bowing to their Japanese counterpart. Among the Japanese, the bow is a finely honed art, practiced from childhood, that acknowledges status differentials and communicates respect for the other person. Because the junior person must always bow lower than his or her senior, U.S. delegates should not bow too deeply when greeting someone of junior status.

While bowing (or shaking hands), business cards (*meshi*) should be exchanged. *Meshi* are an extremely important and integral part of the greeting ritual in Japan. They are used to determine the status of the other person and the necessary degree of respect that should be accorded. The cards indicate the bearer's company and position, each of which carries a hierarchical standing. For example, a vice-president from IBM would have a higher status than a Taco Bell VP. The visitor's status determines not only the treatment he or she will receive in Japan but also even the level of polite language the Japanese will use.[3]

Personal Appearance. Just as in the United States, personal appearance is an important aspect of the Japanese business community, but with a few subtle twists. Generally speaking, business attire should be conservative. A dark blue, tailored suit has long been the standard insignia of the Japanese corporate salary man (*sariman*). Clothes that differentiate an individual from the majority are usually frowned upon because the Japanese predilection for harmonious relations and group membership discourages behaviors that will single out an individual. Although younger Japanese employees have begun to wear a greater variety of colors and styles, conservative dress is still the rule for management and executives.

Many Japanese businessmen wear small, discrete lapel pins that identify their company of employment. Japanese corporations are ranked according to their prestige, and the company (group) actually becomes a part of the worker's personal identity. The appropriate level of respect the Japanese afford each other and visitors is predicated in part on the hierarchical status of their corporate employer.

To enhance institutional identity (group membership), Japanese businesses usually provide service and production area workers with distinctive company uniforms. When working in these areas, even managers will don a uniform. One of the authors actually observed the president of a Japanese manufacturing firm put on a company smock just before entering the assembly line area.

Where to Sit. When visiting a U.S. corporate meeting room, visitors commonly ask about any special seating arrangements and are usually told, "The boss sits here, but you can sit anywhere else." This is yet another manifestation of equality and individual freedom of choice.

Positioning in Japan is not quite that simple. As with almost every aspect of Japanese society, in a business setting where one sits or stands is dictated by status. At a Japanese meeting, the position of honor is normally the seat farthest away from the door (De Mente, 1993). This makes it quite easy for one to determine who is the highest-ranking individual, or guest of honor, when entering a room full of Japanese businessmen.

Communication Content. As suggested by Hall and Hall (1987) and exemplified by the authors' personal experiences, in their early meetings the U.S. business delegates should expect the Japanese to ask numerous and probing questions about the proposal. These requests for explanations and additional details seemingly defy the large body or research that posits the Japanese as being a high-context culture, reliant on intuition and nonverbal exchange rather than oral communications.

The contradictory behavior exhibited by Japanese during initial interactions with international representatives is easily explained by recalling the structured, hierarchical society of the Tokugawa Era and applying Gudykunst's (1995) theory of Anxiety Uncertainty Management (AUM). The tireless Japanese proclivity for group association and status differentiation has produced a society in which members adhere to rigidly proscribed social protocols of deportment and interaction. Coupled with strong in-group affiliation and little or no association with out-groups, this has facilitated a high degree of predictability among Japanese in-group members.

However, when forced to interact with individuals from an out-group, such as U.S. business representatives, the Japanese are confronted with a high level of uncertainty. They have little personal information about the U.S. Americans and are consequently unable to predict the behaviors of these visitors from across the Pacific. Is an association with these U.S. businessmen or women worthwhile? Can they be trusted? Will they make reliable partners for the proposed commercial project? To resolve these questions and abate the rising levels of anxiety, the Japanese attempt to gather as much information as possible. Quite simply, the quest for information is a means of establishing the social (and commercial) credibility of the strangers. Once they are comfortable with the new in-group members, the Japanese will return to their usual high-context communication patterns.

The highly proscribed protocols surrounding an initial business meeting in Japan are designed to help determine the social position of the different individuals, which will dictate the proper level of deportment and language. The importance of knowing the proper social standing of an individual in Japan cannot be over emphasized. Nakane (1970) has posted that a fundamental basis of Japanese social interaction is discerning and responding to these ranked differences. For example, if a Japanese does not know the social position of a business counterpart, he or she may well be unable to sit or even speak!

This need to put everything in a hierarchical order may seem strange to the freedom-loving U.S. businessman or businesswoman. But to understand the motive of this need, one only has to examine Tokugawa society, where the entire Japanese population was divided into ranked social categories, each with different degrees of privilege.

Japanese Concept of Face. Before proceeding to the negotiating and conflict phases of our Japanese–U.S. business interaction, the role of "face" in Japan and the United States must be explained, for it exerts an especially puissant influence on Japanese communicative behaviors. Facework involves those human efforts exerted in the presentation of a civil front during social interaction. More simply put, facework is the construction and communication of *face*, that image of ourselves we want others to see.

An individual's concept of face and facework is also sensitive to a society's underlying values and norms (Ting-Toomey, 1988, 1994). In individualistic cultures, for example, people are more concerned with maintaining their own face. A person's face in the United States is normally independent of others and assumes an individualistic quality. Collectivistic cultures, however, tend to focus more on mutual and other face maintenance. In Japan, for example, face is characteristically a function of group association and acquired through an interdependent process (Morisaki & Gudykunst, 1994).

Because face is usually independent of the group in the United States, individuals are not overly concerned with how they influence another's face. This leads to a more direct, forthright style of communication. The old adages "Tell it like it is" and "Don't beat around the bush" exemplify the value placed on candid, straightforward communication. Positive, cordial relations are often secondary to frankness. For a U.S. American, loss of face is a personal affront, usually interpreted as a threat to personal credibility (Gudykunst & Nishida, 1994).

Face in Japan is normally an integral part of group association, and the Japanese employ concerted efforts to avoid activities that would potentially denigrate the face of their associates or in-group members. There exists a great reluctance to directly address an issue that may produce controversy. Social actions that lead to a loss of face are considered rude and insulting as they carry the potential for disrupting the social balance. This results in a Japanese preference for reticence and indirect communication styles.

Face and Communication Strategies. In Japan, a dichotomy exists between the actions reserved for public consumption (*tatemae*) and those used for genuine, or personal, opinions (*honne*) (Hendry, 1989; Lebra, 1976). *Tatemae* adheres to the principles and expectations of the group and extends to apologies, feigning sincerity, and even remorse. At times, it is a gentle substitute for the harsh words one may actually be thinking and is used to mask these antagonistic thoughts. Although not sinister or deceptive by nature, *tatemae* is merely a method used by the Japanese to seek acceptance, avoid confrontation, and maintain a degree of quietude in the conduct of daily activities. In modern Japanese society, the use of *tatemae* to preserve face is considered a virtue.

Beneath the surface of *tatemae* rests *honne*, the individual's true intentions or personal feelings. Although the employment of *honne* is especially limited within the corporate environment, opportunities for honest expression exist at the conclusion of the workday. Tenhover (1994) posits that the most common place to find *honne* in Japan is in the company of alcohol. Functioning as a social lubricant, alcohol liberates many Japanese from the culturally imposed restraints of *tatemae*. Happy hour is a time to release inhibitions and voice one's real opinions, and it provides an ideal opportunity for co-workers to bond.

Someone unfamiliar with the Japanese social structure, such as a U.S. businessperson, may well consider the functionality of *tatemae* superficial, but within the Japanese mindset it is an integral part of a collectivistic based value system. *Tatemae* provides a valuable social mechanism for avoiding confrontation or embarrassment, and conversations are adapted accordingly. A Japanese recipient will understand that *tatemae* is being used to advert disagreement, ensure group integrity, exhibit deference to a superior or guest, or maintain social cordiality.

For a U.S. American imbued with a tradition of personal expression, *tatemae* can appear evasive at best and duplicitous at worst. Moreover, *tatemae* can be the cause of serious misunderstanding between Japanese and non-Japanese business personnel. For example, in Japan, the use of "yes" is not necessarily a sign of agreement and in some instances can actually mean "no" (March, 1996). The Japanese often use "yes" to indicate the listener merely comprehends what the speaker is saying. "Yes" does not guarantee agreement with what has been said. In addition, "no" is used far less in Japanese than in English. To come right out and say "no" to another person is considered too direct and carries the possibility of conflict. Other Japanese words, such as "difficult" or "maybe," which are softer and less confrontational, are used in place of "no."

Body language can also be used to express dissent. Often, a Japanese will tilt the head to one side and suck air through his or her teeth, an action that equates to an unequivocal no. Among Japanese speakers, this nonverbal response would be immediately understood, but from a U.S. American cultural perspective would appear vague or even indecipherable.

In our Japanese–U.S. business meeting, the Japanese would be reluctant to offer a direct no (*honne*) to a proposal, preferring instead to find the idea "interesting" but needing additional "study" (*tatemae*). The U.S. representatives, enculturated to expect an open, direct communication style, could well take the Japanese response at face value and believe the two sides were close to reaching an agreement. Only much later, when there was no further response from the Japanese company, would the Americans realize that what had been perceived as a "yes" was actually a "no." For the Japanese, the use of *tatemae* has saved the faces of both sides and preserved amiable relations. But on the U.S. side, the use of indirect communication has created misunderstanding and uncertainty, conditions that often produce considerable ill will toward the other side.

These differences arising from varying culturally patterned communication styles can result in misinterpretation, confusion, strained relations, or even animosity, any one of which can produce some degree of social disunity. In our business example, the Japanese adherence to indirect communication as a means of sustaining amicable relations can actually produce the exact opposite effect among the U.S. audience. On the other side, employment of open, direct communication styles of U.S. representatives can be perceived as rude and inconsiderate, resulting in a loss of face for the Japanese.

Decision Making

Decision making is a particularly critical aspect of the commercial world, affecting both the internal and external operations of an organization. The decision to launch a new product line or expand into another market carries fundamental external risks. Internally, successful implementation of any organizational change requires a degree of employee cooperation. As in almost every social endeavor, culture influences and shapes the process used in decision making.

Not unlike other areas of business, the Japanese decision-making procedure is at odds with that employed in the United States. In U.S. companies, decisions are usually a top-down process, disseminated downward through an authoritarian corporate structure. Subordinate employees may or may not be consulted by their corporate leaders. These decisions made by individuals, or simple majorities, can be seen as a continued reflection of a cultural heritage that emphasizes egalitarianism, independence, and frequent change.

In traditional U.S. organizations, decision making is vested in a few individuals and is usually a quick process, requiring only minimal discussion once the appropriate studies (environmental, market survey, etc.) have been completed. Implementation, however, may take much longer. Without prior knowledge, subordinate employees usually need time to understand and accept the new changes and may be slow to acquiesce. This resistance can slow, or even derail, the decision's objective.

As with the United States, the legacy of Japan's historical circumstances and cultural traditions continue to influence contemporary decision making. The Japanese collectivistic nature and desire for social stability is reflected in the group-centered corporate decision process. The Japanese bottom-up procedure (*ringi seido*) usually starts at the middle management level, where a few employees may prepare a memo (*ringi sho*) that suggests a new direction or endeavor for the organization. The document is then circulated through all branches of the company, and at each level, managers have an opportunity to examine and discuss the potential impact of the suggestion. Agreement is indicated by a manager's personal stamp,[4] and disagreement by the absence of the stamp. Ultimately, the document reaches the head of the organization, and if a clear consensus exists the proposal becomes policy (Abegglen & Stalk, 1985; Stewart, 1993).

This communal procedure requires considerable time and employee involvement. Information relating to the proposal must be widely disseminated and studied. Where dissent is encountered, discussions and consultation (*nemawashi*) must be conducted in an effort to find a consensual agreement. These discussions, of course, involve *honne* and *tatemae* and will take place at the office during the workday and continue in bars and restaurants after working hours.

Once a decision is made, however, implementation is rapid and pervasive, a result of wide involvement in the decision process from inception to finish. Everyone had the opportunity to voice an opinion and discuss the various options before the proposal became policy. Thus, employees are already familiar with the decision, its ramifications, and actions needed for implementation.

Negotiations

Over the past decade, the difficulties surrounding Japanese–U.S. trade negotiations have been a frequent feature of U.S. business journals and newspapers. Not unexpectedly, the two nations approach the negotiating table with very different sets of culturally instilled bargaining styles, which further exacerbates and often obscures the substantive differences of the issues under consideration.

The U.S. concept of negotiation is strongly grounded in the classical Greek tradition of rhetorical eloquence, argumentation, debate, and persuasion (Goldman, 1994). The Aristotelian legacy has produced a direct, somewhat confrontational approach to negotiations for U.S. corporate representatives. Often, the negotiation process is seen as adversarial in nature, driven by the underlying objective of "winning." Further, a short- or near-term perspective is produced by the overemphasis on profit maximization, which is usually the principle motivation behind commercial negotiations in the United States.

U.S. negotiators normally come to the table with a predetermined agenda, or "game plan," that includes a specific list of topics for discussion. Negotiations will then proceed in a linear manner, with each proposed discussion topic being addressed point by point. For U.S. business members, negotiations are a time to discuss the proposal, examine and resolve differences, make decisions, and agree to commitments.

This style of negotiation is in direct contrast to the Japanese notion. First, the motives behind Japanese negotiations are more complex. Driven by the pervasive influence of collectivism, Japanese companies approach business with a long-term view. The desire for corporate growth, increased market share, and an expanded employee base takes precedence over short-term profit gains.

Unlike the confrontational character of U.S. negotiations, Japanese negotiations are designed to permit everyone to present their ideas, examine

alternatives, and obtain the most productive consensus. The process is one of continuous modification and compromise. Among the Japanese, negotiations are nonconfrontational, filled with indirect references, and, often, deferred decisions. The underlying objective is to maintain group cohesion and avoid direct, open conflict.

When Japanese businessmen sit down at the bargaining table, they do not expect a rapid decision. The first session should involve a comprehensive overview of the proposed project. The proposal will then be divided into smaller segments for individual in-depth discussions. This process will also require considerable behind-the-scenes discussions (nemawashi) among the Japanese so that they can present a united front.

These differing negotiation styles can produce considerable consternation on both sides of the table. In an attempt to evoke a quick decision, U.S. business personnel are accustomed to presenting their proposal and employing linear, logical arguments to dispel any doubts the other side may have. The veracity of their proposal is thought to be self-evident by the anticipated near-term profit yield. The Japanese, however, are more concerned with the type and quality of the relationship between the two organizations, how will the proposal affect company employees, and, while short-term goals may be attainable, what will be the long-term impact? Even at initial meetings, the U.S. side commonly enters negotiations prepared and wanting to make decisions, but the Japanese may need additional information and time to help achieve a consensus. For U.S. representatives, the need for additional private discussions unnecessarily drag out the negotiations and may even be misinterpreted as indecisive or evasive behavior on the part of the Japanese.

Disparate nonverbal communication behaviors can also exasperate Japanese–U.S. business negotiations. The Japanese, for instance, traditionally employ long periods of silence, often shutting their eyes and leaning back in their chairs. During these periods, they simply want to contemplate the point being discussed, but U.S. negotiators, unaccustomed to prolonged silence, will frequently become agitated and begin reiterating their offer (De Mente, 1993). Sometimes, the Japanese use of silence will even elicit unexpected concessions from the U.S. side.

To emphasize a point, evoke a decision, or express their conviction, U.S. negotiators will quite often become demonstrative, using raised, combative tones and liberal hand and arm gestures. These behaviors can leave the Japanese with the impression that U.S. negotiators are blunt, impatient, and even rude.

As with other components of Japanese–U.S. business interactions, the two nation's dissimilar historical experience and cultural background can be used to explain their contrasting negotiation styles. By allowing everyone to participate in discussions, making necessary compromises, and arriving at a mutually agreeable decision, the Japanese avert open confrontations, maintain amiable relations, and sustain group unity. They want to reach a "win–win" agreement with the U.S. side (Hall & Hall, 1997).

U.S. negotiators, however, enter the process with a them-or-us perception, an attitude frequently attributed to the lingering American frontier mentality. The business proposal is another challenge to be conquered, and there can only be one winner. Concern for the self creates a drive for individual achievement and short-term profits; corporate longevity and employee well-being are not particularly salient considerations.

Conflict Management

Conflict is an inescapable concomitant of relationships and, if managed improperly, can lead to irreparable breakdowns—divorce at the interpersonal level and war on a national scale. How conflict is seen and managed within a society is also a function of cultural values. For example, Japan's collectivistic inclinations have inculcated the population with an aversion to conflict. In contrast, the individualistic values of the United States make dissent a natural part of social life (Barnlund, 1989).

International business, marked by the participants' varying values, ideals, beliefs, and behaviors, provides a rich medium for discord. An awareness of how conflict is perceived by, and managed in, the other culture offers business representatives a substantial benefit in any commercial endeavor.

The potential for disagreement is particularly salient in Japanese–U.S. corporate transactions.

Because the Japanese consider conflict to be socially disruptive and a direct threat to group cohesion, measures have been devised and woven into the social fabric to mitigate the potential for open, direct antagonism.[5] Japanese organizations are especially sensitive to the perils of discord and employ a variety of means to help avoid or reduce the incidence of disagreement. These measures include programs to socialize employees so that they consider the organization part of their "professional and personal fulfillment" (Krauss, Rohlen, & Steinhoff, 1984, p. 382). Because the individual's identity will be derived in part from the organization, there is little incentive toward disruptive organizational activities. Companies will also employ small group discussions, personal communication, and trusted intermediaries to help avoid or resolve conflicts (Krauss, Rohlen, & Steinhoff, 1984). Other methods include the use of prior consultation before meeting formally and an unquestioning acceptance of authority (Befu, 1990).

On an individual basis, the Japanese strive to avoid conflict or, if it is inevitable, search for avenues of accommodation. According to Barnlund (1989), areas of agreement are emphasized and points of disagreement are minimized. The use of *tatemae* and *honne*, coupled with a complex system of reciprocal obligations (*giri* and *on*), provides an effective impediment to interpersonal strife. Criticism, a potent source of disagreement, is expressed in passive, accommodating styles. Faced with the specter of conflict, the Japanese might choose to remain silent or use nonverbal means to express their disapproval. Complaints may be voiced through humor or jokes or by way of a third person. In the United States, however, criticism is expressed more harshly and more pointedly (Nomura & Barnlund, 1983).

Conflict, disagreement, and dissent do not carry negative connotations in the United States, where differences are considered both inevitable and valuable. Here, the strong doctrine of individual freedoms has perpetuated the open and unrestricted exchange of ideas. The ability to argue one's convictions in a strong, eloquent manner is a highly admired trait. Indeed, the dialectic process is commonly used to test and advance new ideas. The acceptance and use of disagreement is exemplified in U.S. schools, where students are taught to engage topics from a critical perspective. Conflict thus becomes a part of daily life, and debates on differences of opinions can frequently prove stimulating and entertaining (Barnlund, 1989). The intense competitiveness that permeates both work and play attests to U.S. acceptance and use of conflict as a positive experience.

In comparison to Japan, social acceptance of interpersonal and institutional disagreement in the United States has promoted methods of conflict management that are usually more institutionalized and applicable to a broad selection of situations. Indeed, one reason for the plethora of U.S. lawyers is the common and frequent use of laws to manage and resolve conflict. Majority rule and unilateral decisions, passed down vertically from higher authority, for example, are common management techniques in the United States. If employees disagree with the decision, they have several options—openly express their dissent to management, fight the decision through legal or arbitration channels, or just quit. None of these options, however, is concerned with harmony or cohesion; individual self-interest overrides matters of organizational stability and group continuity (Barnlund, 1989; Krauss, Rohlen, & Steinhoff, 1984).

The contrasting Japanese and U.S. attitudes toward conflict and styles of managing differences set the stage for a broad range of culturally based misunderstandings and disagreements. In the business environment, the Japanese can be expected to advance their position by careful, indirect methods as they search for a prospective consensus. Euro-Americans, however, will normally view the situation through a more confrontational lens and engage their Japanese counterparts with direct, forthright language in an effort to "win" their objective. To sustain cordial relations, Japanese business representatives will avoid directly addressing controversial topics. The U.S. members, however, may see this reluctance as a sign of weakness and a possible opportunity to gain an advantage. Also, Japanese reticence in the face of blunt, aggressive discourse by U.S. businessmen or women might be misinterpreted as agreement. For the Japanese, the U.S. penchant for directness and confrontation would be considered rude and might well cause a reevaluation of the prospective relationship.

Interpreters

International business communication requires that participants engage in the exacting process of transferring meaning from one party to another through the conduit of two or more different languages. This commonly requires the use of interpreters, an important but often overlooked or underemphasized area of intercultural communication. This is especially true of U.S. Americans, who usually speak only English and see engagement of interpreters as the end of the problem (Stewart & Bennett, 1991). The most frequent shortfall is assuming that the meaning attached to a word in one language carries an identical meaning in another language. Unfortunately, this attitude can lead to irreparable divisions during international interactions.

Competent intercultural communicators recognize that language and culture are inseparable and that the meaning conveyed by words is culturally bound and historically influenced. On some occasions, we may understand the words but not the context. There are also instances where words from one language simply have no translatable equivalent. Moreover, literal translations can sometimes become nonsensical in the other language (Samovar, Porter, & Stefani, 1998).

The Japanese emphasis on indirectness and face-saving tactics can create considerable difficulties for translators attempting to convey meaning to U.S. businesspeople, who value and are accustomed to directness, openness, and often excruciating honesty. Conversely, a translator may encounter problems when trying to impart the candid, to-the-point style used by the U.S. delegates.[6]

Most Japanese businessmen have only a limited or rudimentary English speaking ability. Although they begin studying English in junior high school, until recently instruction has been geared more toward passing high school and university entrance exams, which concentrate on reading and writing. During meetings, however, Japanese business delegates may give the impression of understanding much more than they actually do, because pretending to understand ensures the meeting is conducted in a congenial manner and no one loses face.

To help alleviate these culturally motivated problems, it is necessary to ensure that translators are culturally knowledgeable, as well as linguistically fluent.

U.S. business representatives should engage their own interpreter and never rely on the host company to provide the service. The U.S. delegates should meet with their translator (or translators if meetings are expected to go on all day) one or two days before the scheduled business appointment and go over the planned agenda topics. This will allow the interpreter time to review vocabulary specific to the intended discussions. The ability to translate highly technical subjects (telecommunications, genetic engineering, etc.) requires considerable skill and years of study. If the meeting will involve technical discussions, an appropriate interpreter should be identified and engaged well in advance.[7]

CONCLUSION

The interaction between two or more individuals is an extremely complex and multifaceted enterprise, even when they are from the same culture. Communication between individuals from different nations significantly compounds the enterprise. Varying cultural backgrounds exacerbate language and individual differences. The business setting can often magnify these problems by imposing additional impediments, such as time requirements, organizational preconditions, and monetary considerations.

The communicative aspects of Japanese business that have been described in this chapter are broad generalizations, drawn from academic writings and our personal experiences.[8] Those few areas of business communication discussed in this chapter are intended to heighten the student's awareness of how culture can influence international business communication. They are by no means inclusive. We have not examined many other topics that affect Japanese–U.S. commercial activities. These include, for example, the role of gift giving, dissimilar concepts of time, the influence of gender roles and gender communication, varying attitudes toward praise and complements, disparate nonverbal behaviors, and views of humor.

Our world is undergoing a period of dynamic transition, often referred to as "globalization." The influence of globe-spanning telecommunications networks, modern transportation capabilities, and growing economic interdependencies are bringing people from different nations and cultures into more frequent and prolonged contact. In some instances this contact is tangible and in others virtual via telecommunications. Through travel and multimedia access, people are becoming more aware of the different values, attitudes, and behaviors of other cultures.

This intercultural awareness is particularly salient in Japan, where some university graduates, especially recent ones, have begun to question the values of the nation's tightly wound corporate structure. While that outward structure may appear to be shifting as a result of globalization and the bursting of the "bubble economy," the cultural decorums of Japanese society are changing at a more glacial pace. Contemporary Japan's enduring values, an outgrowth of historical era sociopolitical events, will continue to motivate the methods of discourse explained in this chapter, along with the socioeconomic infrastructure, as the nation struggles for a new identity in the next century.

Notes

1. For this illustration, the authors will draw from their own experiences of living and working in Japan, as well as from those of their expatriate colleagues.
2. The authors are aware of the patriarchal connotation behind the term *businessmen* but feel it is appropriate in the case of Japan, where the number of women serving in executive level positions is still miniscule.
3. The Japanese language contains many conventions for displaying respect and deference. Juniors commonly use honorifics (*keigo*) when addressing seniors.
4. The Japanese do not actually "sign" documents. Rather, they place their personal stamp on a document using an *inkan*, a small device that has the owner's stamp carved into one end. This stamp is usually the individual's name in stylized Japanese.
5. Conflict does, of course, exist in Japan, but it has been found to be less prevalent and intense than in the United States (Krauss, Rohlen, & Steinhoff, 1984).
6. The sentence structure of Japanese (subject–object–verb) facilitates indirectness. By placing the verb at the end of the sentence, a Japanese

speaker can gauge the reactions of the recipient and make appropriate adjustments before revealing the desired action. Compare this with the more direct structure of English (subject–verb–object).

7. There are a host of other considerations attendant to using interpreters. Harris and Moran (1991) and De Mente (1993) provide an excellent discussion of these points.

8. Collectively, the authors have been studying, living, and working with the Japanese for more than thirty years.

References

Abegglen, J. C., & Stalk, G., Jr. (1985). *Kasha: The Japanese corporation*. New York: Basic Books.

Barnlund, D. C. (1989). *Communicative styles of Japanese and Americans*. Belmont, CA: Wadsworth.

Befu, H. (1990). Four models of Japanese society and their relevance to conflict. In S. N. Eisenstadt & E. Ben-Ari (Eds.), *Japanese models of conflict resolution* (pp. 213–238). New York: Keagan Paul International.

De Mente, B. L. (1993). *How to do business with the Japanese* (2nd ed.). Lincolnwood, IL: NTC Business Books.

Goldman, A. (1994). *Doing business with the Japanese*. Albany: State University of New York Press.

Gudykunst, W. B. (1995). Anxiety Uncertainty Management theory: Current status. In R. L. Wiseman (Ed.), *Intercultural communication theory* (pp. 8–58). Thousand Oaks, CA: Sage.

———, & Nishida, T. (1994). *Bridging Japanese/North American differences*. Thousand Oaks, CA: Sage.

Hall, E. T., & Hall, M. R. (1987). *Hidden differences: Doing business with the Japanese*. New York: Anchor Books.

Harris, P. R., & Moran, R. T. (1991). *Managing cultural differences* (3rd ed.). Houston, TX: Gulf Publishing.

Hendry, J. (1989). *Understanding Japanese society*. New York: Routledge.

Hirschmeiier, J., & Yui, T. (1981). *The development of Japanese business* (2nd ed.). Boston: George Allen & Unwin.

Japan on the brink. (1998, April 11). *The Economist*, pp. 15–17.

Krauss, E. S., Rohlen, T. P., & Steinhoff, P. G. (1984). Conflict and its resolution in postwar Japan. In E. S. Krauss, T. P. Rohlen, & P. G. Steinhoff (Eds.), *Conflict in Japan* (pp. 375–397). Honolulu: University of Hawaii Press.

LaFeber, W. (1997). *The clash: U.S.–Japanese relations throughout history*. New York: W. W. Norton.

Lebra, T. S. (1976). *Japanese patterns of behavior*. Honolulu: University of Hawaii Press.

March, R. M. (1992). *Working for a Japanese company: Insights into the multicultural workplace*. Tokyo: Kodansha International.

———. (1996). *Reading the Japanese mind*. Tokyo: Kodansha International.

Morisaki, S., & Gudykunst, W. B. (1994). Face in Japan and the United States. In S. Ting-Toomey (Ed.), *The challenge of facework* (pp. 47–93). Albany: State University of New York Press.

Nakane, C. (1970). *Japanese society*. Berkeley: University of California Press.

Nomura, N., & Barnlund, D. (1983). Patterns of interpersonal criticism in Japan and the United States. *International Journal of Intercultural Relations*, 7, 1–18.

Samovar, L. A., Porter, R. E., & Stefani, L. A. (1998). *Communication between cultures* (3rd ed.). Belmont, CA: Wadsworth.

Stewart, E. C., & Bennett, M. J. (1991). *American cultural patterns* (rev. ed.). Yarmouth, MA: Intercultural Press.

Stewart, L. P. (1993). Organizational communication in Japan and the United States. In W. B. Gudykunst (Ed.), *Communication in Japan and the United States* (pp. 215–248). Albany: State University of New York Press.

Tenhover, G. R. (1994). *Unlocking the Japanese business mind*. Washington, DC: Transemantics.

Ting-Toomey, S. (1988). Intercultural conflict styles: A face-negotiation theory. In Y. Y. Kim & W. B. Gudykunst (Eds.), *Theories in intercultural communication* (pp. 213–235). Newbury Park, CA: Sage.

———. (1994). Face and facework: An introduction. In S. Ting-Toomey (Ed.), *The challenge of facework* (pp. 47–93). Albany: State University of New York Press.

Concepts and Questions

1. What are the fundamental historical differences between Japanese and U.S. American cultural values? Why did these differences evolve in the two cultures?

2. Compare and contrast Japanese and U.S. American business concerns with profit?

3. What do the "command" and "argumentation" aspects of business communication mean? How do Japan and the United States differ in their uses?

4. Why is the first meeting between Japanese and U.S. business representatives considered a "critical period"? What major differences are there

between Japanese and U.S. perceptions of the purpose of initial meetings?

5. Based on your own experiences, how do the Japanese concepts about greeting behaviors, personal appearance, and seat arrangements differ from what you would expect in a U.S. business meeting?

6. During the initial stages of business meetings, Japanese representatives may be found to ask numerous probing questions about the business proposal. This behavior seems to defy the notion that Japan is a high-context culture. How do you explain the discrepancy?

7. What is the Japanese concept of *face*? How does it affect business communication strategies?

8. What are the fundamental differences in the ways in which business decisions are reached in Japan and in the United States? How might these differences affect expectations during business discussions?

9. How do the Japanese and the United States differ in their fundamental concepts of negotiations? How could these different approaches affect negotiations between U.S. and Japanese negotiators?

10. Compare and contrast the Japanese and U.S. approaches to conflict management.

Contrasts in Discussion Behaviors of German and American Managers

ROBERT A. FRIDAY

AMERICAN MANAGERS' EXPECTATIONS

Business Is Impersonal

In any business environment, discussion between colleagues must accomplish the vital function of exchanging information that is needed for the solution of problems. In American business, such discussions are usually impersonal.[1] Traditionally the facts have spoken for themselves in America. "When facts are disputed, the argument must be suspended until the facts are settled. Not until then may it be resumed, for all true argument is about the meaning of established or admitted facts" (Weaver, 1953) in the rationalistic view. Much of post–WWII American business decision making has been based on the quantitative MBA approach which focuses on factual data and its relationship to the ultimate fact of profit or loss, writing strategy plans, and top-down direction. After all of the facts are in, the CEO is often responsible for making the intuitive leap and providing leadership. The power and authority of the CEO has prevailed in the past 40 years, with no predicted change in view (Bleicher & Paul, 1986, pp. 10–11). Through competition and contact with West Germany and Japan, the more personal approach is beginning to enter some lower level decision-making practices (Peters & Waterman, 1982, pp. 35–118).

Another reason for the impersonal nature of American business is that many American managers do not identify themselves with their corporations. When the goals and interests of the corporation match up with those of the American manager, he or she will stay and prosper. However, when the per-

From *International Journal of Intercultural Relations*, Vol. 13, 1989, pp. 429–455. Reprinted by permission of Pergamon Press, Inc., and the author.

sonal agenda of the American manager is not compatible with that of the corporation, he or she is likely to move on to attain his or her objective in a more conducive environment. Most American managers can disassociate themselves from their business identity, at least to the extent that their personal investment in a decision has more to do with their share of the profit rather than their sense of personal worth.

In contrast, "the German salesman's personal credibility is on the line when he sells his product. He spends years cultivating his clients, building long-term relationships based on reliability" (Hall, 1983, p. 67). This tendency on the part of Germans is much like American business in the early part of this century.

The cohesiveness of the employees of most German businesses is evidenced in the narrow salary spread. Whereas in the United States the ratio of lowest paid to highest paid is approximately 1 to 80, in Germany this ratio is 1 to 25 (Hall, 1983, p. 74).

GERMAN MANAGERS' EXPECTATION

Business Is Not as Impersonal

The corporation for most Germans is closely related to his or her own identity. German managers at Mobay are likely to refer to "Papa Bayer" because they perceive themselves as members of a corporate family that meets most of their needs. In turn, most German managers there, as elsewhere, have made a lifelong commitment to the larger group in both a social and economic sense (Friday & Biro, 1986–87). In contrast to the American post–WW II trend is "the German postwar tradition of seeking consensus among a closely knit group of colleagues who have worked together for decades [which] provides a collegial harmony among top managers that is rare in U.S. corporations" (Bleicher & Paul, 1986, p. 12). Our interviews suggested that many German managers may enter a three-year-plus training program with the idea of moving on later to another corporation. This move rarely occurs.

While a three-year training program appears to be excessively long by American standards, one must understand that the longer training program works on several levels that are logical within the German culture. The three or more years of entry level train-

ing is a predictable correlation to the German and USA relative values on the Uncertainty Avoidance Index[2] (Hofstede, 1984, p. 122). The longer training period is required to induct the German manager into the more formal decision-making rules, plans, operating procedures, and industry tradition (Cyert & March, 1963, p. 119), all of which focus on the short-run known entities (engineering/reliability of product) rather than the long-run unknown problems (future market demand).

On another level the "strong sense of self as a striving, controlling entity is offset by an equally strong sense of obligation to a code of decency" (McClelland, Sturr, Knapp, & Wendt, 1958, p. 252). Induction into a German company with an idealistic system of obligation requires a longer training period than induction into an American company in which the corporate strategy for productivity is acquired in small group and interpersonal interaction.[3] The German manager who moves from one corporation to another for the purpose of advancement is regarded with suspicion partly because of his lack of participation in the corporate tradition, which could prove to be an unstabilizing factor.

Our preliminary interview results suggested uncertainty avoidance (Hofstede, 1984, p. 130) in everyday business relationships, especially the German concern for security. For example, most of the transfer preparation from the German home office to the [United States] consists of highly detailed explanations of an extensive benefits package. Since the German manager sees a direct relationship between his or her personal security and the prosperity of his or her company, business becomes more personal for him or her. Similarly, Americans who work in employee-owned companies are also seeing a clear relationship between personal security and the prosperity of their company.

AMERICAN MANAGERS' EXPECTATIONS

Need to Be Liked

The American's need to be liked is a primary aspect of his or her motivation to cooperate or not to cooperate with colleagues. The arousal of this motivation occurs naturally in discussion situations when direct feedback gives the American the desired response, which indicates a sense of belongingness or acceptance. The American "envisions the desired responses and is likely to gear his actions accordingly. The characteristic of seeing others as responses is reflected in the emphasis on communication in interaction and in the great value placed on being liked. . . . [The] American's esteem of others is based on their liking him. This requirement makes it difficult for Americans to implement projects which require an 'unpopular' phase" (Stewart, 1972, p. 58).

For Americans, the almost immediate and informal use of a colleague's first name is a recognition that each likes the other. While such informality is common among American business personnel, this custom should probably be avoided with Germans. "It takes a long time to get on a first-name basis with a German; if you rush the process, you may be perceived as overly familiar and rude. . . . Germans are very conscious of their status and insist on proper forms of address. Germans are bewildered by the American custom of addressing a new acquaintance by his first name and are even more startled by our custom of addressing a superior by first name" (Hall, 1983, pp. 57–58). When such matters of decorum are overlooked during critical discussions, an "unpopular phase" may develop.

> The need to be liked is culturally induced at an early age and continued throughout life through regular participation in group activities. They [Americans] are not brought up on sentiments of obligation to others as the Germans are, but from kindergarten on they regularly participate in many more extracurricular functions of a group nature. In fact, by far the most impressive result . . . is the low number of group activities listed by the Germans (about 1, on the average) as compared with the Americans (about 5, on the average). In these activities the American student must learn a good deal more about getting along with other people and doing things cooperatively, if these clubs are to function at all. (McClelland et al., 1958, p. 250)

This cultural orientation in relation to group participation will be revisited later in the closing discussion on "learning styles, training, instruction, and problem solving."

GERMAN MANAGERS' EXPECTATIONS

Need to Be Credible

The German counterpart to the American need to be liked is the need to establish one's credibility and position in the hierarchy. The contrast between American informality and mobility and German formality and class structure is a reflection of the difference between these two needs. In the absence of a long historical tradition, Americans have developed a society in which friendships and residence change often, family histories (reputations) are unknown, and, therefore, acceptance of what one is doing in the present and plans to do in the future is a great part of one's identity. In order to maintain this mobility of place and relationships, Americans rely on reducing barriers to acceptance through informality.

Germans, with their strong sense of history, tradition, family, and life-long friendships, tend to move much less often, make friendships slowly, and keep them longer than Americans. Because one's family may be known for generations in Germany, the family reputation becomes part of one's own identity, which in turn places the individual in a stable social position.[4]

The stability of the social class structure and, thus, the credibility of the upper class in Germany are largely maintained through the elitist system of higher education.

> Educational achievement has been a major factor in determining occupational attainment and socioeconomic status in the post–World War II era. University education has been virtually essential in gaining access to the most prestigious and remunerative positions. Some of the most enduring social divisions have focused on level of education. (Nyrop, 1982, p. 113)

A German's education most often places him or her at a certain level which, in turn, determines what they can and can't do. In Germany, one must present credentials as evidence of one's qualification to perform *any* task (K. Hagemann, personal communication, May–September, 1987). Thus, the German societal arrangement guarantees stability and order by adherence to known barriers (credentials) that confirm one's credibility. In Germany, loss of credibility would be known in the manager's corporate and social group and would probably result in truncated advancement (not dismissal since security is a high value).

The rigid social barriers established by education and credentials stand in direct contrast to the concepts of social mobility in American society. "Our social orientation is toward the importance of the individual and the equality of all individuals. Friendly, informal, outgoing, and extroverted, the American scorns rank and authority even when [he or she] is the one with the rank. American bosses are the only bosses in the world who insist on being called by their first names by their subordinates" (Kohls, 1987, p. 8). When Germans and Americans come together in discussion, the German's drive is to establish hierarchy, the American's is to dissolve it.

AMERICAN MANAGERS' EXPECTATIONS

Assertiveness, Direct Confrontation, and Fair Play

In comparing Americans with Japanese, Edward Stewart relates the American idea of confrontation as "putting the cards on the table and getting the information 'straight from the horse's mouth.' It is also desirable to face people directly, to confront them intentionally" (Stewart, 1972, p. 52). This is done so that the decision makers can have all of the facts. Stewart contrasts this intentional confrontation of Americans to the indirection of the Japanese, which often requires the inclusion of an intermediary or emissary in order to avoid face to face confrontation and thus, the loss of face. However, this view may leave the American manager unprepared for what he or she is likely to find in his or her initial discussion with a German manager.

The American manager is likely to approach his or her first discussion with German managers in an assertive fashion from the assumption that competition in business occurs within the context of cooperation (Stewart, 1972, p. 56). This balance is attained by invoking the unspoken rule of fair play.

> Our games traditions, although altered and transformed, are Anglo-Saxon in form; and fair play does mean for us, as for the English, a standard of behavior

between weak and the strong—a standard which is curiously incomprehensible to the Germans. During the last war, articles used to appear in German papers exploring this curious Anglo-Saxon notion called "fair play," reproduced without translation—for there was no translation.

> Now the element which is so difficult to translate in the idea of "fair play" is not the fact that there are rules. Rules are an integral part of German life, rules for behavior of inferior to superior, for persons of every status, for every formal situation. . . . The point that was incomprehensible was the inclusion of the other person's weakness inside the rules so that "fair play" included in it a statement of relative strength of the opponents and it ceased to be fair to beat a weak opponent.

> . . . Our notion of fair play, like theirs [British], includes the opponent, but it includes him far more personally. . . . (Mead, 1975, pp. 143–145)

I am not implying that the American is in need of a handicap when negotiating with Germans. It is important to note however, that the styles of assertiveness under the assumption of American equality (fair play) and assertiveness under the assumption of German hierarchy may be very different. The general approach of the German toward the weaker opponent may tend to inspire a negative reaction in the American, thus reducing cooperation and motivation.

GERMAN MANAGERS' EXPECTATIONS

Assertiveness, Sophistication, and Direct Confrontation

The current wisdom either leaves the impression or forthrightly states that Americans and Germans share certain verbal behaviors which would cause one to predict that discussion is approached in a mutually understood fashion.

> If North Americans discover that someone spoke dubiously or evasively with respect to important matters, they are inclined to regard the person thereafter as unreliable, if not dishonest. Most of the European low-context cultures such as the French, the Germans, and the English show a similar cultural tradition.

These cultures give a high degree of social approval to individuals whose verbal behaviors in expressing ideas and feelings are precise, explicit, straightforward, and direct. (Gudykunst & Kim, 1984, p. 144)

Such generalizations do not take into account the difference between *Gespräch* (just talking about—casually) and *Besprechung* (discussion in the more formal sense of having a discussion about an issue). *Besprechung* in German culture is a common form of social intercourse in which one has high level discussions about books, political issues, and other weighty topics. This reflects the traditional German values, which revere education. Americans would best translate *Besprechung* as a high level, well-evidenced, philosophically and logically rigorous debate in which one's credibility is clearly at stake—an activity less familiar to most Americans.

The typical language of most Americans is not the language many Germans use in a high level debate on philosophical and political issues.

In areas where English immigrants brought with them the speech of 16th and 17th century England, we find a language more archaic in syntax and usage than [sic] present-day English. Cut off from the main stream, these pockets of English have survived. But the American language, as written in the newspapers, as spoken over the radio (and television), . . . is instead the language of those who learned it late in life and learned it publicly, in large schools, in the factory, in the ditches, at the polling booth. . . . It is a language of public, external relationships. While the American-born generation was learning this public language, the private talk which expressed the overtones of personal relationships was still cast in a foreign tongue. When they in turn taught their children to speak only American, they taught them a one-dimensional public language, a language oriented to the description of external aspects of behavior, weak in overtones. To recognize this difference one has only to compare the vocabulary with which Hemingway's heroes and heroines attempt to discuss their deepest emotions with the analogous vocabulary of an English novel. All the shades of passion, laughter close to tears, joy tremulous on the edge of revelation, have to be summed up in such phrases as: "They had a fine time." Richness in American writing comes from the invocation of

objects which themselves have overtones rather than from the use of words which carry with them a linguistic aura. This tendency to a flat dimension of speech has not been reduced by the maintenance of a classical tradition. (Mead, 1975, pp. 81–82)

Since many Americans tend not to discuss subjects such as world politics, philosophical and ethical issues with a large degree of academic sophistication, a cultural barrier may be present even if the Germans speak American style English. In a study of a German student exchange program, Hagemann observed that "it was crucial for the Germans, that they could discuss world-politics with their American counterparts, found them interested in environmental protection and disarmament issues and that they could talk with them about private matters of personal importance. . . . If they met Americans who did not meet these demands the relationships remained on the surface" (Hagemann, 1986, p. 8).

This tendency not to enter into sophisticated discussions and develop deeper relationships may be a disadvantage for many Americans who are working with Germans (see Figure 1). In addition, in a society in which one's intellectual credibility[5] establishes one's position in the group and thus determines what one can and can't do, *Besprechung* can become quite heated—as is the case in Germany.

FOCUS: WHEN BESPRECHUNG AND DISCUSSION MEET

The management style of German and American managers within the same multinational corporation is more likely to be influenced by their nationality than by the corporate culture. In a study of carefully matched national groups of managers working in the affiliated companies of a large U.S. multinational firm, "cultural differences in management assumptions were not reduced as a result of working for the same multinational firm. If anything, there was slightly more divergence between the national groups within this multinational company than originally found in the INSEAD multinational study" (Laurent, 1986, p. 95).

On the surface we can see two culturally distinct agendas coming together when German and Amer-

Figure 1 *Development of Discussion Behavior at a Glance*

American	Focus	German
Impersonal—act as own agent—will move on when business does not serve his/her needs or when better opportunity arises	Relationship to business	Not as impersonal—corporation is more cohesive unit—identity more closely associated with position, and security needs met by corporation
Need to be liked—expressed through informal address and gestures	Personal need	Need for order and establishment of place in hierarchy—expressed through formal address and gestures
Short-term—largely informal—many procedures picked up in progress	Orientation to corporation	Long-term training—formal—specific rules of procedure learned
Based on accomplishment and image—underlying drive toward equality	Status	Based on education and credentials—underlying drive toward hierarchy
Assertive, tempered with fair play—give benefit of doubt or handicap	Confrontation	Assertive—put other in his/her place
Discussion about sports, weather, occupation: what you do, what you feel about someone. Logical, historical analysis rarely ventured. Native language sophistication usually low.	Common social intercourse	Besprechung—rigorous logical examination of the history and elements of an issue. Politics favorite topic. Forceful debate expected. Native language sophistication high.

ican managers "discuss" matters of importance. The American character with its need to remain impersonal and to be liked avoids argumentum ad hominem. Any attack on the person will indicate disrespect and promote a feeling of dislike for the other, thus promoting the "unpopular phase," which, as Stewart indicates, may destroy cooperation for Americans.

In contrast, the German manager, with his personal investment in his position and a need to be credible to maintain his or her position, may strike with vigor and enthusiasm at the other's error. The American manager with his lack of practice in German-style debate and often less formal language, education, and training, may quickly be outmaneuvered, cornered, embarrassed, and frustrated. In short, he or she may feel attacked. This possible reaction may be ultimately important because it can be a guiding force for an American.

Beyond the question of character is the more fundamental question of the guidance system of the individual within his or her culture and what effect changing cultural milieu has on the individual guidance system. I define guidance system as that which

guides the individual's actions. In discussing some of the expectations of German and American managers, I alluded several times to what could be construed as peer pressure within small groups. How this pressure works to guide the individual's actions, I will argue in the next section, has great implications for developing programs for American success in Germany.

Viewed as systems of argumentation, discussion and *Besprechung* both begin a social phase even though Americans may at first view the forcefulness of the Germans as anti-social (Copeland & Griggs, 1985, p. 105). However, a dissimilarity lends an insight into the difference in the guidance systems and how Germans and Americans perceive each other.

American discussion, with the focus on arriving at consensus, is based on the acceptance of value relativism (which supports the American value of equality and striving for consensus). The guidance system for Americans is partly in the peer group pressure, which the individual reacts to but may not be able to predict or define in advance of a situation. Therefore, some Americans have difficulty articulating, consciously conceiving, or debating concepts in their guidance system but rather prefer to consider

Figure 2 *Manager Background at a Glance*

American	Focus	German
Peer pressure of immediate group—reluctant to go beyond the bounds of fair play in social interaction—backdrop is social relativism	Guidance system	Peer pressure from generalized or larger social group—forceful drive to conform to the standard—backdrop is consistent and clearly known
Generally weaker higher education—weak historical perspective and integrated thought—focus is on the future results—get educational requirements out of the way to get to major to get to career success	Education	Higher education standards generally superior, speak several languages, strong in history, philosophy, politics, literature, music, geography, and art
More group oriented—social phase develops into team spirit—individual strengths are pulled together to act as one	Problem solving	More individualized and compartmentalized—rely on credentialed and trained professional
Informal awareness—get the hang of variations—often unconscious until pointed out	Learning	Formal awareness—specific instruction given to direct behavior—one known way to act—highly conscious

feedback and adjust their position to accommodate the building of consensus without compromising their personal integrity.

German *Besprechung*, with the focus on arriving at truth or purer concepts, rejects value relativism in support of German values of fixed hierarchy and social order. The German *Besprechung* is argumentation based on the assumption that there is some logically and philosophically attainable truth. The guidance system for Germans is composed of concepts that are consciously taken on by the individual over years of formal learning (à lá Hall) and debate. While a German makes the concepts [his or her] own through *Besprechung*, [his or her] position is not likely to shift far from a larger group pressure to conform to one hierarchical code.

The peer pressure of the immediate group can often become a driving force for Americans. The irony is that many Germans initially perceive Americans as conformists and themselves as individualists, stating that Americans can't act alone while Germans with their clearly articulated concepts do act alone. Americans, on the other hand, often initially perceive Germans as conformists and themselves as individualists stating that Germans conform to one larger set of rules while Americans do their own thing.

LEARNING STYLES, TRAINING, INSTRUCTION, AND PROBLEM SOLVING

Education and Training

The ultimate function of group process in American corporations is problem solving and individual motivation (being liked). For Germans motivation is more of a long-term consideration such as an annual bonus or career advancement. Problem solving for Germans is more compartmentalized and individualized.

The contrasting elements discussed earlier and outlined in both "At a Glance" summaries (Figures 1 and 2) indicate that considerable cultural distance may have to be traveled by Germans and Americans before they can be assured that cooperation and motivation are the by-products of their combined efforts. The contrasting elements are, of course, a result of the organization and education—the acculturation—of the minds of Germans and Americans. In this section I will examine the different cultural tendencies from the perspective of Hall's definitions of formal and informal culture and discuss some implications for intercultural training and education.

The first level of concern is general preparation for the managerial position. As an educator I must take a hard look at the graduates of our colleges and universities as they compare to their German counterparts. I am not attempting to imply that Germans are better than Americans. All cultural groups excel in some area more than other cultural groups.

> Germans are better trained and better educated than Americans. A German university degree means more than its U.S. equivalent because German educational standards are higher and a smaller percentage of the population wins college entrance. Their undergraduate degree is said to be on par with our master's degree. It is taken for granted that men and women who work in business offices are well educated, able to speak a foreign language, and capable of producing coherent, intelligible, thoughtful communications. German business managers are well versed in history, literature, geography, music and art. (Hall, 1983, p. 58)

Americans tend to focus on the present as the beginning of the future, whereas Germans tend to "begin every talk, every book, or article with background information giving historical perspective" (Hall, 1983, p. 20). While Hall makes a strong generalization, a contrary incident is rare. American college graduates are not known for having a firm or detailed idea of what happened before they were born. While some pockets of integrated, sophisticated thinking exist, it is by no means the standard. Indeed, many American college students are unable to place significant (newsworthy) events within an over-all political/philosophical framework two months after the occurrence.

In contrast, college educated Germans tend to express a need to know why they should do something—a reasoning grounded in a logical understanding of the past. Compared to the rigorous German theoretical and concrete analysis of past events, Americans often appear to be arguing from unverifiable aspirations of a future imagined. While such vision is often a valuable driving force and the basis for American innovation and inventiveness, it may not answer the German need to explicitly know why and, thus, may fall short (from a German perspective) in group problem solving when these two cultures are represented. From the educational perspective, one must conclude that more than a few days of awareness

training is needed before successful discussions can result between German and American managers, primarily because of what is not required by the American education system. The contrary may also be true in the preparation of Germans to work with Americans. Tolerance for intuitive thinking may well be a proper focus in part of the German manager's training prior to working with American managers.

Formal and Informal Culture

The unannounced and largely unconscious agenda of small group process among Americans is usually more subtle than the German formal awareness but equally as important. American individuals come together in the initial and critical social phase, "size up" each other, and formally or informally recognize a leader. In a gathering of hierarchical equals the first to speak often emerges as the leader. At this point the embers of team spirit warm once again. As the group moves through purpose and task definition, members define and redefine their roles according to the requirements of the evolving team strategy. Fired with team spirit, inculcated through years of group activity and school sports, the group produces more than the sum of their individual promises.

"In the United States a high spontaneous interest in achievement is counterbalanced by much experience in group activities in which the individual learns to channel achievement needs according to the opinions of others. . . . Interestingly enough, the American 'value formula' appears to be largely unconscious or informally understood, as compared to the German one, at any rate" (McClelland et al., 1958, p. 252). Though this observation is 30 years old, it still appears to be quite accurate. The use of modeling (imitation) as a way of acquiring social and political problem-solving strategies is also a way of adjusting to regionalisms. In taking on different roles, Americans become adept at unconsciously adjusting their character to meet the requirements of different situations. In short, says Hall, "Compared to many other societies, ours does not invest tradition with an enormous weight. Even our most powerful traditions do not generate the binding force which is common in some other cultures. . . . We Americans have emphasized the informal at the expense of the formal" (Hall, 1973, p. 72).

The German learning style is often characterized by formal learning as defined by Hall (Hall, 1973, p. 68). The characteristics of German frankness and directness are echoed in Hall's example of formal learning: "He will correct the child saying, 'Boys don't do that,' or 'You can't do that,' using a tone of voice indicating that what you are doing is unthinkable. There is no question in the mind of the speaker about where he stands and where every other adult stands" (Hall, 1973, p. 68). German formal awareness is the conscious apprehension of the detailed reality of history which forms an idealistic code of conduct that guides the individual to act in the national interest as if there was no other way.[6]

American informal awareness and learning is an outgrowth of the blending of many cultural traditions, in an environment in which people were compelled to come together to perform group tasks such as clearing land, building shelter, farming, and so on. The reduction of language to the basic nouns and functions was a requirement of communication for the multilingual population under primitive conditions. Cultural variations will always be a part of the vast American society. Americans have had to "get the hang of it" precisely because whatever *it* is, *it* is done with several variations in America.

In a sense, the informal rules such as "fair play" are just as prescriptive of American behavior as the system of German etiquette is prescriptive of much of German social interaction, including forms of address (familiar *Du* and the formal *Sie*). Even the rules for paying local taxes, entering children in schools, or locating a reputable repair person vary by local custom in America and can only be known by asking.[7] The clear difference is that the rules are not overtly shared in America.

The American expectations or informal rules for group discussion are general enough to include the etiquette of American managers from different ethnic backgrounds. As long as notions of equality, being liked, respect, fair play, and so on guide behaviors things run smoothly. "Anxiety, however, follows quickly when this tacit etiquette is breached. . . . What happens next depends upon the alternatives provided by the culture for handling anxiety. Ours include withdrawal and anger" (Hall, 1973, p. 76). In the intercultural situation, the American who participates informally in group behavior may feel that something is wrong but may not be able to consciously determine the problem. Without the ability of bringing the informal into conscious awareness, which is a function of awareness and education, many Americans may flounder in a state of confusion, withdrawal, and anger.

CONCLUSION

What should become apparent to intercultural trainers working with companies that are bringing German and American personnel together is that they are working with two populations with distinct learning and problem-solving styles. The American is more likely to learn from an interactive simulation. Within the situation the American can "get the hang of" working with someone who has a German style. Trainers and educators of American managers know that the debriefing of the role play, which brings the operative informal rules into conscious awareness, is the focus of the learning activity. The short-term immersion training so often used today can only supply some basic knowledge and limited role-play experience.

What must never be forgotten in the zeal to train American managers is that their basic guidance system in America is a motivation to accommodate the relative values of the immediate group. While the general cultural awareness exercises that begin most intercultural training may make Americans conscious of their internal workings, much more attention must be given to inculcate an understanding of German social order and the interaction permitted within it.

Knowledge of the language and an in-depth orientation to the culture for the overseas manager and spouse should be mandatory for American success in Germany and German success in the United States. "The high rate of marital difficulties, alcoholism and divorce among American families abroad is well known and reflects a lack of understanding and intelligent planning on the part of American business" (Hall, 1983, p. 88). In our pilot program we became quite aware of the fact that German spouses require much more preparation for a sojourn to America. American short-term planning is in conflict with the long-term preparation needed for most Americans who are going to work with Germans. In Germany the role of the spouse (usually the female) in business includes much less involvement than in the United States. We suspect this has much to do with the lack of attention to spouse preparation that we have observed thus far.

RECOMMENDATION

Long-term programs should be established that provide cultural orientation for overseas families at least three or four years before they start their sojourn with beginning and increasing knowledge of the language as a prerequisite for entry. Such programs should attend to the general instructional deficiencies of Americans in the areas of history, philosophy, and politics as studied by Germans, prepare Germans to expect and participate in an informal culture guided by value relativism in a spirit of equality, incorporate cultural sharing of German and American managers and their families in social settings so the sojourners can come together before, during, and after their individual experiences to establish a formal support network. Segments of such programs could be carried on outside the corporate setting to allow for a more open exchange of ideas. In America, colleges and universities could easily establish such programs. Many American colleges and universities that have served as research and development sites for business and industry are also developing alternative evening programs to meet the educational needs in the community. Also, corporate colleges are an ideal setting for extended in-house preparation. In such learning environments, professors can come together with adjunct faculty (private consultants and trainers) to produce a series of seminars that combine lecture instruction, small group intercultural interaction, networking, media presentations, contact with multiple experts over time, and even a well planned group vacation tour to the sojourner's future assignment site.

Part of the programs should be offered in the evening to avoid extensive interference with the employee's regular assignments and to take advantage of the availability of other family members who should be included in intercultural transfer preparation. Cost to the corporation would be greatly reduced in that start-up funds could be partly supplied through federal grants, travel costs would be lessened, and program costs would be covered under regular tuition and materials fees. As a final note, I strongly recommend that such programs for American managers be viewed as graduate level education since they will be entering a society in which education is a mark of status.

Notes

1. Future references to America and Americans should be understood as referring to the North Eastern United States and the citizens thereof, while references to Germany and Germans should be understood as West Germany and the citizens thereof.
2. Actual German values were 65, with a value of 53 when controlled for age of sample, while the actual USA values were 46, with a value of 36 when controlled for age of sample.
3. For a quick overview of how small group and interpersonal communication is related to corporate success in America see Peters and Austin, 1985, pp. 233–248.
4. These comparative descriptions correspond to the German social orientation and the American personal orientation discussed by Beatrice Reynolds (1984, p. 276) in her study of German and American values.
5. "In Germany, power can be financial, political, entrepreneurial, managerial or intellectual; of the five, intellectual power seems to rank highest. Many of the heads of German firms have doctoral degrees and are always addressed as 'Herr Doktor.'" (Copeland & Griggs, 1985, p. 120). While there may be exceptions to this rule, exceptions are few and hard to find.
6. "Yet this rigidity has its advantages. People who live and die in formal cultures tend to take a more relaxed view of life than the rest of us because the bound-aries of behavior are so clearly marked, even to the permissible deviations. There is never any doubt in anybody's mind that, as long as he does what is expected, he knows what to expect from others" (Hall, 1973, p. 75). "In Germany everything is forbidden unless it is permitted" (Dubos, 1972, p. 100).
7. The perplexing problem for German executives who are new in the United States is that in Ger-

many everything is known thus, you should not have to ask to find your way around. But in the USA where change is the watch word, one has to ask to survive.

References

Bleicher, K., & Paul, H. (1986). Corporate governance systems in a multinational environment: Who knows what's best? *Management International Review, 26* (3), 4–15.

Copeland, L., & Griggs, L. (1985). *Going international: How to make friends and deal effectively in the global marketplace.* New York: Random House.

Cyert, R. M., & March, J. G. (1963). *A behavioral theory of the firm.* Englewood Cliffs, N.J.: Prentice-Hall.

Dubos, R. (1972). *A god within.* New York: Charles Scribner's Sons.

Friday, R. A., & Biro, R. (1986–87). Pilot interviews with German and American personnel at Mobay Corporation (subsidiary of Bayer), Pittsburgh, PA. Unpublished raw data.

Gudykunst, W. B., & Kim, Y. (1984). *Communicating with strangers: An approach to intercultural communication.* Reading, Mass.: Addison-Wesley.

Hagemann, K. (1986). *Social relationships of foreign students and their psychological significance in different stages of the sojourn.* Summary of unpublished diploma thesis, University of Regensburg, Regensburg, Federal Republic of Germany.

Hall, E. T. (1973). *The silent language.* New York: Doubleday.
———. (1983). *Hidden differences: Studies in international communication—How to communicate with the Germans.* Hamburg, West Germany: Stern Magazine Gruner + Jahr AG & Co.

Hofstede, G. (1984). *Culture's consequences: International differences in work-related values.* Beverly Hills: Sage Publications.

Kohls, L. R. (1987). *Models for comparing and contrasting cultures,* a juried paper, invited for submission to National Association of Foreign Student Advisors, June, 1987.

Laurent, A. (1986). The cross-cultural puzzle of international human resource management. *Human Resource Management, 25,* 91–103.

McClelland, D. C., Sturr, J. F., Knapp, R. N., & Wendt, H. W. (1958). Obligations of self and society in the United States and Germany. *Journal of Abnormal and Social Psychology, 56,* 245–255.

Mead, M. (1975). *And keep your powder dry.* New York: William Morrow.

Nyrop, R. F. (Ed.) (1982). *Federal republic of Germany, a country study.* Washington, D.C.: U.S. Government Printing Office.

Peters, T., & Austin, N. (1985). *A passion for excellence.* New York: Warner Communication.

Peters, T., & Waterman, R. (1982). *In search of excellence.* New York: Warner Communication.

Reynolds, B. (1984). A cross-cultural study of values of Germans and Americans. *International Journal of Intercultural Relations, 8,* 269–278.

Stewart, E. C. (1972). *American cultural patterns: A cross-cultural perspective.* Chicago: Intercultural Press.

Weaver, R. M. (1953). *The ethics of rhetoric.* South Bend, Ind.: Regnery/Gateway.

Concepts and Questions

1. How does the American expectation that business is impersonal differ from the corresponding German expectation? How might these differing expectations affect discussion behavior during American–German business discussions?

2. How does the German concept of corporate identity differ from the American? How does this affect entry-level training and career goals?

3. Compare and contrast an American manager's need to be liked with the German manager's need to be credible.

4. How might American and German styles of assertiveness differ? What cultural dynamics might account for these differences?

5. What is the German concept of *Besprechung?* How might Americans perceive its practice by Germans during business discussions? Do you believe the typical American businessperson is adequately prepared to engage in *Besprechung?*

6. How do American and German managers differ in terms of the focus of their fundamental educational backgrounds? How does this influence their approaches to business discussions?

7. Compare and contrast the formal and informal aspects of the German and American cultures as they relate to the conduct of business.

8. Differentiate between German "formal learning" and American "informal awareness and learning." How do these cultural dynamics affect each other's approaches to business discussions?

9. What kind of training program do you believe would be most effective in training American businesspeople to interact effectively with German counterparts?

U.S. Americans and Mexicans Working Together: Five Core Mexican Concepts for Enhancing Effectiveness

SHERYL LINDSLEY

I was disadvantaged when I first came down here because I didn't have the class [intercultural training]. I'm probably still doing some things wrong now. When I go to business meetings, I was raised in a culture where you just get out your reports and start talking about them and that's not how it is here. You talk about family and other things first. I often forget this and so one of my Mexican colleagues will remind me that I'm violating this tradition by saying, "So [name], how is your dog?" When I hear this then I know I'm not supposed to be talking about business.

LINDSLEY & BRAITHWAITE, IN PRESS

This account by a U.S. American who lives and works in Mexico reflects the importance of adapting cultural behaviors to achieve communication competency in organizational settings. As an administrator who was transferred to Mexico more than eight years ago without any intercultural training, he's learned the hard way that lack of cultural knowledge and skills negatively affects organizational relationships, goals, and productivity. In this account, it appears that he still struggles to put aside that U.S. American "Let's get right down to business" orientation to prioritize personal relationships in meetings with his Mexican associates. A look at the literature on U.S. American experiences abroad tells us that his problems in intercultural communication are not unique.

Although U.S. American organizations are increasingly reliant on international liaisons to compete in the global economy, many have suffered failures due to inadequate managerial training for work abroad (Albert, 1994). These problems have resulted in tremendous financial losses to organizations as well as human costs by undermining job successes and increasing personal and familial suffering (Mendenhall et al., 1987). These international experiences demonstrate that one cannot simply export U.S. American ways of doing business to other countries. Rather, it is essential that personnel in international organizations understand the histories, cultures, and languages of the people with whom they work. This essay will review recent events affecting U.S.–Mexican economic relationships and then examine five Mexican cultural concepts influencing organizational effectiveness.

The historical ratification of the North American Free Trade Agreement between the United States, Canada, and Mexico embodied both promises and problems. Government leaders who supported the bill promised increased competitiveness with other trade blocs such as the European Economic Community and the Pacific Rim nations, along with larger consumer markets for goods and services and, ultimately, increased prosperity (Weintraub, 1991). At the same time, this alliance created new problems and highlighted old ones that remain unresolved. Critics have charged that the agreement promotes the interests of only large international and multinational firms, at the expense of smaller businesses and ordinary people in all three nations (Castañeda, 1995). In the United States, domestic manufacturers have problems competing with products made with inexpensive Mexican labor, and many citizens have lost jobs when factories relocated south of the border. In Mexico, many people fear increased national dependency on the United States for employment (Hansen, 1981; Sklair, 1993) and difficulties in competing with large U.S. multinationals in many service and product sectors (Batres, 1991; Hellman, 1994). Finally, critics on both sides of the border have pointed to problems with several U.S.-owned assembly plants in Mexico that have exploited inexpensive labor, failed to provide adequate health and safety conditions for workers, and polluted the borderlands and waterways (Fernandez-Kelly, 1983).

Although a comprehensive review of international relationships between these two countries is beyond the scope of this article, it is important to understand these issues because they contribute to the conditions in which businesses operate and the way people from both countries interpret each other's behaviors in everyday work relationships.

In an environment characterized by anxiety about ongoing economic changes, the need for mutual understanding and respect is critical. One way for those who are unfamiliar with Mexican culture to begin to understand is to examine some of the core cultural concepts that guide organizational relationships. Of course, it's essential to keep in mind that there is diversity within both U.S. American and Mexican societies related to socioeconomic class, ethnic origin, regional affiliation, gender, personal ideologies, and character. Thus, when I use the term *U.S. American* or *North American* culture, I'm referring to dominant cultural characteristics—typically, middle-class, European American male. Among Mexicans, too, it's important to recognize that adherence to dominant cultural characteristics varies within the population, and although most Mexicans are mestizos, of both Spanish and indigenous origin, several ethnic groups have maintained aspects of their precolonial traditions. For example, more than 600,000 people who live on the Yucatan peninsula today speak predominantly Mayan languages among their family, friends, and community members. Because many Mayans learn Spanish as a second language to interact with other Mexicans, they often do not speak it with the same fluency as their first tongue, which likely influences satisfaction and effectiveness in interethnic work relationships (Love, 1994). Regional and ethnic differences also affect the structures of modern-day businesses. Although indigenous Mayans from Mexico's southern highlands emphasize corporate organization, northern Mexican businesses embody characteristics of traditional patronage systems (Alvarez & Collier, 1994).

Diversity notwithstanding, there are many ways of behaving that are typical of dominant cultural patterns in each country that provide a useful starting point for developing intercultural awareness. These shared cultural patterns have been referred to as *core concepts*. Core concepts provide us with knowledge about appropriate and inappropriate cultural interaction in specific relationships and contexts. Through an understanding of these, one can choose from a myriad of ways of behaving in order to enhance intercultural work relationships and goals. Core concepts derived from research on doing business in Mexico include: *confianza, simpatía, palanca, estabilidad*, and *mañana*. Through the discussion, it will be apparent that these are not mutually exclusive categories but overlapping concepts that reflect deeply held values for many Mexicans.

CONFIANZA

In an interview with a Mexican production manager about communication with U.S. home office personnel, I asked her what she does when she thinks someone is wrong. She responded,

> Well, it's hard at first if someone is new, but after you establish trust and confidence, then it's easier. . . . I just make suggestions about things, but I don't tell people they are wrong. I just give them information to make the decisions and then they are grateful and the relationship benefits from this. . . . When you just make suggestions and don't tell people what to do and let them learn and make decisions for themselves, then more confidence in the relationship develops and then they owe you. You didn't confront them, you treated them well, with respect, and now they owe you (Lindsley & Braithwaite 1996, p. 215).

According to this account, indirectness is appropriate in a situation in which another's face (or self-presentation) is vulnerable. Because relationships are generally more central to Mexican than U.S. American organizations, it is no surprise that relationships are carefully nurtured and safeguarded. One of the core aspects of a good relationship is the co-creation of *confianza*, or "trust," which is built through communicative behaviors that adhere to cultural norms for face saving. In addition, the aforementioned production manager's account reveals cultural norms for mutual obligation. There is an explicit reference to reciprocity—each party should protect the other's positive face in interaction.

The kinds of situations in which face concerns are primary include those that could possibly be threatening to one's own image or the other party with whom one is interacting. This means that communication of negative information (e.g., I don't understand; I made a mistake; I disagree with you; You made a mistake) is avoided or communicated indirectly. For example, a person's tone of voice may indicate they are reticent to adopt a new plan, even though they may not state it explicitly. Among the ways that U.S. American managers can adapt their own behaviors are avoiding displays of negative emotions, especially direct criticism, conveying receptivity to negative information, asking how they can help their employees, and paying close attention to nonverbal behaviors.

SIMPATÍA

In an interview with another Mexican production manager, he discussed the importance of good communication between managers and employees is not only maintaining positive working relationships, but also meeting productivity goals. He explained to me:

> When I have to discipline an employee, I start off by talking about the person's place in the corporation and what they are there for . . . what their role is in the plant. Then I talk to them about what they need to do. It is important not to hurt the employee, because once you do—(he shrugs, as if to say, "it's the end." (Lindsley, 1996, p. 32)

It is evident that this situation, in which the employee's behavior was not meeting organizational standards, was potentially face-threatening. In addressing the situation, the manager demonstrated adherence to the cultural script of *simpatía*, which emphasizes emotional support and self-sacrifice for the good of the group (Triandis, Marin, Lisansky, & Betancourt, 1984). The effects of this cultural script on communication include culturally normative behaviors that stress commitment to harmony and cooperation. Thus, there is an emphasis on communication that stresses the positive and minimizes negative feedback. In this case, criticism is couched in terms of the individual's importance to the group (his or her role in the organization), which is stated in

positive terms, showing concern for the employee's feelings. In Mexico, a person who is considered *simpático* "is sympathetic, understanding, pleasing, friendly, well-behaved, [and] trustworthy" (DeMente, 1996, p. 278). Being *simpático* is something to strive for in organizational relationships and is demonstrated through communication behaviors that show positive emotional connection with others.

PALANCA

The concept of *palanca* refers to leverage, or power derived from affiliated connections. It affects organizational relationships in terms of one's ability to get things done by virtue of one's official authority as well as through one's contacts with extensive networks of relationships among family members, relatives, former classmates, friends, and business associates. These connections are often built over many years and enable one to obtain favors that may transcend institutional rules and procedures or overcome scarcity of resources and services (Archer & Fitch, 1994). For example, interpersonal connections may allow one to receive "special" consideration for business transactions, faster service in obtaining government services, and personal recommendations for new jobs.

U.S. Americans may tend to evaluate these practices negatively as "corrupt" without reflecting on the similarities with their own organizational behaviors, or without understanding the rationale for why these behaviors are functional in Mexican culture. It is typical in the United States for businesspeople to say, "Who you know is just as important, if not more so, than what you know," and to rely on personal affiliations for special introductions, advice, and information to promote their business goals. In Mexico, the importance of these interpersonal affiliations in business have been described as evolving from a history in which official authority for hundreds of years was held by descendants of Spanish colonial conquerors and government that were not representative of the majority of the people, but which served the interests of a small elite. Even today, one of the challenges of President Ernesto Zedillo's administration is to establish a true representative democracy (Castañeda, 1995). Therefore, one of the ways that people work to protect themselves and promote their interests is through informal systems of affiliated connection. U.S. Americans often rely on a system of written laws and rules, but history has taught Mexicans that it is often more effective to rely on personal connections for social negotiation of written laws and rules to accomplish desired objectives.

Although the use of *palanca* is typical throughout Central and Latin America, it is important to differentiate from the *mordida* (paying a bribe) and to understand both Mexican laws and U.S. American international laws (e.g., the Foreign Corrupt Practices Act), which prohibit payments for certain kinds of services. Although the differentiation is murky, *palanca* embodies a system of mutual obligation and reciprocated favors, not necessarily money or gifts. In this matter, like all other aspects of culture, Mexican business practices are changing. In addition, there are differences among Mexicans in the way any particular behavior is evaluated. For example, some individuals perceive that giving a small fee to a government worker for processing paperwork expeditiously is something positive and similar to the U.S. practice of tipping a waiter or waitress for good service. Others might think it's inappropriate to give a "tip" but appropriate to reward good service by giving a gift afterward, or simply making a point to tell that person's boss about how satisfied they are with the employee (Lindsley, 1995). In consideration of these issues, U.S. Americans need to be aware not only of the power of affiliated connections, but also of current laws and Mexican's individual attitudes about special favors and consideration.

ESTABILIDAD

A common sentiment among many Mexicans is, "The family is our first priority and must remain so for the future stability of our country" (Kras, 1989, p. 27). The need for *estabilidad* or "stability" reinforces the value of personal relationships and permeates organizational behaviors. It is reflected in the tendency for Mexicans to place relationships before tasks. This is communicated through a wide range of behaviors, including asking questions about colleagues' families, discussing personal matters before business (e.g., at the beginning of a meeting), taking action to promote employees' personal well-being, including families in organizational activities, taking time off work to assist family members in need, and establishing, developing, and maintaining long-term interconnected networks of personal relationships.

Some of the ways that managers show responsibility for employees' well-being may be through *compradrazgo* and *comadrazgo* systems in which they become godfathers, godmothers, and mentors for their employees' children. This type of relationship, which dates back to the sixteenth century, is viewed as mutually beneficial, because young people can rely on their mentors for advice, guidance, and financial, spiritual, and social support. In return, mentors can count on the loyalty of the young people throughout their lives.

These types of relationships exemplify the extent to which Mexican personal and organizational roles overlap in contrast to U.S. roles that are typically more separate. The often blurred distinction between familial and organizational life also means that Mexicans may give preference to hiring relatives over strangers, helping employees get a better education, or giving them small personal loans. These favors are often reciprocated with strong employee support and loyalty to the manager. For example, during financial hardships, the employee might continue working for his or her manager without a paycheck (Alvarez & Collier, 1994). Like other aspects of culture, this is an adaptive mechanism in Mexico—building stability through interconnected networks of familial and organizational relationships provides "social insurance" against the vagaries of uncertainty in economic and political structures.

Concerns for stability are also manifest in some Mexicans' negative attitudes about U.S. American investment in Mexico. Historically, U.S. Americans have often acted in ways that promoted their own interests at the expense of Mexicans, which has led to criticism that U.S. involvement in Mexico threatens Mexican economic, political, and cultural stability. When U.S. American organizational personnel go to Mexico with attitudes of cultural superiority (e.g., We're going to teach Mexicans how to do business), negative stereotypes are reinforced about U.S. Americans as arrogant, exploitive, and self-centered. In this case, fear about threats to stability may emerge when U.S. Americans are in higher power positions and try to use their authority to change Mexican culture, laws, policies, and so on. To establish positive working relationships, these stereotypes and the behaviors that reinforce them must be addressed. Although there are no guaranteed ways to combat stereotypes, a good beginning is awareness that these stereotypes exist. The next step, of course, is developing intercultural awareness and skills in order to adapt behaviors in ways that show understanding of and respect for Mexican culture and language. Mexicans and U.S. Americans can and do learn to appreciate aspects of each other's cultures, but this cannot be accomplished without mutual openness and trust based on true respect and understanding, not one-sided opportunistic motives.

MAÑANA

In intercultural interaction in organizations, Mexicans and U.S. Americans often find themselves at odds over different understandings and attitudes surrounding the concept of time. Misunderstandings may arise in intercultural interpretations of language:

> Spanish language dictionaries say that *mañana* means "tomorrow," and that is the meaning taught to foreign students in the language. But "tomorrow" is a literal translation, not the true cultural meaning of the word. In its normal cultural context *mañana* means "sometime in the near future, maybe." Behind the term are such unspoken things as "If I feel like it," "If I have the time," or "If nothing unexpected happens." (DeMente, 1996, p. 183)

U.S. Americans have the tendency to think about *mañana* as referring to some specific time period beginning at 12 A.M. and running for twenty-four hours, due to a primarily external orientation toward time (clocks guide activities). Most Mexicans use time clocks but also consider time to be more interpersonally negotiable (relationships guide activities) and mediated by unexpected events beyond one's control. In Mexico, organizational tasks are often not accomplished as quickly as in the United States because of infrastructural conditions (e.g., telephone, roads, electricity, water, mail) and other structural elements (e.g., government bureaucracy) that slow progress. Moreover, beyond the physical world, there are metaphorical forces that influence people's lives. For example, events occur "*Si Dios quiere*" (God willing). Therefore, for Mexicans it's very adaptive in interaction to acknowledge that events occur that one cannot control and which influence the flow of organizational processes. In addition, Mexican attitudes toward time differ from U.S. Americans because of relatively differing values that influence how one organizes one's behaviors. One Mexican manager explained to me, "In Mexico we have a saying, '*Salud, dinero, amor y tiempo para disfrutarlos*' [Health, wealth, love and time for enjoying them]." He contrasted this with such American sayings as "Time is money" (Lindsley & Braithwaite, in press). Thus, while Mexicans perceive time as functioning in a way that allows one to engage in behaviors that are part of a desirable life, U.S. Americans quantify time as a commodity that is most importantly viewed as related to profits.

These contrasts in cultural orientation toward time can exacerbate problems in intercultural interaction. When U.S. Americans do not take time to develop and maintain good interpersonal relationships in business, Mexicans may think they do not care about people, only money. Likewise, when Mexicans do not complete tasks "on time," U.S. Americans may think they're lazy. To overcome these misunderstandings, U.S. Americans need to adapt their behaviors to respond to the recognition that personal relationships are the foundation of good business in Mexico, and also adjust their attitudes to recognize that Mexicans work very hard but have other priorities in life, too.

SUMMARY

U.S. organizations often have given employees foreign assignments based on technical expertise. However, experience shows that intercultural communication competency is critical to organizational success. Through an understanding of the concepts of *confianza*, *simpatía*, *palanca*, *estabilidad*, and *mañana*, one can better adapt to working in Mexico. In business, cultural diversity can be a strength that managers can build on when personnel understand the ways that culture affects organizational lives. Thus, cultural contrasts in ways of doing business should not be viewed as simply a problem but as an advantage in contributing to new understandings about ways of conducting business. Significantly, U.S. Americans who learn to adapt their behaviors have reported enjoying the closeness of Mexican relationships, their emphasis on family values, as well as their hard work ethic and employee loyalty. Mexicans working in U.S. organizations have reported enjoying their career opportunities, learning efficiency in developing schedules, and training in new kinds of management philosophies (Lindsley & Braithwaite, in press).

References

Albert, R. D. (1994). Cultural diversity and international training in multinational organizations. In R. L. Wiseman & R. Shuter (Eds.) *Communicating in multinational organizations* (pp. 153–165). Thousand Oaks, CA: Sage.

Alvarez, R. R., & Collier, G. A. (1994). The long haul in trucking: Traversing the borderlands of the North and South. *American Ethnologist, 21*(3), 606–627.

Archer, L. & Fitch, K. L. (1994). Communication in Latin American multinational organizations. In R. L. Wiseman & R. Shuter (Eds.) *Communicating in multinational organizations* (pp. 75–93). Thousand Oaks, CA: Sage.

Batres, R. E. (1991). A Mexican view of the North American Free Trade Agreement. *Columbia Journal of Business, 26*(2), 78–81.

Castañeda, J. G. (1995). *The Mexican shock: The meaning for the U.S.* New York: The New Press.

DeMente, B. L. (1996). *NTC's Dictionary of Mexican cultural code words*. Lincolnwood, IL: NTC Publishing Group.

Fernandez-Kelly, M. P. (1983). *For we are sold, I and my people: Women and industry in Mexico's frontier*. Albany: State University of New York Press.

Hansen, N. (1981). *The border economy*. Austin: University of Texas Press.

Hellman, J. A. (1994). *Mexican lives*. New York: The New Press.

Kras, E. S. (1989). *Management in two cultures*. Yarmouth, ME: Intercultural Press.

Lindsley, S. L. (1995) *Problematic communication: An intercultural study of communication competency in maquiladoras*. Unpublished doctoral dissertation. Arizona State University, Tempe, AZ.

———. (1996). *Communication and "The Mexican way": Stability and trust as core symbols in maquiladoras*. Top competitive paper presented to the Language and Social Interaction Interest Group of the Western States Communication Association Convention, February 16–20.

———, & Braithwaite, C. A. (1996). *"You should 'wear a mask'"*: Facework norms in cultural and intercultural conflict in maquiladoras. *International Journal of Intercultural Relations, 20*, 199–225.

———. & Braithwaite, C. A. (in press). Problematic communication: An intercultural study of communication competency in *maquiladoras*. In P. Lawrence and G. Power (Eds.) *A sense of place: Communication issues and perspectives on the U.S.–Mexico border*. El Paso: Texas Western Press.

Love, B. (1994). *Mayan culture today*. Valladolid, Yucatan: ServiGraf Peninsular.

Mendenhall, M. E., Dunbar, E., & Oddou, G. R. (1987). Expatriate selection, training, and career-pathing: A review and critique. *Human Resource Management, 26*, 331–345.

Sklair, L. (1993). *Assembling for development: The maquila industry in Mexico and the United States*. San Diego: Center for the U.S. Mexican Studies, University of California at San Diego.

Triandis, H. C., Marin, G., Lisansky, J. & Betancourt, H. (1984). Simpatía as a cultural script of Hispanics. *Journal of Personality and Social Psychology, 47*(6), 1363–1375.

Weintraub, S. (1991). *Trade opportunities in the Western hemisphere*. Washington, DC: Woodrow Wilson Center for International Scholars.

Concepts and Questions

1. Describe a few aspects of cultural diversity as it exists in Mexico.

2. How is the core value of *confianza* or trust manifest in Mexican human resources management?

3. How can an American manager manifest *confianza* when dealing with Mexican workers?

4. What role does *simpatía* play in interpersonal relations among Mexicans?

5. What communication behaviors must an American manager manifest to establish that he or she is *simpático*?

6. *Palanca* refers to one's power derived from extensive networking among family members, relatives, former classmates, friends, and business

associates. How does Mexican *palanca* differ from the American concept of the "good old boys" network?

7. How could an American manager in Mexico develop the relationships necessary to employ *palanca* as a management tool?

8. How does *estabilidad* or stability reinforce the value of personal relationships and affect organizational behavior?

9. How do Mexican and American concepts toward time differ?

10. List several ways in which an American manager might misconstrue Mexican workers' behavior that reflects the cultural value of *mañana*.

Communicating Health and Understanding in the Borderlands of Co-Cultures

PATRICIA GEIST

Cultures are now less bounded and homogeneous and more porous and self-conscious than ever before, and cultural differences—of religion, gender, language, class, ethnicity, sexual orientation, and so on—are no longer contained within old geopolitical boundaries. Subcultures, cultures, [co-cultures], and supercultures merge and emerge anew, ceaselessly. In the rough-and-tumble of transnational migration and capitalism, what was exotic yesterday may be domestic today. And what is domestic today may be exotic tomorrow.

BARBASH & TAYLOR, 1997, P. 5

Complex layers of meaning accompany anyone's conversations about health, wellness, illness, and medicine. At home, at work, at the gym, at the hospital, in providers' offices, and in emergency rooms, people talk about their health, their illnesses, and their healthy and unhealthy behaviors. Conversations may concern smoking, not smoking, exercising, not exercising, feeling depressed, feeling energized; or they may concern prescriptions, home remedies, what works, what doesn't work, and generally what we consider to be our state of health and what we believe affects our health the most.

The best we can aim for in any of these conversations about health and illness is some type of shared understanding. However, the complex layers of meaning are complicated further by a wide variety of cultural differences as we communicate across, between, and within cultures. The reality of our contemporary society is that it is a cultural melting pot of individuals with many different national, regional, ethnic, racial, socioeconomic, and occupational orientations that influence interactions in health care settings (Kreps & Thornton, 1992). Because we live, work, and play in the borderlands of communities and co-cultures, and are diverse in genders, ethnicities, religions, sexual orientations, and languages, our conversations about our health and our efforts to sustain or improve our health are complicated by diverse health beliefs, practices, and concerns.

Increasingly, we are taking seriously the need for developing effective multicultural relations in health care system. *Healthy People, 2000*, a document published by the U.S. Department of Health and Human Services, provides national health-promotion and disease-prevention objectives for our diverse populations. The document suggests that special population groups "need targeted preventative efforts, and such efforts require understanding [of] the needs and the particular disparities experienced by these groups" (p. 29).

Communication is a critical bridge across these cultural borderlands. We now know that a person's recovery "can be enhanced or hindered, depending on the communication that takes place between care giver and patient" (Bowman, 1995). However, while knowledge and appreciation of cultural diversity is growing in all types of contexts, providers in the health care setting have more to learn about the cultural influences on individuals' perceptions and communications about their symptoms (Littlewood, 1991). As a result, communication in the health care context needs to consider this kaleidoscope of cultural beliefs, expectations, and behaviors.

This essay begins by linking culture, health, and communication. It then continues by discussing how the vital role of communication is enhanced when we incorporate cultural knowledge in health care interactions. A culturally sensitive model of communication is offered as a model for educating health care providers, for clinical practice, and for patient empowerment (Sharf & Kahler, 1996). The utility of this model for understanding culturally sensitive communication is elaborated through discussion of three dialectics that can become both barriers to and avenues for understanding in the borderlands. What we discover is that the movement to communicate in culturally sensitive ways is often constrained by inattention to layers of meaning described in the

model. Seeking understanding in these borderlands means embracing a definition of health that balances the concern of biological survival with psychological, social, and spiritual concerns.

Next, specific case examples are presented to demonstrate the difficulties providers and patients face when the culturally specific beliefs and practices of patients are not discussed or considered in diagnosing and determining appropriate treatment. Finally, the article concludes with avenues for overcoming the obstacles revealed in programs for expanding our notions of culture and culturally sensitive health care.

LINKING CULTURE, HEALTH, AND COMMUNICATION

By year end 1996, the United States population included close to one million immigrants from around the world (see Table 1). In the coming decades, in fact, California is expected to be the first mainland state with a nonwhite majority (Howe-Murphy, Ross, Tseng, & Hartwig, 1989). With the rising cultural diversity of individuals entering the United States comes increasing diversity in the health care beliefs and practices of those seeking health care.

Understanding and addressing the diversity of health care beliefs and behaviors of immigrants to the United States becomes a major priority. Another significant priority is deepening our understanding of the health beliefs and practices of individuals who are members of a wide array of other co-cultures. The diverse, and often unmet, health care needs and expectations of individuals is what defines their membership in co-cultures. For example, each of us may find ourselves becoming members in numerous co-cultures based on multiple identities, including our gender, religion, sexual orientation, single parenthood, caregiving to an elderly parent, diagnosis with a particular disease, economic status, and even philosophy of wellness. More so in the last decade than ever before, research has turned its attention toward these varied co-cultures, whose health care needs are not being met for a wide variety of reasons related to the health care system, family systems, personal histories, and political systems.

Table 1 Immigrants to the United States in 1996		
Country or Region	Number of Immigrants	Percentage of Immigrants
1. Mexico	163,572	17.9
2. Philippines	55,876	6.1
3. India	44,859	4.9
4. Vietnam	42,067	4.6
5. China	41,728	4.6
6. Dominican Republic	39,604	4.3
7. Cuba	24,666	2.9
8. Ukraine	21,079	2.3
9. Russia	19,668	2.1
10. Jamaica	19,089	2.1
11. Haiti	18,386	2.0
12. Korea	18,185	2.0
13. El Salvador	17,903	2.0
14. Canada	15,825	1.7
15. Poland	15,772	1.7
16. Columbia	14,283	1.6
17. United Kingdom	13,624	1.5
18. Taiwan	13,401	1.5
19. Peru	12,871	1.4
20. Pakistan	12,519	1.4
21. Iran	11,084	1.2
22. Yugoslavia (former)	11,854	1.3
23. Nigeria	10,221	1.1
24. Guyana	9,489	1.0
25. Guatemala	8,763	1.0
26. Ecuador	8,321	0.9
27. Bangladesh	8,221	0.9
28. Hong Kong	7,834	0.9
29. Trinidad & Tobago	7,344	0.8
30. Ethiopia	6,914	0.8
Others & Unknown	199,078	21.7
All Countries	915,900	100.0

Today, the significant influence of culture on health perceptions, treatments, and interactions is being recognized and written about in a wide array of disciplines, including communication, social work, nursing, medical anthropology, sociology, literature, allied health, and medicine. The importance of understanding the link between health and culture is being explored in articles published in journals such as *Health Education Quarterly* (Bird, Otero-Sabogal, Ha, & McPhee, 1996; Pasick, 1996), *Journal of Holistic Nursing* (Sanchez, Plawecki, & Plawecki, 1996), *Journal of Cross-Cultural Psychology* (Edman & Kameoka, 1997), *Health Communication* (Myrick, 1998), *Qualitative Health Research* (Davis & Joakimsen, 1997), and *Journal of Transcultural Nursing* (Thomas, 1995). In addition, more books are being published on this topic, including *Patients and Healers in the Context of Culture* (Kleinman, 1980), *Culture and Depression* (Kleinman & Good, 1985), *Medicine and Culture* (Payer, 1988), *Culture, Health and Illness* (Helman, 1990), *Caring for Patients from Different Cultures* (Galanti, 1991), *Cross-Cultural Caring* (Waxler-Morrison, Anderson, & Richardson, 1991), *Effective Communication in Multicultural Health Care Settings* (Kreps & Kunimoto, 1994), and *Race, Gender, and Health* (Bayne-Smith, 1996).

What is clear in just about every examination of health and culture is that "miscommunication, noncompliance, different concepts of the nature of illness and what to do about it, and above all different values and preferences of patients and their physicians limit the potential benefits of both technology and caring" (Payer, 1988, p. 10). Cross-cultural caring considers health care to be a social process in which professionals and patients bring a set of beliefs, expectations, and practices to the medical encounter (Waxler-Morrison, Anderson, & Richardson, 1991).

Negotiating cultural understanding in the health care context necessitates willingness on the part of providers and patients to communicate honestly—to build a supportive, trusting relationship—"a relationship based not on unrealistic certainty, but on honesty in facing the uncertainty in clinical practice" (Inlander, Levin, & Weiner, 1988, p. 206). We need to understand illness and care as embedded in the social and cultural world (Kleinman, 1980). For Kleinman, "medicine is a cultural system, a system of symbolic meanings anchored in particular arrangements of social institutions and patterns of interpersonal interactions" (p. 24). He uses the term **clinical reality** to describe health-related aspects of social reality—especially attitudes and norms concerning sickness and health, clinical relationships, and treatment or healing activities (p. 37).

The call to expand our understanding and appreciation of clinical realities implies we need to acknowledge our ethnocentrism in dictating the proper way to provide care (Leininger, 1991), internationalize our professional education system (Lindquist, 1990), consider the sociocultural background of patients (Boyle, 1991; Giger & Davidhizar, 1991), develop our cultural sensitivity (Waxler-Morrison et al., 1991), understand traditional (folk-healing) health care beliefs and incorporate them into care (Krajewski-Jaime, 1991), and generally communicate interculturally, recognizing the problems, competencies, prejudices, and opportunities for adaptation (Barna, 1993; Brislin, 1991; Kim, 1991; Spitzberg, 1991).

The task of negotiating an understanding of wellness, disease, illness, diagnosis, or treatment often is complicated by these cultural differences. Communicating health and understanding in the borderlands of co-cultures is not a matter of learning everything there is to know about every co-culture prior to providing care or lending support. It means developing a sensitivity to communicating in ways that we may learn from one another and, in that process of communicating, provide the care, support, and understanding people tell us they need. A significant contribution to our understanding of culture and caring is the culturally sensitive model of communicating.

SHARED UNDERSTANDING OF DESIRED HEALTH CARE OUTCOMES: A CULTURALLY SENSITIVE MODEL OF COMMUNICATING

Barbara Sharf and John Kahler (1996) have devised a culturally sensitive model of patient–physician communication. Although this model is specifically designed to increase understanding between patients and physicians, it is clearly relevant to what we may experience in our attempts to make sense of our conversations about health with anyone—family, friends, providers, and even acquaintances and strangers.

The culturally sensitive model (Sharf & Kahler, 1996) provides insight into the complex and multiple layers of meaning all participants bring to their relationships and to their conversations about health and illness. The five layers are as follow:

1. **Ideological Layer of Meaning:** the philosophical "truths" or the ethical underpinnings of society.

2. **The Sociopolitical Layer of Meaning:** the politics surrounding the primary social bases of power—for example, race, class, and gender.
3. **The Institutional and Professional Layer of Meaning:** the organization of health care and related services by professional and corporate categories—for example, the American Medical Association, federal and state governments, the pharmaceutical industry, health maintenance organizations (HMOs), and professions such as medicine, nursing, and social services.
4. **The Ethnocultural and Familial Layer of Meaning:** the cultural or familial traditions, styles, customs, rituals, and values that form patterns of everyday living, expression, and social interaction.
5. **The Interpersonal Layer of Meaning:** the dynamics of style, intimacy, and roles played out in human interactions.

The five layers of the model indicate (1) sources of meaning that underlie people's communication and (2) sources of understanding for clinical practice, for teaching health professionals, and for patient, family, and community empowerment. In essence, the model has utility for anyone who engages in communicating about health and illness: patients, families, health care policy makers, professionals, and administrators.

Each layer of the model reciprocally influences other layers in the process of communicating. For example, **ideologies** of quality of life versus quantity of life clearly affect the **sociopolitical** and ethical debates surrounding the use of life-support systems in hospitals. **Institutional** and **professional** personnel enter into these discussions, clearly affecting decisions regarding whether to or when to withdraw life support. Simultaneously, **family** members discuss the dilemma with each other, considering their own spiritual, cultural, and personal beliefs in negotiating this difficult decision.

The model focuses our attention on the five layers to assist us in considering what meanings we need to consider to be culturally sensitive in conversing about health and illness. Importantly, the model helps us to see the powerful influence **ideologies** have on our communication and the way ideological layers of meaning permeate the other four layers of meaning. Before moving to an exploration of specific cases, this article discusses dialogically oriented dialectics (Baxter & Montgomery, 1997) as an avenue for understanding the powerful influence of traditional ideologies (Geist & Dreyer, 1993) in permeating the other layers of meaning.

DIALOGIC DIALECTICS

The traditional ideology of health care treats disease mechanistically as a biological problem to be treated objectively and technically (Geist & Dreyer, 1993; Waitzkin, 1979, 1983, 1991). Frequently, the multiple ideologies of the patients, families, and friends are not considered, negotiated, or solicited. The voice of medical science dominates in ways that suppress the types of dialogue that facilitate understanding of the ideologies of diverse co-cultures (Geist & Dreyer, 1993).

Dialogic theory as presented by Bakhtin (1986) offers a critique of idealistic and traditional notions of relationships. A dialogic perspective emphasizes communication as a dialogue, not monologue, where people co-construct in conversation a multivoiced unity that recognizes and appreciates each of their differentiated voices (Baxter & Montgomery, 1997). Importantly, the differences we face in communication are not to be seen as dualisms, emphasizing opposites in parallel, but dialectics, emphasizing the interplay of opposites (Baxter & Montgomery, 1997, p. 328). The point of the dialogue therefore, "is not to persuade, and it is not to produce coherence or convergence into a single point of view. Rather, the point is to elaborate the potential for coordination . . . a kind of interaction that brings about an event that the participants interpret as meaningful from their own particular perspective" (p. 347). The implications of dialogic dialects for communicating about health and illness in the borderlands of co-cultures are that the voices of providers, patients, families, and others must be represented in the multivoiced perspective on illness and wellness. This means that the subtle nuances of contradiction and disagreement in dialogues across and between borderlands are not to be ignored or glossed over as unimportant but instead are listened to, talked about, and considered in health care decisions.

A shift to a dialogic view undoubtedly will be met with resistance on the part of the provider or the patient. Providers may be unresponsive to dialogue because their training in science rather than humanities focuses their attention on technical maneuvers rather than the personal, emotional, or cultural perspectives of the patient (Dobbin, 1990; Geist & Dryer, 1993). Providers may be reluctant to engage in dialogue because they are often expected to be "unfailing gods of healing in a bureaucratized industry jammed with patients, bounded by insurance inflation, swarmed by epidemic diseases and urban breakdown" (Elliott, 1991, p. E9).

Patients may be reluctant to participate, negotiate, or dialogue with health care providers because they do not possess the education or assertiveness to question the physician or to provide in-depth explanations. In today's managed care environment, transformations in the relationship between providers and patients often leave patients in the dark about options and make it difficult or impossible for patients to clearly communicate the kind of health care they need or want (Lammers & Geist, 1997).

We may begin to better understand impediments to a dialogic dialectic in cultural understanding by considering three ideological dialectics that are often prevalent in health dialogues. More often than not, the voice of medicine predominates in ways that construct providers' and patients' concerns as dualisms to be resolved and not dialectics to be discussed in ways that construct multivoiced cultural understandings. Considering dialectics of self, dialectics of knowledge, and dialectics of participation may facilitate communicating about health in the borderlands of co-cultures.

Dialectics of Self (Biological and Biographical Concerns)

Assessment is a clinical art that combines sensitivity, clinical judgment, and scientific knowledge (Anderson, Waxler-Morrison, Richardson, Herber, & Murphy, 1991). Rather than using phrases such as "taking the history," "physical examination," or "case management," health care providers negotiate a plan that will be acceptable to both themselves and their patients. In this way, "a curative emphasis gives way to care, and attention turns to facilitating self-narratives that make sense of biographical turning points members of co-cultures experience in sickness and health (Zook, 1994, p. 355).

In this way, providers recognize that an important part of healing has to do with biography, not just biology. Patients come to medical encounters saying, "Doctor I am sick," and asking "Can you heal my story?" (Zook, 1994, p. 355). Disease then, is the biological disruption, but illness is the process of individual interpretation and response to dysfunctional states (Zook, 1994). Improving our health condition is not just "fixing" our disease but addressing illness as a rupture that disintegrates our embodiment of biological, psychological, social, and spiritual health (Gonzalez, 1994; Zook, 1994).

This philosophy is well represented in Jane Delgado's new book, *Salud! A Latina's Guide to Total Health—Body, Mind and Spirit* (1998). In Delgado's view, we need to cultivate trust and respect for Latina women, not discourage their belief systems. In a review of her book, Condor (1998) describes how Delgado's book encourages the spiritual tendencies and personal instincts of Latinas as applied to health: "She said *consejos* (loosely translated to "the wisdom we gain from experiencing and living life") can be a powerful agent of healing. Everything from prayer to gut feelings to warding off the *mal de ojo* (evil eye) should be welcomed as part of the culture" (p. E-3). Delgado indicates that more and more health organizations are marketing to Hispanic communities. One program in particular in San Diego County is the Community Health Group Foundation of Chula Vista's "Salud, Divino Tesoro" ("Health, A Precious Treasure"). Geared toward both female and male Hispanic community members, it has the goal of minimizing the effects of diabetes and cardiovascular disease (Condor, 1998, p. E-3).

In the same way that it is essential to interplay the biological and biographical selves in communicating about health and illness, humanistic concerns must be balanced with technological concerns if we are to embrace a dialogic dialectic of knowledge.

Dialectics of Knowledge (Humanistic and Technological Concerns)

All cultures have knowledge and beliefs about health and illness that have been passed down from genera-

tion to generation (Galanti, 1991; Krajewski-Jaime, 1991). The difference between the belief system of the Western biomedical model and that of other cultures can result in inappropriate assessment or complications in treatment and communication in the provider–patient relationship. The research investigating the intersection of health and culture abounds with vivid examples of these challenges and the successes and failures in negotiating understandings acceptable to both providers and patients.

In the United States, the emphasis on technological progress and the biomedical model complicates the task of communicating to negotiate cultural understandings. A progressive ideology has produced a society of experts who possess the technical knowledge, not social [and cultural] knowledge, and whose communication to the public places priority on the "body" not the "person" (Hyde, 1990). This progressive ideology places great emphasis on the functioning and malfunctioning of the human machine. One physician points out that this emphasis permeates medical education. "Disease, we were told [in medical school] was caused by a malfunction of the machine, the body. . . . The emphasis began and ended with the body. . . . For this reason the modern medical model is called the molecular theory of disease causation. . . ." (Dossey, 1982, pp. 6–8). But, as a growing number of providers are discovering, this model does not account for the part of the human psyche that is most centrally involved in the cure of illness, namely, varying perceptions of what constitutes health, illness, treatment, and the appropriate interaction between provider and patient (Lowenberg, 1989; Needleman, 1985). In fact, many would argue as Lowenberg (1989) does that the single, most overriding conflict in the health care system is the polarization between humanistic and technological advances in health care. Fisher (1986) suggests that crosscutting all interactions between providers and patients is an ideology that supports the authority of the medical perspective over the patient's perspective. Consequently, the asymmetry of the medical relationship creates difficulties for patients from diverse co-cultures in raising topics of interest to them or providing information they see as relevant (Fisher, 1986; Mishler, 1984).

This dialectic becomes more vividly clear when conducting comparisons of health care diagnostic and treatment decisions in different countries. As Payer (1989) indicates, "many of the medical mistakes made in each country can be best understood by cultural biases that blind both the medical profession and patients, causing them to accept some treatments too quickly and other treatments reluctantly or not at all" (p. 34). These cultural blind spots are often exacerbated by cultural norms of behavior that relegate patients to a passive role in communicating about health.

Dialectics of Participation (Passive and Active)

The very term *patient* is a problem-laden word in that it denotes illness instead of health and recovery, while it connotes a stance of passivity or helplessness where the person is a compliant recipient of medical directives (Sharf & Street, 1997, p. 4). Instead, we need to redefine the patient role as including active participation "in activities focused on disease prevention, health promotion, and maintenance of physical, emotional, and spiritual well-being" (Sharf & Street, 1997, p. 4). In this way, a person with health concerns could be someone who "strives to form a more collaborative partnership with a physician or other clinician, taking an active role in his or her own medical care decision making" (Sharf & Street, 1997, p. 4).

However, it is important to realize that not all co-cultures seek the formation of a collaborative partnership with their providers. Often there exist cultural barriers to patient participation (Young & Klingle, 1996). Research indicates that "cultural forces can foster silent and submissive communicative behaviors that are not conducive to collaborative practice. Cultural norms influence an individual's ability to be assertive and his or her belief regarding the effectiveness of assertive communication" (Young & Klingle, 1996, p. 35). These researchers suggest that patient assertiveness training is not the answer. Instead, discussions with patients need to focus on persuading patients that participation will improve health care delivery and that they can and should participate.

Communicating health and understanding in the borderlands of co-cultures depends on how open we are to the interplay of selves, knowledge, and partic-ipation. Consideration must be given to the complex interdependence of these three dialects in all five layers of meaning in the model of culturally sensitive model. The following cases reveal the importance of the five layers, particularly the ethnocultural and familial layer of meaning.

EXPANDING CULTURAL SENSITIVITY IN THE HEALTH CARE CONTEXT

A growing crisis in the United States health care system is the cultural gap between the medical system and the huge number of ethnic minorities it employs and serves (Galanti, 1991). The following cases reveal the difficulties that providers and patients face negotiating appropriate care. Differences in beliefs about health and illness, perceptions of appropriate treatment, and expectations about interaction in the medical setting complicate the communication process in health care delivery.

One source of misunderstanding in health care delivery stems from the practice of folk-healing medicine. Some practices can result in misdiagnosis, others simply contradict scientific medicine, and still others can result in improper medical treatment (Galanti, 1991). *Curanderismo*, a Hispanic folk-healing belief system originating in Europe, is the treatment of a variety of ailments using a combination of psychosocial interventions, mild herbs, and religion (Chesney, Thompson, Guevara, Vela, & Schottstaedt, 1980; Comas-Diaz, 1989; Krajewski-Jaime, 1991; Maduro, 1983). The three most common beliefs about the causes of disease are (1) natural and supernatural forces, (2) imbalances of hot and cold, and (3) emotions (Krajewski-Jaime, 1991, p. 161). Three practices central to this believe system are (1) the role of the social network, particularly kin, in diagnosing and treating illness; (2) the relationship between religion and illness, which includes the use of religious ritual in many healing processes; and (3) consistency (but not uniformity) of beliefs among Hispanic communities about symptoms and regimens of healing (Krajewski-Jaime, 1991, p. 160).

Knowledge of folk-healing beliefs and practices enable providers to communicate with empathy, sensitivity, and open-mindedness. Social workers, physicians, and nurses who receive special training in interviewing and communication may build trust and mutual sharing of cultural information in their relationships with their patients (Krajewski-Jaime, 1991). When this training has not been part of medical education, differences in health beliefs between predominant-culture providers and minority patients may result in inappropriate assessment. Providers may interpret folk healing beliefs and practices as ignorance, superstition, abuse or neglect because patients do not follow prescribed treatments (Krajewski-Jaime, 1991). In the following case, described in her research on folk-healing beliefs and practices among Mexican-American families, Krajewski-Jaime reveals how a non-Hispanic caseworker's recommendations could have resulted in the unnecessary removal of a Mexican-American child from his caring and nurturing family:

> The assessment indicated that the child in question was ill and in need of medical care, but the mother had obvious emotional problems and appeared to be irrational: the mother had kept on saying, in broken English, that she could not allow any evil spirits to come near her child and had locked the child in his room; hung from the ceiling a pair of sharp scissors just above his head, and would not allow anyone, including the caseworker and the doctor, to enter the child's room. The caseworker's supervisor, who had some knowledge of folk-healing practices among some of the agency's Mexican-American clients, asked a Mexican-American child protective service worker to reinvestigate the case. The worker visited the mother, who, while upset about the child's illness, welcomed someone who spoke Spanish. The mother explained that she had used several home remedies to help her child's fever go away, but evil spirits had already taken possession of her child and the usual remedies no longer helped. The only thing left to do was to prevent new spirits from entering the child's body. The scissors would immediately cut any spirits that would try to enter the child's body. Since evil spirits could attach to anyone who entered the room, she could not allow anyone to enter the room, thus preventing any further harm to her child. The Mexican-American worker, although familiar with folk-healing practices had not seen this particular cure before. She understood the validity of this belief within the client's cultural context, but to successfully obtain the mother's

permission to see the child, to remove the dangerous scissors, and to see that the child received medical attention, she had to validate the mother's beliefs and gain her trust. She told the mother that although she had not seen anyone use this cure before but she had heard her grandmother talk about it. To protect the patient and his or her entire surroundings, however, the grandmother usually nailed the scissors on the room's entrance door. The worker explained that, should the spirits attach themselves to anyone who wished to enter the room, the scissors on the entrance door would immediately prevent them from doing so and thus provided stronger protection to the patient. The Mexican-American worker went on to ask the mother if this made sense to her. She asked the mother if she thought this would be more beneficial since it would allow her child to be seen by the caseworker and the doctor. The mother agreed and emphasized that she wanted only what was best for her child. She changed the location of the scissors and welcomed the caseworker and the doctor to examine the child. (pp. 158–159)

As Krajewski-Jaime points out, although this is an extreme example because of the dangerousness of the practice, most folk-healing practices are harmless. This case demonstrates how folk healing, if understood, can become a resource on which to capitalize in building rapport in relationships with patients or families and negotiating appropriate diagnosis and treatment.

Similar to *curanderismo*, Chinese folk medicine bases many of its beliefs on maintaining a harmonious balance between the two opposing forces of "hot" and "cold," often substituted for yang and yin (Lai & Yue, 1990). Illness may be seen as an imbalance in hot or cold foods and thus people may seek cures from food substances they associate with their own deficiency.

> For instance, a traditional Chinese may eat animal's brains in order to grow wiser. A diabetic may eat an animal's pancreas in hope of cure. People thought to be anemic often eat red foods. These examples illustrate why traditional Chinese may have difficulty in regarding plastic capsules as a cure. (Lai & Yue, p. 80)

These beliefs and practices provide evidence of the Chinese people's great concern about questions of health and health care, more so than Americans (Kleinman, 1980). However, along with this emphasis comes a belief in self-medication that may cause serious health problems.

Three specific examples of health practices reveal the problems that may develop with a patient's self-medication. First, Chinese, embracing the maxim of "all things in moderation," may believe that taking medicine over an extended period of time may weaken their bodies (Li, 1987). As a result, they often feel that "Western medicine is too potent for them or their small bodies and they may reduce dosages to a quantity they believe suitable. For example, an elderly Chinese with diabetes may reduce his insulin because it is 'foreign' and jeopardizes his health" (Lai & Yue, 1990, pp. 83–84). In fact, Chinese may refuse blood tests, believing that loss of blood will weaken their bodies or that the tests are too invasive (Lai & Yue, 1990). Second, dual use of Western medicine and folk medicine is common in the Korean, Bahamian, Haitian, Puerto Rican, Cuban, and Southern U.S. black cultures (Scott, 1974). However, Western prescriptions may contain the same chemical ingredients as herbal prescriptions patients are now consuming; consequently, patients may experience overdose or adverse reactions (Park & Peterson, 1991). Finally, in this third example, we see how the beliefs of a Guatemalan patient's husband led to double dosages of birth control pills:

> One couple that came together for family planning counseling returned in only two weeks asking for more pills. The husband responded to all the questions for his wife regarding how she felt, if she was experiencing any irregular bleeding or pain, without consulting her even though she did understand enough Spanish to know what was being asked. She sat next to him silently as he explained that apparently the woman had taken two pills a day, thinking that they work better if the dosage is doubled. During the initial counseling, the husband also responded to all the questions by the female nurse and translator and stated he understood the procedures required for use of the Pill. However, the subsequent visit indicated that he did not fully understand why he had to take extra precaution during the first few weeks, and thus he had encouraged his wife to double the dosage. (Miralles, 1989, pp. 102-103)

In these three examples, the significance of communication in the provider–patient relationship is pronounced. And it is clear that providers who lack knowledge of health care beliefs and practices must negotiate and construct understanding during their interactions with patients.

The advice to health care providers in communicating with individuals from diverse cultures is to ask specifically about their beliefs and practices concerning herbal medicines or folk-healing practices (Park & Peterson, 1991). Asking these questions directly, rather than waiting for patients to volunteer the information or to ask about such issues, is especially important considering that Chinese and other immigrant groups generally have been taught to respect doctors and not to ask questions (Lai & Yue, 1990). In fact, for many Chinese, agreement and use of the word "yes" help to avoid the embarrassment of saying "no," as the following case illustrates:

> Linh Lee, a sixty-four-year-old Chinese woman [was] hospitalized for an acute evolving heart attack. At discharge, her physician suggested that she come back in two weeks for a follow-up examination. She agreed to do so, but never returned. It is likely that she never intended to do so but agreed because he was an authority figure. Chinese are taught to value accommodation. Rather than refuse to the physician's face and cause him dishonor, Mrs. Lee agreed. She simply did not follow through, sparing everyone embarrassment. When Nancy, her Chinese-American nurse, saw her in Chinatown several weeks later, Mrs. Lee was very cordial and said she was feeling fine. (Galanti, 1991, p. 21)

In a case such as this we find that negotiating an agreed-upon "yes" cannot be taken at face value. Providers who understand how cultural values can lead patients to communicate in prescribed ways will be sensitive to different communication styles in order to avoid the difficulties created by situations such as the one described above.

One additional factor complicating efforts to construct understanding in the provider–patient relationship is the common problem of patients not possessing English language competence. And, although the use of translators can help to mitigate this problem, for a variety of reasons, translators, patients, or family members can complicate and obstruct efforts to negotiate understanding (Fitzgerald, 1988; Galanti, 1991; Hartog & Hartog, 1983; Miralles, 1989).

Miscommunication is a frequent problem with the use of translators (Fitzgerald, 1988; Galanti, 1991; Miralles, 1989). Even with expert translation, problems such as linguistic differences between the terms in English and other languages can present difficulties, especially languages such as Vietnamese, which includes diverse dialects.

[Vietnamese] words that translate "feeling hot" don't mean "fever." What they mean is "I don't feel well" and generalized malaise. And if you should ask your Vietnamese patients, "Have you ever had hepatitis?" the translator [may] translate that into "liver disease," and liver disease in Vietnam means itching. . . . Similarly, the kidney is the center of sexual potency to Indochinese and Vietnamese, and therefore "kidney trouble" may really mean decreased libido or other sexual difficulty. (Fitzgerald, 1988, p. 67)

In addition, translators sometimes choose not to translate exactly what the patient says for any number of reasons—embarrassment, desire to portray the culture in a certain light, or lack of understanding:

[Translators] are sometimes reluctant to translate what they think is ignorance or superstition on the part of the patient. So they are sophisticated and tell you what *they* think rather than what the patient said. [Or the provider may ask] "How do you feel?" The translator then spends five to ten minutes in discussion with the patient and comes back and says, "Fine." (Fitzgerald, 1988, p. 65)

Linguistic variations, slang, and culturally specific terminology existing within any culture can create communication difficulties even for an excellent translator. In addition, translators often selectively choose what to communicate from the patient's or provider's narratives, giving a précis of what the patient says or grossly altering the meaning of the communication (Anderson et al., 1991).

A translator's use of medical jargon and technical vocabulary also may contribute to communication difficulties. In the following case, the provider and patient *appeared* to have negotiated understanding, but unfortunately this was not the case:

Jackie, an anglo nurse, was explaining the harmful side effects of the medication [that] Adela Samillan, a Filipino patient, was to take at home after her discharge. Although Mrs. Samillan spoke some English, her husband, who was more fluent, served as interpreter. Throughout Jackie's explanation, the Samillans nodded in agreement and understanding and laughed nervously. When Jackie verbally tested them on the information, however, it was apparent that they understood very little. What had happened? Dignity and self-esteem are extremely important for most Asians. Had the Samillans indicated they did not understand Jackie's instructions, they would have lost their self-esteem for not understanding or they would have caused Jackie to lose hers for not explaining the material well enough. By pretending to understand, Mr. and Mrs. Samillan felt they were preserving everyone's dignity. Jackie's first clue should have been their nervous laughter. Asians usually manifest discomfort and embarrassment by giggling. Once Jackie realized they had not understood the material, she went over it until they were able to explain it back to her. (Galanti, 1991, p. 20)

This case, as well as other previous cases, demonstrates how important it is not to take smiles and nods of agreement as understanding when communicating with Asian patients (Galanti, 1991). The nurse in this case communicated with the patients to assess their understanding, and it was only through her continued time, patience, and effort that they were able to negotiate understanding.

And still another complicating factor is the fact that professional translators often are not available in the medical setting and the patient's friends or family members are asked to serve as translators. For a wide variety of reasons, these circumstances can contribute to miscommunication. In the following case, we begin to understand how awkward, embarrassing, or difficult it might be for family members to communicate what they are being asked to translate.

A Hispanic woman, Graciela Garcia, had to sign an informed consent for a hysterectomy. Her bilingual son served as the interpreter. When he described the procedure to his mother, he appeared to be translating accurately and indicating the appropriate body parts.

His mother signed willingly. The next day, however, when she learned that her uterus had been removed and that she could no longer bear children, she became very angry and threatened to sue the hospital. What went wrong? Because it is inappropriate for a Hispanic male to discuss private parts with his mother, the embarrassed son explained that a tumor would be removed from her abdomen and pointed to that general area. When Mrs. Garcia learned that her uterus had been removed, she was quite angry and upset because a Hispanic woman's status is derived in large part from the number of children she produces. (Galanti, 1991, p. 15)

There are a whole set of issues complicating communication in the health care setting when children serve as translators. In the case above, cultural rules dictate who can discuss what with whom (Galanti, 1991). In other cases, asking a patient's child to interpret can undermine the parents' competence in the eyes of the child, creating tensions in their relationship (Anderson et al., 1990). Once again we find that selection and use of translators is a complex issue that can interfere with providers' and patients' efforts to negotiate cultural understanding. The final section of this article explores the avenues for overcoming the obstacles faced in negotiating cultural understanding and for expanding our notions of culturally sensitive health care.

APPLYING THE MODEL

One useful starting point for health professionals is **training** that assists individuals in examining their own cultural beliefs and values as a basis for understanding and appreciating other cultural beliefs and values (Gorrie, 1989). At the University of Southern California, a course in cross-cultural communication sensitizes physician assistants to their personal biases and prejudices through videotaped mock interviews (Stumpf & Bass, 1992). Believing that self-awareness of personal discomfort can become a tool for promoting sensitive cross-cultural communication, the curriculum is based on the model "Differences + Discomforts = Discoveries" (Stumpf & Bass, 1992). Critiquing the interviews, students are encouraged to

investigate their own feelings of prejudice and bias and to use their sensitivity to discomfort as "a cue that they are perceiving a difference and to inquire further rather than seek safety in the harbor of fear and prejudice" (Stumpf & Bass, 1992, p. 115).

In a systemwide approach, Howe-Murphy et al. (1989) describe the Multicultural Health Promotion Project, a multidisciplinary, multicultural, and participative model designed to address the need for changes in allied health service delivery to minority populations. Their training efforts are focused on faculty from three allied health departments (health science, nutrition and food science, and occupational therapy), students preparing for careers in these three professions, and community health care practitioners—all of whom face issues of health promotion in the multicultural environment.

Viewing cultures as dynamic and not static unified wholes means that variations exist among individuals of any one culture. Accordingly, health care providers need to assess each patient individually before deciding on a plan of care (Park & Peterson, 1991). Taking a more holistic approach, concentrating on "individual's own experience and understanding of illness" may assist in this assessment (Littlewood, 1991). Providers should acquire a knowledge of the specific language of distress utilized by patients, and the providers' diagnosis and treatment must *make sense* to patients, acknowledging their experience and interpretations of their own condition (Helman, 1990). Individuals from similar cultural groups often share metaphors (sayings or idioms) that express their perspective on situations, problems, and dilemmas (Zuniga, 1992). Providers may use these metaphors in the form of anecdotes, stories, or analogies to build rapport in relationships with patients and to magnify the patient's need to make the changes recommended in treatment plans (Zuniga, 1992).

Listening to the patient's stories (Kreps & Thornton, 1992), soliciting their illness narratives (Kleinman, 1988), considering the poetics and politics of interaction (Geist & Gates, 1996), and building partnerships (Geist & Dreyer, 1993) will facilitate communicating health and understanding in the borderlands of co-cultures. We all bring diverse and multiple beliefs and identities to our conversations about health and illness. Learning to communicate our expectations and preferences and learning to listen to individuals whose beliefs and identities differ from our own is essential if we are to live healthy and supportive lives.

References

Anderson, J. M., Waxler-Morrison, N., Richardson, E., Herbert, C., & Murphy, M. (1991). Conclusion: Delivering culturally sensitive health care. In N. Waxler-Morrison, J. M. Anderson, & E. Richardson (Eds.), *Cross-cultural caring: A handbook for health professionals in Western Canada.* Vancouver: University of British Columbia.

Bakhtin, M. M. (1986). *Speech genres and other late essays.* C. Emerson & M. Holquist (Eds.), V. McGee (Trans.). Austin: University of Texas Press.

Barbash, I., & Taylor, L. (1997). *Cross-cultural filmmaking.* Berkeley: University of California Press.

Barna, L. M. (1993). Stumbling blocks in intercultural communication. In L. A. Samovar & R. E. Porter (Eds.), *Intercultural communication: A reader* (6th ed.) (pp. 345–353). Belmont, CA: Wadsworth.

Baxter, L. A., & Montgomery, B. M. (1997). Rethinking communication in personal relationships from a dialectical perspective. In S. Duck (Ed.), *Handbook of personal relationships* (pp. 325–349). Sussex, England: John Wiley.

Bayne-Smith, M. (Ed.). (1996). *Race, gender, and health.* Thousand Oaks, CA: Sage.

Bird, J. A., Otero-Sabogal, R., Ha, N. T., & McPhee, S. J. (1996). Tailoring lay health worker interventions for diverse cultures: Lessons learned from Vietnamese and Latina communities. *Health Education Quarterly, 23,* 105–133.

Bowman, D. (1995). Nurses build cultural bridges with patients. *University of Iowa Spectator, 28*(2), 2.

Boyle, J. S. (1991). Transcultural nursing care of Central American refugees. *Imprint, 38,* 73–79.

Brislin, R. W. (1991). Prejudice in intercultural communication. In L. A. Samovar & R. E. Porter (Eds.), *Intercultural communication: A reader* (6th ed.) (pp. 366–370). Belmont, CA: Wadsworth.

Chesney, A. P., Thompson, B. L., Guevara, A., Vela, A., & Schottstaedt, M. F. (1980). Mexican-American folk medicine: Implications for the family physician. *The Journal of Family Practice, 11,* 567–574.

Comas-Diaz, L. (1989). Culturally relevant issues and treatment implications for Hispanics. In D. R. Kowlow & E. P. Salett (Eds.), *Crossing cultures in mental health* (pp. 31–48). Washington, DC: Sietar.

Condor, B. (1998, February 23). Salud! Latinas and medical establishment: They're learning more about each other. *San Diego Union Tribune,* pp. E-1, E-3.

Davis, D. L., & Joakimsen, L. M. (1997). Nerves as status and nerves as stigma: Idioms of distress and social action in Newfoundland and Northern Norway. *Qualitative Health Research, 7,* 370-390.

Delgado, J. (1998). *Salud! A Latina's guide to total health—Body, mind and spirit.* New York: Harper Perennial.

Dobbin, M. (1990, February 28). Closing the doctor–patient communication gap. *Sacramento Bee,* pp. E1, E3.

Dossey, L. (1982). *Space, time, and medicine.* Boston: New Science.

Edman, J. L., & Kameoka, V. A. (1997). Cultural differences in illness schemas: An analysis of Filipino and American illness attributions. *Journal of Cross-Cultural Psychology, 28,* 252–266.

Elliot, D. (1991, August 2). The doctor touches nerve in solid story of mortality. *The San Diego Union,* pp. E1, E9.

Fisher, S. (1986). *In the patient's best interest: Women and the politics of medical decisions.* New Brunswick, NJ: Rutgers University Press.

Fitzgerald, F. T. (1988). How they view you, themselves, and disease. *Consultant, 28,* 65–77.

Galanti, G. (1991). *Caring for patients from different cultures: Case studies from American hospitals.* Philadelphia: University of Pennsylvania Press.

Geist, P., & Dreyer, J. (1993). Juxtapositioning accounts: Different versions of different stories in the health care context. In S. Herndon & G. Kreps (Eds.), *Qualitative research: Applications in organizational communication* (pp. 79–105). Cresskill, NJ: SCA Applied Communication Series/Hampton Press.

Geist, P., & Gates, L. (1996). The poetics and politics of recovering identities in health communication. *Communication Studies, 47,* 218–228.

Giger, J. N., & Davidhizar, R. E. (1991). *Transcultural nursing: Assessment and intervention.* St. Louis: Mosby-Year Book.

Gonzalez, M. C. (1994). An invitation to leap from a trinitarian ontology in health communication research to a spiritually inclusive quatrain. In S. A. Deetz (Ed.), *Communication yearbook 17* (pp. 378–387). Thousand Oaks, CA: Sage.

Gorrie, M. (1989). Reaching clients through cross cultural education. *Journal of Gerontological Nursing, 15*(10), 29–31.

Hartog, J., & Hartog, E. A. (1983). Cultural aspects of health and illness behavior in hospitals. *The Western Journal of Medicine, 139,* 106–112.

Helman, C. G. (1990). *Culture, health, and illness: An introduction for health professionals*. Boston: Wright.

Howe-Murphy, R., Ross, H., Tseng, R., & Hartwig, R. (1989). Effecting change in multicultural health promotion: A systems approach. *Journal of Allied Health, 18*, 291–305.

Hyde, M. J. (1990). Experts, rhetoric, and the dilemmas of medical technology: Investigating a problem of progressive ideology. In M. J. Medhurst, A. Gonzalez, & T. R. Peterson (Eds.), *Communication and the culture of technology* (pp. 115–136). Pullman: Washington State University Press.

Inlander, C. B., Levin, L. S., & Weiner, E. (1988). *Medicine on trial: The appalling story of medical ineptitude and the arrogance that overlooks it*. New York: Pantheon.

Kim, Y. Y. (1991). Communication and cross-cultural adaptation. In L. A. Samovar & R. E. Porter (Eds.), *Intercultural communication: A reader* (6th ed.) (pp. 401–411). Belmont, CA: Wadsworth.

Kleinman, A. (1980). *Patients and healers in the context of culture: An exploration of the borderland between anthropology, medicine, and psychiatry*. Berkeley: University of California Press.

————. (1988). *The illness narratives: Suffering, healing, and the human condition*. New York: Basic Books.

————, & Good, B (Eds.) (1985). *Culture and depression: Studies in the anthropology and cross-cultural psychiatry of affect and disorder*. Berkeley: University of California Press.

Krajewski-Jaime, E. R. (1991). Folk-healing among Mexican-American families as a consideration in the delivery of child welfare and child health care services. *Child Welfare, 70*, 157–167.

Kreps, G. L., & Kunimoto, E. N. (1994). *Effective communication in multicultural health care settings*. Thousand Oaks, CA: Sage.

Kreps, G. L., & Thornton, B. C. (1992). *Health communication: Theory and practice*, 2nd ed. New York: Longman.

Lai, M. C., & Yue, K. K. (1990). The Chinese. In N. Waxler-Morrison, J. A. Anderson, & E. Richardson (Eds.), *Cross-cultural caring: A handbook for health professionals in Western Canada* (pp. 68–90). Vancouver: University of British Columbia Press.

Lammers, J. C., & Geist, P. (1997). The transformation of caring in the light and shadow of "managed care." *Health Communication, 9*, 45–60.

Leininger, M. (1991). Transcultural nursing: The study and practice field. *Imprint, 38*(2), 55–66.

Li, K. C. (1987, February). *The Chinese perspective towards mental illness and its implications in treatment*. Paper presented at Haughnessy Hospital, Vancouver.

Lindquist, G. J. (1990). Integration of international and transcultural content in nursing curricula: A process for change. *Journal of Professional Nursing, 6*, 272–279.

Littlewood, R. (1991). From disease to illness and back again. *The Lancet, 337*, 1013–1015.

Lowenberg, J. S. (1989). *Caring and responsibility: The crossroads between holistic practice and traditional medicine*. Philadelphia: University of Pennsylvania Press.

Maduro, R. (1983). Curanderismo and Latino views of disease and curing. *The Western Journal of Medicine, 139*, 868–874.

Miralles, M. A. (1989). *A matter of life and death: Health-seeking behavior of Guatemalan refugees in South Florida*. New York: AMS Press.

Mishler, E. G. (1984). *The discourse of medicine: Dialectics of medical interviews*. Norwood, NJ: Ablex.

Myrick, R. (1998). In search of cultural sensitivity and inclusiveness: Communication strategies used in rural HIV prevention campaigns designed for African Americans. *Health Communication, 10*, 65–85.

Needleman, J. (1985). *The way of the physician*. San Francisco: Harper & Row.

Park, K. Y., & Peterson, L. M. (1991). Beliefs, practices, and experiences of Korean women in relation to childbirth. *Health Care for Women International, 12*, 261–267.

Pasick, R. J. (1996). Similarities and differences across cultures: Questions to inform a third generation for health promotion research. *Health Education Quarterly, 23*, 142–162.

Payer, L. (1989). *Medicine and culture: Notions of health and sickness in Britain, the U.S., France, and West Germany*. London: Victor Gallancz LTD.

Sanchez, T. R., Plawecki, J. A., & Plawecki, H. M. (1996). The delivery of culturally sensitive health care to Native Americans. *Journal of Holistic Nursing, 14*, 295–308.

Scott, C. (1974). Health and healing practices among five ethnic groups in Miami, Florida. *Public Health Report, 89*, 524–532.

Sharf, B. F., & Kahler, J. (1996). Victims of the franchise: A culturally sensitive model of teaching patient-doctor communication in the inner city. In E. B. Ray (Ed.), *Communication and disenfranchisement: Social health issues and implications* (pp. 95–115). Mahwah, NJ: Lawrence Erlbaum Associates.

Sharf, B. F., & Street, R. L. (1997). The patient as a central construct: Shifting the emphasis. *Health Communication, 9*, 1–11.

Spitzberg, B. H. (1991). Intercultural communication competence. In L. A. Samovar & R. E. Porter (Eds.), *Intercultural communication: A reader* (6th ed.) (pp. 353–365). Belmont, CA: Wadsworth.

Stumpf, S. H., & Bass, K. (1992). Cross cultural communication to help physician assistants provide unbiased health care. *Public Health Records, 107,* 113–115.

U.S. Department of Health and Human Services. (1995). *Healthy people, 2000.* Washington, DC: U.S. Government Printing Office.

Waitzkin, H. (1979). Medicine, superstructure and micropolitics. *Social Science and Medicine, 13a,* 601–609.

———. (1983). *The second sickness: Contradictions of capitalist health care.* New York: The Free Press.

———. (1991). *The politics of medical encounters: How patients and doctors deal with social problems.* New Haven, CT: Yale University Press.

Waxler-Morrison, N., Anderson, J., & Richardson, E. (1991). *Cross-cultural caring: A handbook for health professionals in Western Canada.* Vancouver: University of British Columbia Press.

Young, M., & Klingle, R. S. (1996). Silent partners in medical care: A cross-cultural study of patient participation. *Health Communication, 8,* 29–53.

Zook, E. G. (1994). Embodied health and constitutive communication: Toward an authentic conceptualization of health communication. In S. A. Deetz (Ed.), *Communication yearbook 17* (pp. 344–377). Thousand Oaks, CA: Sage.

Zuniga, M. E. (1992). Using metaphors in therapy: Dichos and Latino clients. *Social Work, 37,* 55-60.

3. How might cultural diversity in the ideologies of quality of life influence decisions regarding whether or when to withdraw life support?

4. What are "dialogic dialectics," and how are they employed in health care communication?

5. How should a caregiver make use of the "dialectics of self" in establishing an initial communicative relationship with a patient?

6. In what manner is the term *patient* a problem-laden word?

7. How does the practice of folk-healing medicine influence communication in the health care setting?

8. Discuss some of the problems inherent in the use of language translators in the health care setting. How can these problems be minimized?

9. What recommendations would you make to a health care provider who encounters a situation in which a male family member assumes the role of speaking for a female patient?

10. What recommendations about communication would you make to a health care provider who encounters a Hmong family with an ill child whom the parents claim is afflicted by a *qaug dap peg,* that is, a spirit that catches you and makes you fall down?

Concepts and Questions

1. How does the type of communication between caregivers and patients affect a patient's recovery?

2. What is required of health practitioners in order for them to develop a cultural understanding of health?

Intercultural Communication in the University Classroom

LISA M. SKOW
LAURIE STEPHAN

INTRODUCTION

The university is a setting in which, for the first time in their lives, most students will encounter a community comprising people from many different countries and ethnic communities in the United States. Many of your own classmates may be from Japan, Denmark, Poland, India, or Australia, or from areas of the United States about which you've only heard or read. You might be an international student studying in the United States as a member of the multinational university community on your campus. Some of your instructors, too, may be from diverse countries and cultural communities, and they often bring to their classrooms a host of experiences and views that contribute in significant and unique ways to your learning. It is nearly impossible that university students in the United States would finish their degrees without meeting and interacting with people from countries and cultures other than their own.

With such a diverse community of learners and teachers, communication in the classroom can be exhilarating and yet sometimes problematic. At times, the best intentions of teachers to reach their students are ineffective because their methods of instruction may not reach certain groups in multicultural classrooms. And of equal concern is when students lack an understanding of the teaching methods or communication style used by interna-

tional college instructors. Culture strongly influences how we learn and teach, and it is a significant factor in shaping how students and teachers communicate to accomplish teaching and learning. Educational systems are developed based on norms of communication practiced by individual societies. In an international and multicultural classroom, students and teachers may disagree on appropriate ways of engaging in discussion, or even about whether to discuss at all. Rules of formality versus informality (i.e., raising hands to speak) or nonverbal ways of signaling confusion to the teacher (i.e., silence or inquisitive looks) are often culturally determined. Thus, although the international and multicultural university classroom offers a variety of benefits to students, students and teachers need to make greater efforts to understand how cultural differences influence communication and learning processes. This article has been written with this goal in mind.

Note that we have included increasing understanding for *both* students and teachers in our objective. As with any form or context of communication, the classroom is a place where communication occurs among many people and, therefore, the communication that is created and the relationships that are built are the responsibility of all members of a classroom. Each day in the multicultural classroom is an intercultural event that includes teachers and students trying to teach and learn from one another; when we are involved in an event, we each have a stake in the outcome. So as you read this article, think about your own role in the intercultural events you engage in each time you walk into a college classroom. What is happening communicatively to promote or hinder learning? Are there cultural ways of understanding what is taking place among students and teachers? What are you doing to contribute to this cross-cultural understanding?

First, we will take a look at the trends in the United States that have seen increasing numbers of international graduate students and international teaching faculty on U.S. campuses. You will notice that it is increasingly likely that undergraduates at major universities will have instructors from other countries at some point during their educational careers. Then we will move into a discussion of the variety of dynamics that can come into play in the intercultural classroom and provide opportunities for you to apply what you've learned to actual intercultural scenarios.

THE INTERNATIONAL PRESENCE ON U.S. CAMPUSES

We've stated the importance of examining intercultural communication in university classrooms because of the strong likelihood that undergraduates will have teachers from other cultures and nations. But just how internationalized are our universities in the United States? From what countries and cultures do international instructors arrive?

In the past twenty-five years, there has been a general increase in the number of international students studying at U.S. universities. Whereas 489,000 international students were enrolled during the 1992–93 academic year, only slightly more than 34,000 international students were studying in the United States in 1955 (Institute of International Education, 1992–93). Although this may sound like a substantial increase, international students today represent only approximately 3 percent of the total U.S. university student population (Goodman, 1996). When we compare this figure to France, where international students make up approximately 12 percent of the total university student population, the United States can be seen overall to have a significantly lower international student body attending its universities (Crossing pedagogical oceans, 1991). Still, a crucial, undeniable international presence is evident on university campuses throughout the United States. "From the perspective of a teacher . . . foreign students are vital to the quality of teaching and to the learning process itself" (Goodman, 1996, p. A52).

During the 1992–93 academic year, approximately 44 percent of the international students in the United States were enrolled in graduate programs. Furthermore, more than 65 percent of these graduate students come from the Asian countries of China, Japan, Taiwan, and Korea. European graduate students from Germany, France, Spain, and Greece make up the second largest group of international graduate students. With the number of U.S. citizens studying for advanced degrees in business administration, mathematics, and the sciences steadily decreasing, international graduate students have filled the resulting gaps. For example, the number of U.S. citizens receiving doctorates in mathematics has decreased by 50 percent in the last twenty years; as a result, "in 1989, most of the Ph.D.s in mathematics awarded by U.S. universities went to citizens of other countries" (Crossing pedagogical oceans, 1991, p. 3). Undergraduates will take the majority of their introductory courses in the sciences and mathematics at the same institutions where international graduate students are studying, and many of these graduate students will teach as international teaching assistants (ITAs) while engaged in their studies. Although most of the courses undergraduates take will be with native English-speaking instructors, they "are likely to have comparatively limited but intensely important contact with ITAs" (Crossing pedagogical oceans, 1991, pp. 6–7).

Another important part of the international presence on U.S. university campuses is the hiring of faculty members from other countries. U.S. colleges and universities are hiring greater numbers of faculty members from other countries, especially in the areas of mathematics and engineering. In 1987, 40 percent of the assistant professors teaching mathematics and 35 percent of those assistant professors teaching engineering were graduates of foreign universities. Again, these international professors have filled the gap left by the decreasing number of U.S. citizens studying for advanced degrees in mathematics and engineering, because only approximately 40 percent of new engineering Ph.D.s granted by U.S. universities from 1983 to 1985 were U.S. citizens (Crossing pedagogical oceans, 1991). That number might be even lower today.

All of these statistics combine to mean that at some point in the academic careers of most undergraduates, they will have classes and communicate with instructors who are from other countries and cultures. Although we cannot generalize about these experiences because international instructors have a wide diversity of backgrounds and experiences, one thing is certain: The university has become an intercultural environment. And within such an environment, each day in the college classroom is an intercultural event. The experience of learning and communicating in an intercultural environment is an exciting one with rich possibilities, and improving communication skills and learning to work with people from diverse backgrounds are just two of the benefits. But to succeed in and benefit from the numerous intercultural events of which you will be a part while studying for your degree, it is helpful to have some knowledge of the dynamics that are often present in intercultural classrooms. These dynamics are often grounded in differences in cultural values, learning and teaching styles, and verbal and nonverbal ways of speaking.

CULTURE AND CLASSROOM COMMUNICATION

Although the presence of culture is pervasive in any educational setting, as people interested in studying intercultural communication, we cannot examine everything in the classroom. We are most interested in those particular aspects of culture that greatly influence classroom communication. We will first look at how *values* influence intercultural communication. Then we will examine how culture can determine the different *learning and teaching styles* found in multicultural classrooms. The two final issues we will discuss will be how culture-specific *verbal and nonverbal ways of speaking* influence communication between students and teachers.

The Influence of Values on Classroom Communication

One of the primary ways that culture can influence teaching and learning is through the communication of cultural values and attitudes in the classroom. Although Maslow (1971) described a value system as simply a big container of miscellaneous, vague things, values are quite specific and dominant in our lives. Derived from the deep philosophical underpinnings that shape a culture, values are organized rules that help individuals in a given culture make choices and reduce conflicts (Samovar & Porter, 1997). Although we each hold a unique set of values that characterizes us as individuals, we all carry with us a set of values that we share with others within our culture (Minnick, 1968). Value systems are sets of strong preferences held by cultures that assist their members in knowing right from wrong, appropriate versus inappropriate behavior, and how the world *should be*. For example, four dominant U.S. cultural values can be seen clearly in the development of its current educational system (Robinson, 1992). The U.S. values *individualism* and *competition* among individuals, a value that is manifested in its system of grading and its focus on independent learning and thinking. The *philosophy of knowledge* that shapes our concerns about plagiarism and the emphasis we place on students completing individual course work reflect our concerns about individualism and individual competition as well. U.S. values associate knowledge with the individual, as opposed to other cultures that may assign knowledge to the public domain, and concerns about plagiarism and sharing knowledge in study sessions or on tests are of much less concern.

Equal access to education, the use of multiple forms of evaluation, and the often relaxed relationship between teachers and students demonstrate the values of *equality* and *informality* within U.S. society. This tendency to see education as something equally due to all and that encourages equality in the classroom is quite different from most educational systems in the world. Crittenden (1994) explains this more common approach to higher education:

> The elite systems that typify much of higher education in the world . . . are intended to perpetuate or develop a small elite in society. Selection of students is by birth or more typically by merit, usually defined in terms of scores on competitive exams. Admission requires extreme talent and/or extreme prior investment in the education process on the part of the student. (p. 6)

In such a system, where students are privileged to be selected for higher education and accustomed to working extremely hard to gain that privilege, student responsibility for acquiring knowledge overshadows the role of teacher. Students seem to take much more responsibility for their learning and accomplishment in such a system than they do in a more egalitarian educational system. This means that teachers in these systems may have very different attitudes about teacher and student responsibilities and roles than those of U.S. teachers.

The American educational system is one that tends to emphasize the pragmatic application of learning to real world examples. Thus, many students and teachers in the United States may expect

Table 1 Value Differences in Teaching and Learning

Collectivistic Societies (Arab countries, African, Mexico, Portugal, Taiwan, Japan)	Individualistic Societies (Great Britain, United States, Norway, Germany, Spain, France)
• Young should learn; adults cannot accept student role. • Students will speak only when called upon by teacher; harmony in learning situations should be maintained at all times. • Education is way of gaining prestige, getting into higher social class. • Teachers expected to give preferential treatment to some students.	• One is never too old to learn. • Individual students will speak up in response to general invitation of teacher. • Education is way of improving economic worth and self-respect based on ability and competence. • Teachers expected to be strictly impartial.
Small Power Distance Societies (Costa Rica, Sweden, United States, Australia, Canada, Netherlands)	**Large Power Distance Societies (France, South Africa, African countries, Arab countries, Japan, Korea, Thailand)**
• Teachers should respect independence of students. • Student-centered education • Teacher expects students to find their own paths. • Students allowed to contradict teacher. • Effectiveness of learning related to amount of two-way communication in class. • Outside class, teachers are treated as equals.	• Teacher merits the respect of students. • Teacher-centered education • Students expect teacher to outline paths to follow. • Teacher is never contradicted. • Effectiveness of learning related to excellence of teacher. • Respect for teachers shown outside of class; they maintain authority.
Weak Uncertainty Avoidance Societies (Canada, Hong Kong, India, Sweden, Philippines)	**Strong Uncertainty Avoidance (Japan, Greece, Peru, Korea, Austria, Equador)**
• Students feel comfortable in unstructured learning situations. • Teachers are allowed to say "I don't know." • Good teacher uses plain language. • Students rewarded for innovative approaches to problem solving.	• Students feel comfortable in structured learning situations (precise objective, detailed assignments, strict timetables). • Teachers expected to have all the answers. • Good teacher uses academic language. • Students rewarded for accuracy in problem solving.
Feminine Societies (Sweden, Denmark Costa Rica, Chile, Spain, France, Finland)	**Masculine Societies (Jamaica, Austria, Mexico, Japan, Ireland, U.S., Australia, Venezuela)**
• Teachers avoid openly praising students. • Teachers use average student as the norm. • System rewards students' social adaptation. • Students admire friendliness in teachers. • Students try to behave modestly. • Male students may choose traditionally feminine academic subjects.	• Teachers openly praise good students. • Teachers use best students as the norm. • System rewards students' academic performance. • Students admire brilliance in teachers. • Students try to make themselves visible. • Male students avoid traditional feminine academic subjects.

From G. Hofstede's "Cultural Differences in Teaching and Learning," 1986, *International Journal of Intercultural Relations, 10*, 301–319.

that lessons relate to real world situations and require creative, critical thinking on the part of the individual. Educational systems in other parts of the world may be less focused on individuals applying their knowledge critically to problems in the real world and more focused on imparting a great deal of information, with groups of students working together to learn as much of the information as possible.

Although students are certainly studying and learning practical information and using creative, critical thinking in these systems, these learning goals and methods may take on different forms with quite different functions. For example, learning how to work collaboratively to solve problems may sometimes be more practical and important within particular cultures than having students work independently to accomplish the same kind of task.

Other culturally derived values help shape and maintain educational systems. The work of Geert Hofstede (1986) lends insight into the influence that cultural values has on communication between students and teachers. Based on his well-known study on work-related values in more than 50 countries, Hofstede applied his four-value scheme to the educational setting. He described cultural differences in teacher–student and student–student interaction according to four dimensions: individualism–collectivism, power distance, uncertainty avoidance, and masculinity–femininity (see Table 1). Each of these values manifests itself in culturally specific ways in the classroom. Hofstede claims that, to a large extent, these four values influence the nature of the relationship that develops between teachers and students and help to shape the communication that goes on in classroom settings. We suggest that Hofstede's model should be applied to intercultural classroom communication using a critical lens. As you read our overview of this model, be aware of places where you do not agree with his description of what you have experienced or know about various cultures and their ways of learning and communicating, including your own. We believe that the value of models such as Hofstede's lie less in telling us what cultures *are* and more in helping us develop sets of questions about cultures. We especially encourage you to use Hofstede's model to help you formulate questions about your own cultural values and expectations in relation to learning and classroom communication.

Collectivism Versus Individualism. Hofstede described strong individualistic societies such as Great Britain, the United States, and Germany as those that tend to believe that one is never too old to learn and encourage individual students to speak up freely in class. Strong collectivist societies such as Taiwan,

Mexico, and many African countries, however, tend to believe that it is the young who should learn because adults cannot accept the less powerful role of the student, and students are often encouraged to speak only when called upon. How societies conceive of the individual has a profound effect on how educational systems are structured. For example, educational theories and practices developed by the Chinese are much less interested in individual differences of students; they focus more of their attention on those educational procedures that will transform whole groups of students (Munro, 1977). In the United States, the focus or center of teaching is the individual learner, whereas within Chinese society the collective or a classroom of students is the focal point. This focus on the individual student in U.S. education mirrors the strong cultural value of personal autonomy and individual rights so deeply entrenched in the American psyche. Although traditional Chinese philosophies may mention individual freedoms and rights, these are "subordinate to ideas of duty, ethical conduct, public benefit, and social responsibility—all in pursuit of social harmony" (Pratt, 1991, p. 298). How Chinese college students perceive themselves is also in line with a strong collectivist society as they tend to describe themselves with significantly more collectivist characteristics (e.g., family, ethnicity, occupational groups) than U.S. students (Triandis, 1989).

Communication in the classroom is greatly shaped according to whether a culture tends to be more collectivistic or individualistic. Teachers from individualistic cultures teaching in China or Japan may find it difficult to get their students to discuss their ideas in class because to do so would be to spotlight one's individuality and autonomy by expressing a personal opinion. Whereas American students might feel comfortable and even encouraged to ask a question if they have not understood something a teacher has said, Japanese students are much less likely to do so because of their desire "to secure harmony and to save their face as well as that of their instructor" (Neuliep, 1997, p. 448). Indeed, when students do not ask questions in the United States, it may be seen as a sign of indifference or disinterest (Althen, 1988). Again, in educational settings the focus for more collectivist cultures is being a member of a class and teaching a group of students, whereas in more individualistic societies individual students are encouraged to stand out and be heard, and individual learning needs of students are considered.

Power Distance. The value that a society places on hierarchical relationships among its people determines the extent to which it sanctions or discourages relationships based on power and status. In countries that value larger power distance among people, such as South Africa, Korea, and Arab countries, education tends to be teacher-centered and the teacher controls much of the classroom communication that takes place. In small power distance countries, however, such as Sweden, Canada, and Australia, student-centered education is the norm and students are encouraged to engage in two-way communication with the teacher. In the United States, the university teacher is often portrayed as a facilitator who shares control of classroom communication and encourages collaborative methods. Rural Filipino students may negatively perceive the relaxed, egalitarian nature of many U.S. classrooms because they are more accustomed to the highly structured, teacher-dominated classrooms of their country (Bail & Mina, 1981). International teaching assistants from Asian countries often have difficulty making the transition to the more student-centered classrooms of the United States. An ITA from Japan himself, T. Kuroda explained a more teacher-centered view of education: "Above all, the fundamental concept among Asian people is that education is not anything to be acquired or to be learned by students, but something to be taught by teachers" (p. 16).

The value that a culture places on power distance determines the nature of relationships between students and teachers. One significant factor in defining such a relationship is the amount of social distance that instructors and students maintain, which is dictated by the cultural norms and values of a society. The amount of social distance between teachers and students greatly influences the kind of communication in which they engage. In societies such as the Netherlands and Australia, teachers and students might be treated as equals, and it is not necessarily seen as disrespectful if a student expresses an opinion that is different from the teacher's. In many African, Arab, and Asian countries, however, the status of teachers is distinctly higher than that of students, and teachers are never contradicted. ITAs from Asian countries often come from educational systems

> with considerable social distance between instructors and students, in which classrooms are characterized by formality and one-way flow of information, with the expectation that students will defer to the professors, and will not ask questions or otherwise challenge their authority. American students, on the other hand, represent more egalitarian and informal society. As products of a less selective educational system and often forced to contribute financially to their own schooling, their commitment to education must compete with other roles and responsibilities. They expect to ask questions and have them answered, and they expect instructors to assume greater responsibility for the learning process. (Crittenden, 1994, p. 7)

This view of the U.S. educational system describes relationships between students and teachers much like that of a customer–service provider relationship. Students pay for their education and expect a quality "product" (i.e., education) in return. Such a perspective mirrors the strong capitalist value system held by the United States.

In stark contrast to the student-as-customer view of education is the case of an ITA from the People's Republic of China (Christy & Rittenberg, 1988). Mr. Chou had received complaints from his U.S. students that he was rather aloof, arrogant, and made no attempt to explain material in an interesting way. He wrote on the chalkboard without explanation, used no gestures or eye contact, and spoke with an expressionless voice. From Mr. Chou's cultural frame of reference, it was important to maintain social distance from his students. Whether he spoke in an interesting manner was irrelevant because it was his duty to present the material competently. And speaking with expression and using regular eye contact, ways of communicating that may be perceived as "friendly" by his students, might compromise the social distance that he believed should be maintained. In Chinese society, however, loyalty and deep fondness are often found between teachers and students after a long process of mentorship, although such a relationship is usually not demonstrated in a classroom setting (Christy & Rittenberg, 1988).

Femininity Versus Masculinity. Another way Hofstede claims educational systems and classroom communication differs culturally is according to whether societies tend to be more feminine or masculine. Masculine and feminine do not correspond to "male" and "female" but, like the term *gender*, they are characteristics with often culturally derived meanings (Wood, 1997), and therefore can differ greatly across cultures. Whether a society sanctions more masculine or feminine values in its educational practices is, according to Hofstede, often determined by the status accorded to women and the extent to which men and women are educated together. For example, in countries such as Denmark, Costa Rica, and France, there seem to be relatively overlapping social roles for the sexes with neither gender valued greatly over the other. Hofstede claims that in these countries students tend to admire friendliness a great deal in teachers and that teachers may avoid openly praising students out of concern that such comments may contribute to a more competitive, unequal learning environment. Hofstede contrasts such societies with those where stereotypically masculine behavior such as assertiveness, ambition, and competition are highly regarded. He identifies Venezuela, Ireland, and the United States as countries where such characteristics are strongly manifested and may influence communication in the classroom. In these countries, teachers may openly and frequently praise good students, and students may tend to admire intelligence and competence more than friendliness in teachers (Hofstede, 1986).

It is possible that students from particular cultures or countries may prefer feminine or masculine ways of communicating in the classroom. For example, in a study done by Sanders and Wiseman (1990), "immediacy behaviors" such as eye contact, humor, and the use of personal examples were found to be especially helpful to Hispanic and African American students in their learning. In an additional study, African American students perceived an effective teacher as one who was expressive and immediate (Collier & Powell, 1990). These two studies point to more feminine communication methods that teachers have available to them that might be more effective with certain groups of students.

It is important to be wary of unintended implications of Hofstede's model as we have explained here.

The model may set up a dichotomy between friendliness, which is a trait of "feminine" cultures, and intelligence, a trait of "masculine" cultures. However, friendliness is often used to characterize good teaching in the United States, a supposedly masculine culture. For instance, the authors of this article have found in their work with undergraduate students in the United States that friendliness and approachability are among the most frequently mentioned teacher behaviors that students identify when they describe good teaching. If we wish to use Hofstede's model to help us think about the variety of teaching behaviors exhibited across cultures, it is wise to remember that we should use Hofstede's categories as heuristics—that is, as starting points for thinking about what kinds of questions to ask about communicating in our own classrooms and those in other cultures. We may find that both masculine and feminine traits apply in describing our culture, but to greater or lesser degrees depending on the situation. Thus, taking such variables into consideration may not mean assuming that cultures either exhibit these traits or they don't—rather, it may mean noticing that such variables occur in different combinations in a variety of situational contexts within the same culture and across cultures.

Uncertainty Avoidance. In countries that tend to tolerate uncertainty in life (e.g., Canada, Hong Kong, India) teachers can say "I don't know" without losing the respect of their students. Conversely, in those countries that Hofstede identifies as having strong uncertainty avoidance such as Greece, Korea, Austria, and Ecuador, teachers are expected to have all the answers. In these countries, students may feel more comfortable in more structured learning situations where precise objectives are identified and strict timetables determine the beginning and end of instruction. In the United States and other countries that Hofstede claims do not mind uncertainty, students may feel more comfortable participating in loosely structured lessons. Although the fifty-minute lecture is still presented on university campuses, the U.S. educational system tends to favor a more interactive classroom (Twale, Shannon, & Moore, 1997), which provides for less teacher control and less certainty about what will happen during a lesson. Thus, we could say that more interactive, loosely structured classrooms are a typical feature of the U.S. educational system as a whole. However, before we assume that these are typical features of individual U.S. classrooms, we should note that these approaches to classroom teaching and learning have gained in popularity only in the last thirty years. More "loosely structured" learning methods such as collaborative groups and class discussion are greatly debated in academic circles, and they regularly pose difficulties for U.S. teachers and students who are not used to such open-ended teaching methods and who may not agree about the benefits of such approaches. It is therefore wise to state that, although the United States might as a society rate low in uncertainty avoidance using Hofstede's findings, uncertainty avoidance may be very high for students and teachers within many classroom settings throughout the United States.

Keep in mind that Hofstede's four-value system for describing differences in educational practices across cultures is only one way to describe how cultures *tend* to be and is not meant to pigeonhole entire societies as masculine versus feminine, or collectivistic versus individualistic. His scheme does, however, provide us with a set of possible perspectives from which to think about how values can shape the kind of educational system and classroom communication a society chooses to adopt.

Learning and Teaching Styles

A learning style is a preference for how we go about the business of internalizing and understanding ideas and concepts. Learning styles can be individual, with some people preferring to read about news events and others choosing to learn about the day's happenings by watching Tom Brokaw on NBC or by listening to National Public Radio. Our preferences for learning can also reflect the dominant learning style that our society has sanctioned and used to develop and implement its educational system. Thus, while we may have our own ways of learning, we also have those culturally defined ways of learning that influence us just as profoundly. In the multicultural classroom, especially when a teacher is from another country, teaching methods and ways of communicating in the classroom do not always mesh with the

mode of learning to which most students might be accustomed.

Let's take the example of Mr. Chou whom we introduced earlier in this chapter. Mr. Chou was described by his students as being unexpressive in his ways of explaining material and that he did not explain what he was writing on the board. In China, a dominant style of learning is one in which students are expected to wrestle with the incompleteness of a lesson because "if one is to gain as much knowledge as the mentor [teacher], one must accept the need to piece it together for oneself through collective effort with one's peers" (Christy & Rittenberg, 1988, p. 118). Given this view of how students are expected to learn in China, if Mr. Chou thoroughly explained what he was writing on the board, he would not be allowing his students to struggle with the material but would be, in a sense, giving them the answers. This method of teaching would prevent students from learning as much as possible. Mr. Chou's noble intentions, however, have the opposite effect with his students in the United States because the majority of them are accustomed to instructors who attempt to explain concepts as thoroughly as possible and allow for questions if students do not understand.

Within the United States, there are equally diverse culturally determined ways of learning that can help us explain the problems that students and teachers often have when their methods of teaching and learning do not blend amicably. Traditional Native American styles of learning often do not match university faculty ways of communicating; most of them are of various Anglo-American heritages (Scollon, 1981). Native students at an Alaskan university, for example, described the deductive way of presenting a point (beginning with a general, abstract theory and then moving to specific examples) often used by non-Native teachers as "often misunderstood (by students) as not getting to the point" (Scollon, 1981, p. 10). Whereas a typical Anglo style of presenting an argument or point of view resembles a debate—in which a position is directly stated, the opposing side is described as incorrect, supporting evidence is provided, and a conclusion offered—other cultures may neither seek combat nor come to the point directly (Condon & Yousef, 1988). One method of teaching and a preferred way of learning for some societies is to weave stories as a way to present one's "argument." The first author of this article witnessed such a style during a debate in a small village high school in Nairagi Enkare, Kenya. One of the finest speakers in the school was a first year Maasai student named Obote Uka. Obote would pace at the front of the auditorium and "argue" his point by telling a story or legend that illustrated the point he was trying to make. Few speakers were able to catch the students' attention or persuade them toward their side like Obote, because many of them attempted to mirror the style of argument that their Anglo-American teacher tended to emphasize.

Although there is not one specific way of learning for Native Americans, common patterns of learning have been found across tribal groups (More, 1989). In some exciting work done by Susan Phillips (1983) on the Warm Spring Indian Reservation in Oregon, Native American children tended not to respond when their Anglo teachers asked them questions in front of their peers but did so more frequently when the children initiated conversation with the teacher. How can we explain this according to the cultural ways of learning and communicating amongst the Warm Springs Indian community? In addition to Phillips's work with the Warm Springs children, studies examining the learning styles of children from the Navajo (Longstreet, 1978), Oglala Sioux (Brewer, 1977), and Yaqui (Appleton, 1983) tribes have come to a similar conclusion. Children from these Native American groups tend to develop a learning style in the home that corresponds to the following pattern:

1. Child watches parent, grandparent, or elder sibling do a task.
2. Child receives minimal verbal instruction but self-reflects on the proper way to accomplish the task.
3. Child tries to accomplish the task through self-testing, often alone.
4. Child is ready to perform task in front of others.

Compared to the question-and-response method of teaching and learning carried out by Warm Springs teachers, the above process differs greatly. Observa-tion is the first and most important step, with attempts to accomplish the task taking place only within the safe confines of solitude, not in front of one's peers where a student may not be prepared to perform competently for others. Instead of using the trial-and-error and "If at first you don't succeed, try, try, again" method of learning, children from many Native American communities prefer to follow the watch-and-do and "If at first you don't think, and think again, don't bother trying" philosophy of learning (More, 1989; Werner & Begishe as cited in Swisher & Deyhle, 1989).

Verbal Ways of Speaking in the Classroom

The most obvious cultural difference that can be found in any multicultural classroom, especially on a university campus with a significant international student and faculty presence, is in the area of language. But identifying language differences among culturally diverse peoples is not as obvious as one might think. Unless you are in a foreign language class, English is usually spoken in every university classroom in the United States; thus people are typically speaking the same language in multicultural university classrooms. It is the nuances of language, those less obvious linguistic subtleties that can both enhance and make problematic the teaching and learning that takes place in college multicultural classrooms. In the following section we will examine how culture influences such language issues as idiomatic expressions, rules for politeness, and communication content. As you read, think about your own experiences with language differences in the classroom. How did they manifest themselves? How did you react?

Idiomatic Expressions. A Middle Eastern student attempted to use the idiom "laid back" and ended up mistranslating the phrase from Turkish, causing himself embarrassment as a result. Another student from the Middle East had learned to greet his U.S. friends with "Hey!" followed by the person's last name. When he tried out this idiom to get his instructor's attention during an examination, he exclaimed, "Hey, Smith!" Mr. Smith was not amused and was offended by the rather exuberant, informal greeting during a very serious occasion (Magrath, 1981). Even regional differences in the English language can cause moments of confusion in the classroom. When one of the authors of this article (born and raised on the West Coast) was teaching in Terre Haute, Indiana, one of her students used the idiom "honked off"[1] while relaying an experience. The phrase "honked off" is a decidedly Midwestern phrase, and she had to ask for a definition before the class could continue. These are all examples of how the use of idioms can cause confusion when they are used improperly or in the presence of someone who is not privy to their definition. Usually, any confusion surrounding idioms can be addressed quite easily and swiftly by defining them for the person who does not understand or using contextual cues to interpret them. In addition, those of us who hear idioms that are being used incorrectly can be more understanding of others who may not know the "rules" surrounding particular idiomatic phrases. More than any aspect of language, idioms and metaphors probably make the point most clearly that language is developed and constructed by a people for their own particular purposes and based on objects and experiences specific to a nation, culture, or region. Halliday (1970) has suggested that "the nature of language is closely related to the demands that we make on it, the functions it has to serve. In the most concrete terms, these functions are specific to a culture" (p. 141). It is their culturally specific function that often explains why idioms do not always translate well and are oftentimes difficult to decipher by outsiders. For example, directly translating the English "Forgive me" to Arabic is problematic because such a phrase spoken in Arabic means "May God forgive." Idioms are not just words strung together; they carry with them the cultural preferences and beliefs held by the people who speak them. In the multicultural classroom setting, translation problems may occur because idioms are being spoken by people from different cultural vantage points and they are therefore not necessarily privy to their intended definitions (Bentahila & Davies, 1989).

Rules of Politeness. Language difficulties can also manifest themselves in multicultural situations when people use their own cultural rules instead of applying the rules of the culture in which they are communicating. For example, an ITA in chemistry was very diligent about checking with students to see how their experiments were progressing. She would approach each group of students and ask, "What are you doing?" Students were startled at what they perceived as an abrupt, even accusatory statement, a message that she did not intend to convey (Hoekje & Williams, 1992). A U.S. American TA would probably have said something like, "So, how are things going?" as a way to find out where the students were in the experiment. Sometimes what appears to be a perfectly acceptable question can actually be interpreted as accusatory and combative given a particular situation. Although this can happen in monocultural situations, intercultural communication settings are especially susceptible to such misunderstandings. An opposite dilemma is often faced by many ITAs from Asian cultures such as Japan who might use roundabout, indirect ways of expressing an opinion and go to great lengths to be polite and maintain harmony (Kuroda, 1986). The more direct style of speaking used by U.S. students may appear offensive to these instructors. To U.S. students unaccustomed to extreme efforts to be polite, communication by Japanese teachers may be perceived as inarticulate, disingenuous, or even deceptive.

Translating requests from one language to the next can be problematic when different rules of politeness are working. For example, British English emphasizes what Brown and Levinson (1978) describe as "negative politeness," or a concern for not being an imposition on another person. Thus, British and Americans speaking English might say, "Would you like some more?" But Moroccans use "positive" politeness, which displays a concern for another's welfare and therefore they might use the imperative "Take some more." Although the same message is conveyed ("I would like you to have some more"), whether the message is communicated using a question or an imperative, and how the message is interpreted, depends on the cultural background of the speaker and listener. The necessity of teaching the culturally specific aspects of a language is something with which foreign language instructors often struggle. What cultural rules do they teach students about when to speak and how? In a Spanish class, a teacher could choose to teach the communication rules of Mexico, Spain, or many other South or Central American countries, and each set of rules might be different from the others. Students need to understand that learning a language does not necessarily mean they have learned the rules for communicating in that language in every society that speaks it.

Content of Communication. A U.S. university professor was talking in his office with a visiting student from Russia. The student noticed pictures of the professor's family on his desk and asked, "Why make your family pictures available? You devalue your family and experiences and memories by doing this" (Carbaugh, 1993, p. 169). The student went on to explain that people in Russia do not discuss personal experiences in public, "whatever they are . . . love, sex, relations with God, we cannot express these in words. You make it shallow if you speak it in public." This student's mild admonishment of Professor Carbaugh's display of personal artifacts and his follow-up explanation do much toward our understanding that what we talk about in public settings, including classroom time and office hours, is partially culturally determined. Although we have our own preferences for how much to reveal within educational contexts, what is defined as "public" and "private" in the classroom is not the same across cultures. It may be appropriate to discuss politics in the United States, but in less open societies, such talk in a classroom might mean the loss of a job. Thus, even though talk is a universal occurrence found in every culture, what students and teachers talk about in the classroom depends on where that classroom is in the world and who's doing the talking.

Nonverbal Ways of Speaking in the Classroom

Qiong-ying is a TA from the People's Republic of China. Qiong-ying does not look at her students during the class period and speaks in a voice that students must strain to hear. In the United States, these nonverbal ways of speaking communicate a message to students that is quite different than if Qiong-ying were teaching in China. Confucian standards of hierarchy have strongly influenced the nature of relationships among students and teachers, and

Qiong-ying is using nonverbal ways of communicating to her students that maintain the social distance prescribed by such standards. In addition, using communication that may draw attention toward her physical self could reduce the focus on her intellectual abilities (Christy & Rittenberg, 1988). But status differences between students and teachers are much more relaxed in U.S. classrooms, and not to look at someone or speak using an adequate amount of volume are seen as signs of disinterest and even rudeness by Qiong-ying's students. This example points dramatically to the vastly different interpretations our nonverbal behavior can communicate to people who do not share our cultural experiences and philosophies, and the problems it can create for students and teachers when engaged in the intercultural event of teaching and learning in a multicultural classroom.

Nonverbal ways of speaking encompass a wide array of communicative behaviors, from tones of voice and eye contact to our use of hand gestures and the physical environment in which we communicate. In this section, we will examine how tone of voice, pronunciation, accent, and silence influence communication in the multicultural university classroom.

Paralinguistics. *Paralinguistics* refer to qualities of our voice such as tone, volume, rate of speech, and intonation. These characteristics of our voices also include pronunciation of words and accent. The paralinguistic characteristics of our communication is such a major part of how a message is interpreted that sometimes it overwhelms the words we are uttering and misunderstanding can result. Middle Eastern students may find that others believe they are angry or hostile because their way of speaking appears loud and their intonation similar to what a person would use if they were angry in another culture. This misunderstanding is a function of others' unfamiliarity with the intonation patterns of Arabic and Turkish (Magrath, 1981). When we "hear" another language with the same cultural ear we use to hear our own language, the rules do not always transfer. This dynamic of listening with our own language ear can result in some uncomfortable situations. For instance, in one classroom, an East Indian instructor would call on his students frequently because he wanted to encourage participation in the classroom. However, the intonation of his voice made students feel like he was calling on them in a scolding manner and talking down to them. The instructor was appalled when he found this out, and worked very hard to try and change his intonation so that his positive intentions of wanting to help the students learn could become more apparent. Learning about differences in intonation would have been a very valuable lesson for everyone in this classroom.

How we pronounce our words is also included in the paralinguistic qualities of our voice. As those who have studied a second or third language know, learning a language is not just about picking up vocabulary and using correct grammatical structure. It also involves the vocalized stress we put on certain syllables and the sounds of letters. Even the slightest variations in pronunciation can lead to miscommunication. For example, Hardjo, an Indonesian student learning English, lamented to his tutor, "What is my problem?" because he was having an increasingly difficult time learning the language. Hardjo was having difficulty in part because his mouth was simply unaccustomed to forming certain sounds. Sounds like "g" and "k" were indistinguishable to his ear, which prevented him from pronouncing "dog" and "dock" as two different words (Hoven, 1987).

The accent of our speech—that is, those qualities that can often indicate what country or region a person is from—is also a nonverbal characteristic of communication that can influence classroom communication. When hearing an accent with which we are unfamiliar, it can be difficult to adjust immediately to this new sound of speaking. Just as English speakers may never become native-like in their ability to speak other languages, Hardjo's accent may never become native-like simply because he grew up without utilizing the muscles required to make certain consonantal or vocalic sounds. However, this does not mean that Hardjo's English is inaccurate or inadequate. In fact, as English increasingly becomes the *lingua franca* throughout the world, there are growing numbers of what are becoming known as "world Englishes." These are developing in nonnative English speaking countries where the majority of official educational systems and international business transactions are increasingly conducted in English. As this transition occurs, new brands of English are developed that adhere to grammatical and pronunciation rules that are an amalgamation of the native language of that country and a particular type of English (be it British English, Australian, U.S., or other). Thus, English is no longer seen as only that type of English spoken in Canada or New Zealand. In this increasingly international world in which we must all have some knowledge of each others' ways of speaking to ensure effective communication, native English speakers are finding themselves becoming more familiar with world Englishes from around the globe. The university classroom is a place in which such familiarity can be learned and an appreciation of world Englishes can be celebrated.

Silence. Although silence may be commonly understood as the absence of communication, such a conceptualization ignores silence as the definitive form of nonverbal expression. Western cultures largely view silence as asocial or even antisocial (Johannesen, 1974). The significance of silence among many people in the United States is best exemplified in the U.S. Constitution's Fifth Amendment, which guarantees every citizen the right to remain silent. And yet when this right is invoked, there is usually suspicion and the assumption of wrongdoing. Simply put, silence is suspect in individualistic cultures, "something to be filled in conversations" (Gudykunst, 1994, p. 140). Silence among the Japanese, however, is thought to convey truthfulness because spoken words can often involve distortion and deception (Lebra, 1987).

In the intercultural classroom, silence may be used by a teacher in ways that are useful yet sometimes problematic. In her study of the characteristics of successful classroom discourse, Patricia Rounds (1987) identified three categories of silence in the classrooms of ITAs teaching mathematics: administrative, strategic, and empty. *Administrative silences* included times when a teacher was reading a math problem in the book, writing on the chalkboard, erasing the chalkboard, and handing out papers. *Strategic silences* were those moments when a teacher wanted to create "a certain rhetorical or dramatic effect . . . such as the pregnant pause that comes just before a punch line is delivered or a major point is made" (Rounds, 1987, p. 653). It was the use of *empty silences* that proved problematic for students and ITAs. For example, when Rounds analyzed "Lee's" talk in the classroom, she found that sometimes his pauses occurred in the middle of sentences and created a haphazard effect. In the following example of Lee's communication, the periods in parentheses represent untimed pauses: "And because this (.) concept (.) are very important (.) so (.) we give (.) some (.) names (.) for the (.) quotient (.) and of the limit" (Rounds, 1987, p. 654). Rounds suggests that such uses of silence, unlike administrative and strategic silences, serve to "diffuse attention rather than focus it" (p. 654). Some students in this classroom explained that they had difficulty concentrating on what Lee was saying because his use of silence made it difficult to maintain their train of thought.

Was Lee not communicating effectively with his math students because of his use of empty pauses? Obviously, for some of them this particular use of silence was problematic, whereas other forms of silence were helpful to their learning. As a non-native English speaker, Lee's frequent use of silence can be understood as a struggle to find the right words to convey a thought. These linguistic challenges can be common events in intercultural classrooms, and although they may be cause for frustration among students, they are even more so for non-native English-speaking instructors.

IMPROVING COMMUNICATION IN THE INTERCULTURAL CLASSROOM

Remember that our goal in writing this article was to help students and teachers understand the influence that culture and national origin can have on classroom communication dynamics. We would like to end this essay by challenging you to analyze some intercultural classroom situations on your own. Each scenario below is based on actual experiences of university ITAs and their students. We invite you to read them and consider the following four questions:

1. How is culture influencing the perspectives of education held by the students and ITAs in these scenarios?
2. How is culture influencing the teaching and learning styles described in the scenarios?

3. How is culture being manifested through the verbal and nonverbal behavior and communication of the students and ITAs?
4. What suggestions do you have for the ITAs and students in these scenarios that would positively influence or even improve the classroom communication?

Intercultural Classroom Scenario One: Conflicting Expectations

Imagine that you are an instructor from Russia who teaches entry-level calculus to undergraduates at a large U.S. university. You are frustrated with your students and feel as if you cannot help them. Your students are at all different levels of background knowledge, many of them don't do their homework, and some of them ask the most simplistic questions in class that they could have answered if they'd just done their homework. They've also asked for homework solution handouts with the solutions all carefully worked out and reviews for the tests that have problems on them that look like those that are likely to be on the test. You can't decide if giving all this extra help will really contribute to their learning. In addition, it tends to keep you much busier than you can afford to be, what with all of the demands being placed on you with your rigorous graduate work. You wonder if there is a way to determine which students really belong in the classroom and if there is a way to get them to do more of their own problem solving on the homework.

You invite one of your colleagues to visit the class and ask the students questions about how the course is going. There seems to be a split opinion about your teaching among the students. About half of them think that you are working hard to help them learn calculus. The other half, however, feels that you are condescending and move too quickly through some of the problems. These students are afraid to ask questions, and some are even afraid of visiting your office hours for fear that you'll make them feel less capable. All of the students feel that you could spend more time letting them solve problems and ask questions in class. Right now, you tend to just write all the problems on the board and go through the solutions without giving them enough time to ask questions. What could you do to address the students' concerns without compromising your own teaching standards?

Intercultural Classroom Scenario Two: Issues of Privacy

You are a student in a German conversation class. Your instructor, Anna, is an ITA from Germany. Anna handed out everybody's grades on the last day of class and proclaimed, "Now let's discuss your grades." There was absolute silence in the classroom.

"What? What's wrong?" Anna asked.

"We don't do that here. We don't share our grades," said one of your classmates.

"Well in Germany you do. In Germany you hand out the grades and you discuss it as a class and you negotiate with the professor whether you can change it or not. If you don't think it's fair, you challenge the professor and the whole class decides whether it's fair or not."

No one in the class said a word. "So, anybody not happy with their grade?" Anna asked.

One of the students raised her hand and said, "I don't think that's gonna work here."

"Well, just pretend like it's Germany. This is a class on German. . . . We'll just pretend like it's in Germany," explained Anna.

"I just don't think it's gonna work," said one student.

It was a tense situation and no one was sure what to say next. How could this classroom interaction continue in a more positive direction?

Intercultural Classroom Scenario Three: Voices in the Classroom

Raj was a mathematics teacher who had taught for a few years in India before coming to the United States. He was now a teaching assistant for a math quiz section at the same university in which he was studying for his doctoral degree. When he asked his students for feedback during the middle of the quarter, Raj received complaints about his classroom communication. Many students said that it was difficult to understand what he was saying and a handful believed his accent was the primary problem. Others said that he rarely looked at them and often spoke toward the board as he was explaining problems. But almost all of them described him as knowledgeable and willing to answer questions throughout the class period. Raj was perplexed. He had no idea that his students were having a problem understanding him; no one had mentioned it until now. He didn't know what he could do about his accent, or even if he wanted to change that part of his Indian heritage. He had been speaking English since he was five years old and was a fluent English speaker. No one in his life had ever said they could not understand his communication. Why didn't they understand him?

SUGGESTIONS FOR STUDENTS IN INTERCULTURAL CLASSROOMS

It was our intent to provide you with some insight into the communication dynamics of intercultural and international university classrooms. You may have already experienced some of the issues we have identified, and perhaps you have developed your own ways of adapting to the changes and adjustments that are often needed in your own classes. We applaud such efforts to raise awareness of possible communication differences and to improve interactions in what can be challenging—but exciting—circumstances for learning. The following are some ideas that we hope will assist you further as you continue to learn and communicate in intercultural classrooms.

First, we suggest that you try analyzing the communication in your classes to find out how culture might be influencing interactions among students and teachers. By taking a second look at what is happening in your own classrooms, you might come to understand more fully how culture influences teaching and learning. Two questions to ask yourself as you reflect on classroom interaction are: (1) What comes "naturally" for you? (2) How does this contribute to what you expect in the class? Answers to these questions can help you understand how your own ways of learning and communicating might not be considered natural or even desirable to others. Your reflections can also help you form a wisdom you will be able to rely on for successful intercultural interactions in the future. Second, we suggest you focus on listening to a way of speaking with which you might be unfamiliar. Be patient with the unfamiliar accents, body language, or intonation of your teachers and fellow students. It might take a few weeks until your ear and your expectations have adjusted to new ways of communicating. The payoff, however, is improved communication not only in the present, but also in the future when you meet others who have similar ways of communicating. Our third suggestion is related to the second: Do not hesitate to ask your instructor to repeat information or questions. This is one of the primary ways that teachers of any nationality have of finding out if they have been understood. Fourth, we suggest that you ask your international instructors about their home countries. It has been our experience that most ITAs like to talk about life in their home countries and appreciate the show of interest in their background and experience. A final suggestion we have is probably the most important idea to remember when studying and taking part in any communication situation, but of particular importance in intercultural interactions: Remember that communication in any classroom setting requires people to work together to reach understandings. Sometimes that work is a bit more challenging when people are trying to negotiate their own cultural notions of teaching and learning.

Note

1. The idiom "honked off" is similar to the more crude idiom "pissed off," and means to get angry or upset.

References

Althen, G. (1988). *American ways: A guide for foreigners in the United States.* Yarmouth, ME: Intercultural Press.

Appleton, N. (1983). *Cultural pluralism in education.* New York: Longman.

Bail, F. T., & Mina, S. S. (1981). Filipino and American student perceptions of teacher effectiveness. *Research in Higher Education, 14,* 135–145.

Bentahila, A., & Davies, E. (1989). Culture and language use: A problem for foreign language teaching. *IRAL, 27,* 99–112.

Brewer, A. (1977). On Indian education. *Integrateducation, 15,* 21–23.

Brown, P., & Levinson, S. (1978). Universals in language use: Politeness phenomena. In E. N. Goody (Ed.), *Questions and politeness.* Cambridge, UK: Cambridge University Press.

Carbaugh, D. (1993). Competence as cultural pragmatics: Reflections on some Soviet and American encounters. In R. L. Wiseman and J. Koester (Eds.), *Intercultural communication competence* (pp. 168–183). Newbury Park, CA: Sage.

Christy, E. E., & Rittenberg, W. (1988). Some typical problems in the training of Chinese teaching assistants: Three case studies. In J. C. Constantinides (Ed.), *Wyoming/NAFSA Institute on Foreign TA Training: Working papers* (pp. 111–127). Washington, DC: National Association for Foreign Student Affairs.

Collier, J. J., & Powell, R. (1990). Ethnicity, instructional communication and classroom systems. *Communication Quarterly, 38,* 334–349.

Condon, J. C., & Yousef, F. (1988). *An introduction to intercultural communication.* New York: Macmillan.

Crittenden, K. S. (1994). The mandate to internationalize the curriculum. *Teaching Sociology, 2,* 1–9.

Crossing pedagogical oceans: International teaching assistants in U.S. undergraduate education. (1991). *ASHE-ERIC Higher Education Report No. 8.* Washington, DC: The George Washington University School of Education and Human Development.

Goodman, A. E. (1996, February 16). What foreign students contribute. *The Chronicle of Higher Education,* p. A52.

Gudykunst, W. B. (1994). *Bridging differences: Effective intergroup communication,* 2nd ed. Thousand Oaks, CA: Sage.

Halliday, M. A. K. (1970). Language structure and language function. In J. Lyons (Ed.), *New horizons in linguistics.* Harmondsworth, UK: Penguin Books.

Hoekje, B., & Williams, J. (1992). Communicative competence and the dilemma of international teaching assistant education. *TESOL Quarterly, 26,* 243–269.

Hofstede, G. (1986). Cultural differences in teaching and learning. *International Journal of Intercultural Relations, 10,* 301–319.

Hoven, D. (1987, August). *"What is my problem?" A case study of an adult Indonesian ESL learner in Australia.* Paper presented at the conference of the International Association of Applied Linguistics, New South Wales, Australia.

Institute of International Education. (1993). *Open doors 1992–93.* New York: Author.

Johannesen, R. L. (1974). The functions of silence: A plea for communication research. *Western Journal of Speech Communication, 38,* 25–35.

Kuroda, T. (1986). Overcoming the conflict between Asian TAs and Americans. In J. L. Gburek & S. C. Dunnett (Eds.), *The foreign TA: A guide to teaching effectiveness* (pp. 16–17). Buffalo: State University of New York Press.

Lebra, T. S. (1987). The cultural significance of silence in Japanese communication. *Multilingua*, 6, 343–357.

Longstreet, E. (1978). *Aspects of ethnicity*. New York: Teachers College Press.

Magrath, D. (1981). *Culture and language learning: Middle Eastern students*. Paper presented at the TESOL summer meeting, New York, NY.

Maslow, A. H. (1971). *The farther reaches of human nature*. New York: Viking Press.

Minnick, W. C. (1968). *The art of persuasion* (2nd ed.). Boston: Houghton Mifflin.

More, A. J. (1989). Native Indian learning styles: A review for researchers and teachers. *Journal of American Indian Education, Special Issue*, 15–28.

Munro, D. (1977). *The concept of man in contemporary China*. Ann Arbor: University of Michigan Press.

Neuliep, J. W. (1997). A cross-cultural comparison of teacher-immediacy in American and Japanese college classrooms. *Communication Research*, 24, 431–451.

Phillips, S. (1983). *The invisible culture: Communication in classroom and community on the Warm Springs Indian Reservation*. New York: Longman.

Pratt, D. D. (1991). Conceptions of self within China and the United States: Contrasting foundations for adult education. *International Journal of Intercultural Relations*, 15, 285–310.

Robinson, J. (1992, October). *International students and American university culture: Adjustment issues*. Paper presented at Washington Area Teachers of English to Speakers of Other Languages, Arlington, VA.

Rounds, P. L. (1987). Characterizing successful classroom discourse for NNS teaching assistant training. *TESOL Quarterly*, 21, 643–671.

Samovar, L. A., & Porter, R. E. (1997). An introduction to intercultural communication. In L. A. Samovar & R. E. Porter (Eds.), *Intercultural communication: A reader* (8th ed.) (pp. 5–27). Belmont, CA: Wadsworth.

Sanders, J. A., & Wiseman, R. L. (1990). The effects of verbal and nonverbal teacher immediacy on perceived cognitive, affective, and behavioral learning in the multicultural classroom. *Communication Education*, 39, 341–353.

Scollon, S. B. K. (1981, April). *Professional development seminar: A model for making higher education more culturally sensitive*. Paper presented at the National Association of Asian and Pacific American Education, Honolulu, HI.

Swisher, K., & Deyhle, D. (1989). The styles of learning are different, but the teaching is just the same: Suggestions for teachers of American Indian youth. *Journal of American Indian Education, Special Issue*, 1–14.

Triandis, H. (1989). The self and social behavior in differing cultural contexts. *Psychological Review*, 96, 506–520.

Twale, D. J., Shannon, D. M., & Moore, M. S. (1997). NGTA and IGTA training and experience: Comparisons between self-ratings and undergraduate student evaluations. *Innovative Higher Education*, 22, 61–77.

Wood, J. T. (1997). Gender, communication, and culture. In L. A. Samovar & R. E. Porter, (Eds.), *Intercultural communication: A reader* (8th ed.) (pp. 164–174). Belmont, CA: Wadsworth.

Concepts and Questions

1. Describe several ways in which the international presence on U.S. university campuses have affected the learning process.
2. How does the communication of cultural values and attitudes influence teaching and learning?
3. What differences might you find between collective and individualistic cultures in the structure of the classroom and the learning process?
4. How might a student from a culture in which hierarchies and respect for elders are strong cultural values perceive the relaxed relationship between teachers and students often reflected in U.S. universities?
5. What role does power distance play in determining the forms of communication that are appropriate to the teaching and learning process?
6. How does the gender orientation of a culture affect the forms of communication in the classroom?
7. How might a student from a culture that is high in uncertainty avoidance react to a U.S. professor who answers a student question by saying, "I don't know"?
8. Based on your own observations, detail as many learning styles as you can. How do these various styles merge in a college classroom environment?
9. In what ways do cultural differences in ways of speaking affect learning in a multicultural learning environment?
10. How does cultural diversity in nonverbal behavior affect interactions in a multicultural learning setting?

part 4

Intercultural Communication: Seeking Improvement

Happy are they that hear their detractions and can put them to mending.

WILLIAM SHAKESPEARE

Understanding is the beginning of approving.

ANDRÉ GIDE

In a sense, this entire volume has been concerned with the practice of intercultural communication. We have looked at many diverse cultures and a host of communication variables that operate when people from different cultures attempt to interact. Our analysis thus far, however, has been more theoretical than practical. Previous selections have concentrated primarily on the task of understanding the nature of intercultural communication. We have not yet dealt with the act of practicing intercultural communication.

We have already pointed out many of the problems that cultural diversity introduces into the communication process. And we have shown how awareness not only of other cultures but also of one's own culture can help mediate some of those problems. But intercultural communication is not exclusively a single-party activity. Like other forms of interpersonal communication, it requires for its highest and most successful practice the reciprocal and complementary participation of all parties to the communication event.

When elevated to its highest level, intercultural communication becomes an act in which participants make simultaneous inferences not only about their own roles but also about the role of the other. This act of mutual role taking must exist before people can achieve a level of communication that results in mutual understanding. In intercultural communication, this means that you must know about your own culture and the culture of the one with whom you are communicating. And that person also must know about his or her own culture and about your culture as well. Unless there is mutual acknowledgment of each other's cultures and a willingness to accept those cultures as a reality governing communicative interactions, then intercultural communication cannot rise to its highest potential.

In this final section, we have slightly modified our orientation to discuss the activity of communication. For although the readings in this portion of the book will still increase your understanding, their main purpose is to improve your behavior during intercultural communication.

The motivation for this particular section grows out of an important precept found in the study of human communication. It suggests that human interaction is a behavior in which people engage for the purpose of changing their environment. Inherent in this notion is the idea that communication is something people do—it involves action. Regardless of how much you understand the concepts of intercultural communication, when you are communicating with someone from another culture, you are part of a behavioral situation. You and your communication counterpart are doing things that affect each other. This final part of the book deals with that "doing." In addition, it is intended to help your communication become as effective as possible.

As you might well imagine, personal contact and experience are the most desirable methods for improvement. Knowledge and practice tend to work in tandem. The problem, however, is that we cannot write or select readings that substitute for this personal experience. Therefore, our contribution by necessity must focus on the observations of those who have practiced intercultural communication with some degree of success.

chapter 7

Communicating Interculturally: Becoming Competent

A s we approach the last two chapters of this book, we need to remind you that our primary purpose is to help you become a more effective intercultural communicator. To this end, the readings throughout the text have offered you material that will increase your knowledge about culture in general and also introduce you to many specific cultures. In this chapter we continue with these two themes by offering you advice and counsel that applies to all cultures and to specific cultures: That is to say, the essays in Chapter 7 were specifically selected because the suggestions advanced are both universal and specific. Most of the selections discuss problems as well as solutions. Being alert to potential problems is the first step toward understanding. Once problems have been identified, it is easier to seek means of improvement—and it is improvement that is at the heart of this chapter.

Our first essay moves us from potential problems to possible solutions. In "A Model of Intercultural Communication Competence," Brian W. Spitzberg offers a profile of the effective intercultural communicator. More specifically, he suggests a course of action that is likely to enhance our competence when we are in an intercultural situation. His suggestions take the form of propositions that can be used to guide our actions. We are told that intercultural competence is increased if we (1) are motivated, (2) are knowledgeable, (3) possess interpersonal skills, (4) are credible, (5) meet the expectations of our communication partner, (6) can strike a balance between autonomy needs and intimacy needs, (7) reflect similarities, (8) manifest trust, (9) offer social support, and (10) have access to multiple relationships.

In our next reading, "Managing Intercultural Conflicts Effectively," Stella Ting-Toomey moves us from a general analysis of communication competency to a specific topic associated with intercultural communication: intercultural conflict. The rationale behind this selection is clearly stated in the opening line of the essay: "Conflict is inevitable in all social and personal relationships." To preempt the problems created by interpersonal disharmony, particularly in the intercultural setting, Ting-Toomey maintains that conflict must be defined and managed. To help us improve our capacity to clarify and regulate conflict, the author explains three significant features of intercultural conflict. First, a framework that uses low-context versus high-context and monochronic and polychronic time is advanced to demonstrate why and how cultures are different and similar. Second, some basic assumptions and factors that contribute to conflict are discussed. Finally, Ting-Toomey offers a series of skills that can help individuals manage conflict when it develops in the intercultural encounter.

When we travel to a foreign culture, we often encounter for the first time a new and often-confusing environment. Our ability to interact effectively in a new cultural environment depends on our abilities to adapt. In our next article, "Sojourner Adaptation," Polly Begley draws on her extensive international travel experiences to offer insights and strategies for living, learning, and adapting in global communities. After introducing us to both the characteristics and effects of culture shock and the challenges associated with adapting to another cultural environment, she reviews the changes and adaptations one must make as a sojourner in another culture. Begley suggests that ethnocentrism, language disequilibrium, length of stay, and level of knowledge are the major factors that affect our ability to adapt to a foreign culture. She then provides us with several useful strategies to assist in cultural adaptation.

Two themes recurring throughout this book have been the notions that our world is figuratively shrinking and that the U.S. population is rapidly becoming more diverse and multicultural. Worldwide, as the figurative distance between diverse cultures continues to decrease, and as our own population continues to reflect greater cultural diversity, our proximity to cultural differences grows closer. This nearness demands that we develop intercultural understanding and sensitivity if we are to live peacefully among and interact successfully with others who reflect unique and different cultures. In their essay "Intercultural Sensitivity," Guo-Ming Chen and William J. Starosta provide us with knowledge and insights that help us "develop a positive emotion toward understanding and appreciating cultural differences in order to promote appropriate and effective behavior in intercultural communication." They identify six components of intercultural sensitivity: *self-esteem, self-monitoring, open-mindedness, empathy, interaction involvement,* and *suspended judgment.* Through an analysis and discussion of these components, Chen and Starosta provide us with a clear, systematic approach to improving our intercultural skills and capabilities.

One of the many consequences of a culturally diverse society is a culturally diverse workforce. The composition of the U.S. workforce has shown increasing change for several decades. For the U.S. economy to provide necessary employment for workers and to competitive in world markets, the U.S. business community must create a workplace that values and fully utilizes the skills and talents of a culturally diverse workforce. In our final essay, "Managing Cultural Diversity in the American Workplace," Mohan R. Limaye looks at how the U.S. business community is attempting to deal with diversity in the workforce. He concludes that, for the most part, it is failing. After examining current diversity training programs (DTPs) and revealing their shortcomings, Limaye proposes a model for diversity training that involves the democratization of the American workplace and the use of Spanish as a co-language. He considers the probability that the business community will willingly adopt his kinds of recommended changes and determines that they will not. This apparent unwillingness on the part of the business committee leads Limaye to conclude that the battle for change in the American workplace must, therefore, be political in order to succeed.

A Model of Intercultural Communication Competence

BRIAN H. SPITZBERG

The world we live in is shrinking. Travel that once took months now takes hours. Business dealings that were once confined primarily to local economies have given way to an extensively integrated world economy. Information that once traveled through error-prone and time-consuming methods now appears in the blink of an eye across a wide range of media. People in virtually all locations of the globe are more mobile than ever and more likely to traverse into cultures different than their own. Literally and figuratively, the walls that separate us are tumbling down. Though we may not have fully become a "global village," there is no denying that the various cultures of the world are far more accessible than ever before, and that the peoples of these cultures are coming into contact at an ever-increasing rate. These contacts ultimately comprise interpersonal encounters. Whether it is the negotiation of an arms treaty, or the settlement of a business contract, or merely a sojourner getting directions from a native, cultures do not interact, people do.

The purpose of this essay is to examine the concept of interactional competence in intercultural contexts. *For the purposes of this essay, intercultural communication competence is considered very broadly as an impression that behavior is appropriate and effective in a given context.* Normally, competence is considered an ability or a set of skilled behaviors. However, any given behavior or ability may be judged competent in one context, and incompetent in another. Consequently, competence cannot be defined by the behavior or ability itself. It must instead be viewed as a social evaluation of behavior. This social evalua-

tion comprises the two primary criteria of appropriateness and effectiveness.

Appropriateness means that behavior is viewed as legitimate for, or fitting to, the context. To be appropriate ordinarily implies that the valued rules, norms, and expectancies of the relationship are not violated significantly. Under some circumstances, however, a person violates existing norms to establish new norms. A colleague with whom you work and almost exclusively exchange task information may one day take you aside to talk about a personal problem. This violation of norms, however, may not seem inappropriate as you come to see this person as a friend rather than just a colleague.

Effectiveness is often equated with competence (Bradford, Allen, & Beisser, 1998). Here *effectiveness* is viewed as the accomplishment of valued goals or rewards relative to costs and alternatives. Effectiveness is relative to the available options. For example, effectiveness often implies satisfaction, but there are times when all reasonable courses of action are dissatisfying or ineffective. In such a context, the most effective response may be simply the least dissatisfying. For example, many people find virtually all conflict dissatisfying. If your partner breaks up with you, you may find there is no "effective" response (i.e., something that would "win" this person back). But there are reactions that may be more or less effective in achieving other objectives (e.g., maintaining a friendship, getting your compact discs back, etc.). Effectiveness is also related to, but distinct from, efficiency. *Efficiency*, or expediency, is concerned with communication that is "direct, immediate, and to the point" (Kellerman & Shea, 1996, p. 151). Generally, more efficient communication is considered more effective because it presumes less effort. However, obviously efficient behavior is not always the most effective in obtaining preferred outcomes.

Communication in an intercultural context, therefore, is competent when it accomplishes the objectives of an actor in a manner that is appropriate to the context. *Context* here implies several levels, including culture, relationship, place, and function (Spitzberg & Brunner, 1991). The chapters of this book all illustrate the importance of culture to the use and evaluation of behavior. The competence of behavior also depends significantly on the type of relationship between the interactants. What is appropriate for spouses is not always appropriate for colleagues or friends. Competence also depends on place, or the physical environment. Behavior appropriate for fans at a sporting event will rarely be appropriate at a funeral. Finally, the competence of behavior is influenced by function, or what the communicators are attempting to do. Behavior appropriate for a conflict is often quite different than behavior appropriate for a first date.

The two standards of appropriateness and effectiveness also depend on interaction quality. Quality can be defined by these two criteria by examining the four possible communication styles that result. Communication that is inappropriate and ineffective is clearly of low quality and is referred to as *minimizing*. Communication by someone that is appropriate but ineffective suggests a social chameleon who does nothing objectionable but also accomplishes no personal objectives through interaction. This suggests a *sufficing* style, or one that is sufficient to meet the minimum demands of the situation but accomplishes nothing more. Communication that is inappropriate but effective includes such behaviors as lying, cheating, coercing, forcing, and so forth, which are messages that are ethically problematic. This *maximizing* style reflects a person who attempts to achieve everything, even if it is at the expense of others. While there may be instances in which such actions could be considered competent, they are rarely the ideal behaviors to employ in any given circumstance. Interactants who achieve their goals in a manner that is simultaneously appropriate to the context are competent in an *optimizing* way.

A MODEL OF INTERCULTURAL COMPETENCE

Most existing models of intercultural competence have been fairly fragmented (Lustig & Spitzberg, 1993; Martin, 1993). Typically, the literature is reviewed and a list of skills, abilities, and attitudes is formulated to summarize the literature (Spitzberg & Cupach, 1989). Such lists appear on the surface to reflect useful guidelines for competent interaction and adaptation. For example, Spitzberg's (1989) review of studies reveals dozens of skills, including

ability to deal with stress, understanding, awareness of culture, cautiousness, charisma, cooperation, conversational management, empathy, frankness, future orientation, flexibility, interest, managerial ability, opinion leadership, task persistence, self-actualization, self-confidence, self-disclosure, and strength of personality. Although each study portrays a reasonable list of abilities or attitudes, there is no sense of integration or coherence across lists. It is impossible to tell which skills are most important in which situations, or even how such skills relate to each other. In addition, such lists become cumbersome, as it is difficult to imagine trying to learn dozens of complex skills to become competent.

A more productive approach would be to develop an integrative model of intercultural competence that is both consistent with the theoretical and empirical literatures and provides specific predictions of competent behavior. This approach is reflected in basic form in Figure 1 and elaborated by means of a series of propositions below. The propositions are broken down into three levels of analysis: the individual system, the episodic system, and the relational system. The *individual system* includes those characteristics an individual possesses that facilitate competent interaction in a normative social sense. The *episodic system* includes those features of a particular Actor that facilitate competence interaction on the part of a specific Co-actor in a specific episode of interaction. The *relational system* includes those components that assist a person's competence across the entire span of relationships rather than in just a given episode of interaction. Each successive system level subsumes the logic and predictions of the former. The propositions serve both to provide an outline of a theory of interpersonal competence in intercultural contexts and offer practical advise. To the extent interactants analyze intercultural situations sufficiently, then each proposition suggests a course of action that is likely to enhance their competence in the situation encountered.

By way of overview, the model portrays the process of dyadic interaction as a function of two individuals' *motivation* to communicate, *knowledge* of communication in that context, and *skills* in implementing their motivation and knowledge. Over the course of the interaction both within and across episodes, behavior is matched to expectancies each

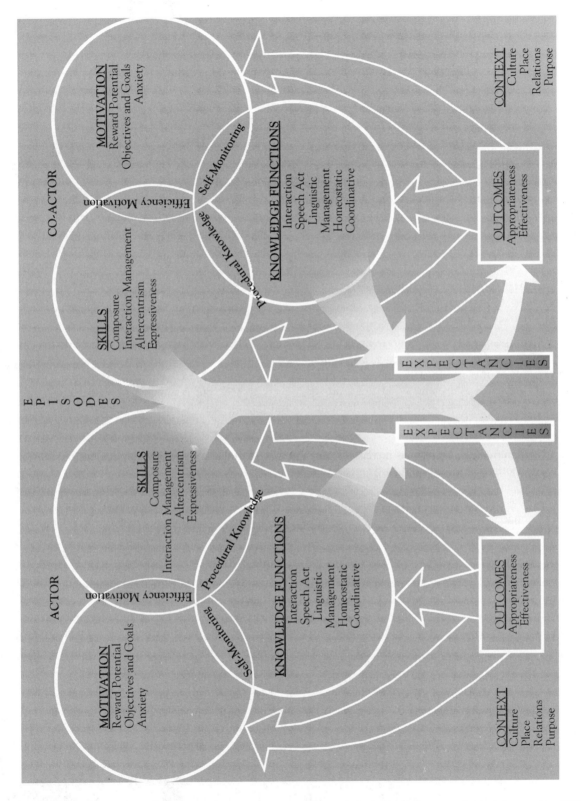

person has of the other and of the interaction process. If expectancies are fulfilled in a rewarding manner, then interactants are likely to perceive both self and other as communicatively competent and feel relatively satisfied that objectives were accomplished. Interactants may be seen as incompetent because they lack motivation to perform competently, lack knowledge of the competent lines of action in the context concerned, or simply lack the communication skills to carry off a deft interaction. Also, interactants may be viewed as incompetent because their partner has unrealistic expectancies for the person or episode.

INDIVIDUAL SYSTEM

1. As Communicator Motivation Increases, Communicative Competence Increases

Very simply, the more a person wants to make a good impression and communicate effectively, the more likely it is that this person will view self, and be viewed by others, as competent. What constitutes or leads to high levels of motivation? The following propositions address this question.

1a. As communicator confidence increases, communicator motivation increases. Confidence results from several individual experiences. For example, a person who is nervous meeting strangers is likely to be less confident when encountering a new person from a different culture. Further, the more unfamiliar a person is with a given type of situation, the less confident that person is regarding what to do and how to do it. Finally, some situations carry more significant implications and are more difficult to manage than others. For example, getting directions to a major urban landmark is likely to permit greater confidence than negotiating a multimillion dollar contract for your company. Thus, social anxiety, familiarity with the situation, and the importance or consequences of the encounter all influence a person's confidence in a social context.

1b. As reward-relevant efficacy beliefs increase, communicator motivation increases. Efficacy beliefs are self-perceptions of ability to perform a given set

of behaviors (Bandura, 1982). Basically, the more actors believe they are able to engage in a set of valued or positive actions, the more prone they are to do so. A professional arbitrator is likely to have much higher efficacy beliefs in negotiating disputes or contracts than the average person. However, this arbitrator might not have any greater confidence than the average person in developing friendships with others in a different culture. Efficacy beliefs are therefore usually task-specific and depend on familiarity with tasks and contexts.

1c. As communicator approach dispositions increase, communicator motivation increases. Approach dispositions refer to personality characteristics that prompt someone to value communicative activity. Several dispositions have been found to influence motivation. People who are higher in self-esteem, who consistently seek relatively high levels of sensory stimulation, who believe they have high levels of control over their environment, who are low in social anxiety (Neuliep & McCroskey, 1997), and who are generally well adjusted psychologically, are likely to seek out communication encounters and find them positively reinforcing. Furthermore, people who are more interculturally tolerant are more likely to engage in competent interaction across cultures (Mendleson, Bures, Champion, & Lott, 1997).

1d. As the relative cost–benefit ratio of a situation increases, communicator motivation increases. Very simply, every situation can be viewed as having certain potential costs and benefits. Even in no-win situations (e.g., "true" conflicts), the behavior that leads to the least costly or painful outcomes is considered the most preferable or beneficial. Likewise, in a win–win situation, the least desirable outcomes are also the most costly. As the perception of potential benefits increases relative to the potential costs of a course of action, the more motivated a person is to pursue that particular course of action. Obviously, the weighing of costs and benefits must always be done relative to alternatives. Asking directions from someone who does not speak your language may be considered too effortful, but only relative to the alternatives of consulting a map, trial-and-error exploration, seeking someone who speaks your language who might be familiar with the locale, or getting hopelessly lost.

2. As Communicative Knowledge Increases, Communicative Competence Increases

A stage actor needs to be motivated to give a good performance to be viewed as a competent actor. However, merely wanting to perform well and being unhampered by stage fright are rarely sufficient to produce a competent performance. The actor also needs to know the script, the layout of the stage, the type of audience to expect, and so forth. Similarly, the more an interactant knows about how to communicate well, the more competent that person is likely to be.

Knowledge of interaction occurs at several microscopic levels (Greene, 1984). As identified in Figure 1, an actor needs to know the basic goals or *interaction* functions being pursued. These interaction behaviors are combined to fulfill *content* functions, which include the production of speech acts such as asking questions, asserting opinions, and making promises. To perform speech acts in turn requires knowledge of semantics, syntax, and the constituents of a meaningful sentence. In other words, grammatical sentences are formed to fulfill a *linguistic* function. Actual performance of these actions requires adaptation of this behavior to the other person. Such adaptation includes achieving coherence, continuity of topic, and relatively smooth flow of speaking turns (i.e., *management* function), a relative balance of physiological activity level (i.e., *homeostatic* function), and an individual matching of verbal and nonverbal components (i.e., *coordinative* function). Several predictions help specify the relevance of knowledge to competent interaction.

2a. As task-relevant procedural knowledge increases, communicator knowledge increases.
Procedural knowledge concerns the "how" of social interaction rather than the "what." For example, knowing the actual content of a joke would be considered the substantive knowledge of the joke. Knowing how to tell it, with all the inflections, subtle timing, and actual mannerisms, are all matters of the procedural knowledge of the joke. This knowledge is typically more "mindless" than other forms of knowledge. Many skill routines are overlearned to the point that the procedures are virtually forgotten, as in driving a familiar route home and not remembering anything

about the drive upon arrival. You "know" how to drive, but you can use such knowledge with virtually no conscious attention to the process. Thus, the more a person actually knows how to perform the mannerisms and behavioral routines of a cultural milieu, the more knowledgeable this person is likely to be in communicating with others in this culture. In general, as a person's exposure to a culture increases, his or her stores of relevant subject matters, topics, language forms, as well as procedural competencies, are likely to increase.

2b. As mastery of knowledge acquisition strategies increases, communicator knowledge increases.
A person who does not already know how to behave is not necessarily consigned to incompetence. People have evolved many means for finding out what to do, and how to do it, in unfamiliar contexts. The metaphor of international espionage illustrates some of the strategies by which people acquire information about others, such as interrogation (e.g., asking questions), surveillance (e.g., observing others), information exchange (e.g., disclosing information to elicit disclosure from others), posturing (e.g., violating some local custom and observing reactions to assess value of various actions), bluffing (e.g., acting as if we know what we are doing and letting the unfolding action inform us and define our role), or engaging double agents (e.g., using the services of a native or mutual friend as informant). The more of these types of strategies actors understand, the more capable they are in obtaining the knowledge needed to interact competently in the culture.

2c. As identity and role diversity increases, communicator knowledge increases.
In general, the more diverse a person's exposure to distinct types of people, roles, and self-images, the more this person is able to comprehend various roles and role behaviors characteristic of a given cultural encounter. Some people live all their lives in a culture within very narrow ranges of contexts and roles. Others experience a wide variety of societal activities (e.g., jobs, tasks), roles (e.g., parent, worshiper, confidant), groups (e.g., political party, religious affiliation, volunteer organization, cultures and co-cultures). A person who has a highly complex self-image reflecting these social identities (Hoelter, 1985) and has interacted

with a diversity of different types of persons and roles (Havighurst, 1957) is better able to understand the types of actions encountered in another culture.

2d. As knowledge dispositions increase, communicator knowledge increases.

Many personality characteristics are related to optimal information processing. Specifically, persons higher in intelligence, cognitive complexity, self-monitoring, listening skills, empathy, role-taking ability, nonverbal sensitivity, perceptual accuracy, creativity, and problem-solving ability, are more likely to know how to behave in any given encounter. In short, while mere possession of information may help, a person also needs to know how to analyze and process that information.

3. As Communicator Skills Increase, Communicator Competence Increases

Skills are repeatable, goal-oriented actions or action sequences. A person who is motivated to perform well and knows the script well still may not possess the acting skills required to give a good performance. All of us have probably encountered instances in which we knew what we wanted to say but just could not seem to say it correctly. Such issues concern the skills of performing our motivation and knowledge. Research indicates that there are four specific clusters of interpersonal skills and one more general type of skill.

Before specifying the nature of skills that facilitate intercultural communication competence, an important qualifier needs to be considered. There are probably no specific behaviors that are universally competent. Even if peoples from all cultures smile, the smile is not always a competent behavior. However, there may be skills that are consistently competent according to standards of appropriate usage within each culture. For example, probably all cultures value the smooth flow of conversation, even though they may differ in the specific behaviors and cues used to accomplish such interaction management. All cultures apparently value eye contact and the use of questions, even if they vary greatly in the *way* in which these skills are appropriately used. Any skill or ability is constrained by its own contextual rules of expression. Thus, skills are always assessed relative to their *contextual frame*. It is in this sense that the following propositions are developed regarding communication skills.

3a. As conversational altercentrism increases, communicator skill increases.

Altercentrism ("alter" means other, "centrism" means to focus upon) involves those behaviors that reveal concern for, interest in, and attention to another person or persons. Behaviors such as eye contact, asking questions, maintenance of others' topics, appropriate body lean and posture, and active listening all indicate a responsiveness to the other person.

3b. As conversational coordination increases, communicator skill increases.

Conversational coordination involves all those behaviors that assist in the smooth flow of an encounter. Minimizing long response delays, providing for smooth initiation and conclusion of conversational episodes, avoiding disruptive interruptions, providing transitions between themes or activities, and providing informative feedback cues all assist in managing the interaction and maintaining appropriate pacing, rhythms, and punctuation of a conversation.

3c. As conversational composure increases, communicator skill increases.

To be composed in a conversation is to reflect calmness and confidence in demeanor. Composure consists of avoiding anxiety cues such as nervous twitches, tapping of feet, lack of eye contact, and breaking vocal pitch. Conversely, composure also implies behaviors such as a steady volume and pitch, relaxed posture, well-formulated verbal statements, and self-assured tones of verbal and nonverbal expression. The composed communicator tends to appear in control of his or her own behavior.

3d. As conversational expressiveness increases, communicator skill increases.

Expressiveness concerns those skills that provide vivacity, animation, intensity, and variability in communicative behavior. Expressiveness is revealed by such behaviors as vocal variety, facial affect, opinion expression, extensive vocabulary usage, and gestures. Expressive communication is closely associated with the ability to display culturally and contextually appropriate affect and energy level through speech and gesture.

3e. As conversational adaptation increases, communicator skill increases. Adaptation is a commonly noted attribute of the competent intercultural communicator. It typically suggests several characteristics. First, rather than radical chameleon-like change, adaptation implies subtle variation of self's behavior to the behavioral style of others. Second, it implies certain homeostatic, or consistency-maintaining, regulatory processes—that is, verbal actions are kept relatively consistent with nonverbal actions. Similarly, amounts of personal altercentrism, coordination, composure, and expressiveness are kept relatively consistent with personal style tendencies. Third, adaptation suggests accommodation of both the actions of the other person as well as one's own goal(s) in the encounter. Rather than implying completely altercentric or egocentric orientations, adaptation implies altering and balancing self's goals and intentions to those of the other person. Thus, the skill of adaptation implies such behaviors as shifts of vocal style, posture, animation, and topic development, as the behaviors of the other person vary and as changes in self's goals change over the course of a conversation.

The propositions in this section have examined three basic individual components of interculturally competent communication. In general, the more motivated, knowledgeable, and skilled a person is, the more competent this person is likely to be. It is possible that a person can be viewed as highly competent if high in only one or two of these components. For example, a person who is very motivated may compensate for lack of knowledge and skill through perseverance and effort alone. Likewise, someone who is extremely familiar with a given type of encounter may be able to "drift" through an interaction with minimal access to his or her motivation. A salesperson might claim to have "written so many contracts in my life I can negotiate one in my sleep." Nevertheless, across most encounters, the more of each of these components a person possesses or demonstrates, the more competent this person's interaction is likely to be.

EPISODIC SYSTEM

The first three primary propositions represented factors that increase the likelihood an actor will produce behaviors that are normatively competent. However, given that competence is an impression, there is no guarantee that a person who has performed behaviors that normally would be viewed as competent will be viewed as competent by a particular conversational partner in a particular relational encounter. The propositions in this section address this latter issue. These propositions are episodic in the sense that characteristics of an Actor influence the impressions of the Co-actor in a specific episode of interaction. The statements concern those characteristics of an Actor that predict Co-actor's impression of Actor's competence.

4. As Actor's Communicative Status Increases, Co-Actor's Impression of Actor's Competence Increases

Communicative status is meant here to represent all those factors that enhance this person's positive evaluation. Competence is, after all, an evaluation. Generally, as a person's status goes, so goes his or her competence. There are obvious exceptions, but it is instructive to consider those status characteristics particularly relevant to communicative competence.

4a. As Actor's motivation, knowledge, and skills increase, Co-actor's impression of Actor's competence increases. The logic of the individual system also applies to the episodic system—that is, the factors that lead a person to behave competently in a normative sense will usually lead to a competent relational performance as well (Imahori & Lanigan, 1989; Spitzberg & Cupach, 1984). This is true in two slightly different senses. In one sense, norms comprise the majority of people's views and behaviors, so a person who is normatively competent will usually be viewed as competent in any given encounter. In another sense, an Actor who is motivated to interact competently with a particular Co-actor, knowledgeable about this particular Co-actor, and skilled in interacting with this particular Co-actor also is more likely to communicate better and be viewed as competent by this Co-actor in a given encounter.

Factors that facilitate motivation, knowledge, and skill in a particular episodic system are likely to be logical extensions of the individual system components. For example, motivation is likely to increase as attraction to Co-actor increases and as positive reinforcement history with Co-actor increases. Knowledge of Co-actor is likely to increase with duration of relationship, and depth and breadth of self-disclosure between Actor and Co-actor increase. Skill in interacting with Co-actor is likely to increase as adaptation and refinement increase over the lifetime of the relationship.

4b. As contextual obstruction of Actor's performance increase, Co-actor's impression of Actor's competence increase. When forming an impression of an Actor, a Co-actor is left to determine the extent to which the Actor's outcomes are due to the Actor's own abilities and effort, rather than the context or other factors. For example, a physically unattractive Actor who consistently makes friends and has dates is likely to be viewed as more communicatively competent than a person who is physically attractive. The reasoning is that the social context is weighted against the unattractive Actor and in favor of the attractive Actor. Thus, the attractive Actor would achieve the same outcomes due to attractiveness rather than his or her competence, whereas the unattractive actor must overcome the contextual barriers through more competent action. In essence, all other things being equal, an Actor's competence is "discounted" if there are obvious alternative explanations for the Actor's good fortune. Similarly, an Actor's competence is "forgiven" if there are many apparent alternative reasons for his or her failure.

4c. As Actor's receipt of valued outcomes increases, Co-actor's impression of Actor's competence increases. While the discounting effect discussed above influences impressions of competence, it is not likely to outweigh other factors entirely. If an Actor is perceived as consistently achieving positive outcomes, a Co-actor is likely to assume that the Actor has something to do with this success (Kaplowitz, 1978). The negotiator who consistently presides over significant agreements is likely to be viewed as more communicatively competent as a simple result of the tangible outcomes, almost regardless of extenuating circumstances.

4d. As Actor's extant attributed communicative status increases, Co-actor's impression of Actor status increases. An actor who comes into an encounter with an established high level of status is more likely to be viewed as competent in subsequent interactions. In addition, an Actor who has established a satisfying relationship with a particular Co-actor has, in effect, established a reserve of competence in the Co-actor's views. Thus, Nelson Mandella, Boris Yelstin, or even Bill Gates enter any communicative situation with considerable communicative status in tow. In essence, then, the impression we initially have of an Actor is likely to be the basis for our later impressions until such time that significant events alter these impressions. Furthermore, certain cultures develop higher regard for other cultures generally. The mutual regard that Americans and Japanese-Americans may share is probably quite different than that which the South African blacks and whites may share.

5. Co-Actor's Impression of Actor's Competence Is a Function of Actor's Fulfillment of Co-Actor's Expectancies

Over time, interactants develop expectations regarding how interpersonal interaction is likely to and should occur in particular contexts. Not surprisingly, therefore, a person's competence in a given relationship is due partly to expectancy fulfillment and violation. Research indicates that expectancies generally develop along the three fundamental EPA dimensions: *evaluation, potency,* and *activity* (Osgood, May, & Miron, 1975; Spitzberg, 1989); that is, most contexts are viewed in terms of their valence (e.g., good versus bad), power (e.g., dominant versus passive), and animation (e.g., noisy versus quiet). A traditional, noncharismatic church service typically is expected to be good (valence), with the audience passive (potency) and relatively quiet (activity). A typical party, in contrast, is expected to be good (valence), strong (potency), fast, and noisy (activity). Upon being fired, an exit interview is expected to be unpleasurable (valence), and the interviewee as weak (potency) and relatively passive (activity). The point is that experience with interpersonal encounters produces expectancies and evaluations about both anticipated and appropriate behavior. The propositions below elaborate the influence of these expectancies.

5a. As Actor's fulfillment of positive Co-actor expectancies increases, Co-actor's impression of Actor's competence increases. To the extent that Co-actor expects an encounter with Actor to be positive, then Actor is likely to be viewed as competent to the extent that he or she fulfills these expectancies. Because the expectancies typically form a consistent system in a Co-actor's mind, an Actor needs to fulfill each of the EPA dimensions. If an interviewer expects interviews to be good (E), his or her own role to be relatively powerful and the role of the interviewee to be relatively powerless (P), and the encounter to be generally quiet but quick (A), then the Actor is well advised to behave according to these expectancies. Because the interviewer has developed these expectancies along all three dimensions, they tend to be "set" in relationship to each other. Thus, part of what makes the interview "good" in the interviewer's opinion is that the interviewer's role is typically powerful, and the interviews tend to go quietly and quickly.

5b. As Actor's normative violation of Co-actor's negative expectancies increases, Co-actor's impression of Actor's competence increases. The logic of the former proposition reverses itself when a Co-actor expects an encounter to be negative. Consider the previous interview example from the interviewee's perspective. An interviewee may find interviews highly anxiety-producing, threatening, and difficult. As such, the interview context is expected to be uncomfortable, the interviewee's role as submissive, and the encounter as generally slow and inactive. So, if the interviewer wants to make a good impression, then he or she needs to violate the interviewee's expectations in an appropriate manner. Such an interviewer might change the setting to a less formal lunchroom context, dress more casually, tell some stories and initially discuss topics unrelated to the position, and generally spend time putting the interviewee in a good mood. Such an encounter violates the interviewee's expectancies, but does so in a way that is normatively acceptable and positive.

5c. As Actor's fulfillment of Co-actor's competence prototype expectancies increases, Co-actor's impression of Actor's competence increases. A prototype in this usage is basically a cognitive outline of concepts, analogous to a mental map of the competence territory. The prototype of a competent person is likely to consist of several levels of concepts varying in their abstraction. A simplified example of a competent communicator prototype is displayed in Figure 2.

At the highest level is the category label that determines what types of inferences are relevant to a given set of observed behavior. For example, observing someone changing the oil in a car is not relevant to the category of "competent communicator." At the next level are types of inferences or impressions that collectively constitute the label of competent communicator. In this hypothetical example, a competent communicator is someone who is believed to be friendly, trustworthy, and assertive. Each inference, in turn, is based on certain types of behavior. To the extent that these behaviors are observed, the inferences follow. Observed behaviors are matched or compared to those that over time have come to occupy the position of category indicators. If there is a good match, then the inferences and evaluations that make up the label of competent communicator (in this case, friendly, trustworthy, assertive) are attributed to the person observed. If only some of the behaviors match, then the inference of competence is diminished proportionately. Certain behaviors in any given encounter also may be weighted in their importance to the impression. When judging whether or not someone is being deceptive, for example, many people would rely most heavily on that person's eye contact, relative to other behaviors, in assessing his or her competence.

5c. As Actor's normative reciprocity of positive affect and compensation of negative affect increases, Co-actor's impression of Actor's competence increases. Reciprocity implies a matching or similarity of response, whereas compensation suggests an opposite or homeostatic response. Research indicates that across most types of relationships and encounters, interactants are generally considered more competent when they reciprocate positive affect and feel more competent when they compensate for negative affect (Andersen, 1998; Spitzberg, 1989). To the extent that Co-actor expresses positive affect, the Actor's response in kind is likely to produce more positive impressions. When the Co-

Figure 2 *A simplified cognitive prototype of a competent communicator*

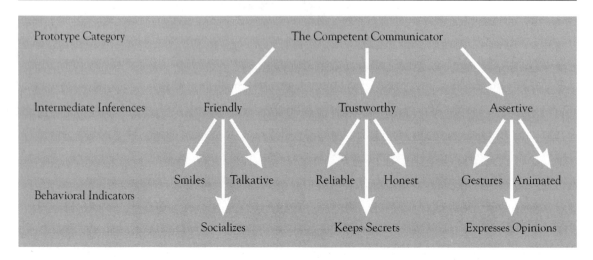

actor expresses negative affect, the Actor is likely to be more competent, responding with more neutral or positive affect.

5d. As Actor's normative compensation of power relations increases, the more Co-actor's impression of Actor's competence increases. Across most types of interpersonal relationships, complementary power relationships tend to produce higher impressions of competence. This is obviously an overstatement in many ways. For example, optimal negotiation outcomes tend to result when parties begin with a competitive and end up in a cooperative orientation. Still, this principle is useful in most types of relations.

Specifically, dominance is more competently met with passivity, and passivity with dominance, than vice versa. The validity of this proposition is best illustrated by considering its alternative. Imagine, for example, reciprocal dominance in work relationships in which every time a superior gives a subordinate orders, the superior is met with counterorders or refusal. Imagine symmetric passivity in married couples in which neither person ever actually makes a decision. In other words, relationships and encounters tend to work more smoothly and comfortably when dominant moves are responded to with complementary passive moves, and passive moves are met with more directive moves. This does not imply

that people should adopt a role of passivity or dominance, but that, in general, on a statement-by-statement basis, most interaction will be viewed as competent to the extent that its power balance is complementary rather than reciprocal.

This section has examined the episodic system of intercultural competence. Specifically, the propositions in this section have involved those characteristics of an Actor that increase the likelihood that Co-actor views Actor as competent in a given episode of interaction. The following section concerns an abbreviated excursion into the relational system, in which characteristics that facilitate competence across the life span of a relationship are considered.

RELATIONAL SYSTEM

Relationships are not simply sums of episodes over time. Certainly, the more competent the average episode of interaction, the more relationally stable and satisfying the relationship is likely to be. In this sense, the logic of the individual system and episodic system also extends to the relational system. However, other factors are at work, and the following section examines some of these features. In this discussion, the phrase "relational competence" refers to the level of communicative quality in an established relationship.

6. As Mutual Fulfillment of Autonomy and Intimacy Needs Increases, Relational Competence Increases

Autonomy and intimacy are two fundamental human needs (McAdams, 1988). Typically, they exist in a form of dialectical tension: Both "struggle" for dominance over the other at any given time, but both are ever-present to some degree. The need for intimacy involves the desire for human contact, connection, belonging, inclusion, camaraderie, communal activity, and nurturance. The need for autonomy, in contrast, is a need for self-control, independence, power, privacy, and solitude. Individuals seem to fluctuate between these two needs over time. And, as with virtually all needs, as each need is fulfilled, it ceases to dominate the individual's behavior. A lonely person continuously thinks about companionship. Once companionship is found, other needs begin to influence this person's thoughts and actions. It follows that if a relationship is competent over the course of its life span, then the members need to fulfill the needs of each other as these dialectical needs fluctuate (Spitzberg, 1993).

7. As Mutual Attraction Increases, Relational Competence Increases

This highly intuitive proposition simply indicates that as partners grow more and more attracted to each other, the more this is likely to reflect and result in mutually competent interaction over time (Eagly, Ashmore, Makhijani, & Longo, 1991). This proposition gains support from the consistent finding that attraction is closely associated, at least initially, with interpersonal similarity (Feingold, 1988). Highly similar persons provide a worldview of similar values and orientations, as well as similar communication skills that facilitate interaction (Burleson & Denton, 1992). In general, we enjoy interacting with those who are similar because they seem to "speak our language." One implication is that initial interactions with culturally dissimilar others should focus on areas of similarity that can support sufficient motivation and reinforcement for continued interaction. This is not to imply that differences are always negatively reinforcing. However, differences tend to make the *process* of communication more effortful and difficult, and thereby generally less rewarding.

8. As Mutual Trust Increases, Relational Competence Increases

Similar to the above proposition, the more partners trust one another, the more competent interaction is likely to be, and the more competent the relationship is likely to be (Canary & Spitzberg, 1989). Trust provides a context in which interaction can be more honest, spontaneous, direct, and open. Over time, such a trusting climate is likely to be mutually reinforcing and lead to a productive and satisfying communicative relationship.

9. As Access to Social Support Increases, Relational Competence Increases

Social support is anything offered by another that assists a person in coping with problematic or stressful situations. Types of support range from the tangible (e.g., lending money) to the informational (e.g., offering advice) to the emotional (e.g., comforting words). Because stresses stimulate personal and often relational crises, anything that diminishes the effects of these stresses is likely to enhance the person's ability to manage the relationship itself. One of the common problems of sojourner couples or families is that the stresses of being in a new culture often cannot be resolved by the social support of a friendship network because it has yet to be established in the new culture.

10. As Relational Network Integration Increases, Relational Competence Increases

When discussing relationships, it is ironically easy to forget that individuals are always simultaneously members of multiple relationships. When two people come together and form a relationship, part of what determines the competence of this relationship is the extent to which each member's personal network integrates with the other person's network of social relationships. Increasingly, as businesses become multinational and move entire management teams to work with labor in other countries, the problems of social network integration will become substantial. The development of common activities and goals that require cooperation or interaction across social networks, and the development of easier access to the network, are likely to facilitate this aspect of intercultural competence.

CONCLUSIONS

Before examining the implications of this essay, an important qualification needs to be considered. Specifically, most of the propositions presented here have what can be considered upper limits. Basically, too much of a good thing can be bad. For example, someone can be *too* motivated, be *too* analytical or knowledgeable, use *too* much expressiveness, or be *too* composed. Virtually any piece of advice, when carried to extremes, tends to lose its functional value. This can be viewed as a *curvilinearity principle*. In essence, as motivation, knowledge, and skill increase, so do impressions of competence, to a point, after which the relationship reverses, and competence impressions decrease.

Sir Karl Popper, an eminent philosopher of science, has warned that theories are only useful if they are in danger of failing. Theories that tell us what we already know must be true, tell us nothing. The point is that theories are only valuable to the extent they make risky predictions that may be disproved. It is in this sense that this essay must be viewed with caution.

Within this cautionary frame, one of the obvious, yet often ignored, lessons is the interdependence of adaptation. It is often assumed, for example, that host cultures possess a position of dominant status, and that visitors or immigrants must bear the responsibility of adapting to the host culture. Ultimately, however, competence in any encounter is contingent on all parties to the interaction. You can be highly motivated, knowledgeable and skilled, and if the co-actors of another culture reject your legitimacy, there may be little chance of a competent interaction (Bourhis, Moïse, Perreault, & Senécal, 1997). The responsibility of adaptation is best shared if competence is a preferred mode of interaction.

The predictions offered in this essay represent statements that, in the daily interplay of lives, are often in danger of being false. None of the predictions should be considered absolutely true or an infallible view of the complex canvas of intercultural relations. Nevertheless, progress in the develop-

ment of knowledge results from such risky propositions, and this essay has attempted to chart a path to progress. In doing so, I have attempted to paint with broad brush strokes the outline of a theory of intercultural competence. The lines of this theory are strained by their abstraction to the point of no longer resembling the vibrant landscape they are meant to represent. Thus, like any theory or work of abstract art, the key is that the benefactor will find some significant personal meaning in it and be ever mindful that the symbol is not the thing to which it refers.

References

Andersen, P. A. (1998). The cognitive valence theory of intimate communication. In M. T. & G. A. Barnett (Eds.), *Progress in communication sciences* (Vol. 14, pp. 39–72). Stamford, CT: Ablex.

Bandura, A. (1982). Self-efficacy mechanism in human agency. *American Psychologist, 37,* 122–147.

Bourhis, R. Y., Moïse, L. C., Perreault, S., & Senécal, S. (1997). Towards an interactive acculturation model: A social psychological approach. *International Journal of Psychology, 32,* 369–386.

Bradford, L., Allen, M., & Beisser, K. (1998, April). *An evaluation and meta-analysis of intercultural communication competence research.* Paper presented at the Central States Communication Association Conference, Chicago, IL.

Burleson, B. R., & Denton, W. H. (1992). A new look at similarity and attraction in marriage: Similarities in social-cognitive and communication skills as predictors of attraction and satisfaction. *Communication Monographs, 59,* 268–287.

Canary, D. J., & Spitzberg, B. H. (1989). A model of the perceived competence of conflict strategies. *Human Communication Research, 15,* 630–649.

Eagly, A. H., Ashmore, R. D., Makhijani, M. G., & Longo, L. C. (1991). What is beautiful is good, but . . . : A meta-analytic review of research on the physical attractiveness stereotype. *Psychological Bulletin, 110,* 109–128.

Feingold, A. (1988). Matching for attractiveness in romantic partners and same-sex friends: A meta-analysis and theoretical critique. *Psychological Bulletin, 104,* 226–235.

Greene, J. O. (1984). A cognitive approach to human communication: An action assembly theory. *Communication Monographs, 51,* 289–300.

Havighurst, R. J. (1957). The social competence of middle-aged people. *Genetic Psychology Monographs, 56,* 297–375.

Hoelter, J. W. (1985). A structural theory of personal consistency. *Social Psychology Quarterly, 48,* 118–129.

Imahori, T. T., & Lanigan, M. L. (1989). Relational model of intercultural communication competence. *International Journal of Intercultural Relations, 13,* 269–286.

Kaplowitz, S. A. (1978). Towards a systematic theory of power attribution. *Social Psychology, 41,* 131–148.

Kellerman, K., & Shea, B. C. (1996). Threats, suggestions, hints, and promises: Gaining compliance efficiently and politely. *Communication Quarterly, 44,* 145–165.

Lustig, M. W., & Spitzberg, B. H. (1993). Methodological issues in the study of intercultural communication competence. In R. L. Wiseman & J. Koester (Eds.), *Intercultural communication competence* (pp. 153–167). Newbury Park, CA: Sage.

McAdams, D. P. (1988). Personal needs and personal relationships. In S. Duck (Ed.), *Handbook of personal relationships: Theory, research and interventions* (pp. 7–22). New York: John Wiley & Sons.

Mendleson, J. L., Bures, A. L., Champion, D. L., & Lott, J. K. (1997). Preliminary development of the intercultural tolerance scale. *Psychological Reports, 80,* 867–876.

Neuliep, J. W., & McCroskey, J. C. (1997). The development of intercultural and interethnic communication apprehension scales. *Communication Research Reports, 14,* 145–156.

Osgood, C. E., May, W. H., & Miron, S. (1975). *Cross-cultural universals of affective meaning.* Urbana: University of Illinois Press.

Pavitt, C. & Haight, L. (1985). The "competent communicator" as a cognitive prototype. *Human Communication Research, 12,* 225–241.

Spitzberg, B. H. (1989). Issues in the development of a theory of interpersonal competence in the intercultural context. *International Journal of Intercultural Relations, 13,* 241–268.

———. (1993). The dialectics of (in)competence. *Journal of Social and Personal Relationships, 10,* 137–158.

———, & Brunner, C. C. (1991). Toward a theoretical integration of context and competence inference research. *Western Journal of Speech Communication, 55,* 28–46.

———, & Cupach, W. R. (1984). *Interpersonal communication competence.* Beverly Hills, CA: Sage.

———, & Cupach, W. R. (1989). *Handbook of interpersonal competence research.* New York: Springer-Verlag.

Concepts and Questions

1. What does Spitzberg mean when he says intercultural competence must be viewed as the social evaluation of behavior?

2. What are the individual, episodic, and relational systems of analysis?

3. What is the relationship between communicator motivation and intercultural communication competence?

4. What is communicator approach disposition, and how does it relate to intercultural communication competence?

5. What is task-relevant procedural knowledge, and how does it relate to intercultural communication competence?

6. How does an actor's communicative status affect interaction? How does it relate to improved communication competence?

7. What are valued outcomes, and how do they affect actors and co-actors?

8. What is relational competence?

9. How does mutual attraction affect relational competence?

10. How can you make personal use of Spitzberg's model of intercultural communication competence?

Managing Intercultural Conflicts Effectively

STELLA TING-TOOMEY

Conflict is inevitable in all social and personal relationships. The Latin root words for conflict, "com" and "fligere," mean "together" and "to strike" or more simply, "to strike together." Conflict connotes a state of dissonance or collision between two forces or systems. This state of dissonance can be expressed either overtly or subtly. In the context of intercultural encounters, *conflict* is defined in this article as the perceived and/or actual incompatibility of values, expectations, processes, or outcomes between two or more parties from different cultures over substantive and/or relational issues. Such differences oftentimes are expressed through different cultural conflict styles. Intercultural conflict typically starts off with miscommunication. Intercultural miscommunication often leads to misinterpretations and pseudoconflict. If the miscommunication goes unmanaged or unclarified, however, it can become actual interpersonal conflict.

This article is developed in three sections: (1) A cultural variability perspective which emphasizes identity construal variations, low-context versus high-context, and monochronic and polychronic time patterns is presented; (2) assumptions and factors leading to conflict induced by violations of expectations are explained; and (3) effective conflict-management skills in managing intercultural conflicts are discussed.

A CULTURAL VARIABILITY PERSPECTIVE

To understand differences and similarities in communication across cultures, it is necessary to have a framework to explain why and how cultures are dif-

This original essay first appeared in the seventh edition. All rights reserved. Permission to reprint must be obtained from the author and the publisher. Dr. Ting-Toomey is a professor at California State University, Fullerton.

ferent or similar. A cultural variability perspective refers to how cultures vary on a continuum of variations in accordance with some basic dimensions or core value characteristics. While there are many dimensions in which cultures differ, one that has received consistent attention from both cross-cultural communication researchers and psychologists around the world is individualism–collectivism. Countless cross-cultural studies (Chinese Culture Connection, 1987; Gudykunst & Ting-Toomey, 1988; Hofstede, 1980, 1991; Hui & Triandis, 1986; Schwartz & Bilsky, 1990; Triandis, Brislin, & Hui, 1988; Wheeler, Reis, & Bond, 1989) have provided theoretical and empirical evidence that the value orientations of individualism and collectivism are pervasive in a wide range of cultures. Ting-Toomey and associates (Ting-Toomey, 1988, 1991; Ting-Toomey, Gao, Trubisky, Yang, Kim, Lin, & Nishida, 1991; Trubisky, Ting-Toomey, & Lin, 1991) related individualism–collectivism to conflict styles, providing clear research evidence that the role of cultural variability is critical in influencing cross-cultural conflict negotiation process.

The cultural socialization process influences individuals' basic assumptions and expectations, as well as their process and outcome orientations in different types of conflict situations. The dimension of individualism–collectivism, as existing on a continuum of value tendency differences, can be used as a beginning point to understand some of the basic differences and similarities in individualistic-based or group-based cultures. Culture is defined as a system of knowledge, meanings, and symbolic actions that is shared by the majority of the people in a society.

INDIVIDUALISM–COLLECTIVISM VALUE TENDENCIES

Basically, *individualism* refers to the broad value tendencies of a culture to emphasize the importance of individual identity over group identity, individual rights over group rights, and individual needs over group needs. In contrast, *collectivism* refers to the broad value tendencies of a culture to emphasize the importance of the "we" identity over the "I" identity, group obligations over individual rights, and in-group–oriented needs over individual wants and desires. An *in-group* is a group whose values, norms, and rules are deemed as salient to the effective functioning of the group in the society and these norms serve as the guiding criteria for everyday behaviors. On the other hand, an *outgroup* is a group whose values, norms, and rules are viewed as inconsistent with those of the in-group and these norms are assigned a low priority from the in-group standard. Macrolevel factors such as ecology, affluence, social and geographic mobility, migration, cultural background of parents, socialization, rural or urban environment, mass media exposure, education, and social change have been identified by Triandis (1988, 1990) as some of the underlying factors that contribute to the development of individualist and collectivistic values. High individualistic values have been found in the United States, Australia, Great Britain, Canada, the Netherlands, and New Zealand. High collectivistic values have been uncovered in Indonesia, Colombia, Venezuela, Panama, Equador, and Guatemala (Hofstede, 1991). In intercultural communication research (Gudykunst & Ting-Toomey, 1988), Australia, Canada, and the United States have been identified consistently as cultures high in individualistic value tendencies, while strong empirical evidence has supported that China, Taiwan, Korea, Japan, and Mexico can be identified clearly as collectivistic, group-based cultures. Within each culture, different ethnic communities can also display distinctive individualistic and collectivistic value tendencies. For example, members of first-generation, Asian immigrant cultures in the United States may retain some basic group-oriented value characteristics.

The core building block of individualism–collectivism is its relative emphasis on the importance of the "autonomous self" or the "connected self" orientation. In using the terms "independent construal of self" and "interdependent construal of self" to represent individualist versus group-oriented identity, Markus and Kitayama (1991) argue that the placement of our sense of self-concept in our culture has a profound influence on our communication with others. They argue that the sense of individuality that accompanies this "independent construal of self" includes a sense of

oneself as an agent, as a producer of one's actions. One is conscious of being in control over the surrounding situation, and of the need to express one's own thoughts, feelings, and actions of others. Such acts of standing out are often intrinsically rewarding because they elicit pleasant, ego-focused emotions (e.g., pride) and also reduce unpleasant ones (e.g., frustration). Furthermore, the acts of standing out, themselves, form an important basis of self-esteem. (p. 246)

Conversely, the self-concept that accompanies an "interdependent construal of self" includes an

attentiveness and responsiveness to others that one either explicitly or implicitly assumes will be reciprocated by these others, as well as the willful management of one's other-focused feelings and desires so as to maintain and further the reciprocal interpersonal relationship. One is conscious of where one belongs with respect to others and assumes a receptive stance toward these others, continually adjusting and accommodating to these others in many aspects of behavior. Such acts of fitting in and accommodating are often intrinsically rewarding, because they give rise to pleasant, other-focused emotions (e.g., feeling of connection), while diminishing unpleasant ones (e.g., shame) and, furthermore, because the self-restraint required in doing so forms an important basis of self-esteem. (p. 246)

Thus, the cultural variability of independent versus interdependent construal of self frames our existential experience and serves as an anchoring point in terms of how we view our communicative actions and ourselves. For example, if we follow an independent construal of self-orientation, our communicative action will tend to be more self-focused, more ego-based, and more self-expressive. Concurrently, the value we place on particular self-conception also influences the criteria we use to perceive and evaluate others' communicative actions. To illustrate, if we follow an interdependent construal of self-orientation, we will tend to use group norms, group interests, and group responsibilities to interpret and evaluate others' conflict behaviors. Overall, the cultural variability dimension of individualism–collectivism and the independent and interdependent construal of self help us to "make sense" or explain why people in some cultures prefer certain approaches or modes of conflict negotiation than people in other cultures.

LOW CONTEXT AND HIGH CONTEXT

In addition to individualism–collectivism, Edward T. Hall's (1976, 1983) low-context and high-context communication framework helps to enrich our understanding of the role of communication in individualistic and collectivistic cultures. According to Hall (1976), human transaction can be basically divided into low-context and high-context communication systems:

> HC [High Context] transactions featured preprogrammed information that is in the receiver and in the setting, with only minimal information in the transmitted message. LC [Low Context] transactions are the reverse. Most of the information must be in the transmitted message in order to make up what is missing in the context. (p. 101)

Although no one culture exists exclusively at one extreme of the communication context continuum, in general, low-context communication refers to communication patterns of linear logic interaction approach, direct verbal interaction style, overt intention expressions, and sender-oriented value (Ting-Toomey, 1985). High-context communication refers to communication patterns of spiral logic interaction approach, indirect verbal negotiation mode, subtle nonverbal nuances, responsive intention inference, and interpreter-sensitive value (Ting-Toomey, 1985). Low-context (LC) communication patterns have been typically found in individualistic cultures and high-context (HC) communication patterns have been typically uncovered in collectivistic cultures.

For individualistic, LC communicators, the bargaining resources in conflict typically revolve around individual pride and self-esteem, individual ego-based emotions, and individual sense of autonomy and power. For collectivistic, HC interactants, the negotiation resources in conflict typically revolve around relational "face" maintenance and group harmony, group-oriented status and self-esteem, face-related emotions, and reciprocal sense of favors and obligations. For individualistic, LC negotiators, con-

flict typically arises because of incompatible personalities, beliefs, or goal orientations. For collectivistic, HC negotiators, conflict typically arises because of incompatible facework or relational management.

The concept of face is tied closely to the need people have to a claimed sense of self-respect in any social interactive situations (Ting-Toomey, 1985, 1988, 1994; Ting-Toomey & Cole, 1990). As human beings, we all like to be respected and feel approved in our everyday communicative behaviors. However, how we manage face and how we negotiate "face loss" and "face gain" in a conflict episode differs from one culture to the next. As Cohen (1991) observes:

> Given the importance of face, the members of collectivistic cultures are highly sensitive to the effect of what they say on others. Language is a social instrument—a device for preserving and promoting social interests as much as a means for transmitting information. [Collectivistic], high-context speakers must weigh their words carefully. They know that whatever they say will be scrutinized and taken to heart. Face-to-face conversations contain many emollient expressions of respect and courtesy alongside a substantive element rich in meaning and low in redundancy. Directness and especially contradiction are much disliked. It is hard for speakers in this kind of culture to deliver a blunt "no." (p. 26)

M-TIME AND P-TIME

Finally, the concept of time in the conflict-negotiation process also varies in accordance with the individualism–collectivism dimension. Time is reflective of the psychological and the emotional environment in which communication occurs. Time flies when two friends are enjoying themselves and having a good time. Time crawls when two enemies stare at each other and have nothing more to say to one another. Time influences the tempos and pacings of the developmental sequences of a conflict-negotiation session. It also influences the substantive ideas that are being presented in a conflict-bargaining episode.

Hall (1983) distinguished two patterns of time that govern the individualistic and collectivistic cultures: Monochronic Time Schedule (M-time) and Polychronic Time Schedule (P-time). According to Hall (1983):

> P-time stresses involvement of people and completion of transactions rather than adherence to preset schedules. Appointments are not taken as seriously and, as a consequence, are frequently broken. P-time is treated as less tangible than M-time. For polychronic people, time is seldom experienced as "wasted," and is apt to be considered a point rather than a ribbon or a road, but that point is often sacred. (p. 46)

For Hall (1983), Latin American, Middle Eastern, African, Asian, French, and Greek cultures are representatives of P-time patterns, while Northern European, North American, and German cultures are representatives of M-time patterns. M-time patterns appear to predominate in individualistic, low-context cultures, and P-time patterns appear to predominate in group-based, high-context cultures. People [who] follow individualistic, M-time patterns usually compartmentalize time schedules to serve individualistic-based needs, and they tend to separate task-oriented time from socioemotional time. In addition, they are more future-conscious of time than centered in the present or the past. People who follow collectivistic, P-time patterns tend to hold more fluid attitudes toward time schedules, and they tend to integrate task-oriented activity with socioemotional activity. In addition, they are more past and present-conscious than future-oriented.

Members of individualistic, M-time cultures tend to view time as something that can be possessed, drained, and wasted, while members of collectivistic, P-time cultures tend to view time as more contextually based and relationally oriented. For individualistic, M-time people, conflict should be contained, controlled, and managed effectively within certain frames or within certain preset schedules. For collectivistic, P-time people, the clock time in resolving conflict is not as important as in taking the time to really know the conflict parties who are involved in the dispute. For P-time individuals, the time spent in synchronizing the implicit interactional rhythms between people is much more important than any preset, objective timetable.

In sum, in individualistic cultures, people typically practice "I" identity-based values, low-context direct interaction, and M-time negotiation schedules. In collectivistic cultures, people typically treasure "we" identity-based values, high-context indirect interaction, and P-time negotiation rhythms.

VIOLATIONS OF CONFLICT EXPECTATIONS

Drawing from the key ideas of the cultural variability perspective, we can now apply these concepts to understanding the specific conflict assumptions, conflict issues and process factors, and the conflict interaction styles that contribute to intercultural miscommunication or intercultural conflict.[1] When individuals from two contrastive cultures meet one another especially for the first time, they typically communicate out of their culturally based assumptions and beliefs, stereotypic images of each other, and habitual communication patterns. These assumptions create expectations for others' conflict behavior.

It is inevitable that we hold anticipations or expectations of how others should or should not behave in any communicative situation. These expectations, however, are grounded in the social norms of the culture and also depend on the symbolic meanings individuals assign to behaviors (Burgoon, 1991). Intercultural miscommunication or intercultural conflict often occurs because of violations of normative expectations in a communication episode. Expectation violations occur frequently, especially if one party comes from an individualistic-based culture and the other party comes from a collectivistic-based culture.

CULTURAL CONFLICT ASSUMPTIONS

Different cultural value assumptions exist as the metaconflict issues in framing any intercultural conflict episode. Based on the individualism–collectivism dimension, we can delineate several cultural assumptions concerning LC and HC communicators' basic attitudes toward conflict. For individualistic, LC communicators, conflict typically follows a "problem-solving" model: (1) Conflict is viewed as an expressed struggle to air out major differences and problems; (2) conflict can be both dysfunctional and functional; (3) conflict can be dysfunctional when it is repressed and not directly confronted; (4) conflict can be functional when it provides an open opportunity for solving problematic issues; (5) substantive and relational issues in conflict should be handled separately; (6) conflict should be dealt with openly and directly; and (7) effective management of conflict can be viewed as a win-win problem-solving game.

For the collectivistic, HC interactants, their underlying assumptions of conflict follow a "face maintenance" model: (1) Conflict is viewed as damaging to social face and relational harmony and should be avoided as much as possible; (2) conflict is, for the most part, dysfunctional; (3) conflict signals a lack of self-discipline and self-censorship of emotional outbursts, and hence, a sign of emotional immaturity; (4) conflict provides a testing ground for a skillful facework negotiation process; (5) substantive conflict and relational face issues are always intertwined; (6) conflict should be dealt with discreetly and subtly; and (7) effective management of conflict can be viewed as a win-win face negotiation game.

From the conflict as a "problem-solving" model, conflict is viewed as potentially functional, personally liberating, and an open forum for "struggling against" or "struggling with" one another in wrestling with the conflict issues at hand. From the conflict as a "face maintenance" model, conflict is viewed as primarily dysfunctional, interpersonally embarrassing and distressing, and a forum for potential group-related face loss and face humiliation. These fundamental cultural conflict assumptions influence the mindsets and attitudinal level of the conflict parties in terms of how they should approach an interpersonal conflict episode. Appropriate and inappropriate conflict behaviors, in short, are grounded in the basic value assumptions of the cultural conflict socialization process.

CONFLICT ISSUES AND PROCESS VIOLATIONS

Every conflict entails both substantive and relational issues. Individualistic conflict negotiators typically attend to the objective; substantive issues more than the relational, socioemotional issues. Collectivistic conflict negotiators, in contrast, typically attune to the relational, affective dimension as the key issue in resolving task-related or procedural-related conflict. When collectivistic communicators are in sync with one another and their nonverbal rhythms harmonize with one another, peaceful resolutions can potentially follow. When individualistic communicators are able to rationalize the separation of the people from the problems, and emphasize compartmentalizing affective issues and substantive issues, conflict can be functional.

In reviewing diplomatic negotiation case studies between individualistic, low-context (United States) and collectivistic, high-context (China, Egypt, India, Japan, and Mexico) cultures, Cohen (1991) concludes:

> Individualistic, low-context negotiators can be described as primarily problem oriented and have the definition of the problem and the clarification of alternative solutions uppermost in their thoughts, [collectivistic] high-context negotiators are seen to be predominantly relationship oriented. For them, negotiation is less about solving problems (although, obviously, this aspect cannot be dismissed) than about attending a relationship. For interdependent cultures it is not a conflict that is resolved but a relationship that is mended. . . . In international relations the consequence is concern both with the international relationship and with the personal ties between the interlocutors. (p. 51)

In individualistic, LC cultures such as Australia and the United States, control of one's autonomy, freedom, territory, and individual boundary is of paramount importance to one's sense of self-respect and ego. In collectivistic, HC cultures such as Japan and Korea, being accepted by one's in-group members and being approved by one's superiors, peers, and/or family members is critical to the development of one's sense of self-respect. Thus, conflict issues in individualistic cultures typically arise through the violation of autonomous space, privacy, individual power, and sense of individual fairness and equity. In collectivistic cultures, conflict issues typically revolve around the violation of in-group or outgroup boundaries, norms of group loyalty and commitment, and reciprocal obligations and trust.

In terms of different goal orientations in intercultural conflict, individualists' conflict-management techniques typically emphasize a win–win goal orientation and the importance of a tangible outcome action plan. For collectivists, typically time and energy are invested in negotiating face loss, face gain, and face protection issues throughout the various developmental phases of conflict. While individualists tend to be highly goal or result-oriented in conflict management, collectivists tend to emphasize heavily the relational or facework process of conflict resolution. This collectivistic conflict facework negotiation process can also take place beyond the immediate conflict situation.

Several writers (Cohen, 1991; Leung, 1987, 1988; Ting-Toomey, 1985) indicate that collectivists tend to display a stronger preference for informal third-party conflict mediation procedure than individualists. For example, for the Chinese culture, conflict typically is diffused through the use of third-party intermediaries. However, there exists a key difference in the use of third-party mediation between the individualistic, Western cultures and the collectivistic, Asian cultures. In the Western cultures, conflict parties tend to seek help with an impartial third-party mediator (such as a professional mediator or family therapist). In many Asian cultures, conflict parties typically seek the help of an older (and hence assumed to be wiser) person who is related to both parties. It is presumed that the informal mediator has a richer database to arbitrate the conflict outcome. Expectations may be violated when an individualistic culture sends an impartial third party to arbitrate an international conflict with no prior relationship-building sessions. Conflict-process violations also arise if an individualistic culture sends an intermediary that is perceived to be of lower ranking or lower status than the representative negotiators of the collectivistic culture. Conversely, a collectivistic culture tends to violate the individualistic fairness norm when it sends an "insider" or in-group person to monitor or arbitrate the conflict outcome situation.

The concept of power in a conflict-negotiation situation also varies from an individualistic culture to a collectivistic culture. Power, in the context of individualistic culture, often means tangible resources of rewards and punishments that one conflict party has over another. Power, in the context of collectivistic culture, often refers to intangible resources such as face loss and face gain, losing prestige or gaining reputation, and petty-mindedness versus benevolent generosity as displayed in the conflict anxiety-provoking situation.

Finally, the interpretation of conflict-resolution rhythm also varies along the individualism–collectivism dimension. For individualistic, M-time people, conflict-resolution processes should follow a clear agenda of opening, expressing conflicting interests, negotiating, and closing sequences. For collectivistic, P-time people, conflict facework processes have no clear beginning and no clear end. For M-time individuals, conflict-resolution time should be filled with decision-making activities. For P-time individuals, time is a "being" construct that is governed by the implicit rhythms in the interaction between people. While M-time negotiators tend to emphasize agenda setting, objective criteria, and immediate, future-oriented goals in the conflict-negotiation process, P-time negotiators typically like to take time to engage in small talk, to delve into family or personal affairs, and also to bring in the historical past to shed light on the present conflict situation. As Cohen (1991) observes:

> [North] Americans, then, are mostly concerned with addressing immediate issues and moving on to new challenges, and they display little interest in (and sometimes little knowledge of) history. The idea that something that occurred hundreds of years ago might be relevant to a pressing problem is almost incomprehensible. . . . In marked contrast, the representatives of non-Western societies possess a pervasive sense of the past. . . . This preoccupation with history, deeply rooted in the consciousness of traditional societies, cannot fail to influence diplomacy. Past humiliations for these societies (which are highly sensitive to any slight on their reputations) are not consigned to the archives but continue to nourish present concerns. (p. 29)

The arbitrary division of clock time or calendar time holds little meaning for collectivistic, P-time people. For them, a deadline, in one sense, is only an arbitrary human construct. For P-time individuals, a deadline is always subject to revision and renegotiation. Graceful handling of time pressure is viewed as much more important than a sense of forceful urgency. In sum, people move with different conflict rhythms in conflict-negotiation sessions. For M-time individuals, a sense of timeline and closure-orientation predominate their mode of conflict resolution. For P-time individuals, a sense of the relational commitment and synchronized relational rhythm signal the beginning stage of a long-term, conflict-bargaining process.

Expectation violations often occur when a person from an individualistic culture engages a person from a collectivistic culture in an interpersonal conflict situation. Different cultural conflict assumptions lead to different attitudes toward how to approach a basic conflict episode. Miscommunication often gives rise to escalatory conflict spirals or prolonged misunderstandings. While common feelings of anxiety, frustration, ambivalence, and a sense of emotional vulnerability typically exist in individuals in any conflict situation, how we go about handling this sense of emotional vulnerability varies from one culture to the next. Individualists and collectivists typically collide over their substantive orientation versus relational face maintenance orientation; goal orientation versus process orientation; formal versus informal third-party consultation process; tangible versus intangible power resources; and different time rhythms that undergird the conflict episode. In addition, the verbal and nonverbal messages they engage in, and the distinctive conflict styles they carry with them can severely influence the overall outcome of the conflict dissonance process.

CROSS-CULTURAL CONFLICT INTERACTION STYLES

In a conflict situation, individualists typically rely heavily on direct requests, direct verbal justifications, and upfront clarifications to defend one's action or decision. In contrast, collectivist typically use qualifiers ("Perhaps we should meet this deadline together"), tag questions ("Don't you think we might not have enough time"), disclaimers ("I'm probably wrong but . . . "), tangential response ("Let's not worry about that now"), and indirect requests ("If it won't be too much trouble, let's try to finish this report together") to make a point in the subtle, conflict face-threatening situation. From the collectivis-

tic orientation, it is up to the interpreter of the message to pick up the hidden meaning or intention of the message and to respond either indirectly or equivocally. In addition, in an intense conflict situation, many collectivists believe that verbal messages can oftentimes compound the problem. However, by not using verbal means to explain or clarify a decision, collectivists are often viewed as "inscrutable."

Silence is viewed as demanding immense self-discipline in a collectivistic conflict situation. On the other hand, silence can be viewed as an admission of guilt or incompetence in an individualistic culture. In addition, while open emotional expression during a stressful conflict situation oftentimes is viewed as a signal of caring in an individualistic culture, proper emotional composure and emotional self-restraint are viewed as signals of a mature, self-disciplined person in most collectivistic, Asian cultures. In comparing verbal and nonverbal exchange processes in Japan and the United States, Okabe (1983) summarizes:

> The digital is more characteristic of the [North] American mode of communication. . . . The Japanese language is more inclined toward the analogical; its use of ideographic characters . . . and its emphasis on the nonverbal aspect. The excessive dependence of the Japanese on the nonverbal aspect of communication means that Japanese culture tends to view the verbal as only a means of communication, and that the nonverbal and the extra-verbal at times assume greater importance than the verbal dimension of communication. This is in sharp contrast to the view of Western rhetoric and communication that the verbal, especially speech, is the dominant means of expression. (p. 38)

In short, in the individualistic cultures, the conflict-management process relies heavily on verbal offense and defense to justify one's position, to clarify one's opinion, to build up one's credibility, to articulate one's emotions, and to raise objections if one disagrees with someone else's proposal. In collectivistic conflict situations, ambiguous, indirect verbal messages often are used with the intention of saving mutual face, saving group face, or protecting someone else's face. In addition, subtle nonverbal gestures or nonverbal silence is often used to signal a sense of cautionary restraint toward the conflict situation.

The use of deep-level silence can also reflect a sense of resignation and acceptance of the fatalistic aspect of the conflict situation. The higher the person is in positional power in a collectivistic culture, the more likely she or he will use silence as a deliberate, cautionary conflict strategy.

In terms of the relationship between the norm of fairness and cross-cultural conflict interaction style, results from past research (Leung & Bond, 1984; Leung & Iwawaki, 1988) indicate that individualists typically prefer to use the equity norm (self-deservingness norm) in dealing with reward allocation in group conflict interaction. In comparison, collectivists oftentimes prefer to use the equality norm (the equal distribution norm) to deal with in-group members and thus avoid group disharmony. However, like their individualistic cohorts, collectivists prefer the application of the equity norm (the self-deservingness norm) when competing with members of outgroups, especially when the conflict involves competition for scarce resources in the system.

Findings in many past conflict studies also indicate that individuals do exhibit quite consistent cross-situational styles of conflict negotiation in different cultures. While dispositional, relationship, or conflict salient factors also play a critical part in conflict-management patterns, culture assumes the primary role of conflict-style socialization process. Based on the theoretical assumptions of the "I" identity and the "we" identity, and the concern of self-face maintenance versus mutual-face maintenance in the two contrastive cultural systems, findings across cultures (China, Japan, Korea, Taiwan, Mexico, and the United States) clearly indicate that individualists tend to use competitive control conflict styles in managing conflict, while collectivists tend to use integrative or compromising conflict styles in dealing with conflict. In addition, collectivists also tend to use more obliging and avoiding conflict styles in task-oriented conflict situations (Chua & Gudykunst, 1987; Leung, 1988; Ting-Toomey et al., 1991; Trubisky, Ting-Toomey, & Lin, 1991).

Different results have also been uncovered concerning in-group and outgroup conflict in the collectivistic cultures. For example, Cole's (1989) study reveals that Japanese students in the United States tend to use obliging strategies more with members of ingroups than with members of outgroups. They also tend to actually use more competitive strategies with outgroup members than in-group members. In addition, the status of the in-group person plays a critical role in the collectivistic conflict process.

Previous research (Ting-Toomey et al., 1991) suggests that status affects the conflict-management styles people use with members of their in-group. For example, in a collectivistic culture, while a high-status person can challenge the position or opinion of a low-status person, it is a norm violation for a low-status person to directly rebut or question the position or the opinion of the high-status person, especially in the public arena. Again, the issue of face maintenance becomes critical in high–low-status conflict interaction. The low-status person should always learn to "give face" or protect the face of the high-status person in times of stressful situations or crises. In return, the high-status person will enact a reciprocal face-protection system that automatically takes care of the low-status person in different circumstances.

Overall, the preferences for a direct conflict style, for the use of the equity norm, and for the direct settlement of disputes reflect the salience of the "I" identity in individualistic, HC cultures; while preferences for an indirect conflict style, for the use of the equality norm, and for the use of informal mediation procedures reflect the salience of the "we" identity in the collectivistic, HC cultures. In individualistic, LC cultures, a certain degree of conflict in a system is viewed as potentially functional and productive. In collectivistic, HC cultures in which group harmony and consultative decision-making are prized, overt expressions of interpersonal conflict are highly avoided and suppressed. Instead, nonverbal responsiveness, indirect verbal strategies, the use of informal intermediaries, and the use of cautionary silence are some of the typical collectivistic ways of dealing with interpersonal conflict.

EFFECTIVE CONFLICT MANAGEMENT

Effective conflict management requires us to communicate effectively, appropriately, and creatively in different conflict interactive situations. Effective conflict management requires us to be knowledgeable and respectful of different worldviews and ways of dealing with a conflict situation. It requires us to be sensitive to the differences and similarities between low-context and high-context communication patterns and to attune to the implicit negotiation rhythms of monochronic-based and polychronic-based individuals.

Effective conflict management also requires the awareness of the importance of both goal-oriented and process-oriented conflict negotiation pathways, and requires that we pay attention to the close relationship between cultural variability and different conflict communication styles. For both individualists and collectivists, the concept of "mindfulness" can serve as the first effective step in raising our awareness of the differences and similarities in cross-cultural conflict-negotiation processes. Langer's (1989) concept of mindfulness helps individuals to tune-in conscientiously to their habituated mental scripts and expectations. According to Langer, if mindlessness is the "rigid reliance on old categories, mindfulness means the continual creation of new ones. Categorization and recategorization, labeling and relabeling as one masters the world are processes natural to children" (p. 63). To engage in a mindfulness state, an individual needs to learn to (a) create new categories, (b) be open to new information, and (c) be aware that multiple perspectives typically exist in viewing a basic event (Langer, 1989, p. 62).

Creating new categories means that one should not be boxed in by one's rigid stereotypic label concerning cultural strangers. One has to learn to draw out commonalties between self and cultural strangers and also learn to appreciate the multifaceted aspects of the individuals to whom the stereotypic label is applied. In order to create new categories, one has to be open to new information. New information relies strongly on responsible sharing and responsive listening behavior.

Some specific suggestions can be made based on differences in individualistic and collectivistic styles of conflict management. These suggestions, however, are not listed in order of importance. *To deal with conflict effectively in the collectivistic culture, individualists need to:*

1. Be mindful of the face-maintenance assumptions of conflict situations that take place in this culture. Conflict competence resides in the strategic skills of managing the delicate interaction balance of humiliation and pride, and shame and honor. The face moves of one-up and one-down in a conflict episode, the use of same status negotiators, and the proprieties and decorum of gracious "face fighting" have to be strategically staged with the larger group audience in mind.

2. Be proactive in dealing with low-grade conflict situations (such as by using informal consultation or the "go between" method) before they escalate into runaway, irrevocable mutual face-loss episodes. Individualists should try to realize that by helping their opponent to save face, they might also enhance their own face. Face is, intrinsically, a bilateral concept in the group-based, collectivistic culture.

3. "Give face" and try not to push their opponent's back against the wall with any room for maneuvering face loss or face recovery. Learn to let their opponent find a gracious way out of the conflict situation if at all possible, without violating the basic spirit of fundamental human rights. They should also learn self-restraint and try not to humiliate their opponent in the public arena or slight her or his public reputation. For collectivists, the concept of "giving face" typically operates on a long-range, reciprocal interaction system. Bilateral face-giving and face-saving ensures a continuous, interdependent networking process of favor-giving and favor concessions—especially along a long-term, historical time sense.

4. Be sensitive to the importance of quiet, mindful observation. Individualists need to be mindful of the historical past that bears relevance to the present conflict situation. Restrain from asking too many "why" questions. Since collectivistic, LC cultures typically focus on the nonverbal "how" process, individualists need to learn to experience and manage the conflict process on the implicit, nonverbal pacing level. Use deep-level silence, deliberate pauses, and patient conversational turn taking in conflict interaction processes with collectivists.

5. Practice attentive listening skills and feel the co-presence of the other person. In Chinese characters, *hearing* or *wun* (聞) means "opening the door to the ears," while the word *listening* or *ting* (聽)

means attending to the other person with your "ears, eyes, and heart." Listening means, in the Chinese character, attending to the sounds, movements, and feelings of the other person. Patient and deliberate listening indicates that one person is attending to the other person's needs even if it is an antagonistic conflict situation.

6. Discard the Western-based model of effective communication skills in dealing with conflict situations in the collectivistic, HC cultures. Individualists should learn to use qualifiers, disclaimers, tag questions, and tentative statements to convey their point of view. In refusing a request, learn not to use a blunt "no" as a response because the word "no" is typically perceived as carrying high face-threat value in the collectivistic culture. Use situational or self-effacing accounts ("Perhaps someone else is more qualified than I am in working on this project"), counterquestions ("Don't you feel someone else is more competent to work on this project . . . "), or conditional statements ("Yes, but . . . ") to convey the implicit sense of refusal.

7. Let go of a conflict situation if the conflict party does not want to deal with it directly. A cooling period sometimes may help to mend a broken relationship and the substantive issue may be diluted over a period of time. Individualists should remember that avoidance is part of the integral, conflict style that is commonly used in the collectivistic, LC cultures. Avoidance does not necessarily mean that collectivists do not care to resolve the conflict. In all likelihood, the use of avoidance is strategically used to avoid face-threatening interaction and is meant to maintain face harmony and mutual face dignity.

In sum, individualists need to learn to respect the HC, collectivistic ways of approaching and handling conflicts. They need to continuously monitor their ethnocentric biases on the cognitive, affective, and behavioral reactive levels, and learn to listen attentively, and observe mindfully and reflectively.

Some specific suggestions also can be made for collectivists in handling conflict with individualists. *When encountering a conflict situation in an individualistic, LC culture, collectivists need to:*

1. Be mindful of the problem-solving assumptions. The ability to separate the relationship from the conflict problem is critical to effective conflict negotiation in an individualistic, LC culture. Collectivists need to learn to compartmentalize the task dimension and the socioemotional dimension of conflict.

2. Focus on resolving the substantive issues of the conflict, and learn to openly express opinions or points of view. Collectivists should try not to take the conflict issues to the personal level, and learn to maintain distance between the person and the conflict problem. In addition, try not to be offended by the upfront, individualistic style of managing conflict. Learn to emphasize tangible outcomes and develop concrete action plans in implementing the conflict-decision proposal.

3. Engage in an assertive, leveling style of conflict behavior. Assertive style emphasizes the rights of both individuals to speak up in a conflict situation and to respect each other's right to defend her or his position. Collectivists need to learn to open a conflict dialogue with an upfront thesis statement, and then develop the key point systematically, with examples, evidence, figures, or a well-planned proposal. In addition, collectivists need to be ready to accept criticisms, counterproposals, and suggestions for modification as part of the ongoing, group dialogue.

4. Own individual responsibility for the conflict decision-making process. Owning responsibility and using "I" statements to describe feelings in an ongoing conflict situation constitute part of effective conflict-management skills in an individualistic, LC culture. Collectivists need to learn to verbally explain a situation more fully and learn not to expect others to infer their points of view. Assume a sender-based approach to resolving conflict; ask more "why" questions and probe for explanations and details.

5. Provide verbal feedback and engage in active listening skills. Active listening skills, in the individualistic, LC culture, means collectivists have to engage in active verbal perception checking and to ensure that the other person is interpreting their points accurately. Collectivists need to use verbal paraphrases, summary statements, and interpretive messages to acknowledge and

verify the storyline of the conflict situation. Learn to occasionally self-disclose feelings and emotions; they cannot rely solely on nonverbal, intuitive understanding to "intuit" and evaluate a situation.

6. Use direct, integrative verbal messages that clearly convey their concern over both the relational and substantive issues of a conflict situation. Collectivists should also not wait patiently for clear turn-taking pauses in the conflict interaction, as individualistic conversation typically allows overlap talks, simultaneous messages, and floor-grabbing behavior. Collectivists also may not want to engage in too many deliberate silent moments as individualists will infer that as incompetence or inefficient use of time.

7. Commit to working out the conflict situation with the conflict party. Collectivists should learn to use task-oriented integrative strategies and try to work out a collaborative, mutual goal dialogue with the conflict party. Work on managing individual defensiveness and learn to build up trust on the one-to-one level of interaction. Finally, confirm the conflict person through explicit relationship reminders and metacommunication talks, while simultaneously working on resolving the conflict substantive issues, responsibly and constructively.

In sum, collectivists need to work on their ethnocentric biases as much as the individualists need to work out their sense of egocentric superiority. Collectivists need to untangle their historical sense of cultural superiority—especially in thinking that their way is the only "civilized" way to appropriately deal with conflict. Both individualists and collectivists need to be mindful of their cognitive, affective, and behavioral blinders that they bring into a conflict-mediation situation. They need to continuously learn new and novel ideas in dealing with the past, present, and the future for the purpose of building a peaceful community that is inclusive in all ethnic and cultural groups.

In being mindful of the potential differences between individualistic, LC and collectivistic, HC conflict styles, the intercultural peacemaking process can begin by affirming and valuing such differences as diverse human options in resolving some funda-

mental, human communication phenomenon. While it is not necessary that one should completely switch one's basic conflict style in order to adapt to the other person's behavior, mutual attuning and responsive behavior in signaling the willingness to learn about each other's cultural norms and rules may be a first major step toward a peaceful resolution process. In addition, conflicting parties from diverse ethnic or cultural backgrounds can learn to work on collaborative task projects and strive toward reaching a larger-than-self, community goal.

To be a peacemaker in the intercultural arena, one has to be first at peace with one's self and one's style. Thus, the artificial switching of one's style may only bring artificial results. Creative peacemakers must learn first to affirm and respect the diverse values that exist as part of the rich spectrum of the basic human experience. They may then choose to modify their behavior to adapt to the situation at hand. Finally, they may integrate diverse sets of values and behaviors, and be able to move in and out of different relational and cultural conflict boundaries. Creative peacemakers can be at ease and at home with the marginal stranger in their search toward common human peace. Peace means, on a universal level, a condition or a state of tranquility—with an absence of oppressed thoughts, feelings, and actions, from one heart to another, and from one nation state to another nation state.

Note

I want to thank Bill Gudykunst for his thoughtful suggestions on an earlier version of the manuscript.

1. Many of the ideas in this section are drawn from Ting-Toomey (in press).

References

Burgoon, J. (1991). "Applying a Comparative Approach to Expectancy Violations Theory." In J. Blumer, J. McCleod, and K. Rosengren (Eds.), *Communication and Culture Across Space and Time*. Newbury Park, CA: Sage.

Chinese Culture Connection. (1987). "Chinese Values and Search for Culture-Free Dimensions of Culture." *Journal of Cross-Cultural Psychology, 18*, 143–164.

Chua, E., and Gudykunst, W. (1987). "Conflict Resolution Style in Low- and High-Context Cultures." *Communication Research Reports, 4,* 32–37.

Cohen, R. (1991). *Negotiating Across Cultures: Communication Obstacles in International Diplomacy.* Washington, D.C.: U.S. Institute of Peace.

Cole, M. (1989, May). "Relational Distance and Personality Influence on Conflict Communication Styles." Unpublished Master's thesis. Arizona State University, Tempe, AZ.

Gudykunst, W., and Ting-Toomey, S. (1988). *Culture and Interpersonal Communication.* Newbury Park, CA: Sage.

Hall, E. T. (1976). *Beyond Culture.* New York: Doubleday.

————. (1983). *The Dance of Life.* New York: Doubleday.

Hofstede, G. (1980). *Culture's Consequences: International Differences in Work-Related Values.* Beverly Hills, CA: Sage.

————. (1991). *Cultures and Organizations: Software of the Mind.* London: McGraw-Hill.

Hui, C., and Triandis, H. (1986). "Individualism-Collectivism: A Study of Cross-Cultural Researchers." *Journal of Cross-Cultural Psychology, 17,* 225–248.

Langer, E. (1989). *Mindfulness.* Reading, MA: Addison-Wesley.

Leung, K. (1987). "Some Determinants of Reactions to Procedural Models for Conflict Resolution: A Cross-National Study." *Journal of Personality and Social Psychology, 53,* 898–908.

————. (1988). "Some Determinants of Conflict Avoidance." *Journal of Cross-Cultural Psychology, 19,* 125–136.

————, and Bond, M. (1984). "The Impact of Cultural Collectivism on Reward Allocation." *Journal of Personality and Social Psychology, 47,* 793–804.

————, and Iwawaki, S. (1988). "Cultural Collectivism and Distributive Behavior." *Journal of Cross-Cultural Psychology, 19,* 35–49.

Markus, H., and Kitayama, S. (1991). "Culture and the Self: Implications for Cognition, Emotion, and Motivation." *Psychological Review, 2,* 224–253.

Martin, J. N. (1993). "Intercultural Communication Competence: A Review." In R. L. Wiseman and J. Koster (Eds.), *Intercultural Communication Competence* (pp. 16–29). Newbury Park, CA: Sage.

Okabe, R. (1983). "Cultural Assumptions of East-West: Japan and the United States." In W. Gudykunst (Ed.), *Intercultural Communication Theory.* Beverly Hills, CA: Sage.

Schwartz, S., and Bilsky, W. (1990). "Toward a Theory of the Universal Content and Structure of Values." *Journal of Personality and Social Psychology, 58,* 878–891.

Ting-Toomey, S. (1985). "Toward a Theory of Conflict and Culture." In W. Gudykunst, L. Stewart, and S. Ting-Toomey (Eds.), *Communication Culture, and Organizational Processes* (pp. 71–86). Beverly Hills, CA: Sage.

————. (1988). "Intercultural Conflict Styles: A Face-Negotiation Theory." In Y. Kim and W. Gudykunst (Eds.), *Theories in Intercultural Communication.* Newbury Park, CA: Sage.

————. (1991). "Intimacy Expressions in Three Cultures: France, Japan, and the United States." *International Journal of Intercultural Relations, 15,* 29–46.

————. (Ed.) (1994). *The Challenge of Facework: Cross-Cultural and Interpersonal Issues.* Albany: State University of New York Press.

————. (in press). *Intercultural Communication Process: Crossing Boundaries.* New York: Guilford.

————, and Cole, M. (1990). "Intergroup Diplomatic Communication: A Face-Negotiation Perspective." In F. Korzenny and S. Ting-Toomey (Eds.), *Communicating for Peace: Diplomacy and Negotiation.* Newbury Park, CA: Sage.

————, Gao, G., Trubisky, P., Yang, Z., Kim, H. S., Lin, S. L., and Nishida, T. (1991). "Culture, Face Maintenance, and Styles of Handling Interpersonal Conflict: A Study in Five Cultures." *The International Journal of Conflict Management, 2,* 275–296.

Triandis, H. (1988). "Collectivism vs. Individualism: A Reconceptualization of a Basic Concept in Cross-Cultural Psychology." In G. Verma and C. Bagley (Eds.), *Cross-Cultural Studies of Personality, Attitudes and Cognition.* London: Macmillan.

————. (1990). "Cross-Cultural Studies of Individualism and Collectivism." In J. Berman (Ed.), *Nebraska Symposium on Motivation.* Lincoln: University of Nebraska Press.

————, Brislin, R., and Hui, C. H. (1988). Cross-Cultural Training Across the Individualism-Collectivism Divide." *International Journal of Intercultural Relations, 12,* 269–289.

Trubisky, P., Ting-Toomey, S., and Lin, S. L. (1991). "The Influence of Individualism-Collectivism and Self-Monitoring on Conflict Styles." *International Journal of Intercultural Relations, 15,* 65–84.

Wheeler, L., Reis, H., and Bond, M. (1989). "Collectivism-Individualism in Everyday Social Life: The Middle Kingdom and the Melting Pot." *Journal of Personality and Social Psychology, 57,* 79–86.

Concepts and Questions

1. How does Ting-Toomey define conflict?
2. In what way does the cultural socialization process relate to different forms of intercultural conflicts?
3. From the perspective of intercultural conflict, how may in-group and out-group differences contribute to such conflict?
4. How can differences between high- and low-context cultures contribute to intercultural conflict?
5. How can an awareness of expectations help mediate intercultural conflict?
6. How do differences along the individualistic–collectivist scale of cultural differences contribute to intercultural conflict? What would you suggest to minimize these influences?
7. In what ways can differences in cross-cultural conflict interaction styles affect intercultural communication?
8. What role does silence play in intercultural conflict reduction?
9. What differences are there between individualistic and collectivist conflict management styles?
10. What does Ting-Toomey suggest is necessary for effective intercultural conflict management?

Sojourner Adaptation

POLLY A. BEGLEY

Former boundaries that mark the edges of a culture on a map have become permeable as countries expand into the international marketplace and individuals invest, work, travel, and live outside their native lands. Every year, more young people are looking for higher-paying jobs outside their countries of origins (Crowell, 1997). Economists predicted significant global economic growth by as much as 3 percent for 1997. With the rise in overseas trade and business ventures, national economies are increasingly connected to the global economy. Foreign investors hold approximately $985.6 billion of the United States' $5.12 trillion debt (Francis, 1997, p. 3).

Exploding global populations also affect every nation with more people in the world, contributing to "political instability, global warming, and resource depletion" (Feldman, 1997, p. 3). Instability stems from clashes between cultures as humankind creates catastrophes that are far worse than natural disasters: "nuclear warfare, acid rain, ocean pollution, extinction of animals, AIDS, or a worldwide recession" (Hofstede, 1997, p. 3). Human beings have to cope with living in harmony on a planet with a volatile international economy, too many people arguing over shrinking resources, humanitarian concerns, and mounting environmental contamination.

This article examines challenges and strategies for living, learning, and adapting in global communities. Specifically, this is a review of the changes or adaptations that occur when a sojourner crosses cultural boundaries. First, the terms *culture shock* and *adaptation* will be defined. Second, this review will focus on the challenges associated with adapting to another cultural environment such as, ethnocentrism, language barriers, disequilibrium, length of stay, and level of knowledge. Finally, previous preparation, fostering certain personality characteristics, personal determination, and amount of time spent communicating are presented as possible strategies for effective adaptation.

SOJOURNERS, CULTURE SHOCK, AND ADAPTATION

People who cross cultural boundaries are referred to as *sojourners*. This term includes immigrants, refugees, business executives, students, and tourists. People enter a cultural region with diverse experiences, backgrounds, knowledge, and goals, but every sojourner must adjust or adapt his or her communication to the particular cultural setting. The term *culture shock* was coined by Oberg (1960) and included a four-stage model of cultural adjustment. These stages referred to the progression of experiences throughout intercultural interactions. Culture shock occurs in the second stage of adjustment and is characterized by hostility and stereotypes. Although it is generally accepted that individuals experience shocks or stress as they learn to communicate with people of another culture, the term *shock* carried a negative connotation. Researchers began to use other terms that described the shocks, stress, rewards, and growth processes of sojourners who work, travel, or live in another country.

Cross-cultural *adaptation* refers to how a sojourner chooses to cope with cultural changes. *Adaptation* is an umbrella term that encompasses culture shock, assimilation, adjustment, acculturation, integration, and coping. A sojourner's coping mechanism can include seeking out specific cultural knowledge, adopting a different style of communication, reserving judgment about unfamiliar cultural practices, or withdrawing from intercultural interactions (Witte, 1993). Adaptation is a complex and dynamic process that is an inevitable part of intercultural interactions. When a sojourner is faced with diverse cultural practices and habits, his or her taken-for-granted cultural training is questioned, reevaluated, and adapted for the cultural environment. The process of learning new greetings, responses, or communication styles while unlearning previous interactive patterns can give rise to some adaptive challenges for the sojourner.

CHALLENGES

Ethnocentrism

Human beings tend to criticize the customs of another culture from the standpoint of their own cultural beliefs, values, and attitudes. Ethnocentrism refers to a cultural bias that leads people to judge another culture's habits and practices as right or wrong, good or bad. Americans are astonished that some people consume dogs or cats. Hindus in India are dismayed by societies that eat cows. Taiwanese prefer jade talismans and are shocked to discover that some Americans carry a severed animal's foot (e.g., a rabbit's foot) in their pockets for good luck. Expelling mucous on a public street corner in China is acceptable behavior. The American practice of blowing the nose into a Kleenex, then saving it in the pocket would astound many Chinese. Islamic countries have been criticized for supposedly subordinating women (e.g., female veiling practices and segregation), but Turkey is a predominantly Muslim country where approximately half of all Turkish stockbrokers, doctors, lawyers, professors, and bankers are women. A young Turkish stockbroker, Esra Yoldas, jokes, "Maybe the abnormal situation is not here, but in Christian countries where stockbrokers are mostly male" (Pope, 1997, p. A8). Ethnocentric attitudes that lead us to evaluate negatively people and cultural diversities influence the adaptation process.

Sojourners must be willing to reserve judgment and to accept that "different" is not automatically negative when they encounter diverse customs and habits. People may choose to eat cows, dogs, cats, or no meat at all. The range of acceptable and unacceptable behavior and communication styles varies from culture to culture. Ethnocentric attitudes can become barriers to the development of international business deals, meaningful relationships, and intercultural understanding. A key to effective adaptation is for a sojourner to not allow his or her own cultural biases to influence communication with people from another culture.

Language

Learning to speak to someone in her or his native language is an indisputable part of the adaptation process. Previous research studies link language skills with adaptation effectiveness (DeVerthelyi, 1995). Long-term sojourners and immigrants in the United States who cannot speak English experience social isolation and are segregated "into fields that require less mastery of the English language and less interpersonal interaction" (Leong & Chou, 1994, p. 165). Likewise, an American is able to order a cup of coffee at a sidewalk cafe in Paris with hand gestures, but philosophical discussions are limited until he or she learns French. Highly touristed areas have bilingual staffs that cater to tourists who cannot speak the local language. Unfortunately, these tourists are gaining a superficial understanding of the culture, and ventures into countryside areas are not possible because of language barriers.

Disequilibrium

Adaptation involves a choice of how or what to adapt to or change to fit into the host culture. An encounter with changing communication patterns, a new language, or ethnocentrism can be a stressful experience. Sojourners are "at least temporarily, in a state of disequilibrium, which is manifested in many emotional 'lows' of uncertainty, confusion and anxiety" (Kim, 1995, p. 177). What if you were working in a country where the word "no" is considered to be insulting? You would have to learn how to say "no" through hesitation or another indirect method. In some countries it is polite to greet someone with "I salute the God within you" instead of asking "How are you?" Learning proper ways to accept or reject requests, local greetings, and polite conversational behavior can be confusing. Our own cultural habits and practices are questioned and modified as we adapt and learn to interact effectively in a different context. The adaptation process is typically characterized by "ups" and "downs" or incidents of effective and ineffective communication as cultural learning advances.

Length of Stay

The length of time spent in a different culture influences the adaptation process. A person who plans a short-term sojourn acquires less-specific cultural knowledge and practical interaction experience and is less motivated to make drastic adaptive changes to fit into the dominant culture. Tourists on a two-week tour need to know an occasional phrase in the local language and only a few details about their destination. In contrast, individuals who seek long-term business relations, work, travel, or residence are motivated to make significant changes in their communicative styles. Longer sojourns are characterized by less "social difficulty" and increasingly effective adaptations (Ward & Kennedy, 1993). Shorter sojourns are characterized by more uncertainty, confusion, or mistakes concerning appropriate communication behavior and practices.

Level of Knowledge

Should I shake hands or bow when I meet them? Should I show enthusiasm when I speak, or control my facial expressions? What kinds of topics are appropriate for initial meetings? A sojourner learns a a long list of cultural customs or norms before and during a sojourn. A person's level of general and specific cultural knowledge can contribute to the adaptation process. For example, a sojourner bargaining in the Middle East should understand when to start with a conservative quote (Bedouin style) or begin with an outrageously high number (*suk* or market style). In China, an altercation should always be in public with plenty of witnesses to preserve the reputation and respect of the concerned parties. Countless international marketing campaigns have failed because companies did not understand local values and beliefs. Negotiations stall between leaders of nations because there is insufficient understanding of appropriate communication or differing interactive styles.

STRATEGIES

Preparation

Previous examples show the importance of acquiring the appropriate knowledge before intercultural contact. Sojourners should never assume that their communicative behavior will be appropriate in every cultural environment. The culture-specific and culture-general are two commonly used approaches to understand interactive customs and behavior. The *culture-specific approach* focuses on one or a limited number of cultures. A *culture-general approach* explores "cultural traits and behaviors that are common to all cultures" (Samovar & Porter, 1995, p. 277).

Communication competence across cultures can benefit from a more general approach. Milhouse (1996) argues that students learn more from general discussions of cross-cultural differences and similarities than from unique cultural details. One must be aware that knowing when to bow or shake hands does not guarantee communicative competence, but understanding that greetings vary according to culture helps us speak with people from diverse backgrounds. The general approach provides students with a broader base of knowledge.

The general approach also can take the focus away from differences. An emphasis on teaching regional differences perpetuates stereotypes and discourages people from realizing that each person is unique. A common focus during culture-specific intercultural training is the characteristics of the group, and individuality is ignored. It would be incorrect to assume that all Americans have blond hair, eat at McDonald's restaurants, wear jeans, and drink Coke. Every population is characterized by diversity, and generalizations can only represent certain tendencies (but not rules) within a group. Individuals are influenced by culture, as well as genetic makeup, personal experiences, and gender. The general approach can teach us to reject false generalizations and to recognize the unique and exceptional characteristics of each person.

Language skills are crucial to learning and adapting to another culture. Classes, books, videos, or tapes are effective ways to study a new language, although common words and slang may have to be learned in the country of origin. The common language and accent may differ slightly according to region. A sojourner who hopes to communicate with people in their own native tongue also must have the tenacity to ask for explanations and be bold enough to make mistakes during interactions. Taiwanese students study English for approximately ten years but frequently admit that communication with speakers of English is difficult. The reason for this difficulty stems from the dichotomy between "textbook language" and the "everyday language" that contains inside references, slang, and other regional differences. The most successful communicators take every opportunity to learn new vocabulary, ask questions, and practice their new language skills. Sojourners also demonstrate an interest in and appreciation for a culture by attempting to learn the language. For example, a well-timed response of *"Inshaallah"* (a common Arabic expression translated as "If God wills it") can elicit applause, lower prices from merchants, or better business relations in Egypt.

Personality Characteristics

Personality characteristics such as openness and strength of personality are influential determinants of cross-cultural adaptation effectiveness. Openness, and the related concept of flexibility, refers to a willingness to suspend judgment about another group's communication habits or practices. This implies a flexible attitude toward change and diverse viewpoints. Openness and flexibility are the antithesis of ethnocentrism and are based on the assumption that there is more than one way to reach our goals. Sojourners must recognize that there is more than one path to truth or understanding. A person may choose to improve his or her life by hiring a *feng shui* (wind and water) expert to rearrange furniture or add elements of wood and water to achieve balance and harmony in the home. Another person buys a red convertible car and an expensive gold watch to improve his or her life. Both people chose different paths to reach the same goal, but only they can judge if their efforts were successful.

Personal Determination

Personal determination can stem from external factors or internal factors. *External factors* refer to length of stay, purpose of visit, or the attitude of the local culture. These factors may or may not be under the sojourner's control. Entry permits limit the amount of time for business or tourist purposes. Companies often decide the agenda for executives. In some cases, cultural differences are tolerated within a society, but in other countries the sojourner is pressured to adapt or change to fit into the dominant culture (Kim, 1995). If the society exhibits high levels of conformity pressure, then visitors have little choice but to adapt their communicative patterns to fit into that cultural group.

Internal factors include strength of personality and adaptive or maladaptive choices. A strong personality is reflected in how a person reacts to challenging or unpredictable communication incidents. Stress or disequilibrium experienced by the sojourner motivates him or her to make adaptive or maladaptive choices. In the face of challenges, "stronger" personalities exhibit more "adaptive outcomes (intercultural adaptation, communicative effectiveness)," and weaker personalities display "maladaptive outcomes (isolation, withdrawal)" (Witte, 1993, p. 206). For example, international students who make friends with members of their own ethnic group and with members of the local culture tend to develop a broader worldview. Although support and information can be gained from people who share a similar cultural background, limiting interactions with students outside one's own culture prevents effective adaptation. The adaptation process is not a predictable or linear experience. A sojourner may experience stressful conditions prompting her or him to withdraw from cross-cultural contact one day, then the next day be able to engage in effective interactions with the local population.

Amount of Time Spent Communicating

The most important factor predicting adaptation is the frequency of host communication participation. Although insight and knowledge can be gained through prior intercultural study, additional practical wisdom is attained through everyday conversations with people from other cultures. Practical interactions or "extroversion" is associated with an increase in "opportunities for cultural learning" (Ward & Kennedy, 1993, p. 240). The implication is that information pertaining to cultural communicative rules, nonverbal, and common customs can be learned and used during communication. Practical communicative experiences contribute to overall understanding and effective adaptations.

Although face-to-face interactions with locals has no substitute, mediated communication also can be an important source of intercultural knowledge and language skills. A sojourner can watch TV programs or listen to radio to learn a language and gain experience about additional cultural situations or events. Popular local programs can be a good topic of conversation. Jordanians especially appreciate the soap opera, *The Bold and the Beautiful*, and they are eager to discuss plot developments with visiting Americans. The Chinese *kung fu* movie star Jackie Chan is well known in Hong Kong, Taiwan, and the United States. The royal family of Britain, world cup soccer, and internationally known pop singer Michael Jackson are all topics that have inspired conversations around the world.

CONCLUSION

An economic recession in one country causes a financial downturn in other countries. The depletion of a rain forest in South America can influence the world's supply of clean air. A nuclear mishap creates a cloud that creates a path of destruction across the globe. Distance and seas no longer keep people at home; more of the world's population is now on the move seeking trade, work, knowledge, and adventure. Sojourners who cross cultural boundaries encounter challenges and initiate strategies to adapt to different cultural settings. This article reviewed the terms that describe the process of cultural change during a sojourn as well as specific challenges and strategies to increase adaptation effectiveness. Intercultural adaptation is a crucial area of interest for people of every nation who wish to live in a healthy and harmonious world.

References

Crowell, T. (1997, January 8). British workers flock to Hong Kong jobs before July handover. *The Christian Science Monitor*, p. 7.

DeVerthelyi, R. F. (1995). International students' spouses: Invisible sojourners in the culture shock literature. *International Journal of Intercultural Relations, 19*, 387–411.

Feldmann, L. (1997, January 31). Debate revives over funds for global family planning. *The Christian Science Monitor*, p. 3.

Francis, D. R. (1997, January 31). Behind bull market fickle foreign money. *The Christian Science Monitor*, p. 8.

Halverson, G. (1997, January 28). Investing overseas balances portfolio. *The Christian Science Monitor*, p. 9.

Hofstede, G. (1997). *Cultures and organizations: Software of the mind*. New York: McGraw-Hill.

Kim, Y. Y. (1995). Cross-cultural adaptation: An integrative theory. In R. L. Wiseman (Ed.), *Theories in intercultural communication* (pp. 170–193). Thousand Oaks, CA: Sage.

Leong, F. T., & Chou, E. L. (1994). The role of ethnic identity and acculturation in the vocational behavior of Asian Americans: An integrative review. *Journal of Vocational Behavior, 44,* 155–172.

Milhouse, V. A. (1996). Intercultural communication education and training goals, content, and methods. *International Journal of Intercultural Relations, 20,* 69–95.

Oberg, K. (1960). Culture shock: Adjustment to new cultural environment. *Practical Anthropology, 7,* 177–182.

Pope, H. (1997, March 14). The new middle: Turks add their voices to contest of generals and fundamentals. *The Wall Street Journal,* pp. A1, A8.

Samovar, L. A., & Porter, R. E. (1995). *Communication between cultures* (2nd ed.). Belmont, CA: Wadsworth.

Ward, C., & Kennedy, A. (1993). Where's the "culture" in cross-cultural transition? Comparative studies of sojourner adjustment. *Journal of Cross-Cultural Psychology, 24,* 221–249.

Witte, K. (1993). A theory of cognition and negative affect: Extending Gudykunst and Hammer's theory of uncertainty and anxiety reduction. *International Journal of Intercultural Relations, 17,* 197–215.

Concepts and Questions

1. What does Begley mean by the term *sojourner?*
2. What is culture shock? How does it affect a sojourner?
3. In what ways can ethnocentrism affect the adaptation of a sojourner to a new cultural environment?
4. How does reserving judgment help a sojourner deal with her or his ethnocentrism?
5. It is unusual for a sojourner to be fully fluent in the language of another culture he or she may be visiting, so what steps may be taken to help overcome language barriers?
6. What characterizes a "state of disequilibrium"? How can a sojourner minimize disequilibrium effect?
7. How does the intended length of stay in a new culture affect a sojourner's experiences in that culture?
8. What strategies does Begley recommend for a sojourner to prepare for entry into a different culture?
9. How does an individual's personality affect interpersonal interactions in another culture?
10. What role can personal determination play in adapting to another culture?

Intercultural Sensitivity

GUO-MING CHEN

WILLIAM J. STAROSTA

Our world is shrinking. Amidst ever-shifting cultural, social, economic, and technological realities, we increasingly depend on one another, and a global community emerges. According to Chen and Starosta (1996), five trends lead us toward a global society: (1) The development of communication and transportation technology links people of different cultural backgrounds from every part of the world together; (2) the globalization of world economy requires employees from multinational corporations to communicate with those in other parts of the world in order to compete successfully in the global economic system; (3) widespread population migration across national borders restructures the fabric of modern society so that it becomes much more culturally diverse than it was in the past; (4) the development of multiculturalism affects every aspect of life in a United States newly emerging workforce of persons who are diverse in race, culture, age, gender, and language; and (5) the deemphasis of nation-state views results in nations forming regional alliances and individuals reasserting ethnic and gender differences within the nation. In this global society, intercultural communication competence becomes an indispensable ability for us to survive and live meaningfully and productively.

Among these trends, widespread population migration and the development of multiculturalism most affect U.S. American society. For example, in 1940, 70 percent of immigrants to the United States originated from Europe. Half a century later, 15 percent came from Europe, 37 percent from Asia, and 44 percent from Latin America and the Caribbean. The current ethnic breakdown for the United States includes 80 percent white, 12 percent black, 6.14

percent Hispanic, and 1.6 percent Asian. Given no new exclusionary legislation, by the year 2050 the population of U.S. white ethnics will decrease to 60 percent, while Asians increase tenfold, Hispanics triple their numbers, and African Americans increase their proportion but slightly (Nieto, 1992).

Shifts in the U.S. population structure influence the U.S. American educational system and organizational life. Educationally, while approximately 27 percent of all U.S. public school students are persons of color, African American and Latino student populations dominate twenty-two of the twenty-five largest central-city school districts. Co-culture majority school systems may increase in number by the year 2000, resulting in a greater proportion of 90 percent nonwhite schools than when the Supreme Court prohibited "separate but equal" schooling in 1954.

Meanwhile, the number of U.S. children who are native speakers of a non-English language will increase from 2 million in 1986 to 5 million by 2020 (Vadivieso & David, 1988). The influx of nonnative speakers of English requires the educational system to develop a curriculum that meets the needs of recent immigrants and their children, promotes learning, and accommodates differing communication styles of recent immigrants that may not match those of teachers and counselors (Sue, 1994).

Persons of co-cultures within the United States consume more goods and services than do any of the United States' trading partners, and their consumption will constitute 25 percent of the U.S. economic market by the year 2000 (Astroff, 1988–89; Foster, Jackson, Cross, Jackson, & Hardiman, 1988). If companies are to attract and retain new workers, then they must recruit persons of varying heritages and ethnicity. Companies that fail to promote minorities and women to higher levels of management will lose their competitive edge (Morrison & Von Glinow, 1990). Companies therefore must begin now to plan creatively and introduce new workplace configurations to make the best use of the talents of nontraditional employees (Goldstein & Gilliam, 1990).

It is clear that cultural diversity of multiculturalism has become the norm rather than the exception in U.S. American life. The changing cultural character of neighborhoods, schools, and the workplace calls on us to adapt to the unfamiliar and to learn to work and live together without being adversely influenced by the differences that people may bring to an encounter. All of these events lead to a strong demand for greater understanding, sensitivity, and competency among people from differing cultural backgrounds. This article proposes to examine one of the most important abilities that help us live successfully in the culturally diverse society: *intercultural sensitivity*. Our discussion is separated into four sections: (1) *What is intercultural sensitivity?* (2) *intercultural sensitivity and training programs;* (3) *components of intercultural sensitivity;* and (4) *conclusion*.

WHAT IS INTERCULTURAL SENSITIVITY?

Intercultural sensitivity is treated as one of the necessary elements for successful communication in intercultural settings, and many intercultural training programs aim to increase the ability of intercultural sensitivity. However, no clear definition of the concept can be found in the existing literature. In addition, we tend to confuse and mingle the meaning of intercultural sensitivity with two other closely related concepts: intercultural awareness and intercultural competence. Such confusion jeopardizes not only the validity and reliability of related research, but also intercultural training programs.

Intercultural awareness is the cognitive aspect of intercultural communication. It refers to the understanding of cultural conventions that affect how people think and behave. Intercultural awareness requires individuals to understand that, from their own cultural perspective, they are cultural beings. They must then use this understanding as a foundation to explore the distinct characteristics of other cultures so that they can effectively interpret others' behaviors in intercultural interactions (Triandis, 1977). Because every culture shows a distinctive thought pattern, misunderstanding reasoning differences often causes serious problems in intercultural communication (Glenn & Glenn, 1981). To be successful in intercultural interactions, we must first demonstrate intercultural awareness by learning the similarities and differences of each other's culture. The process of gaining awareness of cultural similarities and differences, however, is enhanced and buffered by intercultural sensitivity.

Intercultural competence is the behavioral aspect of intercultural communication. It refers to the ability to behave effectively and appropriately in intercultural interactions (Chen & Starosta, 1996). Intercultural competence concerns getting the job done and attaining communication goals through verbal and nonverbal behaviors in intercultural interactions. Effectiveness and appropriateness of behavioral performance are regulated by the cognitive understanding and affective sensitivity of cultural similarity and distinctiveness. In other words, intercultural awareness and intercultural sensitivity are the prerequisites for being competent in intercultural interactions. Thus, intercultural awareness, intercultural sensitivity, and intercultural competence are three separate but mutually dependent elements that combine to lead individuals toward a successfully intercultural interaction. But what is intercultural sensitivity?

Bronfenbrener, Harding, and Gallwey's study (1958) is one early study on sensitivity. The authors propose that *sensitivity to the generalized other* and *sensitivity to individual differences* (i.e., interpersonal sensitivity) are the two major types of ability in social perception. Sensitivity to the generalized other is a "kind of sensitivity to the social norms of one's own group" (McClelland, 1958, p. 241), and interpersonal sensitivity is the ability to distinguish how others differ from us in their behavior, perceptions, or feelings (Bronfenbrener et al., 1958). Bronfenbrener et al.'s *interpersonal sensitivity* parallels what we consider intercultural sensitivity.

Hart and Burks (1972) and Hart, Carlson, and Eadie (1980) treat sensitivity as a mind-set that is applied in one's everyday life. They propose that sensitive persons should be able to accept personal complexity, avoid communication inflexibility, be conscious in interaction, appreciate the ideas exchanged, and tolerate intentional searching. These elements appear to be embedded in the cognitive, affective, and behavioral dimensions of intercultural interaction.

From Gudykunst and Hammer's (1983) three-stage intercultural training model and Hoopes' (1981) intercultural learning model, Bennett (1984) conceives of intercultural sensitivity as a developmental process in which one is able to transform oneself affectively, cognitively, and behaviorally from ethnocentric stages to ethnorelative stages.

This transformation process comprises six analytic stages: (1) *denial*, in which we deny the existence of cultural differences among people; (2) *defense*, in which we try to protect our worldview by countering the perceived threat; (3) *minimization*, in which we attempt to protect the core of our worldview by concealing differences in the shadow of cultural similarities; (4) *acceptance*, in which we begin to accept the existence of behavioral differences and underlying cultural differences; (5) *adaptation*, in which we become empathic to cultural differences and become bicultural or multicultural; and (6) *integration*, in which we are able to apply ethnorelativism to our own identity and can experience "difference as an essential and joyful aspect of all life" (p. 186).

Bennett's model of intercultural sensitivity requires not only gradual change in our affection and cognition, but also our behavioral ability to reach the state of intercultural communication competence. Conceptually, Bennett's perception of intercultural sensitivity seems identical with the concept of intercultural communication competence that has been investigated by other scholars (Chen, 1989, 1990, 1992; Lustig & Koester, 1996; Martin & Hammer, 1989; Ruben, 1976; Spitzberg, 1989).

Finally, Bhawuk and Brislin (1992) offer an instrument for measuring intercultural sensitivity from the perspective of individualism versus collectivism. The authors use the concept of intercultural communication competence to develop intercultural sensitivity measurement based on affective, cognitive, and behavioral dimensions. Those elements used by the authors include: (1) understanding the different ways one can behave, (2) open-mindedness concerning the differences one encounters, and (3) the degree of behavioral flexibility one demonstrates in a new culture.

The above review begins the conceptualization of intercultural sensitivity. Two areas of confusion now need to be clarified before we can generate a working definition of the concept. First, although intercultural sensitivity is related to the cognitive, affective, and behavioral aspects of an interactional situation, it mainly deals with the affect and emotion of the communicators. Second, intercultural awareness (cognition) is the foundation of intercultural sensitivity (affect) that in turn leads to intercultural competence (behavior). In other words, as previously indicated, the three are closely related but separate concepts. Based on these two clarifications, intercultural sensitivity can be considered as *an individual's ability to develop a positive emotion towards understanding and appreciating cultural differences in order to promote appropriate and effective behavior in intercultural communication*. This definition looks at intercultural sensitivity as a dynamic concept. It also reveals that interculturally sensitive persons must have a desire to motivate themselves to understand, appreciate, and accept differences among cultures and to produce a positive outcome from intercultural interactions.

INTERCULTURAL SENSITIVITY AND TRAINING PROGRAMS

The increasing importance of intercultural sensitivity in the global and multicultural society has led many scholars and experts to examine the concept from different perspectives. Practically, the concept has been integrated into intercultural training programs that are initiated to develop the ability of intercultural sensitivity. Those training programs include "T-groups," critical incidents, case studies, role playing, and cultural orientation programs (Brislin, 1981; Cushner & Landis, 1996; Seidel, 1981; Yum, 1989).

Intercultural training commonly aims to develop intercultural sensitivity by increasing awareness of cultural differences and attempts to develop a trainee's communication potential while lessening the likelihood of intercultural misunderstandings (Cargile & Giles, 1996). In other words, intercultural training programs aim to "develop an appreciation and understanding of cross-cultural differences and to acquire some of the necessary abilities, such as an increased awareness and sensitivity to cultural stimuli and better human relations skills" (Seidel, 1981, p. 184). Morgan and Weigel (1988) point out that the major purpose of such training programs is to develop intercultural sensitivity because it is considered a prerequisite for intercultural effectiveness.

As an essential element for positive outcomes in intercultural encounters, sensitivity also can be examined from the six general categories of intercultural training programs: *affective training, cognitive training, behavioral training, area simulation training, cultural awareness training*, and *self-awareness training* (Brislin, Landis, & Brandt, 1983; Gudykunst, Hammer, & Wiseman, 1977).

According to Gudykunst, Ting-Toomey, and Wiseman (1991), affective training should increase trainees' motivation and sensitivity to communication with people from other cultures and ethnic groups. Cognitive training promotes understanding of cultural differences and similarities. Behavioral training provides skill training so that participants learn to communicate more effectively with people of other cultures. Area simulation training requires that participants spend a period of time in a cultural or ethnic neighborhood and interact fully with the residents to gain the real experience of intercultural encounters. Cultural awareness training requires participants to understand the aspects of culture that are universal and specific. Finally, self-awareness training helps participants identify attitudes, opinions, and biases that influence the way they communicate.

Among these training programs, affective training, cognitive training, self-awareness training, and cultural awareness training focus on the cognitive and affective understanding of one's own as well as the host culture. Area simulation training and behavioral training focus on the teaching of specific behaviors that are used to better adjust to a new culture. Seidel (1981) integrates the purposes of these training programs in a sensitivity approach that clearly defines specific spheres of training in the three areas: appreciation and sensitivity (affective), understanding and awareness (cognitive), and skills (behavioral).

Therefore, with the emphasis on an integrated approach, the search for an appropriate conceptualization of intercultural sensitivity should be grounded in the affective aspect and extended to include cognitive and behavioral components. Thus, Parker, Valley, and Geary (1986) reason that intercultural sensitivity can be achieved through a combination of cognitive, affective, and behavioral procedures, because the effectiveness of intercultural communication requires interactants to appropriately demonstrate ability in intercultural awareness, sensitivity, and competence. This is supported by Gullahorn and Gullahorn's (1963) study showing that the problems encountered by people in intercultural interaction are cognitive reorientation (i.e., cognitive), changes

in feelings (i.e., affective), and overt behaviors (i.e., behavioral). Therefore, intercultural training programs concerned with intercultural sensitivity also aim to increase intercultural awareness and develop intercultural competence.

COMPONENTS OF INTERCULTURAL SENSITIVITY

Because intercultural sensitivity focuses on personal affect and emotions that are caused by particular situations, people, and environment (Triandis, 1977), an interculturally sensitive individual should be able to project and receive positive emotional responses before, during, and after intercultural interaction. Intercultural sensitivity especially refers to the attitude of respect (Adler & Towne, 1993). Not knowing how to show respect to others and their cultural differences in the process of intercultural communication usually leads to a lower degree of satisfaction. According to Gudykunst and Kim (1992), a successful integration of affective and cognitive processes can help people achieve an adequate social orientation that enables them to understand both their own and others' feelings and behaviors. Thus, to develop a positive emotion toward understanding and appreciating cultural differences and eventually to promote intercultural competence, interculturally sensitive persons must possess the following abilities: self-esteem, self-monitoring, open-mindedness, empathy, interaction involvement, and suspending judgment.

Self-Esteem

A culturally sensitive person usually shows higher degrees of self-esteem. Self-esteem is a sense of self-value or self-worth. It is based on one's perception of how well one can develop his or her potential in a social environment (Borden, 1991). A person with high self-esteem usually has an optimistic outlook that instills confidence in interactions with others (Foote & Cottrell, 1955). Hamachek (1982) also concludes that persons with high self-esteem are likely to think of others and to expect to be accepted by others. In intercultural encounters, where people inevitably meet psychological stresses when trying to complete their jobs and establish relationships, self-esteem becomes an important variable in the calculation of whether or not they can fulfill their needs. It is self-esteem that enhances the positive emotion toward accurately recognizing and respecting the situational differences in intercultural interactions.

Self-Monitoring

Self-monitoring refers to a person's ability to regulate behavior in response to situational constraints and to implement a conversationally competent behavior. Persons with high self-monitoring are particularly sensitive to the appropriateness of their social behaviors and self-presentation in social interaction (Snyder, 1974). Spitzberg and Cupach (1984) indicate that high self-monitors are more attentive, other-oriented, and adaptable to diverse communication situations. In interaction, high self-monitoring persons are more adept in the use of strategies such as compromise, emotional appeals, coercion, ingratiation, and referent influence (Smith, Cody, Lovette, & Canary, 1990). Berger and Douglas (1982) also report that high self-monitoring helps people better adapt their behaviors to different situations so that they become more competent in communication. Persons who are high in self-monitoring during intercultural communication are also likely to be more sensitive to the expressions of their counterparts and know how to use situational cues to guide their self-presentation (Gudykunst, Yang, & Nishida, 1987). These studies show that self-monitoring equips us with an ability to monitor situational cues sensitively and to develop further a set of appropriate behaviors to fit the situation.

Open-Mindedness

Open-mindedness refers to the willingness of individuals to openly and appropriately explain themselves and to accept other's explanations. This parallels Adler's (1977) concept of "multicultural [hu]man" who accepts the "life patterns different from his or her own and who has psychologically and socially come to grips with a multiplicity of realities" (p. 25). In other words, interculturally sensitive persons understand that an idea can be rendered in mul-

tiform ways (Hart & Burks, 1972). Bennett (1986) also indicates that interculturally sensitive persons possess an internalized, broadened concept of the world. Thus, interculturally sensitive persons are open-minded. Culturally insensitive or narrow-minded persons will not survive their intercultural encounter (Barnlund, 1988).

Ingrained in open-mindedness is the willingness to recognize, accept, and appreciate different views and ideas. Yum (1989) indicates that sensitivity motivates people to understand and acknowledge other people's needs; it also makes them more adaptive to differences in culturally diverse situations. Smith (1966) also points out that being sensitive means having consideration for others, being receptive to others' needs and differences, and being able to translate emotions into actions. It is a process of mutual validation and confirmation of cultural identities that fosters a favorable impression in intercultural communication (Ting-Toomey, 1989).

Empathy

Empathy has been long recognized as a central element for intercultural sensitivity. It refers to a process of projecting ourselves into another person's point of view in which we think the same thoughts and feel the same emotions as another (Adler & Towne, 1993). Empathy allows us to sense what is inside another's mind or to step into another person's shoes. Others call it "affective sensitivity" (Campbell, Kagan, & Krathwohl, 1971), "telepathic or intuition sensitivity" (Gardner, 1962) or "perspective-taking" (Parks, 1976).

According to Barnlund (1988), interculturally sensitive persons tend to look for communication symbols that let them share another's experiences. Interculturally sensitive persons adopt different roles as required by new situations (Hart, Carlson, & Eadie, 1980). Moreover, empathic persons are also judged to be more selfless and to have more concern for the other interactant's feelings and reactions (Davis, 1983). In other words, they are able to accurately estimate the behaviors or internal states of their communication counterparts (Parks, 1994). As a result, empathy allows them to demonstrate reciprocity of affect displays, active listening, and verbal responses that show understanding. It develops a mutual understanding that leads to the establishment of an intercultural rapport (Barnlund, 1988). This is the reason Coke, Bateson, and McDavis (1978) contend that empathy allows a person to possess a higher degree of feeling of sympathy and concern toward others. Hence, the display of identification, understanding, and consideration to others are characteristics of empathy that form the essence of intercultural sensitivity and lead a person to be competent in intercultural communication (Bennett, 1979; Gudykunst, 1993; Yum, 1989).

Interaction Involvement

Interaction involvement is the ability of individuals to perceive the topic and situation that involves their conception of self and self-reward (Spitzberg & Cupach, 1984). It emphasizes a person's sensitivity ability in interaction. Cegala (1981, 1984) considers interaction involvement to be fundamental to the human communication process. His research shows that interaction involvement comprises responsiveness, perceptiveness, and attentiveness.

Being responsive, perceptive, and attentive enables interculturally sensitive persons to better receive and understand messages, to take appropriate turns, and to initiate and terminate an intercultural interaction fluently and appropriately. In other words, interculturally sensitive persons know how to "handle the procedural aspects of structuring and maintaining a conversation" (Spitzberg & Cupach, 1984, p. 46).

Suspending Judgment

Suspending judgment refers to an attitude that allows us to listen sincerely to others during intercultural communication. Nonsensitive persons tend to jump hastily to conclusions without having sufficient data from their interaction (Hart & Burks, 1972). Thus, intercultural sensitivity is the avoidance of rash judgments about the inputs of others. Suspending judgment allows the other party to be psychologically satisfied and happy that she or he has been listened to actively.

In intercultural interaction, being nonjudgmental tends to foster a feeling of enjoyment toward cultural differences. Interculturally sensitive persons need not only to acknowledge and accept cultural differ-

ences, but also to establish a sentiment of enjoyment that promotes a satisfactory feeling toward intercultural encountering. Research has considered several types of enjoyment in intercultural interaction for intercultural sensitivity: (1) the enjoyment of interacting with people from different cultures (Randolph, Landis, & Tzeng, 1977), (2) the enjoyment of increasing good working relations with others from different cultures (Fiedler, Mitchell, & Triandis, 1971), (3) the enjoyment of one's duties in another culture (Gudykunst, Hammer, & Wiseman, 1977), and (4) the enjoyment of sharing a good narrative (Chen & Starosta, forthcoming).

CONCLUSION

Intercultural sensitivity is a precondition for living harmoniously and meaningfully in an increasingly pluralistic world. Together with intercultural awareness and intercultural competence, intercultural sensitivity is a vital element for successful communication in a global village (Barnlund, 1988). Unfortunately, most studies of intercultural sensitivity lack clear conceptualization and are entangled with intercultural awareness and intercultural competence. In this article, we first discuss why it is important to attain intercultural sensitivity in an era of burgeoning multiculturalism and interdependence. We then provide a working definition by conceptualizing intercultural sensitivity as our ability to "develop a positive emotion toward understanding and appreciating cultural differences that promote appropriate and effective behavior in intercultural communication." The relationship between intercultural sensitivity and intercultural training programs is also delineated. Finally, we specify the components of intercultural sensitivity: self-esteem, self-monitoring, open-mindedness, empathy, interaction involvement, and suspending judgment.

References

Adler, P. (1977). Beyond cultural identity: Reflections upon cultural and multicultural man. In R. W. Brislin (Ed.). *Cultural learning concepts, application and research.* Honolulu: University of Hawaii Press.

Adler, R. B., & Towne, N. (1993). *Looking in/looking out.* New York: Holt, Rinehart, & Winston.

Astroff, R. (1988–89). Spanish gold: Stereotypes, ideology, and the construction of a U.S. Latino market. *Howard Journal of Communications, 1,* 155–173.

Barnlund, D. C. (1997). Communication in a global village. In L. A. Samovar & R. E. Porter (Eds.), *Intercultural communication: A reader,* 8th ed. Belmont, CA: Wadsworth.

Bennett, M. J. (1979). Overcoming the golden rule: Sympathy and empathy. In D. Nimmo (Ed.). *Communication Yearbook 3.* Newbury Park, CA: Sage.

———. (1984). *Towards ethnorelativism: A developmental model of intercultural sensitivity.* Paper presented at the Annual Conference of the Council on International Exchange, Minneapolis, MN.

———. (1986). A developmental approach to training for intercultural sensitivity. *International Journal of Intercultural Relations, 10,* 179–196.

Berger, C. R., & Douglas, W. (1982). Thought and talk: "Excuse me, but have I been talking to myself?" In F.E.X. Dance (Ed.), *Human communication theory: Comparative essays.* New York: Harper & Row.

Bhawuk, D.P.S., & Brislin, R. (1992). The measurement of intercultural sensitivity using the concepts of individualism and collectivism. *International Journal of Intercultural Relations, 16,* 413–436.

Borden, G. A. (1991). *Cultural orientation: An approach to understanding intercultural communication.* Englewood Cliffs, NJ: Prentice Hall.

Brislin, R. W. (1981). *Cross-cultural encounters: Face to face interaction.* Elmsford, NY: Pergamon.

———, Landis, D., & Brandt, M. E. (1983). Conceptualizations of intercultural behavior and training. In D. Landis & R. W. Brislin (Eds.), *Handbook of intercultural training,* Vol. 1 (pp. 1–35). New York: Pergamon.

Bronfenbrener, U., Harding, J., & Gallwey, M. (1958). The measurement of skill in social perception. In D. C. McClelland (Ed.), *Talent and society.* New York: Van Nostrand.

Campbell, R. J., Kagan, N., & Krathwohl, D. R. (1971). The development and validation of a scale to measure affective sensitivity (empathy). *Journal of Counseling Psychology, 18,* 407–412.

Cargile, A. C., & Giles, H. (1996). Intercultural communication training: Review, critique, and a new theoretical framework. *Communication Yearbook, 19,* 385–423.

Cegala, D. J. (1981). Interaction involvement: A cognitive dimension of communicative competence. *Communication Education, 30,* 109–121.

———. (1984). Affective and cognitive manifestations of interaction involvement during unstructured and competitive interactions. *Communication Monographs, 51,* 320–338.

Chen, G. M. (1989). Relationships of the dimensions of intercultural communication competence. *Communication Quarterly, 37,* 118–133.

———. (1990). Intercultural communication competence: Some perspectives of research. *Howard Journal of Communication, 2,* 243–261.

———. (1992). A test of intercultural communication competence. *Intercultural Communication Studies, 2,* 62–83.

———, & Starosta, W. J. (1996). Intercultural communication competence: A synthesis. In B. R. Burleson (Ed.), *Communication Yearbook, 19,* 353–384.

———, & Starosta, W. J. (forthcoming). *Foundations of intercultural communication.* Boston: Allyn & Bacon.

Cushner, K., & Landis, D. (1996). The intercultural sensitizer. In D. Landis & R. S. Bhagat (Eds.), *Handbook of intercultural training* (pp. 185–202). London: Sage.

Coke, J., Bateson, C., & McDavis, K. (1978). Empathetic meditation of helping: A two-stage model. *Journal of Personality and Social Psychology, 36,* 752–766.

Davis, M. H. (1983). Measuring individual differences in empathy: Evidence for a multidimensional approach. *Journal of Personality and Social Psychology, 44,* 113–126.

Fiedler, F., Mitchell, T., & Triandis, H. (1971). The culture assimilator: An approach to cross-cultural training. *Journal of Applied Psychology, 55,* 95–102.

Foote, N. N., & Cottrell, L. S. (1955). *Identity and interpersonal competence.* Chicago: University of Chicago Press.

Foster, B. G., Jackson, G., Cross, W. E., Jackson, B., & Hardiman, R. (1988). Workforce diversity and business. *Training & Development Journal,* April, 15–19.

Gardner, G. H. (1962). Cross-cultural communication. *Journal of Social Psychology, 58,* 241–256.

Glenn, E. S., & Glenn, C. G. (1981). *Man and mankind: Conflict and communication between cultures.* Norwood, NJ: Ablex.

Goldstein, I. L., & Gilliam, P. (1990). Training system issues in the year 2000. *American Psychologist, 45,* 143.

Gudykunst, W. B. (1993). Toward a theory of effective interpersonal and intergroup communication: An anxiety/uncertainty management (AUM) perspective. In R. L. Wiseman & J. Koester (Eds.), *Intercultural communication competence* (pp. 33–71). Newbury Park, CA: Sage.

———, & Hammer, M. R. (1983). Basic training design: Approaches to intercultural training. In D. Landis &

R. W. Brislin (Eds.), *Handbook of intercultural training*, Vol. 1 (pp. 118–154). New York: Pergamon.

———, Hammer, M. R., & Wiseman, R. L. (1977). An analysis of an integrated approach to cross-cultural training. *International Journal of Intercultural Relations*, 2, 99–110.

———, & Kim, Y. Y. (1992). *Communicating with strangers*. New York: McGraw-Hill.

———, Ting-Toomey, S., & Wiseman, R. (1991). Taming the beast: Designing a course in intercultural communication. *Communication Quarterly, 40, 272–286.*

———, Yang, S. M., & Nishida, T. (1987). Cultural differences in self-consciousness and unself-consciousness. *Communication Research, 14, 7–36.*

Gullahorn, J. T., & Gullahorn, J. E. (1963). An extension of the U-curve hypothesis. *Journal of Social Issues, 19*, 33–47.

Hamachek, D. E. (1982). *Encounters with others: Interpersonal relationships and you*. New York: Holt, Rinehart, & Winston.

Hart, R. P., & Burks, D. M. (1972). Rhetorical sensitivity and social interaction. *Speech Monographs, 39*, 75–91.

Hart, R. P., Carlson, R. E., & Eadie, W. F. (1980). Attitudes toward communication and the assessment of rhetorical sensitivity. *Communication Monographs, 47*, 1–22.

Hoopes, D. S. (1981). Intercultural communication concepts and the psychology of intercultural experience. In M. D. Pusch (Ed.), *Multicultural education: A cross-cultural training approach*. Chicago: Intercultural Press.

Lustig, M. W., & Koester, J. (1996). *Intercultural competence*. New York: HarperCollins.

Martin, J. N., & Hammer, M. R. (1989). Behavioral categories of intercultural communication competence: Everyday communicators' perceptions. *International Journal of Intercultural Relations, 13*, 303–332.

McClelland, D. C. (1958). Review and prospect. In D. C. McClelland (Ed.), *Talent and society*. New York: Van Nostrand.

Morgan, E., & Weigel, V. (1988). *Credits and credibility: Educating professionals for cultural sensitivity*. Paper presented at the Conference on Science and Technology for International Development, Myrtle Beach, SC.

Morrison, A. M., & Von Glinow, M. A. (1990). Women and minorities in management. *American Psychologist, 45*, 200–207.

Nieto, S. (1992). *Affirming diversity*. New York: Longman.

Parker, V. M., Valley, M. M., & Geary, C. A. (1986). Acquiring cultural knowledge for counselors in training: A multi-faceted approach. *Counselor Education and Supervision, 26*, 61–71.

Parks, M. R. (1976, November). *Communication competence*. Paper presented at the annual meeting of Speech Communication Association, San Francisco.

———. (1994). Communication competence and interpersonal control. In M. L. Knapp & G. R. Miller (Eds.), *Handbook of interpersonal communication* (pp. 589–618). Thousand Oaks, CA: Sage.

Randolph, G., Landis, D., & Tzeng, O. (1977). The effects of time and practice upon Culture Assimilator training. *International Journal of Intercultural Relations, 1*, 105–119.

Ruben, B. D. (1976). Assessing communication competency for intercultural adaptation. *Group & Organization Studies, 1*, 334–354.

———. (1977). Guidelines for cross-cultural communication effectiveness. *Group & Organization Studies, 2*, 470–479.

Seidel, G. (1981). Cross-cultural training procedures: Their theoretical framework and evaluation. In S. Bochner (Ed.). *The mediating person: Bridge between cultures*. Cambridge, UK: Schenhman.

Smith, H. (1966). *Sensitivity to people*. New York: McGraw-Hill.

Smith, S. W., Cody, M. J., Lovette, S., & Canary, D. J. (1990). Self-monitoring, gender and compliance-gaining goals. In M. J. Cody & M. L. McLaughlin (Eds.), *The psychology of tactical communication* (pp. 91–134). Clevedon, UK: Multilingual Matters.

Snyder, M. (1974). Self-monitoring of expressive behavior. *Journal of Personality and Psychology, 30*, 528.

Spitzberg, B. H. (1989). Issues in the development of a theory of interpersonal competence in intercultural context. *International Journal of Intercultural Relations, 13*, 241–268.

Spitzberg, B. H., & Cupach, W. R. (1984). *Interpersonal communication competence*. Beverly Hills, CA: Sage Publications.

Sue, D. W. (1994). A model for cultural diversity training. In L. A. Samovar & R. E. Porter (Eds.), *Intercultural communication: A reader* (pp. 382–391). Belmont, CA: Wadsworth.

Ting-Toomey, S. (1989). Identity and interpersonal bond. In M. K. Asante & W. B. Gudykunst (Eds.), *Handbook of international and intercultural communication* (pp. 151–173). Newbury Park, CA: Sage.

Triandis, H. C. (1977). Theoretical framework for evaluation of cross-cultural training effectiveness. *International Journal of Intercultural Relations, 1*, 195–213.

Valdivieso, R., & David, C. (1988). *Hispanics: Challenging issues for the 1990s*. Washington, DC: Population Trends and Public Policy.

Yum, J. O. (1989). *Communication sensitivity and empathy in culturally diverse organizations*. Paper presented at the 75th Annual Conference of Speech Communication Association, San Francisco.

Concepts and Questions

1. How does intercultural sensitivity differ from intercultural awareness and intercultural competence?
2. What is meant by the statement that intercultural sensitivity is "a development process"? What are the stages of this process?
3. What are the generally accepted categories of intercultural training programs?
4. How does affective training differ from cognitive training?
5. What is area simulation training? How does it contribute to cultural sensitivity?
6. How does self-esteem relate to cultural sensitivity?
7. What is open-mindedness, and how can it facilitate the development of cultural sensitivity?
8. What is empathy essential to developing cultural sensitivity?
9. What is interaction involvement? How does it contribute to cultural sensitivity?
10. How does the suspension of judgment increase one's ability to be culturally sensitive?

Managing Cultural Diversity in the American Workplace

Mohan R. Limaye

The composition of the U.S. workforce has been changing over the last few decades because of differing immigration patterns, the coming of the baby boomers into middle age, and a growing number of women and minorities entering and staying on at the workplace, to name but a few contributing factors. This creates cultural diversity on a scale of magnitude not seen before in the U.S. workplace. The business press frequently refers to the growing diversity of American workers and the necessity for adapting them to U.S. corporate cultures (Loden, 1996; Nemetz & Christensen, 1996; Sussman, 1997; Thiederman, 1991). According to U.S. census data, people of color constituted approximately 18 percent of the total civilian labor force of the country in 1995. Out of a total 132.3 million workers, 23.8 percent were African American and Hispanic or Latino (U.S. Bureau of the Census, 1996). No wonder the U.S. corporate world has taken note of this changing landscape and started examining how this influx of nontraditional people from diverse cultural backgrounds may fit into U.S. businesses and affect corporate productivity and competitiveness.

Instituted by U.S. business organizations as a response to the growing cultural diversity of their employees, most diversity training programs (DTPs) aim to teach management and workers to value diversity through a two-pronged approach—knowledge and sensitivity. The means used by most DTPs is to make employees aware of the *other* (the cognitive approach) and sensitize them to the perils of ethnocentrism (the affective approach). These programs, however, are failing to achieve much progress

This original essay appears here for the first time. All rights reserved. Permission to reprint must be obtained from the publisher and the author. Mohan R. Limaye teaches at Boise State University.

in the retention and promotion of women and people of color. In addition, the number of firms with 100 or more employees sponsoring such programs has dropped from 56 percent in 1994 to 53 percent in 1995 (Gordon, Hequet, Lee, & Picard, 1996).

The thesis of this article is that the current diversity programs are too focused on changing the individual rather than the organization. Their emphasis on cognitive and affective paradigms needs to be supplemented by a more important emphasis: *organizational change*. This article attempts to explain the failure of corporate DTPs and their inherent weaknesses, suggests going beyond the individual-level psychological paradigms currently supreme in various diversity training programs, and makes some recommendations for enabling substantive change in U.S. business organizations.

GOALS OF DIVERSITY INITIATIVES

Scholars, trainers, and businesses generally agree that diversity is desirable, and ethnocentric attitudes and discriminatory behaviors are not just illegal but also counterproductive. Human resource managers and consultants seeking workforce diversity mention the following as desirable goals for DTPs:

1. recruiting and retaining minority workers, including women
2. enhancing employee satisfaction
3. empowering diverse employees
4. promoting or advancing the careers of employees regardless of their color or gender (to name just two dimensions of diversity)
5. increasing organizational innovation and creativity through individual employees' contributions
6. communication synergy

Diversity training in most corporations, unfortunately, has not been successful in attaining most of these goals (Martinez, 1997; Thomas, 1996; Verespej, 1997). Though one reason for such failure might be the lip service paid by management to the concept of valuing diversity—that is, to appear politically correct—the greater share of nonattainment of the goals belongs to the idea held by many trainers that if only individuals change, everything else will fall in place.

COGNITIVE AND AFFECTIVE APPROACHES

Most training consultants come from disciplines such as psychology (industrial or organizational), communication, education, and, at times, anthropology. As such, their intervention preference is for attempting to change the worldview and attitudes of the individual. The individual or interpersonal is most often their focus. The aim to wean the individual from cultural blindness and ethnocentric reactions to intercultural encounters and to teach cross-cultural communication competence (Beamer, 1992; Brislin & Yoshida, 1994; Schaaf, 1981).

Two psychological paradigms, *cognitive* and *affective*, serve as the basis for these programs. The cognitive paradigm maintains, in essence, that the more we learn about others different from us, the more successfully we can cope with and manage diversity. The cognitive paradigm, therefore, emphasizes knowledge about both our own culture and cultures other than ours (Black & Mendenhall, 1990; Bogorya, 1985; Swenson, 1980). The cognitive stages in diversity training attempt to lead corporate participants from an awareness of the primary dimensions of diversity (such as gender, age, race, physical ability, and sexual orientation) to knowledge about the secondary dimensions, including religious beliefs, geography, marital status, family influences, and job context (Loden, 1996; Walker, 1991). As a result of such training, it is hoped that the participants will move from acceptance of differences to adaptation and finally to "integration of differences into one's world view" (Bennett, 1986, p. 179). The cognitive paradigm thus rests on the assumption that the more we learn about others different from us, the more success we may have in coping with diversity at the workplace (Albert, 1983).

The affective portion of most corporate diversity training is aimed at changing the trainee's heart and making him or her sensitive and empathetic toward the culturally different. The goal is to lead the trainee through simulation and role playing to sensitivity toward other cultures (Kolb, 1984; Redmond, 1989). Affective models attempt to imitate as closely as possible the experiences of people who live in a variant culture and expose participants in diversity seminars to approximations of such life situations (Steinkalk & Taft, 1979). These exposures to dramatized situations presumably create empathy for the culturally diverse. Hence, proponents of the affective paradigm emphasize role play and consciousness-raising techniques as effective training methods for preparing trainees to cope with diversity. Shames (1986) summarizes the processes visualized in corporate-sponsored DTPs based on cognitive and affective paradigms: "Readings and self-assessment instruments introduce concepts and trigger insight; case studies and culture assimilators process and apply learning; and role plays and simulation games allow trainees to try out new behavior and develop cultural skills" (p. 27).

REASONS FOR THE CURRENT INDIVIDUAL-LEVEL EMPHASIS

There are several reasons for the emphasis on individual change in corporate training on diversity:

1. The bias of most trainers has already been touched upon. Psychologists and educators are often themselves trained to work with individuals and with employee intervention techniques geared to bring about change in the individual.
2. U.S. business is more interested in employees adapting to the workplace and its culture than modifying the business culture to meet diverse employees halfway (Goddard, 1989; Paskoff, 1996; Ragins, 1997; Thomas, 1996).
3. Organizing a training program is easier than reconfiguring institutional structures and practices.
4. Some diversity programs in U.S. corporations seem to hope that organization-wide equity would result if everybody treated every one else nicely, if human relations improved among all the employees of the organization. This may arguably be treating the symptoms rather than the cause of a disease, which lies deep in the institutional tilt toward those who wield power in the workplace (Scott & Christensen, 1995).

ATTRIBUTION OF DTPs' FAILURE

Why have corporate diversity programs by and large not realized their promise? To what phenomena can we attribute this failure? There are three main reasons. First, diversity workshops have not faced the real problem, namely, the clustering of women and minority at the bottom levels of U.S. corporate hierarchy. One can argue that without the presence of affirmative action and equal employment opportunity legislation, the executive ranks of U.S. businesses would have remained even more dominated by white males than they are today (Ezorsky, 1991; Fine, 1995). As is, only 2.4 percent of top U.S. executives are female (Martinez, 1997), and 9 percent of all U.S. *mid*-level managers belong to minority cultures (Soloman, 1990). Fine, Johnson, and Ryan (1990) report that "at the time of the study [1988 and 1989], no managerial positions were held by minorities" in the federal agency they investigated, which employed more than 500 people. Accelerated advancement for underrepresented employee groups as a planned human resource policy will be one of the solutions, not one of the Pollyannaish "You are OK, I am OK" type of therapy sessions that are conducted in the name of diversity training in many U.S. firms.

Second, most DTPs proceed from the implicit assumption that difference is deficient (Nkomo, 1992). This assumption gives much training a remedial flavor. Even trainers who believe diversity is an asset end up designing programs that aim to remediate. Even today, in many U.S. organizations there is either a denial that differences matter or a pervasive expectation that everybody conform to the organizational norms of behaviors of the top brass. Most DTPs willing to preserve the status quo therefore emphasize acculturation and skill building for diverse or minority employees (Dreyfuss, 1990; Goddard, 1989). In other words, the perception that corporate culture is not going to change results in the entire burden for behavior modification and assimilation being placed on the new recruits who, in a number of cases, either quit or are fired because they could not conform or did not desire to conform.

Third, diversity workshops have to depend for their success on the goodwill of top managers who may not themselves be really committed to change. As mentioned before, they may have approved of training to appear politically correct. Many white males may not be too eager to relinquish the power they have been used to wielding for several generations (Thomas, 1990). After all, why would they be eager to change their organizations' profile when the status quo is in their favor? Incidentally, human history does not reveal cases of powerful groups sharing their power voluntarily with disadvantaged or powerless others. No wonder far-reaching structural and procedural changes have neither been suggested nor frequently implemented in U.S. organizations as a result of diversity training. Training consultants are rarely empowered to recommend sweeping changes or organization-level prescriptions because they are often given a limited charge. How could they dare suggest anything radical enough to limit the power of the top managers when their fees are paid by the top team?

WEAKNESSES OF INDIVIDUAL-LEVEL INTERVENTION

Shallow and Self-Seeking DTPs

Individual-level intervention (based on cognitive and affective theories) as practiced in U.S. corporations often suffers from several problems and weaknesses. To obtain lasting attitudinal and behavioral changes in individual employees, diversity workshops need to be in-depth, frequent, and broadbased. In practice, however, they are shallow and often one-shot deals targeted to lower-level employees. Many diversity workshops and videos deal superficially with issues of interpersonal and group relationships at the workplace rather than probe to find out their deep-seated causes such as prejudice and bigotry. Van Dijk (1993) cites instances of deceptive logic and discourse at various levels of the corporate ladder that go unreproved and are glossed over by trainers. As mentioned above, being employed by top management and hence beholden to corporate executives for their consultancy fees, trainers do not suggest changes that will upset the status quo in organizations. If they are in the regular employ of a corporation (as many diversity workshops are often run by the human resource or personnel departments of business organizations), they are even less likely to recommend to top management radical policy and procedural changes. These organizational realities only reinforce the sycophantic nature of most DTPs.

Low-Level Employee Attendance at Most DTPs

As Fine (1995) indicates, a large majority of training sessions are usually mandatory and attended by the lower strata of employees. Top executives rarely attend such sessions. They quite often give short opening addresses that sing in abstract the praises of diversity. That is where the involvement of most top managers ends. Even for those low-level employees who attend, the training quite often is a one- or two-shot deal; very rarely do corporations engage in frequent reinforcing-training sessions. It is like seminars on sexual harassment awareness that, at most institutions I have researched, are one-time exposures; the only concern that high-level executives seem to have is that all employees have attended at least once so the organization is politically and legally covered.

Absence of Outcomes Assessment

On top of this grudging endorsement of diversity training, in many organizations there is an absence of measurement mechanisms to monitor the outcomes—the "progress"—that are sorely needed (Cox, 1993; Nelton, 1994). Pre- and post-training data and criteria to measure the performance and value of corporate diversity seminars are lacking in training and development literature (Black & Mendenhall, 1990; Elshult & Little, 1990; Lissy, 1993). therefore, it is anybody's guess whether attitudinal changes occurred, to what extent, and how long-lasting they will be. The only apparent outcome is a warm fuzzy feeling on the part of human resource management departments of having done their duty.

INADEQUACY OF INDIVIDUAL-LEVEL PSYCHOLOGICAL APPROACHES

A serious weakness underlying the hyperfocus on individual-level change is the faulty assumption that prejudice can be totally explained by an attitudinal flaw within an individual. Prejudice, according to this school of thought, is an individual aberration, the result of hasty generalization or a deviation caused by overgeneralization (Feagin, 1991). The cure, therefore, is clear and simple: Treat the "diseased" individuals, and the therapy is to provide them with correct knowledge (cognitive approach) and appropriate sensitivities (affective approach). This oversimplification of the problem ignores the influence of groups and social forces on the formation and perpetuation of sexist and racist attitudes. It belittles institutional or systemic impact on the conscious and unconscious attitudes of individuals and their behaviors (Kluegel & Smith, 1986).

The common penchant holds only the individual accountable for her or his beliefs, attitudes, and behaviors. It ignores institutional influences or, as in this case, assigns racial, gender, and age-related prejudices to the individual rather than to the group, which exempts dominant and privileged groups from responsibility for these social maladies and from facing racism and sexism directly. As a result, they do not have to take concerted corrective action to ameliorate the situation on the institutional level. This view holds only the individual as an agent of moral action and lets organizations go without having to bear their fair share of ethical conduct.

Sociologists, however, agree that human actions are in reality often socially driven even though, on the surface, they appear to be individually driven (Boden, Giddens, & Molotch, 1990; Kanter, 1977; Nkomo, 1992). A purely individual approach conceals the fact that inequities are often embedded in social structures and also the fact that "prejudice, discrimination, and racism do not require (individual) intention" (Pine & Hilliard, 1990, p. 595). The most recent example of this phenomenon, one can argue, is the racist rhetoric during early September 1995 by Mark Fuhrman, a former Los Angeles Police Department (LAPD) detective involved in the O. J. Simpson criminal trial. The institutional atmosphere of the LAPD and the milieu of the area in which Fuhrman grew up could be two formative influences (both group or social level phenomena) on his attitudes and beliefs.

BEYOND INDIVIDUAL-LEVEL PARADIGMS

The strongest case for moving beyond cognition and affect, beyond individual-level analysis is provided by the argument that the current diversity training in

U.S. corporations misses the most significant point: The issue of responding to or managing diversity is not merely a matter of knowing the right things and feeling the appropriate sentiments on the individual level but of *willingness* by a group to share power in the organizational setting. Readiness to give up privilege is the best response to the challenges posed by diversity. Power in organizations—how it is acquired and how distributed—is a topic handled by a few academics or organization theorists (Pfeffer, 1981), but business press and corporate trainers rarely deal with it. However, as Russell (1983) states, "the fundamental concept in social science is power, in the same sense in which energy is the fundamental concept in physics" (p. 12). The greatest obstacle to fair and sensitive treatment of diverse employees in an organization is the resistance from those who wield power in that organization and who are unwilling to share it with those who are marginalized (Feagin, 1991; Kanter, 1977; Lissy, 1993).

From the Micro to the Macro Level

Psychological paradigms that are based on cognition and affect and used in diversity workshops direct most training effort at the microlevel toward changing an individual's values and behaviors. A movement is necessary away from individually targeted psychological paradigms to enable trainers to explain change at the macrolevel of organizations. It is reasonable to expect that different effects will result from intervention at the macro or institutional level—effects that are more likely to produce equity, fairness, and decision-making power for women and people of color in U.S. organizations. Although some knowledge about the diverse and sensitivity to cultural difference are prerequisites to positive changes in individuals, they are in themselves inadequate answers to coping with diversity and benefiting by it in an organization.

Responding to diversity, one must realize, is a political issue and the answer therefore is also a political answer. If institutions are allowed to persist in their old forms with traditional systems and structures intact that discriminate in effect (if not by intent), then they will continue reinforcing old attitudes among their employees and subvert changes being promoted on the individual-employee level.

That is why changing group or institutional behaviors is of paramount importance, and this is a political agenda because it strikes at the heart of the power structure of an organization. Institution-level changes therefore must go hand-in-hand with individual-level changes. The use of social science constructs (particularly from sociology and political science) as a powerful framework to study the acquisition and distribution of power in organizations can be a first move to complement the individual psychological approaches that have so far formed the basis of most DTPs. This argument provides the logic behind the thesis of this article.

I therefore suggest two macro or organization-level changes.

DEMOCRATIZATION OF THE U.S. WORKPLACE

To respond positively to diversity in the workforce, U.S. organizations must be willing to share power and resources with employees at all levels of hierarchy. Because I am advocating sociopolitical perspectives to respond to diversity, it is in line with that advocacy to recommend distribution of authority and decision-making power among all employees down the ladder of the organization. On serious issues such as organizational mission and goals, conflicts or differences of opinion are bound to occur in a diverse organization. Consensual decision making about such issues should be encouraged in U.S. organizations. Operationalizing the political principle of equality in the world of business would translate into encouraging and ensuring participation in organizational decision making by *all* employees (traditional as well as nontraditional) regardless of their race, gender, age, ethnicity, national origin, or physical disability. This would mean culturally diverse employees being authorized to influence institutional behaviors. This is empowerment in action, not just the rhetorical or euphemistic buzzword popular in management literature and in the exhortations by top executive officers of U.S. business.

Currently, low-level employees do not have a voice in the day-to-day management of most U.S. organizations, let alone any voice in the formation of strategies and mission or goals for organizations.

Importing the political concept of empowerment into the body economic—that is, applying the principles of proportionate representation and distribution of authority to business organizations—will confer meaningful voice to the lowly. Such power sharing will most likely boost employee morale and enhance their loyalty to the employing organizations.

Along with precedents in the political sphere (one person, one vote) that attempt to guard every individual's rights, there are also precedents in the industrial sphere for such practices. Co-determination in German industry is one such precedent from which the United States can learn (Bridgford & Stirling, 1994). It is a legally established practice that allows workers a meaningful voice in the management of the organization. The German mandate allows a fully developed system of employee participation in management. "Germany . . . has works councils which grant to employees a strong or *equal* voice in a number of matters relating to employee affairs, such as the beginning and end of the working day, distribution of work time, and wage policy. Co-determination also enables the direct participation of worker representatives in the management bodies of the corporation" (August 1993, p. 156).

USE OF SPANISH AS CO-LANGUAGE

The issue of language is germane or central to diversity in the workplace. The role of minority languages such as Spanish is of utmost relevance to synergizing diverse workers' talents and abilities in U.S. business organizations. The language issue is even more closely bound up with power, control, and justice than, for instance, the issues of decentralization of authority and consensual decision making. In the case of language, power has been traditionally retained in the United States by those who speak English as their native language and use it expertly. Incidentally, the case of Canada is similar: The Anglophone Canadians historically (and until recently) have held more economic power and dominance than French-speaking Canadians from the province of Quebec. The exclusive use of English in the United States as a language of government, education, law courts, and business (to mention prominent uses) was not such a hardship to the European immigrants after their second generation assimilated into the melting pot. The use of English as the de facto sole official language of the United States in all substantive aspects of American life has continued to be a liability for the Spanish-speaking population in this country.

The Unique Case of Spanish in the United States

For several reasons, the case of Spanish speakers in the United States is different from the case of the European immigrants who came to the United States. The Europeans came from elsewhere, while Spanish speakers were already living in the lands that the United States acquired from Spain or Mexico. Second, the Europeans lost contact with the Old World and, in most cases, did not desire any contact with the countries of their birth once they literally turned their backs on Europe. Because of continuing legal and illegal immigration, for instance, of Mexicans in this country and the long land border between the United States and Mexico, there is a back-and-forth cultural and linguistic movement across the border. The "Spanish problem" is not, therefore, going to go away even though many second-, third-, and fourth-generation Hispanics only speak English. Fresh reinforcements of people from south of the U.S. border and modern mass media (Spanish radio stations and television channels) are likely to keep Spanish alive, at least, in states such as California, Arizona, New Mexico, Texas, and Florida. The Hispanic population is large enough to affect the demand for Spanish in the southern United States.

An argument that a large linguistic minority has a right to its language is buttressed by demands based on justice or fairness. Bilingual education misses the point that once a language is lost, a culture is lost. Because bilingual education aims to wean students (in this case, Spanish speakers) from their native language and teach them to use English fluently, if such programs are successful, they are eventually likely to replace Spanish with English. By definition, bilingual education is a transitional stage and is unfair because it violates people's rights to their language. The use of Spanish along with English in organizations with a sizable proportion of Spanish-speaking employees and operating in Hispanic areas of this country will boost minority workers' self-respect and morals, as well as strengthen the chances of a peaceful coexistence among people of diverse cultures in the U.S. workplace. The specter of high costs associated with the use of two languages may deter organizations from following such a course, but the benefits, though in some cases intangible, are nonetheless real and long-lasting in terms of communal and linguistic harmony in states where Hispanics constitute a large minority, if not a majority.

Anglo-Americans need to recognize that the argument for recommending the use of Spanish along with English as a guaranteed right in business organizations operating in Hispanic areas has a strong ethical basis. Spanish speakers have gotten a raw deal at the U.S. workplace. Insisting only on English in the workplace, as all Anglo-dominated U.S. companies do, is a mark of colonial and ethnocentric behavior. The fact that the American Southwest was acquired through aggression against Mexico makes the proposal for Spanish as a co-language a moral imperative for Anglo-American businesses to adopt, a sort of atonement for sins or a reparation for damages.

PROBABILITY OF IMPLEMENTATION OF THE RECOMMENDATIONS

Even though I have suggested only two changes, they are far-reaching and would necessitate sweeping reforms in the ways organizational power brokers think and operate. Cox (1993) also suggests a reconfiguration of affirmative action that just falls short of the label "quota." Because both the changes I have recommended require or presuppose sharing of power, I see no hope of proactive moves by business organizations to embrace the recommended changes. Human history does not offer examples of power shared or privilege renounced voluntarily. Business is no exception. Van Dijk (1993) reports a trade-union perception that "most employers will only comply with AA [affirmative action] policies when there is legal pressure on them, and even then they will hire minorities for only the worst jobs" (p. 150). Kavanaugh and Retish (1992) trace the history of how exploitation of workers of Mexican origin became institutionalized soon after the Mexican-

American War ended. They only hope that U.S. business would not repeat history and confirm "Mexico's worst fears with regard to the proposed [now already in effect] free trade agreement [NAFTA]" (p. 94).

The Myth of the Business Case of Diversity

The popular business press and those who advocate diversity measures (Loden, 1996; Thomas, 1996) in U.S. organizations tirelessly offer corporations the carrot that encouraging diversity makes business sense and is profitable. They maintain that they can sell enhancement of creativity and adaptiveness to change as benefits of diversity, as the qualities that diverse workers will bring with them, making businesses increasingly competitive (Herriot & Pemberton, 1995). They point out that the different worldviews that nontraditional employees bring with them will be an asset to companies that are proactive in recruiting and retaining women and people of color. Though sporadic self-reports of a proactive stance toward diversity initiatives by such U.S. business corporations as Avon, U.S. West, and Pepsico are narrated by trade writers as success stories (Nelton, 1994; Shames, 1986; Thomas, 1996), a dearth of empirical findings substantiate the claims of benefit from diversity. Because businesses are persuaded by the bottom line, corporations are unlikely to undertake massive efforts to implement diversity-related changes in their organizations until hard data about the profitability of diversity come up. Until then, they will only do whatever is politically correct and only to the minimum degree necessary. Loden (1996) strongly urges DTPs to make the business case for diversity; however, in her book of 184 pages there is not even half a page of data-driven, bottom-line argument. In fact, not one instance can be found that makes the business case.

If a claim or case for diversity cannot be made based on economic imperative or profit motive, then what is the probability of U.S. businesses adopting the change measures recommended in this essay? Not much, unless the pressure to do so becomes unbearable for them as in the case of affirmative action and equal employment initiatives. These initiatives in the form of enabling legislation during President Lyndon Johnson's administration were not enacted voluntarily by legislators in Congress out of the goodness of their hearts, but only under the moral and political pressure brought about by the African American activism of the 1950s and early 1960s. Businesses are even less susceptible to moral pressure or ethical considerations. The battle for winning the changes recommended here will again have to be a political one, like the civil rights battle of the 1960s. Nondominant groups or castes have to fight for their rights, for an equitable share of the pie. And, as Professor Folb observes, "In the United States, the most visible marks of caste relate to gender, race, age, and the degree to which one is able-bodied" (1997, p. 142).

CONCLUSION

The political and moral atmosphere in the United States in the late 1990s is not very favorable for the adoption of the organization-level changes recommended in this essay. Fresh attacks on affirmative action from the majority party in Congress and even judicial verdicts against people's right to their language have created a dismal landscape for the future of diversity programs and meaningful respect for women and people of color. The Texas judge "who told a Mexican native that she was dooming her daughter to life as a housemaid by speaking only Spanish to her" (Idaho Statesman, 1995) was only reflecting the mood of the country, flooded with English-only official-language propositions. All the woman was doing was passing her ancestral culture and language to her daughter who would have been exposed to the English language anyway as soon as she left her house. Nkomo (1992) refers to the white elite that is unwilling to own or admit the existence of institutional racism in the midst of the United States. In such a climate, the suggested changes have a chance for adoption by U.S. business organizations only if the arguments for justice, equity, and democracy are buttressed by the will of the people to fight for them and only if the political activism of the 1960s surges again among women and people of color. The institution-level changes recommended here are otherwise too sweeping and radical for those in power who will not be happy at the prospect of the diminution of their hold on organizational resources and decision making. But "hope springs eternal in the human breast," and people have fought for justice against all odds and won.

References

Albert, R. D. (1983). The intercultural sensitizer or culture assimilator: A cognitive approach. In D. Landis & R. W. Brislin (Eds.), *Handbook of intercultural training,* Vol. 2 (pp. 186–217). New York: Pergamon.

August, R. (1993). *International business law: Text, cases, and readings.* Englewood Cliffs, NJ: Prentice-Hall.

Beamer, L. (1992). Learning intercultural communication competence. *Journal of Business Communication, 29,* 285–303.

Bennett, M. J. (1986). A developmental approach to training for intercultural sensitivity. *International Journal of Intercultural Relations, 10,* 179–196.

Black, J. S., & Mendenhall, M. (1990). Cross-cultural training effectiveness: A review and a theoretical framework for future research. *Academy of Management Review, 15,* 113–136.

Boden, D., Giddens, A., & Molotch, H. L. (1990). Sociology's role in addressing society's problems is undervalued and misunderstood in academe. *Chronicle of Higher Education, 36*(23), B1, B3.

Bogorya, Y. (1985). Intercultural training for managers involved in international business. *Journal of Management Development, 4*(2), 48–56.

Bridgford, J., & Stirling, J. (1994). *Employee relations in Europe.* Oxford, UK: Blackwell.

Brislin, R.W., & Yoshida, T. (1994). *Intercultural communication training: An introduction.* Thousand Oaks, CA: Sage.

Cox, T. H., Jr. (1993). *Cultural diversity in organizations.* San Francisco: Berrett-Koehler Publishers.

Dreyfuss, J. (1990, April 23). Get ready for the new work force. *Fortune,* pp. 165–181.

Elshult, S., & Little, J. (1990). The case for valuing diversity. *HR Magazine,* pp. 50–51.

Ezorsky, G. (1991). *Racism and justice: The case for affirmative action.* Ithaca, NY: Cornell University Press.

Feagin, J. R. (1991). Blacks still face the malevolent reality of white racism. *Chronicle of Higher Education, 38*(14), A44.

Fine, M. G. (1995). *Building successful multicultural organizations: Challenges and opportunities.* Westport, CT: Quorum Books.

————, Johnson, F. L., & Ryan, S. M. (1990). Cultural diversity in the workplace. *Public Personnel Management, 19,* 305–319.

Folb, E. A. (1997). Who's got the room at the top? Issues of dominance and nondominance in intracultural communication. In L. A. Samovar & R. E. Porter, *Intercultural communication: A reader,* 8th ed. (pp. 138–146). Belmont, CA: Wadsworth.

Goddard, R. W. (1989). Workforce 2000. *Personnel Journal, 68,* 64–71.

Gordon, J., Hequet, M., Lee, C., & Picard, M. (1996). Is diversity training heading south? *Training, 33*(2), 12–14.

Haight, G. (1990). Managing diversity. *Across the Board, 27*(3), 22–29.

Herriot, P., & Pemberton, C. (1995). *Competitive advantage through diversity: Organizational learning from difference.* Thousand Oaks, CA: Sage.

Idaho Statesman. (1995, Sept. 9). Nation roundup.

Kanter, R. M. (1977). *Men and women of the corporation.* New York: Basic Books.

Kavanaugh, P., & Retish, P. (1992). An abused labor pool: Workers of Mexican origin in the U.S. economy. *Human Resource Development Quarterly, 3*(1), 89–95.

Kluegel, J. R., & Smith, E. R. (1986). *Beliefs about inequality: Americans' views of what is and what ought to be.* New York: De Gruyter.

Kolb, D. A. (1984). *Experiential learning.* Englewood Cliffs, NJ: Prentice-Hall.

Limaye, M. R. (1994). Responding to workforce diversity: Conceptualization and search for paradigms. *Journal of Business and Technical Communication, 8,* 353–372.

Lissy, W. E. (1993). U.S. female executives see improvements in pay and job status but say they still hit a glass ceiling. *Compensation and Benefits Review, 25*(6), 9–10.

Loden, M. (1996). *Implementing diversity.* Chicago: Irwin Professional Publishing.

Martinez, M. (1997). Prepared for the future. *HR Magazine, 42*(4), 80–84.

Nelton, S. (1994). Meet your new work force. In *Race and gender in the American economy: Views from across the spectrum* (pp. 72–77). Englewood Cliffs, NJ: Prentice Hall.

Nemetz, P., & Christensen, S. (1996). The challenge of cultural diversity: Harnessing a diversity of views to understand multiculturalism. *Academy of Management Review, 21,* 434–462.

Nkomo, S. M. (1992). The emperor has no clothes: Rewriting race organizations. *Academy of Management Review, 17,* 487–513.

Olsten Corporation. (1995). Managing and developing the new work force. *Olsten Forum on Human Resource Issues and Trends,* 1–10.

Paskoff, S. M. (1996). Ending the workplace diversity wars. *Training, 33*(8), 42–47.

Pfeffer, J. (1981). *Power in organizations.* Marshfield, MA: Pitman.

Pine, G. J., & Hilliard, A. G., III. (1990). Rx for racism: Imperatives for America's schools. *Phi Delta Kappan*, 71, 593–600.

Ragins, B. R. (1997). Diversified mentoring relationships in organizations: A power perspective. *Academy of Management Review*, 22, 482–521.

Redmond, M. V. (1989). The functions of empathy (decentering) in human relations. *Human Relations*, 41, 593–605.

Russell, B. (1983). *Power: A social analysis*. New York: Norton.

Schaaf, D. (1981). The growing need for cross-cultural and bilingual training." *Training/HRD* (January), 85–86.

Scott, W. R., & Christensen, S. (1995). *The institutional construction of organizations: International and longitudinal studies*. Thousand Oaks, CA: Sage.

Shames, G. (1986). Training for the multicultural workplace. *Cornell Hotel and Restaurant Administration*, 26(4), 25–31.

Slater, P., & Bennis, W. G. (1991). Democracy is inevitable. In *Harvard Business Review*, *Participative Management*, 3–12. Cambridge, MA: Harvard Business School.

Soloman, C. (1990). Careers under glass. *Personnel Journal*, 69(4), 96–105.

Steinkalk, E., & Taft, R. (1979). The effects of a planned intercultural experience on the attitudes and behaviors of the participants. *International Journal of Intercultural Relations*, 3, 187–197.

Sussman, L. (1997). Prejudice and behavioral archetypes: A new model of cultural-diversity training. *Business Communication Quarterly*, 60, 7–18.

Swenson, L. L. (1980). *Theories of learning*. Belmont, CA: Wadsworth.

Thiederman, S. (1991). *Bridging cultural barriers for corporate success: How to manage the multicultural workforce*. New York: Lexington Books.

Thomas, R. R., Jr. (1996). *Redefining diversity*. New York: American Management Association.

———. (1990). From affirmative action to affirming diversity. *Harvard Business Review* (March-April), 107–117.

U.S. Bureau of the Census. (1996). *Statistics bulletin 2307*. Washington, DC: U.S. Government Printing Office.

Van Dijk, T. A. (1993). *Elite discourse and racism*. Newbury Park, CA: Sage.

Verespej, M. (1997). Zero tolerance. *Industry Week*, 246(1), 24–28.

Walker, B. A. (1991). Valuing diversity: The concept and a model. In M. A. Smith & S. J. Johnson (Eds.), *Valuing difference in the workplace* (pp. 7–17). Alexandria, VA: ASTD Press.

Concepts and Questions

1. What major difficulty does Limaye have with current diversity programs?

2. What six goals for diversity training programs seem to be commonly accepted by human resource managers and consultants?

3. Distinguish between cognitive and affective approaches to diversity training.

4. Why do current diversity training programs seem to emphasize individual-level changes?

5. What weaknesses does Limaye find in the individual-level intervention approach to diversity training?

6. What is the weakness in the approach to diversity training that assumes that prejudice is an attitudinal failure on the part of the individual?

7. What is wrong with the notion that managing diversity is merely a matter of knowing the right things and feeling the appropriate sentiments on the individual level?

8. What changes does Limaye want to occur when he calls for the democratization of the U.S. workplace?

9. Why does Limaye call for Spanish as a co-language in the U.S. workplace? Why does he not include languages other than Spanish?

10. How does Limaye propose that the needed changes in the U.S. workplace be accomplished? What actions may be expected from management? What actions will be required of workers?

chapter 8

Ethical Considerations: Prospects for the Future

The goal of this book is to help you understand intercultural communication and to assist you in appreciating the issues and problems inherent in interactions involving people from cultures that are different from your own—whether those cultures be across the street or across the ocean. To this end, we have presented a series of diverse essays that examine a variety of variables operable during intercultural encounters. In previous chapters we have looked at what is already known about intercultural communication. We now shift our emphasis and focus on issues that are much more speculative and harder to pin down. These are the ethical considerations that are part of every intercultural encounter. In short, this chapter examines some of the questions we all must confront as we interact with cultures that are different from our own. This contact raises both ethical and philosophical issues about the question of how people from divergent cultures can live together without destroying themselves and the planet. In short, what sort of interpersonal and intercultural ethic must we develop if we are to improve the art and science of intercultural communication?

To set the tone for this final chapter, we begin with an essay by Harlan Cleveland titled "The Limits to Cultural Diversity." Cleveland eloquently alerts us to some of the problems associated with cultural diversity while offering us guidance for the future. The basic problem brought about by increased cultural contact is clear for Cleveland: "Ethnic and religious diversity is creating painful conflicts around the world." Too often these clashes turn one culture against another in ideological disputes. When this happens, according to Cleveland, "culture is being used as an instrument of repression, exclusion, and extinction." Cleveland fears that when people see the chaos created by alien cultures, they "believe that their best haven of certainty and security is a group based on ethnic similarity, common faith, economic interest, or political like-mindedness." Cleveland rejects this "single culture" hypothesis. What he recommends is a counterforce of wider views, global perspectives, and more universal ideas. This universal view, according to Cleveland, rests in a philosophy that has civilization (universal values, ideas, and practices) as the basic core for all humanity. In this analysis, culture represents the "substance and symbols of the community," while civilization is rooted in compromise and built on "cooperation and compassion." With this orientation, people can deal with each other in ways that respect cultural differences while granting essential overarching values. Cleveland's optimism is clearly stated in his conclusion: "For the twenty-first century, the cheerful acknowledgment of differences is the alternative to a planet-wide spread of ethnic cleansing and religious rivalry."

Our next essay, "Intercultural Personhood: An Integration of Eastern and Western Perspectives" by Young Yun Kim, is based on one of the central themes of this book—the idea that today's interconnected and fast-changing world demands that we all change our assumptions about culture and our individual places within that culture. Recognizing these changes, Kim advances a philosophical orientation that she calls "intercultural personhood." For Kim, intercultural personhood combines the key attributes of Eastern and Western cultural traditions. She presents a model that uses these attributes and considers the basic modes of consciousness, cognitive patterns, personal and social values, and communication behavior. The notion of intercultural personhood also leads us into the concept of the multicultural person, as set forth in the next essay.

Communication in any form has the potential to affect others. An ethical dimension therefore must be present in communication to minimize the chance of causing harm to others. In intercultural settings where our ethnocentrism, prejudices, and lack of understanding about other cultures may influence our perceptions of others, the need for an ethical dimension in communicative interaction is paramount.

We begin our exploration of the ethical dimensions of intercultural communication with Robert Shuter's essay "Ethics and Communication: An Intercultural Perspective." Shuter holds the opinion that previous works on ethics and communication have more often than not ignored the issue of culture. To help us gather insight into ethical intercultural communication, Shuter uses an intracultural communication perspective to examine worldviews, values, and communication patterns within a culture to examine cultural ethics. He then explores Confucian and Hindu ethical systems in order to speculate about communication ethics within those systems. Lastly, Shuter discusses communication and demonstrates how communication ethicists have maintained an intracultural bias in their research by focusing on U.S. and Western communication ethics.

Next, David W. Kale, in his essay "Peace as an Ethic for Intercultural Communication," offers several specific challenges. The future is made real by Kale as he presents us with current examples, ranging from our role in the rain forests of Brazil to events taking place in Eastern Europe. Kale begins by acknowledging that most people feel uncomfortable addressing cultural beliefs about what is right and wrong. He reminds us that most of these beliefs are at the very foundation of our lives and our culture. In spite of this uneasiness, increased contact with diverse cultures, combined with the problems that can occur when cultures clash, demand that we examine the issues associated with questions of right and wrong. To help us in that examination, Kale asks that we begin by looking at five interrelated issues directly associated with any evaluation of intercultural ethics: (1) a definition of communication ethics, (2) cultural relativity versus universal ethic, (3) the concept of spirit as a basis for intercultural ethics, (4) peace as the fundamental value in intercultural ethics, and (5) a universal code of ethics in intercultural communication. Kale amplifies the fifth issue by urging us to follow a specific code that is predicated on four principles that should guide the actions of ethical communicators: (1) Address people of other cultures with the same respect that you would like to receive yourself; (2) seek to describe the world as you perceive it as accurately as possible; (3)

encourage people of other cultures to express themselves in their uniqueness; and (4) strive for identification with people of other cultures.

We end this chapter and the book with a final essay by Tom Bruneau. In "Peace Communication: The Ethics of Caring Across Cultures," Bruneau continues the peace theme developed in the previous essay by Kale. Bruneau begins with a discussion of the human image of peace and demonstrates that "in most of humankind's religious and humanitarian traditions, peace is about hopeful, not hopeless, efforts." Using this hopeful perspective as a basis, Bruneau then discusses the image of peace constructed in terms of holy or sacred places, silence, and temporal dimensions. From this philosophic image of peace, he then focuses on peace communication, which is concerned with replacing violence and war with peaceful means of dealing with conflict.

Bruneau holds that "the essence of peace communication concerns those communicative processes that can be termed *empathic*." For Bruneau, empathy means to "feel into" another's feelings. He proceeds with an in-depth discussion of empathy in which he details the affective, imitative, and reflective kinds of empathy. He holds that it is important to recognize "that the processes and types of empathy are different in different social and cultural orders," which adds great complexity to the arena of intercultural communication. Bruneau ends his discussion of empathy by suggesting that the highest form of empathic communication involves mutual empathy in which the parties to peace communication have "shared empathic" abilities.

As we end our readings in this chapter, it might be well to view both Kale's and Bruneau's contributions as well as all the other selections included in this chapter as only a sampling of the many issues that confront those who are involved in intercultural communication. The field is relatively new and the challenges are so varied that it is impossible to accurately predict future directions. Our intent in this chapter, therefore, is simply to introduce you to a few of the concepts that await further discussion as we move into the twenty-first century.

One final note: Much of what we offer in this chapter is subjective and may even appear naive to some of us. Neither we nor the authors of the articles apologize for maintaining that in intercultural contacts each person should aim for the ideal. What we introduce here are suggestions for developing new ways of perceiving oneself and others. In so doing, we can all help make this complex and shrinking planet a more habitable and peaceful place for its nearly six billion residents.

The Limits to Cultural Diversity

HARLAND CLEVELAND

I'm engaged just now in an effort to think through the most intellectually interesting, and morally disturbing, issue in my long experience of trying to think hard about hard subjects. I call it The Limits of Cultural Diversity. If that seems obscure, wait a moment.

After the multiple revolutions of 1989, it began to look as if three ideas we have thought were Good Things would be getting in each other's way, which is not a Good Thing. What I have called the "triple dilemma," or "trilemma," is the mutually damaging collision of individual human rights, cultural human diversity, and global human opportunities. Today the damage from that collision is suddenly all around us.

In 1994, in the middle of Africa, ethnicity took over as an exclusive value, resulting in mass murder by machete. In ex-Yugoslavia (and too many other places), gunpowder and rape accomplish the same purpose: trampling on human rights and erasing human futures.

Even on the Internet, where individuals can now join global groups that are not defined by place-names or cordoned off by gender or ethnicity, people are shouting at each other in flaming, capital-letters rhetoric.

Look hard at your hometown, at the nearest inner city; scan the world by radio, TV, or newspapers and magazines. What's happened is all too clear: Just when individual human rights have achieved superstar status in political philosophy, just when can-do information technologies promise what the U.N. Charter calls "better standards of life in larger freedom," culture and diversity have formed a big, ugly boulder in the road called Future.

"If we cannot end now our differences, at least we can help make the world safe for diversity." That was the key sentence in the most influential speech of

John F. Kennedy's presidency: his commencement address at American University on June 10, 1963. That speech led directly (among other things) to the first nuclear test ban treaty.

For most of the years since then, we were mesmerized by the threat of strategic nuclear war. But now a big nuclear war has become the least likely eventuality among the major threats to human civilization. And that brings us face to face with the puzzle identified in Kennedy's speech: how to make diversity safe.

But is "cultural diversity" really the new Satan in our firmament? Or does it just seem so because "culture" is being used—as Culture has been used in other times and places—as an instrument of repression, exclusion, and extinction?

AN EXCESS OF CULTURAL IDENTITY

In today's disordered world, the collision of cultures with global trends is in evidence everywhere. Ethnic nations, fragmented faiths, transnational business, and professional groups find both their inward loyalties and their international contacts leading them to question the political structures by which the world is still, if tenuously, organized. The results are sometimes symbolic caricatures ("In Rome, can a Moslem minaret be built taller than St. Peter's dome?") and sometimes broken mosaics like the human tragedy in what used to be Yugoslavia.

More people moved in 1994 than ever before in world history, driven by fear of guns or desire for more butter and more freedom. (This was true even before a couple of million Rwandans left their homes in terror—and some were floated out of the country as cadavers.) This more-mobile world multiplies the incentives for individuals to develop "multiple personalities," to become "collages" of identities, with plural loyalties to overlapping groups. Many millions of people believe that their best haven of certainty and security is a group based on ethnic similarity, common faith, economic interest, or political like-mindedness.

Societies based on fear of outsiders tend toward "totalitarian" governance. Fear pushes the culture beyond normal limits on individuals' behavior. "To say that you're ready to *die* for cultural identity," said

From *The Futurist*, March–April, 1995, pp. 23–26. Reprinted by permission of the World Future Society. Harlan Cleveland is president of the World Academy of Art and Science.

one of my colleagues at a workshop of the World Academy of Art and Science in Romania last year, "means that you're also ready to *kill* for cultural identity." Said another: "The ultimate consequence of what's called 'cultural identity' is Hutus and Tutsis murdering each other."

The fear that drives people to cleave to their primordial loyalties makes it harder for them to learn to be tolerant of others who may be guided by different faiths and loyalties. But isolating oneself by clinging to one's tribe is far from a stable condition; these days, the tribe itself is highly unstable. Differences in birth rates and pressures to move will continue to mix populations together. So ethnic purity isn't going to happen, even by forcible "cleansing."

Besides, cultures keep redefining themselves by mixing with other cultures, getting to know people who look, act, and believe differently. In today's more-open electronic world, cultures also expose themselves to new faiths and fashions, new lifestyles, workways, technologies, clothing, and cuisines.

The early stage of every realization of "cultural identity," every assertion of a newfound "right" of differences, does create a distinct group marked by ethnic aspect ("black is beautiful"), gender ("women's lib"), religion ("chosen people"), or status as a political minority. But when members of a group insisting on the group's uniqueness do succeed in establishing their own personal right to be different, something very important happens: They begin to be treated *individually* as equals and tend to integrate with more inclusive communities.

Traditions of separateness and discrimination are often persistent, but they are never permanent and immutable. The recent history of South Africa bears witness.

Before the fighting in Yugoslavia, the most-tolerant people in that part of the world were seen by their close neighbors to be the Serbs, Croats, and Moslems living together in Bosnia and Herzegovina, with the city of Sarajevo as a special haven of mutual tolerance.

The problem does not seem to be culture itself, but cultural overenthusiasm. Cultural loyalties, says one European, have the makings of a runaway nuclear reaction. Without the moderating influence of civil society—acting like fuel rods in a nuclear reactor—the explosive potential gets out of

hand. What's needed is the counterforce of wider views, global perspectives, and more-universal ideas.

Post-communist societies, says a resident of one of them, have experienced a loss of equilibrium, a culture shock from the clash of traditional cultures, nostalgia for the stability of Soviet culture, and many new influences from outside. What's needed, he thinks, is cultural richness without cultural dominance, but with the moderating effect of intercultural respect.

CULTURE AND CIVILIZATION

We have inherited a fuzzy vocabulary that sometimes treats *culture* as a synonym for *civilization*. At a World Academy workshop, my colleagues and I experimented with an alternative construct.

In this construct, *civilization* is what's universal—values, ideas, and practices that are in general currency everywhere, either because they are viewed as objectively "true" or because they are accepted pragmatically as useful in the existing circumstances. These accepted "truths" offer the promise of weaving together a civitas of universal laws and rules, becoming the basis for a global civil society.

What is sometimes called "management culture" appears to be achieving this kind of universal acceptance, hence becoming part of global "civilization." But nobody has to be in charge of practices that are generally accepted. For instance, the international exchange of money—a miracle of information technologies—is remarkably efficient, daily moving more than a trillion dollars' worth of money among countries. Yet, no one is in charge of the system that makes it happen. Recently, the puny efforts of governments to control monetary swings by buying and selling currencies have only demonstrated governments' incapacity to control them.

If civilization is what's universal, *culture* is the substance and symbols of the community. Culture meets the basic human need for a sense of belonging, for participating in the prides and fears that are shared with an in-group.

Both culture and civilization are subject to continuous change. In our time, the most-pervasive changes seem to be brought about by the spread of knowledge, the fallout of information science and information technologies.

Civil society consists of many structures and networks, cutting across cultural fault lines, brought into being by their ability to help people communicate. They are not very dependent on public authority for their charters or their funding, increasingly taking on functions that used to be considered the responsibility of national governments.

Many of these "nongovernments"—such as those concerned, with business and finance, scientific inquiry, the status of women, population policy, and the global environmental commons—have become effective users of modern information technologies. In consequence, they are providing more and more of the policy initiative both inside countries and in world affairs.

Civilization is rooted in compromise—between the idea of a democratic state and a strong state, between a free-market economy and a caring economy, between "open" and "closed" processes, between horizontal and vertical relationships, between active and passive citizenship. The required solvent for civilization is *respect for differences*. Or, as one of my World Academy colleagues puts it, we need to learn *how to be different together*.

Civilization will be built by cooperation and compassion, in a social climate in which people in differing groups can deal with each other in ways that respect their cultural differences. "Wholeness incorporating diversity" is philosopher John W. Gardner's succinct formulation. The slogan on U.S. currency is even shorter, perhaps because it's in Latin: *E pluribus unum* ("from many, one").

LESSONS FROM AMERICAN EXPERIENCE

We Americans have learned, in our short but intensive 200-plus years of history as a nation, a first lesson about diversity: that it cannot be governed by drowning it in "integration."

I came face to face with this truth when, just a quarter century ago, I became president of the University of Hawaii. Everyone who lives in Hawaii, or even visits there, is impressed by its residents' comparative tolerance toward each other. On closer

inspection, paradise seems based on paradox: Everybody's a minority. The tolerance is not in spite of the diversity but because of it.

It is not through the disappearance of ethnic distinctions that the people of Hawaii achieved a level of racial peace that has few parallels around our discriminatory globe. Quite the contrary. The glory is that Hawaii's main ethnic groups managed to establish the right to be separate. The group separateness in turn helped establish the rights of individuals in each group to equality with individuals of different racial aspect, different ethnic origin, and different cultural heritage.

Hawaii's experience is not so foreign to the transatlantic migrations of the various more-or-less-white Caucasians. On arrival in New York (passing that inscription on the Statue of Liberty, "Send these, the homeless, tempest-tost, to me"), the European immigrants did not melt into the open arms of the white Anglo-Saxon Protestants who preceded them. The reverse was true. The new arrivals stayed close to their own kind, shared religion and language and humor and discriminatory treatment with their soul brothers and sisters, and gravitated at first into occupations that did not too seriously threaten the earlier arrivals.

The waves of new Americans learned to tolerate each other—*first* as groups, only thereafter as individuals. Rubbing up against each other in an urbanizing America, they discovered not just the old Christian lesson that all men are brothers, but the hard, new, multicultural lesson that all brothers are different. Equality is not the product of similarity; it is the cheerful acknowledgment of difference.

What's so special about our experience is the assumption that people of many kinds and colors can together govern themselves without deciding in advance which kinds of people (male or female, black, brown, yellow, red, white, or any mix of these) may hold any particular public office in the pantheon of political power.

For the twenty-first century, this "cheerful acknowledgement of difference" is the alternative to a planet wide spread of ethnic cleansing and religious rivalry. The challenge is great, for ethnic cleansing and religious rivalry are traditions as contemporary as Bosnia and Rwanda in the 1990s and as ancient as the Assyrians who, as Byron wrote, "came down like a wolf on the fold" but says the biblical Book of Kings, were prevented by sword-wielding angels from taking Jerusalem.

In too many countries there is still a basic if often unspoken assumption that one kind of people is anointed to be in general charge. Try to imagine a Turkish chancellor of Germany, an Algerian president of France, a Pakistani prime minister of Britain, a Christian president of Egypt, an Arab prime minister of Israel, a Jewish president of Syria, a Tibetan ruler in Beijing, anyone but a Japanese in power in Tokyo.

Yet in the United States during the twentieth century, we have already elected an Irish Catholic as president, chosen several Jewish Supreme Court justices, and racially integrated the armed forces right up to chairman of the Joint Chiefs of Staff. We have not yet adjusted, as voters in India, Britain, and Turkey have done, to having a woman atop the American political heap. But early in the twenty-first century, that too will come. And during that same new century, which will begin with "minorities" as one in every three Americans, there is every prospect that an African American, a Latin American, and an Asian American will be elected president of the United States.

I wouldn't dream of arguing that we Americans have found the Holy Grail of cultural diversity when in fact we're still searching for it. We have to think hard about our growing pluralism. It's useful, I believe, to dissect in the open our thinking about it, to see whether the lessons we are trying to learn might stimulate some useful thinking elsewhere. We do not yet quite know how to create "wholeness incorporating diversity," but we owe it to the world, as well as to ourselves, to keep trying.

Concepts and Questions

1. What does Cleveland mean when he speaks of making diversity safe?
2. What does Cleveland imply when he refers to "an excess of cultural identity"?
3. How does loyalty to one's own cultural identity make it difficult to be tolerant of others?
4. What is meant by the term *cultural overenthusiasm?* How does it affect intercultural relations?
5. How does Cleveland differentiate between the concepts of *culture* and *civilization?*
6. What are the hallmarks of civilization? How can they be maintained?
7. What does Cleveland imply when he states that diversity cannot be governed by drowning it in integration?
8. What does Cleveland mean when he argues that there are limits to diversity?
9. What principles must be followed in order for diversity to flourish in American society?

Intercultural Personhood: An Integration of Eastern and Western Perspectives

YOUNG YUN KIM

We live in a time of clashing identities. As the tightly knit communication web has brought all cultures closer than ever before, rigid adherence to the culture of our youth is no longer feasible. Cultural identity in its "pure" form has become more a nostalgic concept than a reality. As Toffler (1980) noted, we find ourselves "[facing] a quantum leap forward. [We face] the deepest social upheaval and creative restructuring of all time. Without clearly recognizing it, we are engaged in building a remarkable new civilization from the ground up" (p. 44). Yet the very idea of cultural identity, coupled with rising nationalism and xenophobic sentiments, looms over much of today's fractious world landscape. Can the desire for some form of collective uniqueness be satisfied without resulting in divisions and conflicts among groups? Can individuals who are committed to one identity render support and confidence to other groups while upholding the communal values and responsibilities that transcend allegiance to their own people?

This essay addresses these issues by proposing the concept of *intercultural personhood*—a way of life in which an individual develops an identity and a definition of self that integrates, rather than separates, humanity. Intercultural personhood projects a kind of human development that is open to growth—a growth beyond the perimeters of one's own cultural upbringing.[1] In making a case for the viability of intercultural personhood, we will first survey some of the core elements in the two seemingly incompatible cultural traditions of the East and the West. We will focus on the cultural apriority, or "root ideas" that define these philosophical perspectives. An argu-

ment will be made that certain aspects of these two traditions, often considered unbridgeably incompatible, are profoundly complementary and that such complementary elements can be creatively integrated in a ground-level consideration of human conditions. We will then examine how the process of building an intercultural personhood is actually played out in the lives of people whose life experiences span both cultural worlds.

The current discussion of intercultural personhood owes much to the writings of several prominent thinkers of this century who have explored ideologies larger than national and cultural interests and which embrace all humanity. One such work is Northrop's *The Meeting of East and West* (1966), in which an "international cultural ideal" was presented as a way to provide intellectual and emotional foundations for what he envisioned as "partial world sovereignty." Inspiration has also been drawn from the work of Thompson (1973), which explored the idea of "planetary culture," or how Eastern mysticism was integrated with Western science and rationalism. The primary sources for the current analysis of the Eastern and the Western cultural traditions also include Nakamura's *Ways of Thought of Eastern People* (1964), Campbell's *The Power of Myth* (1988), Gulick's *The East and the West* (1963), Oliver's *Communication and Culture in Ancient India and China* (1971), Capra's *The Tao of Physics* (1975), and Hall's *Beyond Culture* (1976) and *The Dance of Life* (1983).

EASTERN AND WESTERN CULTURAL TRADITIONS

Traditional cultures throughout Asia—including India, Tibet, Japan, China, Korea, and those in Southeast Asia—have been influenced by such religious and philosophical systems as Buddhism, Hinduism, Taoism, and Zen. On the other hand, Western Europe has mainly followed the Greek and Judeo-Christian traditions. Of course, any attempt to present the cultural assumptions of these two broadly categorized civilizations inevitably sacrifices specific details and the uniqueness of variations within each tradition. No two individuals or groups hold identical beliefs and manifest uniform behaviors, and whatever characterizations we make about one culture or cultural group must be thought of as normative tendencies that vary rather than monolithic and uniform attributes. Nevertheless, several key elements distinguish each group from the other. To specify these elements is to indicate the general interconnectedness of different nations that constitute either the Eastern or the Western cultural world.

Universe and Nature

A fundamental way in which culture shapes human existence is through the explicit and implicit teachings about our relationships to the nature of the universe and the human and nonhuman realms of the world. Traditional Eastern and Western perspectives diverge significantly with respect to basic premises about these relationships. As Needham (1951) noted in his article "Human Laws and the Laws of Nature in China and the West," people in the West have conceived the universe as having been initially created and, since then, externally controlled by a Divine power. As such, the Western worldview is characteristically dualistic, materialistic, and lifeless. The Judeo-Christian tradition sets "God" apart from this reality; having created it and set it into motion, God is viewed as apart from "His" creation. The fundamental material of the universe is conceived to be essentially nonliving matter, or elementary particles of matter, that interact with one another in a predictable fashion. It is as though the universe is an inanimate machine wherein humankind occupies a unique and elevated position among the life-forms that exist. Assuming a relatively barren universe, it seems only rational that humans make use of the lifeless material universe (and the "lesser" life-forms of nature) on behalf of the most intensely living—humankind itself.

Comparatively, the Eastern worldview is more holistic, dynamic, and inwardly spiritual. From the Eastern perspective, the entirety of the universe is viewed as a vast, multidimensional, living organism consisting of many interdependent parts and forces. The universe is conscious and engaged in a continuous dance of creation: The cosmic pattern is viewed as self-contained and self-organizing. It unfolds itself because of its own inner necessity and not because it is "ordered" by any external volitional power. What exist in the universe are manifestations of a divine

life force. Beneath the surface appearance of things, an "Ultimate Reality" is continuously creating, sustaining, and infusing our worldly experience. The all-sustaining life force that creates our manifest universe is not apart from humans and their worldly existence. Rather, it is viewed as dynamic and intimately involved in every aspect of the cosmos—from its most minute details to its grandest features.

The traditional Eastern worldview, then, reveres the common source out of which all things arise. As Campbell (1990) noted, people in the Eastern cultures—whether they are Indians, Japanese, or Tibetans—tend to think that

> the real mystery is in yourself. . . . Finding the divine not only within you, but within all things. . . . And what the Orient brings is a realization of the inward way. When you sit in meditation with your hands in your lap, with your head looking down, that means you've gone in and you're coming not just to a soul that is disengaged from God: you're coming to that divine mystery right there in yourself. (p. 89)

This perspective recognizes that everything in this world is fluid, ever-changing, and impermanent. In Hinduism, all static forms are called *maya*, that is, existing only as illusory concepts. This idea of the impermanence of all forms is the starting point of Buddhism. Buddhism teaches that "all compounded things are impermanent," and that all suffering in the world arises from our trying to cling to fixed forms—objects, people, or ideas—instead of accepting the world as it moves. This notion of impermanence of all forms and the appreciation of the aliveness of the universe in the Eastern worldview contrasts with the Western emphasis on the denitive forms of physical reality and their improvement through social and material progress.

Knowledge

Because the East and the West have different views of cosmic patterns, we can expect them to have different approaches to knowledge. In the East, because the universe is seen as a harmonious organism, there is a corresponding lack of dualism in epistemological patterns. The Eastern view emphasizes perceiving and knowing things synthetically, rather than analytically. The ultimate purpose of knowledge is to transcend the apparent contrasts and "see" the interconnectedness of all things. When the Eastern mystics tell us that they experience all things as manifestations of a basic oneness, they do not mean that they pronounce all things to be same or equal. Instead, they emphasize that all differences are relative within an all-encompassing phenomenon. Indeed, the awareness that all opposites are polar and, thus, a unity, is one of the highest aims of knowledge. As Suzuki (1968) noted, "The fundamental idea of Buddhism is to pass beyond the world of opposites, a world built up by intellectual distinctions and emotional defilements, and to realize the spiritual world of non-distinction, which involves achieving an absolute point of view" (p. 18).

Because all opposites are interdependent, their conflict can never result in the total victory of one side but will always be a manifestation of the interplay between the two sides. A virtuous person is not one who undertakes the impossible task of striving for the "good" and eliminating the "bad," but rather one who is able to maintain a dynamic balance between the two. Transcending the opposites, one becomes aware of the relativity and polar relationship of opposites. One realizes that good and bad, pleasure and pain, life and death, winning and losing, light and dark, are not absolute experiences belonging to different categories, but merely two sides of the same reality—extreme parts of a single continuum. This point has been emphasized extensively by the Chinese sages in their symbolism of the archetypal poles, *yin* and *yang*. And the opposites cease to be opposites is the very essence of *Tao*. To know the Tao, the illustrious way of the universe is the highest aim of human learning.

This holistic approach to knowledge in the East is pursued by means of "concepts by intuition," a sense of the aesthetic components of things. A concept by intuition is something immediately experienced, apprehended, and contemplated. Northrop (1966) described it as the "differentiated aesthetic continuum" within which there is no distinction between subjective and objective. The aesthetic continuum is a single all-embracing continuity. The aesthetic part of the self is also an essential part of the aesthetic object, whether the object is a flower or a person. Taoism, for example, pursues undifferentiated aesthetic continuum as it is manifested in the differen-

tiated, sensed aesthetic qualities in nature. The Taoist claim is that only if we take the aesthetic continuity in its all-embracing-ness as ultimate and irreducible, will we properly understand the meaning of the universe and nature. Similarly, Confucianism stresses the all-embracing aesthetic continuum with respect to its manifestations in human nature and its moral implications for human society: Only if we recognize the all-embracing aesthetic manifold to be an irreducible part of human nature will we have compassion for human beings other than ourselves.

As such, the undifferentiated aesthetic continuum is the Eastern conception of the constituted world. The differentiations within it—such as particular scenes, events, or persons—are not irreducible atomic identities, but merely arise out of the undifferentiated ground-level reality of the aesthetic continuum. Sooner or later, they fade back into it again. They are transitory and impermanent. Thus, when Eastern sages insist that one must become *selfless*, they mean that the self consists of two components: one, a differentiated, unique element, distinguishing one person from any other person, and the other the all-embracing, aesthetically immediate, compassionate, and undifferentiated component. The former is temporary and transitory, and the cherishing of it, the desire for its immortality, is a source of suffering and selfishness. The part of the self that is not transitory is the aesthetic component of the self, which is identical not merely in all persons, but in all aesthetic objects throughout the universe.

While the Eastern knowledge tradition has concentrated its mental processes on the holistic, intuitive, aesthetic continuum, the Western pursuit of knowledge has been based on a doctrinally formulated dualistic worldview. In this view, because the world and its various components came into existence through the individual creative acts of a god, the fundamental question is, How can I reach out to the external inanimated world or to other people? In this question, there is a basic dichotomy between the knower and the things to be known. Accompanying this epistemological dualism is the emphasis on rationality in the pursuit of knowledge. Since the Greek philosopher Plato "discovered" reason, virtually all subsequent Western thought—its themes, questions, and terms—relies on an essential rational basis (Wei, 1980). Even Aristotle, the great hero of all anti-Platonists, was not an exception. Although Aristotle did not propose, as Plato did, a realm of eternal essences ("really real") to justify the primacy of reason, he was by no means inclined to deny this primacy. This is an indication that, while the East has tended to emphasize the direct experience of oneness via intuitive concepts and contemplation, the West has viewed the faculty of the intellect as the primary instrument of worldly mastery. While Eastern thought tends to conclude in more or less vague, imprecise statements, consistent with its existential flexibility, Western thought emphasizes clear and distinct categorization and the linear, analytic logic of syllogism. While the Eastern cultural drive for human development is aimed at spiritual attainment of oneness with the universe, the Western cultural drive finds its expression in its drive for material and social progress.

Time

Closely parallel to differences between the two cultural traditions regarding the nature of knowledge are differences in the perception and experience of time. Along with the immediate, undifferentiated experiencing of here and now, the Eastern time orientation can be portrayed as a placid, silent pool within which ripples come and go. Historically, the East has tended to view worldly existence as cyclical and has often depicted it with metaphors of movement such as a wheel or an ocean: The "wheel of existence" or the "ocean of waves" appears to be in a continual movement but is "not really going anywhere." Although individuals living in the world may experience a rise or fall in their personal fortunes, the lot of the whole is felt to be fundamentally unchanging. As Northrop (1966) noted, "the aesthetic continuum is the greater mother of creation, giving birth to the ineffable beauty of the golden yellows on the mountain landscape as the sun drops low in the late afternoon, only a moment later to receive that differentiation back into itself and to put another in its place without any effort" (p. 343).

Because worldly time is not experienced as going anywhere and because in spiritual time there is nowhere to go but the eternity within the now, the future is expected to be virtually the same as the past. Recurrence in both cosmic and psychological realms is very much a part of the Eastern thought. Thus, the individual's aim is not to escape from the circular movement into linear time, but to become a part of the eternal through the aesthetic experience of the here and now and the conscious evolution of spirituality to "know" the all-embracing, undifferentiated wholeness. In contrast, the West has represented time either with an arrow or as a moving river that comes out of a distant place and past (which are not here and now) and that goes into an equally distant place and future (which also are not here and now). In this view of time, history is conceived of as goal-directed and gradually progressing in a certain direction (toward the universal salvation and second coming of Christ or, in secular terms, toward an ideal state such as boundless freedom or a classless society).

Closely corresponding to the above comparison is Hall's (1976, 1983) characterization of Asian cultures as "polychronic" and Western cultures as "monochronic" in their respective time orientations. Hall explained that individuals in a polychronic system are less inclined to adhere rigidly to time as a tangible, discrete, and linear entity; instead, they emphasize completion of transactions in the here and now, often carrying out more than one activity simultaneously. Comparatively, according to Hall, a monochronic system emphasizes schedules, segmentation, promptness, and standardization of activities. We may say that the Eastern polychronic time orientation is rooted in the synchronization of human behavior with the rhythms of nature, whereas the Western time orientation is driven by the synchronization of human behavior with the rhythms of the clock or machine.

Communication

The historical ideologies examined so far have shaped the empirical content of the East and the West. The respective Eastern and Western perspective on the universe, nature, knowledge, and time are reflected in many of the specific activities of individuals as they relate themselves to fellow human beings—how individuals view self and the group, and how they use verbal and nonverbal symbols in communication.

First, the view of self and identity cultivated in the Eastern tradition is embedded within an immutable social order. People tend to acquire their sense of identity from an affiliation with, and participation in, a virtually unchanging social order. As has been pointed out in many of the contemporary anthropological studies, the self that emerges from this tradition is not the clearly differentiated *existential ego* of the West, but a less distinct and relatively unchanging *social ego*. Individual members of the family tend to be more willing to submit their own self-interest for the good of the family. Individuals and families are often expected to subordinate their views to those of the community or the state.

The Eastern tradition also accepts hierarchy in social order. In a hierarchical structure, individuals are viewed as differing in status, although all are considered to be equally essential for the total system and its processes. A natural result of this orientation is the emphasis on authority—the authority of the parents over the children; of the grandparents over their descendants; of the official head of the community, the clan, and the state over all its members. Authoritarianism is an outstanding feature of Eastern life, not only in government, business, and family, but also in education and in beliefs. The more ancient a tradition, the greater its authority. The Eastern view further asserts that who "we" are is not limited to our physical existence. Consciousness is viewed as the bridge between the finite and differentiated (one's sense of uniqueness) and the infinite and undifferentiated (the experience of wholeness and eternity). With sufficient training, each person can discover that who he or she is correlates with nature and the divine. All are one and the same in the sense that the divine, undifferentiated, aesthetic continuum of the universe is manifested in each person and in nature. Through this aesthetic connection, individuals and nature are no other than the Tao, the Ultimate Reality, the divine life force, Nirvana, God.

Comparatively, the Western view, in which God, nature, and humans are distinctly differentiated, fosters the development of autonomous individuals with strong ego identification. The dualistic worldview is manifested in an individual's view of his or her relationship to other persons and nature. Interpersonal relationships are essentially egalitarian—cooperative arrangements between two equal partners in which the personal needs and interests of each party are more or less equally respected, negotiated, or resolved by compromise. Whereas the East emphasizes submission (or conformity) of the individual to the group, the West encourages individuality and individual needs to drive the group. If the group no longer serves the individual needs, then it (not the individual) must be changed. The meaning of an interpersonal relationship is decided upon primarily by the functions that each party performs in satisfying the needs of the other. A relationship is regarded as healthy to the extent that it serves the expected function for all parties involved. As extensively documented in anthropology and cross-cultural psychology (e.g., Hsu, 1981; Kluckhorn & Strodtbeck, 1960; Triandis, 1995), individualism is the central theme of the Western personality distinguishing the Western world from the collectivistic non-Western world.

This pragmatic interpersonal orientation of the West can be contrasted with the Eastern tradition, in which group membership is taken as given and therefore unchallenged, and in which individuals must conform to the group in case of conflicting interest. Members of the group are encouraged to maintain harmony and minimize competition. Individuality is discouraged, while moderation, modesty, and the bending of one's ego are praised. In some cases, both individual and group achievement (in a material sense) must be forsaken to maintain group harmony. In this context, the primary source of interpersonal understanding is the unwritten and often unspoken norms, values, and ritualized mannerisms pertinent to a particular situation. Rather than relying heavily on explicit and logical verbal expressions, the Eastern communicator grasps the aesthetic essence of the communication dynamic by observing subtleties in nonverbal and circumstantial cues. Intuition, rather than rational thinking, plays a central role in the understanding of how one talks, how one addresses the other, under what circumstances, on what topic, in which of various styles, with what intent, and with what effect.

These implicit communication patterns are reflected in the Eastern fondness for verbal hesitance and ambiguity—out of fear of disturbing or offending others (Cathcart & Cathcart, 1982; Doi, 1982; Kincaid, 1987). Even silence is sometimes preferred to eloquent verbalization in expressing strong compliments or affection. Easterners are often suspicious of genuineness of excessive verbal praises or comple-ments because, to their view, truest feelings must be intuitively apparent and therefore do not need to be, and cannot be, articulated. As a result, the burden of communicating effectively is shared by both the speaker and the listener, who is expected to "hear" the implicit messages through empathic attentive-ness. In contrast, the Western communicative mode is primarily direct, explicit, and verbal, relying on logic and rational thinking. Participants in commu-nication are viewed as distinctly different individu-als, and their individuality has to be expressed through accurate verbal articulation. Inner feelings are not to be intuitively understood but to be hon-estly and assertively verbalized and discussed. Here, the burden of communicating effectively lies prima-rily with the speaker.

The preceding characterization of Eastern and Western communication patterns is largely consis-tent with observations made by other scholars such as Kincaid (1987), Yum (1994), and Hall (1976, 1983). Hall, in particular, has depicted Asian cul-tures as *high-context* in comparison with the low-con-text cultures of the West. The focal point of Hall's cross-cultural comparison is "contexting," that is, the act of taking into account information that is either embedded in physical or social context (which includes nonverbal behaviors) or internalized in the communicator. In this scheme, low-context commu-nication, which is more prevalent in the West, is observed when the majority of interpersonal infor-mation is expressed by explicit, verbalized codes.

BEYOND CULTURAL DIFFERENCES

As has been pointed out, many of the specific differ-ences that we observe between Eastern and Western societies hinge upon their respective worldviews. Based on an organic, holistic, and cyclic worldview, the East has followed an epistemology that empha-sized direct, immediate, and aesthetic components in human experience of the world. The ultimate aim of human learning was to transcend the immediate, dif-ferentiated self and to develop an integrative percep-tion of the undifferentiated universe. The goal is to be spiritually one with the universe and to find the eternal within the present moment. The present moment is a reflection of the eternal. Alternatively, the eternal resides in the present moment. The Western tradition, in contrast, is rooted in the cos-mology of dualism, determinism, and materialism. It engenders an outlook that is rational, analytic, and indirect. History is conceived as a linear progression from the past into the future. The pursuit of knowl-edge is not so much a pursuit of spiritual enhance-ment as a quest to improve the human condition.

These different worldviews, in turn, are reflected in the individual's conception of the self, the other, and the group. While the East has stressed the pri-macy of the group over the individual, the West has stressed the primacy of the individual over the group. Interpersonally, the East views the self as deeply merged in the group ego, while the West encourages distinct and autonomous individuality. Explicit, clear, and logical verbalization is a salient feature in the Western communication system, as compared to the emphasis on implicit, intuitive, and nonverbal messages in the Eastern tradition.

The cultural premises of the East and the West that we have examined suggest the areas of vitality, as well as areas of weakness, that are characteristic of each civilization. The Western mechanistic and dualistic worldview has helped to advance scientific efforts to describe systematically and explain physical phenomena, leading to extremely successful techno-logical advancements. The West has learned, how-ever, that the mechanistic worldview and the corresponding communication patterns are often inadequate for understanding the rich and complex phenomena of human relationships and that this lack of understanding can cause alienation from self and others. The West has seen that its dualistic dis-tinction between humanity and nature brings about alienation from the natural world. The analytical mind of the West has led to modern science and technology, but it also has resulted in knowledge that is often compartmentalized, fragmented, and detached from the fuller totality of reality.

In comparison, the East has not experienced the level of alienation that the West has. At the same time, however, the East has not seen as much mate-rial and social development. Its holistic and aesthet-ic worldview has not been conducive to the development of science or technology. Its hierarchi-cal social order and binding social relationships have not fostered the civic-mindedness, worldly activism, humanitarianism, and volunteerism that flourish in the West. Many of the Asian societies continue to struggle to bring about democratic political systems that are based on the rights and responsibilities of individuals.

It should be stressed at this time that the Western emphasis on logical, theoretic, dualistic, and analytic thinking does not suggest that it has been devoid of intuitive, direct, purely empirical, aesthetic elements. Conversely, emphasizing the Western contributions of sociomaterial development is not meant to suggest that the East has been devoid of learning in these areas. The differences that have been pointed out do not represent diametric opposition, but rather differences in emphasis that are nonetheless significant and observable. Clearly, the range of sophistication of Western contributions to the sociomaterial domain far exceeds that of contributions from the East. However, the Eastern emphasis on aesthetic and holistic self-mastery has offered a system of life philosophy that touches on the depth of human experience vis-à-vis other humans, the natural world, and the universe.

Indeed, increasing realization of limitations in the Western worldview has been expressed by many. Using the term "extension transference," for instance, Hall (1976) pointed out the danger of the common intellectual maneuver in which technological "extensions"—including language, logic, technology, institutions, and scheduling—are confused with or take the place of the process extended. We observe the tendency in the West to assume that the remedy for problems arising from technology should be sought not in the attempt to rely upon an ideal minimum of technology, but in the development of even more technology. Burke (1974) called this tendency "technologism": "[There] lie the developments whereby 'technologism' confronts its inner contradictions, a whole new realm in which the heights of human rationality, as expressed in industrialism, readily become 'solutions' that are but the source of new and aggravated problems" (p. 148).

Self-criticisms in the West have also been directed to the rigid scientific dogmatism that insists on the discovery of truth based on the mechanistic, linear causality, and objectivity. In this regard, Thayer (1983) commented:

What the scientific mentality attempts to emulate, mainly, is the presumed method of laboratory science. But laboratory science predicts nothing that it does not control or that is not otherwise fully determined. . . . One cannot successfully study relatively open systems with methods that are appropriate only for closed systems. Is it possible that this is the kind of mentality that precludes its own success? (p. 88)

Similarly, Hall (1976) has pointed out that the Western emphasis on logic as synonymous with the "truth" denies that part of human self that integrates. Hall sees that logical thinking is only a small fraction of our mental capabilities and that there are many different and legitimate ways of thinking that have tended to be less emphasized in Western cultures (p. 9).

The criticisms raised by these and other critics of scientific epistemology do not deny the value of the rational, inferential knowledge. Rather, they are directed to the error of Western philosophy in regarding concepts that do not adhere to its mode as invalid. They refer to the arrogance or overconfidence in believing that scientific knowledge is the only way to discover truth, when, in reality, the very process of doing science requires an immediate, aesthetic experience of the phenomenon under investigation. Without the immediately apprehended component, the theoretical hypotheses proposed could not be tested empirically with respect to their truth or falsity and would lack the relevance to the corresponding reality. As Einstein once commented:

Science is the attempt to make the chaotic diversity of our sense-experience correspond to a logically uniform system of thought. In this system single experiences must be correlated with the theoretic structure in such a way that the resulting coordination is complete and convincing. (Quoted in Northrop, 1966, p. 443)

In this description of science, Einstein is careful to indicate that the relation between the theoretically postulated component and the immediately experienced aesthetic component is one of correspondence. The wide spectrum of our everyday life activities demands both scientific and aesthetic modes of apprehension: critical analysis as well as perception of wholes; doubt and skepticism as well as unconditional appreciation; abstraction as well as concreteness; perception of the general and regular as well as the individual and unique; the literalism of technical terms as well as the power and richness of poetic language, silence, and art; relationships with casual acquaintances as well as intimate personal engagement. If we limit ourselves to the dominant scientific mode of apprehension and do not value the aesthetic mode, then we would be making an error of limiting the essential human to only a part of the full span of life activities.

As such, one potential benefit of incorporating the Eastern aesthetic orientation into Western cultural life is a heightened sense of freedom. The aesthetic component of human nature is in part indeterminate, and the ambiguity of indetermination is the very basis of our freedom. We might also transcend the clock-bound worldly time to the "Eternal Now," the "timeless moment" that is embedded within the center of each moment. By occasionally withdrawing into the indeterminate, aesthetic component of our nature, away from the determinate, transitory circumstances, we could overcome the pressures of everyday events into a basis for renewal of our human spirit. The traditional Eastern practice of meditation is designed primarily for the purpose of moving one's consciousness from the determinate to the indeterminate, freer state.

Second, incorporation of the Eastern view could bring the West to a greater awareness of the aliveness and wholeness of the universe we inhabit and the life we live. The universe is engaged in a continuous dance of creation at each instant of time. Everything is alive—brimming with a silent energy that creates, sustains, and infuses all that exists. With the expanded perspective on time, we would increase our sensitivity to the rhythms of nature—such as the seasons and the cycles of birth and decay. This integrative worldview is one that pacifies us. Because of its all-embracing oneness and unity, the indeterminate aesthetic continuum helps us to cultivate compassion and intuitive sensitivity—not only for other humans but also for all of nature's creatures. In this regard, Maslow (1971) referred to Taoistic receptivity or "let-be" as an important attribute of self-actualizing persons:

> We may speak of this respectful attention to the matter-in-paradigm as a kind of courtesy or deference

(without intrusion of the controlling will) which is akin to "taking it seriously." This amounts to treating it as an end, something per se, with its own right to be, rather than as a means to some end other than itself; i.e., as a tool for some extrinsic purpose. (p. 68)

Such aesthetic perception is an instrument of intimate human meeting, a way to bridge the gap between individuals and groups. In dealing with each other aesthetically, we do not subject ourselves to a rigid scheme, but do our best in each new situation, listening to the silence as well as the words, and experiencing the other person as a whole living entity with less infusion of our own egocentric and ethnocentric demands. A similar attitude can be developed toward the physical world, as is witnessed in the rising interest in the West in ecological integrity and holistic medicine (see Brody, 1997; Wallis, 1996).

What the preceding considerations suggest is that many Eastern and Western philosophical premises offer views of reality that are not competitive, but complementary. Of course, the entire values, norms, and institutions of the West cannot, and should not, be substituted for their Eastern counterparts, and vice versa. The West may no more adopt the worldview of the East than the East may adopt the worldviews of the West. Rather, we need to recognize that a combination of rational and intuitive modes of experiencing life leads to a life that is more real and more meaningful. With this understanding, we see the interrelatedness and reconciliation of the two seemingly incompatible perspectives.

Our task, then, is to reach for the unity in human experiences and simultaneously to express diversity. A general synthesis of East and West is neither possible nor desirable: The purpose of evolution is not to create a homogeneous mass, but to continuously unfold an ever diverse and yet organic whole. Yet knowledge of differing cultural traditions can help each society move toward greater collective self-understanding—especially by revealing blind spots that can be illuminated only by adopting a vastly different way of seeing. Each tradition can play a necessary and integral part in the continuing evolution of humanity, out of which another birth, a higher integration of human consciousness, may arise.

EMERGENCE OF INTERCULTURAL PERSONHOOD

The task of synthesizing elements of Eastern and Western cultural traditions is taken not merely to satisfy an esoteric academic curiosity but also out of keen relevance to the everyday realities of numerous individuals whose life experiences extend beyond their primary cultural world. Through extensive and prolonged experiences of interfacing with other cultures, they have embarked on a personal evolution, creating a new culture of their own, fusing diverse cultural elements into a single personality. As Toffler (1980) noted, they have created a new personal culture that is "oriented to change and growing diversity" that attempts "to integrate the new view of nature, of evolution and progress, the new, richer conceptions of time and space, and the fusion of reductionism and wholism, with a new causality" (p. 309).

Identity Transformation

The emergence of intercultural personhood is a direct function of dramatically increasing intercultural communication activities—from the personal experiences of diverse people and events through direct encounters to observations via various communication media such as books, magazines, television programs, movies, magazines, art museums, music tapes, and electronic mail. Communicating across cultural identity boundaries is often challenging because it provokes questions about our taken-for-granted cultural premises and habits, as well as our inevitable intergroup posturing and the us-and-them psychological orientation (Kim, 1991). Yet it is precisely such challenges that offer us openings for new cultural learning, self-awareness, and personal growth (Adler, 1982; Kim, 1988, 1995, in press). The greater the severity of intercultural challenges, the greater the potential for reinvention of an inner self that goes beyond the boundaries of our original cultural conditioning. In this process, our identity is transformed gradually and imperceptibly from an ascribed or assigned identity to an achieved or adopted identity—an emergent intercultural personhood at a higher level of integration (Grotevant, 1993). Such an identity transformation takes place in a pro-

gression of stages. In each stage, new concepts, attitudes, and behaviors are incorporated into an individual's psychological makeup. As previously unknown life patterns are etched into our nervous systems, they become part of our new psyches.

The evolution of our identity from cultural to intercultural is far from smooth or easy. Moments of intense stress can reverse the process at any time, because individuals may indeed regress toward re-identifying with their origins, having found the alienation and malaise involved in maintaining a new identity too much of a strain (De Vos & Suárez-Orozco, 1990). Such strain may take various forms of an identity crisis (Erickson, 1968) and cultural marginality (Stonequist, 1964; Taft, 1977). Yet the stress experience also challenges individuals to accommodate new cultural elements and become more capable of making deliberate and appropriate choices about action as situations demand.

The emerging intercultural personhood, then, is a special kind of mind-set that promises greater fitness in our increasingly intercultural world (Kim, 1995, in press; Kim & Ruben, 1988). It represents a continuous struggle of searching for the authenticity in self and others within and across cultural groups. It is a way of existence that transcends the perimeters of a particular culture and is capable of embracing and incorporating seemingly divergent cultural elements into one's own unique worldview. The process of becoming intercultural affirms the creative courage and resourcefulness of humans as it requires discovering new symbols and new patterns of life. This creative process of identity development speaks to a uniquely human plasticity, "our relative freedom from programmed reflexive patterns . . . the very capacity to use culture to construct our identities" (Slavin & Kriegman, 1992, p. 6). It is the expression of normal, ordinary people in the act of "stretching" themselves out of their habitual perceptual and social categories. In Adler's (1982) words, the development of an intercultural identity and personhood places strangers at a position of continually "negotiating ever new formations of reality" (p. 391).

This kind of human development echoes one of the highest aims of humans in the spiritual traditions of the Eastern cultures. Suzuki (1968) writes, "The fundamental idea of Buddhism is to pass beyond the world of opposites, a world built up by intellectual distinctions and emotional defilements, and to realize the spiritual world of non-distinction, which involves achieving an absolute point of view" (p. 18). A virtuous person in this tradition is not one who undertakes the impossible task of striving for the good and eliminating the bad, but rather one who is able to maintain a dynamic balance between good and bad. This Eastern notion of dynamic balance is reflected in the symbolic use by Chinese sages of the archetypal poles of *yin* and *yang*. These sages call the unity lying beyond *yin* and *yang* the *Tao* and see it as a process that brings about the interplay of the two poles. Yoshikawa (1988) described this development as a stage of "double-swing" or "transcendence of binary opposites" (p. 146). With this transcendental understanding, intercultural persons are better able to conciliate and reconcile seemingly contradictory elements and transform them into complementary, interacting parts of a single whole.

An Illustration

Indeed, many people have been able to incorporate experiential territories that have seldom been thought possible, attainable, or even desirable. In doing so, they have redrawn the lines of their original cultural identity boundary to accommodate new life patterns. They remind us of the fact that we humans are active, if not always successful, strategists of our own development in a world of competing and overlapping interests. Although few theories and empirical studies have systematically examined the phenomenon of identity development, many first-hand accounts are available that bear witness to the reality of intercultural personhood. Such accounts have appeared in case studies, memoirs, biographical stories, and essays of self-reflection and self-analysis (see, for instance, Ainslie, 1994; Copelman, 1993; Keene, 1994; O'Halloran, 1994). Many of these accounts present vivid insights into the emotional ebb and flow of the progress toward an eventual realization of intercultural transformation.

One example of a personal fusion of Eastern and Western cultural elements can be seen in the canvases of the artist C. Meng. Since leaving Shanghai in 1986, Meng has earned a Master of Fine Arts degree in the United States and has been teaching at

a university in Texas. In response to Meng's recent exhibit in Dallas, art critic and reporter C. Mitchell characterized Meng's painting as masterful expressions of "the contrast between Eastern and Western modes of thought." Mitchell (1992) noted the unique synthesis of the two sensibilities in Meng's method, which used both Chinese calligraphy and Western-style abstraction techniques.

An illustration of intercultural synthesis is also offered by Duane Elgin, who was born and raised in the United States as a Christian and studied Buddhism in Tibet and Japan for many years. In his book *Voluntary Simplicity* (1981), Elgin integrated the philosophical ideas of Eastern and Western worldviews into his concept of voluntary simplicity. He presented this idea as global common sense and as a practical lifestyle to reconcile the willful, rational approach to life of the West with the holistic, spiritual orientation of the East. Examining historical trends, cycles of civilizations, and related ecological concerns, Elgin proposed voluntary simplicity as a goal for all of humanity. The main issue Elgin addresses is how humans can find ways to remove, as much as possible, the nonessential clutters of life. He suggests, for example, that one owns or buys things based on real need and consider the impact of one's consumption patterns on other people and on the earth. Before purchasing nonessential items, one should ask oneself if these items promote or compromise the quality of one's nonmaterial life. One could also consciously simplify communications by making them clearer, more direct, and more honest, eliminating idle, wasteful, and manipulative speech. One should also respect the value of silence and nonverbal actions.

Perhaps one of the most succinct and eloquent testimonials to the present conception of intercultural personhood was offered by Muneo Yoshikawa (1978). As one who had lived in both Japan and the United States, Yoshikawa offered the following insight into his own psychic development—an insight that captures the very essence of what it means to be an intercultural person:

> I am now able to look at both cultures with objectivity as well as subjectivity; I am able to move in both cultures, back and forth without any apparent conflict. . . . I think that something beyond the sum of each

[cultural] identification took place, and that it became something akin to the concept of "synergy"—when one adds 1 and 1, one gets [3], or a little more. This something extra is not culture-specific but something unique of its own, probably the emergence of a new attribute or a new self-awareness, born out of an awareness of the relative nature of values and of the universal aspect of human nature. . . . I really am not concerned whether others take me as a Japanese or an American; I can accept myself as I am. I feel I am much freer than ever before, not only in the cognitive domain (perception, thoughts, etc.), but also in the affective (feeling, attitudes, etc.) and behavioral domains. (p. 220)

Emerging from these and other personal stories are common patterns associated with the development of intercultural personhood. One such pattern is a mind-set that is less parochial and more open to different perspectives. This outlook has been referred to as a "third-culture" orientation that enables us to transcend the "paradigmatic barrier" (Bennett, 1976) between divergent philosophical perspectives. Development of an intercultural personhood leads to a cultural relativistic insight (Roosens, 1989) or moral inclusiveness (Opotow, 1990) that is based on an understanding of the profound similarities in human conditions as well as recognition of important differences between and among human groups. In becoming intercultural, then, we can rise above the hidden grips of our childhood culture and discover that there are many ways to be good, true, and beautiful. In this process, we attain a *wider circle of identification*, approaching the limits of many cultures and, ultimately, humanity itself. This process is not unlike climbing a mountain. As we reach the mountaintop, we see that all paths below lead to the same summit and that each path offers unique scenery. Likewise, the process of becoming intercultural leads to an awareness of ourselves as being part of a larger, more inclusive whole and gives us a greater empathic capacity to "step into and imaginatively participate in the other's world view" (Bennett, 1977, p. 49).

Such developments, in turn, endow us with a special kind of *freedom and creativity*, with which we can make deliberate choices about action in specific situations rather than to have these choices simply be dictated by habitual conventions of thought and action. This psychic evolution presents the potential for achieving what Harris (1979) defined as "optimal communication competence." An optimally competent communicator, according to Harris, has a sophisticated "meta system" for critiquing his or her own managing system and interpersonal system. The very existence of the meta system makes the difference between the optimal level and the other two levels of competence a qualitative one (p. 31).

In the end, it is people such as Meng, Elgin, and Yoshikawa who constitute the sustaining core or cross-links of our intercultural world. They provide an infrastructure of moral cement that helps hold together the human and planetary community, and discourage excessive identity claims at the exclusion of other identities. They are the ones who can best meet the enormous challenge that confronts us all—that is, "to give not only yourself but your culture to the planetary view" (Campbell, 1990, p. 114).

Note

1. The term "intercultural personhood" represents other similar terms such as "multicultural man" (Adler, 1982), "universal man" (Tagore, 1961; Walsh, 1973), "international man" (Lutzker, 1960), and "species identity" (Boulding, 1990), as well as "meta-identity" and "transcultural identity."

References

Adler, P. (1982). Beyond cultural identity: Reflections on cultural and multicultural man. In L. Samovar & R. Porter (Eds.), *Intercultural communication: A reader*, 3rd ed. (pp. 389–408). Belmont, CA: Wadsworth.

Ainslie, R. (1994, May). Notes on the psychodynamics of acculturation: A Mexican-American experience. *Mind and Human Interaction*, 5(2), 60–67.

Bennett, J. (1976). *The ecological transition: Cultural anthropology and human adaptation*. New York: Pergamon.

Boulding, E. (1990). *Building a global civic culture*. Syracuse, NY: Syracuse University Press.

Brody, J. (1997, November 6). U.S. panel on acupuncture calls for wider acceptance. *The New York Times*, p. A10.

Burke, K. (1974). Communication and the human condition. *Communication*, 1, 135–152.

Campbell, J. (1988). *The power of myth* (with B. Moyers). New York: Doubleday.

————. (1990). *An open life* (in conversation with M. Toms). New York: Harper & Row.

Capra, F. (1975). *The Tao of physics*. Boulder, CO: Shambhala.

Cathcart, D., & Cathcart, R. (1982). Japanese social experience and concept of groups. In L. Samovar & R. Porter (Eds.), *Intercultural communication: A reader*, 3rd ed. (pp. 120–127). Belmont, CA: Wadsworth.

Copelman, D. (1993, April). The immigrant experience: Margin notes. *Mind and Human Interaction*, 4(2), 76–82.

De Vos, G., & Suárez-Orozco, M. (1990). *Status inequality: The self in culture*. Newbury Park, CA: Sage.

Doi, T. (1982). The Japanese patterns of communication and the concept of amae. In L. Samovar & R. Porter (Eds.), *Intercultural communication: A reader*, 3rd ed. (pp. 218–222). Belmont, CA: Wadsworth.

Elgin, D. (1981). *Voluntary simplicity*. New York: Bantam Books.

Erickson, E. (1968). *Identity, youth, and crisis*. New York: Norton.

Grotevant, H. (1993). The integrative nature of identity: Bridging the soloists to sing in the choir. In J. Kroger (Ed.), *Discussions on ego identity* (pp. 121–146). Hillsdale, NJ: Lawrence Erlbaum.

Gulick, S. (1963). *The East and the West*. Rutland, VT: Charles E. Tuttle.

Hall, E. (1976). *Beyond culture*. Garden City, NY: Anchor Books.

————. (1983). *The dance of life: The other dimension of time*. Garden City, NY: Anchor Press.

Harris, L. (1979, May). *Communication competence: An argument for a systemic view*. Paper presented at the annual meeting of the International Communication Association, Philadelphia, PA.

Hsu, F. (1981). *The challenges of the American dream*. Belmont, CA: Wadsworth.

Keene, D. (1994). *On familiar terms: A journey across cultures*. New York: Kodansha International.

Kim, Y. (1988). *Communication and cross-cultural adaptation: An integrative theory*. Clevedon, UK: Multilingual Matters.

————. (1991). Intercultural communication competence. In S. Ting-Toomey & F. Korzenny (Eds.), *Cross-cultural interpersonal communication* (pp. 259–275). Newbury Park, CA: Sage.

————. (1995). Cross-cultural adaptation: An integrative theory. In R. Wiseman (Ed.), *Intercultural communication theory* (pp. 170–193). Thousand Oaks, CA: Sage.

————. (in press). *Becoming intercultural: An integrative theory of communication and cross-cultural adaptation*. Thousand Oaks, CA: Sage.

————, & Ruben, B. (1988). Intercultural transformation. In Y. Kim & W. Gudykunst (Eds.), *Theories in intercultural communication* (pp. 299–321). Newbury Park, CA: Sage.

Kincaid, L. (1987). Communication East and West: Points of departure. In L. Kincaid (Ed.), *Communication theory: Eastern and Western perspectives* (pp. 331–340). San Diego: Academic Press.

Kluckhohn, F., & Strodtbeck, F. (1960). *Variations in value orientations*. New York: Row, Peterson.

Lutzker, D. (1960). Internationalism as a predictor of cooperative behavior. *Journal of Conflict Resolution*, 4, 426–430.

Maslow, A. (1971). *The farther reaches of human nature*. New York: Viking.

Mitchell, C. (1992, June 15). Review. *The Dallas Morning News*, p. C6.

Nakamura, H. (1964). *Ways of thought of Eastern peoples*. Honolulu: University of Hawaii Press.

Needham, J. (1951). Human laws and laws of nature in China and the West. *Journal of the History of Ideas, XII*.

Northrop, F. (1966). *The meeting of the East and the West*. New York: Collier Books. Originally published 1946.

O'Halloran, M. (1994). *Pure heart, enlightened mind*. Boston: Charles E. Tuttle.

Oliver, R. (1971). *Communication and culture in ancient India and China*. Syracuse, NY: Syracuse University Press.

Opotow, S. (1990). Moral exclusion and inclusion. *Journal of Social Issues*, 46(1), 1–20.

Roosens, E. (1989). *Creating ethnicity: The process of ethnogenesis*. Newbury Park, CA: Sage.

Slavin, M., & Kriegman, D. (1992). *The adaptive design of the human psyche*. New York: Guilford.

Stonequist, E. (1964). The marginal man: A study in personality and culture conflict. In E. Burgess & D. Bogue (Eds.), *Contributions to urban sociology* (pp. 327–345). Chicago: University of Chicago Press.

Suzuki, D. (1968). *The essence of Buddhism*. Kyoto, Japan: Hozokan.

Taft, R. (1977). Coping with unfamiliar culture. In N. Warren (Ed.), *Studies in cross-cultural psychology*, Vol. 2 (pp. 121–153). London: Academic Press.

Tagore, R. (1961). *Toward universal man*. New York: Asia Publishing House.

Thayer, L. (1983). On "doing" research and "explaining" things. *Journal of Communication*, 33(3), 80–91.

Thompson, W. (1973). *Passages about earth: An exploration of the new planetary culture*. New York: Harper & Row.

Toffler, A. (1980). *The third wave*. New York: Bantam Books.

Triandis, H. (1995). *Individualism and collectivism*. Boulder, CO: Westview Press.

Wallis, C. (1996, June 24). Healing. *Time*, pp. 58–64.

Walsh, J. (1973). *Intercultural education in the community of man*. Honolulu: University of Hawaii Press.

Wei, A. (1980, March). *Cultural variations in perception*. Paper presented at the 6th Annual Third World Conference, Chicago, IL.

Yoshikawa, M. (1978). Some Japanese and American cultural characteristics. In M. Prossor, *The cultural dialogue: An introduction to intercultural communication* (pp. 220–239). Boston: Houghton Mifflin.

———. (1988). Cross-cultural adaptation and perceptual development. In Y. Kim & W. Gudykunst (Eds.), *Cross-cultural adaptation: Current approaches* (pp. 140–148). Newbury Park, CA: Sage.

Yum, J. (1994). The impact of Confucianism on interpersonal relationships and communication patterns in East Asia. In L. Samovar & R. Porter (Eds.), *Intercultural communication: A reader*, 7th ed. (pp. 75–86). Belmont, CA: Wadsworth.

Concepts and Questions

1. What is meant by the term "intercultural personhood"?

2. How do Eastern and Western teachings about humankind's relationship to the nature of the universe differ?

3. In what major ways do Eastern and Western approaches to knowledge differ?

4. How do Eastern time orientations differ from those found in the West?

5. How do differences in Eastern and Western views of self and identity affect intercultural communication?

6. What are the major differences between Eastern and Western modes of communication?

7. What strengths and weaknesses are found in Eastern and Western worldviews?

8. How could an integration of Eastern and Western perspectives benefit both Eastern and Western cultural life?

9. What conditions are requisite for the emergence of intercultural personhood?

10. What benefits accrue to both society and the individual from the development of an intercultural personhood perspective?

Ethics, Culture, and Communication: An Intercultural Perspective

Robert Shuter

Ethics, culture, and communication are woven together in a cultural mosaic that make them inseparable and yet distinct elements of each and every society. The inseparability has been alluded to in ethical and communication literatures (Condon, 1977; Howell, 1986; Johannesen, 1990, 1994; Makau & Arnett, 1997), but the fusion has not been adequately articulated. In fact, books and articles on ethics and communication more often than not ignore the issue of culture or offer little more than clichés about culture and communication—values are different worldwide; ethical systems are not easily compared. As a result, leading books on ethics and human communication are essentially written from a Western perspective with U.S. values and norms driving the ethical models and prescriptions provided in these texts (Jaska & Prichard, 1994; Johannesen, 1990; Nilsen, 1966). Even Makau and Arnet's (1997) edited text focuses almost exclusively on diversity and ethics in the United States. This is a major weakness in the literature because it provides little or no understanding of ethical systems that influence communication in social systems outside Western society or, more limited yet, the United States. It also can be argued that the literature on ethics and communication popularized in the field of communication studies have limited application to Europe and South America.

Using an intracultural communication perspective (Shuter, 1990, 1998), this essay examines the cultural myopia of current literature on communication ethics. Shuter's (1990, 1998) intracultural perspective uncovers worldviews, values, and communication patterns within a culture, and it should

This original essay appears here for the first time. All rights reserved. Permission to reprint must be obtained from the publisher and the author. Robert Shuter teaches at Marquette University, Milwaukee, Wisconsin.

be quite revealing when used to examine communication ethics. Confucianist and Hindu ethical systems are also explored intraculturally with the aim of speculating on communication ethics in these systems. Lastly, the essay discusses communication ethics from an intercultural perspective (Shuter 1990, 1998).

ETHICS AND HUMAN COMMUNICATION: CURRENT PERSPECTIVES

Although literature abounds on ethics and communication, the authors and their works clearly reflect Western ethical premises with an implicit U.S. orientation. Evidence for this assertion can be found in analyzing communication ethics literature with the following framework: (1) communicator ethics, (2) message ethics, and (3) receiver or audience ethics. With respect to communicator ethics, Nilsen (1966) summarizes a common view advanced by communication ethical theorists on what constitutes morally right speech when he writes that ethics is "that which contributes to the well-being of others, to their happiness and fulfillment as human beings" (p. 13). Melvin Rader (1964) echoes Nilsen's (1966) perspective: "Only ethics that does justice to every essential side of human nature, as both individual and social, as mind and body, as thinking and feeling and desiring, is complete and complex enough to be the basis of valued ideals" (p. 435). Richard Johannesen (1990, 1994) adds to Nilsen and Rader's ethical criteria the concept of an "ethical contract" that requires "a fundamental implied and unspoken assumption that words can be trusted and people will be truthful" (p. 15). This is consistent with Jaska and Pritchard's (1994) notion that truthfulness is a significant ethical criterion for determining morally right communication.

Implicit in the ethical criteria offered by all these communication theorists is the notion that the center of ethical decisions is the impact of behavior on human beings—their happiness, their feelings and thoughts, their personal and social relations. Similarly, the ethical criterion of truthfulness suggests that human beings can choose their course of action and be judged right or wrong on the basis of those choices. Robert Wargo (1990) argues that these

implicit assumptions spring from a Judeo-Christian tradition that bifurcates the relationship between God, people, and nature. In the Judeo-Christian view, God is infinite, while people and nature are finite. As finite beings, humans have a soul while nature has no soul and is material. As a result, a hierarchy arises that places God at the apex followed by human beings and lastly material nature. It is the human soul—the spiritual side of being—that gives rise to ethics and ethical judgment (Wargo, 1990).

However, in the Judeo-Christian perspective, only human beings possess reason and can choose to make good or bad decisions. It is free will—the possession of an intellect—that separates humans from the rest of nature and makes ethical choices possible. A sin, then, is a human being's choice to commit an offense against God; however, culpability requires knowledge, volition, and capacity (Wargo, 1990).

Although communication ethicists do not generally ground their theories in Judeo-Christian doctrine, it is apparent they are linked. They place human beings at the center of their ethical constructs, and reason, free will, and the intellect are essential to making good ethical choices. As you will see later in this article, many Eastern ethical systems neither bifurcate human beings and nature nor reserve soul (spirit) for humans or make reason and free will an essential human capacity. In fact, Shintoism—a dominant ethical system in Japan—has no concept of good or evil, invests humans and the natural order with spirits, and removes reason and free will from ethical choices (Little, 1974).

A Western and U.S. cultural bias is also revealed in the ethical requirements of messages transmitted to others. Communicators are judged to be ethical depending on their truthfulness, as indicated earlier, and their willingness to provide significant choices to their audience.

"It is choice making that is voluntary, free from physical or mental coercion. It is choice based on the best information available when the decision must be made. It includes awareness of the motivation of those who want to influence the values they serve, the goals they seek" (Nilsen, 1966, p. 45). Information, then, is key to developing ethical messages, for it provides listeners with the ability to make voluntary choices based on the facts. Similarly, the willingness of communicators to disclose their intentions and goals helps to expand listener choice. Johannesen (1990) cites Buber's dialogue as an example of an ethical interpersonal model because it emphasizes authenticity of the communicator and inclusion—exposing the listener to both sides of an argument.

For communication theorists, reason and logic are critical dimensions of ethical messages. The importance of reason and logic have developed from Aristotelian philosophy, which also has diminished the ethical value of emotional appeal. While Johannesen (1990, 1994) is among the only communication ethicists who suggests that cultures may have different logics, even his work fails to identify how culturally incompatible these communication caveats are in most regions of the world.

The preeminence of intellect and reason—hallmarks of Western civilization—are, for example, rejected in traditional Islamic ethical philosophy (Gibb, 1964; Hourani, 1971; Rahman, 1984). Intellectualism for its own sake in Islamic ethics is "a sin against human nature—maybe even a crime" (Hovannisian, 1985, p. 8). Similarly, openness, disclosure, and authenticity—important Western communicator ideals—are simply not valued in Islamic and Hindu ethical systems. Unlike Western cultures and particularly the United States, Hindu and Islamic societies do not revere the individual; hence, they are not grounded in an ethical communicative assumption that each person ought to have optimum information to choose logically between alternative positions.

Finally, communication ethics in Western culture and particularly the United States are grounded in an implicit assumption that listeners, regardless of their ethnicity, social class, race, or gender, ought to have equal access to information to make choices. Equal and universal access to information is an essential component of a participatory democracy according to Jaska and Pritchard (1994). As Nilsen (1966) writes: "The ethical touchstone is the degree of free, informal, rational, and critical choice—significant choice—that is fostered by our speaking" (p. 46). As a result, sexism, classism, ageism, or other forms of discriminatory language and messages are considered unethical. These messages, according to Johannesen (1990), "intentionally demean other people through embodying unfair negative value judgments concerning traits, capacities, and accomplishments" (p. 129).

Listener quality is not a fundamental value in many ethical systems outside the United States as detailed later in this essay. Suffice to say that Confucianism, Hinduism, and Islamic philosophy implicitly give certain listeners and audiences more social value than others (Little & Sumner, 1978). Often these social hierarchies are based on age, class, gender, and familial affiliation, and they regulate the frequency and content of listener and audience communication.

If communication ethics described in the literature is grounded in Western and U.S. ethical values, then what can be said about communication ethics in other societies? The next section of the article develops major principles of communication ethics associated with Confucianism and Hinduism. Because communication literature is devoid of published articles or texts that specifically analyze communication ethics in Confucianism and Hinduism, the communication ethical insights offered here are derived from general ethical theory associated with each of these major philosophies or religions.[1] Hence, this section is exploratory and integrative, offering communication ethical principles that influence world cultures beyond Western society and the United States.

AN INTRACULTURAL ETHICAL FRAMEWORK FOR COMMUNICATION: CONFUCIANISM AND HINDUISM

East Asia, Southeast Asia, and South Asia have been influenced quite dramatically by Confucianism and Hinduism (Little & Sumner, 1978). With respect to Confucianism, Taiwan, Korea, Japan, and People's Republic of China have had significant involvement with Confucian thought and tradition that has influenced the ethical traditions of these societies to varying degrees. Hinduism has had enormous influence in South Asia, particularly India, and has affected the rest of the region as well—Sri Lanka, Nepal, Bangladesh, and Pakistan. Because Confucianism and Hinduism are so integral to Asia in terms of its historical, cultural, and ethical development, it is quite logical that communication ethics in each of these world regions ought to reflect the dominant philosophy or religion (Chan, 1963; Chang, 1962). Confucianism and Hinduism—the latter being a religion and the former a philosophy of life—will be discussed in terms of communication ethics in the following areas: (1) communicator ethics, (2) message ethics, (3) receiver and audience ethics.

CONFUCIANISM

Communicator Ethics

Communicator ethics in Confucian philosophy is intimately tied to the concept of *Li*, a set of rituals and social practices defined by Confucius. These rights and practices are derived from a central premise in Confucian thought: Obligation to parents and family is the *raison d'être* of human existence. The family, then, is at the center of Confucian thought and practice, and all rights and rituals spring from this value (Tu Wei-ming, 1976).

The ethical communicator is someone motivated by proper duty (*yi*) to one's parents and family first, and then the society at large. The Chinese concept of *Jen*—translated as benevolence—guides the ethical communicator to choose actions and attitudes that reveal a general concern for all people while reserving the greatest *Jen* for the family.

The ethical communicator also displays *ksiao* (filial piety) and *ti* (respect for an elder brother). Reverence for parents and elders is central to Confucianism, and communicators are judged as moral or ethical based on this criterion.

In summary, communicator ethics in Confucian philosophy is based on exhibiting appropriate communicative behavior that reflects a keen family commitment to parents, elders, and the larger society. Confucian thought is so rooted in duty that the ethical communicator is obligated to display appropriate attitudes and actions in all settings.

Message Ethics

Reason, logic, evidence, and truthfulness are *not* the criteria for determining whether or not a message is ethical in Confucian philosophy (Ivanhoe, 1990). These standards would be considered morally insufficient because they don't focus on the nature of the message; that is, because Confucian philosophy is grounded in community or family obligations and duties, any message can only be judged ethical if it displays *Jen* (benevolence) for the community and family. Messages that focus on personal profit or benefit are too self-centered to be considered ethical. Hence, messages that are community- or family-centered are more ethical than arguments that focus on enlightened self-interest. Similarly, messages that communicate filial piety and respect for elder brothers are most compatible with Confucian philosophy. In fact, Confucianism obligates people to respect and follow elders, particularly male family members. As a result, all messages should demonstrate a reverence for aging and the aged to be considered ethical.

Confucian philosophy values a heart and mind (*hsin*) approach to evaluating ethical behavior (Ivanhoe, 1990). Confucian thought does not elevate reason and logic to the sublime; on the contrary, it places the heart—the essence of human nature—at the center of ethical behavior. It is the heart and mind—the total human being—that can judge ethical behavior, and by extension, ethical messages. Reason alone is insufficient because it fosters independent thinking and action rather than relying on a "sovereign"—a respected elder who guides one's behavior and messages.

Receiver and Audience Ethics

All listeners are not equal in Confucian philosophy—there is clearly a hierarchy of listener importance based on a listener's age, gender, family status, and authority role (Tu Wei-ming, 1976). Parents and elder brothers are the most revered. Males, older persons regardless of family status, and selected authority figures such as teachers are also highly regarded in Confucian philosophy. As a result, communication must be adapted to listeners in conformity with the ethical requirements of age, gender, family status, and authority role. This means that *who* the listener is ought to determine *what* is communicated, how much is revealed, the level of respect accorded to the receiver, and whether communication is a one-way or two-way process. For example, communicators are ethically required to communicate respectful messages bereft of challenges and disagreements to parents, elder brothers, and teachers. And because women in Confucian philosophy are subordinate to men, there are gender implications for information access and receiver credibility and respect (Ivanhoe, 1990).

The preceding analysis of Confucianism serves as a foundation and catalyst for initiating further intercultural study of communication ethics in societies imbued in Confucian philosophy. Turning to Hinduism, the paper speculates on communication ethics in this dominant Eastern religion.

HINDUISM

Communicator Ethics

Dharma is Hindu ethics, and it is the foundation of all Indian thought and action (Crawford, 1974; Sharma, 1965; Walker, 1986). It prescribes the ideals for human life in this world, people's relations with others, the duties of caste, and the stages of life. *Dharma* for Hindu scholars is the ethical glue that regulates human affairs including bad habits to be broken *(yamas)* and good habits to be established *(niyamas)*. As one studies *Vedas*—the inquiry into *dharma*—one learns Hindu ethical behavior that can purify individuals in this life and the lives to come.

The ethical communicator, then, ought to be influenced by *dharma* in thought and action. Although *dharma* does not directly focus on communicative action, it does comment implicitly on duties required of individuals in their different stages of life as students, family members, and retirees as well as the obligations attending to one's caste—social position within Indian society. For communicators, it is critical to understand one's own role in social institutions and the roles of others to formulate ethical messages and behave ethically (Dasgutta, 1961).

For example, the ethical communicator should construct messages that are appropriate for the caste one represents and the caste with which one is communicating. Similarly, family and gender duties required in *dharma* ought to affect the behavior of communicators when they encounter women and older persons who, according to Hindu ethics, must be treated in certain ways. Class, gender, age, and social position play important roles in *dharma* and,

by extension, require communicators to be rhetorically sensitive.

Dharma also requires that communicators be a role model and live this code of conduct in all dimensions of life. *Karma,* an important Hindu concept that refers roughly to moral climate, is influenced by personal actions that are either compatible or incompatible with *dharma.* Like all human beings according to Hinduism, communicators ought to be conscious of their behavior to influence *karma* positively and achieve the ultimate end of human existence: extricating oneself from the baser instincts of human kind.

Message Ethics

Like Confucianism, reason is not celebrated in Hindu thought—it is not the touchstone for determining value or truth. In fact, emotion, subconscious connections through yoga, and deep spiritual reflection are truly the paths to truth and enlightenment. Reason is a temporal tool to be used in social relations but is limited in utility and scope (Coward, 1989).

As a result, messages that rely principally on reason to inform or persuade would not truly be ethical particularly if they were not in concert with *dharma.* The normative requirements of *dharma* articulates in general terms what a person is obligated to do in each stage of life, and ethical messages ought to reflect this.

Central to Hinduism is reaching *moksha,* roughly translated as liberation or salvation. There are many possible yoga or paths to liberation, but each combines spiritual self-reflection with some degree of intellectual understanding. Hence, ethical messages within Hindu thought should in some way move people closer to *moksha.*

Finally, ethical messages in Hinduism differentiate between listeners and should be adapted to a receiver's position, class, caste, gender, and age. This is central to *dharma* and Hindu thought and is examined in the next section of the article.

Receiver and Audience Ethics

Like Confucianism, Hinduism is not based on the concept that all listeners are or ought to be equal.

To the contrary, *Varna dharma* prescribes duties that are caste- and class-related, and it defines the relationship and communication between castes. Similarly, Hinduism defines the roles of men and women quite clearly in *dharma* and *Yoga Sutras*, with women being considered more impure than men and thus "seen to be of a lower quality (lower class)" (Coward, 1989, p. 3).

Note that purity is a central concept in Hinduism and can be sought through right action (*dharma*); nevertheless, purity is influenced by past lives (reincarnation) and bodily functions. Because women are considered to have more bodily discharges than men, they are viewed as being more impure (Coward, 1989).

According to Hinduism, the social behaviors of caste and gender emerge from inborn qualities of these groups; that is, women and *Harigans* (the untouchable class), for example, are born with qualities that relegate them to subordinate positions in the culture. Even right conduct will not shield individuals from caste or gender distinctions (Crawford, 1974).

Communicators, then, are obligated to interact differently with castes and genders. For example, individuals from lower castes and women in general are neither supposed to receive the same type of information as men or people from higher castes nor to be treated as equals. Coward (1989) details the clash between traditional Hinduism and the new Indian constitution, which guarantees rights to all regardless of caste or gender.

AN INTERCULTURAL COMMUNICATION ETHIC: POSSIBILITY?

While there are more dimensions to a Hindu communication ethic, clearly much of it is fundamentally incompatible with Western communication ethics. Confucian communication ethics is also on a collision course with Western ethical principles. The question remains: Can a communication ethics emerge that transcend culture and serve as a guideline when communicating interculturally?

Because an intracultural analysis uncovers deep structures in a society and its communication, it obviates easy cultural answers such as those traditionally offered about intercultural ethics: Be empathetic, understand people are different, values vary from society to society, ad infinitum. In truth, one could attempt to follow all these intercultural caveats and still reject the ethical premises that regulate a society's communication and relationships. At the base of rejection may be systemic cultural differences that are fundamentally at odds. In the case of Confucianism, Hinduism, and Western and U.S. communication ethics, there are such fundamental differences that it is difficult to conceive of a substantive and acceptable intercultural ethic that transcends banal intercultural caveats.

The intercultural ethical challenge, then, is to understand truly how deeply communication ethics are grounded in culture. With an intracultural perspective, people, society, and their communication can be approached and possibly understood from each culture's terms. As a result, an intracultural analysis probes the essence of communication ethics because it is so deeply rooted in culture. Contradictions, paradox, and social conflict are inevitably revealed when ethics and communication are examined within a society.

The intercultural goal is to develop an increasingly intimate understanding of the complexities of each society and its communication ethics. Communicators need to know and feel the ethical values and moral constraints of a society, the deeply held cultural beliefs and communication expectations that regulate human affairs. Authentic intracultural journeys challenge sojourners, exposing them to ethical and communication systems that may seem so different from their own. It is only through multiple intracultural journeys that communicators can achieve intercultural ethical enlightenment—a personal awareness of just how accepting one can be of ethical systems different from one's own. Intercultural prescriptions and caveats are nothing more than clichés unless communicators have a deep understanding of culture, ethics, and communication.

How do communicators journey intraculturally if the literature on communication ethics is so tied to Western and U.S. cultural ethics? First, communication ethicists need to admit that their research has an intracultural bias; that is, they are not writing about ethics per se but rather about U.S. and Western communication ethics. Next, the research focus must expand with scholars studying communication ethics in societies outside the United States. Africa, Asia, Latin America, and Europe should be explored intraculturally with the aim of articulating the ethical communication systems of countries within these global regions. With scores of intracultural insights, communicators may one day be able to predict, unravel, and maybe even resolve the ethical collisions that inevitably occur when cultures communicate cross-nationally.

Note

1. Although there are several articles and books on Confucianism and communication, no single article or text specifically examines communication ethics and Confucianism. Key articles on Confucianism and communication include:

Chao, Y. R. (1956). Chinese terms of address. *Language, 32*, 217–241.
Chang, C. Y. (1987). Chinese philosophy and contemporary communication theory. In D. L. Kincaid (Ed.), *Communication theory: Eastern and Western perspectives*. New York: Academic Press.
McBrian, C. (1978). Language and social stratification: The case of a Confucian society. *Anthropological Linguistics, 2*, 320–326.
Yum, J. O. (1997). The impact of Confucianism on interpersonal relationships and communication patterns in East Asia. In L. Samovar & R. Porter (Eds.), *Intercultural communication: A reader* (pp. 75–88). Belmont, CA: Wadsworth Publishing.

References

Chan, W. (1963). *Sourcebook in Chinese philosophy*. Princeton, NJ: Princeton University Press.
Chang, C. (1962). *The development of Neo-Confucian thought*. New York: Bookman Associates.
Condon, J. C. (1977). *Intercultural communication*. New York: MacMillan.
Coward, H. G. (1989). Purity in Hinduism. In H. Coward, J. Lipner, & K. Young (Eds.), *Hindu ethics* (pp. 9–40). Albany: State University of New York Press.
Crawford, S. C. (1974). *The evolution of Hindu ethical ideals*. Calcutta: Firma K.L. Mukhopadhyay.
Dasgutta, S. (1961). *Development of moral philosophy in India*. Calcutta: Orient Longmans.
Gibb, A. R. (1964). *Modern trends in Islam*. Chicago: University of Chicago Press.
Hourani, G. (1971). *Islamic rationalism*. New York: Oxford University Press.
Hovannisian, R. G. (1985). *Ethics in Islam*. Malibu, CA: Undena Publications.
Howell, W. S. (1986). "Forward." In N. Asuncion-Lande (Ed.), *Ethical perspectives and critical issues in intercultural communication*. Falls Church, VA: Speech Communication Association.
Ivanhoe, P. J. (1990). *Ethics in the Confucian tradition*. Atlanta: Scholars Press.
Jaska, J. A., & Pritchard, M. S. (1994). *Communication ethics: Methods of analysis*. Belmont, CA: Wadsworth.
Johannesen, R. L. (1990). *Ethics and human communication*. Prospect Heights, IL: Waveland Press.
———. (1994). *Ethics and human communication*. Prospect Heights, IL: Waveland Press.
Little, D. (1974). Max Weber and the comparative study of religious ethics. *Journal of Religious Ethics, 2*(2), 5–40.
———, & Sumner, B. T. (1978). *Comparative religious ethics: A new method*. New York: Harper & Row.
Makau, J., & Arnett, R. (1997). *Communication ethics in an age of diversity*. Urbana: University of Illinois Press.
Nilsen, T. R. (1966). *Ethics of speech communication*. Indianapolis: Bobbs-Merrill.
Rader, M. (1964). *Ethics and the human community*. New York: Holt, Rinehart, & Winston.
Rahman, F. (1984). *Introduction to Islam and modernity*. Chicago: University of Chicago Press.
Sharma, I. C. (1965). *Ethical principles of India*. Lincoln, IL: Johnsen Publishing.
Shuter, R. (1990). The centrality of culture. *The Southern Communication Journal, L5*(3), 237–249.
———. (1998). Revisiting the centrality of culture. In J. T. Nakayama & L. Flores (Eds.), *Readings in cultural context*. Mountain View, CA: Mayfield Publishing.
Tu Wei-ming (1976). *Neo-Confucian thought in action*. Berkeley: University of California Press.
Walker, B. (1986). *Hindu world: An encyclopedic survey of Hinduism*. London: George Allen & Unwin.
Wargo, R. J. (1990). Japanese ethics: Beyond good and evil. In D. Smith (Ed.), *Philosophy East and West* (pp. 129–138). Honolulu: University of Hawaii.

Concepts and Questions

1. What are some of the fundamental differences between Western Judeo-Christian–based ethical systems and Shinto-based ethical systems found in Japan?
2. In what ways are Western and U.S. ethical systems culturally biased?

3. What roles do reason and logic play in Western ethical systems? How does Islamic ethical philosophy treat reason and logic?

4. How is listener equality manifest in U.S. ethical systems?

5. What are the responsibilities of communicators in a Confucian-influenced ethical system? What forms of communicative behavior would you expect of communicators under such a system?

6. From a Confucian philosophic perspective, what criteria determine message ethics?

7. How does listener equality function in a Confucian-based ethical system?

8. From a Hindu perspective, what constitutes ethical communication?

9. In the Hindu tradition, what determines an ethical message?

10. Under Hindu ethics, what behaviors might you expect from an ethical receiver and audience?

Peace as an Ethic for Intercultural Communication

David W. Kale

A Ford Foundation executive with over twenty years experience in overseas travel has been quoted as saying that "most problems in cross-cultural projects come from different ideas about right and wrong" (Howell, 1981, p. 3). This executive's statement refers to two problem areas that have caused a great deal of difficulty in intercultural communication. First, many people have been in the uncomfortable position of doing something completely acceptable in their own country, while unknowingly offending the people of the culture they were visiting. This problem arose when I took a group of university students to Guyana in South America. In that warm climate, our students wore the same shorts they would have worn at home, but the Guyanese were offended by what they considered to be skimpy clothing, particularly when worn by the women. A second problem that arises in intercultural situations results when we try to get the rest of the world to live according to our culture's ideas about right and wrong. Interestingly, we get rather upset when people of another culture tell us how to behave. We like to believe that the way our culture chooses to do things is the right way and we do not appreciate people of other cultures telling us we are wrong.

Both of these problems have a bearing on ethics in intercultural communication. Discussing this topic causes stress to people of all cultures. Bonhoeffer suggests this is because we get the feeling that the basic issues of life are being addressed. When that happens, some of our most cherished beliefs may be challenged. When our cultural beliefs about right and wrong are being threatened, we feel the very

This original essay first appeared in the seventh edition. All rights reserved. Permission to reprint must be obtained from the author and the publisher. David W. Kale teaches at the Olivet Nazarene University, Kankakee, Illinois.

foundation of our lives may be under attack (Bonhoeffer, 1965, pp. 267–268).

While such a discussion may be threatening, it must be undertaken nonetheless. With contact among people of various cultures rapidly on the rise, an increase in the number of conflicts over matters of right and wrong is inevitable. This essay addresses the ethics of intercultural communication by developing the following points: (1) a definition of communication ethics, (2) cultural relativity versus universal ethics, (3) the concept of spirit as a basis for intercultural ethics, (4) peace as the fundamental value in intercultural ethics, and (5) a code of ethics in intercultural communication.

A DEFINITION OF COMMUNICATION ETHICS

Richard Johannesen (1978, pp. 11–12) has said that we are dealing with an ethical issue in human communication when

1. People voluntarily choose a communication strategy.
2. The communication strategy is based on a value judgment.
3. The value judgment is about right and wrong in human conduct.
4. The strategy chosen could positively or negatively affect someone else.

It is important to note in this definition that values are the basis for communication ethics. For example, we place a value on the truth and therefore it is unethical to tell a lie to another person. Without this basis in values, we have no ethical system whatsoever.

We face a major problem in our society because some people think they can decide right and wrong for themselves with no regard for what others think. Such a mind-set shows that these people really don't understand ethics at all. If they did they would know that ethics are based on values, and values are determined by culture. Thus, there can be no such thing as a totally individual system of ethics. Such an approach would eventually result in the total destruction of human society (Weaver, 1971, p. 2; Hauerwas, 1983, p. 3).

Within a culture there is a continual dialogue about the things that are the most meaningful and important to the people of that culture. As a result, cultures are continually in a state of change. When cultures change, so do the values that culture holds. Thus, we must acknowledge that there is no fixed order of values that exists within a culture (Brummett, 1981, p. 293). This does not mean, however, that we are free to determine right and wrong for ourselves. It is much more accurate to say that we are shaped by the values of our culture than to say that we shape the values of our culture (Hauerwas, 1983, p. 3).

CULTURAL RELATIVISM VERSUS UNIVERSAL ETHICS

Because the values on which our ethics are built are generated by dialogue within a culture, the question must then be asked whether a person of one culture can question the conduct of a person in another culture. The concept of cultural relativity would suggest that the answer to this question is generally "No." Cultural relativity suggests that a culture will develop the values it deems best for the people of that culture. These values are dependent on the context in which the people of that culture go to work, raise their children, and run their societies. As such, those who are from a different context will develop a different set of cultural values and therefore have no basis on which to judge the conduct of people in any culture other than their own.

However, few would be willing to strictly follow the concept of cultural relativity. To do so would suggest that it was all right for Hitler to murder six million innocent people since the German people did nothing to stop it (Jaska and Pritchard, 1988, p. 10). At the same time, however, few are willing to support the idea that people of all cultures must abide by the same code of ethics. We know cultures develop different value systems and thus must have different ethical codes.

Both Brummett (p. 294) and Hauerwas (p. 9) have argued that because values are derived through dialogue, there is nothing wrong with attempting to persuade people of other cultures to accept our values. Before we do that, however, we must be convinced that our values are worthy and not based on limited self-interest. We must also be willing to work for genuine dialogue; too often these discussions tend to be monologues. We are generally far more willing to present the case for our own value system than we are to carefully consider the arguments for those of other cultures.

At the time of this writing, for example, people of many cultures are attempting to get the people of Brazil to stop cutting down their rain forests. As long as these persuasive efforts are based on a genuine concern for the negative effect cutting these trees is having on the global climate, there is nothing unethical about them. We must, however, also be willing to understand what is motivating the Brazilians' behavior and accept some responsibility in helping them to solve the serious economic problems their country is facing.

SPIRIT AS THE BASIS FOR ETHICAL UNIVERSALS

To develop the next point, how we are to make ethical decisions in intercultural communication, let me suggest that there is a concept on which we can base a universal code of ethics: the human spirit (Eubanks, 1980, p. 307). In the words of Eliseo Vivas,

> The person deserves unqualified respect because he (or she) is not merely psyche but also spirit, and spirit is, as far as we know, the highest form of being. It is through the human spirit that the world is able to achieve cognizance of its status as creature, to perceive its character as valuable, and through human efforts to fulfill a destiny, which it freely accepts. (p. 235)

It is this human spirit which people of all cultures have in common that serves as a basis of belief that there are some universal values on which we can build a universal code of ethics in intercultural communication.

We have watched dramatic changes take place in the world as people in Eastern Europe and the Commonwealth of Independent States (the former Soviet Union) have attempted to improve the quality of life for themselves and their offspring. We identify with their efforts because we share a human spirit that is the same regardless of cultural background. It is this spirit that makes us people who value in the first place. It is from this spirit that the human derives the ability to make decisions about right and wrong, to decide what makes life worth living, and then to make life the best it can possibly be. Therefore, the guiding principle of any universal code of intercultural communication should be to protect the worth and dignity of the human spirit.

PEACE AS THE FUNDAMENTAL HUMAN VALUE

There is a strong temptation for those of us in Western democracies to identify freedom of choice as the fundamental human value. Hauerwas (pp. 9–12) has convincingly argued that freedom of choice is an unachievable goal for human endeavor. He notes that it is not possible for everyone to have freedom of choice. At the time of this writing, some people in Czechoslovakia want to have the country stay together as a whole while others want it to divide into two separate countries, with each being the home of a different ethnic group. It cannot be that both parties will have their choice.

A goal that is possible to achieve, however, is to direct our efforts toward creating a world where people of all cultures are living at peace with one another. This goal consists of three different levels: minimal peace, moderate peace, and optimal peace.

Minimal peace is defined as merely the absence of conflict. Two parties in conflict with each other are at minimal peace when they would be involved in violent conflict if they felt free to act out their hostile feelings. Perhaps there are U.N. peacekeeping forces restraining the two sides from fighting. Perhaps both sides know that continual fighting will bring condemnation from the rest of the world community. Whatever the reason, the peace is only superficial.

Moderate peace results when two conflicting parties are willing to compromise on the goals they want to achieve. In this case, each party has major concessions it is willing to make to reach agreement, but considerable irritation still exists with the opposing party in the conflict. Each party considers its own goals as worthy and justifiable and any of the other party's goals that conflict with its own are clearly unacceptable.

Moderate peace describes the situation that exists today between Israel and its Arab neighbors. Negotiations are proceeding in Washington between Israel and countries such as Syria, Jordan, and Egypt. The fact that these countries are at least willing to sit down at the same table and negotiate indicates that their relationship has developed beyond that of minimal peace. If those negotiations break off and hostile feelings intensify, they could be back to a relationship of minimal peace in a very short period of time.

Optimal peace exists when two parties consider each other's goals as seriously as they do their own. This does not mean that their goals do not ever conflict. The United States and Canada have a relationship that could be considered as optimal peace, yet there is considerable disagreement over the issue of whether acid rain from U.S. factories is destroying Canadian woodlands. Each side pursues its own goals in negotiations, but considers the other party's goals as worthy and deserving of serious consideration.

At the current time the Soviet republics of Armenia and Azerbaijan are locked in a bitter ethnic conflict over a territory within the republic of Azerbaijan that is populated mostly by Armenians. Because the territory is in their republic, the people of Azerbaijan say they should control it; because it is populated largely by Armenians, the Armenians say they should control it. Both groups cannot have freedom of choice in this situation, but they can live in peace if they are willing to submit to reasonable dialogue on their differences.

The concept of peace applies not only to relations between cultures and countries, but to the right of all people to live at peace with themselves and their surroundings. As such it is unethical to communicate with people in a way that does violence to their concept of themselves or to the dignity and worth of their human spirit.

A UNIVERSAL CODE OF ETHICS IN INTERCULTURAL COMMUNICATION

Before launching into the code itself, a "preamble" should first be presented based on William Howell's suggestion that the first step to being ethical in any culture is the intent to do what one knows is right (1982, p. 6). All societies set out rules of ethical conduct for people to follow based on cultural values. The foundation of ethical behavior is that people intend to do what they know is right. To choose to do something that you know to be wrong is unethical in any culture.

Principle #1   Ethical communicators address people of other cultures with the same respect that they would like to receive themselves.

It is based on this principle that I find ethnic jokes to be unethical. Some people may argue that ethnic jokes are harmless in that they are "just in fun," but no one wants to be on the receiving end of a joke in which their own culture is demeaned by people of another culture (LaFave and Mannell, 1978). Verbal and psychological abuse can damage the human spirit in the same way that physical abuse does damage to the body. Verbal and psychological violence against another person, or that person's culture, is just as unacceptable as physical violence. People of all cultures are entitled to live at peace with themselves and the cultural heritage which has had a part in shaping them. It is, therefore, unethical to use our verbal and/or nonverbal communication to demean or belittle the cultural identity of others.

Principle #2   Ethical communicators seek to describe the world as they perceive it as accurately as possible.

While in our culture we might call this telling the truth, what is perceived to be the truth can vary greatly from one culture to another. We know that reality is not something that is objectively the same for people of all cultures. Reality is socially constructed for us by our culture; we live in different perceptual worlds (Kale, 1983, pp. 31–32).

The point of this principle is that ethical communicators do not deliberately set out to deceive or mislead, especially since deception is very damaging to the ability of people of various cultures to trust each other. It is only when people of the world are able to trust one another that we will be able to live in peace. That trust is only possible when the communication that occurs between those cultures is devoid of deliberate attempts to mislead and deceive (Hauerwas, 1983, p. 15; Bok, 1978, pp. 18–33).

Principle #3 Ethical communicators encourage people of other cultures to express themselves in their uniqueness.

This principle is reflected in Article 19 of the Universal Declaration of Human Rights as adopted by the United Nations. It states: "Everyone has the right to freedom of opinion and expression; this right includes the freedom to hold opinions without interferences and to seek, receive and impart information and ideas through any media and regardless of frontiers (Babbili, p. 9).

In his book, *I and Thou*, Martin Buber cogently discusses the need for us to allow the uniqueness of the other to emerge if genuine dialogue is to take place. Frequently, we place demands on people of other cultures to adopt our beliefs or values before we accept them as full partners in our dialogue.

Is it the right of the U.S. government to demand that Nicaragua elect a non-communist government before that country is granted full partnership in the intercultural dialogue of this hemisphere? It is certainly possible that the people of that country will elect a communist government, and if they do, they are still entitled to equal status with the other governments of Central America. At the same time, we celebrate the fact that in central Europe people of several countries are finally being allowed to express themselves by throwing off the stranglehold of communist ideology imposed on them by forces outside their culture. Ethical communicators place a high value on the right of cultures to be full partners in the international dialogue, regardless of how popular or unpopular their political ideas may be. It is the height of ethnocentrism, and also unethical, to accord people of another culture equal status in the international arena only if they choose to express themselves in the same way we do.

Principle #4 Ethical communicators strive for identification with people of other cultures.

Identification is achieved when people share some principles in common, which they can do while still retaining the uniqueness of their cultural identities (Burke, 1969, p. 21). This principle suggests that ethical communicators encourage people of all cultures to understand each other, striving for unity of spirit. They do this by emphasizing the commonalities among cultural beliefs and values, rather than their differences.

At the present time we are, unfortunately, seeing an increasing number of racial incidents occurring on our college and university campuses. Many times these take the form of racist slogans appearing on the walls of campus buildings. The purpose of these actions is often to stir up racial animosity, creating wider divisions among ethnic groups. Such behavior is unethical according to this principle in that it is far more likely to lead to conflict than it is to peace.

Note

The author wishes to thank Angela Latham-Jones for her critical comments of an earlier version of this essay.

References

Babbili, A. S. (1983). *The Problem of International Discourse: Search for Cultural, Moral and Ethical Imperatives.* Paper presented at the convention of the Association for Education in Journalism and Mass Communication, Corvallis, Oregon.

Bok, S. (1978). *Lying: Moral Choice in Public and Private Life.* New York: Random House.

Bonhoeffer, D. (1965). *Ethics.* Eberhard Bethge, ed. New York: Macmillan.

Brummett, B. (1981). A defense of ethical relativism as rhetorically grounded. *Western Journal of Speech Communication,* 45(4), 286–298.

Buber, M. (1965). *I and Thou.* New York: Peter Smith.

Burke, K. (1969). *A Rhetoric of Motives.* Berkeley: University of California Press.

Eubanks, R. (1980). Reflections on the moral dimension of communication. *Southern Speech Communication Journal,* 45(3), 240–248.

Hauerwas, S. (1983). *The Peaceable Kingdom.* South Bend, Ind.: University of Notre Dame.

Howell, W. (1981). *Ethics of Intercultural Communication.* Paper presented at the 67th convention of the Speech Communication Association, Anaheim, California.

Howell, W. (1982). *Carrying Ethical Concepts Across Cultural Boundaries.* Paper presented at the 68th convention of the Speech Communication Association, Louisville, Kentucky.

Jaska, J., and Pritchard, M. (1988). *Communication Ethics: Methods of Analysis.* Belmont, Calif.: Wadsworth.

Johannesen, R. (1978). *Ethics in Human Communication.* Wayne, N.J.: Avery.

Kale, D. (1983). In defense of two ethical universals in intercultural communication. *Religious Communication Today.* Vol. 6, Sept., 28–33.

LaFave, L., and Mannell, R. (1978). Does ethnic humor serve prejudice? *Journal of Communication,* Summer, 116–124.

Vivas, E. (1963). *The Moral Life and the Ethical Life.* Chicago: Henry Regnery.

Weaver, R. (1971). *Ideas Have Consequences.* Chicago: University of Chicago Press.

Concepts and Questions

1. How do culturally different concepts of right and wrong affect intercultural communication?
2. What conditions constitute an ethical issue in human communication?
3. Why does Kale suggest there can be no such thing as a totally individual system of ethics?
4. Given the cultural relativity of ethics, under what conditions is it permissible for people of one culture to attempt to persuade people of other cultures to accept their values?
5. How may the human spirit serve as a basis for a universal ethic?
6. What is minimal peace? How does it differ from moderate peace?
7. Under what circumstances does optimal peace exist? Is optimal peace a realistic goal in international relations?
8. What is the first step to being ethical in any culture?
9. What is the main point associated with the ethical principle that communicators should seek to describe the world as they perceive it as accurately as possible?
10. How can individuals develop the capability to fulfill the ethical principle that ethical communicators strive for identification with people of other cultures?

Peace Communication: The Ethics of Caring Across Cultures

Tom Bruneau

INTRODUCTION

The recognition of the imperative for peaceful, ethical, and respectful relations is as old as the formation of self–other consciousness. Uniqueness and individuality, regardless of strategies to transcend them, are hopelessly nonisometric, nonisomorphic, and rhythmically dissimilar (Bruneau, 1988b). Interpersonally, then, change is the rule and permanent or mutual understandings seldom occur. We unfortunately assume similarities or shared meanings too frequently. Also, we too often see the appearances of change, but not the changes below the appearances. This complexifies individuality and contributes to interpersonal or group conflict or both. Transcending interpersonal or group conflict with empathy becomes both a purpose and a definition of communication.

THE IMAGE OF PEACE

There is a human propensity to reduce the concept of peace to a vague abstraction, as unworthy of further thought, or as an idealistic venture to be pursued by dreamers. The idea of peace, therefore, becomes negated as hopeless. But in most of humankind's religious and humanitarian traditions, peace is about hopeful, not hopeless, efforts. These hopeful images of peace, incidentally, appear to be basic to and subsuming of our concepts and processes of conflict and have persisted for tens of thousands of years. They can be considered "mythemes" or even archetypal images that occur and reoccur spontaneously

This original article appears here for the first time. All rights reserved. Permission to reprint must be obtained from the author and the publisher. Tom Bruneau teaches at Radford University, Radford, Virginia.

throughout the globe. As students of intercultural communication, we must be hopeful and view these old, steady ideas and images of peace as important and worthy of our consideration. With our ever-increasing means of human destruction, we dare not neglect these images.

Throughout the world in "primitive" or traditional societies, according to Eliade (1952, 1960), there is a yearning for paradise, a place of peace, of rest, a place where there is no conflict, only joy, bliss, stillness, tenselessness. These traditional images seem basic to every group on the face of the earth. Eliade has shown convincingly that all religions, (Christian, Buddhist, Islamic, Hindu, etc.) harbor images of peace constructed in "sacred spaces."

These sacred spaces are also "holy" centers that are peaceful and which are believed to connect people with sacred paradises outside of profane time or everyday activities. These centers are tombs, monuments (i.e., the peace statue at Nagasaki), churches, temples, centers of magical or mythic power, and so on. They often are for the select, the chosen few. "Sacred" places are also gardens (Eden), retreats, mountaintops, origin points (where we began, etc.). Peace images, therefore, are places of sacredness; these places can be personal, private places, public memorial places (Vietnam Memorial), places of reverence, and so forth. They are often places where silence is observed, nourished, and where profane, mundane, everyday talk, thought, and action are quieted and stilled.

Silence is directly related to images of peace as well as the sacredness of place. Silence also implies peace in the sense that the reduction of motion, physically or verbally, concerns the reduction of friction (noise) or the profane world of people using words to articulate conflicts, differences, and the struggles of community. Graveyards are silent; death is silent; and, as Aristotle noted, death is the extinction of heat (friction). So, there are millions of gravestones in Christian graveyards inscribed with statements about "eternal rest," "sleep" and "peace at last." As Merton (1949) observed, finding a deeper solitude is a kind of death; "you find solitude by standing still, here you will discover act without motion" (p. 59). Merton (1955) also noted that silence is the "language of God" (p. 254). "If you go into solitude with a silent tongue, the silence of mute beings will share

with you their rest. . . . The silence of the tongue and of the imagination dissolves the barrier between ourselves and the peace of things that exist only for God" (p. 256). It is this generalized silence that concerns sacred mindfulness in sacred places and within the "spatial" image of power. However, a place is not always necessary to silence. As Merton (1955) noted about silence in a crowd, "The true solitary does not have to run away from others: they cease to notice him [her], because he [she] does not share their love for an illusion" (p. 252). A Hindu teacher could well have made this statement.

Several writers on communication and peacemaking have noted the value of quietism and silence as a way of life connected to everyday living. For example, Crawford (1988, 1993) has shown that Taoist silence can be balanced with a peacefulness of communication with others within the profane world of places, spaces, and linear, clock-bound contexts. Anderson (1989) has also shown that a Taoist way of being is not obverse to persons of peaceful communication. He notes that, "Tao is as much silence and void as it is object and voice." Bruneau and Ishii (1988) developed a yin–yang Model of Taoist silence—speech. And Fiordo (1993) has pointed out that Quaker quietism and silence can be extended into everyday life as peaceful communication. So the image of peace as "silence" need not refer to absolute silence (whatever that could be).

The temporal aspects of peace appear to be the most important for understanding the image of peace as well as the nature of conflict and the processes of conflict. Eternal images of peace concern the extension of living into a sacred and total interminable life hereafter, a separation of permanence and nonpermanence. Time as eternity can also concern a cycle of birth–rebirth–birth, an unending and eternal return, recommencement (Eliade, 1952). It is connected, too, to the feeling and idea that the future is not grim, as in death, but is open to the cessation of conflict. So, Hatano (1963) has commented that "eternity is the present which has no past, but only the future . . . eternity must be a perfect fellowship of life with others . . . eternity comes into being only as love" (p. 64). Hatano also notes that a "permanent now (nunc permanens) [is a] forfeiture of all the nows" (p. 90). Paul Tillich referred to this empty and distinctionless time as "the eternal now" (1963). There seems to be little, if any, conflict in eternity in a Buddhist tradition. Suffering inherent in consciousness, however, may or may not be continued after biological death in Hinduism, Christianity, and Islam (a hell on earth can continue—or not continue—depending on negative fate or sin). The Native American "happy hunting ground" appears to be somewhat free from evangelistic death threats to one's afterlife serenity.

This separation of permanence versus impermanence seems to underlie all wishes for peace from conflict and appears basic to most metaphysical thinking. As Coomaraswamy (1947) noted long ago, anyone "who cannot escape from the standpoint of temporal succession so as to see all things in their simultaneity is incapable of the least conception of the metaphysical order" (p. 71).

The image of peace appears to have a definite temporal aspect. Places and spaces of peace appear to be afterimages of transcendental harmonious and synchronous brain states. These afterimages appear to be attempts to describe what is indescribable. They are nonlinear brain energy transformations (Bruneau, 1994a, 1994b, 1997). These transformations often seem to concern the motifs of light, radiance, illumination, brilliance, pure wisdom, and God as light and love, and so on.

The image of peace is thus one of sacred place and space, of silence, and the time of being combined. These images, it is claimed here, provide a ground for understanding human tension and conflict. The image of peace may be considered not only a projected hope for a more peaceful life, but also a driving force for the reduction of conflict. In a hopeless world of conflict people become suicidal, negate the future, or are driven to self–other annihilation. The image of peace sustains us. It brings joy, hope, and an *elan vitale* with zest. Peace also can be defined, however, as the avoidance of conflict by imposing rigid dogma, ideology, or threat, or by destroying the opposition.

PEACE COMMUNICATION

The study of peace and conflict processes as they pertain to communicative interaction is called "peace communication." Peace communication,

therefore, is not necessarily only about the study of communication between nations, cultures, or groups, but between individuals within or between such aggregates. It also may profoundly concern the nature of interaction as empathic. Peace communication inherently concerns intrapersonal patterns of harmony–tension within one's own brain (Bruneau, 1994b, 1997). Peace is also intrapersonal or having "peace of mind."

Peace communication also "involves the study of people, processes, systems and conditions under which violence and war can be replaced by peaceful means of dealing with struggle at any level of society" (Keltner, 1987). Keltner (1987, 1988) also described the scope of peace communication along a "struggle spectrum." According to Keltner, this spectrum or continuum concerns mild differences, disagreements, disputes, campaigns, and litigation, and fight or war. The struggle spectrum seems to acknowledge that an absolute image of peace may be impossible; that differences are inherent whenever two brains are different—which they always must be to effect any sense of individuality or the impossibility of exactness in shared meanings. *Conflict persists; noise is pervasive.*

Keltner (1991) further defines peace communication in terms of conflict reduction and disputes that can be resolved. He notes that, "peacemaking . . . is that process that interferes with the escalating struggle between adversaries and leads to a resolution of the differences between them before the struggle becomes violent and destructive" (p. 78). So Keltner is concerned not with talk about peace or peace as an abstraction; he believes in action toward or processual communication for more peaceful conditions between persons with differences great and small. Our thesis here is that the essence of peace communication concerns those communicative processes that can be termed empathic.

THE CONCEPT OF EMPATHY

Empathy appears to be the basis of all communication processes because it concerns I–thou, self–other efforts to transcend generic differences. The use of empathy seems to be isomorphic with the processes of conflict resolution and concomitant with motion toward the we-ness or us-ness of shared mutuality to prevent conflict escalation. This seems to be the case, for the most part, whether one or both interactants are practicing empathy. One is better than none. The special case of mutual empathy and the development of a milieu of mutual empathy by peacemakers will be considered below.

Empathic concepts and processes are profoundly complex. A summary of ideas taken from previous study (Bruneau, 1988a, 1989a, 1989b, 1993) is all that space will allow here. Empathy is much more than a single variable or factor. A summary of this previous study is initially necessary to the discussion of the peacemaking potentialities of empathic processes. It also seems preliminary to our later discussion on the more complex aspects of "mutual empathy" as basic to preventing conflict, managing conflict, or arresting destructive conflict. Empathy appears to be basic to any point or transition for all participants or mediators in the spectrum of struggle.

Empathy literally means "feeling into" another's feelings with one's own, vicariously, and attempting to achieve some I–thou congruence. Also, empathy means the sensing of and accommodation to each other's biological rhythms in a synchronous or "rhythmic" fashion.

The affective bases of empathy appear to be inactive for people who deny their own positive feelings or are unable to use their feelings in a manner of positive regard. Many seem to practice negation of others as their entire lifestyle. This is almost a definition of interpersonal alienation or an inability or unwillingness to care for and love otherness. It brings up the difficult question, "How do we teach others to love?" Persons who are objectively stiff, rigidly linearizing others in their habitual styles of perceiving and thinking into the nature of otherness, seem to be incapable or retarded in their vain efforts to experience positive affective otherness. Affective otherness concerns the use of narrative consciousness, not objective thinking. This objectivist (nonflowing) problem seems apparent when "thingifying," prejudice, and stereotyping of others occurs. It is also a problem of persons blocking their own showing of affection. We seem to apply so many unwritten restrictions in the revealing of personal affection; showing certain emotions are often unstated taboos that prevent empathy.

Empathy also concerns a cognitive domain that may or may not be congruent with the corresponding feeling, attitudinal, or valuing aspects of "empathic otherness." Empathy can involve deciphering or discriminating the logic, intent, style of thought, critical thinking, and rhetorical probabilities of otherness vis-à-vis one's self. We will discuss "reflective" and "projective" empathy, implying memory-expectation processes, below. Objectively thinking as another thinks, we must assume, is important to most forms of effective, accurate, and strategic symbolic interaction. Empathy is not separated from strategy; caring is often future-oriented.

The processes of empathy are mainly based in biological, perceptual, conceptual, and affective levels of human communication, especially in their interactive and congruent potentialities. Empathic processes can be synthesized into five thematics: (1) empathy as objectification, (2) empathy as imitation, (3) empathy as role taking, (4) empathy as an alternating perception or a step-flow of sequences, and (5) empathy as a psychological mode.

As objectification, empathy is a fairly crude and primitive manner of otherness. Objective consciousness has limitations as empathic feeling. In the early writing about empathy, writers were concerned with one feeling his or her way into the interior and exterior structures of objects, things, nature, and in terms of articulating the structure of artistic products. However, objective empathy also concerns person recognition, identification, and the processing of the surface appearances of others, their assumed physical characteristics. Rigidity in this processing implies the objective perceptual and conceptual categorizing and classifying of others. One can create a "characteristic" mask on the others' surfaces that prevents further need to inquire of the other. Flexibility in objectively processing others implies penetration beyond one's initial objectifications or the masks (images) that we impose on others. One becomes unable to consider the dynamic grounds and substances of one's own objective perceptions and conceptions. Social and cultural insensitivity has been in this world long, and the ignoring of others for much longer.

The imitative bases of empathy concern identification with and replication of another's nonverbal, paralinguistic, linguistic, and psycholinguistic patterns. We become the other as identification through discriminative perception and social comparison—that is, me, not me, him, her, us, them, we, ours, theirs, mine, yours, and so on. Imitation of the various codification systems of others seems to provide for the comparative common grounds of empathy. Howell (1979) elegantly defined the imitative bases of empathy as "the ability to replicate what one perceives" (p. 33).

The imitative bases of empathy extend into a social cognition of caring. This concerns the development of self-as-other or "vicarious otherness" as "me." This process is, of course, common to the purview of "looking glass" theories of social psychology and the formidable influence of George Herbert Mead. By mentally taking or enacting the entire spectrum of the communicative behaviors of others, we gain a comparative basis for our own communication. This is basic to self-identity, conceptually. By mentally projecting ourselves into the role behaviors, role obligations, role expectations, and role discrepancies of others, we learn about them, ourselves, and our mutual, relational similarities and differences. This is "person learning." Role taking involves life roles (understanding mother, father, son, grandmother, sister, etc.) as well as mentally taking on the occupational, social, and organizational roles of others.

Empathic processes also can be understood to involve perceptual viewpoint alternation, code switching in processing otherness, and also creating kinds of step-flow sequential processing, of gliding in and out of another person or person(s) (in a triad or group). One can and often does attempt to see, hear, or perceive from the perceptual viewpoint of the other. Many have trouble in tests of this ability. One attempts to experience the perceptual realities of the other; this can involve the attempt to replicate or experience the specific sensory systems of others. These nonverbal systems also can be somewhat replicated (role-playing) as they are integrated in the other. Empathy as code switching is closely related to perceptual viewpoint taking. Code switching can refer to our various nonverbal communication systems only. For example, one can take the view of another from the others' paralinguistic cues and then take in the kinesic motorality of the other, then switching to the oculesics or eye behaviors of the other, and so on. Constructing otherness in this manner can allow us to synthesize the other—by

comparing their perspectival worlds with our own. Also, one can also alternate one's projective viewpoint taking in terms of switching between another's nonverbal and verbal expressions (e.g., what they are expressing versus how they are saying what they are saying). This inherently concerns acquiring information about otherness in terms of feelings versus thought. It is an important first step in helping others to be empathic.

Another aspect of empathy as an "alternating-of-viewpoints strategy" is the use of steps of this process sequentially. This is common to considerations of empathic strategies in the psychiatric, counseling, and helping professions. For example, a step-flow sequence was used by Bennett (1979) in discussing the use of empathic strategies in intercultural communication contexts: assuming differences, then knowing self, then suspending self, then allowing for the guided imagination of the other, then allowing empathic experience, and then, finally, reestablishing of self (pp. 419–421). This step-flow can also continue as a cycle.

Empathic processes involving conceptual and psychological processes are quite complicated. A wide range of ideas about the psychology of empathic processes come from various schools of psychology. These modes of empathy involve "thinking as another may be thinking." Crude forms of this are adjectival objectifications of the other—for example, smart, dumb, pretty, ugly. Some writers describe processes as concomitant or related to psychological empathizing—for instance, caring, interest in the other, inferring the other's thoughts, intuiting the other, valuing–evaluating–devaluing the other, foreign consciousness, identification, content analyses of another's thought and meanings, and so forth. The study of the processes of psychological empathizing (social cognition) is ripe with potential. It should be noted that forms of mind reading or even telepathy are involved here, as well as what Ishii (1984) referred to as "*Enryo-sasshi* communication," a kind of sensitive guessing about the other's feelings while maintaining silence. Broome (1991) also has suggested a similar process in discussing educating students in empathy and training them for intercultural interactions.

These thematics of the empathic process are related to other ways in which empathy can be understood and experienced. Empathy has also been described as an integrated system of human neurology. This involves the relationships of three major modes of empathy—interactive empathy, reflective empathy, and projective empathy (Bruneau, 1988a, 1989a, 1989b, 1993). Interactive empathy concerns biological, affective, and perceptual processes within the interactive momentary experience. It concerns otherness in terms of the signalics of nonverbal communication and not the interpretation of these signalics; often we are quite unaware of this "narrational world" of information when we are actively thinking or speaking objectively. Interactive empathy also involves the variable, attentional aspects of signal sharing. It implies information processing as transactional, dynamic, and "momentary experience" in face-to-face situations. This "now-ness" is related to the "then-ness" of reflective empathy (below). No nowness, no then-ness. Excellent attention toward the other is necessary to remember the other, later, reflectively.

Reflective empathy concerns afterimages of the other derived from the efficient and caring high attentional processing of the other in the transactional and interactive nowness. Memory processes are involved as well as the ability to construct and retain images of the other. These reflective images imply re-spect (seeing again) auditory images re-hearing the other), as well as re-smelling, re-touching, and so on, and "re-feeling" of the other *as one's self*, later, after interaction. These are our attempts to develop an informational basis for understanding the differences and similarities of the other in terms of those of our own. Re-thinking and analyzing otherness vis-à-vis our own identities are also involved. Reflective empathy is based not only in our biological replication abilities, our perceptual receptive cortical field reactivations, but also our *own* symbolic representations of our images of the other. The assumption here is that to plan for future interaction, one should draw on reflective memory in ongoing or continued interactions. The reflective empathic bases provide the store of information for "projective empathy" (or "predictive empathy") or careful thinking of interactions to come.

Projective empathy concerns anticipatory rehearsal as well as forebrain expectation. It involves seeing ahead, imagination for upcoming interaction,

forecasting in terms of future communication interactions, events, and occasions. It also can be called *predictive empathy*. Planning as an empathic projective process is important to testing out previous reflections of the other as well as interactional experimentation of one's previous accuracy in deciphering and understanding the other. It is certainly one of the most important aspects of audience analyses as preparatory to delivering a speech in any context.

The three major kinds of empathy being discussed here are congruent with the neurological systems of all human beings. These are the past as memory, the present as attention and perception, and the future as psychological expectation. I believe it is best to consider empathy as crossing many disciplines and as congruent with all human experiencing. Further inquiry and investigation of these systems, especially their relatedness, are certainly in order. The main assumption here is that processes and types of empathy are different in different social and cultural orders. This makes for great complexity in intercultural communication. The study of empathic processes is in an infantile stage; the study of empathic processes across cultures has been only newly born, but holds much promise for peaceful sociocultural and international communication.

A few other ideas about empathic processes are important to our attempt to outline briefly the concept here. The use of empathic processes builds trust. During interactive moments this can be considered to be a kind of "mutual sharing" in terms of mirrored reciprocities that are "rhythmic" rather than "dysrhythmic" (or interactively dysfunctional). Rhythmic reciprocities concern the sharing of perceptual synchronicities and biological rhythms. Also, we can and perhaps should recognize that the dynamic perceptual time chronemics of interaction have corresponding neural dynamics.

In the 1960s, these inner and outer rhythmic exchanges were called good or bad "vibes" or vibrations between people. The sharing of personal tempos, however, is highly involved in attempts at empathic sharing in momentary interaction. We all experience the momentary rhythms of interaction differently. The positive "confirmation" of others, as Koper and Nolan (1988) discuss it, certainly involves some relative temporal congruencies enacted in momentary experience. These "good vibes" or congruencies can also be reexperienced or reflected upon as afterimagery or analytical thoughts about the other—that is, reflective empathy.

The ideas of interactional entrainment and synchronicity are very much involved in empathic processing of the other. These are really neurological rhythms, periodicities, eventualities, sequentialities, and cyclicities involving both "feedback and feedforward neural energy process variables" (i.e., definition of "information"). At the microempathic level, subsuming nonverbal interactions are brain energy transformations of considerable complexity (Bruneau, 1988b, 1989b, 1994a, 1994b, 1997). The tensivities and consonances of these energy fields are basic to future studies of personal time sharing or *chronemics*. Mutual empathy inherently involves these temporal similarities and differences. Time sharing or sharing momentary otherness synchronistically concerns mutual empathy. In intercultural interactions entrainment (merging personal rhythms) and then synching are difficult to achieve.

MUTUAL EMPATHY AND PEACE COMMUNICATION

Mutual empathy implies the use of all of the interaction variables related to the empathic processes discussed here so far. Mutual empathy concerns having "shared empathic" abilities. One can assume an extremely wide range of differences in the empathic abilities of people regardless of where they live on this globe. As a person-to-person variable of human communication, mutuality in empathic processes drives the interaction as trust develops concomitantly. If one becomes more empathic, then the other can choose to reciprocate empathetically. Also, one person who has high empathic skill and knowledge is better than two interactants having few or no empathic abilities. Such is a definition of the contexts for warlike, confrontational conflicts. When the interactants in a dispute have few or no empathic abilities, it is really time for the services of an expert who is a mediator skilled in injecting empathy before, during, or after the conflict.

Mutual empathy also implies that interactants are able actually to communicate empathic concern to the other. When sociocultural empathy systems do not match, this is difficult. Different kinds of media and the sensory channels used can be important. Messages in writing can be limiting, compared to the here-and-now situation of interactants conversing face-to-face. The face-to-face situation can potentially activate *all* processes and forms of empathy. Much more empathic information, or potential empathic information, is available for use. Technologically mediated messages present special problems for the development of empathy in interactions or during peace negotiations. The trust built upon face-to-face interactions is usually limited in mediated interactions. Each technology and sensory channel seems to have different potentialities for empathy.

One can never do enough to practice and develop empathic abilities. The courage to do so and one's energy to do so are important. Being empathic not only requires the courage to risk the rejection of our good intentions, but also to be empathically engaged can overload one's information systems. Empathy is hard work; one is not just egocentrically involved, one centers and decenters his or her self or ego over and over. One processes information not for one, but for two people (or more). Quite an incremental increase in personal energy is necessary.

It is in the development of compassion and respect for the other, as well as for one's self, that mutual arising occurs. This mutual arising of *us* as friends of mutual regard and concern is the essence of both peace communication and peacemaking. I believe it should be the evangel or rallying force of peaceful people and peacemakers. But how to achieve mutual empathy is a road to nirvana fraught with conflict and sorrow. We do not seem to know enough about it. I believe, however, that those who are destructive in their relations with others can use any kind of empathy we can teach them. Bruneau (1988a, 1993) and Broome (1991), as well as others, have given some preliminary practical advice for using or teaching about using empathy in intercultural contexts.

The ideas and processes of empathy are complex, and it is a relatively new area of communication study. Those who see only the conflict of the world avoid "peace" negatively. Peace is a contagious process of communication. Those of us who study this process with hopeful romanticism and not hopeless romanticism seem to know the wisdom of Merton's (1955) definition of empathy: "Compassion and respect enable us to know the solitude of another by finding him [or her] in the intimacy of our own interior solitude" (p. 245).

References

Anderson, R. (1989, November). *Mutual arising: Tao, harmony, and a peace ethic for communication*. Paper presented at the Speech Communication Association Conference, San Francisco.

Bennett, M. J. (1979). Overcoming the golden rule: Sympathy and empathy. In D. Nimmo (Ed.), *Communication yearbook 3* (pp. 407–422). New Brunswick, NJ: Transaction Books.

Broome, B. (1991). Building shared meaning: Implications of a relational approach for teaching intercultural communication. *Communication Education, 40,* 235–249.

Bruneau, T. (1973). Communicative silences: Forms and functions. *Journal of Communication, 23*(1), 17–46.

———. (1988a). Conceptualizing and using empathy in intercultural contexts. *Human Communication Studies, 16,* 37–70.

———. (1988b). Personal time and self-identity. In P. Reale (Ed.), *Time and identity (Tiempo e identita)* (pp. 102–115). Milano, Italy: F. Angeli.

———. (1989a). Empathy and listening: A conceptual review and theoretical directions. *Journal of the International Listening Association, 3,* 1–20.

———. (1989b). The deep structure of intrapersonal communication processes. In C. Roberts & K. Watson (Eds.), *Intrapersonal communication processes: Original essays* (pp. 69–86). Scottsdale, AZ: Gorsuch Scarisbrick.

———. (1993). Empathy and listening. In A. D. Wolvin & C. G. Coakley (Eds.), *Perspectives on listening* (pp. 185–200). Norwood, NJ: Ablex Publishing.

———. (1994a). Contemplation: The art of intrapersonal communication. In J. E. Aaitkens & L. J. Shedletsky (Eds.), *Intrapersonal communication processes* (pp. 208–217), Plymouth, MI: Midnight Oil Press.

———. (1994b, December). *Intrapersonal motion: Neurophysiology and philosophizing*. Paper presented at the First International Conference on Deixis (Time, Space, and Identity), University of Kentucky, Frankfort, KY.

———. (1997). Implications of recent brain studies for understanding problems of intercultural communication. *Human Communication Studies,* Vol. 25, pp. 1–41.

———, & Ishii, S. (1988). Communicative silences: East and West. *World Communication, 17*(1), 1–33.

Coomaraswamy, A. K. (1947). *Time and eternity*. Ascona, Switzerland: Artibus Asiae.

Crawford, L. (1988, November). *The stillpoint: Taoist quietism, human communication, and living peacefully*. Paper presented at the Speech Communication Association Conference, New Orleans, LA.

———. (1993, November). *Everyday Tao: Conversation and contemplation*. Paper presented at the Speech Communication Association Conference, Miami.

Eliade, M. (1952). *Images and symbols: Studies in religious symbolism* (Trans. P. Mairet, 1961). New York: Sheed and Ward.

———. (1960). The yearning for paradise in primitive tradition. In H. A. Murray (Ed.), *Myth and mythmaking* (pp. 61–75). Boston: Beacon Press.

Fiordo, R. A. (1993, November). *Sacralizing genuine humane contact: A philosophy of peaceful communication from the silent Quakers*. Paper presented at the Speech Communication Association Conference, Miami.

Hatano, S. (1963). *Time and eternity*. Tokyo: Ministry of Education.

Howell, W. S. (1979). Theoretical directions for intercultural communication. In M. Asante (Ed.), *Handbook of intercultural communication*. Beverly Hills, CA: Sage.

Ishii, S. (1984). *Enryo-sasshi* communication: A key to understanding Japanese interpersonal relations. *Cross Currents, 11*(1), 49–58.

Keltner, J. (1987, November). *Peace communication: Scope and dimensions*. Paper presented at the Speech Communication Association Conference, Boston.

———. (1988, November). *Understanding peace through the experience of mediation*. Paper presented at the Speech Communication Association Conference, New Orleans.

———. (1991). The role of the dispute resolution professional in the peace-making process. In R. Troester & C. Kelly (Eds.), *Peacemaking through communication* (pp. 77–82). Annandale, VA: Speech Communication Association.

Koper, R. J., & Nolan, L. L. (1988, November). *Confirmation of other cultures as a means of optimizing peaceful coexistence*. Paper presented to the Speech Communication Association Conference, New Orleans.

Merton, T. (1949). *Seeds of contemplation*. Norfolk, CT: New Direction Books.

———. (1955). *No man is an island*. New York: Harcourt and Brace.

Tillich, P. (1963). *The eternal now*. New York: Charles Scribner's Sons.

Concepts and Questions

1. What is implied by the statement "peace is about hopeful, not hopeless, effort"?
2. What elements constitute Bruneau's image of peace?
3. Define "peace communication."
4. How does empathy relate to peace communication?
5. What are the five thematics of empathic processes?
6. What is meant by an "alternating-of-viewpoints strategy" in empathic processes?
7. How should you use reflective empathy in intercultural communication?
8. How does cultural diversity affect empathic communication?
9. What is mutual empathy?
10. How does mutual empathy relate to peace communication?

Index

empathy, 272, 410–411, 435–436
    Confucianism and, 305
    gender and, 294–295
    nunch'i, 61–62, 74–80
    peace communication and, 457–462
ethical systems
    communication and, 443–449
    influence of concepts of right and wrong, 450–454
    Irish, 250
    universals in, 451–454
ethnicity
    group identity and, 18–26
    nationalism and, 54–55, 428
    paradigms of, 4, 52–57, 146
    versus culture, 129
    versus race, 44
ethnocentrism, 9–10, 47, 125, 241–242, 343, 380, 401–402
ethnography, 212–215, 231–237
expectancy fulfillment, 382–383
expressiveness, 260–261, 263, 272–273, 291–292, 380
extension transference, 437
eye contact (oculesics), 154–155, 259, 292–293

face-saving, 70, 316–320, 337, 349–350, 390, 396
family, 12–13, 186
    in Confucianism, 304–305
    in Irish culture, 252–253
    the Maasai and, 93
    in Mexican-American culture, 228–229
    in Mexican culture, 338–339
fatalism, 227–228
female communication, 172–178, 242–243
Ferraro, Geraldine, 290
Five Asian Dragons, 301–310
Folb, Edith, 46, 119–127
folk medicine, 347–349
folk tales, 8, 253
Fong, Mary, 211–216
formal/informal communication, 68–69, 331–332
forms of address, 68–69, 93
Friday, Robert A., 324–333
Fuhrman, Mark, 418

Gannon, Martin J., 248–254
Gardner, John W., 429
Gay culture, 25, 48, 123–124, 158–167, 287
gaze, 292–293
Geist, Patricia, 189–204, 341–354
gender
    as a cultural dimension, 170–178, 263–264, 446–448

nonverbal communication and, 170–178, 287–295, 446–448
    versus sex, 22, 171–173
    geopolitics, 125–126
German Americans, 46
German culture, communication themes, 299, 324–333
gestures
    gender and, 293
    See also nonverbal systems
globalism, 55–57
Goodwin, Joseph P., 158–170
graffiti, 168–169
grandparent relationship, 186
Gray Panthers, 183
Greek culture, conflict in, 105–113

Hall, Edward T., 34–42, 280–286
happiness, 263
haptics (touch). *See* touch
Hawaiian culture, on diversity, 429
health care, communication in, 300, 341–352
Hecht, Michael L., 128–134
height perceptions, gender and, 290–291
heteroglossia, 223–224
Hinduism, 81–89, 431–432, 445
    communication ethics in, 447–448
history, in relation to time, 434, 436
    See also time
Hobbes, Thomas, 120
homeless youths. *See* houseless youth culture
homosexual culture, 25, 48, 123–124, 158–167, 287
honorifics, 68–69, 93
houseless youth culture, 230–239
Human Relations Model, 306, 309
humor, as a communication strategy, 159–164

identification with, 454
identity
    bounded, 45–46
    context and, 28–29
    cultural, 16–31, 43–44, 46, 48–49, 427–430, 439–441
    dual culture, 201, 441
    gender and, 22, 171–173
    group, 189–204, 18–26
    power and, 25–26, 30, 45–50
    white, 43–51
idioms, 217–224, 363–364
illness, interpretations of, 346–348
Ilongot culture, 70
immediacy behaviors. *See* expressiveness
immigrants, 343

India, culture of, 81–89
   See also Hinduism
Indians, American. *See* Native Americans
individualism, 48, 63–64, 71, 226–227, 262–263, 359, 435
   American, 330
   conflict management and, 388–391
   German versus American, 330
Irish, 254
   See also collectivism
infinite interpretation, 70–71
information overload, prevention of.
   See culture, functions of
ingroup/outgroup, 66–67
   conflict management and, 395
   Confucianism and, 303–305
   in Greek culture, 107–109
   Japanese, 271
intercultural personhood, 431–441
intermediaries, 67
International Phonetic Alphabet, 213–214
intonation, 161, 265, 274–275
intrusion distance, 39
   See also proxemics
intuition, versus reason, 432–438
   See also Aristotle
inversion, 160–161, 166
   See also nondominance
Irish culture, 46, 247–254
Islamic culture, 99–101
   ethical philosophy in, 445

Jain, Nemi C., 81–89
Janzen, Rod, 52–58
Japanese culture, 63–64, 68–72
   business communication, 71, 297–299, 301–310, 312–322
   nonverbal communication, 270–277, 319–320
judgment, suspended, in peace communications, 411

Kale, David W., 450–455
Kim, Young Yun, 431–443
kinesics, 259–265, 272, 293
   See also nonverbal systems
knowledge, cultural approaches to, 432–434
Korean culture, 63–72, 74–80
Kussman, Ellen D., 81–89

labels, 44, 46, 48–49
Land, Edwin, 38

language
   attitudes about, 243–245, 363–369
   culture and, 243–245, 247, 363–369, 419–420
   discrimination based on, 239–245
   as influence on culture, 419–420
   learning another, 401–403, 419–420
   vocabulary codes, 131, 134, 151–154, 158–170, 202–203, 231–236
      See also verbal systems
Latham-Jones, Angela, 454
latitude, 261, 265–266
learning styles, 300, 355–369
Lee, Wen-Shu, 216–224
lesbian culture, 25, 48, 163
   See also homosexual culture
LIFE (Learning Informally From Elders), 181
Limaye, Mohan R., 414–422
Lindsley, Sheryl, 335–340
linear thinking, 35–36, 267, 432–438
   See also Aristotle; M-time; reason
linguistic codes, 68–69
   See also speech codes
linguistic devices, 159–164, 213–215
logic. *See* reason
Luna, Lucila, 201–204

M-E (man-environment)transaction, 39
M theory, 306
M-time, 280–286, 390–391, 434, 456–457, 461
   conflict management and, 390–391
Maasai culture, 62, 90–98
   debating style, 95, 363
Malagasy communication, 70
marriage, 182
Martin, Judith N., 43–51
masculinity, 172, 174–178, 263–264, 301–302, 361
mau-mauing, 132
McDaniel, Edwin R., 270–277, 312–322
McKay, Valerie C., 180–187
Meade, George Herbert, 459
meaning
   connotative/denotative, 206–207
   context and, 34–42, 160, 267–268
   metatalk and, 219–224
melting pot assimilation, 53–54, 57
Merrill, Lisa, 287–295
message ethics, 446–447
metaphors, 95, 123
Mexican-American culture, proverbs in, 225–229
Mexican business culture, 299, 335–340
Mondale-Ferraro presidential campaign, 290

PUCCINI
AND HIS
OPERAS

JOHN ANKA
I LOVE PUCCINI

JOHN ANKA
I LOVE PUCCINI

Previous page: Giacomo
Puccini (1858-1924).

Puccini

by Timothy Ramsden

**JOHN ANKA
I LOVE PUCCINI**

Proud Supporter of the Wildlife Land Trust
John J. Anka
3772 Mount Acadia Blvd
San Diego, CA 92111

OMNIBUS PRESS

British Library Cataloguing in
Publication Data:
A catalogue record for this book is
available from the British Library.

Copyright © Timothy Ramsden 1996
Order No.OP47815
ISBN 0-7119-5499-2

First published in softback in the UK
in 1996 by Omnibus Press
(a division of Book Sales Limited),
8/9 Frith Street, London W1V 5TZ.

Exclusive Distributors:
Book Sales Limited,
8/9 Frith Street, London W1V 5TZ.
Music Sales Corporation,
257 Park Avenue South, New York,
NY10010, USA.
Music Sales Pty Limited,
120 Rothschild Avenue, Rosebery,
NSW2018, Australia.

To the Music Trade only:
Music Sales Limited,
8/9 Frith Street, London W1V 5TZ.

Cover designed by Michael Bell Design.
Text edited and designed by
Three's Company, 5 Dryden Street,
London WC2.
Cover photograph courtesy of
The Mansell Collection.

Printed and bound in Great Britain by
Butler & Tanner Ltd, Frome and London

Contents

Picture Acknowledgments
Picture research by Image Select
Elizabeth Davis
Alexander Goldberg

Picture credits
Alinari/Art Resource: p. 91
Art Resource: pp. 1, 63
Catherine Ashmore/Zoë Dominic
Photographs: p. 55
Clive Barda: pp. 77, 83, 125, 149
Zoë Dominic Photographs: pp. 105,
150
Mary Evans Picture Library: p. 15
Hulton Deutsch: p. 69
Farabola foto: pp. 26, 27, 37, 45, 86,
93, 94, 133, 137, 139, 145
Image Select: pp. 9, 21 (top), 29, 51,
61, 85, 87, 111, 129, 141
Mansell Collection: pp. 11, 16, 17, 21
(bottom), 25, 60, 151
Popperfoto: pp. 89, 123
Ann Ronan at Image Select: pp. 19,
49, 53, 70, 75, 79, 99, 103, 147

The Strange Case of Giacomo Puccini

Puccini did not much favour prologues. After a few brief bursts of youthful orchestral energy in *La Bohème*, his bohemians are singing of the problems of art and low temperatures. A few seconds' fireworks display of notes at the beginning of *Tosca*, and the escaped prisoner Angelotti is cowering in the church of Sant' Andrea della Valle. A few flowery phrases, and the marriage-broker Goro is showing Lieutenant Pinkerton around the premises he is taking for himself and his wife Butterfly. Puccini tends to be well into the action before he steps back, sure of our attention, and lets us survey the scene – usually it is before the third act where we find his orchestral pictures.

Action is a key to his success as an opera composer; action and wonderfully composed melodies which breathe the identity of their creator in their sweep, their ravishing shape and their distinctive flavour.

Puccini knew where his great talent lay. Late in his life, when he was working on his last opera *Turandot*, he wrote to Giuseppe Adami, one of its librettists:

> the Almighty touched me with His little finger and said, 'Write for the theatre – mind well, only for the theatre!'

It was a command he obeyed. There were a few religious and orchestral works, written mainly in his youth or student days (some will be mentioned because he recycled their melodies in works such as *La Bohème* and *Tosca*); but it is for his operas that he will be remembered. He wrote ten operas – twelve if the three one-act pieces that make up *Il Trittico* are counted separately, and they might well be, for they are often performed separately. These three include his only comedy, the genuinely funny *Gianni Schicchi*, which is known most widely for the glorious 'O, mio babbino caro!'

In the midst of these works are three of the perennial favourites of any major opera house. No company could survive long without offering the youthful joys and heartaches of *La Bohème*, with its wonderful love sequence, *Tosca*, with its stirring passions and *Madama Butterfly*, a heartrending tale of devotion and betrayal set to some of the most exalted and intense music ever known on the operatic stage. Not that they were considered masterpieces when they appeared: far from it. Nor does Puccini today hold the same high position in the musical firmament as Mozart, Verdi or Wagner. Somehow, it is felt, his music is too instinctively melodic, too blatant in its tugging at our emotions. His works lack musical logic, do not delve into character and have no profundity say the critics.

The situation was not helped by the opposing camps which developed during the later, famous years of his life. On the one side, critics such as Fausto Torrefranca, in his 1912 book *Puccini and International Opera*, castigated Puccini's old ways. Young composers demanded an end to the enslavement of Italian music by the opera house. The tradition of Rossini, Bellini, Donizetti and Verdi should be discarded in favour of a return to the glories of the eighteenth century, the age of Vivaldi. Meanwhile admirers such as Puccini's librettist Giuseppe Adami were determined to keep alive the sacred flame of the composer's reputation. They invented the unrealistic picture of Puccini as saint, and overpraised his music.

Two points emerge when Puccini is looked at in a clearer light. Any composer who lives a reasonable time (Puccini died aged sixty-five) sees changes during his career; but Puccini lived through a period of extreme political and cultural upheaval. When he was born Italy was still not unified and Garibaldi was the political figure of the age. When he died he was a member (however uncommitted) of the Fascist party, hoping Mussolini would reform Italian society. Puccini's first opera *Le Villi* (The Witches) was premièred in 1884. Verdi, Massenet and Dvorak were still writing operas, and Brahms' Double Concerto and Tchaikovsky's final, famous final symphonies, such as the *Pathétique*, lay in the future. He died in 1924, in the musical world of Stravinsky and Schoenberg.

Of course Puccini was not the only 'traditional' composer who spanned this period. Edward Elgar was born a year earlier and died a decade later. Nor do we expect people in their sixties to dress in the fashion of teenagers. But Puccini was always keen to keep up with musical developments. Elements of Debussy, Stravinsky and others were absorbed into his work. He could not have written *Turandot*, the last opera, which was performed posthumously, at the time he wrote *La Bohème* (1896), because other composers had not yet created aspects of musical language, such as the whole-tone scale, which are present in *Turandot*. Yet for all these influences there is never any doubt about the identity of a Puccini opera – he did not take others' ideas because he had none of his own, rather because he could use them creatively to extend his own vocabulary of sounds.

Perhaps we assume that the artist who develops a new language is the better for it, that art must move forward. But there is considerable value too in the consolidator – who is not the same as the plagiarist. If we listen to Puccini alongside the once fashionable composers of realistic verismo operas, Giordano (*Andrea Chénier*), Leoncavallo or Mascagni – whom we will meet again in this study – we will soon see why it is his works that have lasted.

For this is the strange case of Giacomo Puccini: reviled and despised by so many, he remains in constant popular demand. Audiences will not allow *La Bohème*, *Tosca* and *Madama Butterfly* to escape from the repertoire. To these may be added *Manon Lescaut* and *Turandot*. That is five out of ten; not bad when we consider how many little-known Verdi and even early Wagner pieces there are. Yet outbursts as severe as those of Torrefranca continue to emerge from the opposition.

Most famous of these voices is probably the American critic Joseph Kerman, especially as heard in the first edition of his book *Opera as Drama* (1956). Unlike many earlier critics, Kerman is not partisan. He is shrewd and perceptive. He does not devote a chapter to Puccini; rather he quotes his works in discussing other composers, as a principal example of how not to

Gioacchino Rossini (1792-1868), composer of many comic and serious operas, including *The Barber of Seville* and *William Tell*, transformed Italian opera in the period before Verdi.

do it. In particular he denounces *Turandot* – which many believe is Puccini's masterpiece – and attacks *Tosca* as a 'shabby little shocker'. He is particularly critical of the end of that opera, as we shall see.

Even supporters admit to shortcomings. Mosco Carner, author of the standard biography of Puccini and a lifelong student of the composer, confesses he is a borderline case for greatness, and that his music, thrilling, tender and comic as it is, still does not delve into character like that of Mozart or Verdi, or develop symphonically like Wagner's. But if Puccini's characters cover a restricted range, and are limited in the depth of their musical expression, their creator was far more than the cynical manipulator some have presented him to be. He was a scrupulous composer, worrying away at details of the libretto, aware of the need to shape and structure each scene and the overall work.

As for his being manipulative, in a sense, all art is just that, for it works by consciously shaping sensual things – words, sounds, images – to bring about certain effects. Cheap art is done without conviction by someone who wants simply to provoke the most easily stimulated responses. It uses means that the artist knows people will easily absorb. Fame or money are its frequent goals. It can be extremely successful but it rarely lasts long.

Puccini believed in his work. Some of the pieces that are now best loved were far from easily accepted in their own day. At least twice he purposely trod new paths when a repetition of previous ways would have been easier. He did not bother about large issues which did not matter to him as a person. Spirituality very rarely concerned him (when he wrote *Suor Angelica*, with its convent setting, he tested its theology on the nuns of his sister's convent). Only twice does anything like political or social interest disturb his operas, both times with extreme brevity. Cavaradossi's cry of victory at news of Napoleon's success in battle is merely a plot device. The other occasion, when Luigi in *Il Tabarro* cries out at the tough lot of the working man, is more a protest from a lover bound by toil than a political statement. We are very soon back to love and passion in both cases.

Love is where Puccini's real interest lay, and because he wrote about it with conviction; because he cared for the suffering young women who die or disappear from the scene in his operas; because he understood and felt for his Manon, Mimi, Tosca and Butterfly, the music he produced is above cheap emotionalism. It is something far better: it is deeply moving. As unfortunate young women dominate his work, perhaps we can begin by considering one theory as to why they were so important, before returning to the music of this man whose operas are the last resplendent flowering of a great musical tradition.

The first and last two chapters in this book outline the key events in the earlier and later parts of Puccini's life, and discussion of the operas he wrote during the period covered, together with some comments on their main features. Between these, a chapter is given to his first success, followed by more detailed examination of each of the three most celebrated operas. Again each begins with some contemporary biographical events, followed by an account of the composition of the opera. In looking with some detail at the way it adapts the source book or play, we might be thought to be straying from Puccini himself, but he was extremely interested in the words he was going to set and, if his librettists failed to provide the right ones, he was capable of writing his own. We can be sure that nothing would be in a libretto if Puccini had not wanted it there. Very often he argued and insisted upon changes. To ignore the stories and words of these operas would be to miss out a vital aspect of Puccini's achievement. There is also a guide to some of the musical devices and details employed in these works.

Chapter 1

Early Successes

Puccini was a name long linked with music in the old Tuscan capital of Lucca. An important trade centre, Lucca possessed three churches, the grandest being San Martino Cathedral. It was there that the Puccinis had filled the post of organist back to the early eighteenth century. First there had been Giacomo Puccini, then his son Antonio, followed by *his* son Domenico, whose son Michele was occupying the post in 1858 when his wife Albina gave birth to their son on 22nd December. Music flowed in the boy's veins. His mother, too, came from a musical family, the Magi.

San Martino Cathedral was the largest of the many churches in Lucca, where the Puccini family had been organists for several generations.

As if it was known the new child would be the great inheritor of the family's musicianship, his parents had him baptised Giacomo Antonio Domenico Michele Secondo Maria Puccini. There was operatic tradition in the family too, for the eighteenth-century Puccinis had contributed to the Lucca practice of celebrating elections with opera-like works called *tasche*, always the work of local composers.

Puccini's grandfather wrote comic operas, though his own life – or death – was more like melodrama. In 1815 the Austrians had control of Lucca. Domenico was singled out as politically subversive, inveigled to an aristocratic party and handed a cup of poisoned sherbet. So the story goes. Michele Puccini had also composed successful operas, but he died in 1864, leaving Giacomo and five sisters to be brought up by their mother, who – to add to her burden – was pregnant with Giacomo's only brother, Michele.

Giacomo's childhood and youth were spent in a largely female household. He was very close to his mother and overwhelmed by her death when he was only twenty-five. His operas are principally concerned with women. From his third opera, in which he began to assert himself in the choice and treatment of his subjects, most Puccini operas are named after a young female character. True, the title *La Bohème* refers to bohemian lifestyle in general, but even here the angle taken by Puccini focuses attention on the young Mimi. And the trilogy *Il Trittico* keeps to the rule with its middle opera *Suor Angelica*, while, of the outer panels in this triptych, *Il Tabarro* (The Cloak) reflects the title of the original French play – it still concerns a young woman and love – and the final short opera is *Gianni Schicchi*. Schicchi is a male, and a father and provokes ridiculous situations. Comedy is all right for men. Women, their lives, loves and deaths, were serious matters to Puccini.

Was there any connection between this constant theme and the composer's background? The late Mosco Carner believed there might have been. Puccini's early years were dominated by his love for his mother. How could he be free of such ties when he grew up? One way was to avoid strong-willed women who might land him back in the subservient role. In 1884 Puccini set up home with Elvira Gemignani, whose husband was in the grocery trade. Under Roman Catholic rules the pair could not marry while Gemignani was alive. Only years later could they become man and wife, by which time Puccini was a world-famous composer. Elvira might have been strong-willed, but though Puccini stayed with her, he also had many brief flirtations with admiring women. As he became more famous, there were more of these, more willing and increasingly awestruck. Their admiration, Carner claimed, allowed Puccini to experience the upper hand he never had with his mother. No longer did he need to feel dependent.

But all these affairs with insignificant, socially inferior or weaker-willed women left him feeling guilty. They were not like his mother. He had what he wanted in ruling the roost, but he lacked what he needed and had received from that early bond. Guilt is a deeply unpleasant feeling, so it became necessary to dump it, to put the blame elsewhere. And if he was not to blame, it could only be these women who were at fault. From this guilt perhaps there came the 'large load of sadness' which Puccini later said he could find no reason for.

His operas are another parade of blameworthy women: Manon the faithless fortune-hunter, Mimi, who is unfaithful to Rodolfo, the free-living Tosca, Butterfly the geisha, the adulterous Giorgetta, Angelica the unmarried mother. As they are all to blame, he is not. Guilt-free, he can consummate the musical relationship, free to love them in his composition. This is why they are so sympathetic; we forgive – or hardly notice – their moral short-comings. Love, after all, is blind.

Certainly Puccini's heroines are far more sharply drawn than many of their male companions. Cavaradossi is easily the least characterised of the central trio in *Tosca*, while Pinkerton virtually ceases as a role after Act One of *Madama Butterfly*. Only Gianni Schicchi in the comedy, and Michele in *Il Tabarro*, really match the women for interest. Calaf in *Turandot* is the other possible contender.

Puccini found his way into the family musical tradition as choirboy then organist at several churches, while also playing the piano in inns and a brothel. Perhaps this is where he picked up his heavy smoking habit, which combined with the possible inheritance through his mother of a tendency to cancer, contributed to his final illness and death. For young Puccini, though, cigars were a pleasure and a style accessory. Money was a problem so, it was rumoured, he arranged for the removal of pipes from the church organ he was playing to sell for extra lire to turn into tobacco. The young musical genius would then disguise the loss by improvising harmonies that did not require the missing notes.

By his late teens, Puccini was writing his own organ music for the services (no-one has analysed it to see if there are certain notes which never crop up). Congregations would often be surprised to hear phrases of folk tunes and songs from well-known operas coming from the organ loft. In 1876 he went with friends the eighteen-mile-round journey to Pisa to see Verdi's *Aida*, an opera then just five years old. Somehow they bluffed their way in for free. Though he was still to write church music, including a mass in 1880, the Pisa experience helped him decide that the theatre, not the church, was to be his musical future.

Meanwhile he studied at Lucca's Pacini Institute. Despite his failing in a musical composition competition (partly because of his unreadable writing, something that never improved), it was clear Giacomo Puccini needed the most advanced teaching; whether he could afford it was another matter. Milan, home of Italy's leading opera house, Il Teatro alla Scala, and the attached Royal Conservatory, was the place for the next generation of the country's musicians to be educated. It was made available to Puccini by a loan from a relative, Dr Cerù, and a scholarship funded by Queen Margherita. Significantly, the only people not to help Puccini on his musical way were the town council in Lucca. Maybe a less gifted organist had led to the discovery of the missing organ pipes. If not, there were other youthful wild ways that could have been held against him.

Letters to his mother give an idea of Giacomo's student days, though it is possible they were written to please her, both because he wanted to gratify her and because a little extra from the family would always be welcome to top up the scholarship and loan:

I am not starving. I don't eat so very well, but I fill up with minestrone or thick broth etc. etc. My belly is satisfied. Today is a terrible day, awful weather. I went to hear *L'Etoile du Nord* [Meyerbeer's opera *The North Star*] with Donadia and Auber's *Fra Diavolo* with the famous tenor Naudin. However, I did not spend much. For *The Star* I spent just a few pence in the gallery and for *Fra Diavolo* nothing – thanks to free tickets from the manager, who was also from Lucca.

Puccini's working day is described in a letter he wrote home on 19th December 1880:

In the morning, I get up at 8.30. When I have a lesson I go to it. If I have no lesson, I practise the piano a little. I can get along with little practising, but it is necessary that I do a little . . . At 10.30 I have breakfast. I then go out. At one I come home and study for Bazzini for a couple of hours. Then from three to five I return to the piano for some study of classical music. I would like to take out a subscription for musical scores, but I haven't got the money . . . At five I go to take my frugal – but very frugal – dinner. I have *minestrone alla milanese* which to tell the truth is quite good. I have three ladles of that, then some other mess, a little bite of cheese and half a litre of wine. Then I light a cigar and off I go to the Galleria to take my walk, up and down as usual. I remain there until nine and come home dog-tired. I arrive home, I do a little counterpoint, but I don't play. I am not allowed to play at night. Then I climb into bed and put myself to sleep by reading seven or eight pages of a novel. And that is my life.

And this is Puccini to the life, already keen to keep up with the world of opera and conscious of money draining away, something that continued into his later, vastly wealthier, days. As for the regular routine, we should realise this was written when he had been studying for all of three days. The Bazzini he describes himself working for was one of his teachers, soon to become Director of the Conservatory. A violinist turned teacher of music composition, he had written an opera based on the same Italian play as Puccini's last, incomplete work *Turandot*.

His other teacher has a small place in the history of music. Amilcare Ponchielli's first opera *I Promessi Sposi* had been produced as long ago as 1856, since when he had continued to have success with four more works. When we recall the nineteenth century tradition of Italian opera through its greatest exponents, Rossini, Donizetti, Verdi and Puccini, we should remember there were dozens of lesser figures who had varying successes in their own time but are now completely forgotten. That could have been the case with Ponchielli were it not for *La Gioconda*. Its singer heroine's last act aria 'Suicidio' is still occasionally heard, while its ballet music, the *Dance of the Hours*, is a classic pop. It was first heard in 1876 and so was quite a recent hit when Puccini arrived in Milan.

One subject studied at the Conservatory was poetry and drama. As a student keen to write operas, as someone who was to show a fine sense of what would work on stage, somebody who would worry his librettists often to the point of resignation, Puccini ought to have lapped this subject up. Not a bit. Perhaps it was not well taught. Maybe his instincts were already ahead of the rules. In any case, Puccini's comments on these lessons were: 'I'm asleep . . . Help . . . It's too much. It's killing me'.

Equally unsatisfactory were his lodgings. Apart from not being allowed to play, or indeed cook, at night (reasonable enough in a family home), Puccini could not even indulge in the kind of financial juggling that was so to occupy his impoverished bohemians. They would manage any trick to cheat their landlord of his rent. But Puccini's landlord worked for the post office and could extract the rent due as the money arrived from the Queen's scholarship. Puccini's protests were silenced by the argument that, well he was going to pay anyway wasn't he . . . ?

He was due to graduate in 1883, and that meant a graduation composition. This turned out to be neither operatic nor even vocal, but a thirteen-

Gaetano Donizetti (1797-1848), along with Vincenzo Bellini, was the master of 1830s Italian opera. His bel canto works, such as *L'elisir d'amore* and *Lucia di Lammermoor* demanded sophisticated technique from singers.

minute orchestral piece, *Capriccio Sinfonico*. Ideas for it cropped up at various times and were written down on whatever was available. Some of the music was even written around the print on newspapers. It was played by the conservatory students with the leading Italian conductor Franco Faccio and it took Puccini the first positive step in his career. First there was a favourable review by a leading critic. Not only did this praise the *Capriccio Sinfonico*, it gave the work a most precious commodity for a young artist: the kind of detailed consideration that demands public attention, particularly the attention of people who are in a position to further the artist's progress.

Giovannina Lucca, controller of the music publishing business that bore her name, picked up the work and published it in an arrangement for piano duet. Meanwhile, Faccio gave further performances of the original orchestral version in public concerts. As an orchestral piece it was not published until 1978, largely because Puccini suppressed it. He did this less because he was ashamed of his early work, than to prevent people realising he had mined the *Capriccio* for two of his operas. One of these self-plunderings was for his second opera *Edgar*. Nowadays, audiences are far more likely to prick up

Ruggero Leoncavallo (1857-1919) spotted a market niche for one-act operas, leading to the composition of his best known work, *I Pagliacci* (The Clowns) in 1882. Five years later his *La Bohème* met with a greater initial success than had Puccini's.

their ears some way into the work when they hear what became the energetic opening theme from *La Bohème*.

Among the composers Puccini knew was Alfredo Catalani, also from the town of Lucca but four years older and starting his brief operatic career during Puccini's student days (Catalani died in 1893), and Pietro Mascagni (1863-1945), who as a student lodged with Puccini. Only once or twice in their careers did they have any success, Catalani with *Loreley* and *La Wally*, Mascagni with *L'Amico Fritz* and, of course, *Cavalleria Rusticana*. In the future both were to quarrel with Puccini but in the early 1880s, before his rise to what would now be labelled operatic superstardom gave grounds for envy, both were his friends.

There are two reasons for mentioning them here. Firstly, it emphasises the achievement of Puccini. Very many composers never even manage one or two enduring works. Catalani and Mascagni were among the more successful of their time. The first might have achieved more had he not died young, but apart from their successes both produced operas unheard today. By contrast Puccini's output has left an extraordinary legacy of operas that bear repeated hearings. We must remember this when considering his limitations. It is easy to forget the numerous composers he easily outstrips, in his ability to create an individual musical world. He is one of the very limited number of composers whose names become signposts by which we map our route through musical history.

Pietro Mascagni (1863-1945) had a knack for setting new trends; with his 1890 tale of rural revenge, *Cavalleria Rusticana*, he led the way in verismo opera, while in 1898 *Iris*, with its Japanese setting, blazed the trail for the oriental operas which led to *Madama Butterfly*.

Secondly, major composers may be influenced by the music of the age in which they live, but they will not be bounded by it. The key development in Italian opera when Puccini was young was called verismo, which in general means 'truth to life'. Veristic operas tended to deal with ordinary people, often in sordid situations, and to express their lives in a range of realistic-sounding musical effects. Catalani, and even more Mascagni, were part of the drive towards verismo, as was the composer often linked with Mascagni on opera programmes, Ruggero Leoncavallo (1857-1919), composer of *I Pagliacci* (The Clowns). He too was to come into contact, and quarrel, with Puccini. Unlike these three, Puccini cannot be bounded by any school of composition or any adjective – except perhaps 'Puccinian'.

Another feature of veristic operas was often their brevity; hence the '*Cav. and Pag.*' double-bill. As Puccini was turning to face the outside world with his royal scholarship at an end, Dr Cerù in Lucca waiting to be repaid the money he had lent, and Albina poor in finances and in health, along came a competition for a new, one-act opera. His teacher Ponchielli used his influence to persuade the established librettist Ferdinando Fontana to write the words, and in the second part of 1883 – the competition deadline was the end of the year – Puccini composed a short opera named after the sinister female spirits who inhabit the story, *Le Villi*.

On the final day for entries, Puccini submitted his first opera. Its sketches may not have been as ill-assorted as the newspaper margins of the *Capriccio*, but at least he had been able to make a fair copy of that. Time ran out on *Le Villi* and considering the scrawl, annotations and rewrites we can see in his later scores, it is highly likely the judges would have been unable to read it, let alone like it.

No prize, no place among the winners, for *Le Villi* then. However, a number of influential people were persuaded to subscribe towards a production. Fontana, for one thing, was not going to see his libretto go unperformed. And Italy's foremost music publisher, Giulio Ricordi, offered to print the libretto without charge. It was the first of innumerable times he acted as Puccini's good angel – if one with a strong business sense. The first ever performance of a Puccini opera, the one-act *Le Villi*, took place on 31st May 1884 at the Teatro dal Verme in Milan.

The comment that followed did not focus on the features that now seem important to us in Puccini – melody, lyricism, orchestral colours – but on its symphonic tendencies. This led Verdi, who had heard talk about Puccini, to warn:

> Opera is opera and symphony is symphony; and I don't believe that opera should contain symphonic music just so as to let the orchestra have a fling.

There is a ballet within *Le Villi* – common enough in nineteenth-century operas – but it seems strange to find symphonic music drawing the attention in a Puccini work. A lot of the response in the press was very favourable but it is worth considering what Verdi, the giant of Italian opera, meant.

The music of an opera is made up of two elements: voices and instruments. During the nineteenth century the balance between these grew apart in the two chief opera-producing countries of Europe. In Germany the orchestra became more important. This was largely under the influence of Richard Wagner, who also developed the 'leitmotif' as a way of unfolding his plot and giving dramatic and musical unity to his works. A 'leitmotif', or 'leading motif', is a musical phrase – often quite brief – which is linked with a particular character, object or idea and tends to recur whenever they appear, are referred to or become significant in the story.

Wagner used leitmotifs in a subtle way. One of the problems in adapting a novel to the stage is that you lose the tone and comment of the author's storytelling. Leitmotifs are an operatic equivalent to these novelistic features. They can comment on a character, or express what they might be thinking or feeling but not saying. They can refer back to help us link the present with significant previous events, and they can be moulded musically to suit the mood. They may be played faster or slower, distorted by new harmonies, combined with other leitmotifs and, although they do crop up in the vocal line, a lot of their development has to be in the orchestra with its ability to comment on action and provide multiple instrumental lines. If, for example, the words being sung are what characters tell each other, leitmotifs in the orchestra can simultaneously represent unspoken thoughts.

Wagner's emphasis on continuous music drama rather than the set pattern of recitative and arias, plus his use of leitmotifs, gave the orchestra a new importance in opera. It no longer just accompanied the voices; it played an equal part in the action, and the merging and musical development of a continuous instrumental texture, with leitmotif development woven in, meant the orchestra could be used to develop the action by itself. This had a profound effect on the course of opera, and many twentieth-century operas

Richard Wagner (1813-1883) created the 'total art work' by taking sole responsibility for words, music and scenery. His vast music dramas include the love story *Tristan und Isolde* and the four-opera *Ring of the Nibelung* as well as the comedy, *The Mastersingers of Nuremberg*.

make a more immediate appeal through the orchestra than through the vocal lines on stage.

Wagner's influence was enormous, both through those who followed and those who rejected him. But Italy had a very strong tradition of singing, and it had audiences who expected vocal displays in their opera houses. Earlier in the nineteenth century this had reached a height with the bel canto (or 'beautiful singing') composers such as Rossini and Donizetti. There was no question of a dominant orchestra in bel canto: the singing was all. Vocal lines demanded supple, flexible voices that could shoot into cascades of notes and shape elaborate decorations of tunes in display arias. Singers trained for these arias learned nuances of shaping and shading musical phrases and were applauded for a musical skill equivalent to that of a juggler or magician.

Puccini was heir to this tradition – the sung line remains of vital importance in his work – but he adopted at least the idea, if not the full practice, of

19

the leitmotif. In one case at least he came close to the kind of orchestral plot development which can be found in Wagner. The intermezzo, or orchestral movement, between the second and third acts of *Manon Lescaut* helps move the story from Parisian high life to prison in Le Havre, while portraying the characters' feelings. Like Wagner, and the verismo composers in his own country, Puccini moved away from the set pattern of recitative, which pushed the story on, and aria, which developed emotions, varied with duets, trios and other combinations of voices. By the time of his fourth opera, *La Bohème*, Puccini was composing a continuous flow of music through each scene, fusing story and lyrical expression.

No doubt the success of *Le Villi* was the more pleasing to Puccini after its rejection by the competition judges. But that rejection involved an advantage. The competition had been organised by the publishing house of Sonzogno. There was a far more important music publisher, the long-established House of Ricordi. Giulio Ricordi had already contributed to the costs of *Le Villi*. Seeing its success, he acquired the rights and commissioned a new, full-length opera from Puccini.

What was more, he helped the young composer, bathed in the lustre of early success but lacking in lire, by awarding him a monthly payment. And Ricordi had the power to ensure the new opera would see the light of day – or the limelight of the footlights – at La Scala itself. He engaged Fontana once again as Puccini's librettist. Further, Ricordi advised the composer to expand *Le Villi* into two acts. So arrived the first full-length Puccini opera.

Le Villi

First performed at the Teatro Regio, Turin on 26th December 1884.
Conductor: Giovanni Bolzoni.

ACT I: *A clearing in the Black Forest. Spring.*
The Foresters are celebrating the engagement of Anna Wulf, daughter to Guglielmo, to Roberto, who has to leave in order to claim an inheritance from his aunt in the city of Mainz. He swears he will stay faithful to Anna, who has given him a posy of forget-me-nots as a love token.
INTERMEZZO 1: the orchestra portrays how Roberto falls for a society lady in Mainz. Anna dies of grief; her funeral is portrayed at the end of the intermezzo.
INTERMEZZO 2: a second orchestral piece portrays the spirits of young women who died after their lovers deserted them. These spirits – the Villi – take revenge by forcing the men to dance until they drop dead. Meanwhile Roberto, himself deserted by the lady, returns to the Forest.
ACT II: Guglielmo demands Anna's ghost take revenge. The Villi arrive. Roberto enters, hoping Anna will forgive him. He meets her spirit, which he sees as the living Anna. The Villi turn their embrace into a compulsive dance until Roberto lies dead, to their great satisfaction.

Ballet lovers will recognise the same story that gave us *Giselle*. Apart from a couple of very minor plot elements in later works, this was Puccini's only fling with the supernatural.

The short time he was given to expand the opera is the only reason why

Giulio Ricordi (1840-1912), head of the firm which still bears his name, supported the young Puccini.

Opened in 1778, within fifty years Il Teatro alla Scala, Milan had become Italy's leading opera house.

so much of the story is compressed into the intermezzi (orchestral pieces between scenes, a device Puccini was to use more successfully in *Manon Lescaut)*. In its fuller form *Le Villi* is a three-act opera compressed into two – and a contrasting act showing Roberto in Mainz society could have dramatised the story more completely. As it is, the intermezzi are 'explained' by poems printed in the score: 'The Desertion' and 'The Spirit', but that is the method of the concert hall not the opera house, even though an on-stage funeral procession accompanied part of this music. Hence Verdi's concern that a new composer for the stage seemed to be relying on symphonic music.

In *Le Villi* Puccini adheres to the old pattern of separate musical numbers, arias and choruses. Yet there is already the start of the Puccini melodic style, particularly in Anna's aria from Act One as she offers the flowers to Roberto, and his extensive Act Two monologue, in which he expresses his guilt and remorse. In the suffering Anna we also see the first of Puccini's young women victims, though as the vengeful end approaches she gains strength in a way later heroines rarely did.

We tend nowadays to search out such hints of the mature Puccini. At the time audiences were aware only of a new, melodically interesting composer whose music they cheered and encored. In line with Italian practice at premières of the time, the composer came on stage to acknowledge particularly enthusiastic applause. This fitted the old operatic style, with its separated segments, better than the continuous weave of Puccini's later works, but we will find him still coming on for several bows at a time. Audiences liked plenty of chances to applaud, so long as they approved. The audience at La Scala in Milan were not to be so keen on *Le Villi* as Turin had been: too much music, not enough singing. And the immediate consideration was not how little time Puccini had had to compose the work, but how far this new

young composer was guilty of biting off more than he could chew of the Wagner approach to music theatre.

Worse followed in early 1885 at the San Carlo opera house in Naples, where the audience booed and jeered, but this did not stop *Le Villi* being seen in Buenos Aires (where the Teatro Colon became a home for most Puccini operas), Hamburg, Manchester and – though not until 1908, when the composer was a major figure – New York.

His immediate success was soon overshadowed by the death of his mother Albina on 17th July 1884. Then his life was complicated by setting up house with Elvira Gemignani, a relationship that far outlasted the love that led to its formation. One of her two children by her husband, a daughter called Fosca, lived with Giacomo and Elvira, and was with her step-father in Brussels when he died. In 1886 Elvira gave birth to Puccini's only child, his son Antonio (Tonio).

Scandal ensued at home in Lucca when this extra-marital set-up was discovered. An outraged Dr Cerù told Puccini if he could afford to keep a woman he could afford to repay his student loan – at once. Puccini in fact could afford neither. His younger brother Michele had emigrated to South America (where he was to die of yellow fever in 1891) and as late as 1890 Giacomo was considering fleeing his debts and joining him, writing to say:

> Dr Cerù . . . claims I have made 40,000 lire for *Le Villi*. I shall send him my monthly royalty statement from Ricordi to show my share only comes to 6000 lire . . . I'm in desperate straits.

Le Villi apart, his only income was an allowance given by Ricordi of 300 lire a month from July 1884. This was for one year only, but upon Puccini's begging insistence and against the judgement of his fellow directors (whom fortunately he could outvote) Giulio Ricordi extended the payment for several years. Puccini needed it, as it was five years before his next opera *Edgar* finally appeared at La Scala in April 1889. His mother's death and his new household can only be a small part of the reason for this delay in a young, ambitious composer. He was not yet able to assert himself against an established librettist.

A look at the story Fontana provided and a comparison with the later Puccini opera, and their carefully-shaped stories, shows how unattractive the material of *Edgar* must have seemed to Puccini. A few years later he could have demanded extensive changes or, more likely, have thrown over the project for one more to his taste, but for now he could only try to cope, and hope he could retain his publisher's confidence – and subsidy.

Edgar

First performed at the Teatro alla Scala, Milan, on 21st April 1889.
Conductor: Franco Faccio.

ACT I: *A village square, Flanders. 1302. Sunday morning in spring.*
As the angelus sounds peasants move to their day's work. Fidelia wakes Edgar, asleep at the inn, and leaves him, as a sign of her love, an almond-blossom. Tigrana waylays him, laughing at Fidelia's love and trying to seduce him (Tigrana is a Moorish orphan raised alongside Fidelia by the latter's father). When Edgar rejects her, Tigrana laughs mockingly, knowing his

Puccini's second opera was set to an improbable text, but he mined it for future works.

desire for her will overcome his love for Fidelia.

Frank (Fidelia's brother) is infatuated with Tigrana, but she despises him when he complains about her refusal to meet him. She then infuriates the congregation by singing a rude song as they leave church.

Edgar supports Tigrana. The crowd turn against him and in fury he sets fire to his home and declares he will take Tigrana away with him. Frank is jealous and challenges Edgar to a duel. Fidelia and their father Gualtiero fail to prevent Frank being injured and Edgar runs away with Tigrana.

ACT II: *Outside a palace. Night.*
Edgar is disillusioned with Tigrana and regrets leaving Fidelia. He repulses Tigrana, then becomes reconciled with Frank, now a troop leader. Cursed by Tigrana, Edgar decides to enlist in the army, leaving her to swear she will have vengeance.

ACT III: *Near Courtray, a fortress.*
A funeral procession with Frank and a shadowy monk. A requiem is sung for an heroic soldier killed in battle: Edgar. The monk accuses the deceased Edgar for his faults but Fidelia defends her ex-lover. When Tigrana joins in the mourning, the monk and Frank bribe her to accuse Edgar. She is persuaded to do so and whips the soldiers to such a frenzy they attack the coffin and rip it open to find it empty except for a suit of armour. Amid superstitious fear, the monk reveals himself as Edgar and in turn he accuses Tigrana. Fidelia embraces him but she is stabbed by Tigrana, at which Edgar collapses of shock and grief while the army marches Tigrana off to be executed.

Fontana provided a libretto as overt – Fidelia the faithful, Tigrana the tigress – as it is contrived and melodramatic. Still, Puccini had to do what he could with this material. He failed to gain the great tenor Francesco Tamagno to sing Edgar. Maybe the singer's style would have covered the substantial absurdities to some extent. At La Scala there was, however, a strong cast, and Franco Faccio to conduct. Apart from his regular work at La Scala, Faccio had offered to conduct Puccini's graduation work, the *Capriccio Sinfonico*, and had twice played it in concerts during 1884.

Edgar made only a very moderate impression. A good measure of a new work, in days when schedules were not fixed far in advance, was the number of further performances. In this case it was just two.

The first night gave the opera in its original four-act version (the three-act outline given above results from Puccini's reworking later that year, at Ricordi's suggestion). A long post-mortem followed with librettist, composer and publisher. Ricordi brought his experience into play, praised the better part of the opera and warned Puccini he was at a vulnerable stage in his career. The artists' instinct to revise and reopen the work would have to be acted upon hurriedly; and what could be done in five weeks or so that had not been done in close on five years? For the time being Puccini followed Ricordi's advice to forget *Edgar*. It was a wise decision that probably convinced Ricordi to maintain his essential, if meagre, support.

At least one review, in the influential *Corriere della Sera* newspaper, picked two significant points out for mention – the passion of Edgar's 'O soave vision' (O gentle vision) and the general quality of the orchestration. Passion and fine use of the orchestra were indeed two features of the mature

Puccini style already emerging as evidence that *Edgar*, for all its faults, showed the composer's potential.

As an apprentice work, *Edgar* at least allowed Puccini to work on a full-length opera from scratch. Whatever the influences – his teacher Ponchielli, Verdi, plus a first borrowing from his own *Capriccio Sinfonico* – he had now had the chance to compose a full-length work, to consider the portrayal and development of character, the use of variety in voice and orchestra, and how to hold a dramatic structure together through music, as well as to endow the chorus with character. The angry congregation in Act One, the furious soldiers of Act Three, are not mere conventional choruses, but people in their own right expressing emotions and moving the plot forward. The question remained: still poor, with judgement suspended on his quality as a composer for the operatic stage – how could Puccini make any further progress?

Chapter 2

Manon Lescaut

Among the operas Puccini would have known was one produced in France in 1884, the same year as his *Le Villi*. *Manon*, by Jules Massenet (1842-1912), was an acclaimed work by a leading French composer and professor of composition at the Paris Conservatoire. Massenet had also composed *Le Cid*. His career might have seemed in decline around the time of *Edgar* but the early 1890s were to bring him triumphs with *Werther* (1892), *Thaïs* (famous for its 'Meditation') and the short verismo work *La Navarraise* (both 1894).

Massenet's *Manon* attracted Puccini to the story, but he was well aware that he, as a young composer whose second opera was hardly a great success, would be accused by critics and the public of stealing a senior French composer's musical clothes. The French *Manon* had its Italian première in 1893, the year Puccini's *Manon Lescaut* was also first performed.

Jules Massenet (1842-1912) was the leading composer of French opera between Bizet and Debussy. His *Manon* had been a success in Paris almost a decade before Puccini wrote *Manon Lescaut*.

Giuseppe Giacosa (1847-1906) was already author of several serious dramas when Giulio Ricordi brought him together with Puccini. Less fiery-tempered than his fellow-librettist, Luigi Illica, Giacosa's calm manner and appearance earned him the nickname 'Buddha' in the Puccini circle.

At the start of the creative process Puccini took an interest in shaping the story of Manon – 'a heroine I believe in, so she must gain the public's affections'. This was in contrast to a proposed opera set in Russia, the libretto of which Ricordi was having prepared for him – 'How is it possible to compose on a subject one does not fully feel for?' And why not Manon? After all, Massenet was by no means the first artist to exploit the original novel. For the first time Puccini experienced the excitement of contemplating an opera on a subject of his choice.

The gestation of the new Manon opera was to be a complex one. At first Ricordi set the librettist and composer Leoncavallo on the text. Puccini criticised the result and Leoncavallo retired, to write words and music for *I Pagliacci* (1892). A successful young writer, Marco Praga, next worked on *Manon Lescaut*, insisting that the versification, that is turning story and dialogue into precise metrical language, be given to a poet of his generation called Domenico Oliva. Ricordi and Puccini both liked the work Praga and Oliva presented to them in mid-1890.

Puccini started composing in a small village called Vacallo near the border with Switzerland. Who should be working there also but Leoncavallo, who welcomed Puccini with a huge drawing of a clown (*pagliacco*) hung outside his house. The next day he was greeted from the home Puccini was renting with a picture of a white hand (*manon*).

Such merriment did not extend to the libretto. Puccini wanted changes, which Praga refused to consider. This left Puccini and Oliva working together. They achieved what is possibly the opera's finest scene: the present Act Three, set at Le Havre. Puccini meanwhile composed the opening scene, where Manon appears on her way to a convent. But as he composed, he found further faults. Exit Oliva. Puccini's comments have point – most of what he objected to was altered eventually, but he had no way of finding new collaborators. That was done by Giulio Ricordi, who at this time made one of the most fortunate choices of his career.

An operatic subject turned down by Puccini in favour of the Manon story was the Russian tale which Ricordi had asked the well-known playwright Giuseppe Giacosa (1847-1906) to work on. Giacosa was in the forefront of the Realist movement. He was also professor of literature and dramatic art at the Milan conservatory at the time Puccini became connected with it. With such a reputation, Giacosa fortunately considered such play-doctoring on a mere libretto beneath him and in turn he referred Ricordi to a rising young left-wing librettist called Luigi Illica (1857-1919). This made five contributors – six if we count insertions made by Ricordi himself (who was also an amateur composer under the name J. Burgmein). It should have been a disastrous formula, with various minds pulling different ways, and the writers all decided they would prefer to be removed from the credit list. The score appeared with only Puccini named. There was a kind of logic about this for, between them, this crew had helped bring about the first fully recognisable Puccini opera.

Manon Lescaut

First performed at the Teatro Regio, Turin on 1st February 1893.
Conductor: Alessandro Pome.

Turin's Teatro Regio saw the first nights of *Le Villi*, *Manon Lescaut* and *La Bohème*. The building Puccini knew was destroyed by fire in 1936; a new building opened in 1973.

ACT I: *The square, Amiens. Eighteenth century.*

Students sit and play cards as one of their number, Edmondo, sings a madrigal. The Chevalier Des Grieux arrives. The regular coach from Arras brings a young man called Lescaut, accompanying his sister Manon to a convent, and a rich old official Géronte di Ravoir. Des Grieux is attracted to Manon and asks her to tell him about herself, until her brother calls to her to go inside. Géronte bribes Lescaut to let him abduct Manon, and the inn-keeper to provide a coach for them. Edmondo overhears and tells Des Grieux of the plot – he and Manon then escape in Géronte's coach. The old man wants to chase after them, but Lescaut says it is not necessary. He knows his sister, and she will soon leave an impoverished lover. They will just wait for her to come to them in Paris.

ACT II: *A room in Géronte's mansion, Paris.*

Manon has done as her brother predicted but regrets leaving Des Grieux. Lescaut goes to fetch her lover as the bored Manon listens to the madrigal Géronte has composed for her. Géronte enjoys watching Manon put through a dancing lesson. Left alone, Manon is delighted when Des Grieux is brought in by her brother. In her happiness she mocks Géronte when he finds the two of them together. The young lovers decide to elope, but Manon spends so long gathering jewels to take with her that Géronte has time to fetch the guard. Manon is arrested as a thief and prostitute.

INTERMEZZO: *The journey to Le Havre* (orchestra).

ACT III: *The quay at Le Havre. Dawn.*

Des Grieux and Manon are hoping to spring Manon from the harbourside prison where she awaits deportation to America. Des Grieux manages to speak with her through a barred window. Lescaut returns to say that escape is hopeless; the guard they bribed has been found out. Manon and the other women deportees, in their various moods, cross the stage to board the prison ship. Des Grieux cannot bear to be parted from his love and persuades the captain to let him travel with her.

ACT IV: *America: the desert near New Orleans.* Tired and thirsty, Manon collapses and cannot be cheered by Des Grieux. She faints as he searches unsuccessfully for water. Manon has been sleeping; she wakes while he is gone and thinks he has abandoned her. He returns; she assures him of her love, then dies.

Though it had been known as *Manon Lescaut* virtually since its publication in 1731, the title of the novel by the Abbé Prévost was actually *The Story of the Chevalier Des Grieux and Manon Lescaut*. The story in Prévost's novel is told by Des Grieux to the narrator, who is known as The Man of Quality. Regular readers would have known this person already, for the whole tale of Manon Lescaut is an addition to the several volumes of this Man's adventures.

The opera excludes Des Grieux's father and brother, who try to restore him to a sensible life without Manon, and his loyal friend Tiberge, who is the voice of conscience as well as a source of free loans, also disappears. Audiences respond in a different way from readers; there is only time to become acquainted with so many people embodied before us. But the omission of Des Grieux's family and Tiberge also removes the voices warning Des Grieux of his foolishness in following Manon Lescaut, whereas Prévost shows him increasingly aware of his folly, until in the later section of the novel he acknowledges his faults, telling his father: 'You know that the cause of all my misdeeds is love. What a fatal passion it is!' (translated L.W. Tancock, Penguin Classics, 1949).

Love turns Prévost's Des Grieux into a hypocrite, who uses his natural qualities as a mask to exploit others in satisfying Manon. He exploits Tiberge, joins a gang of card sharps, lies to prison authorities to be with her and shoots a prison guard during an escape. His behaviour is that of a drug addict for whom everything is sacrificed to obtain one precious substance. Manon is less heroine than heroin.

Not that any of this revision would be apparent to audiences. The most serious result of all the changes (and the multi-authorship) is the inexplicable last act. What are these two doing in a desert? Prévost's novel offers explanations missing in the opera. The lovers had passed themselves off as man and wife. Now wiser, Manon had wanted to marry Des Grieux, but the Governor's nephew, Synnelet, finding the lovely Manon unattached by law, persuaded his uncle to let him marry her. A duel followed; Des Grieux believed he had killed Synnelet, and escaped across the desert towards the English colony.

Because opera singers take time to train and then to reach the eminence of lead roles, it is very easy not to realise how young many of the Puccini females are. His Manon is eighteen; in the novel she is, if anything slightly younger. She seems not far from being a child prostitute. And her motive is clear; as Des Grieux comes to realise, Manon lusts after Mammon. She must have money and luxury and she will attach herself to anyone who offers it, as a kleptomaniac will pick up anything left lying around. This is largely lost in Puccini. Though her brother tells old Géronte not to worry because his sister will easily be attracted by money, we do not see her desert her lover; we only see her bored with the affluent old man. And in the theatre what we see has more impact than what we are only told about.

There is one practical reason for the jump from the first meeting to

Belgian soprano Fanny Heldy (1888-1973) sang Mimi in Monte Carlo, and besides the role of Manon Lescaut, pictured here, sang Tosca and Madama Butterfly at the Opéra Comique in Paris.

Géronte's house. A proposed scene, which would have come between the present first and second acts, showing Manon and Des Grieux living in happy poverty, was cut because it was felt the opera was becoming too similar to Massenet's successful *Manon*. It is easy to understand Puccini's keenness in what could be his make-or-break opera with Ricordi and the public, not to be written off as a mere imitator. But practicalities like that have a way of aligning themselves with artistic inclinations. What we see in his Manon is the type of Puccini's poor, lost, innocent young women, women turned into big girls. What we might call – if it were not inappropriate – the emasculation of women in Puccini's operas.

Lescaut himself is softened. In the novel he lives off his sister, suggests Des Grieux use Manon as a sexual source of income or turn gigolo himself, then introduces him to card cheats. He is finally murdered by his cronies.

Old Géronte, Manon's rich sugar-daddy, includes elements of three people in Prévost. One of these is an unnamed Italian prince; the one man Manon rejects. She arranges for him to come to her when Des Grieux is there and thrusts his ugliness in the prince's face with a mirror, as Puccini's Manon does to Géronte. The novel shows the mirror incident as carefully plotted by Manon to produce the desired effect on Des Grieux (that he can trust her). Being calculated it is crueller, and hypocritical considering how many older men Manon has gone with. In the opera the incident becomes the spontaneous overflow of young love rejoicing in its suddenly found freedom.

Every change in the adaptation of the novel into the opera works in the same direction, shifting Prévost's story of a young man whose nature is corrupted by an extremely attractive woman of no principles into that of a young woman put upon by parents, brother and the rich admirers who want to buy her beauty and then punish her for it when they cannot possess her. Her flaws are minimised, her vulnerability maximised. She becomes a Puccini heroine.

The original Manon is amoral, not immoral. Her behaviour stems from her nature, not deliberate decisions she knows to be wrong. She is no more culpable than a river would be for running downhill. She has a dramatic and operatic descendant of sorts. In 1937 Alban Berg's opera *Lulu* set two plays by Frank Wedekind about the incarnation of sexuality, her social rise and fall, that show what a Manon might have become in a franker age.

Manon Lescaut: the music

Act One of Puccini's opera opens in lively, bustling style, though after the orchestra's first outburst there is almost at once a quieter, more romantic tune. Edmondo's high-flown sentiments, which we soon hear, are undercut by his fellow students. He is soon leading another song, 'Youth is our name,' fitting for this story of young love and old wealth. The women talk of the perfume scenting the air. Only Des Grieux does not join in the mood. Quizzed by Edmondo, he says he knows nothing of love. As the music slows and the harp sweeps upwards he dreams of an idealised female to be found somewhere:

> Tra voi, belle, brune e bionde
> (Among you, beauties, dark and fair)

Despite his lovely melody the women turn from such dreaming. They want more physical pleasures. At which point, physical pleasure starts coming Des Grieux's way. A cornet announces the coach from Arras. There is scurrying to greet it and a dark, deep chord as Lescaut and Manon appear from it. It would be easy to miss the woodwind phrase that accompanies Manon, but it will soon reappear, adapted and more noticeable when she tells Des Grieux her name. Certainly everyone admires her, even Des Grieux is much taken and his admiration almost conceals the entrance of an older man, Géronte di Ravoir.

As Lescaut enters the inn to fix accommodation, Des Grieux continues to admire Manon. She is used to male attention and it is some time before she notices the student watching her. The yard now lies conveniently empty apart from the two of them and the strings give a soft hint of a tune to be heard from Des Grieux very soon. Meanwhile he asks her name and she tells him:

Manon Lescaut mi chiamo
(Manon Lescaut I'm called)

the music here being based on the woodwind phrase heard as she entered. Des Grieux sees spring unfolding in her face. As he asks about her there is a leaping flute phrase, though she goes on to say, 'My star is sinking.'

Manon thanks him for his compassion – hinting perhaps she has experienced less of that than of passion from men. In turn she asks his name before her brother calls her; she promises to return after sunset. The flute again leaps, no doubt like Des Grieux's heart and the tune that has been hinted at in the orchestra emerges in his song:

Donna non vidi mai simile a questa
(I have never seen a woman like this)

during which the orchestra cannot wait for him to repeat words and music of her 'Manon Lescaut mi chiamo'. It washes waves of sound over his wish to be with her forever and he repeats her name over again.

As the crowd pours back into the yard, Edmondo lightly congratulates Des Grieux on his liaison but a more ominous sound from the lower strings brings back Lescaut and Géronte, plotting. Keen to help a great man, Lescaut assures Géronte it is only his duty that makes him escort his sister to a convent. Géronte reveals he is a tax-farmer, making his fortune by demanding huge taxes. His descendants would be in the first tumbrils of the French Revolution and it would be hard to find a better figure to attract public odium, certainly in the time of Prévost's novel, when tax-farming was regular practice.

Lescaut encourages the old man by saying Manon is only eighteen. He feels he is lucky being able to help such a rich man, so to extend his luck he joins the hard-drinking card game that is now going on in the yard, while Géronte bribes the landlord to have a coach and two horses ready an hour hence to take him and Manon to Paris.

Edmondo has overheard and tells Des Grieux. The orchestra recalls 'Donna non vidi mai' with high string decoration as Manon returns. Des Grieux contrasts her youthful face and serious words. Accompanied by the delicacy of flute and harp Manon remembers how she used to be happy – her little home used to ring with her laughter and she danced with her brothers. No more.

He sees the desire for love in the depths of her eyes and as the orchestra surges in a wild string passage he confesses his love for her. Both Manon's vocal line and the orchestra become more reticent as she talks of her sorrow, but as the duet moves to its climax, introducing a dramatic, tragic phrase, Des Grieux asserts that love will conquer all. The card players call for wine; the interruption reminds him of Géronte's plot. He tells her of this and, to loud hammering orchestral chords, he persuades Manon to go away with him. The orchestral line runs downwards to a more sinister tone, and to a hurried accompaniment Edmondo rejoices in Manon's escape. The act ends busily and loudly, Lescaut trying to calm Géronte in the certainty of eventually obtaining Manon, while the students mock old age in a version of Des Grieux's 'Tra voi belle'.

As the curtain goes up for Act Two on a room in Géronte's magnificent Paris home, we see Lescaut's prediction fulfilled. Manon sits in luxury, being tended to with every physical accessory then imaginable. Powdered, bewigged, bejewelled, she is also bored. Delicate eighteenth-century-style music on flute and harp accompanies the scene. To a large extent this act is built round the artificial, elegant world Géronte has provided as a cocoon for Manon. The music is redolent of the eighteenth century classical period, while the wild emotions of Manon's love and regrets plus Des Grieux's bitterness and passion, are represented with the power, harmonies and expressive range of the late nineteenth century.

Manon has become a complete fabrication, and her life is just as artificial. She all but ignores her brother when he visits her. He is dressed in finery that is probably the result of Géronte's financial gratitude. He reminds his sister that he saved her from a student's love, but sees her regret, expressed in her song:

In quelle trine morbide
nell' alcova dorata
v' è' un silenzio, un gelido, mortal.
(In these soft hangings of the gilded alcove there is a silence,
a deathly ice.)

To a soft woodwind, then string, accompaniment she compares this glacial life of the heart with the love she had in her humble home with Des Grieux – the line rising to a climax as she recalls it. It was of course her choice – or the compulsion of her nature – to leave, as Prévost makes clear and Massenet's opera shows. But in Puccini the falling phrases of the melody work to arouse pity for Manon. Two-thirds of the way through this song, saying she now has everything except affection: 'or ho tutt' altra cosa!'

Manon sings a phrase which descends through an octave from the highest note in the tune. Reworked, that phrase becomes what, for convenience, I characterise as the 'fanfare' theme. It is linked to the love of Manon and Des Grieux and is suitably energetic and flowing. Lescaut points out he is still friendly with Des Grieux and Manon wants to know whether her lover has forgotten her; the orchestra refers to her name as sung in the 'Manon Lescaut mi chiamo' phrase and her vocal line soars as she asks to be given back the past. But the orchestra, having thundered out her feelings for her lover, returns to the eighteenth century elegance of Géronte's house as her mind switches to her gown and wig.

Musicians present her with a madrigal Géronte has written for her, in which he can cast himself conveniently as the lover Phileneus and she as Chloris (there were two classical figures called Chloris: the goddess of flowers and a prostitute). As Phileneus asks whichever Chloris to take pity on him and inquires whether she has a heart, we can assume Géronte is not getting his money's worth.

Saying that a bored young person is a terrifying thing, Lescaut goes to fetch Des Grieux. Meanwhile artificiality prevails as Géronte watches Manon go through her paces and poses in a dancing lesson. However, nothing will keep him from joining the fashionable crowd at the promenading hour. Bored, Manon says she will join him but – as with Rodolfo in *La Bohème*, a five-minute delay leads to her being surprised by love:

> Tu, tu, amore? tu?
> (You! You! My love. It's you?)

she cries as Des Grieux bursts in. Lescaut has brought him. In the long passage that follows, 'You used to love me so much,' she sings with a release of passion lacking in her glacial politeness to Géronte. Unsurprisingly, Des Grieux is angry – this is the woman who walked out on him – but it is the anger of a man in love. Manon tries to explain in terms of the once-tempting luxury; the music here offers a series of three two-note phrases followed by a run up and down, then leaps up. This sense of striving will be heard later.

Her most effective assertion is that he no longer loves her because she is no longer beautiful. Of course, he assures her she is as lovely as ever and he still loves her. To emphasise their love Puccini incorporates music from 'Donna non vidi mai' with Manon's words. At the climax we hear the first, triumphant singing of the 'fanfare' theme (it was heard before in the orchestra – Puccini often lets us hear an important vocal phrase on instruments first). It has the quality of a clarion call, awakening them to the joys of passion and a triumphant trumpeting of their love. After this they sink to a tender embrace interrupted by the returning Géronte. The orchestra greets him with its lower register; he treats the lovers with insolence.

Happy in her temporary triumph and used to having Géronte at her feet, Manon does not see the danger she is in, even mocking the old man by pushing a mirror in front of his wrinkled features. Des Grieux sees the urgency in leaving. There is a moment when Géronte goes, but the Manon whose passion and tenderness Des Grieux loves is taken over by her love of wealth, and in the time it takes her to gather her treasures, Géronte returns with armed policemen, which in that age meant archers. They drag Manon away at his command, while Lescaut prevents Des Grieux trying to rescue her. It would only lead to his arrest and he needs to be free to help her escape. This ruined attempt at flight is set to screeching and rushing strings with hammer-blow chords as escape is cut off.

Before Act Three comes the short orchestral intermezzo. Though he never used this particular device again, Puccini remained fond of orchestral introductions to his third act to paint pictures in sound. But this intermezzo is more than just scene-painting. It depicts Manon's journey as a prisoner to Le Havre, convicted as a thief and prostitute on Géronte's word alone. Des Grieux follows, and rising from regretful viola and cello music come tunes from Act One – a slow version of the once happy 'Manon Lescaut mi chiamo' and a phrase from the moment Des Grieux told Manon of the attempt to kidnap her by coach. The sad development of one theme associated with each of them, and the link to the earlier plan to take Manon away by force, are appropriate. The act two theme of two-note phrases and scale music joins in, reminiscent of her talk of the wealth amongst which she lived

– ironic in the low condition we shall find her in for Act Three. In an even sadder irony, there is a new version of the tune to which near the end of Act Two she sang of her faithfulness to Des Grieux. Now it is he who is staying faithful to her. These tunes build to a climax expressing the anguish of the two lovers, one a captive, the other following her. As the intermezzo closes the once climactic 'fanfare' theme appears, soft and sad. They triumph no more, but in this reduced state arrive at the docks of Le Havre, as the action moves from orchestra pit back to the stage with Manon in prison and Lescaut putting his hope in a bribed guard.

Opening as dawn arrives, the act begins with suitably sombre music, a low clarinet note giving a pulse as rhythmic as a lighthouse beam. Des Grieux feels ever more bleak about the future – which keeps fading like a desert mirage. This act opens up a more personal, searching side to Puccini's music, a change that began in the intermezzo. On viola a baleful-sounding motif, heard earlier several times on various instruments, sounds and Manon comes to the prison window. At the brief, desperate meeting the strings faintly offer 'Donna non vidi mai', now a shadow of its once happy self. There is an echo too in Manon's music of the love duet from the previous act, but the moment together is interrupted as the Lamplighter (or at this time of day, Extinguisher) does his round. This contented individual sings as he works about a young woman called Kate who turned down a king's tempting offer and was rewarded with money and the husband she loved.

Not a subject likely to be music to Manon's ears, for she is in a much less happy situation. She has never shown Kate's moral resolution either. Fearfully she says she will do whatever Des Grieux asks; she has learned more of life and would never be so blind to danger as she was in Géronte's house an act ago. At this moment the strings sound a tune adapted from Puccini's brief string quartet *Crisantemi* (Chrysanthemums).

The 'fanfare' theme gives hope for a moment, but a sudden shot and argument offstage indicate the escape has gone wrong. Lescaut dashes on to confirm this. Des Grieux refuses to run for cover, even when Manon in a new unselfishness tells him to. Locals in Le Havre know what sort of spectacle is on offer when convicted women board the prison-ship, and turn out to watch. A drum-roll announces the parade; insolent, scared, demented, they pass across the stage as their names are read out. Manon is called and as she timidly emerges, Des Grieux rushes to her. A melancholy melody accompanies the women's parade. Having seen young Manon in Act One and Manon in her rich home in Act Two, the sight of her in chains and the wild company of these women is pitiful. Des Grieux offers to sail as the lowliest of sailors and is allowed on board as the act ends with a restatement of the melancholy parade tune.

All three acts so far have included group or crowd scenes. The last act places Manon and Des Grieux alone in the New Orleans desert. There is only the slightest hint given as to why they are there: a reference to Manon's beauty still causing trouble. As there is no mention of her behaviour, it can be assumed that any problem lies now with the behaviour of men in reaction to her rather than her own impulses. A clearer sense of her moral growth or maturity, even if it has come too late, would strengthen this act, which otherwise is a brief mood piece and pathos-raising death scene.

Sombre chords, in which might be detected the name 'Manon' as sung in the Act One line 'Manon Lescaut mi chiamo' introduce the tired, battered pair. Puccini then uses a rising tune, again from *Crisantemi*, as Des Grieux tries to encourage Manon to keep going, but she only speaks of everything growing darker.

In Prévost the two have a definite destination; in the opera the desert seems more a symbol of their despair, suggesting that things have come to an end. Manon, having learned about power, love and moral responsibility, is almost a different person, so it is ironic that the 'Manon Lescaut mi chiamo' tune returns in elegaic mood and a sad strain is recalled from the intermezzo. At times the orchestral sound is as dry as Manon's throat. She asks for water before collapsing into sleep. When she wakes she takes Des Grieux's absence – he is looking for water – as desertion. Maybe she assumes he would behave as she did in happier days.

Hardly anything happens in Act Four; the story is effectively over, but it is a conclusion that asks questions about Manon's character. Were some sudden good fortune to place her safe back in Parisian society, would the experience of her ordeal survive the renewed temptations? Has she really learned better, if too late for her own good? Not that there is any chance of her returning. A series of separate chords, alternating between distant high and low, musically expresses her isolation. Manon collapses to the plaintive tune from the intermezzo and the 'fanfare' theme is heard, now slow and subdued. It is only now, as she wakes and finds herself alone that Manon has an extended soliloquy. There is a new depth inside her to be expressed:

Sola! Perduta! Abandonnata!
(Alone! Lost! Abandoned!)

This is introduced by a grim, low little march rhythm. The main tune consists of slow descents over most of a scale, echoed bleakly by a plangent oboe and offstage flute. It is the orchestral flutes, at low pitch, that play as she finally realises, unwillingly, she is dying. Manon the gadfly regrets she has not found the peace she had thought America could offer, and she becomes agitated as she says her beauty has caused yet more trouble. Ironically, she begins blaming herself just when it may no longer be her responsibility. Des Grieux returns and tries to comfort her but, as the orchestra offers brief outbursts alternating with quiet regret, she asks 'Was your Manon loving? . . . My sins will be forgotten – my love will never die'.

As the orchestra offers a sustained chord then builds to a climax, ending the opera on chords that grow loud then soft, with three quiet chords inserted just before the end, Manon's epitaph for herself fits the whole work. She is given dramatic and musical sympathy way beyond what her 'sins' would suggest she might deserve.

Manon Lescaut was Puccini's first unqualified success. A continuously spun musical thread, where themes were treated symphonically and adapted to suit the characters' development, it is his first major opera. The varied use of the 'Manon Lescaut mi chiamo' motif or the 'fanfare' theme, the interweaving of tunes in the intermezzo, show his mastery of a full-length structure. In some ways, *Manon Lescaut* is more symphonic than his future operas, for Puccini was not about to become an Italian Wagner.

Meanwhile from the brew of writers working at one time or another on the libretto he had found in Giacosa and Illica two men who were to provide him – through a series of stormy processes – with the fine libretti of the three great operas he was about to write.

Chapter 3

La Bohème

La Bohème, premièred in 1896, brought together the team of Giuseppe Giacosa, Luigi Illica and Giacomo Puccini. Despite a mixed reception at its first production, the opera has become especially popular for its mix of high spirits and deep feeling.

La Bohème

First performed at the Teatro Regio, Turin on 1st February 1896.
Conducted by Arturo Toscanini.

ACT ONE: *A Paris attic, 1830s. Christmas Eve.*
A poet, Rodolfo, and a painter, Marcello, share the room. Their efforts to work are hampered by the cold. Being penniless they resort to burning the manuscript of a play Rodolfo has written. Their equally poor friend, the philosopher Colline, enters. Then to their surprise the fourth member of their bohemian group, the musician Schaunard, arrives with food, wine and money. He tells his friends not to eat the food, for on Christmas Eve they must dine out. Their landlord M. Benoit arrives to collect rent arrears. Concealing the signs of their affluence they trick him into revealing his philanderings and, pretending to be shocked by what he says, throw him out, of course without paying.

When his three friends go out to eat Rodolfo stays behind to finish a piece of journalism for the magazine he edits. While he is trying to write there is a knock at the door announcing his female neighbour. She needs a light for her candle, which has blown out. They are soon attracted to each other; the scene is prolonged by the loss of her door key. As they search for it their hands touch; hers is very cold and Rodolfo offers to warm it for her. He introduces himself as a poet. She says her name is Lucia but she is generally known as Mimi. The bohemians call to Rodolfo to hurry up. He and Mimi declare their love for each other and leave to join the others.

ACT TWO: *Paris, the Latin Quarter.*
Amid the pre-Christmas bustle, traders try to sell, children urge their parents to buy and the bohemians join the market. Schaunard buys a horn, Rodolfo buys Mimi a bonnet and they enjoy a festive meal outside the crowded Café Momus. Marcello's old flame Musetta turns up with her rich old admirer Alcindoro. Musetta sets out to re-attract Marcello, despatching Alcindoro to carry out a shoe repair for her. Soldiers march past and the six young people leave. Musetta arranges for the bohemians' bill to be added to hers and the waiter presents Alcindoro with it when he returns.

ACT THREE: *The Barrière d'Enfer, a city gate on the outskirts of Paris. A February morning.*
People wait in the cold for the gate to be opened. Mimi asks if the nearby inn is the one where the painter (Marcello) is working. Musetta is inside singing. Marcello comes out and talks to Mimi. She tells him there has been a rupture between her and Rodolfo caused by the poet's jealous fears that she is seeing

another man.

As Rodolfo emerges, Mimi hides behind a tree. When Marcello blames him for his treatment of Mimi, Rodolfo admits his real fears are for her health and he is afraid that a person with more money could look after her better. Mimi tries to say good-bye to Rodolfo, but they decide they need each other. By contrast Musetta and Marcello show their mutual dependence by continuing to argue.

ACT FOUR: *The attic. Springtime.*
Neither Rodolfo nor Marcello can concentrate on their work because they keep thinking of their lovers. Colline and Schaunard come in and lighten the mood by horseplay and dancing until they are interrupted by Musetta's entry with the news that Mimi, now seriously ill, has returned to Rodolfo but can hardly climb the stairs. She is helped in and put to bed but is still cold. Musetta and Colline offer to sell their valued earrings and greatcoat to fetch medical help. Mimi asks for a muff to warm her hands. As they leave, Marcello runs out to fetch a doctor.

Mimi tells Rodolfo she had only pretended to fall asleep until the others had gone. She tells him how much she loves him, and he expresses his love for her. Their friends return with a muff, some medicine and news that the doctor is coming. Rodolfo shields Mimi's face from the sunlight, but she dies. The opera ends with Rodolfo expressing his grief.

La Bohème: The libretto

With his increased status after *Manon Lescaut*, Puccini cast around for a new subject that would suit him. The likeliest contender looked like being a story of Sicilian peasant life. Giovanni Verga was a writer who specialised in such tales; one of them had already proved a useful source for Mascagni's opera *Cavalleria Rusticana*. Puccini was attracted to *La Lupa* (The She-Wolf), began work on it and went so far as to visit Verga to discuss an adaptation. It was also a chance to take in the Sicilian atmosphere and folk music. Had he travelled home on a different ship, opera houses might now be resounding to the melodies of a grim tale of rural life. But on board he met the step-daughter of the composer Wagner, the Countess Blandine Gravina, who successfully discouraged him. Ricordi could only shrug his shoulders in acceptance and murmur about the publicity already given to the abandoned project.

Somehow Puccini came upon a French period piece, a once famous book of stories set in the 1830s. Instead of Sicily and peasants, this offered Paris and students. In place of grim murder, it had the pathos of young death from the romantic (considered from the safe distance of prosperity) illness of tuberculosis already 'celebrated' in Dumas' *La Dame Aux Camélias* and Verdi's opera from that novel, *La Traviata*. The stories, by a writer called Henry Mürger, were also jocular and lively.

Leoncavallo might well have steered Puccini's attention towards Mürger. Ricordi knew both composers had an interest in the subject. If the publisher sided with Puccini, it was a move which helped his firm's accounts for years to come, and much benefited opera audiences. Leoncavallo went on to write his own *Bohème*. It was initially successful but is rarely heard now.

A confrontation between the two composers occurred in March 1893 when they met in a café in Milan. Each rushed off to be first to tell his story

Puccini (left) with Giuseppe Giacosa (centre) and Luigi Illica (right). Illica (1857-1919) was a left-wing writer and author of thirty-five opera libretti, including the three famous Puccini works he wrote with Giacosa.

in print, the standard way to claim rights in a subject. Leoncavallo came first, in the 20th March issue of *Il Secolo* (owned by Sonzogno, Ricordi's rival and Leoncavallo's publisher). On 21st March the leading paper *Il Corriere Della Sera* carried Puccini's announcement, followed up by a letter from the composer in which he challenged Leoncavallo to a duel of scores, with the public deciding whose opera should come first.

So easy is Puccini's opera to listen to, so delightful in its episodes of joy and grief, that it is hard to imagine the difficulties involved in its creation. Luigi Illica and Giuseppe Giacosa, two of the many people who had worked on the *Manon Lescaut* libretto, were brought in to provide the words for the new opera. Roughly, Illica can be thought of as the dramatic craftsperson, Giacosa the artist. Illica could carpenter a novel or play so that it fitted the needs of the operatic stage, shaping his source material into a suitable, coherent pattern; to this the poet and dramatist Giacosa would give poetic colouring and depth, building the characters and providing for Puccini the luminosity the composer wished to portray in his music. It was the lack of luminosity in Verga's stories that Puccini had given as his final reason for not proceeding with *La Lupa*.

With Puccini's demands on his librettists and Giacosa's extreme self-criticism, not to mention Illica's shortness of temper, it is amazing any of their joint ventures saw the light of day. As it was the three produced the great trio of *La Bohème*, *Tosca* and *Madama Butterfly*. Shortly after the last of these was written, Giocosa died, in 1906. Had he lived longer (Illica survived until 1919) there is no saying what further fine operas might have been produced (if the three-way rope which bound the artists had continued to survive the strain).

That it did so was largely due to the mollifying, vanity-salving, encouraging hand of Giulio Ricordi, who was at the receiving end of any complaints and who often had to prevent one of them giving up on the collaboration. Nicknaming the autocratic composer the 'Doge', after the rulers of Venice, Ricordi managed to insert good-natured humour into many of the apparently irreconcilable arguments.

Bohemianism was a phenomenon which could probably have grown only in France. Germany and Italy did not exist as integral countries in the first half of the nineteenth century, while in England the main university cities of Cambridge and Oxford were distanced from the capital. In France, Paris was both the intellectual and political centre and its students, bringing their many languages from around the continent, found the only way to communicate was in the lingua franca of the educated, Latin. Hence the area where they congregated became known as the Latin Quarter. There they crowded into cheap lodgings, eating and drinking in their favourite cafés and taverns. The name 'bohemian' became attached to the unconventional lifestyle some of them led, from a link with travelling gypsies believed to have made their way from Bohemia. This lifestyle ran along, and often enough crossed, the lines of poverty, promiscuity and conniving to get by from day to day. Students then were all male; the women they brought into their lives came mainly from the poor quarters of the city, or were lively-minded fortune seekers, in the capital to search for adventure and money. Such a life is a passing phase. Only an opera like *La Bohème* can freeze it and make it seem eternal.

Among the struggling artists in 1840s Paris was Henri Murger, who altered his name to the English Henry and added a German accent to become Mürger. For years he fed profound poems and dramas to a world which declined to take any interest. Then, as desperate as any bohemian condemned to the 'open-air inn' of homelessness, he decided to prostitute his high talent with a few stories of everyday, and night, life in the Latin Quarter. A magazine called *Le Corsaire* printed one in March 1845. Almost a year later a second appeared. More were published over the following months and were quietly enjoyed by friends, fellow writers and a limited readership. It might have ended there, had not another keen young writer approached Mürger and suggested writing the play of the stories (as yet they had not appeared in book form). He was called Theodore Barrière, and together the two had *La Vie De Bohème* produced at the Théâtre des Variétés in Paris in November 1849.

Young, rebellious bohemians were bound to attract at least the reputation of being politically subversive. In fact Mürger, like Puccini, was distinctly uninterested in political matters. His bohemians do not sneak off to secret socialist meetings or carry the quite recently published Communist Manifesto in their pockets. But popular images are rarely precise or factual. 1848 had seen revolutions and political protests throughout Europe. A new play about youngsters on the fringe of society, living in streets unknown to respectable theatregoers, had become by 1849 much more topical than were the magazine stories a few years earlier.

Its success led to a commercial demand for more of the same, and in 1851 the collected stories came out as *Scénes De La Bohème*. Illica and Giacosa's libretto has only one fifth the number of pages of the book and the adapta-

The Club at Torre del Lago, named after the opera Puccini was writing, where the composer and friends could base their social activities. Shooting wildfowl was one of Puccini's non-musical obsessions.

tion of what is used shows dramatic economy, as the characters were moulded to become people Puccini would wish to bring to musical life.

An example of the way the librettists shaped and cut the stories comes early in Act One, when Schaunard the musician bursts in on his three hungry, freezing friends with money, food and fuel. He has been hired to play the piano in order to bring about the death of a parrot. For Mürger this was a complete comic chapter. An Englishman – Mürger has fun with his attempts at speaking French – is sick of a parrot owned by his neighbour downstairs. He explains that he wants Schaunard to hammer out scales and vanquish the bird with the noise. Musicianly sentiments do not prevent Schaunard accepting the job and after three days of unsuccessful murder by noise he poisons the parrot with some parsley.

From this the librettists created a scene showing the delight of the other bohemians with the food and fuel; they have limited interest in Schaunard's account. In fact, they all but ignore him, for all Illica and Giacosa needed was a reason for plenty and merriment to enter the opening picture of poverty, and something to bring the four friends together. The money that allows them to eat out gives a good opening for Rodolfo to be left alone to meet Mimi. By adding the joke that the others are not in the least interested in Schaunard's story the writers swiftly create the casual, never-be-serious atmosphere of bohemian life.

Before becoming enmeshed with Puccini and his sad Mimi, it is worth noting another side of his character. His main interest in life outside opera was hunting wild-fowl. He chose Torre del Lago, the home in which he spent most of his adult years, partly for its isolation – he left when industry finally encroached – but also because of the large Lake Massaciuccoli right by it, giving him plenty of hunting opportunities.

Puccini, therefore, was no artist refined out of contact with active life. In the Bohemian Club he formed with friends at Torre, strict rules insisted that anyone serious or pedantic, or who failed to be a hearty eater and drinker would be chased off. The president's decision was final, though he promised to do everything he could to stop the Treasurer collecting subscriptions. This was probably just as well, for another rule declared that

The Treasurer should make off with all the money.

Finally:

Silence is Forbidden

and:

Wisdom is not allowed, unless in special situations.

It's all in the mood of the literary bohemians. One thing used to cut through Puccini's bonhomie, however. After sessions at the club the group would return *chez* Puccini to drink and play cards while he composed in the same room. He ignored them; they ignored him. But Puccini could fly into a rage if anyone started whistling or humming the music he tried out on his piano, for that broke his concentration. Otherwise, it seems the background hubbub helped him.

An image of Puccini sitting indoors yet wearing a hat, composing amid strands of cigar smoke, the whiff of whisky and the rhythms of whist and poker is not surprising when we hear the first parts of the outside acts of *La Bohème*, or indeed the whole of its short second act. But it was not only such sympathetically sociable music that he composed in this way. Mimi's death also came about thus, complete in the score with a skull and crossbones.

All four bohemians have mistresses in Mürger. Colline's is a wifely sort, befitting the bookman; she is never seen. But we do have sightings of Phémie Tienturière. She is a lively woman, and when Schaunard and she move into the same tenement house as Rodolphe and Marcel, the poor neighbours through the thin walls prefer even the nights the pair argue noisily to their nights of reconciliation and far from silent passion.

One thing we lose in the opera is the transience of bohemian life, the way characters move around, move in with or near each other, and of course, in and out of love. But the economy all has a point. Phémie is discarded because Musetta is the only person needed to contrast with Mimi. The promiscuity and one-night stands of bohemian life are not what Puccini wanted at all, despite the fact that the very respectable, and increasingly rich, composer had similar affairs himself.

His Mimi is decidedly not Mürger's: Mimi in Mürger is adorable, but with a voice like the clash of cymbals. When he meets her, Rodolphe is all of twenty-four and convinced love is over for him. Mimi is a petite, delicate eighteen-year-old, but when bored or angry she can flash out in a savage way. Her hands are always white but she is red-blooded and, far from being the shy girl of the opera, she loves gossiping with other mistresses in the area, who give her ideas that need money to fulfil them. As Rodolphe is poor, she begins to look elsewhere. The binding jealousy this causes Rodolphe is more like the Marcello-Musetta relationship in the opera.

The last main chapter in Mürger tells of Mimi's death. Rodolphe has had an affair with the self-centred and exploitative Juliette. He happens to meet Mimi, who is finely dressed courtesy of her latest lover, the Viscount Paul. Rodolphe goes home and writes poems about her; his surface indifference cannot fool Marcel, who himself still pines for Musette. Mimi is no intellectual, so when she returns to work for two days in a flower shop in order to earn the money to buy a copy of the magazine containing Rodolphe's poem about her and learns all thirty-two verses of it, we can assume she has some feeling left for him. Christmas Eve arrives, but not the bustling scene of the opera's opening acts. Instead, Mimi quietly comes to Rodolphe and Marcel's apartment, having been evicted for non-payment of rent. It seems the Viscount became annoyed at Rodolphe's poem and threw Mimi out. Deprived of his support she is hungry but too weak to eat. Grief has taken the bounce and fight from her, but when Marcel suggests she might return to Rodolphe she says she will be going far away – meaning her death is near. She has already tried suicide and is evidently sick.

So, in Mürger it is Mimi herself who knows and declares her death is near. The opera makes her a more passive victim, who hides behind a tree and overhears Rodolphe saying she will die. Mürger continues his story with a harrowing scene, set in a hospital where Mimi is mistakenly thought to be dead. When Rodolphe hears she is in fact alive, he rushes to the hospital, only to find she has really died.

At last we find some of the pathos of Puccini's Mimi, but hardly a close source. Yet, when he devised the libretto he did not needlessly invent. The Café Momus, centre of the bustling pre-Christmas second act, is there in Mürger, as it was also there in Paris. Similarly, when it comes to characters, the origins of Mimi are all in Mürger, but not entirely among Rodolphe's lovers.

Two-thirds of the way through comes an odd chapter called 'Francine's Muff'. Francine lives in the same apartment as Jacques (who meets Mürger in hospital and tells this story). She is a seamstress, escaping the clutches of an evil stepmother by living alone. She survives on little and asks for no more. If that sounds familiar, consider their meeting. Francine comes home cheerful. As she is about to open her door, a gust of wind extinguishes her candle. To avoid a six-flight descent, and seeing a light under Jacques' door, she dares to knock and ask for a light. The great scene of 'Your tiny hand is frozen' and 'Yes, they call me Mimi' is here waiting in the story of Jacques and Francine. And so the opera's great love story is created out of the one chapter not about Rodolphe, Mimi or any other of his girlfriends.

Tired, apologetic Francine is Puccini's kind of girl. Jacques hides his matches to prevent her leaving too soon, they search in the dark for the key and their hands touch often. Yet even Francine is more assertive than the opera's Mimi. She finds the key but deliberately hides it under the bed to maintain their happy vigil. She is, however, inexperienced in love. Aware of her very brief life expectancy – she suffers from tuberculosis – she wants to experience love before she dies and her six months' love affair with Jacques is ended by death.

Another detail is changed for the opera. Mürger's pair meet in spring and Francine dies in the autumn. By putting Rodolfo and Mimi's meeting on Christmas Eve and having her die in spring, the librettists avoid the obvious seasonal correspondences (spring=blossoming love; autumn=decay) for a strange irony. Rodolfo and Mimi's love is given birth next to the Nativity, in a quiet moment amid the festivities which they are enjoying. They are parted at the very moment when life is supposed to be emerging from winter cold. The opera catches this irony in two beautiful details. In the first act, moonlight romantically illuminates Mimi (we remember Puccini turned down *La Lupa* because it had no 'luminous' character). Then in the last act the spring sun shines but it is too strong for Mimi's draining energies and she has to be hidden from it.

It is true that vestiges of other Mimis remain in the opera, but they hardly register; they are mentioned but hardly discussed and never shown. When, early in Act Three, Mimi tells Marcello that Rodolfo is avoiding her because he is jealous she seems genuinely perplexed and his jealousy seems unjustified to us too. Nothing about the Mimi we see gives any cause for it. She tells her story first so when Rodolfo later claims she is: 'always flirting with someone. A scented dandy of noble family tried to win her caresses' it seems his own wild fear, something he has imagined in order to cover the grief he feels because he knows Mimi is dying and that he is too poor to provide the care she needs. That is, he seems to be compensating for his own sense of inadequacy by transferring blame to her, as he soon admits.

Admittedly the final act does indicate Rodolfo might have a point but, as we shall see, it does so only in a muted way. And anyway, after the third act has just ended with a love duet of reconciliation, set against the contrast of Marcello and Musetta's bickering, it would be hard for a momentary pang of jealousy to dent our opinion of the heroine.

Yet there *is* a moment of a different Mimi at the start of Act Four when Marcello tells Rodolfo he has seen her 'out in her carriage arrayed in splendour just like a duchess.' But, after a brief pretence of indifference, Rodolfo abandons his jealousy and recalls her 'hands pale and slender', and when she returns sick all is love and grief.

At one point in the opera's creation however, we were to have seen a Mimi full of life picking up a new love – the one who would give her that carriage to ride in for a time – but this proposed scene was cut. It is an aspect of Mimi Illica wanted to include. It makes her a more varied character, much less the passive victim, and it helps the story unfold – something which was Illica's special skill. It explains how the lovers came to be parted and makes their last act reunion more touching.

However it is hardly surprising if Puccini did not share this enthusiasm: such a Mimi was not the heroine for him. There were many other changes during the making of *La Bohème*. This most accessible opera was hard to knock into shape. Illica had devised the plot early in 1893 and by April Giacosa had set to work creating the precise text. By 28 July most of the libretto was ready; then he had a crisis of confidence in his work and seems to have begun all over again. By early October he had had enough – he just could not find the understanding of the characters that any successful dramatist needs. In addition, Puccini was chasing him for words to start setting them to music.

Giacosa eventually persisted but within a few months – February 1894 – Illica was upset. He had performed a dizzying task shaping Mürger's anecdotes and portraits into a continuous story, and now Puccini was objecting to what he had done. This was the period when Illica was holding out for a more fiery Mimi, while Puccini was insisting on a softer figure. The composer did not like the lovers' separation; the librettist saw the theatrical benefit in having complexity. His pleas to Ricordi, an ever-present pacifier, helped Illica keep at least a glimmer of complexity. He argued that her return to the poverty which had bred her fatal disease in order to be with her real love at the last makes her a dramatically richer character. Even Illica's moderated approach caused Puccini problems, but without the sense of separation which just about remains in the opera, the story would be less affecting. Yet through the year and into the next, Puccini insisted on further changes, especially in the third, Barrière d'Enfer, act. He wanted this to be kept as simple as possible.

Puccini managed to upset Giacosa again by demanding changes in the detail of Mimi's death scene. He wanted Mimi to speak of her love and care for Rodolfo as she died. Her last words breathed in short spasms became:

Qui amor – sempre con te!
Le mani – al caldo – e – dormire
(My love – always with you! My hands – warmer – and – sleep)

This derives from Francine's thinking as she dies of Jacques and is a sure theatrical touch, to catch the audience's sympathy. Whatever shortcomings he may have as a composer, Puccini never lost his sense of what worked well on stage. Nor did he ever lack the melodic gift to make the most of moments of high pathos.

La Bohème was finished on 10th December 1895 at the composer's home in Torre del Lago. He wanted an all-star première in Naples, followed by performances in Rome; but Ricordi recalled the success *Manon Lescaut* had been three years earlier (to the day, as it turned out) in Turin and pushed successfully for the new opera to be premièred in the same city. The businessman in Ricordi could not stomach the cost of stellar casting and argued, in quite a modern way, for an ensemble approach. Rather than go for individually famous singers, he said, this opera would benefit from a cast who could work as a team. While it is possible to sympathise with Puccini, waiting to take the operatic world by storm, his publisher was right, for *La Bohème* needs a strong group on stage. It is a piece about people who live in each others' pockets; the performers need to trust and relate well to each other.

Perhaps the greatest favour Ricordi did Puccini was to argue against the composer's preference for a firmly established big name conductor, and in favour of the resident Turin conductor, still in his twenties, a man called Arturo Toscanini. Puccini needed only a short time at rehearsals to become deeply impressed with Toscanini, who was to be associated with his operas way into the next century – and who was to conduct the première of the last, never-completed, Puccini opera, *Turandot*. Puccini was less happy with the quality of some of the singers, notably the Rodolfo and Marcello.

There was a divided reaction to the first night; the audience was satisfied, the critics were uncertain. Various newspapers told Puccini he had lost his way, gone off the rails since *Manon Lescaut* and given up the cause of art. It has been suggested they were still reeling from the recent Wagnerian assault, when Toscanini had conducted the Italian première of *Götterdammerung*. Seen in its separate glory away from its three predecessors in the Ring cycle, it still ran an impressive, doom-laden six hours with intervals.

Compared with such cosmic significance, ending with flood, fire and the end of civilisation as the ancient Teutons knew it, Puccini's brief sad tale of a dying seamstress must have seemed almost frivolous. Its quick mix of comedy, vivacity and everyday vulnerabilities must have appeared trivial alongside the tidal wave of Wagnerian-scale love, betrayal and revenge.

La Bohème is a rarity in the world of opera, indeed, in the world of drama in general, a world that thrives on conflict and duplicity. It is full of genuine, good-hearted people. Compare it with other Puccini operas. *Manon Lescaut* has barely a decent human being in it (though to be fair, one should not cast aspersions on the Lamplighter). *Tosca* is presided over by the malevolent Scarpia. *Madama Butterfly* has the two-timing Pinkerton, *La Fanciulla del West* the jealous sheriff Rance and so on to *Turandot*, whose eponymous character is someone to freeze all affection. Even the comedy *Gianni Schicchi* is a tale of mean cupidity and scheming rascality. But *La Bohème* is full of good intentions, and this has helped give its joys and griefs a particularly warm place in the heart of opera-goers since its first production.

Throughout his life, Puccini continued working on his operas and supervising major new productions. To do this he would travel between countries and even continents. If some aspect of the work in performance troubled him, he would try to compose a better alternative. He was for some time unhappy with the end of what had become the separate second act, the Café Momus scene. Throughout the discussions with Illica and Giacosa, Puccini – often wisely – had wanted to simplify the stage action. Having seen *La Bohème* in performance he realised there was no need for Alcindoro, Musetta's aged lover, to complain when he returns to find everyone has left the Momus, leaving him to foot the bill. His look, and the gesture in which the proprietor offers him the account, together with the bustle in the orchestra, which does so much to create this act's atmosphere, makes the point. Nothing needed to be said, so the lines were cut to give the snap ending we know.

La Bohème: The music

The bohemian atmosphere is established at the very opening of the opera with the energetic theme Puccini took from his student *Capriccio Sinfonico*, and as it settles down Marcello sings that his picture 'The Crossing of the Red Sea' correlates with the damp, cold room. In revenge he drowns a painted Pharaoh. Further spurts of creative bohemian energy sound in the orchestra and lead to the poet Rodolfo contrasting the smoke from chimneys across Paris with their own unlit stove. His lines 'Nel cieli bigi' introduce the first vocal tune of note, lightly accompanied by a woodwind chord and plucked strings, with no bass notes for several bars. Even then the lower notes are only lightly touched in. Rodolfo's tune is another of Puccini's self-borrowings (from music planned for *La Lupa*) and its striking appeal marks him out as a significant character.

Marcello decides to break up a chair for firewood; even his picture might have to be sacrificed; but Rodolfo has a better idea – to burn the manuscript of his play. This will make less of a stink than the 'Red Sea'. As they talk of Rodolfo's sacrifice and the stove is lit, a flute carries the melody, high strings shimmer and spread chords provide harmony on the harp, an instrument Puccini often used to colour his scenes.

Colline enters, having failed to pawn any of the books he keeps in the vast pockets of his great coat. After some mock high-flown talk as the play crackles on the stove, errand boys bring in food, drink, cigars and firewood, and Schaunard enters to a positive yet carefree tune introduced on woodwind plus violas and cellos. His three friends combine to celebrate:

> Le dovizi e d'una fiera
> il destin ci destino
> (All the luxury of Christmas we are fated now to know)

Colline's Act Four farewell to his favourite coat, *Vecchia zimarra*, was added to the score to give the bass a solo. Puccini was fond of adding sketches to his manuscripts; they also include a skull and crossbones on the page of Mimi's death.

– all singing, if not in unison, at least in the same rhythm, giving a choral effect. Schaunard tells how he could afford all this – the story of the Englishman and the parrot – and feeling confident he has enough cash left still to splash out, he insists they keep the food he has brought for later. This is Christmas Eve; they *must* dine out at the Café Momus in the busy Latin Quarter. At this, the orchestra moves from the theme Schaunard brought in with him to a busy tune which refers to the Quarter and its activity. Here it is introduced softly on flute and clarinet, with the harp spreading out the common chords on which it is built.

Schaunard's tune returns, played loudly on woodwind and horns. As he speaks there is a knock at the door; it is the landlord, M. Benoit. First, they try locking Benoit out, but he asks for just one word. Unfortunately when they let him in, the word turns out to be 'rent'. Bohemian wits are called for. With elaborate politeness Benoit is seated and plied with drink, while being lulled by the sight of Schaunard's earnings. The others are alarmed as Marcello seems to offer money to the landlord, addressing him in polite terms with a gentle insinuating melody that has a falling close. As Benoit drinks he starts boasting of his success with women: and he a married man! Feigning outraged morality, the friends throw him out without a franc. After which successful ruse, they leave, except for Rodolfo who has an article to complete for his latest little magazine. He promises to be along in five minutes.

Two universal truths apply here. The first is that when anybody says they will be only five minutes finishing an article, they can be given up for most of the day. The second is that when anybody decides to stay in alone so as to be uninterrupted, the first thing that will happen is an interruption. It happens in life; it happens in *La Bohème* and, this being an opera, a young woman forms the interruption.

So far the tone of the scene has been spirited and comical. It has also been exclusively male. It is a feature of Puccini's operas that, while the male leads can be introduced early on, the heroine's entry is postponed. This allows her importance to be built up by talk about her, as with *Butterfly* and, supremely, *Turandot*, but it also means the feminine voice comes late to stage and orchestra. When it does arrive it seems to fill a human void, creating a warmth and tenderness whose presence is felt more strongly for its late arrival.

Rodolfo's three friends leave, Schaunard's references to the Latin Quarter and the Café Momus being accompanied by their theme, now played on soft, detached chords from flute and piccolo. The pace slows down, there is an extremely soft, warm string chord and a knock at the door. 'Who is it?' Rodolfo asks. 'Sorry,' says Mimi – her first word being, typically, an apology. And as Rodolfo in surprise says, 'A woman,' two clarinets an octave apart, then the violins, play over a warm bed of string sounds, Mimi's theme – which she will sing to the words 'Mi chiamano Mimi' (They call me Mimi). The tune, like the character, enters the opera gently, but it is a gentleness that flows through the rest of the act. It will burst into passionate expression and there will be a glorious flow of melodies, but the new sound begins here. Mimi may not be personally assertive, but her musical personality grows on us through the rest of this act.

Mimi needs a light for her candle, which has blown out. She drops her key. And there is a first hint of the illness developing inside her, though her coughing and collapse could still be attributed to the stairs she has climbed. She remembers her lost key; her candle goes out. His goes out. They try to find the key in the dark, though the hesitant, then suddenly swift phrases in the orchestra make it clear they are fascinated with each other. This all builds through a lightly scored conversational passage towards the emotional expressions that we know must arrive soon.

In Mürger, of course, it was Francine who kicked the key out of reach. Puccini's Mimi does slide her feet over it but the situation is really sustained by Rodolfo finding it then hiding it in a pocket. This Mimi is too shy even for such a little trick. Then the moment we have all been waiting for – including Rodolfo and Mimi – arrives as their hands meet in the dark. Mürger mentions their hands touching ten times, but once is enough in the theatre, where repetition becomes tedious.

Puccini, like Wagner, had moved away from separate musical 'numbers', but he still marks the big moments clearly, so the movement in the orchestra is stilled to a single note on clarinet, horn and harp. There follows a love duet, one of the most famous passages in all opera, separated out into first a song for him, then one for her, before the two voices combine ecstatically. Rodolfo's famous 'Che gelida manina, se la lasci riscaldar' (Your tiny hand is frozen, let me warm it into life) was, incredibly, not in the first drafts of the scene. It is a perfect piece for its setting, beginning not in the grand manner of an opera set among kings and countesses, but in a plain sense of wonder; the first nine syllables are all sung on the same note. A few muted strings enter after the vocal line has begun; a harp poignantly picks out the early phrases of the melody.

The composer captures the earnest getting-to-know-you aspect of the scene – the short, barely accompanied phrases in which Rodolfo tells Mimi he is a poet, poor but happy. There is an almost shoulder-shrugging deprecation to this: 'How do I manage? I get by.' His poverty is soon ennobled; as he talks of great ladies inspiring him, the strings play assertively. But the surge of passion really comes as he talks of his feeling for Mimi. The words:

Talor dal mio forziere
ruban tutti gioielli
due ladri: gli occhi belli.
(Everything has been stolen from me by two lovely eyes)

are set to a new, beautiful, heart-stopping tune accompanied by surging harp chords. To show that even in a garret, love is still a mighty force, the orchestra swells forth, strings playing the tune from 'Talor dal mio forziere' in romantic heights while woodwind and harp add frenzied rushing musical cascades. It is, of course, physically exciting, but it is not just there to raise applause, for it expresses the truth of a young lover rejoicing in the shock of love. Rodolfo is here the virginal Jacques D– of Mürger and no longer the happy bohemian. After the energy of such a love declaration, Rodolfo and his music descend to a calmer level.

Again Puccini, for all his continuous musical texture, marks out a separate song, with a moment's silence and a single violin note. Slowly, accompanied only by violins with soft chords underlying on other strings, Mimi introduces herself in a vocal line that rises only to fall, reflecting her lowly opinion of herself:

Si. Mi chiamano Mimi,
 ma il mio nome è Lucia
(Yes. I'm called Mimi but my name is really Lucia).

Humbly – eleven syllables repeat the same note – she tells Rodolfo she has little to say of herself. She embroiders silk and satin and is, she claims, happy in her work. Her artistic outlet is embroidering roses and lilies. The vocal line sings as she speaks of the way the flowers remind her of spring. Here the string chords thicken and the reference to *primavera* (spring) is enhanced with woodwind chords. So low is her self-esteem she has to ask this man, who is clearly besotted with her, if she has his attention. Of course it is dark, but surely she picked up the interest in his voice? Or maybe not; perhaps Mimi has never seen herself as loveable. In a repeat of the words and tune of her first line, now accompanied softly by a solo cello – the ultimate romantic sound – she says she is called Mimi but does not know why.

Someone so little in control of her life as not even to understand her nickname must be an ideal, passive Puccini heroine. Certainly she is removed from the real-life women of spirit Mürger put into his pages. She is like a Dickensian heroine, or a waif from a Chaplin movie. Then, as she gets into her stride, knowing Rodolfo is listening to her, she acquires a more confident tune:

Sola, mi fo
il pranzo da me stessa.
(Alone, I eat my little supper)

The orchestra is still sparely used but the speed picks up on these words and a flute bubbles happily. Emotion is rising as the possibility of love comes to life inside her. As she describes the sky seen through her dormer window:

> ma quando vien lo sgelo
> il primo sole è mio
> (But, when the frost has gone the sunlight reaches me first)

her timidity melts like frost in the sun. She sings a new tune 'con molta anima' (with great spirit). Each phrase may descend in pitch, but in mounting excitement it is succeeded by a new phrase starting even higher. What is more, her line is surrounded by an aureole of warm sound, flute, clarinet and violins doubling the melody in different octaves; the second violins add excitement as they play the tune in repeated short notes while horns and other strings offer an insistent chordal accompaniment. This is a Mimi unknown even to herself. It is the capability for joy emerging from a chrysalis of denial and like all great surges of feeling it soon fades. But it leaves a new excitement as she goes on to speak of the rosebud opening.

After which, she excuses herself. She's just a nuisance of a neighbour, she says, in a plain, conversational way, with many repeated notes making the melodic outline plainer. Again Puccini marks the end of the scene by a brief pause, then interrupts the lovers by offstage shouts from the other bohemians, who are sick of waiting. Rodolfo discreetly points out to them through the window that he is no longer alone.

As soon as he can, Rodolfo turns to Mimi and the interrupted love scene continues, becoming an actual duet:

> O soave fanciulla, o dolce viso
> (O gentle girl, o sweet face).

Puccini sets this against the last words of the departing Marcello – 'Trovo la poesia' (Finding poetry) – which the bohemians will be doing in wine. Rodolfo finds his poetry in Mimi. Softly, strings create a tremulous atmosphere as the harp picks out Rodolfo's climactic tune from his earlier declamation 'Talor dal mio forziere', and, fortissimo, the orchestra blasts the tune forth as both lovers sing the melody an octave apart – a fine climax – to different words. The orchestral texture thins, their passion quietens into tenderness and with fragments of 'Che gelida manina' they leave to join the others at the Café Momus over quiet sustained chords, and in the last moments of the act flute and harp colour the mood. The sound of their voices fades offstage in musical and emotional harmony to near-silent woodwind and string chords decorated, again, by the harp.

There could scarcely be a greater contrast with this intimacy than the public crowds and loud bold chords which start Act Two. Christmas Eve was clearly a time of frantic late-night shopping in 1830s Paris. The Momus was a real Parisian café where Mürger/Rodolphe and his friends managed to gain private rights to a room that could accommodate forty by simply smoking and talking any intruder out. In the opera they are not so lucky; the Momus is crowded so they have to sit outside. This allows the colour of city life to flow through the scene. Oranges, chestnuts, toffee and flowers are among the goods on sale and crowds of adults and children are buying. Their vocal lines create a busy atmosphere rather than individual musical interest. It is possible to recognise the tune blared out by trumpets at the opening as the one linked with talk of the Latin Quarter in Act One.

Schaunard has been spending some of his 'parrot money' buying a horn which unfortunately plays out of tune (a neatly portable adaptation of the

Alma Gluck as Musetta in a 1920s American production of *La Bohème*. Mürger based Musetta on Marie-Christine Roux, who built a small fortune while singing in Paris, but then drowned in 1863 when the ship on which she was sailing to a new life in Algiers sank.

faultily-tuned piano he suffers in Mürger's stories). Tiny cells of music are repeated and adapted to build the sense of the moving crowd, the children's voices giving a piquancy to the sound and another layer to the presence of youth in the opera.

Mimi and Rodolfo are window-shopping. He talks of the luxuries he will buy her when he becomes rich. For now he buys her a bonnet. We see the lovers in society as Rodolfo introduces Mimi to his friends. 'I am the poet but she is my inspiration,' he tells them. Marcello mocks his friend's high-flown mood as a toy-seller called Parpignol arrives and immediately attracts a young clientele, whose mothers are less happy than their offspring at the toy-seller's appearance. The bohemians order mutton, turkey, lobster and wine. Marcello asks Mimi what Rodolfo has bought her and in a bright, delicate way she describes the hat, as the clarinets double her tune. It is a happy time for her, and the happy musical line is taken up by Colline and extended with a rising, romantic turn by Marcello as he looks at Mimi and sings of love's dreams and hopes – ironically, in view of what is about to happen to him.

An old man pompously entitled Alcindoro de Milonneux, whose grand name is hardly matched by his person, tries to keep up with the young woman who has him – and his purse – in tow. Everyone at the Momus recognises Musetta, who impertinently calls Alcindoro by his nickname 'Lulu'. He sits by her, his coat collar up, for he does not want anyone in this disreputable company to recognise a man of his standing.

Only Mimi is in the dark. Who better to enlighten her than Marcello, who once had a relationship with Musetta, 'surname Temptation' as he says of her. In true bohemian style he hides his interest in her by scorn and apparent indifference. This annoys Musetta, who puts on a noisy display by smashing a plate which, she complains, smells of onions. Ignoring Alcindoro's embarrassment, she is determined to grab Marcello's attention (she already has everyone else's). She has been equally noticeable in the music.

Mimi's bonnet tune has reached a climax as she, Rodolfo and Marcello drink. They sing in unison, unaccompanied, then on the last syllable they are supported by a long sustained orchestral chord. This is interrupted as Marcello asks for a glass of poison; the orchestra explains why as it leaps into a bright, insistent theme to introduce Musetta. Flute, oboe and clarinet plus violins hammer this out and fragments of the theme keep bubbling away in the scene described above. When Musetta's first ploy fails, she demands attention in a splendid waltz tune, singing of how heads turn when she walks down the street. Puccini had composed the waltz earlier. To give his librettists an idea of the rhythm he wanted them to provide he sang them the nonsense words:

Cocorico, cocorico bifsteaka
(Cock-a-doodle-doo, cock-a-doodle-doo, beefsteak)

A brief preparatory pause marks out the song: two bars with just a low, soft harp harmonic. Characteristically Puccini adds realism by having other, less important, musical phrases sung during Musetta's waltz. 'Tie me down,' Marcello instructs his friends, determined he will not show Musetta he is still attracted. 'What will people say?' Alcindoro pleads.

After two attempts, Musetta screams: a ruse to be rid of the old man. She pretends her shoe is broken and sends him hurrying off for a repair. But the idea of Musetta in pain overcomes Marcello. An excited upward rush of strings leads to him singing of his youth not being dead, to Musetta's waltz tune. By submitting to her tune he is admitting her power over him, but in such a burst of feeling it is hard not to see also the release of his real self. Like Rodolfo and Mimi, he finds himself in his love, even if the nature of his relationship is very different.

A band is heard; in a touch of realism, the composer uses an actual military march tune. The band crosses the stage, causing great excitement around the Momus, and the bohemians follow it. Musetta, in her one shoe, is carried in triumph aloft by Marcello and Colline; the loving couple Mimi and Rodolfo follow arm in arm. Musetta has solved a problem for the bohemians. Schaunard's funds had run out with the bill still to be paid – as a good bohemian he of course waited until after eating and drinking to discover this. Musetta has had their bill added to Alcindoro's and the act ends noisily as

In Act Two of *La Bohème,* Musetta leads on her 'Lulu', the rich and fond Alcindoro, while making a play for her true love, Marcello.

the old man returns to an empty Momus; empty, that is, except for the waiter and his sizeable demand for payment.

We know that Puccini had a liking for orchestral scene-painting at the start of his third acts. It allowed reflection on the audience's part. In *La Bohème* the device is used brilliantly. The curtain rises on a Paris toll-gate one freezing winter's morning as a huddled crowd wait to be allowed through the Barrière d'Enfer. A unison cadence covering several octaves loudly snaps our attention to order, then, in place of the bright, continuous full chords that introduced the cheery Momus, there come soft, detached, bare chords – cold, icy, damp, on flutes and harp over a trembling cello drone. The harp then plays, expressing the mood of the cold, huddled working people. An occasional note from the triangle emphasises the mood. Marcello's retitled painting hangs outside the inn, inside which Musetta is singing her waltz tune, now become a toast to wine and love.

Mimi enters, as violins softly play her theme, 'They call me Mimi' – a precarious note of warmth in all this cold. She coughs violently and asks for the inn where there is a painter working; a guard points out the place. She asks a servant to send Marcello out to her.

So, following her brief joy and confidence in the warmth of Rodolfo's love, Mimi is again the sick, lonely, reticent girl. Marcello enters, announced by the bohemians' opening theme high on woodwind over a bare-sounding string chord. He is surprised to see her and says they are staying at the inn where Musetta earns money by giving singing lessons (Musetta's theme is heard on the oboe). As Mimi coughs, Marcello invites her in but she says she cannot enter if Rodolfo is there.

As we last saw them walking off arm in arm, this may seem surprising – or a sign of a lovers' tiff. Mimi's worsening cough darkens the mood; that and the cold atmosphere on stage and in the orchestra make clear we are no longer in the land of lovers' comedies, and the workaday world has replaced Christmas cheer. If that were not enough, the sight of Mimi alone and diffident would make the scene chilly. Most of all there is her music, to be sung, Puccini instructs, in desperation as she begs for Marcello's help: .

O buon Marcello, aiuto! Aiuto!
(O good Marcello, help me! Help me!)

The youthful hopes and energies of the first two acts are to be paid for through the bitter experience of the fears and illness in the last two, and in some ways Act Three is the bleakest of all. Mimi describes Rodolfo's extreme jealousy. Marcello can only advise they live apart. He contrasts his own happiness with Musetta.

In view of his past quarrels and future bickering with her , this joy of his can only be put down to a sunny temperament. More difficult to understand is where Rodolfo's jealousy has come from. Nevertheless, jealous Rodolfo certainly is, as Mimi tells Marcello:

Mi grida ad ogni istante:
Non fai per me, ti prendi un altro amante
(He is forever telling me: You're not mine, get yourself another lover)

But when Rodolfo comes out, Mimi hides behind a tree, so he has no idea she is present. The gentle sound on violins of his Act One outburst of love 'Talor dal mio forziere' and the bohemians' theme suggest he is more in love than she believes. Speaking to Marcello, it does not take long for Rodolfo to say his anger is rooted in his fear for Mimi's health. He loves her like a flower, but she grows sicker day by day. His grief is expressed in a sad monotone which, unlike the repeated opening notes of 'Che gelida manina', does not burst into melodic warmth and life. His music seems to be dragged reluctantly from him as he sings of her illness:

Una terribil tosse
l'esil petto le scuote
(A terrible coughing shakes her delicate body)

and, despite his opening image of a fickle Mimi, he ends blaming himself. It is as if he is trying to find a way of putting distance between them for her good but needs to convince himself she is not worth his attention. Perhaps he even realises that a bit of infidelity with a rich lover might bring the means to save her, but he cannot bear to think of it in that way.

A fierce cough is unpleasant in any circumstance, but it is particularly inconvenient if you are trying to hide behind a tree, especially on a winter day. So it is not long before Mimi is discovered, as the orchestra in a mighty

Austrian soprano Lotte Schone as Mimi. She was also one of the first singers to play another of Puccini's girl-victims, Liù in *Turandot*, which she sang at Covent Garden, London, in 1927.

whisper plays Rodolfo's tune from his 'terrible coughing' lines, with the harp noticeably rushing up and down the chordal harmony. At just this moment the professedly happy Marcello hears Musetta's laugh – the woodwind merrily play her line – and assuming at once she is up to no good, he rages back into the inn while Mimi and Rodolfo embrace before she says farewell to him – to his surprise, it seems, even though he had seemed to think she would be off any moment.

Mimi says she will go back to her embroidery; but now the roses and lilies she had described in Act One as sources of joy are 'Flowers without life'. Even the source of her joy in life, Rodolfo, has just implicitly pronounced her death sentence. In a slow passage the violins repeat the tune of 'They call me Mimi'. The music slows and is subdued to nearly nothing as she tells Rodolfo:

Addio, senza rancor
Ascolta, ascolta
Le poche robe a duna che lasciai sparse
(Farewell without bitterness
Listen, listen
Gather up what little belongs to me there)

She lists what she has left with him; a small gold chain, a prayer book, her apron – and the bonnet which was bound up with her second act happiness. It is an old dramatic trick, to use inanimate objects invested with strong associations as a way to increase emotion. And here these memories produce the effect that is traditionally held to be the source of greatest sorrow, the memory of happy days in sad times; nostalgia and grief combined. Puccini uses an elegiac tune that leaps up midway only to fall slowly again. It is very lightly accompanied, with soft violin and viola chords as it opens (no lower strings to give their weight). A flute also offers a light, distant decoration to the list of objects which recall the lovers' happiness together as Mimi's vocal line attempts a lightness but is kept within quite a small range. Soon we are back to the bare anchor of string chords and the tune on low clarinet. Then a sudden brief, loud chord expresses her anguish as she nervously asks if he would like to keep the bonnet to remember her by.

A tune follows whose brightness has a forced quality. It dives down every few notes and is brought to a swift, firm conclusion. She repeats her goodbye: farewell to the joy of waking by his side, and farewell to his suspicions. By now Rodolfo and Mimi are recognisably the shy Act One lovers, while Marcello and Musetta are recognisably the fiery couple of Act Two.

The act moves towards its close with the contrasting pairs on stage; it ends with Mimi and Rodolfo leaving tenderly together, as they have done at the close of each act so far. They will stay together – 'For ever,' says Mimi; 'Till spring comes,' says Rodolfo. The delicate orchestral writing matches the mood of love that feels eternal in a life that is only too mortal. The two loud notes that close the act as it began perfectly snap shut the strong emotional space in which this long lovers' scene (again, not a formal duet) has taken place. Although Rodolfo's suspicions remind us of Mürger's Mimi and her friends, what Puccini has made of the act is a song of love and death which anticipates the final separation in Act Four.

Among the devices which give a sense of unity to material drawn from Mürger's kaleidoscope is the return to the scene of the first act for the last.

This also makes for a structure with two outdoor scenes surrounded by two confined indoors. And as the Latin Quarter and Barrière d'Enfer scenes contrast in mood, so there is a difference in mood at the start of the scenes in the artists' room. The music recalls us there with the bohemians' theme, but now shortened. Once again, Rodolfo and Marcello are there – but no 'Red Sea'. In fact, no work going on at all. No wonder Marcello tries to laugh off his friend's sighting of Musetta in a carriage. Rodolfo sees he is really angry, but then is taken aback when Marcello says he has also seen Mimi in a carriage, 'Like a queen'. Musetta and Mimi's themes underlie these references.

A moment's attempt at work soon wears thin and they blame their pen and brush respectively. The strings reveal the truth, bursting out with Rodolfo's Act One 'Talor dal mio forziere', the passionate theme set in the midst of 'Che gelida manina'. Then he softly sings, to a sad yet soaring line, about his loss:

O Mimi, tu più non torni
(O Mimi, you will never return).

As Rodolfo sings of her bonnet, clasping it to his heart, Marcello joins in, saying his attempts at landscapes are invaded by Musetta. The theme expressing their loves is echoed as they cease singing and is played high on a solo violin, lower on a solo cello, with harp chords punctuated by gentle woodwind. It is a sad and beautiful sound, just one example of how Puccini's sense of what works on stage is matched by both his supreme ability in melody and skilful orchestration.

Their attempts to cheer themselves up are helped by sudden upward rushes in the orchestra as Schaunard and Colline arrive – on cue, since Rodolfo was asking, 'Schaunard's not back yet?' In Act One the musician brought abundant food, now he arrives with just bread and a herring; a light yet suitable example of the way elements from the first act are recalled less happily in this final one. As good bohemians they make a joke of poverty and pretend to eat lobster and drink champagne. Sorrow in love is submerged in rumbustious company. They address each other as aristocrats. Schaunard is prevented from proposing a toast. Then the non-banquet is followed by a mock ball, the bohemian signature tune opening a fast dance section. The party is at its height as they clear tables and chairs. Schaunard provides musical accompaniment by singing to 'La', Marcello imitates a woman's voice, Colline leads the dance, then starts a duel with Schaunard involving cutlery as weapons. It all becomes very silly – and loud – when the party atmosphere is shattered by Musetta's urgent entry. Over a trembling drum and low strings she says Mimi is here and is very ill.

Rodolfo's concern is immediate and echoed in the screeching horror of the violins, for Musetta says Mimi cannot even climb the stairs. Rodolfo runs out to her. Schaunard and Colline settle the bed ready for her to lie upon as the trembling sounds in the orchestra rise and fall in dynamic. When she is told to rest, the cor anglais softly repeats, 'Si. Mi chiamano Mimi', its final note trapped in a sudden loud chord.

In the next few minutes a number of musical phrases will be wistfully recalled from earlier in the opera, depicting the stress of the moment, heightening the sense of sad loss and making more poignant, when it comes, the switch to new melodic material. After all the talk of parting in Act Three,

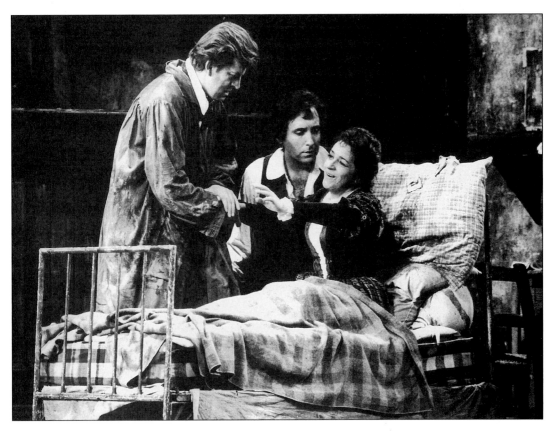

Mimi's death-bed reconciliation with Rodolfo, the famous final scene of *La Bohème*, an opera which also includes plenty of youthful life and high spirits.

now Mimi wants only to stay with Rodolfo and his agreement is immediate. Illica had fought for the poignancy of this reconciliation. It is why the librettist had insisted on the lovers parting, and this moment shows him to have been right.

Everyone is sympathetic. Schaunard laments aside to Colline that it looks as if Mimi will be dead in half an hour. Mimi's hands again are cold, now from sickness as well as room temperature. No delicate touching now; Rodolfo tries to rub them back to warmth; Mimi is beyond recovery. She forces herself to be bright in manner. Musetta offers to sell her earrings to buy medicine and to pay for a doctor. Apart from the flute giving life to Musetta's theme, the orchestra is reduced to almost nothing until Musetta decides to go and fetch Mimi's muff. It may, she says, be Mimi's last request.

Two new, sad, minor key tunes follow in quick succession. The first is a mixture of real sorrow and bohemian-like playing at sorrow. It is Colline's farewell to his great coat, with its vast, book-filled pockets. He sings:

Vecchia zimarra, senti
io resto al pian, tu ascendere
il sacro monte or devi.
(Dear old garment, attend, we must part. I stay here, you climb the sacred mount).

One reason for this aria is to give the singer playing Colline a solo; he has had little enough to do. But the best composers will make such practical considerations serve the work as a whole. Colline here helps bring about a situation where the lovers Rodolfo and Mimi are again left alone. It is another reflection of Act One, distorted by new circumstances. And its mock-tragic aspect sets off the more deeply tragic lines that Mimi is about to sing.

As Schaunard and Colline leave, tunes from Act One are repeated softly in an orchestral passage, again with harp chords. As they come to a rest Mimi asks:

Sono andati? Fingevo di dormire
(Have they gone? I was only pretending to sleep)

because she has so many things to say to him, or rather:

O una sola, ma grande come il mare,
come il mare profunda ed infinita
(One only, but great as the ocean, as the ocean deep and infinite.)

Though the melody of 'Sono andati' curls around, its tendency is to step down through an octave. This gives a poignant effect, emphasised by the string chords working under the tune and also stepping downwards under Mimi's words until at 'Come il mare profunda ed infinita' she leaps, vocally, up in her passion, a brief energy in which Rodolfo as passionately joins her.

Sei il mio amore e tutta la mia vita!
(You are my love and all my life)

She sings as she embraces him; he calls her his beautiful Mimi. But it has been her last burst of energy 'Do you still think I'm beautiful?' she asks and repeats her first act words to him: 'They call me Mimi – I don't know why,' to the familiar tune. As her energy fades her final words become detached. Rodolfo picks up another part of her first act song to sing of the swallow returning to its nest in spring, as he hands the bonnet, symbol of their love, to her and puts it on her head when she asks him to. As they recall their first meeting she sings 'Che gelida manina' but an attack of coughing suddenly interrupts the tender melody. Schaunard returns, soon followed by Musetta and Marcello with the muff, medicine and news – useless as it turns out – that the doctor will be coming. As she warms her hands in the muff Mimi is accompanied by flute and harp softly remembering 'Che gelida manina'.

Musetta heats the medicine – in this cold world there is just a spirit lamp for this – praying as she does so. Marcello shades the lamp to stop it being too bright for Mimi and Rodolfo, buoyed in his desperate hope by Musetta, sees a ray of sunshine fall on his beloved's face. He had first loved her in the cold moonlight; now he has to protect her from the sun which burns too fiercely for the dying girl. She slips into a greater darkness; amid all the activity Schaunard notices Mimi has died. Her last hesitant phrases have ceased. Rodolfo's protective screening, now useless, is accompanied by a single bass and a sustained low woodwind chord until four violins enter softly with a phrase from 'Mi chiamano Mimi'. Rodolfo senses from the others that something is wrong.

'Have courage,' says Marcello embracing his friend as the orchestra loudly declaims the tragic melody of Mimi's last song 'Sono andati?' and a phrase from Colline's 'Vecchia zimarra'. The opera ends on long, sad fading chords.

Chapter 4

Tosca

Tosca

First performed: Teatro Costanzi, Rome on 14th January 1900.
Conductor: Leopoldo Mugnone.

ACT ONE: *Rome, June 1800. Inside the church of Sant' Andrea della Valle.*
Angelotti, an escaped political prisoner, runs fearfully in, searching for the
key to his family chapel. His blond, blue-eyed sister Marchesa Attavanti has
left him female clothes as a disguise in which to escape. She has smuggled
these in while ostensibly coming to pray. While praying, though she does not
know it, she has been used as the model for a painting of Mary Magdalene
by the aristocratic artist Mario Cavaradossi.

As Angelotti hides in the Attavanti chapel, the church's Sacristan comes in
grumbling about having to clean Cavaradossi's brushes. He hungrily notices
the painter has not eaten his lunch yet – the basket is still there, full of food.
Cavaradossi returns and works on his picture, remarking how beauty can be
found in faces as different as those of the fair Marchesa Attavanti and his
own love, the dark-eyed opera singer Floria Tosca. Asking eagerly about the
food, the Sacristan leaves and Angelotti comes out, unaware anyone is
around. He recognises Cavaradossi; eventually the artist remembers the
fugitive. Both have progressive political sympathies.

Tosca's voice is heard; Angelotti hides – with the food Cavaradossi gives
him. When Tosca comes in, her notable jealousy has been aroused: the door
was locked, she heard voices. Was it a woman? She becomes even more suspicious when she sees the painting. Recognising the model, she suspects the
Marchesa has been with her Mario. He assures Tosca he loves her and she
admits it is love that makes her jealous.

When Tosca goes Angelotti returns. Cavaradossi tells him that instead of
disguising himself, he can go to the painter's estate and, in case of danger, can
hide in the well. They leave and the Sacristan prepares the choir for a service
to celebrate Napoleon's defeat. As they rush around, the new police chief,
Scarpia, enters with his men to search for Angelotti. The Sacristan is surprised to find the Attavanti chapel unlocked. The Marchesa's fan is discovered there. Scarpia is interested when he is told her picture is being painted by
Cavaradossi, a politically suspect character. The Sacristan notices the lunch
basket is now empty, and Scarpia deduces Angelotti has been there. When
Tosca returns, Scarpia uses the fan to rouse her jealousy. When she leaves he
has her followed. She will lead them to Cavaradossi, and Scarpia is convinced that he will lead them to Angelotti.

As the congregation gathers, Scarpia determines to execute Cavaradossi. This will rid him of a political opponent and help him conquer Tosca. Political will and sexual desire point the same way. Eventually he snaps out of these musings and joins the devotions of the congregation's Te Deum.

ACT TWO. *The Farnese Palace. Scarpia's room on an upper floor. Evening.*
Scarpia sits at supper, waiting for Tosca to be brought to him. Through the window is heard the concert the Queen of Naples is holding for General Mélas, who beat Napoleon. The policeman Spoletta reports they have not found Angelotti, but Cavaradossi has been arrested. When he is brought in, the artist mocks their failure to prove any charge; he also denies knowledge of Angelotti. Tosca arrives and is surprised to see Cavaradossi, who manages to tell her not to reveal anything of what she saw or was told in the church.

He is taken next door for torture. Scarpia says Tosca can prevent this. Eventually, despite Cavaradossi telling her not to reveal anything, she can no longer stand the thought of his pain and tells Scarpia about the well. Cavaradossi is angry with her, but when another of Scarpia's henchmen, Sciarrone, says the news from the front was wrong, that really Mélas has been defeated and Napoleon is triumphant, Cavaradossi lets out a joyful cry of 'Victory'. Scarpia denounces this as an act of treachery and says the painter will be executed for it. Cavaradossi is taken away.

Tosca pleads for his life but Scarpia makes it clear only her physical submission to him will save her lover. She is revolted and asks God why this is happening to her, as the drums roll and the gallows are built. Spoletta brings a report that Angelotti has killed himself to escape capture. Scarpia tells him to wait before proceeding with Cavaradossi's execution. He wants Tosca's answer. She silently agrees to Scarpia's sexual demand and Scarpia says the gallows will be replaced by a firing squad. There has to seem to be an execution but the bullets will be blanks. He tells Spoletta to prepare things as they once did for the execution of Count Palmieri.

Tosca demands a safe conduct for herself and Cavaradossi. While Scarpia is writing it she picks up a knife and kills him. She wrests the conduct from his hand and arranges the body with candles and crucifix.

ACT THREE. *The battlements of Castel Sant'Angelo prison, just before dawn.*
An unseen Shepherd sings a song of love and death. Cavaradossi is led up to the battlements. He declines religious confession but bribes the Gaoler to let him write to Tosca. Memories of their love overcome him. Spoletta brings Tosca in, then speaks to the Gaoler. Tosca meanwhile runs to her lover and shows him the safe conduct, and tells him how she killed Scarpia. She also tells him she has a carriage waiting for after the mock-execution. Again they declare their love and she tells Cavaradossi to make sure he falls in a realistic way. As the firing-squad line up she again urges him to act death well. He will, he says, copy her stage performance.

Cavaradossi is shot; Tosca admires his artistic fall. Spoletta keeps up a pretence by preventing the sergeant carrying out the shot to the head which assures the prisoner's death. When she is sure everyone has gone she goes to Cavaradossi and tells him he can stand up now and discovers he is dead. Spoletta returns to arrest Tosca for Scarpia's death. To prevent this she makes a death leap over the high battlements.

Tosca: The libretto

While he was working hard on the score of *La Bohème*, Puccini took time off to go with his partner Elvira to the theatre in Florence. The play they saw was by a long-established favourite of the popular stage, the French playwright Victorien Sardou. Set during the turmoil of the Napoleonic Wars it was called, after its lead character, *La Tosca*. The part had been written for the star actress Sarah Bernhardt, who was still performing it in Florence – not much to Puccini's liking. However he had expressed an interest in the subject some seven years earlier, in May 1889, only a couple of years after the play's première. At the same time he was also casting around among the leading writers of the time for a subject. He thought of Maurice Maeterlinck (*Pelléas and Mélisande* – snapped up by Debussy) and Emile Zola (*La Faute de l'Abbé Mouret*/'The Sin of Father Mouret'), as well as considering an opera on the life of Marie Antoinette.

Puccini had set *Manon Lescaut*, despite his rival Massenet. Then he had taken up *Scènes de La Bohème*, which Leoncavallo had claimed. In the case of *Tosca*, the subject was in the hands of a minor, if successful composer called Franchetti. Ricordi had already signed a contract with Franchetti and now tried to have it unsigned. Illica and he set up a meeting at which much shaking of heads, much tutting probably ensued as they tried to discourage the composer. They did not of course tell him they wanted the subject for someone else. No, they made the whole idea of an opera from *La Tosca* seem out of the question: all that historical background to explain, and a killer for a heroine. It would never do. No sooner had Franchetti surrendered *La Tosca* than Puccini took it up. It was a despicable trick, but it gave the world one of its most popular operas. Who can believe that nowadays audiences would be flocking to see Franchetti's *Tosca*?

In fact the dark passions of both Tosca and Scarpia were suited to the direction Italian opera was then taking. Verismo – realism, truth to life – was to opera what film noir became to 1940s American cinema: brooding, morbid, fuelled by hidden passions.

Realism itself, as an artistic movement, started off innocently enough in the nineteenth century, but once the idea of depicting the real surfaces of actual life took hold, two new tendencies developed. One was the insistence on exploring all the dark corners of human existence: realism meaning the kitchen sink instead of the drawing-room. Then it was discovered there is outer realism and inner realism. For example, a person receiving disastrous news might try to stay calm on the surface, while inside there is emotional turmoil. Depict the exterior and you are being true to the person's appearance but missing out their essential experience. Depict the interior and you need methods which will not reproduce the external surfaces of life. The depiction of this inner realism may not have a realistic surface at all.

In the preface which Émile Zola added to the second (1868) edition of his novel *Thérèse Raquin*, he outlined a kind of 'son of Realism' called Naturalism. In pursuit of this he created characters who had no free will at all, their actions being determined by their animal natures. Heredity, environment and circumstances, he believed, determine character and behaviour. The naturalistic artist is like a scientist; Zola examined his characters in the way a doctor might examine a corpse.

The preface was written to answer critics who attacked the novel for

In the preface to *Thérèse Raquin*, the French novelist Émile Zola set out the theory of literary Naturalism, which he went on to expound in his twenty-novel *Rougon-Maquart* series. Puccini for a time considered using one of these, *The Sin of Father Mouret*, as the basis for an opera.

immorality when it was first published in autumn 1867. Zola mines the depths of human emotions. Sardou, the prince of popular theatre, skirts about their dark side while wrapping them up in acceptable theatrical tinsel. He titillates audiences, but does not disturb them. It would be easy to criticise Puccini for choosing the synthetic alternative rather than the real, but Verdi himself had said that, had he been younger, he would have liked to compose a *Tosca*.

At any rate Sardou's play seemed to fit the mood and techniques of verismo. That movement itself began, coincidentally, in bohemianism, or as its restless Italian derivative was called, *scapigliatura*. This term meant 'untidy youth' but its overtones glanced back as far as Mürger's bohemians. Among the writers belonging to this rebellious artistic movement were Praga, one of the many librettists of *Manon Lescaut*, and Franco Faccio, who had also been involved with Puccini early in his career. Such *scapigliati* bequeathed to verismo its sense of rebellion and a fascination with morbid subjects.

The move from palaces to back streets in operatic subjects goes back at least to 1853 and Verdi's *La Traviata*, though the idea was really set going by Bizet in *Carmen* (1875). Verismo accordingly emerged in Italy in the 1870s and was in many ways an Italian equivalent to Zola: crime, sex, perversity, obsession and idiocy feed its plots on page and stage. This literary movement only hit opera in the 1890s, following Pietro Mascagni's adaptation of Giovanni Verga's story of rural jealousy and murder, *Cavalleria Rusticana* (the translation of its title as 'Rustic Chivalry' has an ironic suggestion of romance and nobility, neither of which is evident in the story). By this time

Giuseppi Verdi (1813-1901) was the undisputed master of Italian opera in Puccini's youth and early middle-age. His operas, from *Oberto* in 1839 to *Falstaff* in 1893, include *Aida*, *Rigoletto* and, in 1853, *La Traviata*, which introduced the promiscuous, consumptive heroine to the operatic stage, so prefiguring *La Bohème*.

literature itself was already moving away from verismo.

The low-life, often regional, settings of verismo operas led to the inclusion of popular musical styles in song and dances. Its violent, disturbing subject-matter led also to music of violent contrasts, sudden brief outbursts, vocal lines that follow the dramatic sense rather than decorate the words, and a continuous musical thread binding together elements of the various musical forms that had generally been separated in earlier operas. These included recitative, arias, duets, trios and choruses. The orchestra often commented on the emotions arising in the action. Musical lines were often brief, and interrupted before they reached an end. They often swung wildly in pitch, while vocal lines tended to include spoken or half-spoken exclamations.

Lesser composers follow the predominant style of the day (or one of its styles in the late twentieth century, which has seen so many schools coexist). Better composers absorb what they want for their own musical personality. This is why dozens of undistinguished operas would be merely labelled 'verismo' while *Tosca* is clearly Puccini, even though it uses some veristic techniques. On one other occasion at least he was to use these techniques, but he was never limited by them, just as Zola's novels rise beyond the limiting theory of Naturalism.

However much musical fashion may have helped swing Puccini towards a suitable verismo subject, we should remember that only a few years earlier, when the movement was already strong, he had turned away from *The She-Wolf* by the verismo writer Giovanni Verga because he felt that the story contained not a single luminous character. Sardou was too cunning a dramatist to deny his audiences the joy of such luminosity, and he certainly knew that to attract a major actress like Bernhardt he would need to provide a role with its moments of glory. Puccini might have been willing to wade into the mire of human vice, and indeed to have been fascinated by it; but he still wanted to have a star shining brightly somewhere. Sardou provided him with a perfect compromise.

Yet the dark side of human nature interested him too. It was a part of his own personality he called, in a classical term, Neronic. Cruelty, and sexual power in particular, fascinated Puccini; perhaps verismo was a good cover for exploring his personal interest in these things. There is a macabre face to the second act of *Tosca* which many have found distasteful. With the exception of one interlude, Tosca's prayer 'Vissi d'arte', which Puccini talked of removing because he felt it was too much of a set piece holding up the action, the act contained none of the famous tunes now considered the opera's highlights. Even the orchestral themes introduced in this act tend to be dramatic rather than melodic, or macabre like the death march that becomes important in the later part of the act. The outer acts are lit by the love duets of Tosca and Cavaradossi, but the central act is the black exposition of Scarpia's secret soul, and an important part of this is his sexual exploitation of Tosca. He is driven by his madly selfish desire for her.

Many women fell under the spell of the handsome, confident–seeming and famous Puccini during his middle years. Though he had many brief relationships, there is no evidence Puccini ever behaved in life as his Scarpia does on stage. But his Neronic tendency lies behind the series of vulnerable, emotionally manipulated heroines that runs through the operas. The major exception is the one-act *Gianni Schicchi*, which significantly is his only comedy.

Tosca is a highly religious woman – she even arranges a crucifix and candles around the body of the man she has just murdered – but she is in the middle of a passionate affair with a fellow artist and cannot wait until she has finished her vocal duties for the day so that she can hurry off to their little love nest. For a religious woman of 1800 on the stage of 1900 this was very free behaviour. Yet Puccini does not dwell on her faults, any more than he did with Mimi. Instead, he soon plunges his heroine into a nightmare where she is a sexual victim, while her own love is always presented as pure, spontaneous and deep. We remember again Mosco Carner's theory: Puccini needed to dominate and blame. Yet he did so where he loved.

Illica may have helped Ricordi make the play available for Puccini, but Giacosa was far from sure there was any point in using it. He found it strong in action (Illica's province) but thin on character and emotional detail (his own province). For all its theatrical grandeur, it was, he said, a mere series of duets. By August 1896 he was offering to resign from the project.

Deliver – or else, was Ricordi's reply, metaphorically waving the contract

A man about many towns, in many countries, Puccini was always an elegant, attractive figure, who had many brief affairs while his partner, Elvira, stayed at home at Torre del Lago

in the writer's face. Giacosa's next scheme was to blame Puccini for any delays. By 1898 he was complaining he was not being allowed to hear any samples of the music and offering a disclaimer: 'I've given you the lyrical expressions of feelings you demand but don't expect them to be dramatic, reveal character or further the action.' He correctly picked on the least interesting of the three central characters, Cavaradossi, for particular complaint about lack of depth. Cavaradossi may be the least interesting character, but he has some of the opera's finest tunes, from 'Recondita armonia' to 'E lucevan le stelle', plus the two love duets with Tosca. The co-creator of *Tosca* was the first of many people to say that the characters are unconvincing pasteboard types who could never hold a position on the stage without Puccini's music.

Puccini was working keenly on the score meanwhile. As always, he brought a musician's ear to the text, in July 1898 for example, turning a question into a more forceful exclamation in Act Two: 'Tu mi odii?' (You hate me?) became 'Come tu mi odii!' (How you hate me).

He also insisted on keeping the last line of Act Two, against his librettists' wishes; it is a line he had himself added. Looking at Scarpia's dead body, Tosca says:

E avanti a lui tremava tutta Roma!
(And before him all Rome trembled!)

The following month the composer was writing to Ricordi, insisting on some lines in the libretto being in a precise metre and saying that, whatever happened, certain lines must not be changed. Signs of the stresses between Puccini and his two librettists, and a tribute to Ricordi's diplomacy, can be read into Puccini's comment to his publisher that:

You have more success in receiving what you ask for, and more speedily than I do.

(Incidentally, in the same letter he also refers to alterations to the last act of *La Bohème*, an example of Puccini's continued interest in, and willingness to work upon, his operas after their opening.) He also wrote to a Roman priest, Don Pietro Panichelli, asking for help with the grand Te Deum which ends Act One of *Tosca*. As the clergy processed to the altar, Puccini wanted the crowd to be muttering prayers in a realistic fashion. What prayers, he asks the priest, would be used in such a service? His interest in realism goes, as always, with a concern for what is theatrical. Given a choice between clergy or congregation muttering these prayers, he chooses the congregation because their greater number will make a bigger impact. The lines spoken are:

Adjutorum nostrum in nomine Domini
Qui fecit coelum et terram
Sit nomen Domini benedictum
Et hoc nunc et usque in saeculum.
(Our help is in the name of the Lord
Who made heaven and earth
May the name of the Lord be blessed
Now and evermore.)

In the end Puccini found them for himself, but his contact with Father Panichelli produced information on ecclesiastical parades and costumes which was to be useful in the staging of *Tosca*. The *pretino*, or little priest, as Puccini came to call him, helped with a chant for the Te Deum and gave the composer a contact at St Peter's in Rome for advice on the bells to be used in the opera. Puccini was considerably mocked for his insistence on reproducing actual bell-ringing patterns for matins and for establishing the precise pitch of the deep-ringing bell, the *camparone*, in St Peter's belfry. It is so large that it is rarely used, even in major opera house performances.

A visit to Sardou in Paris on 13th January 1899 must have surprised the composer. Sardou was obsessed with the huge flag he wanted on the battlements of the Castel Sant' Angelo in his latest revival of the play, and clearly thought the opera should end with a bang rather than a whimper:

He wants that woman dead at all costs! . . . But I am still . . . for the end – well, rather delicate.

wrote Puccini. Sardou had been insisting Tosca should throw herself into the River Tiber. Puccini pointed out that, inconvenient though it undoubtedly was, the Tiber failed to flow past the appropriate side of the Castel Sant' Angelo. This mere matter of fact Sardou quickly brushed aside. Puccini was bemused:

> Curious fellow, all life and fire and full of historico- topo-panoramic inexactitudes.

On one level a realist, every plot step, entry and exit explained to the audience, Sardou was beneath the surface a creator of artificial confections. Yet he had encouraged Puccini all along and in the end was generous enough to say the libretto was an improvement on his own play.

Such congratulations were not universal and Puccini received an unpleasant shock when, in the afterglow of Ricordi's approval of both the first two acts, he sent the publisher most of the short Act Three for comment. The composer was very pleased with this act, a dangerously complacent state to be in as it turned out – and as his next opera would prove on a much more massive scale. Ricordi put it as politely as he could, which still left plenty of room for severity in a detailed critique such as no artist could be glad to receive – especially one who had a good opinion of the work being savaged.

What were Ricordi's objections? It is important to point out that he had not been sent the whole act: the opening section was still to be composed. So he was looking mainly at the Tosca-Cavaradossi duet. He thought it too broken up into small segments. And when he did come to a more smoothly flowing section, when Cavaradossi says that Tosca's hands, though they killed Scarpia, are sweet and merciful, the publisher recognised the tune as one taken from *Edgar*. Surely Puccini had progressed beyond such early work?

It took Puccini almost a fortnight to bring himself to reply. On 11 October 1899 he expressed his continuing surprise at Ricordi's comments. The *Edgar* criticism was easily disposed of. Only a few people would even recognise the borrowing, and the melody fitted the new situation better than Ricordi supposed. As for the duet, this no longer expressed the carefree meeting of two lovers, as in Act One. Tosca is preoccupied with the mock-execution. If any detail should go wrong, if any of the soldiers notice anything amiss, questions would be asked; real shots would be fired, and at any moment Scarpia's dead body might be discovered. No wonder Tosca cannot give all her mind to love.

The problems continued. Puccini himself was not happy with Illica and Giacosa's script for this section. It was too conventional, too fanciful, too divorced from reality. As for Ricordi's complaints about the music, Mugnone, who was to conduct the première of the new work, had approved of the score when he heard it. Perhaps that was the problem – Ricordi had only read the third act music; he needed to hear it. Puccini offered to run up and play through it on the piano.

The comments about the love duet are particularly interesting. No doubt Puccini could have provided long, glorious melodies and have pleased the public as well as his publisher; but he needed to be true to the psychology of the drama. Such compulsion marks out the artist from the opportunist. Because Puccini was able to fulfil his artistic response and still please opera audiences, he has been unreasonably accused of fakery. A rumour even grew up he composed his 'big' tunes to fit the sides of 78 rpm records. In fact it was just as recordings began to become a popular phenomenon that he stopped composing so many of these tunes.

Act Three had also caused a confrontation with Illica over a song that continues to be a point of contention, although for a different reason. Near the start of the act Cavaradossi is brought on to the ramparts and, before Tosca arrives, he sings what are almost his last words. They are set to one of the finest tunes in the opera: 'E lucevan le stelle' (And the stars were shining), in which he remembers meeting Tosca and how she ran up to him. His last thoughts are of sex and his girlfriend. Not at all the thing, thought Illica, for an aristocrat, an artist and a figure in an historical drama. What was wanted was a more formal statement, a philosophy of life and art. That was what Illica had provided, what the great Verdi had particularly approved and what the librettist was determined would stay.

No doubt his lines would have been perfect for Verdi's *Tosca*. But this was Puccini's *Tosca* and Puccini not only had ready the tune he wanted, he had supplied his own words to go with it. It was the sound of the song rather than the theoretical arguments that won the case for the composer; though only two of his words eventually survived when Giacosa penned the existing 'E lucevan'. In the penultimate line Cavaradossi sings 'muoio disperato' (I die in despair) – a suitably Puccinian sentiment.

For the première the singers had been selected as much for their acting as their musical abilities. They were of course good opera singers, but not all of the very high standard a Puccini first performance might by now have commanded. The composer did not want a stilted concert performance but a dramatic event. Hariclea Darclée (Tosca) was a good stage performer and a fine looking woman – Puccini had spotted her in the 1898 production of Mascagni's *Iris* in Rome; Darclée had also sung *Manon Lescaut* in 1894 at La Scala. As Tosca she wore an extravagant costume, the long silk dress rustling impressively as she moved, with a bouquet and imposing walking-stick. Nowadays, used to the less formal appearance of modern artists, we might find this excessively statuesque. It fitted the image better in 1900.

The stage director was Giulio Ricordi's son Tito, whose quick temper and self-assurance would cause problems later on between Puccini and the firm of Ricordi. But he was, in a time when theatre directors as we know them hardly existed (often the basic rule of stage movement was simply to give a wide berth to the star, whose brightness must be left to shine in isolated splendour), a conscientious, meticulous worker who took immense care over production effects, and who also rehearsed the performers into an understanding of their characters.

Like many directors he liked to work regularly with the same designer, in this case from La Scala. This meant Roman audiences being expected to spend the evening looking at sets designed by someone from Milan. Metropolitan indignation ran high. Unease grew and tensions heightened as egos off and on stage ground together in increasing conflict. Then some of the cast were sent poison pen letters threatening beatings up if the première went ahead. Mugnone, a senior Italian conductor, was not used to receiving a visit from the police a quarter of an hour before the performance was due to start. He had one on the first night of *Tosca* because of a rumour that someone was planning to throw a bomb in the theatre. If that happened, said the officer, Mugnone was to play the national anthem. If that happened,

Mugnone must have thought, he might well be dead. As the queen and leading politicians were going to be in the audience, stories about assassination attempts naturally started circulating. Unselfishly, Mugnone kept the police news from the composer.

Within seconds of the opera opening there was unusual noise in the stalls. This grew; Mugnone in the pit was scarcely less frightened than Angelotti on the stage. Before long there were audience cries to stop and bring down the curtain. Mugnone's nerve unsurprisingly snapped and he made his escape back stage.

It soon became clear that the disturbance had been caused, not by people intent on wrecking the performance, but by those intent upon watching it. Latecomers had insisted on edging along the rows to their seats. The early birds had strongly defended their right to see the opera undisturbed and the outcome had been a decision on the part of the audience to start all over again. When this happened, peace reigned in the auditorium and murder was properly confined to the stage. The queen turned out to be the latest comer of all, not arriving until Act Two. Puccini may have forgiven her; it was her bursary that had financed his Milan studies some twenty years before.

Although no bomb was thrown, some of those in the audience might have relished the chance. The crowd included Franchetti, who had been tricked out of writing his own *Tosca*, and Mascagni, who must have recalled that ten years earlier this theatre had seen his triumph with *Cavalleria Rusticana*. When he had been struggling to write this piece for a one-act opera competition organised by Ricordi's publishing rival Sonzogno, the only help Puccini had offered was the advice, 'Don't trust competitions.'

The whole experience hardly provided the security in which performers could fling themselves single-mindedly into their parts. This was no doubt one reason for the mixed press the opening received, though it was pointed out in *Il Corriere Della Sera* that Sardou's play, with its rapid action and morbid material, set Puccini a number of major problems. These, said the paper, he had overcome more successfully than he had the thinness of the characters and the melodrama of their situations. This last point is not always a drawback for an audience (melodrama had always been a popular form). And Puccini achieved far more with his music than covering the thinness of the characters.

Tosca was a popular hit at once, with a further twenty sold-out performances in Rome and an early entry into repertoires across Italy and abroad. It has remained a favourite with audiences and an attraction for sopranos (Tosca) and baritones (Scarpia). One of the most famous Scarpias of this century, Tito Gobbi, has written about the part's challenges and satisfactions.

The historical setting seems to have mattered little to Sardou, except as a theatrically colourful background, and even less to Puccini. He was never bothered by political matters. Still, it is there and the details help explain the significance of a lot that happens in the story. During the eighteenth century social pressures were increasing resentment against traditional authority by the mass of the people. This was partly the result of science's increasing importance. It was slowly putting God in the back seat. Belief in God was dependent upon the order of the universe. Because the stars were in the right places, God existed. In people's minds it was no longer the biblical God saying, 'Let there be light,' but the regular return of the sun's light declaring, 'Let there be God.'

If divinity was put in the broom-cupboard, so was the divine right of kings. Traditional religious props to royalty and aristocracy weakened. How, then, was society to be organised – what should be its basis? Reason came into play, and often suggested things might be organised very differently than, in fact, they were. This eighteenth century Enlightenment made religion and authority subject to scrutiny by scientific criteria.

If one group especially represented the new way of thinking it was the Frenchmen who collated the new knowledge into the bible of the scientific age, the *Encyclopaedia*. Of the men involved in this, one above all became for a long time linked with the spirit of critical, independent thinking. He was admired, hated and feared for his frequent outspoken defence of liberty, justice and reason.

François-Marie Arouet lived from 1694-1778 and became known by the name he gave himself, Voltaire. As a young man he was imprisoned for his attacks on the monarchy. Later his *Philosophical Letters* were banned in pre-revolutionary France, from which he was effectively exiled for much of his life. His scorn for the political and religious establishments was made more searing by his inventive wit and powerful mockery. For an upholder of state power like Scarpia, even a good twenty years after Voltaire's death, there could be no greater way of condemning someone than to say he was a follower of Voltaire. It is with this force that Scarpia talks of Cavaradossi in Act One:

Lui! L'amante di Tosca. Un uom sospetto!
Un volterrian!
(Him! Tosca's lover. A suspected man! A follower of Voltaire!)

---

neatly combining Scarpia's double motive for doing away with Cavaradossi: sex and politics.

The broad results of these eighteenth-century pressures can be summarised in two Beethoven works: *Fidelio* (his opera) and the 'Eroica' (the third symphony). In *Fidelio*, though the local representatives of authority may be evil, the ultimate power in the nation is held by a wise ruler who is a source of light and hope. And the later eighteenth century had given rise to such rulers, those who held on to power but wished to use it with justice: the enlightened, or benevolent despots.

As for the 'Eroica', Beethoven dedicated it to Napoleon as a hero of liberty; though he is said to have destroyed the dedication when he decided Bonaparte was becoming power-mad. It is hard now, especially outside France, to recover a full sense of what Napoleon stood for in the minds of political progressives throughout Europe in 1800, when *Tosca* is set. For many the French general carried the ideal of freedom against the forces of dark reaction, bringing a new era of liberty, equality and fraternity to Europe. The forces hostile to him represented the repressive old guard.

Scarpia's Italy was infected by the ideals of the French Revolution and Napoleon's onward march in its name. He had invaded Italy in 1796 and with the support of sympathetic Italians had maintained control for three years. However, the expense of feeding his army, combined with hostility from the Catholic church, resulted in his defeat.

In June 1800, when the opera is set, the anti-French Austrian army under General Mélas had made gains in battle but on June 14 Napoleon met the Austrians in the vital Battle of Marengo, mentioned in the first two acts of

Though Turandot was one of her early roles, Greek-born soprano Maria Callas later specialised in bel canto parts. In the 1960s she returned to Covent Garden as a splendid Tosca, a part suited to her fiery personality and skilful acting.

Tosca. In Act One the reactionary Sacristan enjoys gloating over Cavaradossi by telling him the 'good' news of Napoleon's supposed defeat; the apparent victory of the old forces is the reason for the Te Deum. It is also the cause of the celebration concert which is heard offstage at the start of Act Two. Then the police agent Sciarrone bursts in with the news:

A Marengo . . . Bonaparte è vincitor
(At Marengo . . . Bonaparte has won)

This is not just a theatrical trick; Marengo did originally go in the Austrians' favour and the French victory only became a possibility late in the battle. News travelled more slowly but no more reliably then than now. As a result of Marengo, Rome stayed under French influence until Napoleon's first defeat in 1814.

Sardou was used to writing on a grand scale. Puccini's three acts with nine characters were carved out of a five act play with twenty-three characters. Though much detail had to disappear, more than enough remained to cram into what is quite a brief opera.

Mosco Carner has detailed the changes made by Illica and Giacosa. The

The Corsican who became an emperor, Napoleon Bonaparte was in 1800 the most admired and feared person in Europe. His temporary conquest of Italy forms the political background to the intrigues of *Tosca*.

main plotting was the work of Illica, but in such a breathless rush of events it may well have been Giacosa, who turned his partner's work into verse and created the details of character, who was most frustrated by the continual need to move on to the next bit of action.

One way of abridging the dialogue was to précis a long speech into a short one. Carner's biography of Puccini places an extract from the play and its operatic equivalent side by side. The many blank spaces in the libretto column show how succinct the librettists were. Music creates its own pace and occupies the mind, so audiences do not ask about matters that otherwise might need explanation. And music can provide a sense of place, character and mood. Sardou's fame rested on a style of theatre, the 'well-made play', which expected every incident to connect, every exit and entrance to be motivated. He spelled everything out. Puccini did not have to.

The play describes Cavaradossi's background: he is an aristocrat, he is addressed as such and has inherited a fortune. His intellectual, left-wing credentials are summed up in the opera by Scarpia's one reference to Voltaire.

Illica and Giacosa were very skilful at fitting five acts into three. Act One of the opera is Sardou's opening act minus much of the circumstantial detail. Yet no-one who watches Puccini's *Tosca* ever asks why it takes such a short time from the discovery of Angelotti's escape to Scarpia and the police turning up at the innocent-looking Church of Sant' Andrea dell Valle. When he arrives Scarpia does not even know Cavaradossi is working there. Sardou, of course, explains all. It seems Angelotti bribed a prison guard to help him escape. Under torture this man revealed his escape plans. The playwright was undoubtedly correct to suppose his audience might ask about these things.

The writers of the opera showed a sure instinct in realising that their audience would not.

The opera largely ignores Sardou's Act Two, which takes place in another part of the Farnese Palace, away from Scarpia's quarters. Having rejected this large-scale act, the opera mainly relies, in Act Two, upon Acts Three and Four of the play, which focus upon Scarpia. Puccini's final act condenses the two scenes of Sardou's Act Five. In the first, Cavaradossi is in his condemned cell, refusing any religious rites. Tosca comes to him and tells him – as she does on the ramparts in the opera – of Scarpia's death, their safe conduct out of Rome and the need for him to fake his death convincingly. Then Cavaradossi is lead away, but Tosca and the audience stay in the cell, from where we hear the firing-squad's shots offstage. In the last scene Sardou creates the shock of the dead Cavaradossi's body and the final events as in the opera, except that in the play Spoletta refuses to believe Tosca when she tells him she has killed Scarpia. When he finds it is true and tries to arrest her, Tosca flings herself over the wall with a final taunt in the spirit of, 'You'll never catch me, fools.' The opera gives her the more religious and judicial:

O Scarpia, avanti a Dio!
(O Scarpia, before the throne of God!)

Tosca: The Music

Tosca has one of the most startling openings in all opera. The very loud chords of the first three bars have a cruel and oppressive quality even before they become associated with Scarpia. And it is right they assert his nature from the start; his presence will loom over all that follows. It would have been easy to express his character by music built on the more sombre-sounding minor chords; these are major chords, but given a relentless force and timbre. This is partly the orchestration, plenty of brass along with woodwind and strings, and it is partly a matter of the harmonic relations between each chord and its neighbours. Although they are hardly felt as a melody, they outline an interval in musical pitch known as an augmented fourth. It is equal to half an octave, but no major or minor scale uses it and the discordant effect it produces in traditional harmonies gave it from medieval times the name of 'the devil in music'. The twentieth century has incorporated it more into common musical language but previously its bare sound was particularly harsh; Saint-Saens used it as the sound of Death tuning his fiddle at the start of his *Danse Macabre*. And in *Tosca* it is the total distance between the notes at the top of the first and last of the 'Scarpia chords'.

After these, the music is faster and almost as loud – and action-packed – as Angelotti tumbles in confusion onto the stage. The rhythm linked with Angelotti is urgent and uneven until the music quietens and over a long held note on clarinet, bassoon and violas he sings of his fear, echoed in a brief, loud burst of the same hurried theme from the orchestra.

He finds the Attavanti Chapel and hides there, the long held notes being several times disturbed by scraps of rushing three-note figures on clarinets, then strings. As he hides there is another brief outburst, after which things calm down; there is no stage action until the pace quickens and violins step up to a bright, lolloping tune heard on the woodwind and representing the

Sacristan. A bit like the old courtier Polonius in *Hamlet*, this character can be played as all buffoon, or as someone with a more sinister side. He is returning Cavaradossi's paint-brushes. As the painter is working for the church, it falls within the Sacristan's duties to do this; but because Cavaradossi is a representative of all that the Sacristan hates and, probably, fears, he complains about his task while the orchestra plays on brightly enough. His tune also hints at his nervous facial tic.

As he notices the basket containing Cavaradossi's uneaten lunch, the Sacristan's greed becomes apparent. However, spiritual matters take over as three notes tolling on the bells indicate it is time for one of the set prayers of the day, the angelus, which the Sacristan dutifully intones over further bell notes, long harp notes and a light accompaniment. When Cavaradossi returns, asking him what he is doing, the Sacristan is able to assert his religious credentials by saying he is reciting the angelus – it is a matter of choice in each production whether his attention at this moment is on prayer, food or even the fair-haired Magdalene whom Cavaradossi is painting.

As violins and violas give a rapid, trembling accompaniment, oboe, cor anglais and clarinet play a short theme, opening with four equal descending notes followed by a quick three-note descent, associated through the opera with Cavaradossi – in the second act, it is even heard when Scarpia tries to force himself upon Tosca, taking Cavaradossi's place. It is a theme suggesting vigour and boldness more than art and beauty – these are reserved for Tosca's music. The urgency of his theme links Cavaradossi with his main part in the action as a radical political sympathiser rather than an artist. Horns and harp repeat the theme with some scurrying phrases from the strings, rising to a hint of what will become the love music.

Over a light string accompaniment – suggesting he wants to make the question seem casual – the Sacristan asks Cavaradossi about the unknown woman who has come and knelt before the Madonna on each of the last few mornings. It is, of course, the Marchesa Attavanti, covering her smuggling of escape materials for her brother. Cavaradossi smilingly recalls the lady's religious contemplation, with a pleasure which the Sacristan interprets as very physical. Then, as the Sacristan fetches a bowl of water to continue cleaning the paint brushes, Cavaradossi works on his painting of the fair lady. Her beauty makes him think of his own love, the dark-complexioned Tosca, whose image he has in a medallion. He compares the two and as he does so the music moves for the first time from a realistic description of events to a portrayal of feelings. How strange, Cavaradossi says, that beauty can be so apparent in faces so different:

> Tu azzurro hai l' occhio e Tosca ha l' occhio nero!
> L' arte nel suo mistero
> le diverse bellezze insiem confonde:
> (You have blue eyes and Tosca's are black!
> Art is a mystery which can mix different beauties.)

This song, 'Recondita armonia' (Strange harmony), is introduced by an orchestral passage with a lively yet wistful tune heard first on flutes then repeated on flute, clarinet and harp as Cavaradossi reflects on different styles of beauty. The harp remains prominent through the song, as so often in Puccini's many warmer moments. And as so often, what starts out seeming like a set-piece solo aria is interrupted as the Sacristan tuts over Cavaradossi's 'blasphemies'. These mutterings, each on a single repeated note, do not disrupt but reinforce Cavaradossi's soaring melodic line, which reaches its heroic top note as he finally says Tosca is his sole love.

Apart from being a fine singing opportunity, this statement that he loves only Tosca is made when he is effectively alone and able to tell the truth. It can assure us that there is no ground for her suspicions of him. We will be able to see how entirely these suspicions are whipped up by Scarpia's devious manipulation.

Violins, with chordal movement on the harp, continue the warm-hearted melody even as the Sacristan complains about atheistic dogs. The Sacristan finally manages to leave; clearly he wishes to have done with non-believers' paint brushes. He cannot resist a parting look at the enticing lunch-basket, though. This touches on his own appetite while enforcing the point that Cavaradossi is not hungry, for future plot reference.

When all has gone quiet in the church (violins repeat the four-note opening of Cavaradossi's theme) Angelotti comes out of hiding to a suddenly vehement orchestra. He gratefully recognises Cavaradossi, though it takes more time for the recognition to become mutual. Cavaradossi's greeting to him as ex-Consul of the Roman Republic briefly established under Napoleon's influence is echoed by the orchestra's loud statement of the Angelotti theme. Bassoon and cellos enforce the motif linked to the prison of Castel Sant' Angelo as Angelotti says he has escaped from there, but at once the other call on Cavaradossi's attention is heard. Tosca, from offstage, calls his name, 'Mario', flutes and clarinets hinting at the love music to come as she does so. Her presence brings a warmer timbre, gently curving themes which contrast with the male vigour and urgency so far dominant in the story. Warning Angelotti to hide, the first thing Cavaradossi tells him about Tosca is: 'È una donna . . . gelosa' (She's a jealous woman).

Again she calls, 'Mario' and woodwind offer the same three-note hint at the love music. To more hurried music Angelotti hides, taking the food his friend offers him. By now Tosca has found the door locked and is growing jealous; hence her forceful, unaccompanied repeating of Mario's name three times. However she enters to a new sound in the music, a warm, broad, gently curling tune on flute and cellos, which violins and violas accompany with lightly plucked chordal patterns, while other woodwind and the harp add harmonies. As this tune continues, Tosca asks why the door was bolted and, having heard whispering, she suspects a rival. She takes her flowers to the Madonna – so showing her other characteristic, religious devotion – as cellos and violins, two octaves apart, repeat the tune just heard while flute and clarinets now lightly offer the chord patterns.

She hopes to meet him after her evening performance; a brief glimpse of the Angelotti music recurs across the woodwind to show Cavaradossi's divided loyalties. She is unaware of his dilemma and simply feels happy, though in asking him to repeat that he is happy too, perhaps she notices something unusual.

Tosca goes on to speak of the small country house she has taken for them – 'la nostra cassetta' – and describes its idyllic qualities. There is a joyful drive to the tune she sings, with a characteristic turn when she speaks of it as a place of love and secrets: 'd' amore e di mister'. He clearly longs to join her, judging by his full-throated tagging on to her tune. For a time this mood continues but with Angelotti's music briefly interrupting the idyll is never secure.

This alternation – Angelotti v Tosca – continues as she notices the bright-eyed painting and recognises the Marchesa Attavanti as the model. Violins tremble low down as she asks if he loves the Marchesa and we see – and hear – Tosca in full fury.

Preparing for a big tune the orchestra hushes to a long-held string chord and Cavaradossi starts a new version of the lovers' music as he sings of Tosca's eyes:

> Quale occhio al mondo può star di paro
> all' ardente occhio tuo nero?
> (What eyes in the world can equal your fiery dark eyes?)

A single flute and horn play the tune as Cavaradossi sings it, and among the accompaniment there are periodic harp chords. As it proceeds, violins and oboe join the melody with contributions from other instruments. This sees Tosca overcoming her suspicions and the scene reaches a climactic love duet – the tune is the one hinted at earlier along with her cries of 'Mario'. It is first heard as Cavaradossi calls her his idol, whose every mood he adores:

> Mia Tosca idolatra,
> Ogni cosa in te mi piace;
> (My adored Tosca, your every passion delights me.)

Violins and violas enforce this, alongside spread-out rushes of flutes and clarinets and big harp chords. Once the beautiful tune is established it receives less support in the orchestra until the very end of the passage when strings, then harp also, help bring it to a strong close. Happy, Tosca leaves as the violins and violas play on the bridges of their instruments – to suggest her rustling skirt, said Puccini.

Cavaradossi – and the orchestra – turn to Angelotti in a fast passage with rushing woodwind and strings presenting the Angelotti theme. The love duet is softly hinted at as Cavaradossi warns that Tosca's honesty and devotion to religion make her a dangerous witness; she could not keep anything from her Confessor. Clearly the atheistic artist has no faith in the secrecy of the confessional. He then suggests Angelotti abandon his sister's plan for him to escape in the women's clothing she has smuggled into the Chapel – complete with fan – and that instead he hide on Cavaradossi's estate; they will meet after dark. Cavaradossi now has two appointments at night, with the demands of love and political sympathy pushing him two ways. As he speaks of the well they hear the Castel Sant' Angelo cannon fire. It is the signal of an escape. In the alarm this gives they do not notice that Angelotti has dropped the fan.

In this section too, Cavaradossi expresses his appreciation of the Marchesa's bravery. To repeated, quick woodwind chords violins, violas and cor anglais emphasise his sincerity by playing his theme. Then, as Angelotti specifically tells how she rescued him from Scarpia, the 'Scarpia chords' from the very start of the opera surge in and are repeated with soft menace as Cavaradossi prophetically denounces the sexual passion under the police chief's religious exterior.

Cavaradossi runs off with Angelotti, denying the Sacristan the pleasure of telling him the anti-Napoleon forces have (as it seems) won at Marengo. It is a very busy scene as the choir enter for the victory service. Clearly they are outside the Sacristan's control and are mainly happy that an extra service means extra earnings. But they are silenced surely enough – and the Sacristan

Antonio Scotti was a famous Scarpia, the character whose desire for sexual domination of Tosca is at first concealed beneath a cloak of urbane respectability.

reduced to a trembling jelly – when the now well established chords announce Scarpia's arrival with his police henchmen. He is the last of the three main characters to be seen and the one who is most heralded by music. When Scarpia complains the church is being treated like a fairground, the Sacristan's lollop of a tune is reduced to hurried scraps.

As the choir are sent to prepare and the policeman Spoletta searches the holy premises, Scarpia interrogates the quivering Sacristan, telling him there has been an escape (the Castel Sant' Angelo theme is heard again). Scarpia asks about the Attavanti Chapel and the Sacristan is amazed to find it unlocked and that there is a new key. Scarpia finds the fan, which he holds onto; then he notices the painting of the Marchesa/Magdalene and is interested to hear the name of the painter – Cavaradossi, the follower of Voltaire. The suspicious circumstances increase as a policeman brings in the now empty lunch-basket, which has been found in the chapel. Curiouser and curiouser. The Sacristan, fearful and no doubt feeling he has been denied the prospect of a bite to eat, splutters out that Cavaradossi had no key to take it into the chapel even had he wanted to – and he had said that he was not hungry.

Scarpia immediately realises what has happened: Angelotti came, saw and consumed. An upward rush of violins leads to the Angelotti theme. It is Scarpia's lucky day for now Tosca returns – to the love duet tune – looking for Cavaradossi but finding the police chief at his most unctuous:

Tosca divina
la mano mia
la vostra aspetta – piccola manina
(Divine Tosca, my hand awaits your tiny little hand.)

Then a soft, bell-like pattern on flute, clarinet, violins and violas hints at the church ceremony that is about to start. As the congregation assembles Scarpia drops hints about the painting and the fan (which he pretends was found where Cavaradossi had been working), provoking her jealousy. He wishes – with an underlying depth the innocent Tosca does not recognise in his apparent politeness – he could cheer her, though it cost him his life. He is far from cheering her up, but his life, did he but know it in this hypocritical moment, his efforts will certainly cost him. As Tosca becomes more furious the orchestra continues an onward surge to the climax where – the Angelotti theme reminding us how wrong she is – she calls her lover a traitor.

Scarpia pretends shock at her immoderate language in church, but as soon as she has left – the love music pointing out she is an innocent pawn – he has Spoletta follow her, to find Cavaradossi and therefore, he is sure, Angelotti.

Va Tosca! E Scarpia che scioglie a volo il falco
della tua gelosia. Quanta promessa
nel tuo pronto sospetto!
(Go, Tosca. And Scarpia lets fly the falcon of your jealousy. There is
great hope to be gained from your suspicions)

A theme swings in on strings and builds through the mighty Te Deum. 'We praise you O God' sing the congregation as Scarpia dreams of physically subduing Tosca, emphasizing that he is the real blasphemer. And, of course, he blames Tosca for turning his thoughts from God, before joining in the public praise as his brutal chords bring the act to a crashing end.

When Scarpia sent Spoletta after Tosca he arranged to meet his henchman in his rooms at the Farnese Palace, and there we find him, taking his supper, in Act Two. A brief theme – three descending notes heard three times at lower pitches – creates a sense of unease. Scarpia keeps breaking off from his meal. Fragments of the Act One love music suggest Tosca is on his mind, though the music itself cannot be on his mind as he has never heard it. Puccini's use of a tune with a character hitherto unconnected with it will emerge again in the final moments of the opera.

Scarpia has a window open. Dance music from the victory concert is heard through it, and he sends a note to Tosca to visit him. Love music is hinted at, but Scarpia sings in a scornful tone – she will come for her Mario's sake – it is a dry, lively accompanied passage, Scarpia's chords intruding. Then to a new tune he describes the kind of liaison he likes: a violent, power-seeking possession. God made various wines and women; Scarpia wants to sample them all, then be done with them. And he takes a glass of wine, as casually as he might a woman, for his pleasure. The climax to which this builds peters out as Spoletta returns to face his boss's anger for failing to find Angelotti.

Fortunately for himself, Spoletta arrested Cavaradossi, apparently for no better reason than that he was around at the time. Scarpia ominously demands the torturer Roberti be summoned, as well as a judge. As the prisoner and the others arrive, two soft, yet contrasting, sounds are struck up. The second is the off-stage chorus, representing life and public celebration going on unaware of the dark passions and deeds in Scarpia's room. And representing that darkness and its morbid outcome, just before we hear the offstage chorus, the flutes offer a low, silvery yet ominous tune that will be heard many times again: a kind of tiny death march. The tune covers very little space in terms of musical pitch, something that increases its enclosed, forbidding effect.

There is very spare orchestral accompaniment here – a few lower string notes and, mainly, repeats of the flute tune. The main effect is the contrast of the enjoyment offstage and the interrogation onstage proceeding independently of each other. Cavaradossi denies the unsubstantiated charges made against him and laughs at the police.

Violins join in with a restless musical figure. Flute and clarinet add the death march as Scarpia grows angry at his prisoner's mockery. For a few seconds the orchestra lies silent as the offstage chorus ends. When it returns it is with a loud growl and trembling strings. The low woodwind and string basses add to that an unpleasant three-note descent which is almost a back-to-front version of the Scarpia chords. As the verbal combat proceeds, strings continue trembling and the threatening phrase is heard going up and down. Then Tosca runs in – one of the love themes is heard, but subjected to the violins' trembling – and Cavaradossi manages to warn her against telling what she heard in the church earlier. 'Or they'll kill me,' he warns, and indeed as Scarpia solemnly advises him:

Mario Cavaradossi
qual testimonio il Giudice v' aspetta.
(Mario Cavaradossi, the judge waits for your testimony).

the dead march is announced loud for the first time, on oboe, cor anglais, horn, trumpet and trombone, with strings adding detached, scurrying figures. It is the dramatically terrifying sound of doom. Scarpia tells the torturer to proceed as normal but also to expect special further instructions. As the prisoner is led off, all grows calm. In this mood the police chief offers a friendly chat to Tosca, presenting a forthright surface:

Ed or fra noi parliam da buoni amici. Via quell' aria sgomentata . . .
(So, let's talk like good friends)

and to the same tune he asks her about the fan. It's forgotten, says Tosca, her jealous fit over. When his questions produce nothing, Scarpia puts pressure on her by calling his henchman, Sciarrone, and dropping into his civilised chat with Tosca the fact that next door her lover is being tortured.

She has naively assumed Mario is having a similarly civilised questioning next door, and is horrified. 'What's happening in there?' she demands. Scarpia luridly describes Cavaradossi tied, his head being crunched by spikes. Violas dash out an urgent rhythm, while a low, sinister theme, repeating Scarpia's vocal line, sounds on violins, cellos, cor anglais, bassoon and trombone, its melody also picked up by other woodwind.

'What's happening?' Tosca repeats, near panic, her voice flying up an

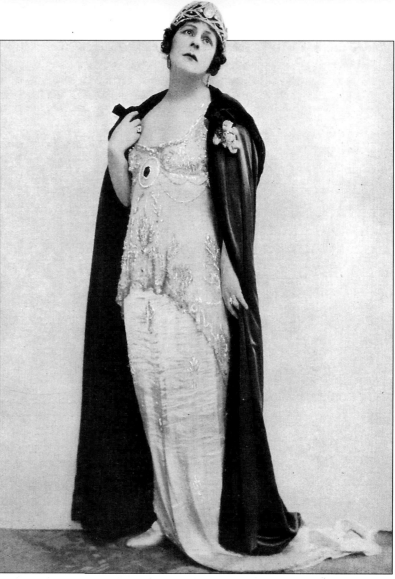

Besides her American engagements, Canadian soprano Louise Edvina was a regular performer at Covent Garden before and after World War I. Her main Puccini role was Tosca (pictured here), which she sang at the Metropolitan Opera House, New York, and used for her farewell performance at Covent Garden.

urgent octave. Then Cavaradossi is heard calling out in true verismo agony from the torture chamber. When Tosca cries out for mercy, Scarpia tells her she can bring it all to an end and he orders Sciarrone to desist.

But Cavaradossi calls to Tosca to continue saying nothing. By now she is under no delusion that Scarpia is a decent person, though she still has not realised the extent of his viciousness. He, meanwhile taunts her:

> Mai Tosca alla scena
> più tragica fu!
> (But Tosca on stage was never more tragic.)

In fury as she backs away from him, Scarpia orders the door to be opened so she will hear Cavaradossi's agony more clearly. He urges Roberti on to more severe action as the sinister theme returns. It is the more alarming, this time, for its relentless, even pace and, like the dead march, it is bound within a small range in pitch, though as it proceeds the orchestra includes rushing scales, scurrying figures between each note of the theme building a tension which reflects the turmoil Tosca is experiencing. Finally she bursts out:

> Ah! . . . cessate il martir!
> è troppo soffrir!
> (Ah! . . . stop the torture. It's too much to bear.)

This is sung to a tearing, violent tune that leaps an octave down and them not quite an octave back in each phrase, theatrically displaying Tosca's torment, her cries also being screamed out by woodwind, horn and strings.

She is shown her bloodstained Mario, who still refuses to let her tell anything – though by asking his permission she is inadvertently confirming Scarpia's suspicion that Cavaradossi has something to hide.

Tosca is learning about the real world of power politics, but she tries to redress things with an innocent plea, 'What harm have I ever done you?' as she breaks down. Spoletta prays, but as the torture starts again – Scarpia is using it now more for its effect on her than on Cavaradossi – five loud orchestral chords lead to a shuddering on strings against which the demoralised Tosca reveals that Angelotti is hiding in the well. The spare orchestra, with thudding timpani, fades out.

Only for a moment, though. The dead march returns on bassoons and violas, with flutes and oboes soon joined by other woodwind and plucked low strings offering accompaniment as Cavaradossi is dragged in, for he is no longer able to walk. Even now the violins manage softly to reintroduce a line from the love music, Cavaradossi's first act praise of Tosca's beautiful eyes. The harp and a cello decorate this with spread chords. It is disrupted when Scarpia sends his men to arrest Angelotti, making Cavaradossi realise Tosca has given him the secret. The orchestra bursts out violently at his realisation. But there need be no more than a lovers' quarrel to end the story. Scarpia might arrest Cavaradossi for assisting an escaped prisoner, but he has achieved his immediate purpose. It is an awkward moment. Somehow the story needs to lead Cavaradossi to his death.

The device used is the sudden, coincidental arrival of news from Marengo. Sciarrone announces Napoleon has, after all, been victorious. This puts new strength into Cavaradossi, who celebrates by a victory shout: 'Vittoria! Vittoria!' at, or near, the top of his voice, and with much orchestral support he invites vengeance against tyranny. Even Tosca sees the danger and tries to quieten him. Tyranny's representative is there in the room, and takes the chance to sentence him to death for treachery in supporting Napoleon, the enemy of the state.

Once again the prisoner is taken away, but Tosca is told to stay. During the Cavaradossi/Scarpia confrontation the orchestra has provided suitable loud, busy sounds; now it quietens for the intimate horror of Scarpia's bargain. He returns to his meal, thereby focusing attention on the table, which will soon play an important part in the action. Earlier music – the three descending three-note phrases linked at the start of the act with Scarpia's meal, the conversational tune used before Tosca became aware of the torture – reappear. Scarpia can afford to spend time letting Tosca's nerves wear thin. He seems to have forgotten the Marengo news, which is surprising because it could have a severe effect on his own future. Or rather Sardou or Puccini has forgotten it. It has served its turn; passions, not politics, are the interest here.

Tosca is not fooled by his casual manner any longer. 'How much?' she asks, expecting him to name his bribe. He just laughs and in a wide-ranging tune that opens up his feelings he reveals his desire for her:

Già mi struggea
l' amor della diva!
(How I have groaned with love for the diva!)

– though he does not tell her how destructive and egotistical his passion is; there will be no wooing and winning, just conquering and abandoning. What he says is enough to make Tosca, to the leaps of the 'tearing' tune, threaten to jump out of the window. This of course is prophetic of her final fate, though she does not know it. What stops her now is the reminder she would be leaving her Mario in Scarpia's deadly hands.

So she decides to appeal to the queen. That, says Scarpia, will do no good. The queen has no power to prevent the execution. Defeated at each turn, Tosca collapses. Scarpia comments:

Così, così ti voglio!
(That – that is how I want you!)

– defeated, loathing and despising him, but unable to put up any resistance. As she calls for help, emphatic violins, high woodwind and trumpet blast out again – uselessly – the tearing theme. To stress her predicament, the sounds of an execution in preparation emerge in a sudden menacing quiet – a march-like percussive rhythm and a detached, fatal-sounding figure on cellos and basses. Time is ticking away, as Scarpia reminds her, and as these rhythmic figures insist.

Scarpia leans casually against his table observing Tosca. The orchestra dies away, with just two clarinets fading out on a long chord – a sign Puccini is coming to a set piece. This particular piece he once thought was too set and considered removing it. Yet the words Tosca is about to sing justify themselves in the dramatic action. Having found all human powers against her, she turns to prayer. Amid aggression and urgency, she provides a quiet contrast and the still, sad music of humanity.

Her song starts with a descending four-note phrase, a different version of the pattern beginning the theme linked with her lover and fellow-artist Cavaradossi. And art is part of her subject:

Vissi d' arte, vissi d' amore
non feci mai male ad anima viva!
Con man furtiva
quante miserie conobbi, aiutai . . .
(A life of art, a life of love has not made me do evil to any creature!
And in secret the poor and needy I have helped.)

After the first lines, as if to remind us Tosca's life is indeed bound by art and love, flute and cello play the warm tune which accompanied her first appearance. The harp typically sprinkles chordal patterns across the music, then violins and violas join the tune. Tension rises as she asks God why he rejects her in her suffering and her voice rises to high notes of pain as the tearing theme with its octave and near-octave leaps makes a brief appearance.

Scarpia lets her talk, unmoved. 'Decided?' he asks. After we have just heard Tosca's feelings so eloquently expressed, his cold response is brutal, although it may not be true coldness. He may be exulting in her powerless writhing.

After the lushness of 'Vissi d' arte', Scarpia's response and her pleas to him are lightly, desolately accompanied. Her plea, 'Vedi' (Mercy) is a falling phrase echoed by bassoon then harp (which has naturally been busy rippling harmonies through 'Vissi d' arte') and repeated in Tosca's melodic line.

A true verismo passage follows, all trembling strings and sudden loud chords, as Scarpia's confidence is expressed in leaping fragments and he tells her she can gain so much – her lover's life – by so little, her body. So obsessed is he with his prey that even Spoletta's news of Angelotti's suicide barely concerns him, though the orchestra pays tribute with a sudden burst of Angelotti's music. Scarpia detains Spoletta, giving Tosca her last moment to decide. She cannot speak but nods agreement, hiding her face in tears.

Scarpia explains it must seem as if there has been an execution, but instead of a hanging there will be a firing-squad. He gives her to understand that will mean blank bullets, although anyone less grief-struck than Tosca might notice an unsettling significance in the way both men emphasise it will be handled, 'as was the case with Count Palmieri' – 'Come facemmo del conte Palmieri' – all this over shuddering strings and a series of low wind chords.

From the dead march on, the tunes in this act have been agonised or ominous, apart from the interlude of 'Vissi d' arte'. As Scarpia turns to Tosca, ready to take his prize, the violins and violas begin a new, funereal theme reflecting Tosca's misery. Little is said – or sung – as might be expected in such a situation. He is writing the safe conduct, which Tosca has demanded and which will see her and Mario out of Rome. And as he writes she notices a knife on his table. Very carefully she picks it up and hides it about her. As he hands her the safe conduct she stabs him. The orchestra, of course, screams out with him – no harp here – and both her cry of revenge: 'Questo è il bacio di Tosca!' (That's Tosca's kiss for you) and Scarpia's calls for help are spoken – or shouted. Things quieten as he grows weaker and Tosca gloats in hatred and revenge, the recently heard 'misery' theme now hurled out violently on cor anglais, clarinets, bassoon and strings.

As she stands over him Tosca sings, on one note, the last line of the act; Puccini's own words, which he retained despite his librettists' doubts:

E avanti a lui tremava tutta Roma
(And in front of him all Rome trembled.)

a line either of wonder such a thing could have been, or contempt for the sort of person he was. The act ends with two finely contrasted actions. First Tosca has to force Scarpia's dead hand open to retrieve the safe conduct. Then before leaving, her religious faith takes over and she arranges candles and crucifix around the body. A series of soft chords create the time for her to do all this, interrupted by one thrillingly loud orchestral chord.

Once again Puccini opens the third act with a prelude. Horns boldly announce a striding theme, but the martial effect gives way to a pastoral feel as an unseen Shepherd Boy sings innocently of love and death to a tune introduced by a gentle orchestral sound. Dawn starts to break as he sings and the carefully researched matins bells are heard in the distance. But reality returns with the dawn, and the Scarpia chords keep intruding unexpectedly despite the fact that Tosca, who might be thought to be preoccupied with the important official she has just murdered, is not there. But Puccini's method is to point the situation out to us, not to explore the mind of a specific character.

The closing moments of *Tosca*, Act II, at Covent Garden: Scarpia's body, bearing a crucifix and surrounded by candles placed by the religious Tosca, who has been driven to stab him to death and now looks back in horror as she flees the scene of the crime.

Cavaradossi is brought up. The Gaoler who comes too carries a lantern, so it is not yet fully day. As the procession arrives, the strings quietly introduce the melody of Cavaradossi's next song. Puccini often uses the orchestra to prepare for a vocal melody, and this one has become quite an old friend by the time it is sung. To keep the vocal interest, the offer and refusal of a priest is handled simply, though a cello reminds us – and Cavaradossi – of his love. A couple of solo violas recall the first act love duet, before shifting to the leaping 'tearing' tune of Act Two.

Then a clarinet picks up the tune heard earlier on violins – Cavaradossi's first words are uttered on a single tone while the melody stays on the clarinet: 'E lucevan le stelle' (The stars were shining) and he recalls his meeting with Tosca. It was here that Verdi, and others, had wanted a reflection on life and art. More realistically, if less nobly, Puccini chose to give his hero some romantic memories before he dies. As he drifts from his last letter to Tosca into his memories, his mind becomes more fully preoccupied and he takes over the magnificent tune of love and regret, with Puccini's own two words 'muoio disperato' (I die despairing) near the end. It is the raging cry of a man forced to leave a life he enjoys, and more exactly, the woman he loves.

Loud, urgent orchestral chords depict Tosca's hurried entry and Cavaradossi's surprise at her manner and the safe conduct. The love duet is referred to in frantic orchestration. Scarpia's chords sound quietly as Cavaradossi finds it difficult to believe in Scarpia's first-ever humane act.

Tosca quickly tells him it was Scarpia's last act too and describes the murder. As she says the Madonna did not help her – Tosca retains her religious scruples – woodwind and violins briefly remind us of her first appearance, when she was still naive. Violas, cellos and basses recreate the drum effect as Tosca talks of hearing the execution drum roll. Scarpia's leaping confidence and her own misery are also recalled by the orchestra. When she says her hands were spattered with blood, Cavaradossi says they are pure and white, in the tune taken from the last act of *Edgar*: 'O dolce mani' (O sweet hands). It forms a lyrical serenade, until woodwind and strings repeat the misery theme as Cavaradossi concludes his praise of her hands by hailing them as victorious.

Tosca turns to practicalities, in a forthright, hopeful tune:

> Senti . . . l' ora è vicina; io già raccolsi
> oro e gioielli . . . una vettura è pronta.
> (Listen . . . dawn is coming; I have collected my gold and jewels
> . . . a carriage is ready).

– and she tells him about the false execution. For a time, matters seem hopeful. He tells her it was the thought of leaving her that made death seem so terrible. She looks to happy times ahead, away from Rome. But this love scene is also played out amid an anxiety not there in the innocent hour of Act One. Tosca keeps repeating the need for his fall to look like a real death.

The firing-squad arrives, its proximity signalled in a brief, sombre falling figure heard first on flute, joined by clarinet. This is the last of the brief, curling minor key musical figures that have built up the sombre mood of the latter part of the opera – the dead march and the misery theme among others.

Cavaradossi refuses a blindfold – he wants to see his Tosca. She cannot wait for the charade to be over. Spoletta stops the Sergeant delivering the final shot to the head in order to assure death and Tosca's impatience takes her racing up to her lover as the new death figure in the music is blasted out by clarinet, horns and upper strings. This tune quietens as the firing-squad recedes and the still confident Tosca warns Mario not to move yet. When the coast is clear, Puccini lets her sing her exhortation to Cavaradossi, 'Quick. Mario. Mario. Be quiet. Let's go,' unaccompanied. It helps to make her more exposed when she kneels and discovers what 'Like Count Palmieri' really means; her Mario is dead. As she cries out the orchestra weighs in with a huge chord and rushed, repeated upper string notes.

Sciarrone arrives with news of Scarpia's death. Spoletta runs to arrest Tosca, but she evades him by throwing herself over the battlements with the final challenging cry :

> O Scarpia, avanti a dio.
> (O Scarpia, before the throne of God.)

As she sings her last, high note the orchestra – woodwind, horn, trumpet and strings – play with maximum force the tune of 'E lucevan le stelle'.

Musically, this ends Tosca on a tragic yet exalted note; what a tune it is! But it has caused dramatic problems for some people. The argument is that 'E lucevan' has been Cavaradossi's tune. He sang it when Tosca was not present. It has no connection with her; she has never heard it, so it should not be her epitaph now. Some go further and tell us that Puccini ought to have ended with a repeat of the Scarpia chords. This would fit the dramatic situation, for Tosca has just hurled a defiant challenge to meet him in front of God, and from the opening chords of Act One Scarpia does permeate the action.

More candles for Tosca: the Italian soprano Renata Tebaldi was also a notable Mimi at the post-war La Scala, Milan. She sang Tosca at Covent Garden in the mid-1950s.

But the opera is not called 'Scarpia'. Puccini could find plenty in Scarpia's dark passions to identify with, but Tosca is his luminous heroine and her dying thoughts are very likely to be of her lover. Her bold leap requires strong music, but the crushing chords would have suggested Scarpia triumphant; the point is lovers may be killed but the capacity for love cannot. Even in their contrasting deaths, Cavaradossi's through shameful deception, Tosca's in defiant independence, liberty and life cannot be finally overcome.

Perhaps if Puccini had given Cavaradossi a long song on life and art he would have written a better Verdian Act Three. If he had made the closing bars of music reflect a theme previously associated with Tosca, he would have written a better Wagnerian Act Three. But people who want last acts by Verdi or Wagner would do better looking in operas by those two composers. Puccini offers an exhilarating finish which is true to his own concerns.

Surely this opera marks a difference, though? Tosca is no wayward Manon Lescaut nor a vulnerable Mimi. On the surface she is more assured,

Luigi Illica (1857-1919) had a fiery temperament and several times during their collaboration came close to parting company with Puccini. After the death of Giuseppe Giacosa in 1906, Illica never worked with the composer again.

but in the world of Scarpia's politics she is innocent and vulnerable. Beneath apparent differences, the common pattern of the Puccini heroine continues.

Chapter 5

Madama Butterfly

Madama Butterfly

First performed: Teatro alla Scala, Milan on 17 February 1904.
Conductor: Cleofonte Campanini.

The leading opera house in Italy, Il Teatro alla Scala was the great institution hovering over Puccini's Milan student days. Later it was the scene of his greatest humiliation with *Madama Butterfly*, but when he died La Scala closed in tribute.

ACT I: *A house on a hill, Nagasaki, 1904.*

A marriage-broker, Goro, shows US naval lieutenant Benjamin Franklin Pinkerton round the house he has taken on a 999 year lease, for himself and young Cio-Cio-San, also known as Butterfly, whom he is marrying. When the American consul, Sharpless, arrives, Pinkerton makes it clear he regards the marriage as temporary and Sharpless warns him not to trifle with Butterfly's affections. The bride arrives, with friends and relations, but as the marriage ceremony proceeds her uncle, the Bonze, enters and curses her for deserting her religion. Pinkerton orders him out, but Cio-Cio-San's family are shocked

by the curse and the news that she has taken up her husband's religion. At their departure, she and her husband are blissfully happy together and in love.

ACT II, PART ONE

Three years later Pinkerton, who left soon after the wedding day, has not returned. Cio-Cio-San's maid Suzuki tries to persuade Butterfly that he never will, but she cannot believe this. She is confident he will come back, as promised, when the robins make their nest. Goro is also aware of the reality and tries to induce Butterfly to marry a rich Japanese suitor, Prince Yamadori. Sharpless is concerned for her, and tries to persuade her the new marriage would be a good idea; but Butterfly maintains Pinkerton will return and is interested only in things American. Sharpless produces a letter from Pinkerton; he wants to break gently the news that the lieutenant now has a 'real', American wife, Kate, but as soon as she hears of the letter Butterfly becomes so excited Sharpless has no time to tell her this before she reveals that her brief time with her husband has produced a child. He is called Trouble, but when Pinkerton returns, he will be renamed Joy. An American ship arrives in Nagasaki harbour; she sees it is the *Abraham Lincoln*, her husband's ship and Butterfly calls Suzuki to bring flowers to spread over the floor of the house to greet her husband. Behind the *shosi*, or screen, Butterfly, Suzuki and Trouble wait for Pinkerton to climb the hill to their house. Offstage, a chorus of humming can be heard as time passes.

ACT II, PART TWO: *Dawn.*

The vigil continues and Pinkerton does not arrive. Suzuki manages to persuade her mistress to go and lie down, just before Pinkerton and Sharpless come in. Kate, the Lieutenant's wife, is with them but stays discreetly outside. Having told Suzuki what she already suspects, they ask her to help them persuade Butterfly to give up Trouble so Pinkerton's boy can have a secure, American upbringing. Overcome by shame, Pinkerton goes. Butterfly comes in, wonders who the strange woman is, then realises the truth. When Kate asks for the boy, Cio-Cio-San replies his father must collect him in half an hour. She sends Suzuki and the boy outside, but suspecting what might happen Suzuki pushes him back in. Butterfly blindfolds him and kills herself with the same ceremonial sword her father had used for his own death.

Madama Butterfly: The Libretto

It is all too easy to see a dead composer's career as a smooth progression – as if each work led naturally to its successor and subjects were picked like the ripest cherries from an abundant tree. In fact the excitement and fatigue of bringing a full-length opera to completion can leave the composer exhausted, yet eager to begin the creative process again. But the early stages have little of the sense of purpose being fulfilled that grows later on. Ideas that seem to offer scope turn out to be blind alleys, to give rise to overwhelming problems or simply to lose their initial interest.

Puccini's projected operas after *Tosca*, in the dawn of the twentieth century, ranged from ancient Rome to a Russian prison camp. He considered a modern play, *The Weavers*, by a German realist playwright Gerhart Hauptmann. Ricordi, possibly thinking there was a useful blend of creative

Speed and mechanical vehicles delighted Puccini, here slicing through the waves of Lake Massaciuccoli near his home in Torre del Lago.

and commercial scope left in the French Revolution, reintroduced the idea of an opera about Marie Antoinette. The composer – for neither the first time nor the last – tried working with the leading Italian poet Gabriele D'Annunzio. This time, as always, the plans came to nothing.

Perhaps it says something about limitations in Puccini's taste that as well as D'Annunzio he turned down projects based on respected classic and modern authors in favour of a one-act play by a confectioner of high-emotion, insubstantial pot-boilers, an American equivalent to Sardou called David Belasco. By doing so Puccini exploited a popular vogue of some years' standing, a taste for sob stories from the orient.

Belasco's play had already been a success in New York when it opened at the Duke of York's theatre in London's West End in late April 1900. It was still running there when Puccini visited London to work on the Covent Garden production of *Tosca*. In a double-bill with a flighty little piece by Jerome K. Jerome (of *Three Men in a Boat* fame), Belasco's *Madam Butterfly* made an instant impact on the composer, whose lack of English meant he probably understood virtually none of the dialogue. It was the look of the thing. If it managed to work a powerful spell on him in these circumstances, it was clear he had found a story with undoubted theatrical force.

In every way – its title, its story, its music, its hit song 'Un bel di' (One Fine Day) – *Madama Butterfly* is the very essence of popular opera. *Tosca's* closing moments may provide a more celebrated, spectacular death scene, but *Butterfly* is more consistently moving, even more than *La Bohème* where grief takes its place alongside scenes of genuine merriment in roughly equal proportions. While *Bohème* ends sadly, it is not tragic, for tragedy implies that the unhappy ending arises from the personalities of the major characters. The bohemians suffer through poverty, cold and disease. Butterfly's death comes because of the sort of people she, and Lieutenant Pinkerton, are.

Puccini had expressed his 'neronic' side in *Tosca*. With the new opera he was about to return to the innocent girl victim he had already created in Mimi. Cio-Cio-San (Madam Butterfly) is only fifteen when the opera opens – younger even than Manon Lescaut.

Madama Butterfly is the last of the three most famous, and best loved, Puccini operas. As if the new century was making its presence felt, or as if the composer decided he needed a new artistic language, once he had completed *Butterfly* he began to search for new ways of composing.

Only two operas can rival *Butterfly* in popularity: *La Traviata* and *Carmen*. All three share the distinction of having been disasters at their first performances. The result in the case of *Madama Butterfly* is that the version usually heard today contains at least two major revisions. Between 1904 and 1906 there were, in a sense, three premières of the opera: at Milan, Brescia and Paris. Little was certain about this work in its early days, even the number of acts it should have.

The basis of the problem was the brevity of the play. Belasco's single act was based upon a short story by a Philadelphia lawyer called John Luther Long. He did not do a straightforward dramatisation of Long's story, but plucked out of it what he wanted for his own, tear-jerking purposes and concentrated the action into a single day.

There was now no doubt who would write the libretto, and as soon as a contract came through from America giving the rights in the adaptation – almost a year after Puccini had first seen the play – Illica and Giacosa were set to work, the former producing a first version of Act One. It was just in time; Illica and Puccini had been irritated with each other for several months and needed to work on something new.

This was Illica's version of Long's story, not the Belasco play which he, unlike Puccini, had not seen or even been able to read in an Italian translation. So it was Long's story that was the starting point for Puccini's *Madama Butterfly*.

While Illica was at work Puccini, as usual, vacillated over the shaping of the opera. At first it was to be in two acts; then he decided on three, before changing back to two. This question of the act structure in *Madama Butterfly* was to remain a vexation even beyond the first night.

Just as *Tosca* had driven Puccini to searching out authentic prayers and bell patterns, so for *Butterfly* he researched Japanese folk and national tunes, arranged a meeting with a famous Japanese actress who happened to be visiting Italy, and held a number of conversations with the wife of the Japanese ambassador, in order to capture the voice patterns and intonations of the Japanese female speaking voice. He also investigated any books he could find on Japan and its music .

It seems that Act One – Butterfly's wedding with Pinkerton and their moment of exalted love – was the easiest section to work on. It neatly fitted the pattern and length of the acts in previous Puccini operas: roughly fifty minutes, with a male opening modified by a later female presence and leading to an extended love scene. The second act, which takes place three years later, has to cover more events and allow for a night to pass during which nothing happens right in the centre of events. It also has to introduce two new characters who are important but are only seen for a short time: Prince Yamadori, the Japanese suitor to Butterfly, and Kate, the American wife to Pinkerton. The music has little time to establish their personalities, while accommodating the move to the tragic dénouement. Moreover, although Trouble, the child of Butterfly and Pinkerton, does not sing, the music has to acknowledge his presence.

Illica drafted Act One of the libretto between March and May 1901. He

did not see the script of Belasco's play in Italian until June. So it was not surprising that he had decided on a three-act structure (like that of *Tosca*) and begun to plan a middle act taken from a section of Long's story in which Butterfly visits the American embassy. Late in 1902 Puccini seems to have decided he did not want the opera to have three acts, and battled with his librettists over the matter.

Otherwise work generally went smoothly, until one of Puccini's hobbies caused a major setback. Besides terminating the existence of as many wildfowl as he could around Torre del Lago, he had a fascination with new mechanical devices and none gave him more pleasure than his motor-car. He was the first in the town to own one. He was also, of course, a keen smoker, especially of cigars. They may have contributed towards the pain in his throat which he could not shake off with any of the usual remedies and which afflicted him during work on *Madama Butterfly*. By February 1903 he had to visit a throat specialist in his native town of Lucca and it was natural he should decide to travel there by car, along with Elvira and their son Tonio. After the consultation, the three went to a friend's house for dinner. By the time they left, the weather was cold, frosty and foggy but Puccini turned down the offer of an overnight stay.

The car managed about four miles, reaching a village called Vignolo di San Macario. Then it came to a sharp bend, skidded and careered down the hillside, ending up on its roof some fifteen feet below. Of the four occupants, only one was seriously hurt: the chauffeur broke his thigh, Elvira and Tonio mainly suffered shock but Puccini himself was trapped under the vehicle, his mouth dangerously close to the petrol fumes. Luckily a doctor with sharp hearing lived nearby and was able to administer some early treatment.

Allowing also for a badly-set shin fracture that had to be broken and re-set, Puccini was out of action so far as composition was concerned until well into the autumn of 1903. He tried a small amount of work, but cannot have been helped by a ticking-off from Ricordi, who seems to have assumed the composer's gradual recovery was being hampered by the effects of venereal disease. In fact, the only disease discovered during treatment after the accident was diabetes. There was certainly enough in Puccini's amorous past to make his publisher suspicious. Yet at the very start of the following year, when the death of Elvira's husband Gemignani allowed it within the Roman Catholic Church, Puccini and Elvira were married, on 3rd January 1904. Only a week earlier he had finished composing *Madama Butterfly*.

Its first performance was set for 17th February 1904 at La Scala in Milan. Puccini was conscious he had written a major new work – and the death of Giuseppe Verdi on 27th January 1901 meant he was now the leading composer of Italian opera in the new century. Puccini, Mascagni and Leoncavallo had all been at the funeral, but there was no doubt which of the three was the leading opera composer of the new age.

The new opera was to be produced by Giulio Ricordi's son Tito. He was a demanding director, but extremely conscientious and concerned that every detail of the stage action should be right. A top-rank cast was assembled. Puccini might well have been nervous. His work now would be judged by the severest critics expecting the highest level of achievement. Besides, neither *La Bohème* nor *Tosca* had been runaway critical successes; why should this be any different?

Nevertheless he seemed happy and confident about *Madama Butterfly* as

Opera-makers being taken for a ride. Alongside Luigi Illica (with cigar) are Umberto Giordano (1867-1948), whose successes included *Andrea Chénier* in 1896, Baron Alberto Franchetti (1860-1942) who lost the composition of *Tosca* to Puccini and gave the right to set *Chénier* to Giordano, and Signor Galeotti.

the opening approached and was encouraged by the singers' enthusiasm for his score. Instead of urging friends and family to stay away – who likes a professional débâcle to be seen by those we meet at home? – Puccini for once asked members of his family to attend the première. This was to be a night of triumph.

It was certainly a remarkable evening. For the first scene: silence. This was not a good sign in Italian opera houses of the time, where audiences pleased with the work called out their approval and were happy to interrupt the performance with encores, special bows for the singers and, in the case of a new work, multiple appearances on stage by the composer to acknowledge their appreciation. Then as Butterfly sang her first words – they are sung offstage and Rosina Storchio as Cio-Cio-San had not even had the opportunity to step into view:

Spira sull mare e sulla
terra un primaveril soffio giocondo.
(There blows over sea and land a springtime-scented breeze.)

voices in the audience declared out loud 'That's from *Bohème*'. More silence; barely a sound of applause even after the long, rapturous love duet which ends the first act. Instead, mockery and jeering as the curtain fell.

That was nothing to what happened during the long second act, when the audience's patience and sitting power was tested up to, and in many cases clearly well beyond, their limit. Today when 'Un bel di' (One Fine Day) is a heart-throbbing part of any opera gala night it is hard to imagine that on its first performance it was greeted with – well, no greeting at all, despite the

Rosina Storchio in 1920. Sixteen years earlier, she was the 'pregnant' Butterfly at the opera's disastrous La Scala première.

demonstrative Italian tradition. Worst of all, a gust of wind managed to sail in through an open door while Storchio was on stage and billow under her kimono. 'Butterfly's pregnant,' somebody shouted, to great cheers. (There were rumours circulating about Storchio's relationship with La Scala's music director, Arturo Toscanini.) So when Butterfly came on to show Sharpless her child there was fine merriment.

As the first scene of Act Two finished, the sustained softness of the offstage humming chorus was followed directly by the next scene, beginning at dawn. Tito seems to have been aware of the realistic work of such directors as Ludwig Cronegk, famous throughout Europe, and perhaps he had heard of Konstantin Stanislavsky's recent realistic storm scene in *Uncle Vanya*. Tito arranged a symphony of mechanical birdsong effects for the dawn chorus. It brought the house down. The fashionable Milanese joined in with their own impromptu impressions and La Scala was turned into an aural aviary. By now melodrama, pounding minor key chords and a tragic suicide had little chance of making their impression. The very first night of one of the best-loved tear-jerkers of the operatic repertoire ended in a cacophony of mockery, and with tears of laughter rolling down its audience's faces.

The last laugh has been on the Milanese audience for a long time now, but the first-night disasters of *Madama Butterfly*, not to mention *Fidelio*, *The*

Barber of Seville and other masterpieces are a useful caution when we stand ready to condemn a difficult-seeming new work. No doubt some of the fiasco was due to an organised anti-Puccini faction. Critically, the work was accused of making too many demands on audiences by following a substantial first act with a second act twice as long.

We need to remember that the *Butterfly* howled down in history is not quite the opera we know today. The changes that were to occur over the following two years improved it considerably. It is fortunate that Puccini was used to reworking his operas. He and the librettists honourably returned the fees which La Scala had paid them, then set to work revising the opera.

For the second production, a three-act version was arranged. This took place only three months later, on 28 May 1904 at the Teatro Grande in Brescia. The first act was cut down and a lot of incidental action, especially involving Butterfly's relations at the wedding, was struck out. Perhaps Brescia's smaller theatre suited the personal story of Butterfly better, perhaps the Milan operagoers who journeyed to Brescia for the second first night of *Butterfly* felt repentant, or were more appreciative when free of a set of determined wreckers. Perhaps, too, a second hearing made the novel elements in the score sound more coherent. Or perhaps the new-model *Madama Butterfly* was a better, more shapely creation than its predecessor. At any rate, in late May Brescia at last gave Puccini's favourite opera the success he was so sure it deserved.

Reworking did not stop there. Another major overhaul was made for the 1906 production at the Opéra-Comique in Paris. This was the theatre whose audience a generation before had slaughtered the première of *Carmen* in 1875. Puccini, very used to making changes by now, probably saw good sense in the proposals of the manager, Albert Carré.

Long's story of 1898 was not the the first of its type. In 1887 Pierre Loti had published *Madame Chrysanthème* (made into an opera by the composer-conductor André Messager in 1893). Loti (unlike any of the people involved in the various *Butterfly*s) knew Japan at first hand through voyages made while he was a lieutenant in the US Navy.

In Loti's story, a Pinkerton equivalent looks for a temporary Japanese wife, a process that involves paying a negotiated price to a marriage broker and which brings him a flighty girl called Chrysanthemum. Before long, he has had enough of her and pays her off when his ship is about to leave. Chrysanthemum seems distressed, with considerable wailing and gnashing of teeth, but when he happens to go back for something he has left behind, she is sitting there tearless, counting the money he has left her.

This is far removed from Long's Butterfly, even more from Puccini's. It was loss of her family's money that originally forced the well brought up Cio-Cio-San into the world of the geisha. When Sharpless asks Butterfly what she will do if Pinkerton never returns she tells him she can go back to entertaining people with her singing and dancing, or die. Yet in Act Two the money Pinkerton left when he went three years before is almost exhausted and Butterfly is clinging to the model existence of an American wife.

Loti's casual dismissal of Japanese attitudes and feelings is reflected in Pinkerton, especially the harsher Pinkerton of the first version of the opera. In Loti, the Japanese are referred to as monkeys; Pinkerton calls Butterfly's servants, including Suzuki, Mugs. The difference is that in *Chrysanthème* we are expected to go along with these names; in *Butterfly* we feel a distance from Pinkerton's callous attitude. By the 1906 Paris production Pinkerton's name-calling had been cut.

When John Luther Long's *Madam Butterfly* appeared in 1898, it could have been read as a corrective to Loti's dismissive approach. Western attitudes towards the East are important to Puccini's opera. Act One is derived from the Long story and not Belasco's play, as we have seen. And the story – though not the play – is concerned with cultural relations between the two nations – forward-looking America and (from the Americans' viewpoint) backward-seeming Japan. In Long's story Pinkerton is fed up with being consigned to naval duties in the east. 'Banishment' is how he thinks of it. His friend Sayre suggests marriage as a distraction. Significantly he puts the matter as a joke, 'with a laugh'. Illica picked this up in his first version of Act One, where the American characters are consistently laughing.

Long's Pinkerton follows up the idea, using a marriage-broker to go one better and find a wife *and* a house. He accepts the 999 year lease and uses it as a proof to Butterfly that he means to be faithful to her, not pointing out that as a foreigner he could end the agreement simply by walking out and not paying. Deception and condescension lie at the base of Pinkerton's behaviour from the start. No doubt he thinks them quite justified because he is 'only' dealing with the Japanese.

Because Long is interested more in the question of cultural relations than one woman's tragedy, the focus is on Pinkerton. And Pinkerton's assumption of American superiority stretches to the house he has had built. He 'Americanises' the paper-built structure, giving it opaque walls and lockable doors. Butterfly accepts these foreign adaptations happily – 'and [goes] about jingling her new keys and her new authority like toys,' until she finds out that among those to be locked out are, in Pinkerton's terms, 'the appalling horde' of her own family.

From this hint Illica took the opera's wedding scene, which in its first, Milan, form was longer than in later versions, with clowning by the drunken uncle Yakusidé. Illica also took over the unsympathetic Pinkerton, who in the first draft of the libretto calls Cio-Cio-San's family a bunch of 'noisy frogs'. The Lieutenant we meet in the opera today, while he remains a cad, is both less abusive and, in the end, more guilt-stricken than in either the story or the first version of the libretto.

Long also tells us that Butterfly's family did not approve of her marriage. This is represented operatically when the Bonze, one of her uncles, interrupts the wedding with his curse, like the Wicked Fairy at Princess Aurora's wedding in *The Sleeping Beauty*. Puccini uses the brief, threatening curse theme frequently through the rest of the opera, reflecting its importance to the story. It is one of the few themes he uses in the way Wagner did his leitmotifs. It is a theme that connects with both aspects of the Butterfly story: on the one hand, it shows a traditional society's hostility to outside influences; on the other it intensifies the pressure on Butterfly herself. It is the Bonze who truly splits her from her family. Because of him, Butterfly is stranded when her husband deserts her. She has left the security of her own culture in the belief she has found another, but she is mistaken, for the other culture has not adopted her, nor has she been able fully to adapt to it.

The way she is deserted is the more cruel because it is so thoughtless. Any of Long's readers who knew either version of Loti's *Madame Chrysanthème* would assume the story might end as a joke: another foreign lady has been left counting her gains. They discover Butterfly has nothing left to count but the cost of her love and trust. Far from waiting, like Chrysanthemum, for another profitable temporary match to come along, Butterfly insists on keeping up her American dream lifestyle. When she visits the consul, though, we see how he regards her as non-American: by name, family and occupation. 'You are Cio-Cio-San, the daughter . . . You used to dance, did you not?' Butterfly strugglingly asserts her American credentials: 'I nobody's daughter; jus' Missus Ben-ja-no! Missus Frang-a-leen Ben-ja-meen – no, no, no! Missus Ben-ja-meen Frang-a-leen Pikkerton. Aeverybody else outcast me.' (One thing we can be glad the libretto did not adopt is Butterfly's broken English There is no evidence Long used realistic speech patterns and the opera rightly gives Butterfly the dignity of clear speech.) Secure, as she thinks, as Mrs Pinkerton, she can take the outcast status lightly.

Two things here reached the opera. In Act Two Sharpless, the consul, visits Butterfly in her home: 'Please excuse me. Madam Butterfly,' he starts. 'My name is Pinkerton, please,' she answers at once.

As has been said, Illica worked from John L. Long's story and planned an act set in the American consulate, where Butterfly learns that Pinkerton has a new wife. Illica could see the stage possibilities in the scene. Butterfly feels faint; Sharpless seats her behind a screen. Then Kate Pinkerton (Adelaide in Long's story) enters to send a telegram to 'My husband . . . Lieutenant Pinkerton'. Unwittingly adding insult to injury, she notices Cio-Cio-San, and (not knowing who she is) says with the best intentions, 'How very charming – how *lovely* – you are, dear! Will you kiss me, you pretty – *plaything*!' The consul's words make Butterfly feel faint. It is then she is given a seat and a screen placed in front of her, for the fateful scene with Mrs Pinkerton.

After Mrs Pinkerton has left, Butterfly staggers weakly up to the consul and returns the few coins remaining from Pinkerton's allowance to her. This is the final thread of the financial contrast to the Chrysanthemum story. Although story – and play – end with Butterfly's use of the sword the Mikado had sent her father when demanding his ritual suicide, her death is not recorded. All we are told by Long is that Butterfly's maid bound up the wound and that: 'When Mrs Pinkerton called next day at the little house on Higashi Hill it was quite empty.'

Between Milan and Paris the opera lost some of its extraneous details, passages that did not drive the story forward. The work was divided for a time into three acts, before the last two became two continuous scenes in Act Two, and the Pinkertons were given more humanity. Both Italian posteriors and American sensibilities were accommodated in the process.

Madama Butterfly: The Music

In the version of the opera which became standard (and is represented in the published Ricordi score) the action all takes place in a house on a hill overlooking the major Japanese port of Nagasaki. The house has a terrace and a garden. There is delicacy suggested in the brief orchestral introduction, in which a short phrase is expanded into a longer melodic sequence on the violins before being introduced also on violas, cellos and bassoons, flutes joining in with violins for occasional phrases and building very soon to a series of four-note phrases played by full orchestra. It is a good example of Puccini's careful orchestration in the creation of beautiful and appropriate sound.

As the music repeats the opening phrase, Pinkerton is seen being shown round the house by the marriage-broker Goro. While phrases of Japanese delicacy continue, Pinkerton is shown to be ignorant of Japanese house construction. Goro shows him how the sliding screens move to create various living compartments. Pinkerton's interest in the arrangement is clear: he asks where the bedroom is. These opening lines are sung over distinctive orchestral phrases involving an octave's drop on woodwind and reminders of the opening phrase from violins.

Used to solid American structures, Pinkerton cannot believe this delicate building will stand up. Is it strong enough? From ground to roof, Goro assures him, then claps his hands to summon the houseboy, cook and, most important to the story, Butterfly's loyal maid Miss Light Morning Breeze, or Suzuki. In the first version of the opera, this is where Pinkerton rudely called their Japanese names silly and decided to call them Mugs One, Two and Three. With this cut the music now moves through four repeats of the very opening phrase, then continues into a broad phrase on oboe; clarinet and bassoon cluck out that opening phrase at various times by way of contrast. Suzuki speaks of smiles but Pinkerton becomes impatient at her chatter:

A chiacchiere costei
mi par cosmopolita.
(When women start to talk I find them the same all over.)

Meanwhile Goro is on the lookout for the bride, helping to build the audience's interest in and expectations of her. Goro lists the people to be expected – the registrar of marriages, the bride's relations, the American consul and Pinkerton's bride herself. Pinkerton is happy enough at the necessary officials, less so at the family:

E son molti i parenti?
(Are there many of these relatives?)

he asks.

While Goro has been describing the wedding party the bassoon, over a light string accompaniment, has introduced a new tune, a kind of limping march to indicate the family making their way up the hill. A slightly varied version is given out on the violins as Goro lists the expected people. High violins and cellos sing out the same tune as Goro lists Butterfly's family: mother, grandmother, her uncle the Bonze (who is unlikely to turn up), cousins, ancestors – two dozen, most likely, in all. All this stops as the broker breaks off to point out that ancestors there may be, but the matter of descendants can safely be left to the Lieutenant and his wife. This is said over a sustained chord on horns, a sweep upwards on harp and a busy Japanese theme from woodwind and strings at the reference to the wedding night. (The joke about descendants is later seen in a new light when Butterfly's child is about to be prised away from her).

A voice is heard off stage – someone unused to climbing hills. It is Sharpless, the American Consul in Nagasaki. His first words, about the troublesome climb:

E suda e arrampica!
e sbuffa e inciampica!
(It can't be much further now! Stumbling! And spluttering!)

Pinkerton – here the
Irish-American tenor
John McCormack
(1884-1945).

repeat, with violins and cellos, the last phrase sung by Goro; the effect is to work a transition before Sharpless' second, short speech. His words are sung to a musical line which includes a phrase soaring almost an octave up over four notes. This is heard also on the violins and split between an oboe and a flute. It is a little tune that remains associated with Sharpless throughout the opera, a bright, optimistic theme suited to the kindly and efficient consul. The violins, oboes and clarinets give us a further chance to become acquainted with it before the woodwind recalls the decorative four-note phrases from near the opening – no doubt as Sharpless acclimatises himself to the height and the view. The opera's first phrase is recalled on strings, then oboe as he looks at the scene.

Pinkerton talks to him man to man and speaks in a condescending way about the house:

E una casetta
che obbedisce a bacchetta.
(It's a house so fragile it stands up by magic).

and he goes on from this idea of fragility to laugh at the elasticity of Japanese contracts – as long as 999 years, but snapping shut in a month if he chooses. Along with the view of the Japanese as delicate and toylike, these ideas show Pinkerton sees nothing fine, lasting or valuable in the country. Ironically, it is his faith that is fragile, not the Japanese or their buildings. Even Sharpless adds the comment that a person without conscience would look at things in such a way. His line follows a brief ferocious orchestral outburst after Pinkerton's speech.

Drinks are brought by Goro; the music stops. Since Puccini uses several genuine Japanese tunes to build his oriental atmosphere, it should be no surprise he uses an American tune to reinforce the US presence. Of course the original audiences (like most today) in Italy, France, Britain and America would be unlikely to recognise Japanese melodies from outside the opera – a general Japanese feel would be the result. But most would recognise the tune which is blazed forth by brass and woodwind after a brief silence. It is 'The Star Spangled Banner' and from the first its use was controversial. Americans were upset; presumably an American anthem should not have been treated like a mere Japanese tune. Pinkerton clearly did represent an element in his nation.

The use of 'The Star Spangled Banner' creates a contrast which emphasises the wide gap between the sounds of America and Japan. And as the toast to which Pinkerton and Sharpless will shortly drink is 'America for ever' (they sing it in English) a bit of patriotism in the music fits the moment well. The rhythm of a three-note musical 'cell' in the tune is repeated by flutes and taken up by violins as Pinkerton begins singing to a new tune about the Yankee travelling the world, stopping off where he pleases, entrancing a girl in every port. Casually he breaks off this statement to offer (the libretto once again uses the English names) milk punch or whisky to Sharpless. The Consul tries to insert a caution:

È un facile vangelo
che fa la vita vaga
ma che intristisce il cuor.
(That's an easy gospel which makes life pleasant
but finally sours the heart.)

Pinkerton swaggers on arrogantly:

Così mi sposo all'uso giapponese
per novecento
novantanove
anni. Salvo a prosciogliermi ogni mese.
(So I'm taking a wife Japanese fashion for 999 years.
Able to end the marriage monthly.)

'America for ever,' he triumphantly adds and Sharpless repeats the toast.

The instrumental scoring for this section is generally light – what matters is that the melodies should bounce along, like Pinkerton's easy self-confidence. When Sharpless asks if the bride is beautiful, Goro cannot help coming forward to pursue his trade: fair as a flower, bright as a star – dirt cheap at a hundred yen – he all but offers his services to Sharpless too. Softly and delicately, woodwind play the phrase Goro had earlier sung (and Sharpless' musical line had picked up) about Butterfly and Pinkerton adding a new generation to the family. Strings soon join in, violins offering a reminder of the main musical figure from the opening bars of the opera.

When Pinkerton has sent Goro to search for Butterfly, Sharpless uses the opportunity to criticise his fellow American more directly:

Quale smania vi prende!
Sareste addirittura
cotto?
(Have you taken leave of your senses? Or are you infatuated?)

Unaccompanied apart from a soft, sustained woodwind chord, Pinkerton replies that it depends how you define infatuation. And he openly states he has no idea whether he loves Butterfly or merely fancies her for the moment:

Amore o grillo,
dir non saprei.
(Love or fancy I cannot say.)

He sings this to a new tune, but again it is a confident, swaggering one which tramples over any suggestion of real affection, the kind of tune that might more usually be found as a drinking song among comrades. If he does not call her a plaything he certainly regards her as somehow unreal, out of the quaint Japanese world – like a design on a screen, he says. And a lot of this description is rattled out in phrases on a single pitch before he returns to the confident, masculine tune, made more forceful as it is played also on violins, several woodwind and horns when it returns, then on violins over two octaves on its immediate repeat. When Pinkerton's sung line finally rises to passionate heights it is only to express his own sexual desire. Harp chords enrich the loud orchestral reinforcement of his high phrase. But no sooner has he spoken than the passion quietens and another new tune enters on oboe, clarinet and violas as Sharpless 'seriously and good-naturedly' tells how Butterfly had come to the consulate ('I did not see her, but I heard,' he says, echoing Long's detail that she saw the vice-consul on this first visit). He speaks more feelingly of Butterfly as an individual:

Di sua voce il mistero
l' anima mi colpi.

(Her voice in its mystery touched my soul.)

Woodwind and string chords provide the gentle harmony as we hear Butterfly talked about for the first time as a real person. And the Consul offers a warning, extending her name into metaphor:

Sarebbe gran peccato le lievi ali strappar
e desolar forse un credulo cuor.
(It would be a great wrong to tear such fragile wings
and desolate a trusting heart.)

In a lively passage, with no sincerity, Pinkerton says that of course he means no harm – and turns to the serious subject of offering Sharpless another glass of whisky. The Consul accepts and toasts Pinkerton's American friends and relatives. Having moved Sharpless from thinking about Butterfly, Pinkerton can now toast his real, American wedding day, which will occur at some unspecified time in the future. If Sharpless himself expresses no further pity for Butterfly, the strings recall it for him through the tune in which he sang about her a few moments before.

As Goro runs on to say the wedding party is on its way, Butterfly's friends are heard off stage, bringing the first female voices into the opera. Distantly, they sing sustained notes as clarinets and bassoon, joined in part by violas and cellos, play brief staccato notes and the violins offer rapid-note chords. The wordless chorus acquires words and rhythm as they admire sea, sky and flowers and the orchestra reduces to just shimmering violas with a harp harmonic. As the harp then spreads a chord across its strings, and soft violin sounds plus clarinet and horns add harmony, Butterfly herself is heard for the first time, off stage:

Ancora un passo or via
(One more step and we're there).

As this, sung at a single pitch, broadens into a tune associated with Butterfly herself, the harp ripples out repeated harmonies, her friends sing a blessing and the violins, softly at first, hint at the Butterfly tune. At:

Amiche, io son venuta
al richiamo d' amor
venni alle soglie
ove s' accoglie
il bene di chi vive e di chi muor.
(Friends, I am brought by the sweet call of love. I come to the threshold
to find what life or death has waiting for me.)

the tune is heard in Butterfly's voice in its full glory.

After this rapturous entrance, Butterfly introduces her friends to her husband-to-be, F. B. Pinkerton as she refers to him, in a tune that is Japanese in shape but which is capable of being played in a slow, smooth way and sounding like nothing other than a Puccini melody of the utmost tenderness. It is used to such effect at the very end of Act One. For now it is in Japanese guise and is heard on flute, piccolo, harp and glockenspiel over a shimmering string sound. She tries to impress him with a series of polite comments but Pinkerton replies awkwardly. Sharpless shows more genuine interest in

Butterfly's past than does the man who is about to become her husband. Something of her life history then emerges: her former family wealth, her impoverished mother and the father who is dead.

Two new tunes occur here, and will recur. Out of a lightly scored passage (a contrast to the recent luscious-sounding entrance scene), oboe, cor anglais, bassoon, a horn and plucked cellos loudly sound a brief, troubled theme. Here it is linked to a comparison, that family misfortunes are like trees uprooted in a storm; such a process forced the genteel Cio-Cio-San to become a geisha. Later it will be associated with her further troubles. At Sharpless' question about her father, low woodwind and strings sound a serious theme as the friends bow their heads and cover their embarrassment with an outbreak of fanning. Even unshockable Goro seems awkward here.

Between them these tunes, in angular shapes and at low pitches, douse the comedy and romance seen so far. A brief section about Butterfly's uncles was cut when the work reached Paris and the Opéra-Comique. She goes on to ask the Americans if they can tell her age. Ten? they suggest. She corrects them: 'Fifteen,' she replies. 'I'm old, aren't I?' Any soprano with the technique and experience required to sing the role of Butterfly is likely to look a good deal older. And in English, at least, the title 'Madame' tends to suggest considerably more than fifteen. But fifteen she is, and in a matter of months will be a mother. She kills herself at the age of eighteen. This is something to be borne in mind when watching the production, or listening to maturer voices on recordings.

Enter Butterfly's relatives to the bumpy march heard near the start of the act. A funny-looking lot, Pinkerton observes to Sharpless, laughing at the prospect of a mother-in-law among them and pointing out the drunken uncle Yakusidé. There is the sort of chatter that could go on at any wedding, including some behind-hand (or behind-fan) disparagement of the bride. Uncle Yakuside looks for the wine.

The original plan was for this wedding scene to be more extensive than it became in the final version. A lot was cut for the second, Brescia production, and there were more cuts for Paris. What has stayed is a wide-ranging tune begun low by Sharpless:

O amico fortunato
(My lucky friend)

its next phrase begun high by Pinkerton, while Sharpless continues:

Pinkerton: Si, è vero, è un fiore, un fiore
Sharpless: O fortunato Pinkerton
(*Pinkerton*: Yes, really, she's a flower, a flower
Sharpless: Lucky Pinkerton)

This passionate outburst continues as both praise Butterfly, but while Pinkerton talks of his desire, Sharpless thinks of Butterfly's trust and warns his compatriot not to betray it.

This section ends quietly with soft echoes of the men's wide-ranging theme and the tune to which Butterfly entered. Then she asks if she can show her husband the few objects she possesses; a simple six-note phrase is repeated on various woodwind, with cellos the first time and glockenspiel later. Her only secret is the content of a sheath she possesses. Her secrecy will help register this sheathed sword in the audience's minds for the end of the opera. For

New Zealander Rosina Buckman (1881-1948) sang Musetta at Covent Garden in 1914; during World War I she added Mimi and Butterfly to her London repertory.

now Goro explains, in Butterfly's absence, that it is the sword sent to her father by the Mikado; in effect an order that her father kill himself.

In a momentary silence, Goro moves away and Butterfly returns with fig-urines representing the souls of her ancestors. Pinkerton is polite but does not consider them for long. However, they have helped Cio-Cio-San introduce her important news: she has become a Christian (this is another passage altered during the early productions). A new religion for a new life, she says. Her speech starts over very sparse orchestration but as she talks of following her new destiny – plunging into an unknown future, we might say – the orchestra bathes her with flute, oboe and harp figures and a delicate, tender tune high on violins and cellos, music which will be heard in the love scene at the end of this act. Here, on the words 'Amore mio' (My love), she embraces Pinkerton in commitment and trust. The danger of this trust is underlined at this moment by low woodwind and strings, plus horns and trombones sounding out the low-pitched angular theme heard earlier.

The official Commissioner performs the civil marriage service over trembling strings, with just a hint of 'The Star Spangled Banner' at his reference to North America. All is going well. The Sharpless tune is played as he arranges to meet Pinkerton the next day, the guests sing a wedding song 'O Kami, O Kami', softly outlined by flutes and violins, with more harp chordal patterns.

Then there is a sudden loud chord as strings start trembling and a deep voice balefully cries out 'Cio-Cio-San'. It is the Bonze, Butterfly's religious uncle. He knows she has been to the Christian Mission. 'What were you doing there?' he demands to know – and everyone on the Japanese side (except possibly uncle Yakusidé who is only bothered about what comes in bottles) wants to know too. Woodwind and violas sound out a low, brief, menacing theme to represent the curse he brings for Butterfly. Its sound, a brief, memorable phrase, is repeated often in her later distress. This menacing sound grows louder as the Bonze takes over the proceedings, until it is hammered out by oboe, cor anglais, horn, trumpet and violins, with a characteristic fist-shaking trill included.

Only Pinkerton is unmoved. If the Japanese generally are playthings and ornaments to him, the Bonze is a side-show freak. But the Japanese join in the Bonze's cursing as the menacing motif is heard again in the orchestra. Faced with the angry Pinkerton the Bonze retreats, using his authority to take the family and other wedding guests with him. He will not even allow Butterfly's mother to stay.

Apart from trembling violas, Pinkerton's order to the Bonze to leave stands out in the silence of the orchestra, but as the guests leave the low theme associated with the death of Butterfly's father is sounded loud – now she is dead to her former life, renounced by her family, as her father had been ordered to give up his own life.

As the guests leave, the curse motif quietens and the orchestral writing becomes more spare. Pinkerton tries to cheer his new wife up, telling her all this cursing is of no importance. He cannot sympathise enough to see how it affects her now. He certainly does not take it into account when he deserts her in the knowledge she has been rejected by her own people. But for now her fear is overcome by his sugared words about her dear, beautiful eyes (this being an endearment of which Illica and Giacosa seem to have been fond).

These comforting words smoothly lead to the long lovers' talk, an extended love duet, which rapturously and tenderly closes the act. It begins as Suzuki, in the house, starts her evening prayer – on single, repeated, unaccompanied notes, as simple as can be. Butterfly changes from her wedding clothes for the night, glad to be unencumbered. Pinkerton orders Suzuki to slide the screens while his wife changes. For now he has assured control of the house he no longer needs to ask what the screens are for. 'Viene la sera' (Evening draws on) sings Pinkerton to a gentle, descending tune. The atmosphere is that of two lovers alone, secluded, the servants sent to sleep. Butterfly still cannot put the thought of the curse out of her mind, but she feels secure in her husband's love, while he adores her movements and her charm. Woodwind and strings gently accompany them. Then he talks to, rather than merely about, her:

Bimba dagli occhi pieni di malia
(Child whose eyes shine with witchcraft).

This starts over soft harp and string chords, then bassoons follow the melody for a phrase; the music builds to a climax as his passion surges through looking at her and talking of her beauty. And she gently describes herself as like 'The little moon goddess'.

As she says he is the most important thing in the world to her, the violins play a rising tune, also heard in the voice. Its urgency combines Butterfly's rapture and her moments of alarm as she recalls her relatives. A new tune intensifies the mood as she sings:

– Vogliatemi bene,
un bene piccolino,
un bene da bambino . . .
(Love me, just a little, as if I were a baby . . .)

It is heard on the violins, but its final notes are echoed by various woodwind as the music builds to passion and tenderness in both lovers.

Pinkerton has mocked elegant Japanese names, but here he says Butterfly is a fine name for someone so fragile. She is more acute than she realises when she takes alarm and says that in America a butterfly that is caught by a man is pierced through the heart with a needle.

East meets West in Covent Garden: the Royal Opera's *Madama Butterfly*. The opera's first act is taken from the original magazine story by John L. Long rather than Belasco's play.

But he soon assures her of his love and as the scene reaches its climax, the music linked to Butterfly herself since her first appearance resounds from the orchestra, the harp being busy with spread chords as Butterfly sings of the romantic setting:

Ah! Dolce notte! Quante stelle!

Non le vidi mai si belle!
(Ah! Sweet night! So many stars! I have never seen such beauty)

until the rapture subsides into tenderness and the pair go into the house – the bedroom of course – as harp chords support woodwind gently playing the erstwhile Japanese theme.

Three years have passed by the time the curtain goes up again for what is usually known as Act Two, part one. The scene is still set in Butterfly's house, and after a short orchestral prelude, where the busy opening tune is soon brought to a halt, Suzuki is heard praying as Butterfly stands, head in hands. There could hardly be a greater contrast with the end of the previous scene, and trouble is suggested as the Bonze's curse theme is heard briefly, reminding us that Butterfly cannot turn to her family. Suzuki prays her mistress will cry no more – which means, that Pinkerton will return. But it is only Butterfly who has any faith in that happening.

Butterfly herself does not blame Pinkerton for her sadness, nor even the God of his religion. Instead she blames her own country's uncaring gods. With a childlike semi-understanding she is confident the American God will do more, but she fears Japan is too remote for Him to hear her prayers. Apart from emotional consolation, there is a more practical concern. The money Pinkerton left will soon have run out. Even here Butterfly takes the blame on herself and Suzuki. It is their fault for spending too much – the curse motif sounds out on clarinets, and the very start of the opera is recalled, its flowery tune now in a less hospitable setting.

As for Suzuki's suggestion Pinkerton will never return, Butterfly refuses even to consider it, producing an argument we already know from Pinkerton himself is invalid: why did he take the house for so long, have locks put on it? A lot of this is set against simple orchestral accompaniment but as she explains it is to protect her, his wife, that he did these things, (therefore he must care for her and will return), the harp begins running up and down various chords as, softly, woodwind and violins play one of the Butterfly tunes. It is a very brief warmth in the sound before Suzuki expresses her doubt. Then Butterfly shuts her up:

Ah! Taci, o t' uccido.
(Ah! Shut up, or I'll kill you.)

After her moment of fury, she gently repeats Pinkerton's promise to return in the spring when flowers bloom and robins nest.

The accompaniment here is slight – only Butterfly's hopeful voice soars, and Suzuki, to please her rather than out of belief, says 'He'll come back'. This effort to please the mistress she knows is being cheated makes Suzuki break into tears and Butterfly offers to convince her all is well. As she does so, long quiet chords fade out and there is a silence before what may be Puccini's best-known melody begins. For all the continuous texture, the pause before it starts and the firm conclusion to which it comes make this clearly a separate aria:

Un bel dì, vedremo
levarsi un fil di fumo s'ull' estremo
confin del mare.
(One fine day, we'll see a thread of smoke rise over the sea's horizon).

The final bars of the great love scene which ends Act One of *Madama Butterfly*. Puccini's scores were untidy from the start; later they grew worse, a fact about which he joked. The House of Ricordi had a Puccini specialist to copy the works out neatly.

At first it is lightly accompanied, and extremely softly as a solo clarinet and violin join the tune while muted violins provide trembling chords of thrilled expectation. She imagines the ship appearing in the distance, sailing into the harbour, its cannon blazing. She will wait, she says, on the hill for him to come out of the crowded city. As she talks of a man climbing the hillside the tune too seems to step uphill and it has an epic quality suggesting how important the event will be to her.

Then soft, muted trumpets provide a rhythm made out of slow chords as she playfully imagines him coming close. When she talks of hiding, not just as a game but to retain the excitement of discovery for as long as possible, there is a sudden orchestral outburst with the opening tune of 'Un bel di'. Just as suddenly, all goes quiet again before building to a final climax as, soaring towards the top of the soprano register, she says all will again be well when he arrives, the orchestra alone thundering out the main tune of this aria, before the sound dissipates into the air. It is, after all, an imagined vision, and soon comes to a close followed briefly by a silence. What else is there to say after such a heartfelt expression of belief? This sudden switching between quiet and loud passages is a verismo technique, but also an apt expression of the young Butterfly's hope and excitement. This is music for an eighteen-year-old. The end also comments on her state of mind. Her hope propels the orchestra into that last climax, but soon it has all died out. This heat of love and hope also leads Suzuki to embrace her mistress before she is sent out.

There follows a quickening of pace in the music and Sharpless is announced by his tune on violins. Goro is with him, and if they had arrived a few moments earlier to hear Butterfly's aria they would have realised their mission was impossible. Flute and clarinet offer a dancing Japanese tune. All is now positive and everyday as the opening music of the opera is heard. Then it introduced Goro with Pinkerton, preparing for Cio-Cio-San's marriage. Now it accompanies Goro with the other American character, but marriage is still in prospect. Not realising what is coming she asserts her American identity. When Sharpless calls her Madama Butterfly she politely corrects him, insisting on the title Madama Pinkerton. 'Welcome to this American house,' she says. Sharpless is surprised she remembers him across the years.

The music becomes almost chatty, with tunes in Japanese style. Butterfly entertains Sharpless and enjoys playing the hostess in as American a way as possible. When finally Sharpless manages to mention Pinkerton's letter, Butterfly asks eagerly how her husband is. The music hints at 'The Star Spangled Banner' and it is clear why Puccini needed to use this tune. It is not just to help describe two American characters, not even to provide a musical expression of Americanism. It is a defiantly, unmistakably American theme by which the alien nature of these westerners is made clear. While we may perceive genuine Japanese tunes as simply atmospheric, when we hear 'The Star Spangled Banner' we are pulled up short. It is not Puccini; it is from else-where. It is American, separate from all the rest of the music. And that expresses how unreachable any real American identity will always remain for Butterfly.

Sharpless produces Pinkerton's letter. She is delighted and asks innocently when robins nest in America. The Consul is puzzled – why does she want to know? She explains Pinkerton's promise to return when the robins nest. Goro laughs, bringing him to her attention. As the robins have nested three times in Japan, they must have different schedules in America, she suggests. Sharpless, awkward and confused in front of this trust, apologises: he is no ornithologist. He tries to return to the letter. During this section the orchestra lightly chats along with Butterfly in delicately scored Japanese melodies until her questions about the robins, sung amid trembling strings and woodwind. Butterfly picks up the Japanese melody as she tells Sharpless how Goro has been trying to marry her off to one of her own countrymen.

Goro adds his voice. The suitor is Yamadori, rich and a prince, while Cio-Cio-San is poor. This point is reinforced by the Bonze's curse, on oboe and clarinet. It is developed by the orchestra into an urgent little rushing phrase leading to high, trembling violins. The situation carries heavy pathos: a sympathetic, vulnerable character who does not realise her danger is surrounded by people who do not wish to be brutal to her. They want to do the best for her but it is at the risk of breaking her heart.

Yamadori enters grandly with his servants; bassoon, horn and cellos loudly introduce him with the Japanese tune we have been hearing, as if to say, like it or not, he is Butterfly's only hope. She greets him, if that is the word, by mocking him: 'Still intend to die, do you, if you cannot have me?' The broad tune to which she sings this has an ecstasy that owes nothing to Yamadori, everything to her confidence in Pinkerton. Did he not say she was safe with him in Act One? This tune is played high on the violins, plus woodwind and lower strings, with accompanying sweeps on the harp.

Over agonised violins Yamadori expresses his plight then replies to her scornful comments about his many wives that he is indeed much-divorced but would stay faithful to her – a trumpet accompanies him with a Japanese tune. This Prince could have his pick of women in Japan. To a large extent he already has done, marrying and leaving many. But he so loves Butterfly he swears continued fidelity to her. Would he turn out to be another Pinkerton? Or is it her bad fortune that her love for the man who deserted her prevents her affluent happiness with a leading Japanese eligible bachelor?

Amid all this Sharpless replaces in his pocket the letter which he fears he will now never be able to deliver. Goro and Yamadori – and the orchestra, high strings and woodwind screaming out their fateful message – cannot persuade her that the marriage with Pinkerton is effectively over. The deserted wife can obtain a divorce Goro tells her. Only in Japan, she replies. Pinkerton encouraged her belief in him by convenient accounts of the American way of divorce; she is convinced husbands can be thrown into jail for seeking divorces over there. And she closes the subject by telling Suzuki to bring tea as Yamadori and Sharpless despair of ever making her realise the situation she is in.

Tea is served to a little waltz on violins that is more European than either Japanese or American. It matches the conversational pleasantries which set off the urgency Goro describes – Pinkerton's ship is approaching. But he will not be climbing the hill to see Butterfly. He will barely think of her, if at all. It is vital she marry again quickly and starts a new life before she is destroyed by the truth. The drama of the scene lies in the contrast between this urgency and Butterfly's naïvety, so well expressed by the charming waltz.

Unsuccessful, Yamadori leaves to a sadder version of his entrance tune. As her only chance departs, his status reinforced by the palanquin on which he is carried, Butterfly's ecstasy tune is ironically heard in the orchestra. It is ironic because this musical representation of her confidence happens as her only chance of avoiding disaster slips away.

Sharpless' tune plays as he takes the letter from his pocket for another try. She takes it and pushes it unread to her heart. As she does this a new tune is quietly plucked on the strings and bassoon. It accompanies Sharpless as he reads the letter to her and is expressive of her simple joy in hearing anything from Pinkerton. The new tune is heard on a single violin and viola while Butterfly cannot believe Pinkerton might think she would not remember him. She becomes excited when she believes he is returning, so that Sharpless cannot bring himself to deliver the blow:

Quel diavolo d' un Pinkerton!
(What a devil Pinkerton is!)

Unadorned by any orchestral accompaniment he asks what she would do if Pinkerton never returned. She just stands, dumbstruck, then quietly says she would either return to entertaining people or, better, die. There is little doubt which she would choose. Her reply is given little orchestral bedding, but there is a soft gloom as she talks of death.

The Consul can only advise her, gently, to marry Yamadori. Woodwind and strings play a tune, to be heard over again, which despite its rising opening phrase is contorted enough to display torment and sadness. This, as much as anger at the proposal, is her mood as Butterfly has Sharpless shown out. She apologises for her comments and tells him of her evil fate. All this time the same anguished tune is played. Swiftly she fetches her son as the orchestra thunders out the Butterfly theme from earlier in the opera. Though he is American in eyes, lips and his fair hair, he is brought on to another Japanese melody. This, like the child, is to become a source of great emotion in the latter part of the opera.

It is the first Sharpless knew of a child. Surely Pinkerton will rush back when he knows – the child was born after he left of course. Butterfly speaks to the boy, telling him that nasty Mr Sharpless wanted them to tramp through the rain looking for the army or the Emperor as a source of money. An imperial march is softly sounded as if distant in her mind. She thinks of herself being forced to sing in sadness, then rejects the idea fatefully:

> No, No! questo mai!
> questo mestier che al disonore porta!
> Morta! Mai piu danzar!
> (No! No! Not that. That dishonourable route I'll never take.
> Death rather than that.)

'Morta!' Morta!' (Death! Death!) she cries, rather than have to face what the future would hold. Her previous confidence is under attack now; the music builds to a climax with harp chords, woodwind and strings before suddenly dying away.

Sharpless comments on the child's golden hair and asks his name. It is another characteristic Japanese name: Trouble, to be renamed Joy when his father returns. And as she mentions that happy day two horns blast out the tune of 'One Fine Day' over a loud orchestral chord. It is a short-lived blaze of optimism, soon fading away. And Sharpless goes, assuring her that Pinkerton will be told about his son.

A mood change has Suzuki drag Goro in, saying he has been gossiping about the paternity of Trouble. Goro claims she has the wrong idea – he had merely said that in America a child born in such a way would be a social outcast; there seem a lot of rumours going around Nagasaki about American life. Butterfly's faith is now under pressure, as the new sadness of her music in the scene with Sharpless has just shown. This pressure is increased by the Bonze's curse recurring extremely loudly on woodwind, trumpets and violins. The mood continues in phrases on clarinet and bassoon, then, during Goro's explanation, on oboe and trumpet.

Putting herself between the child and Goro, as though he might physically harm Trouble, Butterfly angrily calls the broker a liar and threatens him with her father's sword. To no avail; the curse motif is relentless. To a plangent tune, she tries to comfort the child – his father will return.

Right on cue the harbour cannon signals a ship. Softly, muted violins and violas, plus a flute, signal 'One Fine Day'. Butterfly picks up the telescope she keeps ready and rushes to her terrace to identify the arrival. It is the *Abraham Lincoln*: his ship. The melody of 'One Fine Day' persists as

Cio-Cio-San had been eager to remove her ceemonial wedding clothes for her night of love with Pinkerton. Three years later she as eagerly dresses in them, sure that the return of her husband's ship, the *Abraham Lincoln*, will mean he has come home to her. The child she calls Trouble will then be renamed Joy.

strongly as had the Bonze's curse a few moments before. And with Yankee confidence 'The Star Spangled Banner' strides through the orchestra and the voice. Butterfly's own tune is sounded once, then again screwed up a tone in pitch, before a flowing melody of pure happiness runs ahead on clarinet and bassoon, harp rippling an accompaniment, as Butterfly joins the happy melody:

> Scuoti quella fronda
> di ciliegio e lo innonda di fior.
> (Shake the cherry tree branches; let its flowers cover the floor.)

Flute and oboe add their melodic contributions. This is another scene abridged before the Brescia performances.

Suzuki tries to calm Butterfly, who seems near hysteria. Whenever Pinkerton arrives it will be too soon – because Suzuki understands that he will bring disappointment to her mistress. There is no stopping the happy Cio-Cio-San. She tells Suzuki to pick every flower and light every lantern, another happy, rising tune emphasizing her new delirious mood. Suzuki's words sound a sad counterblast:

> Uno squallor d' inverno sarà tutto il giardino.
> (All the garden will have a wintry desolation.)

They scatter flowers over the floor, as the music takes on a more sober manner until their voices harmonise in a happy duet that might seem, in shape and mood, about to soothe away the Bonze's curse:

> Gettiamo a mani piene
> mammole e tuberose,
> corolle di verbene,
> petali d' ogni fior!
> (Let us scatter handfuls of violets and mimosa, branches of roses,
> petals of all flowers.)

– at which, as the sun sets, Suzuki lights two lamps and fetches Trouble. Flute and low violins play the happy tune more soberly and as the child is brought on to the stage, low flute and the harp add a poignant melody over the plucked double basses.

Butterfly puts cosmetics on her own and her son's faces. She feels her looks have faded, but Suzuki says happiness will restore them. Cio-Cio-San is happy. When the curse theme is heard softly it is because she laughs innocently at her uncle and at poor Yamadori, her suitor. (This scene was tightened after the première, where the innocent gloating was perhaps over extended.) One of the Japanese tunes is heard on clarinet and bassoon, then as Butterfly asks for her wedding clothes violins recall the start of the first act love music. Then, happy with her husband, she was keen to take off the ceremonious robes. This time there will be a very different ending.

She sings a lullaby and puts on her wedding clothes while Suzuki dresses the child in another robe. To look precisely as she did on her wedding night Butterfly has a red poppy placed in her hair. As night intensifies they stand behind the shosi, a paper screen that can be used as a window when holes are pierced in it. They begin their vigil, so they can be ready to surprise and delight Pinkerton.

As they wait, the peaceful night is represented by a chorus off stage, humming over delicate orchestral sounds a tune already heard once in this act – when Sharpless tried to tell Butterfly about Pinkerton's letter. Violins and violas pluck a rhythm. Flute, the romantic sounding viola d'amore and occasionally the harp join the melody which then moves to plucked violins before returning to fade out on flute, then harp.

Here an interval could occur. What follows the humming chorus has been either Act Three or, more usually, Act Two, scene two. At the Milan première the action of course was continuous and the already frisky audience, denied an interval, were soon whooping with delight when the coming of dawn brought Tito Ricordi's birdsong.

Taken seriously, this passage can be seen as another of Puccini's 'third act' orchestral scene-paintings. It opens loudly (a shock when it comes immediately after the gentle chorus). There is an oriental flavour and a sense of longing in this, a sense of hope becoming increasingly desperate, until Butterfly's own theme is sounded loudly on woodwind and violins over heavy trumpet and harp chords.

The first voices we hear belong to sailors in the off-stage distance. There are also hints of earlier music with a phrase from 'One Fine Day' creeping unassertively in, and the tune which romantically closed Act One heard in more businesslike guise. Life goes on. And a new, assertive tune makes its way through the orchestra – on bassoon, higher woodwind, horn, violins and woodwind, then with sweeping harp accompaniment until flute and violins begin carrying this tune along and brass offers an assertive continuation of the new melody.

Such gale-force music might easily blow away poor Butterfly ('*povera Butterfly*,' Suzuki calls her). In the revised libretto it is Suzuki who wakes and brings round Butterfly from her waking sleep. She has been so intent to watch for Pinkerton that she has not closed her eyes, but is so tired and drained she can hardly be said to be conscious. Suzuki insists she have some proper sleep. Butterfly takes her child with her, again saying Pinkerton will come. A lullaby, to a tune already heard, sums up her love for her husband and her child.

And Pinkerton does come, quietly knocking at the door as the violins introduce a new tune with considerable melancholy potential. He is anxious Suzuki should not let Butterfly know he is there. The maid points out the flowers her mistress has spread for his return. 'What did I tell you?' Sharpless rebukes him, but the force of Butterfly's love takes Pinkerton by surprise. Suzuki too is surprised, by the sight of a woman in the garden. Despite urging from Sharpless, Pinkerton is too ashamed to tell the truth about her; 'She came with me,' is all he will say and it is Sharpless who has to admit this is indeed Mrs Kate Pinkerton.

Suzuki's questioning, 'Who's that?' is set to forceful stabs of music; her reaction to the truth is a scream of horror calling on her ancestors and declared largely with no orchestra. Puccini reserved these suddenly unaccompanied moments for extremes of passion. She faints and Sharpless helps her, over trembling strings; then there is silence, followed by a plangent chord on horn, before he asks Suzuki for her help in telling Butterfly the true situation. As woodwind and violins quietly take up the melancholy yet dignified tune recently heard, Puccini uses it to express Sharpless' sense of sympathy for Butterfly's agony, yet simultaneously increases the pain she will feel when he says the Americans also want Kate to take the child and give him a secure home. Trouble will never become Butterfly's Joy. The Consul sends Suzuki out to Kate.

The scene that follows between the two men was altered after the first performance, adding a significant line by Pinkerton:

Ma un gel di morte vi sta.
(But a deathly cold waits here.)

and his gesture in handing over money for Sharpless to give to Butterfly before he runs away. Sharpless was allowed a larger role here, reminding Pinkerton in detail how he warned him of Butterfly's trust. And in a move to make Pinkerton seem less callous, the Lieutenant was given a direct expression of remorse:

Si, tutto in un istante
io vedo il fallo mio e sento
che di questo tormento
tregua mai non avrò! no!
(Yes. All in an instant I see my treacherous behaviour and feel that
I shall never be free of this torment I feel.)

113

The torment *he* feels? Still, at least there is some regret, however inadequate or useless. And as Sharpless sends him away, Pinkerton's remorse is given a new tune, over string harmonies and chords spread across harp and clarinet he sings:

> Addio, fiorito asil,
> di letizia e d' amor.
> (Farewell, dear home of happiness and love.)

– her eyes will always haunt him, he says. On this self-absorbed note he leaves the opera accompanied by loud chords, watched by his disapproving Consul. Throughout the history of opera heroes have spent the final act, being killed, assassinated, executed and coming to sundry sad ends, but no other tenor lead can have such a minimal role in the last (long) act of an opera or slink off under such a cloud of disgrace as Lieutenant Pinkerton of the US Navy.

Revisions after the first night also made Kate gentler, as she asks Suzuki to let Butterfly know she can trust her husband's American wife. Suzuki promises to tell Butterfly about the proposed adoption of her son. Butterfly is heard calling Suzuki, over quietly trembling strings. She will not be stopped from coming down – despite three trombones using all their fateful sound in a warning blast – and from running happily round the room, convinced her husband is playing a game and hiding somewhere to surprise her. There is a far less happy shock in store for her, as a repeated orchestral phrase reminiscent of the Bonze's curse suggests with mounting tension. It seems to echo the fading of Butterfly's happy energy. Orchestral forces are reduced too, until as she sees Kate just two clarinets play a low, restless musical pattern.

'Who is this lady?' Cio-Cio-San asks. Suzuki weeps but no-one speaks and Butterfly is anxious, puzzled. Whereas we have just seen Pinkerton off in self-absorbed remorse, Butterfly's anguish is unselfish. 'Is he alive?' she fearfully asks. So much is the focus on Butterfly here that the orchestral writing remains spare, mainly sustained chords to echo her mood, turning to agitated plucked notes on lower strings as her fears rise over who Kate might be.

'Innocently, I am the cause of your sorrow,' Kate originally told her here; but for Paris in 1906 the lines were transferred to the third person and given to Sharpless in his role as patient explainer. He also took over from her the appeal to let the child be adopted. Butterfly says she will hand over Trouble in half an hour, if Pinkerton himself will come and collect him. Though the orchestra remains soft these last words bring a sudden brief warmth of violin sound, while Butterfly recalls the musical phrase in which earlier she had talked of Pinkerton climbing the hill not, as now he will, to collect his son, but to return to her. Yet in her sadness she has the generosity to acknowledge Kate's happiness:

> Sotto il gran ponte del cielo non v' è
> donna di voi più felice.
> (Under the great arch of the sky there is no lady happier than you.)

Before Pinkerton left he gave Sharpless money for Butterfly. In early productions a scene followed where Suzuki takes Kate away and the Consul tries to hand over the money but Cio-Cio-San stubbornly refuses it. This was cut for the Paris performances. Now Sharpless leaves with Kate.

As they go, the orchestra leaves no doubt about the tragic mood that has engulfed Butterfly; it is made all the more tense by the sad chords being contained in a steady rhythm, woodwind and violins outlining an assertively tragic melody. The hill-climb theme easily fits this mould and is heard on lower strings, bassoon then clarinet. Suzuki feels Butterfly's rapidly beating heart. The 'hill' motif is heard again on woodwind over string chords, then on lower strings; there can be no doubting Butterfly's emotional turmoil as the orchestra represents the earlier happy hopes which must now be swimming sourly in her head.

Also from earlier in the act comes the assertive tune heard as morning broke. But now daylight is not for Butterfly; it is heard in a sadder, minor key version as she sings:

Troppa luce è di fuor,
e troppa primavera.
(Too much light shining and too much springtime.)

(There is an echo here of *La Bohème*, where Mimì died in spring as her face was shielded from the sun.) Butterfly *orders* the screen to be closed, one of the screens Pinkerton so lightly shifted around at the very start of the opera and which he himself closed for their wedding night. Now Butterfly, alone, wants only darkness.

As darkness spreads over the stage, movement in the orchestral writing stills. Butterfly asks for Trouble. He is outside, Suzuki says and is sent out to join him. She will not leave Butterfly alone, but gently her mistress reminds her it was Suzuki's own advice she should rest, though '*riposo*' (sleep) takes on a more sinister meaning in this mood, as the rapid beats on the drum (timpani) suggest. A brief reference to a song about love and death was cut before the Paris production but could only have increased the doom-laden atmosphere.

Butterfly forces out the crying Suzuki as the drums beat louder and the orchestra bursts in with a fullness not heard for some time. Then suddenly all is quiet, timpani very faint and soft string phrases and cellos quietly sing out her theme as Butterfly stands in front of the statue of Buddha. This is true music theatre – Suzuki's offstage sobs mixing with music catapulting between loud and soft as with external calm Cio-Cio-San fetches the sword seen in Act One. The Russian playwright Anton Chekhov said that a gun seen in Act One should be fired in Act Three; the sword, we feel, is being used in the same dramatic way. Not only the sword is recalled – but also the Bonze's curse. Butterfly reads the sword's inscription: 'Honourable death is preferable to life without honour'.

Suzuki makes a last attempt; as she is forbidden to enter she sends in the child. 'You must never know,' Butterfly says to her son, 'I die for you.' She does not want him to feel deserted. Sudden loud chords tear into her vocal line until she sings of her child:

O a me, sceso dal trono
dell' alto Paradiso,
(O my child, sent down from high heaven)

to a final, dignified, tragic melody, accompanied by rising figures in the woodwind and strings, with harp chords. In the first version of the opera she asked Trouble to look at her, hoping to imprint a sense of his mother's face on his mind. The final version has her wishing the boy will remember her.

The orchestra fades away to near silent drumbeats and sombre trombone notes while violas continue the melodic lament. After gently blindfolding Trouble, Butterfly stabs herself behind a screen then comes into view, staggering into a brief, final embrace with her son as flute, clarinet and strings build tension to a piercing sound which moves between soft and loud with great rapidity, and trombones intone the 'hill' motif. Pinkerton is heard offstage calling 'Butterfly' three times. The US Navy arrives even later than the US Cavalry. Pinkerton enters with Sharpless; while the Lieutenant falls to his knees, the Consul is once again the person to do something useful and look after the child. As this happens the orchestra thunders out a final tribute to Madama Butterfly with the Japanese tune to which she had earlier said she would prefer death to the life of a geisha.

There is no doubt the close of *Madama Butterfly* represents an excess of melodrama: devoted love, mother and son, desperate (and well-timed) offstage cries, death. Spoken, it would be risible today. What sets it apart is Puccini's score; its fine tunes are never clichéd and give the action a nobility and significance that go beyond the contrived detail. It is not only a matter of the invention of tunes; it is also the way themes and motifs tie together details of the action across the whole opera. For example, it would be possible to chart Butterfly's mood through the use of the Bonze's curse motif and 'The Star Spangled Banner'. The composer's supreme orchestration, building in intensity or at other times reducing to almost nothing, affects the pace at which events seem to move, and with his use of instruments, singly and in combination, combines to form his individual language. This is the art that continues to give life to the death of Butterfly.

Chapter 6

Later Operas

If Mozart had lived beyond the age of thirty-six and survived into a healthy old age, what might he have written? How much we would have lost had Verdi not lived to compose his final great Shakespeare operas *Otello* and *Falstaff* we do know and can only be thankful they were composed. If Puccini had died in 1906 after the major revisions to *Madama Butterfly*, would we now be speculating on how he might have developed as the twentieth century progressed?

Would we have deduced what did happen? For he seems to have determined not to go on producing works in the same style. Ever ready to pick up new musical developments, he wanted to find a new approach to opera. In one way he was forced to do so, for in 1906 Giuseppe Giacosa died. He had been the greater writing talent of the two librettists, and his death meant future collaboration between Illica and Puccini would leave them exposed to each other's fits of temper. They never worked together again.

Puccini soon had other quarrels on his mind, arising from his own household. But even without scandal his days could easily have been filled with overseeing revivals of his previous operas. He and Elvira spent two months in the summer of 1905 attending a Puccini festival in Buenos Aires, for which he provided another revised version of the early *Edgar* to go alongside more recent operas.

Finding a new subject, wishing not to repeat himself and staying open to new musical influences in a period when fundamental changes in style were accelerating in all the arts, was time-consuming. Although Elvira went with him to Buenos Aires, she had not been able to accompany him on many of his journeys. Their domestic situation was a recipe for tension. While Elvira the boldly attractive young woman became plainer and stouter in middle-age her husband was becoming increasingly distinguished in appearance and reputation. He travelled widely and frequently to theatres where he would find plenty of attractive young women. It was Elvira's misfortune that when her jealousy did boil over it did so on to an innocent and vulnerable local teenager. Had Puccini wished to look into his own life for material he could hardly have found a better successor to Mimi or Butterfly than Doria Manfredi, the local girl he had hired as a domestic servant.

But the composer did not want another Mimi, or another anything. He searched widely for a different type of subject among French, Spanish and English literature – helped in the last by a friend in London society, Sybil Seligman. She was one of his short-term lovers who stayed a long-term friend, and her son Vincent later wrote a memoir based on the non-sexual years of the relationship. For a time it looked as though Puccini was going to find inspiration in a modern French novel of – for the period – unusual sexual outspokenness. Pierre Loüys's *The Woman and the Puppet* caused a stir in its day. The opera planned from it was to take the name of a character, *Conchita*, and provide a story of sexual obsession and domination whose anti-heroine worked, like Carmen, in a Seville cigarette factory. Her psycho-sexual tormenting of her rich lover is reversed after he gives her a beating. It would have been fascinating to see how such a story would have survived in the operatic repertoire today.

Not that the opera Puccini *did* write is seen that often. In the end he went back to the source of his previous opera, choosing this time a full-length three-act drama by Belasco called *The Girl of the Golden West* (it retains Belasco's title in English though the 'Golden' was lost in the Italian title *La Fanciulla del West*). But before it was written another girl – in an incident far from golden – disrupted the composer's life.

Puccini had already had one, quite comical, brush with the law. Perpetually fond of hunting wild-fowl he had arranged hunting rights with a local landowner so he could shoot on the lake. One night a keeper failed to recognise Puccini's legitimate shots in the dark and hauled him up before the local constabulary. Luckily order was restored before Italy's leading composer was sent down as a poacher.

What happened in 1909 was far more serious. Ever since the car crash during work on *Madama Butterfly* Puccini had employed Doria Manfredi to help about the house. Quite why Elvira began to suspect a sexual relationship between Doria and Giacomo is unclear; perhaps it was a displacement from her suspicions over his many brief liaisons in distant places. Here was somebody she *could* lay her hands on. However it came about, jealousy led her to a campaign of lies directed both at Doria herself and at anyone else who would listen. She sacked Doria, she attacked her verbally in the street; she tried to have the young woman thrown out of town.

Doria was a mild, impressionable young woman and was not equipped to fight such a grand opponent. From the start her family had not wanted her to work for the Puccinis. Now with Elvira coming up to them and speaking of Doria's 'affair' with her husband, some of the Manfredis began to believe the story. Attacked and humiliated on all sides, Doria gave up and in January 1909 she killed herself, taking most of a week to die painfully of poison.

Events then moved quickly. Her family had her corpse medically examined. She was a virgin; all Elvira's insults had been lies. There had been defamation as well. By 1st February the Manfredis had begun legal proceedings. The people of Torre del Lago turned against the Puccinis and particularly against Elvira. At the trial, held in Pisa that summer, she was found guilty and sentenced to five months and five days in prison, was fined and had costs awarded against her.

Elvira had brought this on herself not only by her jealousy and accusations but by an hysterical certainty she could prove her claims. Her supposed proofs never materialised, leaving her defence a shambles. After the verdict she continued to insist she had documentary evidence of her allegations. None was ever produced. A better organised appeal was arranged, led now by proper legal experts. Puccini raised his offer of an out-of-court settlement. By October 1909 the matter was officially over.

Had his wife actually gone to prison the shame would have been far worse for Puccini. As it was the death of this poor girl of Torre had cost him

most of the year with his *Girl of the Golden West*. And from the time of this death, his heroines began to have a better chance of survival.

La Fanciulla del West

First performed at the Metropolitan Opera House, New York, on 10th December 1910.
Conductor: Arturo Toscanini.

ACT I: *The Polka Saloon, Sierra Nevada, California. 1849.*
As a minstrel sings outside, Sheriff Jack Rance sits smoking. Miners enter, start drinking and gambling. Bartender Nick assures several of them that Minnie, who owns the Polka, will marry them. This proves good for business as the deludedly happy suitors each order cigars or whisky all round. One miner, Larkens, becomes homesick and the others collect for his fare back to Cornwall. An argument over a card cheat is followed by another over who is actually going to marry Minnie. Rance stops the first, Minnie herself enters putting an end to the second. She gathers the miners round for their regular Bible class. Following this, Rance says he loves her as he has never loved anybody before and that he would give all his wealth for a kiss. She declines; then in comes Dick Johnson, a stranger whose imminent arrival has already caused a sensation because he is looking to buy whisky diluted with water (at the Polka they take their whisky neat).

Johnson and Minnie recognise one another; they have met once before and clearly made a mutual impression. Rance is jealous as the pair go next door to dance. Ashby, agent of the transit company Wells Fargo, announces the Mexican bandit Ramerrez is around; one of his gang, a man called Castro, has been captured. Castro is dragged on and recognises Dick Johnson's saddlebags as those of Ramerrez. He assumes his leader has been caught. A few moments later Johnson returns and, seeing him free, Castro passes a message to Johnson/Ramerrez that a whistle from him will be the signal for the gang to rob the Polka, where the miners' gold is stored.

Castro offers to lead the miners to Ramerrez but takes them on a false trail. However, Johnson does not give the signal and, instead of using their absence to rob Minnie's saloon, he stays with her before following her to her mountain cabin.

ACT II: *Minnie's cabin.*
Minnie prepares for Johnson's arrival, sending her Indian servant Wowkle home. During their conversation Johnson asks for a kiss and decides to leave when she declines. But a blizzard is blowing up and she tells him to stay, giving up her bed and lying by the fire. A loud knock at the door announces Rance, Ashby and others searching for Ramerrez. Johnson hides while she lets them in. Rance also shows Minnie a picture of the mysterious Nina Micheltorena who is said to be Ramerrez's lover. And he tells her Johnson is Ramerrez. The search party leaves and despite Johnson's declarations of love, Minnie orders him out. He goes. There is a shot. Johnson returns wounded. She can no longer hide her love for him, but conceals Johnson in her loft. When Rance comes back Minnie repulses his advances and invites him to search the cabin if he is so sure Ramerrez is there. Rance looks but finds nothing; he has not thought of the loft. Then just as he is about to go, blood

from Johnson's wound falls on to the Sheriff's hand. He fetches the bandit down and as Johnson collapses Minnie helps him to the table where he slumps forward unconscious. Minnie offers an all-or-nothing-best-of-three poker game to Rance. If she wins Johnson will be allowed to go free; if Rance wins he can have her as his own. Rance agrees. Each wins one hand. Rance is about to win the third when Minnie causes a distraction and takes the game by cheating.

ACT III: *A forest clearing. Dawn.*
Shouts from the search party closing in on Johnson wake Ashby who rides off to ensure the bandit is taken alive. Johnson is brought on and a lynch mob set about hanging him. He asks only that Minnie is not told about his death, but allowed to go on believing he has left for a new life elsewhere. Rance's jealousy surges; he hits Johnson and demands the execution go ahead at once. But as the noose is being tightened Minnie rides on, pistol in hand, demanding the lynch mob stop. Against Rance, Minnie insists Johnson be given a fresh chance to start a new life. Reminded of all she has done for them, the miners stand back and the two lovers leave together.

La Fanciulla del West: The Libretto

The Californian gold rush of 1849 was half a century in the past when Belasco wrote his play. It had all happened the other side of the continent from New York theatregoers. It was distant enough in time and space to be romanticised. Puccini had liked the Wild West plays he had seen when visiting New York for *Butterfly*. These had included *The Girl of the Golden West*. His English lover and friend Sybil Seligman arranged for an Italian translation to be provided.

La Fanciulla del West is the first full voice of a new, twentieth-century Puccini. Giacosa's death had ended the old angry partnership of Puccini-Giacosa-Illica. Instead there was a new angry partnership. Carlo Zangarini worked steadily – so steadily that despite liking Zangarini's work, Puccini had to insist on a quicker collaborative hand. Ricordi brought in Guelfo Civinini, to Zangarini's intense displeasure. In fact he seems to have finally abandoned the whole job to Civinini.

If Puccini intended his new style to avoid a repeat of the *Madama Butterfly* première, he succeeded. Helped by Belasco's immaculately detailed scenic and staging techniques and the prestige of the New York Metropolitan's first ever world première (the new world stealing a march on the old, safe from the problems and politics of La Scala), *La Fanciulla del West* was a popular and critical success of the first order. Soon it had spread to the major American opera centres – Philadelphia, Chicago, Boston and St Louis among them.

So, after a disaster with one of the most famous-to-be operas of the century, Puccini had a hit with a soon-to-be-all-but-forgotten work. It might be said that the initial success was that of Belasco, for the author knew how to please his fellow Americans and his staging expertise as director played a vital part in the impact of the New York production.

In London, unaccustomed to the Wild West myth (not yet exported through Hollywood), and minus Belasco and the singing of Enrico Caruso as Dick Johnson, *La Fanciulla* had less success. By the time it reached Italy the opera was already reputed to mark a new stylistic path in Puccini's career. A pattern tends to recur in such situations. A composer introduces new elements into his work. At first hearing, these stand out and the comment is all about differences. By the time the news has gone round, or the work been heard several times, these novel features have been absorbed into the overall style. People start noticing the similarities and comment moves to what is consistent across the composer's output.

There are undoubtedly new sounds in this opera. The most anthologised highlight is Johnson's act three plea that Minnie is not told of his fate, 'Ch' ella me creda libere' (I let her believe me free), yet it lasts only two minutes. There are far fewer starry sequences than in Puccini's preceding operas. The tendency to close down the movement in the score and take a breath before a major lyrical piece – seen most clearly in 'Un bel di' – has disappeared. There is a new manner of using woodwind and brass in the orchestra to characterise moments in the action, while the vocal lines of Minnie and Johnson in particular show a wide range in pitch and in mood, from the gentle and restrained to the forceful and declamatory.

Puccini again played a major role in the final shape the opera took. Most significantly he telescoped Belasco's two final acts into one and moved this from the saloon to the outdoors, exploiting the scenic scope of the Sierra. He also shifted Minnie's Bible class from the last act to the first. As the Bible lesson's theme from Psalm 51 is the possibility that anyone may be redeemed, this both establishes Minnie's kindly authority with the miners and her optimism early in the action – an optimism she needs bringing Bible classes to these miners for Mammon – and it shows that her belief in redemption is not just special pleading for the man she loves.

La Fanciulla del West: The Music

So modern is the score, for 1910, that the crash of the opening might well have come from a 1940s gangster film. It is soon swept aside by a warmer tune. As with the two operas he set in the orient, Puccini uses genuine folk tunes in his western, to be sung by the chorus. It is interesting that Sheriff Rance's first part in the action is to stop the miners killing a card cheat. Instead he places a playing card over the man's heart as a warning no-one should trust him. If it is removed, the cheat can be shot. For Rance is the law in California just as Scarpia was in Rome. Both have a personal reason to wish the tenor dead – Cavaradossi or Dick Johnson. But whereas Scarpia is unscrupulous and ruthless, Rance is genuinely in love with Minnie. And for all his fervour in hurrying on the lynch mob when Johnson is to be hanged, he keeps to his second act bargain. It is the Wells Fargo agent Ashby who has hunted Johnson/Ramerrez down. The way Rance uses a card to pinpoint a cheat is reflected in Minnie's cheating at the end of Act Two, for Johnson's sake, and Rance's failure to notice. It is possible to feel sympathy for him. At the very least he is a person struggling with his conscience, not a deliberate villain.

Despite the complexity of his character, Sheriff Rance enjoys less musical sympathy than either Minnie or Johnson. For although the world will always welcome lovers, it still has nothing on Puccini, who composed most of his finest music in his extensive and unconventionally structured love scenes. Yet Rance is given a background: he is a solitary individual seeking solace and

With *La Fanciulla del West*, his second opera derived from a play by the popular American writer/producer David Belasco, Puccini struck out in a new artistic direction. The instant appeal in New York was great, thanks to Belasco's magnificent and detailed stage production, but the work has fared less well subsequently.

fulfilment through love.

So is Minnie, who is given space in the first act to sing about her dirty childhood living in a room over a kitchen in Soledad, and seeking the kind of love her parents had. Rance tries to persuade her she has found such love with him, but he is undercut by the action, as Dick Johnson walks in to the Polka.

If the sheriff is not a villain, can it be that the bandit is a hero? Johnson is of course a very special sort of bandit, a criminal more by inheritance than inclination. In fact he managed to be brought up and enter adulthood without realising his father was in the business of robbery at all. On his father's death the gang announced themselves to him as a legacy. This happened only six months ago. Everything is being done to show that he is

Sheriff Jack Rance at the
Polka Saloon, beside a
'wanted' poster for the
bandit Ramirez, who
turns up as the tenor,
Dick Johnson. As with
Tosca, the lawman has
personal and business
reasons for wanting to
remove the tenor,
though Rance's passion
for saloon-keeper
Minnie is more generous
than Scarpia's for Tosca.

not really a bandit at all. No wonder Minnie sees he is capable of being plucked back to grace by a redemptive hand ('You have the face of an angel,' he tells Minnie at the end of Act One). Indeed Johnson says he accepted criminal status as his destiny, as if it were separate from his own will. Of the three central characters this gang leader is the least violent on stage. Even Minnie produces a handy little Derringer – the western lady's companion – and uses it to discourage Rance's attentions in Act One.

Rance may be the official peacekeeper but he is associated with the shot that wounds Johnson, and the music in Act Two often links him to what is urgent or harsh, as with the loud chords with which Minnie tells him to leave her forever after he has searched her house. Johnson in contrast has some of the warmest, richly harmonised music in the score – swaying, passionate, yearning and reaching its climax in his apparently last words about letting Minnie believe he remains alive and free.

If *La Fanciulla del West* suffers in popularity for its experimentation with the new ways of the music Puccini heard from progressive composers of the day, his next work *La Rondine* (The Swallow) began as an intention to use that conservative form, the operetta. He soon found that it was not something he could turn his musical personality to. This is no surprise, for operettas consisted of separate musical numbers isolated by chunks of spoken dialogue which moved the story forward without the composer's involvement. Puccini could hardly adapt to a way of working so unlike his own use of music for dramatic and character development. And as luck would have it – or as might be expected in someone so sublimely unaware of politics – Puccini found himself working to a commission from the Vienna Karltheater just as the First World War broke out. In 1915 Italy was in conflict with Austria.

Puccini discarded the operetta idea as soon as he saw the libretto. He began talking about a comic opera, specifically mentioning Richard Strauss's *Der Rosenkavalier* – to which *La Rondine* shows no noticeable resemblance. The score was finished in October 1915. Because of the war, the première was moved to Monte Carlo and, its contractual ties broken, the house of Ricordi (run since Julio's death in 1912 by his son Tito, the producer of the original La Scala *Madama Butterfly*) decided not to publish the score. Their rivals Sonzogno did. *La Rondine* was the only Puccini opera not to be published by Ricordi.

La Rondine

First performed at the Théâtre du Casino, Monte Carlo on 27th March 1917.
Conducted by Gino Marinuzzi.

ACT I: *Paris, in the Second Empire. An elegant drawing-room.*
Magda de Civry, the mistress of a wealthy banker called Rambaldo, pours tea for her guests Yvette, Bianca and Suzy as the poet Prunier offers his views on love. Magda adds her own verse to his poem. Rambaldo introduces the son of an old friend. Prunier tells Magda she resembles a swallow (*rondine*) wishing to fly to real love. The friend's son, Ruggero, is taken out to a fashionable dance. Magda decides to go there too, in disguise. Her maid Lisette goes along with Prunier.

ACT II: *The Bal Bullier. Night.*

Avoiding various flirtatious men, Magda approaches Ruggero, calling herself Paulette. As they dance Lisette enters with Prunier. Lisette recognises her mistress despite Magda's disguise. She and Prunier pretend not to know it is Magda, however. Then Rambaldo finds them; Magda admits she loves Ruggero and leaves with him.

ACT III: *The Riviera. A villa terrace. Several months later.*

Ruggero wants to marry Magda but she knows his family would never accept her. Rambaldo is willing to take her back as his mistress. Lisette, fed up with being trained by Prunier to be more ladylike, asks to go back to Magda's service. Magda leaves Ruggero devastated when he finds out her real lifestyle.

Any impression that we are in a world resembling *Die Fledermaus* is accurate. Magda is a stereotype from operetta rather than a real person. The role relies on the performer's charm rather than intrinsic interest. Very little actually happens in *La Rondine*, certainly by comparison with Puccini's other operas. Its main importance lay in bringing the librettist Giuseppe Adami into collaboration with Puccini. Though his work was nowhere near the quality of the fine Illica/Giacosa libretti, Adami was to do better for Puccini, as well as writing an early, enthusiastic biography of the composer and compiling a volume of his letters.

While the music of *La Rondine* has no great character-delving properties, the huge amount of dance, especially waltz, music includes attractive melodies and intriguing orchestrations. Puccini continued to develop the boundaries of his harmonies in a way the old waltz operetta-writers would never have done – there is something of the old style in modern dress that is found in Ravel's *La Valse*. As Magda remembers a fleeting earlier love at a previous Bal Bullier, 'Ora dolci e divine' (Sweet and divine hours), there is a memorable, bittersweet tune to the words of a distant voice:

> Fanciulla, è sbocciato l' amore!
> Difendi, difendi il tuo cuore!
> (Child, love has blossomed! Defend, defend your heart!)

– a haunting phrase that develops in an earnest, energetic, upward-sweeping line.

Although the yearning to compose an operetta had turned out to be an impractical wish, against the grain of Puccini's musical nature, another long-nursed idea was about to develop a powerful outcome. Since the early years of the new century Puccini had talked about an evening made up of three one-act operas. As a fashion, the one-act opera had been popular in the late nineteenth century's brief verismo phase, the one lasting result of which has been the frequent combining of Leoncavallo's *I Pagliacci* with Mascagni's *Cavalleria Rusticana*. Ricordi had dissuaded Puccini at first, more on commercial than artistic grounds, and time had passed on. However in 1913, shortly after Giulio Ricordi's death, Puccini began working on a macabre one-act French play *La Houppelande* (The Cloak) by Didier Gold. Neither of the two pieces he considered as companions for this came to anything. This is probably just as well: one of them was a play about a black African who took revenge on white Europeans who had exhibited him in a Paris funfair, by making a pre-prandial exhibition of some European explorers when they came to his cannibal village. Gold's play, in Italian *Il Tabarro*, stayed with the composer however. It is a dark, realistic piece and Puccini wanted something light and spiritual to follow it. This he found eventually in *Suor Angelica*, though it is the third piece in what became *Il Trittico* (The Triptych, a name that was eventually found for the whole programme) which became the greatest success. The comedy – Puccini's sole comedy – *Gianni Schicchi* – is light but earthy.

The idea of three one-act operas that have no connection in subject and a distinct contrast in atmosphere, was a development in Puccini's theatrical thinking. The scores show changes in his musical ideas too – developments that had begun with *La Fanciulla del West* but were only now to start creating major Puccini works. Europe was entering upon a decidedly new cultural mood, one that was to cock snooks at traditional expectations of culture and lead to a fragmentation of artistic expression. Of course there had always been experimentation and in the late nineteenth century there were challenges to audience expectations. But soon into the twentieth century the new movements drumming away at the limits of accepted artistic expression burst all bounds. Society was no longer sufficiently confident or supple to control the new music, drama, literature and painting.

Puccini was no longer simply the successor to the confident tradition of Verdi and Rossini. He was the only remaining composer of any achievement in Italian opera. Younger critics and musicians attacked all he represented. Meanwhile the composer himself, continually absorbing new influences, was aware of the sounds of Debussy and Stravinsky. In harmony, rhythm and orchestral texture his music was changing. In range of subject his theatrical sights were shifting too. Yet we should not too easily assume that a pattern of cultural or social development was responsible for all Puccini's decisions. He remained a forceful individual.

Composition of *Il Tabarro* began in 1913, was resumed in 1915 and finished late in 1916. A number of hands had a go at the libretto, but it was finally written by Giuseppe Adami. *Suor Angelica* and *Gianni Schicchi* were the work of Giovacchino Forzano. *Gianni Schicchi* was based on a brief mention, in Dante's *The Divine Comedy*, Schicchi being condemned to hell for imitating a dead man in order to create a false will. 20th April 1918 saw Schicchi's fate musically determined and the *Trittico* completed.

Il Trittico

First performed at the Metropolitan Opera House, New York on 14th December 1918.
Conductor: Roberto Moranzoni.

Il Tabarro (The Cloak)
Paris. A quay on the Seine, where Michele's barge is moored. The early twentieth century. Sunset.
Michele smokes a pipe while talking with his young wife Giorgetta. It is plain she does not love him. Michele's men finish unloading the barge and Giorgetta gives them a drink. An itinerant musician passes and Giorgetta dances with some of the men, including the youngest of the workers on Michele's barge, Luigi. Left alone, these two arrange a lovers' assignation for later; the sign for Luigi to approach will be Giorgetta striking a match.

Lovers pass by. La Frugola, wife to another of Michele's men Il Talpa (The Mole) speaks of her dream of a country cottage. Michele tries to reawaken Giorgetta's love and refers to their child who died. He has no success. When she goes down into the barge, Michele speaks to himself of the lover he is sure she has – who could it be? The young Luigi is most likely, but he has asked to leave the barge. As he thinks, Michele strikes a match for his pipe. Luigi takes this for Giorgetta's signal, arrives and is strangled by Michele, who then hides him under his great cloak. When Giorgetta reappears Michele reveals, to her horror, her lover's body.

Suor Angelica
An Italian convent. Late seventeenth century.
Some nuns are late for prayers and receive small punishments. Various nuns talk of their secret desires. There is joy in the effect that happens only for three days when the sun's rays are at the necessary angle to give a wonderful gold complexion to the water in the convent fountain. Sister Angelica has been seven years in the convent and claims to have no secret desire. But her composure is disturbed when a rich carriage arrives and there is a visitor for her. It is the Princess, her aunt, who wants Angelica's signature on a document. Angelica's sister is to marry and her husband is to be Angelica's former lover. But what really consumes the nun is the need for news of the child she bore this man. Severely, the Princess tells her the child is dead. Left alone, Angelica mourns and in her sorrow uses her knowledge of herbs to prepare a poison. No sooner has she drunk it than she realises suicide is a sin – she fears damnation. She prays to the Madonna to save her and is granted a celestial vision of her child, who leads his mother to Paradise.

Gianni Schicchi
The house of Buoso Donati, Florence. Late thirteenth century, or thereabouts.
Buoso has just died and his assembled relatives put on a show of grief. They are alarmed to hear that he has left his fortune to the church and search frantically for the will. They find it, and he has. Young Rinuccio is in love with Lauretta, daughter to the trickster Gianni Schicchi. He hoped the inheritance would free him to marry but now suggests sending for Schicchi to help them – he is the only person cunning enough to devise a plan. The rest of the Donati family want nothing to do with the parvenu Schicchi, but Rinuccio sends for him anyway. When Schicchi and Lauretta turn up, the Donati are curt with him and he turns to leave, but Lauretta appeals to him to stay and help her lover's family. Ascertaining that nobody else knows of Buoso's death, Gianni decides to impersonate the deceased and dictate a new will. A doctor arrives and Gianni sends him away, incidentally trying out his vocal impersonation of Buoso. It works. A notary is called to make a new will but Gianni leaves all the best things, including the house, to himself. Then he orders the family out of his house. Lauretta and Rinuccio are happy with each other, but Gianni Schicchi reminds us he was sent to hell for this trick.

Il Trittico: The Music

As *Il Tabarro* starts, a gently rising theme represents the calmly lapping waters. In some ways things are too calm for Giorgetta. 'Smoke no longer comes from your pipe,' she laments to Michele. This 'smoke' refers to the fires of passion too, but in these first words there is also a link to the end of the opera, where a match will provoke the tragedy. Michele assures her he still loves her, 'Because my pipe is finished doesn't mean my passion is too.' The reserve and caution, the hesitancies between the two tell of their strained relationship. Giorgetta relaxes in other company, none more so than that of Luigi. Of the three barge hands he is the only one without a nickname – the others are Il Tinca (The Tench) and Il Talpa (The Mole). Musically, when Giorgetta changes dancing partners from Il Tinca to Luigi, orchestral strings add a new warmth to the music.

Michele's return brings back the sense of caution and separation. The red sunset Giorgetta notices hints too at passion and violence, while Michele's words, 'People who work, survive,' show the pressure of daily toil on these people. When Luigi protests about the life of a working man, it is less a political outburst than the exuberance of passion. Old men like Michele might be ground into a rut; life has more to offer the young. To see Luigi's words as the anger of love repressed by the need to earn a living, and Michele's as the refuge of someone who has lost love, puts this part of the opera clearly in the mould of Puccini's preoccupation with passions.

Even more than *Tosca*, *Il Tabarro* is Puccini's belated dip into verismo. It is present in the workaday setting, though in this case it is urban rather than rural, in the simmering, ultimately murderous, obsessive passion of Michele

An old man and his pipe; Michele the barge-owner suspects his young wife Giorgetta of having a affair, but does not yet know the identity of her lover. Michele is played by the Italian baritone Tito Gobbi (1913-1984). Gobbi was also an outstanding Scarpia, often singing the part opposite the Tosca of Maria Callas.

and in Giorgetta's frustrated desires. Musically, verismo can be heard in the 'sound effects' of tug hooter and car horn, the realistic effect of the not-quite-octaves on an out of tune barrel-organ and in the use of popular ballad style. Though there is no connection but the name, the ballad-singer's song of the story of Mimi ends each stanza with a speeded-up, rather jolly version of *La Bohème's* 'Si. Mi chiamano Mimi'.

Other musical influences date from after the verismo period, such as the Debussy-like chords that accompany reference to the rummaging through rubbish of La Frugola (Il Talpa's wife; the name means 'The Rummager'). La Frugola's dream of a country cottage idyll, despite its catchy one-note phrase, is linked verbally to the idea of waiting for death. Giorgetta and Luigi's love finds an outlet when they unite in praise of the urban life of their back-grounds in Belleville, in the heart of Paris. The characters who work around the barge add colour but they also reflect the central conflict between Michele and Giorgetta. La Frugola is a cat-lover, a refuge from her awkward relations with her husband. Il Tinca drinks a lot, but Michele defends him because he has an unfaithful wife.

If the first half of the opera presents a rich preparation of character and atmosphere, the second half brings affairs to a swift climax. It is increasingly dominated by brief, fateful-sounding motifs, often at a low pitch. The effect is one of concentration and passion bursting at its bounds. Michele and Giorgetta sing together in what is far from a love duet, but is Michele's attempt to revive love in his wife. The cello theme accompanying this softens his character for us, though a new theme as he talks of how he used to protect Giorgetta in the old days by wrapping her in his cloak brings a sinister foreboding, connected to the great garment.

'Whore!' he calls her after she has left him and gone down into the barge. His gloom is only increased by the happy lovers passing on the road and the evening signal from the army barracks. Michele's introspection takes the form of a soliloquy with a bleak, dark opening: 'Nulla! Silenzio! (Nothing! Silence!). When Luigi arrives, mistaking Michele's match for Giorgetta's signal, the music linked to Michele's cloak becomes increasingly assertive until it dominates the scene.

On-stage murder in *Il Tabarro* is replaced by on-stage suicide in *Suor Angelica* (Sister Angelica), in which the almost entirely female voices express the spirituality Puccini wanted in contrast to the first *Trittico* panel. Though there are secret desires and longings in the second opera, a lightness of manner is set beside the dark passions of the previous opera. Once again there are sad memories of a past love. But Angelica's emotions are those of a mother rather than a lover and the separation is caused by renunciation – by implication the result of severe family pressure.

Soft bells, strings and harp help establish the ordered, spiritual life. Even here, though, the opening presents a minor example of sin and punishment. At the start two nuns are late for service and offer no excuse. There is also the sense of transience in the earthly reflection of spiritual beauty. Time gives but soon takes away. Only for three days a year does the sun create the miracle of the golden fountain. The convent is a kind of death, the death of desires: 'I have no desires,' Angelica lies. We are told too that 'Desires are the flowers of the living'.

The opera shows that passions are a disturbing, inevitable part of life. In *Il Tabarro* there was the self-deception that indifference could lead to a life where passion played no part: that one could get by, as La Frugola put it. In *Suor Angelica* we see that even the best of intentions and a regime of disciplined daily life do not remove all-pervading passions. Such passions can destroy, as Michele destroys Luigi and Giorgetta's love. Turned inwards they can destroy one's self, as happens with Angelica. In the final panel of the triptych the mood swings round to comedy and even the meanest passion, greed, leads unintentionally to two lovers being brought together.

In *Suor Angelica*, it is a long time before the action becomes dramatic – there is a lot of atmospheric preparation. This lack of forward momentum is made tolerable by delicate scoring, particularly among the woodwind. Animal impressions occur, as with La Frugola's cat in *Il Tabarro*. In one case the animal itself, a donkey, puts in an appearance. It is the arrival of the Princess that really begins the action. Angelica, who has claimed she has no desires, asks eagerly about the colour and coat of arms of the carriage that

Three operas in one: Puccini had contemplated such a bill of fare for many years, but the evening's components soon split apart, with the final comedy, *Gianni Schicchi* proving the most popular. However, the opening opera, *Il Tabarro*, has considerable power in its compresssed tragedy.

This Theatre, when filled to its capacity, can be emptied in five minutes. Choose the nearest exit now and in case of need walk quietly (do not run) to that exit in order to avoid panic.

METROPOLITAN OPERA HOVSE

SATURDAY EVENING, DECEMBER 14TH, AT 8 O'CLOCK
FIRST PERFORMANCE ON ANY STAGE
GIACOMO PUCCINI'S

THREE ONE-ACT OPERAS

I.

IL TABARRO

(THE CLOAK)

Book by GIUSEPPE ADAMI after "La Houppelande," by Didier Gold

MICHELE	LUIGI MONTESANTO	GIORGETTA	CLAUDIA MUZIO
LUIGI	GIULIO CRIMI	LA FRUGOLA	ALICE GENTLE
IL TINCA	ANGELO BADA	VENDITORE DI CANZONI	PIETRO AUDISIO
IL TALPA	ADAMO DIDUR	L'INNAMORATA	MARIE TIFFANY

CARRIERS, MIDINETTES, AN ORGAN-GRINDER.

SCENE:—THE SEINE, PARIS. MICHELE'S BARGE.
Painted by Ernest M. Gros after a sketch by Pietro Stroppa.

II.

SUOR ANGELICA

(SISTER ANGELICA)

Book by GIOACHINO FORZANO

SUOR ANGELICA	GERALDINE FARRAR	SUOR DOLCINA	MARIE MATTFELD
LA ZIA PRINCIPESSA	FLORA PERINI	SORELLE CERCATRICI	KITTY BEALE
LA BADESSA	RITA FORNIA		MINNIE EGENER
LA SUOR ZELATRICE	MARIE SUNDELIUS	LE CONVERSE	MARIE TIFFANY
LA MAESTRA DELLE NOVIZIE	CECIL ARDEN		VENI WARWICK
SUOR GENOVIEFFA	MARY ELLIS	UNA NOVIZIA	PHILLIS WHITE
SUOR OSMINA	MARGUERITE BELLERI		

SCENE:—A CONVENT IN ITALY. END OF 1600.
Painted by Frank Platzer after a sketch by Pietro Stroppa.

III.

GIANNI SCHICCHI

Book by GIOACHINO FORZANO

GIANNI SCHICCHI	GIUSEPPE DE LUCA	SIMONE	ADAMO DIDUR
LAURETTA	FLORENCE EASTON	MARCO	LOUIS D'ANGELO
LA VECCHIA	KATHLEEN HOWARD	LA CIESCA	MARIE SUNDELIUS
RINUCCIO	GIULIO CRIMI	SPINELLOCCIO	POMPILIO MALATESTA
GHERARDO	ANGELO BADA	SER AMANTIO DI NICOLAO	ANDRES DE SEGUROLA
NELLA	MARIE TIFFANY	PINELLINO	VINCENZO RESCHIGLIAN
GHERARDINO	MARIO MALATESTA	GUCCIO	CARL SCHLEGEL
BETTO	PAOLO ANANIAN		

SCENE:—THE BEDROOM OF THE LATE BUOSO DONATI. (FLORENCE ANNO 1299.)
Painted by Pieretto Bianco after a sketch by Galileo Chini, Florence.

CONDUCTOR, ROBERTO MORANZONI

STAGE DIRECTOR	RICHARD ORDYNSKI	TECHNICAL DIRECTOR	EDWARD SIEDLE
CHORUS MASTER	GIULIO SETTI	STAGE MANAGER	ARMANDO AGNINI

Costumes executed by Mme. Louise Musaeus.
Properties and accessories by the Siedle Studio.

comes to the convent. Her curiosity seems about to be answered when the convent bell rings and the music takes on a new tune, spiritual delicacy being infused with human passion. The new theme is soon repeated by a solo flute and viola, an octave apart, with pizzicato violins.

Angelica's aunt, the Princess, enters. This stern lady is announced by a phrase heard four times with slight variations. Whatever the rift between Angelica and her family this autocrat has not come to mend it, simply to obtain the nun's necessary signature on a legal document. Music and performances contrast the old Princess and the nun trembling with the life instinct. Angelica's feelings at last burst out when she hears that her former lover is to marry her young sister. The Princess continues to disregard Angelica's feelings. In a firm, rising, repeated theme expressing her unrelenting personality, she condemns Angelica.

Angelica's eager questions about her illegitimate son (it is his father who is about to marry her sister) are accompanied by a short, agitated motif, leading to the news of the child's death. Angelica collapses, and though the Princess seems willing to help her if she has fainted, the first tearful suggestion that her collapse was a sign of distress repels the aunt. Utterly demoralised, Angelica signs the document.

Alone, and with the brief golden sun glow on the fountain having long given way to darkness, Angelica sings a soliloquy in which she imagines herself addressing the baby who never knew her:

Senza mamma, o bimbo, tu sei morto!
(Without your mother, O child, you died!)

Puccini's penchant for the potentially sickly is salvaged by his melodic persuasion and originality, enhanced by sensitivity and individuality in his use of the orchestra. In 'Senza mamma' for example, he switches around the expected relation between harp and violins; it is the harp that carries the tune and violins which provide the accompaniment in spread chords. Few artists have this ability to transform sentimentality into high – if not the highest – art.

Grief is followed by unnaturally heightened spirits, as can happen, and a chorus of nuns increases the effect. Next comes calm, the stage empty, the orchestra hinting that the underlying grief remains – for 'Senza mamma' is recalled. Angelica returns with a jar in which she collects water and herbs for a poisonous pot-pourri. Saying goodbye to the convent and kissing the crucifix, she drinks her lethal concoction to a theme earlier linked with the idea:

La morte é vita bella.
(Death is beautiful life.)

But to a nun suicide is also a sin. With the music that had accompanied her previous anxiety over her son, she asks the Madonna for help. This comes in the form of an off-stage chorus and band including organ, piano and trumpets, representing the voice of heaven. As it moves towards its climax it adds a male element – the only, brief use of male voices in *Suor Angelica*. And, as a fierce light suggests the gates of heaven opening, Angelica is united in death with her son.

In *Gianni Schicchi* the doorway between life and death has already shut with Buoso Donati on the wrong side, although this tale of trickery and the

The first production of *Gianni Schicchi* at the Metropolitan Opera House, New York, in December 1918 with Giuseppe De Luca as Schicchi, Florence Easton as Lauretta and Giulio Crimi as Rinuccio. Within a month it was seen, as part of the full *Il Trittico* programme, in Rome.

outwitting of lesser unworthies by a more cunning rascal is built on an attempt to deny the fact. Death is a common thread through *Il Trittico*, together with love. In *Il Tabarro* an unwise marriage diverts love into adultery and jealousy leading to death. In *Suor Angelica* the birth of a child creates a love which becomes intolerable when it is frustrated (her child clearly matters far more to Angelica than her lover). The birth, marriage, death triptych is completed by *Gianni Schicchi*. But this is a comedy and the death of old Buoso brings young lovers together.

The Donati regard themselves as a truly established pillar of thirteenth century Florentine society. They will have nothing to do with the incomer Schicchi. The story is not about individuals this time so much as types. In this way Forzano drew on the Italian tradition of the *commedia dell'arte*.

Commedia was performed by theatrical families who stuck together, each member performing the same part time and time again. There was no set script, just a convoluted plot outline for each show, around which the actors would weave their much-practised verbal and physical routines as seemed best for each particular audience. Actors generally wore half-masks, covering their faces from nose and cheeks up. All this meant there was no room to build individuality, and the same character types would pop up in every *commedia* performance. Audiences would know whom to expect and how they would, in general terms, behave. There were young lovers, cunning servants, pedantic professors and pompous old men. Some of these types, such as Pulcinella, Harlequin or Columbine, survive in popular entertainments such as pantomime or Punch and Judy shows. They also survive as the three 'Masks' in *Turandot*.

Unlike the *commedia*, Puccini's *Gianni Schicchi* is obviously fully written out by the composer and it is based on a work that pre-dates this comic tradition, but Forzano's libretto contains the types of Italian comedy – young lovers, scheming rogue (usually a servant; Gianni is not a servant but comes from a lowly social class) and greedy old burghers.

133

Another of Puccini's bright and fast openings introduces a clucking little theme. Slower and quieter, it might be quite sad, and it uses the kind of phrase associated with laments in Italian opera; but at this speed it tells that the line of Buoso's weeping relatives have thoughts other than of grief for him. Mixed in with this is a quick six-note figure which heralds the importance of Gianni Schicchi to the plot. Even the drumbeats which funereally join the clucking theme do not stop the comic feel of the music. When one of the family, Betto, puts about the rumour he has heard, that Buoso died leaving his money to the church, the relatives begin a frantic, greed-inspired search for the will. Can the horrid rumour be true? A cor anglais introduces a sad version of the clucking tune, suggesting the loss of the inheritance strikes the family more deeply than the loss of their relative. This section also brings the young Rinuccio to notice, as he talks in his imagination to his love, Gianni Schicchi's daughter Lauretta:

O Lauretta, amore mio, speriam nel testamento dello zio.
(O Lauretta, my love, let us place our hope in this will.)

Meanwhile as the search for the will is interrupted by brief, but false, hopes it has been found, Betto helps himself to the family silver along the way.

Rinuccio finds the will and is so sure of a large inheritance that he sends for Gianni Schicchi so he can arrange a marriage with his daughter. There is a sweeping elation in the music which will be associated with the hopes of the lovers throughout the opera; for now it is linked to Rinuccio's hopes of marrying Lauretta Schicchi. At first the news seems good and as the relatives light candles in memory of Buoso, a brief theme, almost like the elaborated final cadence of a longer tune, brings a dry, legalistic formality as they read on. Then comes the bad news: the real money has been left to the church. The candles get blown out. The music contributes to the absurdity by treating essentially untragic tunes in a dolorous manner. Anger, then misery, follow – though there is a touch of sympathy as Rinuccio sees his means of getting married blown away. At least he did not want the inheritance out of mean-spirited acquisitiveness. To a four-note motto representing 'Gianni Schicchi' Rinuccio says that the well known trickster is the only person who can help them.

No, says Buoso's aged cousin Zita; family pride will not accept help from such a source:

Di Gianni Schicchi, della figliola,
non vo' sentirne parlar maì più!
E intendi bene!
(About Gianni Schicchi, or his daughter, I do not want
to hear any more said! Understood!)

It is now that Rinuccio really emerges as a finer, if still self-interested, character. Love helps him to a more generous view of society. An assertive tune, sung first then heard softly on woodwind and trumpets, represents Gianni's cunning mind. It is followed by Rinuccio's praise of their city, a hearty, uplifting piece apparently in the manner of a Tuscan popular song. Florence has thrived on its acceptance of new inhabitants, Rinuccio says:

Firenze è come un albero fiorito
che in piazza dei Signora ha tronco e fronde

ma le radici forze nuove apportano
dalle convalli limpide e feconde!
(Florence is like a tree in flower which has its trunk and branches in the
Piazza dei Signori but its roots gather new strength from the fertile valleys
with clear rivers).

As long ago as *Manon Lescaut* Puccini had prefigured an important tune
by tucking it in at the end of a verse in a different song. Here the first stanza
of Rinuccio's hymn to Florence ends with the first phrase of the glorious
melody Lauretta will soon sing to her dearly beloved daddy. The same part of
Lauretta's song is repeated low down in the orchestra at the end of Rinuccio's
praise of Florence. The end of his song is also a virtual hip-hip-hooray! in
praise of Gianni Schicchi.

Well, Rinuccio is in love, and his music also has the energy, naïvety and
optimism of youth. They are contrasted with the scepticism of age as Schicchi
arrives, sees them all miserable and assumes Buoso has revived. When he discovers the truth about the will he understands their depression. Cousin Zita
attacks him as a low-born creature who is not going to become connected in
any way with her family. He is just as adamant he is not going to have
anything to do with the Donati and, like a comic Romeo and Juliet, Rinuccio
and Lauretta are caught between the rival factions. As their elders try to pull
them apart, the youngsters sing the sweeping, and by now romantic, music in
which Rinuccio previously sang of his hopes of marrying Lauretta.

As Gianni tries to drag Lauretta away, his daughter comes out with a
heart-stoppingly, show-stoppingly beautiful melody that rivals 'Un bel di'
from *Madama Butterfly* as the most impassioned popular tune in all Puccini's
works:

Oh, mio babbino caro, mi piace, è bello bello;
Vo' andare in Porta Rossa a comperar l' anello!
Sì, sì, ci voglio andare! E se l' amassi indarno,
andrei sul Ponte Vecchio, ma per buttarmi in Arno!
Mi struggo e mi tormento! O Dio, vorrei morir!
Babbo, pietà, pietà! Babbo, pietà, pietà!
(O, my beloved daddy, I love him, he is handsome, handsome;
I want to go to Porta Rossa and buy the wedding-ring!
Yes, yes, I truly love him! And if this love is frustrated
I will go to Ponte Vecchio and throw myself into the Arno!
I struggle and am tormented! O God, I would rather die!
Daddy, take pity, pity! Daddy, take pity, pity!)

It is worth quoting the entire lyric, if only to show how slight a piece can
give rise to a world-famous song. But what is its place in the comedy as a
whole? Is it just that Puccini could never resist a beautiful tune where a pretty
girl was concerned? Or is it a bit of cunning characterisation, showing that
the daughter can manipulate her father as cleverly as he can manipulate
others; that she has inherited the family skill? Her threat – let me marry him
or I drown myself – might suggest this. But the song ends with a heartfelt
confession of her love. She hardly seems in manipulative mood. If she is
showing such a skill, it is like Rinuccio's praise of Florence and Gianni
Schicchi; the self-interest merges into a more generous youthful ardour.
Whatever they might become in later years, for the moment these two are an
open-hearted pair. The sweep of Rinuccio's music shows that as clearly as the

leaping tune of Lauretta's 'Oh, mio babbino caro'. And so it is fitting they should be linked by the phrases of Lauretta's song being mixed in with Rinuccio's. It is her desperation that makes Lauretta mention suicide; the lovers' songs are the testaments of the living; let their elders be obsessed with the will of the dead.

Moved by his daughter, Gianni thinks – no, nothing – yet; wait – maybe – perhaps he can do something. The contemptuous Donati now hang greedily on his every word. To deathlike sounds he prepares the scene.

He is interrupted by the inopportune arrival of Buoso's doctor. Gianni's plan depends upon nobody outside the house realising that Buoso is already dead. In such circumstances, the arrival of a doctor is very inconvenient, so they bundle him out, explaining Buoso has recovered but is resting. This gives Gianni a chance to try out his Buoso Donati impression. The doctor departs convinced he has heard Buoso still alive, but not without testing everybody's patience with a spiel about the value of medicine as practised by doctors from Bologna (he had to come from Bologna, for it was the home of *Il Dottore*, the longwinded pedant in the *commedia dell'arte*).

Instead of a doctor, they need a notary, someone who writes out wills. Gianni will impersonate Buoso and have a new will drawn up. Many tunes heard in this short comic opera are very brief; a new one follows now consisting of just two three-note phrases, little more than brief runs up and down the first five notes of the scale, to signify the new will (this theme for the new will uses the bottom half of the major scale, it matches the formal cadence-like tune for the old will, formed out of the top half).

Three parts of the legacy are the ripest plums for picking: the mule, the house in Florence (where the action is happening) and the mills at Signa. Arguments over these disrupt the fragile family fellow-feeling. Hope is also replaced by a fear even more severe than that caused by the doctor's arrival: a funeral bell is heard. The news of Buoso's death must have leaked out; their plan is hopeless. With great relief they discover the bell is for someone else and happily hope he rests in peace.

During this plotting, innocent Lauretta has been sent out to feed the birds. Her return to say they are replete is met by Gianni's brisk instruction to go and give them a drink. The Donati decide Gianni should choose who is to inherit the mule, house and mills. A quick reminder of the music for Rinuccio's hymn to Florence suggests they are ready now to adopt Schicchi as an ally in their own self-interest. So he puts on Buoso's clothes in case the notary catches a glimpse of him. In helping him dress up, each Donato takes the opportunity to offer him a bribe to leave the properties to him or her. The orchestral temperature rises as Gianni reminds the whole group what the law says: anyone involved in faking a will has his hand cut off and is exiled. Scared, the family echo the musical phrase he uses for this warning.

The notary and the necessary two witnesses arrive and the themes for wills old and new accompany the proceedings in suitably dry form for this legal official, in a mixture that also recalls the clucking theme and six-note 'Gianni Schicchi' figure from the opening of the opera.

As Gianni/Buoso dictates small bequests the relatives put on a front of pious approval. The reason it is being dictated, says the false Buoso, is because his hand is paralysed; this is ironic given the legal threat of amputation now hanging over them all. When he leaves each of mule, house and mills to 'My friend, Gianni Schicchi,' he silences the relatives' protests with

Puccini's study at Torre del Lago, complete with picture of the composer. The piano is the one at which he wrote his operas, sometimes while friends chatted around him.

reminders of this punishment. As a sting in the tail, Gianni orders 'his' cousin Zita to pay the notary and witnesses.

Left alone, the family attack him in fury, but he turns them out of what is now his house. They retreat, gathering whatever they can pick up. The story is over; the stage empty. But there are two epilogues. First, as the quarrelling fades away, the window opens and sunlit Florence is revealed in its magnificence. The lovers embrace and the journey of *Il Trittico* is over.

In its first opera characters longed for different homes, La Frugola the country, Michele a happy life on his barge, Giorgetta and Luigi their urban Belleville. In the middle opera Angelica was in a sense exiled from life. Now Rinuccio and Lauretta find their home and happiness in Florence, where they first swore love and kissed:

Lauretta mia, staremo sempre qui.
(My Lauretta, we will always live here.)

As the second epilogue makes clear, Gianni Schicchi himself was exiled to hell for his sin. Still, he has his proper home – the stage – as he addresses the audience and asks for their applause.

It would be difficult not to offer it readily, for *Gianni Schicchi* is one of the finest of comic operas. It may not match the scope and luminosity (to use a favourite Puccini word) of Wagner's *The Mastersingers of Nuremberg* or Verdi's *Falstaff*, but in it character and situation are presented with a pace and economy rarely met. As Puccini's only comedy, it provides a supreme example of one end of his musical spectrum.

Il Trittico is the most undeservedly unknown of the composer's works. Perhaps the idea of greatness equalling significance and length means that three short operas are felt to be of lesser value. They do demand an interest in three different styles, but they are not odd one-act pieces thrown together for convenience. They have their own unity of strength through contrasting ways of looking at love, death and the need for a place to belong.

Puccini and Toscanini fell out over the work(s), which the latter hated. Toscanini had been due to conduct the London première of *Il Trittico* but, for whatever reason, did not do so. Fortunately the breach was repaired in time for him to conduct *Turandot*.

Chapter Seven:

An Incomplete Last Work

Viareggio, where Puccini
moved for the last years
of his life when
advancing industry and
political discontent
broke the peace of his
beloved Torre del Lago.

By the end of the First World War, Puccini was only a few weeks from his sixtieth birthday, and *Il Trittico* was a month from its New York première. The world was greatly changed. His next composition, the short *Inno di Roma* was a national hymn suggested by Prince Prospero Colonna and dedicated to Princess Jolanda of Savoy. It was first performed in June 1920 in Rome Stadium. Its composer thought very little of it. One person who did appreciate its national fervour was Benito Mussolini, under whose regime it became a Fascist anthem. Puccini applied to become a member of the Fascist party and later accepted Mussolini's offer of the title of Senator. These now seem like acts of political naïvety. The Fascist party of course exploited them, but there is no evidence of any political conviction in Puccini's behaviour other than a general feeling that Italy needed political discipline. It was an unsettled country, a newish nation with Communism licking at its edges, in a

restive Europe. Fascism was not yet the horror it had become a dozen years after Puccini's death.

Yet he feared for the future. The man who had travelled only when necessary and had always loved returning to his home, Lake Massaciuccoli and its latest generation of wildfowl, now even considered emigrating. He never did, but he had to leave Torre del Lago as the once quiet town became subject to the noise and disturbances of industrialisation. A peat factory was built near his house. Then the lake where he had for years enjoyed peaceful hunting became a place where he was verbally assaulted. A fisherman, probably inspired by the left-wing agitation that had conquered Russia and briefly ruled Germany after the war, shook his fist at the composer in his boat with a shout of, 'Wait till we're in power'. It left Puccini feeling like the Tosca of 'Vissi d' arte'. He had lived for music and love, had done no conscious harm and had helped people on occasion. Yet now he was suffering. It was the kind of simple incident that was likely to push an elderly person into the arms of the Fascists.

Puccini already owned land a few miles away, on the coast at Viareggio. The house he built there, in what was still a small fishing village, is now commemorated by the adjoining Via Giacomo Puccini. It was to be his last home, though he would die a long way distant from it.

The usual search for a new opera subject continued. At one point he looked like preceding Lionel Bart by forty years with a version of *Oliver Twist*, which with a typical interest in the female character and some eccentric renaming would have been called *Fanny*. The eventual subject was an eighteenth-century Italian play, Carlo Gozzi's *Turandotte*. One of his teachers at the Milan Conservatory, Bazzini, had written an opera on the subject and Puccini had seen a German production of the play. He mentioned the idea in a letter to the librettist Renato Simoni in March 1920. A few months later, Simoni reminded him of it. Several years earlier he might have turned it down (as he had rejected an *Arabian Nights* proposal). Now its magic and fantasy interested him.

(In the middle of the eighteenth century there had arisen a feeling that the traditional *commedia dell'arte* needed reform; it was a good thing but had gone on long enough. Two rival playwrights developed it in different ways; Carlo Goldoni towards realistic characters and situations; Carlo Gozzi towards fairytale-like fantasy.)

Once the subject had been decided, the music for it obsessed Puccini. Possibly it was his sole consolation in the post-war world. Giacosa, Ricordi and now (in 1919) Illica had died. Of Puccini's sisters, Ramelde had died in 1912, Tomaide in 1917. Soon Iginia (the nun in whose convent he had previewed *Suor Angelica*) would die – in 1922 – and the eldest of the generation, Otilia in 1923. This would leave only Nitteti, who survived until 1928. Family, colleagues and the world he had known, were all gone. No wonder a fantasy set in ancient China was a more welcome domain for the ageing composer's imagination.

And just as, following *Madama Butterfly*, he had taken a deliberate new direction in *La Fanciulla del West*, so now Puccini felt himself working in a new way. It was one which tested his confidence in his own powers as a composer. This is not surprising. It was now the age of Ravel, Stravinsky and Schoenberg. Young Italian composers, little known today but powerful enough forces in their own time, were attacking Puccini and demanding

By the 1920s Puccini was world famous, but World War I had unsettled Europe, and many of his associates were dead. For a time he even thought of emigrating, though eventually he moved only a few miles. He was also facing his final artistic challenge in the story of the ice Princess Turandot, so different from his previous loving heroines.

Italian music forsake the nineteenth century operatic tradition. He was the last of that tradition, at the height of his achievement, and he felt old; but he battled on.

The outline of the new opera, with its libretto to be written by Giuseppe Adami and Renato Simoni, was finished by late 1920. There was uncertainty over the use of the three 'Masks' – *commedia dell'arte* figures who were adapted to create Ping, Pang and Pong. Luckily they remained in the opera.

Puccini himself introduced Liù, the young female slave who sacrifices her life to help save Prince Calaf. There is a distant original in Gozzi's play, Princess Adelma, but she is a very different character. *Turandot's* structure altered; originally it was to be the first of the three acts that had two scenes (it ended up the only act to have just one scene). This act would have taken the story right up to the solving of Turandot's riddles. Both the greatest aria in the opera, Turandot's 'In questa regia' (In that reign), and the most famous, Calaf's 'Nessun dorma' (No–one is to sleep), were added during the progress of work on the opera; neither was in the original scheme.

The final question of Puccini's life relates to his failure to complete *Turandot*. We can look at the artistic aspects of this later; for now the biographical one can complete his life's story. There had been crises of self–confidence and arguments with Adami and Simoni along the way, but work continued until the whole opera was mapped and sketched out and all but the last love duet composed and orchestrated. This love duet, in which Turandot accepts Calaf's love and renounces her hatred of men, existed in the form of untidy sketches.

By September 1924 Puccini and Toscanini were discussing plans for the première of *Turandot*, which was scheduled for spring 1925. They were friends again, the music was going well at last and the composer was awaiting the final form of the words for the closing Turandot/Calaf duet. A month later, the words arrived and Puccini approved. But over the next few weeks an unpleasantly persistent sensation in his throat quickly grew more severe. A local throat specialist advised him to rest, give up smoking and not to worry.

Puccini remained worried enough to visit another specialist, this time in Florence. There the doctor diagnosed advanced throat cancer. Puccini went to Brussels, where a new X–ray treatment was available. By now it was November 1924, the last month of Puccini's life. With him went his son Tonio, a representative of Ricordi – and the manuscript of the closing scene of *Turandot*.

Any hopes of completing the opera proved futile when the doctors in Brussels moved to the second stage of treatment. This involved sticking needles in his neck, and attaching a tube to a hole cut in his throat so he could breathe. It would not hurt a bit, they told him, with their usual optimism. His operation, on 24th November, lasted almost four hours. At first, though in pain and speechless, he rallied. By 28th November his step–daughter Fosca, who had arrived just before the operation, was writing hopefully to Elvira. Two hours later, under the strain of the treatment, Puccini suffered a heart attack; he died in the early hours of 29th November 1924.

After a funeral ceremony held in Brussels on 1st December, his body was returned to Milan where he was buried on 3rd December. Toscanini conducted the theatre orchestra in the Requiem which Puccini had composed years before for *Edgar*. There was national mourning; La Scala, where the composer had been humiliated over *Madama Butterfly*, was closed in respect.

In late 1926 Puccini's body was brought to Torre del Lago and placed in a specially built tomb. He was survived by Elvira, who died in 1930, and Tonio who lived until 1946. Tonio's daughter Simonetta later helped establish the Institute of Puccini Studies in Milan.

At the first performance of *Turandot* in April 1926, Toscanini did something which the composer had himself predicted before his final illness became apparent, realising, for one reason or another, that he would never complete it. After the death of Liù, when he reached the place where the composer's score came to an end, Toscanini brought the orchestra to a halt and announced to the audience that this was the moment where the composer had broken off his work. Subsequent performances have been given with a completion based on Puccini's notes; this was composed by Franco Alfano.

Turandot had to wait seventeen months after Puccini's death for its première, completed by Franco Alfano and conducted by Arturo Toscanini. On the first night Toscanini ended the performance with the death of the slave-girl Liù, announcing that this was where the master had laid down his pen.

Turandot

First performed at the Teatro alla Scala, Milan on 25th April 1926.
Conductor: Arturo Toscanini.

ACT I: *Outside the Imperial Palace, Peking. Ancient times.*
It is proclaimed that Princess Turandot will marry whoever answers her three riddles. Failure to answer means death. The people demand more executions and the slave Liù calls out that Timur, the old man she is accompanying, has been knocked over by the crowd. Calaf helps Liù and Timur, who is ex-king of Tartary. They recognise him as Timur's long-lost son. Liù loves Calaf, who once smiled at her. The Prince of Persia has failed to answer the riddles and,

143

to the crowd's hysterical delight, is taken to execution. However, the sight of the Prince brings out sudden pity, but Turandot – seen but not heard – demands the beheading take place. Calaf falls in love with the beautiful Turandot and despite three ministers, Ping, Pang and Pong, trying to dissuade him, he insists on trying the riddles. He calls out Turandot's name and sounds the great gong as a signal of this intent.

ACT II: SCENE 1: *A pavilion.*
Ping, Pang and Pong deplore the many deaths and wish they could return to the peace of their homes in the country. Trumpets announce the new suitor's test.

ACT II: SCENE 2: *The palace courtyard.*
The feeble emperor Altoum also tries to dissuade Calaf and fails. Turandot speaks for the first time and explains she is revenging herself on men for the rape and murder, in ancient days, of her forebear Lo-u-Ling. When Calaf succeeds in answering her three riddles, Turandot asks Altoum to release her from her marriage obligation. He refuses. She asks Calaf if he wants to take her by force; he replies he wants her love and offers her a way out. If she can discover his name before morning she can execute him.

ACT III: SCENE 1: *The palace garden.*
As night ends there are repeated announcements of Turandot's order that nobody be allowed to sleep until Calaf's name is discovered. Calaf meanwhile looks forward to winning the Princess. The three ministers and the people bribe and threaten him, fearing for their own lives if they fail to find out his name. Timur and Liù are brought in; they will be killed if he does not tell his name. Liù says only she knows it and to prevent herself revealing it under torture, she kills herself. Turandot cannot understand the force of Liù's love, but she still refuses Calaf. She breaks into tears and, ashamed of her weakness, asks him to leave. Instead he tells her his name is Calaf. Now she has it in her power to execute him.

ACT III: SCENE 2: *The palace courtyard.*
Turandot tells her father, in the presence of the crowd that she has learnt the prince's name: it is Love. Everybody is happy.

Madama Butterfly is a late nineteenth century opera that happens to have been composed in the twentieth century, but *Turandot*, Puccini's other opera with an oriental setting, is very definitely twentieth century in its musical language.

    Turandot departs significantly from Puccini's other operas in its treatment of the women characters. The line of poor girls destroyed by their love finds its apogee in Liù, but it also meets its reverse image in Turandot, the stern princess who is fully in control not only politically but in terms of her own emotions. Or so she believes. For she has this control only because she is remote and denies her humanity. Her negativity spreads out into the blood-thirstiness and dissatisfaction in the people around her. By surrendering to love, which she fears and sees as a weakness, Turandot opens herself to the promise of a fuller life, where she can be herself and not hide in the alter-ego of Lo-u-Ling. Alas, this can only happen when she has seen the shocking self-sacrifice with which Liù devastates the people of Peking.

Yet even this suicide is in a sense the fulfilment of Liù. The character is not in Gozzi's play, as we have seen. She was Puccini's idea, and given his operatic history, she might well be seen as a character born to be killed off. She is the culmination of Puccini's heroines. Her whole life is devoted to the love she has for Calaf and she has never received a moment's reciprocation. Puccini's early heroines may be swept along by their feelings, and they may die, but they all make some impact on their own stories. It is only in death that Liù has any impact on events.

Liù often gains audience sympathy and she has some sensuous music which, as we will see, forms an important contrast to the bright, hard edges found in the music elsewhere. The heroic style is used for the brave Calaf.

Turandot herself is briefly seen in Act One, but it is only in the third scene that she is heard. There we finally discover her explanation for hating men, the deadly game she plays to protect her vulnerability without having to deny her sexuality openly, by putting the impassable barrier of the three all-or-nothing questions between herself and any suitor. When Calaf finally breaches that barrier she cannot face the consequences. Turandot will not play her part.

Calaf offers her a new game to play; or rather, the same game in reverse. Now she has to answer just one question: to find out his name. This will restore her ultimate control over him; she can kill him. When she fails to do this, Calaf gives the game away. He tells her his name. The rules allow he can be killed. But they are now his rules. And the mood of the game has been altered by Turandot's amazement at Liù's willingness to suffer torture and kill herself rather than betray Calaf. This leaves Turandot in a moral quandary; now it is she who is in the position of the rapist. Not only would she use unwarranted power against this man who has played by the rules and still abdicated his advantage. She would be violating Liù's love.

Unfortunately, the incomplete state of the opera leaves unanswered the question of what happens to Turandot's mind in the last scene. But it is a sign of the opera's force and scope that many possibilities open up.

Although the character of Liù can be traced back to Gozzi's Adelma, for all practical purposes she is a new character. A similar, if less radical, transformation has undergone the three *commedia dell'arte* characters who are known as the Masks: Ping, Pang and Pong. They are the comic relief from Gozzi's *Turandotte*. They now occupy a place between the original stereotypes and individual human beings. As such they are a link in the structure of Puccini's work. For at one end stand Calaf, Liù and Timur, individuals with full human emotions; at the other Turandot herself, who denies her emotions, and the people of Peking, who are emotionally frozen by her influence. Caught between these extremes, the Masks show human feelings – what could be more natural than their longings for peace and their native homes? Yet they can also be official functionaries, pliantly carrying out Turandot's unbending will.

Turandot: The Music

Musically, *Turandot* declares itself with its mighty oriental orchestral outburst at the very start. A loud, harsh, official proclamation is the first thing to be sung, announcing that Turandot's riddles have claimed another victim, the young Prince of Persia. It is the Princess's hand against the Prince's head, and he has lost. He failed to answer her three cryptic riddles; he will be executed as soon as the moon rises. The moon, as a symbol of Turandot's unrelenting coldness, almost has its own status as a character.

The announcement fires the people of Peking: all they want is blood. What is cold necessity for Turandot – her remorseless revenge against men – flows over to the crowd and becomes violence, reciprocated as the guards push the people back. The first voice raised against all this that of Liù, a stranger uninfected by the plague of cruelty. At her first appearance Liù is already thinking of someone else, for the crowd is crushing her companion, the aged and deposed king Timur. Through her call for help, the two are reunited with Timur's long-lost son, Calaf. Timur's story is told to Calaf in a passage of a gentler, melodic nature. This is the voice that stands in contrast to Turandot's music. Yet the sound of drums and the appearance of the assistant executioners shows, not for the last time, that violence is always close in this land.

Within a few minutes Puccini has portrayed musically most of his chief characters, and the extremes of humanity – cold, cruel and impersonal on the one hand; warm, loving and personal on the other. A dramatic switch comes as the moon rises and the crowd hushes. They address the moon, at first in awe-struck quiet, then with a mounting thrill, reaching a climax as children enter singing. Even the young are caught up in the murderous procedures of Turandot's kingdom. Then the Executioner himself comes in, a great, threatening figure. The music linked here with death is also attached to Turandot. The doomed Persian prince marches sadly to his death. And as he does so, the bloodthirsty crowd suddenly express pity for him. It is a rare moment for them.

It is only now, when music and action have produced a near frenzy, that Turandot herself appears. She says nothing. She remains a figure remote and mysterious for the first half of the opera. For now, despite the crowd's pleas, she makes a mere gesture, the decisive death signal. Yet the sight of her has made love spring up in Calaf. It does so as the death procession fades away, with the music at the extremes of orchestral pitch, a warning to any would-be suitor. There is a sense of a fatal process beginning again as first Calaf, and then the Persian prince, about to die off-stage, call out Turandot's name.

The signal of a new suitor is his striking the great gong. Calaf is about to do this when the three Masks stop him. Puccini uses oriental effects in his orchestral writing, as well as Chinese tunes. The orchestration uses many percussion instruments, both those tuned to give pitched notes, such as xylophone and glockenspiel, and those which create an untuned sound, such as gong and triangle. Nowhere are such effects more noticeable than in the music of the Masks. Their bawdy suggestion – forget Turandot, have fun with a hundred ladies – shows their comic origins. It is also hushed by Turandot's maids saying she is asleep. Eerie music, with modernistic clashing chords, quiet trombones and harp plus strings and percussion, suggests the chilling idea that Turandot has gone calmly to sleep soon after the execution.

Nevertheless, the three Masks again attempt to dissuade Calaf; again Puccini creates an eerie sound as their babble is set against a distant, unseen chorus, singing offstage with hands cupped over their mouths. These are the disembodied voices of the men who died seeking Turandot's hand. It is a brief but vital moment which works because of the strangeness and extremity of the situation and of the general musical expression of this world. In no

Maria Jeritza was the first Tosca to sing 'Vissi d'arte' lying on the floor – initially following an accident during rehearsal. *Turandot* poses the final Puccini enigma; was he unable to complete the opera simply because of the onset of illness, or was he unable to solve the artistic problem of a powerful woman succumbing to love?

other Puccini opera does the music sweep along in quite such a startling way.

The dead voices singing of their love only spur Calaf on to taking Turandot's test. The Masks say, don't do it; the Persian prince's head brought in on a pole gives an awful warning. Most of all, Liù, in her gentle mellifluous manner, asks him to listen to her – 'Signore, ascolta.' She is given a Chinese folk tune here, perfectly fitted to her character and to the situation. Accompaniment includes scale-like harp figures; the song expresses her love for him. What is more, the idea of love is associated with her knowing his name. The linking of naming and loving reaches a climax at the end of the opera when Turandot declares of Calaf, 'His name is love.'

Whereas loud, brash music expresses Turandot's Peking, the whole section of this act between Calaf and Liù is gentle and flowing, including Calaf's reply, 'Non piangere, Liù' (Do not cry, Liù). This mood changes as Turandot obsesses him and, to the sorrow of Timur and Liù, and the mad cackle of the Masks, the act ends in an aggressive blaze as Calaf hits the gong three times to signal his candidature.

It is the Masks we meet in the next scene, and the chinoiserie of their pavilion music resembles that of Ravel in his *Mother Goose* suite. The main action of the opera is effectively suspended in this short scene, just as Ping, Pang and Pong's ancestors in the *commedia dell'arte* used to create self-sufficient comic routines out of their store of gags. These three merrily prepare for Calaf's success or failure, setting up either wedding or funeral. And they lament nostalgically the old, happy days before Turandot and her gong came along. They count up the dead bodies over the years, music from Act One reminding what happened each of these many times. They express a longing to return to their homes, a desire intensified by delicate orchestral decoration.

Back to the present, which makes itself felt by the offstage crowd, in bloodthirsty mood again, supported by brass instruments. The Masks fantasise about Turandot actually giving in to love and giving up her deadly crusade. How happy that would make them. Puccini used the orchestral harp plentifully throughout his operas. Here he tries a new effect; one of the harpists has to put paper between the harp strings to create a mysterious sound. Such a mood is soon threatened by strong hints of the death process starting up again as drums and brass instruments make their presence felt.

And so back to the square outside the palace. The crowd assembles, the scrolls with the correct answers to the three cryptic questions are brought in. The Masks reappear, now in official guise. All is grand and chilling in its impersonal foreboding. The Emperor himself is seen at the climax; he is old and feeble but, in contrast to his dignified position on high and the massed population of the city, the small group of Calaf, Timur and Liù looks forlorn.

Brass and percussion are kept very busy in *Turandot*; they are used with the expressive importance woodwind and strings have held in other Puccini operas. But here the Emperor's feeble voice is only occasionally underlined softly by the orchestra, as he asks Calaf to desist. He too is tired of bloodshed, but bound to continue with the process because he swore long ago to do so. In a contrast created by his firmer voice and increased orchestral support, Calaf insists he will go ahead. It is youth versus age, individual against institution, hope against resignation and despair. It is the insistent renewal of life against mortality.

More ceremonial and, a surprise in this usually oriental instrumentation, the sound of two saxophones concealed on-stage, lead to Turandot's entrance. Scarcely any operatic character can have had such an extended build-up. The problem is to provide the music to meet the expectations raised. Puccini succeeds magnificently with Turandot in her aria 'In questa Reggia'. She explains how she has taken on the mantle of her ancestor Luo-o-Ling, who was raped and murdered by an invading Tartar king. It happened centuries before in this same palace. Luo-o-Ling's unassertive beauty cost her her life; Turandot's assertive beauty will cost many men their lives.

Her music is declamatory, almost spat out at times. She will allow no gap in her defences and is certainly not going to create one by stopping to question herself. Midway through the song a warmer tune arrives in the orchestra, but Turandot never fully relaxes into it. As the melodic line rises Calaf interrupts her certainty. She speaks of her questions bringing death; he associates them with life. By the end of the aria they are singing together but with opposite intentions.

Two British opera companies have presented director Christopher Alden's production of *Turandot* in the 1990s, Welsh National Opera (above) and English National Opera. Alden related the work to its own time, with the Chorus representing the masses who supported fascistic authority – ironicallly, as Puccini was a member of Mussolini's Italian fascist party. The pictures of Turandot's dead suitors also recall the political terror killings of oppressive twentieth century regimes.

Three harsh chords introduce the three questions. The first question demands what flies by night, is looked for by all people, vanishes at dawn and is reborn next night, to die the following day. Calaf's answer is: Hope. He is correct. But Turandot scornfully tells him hopes are dupes.

Tension mounts at each question. Liù encourages him as he searches for the second answer: Blood. Eventually he manages the third answer, which is: Turandot. The three outline the deadly process; a suitor's hope, his spilled blood and the remote Turandot left by herself. Except that this time she is not. And she cannot accept he has won. She asks her father to release her from the rules of the game. But the oath that binds him binds her also. To agitated music, Turandot's fury mounts. She turns to Calaf and asks if he wants her even though she is unwilling. He replies that he wants her love.

As the chords that introduced Turandot's riddles are heard again, Calaf offers her a challenge: just one riddle to free her. Can she discover his name before dawn? If so, she can execute him. She accepts, but it is a step in the wrong direction for her. Now she has to play his game. With the Emperor clearly on Calaf's side, the act ends thunderously.

Again a Puccini third act begins with evocative orchestral music, including some thrillingly high sounds. Offstage yet more proclamations are heard; that no-one is to sleep in Peking this night, on pain of death. All must search for the suitor's name. Calaf listens and takes up the words 'Nessun dorma' (No-one is to sleep). While Calaf, Liù and Timur have always talked to each other as people, the Peking authorities have tended to speak in proclamations or public announcements. The Masks have chatted privately, but spoke in stylised gabble to Calaf. The crowd have tended to offer mass reactions. The effect has been to place Calaf, Liù and Timur closer to us and put Peking at a cold, formal distance.

So now, the words 'Nessun dorma' are turned from a proclamation to a personal statement by Calaf. He addresses Turandot in her absence. He too keeps his secret; at dawn he will be victorious. Meanwhile, his tune is heard

Act One of *Turandot* in Andrei Serban's production at the Royal Opera House, Covent Garden, London. Unlike Alden's contemporary presentation, Serban emphasized the ancient, ritual society – as did the La Scala première in 1926. In both productions the importance of the Chorus as a character in its own right is clear. The chorus concludes the opera, though we can never know how Puccini would have handled their final contribution.

repeated by the Peking women offstage. They fear death if they fail to discover his name. Turandot's fears have led her to terrorise and corrupt the people. Enter the Masks, and others, with bribes – women. money, power. When these fail the people try threats. Then Timur and Liù are dragged in.

Turandot arrives and the Masks are as keen as anyone to torture Timur and Liù; a cruel dictator brings out the worst in fearful people. Liù is tortured but will not speak. And here the two women of this opera, cold and powerful Turandot, warm and vulnerable Liù are directly opposed against each other. Turandot seems far more powerful and in a sense she is. But she cannot understand how Liù can bear this suffering. Love is the reason answers Liù. Surprised by a phenomenon she has never met in her life, Turandot is perplexed, repeating the word softly in wonder.

To gentle music, softened further by a solo violin, Liù speaks of her love for Calaf. Turandot cannot bear the challenge of the strength Liù possesses through love – the emotion she, Turandot, has built her whole identity, her sense of her place in the world, on rejecting. The princess demands the slave be made to tell the secret name, but love gives the prisoner power and, telling Turandot that this suitor will win the princess, she stabs herself. The crowd is horrified; their hope of the discovery has gone, and this is a kind of sacrifice they are not used to in their deadly world. Liù's death is set to a march, grave and dignified yet also heartfelt. It is music Liù deserves and which could not be associated with Turandot.

The poor crowd are torn between fear at Turandot's revenge because they have failed to find the name, and fear that Liù will become an avenging spirit. Liù's body is borne off to tender music. Even the Masks follow the body. Now Puccini's last victim girl is dead. How will he handle the invulnerable, assertive Turandot as the scene approaches where she will accept love?

We will never know, because this is all he composed before his death. It is on this sad, fading death procession that Toscanini stopped the La Scala première in 1926. Puccini's sketches for the rest of the scene are inconclusive.

Arturo Toscanini (1867-1957) has the most enduring reputation of the conductors who premièred Puccini operas – he conducted the first nights of *La Bohème*, *La Fanciulla del West* and the posthumously produced *Turandot*. Puccini admired his conducting, though there were conflicts between them. When he ran La Scala, Toscanini fought hard to reform bad practices, including encores and bows that interrupted the performances. In later life he abandoned opera for symphony concerts – here he conducts with soloist Lotte Lehmann.

Franco Alfano's musical completion rounds off the action effectively and with physical excitement. But it is his ending, not Puccini's. There remain unanswered questions. What would have been the effect on Turandot of discovering Calaf to be a descendent of the murderer of Lou-o-Ling, for example? And, most intriguingly, why and how does Turandot accept Calaf and say his name is love? And did Toscanini cut Alfano's music, making Turandot's sudden turnaround less credible?

The biggest question about this incomplete masterpiece is why it remains unfinished. It could have been an accident of timing. Another few weeks before the onset of serious cancer symptoms and the opera might have been completed. But was it only a matter of time? Or is the very greatness of this score a sign of a deeper, more urgent debate within Puccini's personality? Going back to Mosco Carner's theory, with which this book began, did the Puccini who needed to dominate less powerful women find in the end he could not wrestle, even on the operatic stage, with love among equals?

THE MUSIC OF PUCCINI

1876	*Preludio Sinfonico* for orchestra
1877	*Vexilla Regis prodeunt* for male chorus and organ
	I Figli d'Italia bella cantata for voices and orchestra
1878	*Credo* for voices and orchestra
	Motetto for voices
1880	*Salve del ciel regina* for soprano with harmonium
	Messa di Gloria for four voices and orchestra
1881	*Melancolia* for baritone and piano/orchestra
	Scherzo for string quartet
1882	*Ad una morta* for baritone and piano/orchestra
	Salve Regina for soprano and organ/harmonium
	Trio for two violins and piano
1883	*Adagietto* for orchestra
	String Quartet in D
	Fuga in A, C minor and G for string quartet
	La Sconsolata for violin and piano
	Capriccio Sinfonico for orchestra
1884	LE VILLI (one and two act versions)
1889	EDGAR (four act version)
1890	*Three Minuets* for string quartet
	Crisantemi for string quartet
1892	EDGAR (three act version)
1893	MANON LESCAUT
1896	LA BOHÈME
1900	TOSCA
1904	MADAMA BUTTERFLY (Milan and Brescia versions)
1905	*Requiem* for voices and organ/harmonium
1906	MADAMA BUTTERFLY (Paris version)
1910	LA FANCIULLA DEL WEST
1917	LA RONDINE
1918	IL TRITTICO (IL TABARRO, SUOR ANGELICA, GIANNI SCHICCHI)
1919	*Inno di Roma* for orchestra
1926	TURANDOT

Plus small-scale piano pieces and songs with piano

(Dates vary between those of composition, publication and première. In each case the most significant date for the work concerned has been given).

Some Puccini artistes

Famed for her temperament almost as much as her singing, the American-born Greek soprano Maria CALLAS (1923-1977) first sang Tosca in 1942. She was also a fine Turandot but after her rise to fame in Ponchielli's *La Gioconda* (1947) the conductor Tullio Serafin, whom she greatly admired, steered her from verismo and dramatic roles into the earlier bel canto parts. In 1964 Callas sang Tosca at London's Covent Garden in a production built round her, with Tito Gobbi's Scarpia. This partnership had also been heard in the roles at La Scala. Several of the London opera house's board had been sceptical about her suitability for the part and the production had to be done on less rehearsal time than usual. It was a triumph. Callas had a thrilling, dark voice in the middle range and acted with conviction. The Callas/Gobbi partnership worked so supremely well – even if she did stab him for real one night when the trick knife failed to do its trick. Her Tosca was incandescent in its jealous fury – literally so once when her wig caught fire from a nearby candle. 'With Maria it was not playing but living,' Tito Gobbi said.

Enrico CARUSO (1873-1921) only created one Puccini role, the outlaw hero Dick Johnson in *La Fanciulla del West* at the Metropolitan Opera House, New York on 10th December 1910. 'Magnificent,' acclaimed Puccini – and that was only in rehearsal. But Caruso's involvement with the composer's operas went far wider – and started earlier. When he was starting out as a singer, Caruso was taken to Torre del Lago by a friend of both singer and composer. He sang 'Che gelida manina' from *La Bohème* to Puccini, who uttered the words, 'Who sent you to me? Was it God?' Caruso relayed this to a theatre in Leghorn, who promptly employed him to sing in the same opera.

Years later Puccini's praise was more reserved: 'He won't learn, he's lazy and too pleased with himself – still, he has a magnificent voice.'

Caruso spent years as a struggling young tenor before he was given his first major opportunity in *La Gioconda*. Later, Puccini turned Caruso down for *Tosca* despite the singer's efforts to win the part of Cavaradossi. Neither in singing nor acting, it seemed, was 'the great Caruso' yet so great. Though he could be a rough performer, he won Puccini over eventually when he did come to sing Cavaradossi at Bologna. His success increased after he moved to America and the Metropolitan Opera House where, apart from Dick Johnson, he sang Rodolfo and Cavaradossi. Other Puccini roles included Des Grieux in *Manon Lescaut* and Pinkerton in *Madama Butterfly*. In 1907 four Puccini operas were given in a single New York season – and Caruso sang in them all.

Largely self-taught, Caruso never acquired a firm technique and had problems in his high register which he used to solve by having the music rewritten for performance at a lower pitch. Sometimes he would sing top notes falsetto. But in the lower range his voice was rich and compelling and he learned to control it so as to be fierce or smooth as the character demanded. Like Maria Jeritza, Caruso made many recordings in the early days of the gramophone.

Italian soprano Gilda DALLA RIZZA (1892-1975) was the first Magda in *La Rondine*, at Monte Carlo in the Théâtre du Casino on 27th March 1917. She repeated the role at the Buenos Aires Teatro Colon, and introduced two lead roles in *Il Trittico* to Italy, singing Suor Angelica and Lauretta (in *Gianni Schicchi*) at the Teatro Costanzi in Rome on 11th January 1919. The following year she sang them again at Covent

Garden, with less success. Puccini came to see her as the ideal Minnie in *La Fanciulla del West* and wrote the role of Liù in Turandot for her. But she never sang it, even though she took over the role of Manon Lescaut in the thirtieth anniversary production, conducted by Toscanini in 1923, when the intended soprano Juanita Caracciolo became terminally ill. Her bold acting style led to her being labelled the opera stage's equivalent of the great actor-dancer Eleonora Duse.

Rumanian soprano Hariclea DARCLÉE (1860-1939) first sang in *Faust* at the Paris Opera. She was equally at home in the display coloratura parts and in the deeper character studies of dramatic roles. Her first Puccini role came when she took over as Manon Lescaut from Olga Olghina in 1894 at La Scala. She also sang Mimi and verismo roles in operas by Catalani and Mascagni. Seeing her in the latter's *Iris*, Puccini decided to let her create his Tosca in Rome on 14th January 1900. Her mix of agile voice, smooth legato singing style and physical beauty as an actor made her an operatic and social star. This presumably melted the icy audience at the La Scala opening of *Tosca* on 17th March 1900, when her 'Vissi d' arte' produced the first signs of enthusiasm among spectators. Like Catalani, Puccini found Darclee, for all her qualities, too cold a stage presence and certainly not the tempestuous, emotionally led Tosca he later found in Ternina. However, she brought her acting powers to the role. Unlike older, and older-fashioned, singers Darclee brought strong stage presence to her portrayals.

The final part of Puccini's *Il Trittico* was his only purely comic opera *Gianni Schicchi*. The medieval Florentine trickster of the title role was sung at the New York Metropolitan Opera House world première on 14th December 1918 by the Italian baritone Giuseppe DE LUCA (1876-1950). He portrayed him as a consummate rascal.

De Luca's first Puccini experience had been very brief – the American Consul Sharpless in the single, disastrous La Scala première of *Madama Butterfly* on 17th February 1904. Later he sang Ping, one of the three 'masks' in *Turandot* at the first Metropolitan production on 16th November 1926. De Luca's firm technique enabled him to keep singing important roles into his late fifties.

Later in life Emmy DESTINN (1878-1930) reverted to her Czech origins and insisted on being called Ema Destinnova – though her real name was Kittl. She adopted the name of her teacher, Marie Loewe-Destinn as an act of homage. Experienced in verismo and Wagner, she was considered by Puccini to be one of the best Butterflys he knew. Emmy sang the role in the star-studded London première at Covent Garden on 10th July 1905. She was much more in the dramatic mode of Salomea Krusceniski than the lyrical manner of Rosina Storchio, who had created the part. Destinn's voice was often recorded, allowing us to know she sang Butterfly's dying words to her son, 'fairest, beautiful flower,' an octave lower than it is written. This did not upset Puccini who invited her to create Minnie, the heroine of his next opera *La Fanciulla del West* – at the Metropolitan Opera House on 10th December 1910. Puccini supervised the production – Destinn caused him some anxiety in rehearsals. She seemed to lack energy; but energy was just what the first night critics praised her for, along with her sincerity in this idealised role. She repeated the part at Covent Garden on 29th May 1911 – the only Metropolitan cast member to cross the Atlantic for the occasion.

Florence Gertrude EASTON (1882-1953) hailed from Middlesbrough, on the river Tees in the north of England; the soprano toured Europe and America before staying on at the Metropolitan Opera House, New York from 1917, where she was appreciated as a highly versatile singer, able to give fine performances in parts demanding different sorts of musicianship. On 14th December 1918 she created Lauretta, becoming the first to address Gianni Schicchi with the words 'Oh! mio babbino caro'. Her many Wagnerian roles no doubt helped fit her for Turandot, which she sang at Covent Garden, London a year after the opera's posthumous première. A different soprano had been cast, but found unacceptable to London audiences.

Born in America, soprano Geraldine FARRAR (1882-1967) spent years studying and singing in Germany before returning to New York's Metropolitan Opera House where she sang many parts between 1906 and 1922. A striking figure with a voice that shaped the melodic line clearly, she sang Butterfly. Puccini was less than happy, however, claiming the local heroine had too small a voice and kept singing out of tune: 'The woman was not what she ought to have been,' was his blunt comment. Yet she went on to create Suor Angelica when *Il Trittico* was premièred at the Metropolitan on 14th December 1918. Neither she nor the opera made much impact – she had undergone a throat operation not long before.

Italian soprano Cesira FERRANI (1863-1943) was born in Turin, where she created the roles of Manon Lescaut at the Teatro Regio on 1st February 1893, and Mimi exactly three years later, filling the time between as Puccini's Manon in Rome and Buenos Aires. The role became her favourite and she sang it almost three hundred times before retiring in 1909. Ferrani was very popular in her home town, so she was a wise choice to introduce these roles by the still-developing composer.

Tito GOBBI (1913-1984) the Italian baritone was more frequently found playing Verdi roles, but he was a famous Scarpia and Gianni Schicchi. He combined a fine voice with great acting skill and understanding of the role. Gobbi played Scarpia eight hundred and seventy times and used to practise putting the character's make-up on at home, using three mirrors to see how he appeared from every possible angle – a complexity he brought to his all-round performances too.

Though she never created a new Puccini role, Czech-born Maria JERITZA (1887-1982) was one of the composer's favourite sopranos. She was an admired Tosca, especially in Vienna, where audiences made her a special favourite. She also gave many performances as Minnie in *La Fanciulla del West* and as Turandot, singing in the first U.S. performance of Puccini's last opera at the Metropolitan Opera house, New York on 16th November 1926. She was admired more than the opera itself and would have introduced it to London the following June but fell ill.

Much of her strong appeal came from her magnetic stage presence – her spirited Giorgetta in *Il Tabarro* impressed Puccini on 20th October 1920, when *Il Trittico* received its first Viennese performance. This was the period when Jeritza's upper vocal range was especially sonorous and –

though the role went first to Rosa Raisa – it is possible Turandot, with the high declamatory 'In questa reggia' were written with Jeritza in mind. She had been a favourite of the composer's since her Tosca at Vienna in 1914. Puccini had been at rehearsals when one day, going through the famous aria 'Vissi d' arte', Jeritza fell. Ever the trouper she carried on singing on the floor. The composer liked the effect and Toscas ever since have tended to take the aria lying down – though deliberately.

Puccini admired Jeritza to the end; at a Puccini Festival in Vienna in October 1923 he called her Tosca, 'Sublime. A wild success'. Alas, her recorded legacy also shows vocal flaws which her stage magnetism presumably made forgivable.

Salomea KRUSCENISKI (1872-1952), the Ukrainian soprano, took Italian citizenship when she married in 1910. She sang Manon Lescaut in Cremona and after a successful career in Russia returned to Italy and created the 'new' Butterfly at the Teatro Grande in Brescia on 28th May 1904. A singer of Verdi, Wagner and Richard Strauss, she combined power with restraint; her strong style contrasted with the light voice of the Milan Butterfly, Rosina Storchio.

Leopoldo MUGNONE (1858-1941) was a teenage composer who studied in Naples and turned to conducting. He conducted the world première of *Cavalleria Rusticana* and the London premières of operas by Giordano and Mascagni. Mugnone was responsible for the first performance of *Tosca* at La Scala on 14th January 1900 and the Italian première of *La Rondine* in 1917. He fell out with Puccini over *Madama Butterfly*.

Claudia MUZIO (1889-1936) created the adulterous Giorgetta in *Il Tabarro*, first of the three one-act operas in *Il Trittico* on 14th December 1918 at New York's Metropolitan Opera House – where her father had been a stage director. She had already sung Mimi and Tosca alongside Enrico Caruso, at Covent Garden. Tosca was also her New York début in 1916. Ten years later she sang the role at La Scala. But she also sang many other Puccini and Verdi characters. She brought her unusual refinement to the rough gallery of verismo women and was celebrated for her sweet voice, but she was also a strong dramatic actress. Early audiences at *Il Tabarro* were gripped by her acting and the terrible scream she gave at the end of the opera on discovering her lover's dead body wrapped in her husband's cloak. Muzio later sang in the first *Turandot* outside Italy – on 25th June 1926 at the Teatro Colon, Buenos Aires.

Dalmatian baritone Antonio PINI-CORSI (1858-1918) created the parrot-exterminating musician Alexandre Schaunard in *La Bohème* at the Teatro Regio, Turin on 14th February 1896. He was interesting casting, for he was primarily known for his comic roles. Aptly enough he also created the small character role of Happy in *La Fanciulla del West* in New York on 10th December 1910. A supple, intelligent singer, his other Puccini roles included Lescaut in *Manon Lescaut* at the British première at Covent Garden on 14th May 1894. He did not impress Puccini's publisher Giulio Ricordi who heard Pini-Corsi in Verdi's *Falstaff* – 'Good voice, but like a dozen others and a poor actor.'

Puccini's ice-maiden Turandot was first sung, at La Scala on 25th April 1926 by the Polish-American soprano Rosa RAISA (1893-1963). Raisa trained in Milan and had the dramatic force to play and sing this demanding role. She was also an early Suor Angelica, at Chicago on 6th December 1919.

Antonio SCOTTI (1866-1936) was not the first, but was probably the first great Scarpia in *Tosca*. He sang the part in London opposite Milka Ternina on 12th July 1900. The composer was sufficiently impressed to modify some of the high notes in the part to fit Scotti's voice. Scotti triumphantly introduced the American consul Sharpless in *Madama Butterfly* to London at Covent Garden on 10th July 1905 and two years later to the Metropolitan Opera House in New York in a Puccini season where he also sang Lescaut, Manon's rakish brother. But Scarpia remained a Scotti speciality up to his retirement in 1940.

Venetian soprano Rosina STORCHIO (1872-1945) first sang Musetta in 1897 in her home town – but in Leoncavallo's *La Bohème*. Leoncavallo had chosen her for her quick-sensitivity and the ability to move and speak well on stage. She went on to sing Puccini's Mimì and the composer's favourable opinion of her as Musetta in his *Bohème* in Rome meant he had her in mind while composing *Madama Butterfly*. (It was Toscanini who brought her to La Scala). She sang Cio-Cio-San in the notorious La Scala première of the opera on 17th February 1904, before repeating it far more successfully in Buenos Aires in 1905. Butterfly was a suitable role for Storchio, whose sweet tone and flexibility of voice were not complemented by great power. By the time she sang Butterfly her voice was already thin, particularly in the middle register. But she continued to sing the role until she was in her mid-forties and, in Puccini's view, was too slight and overtly childish in manner. A sad decline for a singer whose lyric soprano and acting ability gave her many qualities to play one of Puccini's most fragile young women.

Croatian Milka TERNINA (1863-1941) had already sung Verdi and Wagner roles before she sang Tosca at both the British (12th July 1900) and American (4th February 1901) premières opposite Antonio Scotti's Scarpia. Puccini preferred Ternina to his original Tosca, praising her as a 'genuine creation'. Ternina, with many Wagner roles in her repertoire, never quite caught the lightness of Tosca in her opening scene, but was compelling in the later dramatic scenes with Scarpia and in the scene of Cavaradossi's death. Her final 'O Scarpia, avanti a Dio!' was truly thrilling.

Arturo TOSCANINI (1867-1957) gave the premières of *La Bohème* at the Teatro Regio, Turin on 1st February 1896 and *Turandot* at La Scala on 25th April 1926. In charge of the orchestra at La Scala, Toscanini improved both playing and production standards – not to mention audiences. He insisted the spectators focus attention on the stage by fading out the house lights throughout the auditorium, and fought a long battle against the numerous encores and on-stage bows which interrupted the dramatic unity and flow of the action. He was to return in 1920, after an absence which included several years trying to improve standards at the Metropolitan opera house in New York. Toscanini spent the 1920s at La Scala, before leaving Fascist Italy and concentrating in later years on conducting symphony concerts.

Further Reading

The standard work on the composer is Mosco Carner's magisterial *Puccini: A Critical Biography* (3rd edition, London 1985), which looks at the life, musical style and individual operas in three sections. A briefer, cogent study is William Ashbrook's *The Operas of Puccini* (2nd edition, London, 1985). Spike Hughes' *Famous Puccini Operas* (London, 1959) concentrates on the handling of the orchestra in seven operas – the two early works and *La Rondine* are omitted. H. Greenfeld: *Puccini* (London, 1980) and Charles Osborne: *The Complete Operas of Puccini* (London, 1981) are among other modern studies, and *The Puccini Companion*, edited by William Weaver and the composer's grand-daughter, Simonetta Puccini (London, 1994), contains essays on various aspects of each opera, non-operatic compositions and family, plus musical backgrounds and documentary information.

Studies of individual operas include, in Cambridge Opera Handbooks: Arthur Groos and Roger Parker *La Bohème* (Cambridge, 1986) and Mosco Carner: *Tosca* (Cambridge, 1985), and in the English National Opera Guides: *La Bohème* (London, 1982), *Tosca* (London, 1982) and *Madam Butterfly* (London, 1984). This series includes parallel Italian and English versions of each opera's libretto. William Ashbrook and Harold Powers examine the last opera in *Puccini's Turandot: The End of the Great Tradition* (Princeton, 1991).

Older studies that still carry interest are Edward Greenfield: *Puccini: Keeper of the Seal* (London, 1958) and, for its quotation of Puccini material, George Marek: *Puccini: A Biography* (New York, 1951). A selection of the composer's letters was published in English translation in Giuseppe Adami, *The Letters of Giacomo Puccini* (London, 1931).

The sources of the operas are not readily available, though John L. Long's story Madame Butterfly is included in the ENO Guide to the opera, and Penguin published L. W. Tancock's translation of Prévost's *Manon Lescaut*. The Folio Society published Mürger's *Vie de Bohème*. Both of these are out of print.

Index

JOHN ANKA
I LOVE PUCCINI

JOHN ANKA
I LOVE PUCCINI